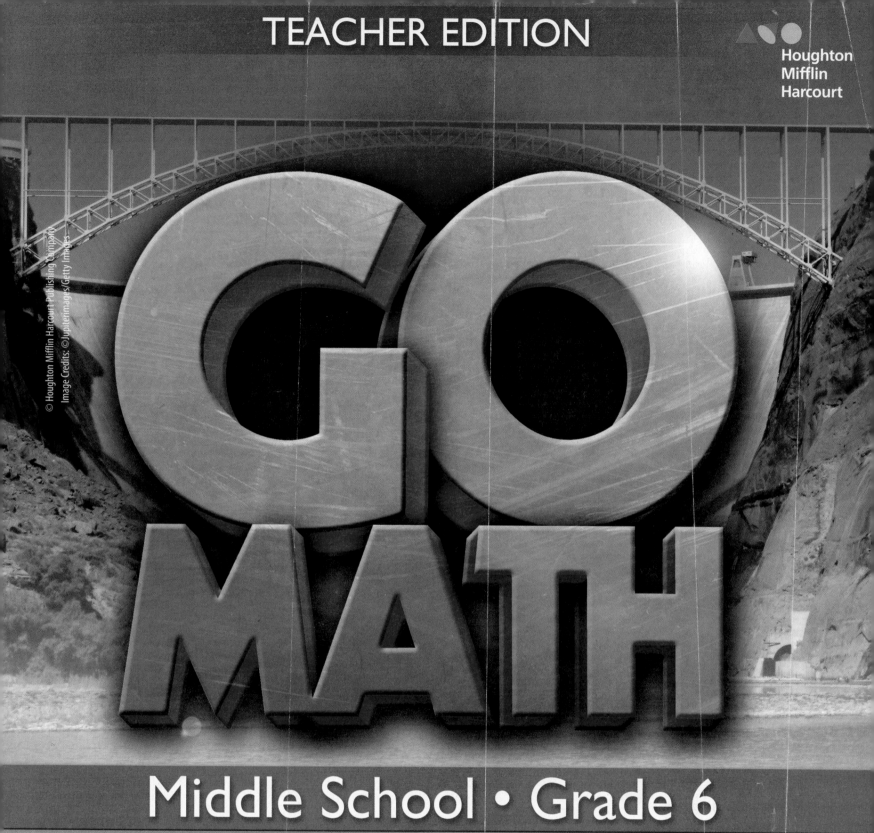

TEACHER EDITION

Houghton Mifflin Harcourt

GO MATH

Middle School • Grade 6

Edward B. Burger

Juli K. Dixon

Timothy D. Kanold

Matthew R. Larson

Steven J. Leinwand

Martha E. Sandoval-Martinez

Printed in the U.S.A

ISBN 978-0-544-06571-0

7 8 9 10 0868 23 22 21 20 19 18 17 16 15 14

4500517249   C D E F G

Authors

Edward B. Burger, Ph.D., is the president of Southwestern University, a former Francis Christopher Oakley Third Century Professor of Mathematics at Williams College, and a former vice provost at Baylor University. He has authored or coauthored more than sixty-five articles, books, and video series; delivered over five hundred addresses  and workshops throughout the world; and made more than fifty radio and television appearances. He is a Fellow of the American Mathematical Society as well as having earned many national honors, including the Robert Foster Cherry Award for Great Teaching in 2010. In 2012, Microsoft Education named him a "Global Hero in Education."

Juli K. Dixon, Ph.D., is a Professor of Mathematics Education at the University of Central Florida. She has taught mathematics in urban schools at the elementary, middle, secondary, and post-secondary levels. She is an active researcher and speaker with numerous publications and conference presentations. Key areas 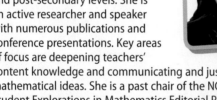 of focus are deepening teachers' content knowledge and communicating and justifying mathematical ideas. She is a past chair of the NCTM Student Explorations in Mathematics Editorial Panel and member of the Board of Directors for the Association of Mathematics Teacher Educators.

Timothy D. Kanold, Ph.D., is an award-winning international educator, author, and consultant. He is a former superintendent and director of mathematics and science at Adlai E. Stevenson High School District 125 in Lincolnshire, Illinois. He is a past president of the National Council of Supervisors of Mathematics (NCSM) and the Council  for the Presidential Awardees of Mathematics (CPAM). He has served on several writing and leadership commissions for NCTM during the past decade. He presents motivational professional development seminars with a focus on developing professional learning communities (PLC's) to improve the teaching, assessing, and learning of students. He has recently authored nationally recognized articles, books, and textbooks for mathematics education and school leadership, including *What Every Principal Needs to Know about the Teaching and Learning of Mathematics*.

Matthew R. Larson, Ph.D., is the K-12 mathematics curriculum specialist for the Lincoln Public Schools and served on the Board of Directors for the National Council of Teachers of Mathematics from 2010-2013. He is a past chair of NCTM's Research Committee and was a member of NCTM's Task Force  on Linking Research and Practice. He is the author of several books on implementing the Common Core Standards for Mathematics. He has taught mathematics at the secondary and college levels and held an appointment as an honorary visiting associate professor at Teachers College, Columbia University.

Steven J. Leinwand is a Principal Research Analyst at the American Institutes for Research (AIR) in Washington, D.C., and has over 30 years in leadership positions in mathematics education. He is past president of the National Council of Supervisors of Mathematics and served on the NCTM Board of Directors. He is the author of numerous articles, books, and textbooks and has made countless presentations with topics including student achievement, reasoning, effective assessment, and successful implementation of standards.

Martha E. Sandoval-Martinez is a mathematics instructor at El Camino College in Torrance, California. She was previously a Math Specialist at the University of California at Davis and former instructor at Santa Ana College, Marymount College, and California State University, Long Beach. In 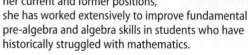 her current and former positions, she has worked extensively to improve fundamental pre-algebra and algebra skills in students who have historically struggled with mathematics.

Program Reviewers

Sharon Brown
Instructional Staff Developer
Pinellas County Schools
St. Petersburg, FL

Maureen Carrion
Math Staff Developer
Brentwood UFSD
Brentwood, NY

Jackie Cruse
Math Coach
Ferrell GPA
Tampa, FL

John Esser
Secondary Mathematics
Coordinator
Racine Unified School District
Racine, WI

Donald Hoessler
Math Teacher
Discovery Middle School
Orlando, Florida

Becky (Rebecca) Jones, M.Ed.
NBCT EA-Math
Orange County Public Schools
Orlando, FL

Sheila D.P. Lea, MSA
Ben L. Smith High School
Greensboro, NC

Toni Lwanga
Newell Barney Jr. High
Queen Creek Unified School District
Queen Creek, AZ

Tiffany J. Mack
Charles A. Lindbergh Middle School
Peoria District #150
Peoria, IL

Jean Sterner
Thurgood Marshall Fundamental
Middle School
Pinellas County Schools
St. Petersburg, FL

Mona Toncheff
Math Content Specialist
Phoenix Union High School District
Phoenix, AZ

Kevin Voepel
Mathematics & Professional
Development Coordinator
Ferguson-Florissant School District
Florissant, MO

© Houghton Mifflin Harcourt Publishing Company

UNIT 1

Numbers

MODULE 1 Integers

COMMON CORE

MODULE 2 Factors and Multiples

COMMON CORE

MODULE 3

Rational Numbers

COMMON CORE

UNIT 2 Number Operations

MODULE 4 Operations with Fractions

COMMON CORE

MODULE 5 Operations with Decimals

COMMON CORE

© Houghton Mifflin Harcourt Publishing Company • Image Credits: (t) Tetra Images/Alamy; (b) ©PhotoDisc/Getty Images

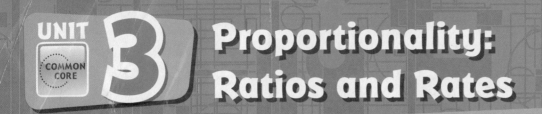

UNIT 3 Proportionality: Ratios and Rates

MODULE 6 Representing Ratios and Rates

MODULE 7 Applying Ratios and Rates

© Houghton Mifflin Harcourt Publishing Company • Image Credits: (t) ©Anne-Marie Palmer/Alamy; (b) ©Bravo/NBCUniversal/Getty Images

MODULE **8** **Percents**

COMMON CORE

UNIT 4

COMMON CORE

Equivalent Expressions

MODULE 9 Generating Equivalent Numerical Expressions

COMMON CORE

MODULE 10 Generating Equivalent Algebraic Expressions

COMMON CORE

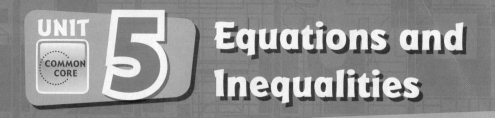

UNIT 5

COMMON CORE

Equations and Inequalities

MODULE 11 Equations and Relationships

COMMON CORE

MODULE 12 Relationships in Two Variables

COMMON CORE

UNIT 6 Relationships in Geometry

COMMON CORE

MODULE 13 Area and Polygons

COMMON CORE

MODULE 14 Distance and Area in the Coordinate Plane

COMMON CORE

© Houghton Mifflin Harcourt Publishing Company • Image Credits: (t) ©Getty Royalty Free; (b) ©Balefire/ Shutterstock.com

MODULE 15 Surface Area and Volume of Solids

COMMON CORE

UNIT 7 Measurement and Data

MODULE 16 Displaying, Analyzing, and Summarizing Data

Working as a Professional Learning Community

Great teaching materials do not provide great education in and of themselves. Educators who collaborate in Professional Learning Communities can have a profound impact on their students. As a middle school mathematics teacher, your grade-level or course-based collaborative team is the engine that can drive your professional learning and the professional learning community (PLC) process. You and your colleagues hold a critical key to helping *all* students successfully learn the Common Core Mathematics Standards in your middle school. Through your hard work and the work of your collaborative team, effective instruction, assessment, and intervention practices become more coherent and focused.

Coherence implies that the standards in each unit are more than a mere checklist of disconnected content; rather, they are organized into meaningful progressions of content that highlight the unity of the mathematics curriculum at your grade level, and throughout each grade of middle school.

Focus is provided in order to allow *time* for your students to master the intricate complexities of the content progressions across grades. Helping your students to better understand the coherent and focused aspects of the standards becomes one of the major benefits of working closely with your colleagues in a PLC school culture.

The National Board for Professional Teaching Standards states the following:

> Seeing themselves as partners with other teachers, [faculty members] are dedicated to improving the profession. They care about the quality of teaching in their schools, and, to this end, their collaboration with colleagues is continuous and explicit. They recognize that collaborating in a professional learning community contributes to their own professional growth, as well as to the growth of their peers, for the benefit of student learning. Teachers promote the ideal that working collaboratively increases knowledge, reflection, and quality of practice and benefits the instructional program. (*Mathematics Standards for Teachers of Students Ages 11–18+*, ©2010, p. 75)

As a highly accomplished middle school mathematics teacher you understand the value in the practice of effective collaboration with your colleagues. Teacher collaboration is not the icing on top of the proverbial cake of your work. Instead, it is the egg in the batter, holding the cake together.

As your school becomes a learning institution for the adults, it also becomes a learning institution dedicated to preparing all students for the future. The process of your collaboration in a PLC culture capitalizes on the fact that you and your colleagues come together with diverse experiences and knowledge to create a whole that is larger than the sum of the parts. Teacher collaboration is the solution to your sustained professional learning—the ongoing and never-ending process of growth necessary to meet the classroom demands of the CCSS expectations and the unit-by-unit mathematics content described in our series.

—Tim Kanold, Program Author

Progressions and Common Core Standards

HMH Go Math is designed to fully address the Common Core State Standards. Concepts within each grade are organized in units that align to major domains and provide focus on key big ideas. Within each unit, concepts are organized into modules that align to clusters and build connections among the individual standards.

HMH Go Math is also designed to provide coherent and focused progressions across the grades. The table below provides an overview of how important topics within each domain are developed across the grades.

	Grade 6	Grade 7	Grade 8
Ratios and Proportionality	• Understand ratio concepts and use ratio reasoning to solve problems.	• Analyze proportional relationships and use them to solve real-world and mathematical problems.	
The Number System	• Apply and extend previous understandings of multiplication and division to divide fractions. • Compute fluently with multi-digit numbers and find common factors and multiples. • Apply and extend previous understandings of numbers to the system of rational numbers	• Apply and extend previous understandings of operations with fractions to add, subtract, multiply, and divide rational numbers.	• Know that there are numbers that are not rational, and approximate them by rational numbers.
Expressions and Equations	• Apply and extend previous understandings of arithmetic to algebraic expressions. • Reason about and solve one-variable equations and inequalities. • Represent and analyze quantitative relationships between dependent and independent variables.	• Use properties of operations to generate equivalent expressions. • Solve real-life and mathematical problems using numerical and algebraic expressions and equations.	• Work with radicals and integer exponents. • Understand the connections between proportional relationships, lines, and linear equations. • Analyze and solve linear equations and pairs of simultaneous linear equations.
Geometry	• Solve real-world and mathematical problems involving area, surface area, and volume.	• Draw, construct and describe geometrical figures and describe the relationships between them. • Solve real-life and mathematical problems involving angle measure, area, surface area, and volume.	• Understand congruence and similarity using physical models, transparencies, or geometry software. • Understand and apply the Pythagorean theorem. • Solve real-world and mathematical problems involving volume of cylinders, cones and spheres
Statistics and Probablilty	• Develop understanding of statistical variability. • Summarize and describe distributions.	• Use random sampling to draw inferences about a population. • Draw informal comparative inferences about two populations. • Investigate chance processes and develop, use, and evaluate probability models.	• Investigate patterns of association in bivariate data.
Functions			• Define, evaluate, and compare functions. • Use functions to model relationships between quantities.

Common Core Standards for Mathematics

Correlations for *HMH Go Math* Grade 6

Standard	Descriptor	Taught	Reinforced
6.RP Ratios and Proportional Relationships			
Understand ratio concepts and use ratio reasoning to solve problems.			
CC.6.RP.1	Understand the concept of a ratio and use ratio language to describe a ratio relationship between two quantities.	SE: 149–150, 152	SE: 153–154, 167–168, 197–198
CC.6.RP.2	Understand the concept of a unit rate $\frac{a}{b}$ associated with a ratio $a{:}b$ with $b \neq 0$, and use rate language in the context of a ratio relationship.	SE: 155–156, 158	SE: 159–160, 167–168
CC.6.RP.3	Use ratio and rate reasoning to solve real-world and mathematical problems, e.g., by reasoning about tables of equivalent ratios, tape diagrams, double number line diagrams, or equations.	SE: 151–152, 157–158, 162–164, 173, 176, 179, 182, 185–188, 193–194, 209–212, 215, 218, 220; *See also below.*	SE: 153–154, 159–160, 165–166, 167–168, 177–178, 183–184, 189–190, 195–196, 197–198, 213–214, 221–222, 223–224; *See also below.*
CC.6.RP.3a	Make tables of equivalent ratios relating quantities with whole-number measurements, find missing values in the tables, and plot the pairs of values on the coordinate plane. Use tables to compare ratios.	SE: 151, 161, 164, 173–176	SE: 153–154, 165–166, 177–178
CC.6.RP.3b	Solve unit rate problems including those involving unit pricing and constant speed.	SE: 155, 157–158, 175, 180–182, 193–194	SE: 159–160, 167–168, 177–178, 183–184, 195–196
CC.6.RP.3c	Find a percent of a quantity as a rate per 100 (e.g., 30% of a quantity means $\frac{30}{100}$ times the quantity); solve problems involving finding the whole, given a part and the percent.	SE: 203–206, 216, 219–220	SE: 207–208, 221–222, 223–224
CC.6.RP.3d	Use ratio reasoning to convert measurement units; manipulate and transform units appropriately when multiplying or dividing quantities.	SE: 185–188, 191–194	SE: 189–190, 195–196, 197–198

Standard	Descriptor	Taught	Reinforced
6.NS The Number System			
Apply and extend previous understandings of multiplication and division to divide fractions by fractions.			
CC.6.NS.1	Interpret and compute quotients of fractions, and solve word problems involving division of fractions by fractions, e.g., by using visual fraction models and equations to represent the problem.	SE: 85–88, 91–94, 97–98	SE: 89–90, 95–96, 99–100, 101–102
Compute fluently with multi-digit numbers and find common factors and multiples.			
CC.6.NS.2	Fluently divide multi-digit numbers using the standard algorithm.	SE: 107–110	SE: 111–112, 135–136
CC.6.NS.3	Fluently add, subtract, multiply, and divide multi-digit decimals using the standard algorithm for each operation.	SE: 113–116, 119–122, 125–128, 131–132	SE: 117–118, 123–124, 129–130, 133–134, 135–136
CC.6.NS.4	Find the greatest common factor of two whole numbers less than or equal to 100 and the least common multiple of two whole numbers less than or equal to 12. Use the distributive property to express a sum of two whole numbers 1–100 with a common factor as a multiple of a sum of two whole numbers with no common factor.	SE: 31–34, 37–38, 79–82	SE: 35–36, 39–40, 41–42, 83–84, 102
Apply and extend previous understandings of numbers to the system of rational numbers.			
CC.6.NS.5	Understand that positive and negative numbers are used together to describe quantities having opposite directions or values (e.g., temperature above/below zero, elevation above/below sea level, credits/debits, positive/negative electric charge); use positive and negative numbers to represent quantities in real-world contexts, explaining the meaning of 0 in each situation.	SE: 7	SE: 11–12, 25–26, 65
CC.6.NS.6	Understand a rational number as a point on the number line. Extend number line diagrams and coordinate axes familiar from previous grades to represent points on the line and in the plane with negative number coordinates.	SE: 7, 10, 47–50, 53, 56, 332, 334; *See also below.*	SE: 12, 17, 25–26, 51–52, 58, 65–66, 335–336, 357–358; *See also below.*
CC.6.NS.6a	Recognize opposite signs of numbers as indicating locations on opposite sides of 0 on the number line; recognize that the opposite of the opposite of a number is the number itself, e.g., $-(-3) = 3$, and that 0 is its own opposite.	SE: 8–10, 54, 56	SE: 11–12, 25–26, 57–58, 66
CC.6.NS.6b	Understand signs of numbers in ordered pairs as indicating locations in quadrants of the coordinate plane; recognize that when two ordered pairs differ only by signs, the locations of the points are related by reflections across one or both axes.	SE: 331, 334, 401–402, 404	SE: 335–336, 357–358, 405–406, 413–414

Standard	Descriptor	Taught	Reinforced
CC.6.NS.6c	Find and position integers and other rational numbers on a horizontal or vertical number line diagram; find and position pairs of integers and other rational numbers on a coordinate plane.	SE: 9–10, 53–54, 56, 331–332, 334	SE: 17, 25–26, 58, 65–66, 335–336, 357–358
CC.6.NS.7	Understand ordering and absolute value of rational numbers.	SE: 13–14, 16, 19, 22, 55–56, 60, 62; *See also below.*	SE: 17–18, 23–24, 25–26, 57–58, 63–64, 65–66; *See also below.*
CC.6.NS.7a	Interpret statements of inequality as statements about the relative position of two numbers on a number line diagram.	SE: 13, 15–16, 59–62	SE: 17–18, 64
CC.6.NS.7b	Write, interpret, and explain statements of order for rational numbers in real-world contexts.	SE: 15–16, 61–62	SE: 17–18, 26, 63–64, 65–66
CC.6.NS.7c	Understand the absolute value of a rational number as its distance from 0 on the number line; interpret absolute value as magnitude for a positive or negative quantity in a real-world situation.	SE: 19–22, 55–56	SE: 23–24, 25–26, 57–58
CC.6.NS.7d	Distinguish comparisons of absolute value from statements about order.	SE: 21–22	SE: 23–24, 25–26
CC.6.NS.8	Solve real-world and mathematical problems by graphing points in all four quadrants of the coordinate plane. Include use of coordinates and absolute value to find distances between points with the same first coordinate or the same second coordinate.	SE: 333–334, 403–404	SE: 335–336, 405–406, 413–414

6.EE Expressions and Equations

Apply and extend previous understandings of arithmetic to algebraic expressions.

Standard	Descriptor	Taught	Reinforced
CC.6.EE.1	Write and evaluate numerical expressions involving whole-number exponents.	SE: 237–240, 243–246, 249–252	SE: 241–242, 247–248, 253–254, 255–256
CC.6.EE.2	Write, read, and evaluate expressions in which letters stand for numbers.	SE: See below.	SE: See below.
CC.6.EE.2a	Write expressions that record operations with numbers and with letters standing for numbers.	SE: 261–262, 265	SE: 266–268, 283–284
CC.6.EE.2b	Identify parts of an expression using mathematical terms (sum, term, product, factor, quotient, coefficient); view one or more parts of an expression as a single entity.	SE: 261, 265, 279–280	SE: 266, 268, 281–282
CC.6.EE.2c	Evaluate expressions at specific values of their variables. Include expressions that arise from formulas used in real-world problems. Perform arithmetic operations, including those involving whole-number exponents, in the conventional order when there are no parentheses to specify a particular order (Order of Operations).	SE: 269–272	SE: 273–274, 283–284, 419

Standard	Descriptor	Taught	Reinforced
CC.6.EE.3	Apply the properties of operations to generate equivalent expressions.	SE: 276–280	SE: 281–282, 283–284
CC.6.EE.4	Identify when two expressions are equivalent (i.e., when the two expressions name the same number regardless of which value is substituted into them).	SE: 263, 265, 275, 280	SE: 266–267, 281–282, 283–284

Reason about and solve one-variable equations and inequalities.

Standard	Descriptor	Taught	Reinforced
CC.6.EE.5	Understand solving an equation or inequality as a process of answering a question: which values from a specified set, if any, make the equation or inequality true? Use substitution to determine whether a given number in a specified set makes an equation or inequality true.	SE: 297, 300, 304–305, 308, 312–313, 316, 319–320, 322	SE: 302, 309, 317–318, 323–324, 343–344
CC.6.EE.6	Use variables to represent numbers and write expressions when solving a real-world or mathematical problem; understand that a variable can represent an unknown number, or, depending on the purpose at hand, any number in a specified set.	SE: 264–265, 298, 300, 303, 306, 308, 311, 316, 321–322	SE: 266–268, 301–302, 309–310, 317–318, 323–324, 343–344
CC.6.EE.7	Solve real-world and mathematical problems by writing and solving equations of the form $x + p = q$ and $px = q$ for cases in which p, q and x are all non-negative rational numbers.	SE: 299–300, 303, 306–308, 314–316, 383–384, 386, 431–432	SE: 301–302, 309–310, 317–318, 343–344, 388, 433–434
CC.6.EE.8	Write an inequality of the form $x > c$ or $x < c$ to represent a constraint or condition in a real-world or mathematical problem. Recognize that inequalities of the form $x > c$ or $x < c$ have infinitely many solutions; represent solutions of such inequalities on number line diagrams.	SE: 319, 321–322	SE: 323–324, 325–326

Represent and analyze quantitative relationships between dependent and independent variables.

Standard	Descriptor	Taught	Reinforced
CC.6.EE.9	Use variables to represent two quantities in a real-world problem that change in relationship to one another; write an equation to express one quantity, thought of as the dependent variable, in terms of the other quantity, thought of as the independent variable. Analyze the relationship between the dependent and independent variables using graphs and tables, and relate these to the equation.	SE: 337–342, 345–348, 351–354	SE: 343–344, 349–350, 355–356, 357–358

6.G Geometry

Solve real-world and mathematical problems involving area, surface area, and volume.

Standard	Descriptor	Taught	Reinforced
CC.6.G.1	Find the area of right triangles, other triangles, special quadrilaterals, and polygons by composing into rectangles or decomposing into triangles and other shapes; apply these techniques in the context of solving real-world and mathematical problems.	SE: 371–374, 377–380, 383–386, 389–392	SE: 375–376, 381–382, 387–388, 393–394, 395–396

Standard	Descriptor	Taught	Reinforced
CC.6.G.2	Find the volume of a right rectangular prism with fractional edge lengths by packing it with unit cubes of the appropriate unit fraction edge lengths, and show that the volume is the same as would be found by multiplying the edge lengths of the prism. Apply the formulas $V = l\,w\,h$ and $V = b\,h$ to find volumes of right rectangular prisms with fractional edge lengths in the context of solving real-world and mathematical problems.	SE: 425–428, 431–432	SE: 429–430, 433–434, 435–436
CC.6.G.3	Draw polygons in the coordinate plane given coordinates for the vertices; use coordinates to find the length of a side joining points with the same first coordinate or the same second coordinate. Apply these techniques in the context of solving real-world and mathematical problems.	SE: 407–410	SE: 411–412, 413–414
CC.6.G.4	Represent three-dimensional figures using nets made up of rectangles and triangles, and use the nets to find the surface area of these figures. Apply these techniques in the context of solving real-world and mathematical problems.	SE: 419–422	SE: 423–424, 435–436
6.SP Statistics and Probability			
Develop understanding of statistical variability.			
CC.6.SP.1	Recognize a statistical question as one that anticipates variability in the data related to the question and accounts for it in the answers.	SE: 469, 473	SE: 474–475
CC.6.SP.2	Understand that a set of data collected to answer a statistical question has a distribution which can be described by its center, spread, and overall shape.	SE: 471, 473	SE: 474–476
CC.6.SP.3	Recognize that a measure of center for a numerical data set summarizes all of its values with a single number, while a measure of variation describes how its values vary with a single number.	SE: 449, 452	SE: 453–454
Summarize and describe distributions.			
CC.6.SP.4	Display numerical data in plots on a number line, including dot plots, histograms, and box plots.	SE: 463, 466, 470, 473, 477–478, 480	SE: 467–468, 474–476, 481–482, 483
CC.6.SP.5a	Summarize numerical data sets in relation to their context, such as by: Reporting the number of observations.	SE: 449, 452, 477–480	SE: 453–454, 481–482
CC.6.SP.5b	Summarize numerical data sets in relation to their context, such as by: Describing the nature of the attribute under investigation, including how it was measured and its units of measurement.	SE: 450, 452, 477, 479–480	SE: 453–454, 481–482

Standard	Descriptor	Taught	Reinforced
CC.6.SP.5c	Summarize numerical data sets in relation to their context, such as by: Giving quantitative measures of center (median and/or mean) and variability (interquartile range and/or mean absolute deviation), as well as describing any overall pattern and any striking deviations from the overall pattern with reference to the context in which the data were gathered.	SE: 449–452, 455–459, 464–466, 472–473, 477, 479–480	SE: 453–454, 460–462, 467–468, 474–476, 481–482, 483–484
CC.6.SP.5d	Summarize numerical data sets in relation to their context, such as by: Relating the choice of measures of center and variability to the shape of the data distribution and the context in which the data were gathered.	SE: 451, 472–473, 477, 479–480	SE: 453–454, 475–476, 481–482

Standard	Descriptor	Citations
MP Mathematical Practices Standards		*The mathematical practices standards are integrated throughout the book. See, for example, the citations below.*
CC.MP.1	**Make sense of problems and persevere in solving them.** Mathematically proficient students start by explaining to themselves the meaning of a problem and looking for entry points to its solution. They analyze givens, constraints, relationships, and goals. They make conjectures about the form and meaning of the solution and plan a solution pathway rather than simply jumping into a solution attempt. They consider analogous problems, and try special cases and simpler forms of the original problem in order to gain insight into its solution. They monitor and evaluate their progress and change course if necessary. Older students might, depending on the context of the problem, transform algebraic expressions or change the viewing window on their graphing calculator to get the information they need. Mathematically proficient students can explain correspondences between equations, verbal descriptions, tables, and graphs or draw diagrams of important features and relationships, graph data, and search for regularity or trends. Younger students might rely on using concrete objects or pictures to help conceptualize and solve a problem. Mathematically proficient students check their answers to problems using a different method, and they continually ask themselves, "Does this make sense?" They can understand the approaches of others to solving complex problems and identify correspondences between different approaches.	36, 97–98, 190, 268, 302, 376, 454

© Houghton Mifflin Harcourt Publishing Company

CC6   Common Core Standards for Mathematics

Standard	Descriptor	Citations
CC.MP.2	**Reason abstractly and quantitatively.** Mathematically proficient students make sense of quantities and their relationships in problem situations. They bring two complementary abilities to bear on problems involving quantitative relationships: the ability to decontextualize—to abstract a given situation and represent it symbolically and manipulate the representing symbols as if they have a life of their own, without necessarily attending to their referents—and the ability to contextualize, to pause as needed during the manipulation process in order to probe into the referents for the symbols involved. Quantitative reasoning entails habits of creating a coherent representation of the problem at hand; considering the units involved; attending to the meaning of quantities, not just how to compute them; and knowing and flexibly using different properties of operations and objects.	64, 90, 193, 254, 320, 382, 462
CC.MP.3	**Construct viable arguments and critique the reasoning of others.** Mathematically proficient students understand and use stated assumptions, definitions, and previously established results in constructing arguments. They make conjectures and build a logical progression of statements to explore the truth of their conjectures. They are able to analyze situations by breaking them into cases, and can recognize and use counterexamples. They justify their conclusions, communicate them to others, and respond to the arguments of others. They reason inductively about data, making plausible arguments that take into account the context from which the data arose. Mathematically proficient students are also able to compare the effectiveness of two plausible arguments, distinguish correct logic or reasoning from that which is flawed, and—if there is a flaw in an argument—explain what it is. Elementary students can construct arguments using concrete referents such as objects, drawings, diagrams, and actions. Such arguments can make sense and be correct, even though they are not generalized or made formal until later grades. Later, students learn to determine domains to which an argument applies. Students at all grades can listen or read the arguments of others, decide whether they make sense, and ask useful questions to clarify or improve the arguments.	24, 112, 208, 248, 318, 406, 468

Standard	Descriptor	Citations
CC.MP.4	**Model with mathematics.** Mathematically proficient students can apply the mathematics they know to solve problems arising in everyday life, society, and the workplace. In early grades, this might be as simple as writing an addition equation to describe a situation. In middle grades, a student might apply proportional reasoning to plan a school event or analyze a problem in the community. By high school, a student might use geometry to solve a design problem or use a function to describe how one quantity of interest depends on another. Mathematically proficient students who can apply what they know are comfortable making assumptions and approximations to simplify a complicated situation, realizing that these may need revision later. They are able to identify important quantities in a practical situation and map their relationships using such tools as diagrams, two—way tables, graphs, flowcharts and formulas. They can analyze those relationships mathematically to draw conclusions. They routinely interpret their mathematical results in the context of the situation and reflect on whether the results make sense, possibly improving the model if it has not served its purpose.	17, 100, 215–216, 249, 324, 385, 468
CC.MP.5	**Use appropriate tools strategically.** Mathematically proficient students consider the available tools when solving a mathematical problem. These tools might include pencil and paper, concrete models, a ruler, a protractor, a calculator, a spreadsheet, a computer algebra system, a statistical package, or dynamic geometry software. Proficient students are sufficiently familiar with tools appropriate for their grade or course to make sound decisions about when each of these tools might be helpful, recognizing both the insight to be gained and their limitations. For example, mathematically proficient high school students analyze graphs of functions and solutions generated using a graphing calculator. They detect possible errors by strategically using estimation and other mathematical knowledge. When making mathematical models, they know that technology can enable them to visualize the results of varying assumptions, explore consequences, and compare predictions with data. Mathematically proficient students at various grade levels are able to identify relevant external mathematical resources, such as digital content located on a website, and use them to pose or solve problems. They are able to use technological tools to explore and deepen their understanding of concepts.	8, 91, 185, 276, 303, 371, 458

Standard	Descriptor	Citations
CC.MP.6	**Attend to precision.** Mathematically proficient students try to communicate precisely to others. They try to use clear definitions in discussion with others and in their own reasoning. They state the meaning of the symbols they choose, including using the equal sign consistently and appropriately. They are careful about specifying units of measure, and labeling axes to clarify the correspondence with quantities in a problem. They calculate accurately and efficiently, express numerical answers with a degree of precision appropriate for the problem context. In the elementary grades, students give carefully formulated explanations to each other. By the time they reach high school they have learned to examine claims and make explicit use of definitions.	13, 93, 214, 242, 336, 424, 452
CC.MP.7	**Look for and make use of structure.** Mathematically proficient students look closely to discern a pattern or structure. Young students, for example, might notice that three and seven more is the same amount as seven and three more, or they may sort a collection of shapes according to how many sides the shapes have. Later, students will see 7×8 equals the well remembered $7 \times 5 + 7 \times 3$, in preparation for learning about the distributive property. In the expression $x^2 + 9x + 14$, older students can see the 14 as 2×7 and the 9 as $2 + 7$. They recognize the significance of an existing line in a geometric figure and can use the strategy of drawing an auxiliary line for solving problems. They also can step back for an overview and shift perspective. They can see complicated things, such as some algebraic expressions, as single objects or as being composed of several objects. For example, they can see $5 - 3(x - y)^2$ as 5 minus a positive number times a square and use that to realize that its value cannot be more than 5 for any real numbers x and y.	18, 118, 214, 263–264, 311, 430, 471
CC.MP.8	**Look for and express regularity in repeated reasoning.** Mathematically proficient students notice if calculations are repeated, and look both for general methods and for shortcuts. Upper elementary students might notice when dividing 25 by 11 that they are repeating the same calculations over and over again, and conclude they have a repeating decimal. By paying attention to the calculation of slope as they repeatedly check whether points are on the line through (1, 2) with slope 3, middle school students might abstract the equation $\frac{(y-2)}{(x-1)} = 3$. Noticing the regularity in the way terms cancel when expanding $(x-1)(x+1)$, $(x-1)(x^2+x+1)$, and $(x-1)(x^3+x^2+x+1)$ might lead them to the general formula for the sum of a geometric series. As they work to solve a problem, mathematically proficient students maintain oversight of the process, while attending to the details. They continually evaluate the reasonableness of their intermediate results.	19, 125, 149, 237, 242, 310, 378, 462

Succeeding with HMH Go Math

Actively participate in your learning with your write-in Student Edition. Explore concepts, take notes, answer questions, and complete your homework right in your textbook!

LESSON 1.1 Identifying Integers and Their Opposites

COMMON CORE 6.NS.5
Understand that positive and negative numbers are used together to describe quantities having opposite directions or values.... *Also* 6.NS.6, 6.NS.6a, 6.NS.6c

? ESSENTIAL QUESTION
How do you identify an integer and its opposite?

EXPLORE ACTIVITY 1 Real World   **COMMON CORE 6.NS.5, 6.NS.6**

Positive and Negative Numbers

Positive numbers are numbers greater than 0. Positive numbers can be written with or without a plus sign; for example, 3 is the same as +3. **Negative numbers** are numbers less than 0. Negative numbers must always be written with a negative sign.

The number 0 is neither positive nor negative.

−5 −4 −3 −2 −1 0 1 2 3 4 5
Negative integers   Positive integers

The elevation of a location describes its height above or below sea level, which has elevation 0. Elevations below sea level are represented by negative numbers, and elevations above sea level are represented by positive numbers.

A The table shows the elevations of several locations in a state park. Graph the locations on the number line according to their elevations.

Location	Little Butte A	Cradle Creek B	Dinosaur Valley C	Mesa Ridge D	Juniper Trail E
Elevation (ft)	5	−5	−9	8	−3

−10 −9 −8 −7 −6 −5 −4 −3 −2 −1 0 1 2 3 4 5 6 7 8 9 10

B What point on the number line represents sea level? _____

C Which location is closest to sea level? How do you know?

Representing Rates with Tables and Graphs

You can use tables and graphs to represent real-world problems involving equivalent rates.

EXAMPLE 1 Real World   **COMMON CORE 6.RP.3a, 6.RP.3b**

The Webster family is taking an express train to Washington, D.C. The train travels at a constant speed and makes the trip in 2 hours.

A Complete the table to show the distance the train travels in various amounts of time.

STEP 1 Write a ratio of distance to time to find the rate.

$$\frac{distance}{time} = \frac{120 \text{ miles}}{2 \text{ hours}} = \frac{60 \text{ miles}}{1 \text{ hour}} = 60 \text{ miles per hour}$$

STEP 2 Use the unit rate to complete the table.

Time (h)	2	3	3.5	4	5.5
Distance (mi)	120	180	210	240	330

B Graph the information from the table.

STEP 1 Write ordered pairs. Use Time as the x-coordinates and Distance as the y-coordinates.

(2, 120), (3, 180), (3.5, 210), (4, 240), (5, 300)

STEP 2 Graph the ordered pairs and connect the points.

YOUR TURN

3. A shower uses 12 gallons of water in 3 minutes. Complete the table a...

Time (min)	2	
Water used (gal)		

EXPLORE ACTIVITY Real World

Explore Activities help you develop a deeper understanding of math concepts.

YOUR TURN

Your Turn exercises check your understanding of new concepts.

Math On the Spot

⟳ my.hrw.com

Scan QR codes with your smart phone to watch Math On the Spot tutorial videos for every example in the book!

UNIT 2 MIXED REVIEW

COMMON CORE

Assessment Readiness

Check your mastery of concepts through review and practice for high stakes standardized tests.

my.hrw.com

Practice skills and complete your homework online with the Personal Math Trainer. Your Personal Math Trainer provides a variety of learning aids that develop and improve your understanding of math concepts including videos, guided examples, and step-by-step solutions.

Personal Math Trainer

Online Assessment and Intervention

my.hrw.com

The Interactive Student Edition provides additional videos, activities, tools, and learning aids to support you as you study!

Math On the Spot

my.hrw.com

Math On the Spot video tutorials provide step-by-step instruction of the math concepts covered in each example.

Animated Math activities let you interactively explore and practice key math concepts and skills.

Animated Math

my.hrw.com

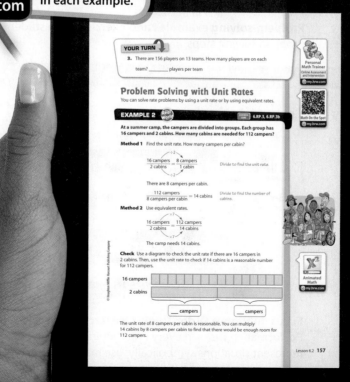

YOUR TURN

3. There are 156 players on 13 teams. How many players are on each team? _____ players per team

Problem Solving with Unit Rates

You can solve rate problems by using a unit rate or by using equivalent rates.

EXAMPLE 2 Real World   6.RP.3, 6.RP.3b

At a summer camp, the campers are divided into groups. Each group has 16 campers and 2 cabins. How many cabins are needed for 112 campers?

Method 1 Find the unit rate. How many campers per cabin?

$$\frac{16 \text{ campers}}{2 \text{ cabins}} = \frac{8 \text{ campers}}{1 \text{ cabin}}$$ Divide to find the unit rate.

There are 8 campers per cabin.

$$\frac{112 \text{ campers}}{8 \text{ campers per cabin}} = 14 \text{ cabins}$$ Divide to find the number of cabins.

Method 2 Use equivalent rates.

$$\frac{16 \text{ campers}}{2 \text{ cabins}} = \frac{112 \text{ campers}}{14 \text{ cabins}}$$

The camp needs 14 cabins.

Check Use a diagram to check the unit rate if there are 16 campers in 2 cabins. Then, use the unit rate to check if 14 cabins is a reasonable number for 112 campers.

16 campers

2 cabins

___ campers   ___ campers

The unit rate of 8 campers per cabin is reasonable. You can multiply 14 cabins by 8 campers per cabin to find that there would be enough room for 112 campers.

Lesson 6.2 **157**

Standards for Mathematical Practice

The topics described in the Standards for Mathematical Content will vary from year to year. However, the *way* in which you learn, study, and think about mathematics will not. The Standards for Mathematical Practice describe skills that you will use in all of your math courses. These pages show some features of your book that will help you gain these skills and use them to master this year's topics.

MP.1 Make sense of problems and persevere in solving them.

Mathematically proficient students start by explaining to themselves the meaning of a problem… They analyze givens, constraints, relationships, and goals. They make conjectures about the form… of the solution and plan a solution pathway…

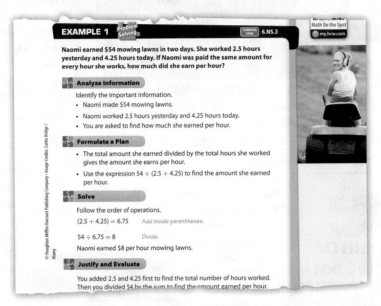

Problem-solving examples and exercises lead students through problem solving steps.

MP.2 Reason abstractly and quantitatively.

Mathematically proficient students… bring two complementary abilities to bear on problems…: the ability to decontextualize— to abstract a given situation and represent it symbolically… and the ability to contextualize, to pause… in order to probe into the referents for the symbols involved.

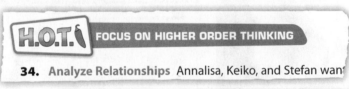

Focus on Higher Order Thinking exercises in every lesson and **Performance Tasks** in every unit require you to use logical reasoning, represent situations symbolically, use mathematical models to solve problems, and state your answers in terms of a problem context.

MP.3 Construct viable arguments and critique the reasoning of others.

Mathematically proficient students... justify their conclusions, [and]... distinguish correct... reasoning from that which is flawed.

Reflect

1. **Critique Reasoning** Jo says she can find the percent equivaler multiplying the percent equivalent of $\frac{1}{4}$ by 3. How can you use bar model to support this claim?

 **ESSENTIAL QUESTION CHECK-IN**

Essential Question Check-in and **Reflect** in every lesson ask you to evaluate statements, explain relationships, apply mathematical principles, make conjectures, construct arguments, and justify your reasoning.

MP.4 Model with mathematics.

Mathematically proficient students can apply... mathematics... to... problems... in everyday life, society, and the workplace.

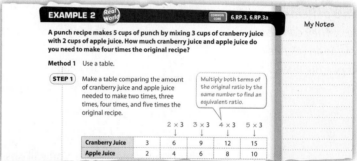

EXAMPLE 2 Real World   COMMON CORE 6.RP.3, 6.RP.3a   My Notes

A punch recipe makes 5 cups of punch by mixing 3 cups of cranberry juice with 2 cups of apple juice. How much cranberry juice and apple juice do you need to make four times the original recipe?

Method 1 Use a table.

STEP 1 Make a table comparing the amount of cranberry juice and apple juice needed to make two times, three times, four times, and five times the original recipe.

> Multiply both terms of the original ratio by the same number to find an equivalent ratio.

		2 × 3	3 × 3	4 × 3	5 × 3
Cranberry Juice	3	6	9	12	15
Apple Juice	2	4	6	8	10

Real-world examples and **mathematical modeling** apply mathematics to other disciplines and real-world contexts such as science and business.

MP.5 Use appropriate tools strategically.

Mathematically proficient students consider the available tools when solving a... problem... [and] are... able to use technological tools to explore and deepen their understanding...

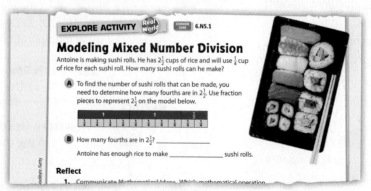

EXPLORE ACTIVITY Real World   COMMON CORE 6.NS.1

Modeling Mixed Number Division

Antoine is making sushi rolls. He has $2\frac{1}{2}$ cups of rice and will use $\frac{1}{4}$ cup of rice for each sushi roll. How many sushi rolls can he make?

A To find the number of sushi rolls that can be made, you need to determine how many fourths are in $2\frac{1}{2}$. Use fraction pieces to represent $2\frac{1}{2}$ on the model below.

B How many fourths are in $2\frac{1}{2}$? _____

Antoine has enough rice to make _____ sushi rolls.

Reflect

1. Communicate Mathematical Ideas Which mathematical operation

Exploration Activities in lessons use concrete and technological tools, such as manipulatives or graphing calculators, to explore mathematical concepts.

MP.6 Attend to precision.

Mathematically proficient students... communicate precisely... with others and in their own reasoning... [They] give carefully formulated explanations...

31. Communicate Mathematical Ideas Write an example of an that cannot be simplified, and explain how you know that it simplified.

Precision refers not only to the correctness of calculations but also to the proper use of mathematical language and symbols. **Communicate Mathematical Ideas** exercises and **Key Vocabulary** highlighted for each module and unit help you learn and use the language of math to communicate mathematics precisely.

MP.7 Look for and make use of structure.

Mathematically proficient students... look closely to discern a pattern or structure... They can also step back for an overview and shift perspectives.

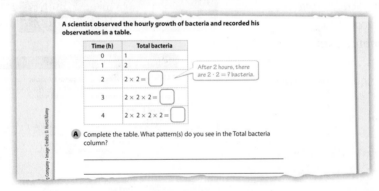

A scientist observed the hourly growth of bacteria and recorded his observations in a table.

Time (h)	Total bacteria
0	1
1	2
2	$2 \times 2 = \square$
3	$2 \times 2 \times 2 = \square$
4	$2 \times 2 \times 2 \times 2 = \square$

After 2 hours, there are $2 \cdot 2 = ?$ bacteria.

A Complete the table. What pattern(s) do you see in the Total bacteria column?

Throughout the lessons, you will observe regularity in mathematical structures in order to make generalizations and make connections between related problems. For example, you can use what you known about multiplication to understand how to use exponents.

MP.8 Look for and express regularity in repeated reasoning.

Mathematically proficient students... look both for general methods and for shortcuts... [and] maintain oversight of the process, while attending to the details.

46. Look for a Pattern Find the values of the powers in the follo pattern: 10^1, 10^2, 10^3, 10^4.... Describe the pattern, and use it 10^6 without using multiplication.

25. Justify Reasoning Determine whether $3x + 12 + x$ is e $4(3 + x)$. Use properties of operations to justify your ans

Reflect

8. Make a Conjecture Use the pattern in the table to make a c about how you can use multiplication to divide one fraction

You will look for repeated calculations and mathematical patterns in examples and exercises. Recognizing patterns can help you make generalizations and obtain a better understanding of the underlying mathematics.

HMH Go Math

Teachers Edition, Grade 6

Contents in Brief

Teacher Material

Selected Answers are provided at the back of the Student Edition.

Review Test

Selected Response

1. Al used the expression $8 + 25 \times 2 - 45$ to find how many CDs he has. How many CDs does he have?

Ⓐ 3   Ⓒ 21
Ⓑ 13   Ⓓ 103

2. Jamie baked 24 biscuits. Her sister Mia ate 3 biscuits, and her brother David ate 2 biscuits. Which expression can Jamie use to find how many biscuits are left?

Ⓐ $24 + (3 + 2)$ Ⓒ $(24 - 3) + 2$
Ⓑ $24 - (3 + 2)$ Ⓓ $24 - (3 - 2)$

3. What is the unknown number in sequence 2 in the chart?

Sequence Number	1	2	3	5	7
Sequence 1	3	6	9	15	21
Sequence 2	15	30	45	75	?

Ⓐ 63   Ⓒ 105
Ⓑ 90   Ⓓ 150

4. Patel hopes to be one of the first fans to get into the stadium for the baseball game because the first 30,000 fans will receive a baseball cap. Which shows 30,000 as a whole number multiplied by a power of ten?

Ⓐ 3×10^1 Ⓒ 3×10^3
Ⓑ 3×10^2 Ⓓ 3×10^4

5. The Davis family pays $200,000 for a new house. They make a down payment that is $\frac{1}{10}$ of the price of the house. How much is the down payment?

Ⓐ $20   Ⓒ $2,000
Ⓑ $200   Ⓓ $20,000

6. Jackie found a rock that has a mass of 78.852 grams. What is the mass of the rock rounded to the nearest tenth?

Ⓐ 78.85 grams   Ⓒ 79 grams
Ⓑ 78.9 grams   Ⓓ 80 grams

7. A company manufactures 295 toy cars each day. How many toy cars does the company manufacture in 34 days?

Ⓐ 3,065   Ⓒ 10,065
Ⓑ 7,610   Ⓓ 10,030

8. There are 6 buses transporting students to a baseball game, with 32 students on each bus. Each row at the baseball stadium seats 8 students. If the students fill up all of the rows, how many rows of seats will the students need altogether?

Ⓐ 22   Ⓒ 24
Ⓑ 23   Ⓓ 1,536

9. The portions of a house that need to be heated can be modeled by one rectangular prism with a length of 45 feet, a width of 20 feet, and a height of 18 feet, and a second rectangular prism with a base area of 350 square feet and a height of 9 feet. What is the total volume?

Ⓐ 12500 cubic feet
Ⓑ 16,200 cubic feet
Ⓒ 16,550 cubic feet
Ⓓ 19,350 cubic feet

10. Marci mailed 9 letters at the post office. Each letter weighed 3.5 ounces. What was the total weight of the letters?

Ⓐ 33.5 ounces   Ⓒ 31.5 ounces
Ⓑ 32.5 ounces   Ⓓ 27.5 ounces

11. Denise, Keith, and Tim live in the same neighborhood. Denise lives 0.3 mile from Keith. The distance that Tim and Keith live from each other is 0.2 times as great as the distance between Denise and Keith. How far from each other do Tim and Keith live?

Ⓐ 0.6 mile   Ⓒ 0.1 mile
Ⓑ 0.5 mile   Ⓓ 0.06 mile

12. Madison needs to buy enough meat to make 1,000 hamburgers for the company picnic. Each hamburger will weigh 0.25 pound. How many pounds of hamburger meat should Madison buy?

Ⓐ 2.5 pounds   Ⓒ 250 pounds
Ⓑ 25 pounds   Ⓓ 2,500 pounds

Mini-Tasks

13. Rayna wrote 260,980 as $(2 \times 100,000) + (6 \times 10,000) + (9 \times 1,000) + (8 \times 100)$. What error did Rayna make? Write the correct expanded form.

She did not use the correct place values in the expanded form for the numbers in the hundreds and tens places; $(2 \times 100,000) + (6 \times 10,000) + (9 \times 1,000) + (8 \times 10)$

14. The highest scores at a gymnastics meet were 9.675, 9.25, 9.325, and 9.5. Write the scores in order from least to greatest.

9.25, 9.325, 9.5, 9.675

15. Ann and Joe's father donated $3 for every lap they swam in a swim-a-thon. Ann swam 21 laps, and Joe swam 15 laps. Use the Distributive Property to find the amount of money their father donated.

Sample answer: The Distributive Property says that $3 \times (21 + 15) = (3 \times 21) + (3 \times 15) = 63 + 45 = 108$. He donated $108.

16. A grain of sand has a diameter of 0.049 millimeter. Write 0.049 in words.

forty-nine thousandths

Performance Task

17. Jennifer has $12 to spend on lunch and the roller rink. Admission to the roller rink is $5.75. Jennifer estimates that she can buy a large drink and a turkey sandwich and still have enough money to get into the rink. Do you agree? Support your answer.

Sandwiches		Drinks	
Tuna	$3.95	Small	$1.29
Turkey	$4.85	Medium	$1.59
Grilled Cheese	$3.25	Large	$1.79

No; sample answer: I rounded each amount to the nearest dollar. The admission is about $6, the large drink is about $2, and the turkey sandwich is about $5. $6 + $2 + $5 = $13, which is more than she has.

Grade 5

Review Test

Use this test to ensure that your students have mastered the concepts from the previous course.

Scoring Guide for Performance Task

2 points for correctly rounding amounts from the table.

2 points for correctly finding an estimated cost and comparing it to the amount Jennifer has.

2 points for describing the reasoning used to solve the problem.

Common Core Standards

Items	Standards	Items	Standards
1	5.OA.1	10	5.NBT.7
2	5.OA.2	11	5.NBT.7
3	5.OA.3	12	5.NBT.2
4	5.NBT.2	13	5.NBT.1
5	5.NBT.1	14	5.NBT.3
6	5.NBT.4	15	5.NBT.6
7	5.NBT.5	16	5.NBT.3a
8	5.NBT.6	17	5.NBT.7
9	5.MD.5c		

Review Test

Personal Math Trainer
Online Assessment and Intervention
@ my.hrw.com

Selected Response

1. Charles bought $\frac{7}{8}$ foot of electrical wire and $\frac{5}{6}$ foot of copper wire for his science project. What is the least common denominator of the fractions?

Ⓐ 14 Ⓒ 24
Ⓑ 18 Ⓓ 48

2. Tom jogged $\frac{3}{5}$ mile on Monday and $\frac{2}{6}$ mile on Tuesday. How much farther did Tom jog on Monday than on Tuesday?

Ⓐ $\frac{1}{30}$ mile Ⓒ $\frac{8}{30}$ mile
Ⓑ $\frac{3}{15}$ mile Ⓓ $\frac{14}{15}$ mile

3. Three fences on a ranch measure $\frac{15}{16}$ mile, $\frac{7}{8}$ mile, and $\frac{7}{16}$ mile. Which is the best estimate of the total length of all three fences?

Ⓐ $1\frac{1}{2}$ miles Ⓒ $2\frac{1}{2}$ miles
Ⓑ 2 miles Ⓓ 3 miles

4. Lawrence bought $\frac{2}{3}$ pound of roast beef. He used $\frac{3}{4}$ of it to make a sandwich. How much roast beef did Lawrence use for his sandwich? You may use a model to help you solve the problem.

Ⓐ $\frac{5}{12}$ pound Ⓒ $\frac{5}{7}$ pound
Ⓑ $\frac{1}{2}$ pound Ⓓ $\frac{6}{7}$ pound

5. Sarah built a table using 6 pieces of wood that were each $3\frac{3}{4}$ inches wide. How wide was the table?

Ⓐ $18\frac{1}{8}$ inches Ⓒ $21\frac{1}{4}$ inches
Ⓑ $18\frac{3}{4}$ inches Ⓓ $22\frac{1}{2}$ inches

6. Vanessa made 6 sandwiches for a party and cut them all into fourths. How many $\frac{1}{4}$-sandwich pieces did she have?

Ⓐ $1\frac{1}{2}$ Ⓒ 4
Ⓑ $2\frac{1}{4}$ Ⓓ 24

7. Dr. Watson combines 400 mL of detergent, 800 mL of alcohol, and 1,500 mL of water. How many liters of solution does he have?

Ⓐ 2.7 liters Ⓒ 270 liters
Ⓑ 27 liters Ⓓ 2,700 liters

8. Give the most descriptive name for the figure.

Ⓐ square Ⓒ parallelogram
Ⓑ rectangle Ⓓ rhombus

9. Find the volume of the rectangular prism.

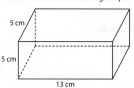

5 cm
5 cm
13 cm

Ⓐ 310 cm³ Ⓒ 325 cm³
Ⓑ 184 cm³ Ⓓ 23 cm³

10. Which ordered pair describes the location of Point A?

Ⓐ (0, 2) Ⓒ (4, 0)
Ⓑ (2, 4) Ⓓ (4, 2)

11. Which ordered pair describes the location of Point A?

Ⓐ (0, 5) Ⓒ (5, 5)
Ⓑ (5, 0) Ⓓ (1, 5)

Mini-Tasks

12. When Bruce started bowling, he won $\frac{1}{4}$ of the games he played. Within six months, he was winning $\frac{7}{16}$ of his games. If he improves at the same rate, what fraction of his games should he expect to win after another six months?

$\frac{5}{8}$

13. Gina wants to ship 3 books that weigh $2\frac{7}{16}$ pounds, $1\frac{7}{8}$ pounds and $\frac{1}{2}$ pound. The maximum weight she can ship is 6 pounds. Estimate to see if Gina can ship all 3 books. Explain your answer.

Sample answer: Yes. I rounded to $2\frac{1}{2}$, 2, and $\frac{1}{2}$. $2\frac{1}{2} + 2 + \frac{1}{2} = 5$ pounds, which is less than the actual weight of 6 pounds.

14. How much trail mix will each person get if 5 people share $\frac{1}{2}$ pound of trail mix?

$\frac{1}{10}$ of a pound

15. Write a story to represent the division problem $6 \div \frac{1}{3}$.

Sample answer: A ribbon is 6 feet long and is cut into pieces that are $\frac{1}{3}$ foot long. How many pieces are there?

16. What is the volume in cubic centimeters of the solid?

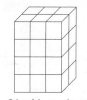

24 cubic centimeters

Performance Task

17. Shia measured the thickness of some buttons. She graphed the results in a line plot.

x x x
x x x
x x x
$\frac{1}{16}$ $\frac{1}{8}$ $\frac{1}{4}$
Button thicknesses (in.)

Part A: Suppose Shia makes a stack of all the buttons. How tall will the stack be?

$1\frac{5}{16}$ in.

Part B: Suppose Shia wants the stack to be 2 inches high. How many buttons that are $\frac{1}{16}$ inch thick must be added to the stack of buttons?

11 buttons

Common Core Standards

Items	Standards	Items	Standards
1	5.NF.1	10	5.G.1
2	5.NF.1	11	5.G.1
3	5.NF.2	12	5.NF.1
4	5.NF.4	13	5.NF.2
5	5.NF.6	14	5.NF.7
6	5.NF.7	15	5.NF.7
7	5.MD.1	16	5.MD.4
8	5.G.4	17	5.MD.2
9	5.MD.5		

Scoring Guide for Performance Task

A. 2 points for correctly reading data from the dot plot.
2 points for correctly finding the height of the stack of buttons.

B. 2 points for correctly finding the number of buttons that must be added to the stack.

COMMON CORE

GRADE 6 PART 1

Benchmark Test

Personal Math Trainer
my.hrw.com
Online Assessment and Intervention

Selected Response

1. Suppose you have developed a scale that indicates the brightness of sunlight. Each category in the table is 9 times brighter than the category above it. For example, a day that is dazzling is 9 times brighter than a day that is radiant. How many times brighter is a dazzling day than an illuminated day?

Sunlight Intensity

Category	Brightness
Dim	2
Illuminated	3
Radiant	4
Dazzling	5

- (A) 2 times brighter
- (B) 729 times brighter
- (C) 81 times brighter
- (D) 9 times brighter

2. Which group of numbers is in order from least to greatest?

- (A) $2.58, 2\frac{5}{8}, 2.6, 2\frac{2}{3}$
- (B) $2\frac{2}{3}, 2\frac{5}{8}, 2.6, 2.58$
- (C) $2\frac{5}{8}, 2\frac{2}{3}, 2.6, 2.58$
- (D) $2.58, 2.6, 2\frac{5}{8}, 2\frac{2}{3}$

3. Which temperature is coldest?

- (A) $-13°F$
- (C) $-20°F$
- (B) $20°F$
- (D) $13°F$

4. Patricia paid $385 for 5 nights at a hotel. Find the unit rate.

- (A) $\frac{\$77}{1 \text{ night}}$
- (C) $\frac{\$385}{1 \text{ night}}$
- (B) $\frac{\$154}{1 \text{ night}}$
- (D) $\frac{\$39}{1 \text{ night}}$

5. The fuel for a chain saw is a mix of oil and gasoline. The label says to mix 6 ounces of oil with 16 gallons of gasoline. How much oil would you use if you had 32 gallons of gasoline?

- (A) 3 ounces
- (C) 18 ounces
- (B) 12 ounces
- (D) 85.3 ounces

6. Lee is putting together fruit baskets for gifts. He has 18 apples, 24 pears, and 30 oranges. What is the greatest number of fruit baskets he can make if he uses all the fruit and each basket is the same?

- (A) 2 baskets
- (C) 4 baskets
- (B) 3 baskets
- (D) 6 baskets

7. It takes light about 134 milliseconds to travel the distance around Earth's Equator. How many seconds is this?

- (A) 0.000134 sec
- (C) 0.134 sec
- (B) 0.0134 sec
- (D) 1.34 sec

8. From the beginning of cross-country season to the end, Tisha reduced her time by 17%, Anchara reduced hers by $\frac{1}{6}$, Juanita reduced hers by $\frac{4}{25}$, and Julia reduced hers from 16:00 to 13:30. Who reduced her time by the greatest percent?

- (A) Tisha
- (C) Juanita
- (B) Anchara
- (D) Julia

9. A stack of blocks is 15.2 inches tall. If there are 10 blocks stacked one on top of the other, how tall is each block?

- (A) 1.62 inches
- (C) 1.72 inches
- (B) 1.52 inches
- (D) 5.2 inches

10. The ratio of students in Jaíme's class who have a dog or cat at home to those who don't is 12 : 8. What percent of the class do NOT have a dog or cat at home?

- (A) $33\frac{1}{3}$%
- (C) 60%
- (B) 40%
- (D) $66\frac{2}{3}$%

11. Ninety percent of a school's students, or 540 students, attended a school assembly. How many students are there at the school?

- (A) 486 students
- (C) 600 students
- (B) 594 students
- (D) 621 students

12. Find the quotient $9\frac{3}{5} \div \frac{8}{15}$.

- (A) 2
- (C) $16\frac{7}{8}$
- (B) 18
- (D) $18\frac{3}{4}$

13. Find the product 4.51×3.4.

- (A) 153.34
- (C) 7.91
- (B) 1.5334
- (D) 15.334

14. Jorge is building a table out of boards that are 3.75 inches wide. He wants the table to be at least 36 inches wide. What is the least number of boards he can use?

- (A) 9
- (C) 10
- (B) 9.6
- (D) 135

Mini-Tasks

15. Nikita is making spaghetti sauce and pizzas for a large party. Her spaghetti sauce recipe calls for $1\frac{3}{4}$ cups of tomato paste, and her pizza recipe uses $\frac{2}{3}$ cup of tomato paste per pizza. She will triple her spaghetti sauce recipe and make 6 pizzas. Write and evaluate an expression for how many $\frac{3}{4}$ cup cans of tomato paste she will need in all.

$$\left(3 \cdot 1\frac{3}{4} + 6 \cdot \frac{2}{3}\right) \div \frac{3}{4} = 12\frac{1}{3},$$

13 cans.

16. Explain how you can use multiplication to find the quotient $\frac{3}{4} \div \frac{3}{16}$. Then evaluate the expression.

Multiply by the reciprocal of the divisor: $\frac{3}{4} \div \frac{3}{16} = \frac{3}{4} \times \frac{16}{3} = 4$

17. A chef has 6 cups of berries and will use $\frac{2}{3}$ cup of berries for each serving of fruit salad. How many servings can be made?

9 servings

Performance Task

18. School A has 480 students and 16 classrooms. School B has 192 students and 12 classrooms.

Part A: What is the ratio of students to classrooms at School A?

Part B: What is the ratio of students to classrooms at School B?

Part C: How many students would have to transfer from School A to School B for the ratios of students to classrooms at both schools to be the same? Explain your reasoning.

Part A: 30 students to 1 classroom

Part B: 16 students to 1 classroom

Part C: 96 students would have to transfer from School A to School B. Since there are 28 classrooms and 672 students at both schools, the ratio of students to classrooms should be 24 : 1. There should be 16 × 24 or 384 students at School A, and 12 × 24 or 288 students at School B.

Grade 6

Benchmark Test

Use this test to assess students' mastery of topics in this course. The test can be used to assist with placement or as a cumulative review before high-stakes tests.

Scoring Guide for Performance Task

A. 1 point for correctly identifying the ratio of students to classrooms at School A.

B. 1 point for correctly identifying the ratio of students to classrooms at School B.

C. 1 point for identifying the ratio of the total number of students to the total number of classrooms. **1 point each** for finding the correct number of students at each school after the transfer. **1 point** for finding the number of students who must transfer.

Common Core Standards

Items	Standards	Items	Standards
1	6.EE.1	10	6.RP.1
2	6.NS.7	11	6.RP.3c
3	6.NS.5	12	6.NS.1
4	6.RP.2	13	6.NS.3
5	6.RP.3	14	6.NS.3
6	6.NS.4	15	6.NS.1
7	6.RP.3d	16	6.NS.1
8	6.RP.3c	17	6.NS.1
9	6.NS.3	18	6.RP.1

Benchmark Test

Personal Math Trainer
Online Assessment and Intervention
@ my.hrw.com

Selected Response

1. Kahlil is recording a beat for a song that he is working on. He wants the length of the beat to be more than 10 seconds long. His friend tells him the beat needs to be 5 seconds longer than that to match the lyrics he has written.

Write an inequality to represent the beat's length. Give three possible beat lengths that satisfy the inequality.

- Ⓐ $t > 5$; 16, 21, 22
- Ⓑ $t > 15$; 16, 21, 22
- Ⓒ $t < 15$; 4, 3, 2
- Ⓓ $t < 10$; 4, 3, 2

2. Write an expression for the missing value in the table.

Tom's Age	Kim's Age
10	13
11	14
12	15
a	?

- Ⓐ $a + 1$
- Ⓒ $a + 3$
- Ⓑ $a + 15$
- Ⓓ $a + 10$

3. What is the area of the polygon?

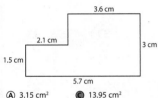

- Ⓐ 3.15 cm²
- Ⓒ 13.95 cm²
- Ⓑ 10.8 cm²
- Ⓓ 1395 cm²

4. A plant's height is 1.4 times its age. Write an equation for this situation.

- Ⓐ h = plant's height; y = plant's age; $h = 1.4y$
- Ⓑ h = plant's age; y = plant's height; $h = 1.4y$
- Ⓒ h = plant's height; y = plant's age; $y = 1.4h$
- Ⓓ h = plant's height; y = plant's age; $1.4 = hy$

5. A rectangular box is $8\frac{1}{2}$ inches long, $5\frac{1}{4}$ inches wide, and 4 inches high. What is its volume?

- Ⓐ 160 cubic inches
- Ⓑ 168 cubic inches
- Ⓒ $178\frac{1}{2}$ cubic inches
- Ⓓ 180 cubic inches

6. Write the phrase as an algebraic expression.

4 times the sum of a number and 20

- Ⓐ $20 \div y$
- Ⓒ $4(y + 20)$
- Ⓑ $20 + y$
- Ⓓ $4y - 20y$

7. Wilson bought gift cards for some lawyers and their assistants. Each lawyer got a gift card worth ℓ dollars. Each assistant got a gift card worth a dollars. There are 14 lawyers. Each lawyer has 3 assistants. The expression for the total cost of the gift cards is $14\ell + 42a$. Write an expression that is equivalent to the given expression.

- Ⓐ $14(\ell + 2a)$
- Ⓒ $14(\ell + 42a)$
- Ⓑ $14(\ell + 3a)$
- Ⓓ $42(\ell + 3a)$

8. At the beginning of the year, Jason had $120 in his savings account. Each month, he added $15 to his account. Write an expression for the amount of money in Jason's savings account each month. Then use the expression to find the amount of money in his account at the end of the year.

Month	January	February	March	m
Amount	$135	$150	$165	$?

- Ⓐ $120 + 12m$; $264
- Ⓑ $135 + 15m$; $315
- Ⓒ $135 + m$; $147
- Ⓓ $15m + 120$; $300

9. Which question is a statistical question?

- Ⓐ What are the ages of schools in the school district?
- Ⓑ How old is the middle school building?
- Ⓒ How many classrooms are there in the elementary school building?
- Ⓓ How many daily class periods are there in the high school?

10. Find the interquartile range for the data set: 10, 3, 8, 6, 9, 12, 13.

- Ⓐ 12
- Ⓒ 6
- Ⓑ 8
- Ⓓ 7

Mini-Tasks

11. Mike was in charge of collecting contributions for the Food Bank. He received contributions of $80, $70, $60, $40, and $80. Find the mean and the median of the contributions.

mean: $66; median: $70

12. One side of trapezoid is 10 inches. The side parallel to this is twice as long as this side. The height is half as long as the given side length. Find the area of the trapezoid.

75 square inches

13. Find the perimeter of the rectangle with vertices at $R(-2, 3)$, $S(4, 3)$, $T(4, -1)$ and $U(-2, -1)$.

20 units

14. Brian is ordering tickets online for a concert. The price of each ticket for the concert is t dollars. For online orders, there is an additional charge of $11 per ticket, and a service charge of $14 for the entire order. The cost for 7 tickets can be represented by the expression $7(t + 11) + 14$.

Write two expressions equivalent to the cost expression. Then, find the total cost of Brian's online order if the price of each ticket for this concert is $33.

$7t + 77 + 14$; $7t + 91$; $322

Performance Task

15. Jillian wants to find the surface area of a pyramid. The base is a square with with sides that are 4 inches long. The other faces are isosceles triangles. The ratio of the height of each triangle to its base is 3 : 2.

Part A: Give the base length and the height of each triangular face.

Part B: Find the combined area of the triangular faces.

Part C: Find the surface area of the pyramid.

Part A: base: 4 inches; height: 6 inches

Part B: 48 square inches

Part C: 64 square inches

Common Core Standards

Items	Standards		Items	Standards
1	6.EE.8		9	6.SP.1
2	6.EE.2		10	6.SP.2
3	6.G.1		11	6.SP.3
4	6.EE.9		12	6.G.1
5	6.G.2		13	6.NS.8
6	6.EE.2a		14	6.EE.3
7	6.EE.4		15	6.G.4
8	6.EE.6			

Scoring Guide for Performance Task

A. 1 point for correctly giving the base length and height.

B. 2 points for correctly finding the combined areas of the faces.

C. 3 points for correctly finding the surface area.

UNIT 1

Numbers

Contents

Unit Pacing Guide

45-Minute Classes

Module 1

DAY 1	DAY 2	DAY 3	DAY 4	DAY 5
Lesson 1.1	Lesson 1.1	Lesson 1.1	Lesson 1.2	Lesson 1.2

DAY 6	DAY 7	DAY 8	DAY 9	
Lesson 1.3	Lesson 1.3	Lesson 1.3	Ready to Go On? Assessment Readiness	

Module 2

DAY 1	DAY 2	DAY 3	DAY 4	DAY 5
Lesson 2.1	Lesson 2.1	Lesson 2.1	Lesson 2.2	Lesson 2.2

DAY 6				
Ready to Go On? Assessment Readiness				

Module 3

DAY 1	DAY 2	DAY 3	DAY 4	DAY 5
Lesson 3.1	Lesson 3.1	Lesson 3.2	Lesson 3.2	Lesson 3.3

DAY 6	DAY 7	DAY 8		
Lesson 3.3	Ready to Go On? Assessment Readiness	Study Guide Assessment Readiness		

90-Minute Classes

Module 1

DAY 1	DAY 2	DAY 3	DAY 4
Lesson 1.1	Lesson 1.2	Lesson 1.3	Ready to Go On? Assessment Readiness

Module 2

DAY 1	DAY 2	DAY 3	DAY 4
Lesson 2.1	Lesson 2.2	Lesson 2.3	Ready to Go On? Assessment Readiness

Module 3

DAY 1	DAY 2	DAY 3	DAY 4	DAY 5
Lesson 3.1	Lesson 3.2	Lesson 3.3	Ready to Go On? Assessment Readiness	Study Guide Assessment Readiness

Program Resources

⏻ Plan

Online Teacher Edition

Access a full suite of teaching resources online—plan, present, and manage classes, assignments, and activities.

ePlanner Easily plan your classes, create and view assignments, and access all program resources with your online, customizable planning tool.

Professional Development Videos

Author Juli Dixon models successful teaching practices and strategies in actual classroom settings.

QR Codes Scan with your smart phone to jump directly from your print book to online videos and other resources.

Teacher's Edition

Support students with point-of-use Questioning Strategies, teaching tips, resources for differentiated instruction, additional activities, and more.

⏻ Engage and Explore

Real-World Videos Engage students with interesting and relevant applications of the mathematical content of each module.

Animated Math Online interactive simulations, tools, and games help students actively learn and practice key concepts.

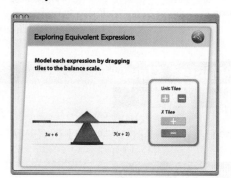

Explore Activities

Students interactively explore new concepts using a variety of tools and approaches.

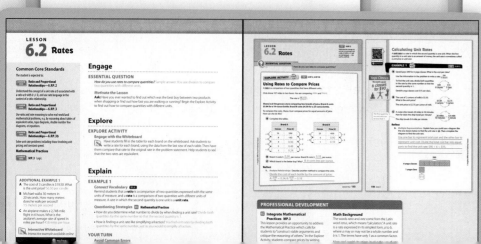

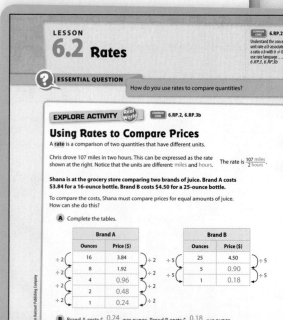

Teach

Math On the Spot video tutorials, featuring program authors Dr. Edward Burger and Martha Sandoval-Martinez, accompany every example in the textbook and give students step-by-step instructions and explanations of key math concepts.

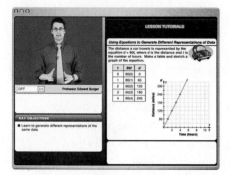

Present engaging content on a multitude of devices, including tablets and interactive whiteboards.

 Continually monitor and assess student progress with integrated formative assessment.

 Look for exercises indicated with this icon to build connections among standards within Common Core clusters.

Differentiated Instruction Print Resources

Support all learners with Differentiated Instruction Resources, including

- Leveled Practice and Problem Solving
- Reteach
- Reading Strategies
- Success for English Learners
- Challenge

Assessment and Intervention

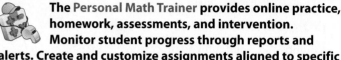

The **Personal Math Trainer** provides online practice, homework, assessments, and intervention. Monitor student progress through reports and alerts. Create and customize assignments aligned to specific lessons or standards.

- **Practice** – With dynamic items and assignments, students get unlimited practice on key concepts supported by guided examples, step-by-step solutions, and video tutorials.
- **Assessments** – Choose from course assignments or customize your own based on course content, standards, difficulty levels, and more.
- **Homework** – Students can complete online homework with a wide variety of problem types, including the ability to enter expressions, equations, and graphs. Let the system automatically grade homework, so you can focus where your students need help the most!
- **Intervention** – Let the Personal Math Trainer automatically prescribe a targeted, personalized intervention path for your students.

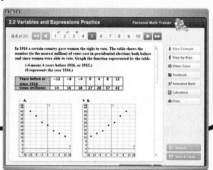

 Raise the bar with homework and practice that incorporates higher-order thinking and mathematical processes in every lesson.

Assessment Readiness
Prepare students for success on tests of the Common Core Standards with practice at every module and unit.

Assessment Resources

Tailor assessments to meet the needs of all your classes and students, including

- Leveled Module Quizzes
- Leveled Unit Tests
- Unit Performance Tasks
- Placement, Diagnostic, and Quarterly Benchmark Tests

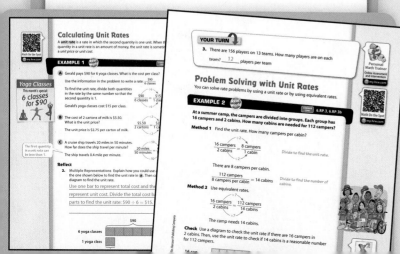

Math Background

Identifying Integers and Their Opposites 6.NS.6a
LESSON 1.1

On a number line, *opposites* are the same distance from 0 but on different sides of 0. For example, 3 and −3 are opposites. Zero is its own opposite. For any real number *a*, its opposite is written −*a*.

The expression −3 can be read as "negative 3" or as "the opposite of 3." The expression −(−3) can be read as "the opposite of negative 3" or as "the opposite of the opposite of 3." Both statements show that the value of the expression −(−3) is 3. In general, the opposite of the opposite of a number is the number itself. That is, −(−*a*) = *a*.

The *integers* consist of the whole numbers, {0, 1, 2, 3, …}, and their opposites, {−1, −2, −3, …}. Informally, integers can be defined as the real numbers that can be written without a decimal or fractional component. Students should become adept at visualizing the location of the integers on a number line. In particular, they should be aware of their symmetry about 0. If the number line is folded on itself at 0, each integer is paired with its opposite.

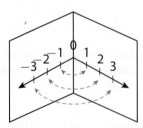

Absolute Value 6.NS.7c
LESSONS 1.3 and 3.2

The absolute value of a real number is its distance from 0 on a number line. Because distance is always nonnegative, the absolute value of any number is nonnegative. Absolute value can also be defined as follows.

$$|a| = \begin{cases} a, & a \geq 0 \\ -a, & a < 0 \end{cases}$$

This definition states that the absolute value of a nonnegative number is the number itself and that the absolute value of a negative number is the number's opposite. Loosely speaking, this means that the absolute value of a number can be thought of as "the number without its sign." That is, taking the absolute value of a negative number simply removes the minus sign.

The following properties of absolute values should seem intuitively reasonable.

- $|a| = 0$ if and only if $a = 0$
- $|ab| = |a||b|$
- $\left|\dfrac{a}{b}\right| = \dfrac{|a|}{|b|}$, for $b \neq 0$
- $|-a| = |a|$

Classifying Rational Numbers 6.NS.6
LESSON 3.1

A rational number can be written as a quotient of two integers, where the divisor is not zero. To show that a number is rational, rewrite the number as an equivalent ratio of two integers. A whole number such as 5 can be rewritten as $\frac{5}{1}$. Negative rational numbers can be written three ways: $-\frac{3}{4} = \frac{-3}{4} = \frac{3}{-4}$.

A decimal like 1.5 that ends, or terminates, is called a *terminating decimal*. If the same block of digits in a decimal repeats without end, like 0.3333…, the decimal is a *repeating decimal*. Both repeating and terminating decimals are rational numbers.

Rational numbers include integers and whole numbers as shown in the Venn diagram.

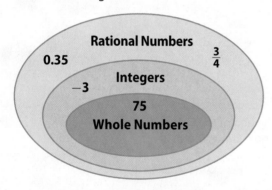

The set of integers includes negative integers, zero, and positive integers. Positive numbers are also known as the counting numbers or *natural numbers*. *Whole numbers* are all nonnegative integers, meaning the natural numbers and zero.

All rational numbers can be represented by a point on a number, whether the number is a whole number, integer, terminating decimal, or repeating decimal. Positioning rational numbers on a number line can help students understand opposites, absolute value, and ordering of numbers.

In Grade 8, students will learn that rational numbers are part of a larger set of numbers called the *real numbers*. Real numbers include the rational numbers and the irrational numbers. Numbers like π and $\sqrt{2}$ are irrational because they cannot be written as quotient of two integers. When an irrational number is written as a decimal, the digits after the decimal point never terminate and have no repeating pattern.

Comparing and Ordering Rational Numbers 6.NS.7a
LESSON 3.3

According to the Law of Trichotomy, given any two rational numbers a and b, exactly one of the following relationships must be true:

- $a < b$
- $a > b$
- $a = b$

Students can visualize the relationships between any two rational numbers by plotting them on a number line. The essential idea is that the value of the numbers increases as you move to the right along the number line. So, if a number a is less than the number b ($a < b$), then a is to the left of b on a number line. This representation also makes clear the equivalent statement that b is greater than a ($b > a$).

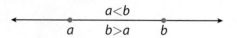

UNIT 1

Numbers

MODULE 1
Integers
COMMON CORE · 6.NS.5, 6.NS.7b, 6.NS.7c

MODULE 2
Factors and Multiples
COMMON CORE · 6.NS.4

MODULE 3
Rational Numbers
COMMON CORE · 6.NS.6, 6.NS.6c, 6.NS.7a

CAREERS IN MATH

Climatologist A climatologist is a scientist who studies long-term trends in climate conditions. These scientists collect, evaluate, and interpret data and use mathematical models to study the dynamics of weather patterns and to understand and predict Earth's climate.

If you are interested in a career in climatology, you should study these mathematical subjects:
- Algebra
- Trigonometry
- Probability and Statistics
- Calculus

Research other careers that require the analysis of data and use of mathematical models.

Unit 1 Performance Task

At the end of the unit, check out how **climatologists** use math.

Careers in Math

Climatologist

Climatology is based on making accurate measurements of various phenomena and creating mathematical models to make predictions. Climatologists analyze data from diverse sources such as ice cores taken from Antarctica or the rings of trees. You will learn more about analyzing tree rings in the Performance Tasks at the end of the unit.

For more information about careers in mathematics as well as various mathematics appreciation topics, visit the American Mathematical Society at www.ams.org

Vocabulary Preview

Use the puzzle to give students a preview of important concepts in this unit. Students may work individually, in pairs, or in groups.

Unit Resources

Go online to access all your unit resources.

⏻ my.hrw.com

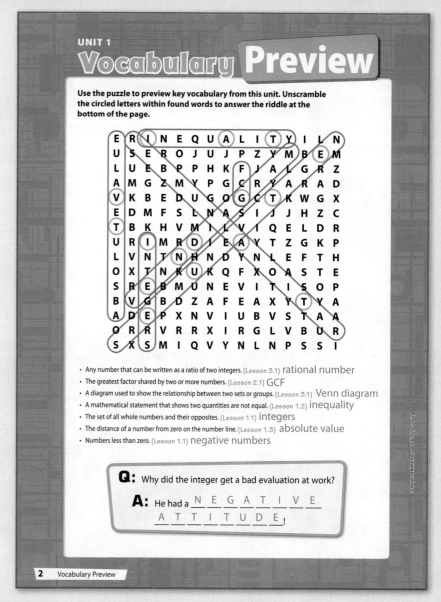

Use the puzzle to preview key vocabulary from this unit. Unscramble the circled letters within found words to answer the riddle at the bottom of the page.

```
E R I N E Q U A L I T Y I L N
U S E R O J U J P Z Y M B E M
L U E B P P H K F J A L G R Z
A M G Z M Y P G C R Y A R A D
V K B E D U G O G C T K W G X
E D M F S L N A S I J J H Z C
T B K H V M I L V I Q E L D R
U R I M R D I E A Y T Z G K P
L V N T N H N D Y N L E F T H
O X T N K U K Q F X O A S T E
S R E B M U N E V I T I S O P
B V G B D Z A F E A X Y T Y A
A D E P X N V I U B V S T A A
O R R V R R X I R G L V B U R
S X S M I Q V Y N L N P S S I
```

- Any number that can be written as a ratio of two integers. (Lesson 3.1) rational number
- The greatest factor shared by two or more numbers. (Lesson 2.1) GCF
- A diagram used to show the relationship between two sets or groups. (Lesson 3.1) Venn diagram
- A mathematical statement that shows two quantities are not equal. (Lesson 1.2) inequality
- The set of all whole numbers and their opposites. (Lesson 1.1) integers
- The distance of a number from zero on the number line. (Lesson 1.3) absolute value
- Numbers less than zero. (Lesson 1.1) negative numbers

Q: Why did the integer get a bad evaluation at work?

A: He had a N E G A T I V E A T T I T U D E !

© Houghton Mifflin Harcourt Publishing Company

Before	In this Unit	After
Students understand whole numbers, fractions, and decimals: • compare and order • relate fractions and decimals	Students will learn about: • integers and their opposites • absolute value • rational numbers and their opposites • comparing and ordering rational numbers • greatest common factors • least common multiples	Students will connect rational numbers and integers: • classify sets and subsets of rational numbers • perform operations with rational numbers

Integers

COMMON CORE

? ESSENTIAL QUESTION

How can you use integers to solve real-world problems?

You can represent real-world quantities such as temperatures, elevations, and gains and losses of money with positive and negative integers.

Real-World Video

Integers can be used to describe the value of many things in the real world. The height of a mountain in feet may be a very great integer while the temperature in degrees Celsius at the top of that mountain may be a negative integer.

my.hrw.com

GO DIGITAL
my.hrw.com

my.hrw.com

Go digital with your write-in student edition, accessible on any device.

Math On the Spot

Scan with your smart phone to jump directly to the online edition, video tutor, and more.

Animated Math

Interactively explore key concepts to see how math works.

Personal Math Trainer

Get immediate feedback and help as you work through practice sets.

Are You Ready?

Assess Readiness

Use the assessment on this page to determine if students need intensive or strategic intervention for the module's prerequisite skills.

 **RtI** Response to Intervention

Intervention	Enrichment

Access Are You Ready? assessment online, and receive instant scoring, feedback, and customized intervention or enrichment.

Online and Print Resources

Personal Math Trainer
Online Assessment and Intervention
⏻ my.hrw.com

Skills Intervention worksheets
- Skill 4 Compare Whole Numbers
- Skill 5 Order Whole Numbers
- Skill 61 Locate Numbers on a Number Line

Differentiated Instruction
- Challenge worksheets **PRE-AP**
- Extend the Math **PRE-AP** Lesson Activities in TE

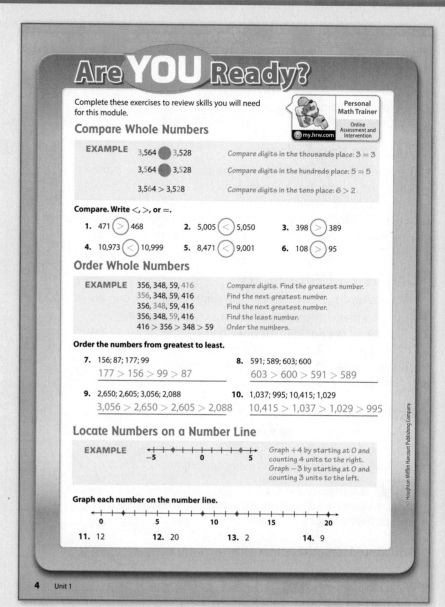

PROFESSIONAL DEVELOPMENT VIDEO

Author Juli Dixon models successful teaching practices as she explores integers in an actual sixth-grade classroom.

Professional Development
⏻ my.hrw.com

GO DIGITAL
my.hrw.com

 Online Teacher Edition
Access a full suite of teaching resources online—plan, present, and manage classes and assignments.

 ePlanner
Easily plan your classes and access all your resources online.

 Interactive Answers and Solutions
Customize answer keys to print or display in the classroom. Choose to include answers only or full solutions to all lesson exercises.

 Interactive Whiteboards
Engage students with interactive whiteboard-ready lessons and activities.

 Personal Math Trainer: Online Assessment and Intervention
Assign automatically graded homework, quizzes, tests, and intervention activities. Prepare your students with updated practice tests aligned with Common Core.

Reading Start-Up

Have students complete the activities on this page by working alone or with others.

Visualize Vocabulary

The definition and example chart helps students learn the symbols used in this chapter. Explain to students that a symbol is a character that represents a mathematical relationship or operation. To help students understand the concept of symbols, write a few symbols from real life on the board, such the symbol for money or dollar sign ($) and the "at" symbol used in e-mail (@).

Understand Vocabulary

Use the following explanations to help students learn the preview words.

On a thermometer, if the temperature is above 0, it is written as a **positive number**. If the temperature is below 0, it is written as a **negative number**. For example, if the temperature is 10 degrees below 0, it is written as –10, or minus 10 degrees.

Active Reading

Integrating Language Arts

Students can use these reading and note-taking strategies to help them organize and understand new concepts and vocabulary.

COMMON CORE **ELA-Literacy.RST.6-8.7** Integrate quantitative or technical information expressed in words in a text with a version of that information expressed visually (e.g., in a flowchart, diagram, model, graph, or table).

Additional Resources

Differentiated Instruction
- Reading Strategies **ELL**

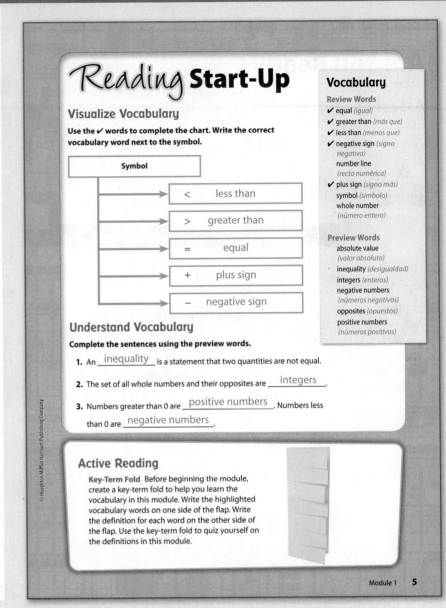

Before	In this module	After
Students understand whole numbers, fractions, and decimals: • compare and order • relate fractions and decimals	Students recognize, order, and perform computations with integers: • identify a number and its opposite • compare and order integers using a number line • find the absolute value of a number	Students work with factors and multiples: • find the greatest common factor • use the distributive property

Unpacking the Standards

Use the examples on this page to help students know exactly what they are expected to learn in this module.

Common Core Standards

Content Areas

 The Number System—6.NS

Apply and extend previous understandings of numbers to the system of rational numbers.

Go online to see a complete unpacking of the Common Core Standards.

my.hrw.com

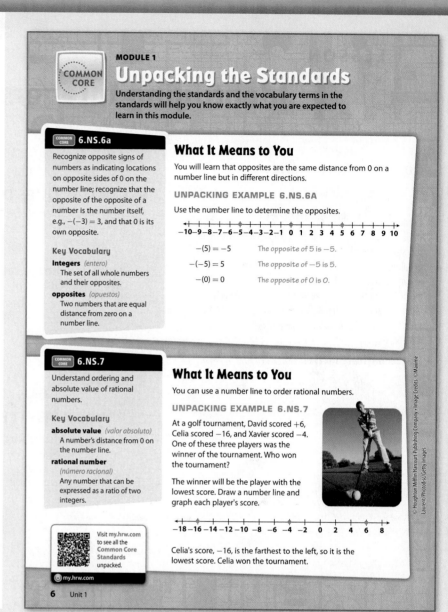

COMMON CORE MODULE 1

Unpacking the Standards

Understanding the standards and the vocabulary terms in the standards will help you know exactly what you are expected to learn in this module.

COMMON CORE 6.NS.6a

Recognize opposite signs of numbers as indicating locations on opposite sides of 0 on the number line; recognize that the opposite of a number is the number itself, e.g., $-(-3) = 3$, and that 0 is its own opposite.

Key Vocabulary

Integers (entero)
The set of all whole numbers and their opposites.

opposites (opuestos)
Two numbers that are equal distance from zero on a number line.

What It Means to You

You will learn that opposites are the same distance from 0 on a number line but in different directions.

UNPACKING EXAMPLE 6.NS.6A

Use the number line to determine the opposites.

$$-10\ -9\ -8\ -7\ -6\ -5\ -4\ -3\ -2\ -1\quad 0\quad 1\ 2\ 3\ 4\ 5\ 6\ 7\ 8\ 9\ 10$$

$-(5) = -5$	The opposite of 5 is -5.
$-(-5) = 5$	The opposite of -5 is 5.
$-(0) = 0$	The opposite of 0 is 0.

COMMON CORE 6.NS.7

Understand ordering and absolute value of rational numbers.

Key Vocabulary

absolute value (valor absoluto)
A number's distance from 0 on the number line.

rational number (número racional)
Any number that can be expressed as a ratio of two integers.

Visit my.hrw.com to see all the Common Core Standards unpacked.

my.hrw.com

What It Means to You

You can use a number line to order rational numbers.

UNPACKING EXAMPLE 6.NS.7

At a golf tournament, David scored $+6$, Celia scored -16, and Xavier scored -4. One of these three players was the winner of the tournament. Who won the tournament?

The winner will be the player with the lowest score. Draw a number line and graph each player's score.

$$-18\ -16\ -14\ -12\ -10\ -8\ -6\ -4\ -2\quad 0\quad 2\ 4\ 6\ 8$$

Celia's score, -16, is the farthest to the left, so it is the lowest score. Celia won the tournament.

Common Core Standards	Lesson 1.1	Lesson 1.2	Lesson 1.3
6.NS.5 Understand that positive and negative numbers are used together to describe quantities having opposite directions or values . . .; use positive and negative numbers to represent quantities in real-world contexts, explaining the meaning of 0 in each situation.	COMMON CORE		
6.NS.6 Understand a rational number as a point on the number line. Extend number line diagrams and coordinate axes . . . to represent points on the line and in the plane with negative number coordinates.	COMMON CORE		
6.NS.7a Interpret statements of inequality as statements about the relative position of two numbers on a number line diagram.		COMMON CORE	
6.NS.7b Write, interpret, and explain statements of order for rational numbers . . .		COMMON CORE	
6.NS.7c Understand the absolute value of a rational number . . .; interpret absolute value as magnitude for a positive or negative quantity . . .			COMMON CORE
6.NS.7d Distinguish comparisons of absolute value from statements about order.			COMMON CORE

© Houghton Mifflin Harcourt Publishing Company • Image Credits: ©Maxime Laurerl/Photodisc/Getty Images

LESSON
1.1 Identifying Integers and Their Opposites

Common Core Standards

The student is expected to:

 The Number System—6.NS.5

Understand that positive and negative numbers are used together to describe quantities having opposite directions or values (e.g., temperature above/below zero, elevation above/below sea level, credits/debits, positive/negative electric charge); use positive and negative numbers to represent quantities in real-world contexts, explaining the meaning of 0 in each situation. *Also 6.NS.6, 6.NS.6a, 6.NS.6c*

Mathematical Practices

 MP.2 Reasoning

Engage

ESSENTIAL QUESTION

How do you identify an integer and its opposite? Look for numbers that are the same distance from zero and on opposite sides of zero on the number line; for example, −4 and 4.

Motivate the Lesson

Ask: What is the coldest weather you have ever experienced? Have you ever experienced a temperature that is below zero? How do you write a temperature that is below zero? Begin the Explore Activity to find out.

Explore

EXPLORE ACTIVITY 1

Focus on Modeling **CC** **Mathematical Practices**

Point out to students that the number line is presented horizontally, but for elevation it is useful to think of it vertically. You may want to draw a vertical number line on the board and label the various locations presented in the table on the vertical number line.

Explain

EXPLORE ACTIVITY 2

Connect Vocabulary **ELL**

To help students understand the concept of **opposite** in math and in other contexts, make a list with students of pairs of opposites, such as hot and cold, black and white, up and down, left and right. Clarify that left and right are used in the math concept of opposite, with negative numbers to the left of 0 and positive numbers to the right. Zero is its own opposite.

Questioning Strategies **CC** **Mathematical Practices**

• Does every integer have an opposite? Explain. Yes, zero is its own opposite. For all other integers, the opposite has a different sign.

• How does a number line help you understand what the opposite of an integer is? I can visually see that 4 and −4 are the same distance from zero.

Connect to Daily Life

Explain that bank statements record amounts of money being withdrawn or spent as negative amounts and amounts of money being deposited as positive amounts.

Talk About It
Check for Understanding

 Ask: How do you find the opposite of an integer? Look for the integer that is the same distance from 0 on the number line, but on the other side of zero.

LESSON
1.1 Identifying Integers and Their Opposites

 COMMON CORE 6.NS.5
Understand that positive and negative numbers are used together to describe quantities having opposite directions or values.... *Also* 6.NS.6, 6.NS.6a, 6.NS.6c

? ESSENTIAL QUESTION

How do you identify an integer and its opposite?

EXPLORE ACTIVITY 1 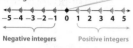 COMMON CORE 6.NS.5, 6.NS.6

Positive and Negative Numbers

Positive numbers are numbers greater than 0. Positive numbers can be written with or without a plus sign; for example, 3 is the same as +3. **Negative numbers** are numbers less than 0. Negative numbers must always be written with a negative sign.

> The number 0 is neither positive nor negative.

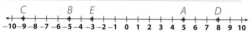

Negative integers ⟵   Positive integers ⟶

The elevation of a location describes its height above or below sea level, which has elevation 0. Elevations below sea level are represented by negative numbers, and elevations above sea level are represented by positive numbers.

A The table shows the elevations of several locations in a state park. Graph the locations on the number line according to their elevations.

Location	Little Butte A	Cradle Creek B	Dinosaur Valley C	Mesa Ridge D	Juniper Trail E
Elevation (ft)	5	−5	−9	8	−3

```
     C        B   E                A      D
  ‹─┼──┼──┼──┼──┼──┼──┼──┼──┼──┼──┼──┼──┼──┼──┼──┼──┼──┼──┼──┼─›
 −10 −9 −8 −7 −6 −5 −4 −3 −2 −1  0  1  2  3  4  5  6  7  8  9 10
```

B What point on the number line represents sea level? _____0_____

C Which location is closest to sea level? How do you know?

Juniper Trail; its elev. is closest to 0 on the number line.

D Which two locations are the same distance from sea level? Are these locations above or below sea level?

Little Butte (above) and Cradle Creek (below)

E Which location has the least elevation? How do you know?

Dinosaur Valley; its elev. is farthest left on the number line.

Lesson 1.1 **7**

EXPLORE ACTIVITY *(cont'd)*

Reflect

1. **Analyze Relationships** Morning Glory Stream is 7 feet below sea level. What number represents the elevation of Morning Glory Stream?

−7

2. **Multiple Representations** Explain how to graph the elevation of Morning Glory Stream on a number line.

Graph a point 7 units to the left of 0 on the number line.

EXPLORE ACTIVITY 2 COMMON CORE 6.NS.6a

Opposites

Two numbers are **opposites** if, on a number line, they are the same distance from 0 but on different sides of 0. For example, 5 and −5 are opposites. 0 is its own opposite.

```
 ‹─┼──┼──┼──┼──┼──┼──┼──┼──┼──┼──┼──┼──┼─›
 −6 −5 −4 −3 −2 −1  0  1  2  3  4  5  6
```

Integers are the set of all whole numbers and their opposites.

> Remember, the set of whole numbers is 0, 1, 2, 3, 4, 5, 6, ...

On graph paper, use a ruler or straightedge to draw a number line. Label the number line with each integer from −10 to 10. Fold your number line in half so that the crease goes through 0. Numbers that line up after folding the number line are opposites.

A Use your number line to find the opposites of 7, −6, 1, and 9. −7; 6; −1; −9

B How does your number line show that 0 is its own opposite?

The crease goes through 0, so 0 lines up with itself.

C What is the opposite of the opposite of 3? _____3_____

Reflect

3. **Justify Reasoning** Explain how your number line shows that 8 and −8 are opposites.

8 and −8 are the same distance from 0 but on different sides of 0.

4. **Multiple Representations** Explain how to use your number line to find the opposite of the opposite of −6.

Fold the number line in half at 0. −6 lines up with 6 so 6 is the opposite of −6 and −6 is the opposite of 6. So −6 is the opposite of the opposite of −6.

8 Unit 1

PROFESSIONAL DEVELOPMENT

CC Integrate Mathematical Practices MP.2

This lesson provides an opportunity to address this Mathematical Practice standard. It calls for students to communicate mathematical ideas using multiple representations, including symbols, graphs, and language as appropriate. In each Explore Activity and Example, students use number lines to represent the integers and opposites that are described with language and/or numbers with or without negative symbols. In this way, students are able to make the connections between and become fluent in using the different representations of integers and their opposites.

Math Background

The opposite of any positive number is negative, and the opposite of any negative number is positive. The sum of a number and its opposite is zero, which is neither positive nor negative.

An integer's distance from zero is said to be non-negative instead of positive. When a distance measurement includes a negative symbol, the symbol describes the direction rather than the distance.

EXAMPLE 1

Questioning Strategies Mathematical Practices

• Is the opposite of a temperature always colder? Explain. No, because if the temperature is negative, say −5°, then the opposite would be 5°, which would be warmer.

• Is the opposite of an opposite always the number you started with? Give an example. Yes. If you start at 3, the opposite is −3, then the opposite of −3 is 3.

Engage with the Whiteboard

Have students take turns graphing an integer and then have another student graph the integer's opposite on the number line.

Focus on Patterns Mathematical Practices

Elicit from students that when finding the opposite of the opposite of a positive number, the pattern of the signs in the steps is +, −, +. When finding the opposite of the opposite of a negative number, the pattern of the signs in the steps is −, +, −.

YOUR TURN

Avoid Common Errors

If students seem to get lost with the notation "the opposite of the opposite of," suggest that they work backward through the sentence. First they find the opposite of 4, which is −4. Then they find the opposite of −4.

Elaborate

Talk About It
Summarize the Lesson

Ask: How do you find the opposite of an integer? The opposite of an integer is the integer the same distance from zero on the number line, but on the other side of 0. If the integer is 5, then the opposite is −5. If the integer is −3, then the opposite is 3.

GUIDED PRACTICE

Engage with the Whiteboard

 For Exercises 1–4, you may want to have students take turns graphing an integer and then have another student graph the integer's opposite on the number lines.

Avoid Common Errors

Exercise 1 Remind students to label the points they graph on the number line carefully, so it is clear which point they intend as the answer.

Exercise 9 Remind students that zero is its own opposite.

Talk About It
Check for Understanding

Ask: I am thinking of a number. The opposite of my number is a distance of 8 units from 0. Do you know what my number is? No, because both 8 and −8 are a distance of 8 units from 0. It could be either 8 or −8.

Integers and Opposites on a Number Line

Positive and negative numbers can be used to represent real-world quantities. For example, 3 can represent a temperature that is 3 °F above 0. −3 can represent a temperature that is 3 °F below 0. Both 3 and −3 are 3 units from 0.

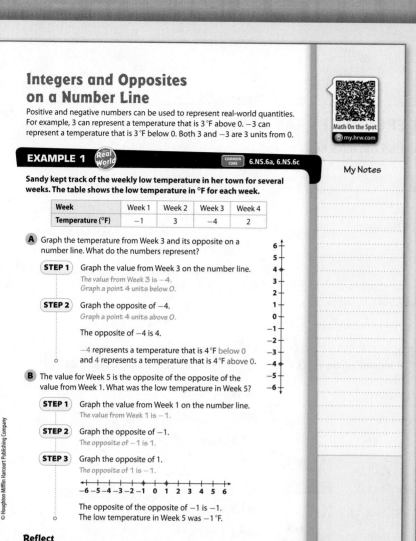

EXAMPLE 1 Real World

COMMON CORE 6.NS.6a, 6.NS.6c

Sandy kept track of the weekly low temperature in her town for several weeks. The table shows the low temperature in °F for each week.

Week	Week 1	Week 2	Week 3	Week 4
Temperature (°F)	−1	3	−4	2

A Graph the temperature from Week 3 and its opposite on a number line. What do the numbers represent?

STEP 1 Graph the value from Week 3 on the number line.
The value from Week 3 is −4.
Graph a point 4 units below 0.

STEP 2 Graph the opposite of −4.
Graph a point 4 units above 0.

The opposite of −4 is 4.

−4 represents a temperature that is 4 °F below 0 and 4 represents a temperature that is 4 °F above 0.

B The value for Week 5 is the opposite of the opposite of the value from Week 1. What was the low temperature in Week 5?

STEP 1 Graph the value from Week 1 on the number line.
The value from Week 1 is −1.

STEP 2 Graph the opposite of −1.
The opposite of −1 is 1.

STEP 3 Graph the opposite of 1.
The opposite of 1 is −1.

The opposite of the opposite of −1 is −1.
The low temperature in Week 5 was −1 °F.

Reflect

5. Analyze Relationships Explain how you can find the opposite of the opposite of any number without using a number line.

The opposite of the opposite of a number is the number itself.

My Notes

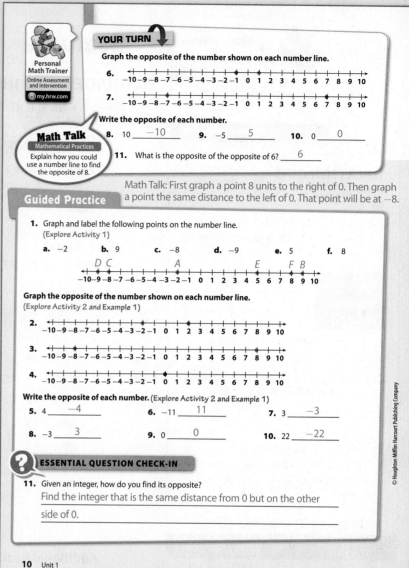

YOUR TURN

Graph the opposite of the number shown on each number line.

6.

7.

Write the opposite of each number.

8. 10 _____−10_____   9. −5 _____5_____   10. 0 _____0_____

11. What is the opposite of the opposite of 6? _____6_____

Math Talk
Mathematical Practices
Explain how you could use a number line to find the opposite of 8.

Math Talk: First graph a point 8 units to the right of 0. Then graph a point the same distance to the left of 0. That point will be at −8.

Guided Practice

1. Graph and label the following points on the number line.
(Explore Activity 1)

   a. −2   b. 9   c. −8   d. −9   e. 5   f. 8

Graph the opposite of the number shown on each number line.
(Explore Activity 2 and Example 1)

2.

3.

4.

Write the opposite of each number. (Explore Activity 2 and Example 1)

5. 4 _____−4_____   6. −11 _____11_____   7. 3 _____−3_____

8. −3 _____3_____   9. 0 _____0_____   10. 22 _____−22_____

 ESSENTIAL QUESTION CHECK-IN

11. Given an integer, how do you find its opposite?
Find the integer that is the same distance from 0 but on the other side of 0.

DIFFERENTIATE INSTRUCTION

World History
The concept of negative numbers can be traced to Hindu mathematicians. They used negative numbers to represent debts, as we do today, and formulated rules for the arithmetic of integers. Their ideas were acquired by Arab mathematicians, who passed the ideas on to European scientists over time.

Manipulatives
For Explore Activity 2, some students have difficulty labeling a number line and folding it so the opposite integers line up. It may be helpful to give them printed number lines with a vertical dashed line through zero.

Additional Resources
Differentiated Instruction includes:
- Reading Strategies
- Success for English Learners **ELL**
- Reteach
- Challenge **PRE-AP**

1.1 LESSON QUIZ

 6.NS.5

Sara keeps a record of the money that she deposits and withdraws from her account each week.

Week	1	2	3
Account entry ($)	$4	$10	−$8

1. Which week(s) does Sara have a negative entry in her account?

2. Graph each value and its opposite on a number line.

3. Which week's entry was the closest to zero?

4. For Week 4, Sara's entry is the opposite of the opposite of her entry on Week 1. What is her Week 4 entry?

Lesson Quiz available online

my.hrw.com

Answers

1. Week 3

2.
−10 −8 −6 −4 −2 0 2 4 6 8 10

3. Week 1

4. $4

Evaluate

GUIDED AND INDEPENDENT PRACTICE

COMMON CORE 6.NS.5, 6.NS.6, 6.NS.6a, 6.NS.6c

Concepts & Skills	Practice
Explore Activity 1 Positive and Negative Numbers	Exercises 1, 12, 23, 24
Explore Activity 2 Opposites	Exercises 2–10, 12, 13, 15, 18, 19–24
Example 1 Integers and Opposites on a Number Line	Exercises 2–10, 14, 16, 17, 20–23

Exercise	Depth of Knowledge (D.O.K.)		**COMMON CORE** Mathematical Practices
12	**2** Skills/Concepts		**MP.4** Modeling
13–18	**1** Recall of Information		**MP.5** Using Tools
19–23	**2** Skills/Concepts		**MP.5** Using Tools
24	**3** Strategic Thinking	H.O.T.	**MP.4** Modeling
25	**3** Strategic Thinking	H.O.T.	**MP.3** Logic
26	**3** Strategic Thinking	H.O.T.	**MP.7** Using Structure
27	**3** Strategic Thinking	H.O.T.	**MP.3** Logic
28	**3** Strategic Thinking	H.O.T.	**MP.5** Using Tools

Additional Resources

Differentiated Instruction includes:

• Leveled Practice Worksheets

Name_____ Class_____ Date_____

1.1 Independent Practice

COMMON CORE 6.NS.5, 6.NS.6, 6.NS.6a, 6.NS.6c

Personal Math Trainer

my.hrw.com

Online Assessment and Intervention

12. **Chemistry** Atoms normally have an electric charge of 0. Certain conditions, such as static, can cause atoms to have a positive or a negative charge. Atoms with a positive or negative charge are called *ions*.

Ion	A	B	C	D	E
Charge	−3	+1	−2	+3	−1

a. Which ions have a negative charge?

A, C, E

b. Which ions have charges that are opposites?

A and D; B and E

c. Which ion's charge is not the opposite of another ion's charge?

C

Name the integer that meets the given description.

13. the opposite of −17 _____17_____

14. 4 units left of 0 _____−4_____

15. the opposite of the opposite of 2 ___2___

16. 15 units right of 0 ___15___

17. 12 units right of 0 _____12_____

18. the opposite of −19 ___19___

19. **Analyze Relationships** Several wrestlers are trying to lose weight for a competition. Their change in weight since last week is shown in the chart.

Wrestler	Tino	Victor	Ramsey	Baxter	Luis
Weight Change (in pounds)	−2	6	2	5	−5

a. Did Victor lose or gain weight since last week? _____gain_____

b. Which wrestler's weight change is the opposite of Ramsey's? _____Tino_____

c. Which wrestlers have lost weight since last week? _____Tino and Luis_____

d. Frankie's weight change since last week was the opposite of Victor's.

What was Frankie's weight change? _____−6_____

e. Frankie's goal last week was to gain weight. Did he meet his goal? Explain.

No; −6 pound change means Frankie lost 6 pounds.

Find the distance between the given number and its opposite on a number line.

20. 6 _____12 units_____

21. −2 _____4 units_____

22. 0 _____0 units_____

23. −7 _____14 units_____

24. **What If?** Three contestants are competing on a trivia game show. The table shows their scores before the final question.

Contestant	Score Before Final Question
Timothy	−25
Shawna	18
Kaylynn	−14

a. How many points must Shawna earn for her score to be the opposite of Timothy's score before the final question?_____7 points_____

b. Which person's score is closest to 0? _____Kaylynn_____

c. Who do you think is winning the game before the final question? Explain.

Shawna; she is the only player with a positive score.

H.O.T. FOCUS ON HIGHER ORDER THINKING

25. **Communicate Mathematical Ideas** Which number is farther from 0 on a number line: −9 or 6? Explain your reasoning.

−9; it is 9 units away from 0 on a number line, and 6 is only 6 units away from 0.

26. **Analyze Relationships** A number is *k* units to the left of 0 on the number line. Describe the location of its opposite.

Its opposite is *k* units to the right of 0 on the number line.

27. **Critique Reasoning** Roberto says that the opposite of a certain integer is −5. Cindy concludes that the opposite of an integer is always negative. Explain Cindy's error.

Cindy assumed the original integer is always positive. But if the original integer is negative, its opposite will be positive. Also, if the original integer is 0, its opposite will be 0.

28. **Multiple Representations** Explain how to use a number line to find the opposites of the integers 3 units away from −7.

The opposites are 10 and 4; −10 is 3 units to the left of −7, and 10 is the opposite of −10. −4 is 3 units to the right of −7, and 4 is the opposite of −4.

Work Area

EXTEND THE MATH PRE-AP

Activity available online my.hrw.com

Activity The lowest and highest places in the contiguous, or adjoining, states of the United States are both in California, as shown in the graph. How can you use the graph to find the difference in elevation between the two locations?

If you start at the lowest point, you need to go up 282 ft to sea level and then another 14,495 ft to get to the top of Mt. Whitney. 282 + 14,495 = 14,777.

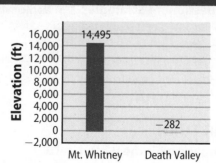

© Houghton Mifflin Harcourt Publishing Company

Common Core Standards

The student is expected to:

 The Number System—6.NS.7b

Write, interpret, and explain statements of order for rational numbers in real-world contexts. *Also 6.NS.7, 6.NS.7a*

Mathematical Practices

 MP.5 Using Tools

Engage

ESSENTIAL QUESTION

How do you compare and order integers? Graph the integers on a number line, and then read the integers in order from left to right to order them from least to greatest.

Motivate the Lesson

Ask: Which temperature is colder: −20° or −8°? How can you decide? Begin the Explore Activity to find out.

Explore

EXPLORE ACTIVITY

Focus on Reasoning

Point out to students that teams with negative win/loss records have more losses than wins, while those with positive records have more wins than losses. So when comparing records, a team with a negative win/loss record is less successful than a team with a positive win/loss record.

Explain

EXAMPLE 1

Talk About It
Check for Understanding

 Ask: How does a number line help you order a set of integers? A number line provides a visual representation of the values of the integers in order from least to greatest from left to right (horizontal number line) or from bottom to top (vertical number line).

Questioning Strategies CC Mathematical Practices

- What is the best score Fred recorded for the week and when does it occur? How do you know? −5 and it occurs on Thursday. −5 has the least value of all the scores recorded and in golf the lowest score, not the highest score, wins the game.

- How do integers change as you move farther left from zero on the number line? They decrease in value.

YOUR TURN

Engage with the Whiteboard

 Have students take turns graphing the numbers on the number line and then have another student list the numbers in order from least to greatest.

Talk About It
Check for Understanding

 Ask: What do the following changes in stock prices mean: −$5, $4, and $0? A change of −$5 means the stock price fell $5, a change of $4 means the stock price rose $4, and a change of $0 means the stock price did not change.

ADDITIONAL EXAMPLE 1
Tia's golf scores during her first five days at a golf academy are shown in the table. Graph the scores on a number line, and then list the numbers in order from least to greatest.

Day	Mon	Tue	Wed	Thu	Fri
Score	5	−1	3	2	−3

−3, −1, 2, 3, 5

Interactive Whiteboard
Interactive example available online

⏻ my.hrw.com

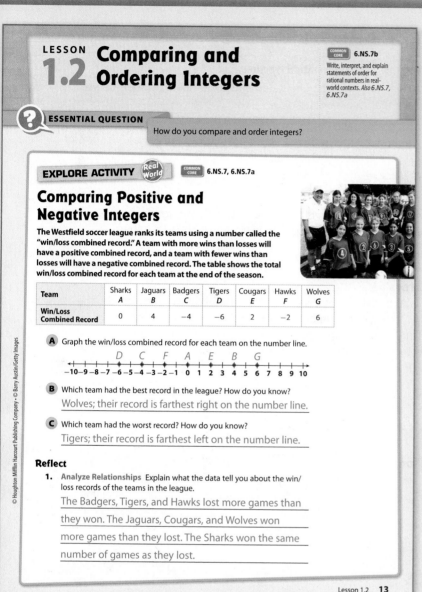

LESSON 1.2 Comparing and Ordering Integers

COMMON CORE 6.NS.7b
Write, interpret, and explain statements of order for rational numbers in real-world contexts. *Also 6.NS.7, 6.NS.7a*

? ESSENTIAL QUESTION

How do you compare and order integers?

EXPLORE ACTIVITY *Real World* **COMMON CORE** 6.NS.7, 6.NS.7a

Comparing Positive and Negative Integers

The Westfield soccer league ranks its teams using a number called the "win/loss combined record." A team with more wins than losses will have a positive combined record, and a team with fewer wins than losses will have a negative combined record. The table shows the total win/loss combined record for each team at the end of the season.

Team	Sharks A	Jaguars B	Badgers C	Tigers D	Cougars E	Hawks F	Wolves G
Win/Loss Combined Record	0	4	−4	−6	2	−2	6

A Graph the win/loss combined record for each team on the number line.

D C F A E B G
−10−9−8−7−6−5−4−3−2−1 0 1 2 3 4 5 6 7 8 9 10

B Which team had the best record in the league? How do you know?
Wolves; their record is farthest right on the number line.

C Which team had the worst record? How do you know?
Tigers; their record is farthest left on the number line.

Reflect

1. **Analyze Relationships** Explain what the data tell you about the win/loss records of the teams in the league.
The Badgers, Tigers, and Hawks lost more games than they won. The Jaguars, Cougars, and Wolves won more games than they lost. The Sharks won the same number of games as they lost.

Lesson 1.2 **13**

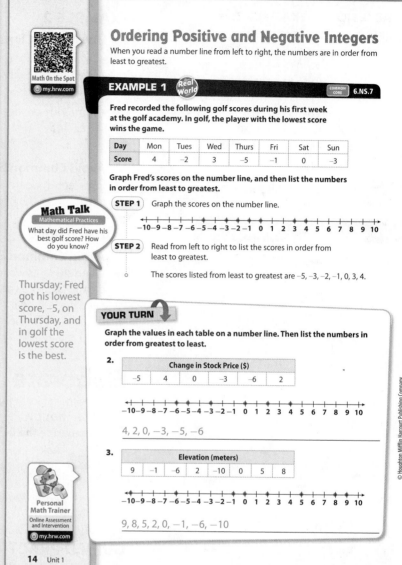

Ordering Positive and Negative Integers

When you read a number line from left to right, the numbers are in order from least to greatest.

EXAMPLE 1 *Real World* **COMMON CORE** 6.NS.7

Fred recorded the following golf scores during his first week at the golf academy. In golf, the player with the lowest score wins the game.

Day	Mon	Tues	Wed	Thurs	Fri	Sat	Sun
Score	4	−2	3	−5	−1	0	−3

Graph Fred's scores on the number line, and then list the numbers in order from least to greatest.

STEP 1 Graph the scores on the number line.

−10−9−8−7−6−5−4−3−2−1 0 1 2 3 4 5 6 7 8 9 10

STEP 2 Read from left to right to list the scores in order from least to greatest.

The scores listed from least to greatest are −5, −3, −2, −1, 0, 3, 4.

Math Talk
Mathematical Practices
What day did Fred have his best golf score? How do you know?

Thursday; Fred got his lowest score, −5, on Thursday, and in golf the lowest score is the best.

YOUR TURN

Graph the values in each table on a number line. Then list the numbers in order from greatest to least.

2.
Change in Stock Price ($)					
−5	4	0	−3	−6	2

−10−9−8−7−6−5−4−3−2−1 0 1 2 3 4 5 6 7 8 9 10

4, 2, 0, −3, −5, −6

3.
Elevation (meters)							
9	−1	−6	2	−10	0	5	8

−10−9−8−7−6−5−4−3−2−1 0 1 2 3 4 5 6 7 8 9 10

9, 8, 5, 2, 0, −1, −6, −10

Personal Math Trainer
Online Assessment and Intervention
my.hrw.com

14 Unit 1

PROFESSIONAL DEVELOPMENT

CC Integrate Mathematical Practices MP.2

This lesson provides an opportunity to address this Mathematical Practice standard. It calls for students to select tools and techniques, including number sense as appropriate, to solve problems. In the Explore Activity and in both Examples, students use a number line to order and compare integers in real-world contexts, such as ordering rankings, golf scores, and comparing annual precipitation. In this way, students are able to see the integers in terms of their relationship to zero, to each other, and to create statements of numerical order in real-world contexts.

Math Background

The integers consist of the whole numbers, {0, 1, 2, 3, …}, and their opposites, {0, −1, −2, −3, …}. Informally, integers can be defined as the real numbers that can be written without a decimal or fractional component. Students should become adept at visualizing the location of the integers on a number line. In particular, they should be aware of their symmetry about 0. If the number line is folded on itself at 0, each integer is paired with its opposite.

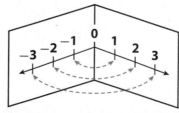

Comparing and Ordering Integers **14**

EXAMPLE 2

Questioning Strategies Mathematical Practices

- Can you always write two different inequality statements to compare two numbers with different values? Explain. Yes, because you can use > to compare the larger number to the smaller number and < to compare the smaller number to the larger number.

- If −1 is the greatest negative integer, is there a least negative integer? Explain. No, the set of negative numbers is infinite, so every negative integer on the number line has an integer of lesser value to its left.

Avoid Common Errors

If students have trouble in determining which inequality sign to use, you may want to remind them that the inequality sign always points to the lesser of two numbers.

YOUR TURN

Avoid Common Errors

When students work with negative numbers, they often think that the number with the greater absolute value is the greater number. You may want to remind them that for negative numbers, the number with the greater absolute value is actually the lesser number because it is farther away from zero in the negative direction.

Elaborate
· ·

Talk About It
Summarize the Lesson

 Ask: How is a number line used to compare and order integers? When the numbers are graphed they are in order of their value. A horizontal number line shows the numbers from least to greatest (left to right) and from greatest to least (right to left). A vertical number line shows the numbers from least to greatest (bottom to top) and from greatest to least (top to bottom).

GUIDED PRACTICE

Engage with the Whiteboard

For Exercise 2, have students use the number line given in Exercise 1 to graph and order the integers.

Avoid Common Errors

Exercise 1 Remind students that the coldest temperature is the least temperature, the one farthest to the left on the number line.

Exercises 2–3 Caution students to pay attention to the signs of the numbers when they create their ordered lists.

Exercise 4 Remind students that when comparing negative integers, the number with the greater absolute value is actually the lesser number because values decrease as one moves left from zero.

Writing Inequalities

An **inequality** is a statement that two quantities are not equal. The symbols < and > are used to write inequalities.

- The symbol > means "is greater than."
- The symbol < means "is less than."

You can use a number line to help write an inequality.

Math On the Spot
my.hrw.com

EXAMPLE 2 (Real World)

COMMON CORE 6.NS.7a, 6.NS.7b

A In 2005, Austin, Texas, received 51 inches in annual precipitation. In 2009, the city received 36 inches in annual precipitation. In which year was there more precipitation?

Graph 51 and 36 on the number line.

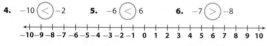

- 51 is to the *right* of 36 on the number line.

  This means that 51 is **greater than** 36.

  Write the inequality as 51 > 36.

- 36 is to the *left* of 51 on the number line.

  This means that 36 is **less than** 51.

  Write the inequality as 36 < 51.

  There was more precipitation in 2005.

B Write two inequalities to compare −6 and 7.
−6 < 7; 7 > −6

C Write two inequalities to compare −9 and −4.
−4 > −9; −9 < −4

Math Talk
Mathematical Practices

Is there a greatest integer? Is there a greatest negative integer? Explain.

No; for any positive integer, you can find greater positive integers to the right of it on the number line; yes, −1.

YOUR TURN

Compare. Write > or <. Use the number line to help you.

4. −10 (<) −2   **5.** −6 (<) 6   **6.** −7 (>) −8

-10 -9 -8 -7 -6 -5 -4 -3 -2 -1 0 1 2 3 4 5 6 7 8 9 10

7. Write two inequalities to compare −2 and −18. −2 > −18; −18 < −2

8. Write two inequalities to compare 39 and −39. −39 < 39; 39 > −39

Personal Math Trainer
Online Assessment and Intervention
my.hrw.com

Guided Practice

1a. Graph the temperature for each city on the number line. (Explore Activity)

City	A	B	C	D	E
Temperature (°F)	−9	10	−2	0	4

A   C D   E   B
-10 -9 -8 -7 -6 -5 -4 -3 -2 -1 0 1 2 3 4 5 6 7 8 9 10

b. Which city was coldest? _____A_____

c. Which city was warmest? _____B_____

List the numbers in order from least to greatest. (Example 1)

2. 4, −6, 0, 8, −9, 1, −3
−9, −6, −3, 0, 1, 4, 8

3. −65, 34, 7, −13, 55, 62, −7
−65, −13, −7, 7, 34, 55, 62

4. Write two inequalities to compare −17 and −22. −17 > −22; −22 < −17

Compare. Write < or >. (Example 2)

5. −9 (<) 2   **6.** 0 (<) 6   **7.** 3 (>) −7   **8.** 5 (>) −10

9. −1 (>) −3   **10.** −8 (<) −4   **11.** −4 (<) 1   **12.** −2 (>) −6

13. Compare the temperatures for the following cities. Write < or >. (Example 2)

City	Alexandria	Redwood Falls	Grand Marais	Winona	International Falls
Average Temperature in March (°C)	−3	0	−2	2	−4

a. Alexandria and Winona _____−3 < 2_____

b. Redwood Falls and International Falls _____0 > −4_____

ESSENTIAL QUESTION CHECK-IN

14. How can you use a number line to compare and order numbers?

The numbers on a number line are in order from least to greatest as you move from left to right.

DIFFERENTIATE INSTRUCTION

Kinesthetic Experience

Have students write the integers being compared on sticky notes and arrange them on a large number line on the board. Ask them to explain why they placed the numbers in the position they did, and encourage them to rearrange the notes if placed incorrectly. Then have students write two inequalities for each comparison they make.

Number Sense

Have students practice comparing numbers without a number line by visualizing them on a number line. For example, **Ask:** *Would −125 be to the left or to the right of −76 on a number line?* Have students challenge one another to tell whether a number is located to the left or right of another number on the number line.

Additional Resources

Differentiated Instruction includes:

- Reading Strategies
- Success for English Learners **ELL**
- Reteach
- Challenge **PRE-AP**

Personal Math Trainer

Online Assessment and Intervention

Online homework assignment available

 my.hrw.com

1.2 LESSON QUIZ

 6.NS.7b

Use a number line to list the numbers in order from least to greatest.

1. 4, −1, 6, 0, −4, 5, −3

2. 9, −12, −5, 8, −15, 0, −2

3. −38, −16, 45, −24, 71, −63, 10

4. Write two inequalities to compare −13 and −26.

5. Write two inequalities to compare 0 and −8.

6. At the end of a golf game, Jared's score was −3 and Ned's score was −5. Who won the game? Explain your reasoning.

Lesson Quiz available online

 my.hrw.com

Answers

1. −4, −3, −1, 0, 4, 5, 6

2. −15, −12, −5, −2, 0, 8, 9

3. −63, −38, −24, −16, 10, 45, 71

4. −13 > −26; −26 < −13

5. 0 > −8; −8 < 0

6. Ned; In golf, the player with the lowest score wins.

Evaluate

GUIDED AND INDEPENDENT PRACTICE

 6.NS.7, 6.NS.7a, 6.NS.7b

Concepts & Skills	Practice
Explore Activity Comparing Positive and Negative Integers	Exercises 1, 15, 19
Example 1 Ordering Positive and Negative Integers	Exercises 2–4, 18, 19
Example 2 Writing Inequalities	Exercises 5–13, 16, 17, 20–23

Exercise	Depth of Knowledge (D.O.K.)	Mathematical Practices
15	**2** Skills/Concepts	**MP.2** Reasoning
16–18	**2** Skills/Concepts	**MP.4** Modeling
19	**2** Skills/Concepts	**MP.2** Reasoning
20–23	**2** Skills/Concepts	**MP.4** Modeling
24	**3** Strategic Thinking H.O.T.	**MP.7** Using Structure
25	**3** Strategic Thinking H.O.T.	**MP.4** Modeling
26	**3** Strategic Thinking H.O.T.	**MP.4** Modeling
27	**3** Strategic Thinking H.O.T.	**MP.8** Patterns

Additional Resources

Differentiated Instruction includes:

• Leveled Practice worksheets

CC CLUSTER CONNECTION **Exercise 19** combines concepts from the Common Core cluster "Apply and extend previous understandings of numbers to the system of rational numbers."

1.2 Independent Practice

COMMON CORE 6.NS.7, 6.NS.7a, 6.NS.7b

Personal Math Trainer
Online Assessment and Intervention
my.hrw.com

15. Multiple Representations A hockey league tracks the plus-minus records for each player. A plus-minus record is the difference in even strength goals for and against the team when a player is on the ice. The following table lists the plus-minus values for several hockey players.

Player	A. Jones	B. Sutter	E. Simpson	L. Mays	R. Tomas	S. Klatt
Plus-minus	−8	4	9	−3	−4	3

a. Graph the values on the number line.

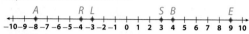

b. Which player has the best plus-minus record? ____E. Simpson____

Astronomy The table lists the average surface temperature of some planets. Write an inequality to compare the temperatures of each pair of planets.

Planet	Average Surface Temperature (°C)
Mercury	167
Uranus	−197
Neptune	−200
Earth	15
Mars	−65
Jupiter	−110

16. Uranus and Jupiter ____$-197 < -110$____

17. Mercury and Mars ____$167 > -65$____

18. Arrange the planets in order of average surface temperature from greatest to least. Mercury, Earth, Mars, Jupiter, Uranus, Neptune

19. Represent Real-World Problems For a stock market project, five students each invested pretend money in one stock. They tracked gains and losses in the value of that stock for one week. In the following table, a gain is represented by a positive number and a loss is represented by a negative number.

Students	Andre	Bria	Carla	Daniel	Ethan
Gains and Losses ($)	7	−2	−5	2	4

Graph the students' results on the number line. Then list them in order from least to greatest.

a. Graph the values on the number line.

b. The results listed from least to greatest are ____$-5, -2, 2, 4, 7$____.

Geography The table lists the lowest elevation for several countries. A negative number means the elevation is below sea level, and a positive number means the elevation is above sea level. Compare the lowest elevation for each pair of countries. Write < or >.

Country	Lowest Elevation (feet)
Argentina	−344
Australia	−49
Czech Republic	377
Hungary	249
United States	−281

20. Argentina and the United States __$-344 < -281$__

21. Czech Republic and Hungary __$377 > 249$__

22. Hungary and Argentina __$249 > -344$__

23. Which country in the table has the lowest elevation? ____Argentina____

24. Analyze Relationships There are three numbers a, b, and c, where $a > b$ and $b > c$. Describe the positions of the numbers on a number line.

The first number, a, will be the farthest to the right on the number line. The third number, c, will be farthest to the left on the number line. The second number, b, will be between a and c on the number line.

H.O.T. FOCUS ON HIGHER ORDER THINKING

Work Area

25. Critique Reasoning At 9 A.M. the outside temperature was −3°F. By noon, the temperature was −12°F. Jorge said that it was getting warmer outside. Is he correct? Explain.

No; $-12°F < -3°F$, so it was getting colder outside.

26. Problem Solving Golf scores represent the number of strokes above or below par. A negative score means that you hit a number below par while a positive score means that you hit a number above par. The winner in golf has the lowest score. During a round of golf, Angela's score was −5 and Lisa's score was −8. Who won the game? Explain.

Lisa won the game because she had the lowest score.

27. Look for a Pattern Order −3, 5, 16, and −10 from least to greatest. Then order the same numbers from closest to zero to farthest from zero. Describe how your lists are similar. Would this be true if the numbers were −3, 5, −16 and −10?

−10, −3, 5, 16 and −3, 5, −10, 16; both lists end with 16 because 16 is the greatest number and is farthest from zero. This would not be true for the second group of numbers because in that list, the least number, −16, would be at the beginning of the first list, not at the end.

EXTEND THE MATH PRE-AP

Activity available online my.hrw.com

Activity In a game on a number line, the starting line is at zero. Each player makes three consecutive jumps. A forward jump is represented by a positive number, and a backward jump is represented by a negative number.

1st jump: The player makes a jump away from the starting line and lands on a point.

2nd jump: From the point where he or she lands, the player makes a second jump towards the starting line.

3rd jump: Now the player makes a third jump away from the starting line.

Rachel makes three consecutive jumps of 8 feet, −5 feet, and 6 feet.

Andy makes three consecutive jumps of −10 feet, 7 feet, and −4 feet.

Who is closer to the starting line at the end of the round? Explain. You may find it helpful to use a counter and a number line to track each player's jumps.

Rachel jumps forward 8 ft, then back 5 ft, and then forward 6 ft. She is now 9 ft in front of the starting line. Andy jumps back 10 ft, then forward 7 ft, and then back 4 ft. He is now 7 ft behind the starting line. Since −7 is closer to zero than 9, Andy is closer to the starting line at the end of the round.

LESSON
1.3 Absolute Value

Common Core Standards

The student is expected to:

 The Number System—6.NS.7c

Understand the absolute value of a rational number as its distance from 0 on the number line; interpret absolute value as magnitude for a positive or negative quantity in a real-world situation. *Also 6.NS.7, 6.NS.7d*

Mathematical Practices

 MP.4 Modeling

ADDITIONAL EXAMPLE 1

A deep-sea diver dived off a boat to a depth of −45 feet. What is the absolute value that expresses the distance the diver went? The absolute value of −45 is 45.

 Interactive Whiteboard
Interactive example available online

 my.hrw.com

 Animated Math
Absolute Values and Opposites

Students explore integers, their opposites, and their absolute values with a dynamic number line.

 my.hrw.com

Engage

ESSENTIAL QUESTION

How do you find and use absolute value? Count the distance from zero to a number on a number line. Absolute value is always nonnegative and is useful for representing distance or an amount of change.

Motivate the Lesson
Ask: Have you ever borrowed money from a friend? How can you mathematically describe owing money? Begin the Explore Activity to find out.

Explore

EXPLORE ACTIVITY 1

Connect to Daily Life
Point out to students that they can use absolute value to describe or compare real-life distances such as how far they ride a bike, dive under water, or ascend in a Ferris wheel.

Explain

EXAMPLE 1

Focus on Communication
Discuss with students why an absolute value of $25 may be used to describe a −$25 change to the balance of a gift card.

Engage with the Whiteboard
 Have students take turns graphing a number on a number line and showing how to use the number line to find the absolute value of the number.

Questioning Strategies CC Mathematical Practices

• How would you define a balance on a gift card? It is the amount of money that is available to the cardholder.

• How would you explain what a balance of $0.00 on a gift card means? It means that the card has no monetary value.

• How can you use absolute value to show the amount Jake has left on his gift card? Find the absolute value of each item Jake bought. Add the two values to find the absolute value of his purchases. Subtract that number from the balance on his gift card.

LESSON

1.3 Absolute Value

COMMON CORE 6.NS.7c

Understand the absolute value of a rational number... interpret absolute value as magnitude... in a real-world situation. Also 6.NS.7, 6.NS.7d

? ESSENTIAL QUESTION

How do you find and use absolute value?

EXPLORE ACTIVITY 1 COMMON CORE 6.NS.7, 6.NS.7c

Finding Absolute Value

The **absolute value** of a number is the number's distance from 0 on a number line. For example, the absolute value of −3 is 3 because −3 is 3 units from 0. The absolute value of −3 is written $|-3|$.

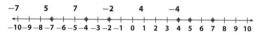

3 units

−5 −4 −3 −2 −1 0 1 2 3

$|-3| = 3$

Because absolute value represents a distance, it is always nonnegative.

Graph the following numbers on the number line. Then use your number line to find each absolute value.

−7   5   7   −2   4   −4

−10 −9 −8 −7 −6 −5 −4 −3 −2 −1 0 1 2 3 4 5 6 7 8 9 10

A $|-7| = \underline{7}$ **B** $|5| = \underline{5}$ **C** $|7| = \underline{7}$

D $|-2| = \underline{2}$ **E** $|4| = \underline{4}$ **F** $|-4| = \underline{4}$

Reflect

1. **Analyze Relationships** Which pairs of numbers have the same absolute value? How are these numbers related?

   −7 and 7; 4 and −4; they are opposites.

2. **Justify Reasoning** Negative numbers are less than positive numbers. Does this mean that the absolute value of a negative number must be less than the absolute value of a positive number? Explain.

   No; −7 < 3 but $|-7| > |3|$; the distance from −7 to 0 is greater than the distance from 3 to 0.

Lesson 1.3 **19**

Math On the Spot
my.hrw.com

X²
Animated Math
my.hrw.com

Absolute Value In A Real-World Situation

In real-world situations, absolute values are often used instead of negative numbers. For example, if you use a $50 gift card to make a $25 purchase, the change in your gift card balance can be represented by −$25.

EXAMPLE 1 Real World COMMON CORE 6.NS.7c

Jake uses his online music store gift card to buy an album of songs by his favorite band.

Find the negative number that represents the change in the balance on Jake's card after his purchase. Explain how absolute value would be used to express that number in this situation.

Music Online

| Account Balance | $25.00 |
| Cart | 1 album | $10.00 |

STEP 1 Find the negative integer that represents the change in the balance.

−$10 *The balance decreased by $10, so use a negative number.*

The balance went down, so the change is a negative number.

Math Talk
Mathematical Practices

Explain why the price Jake paid for the album is represented by a negative number.

Jake pays $10 so there will be a change of −$10 in Jake's gift card balance.

STEP 2 Use the number line to find the absolute value of −$10.

−10 is 10 units from 0 on the number line.

10 units

−10 −9 −8 −7 −6 −5 −4 −3 −2 −1 0 1 2 3 4 5 6 7 8 9 10

The absolute value of −$10 is $10, or $|-10| = 10$.

The balance on Jake's card decreased by $10.

Reflect

3. **Communicate Mathematical Ideas** Explain why the absolute value of a number will never be negative.

   The absolute value of a number is its distance from 0 on the number line. Distance can never be negative.

20 Unit 1

PROFESSIONAL DEVELOPMENT

CC Integrate Mathematical Practices MP.4

This lesson provides an opportunity to address this Mathematical Practice standard. It calls for students to apply mathematics to problems arising in everyday life, society, and the workplace. Example 1 and Explore Activity 2 draw direct connections between absolute value and real-world situations, including the amount owed on a credit card and the amount of money stored on a gift card.

Math Background

You can interpret absolute value as the magnitude of a real number without regard to its sign. It measures the amount of change rather than the direction of change; the farther a number is from 0, the greater its absolute value. This is easy to visualize on a number line. You can also look at it mathematically:

$|n| = n$ if n is ≥ 0

$|n| = -n$ if n is < 0

YOUR TURN

Avoid Common Errors

Make sure that students understand that the absolute value of any negative integer is its *distance* from zero on a number line, which is always expressed as a *nonnegative* number.

Talk About It
Check for Understanding

 Ask: What can you say about the distance of numbers −55 and 55 from 0? Because they are opposites, they are both the same distance from 0 and have the same absolute value.

EXPLORE ACTIVITY 2

Connect Vocabulary

Point out to students that when working with money, a loss or a debt can be represented by a negative number. So, in Explore Activity 2, the negative amounts represent money that you spent, a negative change.

Talk About It
Check for Understanding

 Ask: How can you tell which person owes the most money? His or her balance will have the greatest absolute value.

Questioning Strategies **CC** Mathematical Practices

- If a person has a credit card balance of $50 and has a −$30 change in their balance, how do you find the amount the person owes? Find the absolute value of −$30, which is $30, and add it to $50. The person now owes $80.

- If a person's credit card balance decreases, what happens to the amount the person owes? It decreases.

- When a person makes a payment on their credit card, what happens to the amount of money available on the card (card limit) and to the amount the person owes (card balance)? The amount of money available (card limit) will increase while the amount the person owes (card balance) will decrease.

Elaborate

Talk About It
Summarize the Lesson

 Ask: How do you use absolute value to compare two negative numbers, such as fees, or amounts owed on a credit card or other kind of loan? You compare the absolute values of the negative numbers; the negative number with the greater absolute value is the lesser amount, indicating a greater amount owed.

GUIDED PRACTICE

Engage with the Whiteboard

For Exercise 2, have students count the tick marks to show that the distance from 0 to −10 is 10.

Avoid Common Errors

Exercise 2 If students have difficulty understanding how a credit or a fee affects the bill, remind them that a credit is like a payment, it will decrease the balance, while a fee is like a purchase, it will increase the balance.

YOUR TURN

4. The temperature at night reached −13°F. Write an equivalent statement about the temperature using the absolute value of the number.

   The temperature at night reached 13°F below zero.

Find each absolute value.

5. |−12| __12__   6. |91| __91__   7. |−55| __55__

8. |0| __0__   9. |88| __88__   10. |1| __1__

EXPLORE ACTIVITY 2 *Real World* COMMON CORE 6.NS.7c, 6.NS.7d

Comparing Absolute Values

You can use absolute values to compare negative numbers in real-world situations.

Maria, Susan, George, and Antonio checked their credit card balances on their smartphones. The amounts owed are shown.

You owe: $20   You owe: $25   You owe: $30   You owe: $45

Susan   George   Antonio   Maria

Answer the following questions. When you have finished, you will have enough clues to match each smartphone with the correct person.

Remember: When someone owes a positive amount of money, this means that he or she has a *negative* balance.

A Maria's credit card balance is less than −$30. Does Maria owe more than $30 or less than $30? __more than $30__

B Susan's credit card balance is greater than −$25. Does Susan owe more than $25 or less than $25? __less than $25__

C George's credit card balance is $5 less than Susan's balance. Does George owe more than Susan or less than Susan? __more than Susan__

D Antonio owes $15 less than Maria owes. This means that Antonio's balance is __greater__ than Maria's balance.

E Write each person's name underneath his or her smartphone.

Personal Math Trainer
Online Assessment and Intervention
my.hrw.com

EXPLORE ACTIVITY 2 (cont'd)

Reflect

11. **Analyze Relationships** Use absolute value to describe the relationship between a negative credit card balance and the amount owed.

    The amount owed is the absolute value of the balance.

Guided Practice

1. **Vocabulary** If a number is ____negative____, then the number is less than its absolute value. (Explore Activity 1)

2. If Ryan pays his car insurance for the year in full, he will get a credit of $28. If he chooses to pay a monthly premium, he will pay a $10 late fee for any month that the payment is late. (Explore Activity 1, Example 1)

   a. Which of these values could be represented with a negative number? Explain.

      −$10; it is a fee, so it represents a change of −$10 in the amount of money Ryan has.

   b. Use the number line to find the absolute value of your answer from part a. $|-10| = 10$

      ← −10 −9 −8 −7 −6 −5 −4 −3 −2 −1 0 1 2 3 4 5 6 7 8 9 10 →

3. Leo, Gabrielle, Sinea, and Tomas are playing a video game. Their scores are described in the table below. (Explore Activity 2)

Name	Leo	Gabrielle	Sinea
Score	less than −100 points	20 more points than Leo	50 points less than Leo

   a. Leo wants to earn enough points to have a positive score. Does he need to earn more than 100 points or less than 100 points? __more than 100__

   b. Gabrielle wants to earn enough points to not have a negative score. Does she need to earn more points than Leo or less points than Leo? __less than Leo__

   c. Sinea wants to earn enough points to have a higher score than Leo. Does she need to earn more than 50 points or less than 50 points? __more than 50__

? ESSENTIAL QUESTION CHECK-IN

4. When is the absolute value of a number equal to the number?

   when the number is nonnegative

DIFFERENTIATE INSTRUCTION

Home Connection

Students may be unfamiliar with how loans work. Discuss that many people borrow money they need to buy expensive items like cars, furniture, computers, and homes. Discuss that people pay back the money they borrow over a period of time and they pay fees for that privilege. Invite students to cite some examples with which they are familiar. Then have them define absolute value in their own words and then explain how it is used to express the amount of money borrowed.

Critical Thinking

Ask: How does the relationship between a negative number and its absolute value compare with the relationship between a nonnegative number and its absolute value?

A nonnegative number is *equal to* its absolute value; a negative number is *less than* its absolute value.

Additional Resources

Differentiated Instruction includes:

• Reading Strategies

• Success for English Learners **ELL**

• Reteach

• Challenge **PRE-AP**

1.3 LESSON QUIZ

 6.NS.7c

1. Mia's credit card balance is less than −$85. Does she owe more or less than $85?

2. Leon has a gift card for $100. He spent $65 of it on books. Describe the change in Leon's card balance in two different ways.

3. The record low temperature in Oregon is −54 °F. Use absolute value to express that temperature in degrees below zero.

4. Nick's bank account balance changed by $34 one month and by −$82 the next month. Which amount represents the lesser change?

Lesson Quiz available online

 my.hrw.com

Answers

1. She owes more than $85.

2. Use the negative number −$65 to represent the change in the value of Leon's card; use absolute value to say that his balance will be $65 less.

3. 54 degrees below zero

4. $34

Evaluate

GUIDED AND INDEPENDENT PRACTICE

 6.NS.7, 6.NS.7c, 6.NS.7d

Concepts & Skills	Practice
Explore Activity 1 Finding Absolute Value	Exercises 1, 2
Example 1 Absolute Value in a Real-World Situation	Exercises 2, 5, 8–11
Explore Activity 2 Comparing Absolute Values	Exercises 3, 6, 7

Exercise	Depth of Knowledge (D.O.K.)	**Mathematical Practices**
5	**2** Skills/Concepts	**MP.4** Modeling
6	**2** Skills/Concepts	**MP.7** Using Structure
7	**3** Strategic Thinking H.O.T.	**MP.6** Precision
8	**2** Skills/Concepts	**MP.7** Using Structure
9	**2** Skills/Concepts	**MP.4** Modeling
10	**2** Skills/Concepts	**MP.4** Modeling
11	**2** Skills/Concepts	**MP.4** Modeling
12	**3** Strategic Thinking H.O.T.	**MP.8** Patterns
13	**3** Strategic Thinking H.O.T.	**MP.7** Using Structure
14	**3** Strategic Thinking H.O.T.	**MP.8** Patterns

Additional Resources

Differentiated Instruction includes:

• Leveled Practice worksheets

1.3 Independent Practice

COMMON CORE 6.NS.7, 6.NS.7c, 6.NS.7d

Personal Math Trainer
Online Assessment and Intervention
my.hrw.com

5. Financial Literacy Jacob earned $80 babysitting and deposited the money into his savings account. The next week he spent $85 on video games. Use integers to describe the weekly changes in Jacob's savings account balance.

The first week his balance changed by +$80. The

second week his balance changed by −$85.

6. Financial Literacy Sara's savings account balance changed by $34 one week and by −$67 the next week. Which amount represents the greatest change? −$67

7. Analyze Relationships Bertrand collects movie posters. The number of movie posters in his collection changes each month as he buys and sells posters. The table shows how many posters he bought or sold in the given months.

Month	January	February	March	April
Posters	Sold 20	Bought 12	Bought 22	Sold 28

a. Which months have changes that can be represented by positive numbers? Which months have changes that can be represented by negative numbers? Explain.

February and March represent positive numbers

because Bertrand bought posters. January and April

represent negative numbers because Bertrand sold

posters.

b. According to the table, in which month did the size of Bertrand's poster collection change the most? Use absolute value to explain your answer.

April; He sold 28 posters which can be represented

by −28. The absolute value of −28 is 28, the greatest

of any month.

8. Earth Science Death Valley has an elevation of −282 feet relative to sea level. Explain how to use absolute value to describe the elevation of Death Valley as a positive integer.

The absolute value of −282 is 282 so Death Valley is 282

feet below sea level.

9. Communicate Mathematical Ideas Lisa and Alice are playing a game. Each player either receives or has to pay play money based on the result of their spin. The table lists how much a player receives or pays for various spins.

Red	Pay $5
Blue	Receive $4
Yellow	Pay $1
Green	Receive $3
Orange	Pay $2

a. Express the amounts in the table as positive and negative numbers.

−5, 4, −1, 3, −2

b. Describe the change to Lisa's amount of money when the spinner lands on red.

The spinner landing on red results in a change of

−$5 to Lisa's amount of money.

10. Financial Literacy Sam's credit card balance is less than −$36. Does Sam owe more or less than $36? Sam owes more than $36.

11. Financial Literacy Emily spent $55 from her savings on a new dress. Explain how to describe the change in Emily's savings balance in two different ways.

Use a negative integer to say that Emily's balance

changed by −$55; Use absolute value to say that Emily's

balance is $55 less.

 FOCUS ON HIGHER ORDER THINKING

12. Make a Conjecture Can two different numbers have the same absolute value? If yes, give an example. If no, explain why not.

Yes, it is possible. For example, $|-1| = 1$ and $|1| = 1$.

13. Communicate Mathematical Ideas Does $-|-4| = |-(-4)|$? Justify your answer.

No; $-|-4| = -4$, and $|-(-4)| = |4| = 4$.

14. Critique Reasoning Angelique says that finding the absolute value of a number is the same as finding the opposite of the number. For example, $|-5| = 5$. Explain her error.

Angelique's technique only works if the original number

is negative. The absolute value of a nonnegative number

is equal to the number itself, not its opposite.

Work Area

EXTEND THE MATH PRE-AP
Activity available online ⏻ my.hrw.com

Activity Read each statement carefully. Write *True* or *False*.

1. $|14| > 14$ False

2. $|44| = |-44|$ True

3. $|-17| = 17$ True

4. $|-22| = -22$ False

5. $-n$ and n have the same absolute value. True

6. $|-33|$ is the opposite of -33. True

7. Rewrite one number in Exercises 1–4 above to make each false statement true and each true statement false.

1. $|14| > -14$ True

2. $-|44| = |-44|$ False

3. $|-17| = -17$ False

4. $|-22| = 22$ True

Ready to Go On?

Assess Mastery

Use the assessment on this page to determine if students have mastered the concepts and standards covered in this module.

 **RtI** **Response to Intervention**

Personal Math Trainer

Online Assessment and Intervention

(b) my.hrw.com

Intervention	Enrichment

Access Ready to Go On? assessment online, and receive instant scoring, feedback, and customized intervention or enrichment.

Online and Print Resources

Differentiated Instruction	*Differentiated Instruction*
• Reteach worksheets	• Challenge worksheets
• Reading Strategies **ELL**	**PRE-AP**
• Success for English Learners **ELL**	Extend the Math **PRE-AP** Lesson Activities in TE

Additional Resources

Assessment Resources includes:

• Leveled Module Quizzes

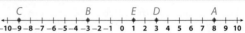

Ready to Go On?

Personal Math Trainer
Online Assessment and Intervention

(b) my.hrw.com

1.1 Identifying Integers and Their Opposites

1. The table shows the elevations in feet of several locations around a coastal town. Graph and label the locations on the number line according to their elevations.

Location	Post Office *A*	Library *B*	Town Hall *C*	Laundromat *D*	Pet Store *E*
Elevation (feet)	8	−3	−9	3	1

```
      C        B      E   D          A
 <─┼──┼──┼──┼──┼──┼──┼──┼──┼──┼──┼──┼──┼──┼──┼──┼──┼──┼──┼──┼─>
 −10−9−8−7−6−5−4−3−2−1  0  1  2  3  4  5  6  7  8  9 10
```

Write the opposite of each number.

2. −22 _____ 22   **3.** 0 _____ 0

1.2 Comparing and Ordering Integers

List the numbers in order from least to greatest.

4. −2, 8, −15, −5, 3, 1 _____ −15, −5, −2, 1, 3, 8

Compare. Write < or >.

5. −3 $>$ −15   **6.** 9 $>$ −10

1.3 Absolute Value

Graph each number on the number line. Then use your number line to find the absolute value of each number.

```
 <─┼──┼──┼──┼──┼──┼──┼──┼──┼──┼──┼──┼──┼──┼──┼──┼──┼──┼──┼──┼─>
 −10−9−8−7−6−5−4−3−2−1  0  1  2  3  4  5  6  7  8  9 10
```

7. 2 _____ 2   **8.** −8 _____ 8   **9.** −5 _____ 5

? ESSENTIAL QUESTION

10. How can you use absolute value to represent a negative number in a real-world situation?

Sample answer: Sam made a $20 payment on his credit card.

This represents a change of −$20 in the amount he owes.

Common Core Standards

Lesson	Exercises	Common Core Standards
1.1	1–3	**6.NS.5, 6.NS.6, 6.NS.6a, 6.NS.6c**
1.2	4–6	**6.NS.7, 6.NS.7a, 6.NS.7b**
1.3	7–9	**6.NS.7, 6.NS.7c, 6.NS.7d**

Assessment Readiness

Assessment Readiness Tip Students can draw a diagram, graph, or picture to help organize information from a test item.

Item 5 If students sketch a number line and plot a point for the temperature of each city, Calgary's point will be the farthest to the left. This means Calgary is the coldest, and therefore the correct answer.

Item 6 If students notice that each answer choice uses the same numbers in a different order, they can sketch a number line and plot the numbers from any of the answer choices. Reading the plotted points from left to right gives the order of the numbers from least to greatest, revealing C as the correct answer.

Avoid Common Errors

Item 2 Students may read the term *opposite* and think that the answer will be negative. Point out that they need to find the opposite of negative 3, which is positive 3.

Item 7 Caution students to read the question carefully so they understand what is being asked. The question asks for the numbers to be ordered from greatest to least rather than from least to greatest.

Additional Resources

Personal Math Trainer

Online Assessment and Intervention

my.hrw.com

MODULE 1 MIXED REVIEW

COMMON CORE

Assessment Readiness

Personal Math Trainer

Online Assessment and Intervention

my.hrw.com

Selected Response

1. Which number line shows 2, 3, and −3?

Ⓐ ── −4 −3 −2 −1 0 1 2 3 4
Ⓑ ── −4 −3 −2 −1 0 1 2 3 4
Ⓒ ── −4 −3 −2 −1 0 1 2 3 4
Ⓓ ── −4 −3 −2 −1 0 1 2 3 4

2. What is the opposite of −3?

Ⓐ 3   Ⓒ $-\frac{1}{3}$
Ⓑ 0   Ⓓ $\frac{1}{3}$

3. Darrel is currently 20 feet below sea level. Which correctly describes the opposite of Darrel's elevation?

Ⓐ 20 feet below sea level
Ⓑ 20 feet above sea level
Ⓒ 2 feet below sea level
Ⓓ At sea level

4. Which has the same absolute value as −55?

Ⓐ 0   Ⓒ 1
Ⓑ −1   Ⓓ 55

5. In Bangor it is −3 °F, in Fairbanks it is −12 °F, in Fargo it is −8 °F, and in Calgary it is −15 °F. In which city is it the coldest?

Ⓐ Bangor   Ⓒ Fargo
Ⓑ Fairbanks   Ⓓ Calgary

6. Which shows the integers in order from least to greatest?

Ⓐ 20, 6, −2, −13   Ⓒ −13, −2, 6, 20
Ⓑ −2, 6, −13, 20   Ⓓ 20, −13, 6, −2

7. How would you use a number line to put integers in order from greatest to least?

Ⓐ Graph the integers, then read them from left to right.
Ⓑ Graph the integers, then read them from right to left.
Ⓒ Graph the absolute values of the integers, then read them from left to right.
Ⓓ Graph the absolute values of the integers, then read them from right to left.

Mini-Task

8. The table shows the change in the amounts of money in several savings accounts over the past month.

Account	Change
A	$125
B	−$45
C	−$302
D	$108

a. List the dollar amounts in the order in which they would appear on a number line from left to right.

−$302, −$45, $108, $125

b. In which savings account was the absolute value of the change the greatest? Describe the change in that account.

Account C; $302 decrease

c. In which account was the absolute value of the change the least?

Account B; $45 decrease

Common Core Standards

Items	Grade 6 Standards	Mathematical Practices
1*	6.NS.6c	MP.6
2	6.NS.5, 6.NS.6a	MP.7
3	6.NS.5	MP.4
4	6.NS.7a, 6.NS.7b	MP.7
5	6.NS.5	MP.5
6	6.NS.7a, 6.NS.7b	MP.5
7	6.NS.7a, 6.NS.7b	MP.5
8	6.NS.7a, 6.NS.7b	MP.4

* Item integrates mixed review concepts from previous modules or a previous course.

Factors and Multiples

? ESSENTIAL QUESTION

How can you use greatest common factors and least common multiples to solve real-world problems?

You can use a GCF to divide two or more amounts into equal groups. You can use an LCM to find when two repeating number patterns match up.

LESSON 2.1
Greatest Common Factor

COMMON CORE 6.NS.4

LESSON 2.2
Least Common Multiple

COMMON CORE 6.NS.4

 my.hrw.com

Real-World Video

Organizers of banquets and other special events plan many things, including menus, seating arrangements, table decorations, and party favors. Factors and multiples can be helpful in this work.

© Houghton Mifflin Harcourt Publishing Company • Image Credits: STOCK4B-RF/Getty Images

GO DIGITAL
my.hrw.com

my.hrw.com	**Math On the Spot**	**Animated Math**	**Personal Math Trainer**
Go digital with your write-in student edition, accessible on any device.	Scan with your smart phone to jump directly to the online edition, video tutor, and more.	Interactively explore key concepts to see how math works.	Get immediate feedback and help as you work through practice sets.

Are You Ready?

Assess Readiness

Use the assessment on this page to determine if students need intensive or strategic intervention for the module's prerequisite skills.

 **RtI** Response to Intervention

Intervention	Enrichment

 Access Are You Ready? assessment online, and receive instant scoring, feedback, and customized intervention or enrichment.

Personal Math Trainer
Online Assessment and Intervention
⏻ my.hrw.com

Online and Print Resources

Skills Intervention worksheets
• Skill 7 Multiples
• Skill 8 Factors
• Skill 49 Multiplication Properties

Differentiated Instruction
• Challenge worksheets **PRE-AP**

Extend the Math **PRE-AP** Lesson Activities in TE

Are YOU Ready?

Complete these exercises to review skills you will need for this module.

Personal Math Trainer
Online Assessment and Intervention
⏻ my.hrw.com

Multiples

EXAMPLE	5×1 $= 5$	5×2 $= 10$	5×3 $= 15$	5×4 $= 20$	5×5 $= 25$	To find the first five multiples of 5, multiply 5 by 1, 2, 3, 4, and 5.

List the first five multiples of the number.

1. 7 __7, 14, 21, 28, 35__   2. 11 __11, 22, 33, 44, 55__   3. 15 __15, 30, 45, 60, 75__

Factors

EXAMPLE	$1 \times 12 = 12$ $2 \times 6 = 12$ $3 \times 4 = 12$ The factors of 12 are 1, 2, 3, 4, 6, 12.	To find the factors of 12, use multiplication facts of 12. Continue until pairs of factors repeat.

Write all the factors of the number.

4. 24 __1, 2, 3, 4, 6, 8, 12, 24__   5. 36 __1, 2, 3, 4, 6, 9, 12, 18, 36__

6. 45 __1, 3, 5, 9, 15, 45__   7. 32 __1, 2, 4, 8, 16, 32__

Multiplication Properties (Distributive)

EXAMPLE	$7 \times 14 = 7 \times (10 + 4)$ $= (7 \times 10) + (7 \times 4)$ $= 70 + 28$ $= 98$	To multiply a number by a sum, multiply the number by each addend and add the products.

Use the Distributive Property to find the product.

8. $8 \times 15 = 8 \times \left(\boxed{10} + \boxed{5} \right)$

$= \left(\boxed{8} \times \boxed{10} \right) + \left(\boxed{8} \times \boxed{5} \right)$

$= \boxed{80} + \boxed{40}$

$= \boxed{120}$

9. $6 \times 17 = 6 \times \left(\boxed{10} + \boxed{7} \right)$

$= \left(\boxed{6} \times \boxed{10} \right) + \left(\boxed{6} \times \boxed{7} \right)$

$= \boxed{60} + \boxed{42}$

$= \boxed{102}$

PROFESSIONAL DEVELOPMENT VIDEO

 Author Juli Dixon models successful teaching practices as she explores the concepts of greatest common factor and least common multiple in an actual sixth-grade classroom.

Professional Development
⏻ my.hrw.com

GO DIGITAL
my.hrw.com

 Online Teacher Edition
Access a full suite of teaching resources online—plan, present, and manage classes and assignments.

 ePlanner
Easily plan your classes and access all your resources online.

 Interactive Answers and Solutions
Customize answer keys to print or display in the classroom. Choose to include answers only or full solutions to all lesson exercises.

 Interactive Whiteboards
Engage students with interactive whiteboard-ready lessons and activities.

 Personal Math Trainer: Online Assessment and Intervention
Assign automatically graded homework, quizzes, tests, and intervention activities. Prepare your students with updated practice tests aligned with Common Core.

Reading Start-Up

Have students complete the activities on this page by working alone or with others.

Visualize Vocabulary

This graphic helps students review the vocabulary associated with factors and multiples. Students should write the word from the Review List in the box that shows an example of the word.

Understand Vocabulary

Use the following explanations to help students learn the preview words.

> When listing the factors of two numbers, the largest number that appears on both lists is the **greatest common factor.**

> When listing the multiples of two numbers, the smallest number that appears on both lists is the **least common multiple.**

Active Reading

Integrating Language Arts

Students can use these reading and note-taking strategies to help them organize and understand new concepts and vocabulary.

COMMON CORE **ELA-Literacy.RST.6-8.7** *Integrate quantitative or technical information expressed in words in a text with a version of that information expressed visually (e.g., in a flowchart, diagram, model, graph, or table).*

Additional Resources

Differentiated Instruction

• Reading Strategies **ELL**

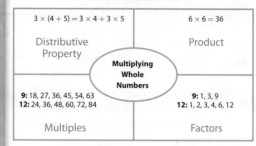

Reading Start-Up

Vocabulary

Review Words

✔ area *(área)*
✔ Distributive Property *(Propiedad distributiva)*
✔ factor *(factor)*
✔ multiple *(múltiplo)*
✔ product *(producto)*

Preview Words

greatest common factor (GCF) *(máximo común divisor (MCD))*
least common multiple (LCM) *(mínimo común múltiplo (m.c.m.))*

Visualize Vocabulary

Use the ✔ words to complete the graphic.

$3 \times (4 + 5) = 3 \times 4 + 3 \times 5$	$6 \times 6 = 36$
Distributive Property	Product
9: 18, 27, 36, 45, 54, 63 **12:** 24, 36, 48, 60, 72, 84	**9:** 1, 3, 9 **12:** 1, 2, 3, 4, 6, 12
Multiples	Factors

(center: Multiplying Whole Numbers)

Understand Vocabulary

Complete the sentences below using the preview words.

1. Of all the whole numbers that divide evenly into two or more numbers, the one with the highest value is called the _____greatest common factor_____.

2. Of all the common products of two numbers, the one with the lowest value is called the _____least common multiple_____.

Active Reading

Two-Panel Flip Chart Create a two-panel flip chart to help you understand the concepts in this module. Label one flap "Greatest Common Factor." Label the other flap "Least Common Multiple." As you study each lesson, write important ideas under the appropriate flap.

© Houghton Mifflin Harcourt Publishing Company

Module 2   **29**

Before	**In this module**	**After**
Students recognize, order, and perform computations with integers: • identify a number and its opposite • compare and order integers using a number line • find the absolute value of a number	Students work with factors and multiples: • find the greatest common factor of two whole numbers less than or equal to 100 and the least common multiple of two whole numbers less than or equal to 12 • use the Distributive Property to express a sum of two whole numbers 1–100 with a common factor as a multiple of a sum of two whole numbers with no common factor	Students will connect rational numbers and integers: • identify opposites and absolute value • locate, compare, and order integers using a number line

Unpacking the Standards

Use the examples on the page to help students know exactly what they are expected to learn in this module.

Common Core Standards

Content Areas

 The Number System —6.NS

Compute fluently with multi-digit numbers and find common factors and multiples.

> **Go online to see a complete unpacking of the Common Core Standards.**
> ⏻ my.hrw.com

MODULE 2

Unpacking the Standards

Understanding the standards and the vocabulary terms in the standards will help you know exactly what you are expected to learn in this module.

COMMON CORE 6.NS.4

Find the **greatest common factor** of two whole numbers less than or equal to 100 and the least common multiple of two whole numbers less than or equal to 12. Use the Distributive Property to express a sum of two whole numbers 1–100 with a common factor as a multiple of a sum of two whole numbers with no common factor.

Key Vocabulary

greatest common factor (GCF)
(máximo común divisor (MCD))
The largest common factor of two or more given numbers.

What It Means to You

You will determine the greatest common factor of two numbers and solve real-world problems involving the greatest common factor.

UNPACKING EXAMPLE 6.NS.4

There are 12 boys and 18 girls in Ms. Ruiz's science class. Each lab group must have the same number of boys and the same number of girls. What is the greatest number of groups Ms. Ruiz can make if every student must be in a group?

Factors of 12: 1, 2, 3, 4, 6, 12

Factors of 18: 1, 2, 3, 6, 9, 18

The GCF of 12 and 18 is 6. The greatest number of groups Ms. Ruiz can make is 6.

COMMON CORE 6.NS.4

Find the greatest common factor of two whole numbers less than or equal to 100 and the **least common multiple** of two whole numbers less than or equal to 12. …

Key Vocabulary

least common multiple (LCM)
(mínimo común múltiplo (m.c.m.))
The smallest number, other than zero, that is a multiple of two or more given numbers.

 Visit my.hrw.com to see all the Common Core Standards unpacked.
⏻ my.hrw.com

What It Means to You

You will determine the least common multiple of two numbers and solve real-world problems involving the least common multiple.

UNPACKING EXAMPLE 6.NS.4

Lydia's family will provide juice boxes and granola bars for 24 players. Juice comes in packs of 6, and granola bars in packs of 8. What is the least number of packs of each needed so that every player has a drink and a granola bar and there are none left over?

Multiples of 6: 6, 12, 18, 24, 30, …

Multiples of 8: 8, 16, 24, 32, …

The LCM of 6 and 8 is 24. Lydia's family should buy $24 \div 6 = 4$ packs of juice and $24 \div 8 = 3$ packs of granola bars.

30 Unit 1

Common Core Standards	Lesson 2.1	Lesson 2.2
6.NS.4 Find the **greatest common factor** of two whole numbers less than or equal to 100.	COMMON CORE	
6.NS.4 Find the **least common multiple** of two whole numbers less than or equal to 12.		COMMON CORE
6.NS.4 Use the Distributive Property to express a sum of two whole numbers 1–100 with a common factor as a multiple of a sum of two whole numbers with no common factor.	COMMON CORE	

LESSON
2.1 Greatest Common Factor

Common Core Standards

The student is expected to:

 The Number System—6.NS.4

Find the greatest common factor of two whole numbers less than or equal to 100 and the least common multiple of two whole numbers less than or equal to 12. Use the distributive property to express a sum of two whole numbers 1–100 with a common factor as a multiple of a sum of two whole numbers with no common factor.

Mathematical Practices

 MP.2 Reasoning

ADDITIONAL EXAMPLE 1

Jill has 12 apples and 16 pears that she wants to arrange in baskets. There needs to be the same numbers of apples and of pears in each basket. What is the greatest number of baskets she can make? How many apples and pears will be in each basket? 4 baskets; 3 apples and 4 pears

 Interactive Whiteboard
Interactive example available online

⏻ my.hrw.com

Engage

ESSENTIAL QUESTION

How can you find and use the greatest common factor of two whole numbers? List the factors of each number, and then identify the factors shared by the numbers. The greatest common factor of two or more numbers is the greatest value that is a factor of each of the numbers.

Motivate the Lesson

Ask: How can math help a florist decide how to arrange flowers or help a baker to package bagels? Begin the Explore Activity to find out.

Explore

EXPLORE ACTIVITY 1

Focus on Patterns

Show students the relationship between the numbers in the table by explaining the relationship between the factors and the number. Every factor of a number has a "partner." For example, if 3 is a factor of 18, to determine its partner students should ask themselves, "what number multiplied by 3 equals 18?" Since the answer is 6, 6 is also a factor of 18.

Explain

EXAMPLE 1

Connect Vocabulary

Remind students that factors are numbers that divide evenly into a number. For example, 4 is a factor of 24 because $24 \div 4 = 6$. Therefore, 24 is divisible by both 4 and by 6 because $4 \times 6 = 24$.

Questioning Strategies CC Mathematical Practices

• How would the boxes change if the baker had 32 sesame bagels instead of 24 sesame bagels? The baker would only be able to make 4 boxes, as 4 is the GCF of 32 and 36. There would be 8 sesame bagels in each box because $32 \div 4 = 8$. There would be 9 plain bagels because $36 \div 4 = 9$.

YOUR TURN

Engage with the Whiteboard

Have student volunteers list the factors of each number on the whiteboard. Then have them circle the common factors using colored markers to make it easier to identify the common factors.

Avoid Common Errors

Some students may find *any* common factor, instead of the *greatest* common factor. Remind them to find the greatest of the common factors.

Greatest Common Factor

COMMON CORE 6.NS.4
Find the greatest common factor of two whole numbers....

? ESSENTIAL QUESTION How can you find and use the greatest common factor of two whole numbers?

EXPLORE ACTIVITY 1 Real World

COMMON CORE 6.NS.4

Understanding Common Factors

The **greatest common factor (GCF)** of two numbers is the greatest factor shared by those numbers.

A florist makes bouquets from 18 roses and 30 tulips. All the bouquets will include both roses and tulips. If all the bouquets are identical, what are the possible bouquets that can be made?

A Complete the tables to show the possible ways to divide each type of flower among the bouquets.

Roses

Number of Bouquets	1	2	3	6	9	18
Number of Roses in Each Bouquet	18	9	6	3	2	1

Tulips

Number of Bouquets	1	2	3	5	6	10	15	30
Number of Tulips in Each Bouquet	30	15	10	6	5	3	2	1

B Can the florist make five bouquets using all the flowers? Explain.

No; 18 (the number of roses) is not divisible by 5.

C What are the common factors of 18 and 30? What do they represent?

1, 2, 3, and 6; the possible numbers of bouquets

D What is the GCF of 18 and 30? _____ 6

Reflect

1. **What If?** Suppose the florist has 18 roses and 36 tulips. What is the GCF of the numbers of roses and tulips? Explain.

Since 36 is a multiple of 18, the GCF is 18.

Finding the Greatest Common Factor

One way to find the GCF of two numbers is to list all of their factors. Then you can identify common factors and the GCF.

Math On the Spot my.hrw.com

EXAMPLE 1 Real World

COMMON CORE 6.NS.4

A baker has 24 sesame bagels and 36 plain bagels to put into boxes. Each box must have the same number of each type of bagel. What is the greatest number of boxes that the baker can make using all of the bagels? How many sesame bagels and how many plain bagels will be in each box?

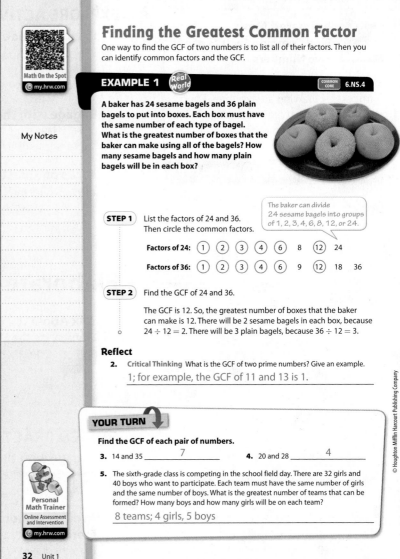

STEP 1 List the factors of 24 and 36. Then circle the common factors.

The baker can divide 24 sesame bagels into groups of 1, 2, 3, 4, 6, 8, 12, or 24.

Factors of 24: ① ② ③ ④ ⑥ 8 ⑫ 24

Factors of 36: ① ② ③ ④ ⑥ 9 ⑫ 18 36

STEP 2 Find the GCF of 24 and 36.

The GCF is 12. So, the greatest number of boxes that the baker can make is 12. There will be 2 sesame bagels in each box, because $24 \div 12 = 2$. There will be 3 plain bagels, because $36 \div 12 = 3$.

Reflect

2. **Critical Thinking** What is the GCF of two prime numbers? Give an example.

1; for example, the GCF of 11 and 13 is 1.

YOUR TURN

Personal Math Trainer
Online Assessment and Intervention
my.hrw.com

Find the GCF of each pair of numbers.

3. 14 and 35 _____ 7

4. 20 and 28 _____ 4

5. The sixth-grade class is competing in the school field day. There are 32 girls and 40 boys who want to participate. Each team must have the same number of girls and the same number of boys. What is the greatest number of teams that can be formed? How many boys and how many girls will be on each team?

8 teams; 4 girls, 5 boys

My Notes

PROFESSIONAL DEVELOPMENT

CC Integrate Mathematical Practices MP.2

This lesson provides an opportunity to address the Mathematical Practice standard that calls for students to "reason abstractly and quantitatively." In Explore Activity 1 and Example 1, students identify common factors and the GCF to make reasonable decisions on arranging items or forming groups. In Explore Activity 2, students use quantitative reasoning to use area models to identify a GCF in an application of the distributive property.

Math Background

Euclid's work *The Elements* contains a method for determining the greatest common factor of two whole numbers that is known as the Euclidean algorithm.

Here is a simple variation of the Euclidean algorithm: If $a > b$, the GCF of a and b equals the GCF of b and $a - b$. For example, the GCF of 48 and 30 equals the GCF of 30 and 18. This process can be continued until one of the terms divides the other: the GCF of 30 and 18 equals the GCF of 18 and 12; the GCF of 18 and 12 equals the GCF of 12 and 6. Because 6 divides 12, the GCF of 48 and 30 is 6.

EXPLORE ACTIVITY 2

Focus on Modeling Mathematical Practices

• **How can you use grid paper to find factors of a number?** By making area models of rectangles that have areas of 45 and 60, you can find the common factors of 45 and 60. The side lengths of these rectangles are the factors of the numbers.

Engage with the Whiteboard

Have students draw area models for the number 60 on the whiteboard. Then ask the students to answer questions C through F, writing their answers on the whiteboard.

Focus on Questioning Strategies Mathematical Practices

• **How would this process change if you were adding three numbers instead of two?** You would still find the GCF for all three numbers, but your addition problem would contain three numbers instead of two to find the other factor.

Elaborate

Talk About It
Summarize the Lesson

Ask: How do you find the GCF of two or more numbers? List the factors of each number and then identify the factors shared by the numbers. The greatest common factor of two or more numbers is the greatest value that is a factor of each of the numbers.

GUIDED PRACTICE

Engage with the Whiteboard

For Exercise 1, have students fill in the table on the whiteboard. Then have them answer each question explaining their reasoning.

Avoid Common Errors

Exercise 2 If students have difficulty writing each number as a product of the GCF and the sum of two numbers, encourage them to make area models to represent the numbers 36 and 45. The side lengths of these rectangles are the factors of 36 and 45.

COMMON CORE 6.NS.4

Using the Distributive Property

You can use the Distributive Property to rewrite a sum of two or more numbers as a product of their GCF and a sum of numbers with no common factor. To understand how, you can use grid paper to draw area models of 45 and 60. Here are all the possible area models of 45.

Animated Math
my.hrw.com

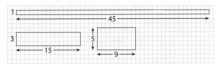

A What do the side lengths of the area models (1, 3, 5, 9, 15, and 45) represent? _factors of 45_

B On your own grid paper, show all of the possible area models of 60.
Check students' work.

C What side lengths do the area models of 45 and 60 have in common? What do the side lengths represent?
1, 3, 5, 15; common factors of 45 and 60

D What is the greatest common side length? What does it represent?
15; GCF of 45 and 60

E Write 45 as a product of the GCF and another number. _15 × 3_
Write 60 as a product of the GCF and another number. _15 × 4_

F Use your answers above to rewrite 45 + 60.

45 + 60 = 15 × _3_ + 15 × _4_

Use the Distributive Property and your answer above to write 45 + 60 as a product of the GCF and a sum of two numbers.

15 × _3_ + 15 × _4_ = 15 × (_3_ + _4_) = 15 × 7

> **Math Talk**
> Mathematical Practices
> How can you check to see if your product is correct?

Make sure the numbers in the sum have no common factors. Then perform the operations to make sure each expression has the same value.

Reflect

Write the sum of the numbers as the product of their GCF and another sum.

6. 27 + 18 _9 × (3 + 2) = 9 × 5_

7. 120 + 36 _12 × (10 + 3) = 12 × 13_

8. 9 + 35 _1 × (9 + 35) = 1 × 44_

---

1. Lee is sewing vests using 16 green buttons and 24 blue buttons. All the vests are identical, and all have both green and blue buttons. What are the possible numbers of vests Lee can make? What is the greatest number of vests Lee can make? (Explore Activity 1, Example 1)

List the factors of 16 and 24. Then circle the common factors.

Factors of 16:	①	②	④	⑧	16			
Factors of 24:	①	②	3	④	6	⑧	12	24

What are the common factors of 16 and 24? _1, 2, 4, 8_

What are the possible numbers of vests Lee can make? _1, 2, 4, 8_

What is the GCF of 16 and 24? _8_

What is the greatest number of vests Lee can make? _8_

Write the sum of numbers as a product of their GCF and another sum.
(Explore Activity 2)

2. 36 + 45

What is the GCF of 36 and 45? _9_

Write each number as a product of the GCF and another number. Then use the Distributive Property to rewrite the sum.

$$\left(\boxed{9} \times \boxed{4}\right) + \left(\boxed{9} \times \boxed{5}\right) = \left(\boxed{9}\right) \times \left(\boxed{4} + \boxed{5}\right)$$

3. 75 + 90

What is the GCF of 75 and 90? _15_

Write each number as a product of the GCF and another number. Then use the Distributive Property to rewrite the sum.

$$\left(\boxed{15} \times \boxed{5}\right) + \left(\boxed{15} \times \boxed{6}\right) = \left(\boxed{15}\right) \times \left(\boxed{5} + \boxed{6}\right)$$

? ESSENTIAL QUESTION CHECK-IN

4. Describe how to find the GCF of two numbers.
Find the common factors of the two numbers; the GCF is the greatest factor both numbers have in common.

DIFFERENTIATE INSTRUCTION

Visual Cues

Some students may benefit from using colored pencils to circle the common factors in the list of factors they generate. This may help prevent them from overlooking a pair when determining the GCF.

Curriculum Integration

Language Arts Explore nonmathematical meanings for the words *greatest* and *common*. Ask students to brainstorm a list of synonyms for each term. Synonyms for *greatest* might include *highest*, *biggest*, and *largest*. Synonyms for *common* might include *same*, *shared*, and *mutual*. Finally, have students define *greatest common factor* using some of the synonyms they listed. Sample answers: largest shared factor; biggest same factor; highest mutual factor

Additional Resources

Differentiated Instruction includes:

- Reading Strategies
- Success for English Learners **ELL**
- Reteach
- Challenge **PRE-AP**

2.1 LESSON QUIZ

 6.NS.4

1. What is the GCF of 36 and 48?

2. Paul has 16 fish pictures and 12 deer pictures to display. He wants to arrange the pictures in rows with the same numbers of fish and of deer pictures in each row. What are the possible numbers of rows Paul will need?

3. Megan has 30 brownies and 42 cupcakes to package. She wants to put the same numbers of brownies and of cupcakes in each box. What is the greatest number of boxes she can make? How many cupcakes and how many brownies will each box contain?

4. Write $54 + 63$ as the product of the GCF of 54 and 63 and another sum.

Lesson Quiz available online

 my.hrw.com

Answers
1. 12

2. 1, 2, and 4

3. 6 boxes; each box will have 5 brownies and 7 cupcakes.

4. $9 \times (6 + 7) = 9 \times 13$

Evaluate

GUIDED AND INDEPENDENT PRACTICE

 6.NS.4

Concepts and Skills	Practice
Explore Activity 1 Understanding Common Factors	Exercises 1, 5–8
Example 1 Finding the Greatest Common Factor	Exercises 1, 9–22
Explore Activity 2 Using the Distributive Property	Exercises 2–3, 23–30

Exercise	Depth of Knowledge (D.O.K.)	COMMON CORE Mathematical Practices
5–18	**2** Skills/Concepts	**MP.6** Precision
19–22	**3** Strategic Thinking H.O.T.	**MP.2** Reasoning
23–30	**2** Skills/Concepts	**MP.2** Reasoning
31–32	**3** Strategic Thinking H.O.T.	**MP.2** Reasoning
33	**3** Strategic Thinking H.O.T.	**MP.1** Problem Solving
34	**3** Strategic Thinking H.O.T.	**MP.2** Reasoning

Additional Resources
Differentiated Instruction includes:

• Leveled Practice Worksheets

CC CLUSTER CONNECTION **Exercise 34** combines concepts from the Common Core cluster "Compute fluently with multi-digit numbers and find common factors and multiples."

2.1 Independent Practice

COMMON CORE 6.NS.4

Personal Math Trainer

Online Assessment and Intervention

my.hrw.com

List the factors of each number.

5. 12 _1, 2, 3, 4, 6, 12_

6. 50 _1, 2, 5, 10, 25, 50_

7. 39 _1, 3, 13, 39_

8. 64 _1, 2, 4, 8, 16, 32, 64_

Find the GCF of each pair of numbers.

9. 40 and 48 _8_

10. 30 and 45 _15_

11. 10 and 45 _5_

12. 25 and 90 _5_

13. 21 and 40 _1_

14. 28 and 70 _14_

15. 60 and 72 _12_

16. 45 and 81 _9_

17. 28 and 32 _4_

18. 55 and 77 _11_

19. Carlos is arranging books on shelves. He has 24 novels and 16 autobiographies. Each shelf will have the same numbers of novels and autobiographies. If Carlos must place all of the books on shelves, what are the possible numbers of shelves Carlos will use?

1, 2, 4, or 8 shelves

20. The middle school band has 56 members. The high school band has 96 members. The bands are going to march one after the other in a parade. The director wants to arrange the bands into the same number of columns. What is the greatest number of columns in which the two bands can be arranged if each column has the same number of marchers? How many band members will be in each column?

8 columns; 19 band members

21. For football tryouts at a local school, 12 coaches and 42 players will split into groups. Each group will have the same numbers of coaches and players. What is the greatest number of groups that can be formed? How many coaches and players will be in each of these groups?

6 groups; 2 coaches and 7 players

22. Lola is placing appetizers on plates. She has 63 spring rolls and 84 cheese cubes. She wants to include both appetizers on each plate. Each plate must have the same numbers of spring rolls and cheese cubes. What is the greatest number of plates she can make using all of the appetizers? How many of each type of appetizer will be on each of these plates?

21 plates; 3 spring rolls and 4 cheese cubes

Write the sum of the numbers as the product of their GCF and another sum.

23. 56 + 64 _8 × (7 + 8) = 8 × 15_

24. 48 + 14 _2 × (24 + 7) = 2 × 31_

25. 30 + 54 _6 × (5 + 9) = 6 × 14_

26. 24 + 40 _8 × (3 + 5) = 8 × 8_

27. 55 + 66 _11 × (5 + 6) = 11 × 11_

28. 49 + 63 _7 × (7 + 9) = 7 × 16_

29. 40 + 25 _5 × (8 + 5) = 5 × 13_

30. 63 + 15 _3 × (21 + 5) = 3 × 26_

31. **Vocabulary** Explain why the greatest common factor of two numbers is sometimes 1.

1 is a factor of all whole numbers, and some pairs of whole numbers have no common factors other than 1. For example, 7 and 16 have no common factors other than 1.

H.O.T. FOCUS ON HIGHER ORDER THINKING

Work Area

32. **Communicate Mathematical Ideas** Tasha believes that she can rewrite the difference 120 − 36 as a product of the GCF of the two numbers and another difference. Is she correct? Explain your answer.

Yes; the GCF of 120 and 36 is 12, so 120 − 36 can be written as 12 × 10 − 12 × 3, which is 12 × (10 − 3) or 12 × 7.

33. **Persevere in Problem Solving** Explain how to find the greatest common factor of three numbers.

Find the factors of all three numbers, and take the greatest factor that is common to all three. For example, for the GCF of 6, 9, and 12, the factors of 6 are 1, 2, 3, and 6; the factors of 9 are 1, 3, and 9; and the factors of 12 are 1, 2, 3, 4, 6, and 12. So, the GCF is 3.

34. **Critique Reasoning** Xiao's teacher asked him to rewrite the sum 60 + 90 as the product of the GCF of the two numbers and a sum. Xiao wrote 3(20 + 30). What mistake did Xiao make? How should he have written the sum?

He found a common factor, but not the greatest common factor. The GCF of 60 and 90 is 30. He should have written the sum as 30(2 + 3).

EXTEND THE MATH PRE-AP

Activity available online my.hrw.com

You can also find the GCF using Euclid's algorithm.

Divide the lesser number into the greater number. If the remainder is 0, the lesser number is the GCF. If the remainder is not 0, keep dividing the remainder into the previous divisor until the remainder is 0. The last divisor is the GCF.

Example: Find the GCF of 128 and 176.

Step 1: 176 ÷ 128 = 1 R48

Step 2: 128 ÷ 48 = 2 R32

Step 3: 48 ÷ 32 = 1 R16

Step 4: 32 ÷ 16 = 2 R0

16 is the last divisor and the GCF of 128 and 176.

Have students try this method for the following:

1. 75 and 120 _15_

2. 105 and 252 _21_

3. 360 and 654 _6_

LESSON
2.2 Least Common Multiple

Common Core Standards

The student is expected to:

 The Number System—6.NS.4

Find the greatest common factor of two whole numbers less than or equal to 100 and the least common multiple of two whole numbers less than or equal to 12. Use the distributive property to express a sum of two whole numbers 1–100 with a common factor as a multiple of a sum of two whole numbers with no common factor.

Mathematical Practices

 MP.8 Patterns

ADDITIONAL EXAMPLE 1
Jack has baseball practice every third day and swimming practice every second day. During a month that has 30 days, how many days will Jack have both practices? 5 days

 Interactive Whiteboard
Interactive example available online

 my.hrw.com

Engage

ESSENTIAL QUESTION

How do you find and use the least common multiple of two whole numbers? List multiples of both numbers. The least common multiple (LCM) will be the least multiple that is common to both numbers. It can be used for determining the least number that both numbers will divide into without a remainder.

Motivate the Lesson
Ask: If an athlete trains for one sport every sixth day and another every eighth day, how can you determine the days on which the athlete will train for both sports? Begin the Explore Activity to find out.

Explore

EXPLORE ACTIVITY

Engage with the Whiteboard
For A, have students list the multiples of 6 and 8 next to the chart. Then have students highlight the common multiples in each list with a colored marker to emphasize that both methods provide the same results. Repeat this activity with the numbers 6 and 9.

Explain

EXAMPLE 1

Connect Vocabulary ELL
Remind students that a *multiple* of a number is the product of the number and any nonzero whole number. There is no limit as to how many multiples you can list for a given number.

Questioning Strategies CC Mathematical Practices
• When finding the least common multiple of a pair of numbers, which number will you more likely need to list more multiples of to find the LCM? The lesser number will require a longer list of multiples than the greater number.

YOUR TURN

Avoid Common Errors
Some students may confuse LCM with GCF. Tell them to concentrate on the words *multiple* and *factor* to keep their meanings straight.

Questioning Strategies CC Mathematical Practices
• When listing multiples to find the LCM, how do you know when to stop? When you find the first common multiple, you can stop.

LESSON
2.2 Least Common Multiple

COMMON CORE 6.NS.4
Find … the least common multiple of two whole numbers….

? ESSENTIAL QUESTION
How do you find and use the least common multiple of two numbers?

EXPLORE ACTIVITY Real World   COMMON CORE 6.NS.4

Finding the Least Common Multiple

A multiple of a number is the product of the number and another number. For example, 9 is a multiple of the number 3. The **least common multiple (LCM)** of two or more numbers is the least number, other than zero, that is a multiple of all the numbers.

Ned is training for a biathlon. He will swim every sixth day and bicycle every eighth day. On what days will he both swim and bicycle?

A In the chart below, shade each day that Ned will swim. Circle each day Ned will bicycle.

1	2	3	4	5	6	7	8	9	10
11	12	13	14	15	16	17	18	19	20
21	22	23	24	25	26	27	28	29	30
31	32	33	34	35	36	37	38	39	40
41	42	43	44	45	46	47	48	49	50
51	52	53	54	55	56	57	58	59	60
61	62	63	64	65	66	67	68	69	70
71	72	73	74	75	76	77	78	79	80
81	82	83	84	85	86	87	88	89	90
91	92	93	94	95	96	97	98	99	100

B On what days will Ned both swim and bicycle?

24, 48, 72, and 96

The numbers of the days that Ned will swim and bicycle are common multiples of 6 and 8.

Reflect

1. Interpret the Answer What does the LCM represent in this situation?

The first day that Ned will both swim and bicycle.

Applying the LCM

You can use the LCM of two whole numbers to solve problems.

EXAMPLE 1 Real World   COMMON CORE 6.NS.4

A store is holding a promotion. Every third customer receives a free key chain, and every fourth customer receives a free magnet. Which customer will be the first to receive both a key chain and a magnet?

STEP 1 List the multiples of 3 and 4. Then circle the common multiples.

Multiples of 3: 3   6   9   (12)   15   18   21   (24)   27

Multiples of 4: 4   8   (12)   16   20   (24)   28   32   36

STEP 2 Find the LCM of 3 and 4.

The LCM is 12.

The first customer to get both a key chain and a magnet is the 12th customer.

Multiply the number by 1, 2, 3, and so on.

Math Talk
Mathematical Practices
What steps do you take to list the multiples of a number?

Math On the Spot
my.hrw.com

Personal Math Trainer
Online Assessment and Intervention
my.hrw.com

YOUR TURN

2. Find the LCM of 4 and 9 by listing the multiples. ___36___

Multiples of 4: 4, 8, 12, 16, 20, 24, 28, 32, 36, 40

Multiples of 9: 9, 18, 27, 36, 45, 54, 63, 72, 81, 90

Guided Practice

1. After every ninth visit to a restaurant you receive a free beverage. After every twelfth visit you receive a free appetizer. If you visit the restaurant 100 times, on which visits will you receive a free beverage and a free appetizer? At which visit will you first receive a free beverage and a free appetizer? (Explore Activity 1, Example 1)

36th and 72nd visits; 36th visit

? ESSENTIAL QUESTION CHECK-IN

2. What steps can you take to find the LCM of two numbers?

Find common multiples of the two numbers; the LCM is the least multiple both numbers have in common.

DIFFERENTIATE INSTRUCTION

Curriculum Integration
Language Arts Explore nonmathematical meanings for the words *least* and *common*. Ask students to brainstorm a list of synonyms for each term. Synonyms for *least* might include *lowest*, *smallest*, and *tiniest*. Synonyms for *common* might include *same*, *shared*, and *mutual*. Finally, have students define *least common multiple* using some of the synonyms they listed. Sample answers: smallest shared multiple; tiniest same multiple; lowest mutual multiple

Critical Thinking
Ask students to find as many pairs of numbers as they can that have the LCM of 48. When they are finished, have students share and compare their answers and their methods. Sample answers: 3 and 16, 12 and 16, 16 and 24

Additional Resources
Differentiated Instruction includes:
- Reading Strategies
- Success for English Learners **ELL**
- Reteach
- Challenge **PRE-AP**

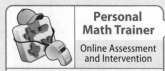

2.2 LESSON QUIZ

 6.NS.4

1. Find the LCM for 7 and 9.

2. Find the LCM for 12 and 15.

3. For the month of March, Kasey plans to vacuum her floor every fourth day and clean her bathroom every seventh day. If she begins this March 1, on what day of the month will she do both jobs?

4. List a pair of numbers that would have 20 as their LCM.

Lesson Quiz available online

 my.hrw.com

Answers

1. 63

2. 60

3. March 28

4. Sample answer: 4 and 5

Elaborate

Talk About It
Summarize the Lesson

 Ask: How do you find the LCM of two numbers? List multiples of both numbers. The least common multiple (LCM) will be the least multiple that is common to both numbers.

GUIDED PRACTICE

Engage with the Whiteboard

 For Exercise 1, have the students create a chart showing the numbers 0-100 on the whiteboard. Then have students highlight or circle the multiples of 9 and 12 using different colored markers. Also, have students make lists of multiples of 9 and 12 next to the chart. Discuss the pros and cons of each method.

Avoid Common Errors

Exercise 1 Point out to students that they can also use repeated addition to help make sure they do not omit a multiple from their lists.

Evaluate

GUIDED AND INDEPENDENT PRACTICE

COMMON CORE **6.NS.4**

Concepts and Skills	Practice
Explore Activity Finding the Least Common Multiple	Exercises 2, 3–11
Example 1 Applying the Least Common Multiple	Exercises 1, 12, 14, 15

Exercise	Depth of Knowledge (D.O.K.)	COMMON CORE Mathematical Practices
3–10	**2** Skills/Concepts	**MP.1** Problem Solving
11	**2** Skills/Concepts	**MP.2** Reasoning
12	**3** Strategic Thinking H.O.T.	**MP.3** Logic
13–15	**2** Skills/Concepts	**MP.8** Patterns
16–17	**3** Strategic Thinking H.O.T.	**MP.2** Reasoning
18–19	**3** Strategic Thinking H.O.T.	**MP.3** Logic
20	**3** Strategic Thinking H.O.T.	**MP.7** Use Structure

Additional Resources

Differentiated Instruction includes:

• Leveled Practice Worksheets

2.2 Independent Practice

 6.NS.4

Personal Math Trainer

Online Assessment and Intervention

my.hrw.com

Find the LCM of each pair of numbers.

3. 8 and 56 ____56____

4. 25 and 50 ____50____

5. 12 and 30 ____60____

6. 6 and 10 ____30____

7. 16 and 24 ____48____

8. 14 and 21 ____42____

9. 9 and 15 ____45____

10. 5 and 11 ____55____

11. During February, Kevin will water his ivy every third day, and water his cactus every fifth day.

    a. On which date will Kevin first water both plants together?

    February 15

    b. Will Kevin water both plants together again in February? Explain.

    No; there are only 28 or 29 days in February, and the next common multiple of 3 and 5 is 30.

12. Vocabulary Given any two numbers, which is greater, the LCM of the numbers or the GCF of the numbers? Why?

LCM; the LCM is a multiple of both numbers, so it is greater than or equal to the greater number; the GCF is a factor of both numbers, so it is less than or equal to the lesser number.

Use the subway train schedule.

13. The red line and the blue line trains just arrived at the station. When will they next arrive at the station at the same time?

In ____40____ minutes

14. The blue line and the yellow line trains just arrived at the station. When will they next arrive at the station at the same time?

In ____60____ minutes

15. All three trains just arrived at the station. When will they next all arrive at the station at the same time?

In ____120____ minutes

Train Schedule

Train	Arrives Every...
Red line	8 minutes
Blue line	10 minutes
Yellow line	12 minutes

16. You buy a lily and an African violet on the same day. You are instructed to water the lily every fourth day and water the violet every seventh day after taking them home. What is the first day on which you will water both plants on the same day? How can you use this answer to determine each of the next days you will water both plants on the same day?

Both will be watered on day 28; the next days will be multiples of 28, so determine the multiples of 28. The plants will be watered together on day 28, day 56, day 84, and so on.

H.O.T. FOCUS ON HIGHER ORDER THINKING

Work Area

17. What is the LCM of two numbers if one number is a multiple of the other? Give an example.

The LCM is the greater of the two numbers. For example, the LCM of 4 and 8 is 8.

18. What is the LCM of two numbers that have no common factors greater than 1? Give an example.

The LCM is the product of the two numbers. For example, the LCM of 4 and 9 is 36.

19. Draw Conclusions The least common multiple of two numbers is 60, and one of the numbers is 7 less than the other number. What are the numbers? Justify your answer.

5 and 12; 60 is a multiple of each of its factors, which are 1, 2, 3, 4, 5, 6, 10, 12, 15, 20, 30, and 60. The factors with a difference of 7 are 5 and 12, and their LCM is 60.

20. Communicate Mathematical Ideas Describe how to find the least common multiple of three numbers. Give an example.

To find the LCM of three numbers, list the multiples of each and take the least multiple that is common to all three. For example, find the LCM of 6, 8, and 12. First, list the multiples of each. The multiples of 6 are 6, 12, 18, 24, …. The multiples of 8 are 8, 16, 24, 32, …. The multiples of 12 are 12, 24, 36, …. The LCM of 6, 8, and 12 is 24.

EXTEND THE MATH PRE-AP

Activity available online my.hrw.com

Activity During its grand opening weekend, a restaurant gave every eighth customer a free appetizer, every twelfth customer a free beverage, and every fifteenth customer a free dish of frozen yogurt.

a. Which customer was the first to receive all three free items? 120

b. Which customer was the first to receive a free appetizer and frozen yogurt? 120

c. If the restaurant served 500 customers that weekend, how many of those customers received all three free items? 4

Ready to Go On?

Assess Mastery

Use the assessment on this page to determine if students have mastered the concepts and standards covered in this module.

 **Response to Intervention**

Intervention	Enrichment

Access Are You Ready? assessment online, and receive instant scoring, feedback, and customized intervention or enrichment.

Personal Math Trainer
Online Assessment and Intervention
⏻ my.hrw.com

Online and Print Resources

Differentiated Instruction
• Reteach worksheets
• Reading Strategies **ELL**
• Success for English Learners **ELL**

Differentiated Instruction
• Challenge worksheets
 PRE-AP
• Extend the Math **PRE-AP**
 Lesson Activities in TE

Additional Resources

Assessment Resources includes:
• Leveled Module Quizzes

Ready to Go On?

Personal Math Trainer
Online Assessment and Intervention
my.hrw.com

2.1 Greatest Common Factor

Find the GCF of each pair of numbers.

1. 20 and 32 ___4___   2. 24 and 56 ___8___

3. 36 and 90 ___18___   4. 45 and 75 ___15___

5. 28 girls and 32 boys volunteer to plant trees at a school. The principal divides the girls and boys into identical groups that have girls and boys in each group. What is the greatest number of groups the principal can make? ___4___

Write the sum of the numbers as the product of their GCF and another sum.

6. 32 + 20 $4 \times (8 + 5) = 4 \times 13$

7. 18 + 27 $9 \times (2 + 3) = 9 \times 5$

2.2 Least Common Multiple

Find the LCM of each pair of numbers.

8. 6 and 12 ___12___   9. 6 and 10 ___30___

10. 8 and 9 ___72___   11. 9 and 12 ___36___

12. Juanita runs every third day and swims every fifth day. If Juanita runs and swims today, in how many days will she run and swim again on the same day? ___in 15 days___

 **ESSENTIAL QUESTION**

13. What types of problems can be solved using the greatest common factor? What types of problems can be solved using the least common multiple?

Sample answer: Problems in which two different amounts must be split into the same number of groups can be solved using the GCF; problems with events that occur on different schedules can be solved using the LCM.

Common Core Standards

Lesson	Exercises	Common Core Standards
2.1	1–7	**6.NS.4**
2.2	8–12	**6.NS.4**

Assessment Readiness

Assessment Readiness Tip Remind students to think about the differences between factors and multiples.

Item 1 A least common multiple cannot be smaller than the larger number given in the question. As the number 150 is larger than 5, the least common multiple must be at least 150.

Item 5 The greatest common factor of a pair of numbers cannot be larger than the smaller number. Since the numbers are 12 and 16, the largest possible factor of both numbers would not be greater than 12. Recognizing this fact may prevent students from selecting 48, which is the LCM of 12 and 16.

Avoid Common Errors

Item 2 If students have difficulty with this problem, remind them to begin by first finding the greatest common factor of the two sets of cards. Then they can determine how many packages can be formed.

Item 8 If students have difficulty with this problem, remind them to begin by first finding the least common multiple of the number of cups and plates that come in each package. Then they can determine how many packages need to be purchased.

Additional Resources

Personal Math Trainer

Online Assessment and Intervention

my.hrw.com

MODULE 2 MIXED REVIEW
COMMON CORE
Assessment Readiness

Personal Math Trainer
Online Assessment and Intervention
my.hrw.com

Selected Response

1. What is the least common multiple of 5 and 150?
   - Ⓐ 5
   - Ⓒ 15
   - Ⓑ 50
   - Ⓓ 150

2. Cy has 42 baseball cards and 70 football cards that he wants to group into packages. Each package will have the same number of cards, and each package will have the same numbers of baseball cards and football cards. How many packages will Cy make if he uses all of the cards?
   - Ⓐ 7
   - Ⓒ 14
   - Ⓑ 10
   - Ⓓ 21

3. During a promotional event, a sporting goods store gave a free T-shirt to every 8th customer and a free water bottle to every 10th customer. Which customer was the first to get a free T-shirt and a free water bottle?
   - Ⓐ the 10th customer
   - Ⓑ the 20th customer
   - Ⓒ the 40th customer
   - Ⓓ the 80th customer

4. The table below shows the positions relative to sea level of four divers.

Kareem	Li	Maria	Tara
−8 ft	−10 ft	−9 ft	−7 ft

   Which diver is farthest from the surface?
   - Ⓐ Kareem
   - Ⓒ Maria
   - Ⓑ Li
   - Ⓓ Tara

5. What is the greatest common factor of 12 and 16?
   - Ⓐ 2
   - Ⓒ 12
   - Ⓑ 4
   - Ⓓ 48

6. Which expression is equivalent to $27 + 15$?
   - Ⓐ $9 \times (3 + 5)$
   - Ⓑ $3 \times (9 + 15)$
   - Ⓒ $9 \times (3 + 15)$
   - Ⓓ $3 \times (9 + 5)$

7. During a science experiment, the temperature of a solution in Beaker 1 was 5 degrees below zero. The temperature of a solution in Beaker 2 was the opposite of the temperature in Beaker 1. What was the temperature in Beaker 2?
   - Ⓐ −5 degrees
   - Ⓒ 5 degrees
   - Ⓑ 0 degrees
   - Ⓓ 10 degrees

Mini-Task

8. Tia is buying paper cups and plates. Cups come in packages of 12, and plates come in packages of 10. She wants to buy the same number of cups and plates, but plans to buy the least number of packages possible. How much should Tia expect to pay if each package of cups is $3 and each package of plates is $5? Explain.

   $45; the LCM of 12 and 10 is 60, so she will have 60 cups, which is 5 packages, and 60 plates, which is 6 packages. The cups cost $15 and the plates cost $30, for a total of $45.

© Houghton Mifflin Harcourt Publishing Company

Common Core Standards

Items	Grade 6 Standards	Mathematical Practices
1	6.NS.4	MP.2
2	6.NS.4	MP.4
3	6.NS.4	MP.4
4	6.NS.5	MP.4
5	6.NS.4	MP.2
6	6.NS.4	MP.7
7*	6.NS.5	MP.4
8	6.NS.4	MP.4

* Item integrates mixed review concepts from previous modules or a previous course.

Rational Numbers

ESSENTIAL QUESTION

How can you use rational numbers to solve real-world problems?

You can represent any real-world quantity that can be written as $\frac{a}{b}$, where a and b are integers and $b \neq 0$, as a rational number.

Real-World Video

In sports like baseball, coaches, analysts, and fans keep track of players' statistics such as batting averages, earned run averages, and runs batted in. These values are reported using rational numbers.

my.hrw.com

GO DIGITAL

my.hrw.com

 my.hrw.com

Go digital with your write-in student edition, accessible on any device.

 Math On the Spot

Scan with your smart phone to jump directly to the online edition, video tutor, and more.

 Animated Math

Interactively explore key concepts to see how math works.

 Personal Math Trainer

Get immediate feedback and help as you work through practice sets.

Are You Ready?

Assess Readiness

Use the assessment on this page to determine if students need intensive or strategic intervention for the module's prerequisite skills.

RtI Response to Intervention

Intervention	Enrichment

Access Are You Ready? assessment online, and receive instant scoring, feedback, and customized intervention or enrichment.

Personal Math Trainer

Online Assessment and Intervention

 my.hrw.com

Online and Print Resources

Skills Intervention worksheets
- Skill 17 Compare and Order Decimals
- Skill 21 Write an Improper Fraction as a Mixed Number
- Skill 22 Write a Mixed Number as an Improper Fraction

Differentiated Instruction
- Challenge worksheets **PRE-AP**
- Extend the Math **PRE-AP** Lesson Activities in TE

Are YOU Ready?

Complete these exercises to review skills you will need for this module.

 Personal Math Trainer
Online Assessment and Intervention
my.hrw.com

Write an Improper Fraction as a Mixed Number

EXAMPLE
$$\frac{11}{3} = \frac{3}{3} + \frac{3}{3} + \frac{3}{3} + \frac{2}{3}$$ Write as a sum using names for one plus a proper fraction.
$$= 1 + 1 + 1 + \frac{2}{3}$$ Write each name for one as one.
$$= 3 + \frac{2}{3}$$ Add the ones.
$$= 3\frac{2}{3}$$ Write the mixed number.

Write each improper fraction as a mixed number.

1. $\frac{7}{2}$ $3\frac{1}{2}$
2. $\frac{12}{5}$ $2\frac{2}{5}$
3. $\frac{11}{7}$ $1\frac{4}{7}$
4. $\frac{15}{4}$ $3\frac{3}{4}$

Write a Mixed Number as an Improper Fraction

EXAMPLE $3\frac{3}{4} = 1 + 1 + 1 + \frac{3}{4}$ Write the whole number as a sum of ones.
$$= \frac{4}{4} + \frac{4}{4} + \frac{4}{4} + \frac{3}{4}$$ Use the denominator of the fraction to write equivalent fractions for the ones.
$$= \frac{15}{4}$$ Add the numerators.

Write each mixed number as an improper fraction.

5. $2\frac{1}{2}$ $\frac{5}{2}$
6. $4\frac{3}{5}$ $\frac{23}{5}$
7. $3\frac{4}{9}$ $\frac{31}{9}$
8. $2\frac{5}{7}$ $\frac{19}{7}$

Compare and Order Decimals

EXAMPLE Order from least to greatest: 7.32, 5.14, 5.16.
7.32 is greatest.
5.14 < 5.16
The order is 5.14, 5.16, 7.32.   Use place value to compare numbers, starting with ones, then tenths, then hundredths.

Compare the decimals.

9. 8.86 $>$ 8.65
10. 0.732 $<$ 0.75
11. 0.22 $>$ 0.022

12. Order 0.98, 0.27, and 0.34 from greatest to least.   0.98, 0.34, 0.27

© Houghton Mifflin Harcourt Publishing Company

PROFESSIONAL DEVELOPMENT VIDEO

Author Juli Dixon models successful teaching practices as she explores rational numbers in an actual sixth-grade classroom.

Professional Development

my.hrw.com

GO DIGITAL
my.hrw.com

Online Teacher Edition
Access a full suite of teaching resources online—plan, present, and manage classes and assignments.

ePlanner
Easily plan your classes and access all your resources online.

Interactive Answers and Solutions
Customize answer keys to print or display in the classroom. Choose to include answers only or full solutions to all lesson exercises.

Interactive Whiteboards
Engage students with interactive whiteboard-ready lessons and activities.

Personal Math Trainer: Online Assessment and Intervention
Assign automatically graded homework, quizzes, tests, and intervention activities. Prepare your students with updated practice tests aligned with Common Core.

Reading Start-Up

Have students complete the activities on this page by working alone or with others.

Visualize Vocabulary

The main idea web helps students learn the vocabulary and organize the concepts related to integers. In each of the outer boxes, students should write one or more review words that describe the numbers.

Understand Vocabulary

Use the following explanations to help students learn the preview words.

Many things are alike in some ways and different in others. For example, a lizard and a snake are both reptiles. They are alike because they are both cold-blooded. But a lizard has legs and a snake does not. In that way they are different. When we think about how things are alike and how they are different, we compare and contrast them.

To help you compare and contrast ideas in this chapter, you will use a **Venn diagram**.

Active Reading

Integrating Language Arts

Students can use these reading and note-taking strategies to help them organize and understand new concepts and vocabulary.

COMMON CORE **ELA-Literacy.RST.6-8.7** Integrate quantitative or technical information expressed in words in a text with a version of that information expressed visually (e.g., in a flowchart, diagram, model, graph, or table).

Additional Resources

Differentiated Instruction

- Reading Strategies **ELL**

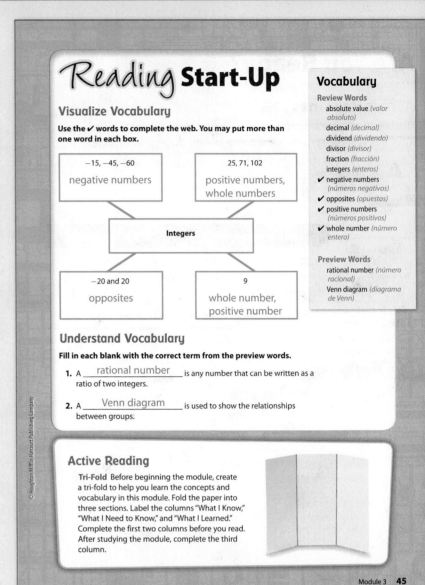

Before	In this module	After
Students work with factors and multiples: • find the greatest common factor • use the distributive property	Students classify, order, and compare rational numbers: • classify whole numbers, integers, and rational numbers using a visual representation such as a Venn diagram to describe relationships between sets of numbers • identify opposites and absolute values of rational numbers • compare and order a set of rational numbers arising from mathematical and real-world contexts	Students will connect rational numbers and integers: • describe relationships between sets and subsets of rational numbers • perform operations with rational numbers • locate, compare, and order rational numbers using a number line

Unpacking the Standards

Use the examples on the page to help students know exactly what they are expected to learn in this module.

Common Core Standards

Content Areas

 The Number System—6.NS

Apply and extend previous understandings of numbers to the system of rational numbers.

Go online to see a complete unpacking of the Common Core Standards.

my.hrw.com

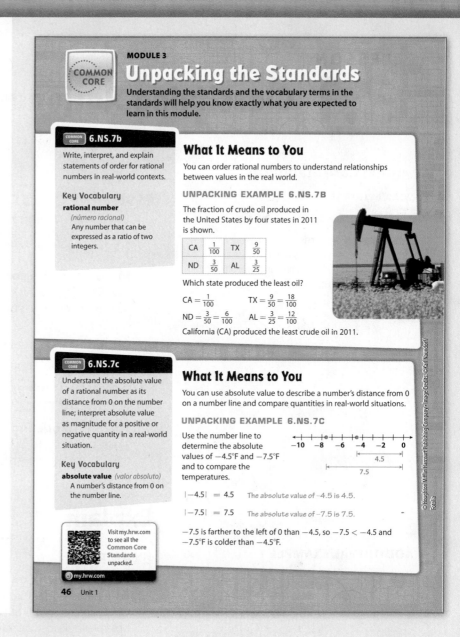

MODULE 3
Unpacking the Standards

Understanding the standards and the vocabulary terms in the standards will help you know exactly what you are expected to learn in this module.

6.NS.7b

Write, interpret, and explain statements of order for rational numbers in real-world contexts.

Key Vocabulary

rational number
(número racional)
Any number that can be expressed as a ratio of two integers.

What It Means to You

You can order rational numbers to understand relationships between values in the real world.

UNPACKING EXAMPLE 6.NS.7B

The fraction of crude oil produced in the United States by four states in 2011 is shown.

| CA | $\frac{1}{100}$ | TX | $\frac{9}{50}$ |
| ND | $\frac{3}{50}$ | AL | $\frac{3}{25}$ |

Which state produced the least oil?

$CA = \frac{1}{100}$ $TX = \frac{9}{50} = \frac{18}{100}$

$ND = \frac{3}{50} = \frac{6}{100}$ $AL = \frac{3}{25} = \frac{12}{100}$

California (CA) produced the least crude oil in 2011.

6.NS.7c

Understand the absolute value of a rational number as its distance from 0 on the number line; interpret absolute value as magnitude for a positive or negative quantity in a real-world situation.

Key Vocabulary

absolute value *(valor absoluto)*
A number's distance from 0 on the number line.

What It Means to You

You can use absolute value to describe a number's distance from 0 on a number line and compare quantities in real-world situations.

UNPACKING EXAMPLE 6.NS.7C

Use the number line to determine the absolute values of $-4.5°F$ and $-7.5°F$ and to compare the temperatures.

$|-4.5| = 4.5$ *The absolute value of -4.5 is 4.5.*

$|-7.5| = 7.5$ *The absolute value of -7.5 is 7.5.*

-7.5 is farther to the left of 0 than -4.5, so $-7.5 < -4.5$ and $-7.5°F$ is colder than $-4.5°F$.

Visit my.hrw.com to see all the Common Core Standards unpacked.

my.hrw.com

Common Core Standards	Lesson 3.1	Lesson 3.2	Lesson 3.3
6.NS.6 Understand a rational number as a point on the number line. Extend number line diagrams and coordinate axes … to represent points on the line and in the plane with negative number coordinates.	COMMON CORE	COMMON CORE	
6.NS.6a Recognize opposite signs of numbers as indicating locations on opposite sides of 0 on the number line; recognize that the opposite of the opposite of a number is the number itself, e.g., $-(-3) = 3$, and that 0 is its own opposite.		COMMON CORE	
6.NS.6c Find and position integers and other rational numbers on a horizontal or vertical number line diagram; find and position pairs of integers and other rational numbers on a coordinate plane.		COMMON CORE	
6.NS.7a Interpret statements of inequality as statements about the relative position of two numbers on a number line diagram.			COMMON CORE
6.NS.7b Write, interpret, and explain statements of order for rational numbers in real-world contexts.			COMMON CORE
6.NS.7c Understand the absolute value of a rational number as its distance from 0 on the number line; interpret absolute value as magnitude for positive or negative quantity in a real-world situation.		COMMON CORE	

3.1 Classifying Rational Numbers

Common Core Standards

The student is expected to:

 The Number System—6.NS.6

Understand a rational number as a point on the number line. Extend number line diagrams and coordinate axes familiar from previous grades to represent points on the line and in the plane with negative number coordinates.

Mathematical Practices

 MP.3 Logic

ADDITIONAL EXAMPLE 1
Write each rational number as $\frac{a}{b}$:

A) $1\frac{3}{8}$ $\frac{11}{8}$

B) 0.75 $\frac{75}{100}$

C) 12 $\frac{12}{1}$

D) -9 $\frac{-9}{1}$

 Interactive Whiteboard
Interactive example available online

 my.hrw.com

Engage

ESSENTIAL QUESTION

How can you classify rational numbers? You classify numbers according to their characteristics. Rational numbers can be written as a quotient of two integers, so rational numbers can be fractions, decimals, integers, or whole numbers.

Motivate the Lesson
Ask: Biologists classify animals based on shared characteristics. For example, the horned lizard is an animal, a reptile, a lizard, and a gecko. How can you classify the number −12?

Explore

EXPLORE ACTIVITY

Focus on Modeling
It may be helpful to give each student 3 paper squares and a pair of scissors to work through the Explore Activity with physical models.

Explain

EXAMPLE 1

Focus on Math Connections
Point out to students that part of the definition of a rational number is that the denominator, *b*, cannot equal zero. This is because division by zero is undefined. It is possible to divide 0 pizza between 3 people; each person would get 0 pizza. But 3 pizzas shared by 0 people is meaningless.

Questioning Strategies **CC** Mathematical Practices

• How do you decide which number to use for the denominator when you are rewriting a decimal as a fraction? You use the place value of the digit farthest to the right. For example, if the decimal has 2 places, use 100 for the denominator.

• What are three equivalent expressions for $3\frac{2}{5}$? You can write it as a mixed number, as an improper faction, and as a decimal. $3\frac{2}{5}$; $\frac{17}{5}$; 3.4

YOUR TURN

Avoid Common Errors
Remind students that when writing a negative integer as a fraction, they need to include the negative sign with the fraction.

Talk About It
Check for Understanding
Ask: How can you show that a number is a rational number? by writing it as a fraction where the numerator and the denominator are both integers, and the denominator is not equal to 0

Classifying Rational Numbers

COMMON CORE 6.NS.6
Understand a rational number as a point on the number line…

? ESSENTIAL QUESTION

How can you classify rational numbers?

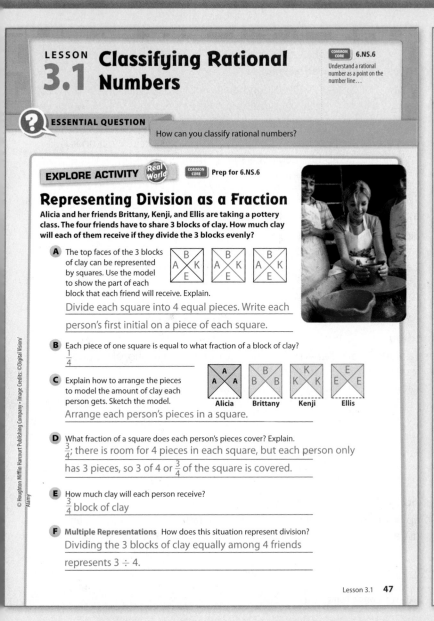

EXPLORE ACTIVITY *Real World*

COMMON CORE Prep for 6.NS.6

Representing Division as a Fraction

Alicia and her friends Brittany, Kenji, and Ellis are taking a pottery class. The four friends have to share 3 blocks of clay. How much clay will each of them receive if they divide the 3 blocks evenly?

A The top faces of the 3 blocks of clay can be represented by squares. Use the model to show the part of each block that each friend will receive. Explain.

Divide each square into 4 equal pieces. Write each person's first initial on a piece of each square.

B Each piece of one square is equal to what fraction of a block of clay?

$\frac{1}{4}$

C Explain how to arrange the pieces to model the amount of clay each person gets. Sketch the model.

Alicia   Brittany   Kenji   Ellis

Arrange each person's pieces in a square.

D What fraction of a square does each person's pieces cover? Explain.

$\frac{3}{4}$; there is room for 4 pieces in each square, but each person only has 3 pieces, so 3 of 4 or $\frac{3}{4}$ of the square is covered.

E How much clay will each person receive?

$\frac{3}{4}$ block of clay

F **Multiple Representations** How does this situation represent division?

Dividing the 3 blocks of clay equally among 4 friends represents $3 \div 4$.

EXPLORE ACTIVITY *(cont'd)*

Reflect

1. **Communicate Mathematical Ideas** $3 \div 4$ can be written $\frac{3}{4}$. How are the dividend and divisor of a division expression related to the parts of a fraction?

The divisor is the denominator of the fraction and the dividend is the numerator.

2. **Analyze Relationships** How could you represent the division as a fraction if 5 people shared 2 blocks? if 6 people shared 5 blocks?

$\frac{2}{5}; \frac{5}{6}$

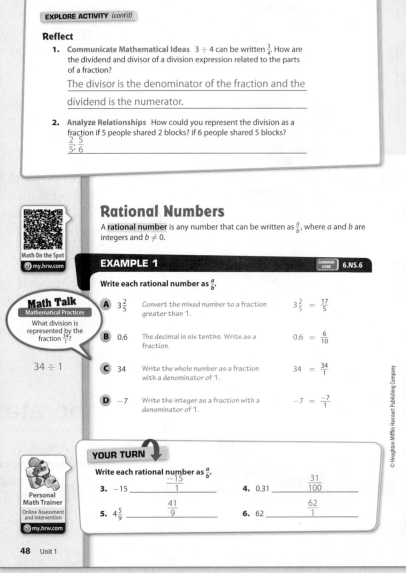

Math On the Spot
my.hrw.com

Rational Numbers

A **rational number** is any number that can be written as $\frac{a}{b}$, where a and b are integers and $b \neq 0$.

EXAMPLE 1

COMMON CORE 6.NS.6

Write each rational number as $\frac{a}{b}$.

Math Talk
Mathematical Practices

What division is represented by the fraction $\frac{34}{1}$?

$34 \div 1$

A $3\frac{2}{5}$ — Convert the mixed number to a fraction greater than 1. — $3\frac{2}{5} = \frac{17}{5}$

B 0.6 — The decimal is six tenths. Write as a fraction. — $0.6 = \frac{6}{10}$

C 34 — Write the whole number as a fraction with a denominator of 1. — $34 = \frac{34}{1}$

D -7 — Write the integer as a fraction with a denominator of 1. — $-7 = \frac{-7}{1}$

YOUR TURN

Write each rational number as $\frac{a}{b}$.

3. -15 $\frac{-15}{1}$

4. 0.31 $\frac{31}{100}$

5. $4\frac{5}{9}$ $\frac{41}{9}$

6. 62 $\frac{62}{1}$

Personal Math Trainer
Online Assessment and Intervention
my.hrw.com

PROFESSIONAL DEVELOPMENT

CC Integrate Mathematical Practices MP.3

This lesson provides an opportunity to address this Mathematical Practice standard. It calls for students to justify mathematical ideas using precise mathematical language. Students use the mathematical definition of a rational number to justify that numbers are rational numbers by rewriting them to meet the requirements of the definition.

Math Background

Rational numbers and Irrational numbers make up the set of Real Numbers. As this lesson states, rational numbers are numbers that can be expressed as a quotient of two integers. Irrational numbers are numbers that cannot be expressed as a quotient of two integers.

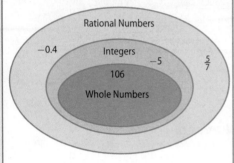
EXAMPLE 2

Questioning Strategies 🆑 Mathematical Practices

- In a Venn diagram, explain what it means when a number is within a particular circle. It means that the number is part of the group represented by the circle. For example, a number within the Integers circle is an integer.

- The Venn diagram shows the Whole Numbers circle within the Integers circle. What does that tell you about whole numbers? about integers? Name an integer that is not a whole number. It means that all whole numbers are integers. Not all integers are whole numbers. −2 is an integer but not a whole number.

Focus on Math Connections 🆑 Mathematical Practices

Point out to students the connections among the sets shown in the Venn diagram. The set of Whole Numbers is shown inside the smallest and most interior oval, so it is part of both of the outer sets, Integers and Rational Numbers.

YOUR TURN

Talk About It
Check for Understanding

Ask: Suppose a student says that −15 is an integer, but it is not a rational number because it is not a fraction. Is the student correct? Explain. The student is not correct. Integers are rational numbers. For instance, you can write −15 as $\frac{-15}{1}$.

Elaborate

. . . .

Talk About It
Summarize the Lesson

Present the graphic organizer showing how to classify a rational number in a Venn diagram. Discuss each box in the graphic organizer and complete it with students.

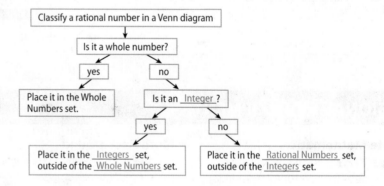

GUIDED PRACTICE

Engage with the Whiteboard

Have students suggest numbers that can be placed within the Venn diagram given for Exercises 5 and 6. Discuss what each placement tells them about the number.

Avoid Common Errors

Exercise 1 Remind students that Sarah counts as one of the classmates sharing the ribbon, so there are 5 students sharing.

Classifying Rational Numbers

A **Venn diagram** is a visual representation used to show the relationships between groups. The Venn diagram below shows how rational numbers, integers, and whole numbers are related.

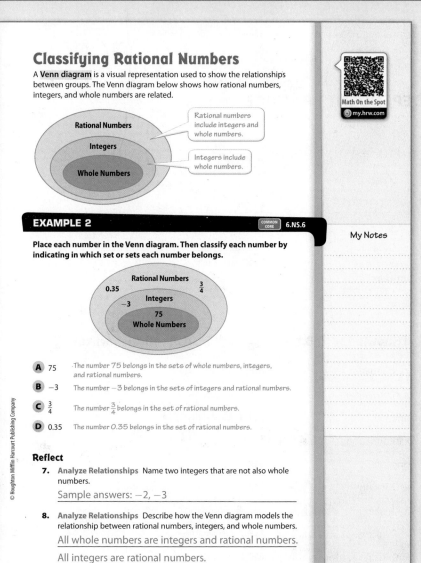

Rational numbers include integers and whole numbers.

Integers include whole numbers.

Math On the Spot
my.hrw.com

EXAMPLE 2
COMMON CORE 6.NS.6

Place each number in the Venn diagram. Then classify each number by indicating in which set or sets each number belongs.

Rational Numbers
0.35 $\frac{3}{4}$
Integers
−3
75
Whole Numbers

A 75   The number 75 belongs in the sets of whole numbers, integers, and rational numbers.

B −3   The number −3 belongs in the sets of integers and rational numbers.

C $\frac{3}{4}$ The number $\frac{3}{4}$ belongs in the set of rational numbers.

D 0.35   The number 0.35 belongs in the set of rational numbers.

Reflect

7. Analyze Relationships Name two integers that are not also whole numbers.

Sample answers: −2, −3

8. Analyze Relationships Describe how the Venn diagram models the relationship between rational numbers, integers, and whole numbers.

All whole numbers are integers and rational numbers.

All integers are rational numbers.

My Notes

Personal Math Trainer
Online Assessment and Intervention
my.hrw.com

YOUR TURN

Place each number in the Venn diagram. Then classify each number by indicating in which set or sets it belongs.

Rational Numbers
14.1 $7\frac{1}{5}$
Integers
−8
101
Whole Numbers

9. 14.1   rational numbers

10. $7\frac{1}{5}$ rational numbers

11. −8   integers and rational numbers

12. 101   whole numbers, integers, and rational numbers

Guided Practice

1. Sarah and four friends are decorating picture frames with ribbon. They have 4 rolls of ribbon to share evenly. (Explore Activity 1)

a. How does this situation represent division?

4 rolls of ribbon divided evenly among the 5 friends. 4 ÷ 5.

b. How much ribbon does each person receive? $\frac{4}{5}$ roll

Write each rational number in the form $\frac{a}{b}$, where a and b are integers. (Example 1)

2. 0.7 $\frac{7}{10}$ **3.** −29 $\frac{-29}{1}$ **4.** $8\frac{1}{3}$ $\frac{25}{3}$

Place each number in the Venn diagram. Then classify each number by indicating in which set or sets each number belongs. (Example 2)

5. −15   integers, rational numbers

6. $5\frac{10}{11}$ rational numbers

Rational Numbers
$5\frac{10}{11}$
Integers
−15
Whole Numbers

❓ ESSENTIAL QUESTION CHECK-IN

7. How is a rational number that is not an integer different from a rational number that is an integer?

When written in the form $\frac{a}{b}$, non integer rational

numbers have a denominator that does not divide

evenly into the numerator.

DIFFERENTIATE INSTRUCTION

Number Sense

Guide students to create a list of names for the different types of numbers. The list should include fractions, decimals, mixed numbers, positive fractions, negative fractions, whole numbers, counting numbers, and improper fractions. Have students give examples of each type that is mentioned. Then relate all the terms to a Rational Number Venn diagram.

Kinesthetic Experience

Give each student an index card. Have them write a rational number on the card. Encourage a variety of rational numbers: whole numbers, integers, fractions, and decimals. Then work with the class to create a Rational Number Venn diagram on which to place the cards. Use yarn to define an area for Rational Numbers, within that an area for Integers, and within the integer area, an area for Whole Numbers.

Additional Resources

Differentiated Instruction includes:
- Reading Strategies
- Success for English Learners **ELL**
- Reteach
- Challenge **PRE-AP**

3.1 LESSON QUIZ

COMMON CORE **6.NS.6**

1. There are 2 pounds of peanuts to be divided evenly into 10 bags.

  a. How does this situation represent division?

  b. What fraction of a pound of peanuts will each bag get?

Write each rational number as $\frac{a}{b}$.

2. −27   **3.** 16   **4.** 0.15   **5.** $7\frac{1}{2}$

Use the Venn diagram to determine in which set or sets each number belongs. Place the numbers in the Venn diagram.

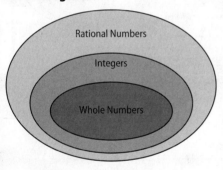

Rational Numbers

Integers

Whole Numbers

6. 18   **7.** −17   **8.** −2.3   **9.** $\frac{3}{8}$

Lesson Quiz available online

 my.hrw.com

Answers

1. a. 2 pounds must be evenly divided among 10 bags. This represents the division 2 ÷ 10.

  b. $\frac{2}{10}$ or $\frac{1}{5}$ pound

2. $\frac{-27}{1}$ **4.** $\frac{15}{100}$

3. $\frac{16}{1}$ **5.** $\frac{15}{2}$

6. Whole Numbers, Integers, Rational Numbers

7. Integers, Rational Numbers

8. Rational Numbers

9. Rational Numbers

Evaluate

GUIDED AND INDEPENDENT PRACTICE

COMMON CORE **6.NS.6**

Concepts & Skills	Practice
Explore Activity Representing Division as a Fraction	Exercises 1, 10, 14–16
Example 1 Rational Numbers	Exercises 2–4, 11
Example 2 Classifying Rational Numbers	Exercises 5, 6, 8, 9, 13, 14–16

Exercise	Depth of Knowledge (D.O.K.)		COMMON CORE Mathematical Practices
8	**1**	Recall of Information	**MP.2** Reasoning
9	**1**	Recall of Information	**MP.2** Reasoning
10–12	**2**	Skills/Concepts	**MP.4** Modeling
13	**1**	Recall of Information	
14–16	**2**	Skills/Concepts	**MP.4** Modeling
17	**3**	Strategic Thinking H.O.T.	**MP.4** Modeling
18	**3**	Strategic Thinking H.O.T.	**MP.6** Precision
19	**3**	Strategic Thinking H.O.T.	**MP.7** Using Structure
20	**3**	Strategic Thinking H.O.T.	**MP.8** Patterns

Additional Resources

Differentiated Instruction includes:

• Leveled Practice worksheets

3.1 Independent Practice

 6.NS.6

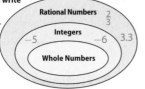 Personal Math Trainer

Online Assessment and Intervention

my.hrw.com

List two numbers that fit each description. Then write the numbers in the appropriate location on the Venn diagram. **Sample answers are given.**

Rational Numbers $\frac{2}{3}$

Integers

-5 -6 3.3

Whole Numbers

8. Integers that are not whole numbers

$-5, -6$

9. Rational numbers that are not integers

$\frac{2}{3}, 3.3$

10. Multistep A nature club is having its weekly hike. The table shows how many pieces of fruit and bottles of water each member of the club brought to share.

Member	Pieces of Fruit	Bottles of Water
Baxter	3	5
Hendrick	2	2
Mary	4	3
Kendra	5	7

a. If the hikers want to share the fruit evenly, how many pieces should each person receive?

$\frac{14}{4}$, or $3\frac{1}{2}$ pieces of fruit

b. Which hikers received more fruit than they brought on the hike?

Baxter and Hendrick

c. The hikers want to share their water evenly so that each member has the same amount. How much water does each hiker receive?

$\frac{17}{4}$, or $4\frac{1}{4}$ bottles of water

11. Sherman has 3 cats and 2 dogs. He wants to buy a toy for each of his pets. Sherman has $22 to spend on pet toys. How much can he spend on each pet? Write your answer as a fraction and as an amount in dollars and cents.

$\$\frac{22}{5}$, or $4.40

12. A group of 5 friends are sharing 2 pounds of trail mix. Write a division problem and a fraction to represent this situation.

$2 \div 5$; $\frac{2}{5}$

13. Vocabulary A ___Venn___ diagram can represent set relationships visually.

Financial Literacy For 14–16, use the table. The table shows Jason's utility bills for one month. Write a fraction to represent the division in each situation. Then classify each result by indicating the set or sets to which it belongs.

March Bills	
Water	$35
Gas	$14
Electric	$108

14. Jason and his 3 roommates share the cost of the electric bill evenly.

$\$\frac{108}{4}$; whole numbers, integers, rational numbers

15. Jason plans to pay the water bill with 2 equal payments.

$\$\frac{35}{2}$; rational numbers

16. Jason owes $15 for last month's gas bill also. The total amount of the two gas bills is split evenly among the 4 roommates.

$\$\frac{29}{4}$; rational numbers

17. Lynn has a watering can that holds 16 cups of water, and she fills it half full. Then she waters her 15 plants so that each plant gets the same amount of water. How many cups of water will each plant get?

$\frac{8}{15}$ cup

 **FOCUS ON HIGHER ORDER THINKING**

Work Area

18. Critique Reasoning DaMarcus says the number $\frac{24}{6}$ belongs only to the set of rational numbers. Explain his error.

$24 \div 6 = 4$, which is a whole number. $\frac{24}{6}$ belongs to the set of whole numbers and the set of integers, as well as the set of rational numbers.

19. Analyze Relationships Explain how the Venn diagrams in this lesson show that all integers and all whole numbers are rational numbers.

The oval representing the set of integers and the oval representing the set of whole numbers are inside of the oval representing the set of rational numbers.

20. Critical Thinking Is it possible for a number to be a rational number that is not an integer but is a whole number? Explain.

No; Every whole number is an integer.

EXTEND THE MATH PRE-AP

Activity available online my.hrw.com

Activity Use this activity to extend student understanding of sets, subsets, and Venn diagrams. Have students complete the Venn diagram by placing the numbers from 1 to 20 in the correct part of the diagram.

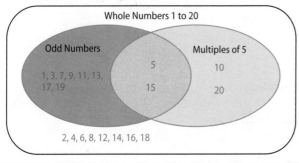

Whole Numbers 1 to 20

Odd Numbers

Multiples of 5

1, 3, 7, 9, 11, 13, 17, 19

5

15

10

20

2, 4, 6, 8, 12, 14, 16, 18

Common Core Standards

The student is expected to:

 The Number System—6.NS.6c

Find and position integers and other rational numbers on a horizontal or vertical number line diagram; find and position pairs of integers and other rational numbers on a coordinate plane. *Also 6.NS.6, 6.NS.6a, 6.NS.7, 6.NS.7c*

Mathematical Practices

 MP.4 Modeling

ADDITIONAL EXAMPLE 1

Alberto's average running time for 100 meters is $17\frac{1}{2}$ sec. Each day after he warms up, Alberto records his run time so he can compare it to his average time.

Day	Monday	Tuesday
Change in time	$2\frac{1}{4}$	$-1\frac{3}{4}$

Graph the change in time for Tuesday and its opposite.

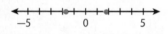

 Interactive Whiteboard
Interactive example available online

 my.hrw.com

Engage

ESSENTIAL QUESTION

How can you identify opposites and absolute values of rational numbers? Opposites are the same distance from 0 on the number line but on different sides of 0. Absolute value is the number's distance from 0.

Motivate the Lesson

Ask: Have you ever seen a picture of Death Valley? Death Valley is 282 feet below sea level. What is the opposite of 282 feet below sea level? How can you use positive and negative numbers to express values and their opposites? Begin the Explore Activity to find out.

Explore

EXPLORE ACTIVITY

Connect to Daily Life

Ask students if they have seen the tide come in, in person or in pictures or video. Point out to students that as the tides change so does sea level. At low tide, land that was below sea level may now be above sea level.

Explain

EXAMPLE 1

Focus on Math Connections CC Mathematical Practices

Emphasize that just as with positive and negative integers, the opposite of any negative rational number is a positive rational number, and the opposite of a positive rational number is a negative rational number.

Questioning Strategies CC Mathematical Practices

• Using the information presented in the table, can you find the price of the stock at the end of Wednesday? No, because the table does not give the starting price on Tuesday.

• How can you tell whether the stock gained value or lost value? Look at the sign of the number on the table. A positive number represents a gain; a negative number represents a loss.

YOUR TURN

Engage with the Whiteboard

 Have a student plot the value for Tuesday, $1\frac{5}{8}$, and its opposite on the vertical number line given in Step 1.

Talk About It
Check for Understanding

Ask: How do you find the opposite of a negative number on a number line? Find the number that is the same distance from 0 on the right hand side of 0 on the number line.

Identifying Opposites and Absolute Value of Rational Numbers

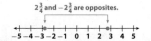

COMMON CORE 6.NS.6c

Find and position integers and other rational numbers on a horizontal or vertical number line diagram... *Also 6.NS.6, 6.NS.6a, 6.NS.7, 6.NS.7c*

 ESSENTIAL QUESTION How do you identify opposites and absolute value of rational numbers?

EXPLORE ACTIVITY **COMMON CORE** 6.NS.6, 6.NS.6c

Positive and Negative Rational Numbers

Recall that positive numbers are greater than 0. They are located to the right of 0 on a number line. Negative numbers are less than 0. They are located to the left of 0 on a number line.

Water levels with respect to sea level, which has elevation 0, may be measured at beach tidal basins. Water levels below sea level are represented by negative numbers.

A The table shows the water level at a tidal basin at different times during a day. Graph the level for each time on the number line.

Time	4 A.M. A	8 A.M. B	Noon C	4 P.M. D	8 P.M. E
Level (ft)	3.5	2.5	−0.5	−2.5	0.5

B How did you know where to graph −0.5? It is halfway between −1 and 0.

C At what time or times is the level closest to sea level? How do you know?
noon and 8 P.M.; they are each 0.5 units from 0.

D Which point is located halfway between −3 and −2? _____D_____

E Which point is the same distance from 0 as D? _____B_____

Reflect

1. **Communicate Mathematical Ideas** How would you graph −2.25? Would it be left or right of point D?
Graph the point halfway between −2.5 and −2; right

© Houghton Mifflin Harcourt Publishing Company • Image Credits: ©Anna Blume/Alamy

---

 Math On the Spot
©my.hrw.com

Rational Numbers and Opposites on a Number Line

You can find the opposites of rational numbers the same way you found the opposites of integers. Two rational numbers are opposite if they are the same distance from 0 but on different sides of 0.

$2\frac{3}{4}$ and $-2\frac{3}{4}$ are opposites.

$$-5\ -4\ -3\ -2\ -1\ \ 0\ \ 1\ \ 2\ \ 3\ \ 4\ \ 5$$

EXAMPLE 1 **COMMON CORE** 6.NS.6a, 6.NS.6c

Until June 24, 1997, the New York Stock Exchange priced the value of a share of stock in eighths, such as $27\frac{1}{8}$ or at $41\frac{3}{4}$. The change in value of a share of stock from day to day was also represented in eighths as a positive or negative number.

The table shows the change in value of a stock over two days. Graph the change in stock value for Wednesday and its opposite on a number line.

Day	Tuesday	Wednesday
Change in value ($)	$1\frac{5}{8}$	$-4\frac{1}{4}$

STEP 1 Graph the change in stock value for Wednesday on the number line.

The change in value for Wednesday is $-4\frac{1}{4}$.

Graph a point $4\frac{1}{4}$ units below 0.

STEP 2 Graph the opposite of $-4\frac{1}{4}$.

The opposite of $-4\frac{1}{4}$ is the same distance from 0 but on the other side of 0.

The opposite of $-4\frac{1}{4}$ is $4\frac{1}{4}$.

The opposite of the change in stock value for Wednesday is $4\frac{1}{4}$.

$-4\frac{1}{4}$ is between −4 and −5. It is closer to −4.

 Personal Math Trainer
Online Assessment and Intervention
©my.hrw.com

YOUR TURN

2. What are the opposites of 7, −3.5, 2.25, and $9\frac{1}{3}$?
$-7, 3.5, -2.25$, and $-9\frac{1}{3}$.

© Houghton Mifflin Harcourt Publishing Company • Image Credits: ©Image Source/Getty Images

---

PROFESSIONAL DEVELOPMENT

CC **Integrate Mathematical Practices MP.4**

This lesson provides an opportunity to address this Mathematical Practice standard. It calls for students to communicate mathematical ideas using multiple representations as appropriate. In the Explore Activity and Example 1, students use number lines to model the relationship between positive and negative numbers and absolute value. Using a number line, students can see that absolute values of opposites are equal because the opposites are the same distance from 0.

Math Background

As with integers, you can interpret the absolute value of any other rational number as the magnitude of the number without regard to its sign. It measures the amount of change rather than the direction of change.

Many real-world situations involve absolute value. For example, the manufacturer of a 32-ounce box of cereal may have a 0.75 ounce tolerance in the weight of the contents of the box. This is an absolute value and means that actual weights of between 32 − 0.75 and 32 + 0.75 ounces are acceptable.

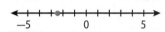
EXAMPLE 2

Questioning Strategies [CC] Mathematical Practices

• Is the point −5.4 above or below −3.2 on a vertical number line? Explain? It is below −3.2, because −5.4 is farther from 0 than −3.2.

• Which number in the table has the least absolute value? Explain. −0.8 because it is the closest number to 0.

Focus on Math Connections [CC] Mathematical Practices

Make sure students understand that distance from zero is always a nonnegative value because distance does not indicate a direction from zero.

YOUR TURN

Talk About It
Check for Understanding

Ask: How do you use a number line to find the absolute value of a number? Graph the number, and find the distance between the number and 0.

Connect to Daily Life [CC] Mathematical Practices

Discuss with students that financial debt is often discussed without any reference to the negative sign. A start-up tech company borrows $50,000 to develop a product. Then the company borrows another $25,000 to complete the project. Point out that the actual debt value is −$75,000 because it is money owed. When you talk about the amount of debt, the negative symbol is dropped because the word *debt* indicates that it is a negative value, an amount owed.

Elaborate

Talk About It
Summarize the Lesson

 Ask: How is absolute value related to the concept of opposites? Opposites are on opposite sides of 0 on the number line, but they have the same absolute value.

GUIDED PRACTICE

Engage with the Whiteboard

 For Exercises 1–4, have students plot each number and its opposite on the number lines.

Avoid Common Errors

Exercises 1–4 If students have trouble estimating the position of a rational number on the number line, encourage them to first identify the two consecutive integers between which it lies.

Exercises 5–18 Caution students to read the directions carefully. For Exercises 5–10, they need to find the opposite, and for Exercises 12–17 they need to find the absolute value.

Absolute Values of Rational Numbers

You can also find the absolute value of a rational number the same way you found the absolute value of an integer. The absolute value of a rational number is the number's distance from 0 on the number line.

Math On the Spot
my.hrw.com

EXAMPLE 2 Real World
COMMON CORE **6.NS.7, 6.NS.7c**

The table shows the average low temperatures in January in one location during a five-year span. Find the absolute value of the average January low temperature in 2009.

Year	2008	2009	2010	2011	2012
Temperature (°C)	−3.2	−5.4	−0.8	3.8	−2

STEP 1 Graph the 2009 average January low temperature.

The 2009 average January low is −5.4°C.
Graph a point 5.4 units below 0.

STEP 2 Find the absolute value of −5.4.

−5.4 is 5.4 units from 0.

$|-5.4| = 5.4$

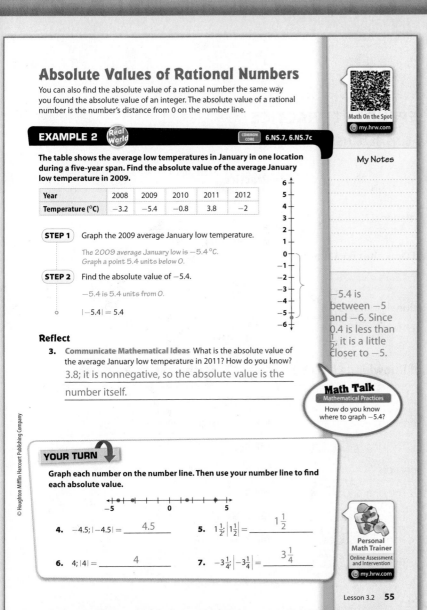

My Notes

−5.4 is between −5 and −6. Since 0.4 is less than $\frac{1}{2}$, it is a little closer to −5.

Math Talk
Mathematical Practices
How do you know where to graph −5.4?

Reflect

3. Communicate Mathematical Ideas What is the absolute value of the average January low temperature in 2011? How do you know?

3.8; it is nonnegative, so the absolute value is the number itself.

YOUR TURN

Graph each number on the number line. Then use your number line to find each absolute value.

4. −4.5; |−4.5| = ____4.5____

5. $1\frac{1}{2}$; $|1\frac{1}{2}|$ = ____$1\frac{1}{2}$____

6. 4; |4| = ____4____

7. $-3\frac{1}{4}$; $|-3\frac{1}{4}|$ = ____$3\frac{1}{4}$____

Personal Math Trainer
Online Assessment and Intervention
my.hrw.com

Guided Practice

Graph each number and its opposite on a number line. (Explore Activity and Example 1)

1. −2.8

2. 4.3

3. $-3\frac{4}{5}$

4. $1\frac{1}{3}$

Find the opposite of each number. (Example 1)

5. 3.78 ____−3.78____

6. $-7\frac{5}{12}$ ____$7\frac{5}{12}$____

7. 0 ____0____

8. 4.2 ____−4.2____

9. 12.1 ____−12.1____

10. 2.6 ____−2.6____

11. Vocabulary Explain why 2.15 and −2.15 are opposites. (Example 1)

They are the same distance from 0 on the number line.

Find the absolute value of each number. (Example 2)

12. 5.23 ____5.23____

13. $-4\frac{2}{11}$ ____$4\frac{2}{11}$____

14. 0 ____0____

15. $-6\frac{3}{5}$ ____$6\frac{3}{5}$____

16. −2.12 ____2.12____

17. 8.2 ____8.2____

? ESSENTIAL QUESTION CHECK-IN

18. How do you identify the opposite and the absolute value of a rational number?

Opposites are the same distance from zero on the number line in the opposite direction. Absolute value is the number's distance from zero.

DIFFERENTIATE INSTRUCTION

Cognitive Strategies

To help students understand the concept of opposite integers, discuss what *opposite* means in contexts other than math. Have students generate a list of opposite terms (e.g., old and new, up and down, tall and short). Then have students name some pairs of opposite integers (e.g., 1 and −1, −13 and 13).

Visual Cues

Draw the absolute value symbols on the board and create a function machine around them. Have students take turns putting in a number and showing the number that comes out. Suggest students think of the absolute value symbols as squeezing the negative sign from negative numbers. **−3.2**

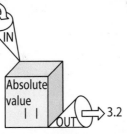

Additional Resources

Differentiated Instruction includes:
- Reading Strategies
- Success for English Learners **ELL**
- Reteach
- Challenge **PRE-AP**

3.2 LESSON QUIZ

 6.NS.6c

1. The table shows how the rainfall varied each of three months compared with the average rainfall for that month.

Month	Jun	Jul	Aug
Rainfall variation (in.)	−1.2	3.25	−0.5

a. Graph each month's rainfall variation and its opposite on a number line.

b. For which month did the variation differ the most from the monthly average? Explain.

Write the absolute value of each number.

2. 9.01   **3.** $-\frac{2}{8}$ **4.** −8.7   **5.** $3\frac{3}{4}$

Lesson Quiz available online

 my.hrw.com

Answers

1. a.

   b. July; because July had 3.25 more inches than the average June had about 1 inch less than average, and August had 0.5 inches less than average.

2. 9.01

3. $\frac{2}{8}$

4. 8.7

5. $3\frac{3}{4}$

Evaluate

GUIDED AND INDEPENDENT PRACTICE

COMMON CORE 6.NS.6, 6.NS.6a, 6.NS.6c, 6.NS.7, 6.NS.7c

Concepts & Skills	Practice
Explore Activity Positive and Negative Rational Numbers	Exercises 1–4
Example 1 Rational Numbers and Opposites on a Number Line	Exercises 1–11, 19, 20
Example 2 Absolute Values of Rational Numbers	Exercises 12–17, 21

Exercise	Depth of Knowledge (D.O.K.)	Mathematical Practices
19	**2** Skills/Concepts	**MP.4** Modeling
20	**2** Skills/Concepts	**MP.7** Using Structure
21	**3** Strategic Thinking H.O.T.	**MP.3** Logic
22	**2** Skills/Concepts	**MP.8** Patterns
23	**3** Strategic Thinking H.O.T.	**MP.3** Logic
24	**3** Strategic Thinking H.O.T.	**MP.7** Using Structure
25	**3** Strategic Thinking H.O.T.	**MP.2** Reasoning
26	**3** Strategic Thinking H.O.T.	**MP.8** Patterns

Additional Resources

Differentiated Instruction includes:

• Leveled Practice worksheets

3.2 Independent Practice

COMMON CORE 6.NS.6, 6.NS.6a, 6.NS.6c, 6.NS.7, 6.NS.7c

Personal Math Trainer

my.hrw.com

Online Assessment and Intervention

19. Financial Literacy A store's balance sheet represents the amounts customers owe as negative numbers and credits to customers as positive numbers.

Customer	Girardi	Lewis	Stein	Yuan	Wenner
Balance ($)	−85.23	20.44	−116.33	13.50	−9.85

a. Write the opposite of each customer's balance.

   Girardi $85.23, Lewis −$20.44, Stein $116.33, Yuan

   −$13.50, Wenner $9.85

b. Mr. Yuan wants to use his credit to pay off the full amount that another customer owes. Which customer's balance does Mr. Yuan have enough money to pay off? **Wenner**

c. Which customer's balance would be farthest from 0 on a number line? Explain.

   Stein; when you find the absolute value of each

   balance, Stein's is the greatest.

20. Multistep Trina and Jessie went on a vacation to Hawaii. Trina went scuba diving and reached an elevation of −85.6 meters, which is below sea level. Jessie went hang-gliding and reached an altitude of 87.9 meters, which is above sea level.

a. Who is closer to the surface of the ocean? Explain.

   Trina; |−85.6| is less than |87.9|

b. Trina wants to hang-glide at the same number of meters above sea level as she scuba-dived below sea level. Will she fly higher than Jessie did? Explain.

   No; the opposite of −85.6 meters is 85.6 meters,

   which is less than 87.9 meters.

21. Critical Thinking Carlos finds the absolute value of −5.3, and then finds the opposite of his answer. Jason finds the opposite of −5.3, and then finds the absolute value of his answer. Whose final value is greater? Explain.

   Jason's; Carlos finds |−5.3| = 5.3. Then he finds the

   opposite, which is −5.3. Jason finds the opposite

   of −5.3, which is 5.3. Then he finds |5.3|, which is 5.3.

22. Explain the Error Two students are playing a math game. The object of the game is to make the least possible number by arranging the given digits inside absolute value bars on a card. In the first round, each player will use the digits 3, 5, and 7 to fill in the card.

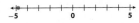

a. One student arranges the numbers on the card as shown. What was this student's mistake?

   The student made the least negative number that could

   be formed with the given digits but did not take into

   account the absolute value symbols.

b. What is the least possible number the card can show? _____ |−35.7|

H.O.T. FOCUS ON HIGHER ORDER THINKING

23. Analyze Relationships If you plot the point −8.85 on a number line, would you place it to the left or right of −8.8? Explain.

   to the left; 8.85 is greater than 8.8, so −8.85 is farther

   from 0 on the number line.

24. Make a Conjecture If the absolute value of a negative number is 2.78, what is the distance on the number line between the number and its absolute value? Explain your answer.

   5.56; both values are 2.78 units from 0, and in opposite

   directions. So the distance is 2(2.78) = 5.56.

25. Multiple Representations The deepest point in the Indian Ocean is the Java Trench, which is 25,344 feet below sea level. Elevations below sea level are represented by negative numbers.

a. Write the elevation of the Java Trench. _____ −25,344 ft

b. A mile is 5,280 feet. Between which two integers is the elevation in miles? _____ −5 and −4

c. Graph the elevation of the Java Trench in miles.

```
◄─●─┼─┼─┼─┼─┼─┼─┼─┼─┼─┼─►
 −5        0        5
```

26. Draw Conclusions A number and its absolute value are equal. If you subtract 2 from the number, the new number and its absolute value are <u>not</u> equal. What do you know about the number? What is a possible number that satisfies these conditions?

   It is greater than or equal to 0 and less than 2; 1 is a

   possible solution.

Work Area

EXTEND THE MATH   PRE-AP

Activity available online my.hrw.com

Activity On Monday morning the opening price of a stock was $10. Complete the table to find the closing price of the stock on Friday afternoon. What was the closing price?

The closing price on Friday was $11.75.

Day	Change	Closing price calculation	Closing price
Monday	$2\frac{1}{8}$	$10 + 2\frac{1}{8}$	$12\frac{1}{8}$
Tuesday	$-1\frac{2}{8}$	$12\frac{1}{8} - 1\frac{2}{8}$	$10\frac{7}{8}$
Wednesday	$-\frac{2}{8}$	$10\frac{7}{8} - \frac{2}{8}$	$10\frac{5}{8}$
Thursday	$\frac{1}{8}$	$10\frac{5}{8} + \frac{1}{8}$	$10\frac{6}{8}$
Friday	1	$10\frac{6}{8} + 1$	$11\frac{6}{8}$

3.3 Comparing and Ordering Rational Numbers

Common Core Standards

The student is expected to:

 The Number System—6.NS.7a

Interpret statements of inequality as statements about the relative position of two numbers on a number line diagram. *Also 6.NS.7, 6.NS.7b*

Mathematical Practices

 MP.4 Modeling

ADDITIONAL EXAMPLE 1

A) Order 0.3, $\frac{2}{5}$, 0.85, 0.09, $\frac{3}{4}$, and $\frac{3}{20}$ from least to greatest.

  0.09, $\frac{3}{20}$, 0.3, $\frac{2}{5}$, $\frac{3}{4}$, 0.85

B) Order 0.4, $\frac{1}{3}$, and $\frac{5}{6}$ from least to greatest.

  $\frac{1}{3}$, 0.4, $\frac{5}{6}$

 Interactive Whiteboard
Interactive example available online

 my.hrw.com

 Animated Math
Ordering Rational Numbers

Students build fluency with ordering rational numbers in an engaging scoring game with a dynamic number line.

 my.hrw.com

Engage

ESSENTIAL QUESTION

How do you compare and order rational numbers? You can write the numbers so they are all in the same form, such as equivalent decimals or fractions, and then compare or order them.

Motivate the Lesson

Ask: Suppose you like to drink iced tea on a hot day. You can choose between two glasses, one with $\frac{1}{2}$ cup of tea or one with 0.6 cup of tea. Which glass contains more tea? Begin the Explore Activity to find out how to compare these rational numbers.

Explore

EXPLORE ACTIVITY

Focus on Modeling Mathematical Practices

Point out to students that the scale used for the number line is tenths. Every other fraction on the number line has a denominator of 5 because the labels are in simplest form. For example, $\frac{2}{10}$ simplifies to $\frac{1}{5}$.

Integrating Language Arts ELL

You may want to pair English learners with a partner for Explore Activity 1 to help them develop their language skills.

Explain

EXAMPLE 1

Questioning Strategies CC Mathematical Practices

• How can you compare two fractions? Compare their equivalent decimals or rewrite them with common denominators and compare the numerators.

• How can you compare a fraction with a decimal? Rewrite them so both are decimals or both are fractions.

• In B Step 2, if you use a common denominator other than 60, will the order be the same? Justify your answer. Yes, as long as the fractions are equivalent to the original value, the order will remain the same.

Engage with the Whiteboard

Have students plot and label the values in A on the given number line with both fractional and decimal equivalents.

YOUR TURN

Connect Multiple Representations CC Mathematical Practices

Point out that writing rational numbers as equivalent decimals or fractions does not change the value of the rational number. It just makes it easier to compare rational numbers.

Comparing and Ordering Rational Numbers

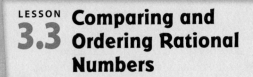

COMMON CORE **6.NS.7a**
Interpret statements of inequality as statements about the relative position of two numbers on a number line diagram. *Also 6.NS.7, 6.NS.7b*

? **ESSENTIAL QUESTION**

How do you compare and order rational numbers?

EXPLORE ACTIVITY COMMON CORE Prep for 6.NS.7a

Equivalent Fractions and Decimals

Fractions and decimals that represent the same value are *equivalent*. The number line shows equivalent fractions and decimals from 0 to 1.

A Complete the number line by writing the missing decimals or fractions.

B Use the number line to find a fraction that is equivalent to 0.25. Explain.

$\frac{1}{4}$; 0.25 and $\frac{1}{4}$ both represent

the point halfway between 0.2 and 0.3.

C Explain how to use a number line to find a decimal equivalent to $1\frac{7}{10}$.

$1\frac{7}{10}$ is a mixed number equal to $1 + \frac{7}{10}$. $\frac{7}{10}$ is equivalent

to 0.7. $1 + 0.7$ is equal to 1.7, so $1\frac{7}{10}$ is equivalent to 1.7.

D Use the number line to complete each statement.

$0.2 = \frac{1}{5}$ $\frac{0.3}{} = \frac{3}{10}$ $0.75 = \frac{3}{4}$ $1.25 = 1\frac{1}{4}$

Reflect

1. **Communicate Mathematical Ideas** How does a number line represent equivalent fractions and decimals?

A decimal and fraction that represent the same point

on the number line are equivalent.

2. Name a decimal between 0.4 and 0.5.

Sample answers: 0.42, 0.47

Ordering Fractions and Decimals

You can order fractions and decimals by rewriting the fractions as equivalent decimals or by rewriting the decimals as equivalent fractions.

Math On the Spot
my.hrw.com

EXAMPLE 1 COMMON CORE **6.NS.7, 6.NS.7a**

A Order 0.2, $\frac{3}{4}$, 0.8, $\frac{1}{2}$, $\frac{1}{4}$, and 0.4 from least to greatest.

STEP 1 Write the fractions as equivalent decimals.

$\frac{1}{4} = 0.25$ $\frac{1}{2} = 0.5$ $\frac{3}{4} = 0.75$

STEP 2 Use the number line to write the decimals in order.

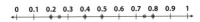

$0.2 < 0.25 < 0.4 < 0.5 < 0.75 < 0.8$

The numbers from least to greatest are 0.2, $\frac{1}{4}$, 0.4, $\frac{1}{2}$, $\frac{3}{4}$, 0.8.

B Order $\frac{1}{12}$, $\frac{2}{3}$, and 0.35 from least to greatest.

STEP 1 Write the decimal as an equivalent fraction.

60 is a multiple of the denominators of all three fractions.

$0.35 = \frac{35}{100} = \frac{7}{20}$

STEP 2 Find equivalent fractions with 60 as the common denominator.

$\frac{1}{12} \overset{\times 5}{=} \frac{5}{60}$ $\frac{2}{3} \overset{\times 20}{=} \frac{40}{60}$ $\frac{7}{20} \overset{\times 3}{=} \frac{21}{60}$

STEP 3 Order fractions with common denominators by comparing the numerators.

$5 < 21 < 40$

The fractions in order from least to greatest are $\frac{5}{60}$, $\frac{21}{60}$, $\frac{40}{60}$.

The numbers in order from least to greatest are $\frac{1}{12}$, 0.35, and $\frac{2}{3}$.

Animated Math
my.hrw.com

Personal Math Trainer
Online Assessment and Intervention
my.hrw.com

YOUR TURN

Order the fractions and decimals from least to greatest.

3. 0.85, $\frac{3}{5}$, 0.15, $\frac{7}{10}$ 0.15, $\frac{3}{5}$, $\frac{7}{10}$, 0.85

PROFESSIONAL DEVELOPMENT

CC **Integrate Mathematical Practices MP.4**

This lesson provides an opportunity to address this Mathematical Practice standard. It calls for students to communicate mathematical ideas using multiple representations as appropriate. In the Explore Activity and both Examples, students compare rational numbers by writing and graphing their equivalent fractions or decimals. Thus students are ordering rational numbers using multiple representations.

Math Background

The process for writing equivalent fractions is based on two properties.

(1) A nonzero number divided by itself is 1,

or $\frac{a}{a} = 1, a \neq 0$.

(2) $1 \cdot x = x$.

The process of writing an equivalent fraction by dividing the numerator and denominator by the same number is also based on the property that $\frac{ac}{bd} = \frac{a}{b} \cdot \frac{c}{d}, (b, d \neq 0)$.

EXAMPLE 2

Avoid Common Errors

Make sure that students understand that the table does not give any information about actual running times. It only shows how each runner's time differs from the average running time. Also be sure students understand that the fastest time is the farthest below the average.

Questioning Strategies **CC Mathematical Practices**

- How can you determine whose time was closest to the average time? Since 0 represents no difference from the average, find the time closest to 0. John's time is closest to 0.

- Why is the average time shown to be 0 on the number line? The numbers on the number line represent differences from the average time. The point 0 on the number line represents 0 or no difference from the average.

Engage with the Whiteboard

Have students take turns writing the converted fractions on the table and plotting points on the graph. As they plot a point, have them write the runner's name below it. Then ask students to list the runners from fastest to slowest according to their time.

YOUR TURN

Focus on Reasoning **CC Mathematical Practices**

Ask students to look at the table and determine who biked fastest and who biked slowest without making any calculations. Ask students to explain their reasoning. Help students see that the fastest biker will have the least time in minutes and the slowest biker will have the greatest.

Elaborate

Talk About It
Summarize the Lesson

Ask: How can a number line help you order rational numbers? Once you have graphed the numbers, the numbers will be in order from least to greatest from left to right on a horizontal number line, or from bottom to top on a vertical number line.

GUIDED PRACTICE

Engage with the Whiteboard

For Exercises 1–9, have students take turns writing an equivalent fraction or decimal for each number, while showing their work and explaining their reasoning. Discuss other possible equivalent fractions or decimals that students may have written.

Focus on Communication **CC Mathematical Practices**

For Exercises 12–20, have students discuss the methods they used to order the numbers.

Avoid Common Errors

Exercise 9 Point out that $\frac{6}{8} = \frac{3}{4}$, and they probably know the decimal equivalent for $\frac{3}{4}$.

Exercises 15–18 Caution students not to drop the negative sign when converting negative rational numbers.

Ordering Rational Numbers

You can use a number line to order positive and negative rational numbers.

EXAMPLE 2   **COMMON CORE** 6.NS.7a, 6.NS.7b

Five friends completed a triathlon that included a 3-mile run, a 12-mile bike ride, and a $\frac{1}{2}$-mile swim. To compare their running times they created a table that shows the difference between each person's time and the average time, with negative numbers representing times less than the average.

Runner	John	Sue	Anna	Mike	Tom
Time above or below average (minutes)	$\frac{1}{2}$	1.4	$-1\frac{1}{4}$	-2.0	1.95

Order the numbers from greatest to least.

STEP 1   Write the fractions as equivalent decimals.

$$\frac{1}{2} = 0.5 \qquad -1\frac{1}{4} = -1.25$$

STEP 2   Use the number line to write the decimals in order.

−2.0   −1.5   −1.0   −0.5   0.0   0.5   1.0   1.5   2.0

★ Average Time

$$1.95 > 1.4 > 0.5 > -1.25 > -2.0$$

The numbers in order from greatest to least are 1.95, 1.4, $\frac{1}{2}$, $-1\frac{1}{4}$, −2.0.

Reflect

4. Communicate Mathematical Ideas Describe a different way to order the numbers.

Convert the decimals to fractions. $1.4 = 1\frac{4}{10}$; $-2.0 = -\frac{2}{1}$;

$1.95 = 1\frac{95}{100}$; find a common denominator and

compare the whole numbers and then the numerators.

YOUR TURN

5. To compare their bike times, the friends created a table that shows the difference between each person's time and the average bike time. Order the bike times from least to greatest.

Biker	John	Sue	Anna	Mike	Tom
Time above or below average (minutes)	−1.8	1	$1\frac{2}{5}$	$1\frac{9}{10}$	−1.25

$-1.8, -1.25, 1, 1\frac{2}{5}, 1\frac{9}{10}$

Math On the Spot ☐ my.hrw.com

Math Talk
Mathematical Practices
Who was the fastest runner? Explain.

Mike; he finished running in the least amount of time.

Personal Math Trainer
Online Assessment and Intervention
☐ my.hrw.com

Find the equivalent fraction or decimal for each number.
(Explore Activity 1)

1. $0.6 = \underline{\frac{3}{5}}$ **2.** $\frac{1}{4} = \underline{0.25}$ **3.** $0.9 = \underline{\frac{9}{10}}$

4. $0.1 = \underline{\frac{1}{10}}$ **5.** $\frac{3}{10} = \underline{0.3}$ **6.** $1.4 = \underline{1\frac{2}{5}}$

7. $\frac{4}{5} = \underline{0.8}$ **8.** $0.4 = \underline{\frac{2}{5}}$ **9.** $\frac{6}{8} = \underline{0.75}$

Use the number line to order the fractions and decimals from least to greatest. (Example 1)

10. 0.75, $\frac{1}{2}$, 0.4, and $\frac{1}{5}$

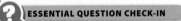

0   0.1   0.2   0.3   0.4   0.5   0.6   0.7   0.8   0.9   1

$\frac{1}{5}$, 0.4, $\frac{1}{2}$, 0.75

11. The table shows the lengths of fish caught by three friends at the lake last weekend. Write the lengths in order from greatest to least. (Example 1)

$12\frac{3}{4}$, 12.7, $12\frac{3}{5}$

Lengths of Fish (cm)		
Emma	Anne	Emily
12.7	$12\frac{3}{5}$	$12\frac{3}{4}$

List the fractions and decimals in order from least to greatest.
(Example 1, Example 2)

12. 2.3, $2\frac{4}{5}$, 2.6

2.3, 2.6, $2\frac{4}{5}$

13. 0.5, $\frac{3}{16}$, 0.75, $\frac{5}{48}$

$\frac{5}{48}$, $\frac{3}{16}$, 0.5, 0.75

14. 0.5, $\frac{1}{5}$, 0.35, $\frac{12}{25}$, $\frac{4}{5}$

$\frac{1}{5}$, 0.35, $\frac{12}{25}$, 0.5, $\frac{4}{5}$

15. $\frac{3}{4}$, $-\frac{7}{10}$, $-\frac{3}{4}$, $\frac{8}{10}$

$-\frac{3}{4}$, $-\frac{7}{10}$, $\frac{3}{4}$, $\frac{8}{10}$

16. $-\frac{3}{8}$, $\frac{5}{16}$, -0.65, $\frac{2}{4}$

-0.65, $-\frac{3}{8}$, $\frac{5}{16}$, $\frac{2}{4}$

17. -2.3, $-2\frac{4}{5}$, -2.6

$-2\frac{4}{5}$, -2.6, -2.3

18. -0.6, $-\frac{5}{8}$, $-\frac{7}{12}$, -0.72

-0.72, $-\frac{5}{8}$, -0.6, $-\frac{7}{12}$

19. 1.45, $1\frac{1}{2}$, $1\frac{1}{3}$, 1.2

1.2, $1\frac{1}{3}$, 1.45, $1\frac{1}{2}$

20. -0.3, 0.5, 0.55, -0.35

-0.35, -0.3, 0.5, 0.55

❓ ESSENTIAL QUESTION CHECK-IN

21. Explain how to compare 0.7 and $\frac{5}{8}$.

Convert the fraction to a decimal. $\frac{5}{8} = 0.625$. Compare

by using place value or graphing both numbers on a

number line. $0.7 > \frac{5}{8}$

DIFFERENTIATE INSTRUCTION

Cooperative Learning

Have students work in pairs to order each set from least to greatest. Instruct the pairs to order one set using decimals and one set using fractions. Invite pairs to explain how they chose which set to order with decimals and which to order with fractions.

Set 1: 0.3, -1.7, $-1\frac{3}{5}$, $-1\frac{7}{20}$, $-\frac{1}{2}$, 0.05

Set 2: -0.2, 0.5, $1\frac{1}{3}$, $-2\frac{1}{6}$, $\frac{4}{15}$, 0.1

Set 1: -1.7, $-1\frac{3}{5}$, $-\frac{1}{2}$, 0.05, 0.3, $1\frac{7}{20}$

Set 2: $-2\frac{1}{6}$, -0.2, 0.1, $\frac{4}{15}$, 0.5, $1\frac{1}{3}$

Multiple Representations

Have students sketch a number line for Exercises 12 and 17 in the Guided Practice. Have them determine what scale and the range of numbers to use on each number line. Then have them plot and label the points on the number line.

Exercise 12

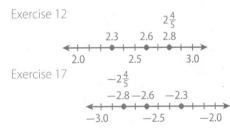

$2\frac{4}{5}$
2.3   2.6   2.8
2.0   2.5   3.0

Exercise 17

$-2\frac{4}{5}$
-2.8 -2.6 -2.3
-3.0 -2.5 -2.0

Additional Resources

Differentiated Instruction includes:

- Reading Strategies
- Success for English Learners **ELL**
- Reteach
- Challenge **PRE-AP**

Personal Math Trainer

Online Assessment and Intervention

Online homework assignment available

 my.hrw.com

3.3 LESSON QUIZ

COMMON CORE 6.NS.7a

Andy, Dana, and Becky each worked on homework for an hour. The table shows what part of homework time each spent on math and English.

	Math	English
Andy	$\frac{1}{2}$	0.2
Dana	0.35	$\frac{3}{5}$
Becky	$\frac{3}{8}$	0.4

1. Who spent the most time on math?

2. Order the times spent on English from least to greatest.

3. List all the fractions and decimals given in the table from least to greatest.

4. Order the set of fractions and decimals below from least to greatest.

$$0.15, -\frac{4}{5}, -1.25, 1.03, 1\frac{5}{6}, -\frac{7}{20}$$

Lesson Quiz available online

 my.hrw.com

Answers

1. Andy

2. $0.2, 0.4, \frac{3}{5}$

3. $0.2, 0.35, \frac{3}{8}, 0.4, \frac{1}{2}, \frac{3}{5}$

4. $-1.25, -\frac{4}{5}, -\frac{7}{20}, 0.15, 1.03, 1\frac{5}{6}$

Evaluate

GUIDED AND INDEPENDENT PRACTICE

 COMMON CORE 6.NS.7, 6.NS.7a, 6.NS.7b

Concepts & Skills	Practice
Explore Activity Equivalent Fractions and Decimals	Exercises 1–9
Example 1 Ordering Fractions and Decimals	Exercises 10–20
Example 2 Ordering Rational Numbers	Exercises 10–20, 22

Exercise	Depth of Knowledge (D.O.K.)	**COMMON CORE** Mathematical Practices
22	**2** Skills/Concepts	**MP.4** Modeling
23	**3** Strategic Thinking	**MP.7** Using Structure
24	**2** Skills/Concepts	**MP.4** Modeling
25	**3** Strategic Thinking H.O.T.	**MP.8** Patterns
26	**3** Strategic Thinking H.O.T.	**MP.8** Patterns
27	**3** Strategic Thinking H.O.T.	**MP.3** Logic

Additional Resources

Differentiated Instruction includes:

• Leveled Practice worksheets

CC CLUSTER CONNECTION **Exercise 24** combines concepts from the Common Core cluster "Apply and extend previous understandings of numbers to the system of rational numbers."

3.3 Independent Practice

COMMON CORE 6.NS.7, 6.NS.7a, 6.NS.7b

Personal Math Trainer
Online Assessment and Intervention
my.hrw.com

22. Rosa and Albert receive the same amount of allowance each week. The table shows what part of their allowance they each spent on video games and pizza.

	Video games	Pizza
Rosa	0.4	$\frac{2}{5}$
Albert	$\frac{1}{2}$	0.25

a. Who spent more of their allowance on video games? Write an inequality to compare the portion spent on video games.

Albert; $\frac{1}{2} > 0.4$ or $0.4 < \frac{1}{2}$

b. Who spent more of their allowance on pizza? Write an inequality to compare the portion spent on pizza.

Rosa; $\frac{2}{5} > 0.25$ or $0.25 < \frac{2}{5}$

c. Draw Conclusions Who spent the greater part of their total allowance? How do you know?

Rosa; she spent $0.4 + \frac{2}{5} = 0.4 + 0.4 = 0.8$;

Albert spent $0.25 + \frac{1}{2} = 0.25 + 0.5 = 0.75$

23. A group of friends is collecting aluminum for a recycling drive. Each person who donates at least 4.25 pounds of aluminum receives a free movie coupon. The weight of each person's donation is shown in the table.

	Brenda	Claire	Jim	Micah	Peter
Weight (lb)	4.3	5.5	$6\frac{1}{6}$	$\frac{15}{4}$	$4\frac{3}{8}$

a. Order the weights of the donations from greatest to least.

$6\frac{1}{6}$, 5.5, $4\frac{3}{8}$, 4.3, $\frac{15}{4}$

b. Which of the friends will receive a free movie coupon? Which will not?

Claire, Peter, Brenda, and Jim; Micah

c. What If? Would the person with the smallest donation win a movie coupon if he or she had collected $\frac{1}{2}$ pound more of aluminum? Explain.

Yes; the smallest donation is $\frac{15}{4}$ pounds. $\frac{1}{2}$ pound is

equal to $\frac{2}{4}$ pound. $\frac{15}{4} + \frac{2}{4} = \frac{17}{4} = 4\frac{1}{4} = 4.25$ lb, which is

just enough to win a free movie coupon.

24. Last week, several gas stations in a neighborhood all charged the same price for a gallon of gas. The table below shows how much gas prices have changed from last week to this week.

Gas Station	Gas and Go	Samson Gas	Star Gas	Corner Store	Tip Top Shop
Change from last week (in cents)	−6.6	5.8	$-6\frac{3}{4}$	$\frac{27}{5}$	$-5\frac{5}{8}$

a. Order the numbers in the table from least to greatest.

$-6\frac{3}{4}$, −6.6, $-5\frac{5}{8}$, $\frac{27}{5}$, 5.8

b. Which gas station has the cheapest gas this week? ___Star Gas___

c. Critical Thinking Which gas station changed their price the least this week?

Corner Store

H.O.T. FOCUS ON HIGHER ORDER THINKING

Work Area

25. Analyze Relationships Explain how you would order from least to greatest three numbers that include a positive number, a negative number, and zero.

Negative numbers are less than zero and positive

numbers are greater than zero, so the order would be

negative, zero, positive.

26. Critique Reasoning Luke is making pancakes. The recipe calls for 0.5 quart of milk and 2.5 cups of flour. He has $\frac{3}{8}$ quart of milk and $\frac{18}{8}$ cups of flour. Luke makes the recipe with the milk and flour that he has. Explain his error.

Luke does not have enough of either ingredient. He has

$\frac{3}{8}$ of a quart of milk, or 0.375. $0.375 < 0.5$. He has $\frac{18}{8}$

cups of flour, or 2.25. $2.25 < 2.5$.

27. Communicate Mathematical Ideas If you know the order from least to greatest of 5 negative rational numbers, how can you use that information to order the absolute values of those numbers from least to greatest? Explain.

The order of the absolute values will be the reverse

of the order of the negative rational numbers. The

least negative number will be the farthest from 0 on

a number line. The greatest negative number will be

closest to 0 on a number line.

EXTEND THE MATH PRE-AP

Activity available online my.hrw.com

Activity Have students use the given information to find the Mystery Number. After students solve the number puzzle, ask them to share the methods they used to identify the number. Then encourage students to write a similar number puzzle and challenge other students to solve it.

The Mystery Number is −0.15 or $-\frac{3}{20}$.

Mystery Number

1. The absolute value of the mystery number is less than $\frac{1}{2}$ but greater than $\frac{1}{10}$.

2. The mystery number is to the left of 0 on the number line.

3. When written as a decimal, the mystery number requires 2 places to the right of the decimal point.

4. As a fraction in simplest form, the denominator is a multiple of 10 and the numerator is an odd number.

Ready to Go On?

Assess Mastery

Use the assessment on this page to determine if students have mastered the concepts and standards covered in this module.

Response to Intervention

Intervention	Enrichment

Access Ready to Go On? assessment online, and receive instant scoring, feedback, and customized intervention or enrichment.

Personal Math Trainer
Online Assessment and Intervention
my.hrw.com

Online and Print Resources

Differentiated Instruction
- Reteach worksheets
- Reading Strategies **ELL**
- Success for English Learners **ELL**

Differentiated Instruction
- Challenge worksheets **PRE-AP**
- Extend the Math **PRE-AP** Lesson Activities in TE

Additional Resources

Assessment Resources includes:
- Leveled Module Quizzes

MODULE QUIZ

Ready to Go On?

Personal Math Trainer
Online Assessment and Intervention
my.hrw.com

3.1 Classifying Rational Numbers

1. Five friends divide three bags of apples equally between them. Write the division represented in this situation as a fraction. $\dfrac{3}{5}$

Write each rational number in the form $\dfrac{a}{b}$, where a and b are integers.

2. $5\frac{1}{6}$ $\underline{\quad \dfrac{31}{6} \quad}$

3. -12 $\underline{\quad \dfrac{-12}{1} \quad}$

Determine if each number is a whole number, integer, or rational number. Include all sets to which each number belongs.

4. -12 $\underline{\quad\text{integer and rational number}\quad}$

5. $\frac{7}{8}$ $\underline{\quad\text{rational number}\quad}$

3.2 Identifying Opposites and Absolute Value of Rational Numbers

6. Graph -3, $1\frac{3}{4}$, -0.5, and 3 on the number line.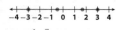

7. Find the opposite of $\frac{1}{3}$ and of $-\frac{7}{12}$. $\underline{\quad -\frac{1}{3}, \frac{7}{12} \quad}$

8. Find the absolute value of 9.8 and of $-\frac{10}{3}$. $\underline{\quad 9.8; \frac{10}{3} \quad}$

3.3 Comparing and Ordering Rational Numbers

9. Over the last week, the daily low temperatures in degrees Fahrenheit have been -4, 6.2, $18\frac{1}{2}$, -5.9, 21, $-\frac{1}{4}$, and 1.75. List these numbers in order from greatest to least.
21, $18\frac{1}{2}$, 6.2, 1.75, $-\frac{1}{4}$, -4, -5.9

? ESSENTIAL QUESTION

10. How can you order rational numbers from least to greatest?
Convert so that all numbers are in the same form.
Order them as they appear on the number line.

Common Core Standards

Lesson	Exercises	Common Core Standards
3.1	1–5	**6.NS.6**
3.2	6–8	**6.NS.6, 6.NS.6a, 6.NS.6c, 6.NS.7, 6.NS.7c**
3.3	9	**6.NS.7, 6.NS.7a, 6.NS.7b**

Assessment Readiness

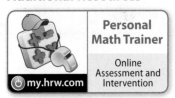

 COMMON CORE

MODULE 3 MIXED REVIEW

Assessment Readiness

Personal Math Trainer
Online Assessment and Intervention
my.hrw.com

Selected Response

1. Suki split five dog treats equally among her six dogs. Which fraction represents this division?

(A) $\frac{6}{5}$ of a treat   (C) $\frac{1}{5}$ of a treat

(B) $\frac{5}{6}$ of a treat   (D) $\frac{1}{6}$ of a treat

2. Which set or sets does the number 15 belong to?

(A) whole numbers only

(B) rational numbers only

(C) integers and rational numbers only

(D) whole numbers, integers, and rational numbers

3. Which of the following statements about rational numbers is correct?

(A) All rational numbers are also whole numbers.

(B) All rational numbers are also integers.

(C) All rational numbers can be written in the form $\frac{a}{b}$, where a and b are integers and $b \neq 0$.

(D) Rational numbers cannot be negative.

4. Which of the following shows the numbers in order from least to greatest?

(A) $-\frac{1}{5}, -\frac{2}{3}, 2, 0.4$

(B) $2, -\frac{2}{3}, 0.4, -\frac{1}{5}$

(C) $-\frac{2}{3}, 0.4, -\frac{1}{5}, 2$

(D) $-\frac{2}{3}, -\frac{1}{5}, 0.4, 2$

5. What is the absolute value of -12.5?

(A) 12.5   (C) -1

(B) 1   (D) -12.5

6. Which number line shows $-\frac{1}{4}$ and its opposite?

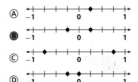

7. Horatio climbed to the top of a ladder that is 10 feet high. Which number is the opposite of the number that represents Horatio's height?

(A) -10 (C) 0

(B) 10   (D) $\frac{1}{10}$

Mini-Task

8. The table shows the heights in feet of several students in Mrs. Patel's class.

Name	Height (ft)
Olivia	$5\frac{1}{4}$
James	5.5
Carmela	4.9
Feng	5

a. Write each height in the form $\frac{a}{b}$.

$\frac{21}{4}, \frac{11}{2}, \frac{49}{10}, \frac{5}{1}$

b. List the heights in order from greatest to least.

$5.5, 5\frac{1}{4}, 5, 4.9$

Common Core Standards

Items	Grade 6 Standards	Mathematical Practices
1	6.NS.6	MP.4
2	6.NS.6	MP.7, MP.8
3	6.NS.6	MP.7, MP.8
4	6.NS.7	MP.7, MP.8
5	6.NS.7c	MP.7, MP.8
6	6.NS.6a, 6.NS.6c	MP.2, MP.4, MP.6
7*	6.NS.5, 6.NS.6a	MP.2, MP.4, MP.6
8	6.NS.7	MP.4

* Item integrates mixed review concepts from previous modules or a previous course.

Study Guide Review

Vocabulary Development

Integrating Language Arts

Encourage students to practice using the unit vocabulary as they talk and write about mathematics. Understanding vocabulary will aid their understanding of the concepts.

 ELA-Literacy.RST.6-8.4 Determine the meaning of symbols, key terms, and other domain-specific words and phrases as they are used in a specific scientific or technical context relevant to grades 6–8 texts and topics.

MODULE 1 Integers

 6.NS.5, 6.NS.6, 6.NS.6a, 6.NS.6c, 6.NS.7, 6.NS.7a, 6.NS.7b, 6.NS.7c, 6.NS.7d

Key Concepts

- Integers are positive and negative whole numbers. *(Lesson 1.1)*
- Inequality symbols include >, or "greater than," and <, or "less than." *(Lesson 1.2)*
- The absolute value of a number is always positive, since it is the number's distance from 0. *(Lesson 1.3)*

MODULE 2 Factors and Multiples

6.NS.4

Key Concepts

- The greatest common factor of two numbers is the greatest factor those two numbers share. *(Lesson 2.1)*
- The least common multiple is the least common multiple of two or more counting numbers. *(Lesson 2.2)*

Study Guide Review

MODULE 1 Integers

? ESSENTIAL QUESTION

How can you use integers to solve real-world problems?

Key Vocabulary

absolute value (valor absoluto)

inequality (desigualdad)

integers (enteros)

negative numbers (números negativos)

opposites (opuestos)

positive numbers (números positivos)

EXAMPLE 1

James recorded the temperature at noon in Fairbanks, Alaska, over a week in January.

Day	Mon	Tues	Wed	Thurs	Fri
Temperature	3	2	7	−3	−1

Graph the temperatures on the number line, and then list the numbers in order from least to greatest.

Graph the temperatures on the number line.

Read from left to right to list the temperatures in order from least to greatest.

The temperatures listed from least to greatest are −3, −1, 2, 3, 7.

EXAMPLE 2

Graph −4, 0, 2, and −1 on the number line. Then use the number line to find each absolute value.

A number and its opposite are the same distance from 0 on the number line. The absolute value of a negative number is its opposite.

$|-4| = 4$ $|0| = 0$ $|2| = 2$ $|-1| = 1$

EXERCISES

1. Graph 7, −2, 5, 1, and −1 on the number line. (Lesson 1.1)

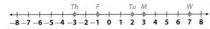

List the numbers from least to greatest. (Lesson 1.2)

2. 4, 0, −2, 3 ___−2, 0, 3, 4___

3. −3, −5, 2, −2 ___−5, −3, −2, 2___

Compare using < or >. (Lesson 1.2)

4. 4 $>$ 1

5. −2 $<$ 2

6. −3 $>$ −5

7. −7 $<$ 2

Find the opposite and absolute value of each number. (Lessons 1.1, 1.3)

8. 6 ___−6, 6___

9. −2 ___2, 2___

MODULE 2 Factors and Multiples

? ESSENTIAL QUESTION

How do you find and use the greatest common factor of two whole numbers? How do you find and use the least common multiple of two numbers?

Key Vocabulary

greatest common factor (GCF) (máximo común divisor (MCD))

least common multiple (LCM) (mínimo común múltiplo (mcm))

EXAMPLE 1

Use the Distributive Property to rewrite 32 + 24 as a product of their greatest common factor and another number.

A. List the factors of 24 and 32. Circle the common factors.

24: ① ② 3 ④ 6 ⑧ 12 24

32: ① ② ④ ⑧ 16 32

B. Rewrite each number as a product of the GCF and another number.

24: 8×3 32: 8×4

C. Use the Distributive Property and your answer above to rewrite 32 + 24 using the GCF and another number.

$32 + 24 = 8 \times 3 + 8 \times 4$

$32 + 24 = 8 \times (3 + 4)$

$32 + 24 = 8 \times 7$

EXAMPLE 2

On Saturday, every 8th customer at Adam's Bagels will get a free coffee. Every 12th customer will get a free bagel. Which customer will be the first to get a free coffee and a free bagel?

A. List the multiples of 8 and 12. Circle the common multiples.

8: 8 16 ㉔ 32 40 ㊽

12: 12 ㉔ 36 ㊽

B. Find the LCM of 8 and 12.

The LCM is 24. The 24th customer will be the first to get a free coffee and a free bagel.

EXERCISES

1. Find the GCF of 49 and 63 (Lesson 2-1) ___7___

Rewrite each sum as a product of the GCF of the addends and another number. (Lesson 2-1)

2. $15 + 45 = $ ___$15 \times (1 + 3) = 15 \times 4$___

3. $9 + 27 = $ ___$9 \times (1 + 3) = 9 \times 4$___

4. Find the LCM of 9 and 6 (Lesson 2-2) ___18___

MODULE 3 Rational Numbers

 6.NS.6, 6.NS.6a, 6.NS.6c, 6.NS.7, 6.NS.7a, 6.NS.7b, 6.NS.7c

Key Concepts
- A rational number is any number that can be written as $\frac{a}{b}$. *(Lesson 3.1)*
- The opposite of a rational number is the number the same distance from 0 on the number line but on the opposite side of 0. *(Lesson 3.2)*
- To compare and order rational numbers, convert them to decimals or fractions. *(Lesson 3.3)*

Unit 1 Performance Tasks

The Performance Tasks provide students with the opportunity to apply concepts from this unit in real-world problem situations.

CAREERS IN MATH

Climatologist In Performance Task Item 1, students can see how a climatologist uses mathematics on the job.

SCORING GUIDES FOR PERFORMANCE TASKS

1. MATHEMATICAL PRACTICES   **MP.4, MP.6**

Task	Possible Points (Total: 6)
a	**2 points** for correct list: 1920, 1900, 1910, 1940, 1930
b	**1 point** for correct year: 1930 **1 point** for explanation: This was the year when the ring was widest, which means that year had the greatest average temperature.
c	**1 point** for correct year: 1920 **1 point** for explanation: This was the year when the ring was narrowest, which means that year had the least average temperature.

2. MATHEMATICAL PRACTICES   **MP.4, MP.5**

Task	Possible Points (Total: 6)
a	**1 point** for listing integers: −4, −3, and 4 **1 point** for explanation: I will use positive and negative integers because some floors are below ground level, and some floors are above ground level. Zero is ground level.
b	**1 point** for graphing all values: −5 −4 −3 −2 −1 0 1 2 3 4 5
c	**1 point** for listing values in order: −4, −3, 0, 1, 4
d	**1 point** for correct number of flights of stairs: 8 flights **1 point** for explanation: Starting at −4, I count integers to the right until I reach 4, for a total of 8, so that means that starting at the fourth floor below ground level, Gala must climb 8 flights of stairs to get to the fourth floor above ground level.

CAREERS IN MATH

For more information about careers in mathematics as well as various mathematics appreciation topics, visit the American Mathematical Society http://www.ams.org

MODULE 3 **Rational Numbers**

Key Vocabulary
rational number *(número racional)*
Venn diagram *(diagrama de Venn)*

? ESSENTIAL QUESTION

How can you use rational numbers to solve real-world problems?

EXAMPLE 1

Use the Venn diagram to determine in which set or sets each number belongs.

A. $\frac{1}{2}$ belongs in the set of rational numbers.

B. −5 belongs in the sets of integers and rational numbers.

C. 4 belongs in the sets of whole numbers, integers, and rational numbers.

D. 0.2 belongs in the set of rational numbers.

EXAMPLE 2

Order $\frac{2}{5}$, 0.2, and $\frac{4}{15}$ from greatest to least.

Write the decimal as an equivalent fraction. $0.2 = \frac{2}{10} = \frac{1}{5}$

Find equivalent fractions with 15 as the common denominator.

$\frac{2 \times 3}{5 \times 3} = \frac{6}{15}$ $\frac{1 \times 3}{5 \times 3} = \frac{3}{15}$ $\frac{4}{15} = \frac{4}{15}$

Order fractions with common denominators by comparing the numerators.

$6 > 4 > 3$ $\frac{6}{15} > \frac{4}{15} > \frac{3}{15}$

The numbers in order from greatest to least are, $\frac{2}{5}$, $\frac{4}{15}$, and 0.2.

EXERCISES

Classify each number by indicating in which set or sets it belongs. (Lesson 2.1)

1. 8 _whole numbers, integers, rational numbers_

2. 0.25 _rational numbers_

Find the absolute value of each rational number. (Lesson 2.2)

3. |3.7| _____ 3.7 _____

4. $\left|-\frac{2}{3}\right|$ _____ $\frac{2}{3}$ _____

Graph each set of numbers on the number line and order the numbers from greatest to least. (Lesson 2.1, 2.3)

5. $-0.5, -1, -\frac{1}{4}, 0$

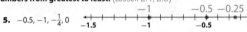

$0, -\frac{1}{4}, -0.5, -1$

Unit 1 Performance Tasks

1. **CAREERS IN MATH** Climatologist Each year a tree is alive, it adds a layer of growth, called a tree ring, between its core and its bark. A climatologist measures the width of tree rings of a particular tree for different years:

Year	1900	1910	1920	1930	1940
Width of ring (in mm)	$\frac{14}{25}$	$\frac{29}{50}$	$\frac{53}{100}$	$\frac{13}{20}$	$\frac{3}{5}$

The average temperature during the growing season is directly related to the width of the ring, with a greater width corresponding to a higher average temperature.

a. List the years in order of increasing ring width.

_1920, 1900, 1910, 1940, 1930_

b. Which year was hottest? How do you know?

1930; its ring is the widest.

c. Which year was coldest? How do you know?

1920; its ring is the narrowest.

2. A parking garage has floors above and below ground level. For a scavenger hunt, Gaia's friends are given a list of objects they need to find on the third and fourth level below ground, the first and fourth level above ground, and ground level.

a. If ground level is 0 and the first level above ground is 1, which integers can you use to represent the other levels where objects are hidden? Explain your reasoning.

−4, −3, and 4; if positive 1 represents the first level above ground,

negative numbers are a good choice to represent levels below ground.

b. Graph the set of numbers on the number line. `−5 −4 −3 −2 −1  0  1  2  3  4  5`

c. Gaia wants to start at the lowest level and work her way up. List the levels in the order that Gaia will search them.

_−4, −3, 0, 1, 4_

d. If she takes the stairs, how many flights of stairs will she have to climb? How do you know?

8 flights; starting at −4 and moving to 4, you pass a total of

8 integers on the number line.

Assessment Readiness

Additional Resources

Personal Math Trainer

Online Assessment and Intervention

my.hrw.com

Assessment Resources
- Leveled Unit Tests: A, B, C, D
- Performance Assessment

Assessment Readiness Tip Students can use number lines or other visual aids to help compare and order numbers.

Item 5   A number line will help students order the integers from greatest to least.

Item 10   Students may have difficulty ordering fractions and decimals. A number line may remind students to convert all numbers to either fractions or decimals before comparing and ordering them.

Avoid Common Errors

Item 4   Some students will ignore the negative sign and choose Albany because it appears to be the smallest number. Remind students that in this context, negative numbers represent colder temperatures as their absolute values get larger, and encourage them to sketch a number line if they need a reminder.

Item 8   Because the number in the problem does not include a negative sign, some students may select answer choice A. Remind students that the language and context of the problem can represent a negative quantity even when a negative sign is not used.

Common Core Standards

Items	Grade 6 Standards	Mathematical Practices
1	**6.NS.6a**	**MP.5** Using Tools
2	**6.NS.6a**	**MP.4** Modeling
3	**6.NS.7**	**MP.5** Using Tools
4	**6.NS.6c**	**MP.4** Modeling
5	**6.NS.1**	**MP.5** Using Tools
6*	**6.NS.6**	**MP.4** Modeling
7	**6.NS.6a**	**MP.8** Patterns
8	**6.NS.6a**	**MP.4** Modeling
9	**6.NS.7**	**MP.2** Reasoning
10*	**6.NS.6a**	**MP.5** Using Tools
11	**6.NS.6a**	**MP.2** Reasoning
12	**6.NS.4**	**MP.7** Using Structure
13	**6.NS.4**	**MP.7** Using Structure
14	**6.NS.4**	**MP.7** Using Structure
15	**6.NS.7**	**MP.4** Modeling
16	**6.NS.4**	**MP.4** Modeling

* Item integrates mixed review concepts from previous modules or a previous course.

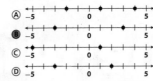
Selected Response

1. What is the opposite of −9?

Ⓐ 9

Ⓑ −$\frac{1}{9}$

Ⓒ 0

Ⓓ $\frac{1}{9}$

2. Kyle is currently 60 feet above sea level. Which correctly describes the opposite of Kyle's elevation?

Ⓐ 60 feet below sea level

Ⓑ 60 feet above sea level

Ⓒ 6 feet below sea level

Ⓓ At sea level

3. What is the absolute value of 27?

Ⓐ −27

Ⓑ 0

Ⓒ 3

Ⓓ 27

4. In Albany it is −4°F, in Chicago it is −14°F, in Minneapolis it is −11°F, and in Toronto it is −13°F. In which city is it the coldest?

Ⓐ Albany

Ⓑ Chicago

Ⓒ Minneapolis

Ⓓ Toronto

5. Which shows the integers in order from greatest to least?

Ⓐ 18, 4, 3, −2, −15

Ⓑ −2, 3, 4, −15, 18

Ⓒ −15, −2, 3, 4, 18

Ⓓ 18, −15, 4, 3, −2

6. Joanna split three pitchers of water equally among her eight plants. What fraction of a pitcher did each plant get?

Ⓐ $\frac{1}{8}$ of a pitcher

Ⓑ $\frac{1}{3}$ of a pitcher

Ⓒ $\frac{3}{8}$ of a pitcher

Ⓓ $\frac{8}{3}$ of a pitcher

7. Which set or sets does the number −22 belong to?

Ⓐ Whole numbers only

Ⓑ Rational numbers only

Ⓒ Integers and rational numbers only

Ⓓ Whole numbers, integers, and rational numbers

8. Carlos swam to the bottom of a pool that is 12 feet deep. What is the opposite of Carlos's elevation relative to the surface?

Ⓐ −12 feet

Ⓒ 12 feet

Ⓑ 0 feet

Ⓓ $\frac{1}{12}$ foot

9. Which number line shows $\frac{1}{3}$ and its opposite?

Ⓐ ![number line from −1 to 1]

Ⓑ ![number line from −1 to 1]

Ⓒ ![number line from −1 to 1]

Ⓓ ![number line from −1 to 1]

10. Which of the following shows the numbers in order from least to greatest?

Ⓐ −$\frac{2}{3}$, −$\frac{3}{4}$, 0.7, 0

Ⓑ 0.7, 0, −$\frac{2}{3}$, −$\frac{3}{4}$

Ⓒ −$\frac{2}{3}$, −$\frac{3}{4}$, 0, 0.7

Ⓓ −$\frac{3}{4}$, −$\frac{2}{3}$, 0, 0.7

11. Which number line shows an integer and its opposite?

Ⓐ ![number line −5 to 5]

Ⓑ ![number line −5 to 5]

Ⓒ ![number line −5 to 5]

Ⓓ ![number line −5 to 5]

12. Which is another way to write 42 + 63?

Ⓐ 7 × (6 + 7)

Ⓒ 7 × 6 × 9

Ⓑ 7 × 15

Ⓓ 7 + 6 + 9

13. What is the LCM of 9 and 15?

Ⓐ 30

Ⓒ 90

Ⓑ 45

Ⓓ 135

14. What is the GCF of 40 and 72?

Ⓐ 2

Ⓒ 8

Ⓑ 4

Ⓓ 12

Mini-Task

15. Stella is recording temperatures every day for 5 days. On the first day, Stella recorded a temperature of 0 °F.

a. On the second day, the temperature was 3 °F above the temperature on the first day. What was the temperature on the second day? _____3 °F_____

b. On the third day, it was 4 °F below the temperature of the first day. What was the temperature? _____−4 °F_____

c. The temperature on the fourth day was the opposite of the temperature on the second day. What was the temperature? _____−3 °F_____

d. The temperature on the fifth day was the absolute value of the temperature on the fourth day. What was the temperature? _____3 °F_____

e. Write the temperatures in order from least to greatest. ____−4, −3, 0, 3____

f. What is the difference in temperature between the coldest day and the warmest day? _____−7 °F_____

16. Marco is making mosaic garden stones using red, yellow, and blue tiles. He has 45 red tiles, 90 blue tiles, and 75 yellow tiles. Each stone must have the same number of each color tile. What is the greatest number of stones Marco can make? _____15_____

a. How many of each color tile will Marco use in each stone? ____3 red, 6 blue, 5 yellow____

b. How can Marco use the GCF to find out how many tiles he has in all? He can multiply the GCF by the sum of the other factors. 15 × (3 + 6 + 15) = 15 × 24

UNIT 2

Number Operations

Contents

Unit Pacing Guide

45-Minute Classes

Module 4

DAY 1	DAY 2	DAY 3	DAY 4	DAY 5
Lesson 4.1	Lesson 4.1	Lesson 4.2	Lesson 4.2	Lesson 4.2

DAY 6	DAY 7	DAY 8	DAY 9	DAY 10
Lesson 4.3	Lesson 4.3	Lesson 4.4	Lesson 4.4	Ready to Go On? Assessment Readiness

Module 5

DAY 1	DAY 2	DAY 3	DAY 4	DAY 5
Lesson 5.1	Lesson 5.1	Lesson 5.2	Lesson 5.2	Lesson 5.3

DAY 6	DAY 7	DAY 8	DAY 9	DAY 10
Lesson 5.3	Lesson 5.4	Lesson 5.4	Lesson 5.5	Lesson 5.5

DAY 11	DAY 12			
Ready to Go On? Assessment Readiness	Study Guide Assessment Readiness			

90-Minute Classes

Module 4

DAY 1	DAY 2	DAY 3	DAY 4	DAY 5
Lesson 4.1	Lesson 4.2	Lesson 4.3	Lesson 4.4	Ready to Go On? Assessment Readiness

Module 5

DAY 1	DAY 2	DAY 3	DAY 4	DAY 5
Lesson 5.1	Lesson 5.2	Lesson 5.3	Lesson 5.4	Lesson 5.5

DAY 6	DAY 7			
Ready to Go On? Assessment Readiness	Study Guide Assessment Readiness			

Program Resources

⏻ Plan

Online Teacher Edition

Access a full suite of teaching resources online—plan, present, and manage classes, assignments, and activities.

ePlanner **Easily plan your classes, create and view assignments, and access all program resources with your online, customizable planning tool.**

Professional Development Videos

Author Juli Dixon models successful teaching practices and strategies in actual classroom settings.

QR Codes **Scan with your smart phone to jump directly from your print book to online videos and other resources.**

Teacher's Edition

Support students with point-of-use Questioning Strategies, teaching tips, resources for differentiated instruction, additional activities, and more.

⏻ Engage and Explore

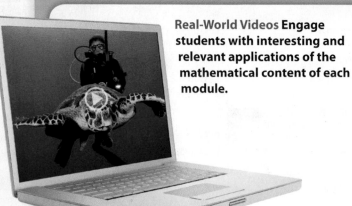

Real-World Videos Engage students with interesting and relevant applications of the mathematical content of each module.

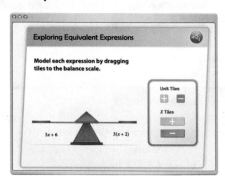

Animated Math **Online interactive simulations, tools, and games help students actively learn and practice key concepts.**

Explore Activities

Students interactively explore new concepts using a variety of tools and approaches.

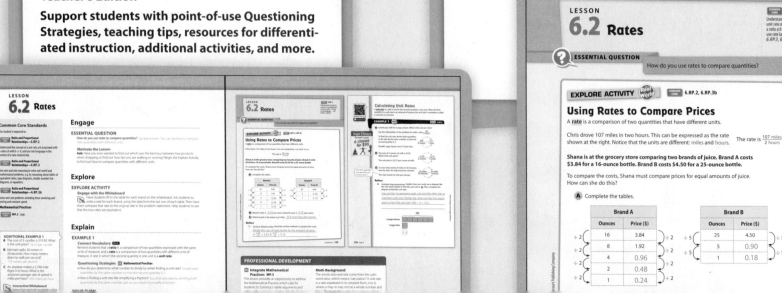

LESSON
6.2 Rates

6.RP.2
Understand the concept of a unit rate a/b associated with a ratio a:b with b ≠ 0, and use rate language.....Also 6.RP.3, 6.RP.3b

ESSENTIAL QUESTION

How do you use rates to compare quantities?

EXPLORE ACTIVITY Real World 6.RP.2, 6.RP.3b

Using Rates to Compare Prices

A **rate** is a comparison of two quantities that have different units.

Chris drove 107 miles in two hours. This can be expressed as the rate shown at the right. Notice that the units are different: miles and hours.

The rate is $\frac{107 \text{ miles}}{2 \text{ hours}}$.

Shana is at the grocery store comparing two brands of juice. Brand A costs $3.84 for a 16-ounce bottle. Brand B costs $4.50 for a 25-ounce bottle.

To compare the costs, Shana must compare prices for equal amounts of juice. How can she do this?

A Complete the tables.

Brand A	
Ounces	Price ($)
16	3.84
8	1.92
4	0.96
2	0.48
1	0.24

÷2 ÷2 ÷2 ÷2

Brand B	
Ounces	Price ($)
25	4.50
5	0.90
1	0.18

÷5 ÷5 ÷5

⏻ Teach

Math On the Spot video tutorials, featuring program authors Dr. Edward Burger and Martha Sandoval-Martinez, accompany every example in the textbook and give students step-by-step instructions and explanations of key math concepts.

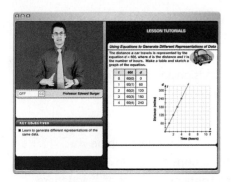

Present engaging content on a multitude of devices, including tablets and interactive whiteboards.

Math Talk Continually monitor and assess student progress with integrated formative assessment.

CC CLUSTER CONNECTION Look for exercises indicated with this icon to build connections among standards within Common Core clusters.

Differentiated Instruction Print Resources

Support all learners with Differentiated Instruction Resources, including

- **Leveled Practice and Problem Solving**
- **Reteach**
- **Reading Strategies**
- **Success for English Learners**
- **Challenge**

⏻ Assessment and Intervention

The **Personal Math Trainer** provides online practice, homework, assessments, and intervention. Monitor student progress through reports and alerts. Create and customize assignments aligned to specific lessons or standards.

- **Practice** – With dynamic items and assignments, students get unlimited practice on key concepts supported by guided examples, step-by-step solutions, and video tutorials.

- **Assessments** – Choose from course assignments or customize your own based on course content, standards, difficulty levels, and more.

- **Homework** – Students can complete online homework with a wide variety of problem types, including the ability to enter expressions, equations, and graphs. Let the system automatically grade homework, so you can focus where your students need help the most!

- **Intervention** – Let the Personal Math Trainer automatically prescribe a targeted, personalized intervention path for your students.

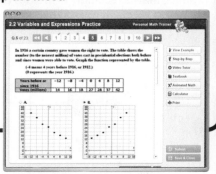

Raise the bar with homework and practice that incorporates higher-order thinking and mathematical processes in every lesson.

COMMON CORE

Assessment Readiness
Prepare students for success on tests of the Common Core Standards with practice at every module and unit.

Assessment Resources

Tailor assessments to meet the needs of all your classes and students, including

- **Leveled Module Quizzes**
- **Leveled Unit Tests**
- **Unit Performance Tasks**
- **Placement, Diagnostic, and Quarterly Benchmark Tests**

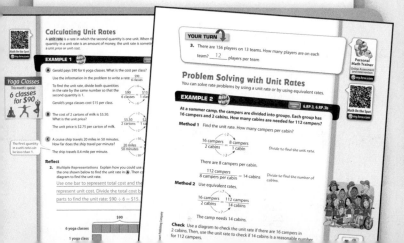

Math Background

Multiplying Fractions Prep for 6.NS.1
LESSON 4.1

The algorithm for multiplying two fractions is easy to use: multiply the numerators, multiply the denominators, and write the resulting fraction in simplest form. Symbolically, $\frac{a}{b} \cdot \frac{c}{d} = \frac{ac}{bd}$, where b and d are nonzero.

Although students may have little difficulty applying this algorithm, they may not understand the underlying rationale. They should recognize that any product $m \cdot n$, for positive real numbers m and n, can be defined as the area of a rectangle with sides of length m and n. Thus, $\frac{a}{b} \cdot \frac{c}{d}$ can be defined as the area of a rectangle with side lengths $\frac{a}{b}$ and $\frac{c}{d}$.

For example, consider the product $\frac{2}{5} \cdot \frac{1}{3}$. To illustrate the product, draw a rectangle with sides of length $\frac{2}{5}$ and $\frac{1}{3}$ inside a square with sides of length 1.

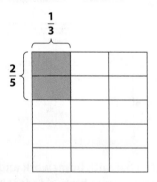

Notice that the square is divided into 15 equal parts, and 2 of these parts are shaded. Therefore, the area of the shaded rectangle is $\frac{2}{15}$ of the area of the square. In other words, $\frac{2}{5} \cdot \frac{1}{3} = \frac{2}{15}$. The product of the denominators is equal to the total number of parts into which the square is divided, and the product of the numerators is equal to the number of shaded parts.

Students who have this model in mind may be less likely to confuse the algorithm for multiplying fractions with those for other fraction operations. Also, the area model of multiplication is quite versatile. It will be extended in future mathematics courses to illustrate multiplication of polynomials.

Dividing Fractions 6.NS.1
LESSON 4.2

Two numbers are *reciprocals* if their product is 1. That is, two numbers are reciprocals if they are multiplicative inverses. In practical terms, the reciprocal of a fraction can be found by interchanging the numerator and denominator.

To multiply two fractions, you multiply the dividend by the reciprocal of the divisor. Symbolically, $\frac{a}{b} \div \frac{c}{d} = \frac{a}{b} \cdot \frac{d}{c}$, where b, c, and d are nonzero. This algorithm makes explicit use of the connection between division and multiplication, and it is worth illustrating how and why this connection comes into play.

Consider the quotient $4 \div \frac{1}{3}$. The quotient can be understood as "How many groups of $\frac{1}{3}$ are in 4?" To answer that question, note that 1 contains 3 groups of $\frac{1}{3}$, and there are 4 groups of 1 in 4. Therefore, the total number of groups of $\frac{1}{3}$ in 4 is simply $4 \times 3 = 12$. This is shown in the figure.

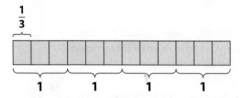

The above example shows why it makes sense to find the quotient $4 \div \frac{1}{3}$ by converting the division problem to the multiplication problem 4×3. In particular, dividing by $\frac{1}{3}$ is equivalent to multiplying by the reciprocal, 3. It is not difficult to extend this line of reasoning to more general situations in which the dividend is not a whole number and the divisor is a fraction that does not have 1 as its numerator.

Adding Decimals 6.NS.3
LESSON 5.2

Understanding decimal addition and subtraction depends upon understanding the connection between decimals and place value. Consider the sum $3.51 + 2.07$. The first addend, 3.51, means 3 ones, 5 tenths, and 1 hundredth. The second addend, 2.07, means 2 ones, no tenths, and 7 hundredths. To find the sum, add like place values: there are 5 ones, 5 tenths, and 8 hundredths. Therefore, the sum is 5.58. Recognizing the role of place values explains why students are told to add by first aligning the decimal points of the addends. Doing so aligns the digits according to place value so that the digits in each column can be added.

It is also useful to recognize that many decimal concepts can be further explained once the relationship between fractions and decimals is clear. For example, the above sum can also be understood by expressing the decimals as fractions.

$$3.51 = 3 + \frac{5}{10} + \frac{1}{100}$$
$$2.07 = 2 + \frac{0}{10} + \frac{7}{100}$$

The sum is $5 + \frac{5}{10} + \frac{8}{100} = 5.58$. The fractional representations are another way to reinforce the importance of place value in decimal calculations.

Multiplying Decimals 6.NS.3
LESSON 5.3

To multiply two decimals, multiply as if the numbers are whole numbers and place the decimal point in the product by finding the total number of decimal places in the factors.

The validity of this algorithm can be shown by using fractions. Consider the following product:

$$2.5 \cdot 4.17 = \frac{25}{10} \cdot \frac{417}{100} = \frac{10,425}{1,000} = 10.425$$

Notice that the number of digits to the right of the decimal point in the product is the sum of the numbers of digits to the right of the decimal point in each of the factors.

The laws of exponents can be used to show that this is always true. If $\frac{a}{10^m}$ and $\frac{b}{10^n}$ represent two decimals with m and n digits to the right of the decimal point, respectively, then $\frac{a}{10^m} \cdot \frac{b}{10^n} = \frac{ab}{10^{m+n}}$. Thus, the product has $(m + n)$ decimal places.

Dividing Decimals 6.NS.3
LESSON 5.4

Fractions can be used to confirm the correct placement of the decimal point when dividing decimals.

$$
\begin{aligned}
4.32 \div 3.6 &= \frac{432}{100} \div \frac{36}{10} \\
&= \frac{\overset{12}{\cancel{4.32}}}{\underset{10}{\cancel{100}}} \cdot \frac{\overset{1}{\cancel{10}}}{\underset{1}{\cancel{36}}} \\
&= \frac{12}{10} \\
&= 1.2
\end{aligned}
$$

When dividing by a decimal, students may wonder why they can multiply both the divisor and the dividend by the same number without changing the value of the quotient. Explain this by reminding students that a division problem can be written as a fraction (for example, $8 \div 4 = \frac{8}{4} = 2$). Multiplying the numerator and denominator by the same number does not change the value of the fraction because doing so is equivalent to multiplying by 1.

$$0.8 \div 0.4 = \frac{0.8}{0.4} = \frac{0.8 \cdot 10}{0.4 \cdot 10} = \frac{8}{4} = 2$$

UNIT 2
Number Operations

MODULE 4

Operations with Fractions

COMMON CORE 6.NS.1, 6.NS.4

MODULE 5

Operations with Decimals

COMMON CORE 6.NS.2, 6.NS.3

CAREERS IN MATH

Chef The role of a chef is diverse and can include planning menus, overseeing food preparation, training staff, and ordering and purchasing food items. Chefs use mathematics when scaling recipes as well as in budgeting and financial planning.

If you are interested in a career as a chef, you should study these mathematical subjects:
- Basic Math
- Business Math

Research other careers that require the use of scaling quantities, and financial planning.

Unit 2 Performance Task

At the end of the unit, check out how **chefs** use math.

Careers in Math

Chef

Chefs often use mathematics in their work. They must have a solid understanding of fractions and scaling. You will learn more about this in the Performance Tasks at the end of the unit.

For more information about careers in mathematics as well as various mathematics appreciation topics, visit the American Mathematical Society at www.ams.org

Vocabulary Preview

Use the puzzle to give students a preview of important concepts in this unit. Students may work individually, in pairs, or in groups.

Unit Resources

Go online to access all your unit resources.

my.hrw.com

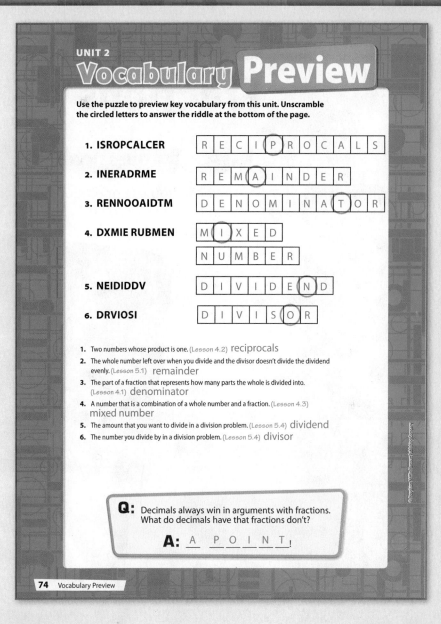

UNIT 2

Vocabulary Preview

Use the puzzle to preview key vocabulary from this unit. Unscramble the circled letters to answer the riddle at the bottom of the page.

1. ISROPCALCER — R E C I (P) R O C A L S
2. INERADRME — R E M (A) I N D E R
3. RENNOOAIDTM — D E N O M I N A (T) O R
4. DXMIE RUBMEN — M (I) X E D / N U M B E R
5. NEIDIDDV — D I V I D E (N) D
6. DRVIOSI — D I V I S (O) R

1. Two numbers whose product is one. (Lesson 4.2) **reciprocals**
2. The whole number left over when you divide and the divisor doesn't divide the dividend evenly. (Lesson 5.1) **remainder**
3. The part of a fraction that represents how many parts the whole is divided into. (Lesson 4.1) **denominator**
4. A number that is a combination of a whole number and a fraction. (Lesson 4.3) **mixed number**
5. The amount that you want to divide in a division problem. (Lesson 5.4) **dividend**
6. The number you divide by in a division problem. (Lesson 5.4) **divisor**

Q: Decimals always win in arguments with fractions. What do decimals have that fractions don't?

A: A P O I N T !

Before	In this Unit	After
Students understand multiplication, division, addition, and subtraction: • multiply and divide whole numbers, fractions, and decimals • add and subtract whole numbers, fractions, and decimals	Students will learn about: • multiplication of fractions and mixed numbers • division of fractions and mixed numbers • multiplication and division of decimals • addition, subtraction, multiplication, and division of integers	Students will connect rational numbers and integers: • perform operations with rational numbers

Operations with Fractions

MODULE 4

COMMON CORE

ESSENTIAL QUESTION

How can you use operations with fractions to solve real-world problems?

You can represent real-world quantities as fractions, and then solve the problems using the appropriate operation(s).

Real-World Video

To find your average rate of speed, divide the distance you traveled by the time you traveled. If you ride in a taxi and drive $\frac{1}{2}$ mile in $\frac{1}{4}$ hour, your rate was 2 mi/h which may mean you were in heavy traffic.

my.hrw.com

© Houghton Mifflin Harcourt Publishing Company · Image Credits: (c)Tetra Images / Alamy

GO DIGITAL

my.hrw.com

my.hrw.com

Go digital with your write-in student edition, accessible on any device.

Math On the Spot

Scan with your smart phone to jump directly to the online edition, video tutor, and more.

Animated Math

Interactively explore key concepts to see how math works.

Personal Math Trainer

Get immediate feedback and help as you work through practice sets.

Are You Ready?

Assess Readiness

Use the assessment on this page to determine if students need intensive or strategic intervention for the module's prerequisite skills.

  **RtI** **Response to Intervention**

Personal Math Trainer

Online Assessment and Intervention

🔘 my.hrw.com

Intervention	Enrichment

Access Are You Ready? assessment online, and receive instant scoring, feedback, and customized intervention or enrichment.

Online and Print Resources

Skills Intervention worksheets	*Differentiated Instruction*
• Skill 21 Write an Improper Fraction as a Mixed Number	• Challenge worksheets **PRE-AP**
• Skill 36 Multiplication Facts	Extend the Math **PRE-AP** Lesson Activities in TE
• Skill 38 Division Facts	

Are YOU Ready?

Complete these exercises to review skills you will need for this module.

 Personal Math Trainer

🔘 my.hrw.com

Online Assessment and Intervention

Write an Improper Fraction as a Mixed Number

EXAMPLE	$\frac{13}{5} = \frac{5}{5} + \frac{5}{5} + \frac{3}{5}$	Write as a sum using names for one plus a proper fraction.
	$= 1 + 1 + \frac{3}{5}$	Write each name for one as one.
	$= 2 + \frac{3}{5}$	Add the ones.
	$= 2\frac{3}{5}$	Write the mixed number.

Write each improper fraction as a mixed number.

1. $\frac{9}{4}$ $2\frac{1}{4}$ 2. $\frac{8}{3}$ $2\frac{2}{3}$ 3. $\frac{23}{6}$ $3\frac{5}{6}$ 4. $\frac{11}{2}$ $5\frac{1}{2}$

5. $\frac{17}{5}$ $3\frac{2}{5}$ 6. $\frac{15}{8}$ $1\frac{7}{8}$ 7. $\frac{33}{10}$ $3\frac{3}{10}$ 8. $\frac{29}{12}$ $2\frac{5}{12}$

Multiplication Facts

EXAMPLE	$7 \times 6 = \blacksquare$	Use a related fact you know.
		$6 \times 6 = 36$
		Think: $7 \times 6 = (6 \times 6) + 6$
		$= 36 + 6$
	$7 \times 6 = 42$	$= 42$

Multiply.

9. 6×5 _30_   10. 8×9 _72_   11. 10×11 _110_   12. 7×8 _56_

13. 9×7 _63_   14. 8×6 _48_   15. 9×11 _99_   16. 11×12 _132_

Division Facts

EXAMPLE	$63 \div 7 = \blacksquare$	Think: 7 times what number equals 63?
		$7 \times 9 = 63$
	$63 \div 7 = 9$	So, $63 \div 7 = 9$.

Divide.

17. $35 \div 7$ _5_   18. $56 \div 8$ _7_   19. $28 \div 7$ _4_   20. $48 \div 8$ _6_

21. $36 \div 4$ _9_   22. $45 \div 9$ _5_   23. $72 \div 8$ _9_   24. $40 \div 5$ _8_

 GO DIGITAL my.hrw.com

PROFESSIONAL DEVELOPMENT VIDEO

 Author Juli Dixon models successful teaching practices as she explores multiplying and dividing fractions in an actual sixth-grade classroom.

 Professional Development

🔘 my.hrw.com

 Online Teacher Edition
Access a full suite of teaching resources online—plan, present, and manage classes and assignments.

 ePlanner
Easily plan your classes and access all your resources online.

 Interactive Answers and Solutions
Customize answer keys to print or display in the classroom. Choose to include answers only or full solutions to all lesson exercises.

 Interactive Whiteboards
Engage students with interactive whiteboard-ready lessons and activities.

 Personal Math Trainer: Online Assessment and Intervention
Assign automatically graded homework, quizzes, tests, and intervention activities. Prepare your students with updated practice tests aligned with Common Core.

Reading Start-Up

Have students complete the activities on this page by working alone or with others.

Visualize Vocabulary

The summary triangle helps students review vocabulary associated with fractions and operations. In or next to each section of the triangle, students should write the review word that fits the description.

Understand Vocabulary

Use the following explanation to help students learn the preview words.

> To help you remember the word **reciprocal**, think about how things go together. For example, visualize two building blocks that fit together. Together they make one whole.

Active Reading

Integrating Language Arts

Students can use these reading and note-taking strategies to help them organize and understand new concepts and vocabulary.

COMMON CORE **ELA-Literacy.RST.6-8.7** Integrate quantitative or technical information expressed in words in a text with a version of that information expressed visually (e.g., in a flowchart, diagram, model, graph, or table).

Additional Resources

Differentiated Instruction

• Reading Strategies **ELL**

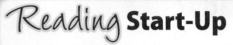

Visualize Vocabulary

Use the ✔ words to complete the triangle. Write the review word that fits the description in each section of the triangle.

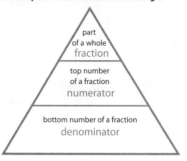

part of a whole
fraction

top number of a fraction
numerator

bottom number of a fraction
denominator

Vocabulary

Review Words
- area *(área)*
- ✔ denominator *(denominador)*
- ✔ fraction *(fracción)*
- greatest common factor (GCF) *(máximo común divisor (MCD))*
- least common multiple (LCM) *(mínimo común múltiplo (m.c.m.))*
- length *(longitud)*
- ✔ numerator *(numerador)*
- product *(producto)*
- width *(ancho)*

Preview Words
- mixed number *(número mixto)*
- order of operations *(orden de las operaciones)*
- reciprocals *(recíprocos)*

Understand Vocabulary

In each grouping, select the choice that is described by the given vocabulary word.

1. reciprocals   Ⓐ 1:15   Ⓑ $\frac{3}{4} \div \frac{1}{6}$ Ⓒ $\frac{3}{5}$ and $\frac{5}{3}$

2. mixed number   Ⓐ $\frac{1}{3} - \frac{1}{5}$ Ⓑ $3\frac{1}{2}$ Ⓒ -5

3. order of operations   Ⓐ $5 - 3 + 2 = 0$ Ⓑ $5 - 3 + 2 = 4$ Ⓒ $5 - 3 + 2 = 6$

Active Reading

Layered Book Before beginning the module, create a layered book to help you learn the concepts in this module. Label each flap with lesson titles. As you study each lesson, write important ideas, such as vocabulary and processes, under the appropriate flap. Refer to your finished layered book as you work on exercises from this module.

Before	**In this module**	**After**
Students understand multiplication and division: • multiply whole numbers • divide whole numbers	Students learn to multiply and divide positive rational numbers fluently: • multiply fractions • multiply mixed numbers • divide fractions • divide mixed numbers	Students will connect rational numbers and integers: • multiply rational numbers fluently • divide rational numbers fluently

Unpacking the Standards

Use the examples on the page to help students know exactly what they are expected to learn in this module.

Common Core Standards

Content Areas

 The Number System—6.NS

Apply and extend previous understandings of multiplication and division to divide fractions by fractions.

 The Number System—6.NS

Compute fluently with multi-digit numbers and find common factors and multiples.

Go online to see a complete unpacking of the Common Core Standards.

my.hrw.com

MODULE 4
Unpacking the Standards

Understanding the standards and the vocabulary terms in the standards will help you know exactly what you are expected to learn in this module.

COMMON CORE 6.NS.1

Interpret and compute quotients of fractions, and solve word problems involving division of fractions by fractions, e.g., by using visual fraction models and equations to represent the problem.

Key Vocabulary

quotient *(cociente)*
The result when one number is divided by another.

fraction *(fracción)*
A number in the form $\frac{a}{b}$, where $b \neq 0$.

What It Means to You

You will learn how to divide two fractions. You will also understand the relationship between multiplication and division.

UNPACKING EXAMPLE 6.NS.1

Zachary is making vegetable soup. The recipe makes $6\frac{3}{4}$ cups of soup. How many $1\frac{1}{2}$-cup servings will the recipe make?

$$6\frac{3}{4} \div 1\frac{1}{2}$$
$$= \frac{27}{4} \div \frac{3}{2}$$
$$= \frac{27}{4} \times \frac{2}{3}$$
$$= \frac{9}{2}$$
$$= 4\frac{1}{2}$$

The recipe will make $4\frac{1}{2}$ servings.

COMMON CORE 6.NS.4

Find the greatest common factor of two whole numbers less than or equal to 100 and the least common multiple of two whole numbers less than or equal to 12. Use the distributive property to express a sum of two whole numbers 1–100 with a common factor as a multiple of a sum of two whole numbers with no common factor.

Visit my.hrw.com to see all the Common Core Standards unpacked.

my.hrw.com

What It Means to You

You can use greatest common factors and least common multiples to simplify answers when you calculate with fractions.

UNPACKING EXAMPLE 6.NS.4

Add. Write the answer in simplest form.

$$\frac{1}{3} + \frac{1}{6} = \frac{2}{6} + \frac{1}{6} \qquad \text{Use the LCM of 3 and 6 as a common denominator.}$$
$$= \frac{2+1}{6} \qquad \text{Add the numerators.}$$
$$= \frac{3}{6}$$
$$= \frac{3 \div 3}{6 \div 3} \qquad \text{Simplify by dividing by the GCF. The GCF of 3 and 6 is 3.}$$
$$= \frac{1}{2} \qquad \text{Write the answer in simplest form.}$$

Common Core Standards	Lesson 4.1	Lesson 4.2	Lesson 4.3	Lesson 4.4
6.NS.1 Interpret and compute quotients of fractions and solve word problems involving division of fractions by fractions, ...		COMMON CORE	COMMON CORE	COMMON CORE
6.NS.4 Find the greatest common factor of two whole numbers and the least common multiple of two whole numbers ... Use the Distributive Property to express the sum of two whole numbers 1–100 with a common factor as a multiple of a sum of two whole numbers.	COMMON CORE			

LESSON
4.1 Applying GCF and LCM to Fraction Operations

Engage

ESSENTIAL QUESTION

How do you use the GCF and LCM when adding, subtracting, and multiplying fractions? You use the GCF to simplify fractions when you find sums, differences, and products of fractions. You use the LCM of the denominators of fractions to add and subtract fractions.

Motivate the Lesson
Ask: Suppose you want to make half a batch of cookies and the recipe calls for $\frac{3}{4}$ cup of pecans. How many pecans should you use? Begin the Explore Activity to find out.

Explore

Connect Multiple Representations
Explain to students that there are two ways to multiply fractions.

- **Method A:** Simplify after you multiply by dividing the numerator and denominator of the product by the GCF.

- **Method B:** Simplify before multiplying by dividing a numerator and a denominator by a common factor.

Explain

EXAMPLE 1

Questioning Strategies Mathematical Practices

- Does the order in which you multiply two fractions matter? Explain. No. The Commutative Property of Multiplication states that changing the order of the factors does not change the product.

- How can you tell when it would be easier to simplify before multiplying than to simplify the product? When one of the factors in the numerator is the same as one of the factors in the denominator, it is easier to simplify before multiplying.

Focus on Communication
Remind students that the multiplication sign means "of." So, $\frac{1}{2} \times \frac{1}{4}$ means "What is $\frac{1}{2}$ of $\frac{1}{4}$?" Use a diagram to help them see that $\frac{1}{2}$ of $\frac{1}{4}$ is $\frac{1}{8}$.

YOUR TURN

Avoid Common Errors
Students often forget to simplify the product after multiplying. Remind students that their final answer should always be in simplest form.

EXAMPLE 2

Questioning Strategies Mathematical Practices

- Why can you write 18 as $\frac{18}{1}$? 18 is a rational number, and you can write every rational number as a quotient of two integers.

Focus on Reasoning Mathematical Practices

Have students relate the Reflect question to the similar question about multiplying two fractions. Remind them that the multiplication sign means "of." So, $\frac{5}{9} \times 18$ means "What is $\frac{5}{9}$ of 18?"; the answer must be less than 18.

Applying GCF and LCM to Fraction Operations

COMMON CORE 6.NS.4
Find the greatest common factor…and the least common multiple of two whole numbers…

? ESSENTIAL QUESTION

How do you use the GCF and LCM when adding, subtracting, and multiplying fractions?

Multiplying Fractions

To multiply two fractions you first multiply the numerators and then multiply the denominators.

$$\frac{\text{numerator} \times \text{numerator}}{\text{denominator} \times \text{denominator}} = \frac{\text{numerator}}{\text{denominator}}$$

The resulting product may need to be written in simplest form. To write a fraction in simplest form, you can divide both the numerator and the denominator by their greatest common factor.

Example 1 shows two methods for making sure that the product of two fractions is in simplest form.

EXAMPLE 1

COMMON CORE 6.NS.4

Multiply. Write the product in simplest form.

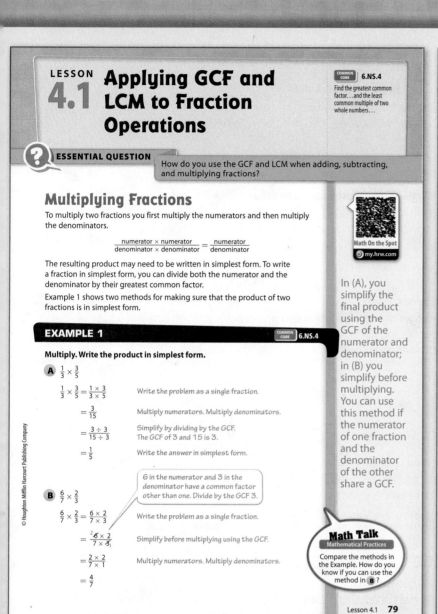

A $\frac{1}{3} \times \frac{3}{5}$

$\frac{1}{3} \times \frac{3}{5} = \frac{1 \times 3}{3 \times 5}$ Write the problem as a single fraction.

$= \frac{3}{15}$ Multiply numerators. Multiply denominators.

$= \frac{3 \div 3}{15 \div 3}$ Simplify by dividing by the GCF. The GCF of 3 and 15 is 3.

$= \frac{1}{5}$ Write the answer in simplest form.

> 6 in the numerator and 3 in the denominator have a common factor other than one. Divide by the GCF 3.

B $\frac{6}{7} \times \frac{2}{3}$

$\frac{6}{7} \times \frac{2}{3} = \frac{6 \times 2}{7 \times 3}$ Write the problem as a single fraction.

$= \frac{\overset{2}{6} \times 2}{7 \times \underset{1}{3}}$ Simplify before multiplying using the GCF.

$= \frac{2 \times 2}{7 \times 1}$ Multiply numerators. Multiply denominators.

$= \frac{4}{7}$

In (A), you simplify the final product using the GCF of the numerator and denominator; in (B) you simplify before multiplying. You can use this method if the numerator of one fraction and the denominator of the other share a GCF.

Math Talk
Mathematical Practices

Compare the methods in the Example. How do you know if you can use the method in **B** ?

Math On the Spot
my.hrw.com

YOUR TURN

Personal Math Trainer
Online Assessment and Intervention
my.hrw.com

Multiply. Write each product in simplest form.

1. $\frac{1}{6} \times \frac{3}{5}$ $\frac{1}{10}$

2. $\frac{3}{4} \times \frac{7}{9}$ $\frac{7}{12}$

3. $\frac{3}{7} \times \frac{2}{3}$ $\frac{2}{7}$

4. $\frac{4}{5} \times \frac{2}{7}$ $\frac{8}{35}$

5. $\frac{7}{10} \times \frac{8}{21}$ $\frac{4}{15}$

6. $\frac{6}{7} \times \frac{1}{6}$ $\frac{1}{7}$

Multiplying Fractions and Whole Numbers

To multiply a fraction by a whole number, you rewrite the whole number as a fraction and multiply the two fractions. Remember to use the GCF to write the product in simplest form.

EXAMPLE 2   Real World

COMMON CORE 6.NS.4

A class has 18 students. The teacher asks how many students in the class have pets and finds $\frac{5}{9}$ of the students have pets. How many students have pets?

STEP 1   Estimate the product. Multiply the whole number by the nearest benchmark fraction.

$\frac{5}{9}$ is close to $\frac{1}{2}$, so multiply $\frac{1}{2}$ times 18.

$\frac{1}{2} \times 18 = 9$

STEP 2   Multiply. Write the product in simplest form.

> You can write $\frac{5}{9}$ times 18 three ways.
> $\frac{5}{9} \times 18$ $\frac{5}{9} \cdot 18$ $\frac{5}{9}(18)$

$\frac{5}{9} \times 18$

$\frac{5}{9} \times 18 = \frac{5}{9} \times \frac{18}{1}$ Rewrite 18 as a fraction.

$= \frac{5 \times \overset{2}{18}}{\underset{1}{9} \times 1}$ Simplify before multiplying using the GCF.

$= \frac{5 \times 2}{1 \times 1}$ Multiply numerators. Multiply denominators.

$= \frac{10}{1} = 10$ Simplify by writing as a whole number.

10 students have pets.

Math Talk
Mathematical Practices

How can you check to see if the answer is correct?

Compare the answer to the estimate. The answer, 10, is close to the estimate, 9.

Math On the Spot
my.hrw.com

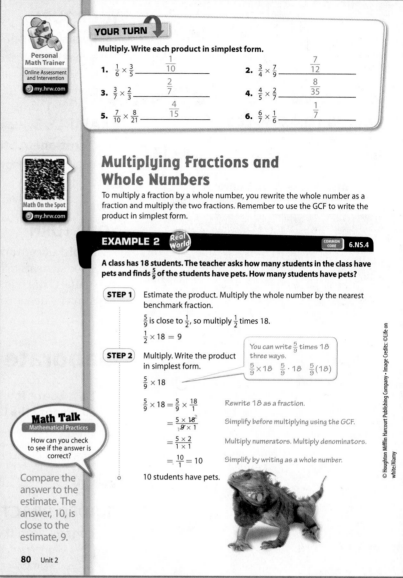

PROFESSIONAL DEVELOPMENT

CC Integrate Mathematical Practices MP.5

This lesson provides an opportunity to address the Mathematical Practices standard that calls for students to use appropriate tools strategically. In Example 1, students use an algorithm to multiply two fractions. Then, in Example 2, students estimate and then use the algorithm to multiply a fraction and a whole number by rewriting the whole number as a fraction. Finally, in Example 3, students use the LCM to rewrite fractions so they have the same denominator to simplify expressions.

Math Background

Although students may have little difficulty applying the multiplication algorithm, they may not understand the underlying rationale. They should recognize that any product $m \cdot n$, for positive real numbers m and n, can be defined as the area of a rectangle with sides of length m and n.

Thus, $\frac{a}{b} \cdot \frac{c}{d} = \frac{ac}{bd}$ can be defined as the area of a rectangle with side lengths $\frac{a}{b}$ and $\frac{c}{d}$. This may be easier for sixth-graders to understand when presented on a labeled model than when presented algebraically as above.

YOUR TURN

Focus on Models CC Mathematical Practices

Remind students to estimate the product first. They may find it helpful to draw a 0 to 1 number line and label it in fourths to decide which benchmark fraction to use as a multiplier.

EXAMPLE 3

Questioning Strategies CC Mathematical Practices

• How do you know that $\frac{16}{30} + \frac{5}{30}$ is equivalent to $\frac{8}{15} + \frac{1}{6}$? $\frac{8}{15}$ is multiplied by $\frac{2}{2}$, or 1. So its value does not change. $\frac{1}{6}$ is multiplied by $\frac{5}{5}$, or 1, so its value does not change. Because the fractions being added are equivalent, the sums are equivalent.

YOUR TURN

Avoid Common Errors

Some students may forget to find a common denominator for the fractions and add or subtract both numerators and denominators. Remind students that you must find a common denominator before adding and subtracting fractions.

Elaborate
....

Talk About It
Summarize the Lesson

Ask: How are adding and subtracting two fractions and multiplying two fractions similar and different? In both types of problems, you can use the GCF to write the answer in simplest form. But when adding or subtracting fractions, you first use the LCM of the denominators to rewrite the fractions so they have the same denominator.

GUIDED PRACTICE

Engage with the Whiteboard

For Exercise 1, have two students come up to the whiteboard. Instruct one student to simplify before multiplying and the other student to simplify after multiplying. Have students compare the two methods and discuss their reasons for preferring one method over the other.

Avoid Common Errors

Exercises 2–10 Some students may not write the product in simplest form. Remind them to check each product to be certain that the numerator and denominator do not have a common factor.

Exercises 11–16 Some students may forget to find a common denominator for the fractions and add or subtract both numerators and denominators. Remind students that you must find a common denominator before adding and subtracting fractions.

Reflect

7. Analyze Relationships Is the product of a fraction less than 1 and a whole number greater than or less than the whole number? Explain.

Less than; a fraction of a whole, if the fraction is less than 1, is always less than the whole.

YOUR TURN

Personal Math Trainer
Online Assessment and Intervention
© my.hrw.com

Multiply. Write each product in simplest form.

8. $\frac{5}{8} \times 24$ ___15___   **9.** $\frac{3}{5} \times 20$ ___12___

10. $\frac{1}{3} \times 8$ ___$\frac{8}{3}$___   **11.** $\frac{1}{4} \times 14$ ___$\frac{7}{2}$___

12. $3\frac{7}{10} \times 7$ ___$25\frac{9}{10}$___   **13.** $2\frac{3}{10} \times 10$ ___23___

Adding and Subtracting Fractions

You have learned that to add or subtract two fractions, you can rewrite the fractions so they have the same denominator. You can use the least common multiple of the denominators of the fractions to rewrite the fractions.

Math On the Spot
© my.hrw.com

EXAMPLE 3
COMMON CORE 6.NS.4

Add $\frac{8}{15} + \frac{1}{6}$. Write the sum in simplest form.

STEP 1 Rewrite the fractions as equivalent fractions. Use the LCM of the denominators as the new denominator.

$$\frac{8}{15} \rightarrow \frac{8 \times 2}{15 \times 2} \rightarrow \frac{16}{30} \qquad \text{The LCM of 15 and 6 is 30.}$$
$$\frac{1}{6} \rightarrow \frac{1 \times 5}{6 \times 5} \rightarrow \frac{5}{30}$$

STEP 2 Add the numerators of the equivalent fractions. Then simplify.

$$\frac{16}{30} + \frac{5}{30} = \frac{21}{30}$$
$$= \frac{21 \div 3}{30 \div 3} \qquad \text{Simplify by dividing by the GCF.}$$
$$= \frac{7}{10} \qquad \text{The GCF of 21 and 30 is 3.}$$

Reflect

14. Can you also use the LCM of the denominators of the fractions to rewrite the difference $\frac{8}{15} - \frac{1}{6}$? What is the difference?

yes; $\frac{11}{30}$

My Notes

© Houghton Mifflin Harcourt Publishing Company

YOUR TURN

Personal Math Trainer
Online Assessment and Intervention
© my.hrw.com

Add or subtract. Write each sum or difference in simplest form.

15. $\frac{5}{14} + \frac{1}{6}$ ___$\frac{11}{21}$___   **16.** $\frac{5}{12} - \frac{3}{20}$ ___$\frac{4}{15}$___

17. $\frac{5}{12} - \frac{3}{8}$ ___$\frac{1}{24}$___   **18.** $1\frac{3}{10} + \frac{1}{4}$ ___$1\frac{11}{20}$___

19. $\frac{2}{3} + 6\frac{1}{5}$ ___$6\frac{13}{15}$___   **20.** $3\frac{1}{6} - \frac{1}{7}$ ___$3\frac{1}{42}$___

Guided Practice

Multiply. Write each product in simplest form. (Example 1)

1. $\frac{1}{2} \times \frac{5}{8}$ ___$\frac{5}{16}$___   **2.** $\frac{3}{5} \times \frac{5}{9}$ ___$\frac{1}{3}$___   **3.** $\frac{3}{8} \times \frac{2}{5}$ ___$\frac{3}{20}$___

4. $2\frac{3}{8} \times 16$ ___38___   **5.** $1\frac{4}{5} \times \frac{5}{12}$ ___$\frac{3}{4}$___   **6.** $1\frac{2}{10} \times 5$ ___6___

Find each amount. (Example 2)

7. $\frac{1}{4}$ of 12 bottles of water = ___3___ bottles   **8.** $\frac{2}{3}$ of 24 bananas = ___16___ bananas

9. $\frac{3}{5}$ of $40 restaurant bill = $ ___24___   **10.** $\frac{5}{6}$ of 18 pencils = ___15___ pencils

Add or subtract. Write each sum or difference in simplest form.

11. $\frac{3}{8} + \frac{5}{24}$ ___$\frac{7}{12}$___   **12.** $\frac{1}{20} + \frac{5}{12}$ ___$\frac{7}{15}$___   **13.** $\frac{9}{20} - \frac{1}{4}$ ___$\frac{1}{5}$___

14. $\frac{9}{10} - \frac{3}{14}$ ___$\frac{24}{35}$___   **15.** $3\frac{3}{8} + \frac{5}{12}$ ___$3\frac{19}{24}$___   **16.** $5\frac{7}{10} - \frac{5}{18}$ ___$5\frac{19}{45}$___

? ESSENTIAL QUESTION CHECK-IN

17. How can knowing the GCF and LCM help you when you add, subtract, and multiply fractions?

Knowing the GCF helps to simplify products, sums, and differences as well as fractions before multiplying. Knowing the LCM is necessary to add and subtract fractions.

© Houghton Mifflin Harcourt Publishing Company

DIFFERENTIATE INSTRUCTION

Manipulatives

Give each student a piece of paper and two colored pencils. Have students fold the paper to find the product of two fractions, such as $\frac{1}{2} \times \frac{3}{4}$.

- Fold the paper vertically in half, unfold it, and color one column to represent $\frac{1}{2}$.
- Fold the paper horizontally into fourths, unfold it, and color over three previously colored sections with a different color.
- The double-colored sections represent the product $\frac{3}{8}$.

Modeling

Students can use graph paper to model multiplying a fraction and a whole number *when the denominator of the fraction is a factor of the whole number.* To model $\frac{2}{3} \times 12$:

- Draw 12 equal-sized squares.
- Divide the 12 squares into 3 equal groups by drawing rings around the groups. (Point out that there are 4 squares in each group.)
- The numerator of the fraction is 2. Shade the squares in 2 of the groups.
- There are 8 shaded squares, so $\frac{2}{3} \times 12 = 8$.

Additional Resources

Differentiated Instruction includes:

- Reading Strategies
- Success for English Learners **ELL**
- Reteach
- Challenge **PRE-AP**

4.1 LESSON QUIZ

COMMON CORE 6.NS.4

In one school, $\frac{5}{6}$ of the sixth-graders take a foreign language. Of these students, $\frac{2}{5}$ take French.

1. What fraction of the sixth-graders take French?

2. If there are 150 sixth-grade students, how many take French?

Multiply. Write each product in simplest form.

3. $\frac{7}{8} \times \frac{2}{5}$

4. $\frac{2}{3} \times 18$

Lesson Quiz available online

 my.hrw.com

Answers

1. $\frac{1}{3}$
2. 50
3. $\frac{7}{20}$
4. 12

Evaluate

GUIDED AND INDEPENDENT PRACTICE

 COMMON CORE 6.NS.4

Concepts & Skills	Practice
Example 1 Multiplying Fractions	Exercises 1–6, 18
Example 2 Multiplying Fractions and Whole Numbers	Exercises 7–10, 19, 21
Example 3 Adding and Subtracting Fractions	Exercises 11–16, 20, 22–23

Exercise	Depth of Knowledge (D.O.K.)	**COMMON CORE** Mathematical Practices
18	**2** Skills/Concepts	**MP.4** Modeling
19	**3** Strategic Thinking H.O.T.	**MP.4** Modeling
20	**2** Skills/Concepts	**MP.4** Modeling
21	**3** Strategic Thinking H.O.T.	**MP.3** Reasoning
22	**2** Skills/Concepts	**MP.4** Modeling
23–24	**3** Strategic Thinking H.O.T.	**MP.4** Modeling
25	**3** Strategic Thinking H.O.T.	**MP.7** Using Structure
26	**3** Strategic Thinking H.O.T.	**MP.3** Reasoning

Additional Resources

Differentiated Instruction includes:

• Leveled Practice worksheets

4.1 Independent Practice

COMMON CORE 6.NS.4

Personal Math Trainer

@ my.hrw.com

Online Assessment and Intervention

Solve. Write each answer in simplest form.

18. Erin buys a bag of peanuts that weighs $\frac{3}{4}$ of a pound. Later that week, the bag is $\frac{2}{3}$ full. How much does the bag of peanuts weigh now? Show your work.

$\frac{2}{3} \times \frac{3}{4} = \frac{2 \times 3}{3 \times 4} = \frac{6}{12} = \frac{1}{2}, \frac{1}{2}$ pound

19. Multistep Marianne buys 16 bags of potting soil that comes in $\frac{5}{8}$-pound bags.

a. How many pounds of potting soil does Marianne buy?

10 pounds

b. If Marianne's father calls and says he needs 13 pounds of potting soil, how many additional bags should she buy?

5 more bags

20. Music Two fifths of the instruments in the marching band are brass, one third are percussion, and the rest are woodwinds.

a. What fraction of the band is woodwinds?

$\frac{4}{15}$

b. One half of the woodwinds are clarinets. What fraction of the band is clarinets?

$\frac{2}{15}$

c. One eighth of the brass instruments are tubas. If there are 240 instruments in the band, how many are tubas?

12

21. Marcial found a recipe for fruit salad that he wanted to try to make for his birthday party. He decided to triple the recipe.

Fruit Salad
$3\frac{1}{2}$ cups thinly sliced rhubarb
15 seedless grapes, halved
$\frac{1}{2}$ orange, sectioned
10 fresh strawberries, halved
$\frac{3}{5}$ apple, cored and diced
$\frac{2}{3}$ peach, sliced
1 plum, pitted and sliced
$\frac{1}{4}$ cup fresh blueberries

a. What are the new amounts for the oranges, apples, blueberries, and peaches?

oranges $= 1\frac{1}{2}$, apples $= 1\frac{4}{5}$,

blueberries $= \frac{3}{4}$ cup,

peaches $= 2$

b. Communicate Mathematical Ideas The amount of rhubarb in the original recipe is $3\frac{1}{2}$ cups. Using what you know of whole numbers and what you know of fractions, explain how you could triple that mixed number.

Sample answer: If you triple 3, it becomes 9. If you triple $\frac{1}{2}$, it becomes $1\frac{1}{2}$. Add $9 + 1\frac{1}{2} = 10\frac{1}{2}$

22. One container holds $1\frac{7}{8}$ quarts of water and a second container holds $5\frac{3}{4}$ quarts of water. How many more quarts of water does the second container hold than the first container?

$3\frac{7}{8}$ quarts

23. Each of 15 students will give a $1\frac{1}{2}$-minute speech in English class.

a. How long will it take to give the speeches? $22\frac{1}{2}$ minutes

b. If the teacher begins recording on a digital camera with an hour available, is there enough time to record everyone if she gives a 15-minute introduction at the beginning of class and every student takes a minute to get ready? Explain.

Yes, there is enough time; 15 min for the teacher's introduction + 15 min for students to get ready + $22\frac{1}{2}$ min for speeches $= 52\frac{1}{2}$ min

c. How much time is left on the digital camera? $7\frac{1}{2}$ minutes

H.O.T. **FOCUS ON HIGHER ORDER THINKING**

24. Represent Real-World Problems Kate wants to buy a new bicycle from a sporting goods store. The bicycle she wants normally sells for $360. The store has a sale where all bicycles cost $\frac{5}{6}$ of the regular price. What is the sale price of the bicycle?

$300.00

$360

25. Error Analysis To find the product $\frac{3}{7} \times \frac{4}{9}$, Cameron simplified $\frac{3}{7}$ to $\frac{1}{7}$ and then multiplied the fractions $\frac{1}{7}$ and $\frac{4}{9}$ to find the product $\frac{4}{63}$. What is Cameron's error?

Cameron divided a factor in one of the numerators by the GCF but did not divide a factor in one of the denominators by the GCF. He should have simplified $\frac{4}{9}$ to $\frac{4}{3}$ and multiplied $\frac{1}{7}$ and $\frac{4}{3}$ to find the product $\frac{4}{21}$.

Work Area

26. Justify Reasoning To multiply a whole number by a fraction, you can first write the whole number as a fraction by placing the whole number in the numerator and 1 in the denominator. Does following this step change the product? Explain.

No; the fraction bar represents division, and dividing the whole number by 1 does not change its value, so the product is the same.

EXTEND THE MATH **PRE-AP**

Activity available online @ my.hrw.com

Activity In the United States, we use the Fahrenheit scale to measure temperature. Other countries use the Celsius temperature scale. The equation $C = \frac{5}{9} \times (F - 32)$ is used to convert a temperature in °F to °C. Show students that if the temperature is 50 °F, the equivalent temperature in °C is $\frac{5}{9} \times (50 - 32) = \frac{5}{9} \times 18 = 10$, or 10 °C. Give students other temperatures to convert and have students check each other's conversions. Start with temperatures that convert to whole numbers, such as 41 °F, 59 °F, 68 °F, 77 °F, 86 °F, and so on.

Common Core Standards

The student is expected to:

 The Number System—6.NS.1

Interpret and compute quotients of fractions, and solve word problems involving division of fractions by fractions, e.g., by using visual fraction models and equations to represent the problem.

Mathematical Practices

 MP.4 Modeling

Engage

ESSENTIAL QUESTION

How do you divide fractions? Multiply the dividend by the reciprocal of the divisor.

Motivate the Lesson

Ask: Suppose you have a $2\frac{1}{2}$-lb package of ground beef and you want to make $\frac{1}{4}$-lb hamburger patties for dinner. How many hamburger patties can you make? Begin the Explore Activity to find out more about dividing fractions.

Explore

EXPLORE ACTIVITY 1

Focus on Modeling [CC] Mathematical Practices

In A, make sure that students realize that the bar model represents 1 whole. Point out that the solid lines represent the division of the bar into 4 equal pieces. Next, point out that each of the shaded sections was divided in half to make a total of 8 sections. Explain that this level of subdivision is necessary, since each burrito requires $\frac{1}{8}$ cup of salsa.

Explain

EXAMPLE 1

Focus on Math Connections [CC] Mathematical Practices

Remind students that two numbers are *reciprocals* if their product is 1. Note also that every number except 0 has a reciprocal.

Questioning Strategies [CC] Mathematical Practices

• If the value of a fraction is less than one, what will be true about its reciprocal? It will be a fraction greater than 1.

• B shows that the reciprocal of the unit fraction $\frac{1}{8}$ is the integer 8. Is the reciprocal of a unit fraction always an integer? Justify your answer. Yes. Because a unit fraction has 1 in the numerator, the reciprocal will have 1 in the denominator.

YOUR TURN

Talk About It
Check for Understanding

 Ask: How do you find the reciprocal of a fraction? Switch the numerator and the denominator.

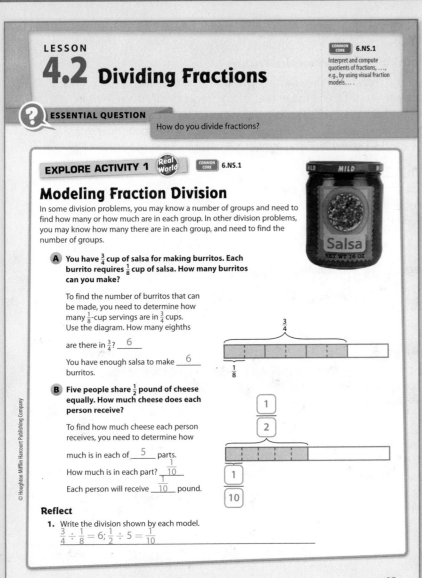

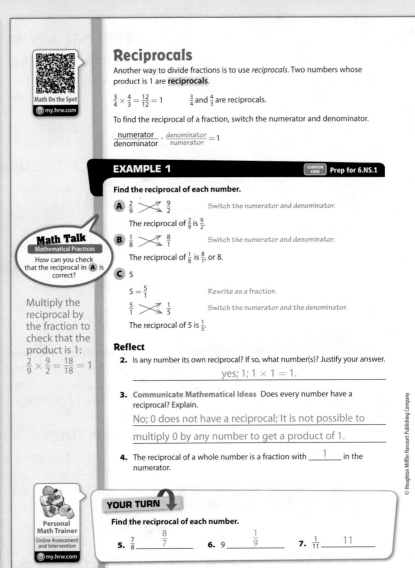

LESSON

4.2 Dividing Fractions

COMMON CORE 6.NS.1
Interpret and compute quotients of fractions, ..., e.g., by using visual fraction models....

? ESSENTIAL QUESTION

How do you divide fractions?

EXPLORE ACTIVITY 1 *Real World* COMMON CORE 6.NS.1

Modeling Fraction Division

In some division problems, you may know a number of groups and need to find how many or how much are in each group. In other division problems, you may know how many there are in each group, and need to find the number of groups.

A You have $\frac{3}{4}$ cup of salsa for making burritos. Each burrito requires $\frac{1}{8}$ cup of salsa. How many burritos can you make?

To find the number of burritos that can be made, you need to determine how many $\frac{1}{8}$-cup servings are in $\frac{3}{4}$ cups. Use the diagram. How many eighths are there in $\frac{3}{4}$? ___6___

You have enough salsa to make ___6___ burritos.

B Five people share $\frac{1}{2}$ pound of cheese equally. How much cheese does each person receive?

To find how much cheese each person receives, you need to determine how much is in each of ___5___ parts.

How much is in each part? $\frac{1}{10}$

Each person will receive $\frac{1}{10}$ pound.

Reflect

1. Write the division shown by each model.

$\frac{3}{4} \div \frac{1}{8} = 6$; $\frac{1}{2} \div 5 = \frac{1}{10}$

Lesson 4.2 **85**

Reciprocals

Another way to divide fractions is to use *reciprocals*. Two numbers whose product is 1 are **reciprocals**.

$\frac{3}{4} \times \frac{4}{3} = \frac{12}{12} = 1$ $\frac{3}{4}$ and $\frac{4}{3}$ are reciprocals.

To find the reciprocal of a fraction, switch the numerator and denominator.

$\frac{numerator}{denominator} \cdot \frac{denominator}{numerator} = 1$

EXAMPLE 1 COMMON CORE Prep for 6.NS.1

Find the reciprocal of each number.

A $\frac{2}{9}$ ⤫ $\frac{9}{2}$ Switch the numerator and denominator.

The reciprocal of $\frac{2}{9}$ is $\frac{9}{2}$.

B $\frac{1}{8}$ ⤫ $\frac{8}{1}$ Switch the numerator and denominator.

The reciprocal of $\frac{1}{8}$ is $\frac{8}{1}$, or 8.

C 5

$5 = \frac{5}{1}$ Rewrite as a fraction.

$\frac{5}{1}$ ⤫ $\frac{1}{5}$ Switch the numerator and the denominator.

The reciprocal of 5 is $\frac{1}{5}$.

Reflect

2. Is any number its own reciprocal? If so, what number(s)? Justify your answer.

yes; 1; $1 \times 1 = 1$.

3. **Communicate Mathematical Ideas** Does every number have a reciprocal? Explain.

No; 0 does not have a reciprocal; It is not possible to multiply 0 by any number to get a product of 1.

4. The reciprocal of a whole number is a fraction with ___1___ in the numerator.

Math Talk
Mathematical Practices

How can you check that the reciprocal in **A** is correct?

Multiply the reciprocal by the fraction to check that the product is 1:
$\frac{2}{9} \times \frac{9}{2} = \frac{18}{18} = 1$

YOUR TURN

Find the reciprocal of each number.

5. $\frac{7}{8}$ ___$\frac{8}{7}$___   6. 9 ___$\frac{1}{9}$___   7. $\frac{1}{11}$ ___11___

Personal Math Trainer
Online Assessment and Intervention
my.hrw.com

86 Unit 2

PROFESSIONAL DEVELOPMENT

CC Integrate Mathematical Practices MP.4

This lesson provides an opportunity to address this Mathematical Practice standard. It calls for students to communicate mathematical ideas using multiple representations as appropriate. In the Explore Activity, students use bar models to model the division of fractions. Using the model, they are able to see that dividing a fraction by a fraction can result in a whole number quotient, a concept that many students do not find intuitive.

Math Background

Being comfortable with dividing fractions and finding the reciprocal will be very helpful for students when it is time to simplify complex fractions such as $\frac{\frac{2}{3}}{\frac{1}{4}}$. A simple fraction, such as $\frac{1}{2}$, can be thought of as a division problem: $1 \div 2$. So, the complex fraction can be simplified by writing it as a division problem:

$$\frac{\frac{2}{3}}{\frac{1}{4}} = \frac{2}{3} \div \frac{1}{4} = \frac{2}{3} \times \frac{4}{1} = \frac{8}{3} = 2\frac{2}{3}$$

Dividing Fractions **86**

EXPLORE ACTIVITY 2

Focus on Critical Thinking Mathematical Practices

Be sure students understand that, when they divide either a fraction by a fraction or a whole number by a fraction, the result will be an answer that is larger than the dividend. Explain that this is because they are finding the number of smaller groups within a large group. For example, in the first division in the table, $\frac{6}{7} \div \frac{2}{7}$, you are asking the question "How many groups of two sevenths are in six sevenths?" The answer is 3 groups.

Engage with the Whiteboard

 Have students sketch a bar model, like the one in Explore Activity 1, to represent each division problem in the table.

EXAMPLE 2

Questioning Strategies Mathematical Practices

- Are the two expressions $\frac{1}{2} \div \frac{5}{6}$ and $2 \times \frac{5}{6}$ equivalent? Explain. No, they are not the same. The wrong number has been replaced by its reciprocal. The reciprocal of the divisor, not the dividend, should be used.

Connect Vocabulary ELL

Stress proper mathematical language to avoid confusion regarding the change to multiplication by the reciprocal. The dividend *divided* by the *divisor* becomes the dividend *multiplied* by the *reciprocal* of the *divisor*.

YOUR TURN

Avoid Common Errors

If students are not sure which number is the divisor and incorrectly find the reciprocal of the dividend, point out that ÷ means "divided by" and the number that follows it is the divisor. It may help it they circle the divisors before they begin the exercises.

Elaborate

Talk About It
Summarize the Lesson

 Ask: How is multiplication related to dividing fractions? You can divide a number by a fraction by multiplying the dividend by the reciprocal of the divisor.

GUIDED PRACTICE

Engage with the Whiteboard

 For Exercises 4–6, have students sketch bar models, like the one in Explore Activity 1, to check their answers.

Avoid Common Errors

Exercise 2 Some students may have difficulty writing the reciprocal of a unit fraction. Remind students that the reciprocal of a unit fraction is always an integer.

Using Reciprocals to Find Equivalent Values

A Complete the table below.

Division	Multiplication
$\frac{6}{7} \div \frac{2}{7} = 3$	$\frac{6}{7} \times \frac{7}{2} = 3$
$\frac{5}{8} \div \frac{3}{8} = \frac{5}{3}$	$\frac{5}{8} \times \frac{8}{3} = \frac{5}{3}$
$\frac{1}{6} \div \frac{5}{6} = \frac{1}{5}$	$\frac{1}{6} \times \frac{6}{5} = \frac{1}{5}$
$\frac{1}{4} \div \frac{1}{3} = \frac{3}{4}$	$\frac{1}{4} \times \frac{3}{1} = \frac{3}{4}$

B How does each multiplication problem compare to its corresponding division problem?

The first fraction is the same. The second fractions are reciprocals of each other.

C How does the answer to each multiplication problem compare to the answer to its corresponding division problem?

The answers are the same.

Reflect

8. Make a Conjecture Use the pattern in the table to make a conjecture about how you can use multiplication to divide one fraction by another.

Multiply the first fraction by the reciprocal of the second fraction.

9. Write a division problem and a corresponding multiplication problem like those in the table. Assuming your conjecture in **8** is correct, what is the answer to your division problem?

Sample answer: $\frac{5}{7} \div \frac{3}{4}, \frac{5}{7} \times \frac{4}{3}, \frac{20}{21}$.

Math On the Spot
my.hrw.com

Using Reciprocals to Divide Fractions

Dividing by a fraction is equivalent to multiplying by its reciprocal.

$\frac{1}{5} \div \frac{1}{4} = \frac{4}{5}$ $\frac{1}{5} \times \frac{4}{1} = \frac{4}{5}$

Animated Math
my.hrw.com

EXAMPLE 2

Divide $\frac{5}{9} \div \frac{2}{3}$. Write the quotient in simplest form.

STEP 1 Rewrite as multiplication, using the reciprocal of the divisor.

$\frac{5}{9} \div \frac{2}{3} = \frac{5}{9} \times \frac{3}{2}$ The reciprocal of $\frac{2}{3}$ is $\frac{3}{2}$.

STEP 2 Multiply and simplify.

$\frac{5}{9} \times \frac{3}{2} = \frac{15}{18}$ Multiply the numerators. Multiply the denominators

$= \frac{5}{6}$ Write the answer in simplest form.

$\frac{5}{9} \div \frac{2}{3} = \frac{5}{6}$ $\boxed{\frac{15 \div 3}{18 \div 3} = \frac{5}{6}}$

Personal Math Trainer
Online Assessment and Intervention
my.hrw.com

YOUR TURN

Divide.

10. $\frac{9}{10} \div \frac{2}{5} = $ _____ $2\frac{1}{4}$

11. $\frac{9}{10} \div \frac{3}{5} = $ _____ $1\frac{1}{2}$

Guided Practice

Find the reciprocal of each fraction. (Example 1)

1. $\frac{2}{5}$ _____ $\frac{5}{2}$

2. $\frac{1}{9}$ _____ 9

3. $\frac{10}{3}$ _____ $\frac{3}{10}$

Divide. (Explore 1, Explore 2, and Example 2)

4. $\frac{4}{3} \div \frac{5}{3} = $ _____ $\frac{4}{5}$

5. $\frac{3}{10} \div \frac{4}{5} = $ _____ $\frac{3}{8}$

6. $\frac{1}{2} \div \frac{2}{5} = $ _____ $1\frac{1}{4}$

ESSENTIAL QUESTION CHECK-IN

7. How do you divide fractions?

Multiply the dividend by the reciprocal of the divisor.

DIFFERENTIATE INSTRUCTION

Manipulatives

Use pattern blocks to model the division $\frac{2}{3} \div \frac{1}{6} = 4$. Remind students that the division is asking "How many one-sixths are in two-thirds?" Point out that the blue rhombus $= \frac{1}{3}$ and the green triangle $= \frac{1}{6}$.

$\frac{2}{3} \div \frac{1}{6} = ?$ $\frac{2}{3} \div \frac{1}{6} = 4$

$\frac{2}{3}$ $\frac{2}{3} = \frac{4}{6}$

Communicating Math

On the board, write $8 \div 2 = 4$ and $8 \times \frac{1}{2} = 4$. Invite students to explain why the two expressions have the same result. Guide students to understand that dividing 8 by 2 is finding the size of each group when 8 is divided into 2 groups. Point out that this is really the same as finding half of 8, or $8 \times \frac{1}{2}$. So, dividing by 2 and multiplying by its reciprocal, $\frac{1}{2}$, gives the same result.

Additional Resources

Differentiated Instruction includes:

- Reading Strategies
- Success for English Learners **ELL**
- Reteach
- Challenge **PRE-AP**

Evaluate

GUIDED AND INDEPENDENT PRACTICE

 COMMON CORE **6.NS.1**

Concepts & Skills	Practice
Explore Activity 1 Modeling Fraction Division	Exercises 4–6
Example 1 Reciprocals	Exercises 1–6
Explore Activity 2 Using Reciprocals to Find Equivalent Values	Exercises 4–6
Example 2 Using Reciprocals to Divide Fractions	Exercises 4–6, 9–16

Exercise	Depth of Knowledge (D.O.K.)	COMMON CORE Mathematical Practices
8–15	**2** Skills/Concepts	**MP.4** Modeling
16	**3** Strategic Thinking H.O.T.	**MP.3** Logic
17	**3** Strategic Thinking H.O.T.	**MP.7** Using Structure
18	**2** Skills/Concepts	**MP.4** Modeling
19	**3** Strategic Thinking H.O.T.	**MP.6** Precision
20	**3** Strategic Thinking H.O.T.	**MP.4** Modeling
21	**3** Strategic Thinking H.O.T.	**MP.3** Logic

Additional Resources

Differentiated Instruction includes:

• Leveled Practice Worksheets

 CC CLUSTER CONNECTION

Exercise 21 combines concepts from the Common Core cluster "Apply and extend previous understandings of multiplication and division to divide fractions by fractions."

4.2 Independent Practice

 6.NS.1

 Personal Math Trainer
Online Assessment and Intervention
my.hrw.com

8. Alison has $\frac{1}{2}$ cup of yogurt for making fruit parfaits. Each parfait requires $\frac{1}{8}$ cup of yogurt. How many parfaits can she make?

4 parfaits

9. A team of runners is needed to run a $\frac{1}{4}$-mile relay race. If each runner must run $\frac{1}{16}$ mile, how many runners will be needed?

4 runners will be needed.

10. Trevor paints $\frac{1}{6}$ of the fence surrounding his farm each day. How many days will it take him to paint $\frac{3}{4}$ of the fence?

It will take him $4\frac{1}{2}$ days.

11. Six people share $\frac{3}{5}$ pound of peanuts equally. What fraction of a pound of peanuts does each person receive?

$\frac{1}{10}$ pound

12. Biology If one honeybee makes $\frac{1}{12}$ teaspoon of honey during its lifetime, how many honeybees are needed to make $\frac{1}{2}$ teaspoon of honey?

6 honeybees

13. Jackson wants to divide a $\frac{3}{4}$-pound box of trail mix into small bags. Each of the bags will hold $\frac{1}{12}$ pound of trail mix. How many bags of trail mix can Jackson fill?

9 bags

14. A pitcher contains $\frac{2}{3}$ quart of lemonade. If an equal amount of lemonade is poured into each of 6 glasses, how much lemonade will each glass contain?

$\frac{1}{9}$ quart

15. How many tenths are there in $\frac{4}{5}$?

8

16. You make a large bowl of salad to share with your friends. Your brother eats $\frac{1}{3}$ of it before they come over.

a. You want to divide the leftover salad evenly among six friends. What expression describes the situation? Explain.

$\frac{2}{3} \div 6$, because if the brother ate $\frac{1}{3}$, then there is $\frac{2}{3}$ of the salad left to split between the six friends.

b. What fractional portion of the original bowl of salad does each friend receive?

$\frac{2}{3} \div 6 = \frac{2}{3} \div \frac{6}{1} = \frac{2}{3} \times \frac{1}{6} = \frac{2}{18} = \frac{1}{9}$, so each friend receives $\frac{1}{9}$ of the original bowl of salad.

---

17. Interpret the Answer The length of a ribbon is $\frac{3}{4}$ meter. Sun Yi needs pieces measuring $\frac{1}{3}$ meter for an art project. What is the greatest number of pieces measuring $\frac{1}{3}$ meter that can be cut from the ribbon? How much ribbon will be left after Sun Yi cuts the ribbon? Explain your reasoning.

Greatest number of pieces: 2; Ribbon left: $\frac{1}{12}$ m; Sample answer: $\frac{3}{4} \div \frac{1}{3} = 2\frac{1}{4}$. The 2 represents 2 pieces that are each $\frac{1}{3}$ m long. The $\frac{1}{4}$ represents $\frac{1}{4}$ of a $\frac{1}{3}$ m piece of ribbon, not $\frac{1}{4}$ m. Sun Yi will have $\frac{1}{4} \times \frac{1}{3} = \frac{1}{12}$ m of ribbon left.

18. Represent Real-World Problems Liam has $\frac{9}{10}$ gallon of paint for painting the birdhouses he sells at the craft fair. Each birdhouse requires $\frac{1}{20}$ gallon of paint. How many birdhouses can Liam paint? Show your work.

$\frac{9}{10} \div \frac{1}{20} = \frac{9}{10} \times \frac{20}{1} = 18$

19. Justify Reasoning When Kaitlin divided a fraction by $\frac{1}{2}$, the result was a mixed number. Was the original fraction less than or greater than $\frac{1}{2}$? Explain your reasoning.

Greater than $\frac{1}{2}$; since the quotient was a mixed number, the original fraction contained more than 1 unit of $\frac{1}{2}$.

20. Communicate Mathematical Ideas The reciprocal of a fraction less than 1 is always a fraction greater than 1. Why is this?

In a fraction less than 1, the numerator is less than the denominator. In its reciprocal, the numerator is greater than the denominator, making it a fraction greater than 1.

21. Make a Prediction Susan divides the fraction $\frac{5}{8}$ by $\frac{1}{16}$. Her friend Robyn divides $\frac{5}{8}$ by $\frac{1}{32}$. Predict which person will get the greater quotient. Explain and check your prediction.

Robyn; Robyn is dividing $\frac{5}{8}$ into smaller groups than Susan; there are more thirty-seconds in $\frac{5}{8}$ than there are sixteenths. $\frac{5}{8} \div \frac{1}{16} = 10$; $\frac{5}{8} \div \frac{1}{32} = 20$.

EXTEND THE MATH PRE-AP

Activity available online my.hrw.com

Activity Have students follow the procedure below to divide fractions.

Begin by dividing the first numerator by the second numerator, and the first denominator by the second denominator.

$$\frac{3}{5} \div \frac{2}{3} = \frac{3 \div 2}{5 \div 3} = \frac{\frac{3}{2}}{\frac{5}{3}}$$

Next, multiply by a fraction that is equal to 1 and results in a whole-number numerator.

$$\frac{\frac{3}{2}}{\frac{5}{3}} \times \frac{2}{2} = \frac{3}{\frac{10}{3}}$$

Finally, multiply by another fraction that is equal to 1 and results in a whole-number denominator.

$$\frac{3}{\frac{10}{3}} \times \frac{3}{3} = \frac{9}{10}$$

Invert and multiply to confirm that this product is correct. Then repeat the procedure for another pair of fractions.

Common Core Standards

The student is expected to:

 The Number System—6.NS.1

Interpret and compute quotients of fractions, and solve word problems involving division of fractions by fractions, e.g., by using visual fraction models and equations to represent the problem.

Mathematical Practices

 MP.4 Modeling

ADDITIONAL EXAMPLE 1

Ryan feeds his chicken $1\frac{1}{3}$ cups of grain per day. The grain container has $6\frac{2}{3}$ cups of grain left. For how many days can Ryan feed the chicken?

5 days

 Interactive Whiteboard
Interactive example available online

⏻ my.hrw.com

Engage

ESSENTIAL QUESTION

How do you divide mixed numbers? Rewrite the mixed numbers as fractions and multiply the dividend by the reciprocal of the divisor. Write the product in simplest form.

Motivate the Lesson

Ask: You have $2\frac{1}{4}$ lb of trail mix and want to know how many $\frac{1}{8}$-lb servings you can make. Begin the Explore Activity to find out more about dividing mixed numbers.

Explore

EXPLORE ACTIVITY 1

Engage with the Whiteboard

 Have students use the whiteboard to explain how the model represents the given situation by showing how the top and bottom rows relate to the question.

Explain

EXAMPLE 1

Focus on Reasoning CC Mathematical Practices

Make sure students understand the problem. Explain that an amount of cereal (given in ounces) is going to be divided into smaller servings (also expressed in ounces). Since the question is how many servings can be made, the answer is the number of servings.

Questioning Strategies CC Mathematical Practices

- Why is $17\frac{1}{2}$ rewritten as $\frac{35}{2}$? Because you need to write the mixed number as a fraction before multiplying: $17 \times 2 = 34$, and $34 + 1 = 35$, so 35 is the numerator.

- What would happen if you did not simplify by using the GCF before multiplying? The product would be $\frac{175}{14}$, which would still need to be simplified.

YOUR TURN

Focus on Critical Thinking CC Mathematical Practices

Encourage students to estimate the answer before actually solving the problem. Each container will hold more than 1 lb but less than 2 lb, so the number of containers should be less than 10 but more than 5. Since $1\frac{1}{4}$ is closer to 1 than to 2, the answer will be closer to 10 than to 5.

 **6.NS.1**

Interpret and compute quotients of fractions, and solve word problems involving division of fractions by fractions....

? ESSENTIAL QUESTION

How do you divide mixed numbers?

 **EXPLORE ACTIVITY** **6.NS.1**

Modeling Mixed Number Division

Antoine is making sushi rolls. He has $2\frac{1}{2}$ cups of rice and will use $\frac{1}{4}$ cup of rice for each sushi roll. How many sushi rolls can he make?

A To find the number of sushi rolls that can be made, you need to determine how many fourths are in $2\frac{1}{2}$. Use fraction pieces to represent $2\frac{1}{2}$ on the model below.

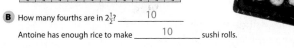

1	1	$\frac{1}{2}$
$\frac{1}{4}$ $\frac{1}{4}$ $\frac{1}{4}$ $\frac{1}{4}$	$\frac{1}{4}$ $\frac{1}{4}$ $\frac{1}{4}$ $\frac{1}{4}$	$\frac{1}{4}$ $\frac{1}{4}$

B How many fourths are in $2\frac{1}{2}$? _____10_____

Antoine has enough rice to make _____10_____ sushi rolls.

Reflect

1. **Communicate Mathematical Ideas** Which mathematical operation could you use to find the number of sushi rolls that Antoine can make? Explain.

   division; You are dividing the total amount of rice by the amount needed for each sushi roll.

2. **Multiple Representations** Write the division shown by the model.

   $2\frac{1}{2} \div \frac{1}{4} = 10$

3. **What If?** Suppose Antoine instead uses $\frac{1}{8}$ cup of rice for each sushi roll. How would his model change? How many rolls can he make? Explain.

   His fraction model would need to be divided in eighths.

   The total number of rolls he can make would be 20, which is twice as many because $\frac{1}{4}$ is twice as large as $\frac{1}{8}$.

Math On the Spot
© my.hrw.com

My Notes

Using Reciprocals to Divide Mixed Numbers

Dividing by a fraction is equivalent to multiplying by its reciprocal. You can use this fact to divide mixed numbers. First rewrite the mixed numbers as fractions greater than 1. Then multiply the dividend by the reciprocal of the divisor.

EXAMPLE 1 *Real World*   **6.NS.1**

One serving of Harold's favorite cereal contains $1\frac{2}{5}$ ounces. How many servings are in a $17\frac{1}{2}$-ounce box?

STEP 1 Write a division statement to represent the situation.

$17\frac{1}{2} \div 1\frac{2}{5}$

> You need to find how many groups of $1\frac{2}{5}$ are in $17\frac{1}{2}$.

STEP 2 Rewrite the mixed numbers as fractions greater than 1.

$17\frac{1}{2} \div 1\frac{2}{5} = \frac{35}{2} \div \frac{7}{5}$

STEP 3 Rewrite the problem as multiplication using the reciprocal of the divisor.

$\frac{35}{2} \div \frac{7}{5} = \frac{35}{2} \times \frac{5}{7}$ The reciprocal of $\frac{7}{5}$ is $\frac{5}{7}$.

STEP 4 Multiply.

$\frac{35}{2} \times \frac{5}{7} = \frac{\overset{5}{35}}{2} \times \frac{5}{\underset{1}{7}}$ Simplify first using the GCF.

$= \frac{5 \times 5}{2 \times 1}$ Multiply numerators. Multiply denominators.

$= \frac{25}{2}$, or $12\frac{1}{2}$ Write the result as a mixed number.

There are $12\frac{1}{2}$ servings of cereal in the box.

Reflect

4. **Analyze Relationships** Explain how can you check the answer.

   Multiplication is the inverse of division. Multiply $12\frac{1}{2} \times 1\frac{2}{5}$. Since $12\frac{1}{2} \times 1\frac{2}{5} = 17\frac{1}{2}$, the answer is correct.

5. **What If?** Harold serves himself $1\frac{1}{2}$-ounces servings of cereal each morning. How many servings does he get from a box of his favorite cereal? Show your work.

   $11\frac{2}{3}$ servings; $17\frac{1}{2} \div 1\frac{1}{2} = 11\frac{2}{3}$ servings.

DIFFERENTIATE INSTRUCTION

CC Integrate Mathematical Practices MP.4

This lesson provides an opportunity to address this Mathematical Practice standard. It calls for students to apply mathematics to problems arising in everyday life. In the Explore Activity, Example 1 and Example 2, students divide mixed numbers to solve real-world mathematical problems involving measures of volume, weight, and area. This helps students understand that the division skills presented are applicable to everyday life.

Math Background

The use of multiplication by the reciprocal to divide by a fraction can be traced to Hindu and Arab mathematicians in the early Middle Ages.

A second method is to first rewrite the dividend and the divisor using a common denominator. Thus, $\frac{5}{6} \div \frac{7}{8}$ could be rewritten as $\frac{20}{24} \div \frac{21}{24}$. Then the quotient of the numerators is found: $\frac{20}{24} \div \frac{21}{24} = \frac{20}{21}$.

This method has the advantage of fitting in nicely with the algorithms learned for addition and subtraction. Its disadvantage lies in the need for a common denominator.

EXAMPLE 2

Questioning Strategies Mathematical Practices

• Why do you use division to find the width? Because area is the product of the length times the width, you can divide the area by the length to find the width.

• Suppose you had been given the width instead of the length. Could you use multiplication to find the length of the sandbox? No; you still need to use division, as area is the product of length times width.

Avoid Common Errors

In Step 2, some students may want to rewrite the expression $\frac{170}{3} \div \frac{17}{2}$ by dividing out the GCF of 2 from the numerator of the dividend and the denominator of the divisor. Remind students that they can simplify only after they have rewritten the division problem as multiplication by the reciprocal.

YOUR TURN

Avoid Common Errors

Exercises 8–9 Students may neglect to include the units when reporting an answer. Remind students that when they solve a problem involving measurements, they need to check to see whether a unit should be included in the answer.

Elaborate

Talk About It
Summarize the Lesson

 Ask: Complete the graphic organizer with students to discuss and summarize lesson concepts.

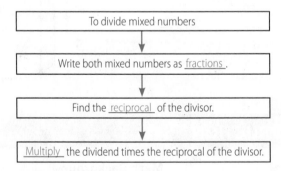

To divide mixed numbers

↓

Write both mixed numbers as <u>fractions</u>.

↓

Find the <u>reciprocal</u> of the divisor.

↓

<u>Multiply</u> the dividend times the reciprocal of the divisor.

GUIDED PRACTICE

Engage with the Whiteboard

For Exercises 3–4, have students use the whiteboard to make models that represent the division of mixed numbers. Then have students explain their reasoning.

Avoid Common Errors

Exercises 7–8 Students may neglect to include the units when reporting an answer. Remind students that when they solve a problem involving measurements, they need to check to see whether a unit should be included in the answer.

YOUR TURN

6. Sheila has $10\frac{1}{2}$ pounds of potato salad. She wants to divide the potato salad into containers, each of which holds $1\frac{1}{4}$ pounds. How many containers does she need? Explain.

   9; $10\frac{1}{2} \div 1\frac{1}{4} = 8\frac{2}{5}$; She will need 9 containers.

Personal Math Trainer
Online Assessment and Intervention
my.hrw.com

Solving Problems Involving Area

Recall that to find the area of a rectangle, you multiply length × width. If you know the area and only one dimension, you can divide the area by the known dimension to find the other dimension.

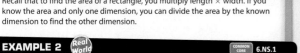

EXAMPLE 2 Real World

COMMON CORE 6.NS.1

The area of a rectangular sandbox is $56\frac{2}{3}$ square feet. The length of the sandbox is $8\frac{1}{2}$ feet. What is the width?

STEP 1 Write the situation as a division problem.

$$56\frac{2}{3} \div 8\frac{1}{2}$$

STEP 2 Rewrite the mixed numbers as fractions greater than 1.

$$56\frac{2}{3} \div 8\frac{1}{2} = \frac{170}{3} \div \frac{17}{2}$$

STEP 3 Rewrite the problem as multiplication using the reciprocal of the divisor.

$$\frac{170}{3} \div \frac{17}{2} = \frac{170}{3} \times \frac{2}{17}$$

$$= \frac{\overset{10}{\cancel{170}} \times 2}{3 \times \cancel{17}_{1}}$$ Multiply numerators. Multiply denominators.

$$= \frac{20}{3}, \text{ or } 6\frac{2}{3}$$ Simplify and write as a mixed number.

The width of the sandbox is $6\frac{2}{3}$ feet.

Math Talk
Mathematical Practices

Explain how to find the length of a rectangle when you know the area and the width.

Divide the area by the width to find the length.

Reflect

7. **Check for Reasonableness** How can you determine if your answer is reasonable?

   Sample answer: Use compatible numbers to estimate.

   Round the area to 56 square feet and the length to 8 feet. $56 \div 8 = 7$. Since $6\frac{2}{3}$ is close to 7, the answer

   is reasonable.

Math On the Spot
my.hrw.com

Personal Math Trainer
Online Assessment and Intervention
my.hrw.com

YOUR TURN

8. The area of a rectangular patio is $12\frac{3}{8}$ square meters. The width of the patio is $2\frac{3}{4}$ meters. What is the length? $4\frac{1}{2}$ meters

9. The area of a rectangular rug is $14\frac{1}{12}$ square yards. The length of the rug is $4\frac{1}{3}$ yards. What is the width? $3\frac{1}{4}$ yards

Guided Practice

Divide. Write each answer in simplest form. (Explore Activity and Example 1)

1. $4\frac{1}{4} \div \frac{3}{4}$

   $\boxed{\dfrac{17}{4}} \div \dfrac{3}{4} =$

   $\boxed{\dfrac{17}{4}} \times \dfrac{\boxed{4}}{\boxed{3}} =$

   $\underline{\quad 5\frac{2}{3} \quad}$

2. $1\frac{1}{2} \div 2\frac{1}{4}$

   $\boxed{\dfrac{3}{2}} \div \boxed{\dfrac{9}{4}} =$

   $\boxed{\dfrac{3}{2}} \times \dfrac{\boxed{4}}{\boxed{9}} =$

   $\underline{\quad \frac{2}{3} \quad}$

3. $4 \div 1\frac{1}{8}$ $\underline{\quad 3\frac{5}{9} \quad}$

4. $3\frac{1}{5} \div 1\frac{1}{7}$ $\underline{\quad 2\frac{4}{5} \quad}$

5. $8\frac{1}{3} \div 2\frac{1}{2}$ $\underline{\quad 3\frac{1}{3} \quad}$

6. $15\frac{1}{3} \div 3\frac{5}{6}$ $\underline{\quad 4 \quad}$

Write each situation as a division problem. Then solve. (Example 2)

7. A sandbox has an area of 26 square feet, and the length is $5\frac{1}{2}$ feet. What is the width of the sandbox?

   $26 \div 5\frac{1}{2}$; The width is $4\frac{8}{11}$ feet.

8. Mr. Webster is buying carpet for an exercise room in his basement. The room will have an area of 230 square feet. The width of the room is $12\frac{1}{2}$ feet. What is the length?

   $230 \div 12\frac{1}{2}$; $18\frac{2}{5}$ feet

? ESSENTIAL QUESTION CHECK-IN

9. How does dividing mixed numbers compare with dividing fractions?

   The process is the same except that you must first

   change the mixed numbers to fractions.

DIFFERENTIATE INSTRUCTION

Number Sense

Encourage students to always estimate the quotients when dividing mixed numbers before they actually solve the problem. Review rounding and using compatible numbers for division. For example, in $27\frac{1}{4} \div 3\frac{1}{5}$ students can simply round to the nearest whole numbers to find $27 \div 3$. For $33\frac{1}{6} \div 5\frac{8}{9}$, they could use compatible numbers and find $30 \div 5$. Remind students that estimating is not exact, so there is more than one right way to estimate.

Critical Thinking

Challenge students to find the missing numbers in the following division problems. Have them check their answers.

1. $\frac{3}{4} \div \underline{\quad\quad} = 3\frac{3}{4}$ $\frac{1}{5}$

2. $\underline{\quad\quad} \div \frac{5}{6} = 1\frac{4}{5}$ $1\frac{1}{2}$

3. $2\frac{1}{2} \div \underline{\quad\quad} = 1\frac{3}{7}$ $1\frac{3}{4}$

4. $\underline{\quad\quad} \div 2\frac{1}{10} = 1\frac{2}{3}$ $3\frac{1}{2}$

For an added challenge, ask students to explain how they found their answers.

Additional Resources

Differentiated Instruction includes:

• Reading Strategies

• Success for English Learners **ELL**

• Reteach

• Challenge **PRE-AP**

4.3 LESSON QUIZ

COMMON CORE **6.NS.1**

Divide.

1. $9\frac{1}{3} \div 1\frac{5}{9}$ **2.** $2\frac{4}{7} \div 3$

3. $4\frac{3}{8} \div 1\frac{2}{5}$ **4.** $15 \div 6\frac{1}{2}$

5. $16\frac{2}{3} \div 4\frac{1}{6}$ **6.** $23\frac{4}{7} \div 3\frac{1}{7}$

7. Melinda is baking Irish soda bread for the PTA bake sale. She has $10\frac{1}{2}$ cups of flour. The recipe for 1 loaf calls for $2\frac{1}{3}$ cups of flour. This is enough flour for how many loaves of bread?

8. The area of a rectangular tablecloth is $4\frac{1}{6}$ square meters. The width of the tablecloth is $1\frac{1}{4}$ meters. What is the length of the tablecloth?

Lesson Quiz available online

 my.hrw.com

Answers

1. 6

2. $\frac{6}{7}$

3. $3\frac{1}{8}$

4. $2\frac{4}{13}$

5. 4

6. $7\frac{1}{2}$

7. 4 loaves

8. $3\frac{1}{3}$ meters

Evaluate

GUIDED AND INDEPENDENT PRACTICE

COMMON CORE **6.NS.1**

Concepts & Skills	Practice
Explore Activity Modeling Mixed-Number Division	Exercises 10–11
Example 1 Using Reciprocals to Divide Mixed Numbers	Exercises 1–6, 12–13, 16
Example 2 Solving Problems Involving Area	Exercises 7–8, 14–15, 17

Exercise	Depth of Knowledge (D.O.K.)	COMMON CORE Mathematical Practices
10–11	**2** Skills/Concepts	**MP.2** Reasoning
12–13	**2** Skills/Concepts	**MP.4** Modeling
14–15	**3** Strategic Thinking **H.O.T.**	**MP.4** Modeling
16–17	**2** Skills/Concepts	**MP.4** Modeling
18	**3** Strategic Thinking **H.O.T.**	**MP.3** Logic
19	**3** Strategic Thinking **H.O.T.**	**MP.7** Using Structure
20	**3** Strategic Thinking **H.O.T.**	**MP.6** Precision

Additional Resources

Differentiated Instruction includes:

• Leveled Practice Worksheets

Name _____ Class _____ Date _____

10. Jeremy has $4\frac{1}{2}$ cups of iced tea. He wants to divide the tea into $\frac{3}{4}$-cup servings. Use the model to find the number of servings he can make.

6 servings

11. A ribbon is $3\frac{2}{3}$ yards long. Mae needs to cut the ribbon into pieces that are $\frac{2}{3}$ yard long. Use the model to find the number of pieces she can cut.

$5\frac{1}{2}$ pieces

12. Dao has $2\frac{3}{8}$ pounds of hamburger meat. He is making $\frac{1}{4}$-pound hamburgers. Does Dao have enough meat to make 10 hamburgers? Explain.

no; He has only enough meat to make $9\frac{1}{2}$ quarter pound hamburgers.

13. Multistep Zoey made $5\frac{1}{2}$ cups of trail mix for a camping trip. She wants to divide the trail mix into $\frac{3}{4}$-cup servings.

a. Ten people are going on the camping trip. Can Zoey make enough $\frac{3}{4}$-cup servings so that each person on the trip has one serving?

No, it only makes $7\frac{1}{3}$ servings.

b. What size would the servings need to be for everyone to have a serving? Explain.

$\frac{11}{20}$ of a cup; $5\frac{1}{2}$ cups ÷ 10 people $= \frac{11}{2} \times \frac{1}{10} = \frac{11}{20}$

c. If Zoey decides to use the $\frac{3}{4}$-cup servings, how much more trail mix will she need? Explain.

She would need $7\frac{1}{2}$ cups total, so she would need 2 more cups of trail mix.

14. The area of a rectangular picture frame is $30\frac{1}{3}$ square inches. The length of the frame is $6\frac{1}{2}$ inches. Find the width of the frame.

$4\frac{2}{3}$ in.

15. The area of a rectangular mirror is $11\frac{11}{16}$ square feet. The width of the mirror is $2\frac{3}{4}$ feet. If there is a 5 foot tall space on the wall to hang the mirror, will it fit? Explain.

yes because the height is $4\frac{1}{4}$ feet

16. Ramon has a rope that is $25\frac{1}{2}$ feet long. He wants to cut it into 6 pieces that are equal in length. How long will each piece be?

$4\frac{1}{4}$ feet

17. Eleanor and Max used two rectangular wooden boards to make a set for the school play. One board was 6 feet long, and the other was $5\frac{1}{2}$ feet long. The two boards had equal widths. The total area of the set was $60\frac{3}{8}$ square feet. What was the width?

$5\frac{1}{4}$ feet

 FOCUS ON HIGHER ORDER THINKING

Work Area

18. Draw Conclusions Micah divided $11\frac{2}{3}$ by $2\frac{5}{6}$ and got $4\frac{2}{17}$ for an answer. Does his answer seem reasonable? Explain your thinking. Then check Micah's answer.

Sample answer: The answer seems reasonable because $11\frac{2}{3}$ can be rounded to 12, and $2\frac{5}{6}$ can be rounded to 3, and $12 \div 3 = 4$, which is close to $4\frac{2}{17}$. $4\frac{2}{17} \times 2\frac{5}{6} = 11\frac{2}{3}$, so Micah's answer is correct.

19. Explain the Error To divide $14\frac{2}{3} \div 2\frac{3}{4}$, Erik multiplied $14\frac{2}{3} \times \frac{4}{3}$. Explain Erik's error.

He used the reciprocal of $\frac{3}{4}$ instead of the reciprocal of $2\frac{3}{4}$. The reciprocal of $2\frac{3}{4}$ is $\frac{4}{11}$.

20. Analyze Relationships Explain how you can find the missing number in $3\frac{4}{5} \div \blacksquare = 2\frac{5}{7}$. Then find the missing number.

Divide $3\frac{4}{5}$ by $2\frac{5}{7}$, since $3\frac{4}{5}$ is the product of $2\frac{5}{7}$ and the missing number. The missing number is $1\frac{2}{5}$.

EXTEND THE MATH   PRE-AP

Activity available online my.hrw.com

Activity Adrian is trying to solve the problem shown at the right. He thinks that more than one answer is possible. Is he right? Justify your answer.

Sample answer: Yes, $9\frac{1}{3} \div 2\frac{2}{3} = 3\frac{1}{2}$ and $9\frac{1}{5} \div 2\frac{4}{5} = 3\frac{2}{7}$. Both meet the conditions of the clues:

• $9\frac{1}{3} + 2\frac{2}{3} = 12$ and $9\frac{1}{5} + 2\frac{4}{5} = 12$
• Both quotients are >3 but <4.
• In $\frac{1}{2}$ and $\frac{2}{7}$, 1, 2, and 7 are prime numbers <10.

What is the mixed number division problem that these clues describe?

A The sum of the dividend and the divisor is 12.

B The quotient is greater than 3, but less than 4.

C The dividend and the divisor in the fractional part of both quotients are prime numbers less than 10.

LESSON 4.4 Solving Multistep Problems with Fractions and Mixed Numbers

Common Core Standards

The student is expected to:

COMMON CORE **The Number System—6.NS.1**

Interpret and compute quotients of fractions, and solve word problems involving division of fractions by fractions, e.g., by using visual fraction models and equations to represent the problem.

Mathematical Practices

COMMON CORE **MP.1** Problem Solving

ADDITIONAL EXAMPLE 1

Jillian bought $\frac{1}{2}$ pound of turkey and $1\frac{1}{3}$ pounds of cheddar cheese at the deli. Both items are on sale for $6 per pound. How much does the turkey and cheese cost? $11

 Interactive Whiteboard
Interactive example available online

 my.hrw.com

Engage

ESSENTIAL QUESTION

How can you solve word problems involving more than one fraction operation? Determine which operations to use; then follow the order of operations.

Motivate the Lesson

Ask: Have you ever used a recipe? Have you ever had to use fractions to measure the ingredients? Begin Example 1 to see how to use fractions to find the total amount of an ingredient needed in a recipe.

Explore

Engage with the Whiteboard

 List the following fractions on the whiteboard. Then have students identify the pairs of fractions with a product of 1. Remind students what a reciprocal is and how to use it when dividing fractions.

$$\frac{2}{3}, \frac{2}{5}, \frac{3}{2}, \frac{3}{4}, \frac{4}{3}, \frac{5}{2}, \frac{5}{6}, \frac{6}{5} \qquad \frac{2}{3} \text{ and } \frac{3}{2}, \frac{2}{5} \text{ and } \frac{5}{2}, \frac{3}{4} \text{ and } \frac{4}{3}, \frac{5}{6} \text{ and } \frac{6}{5}$$

Explain

EXAMPLE 1

Engage with the Whiteboard

In Step 1, under Analyze Information, have students draw bar models to represent the amount of lentils needed, one bar for $\frac{3}{4}$ and another for $1\frac{1}{2}$. Then have students divide the models into eighths to find the number of scoops needed.

Questioning Strategies **CC** Mathematical Practices

• Does the order of the fractions in the parentheses matter? No. Addition is commutative.

YOUR TURN

Avoid Common Error

Some students will want to cancel common factors out of numerators and denominators in a division problem. Remind students that they can only cross out common factors after they have rewritten the division problem as multiplication by the reciprocal.

Solving Multistep Problems with Fractions and Mixed Numbers

 COMMON CORE 6.NS.1
...Solve word problems involving division of fractions by fractions...

? ESSENTIAL QUESTION How can you solve word problems involving more than one fraction operation?

Solving Problems with Rational Numbers

Sometimes more than one operation will be needed to solve a multistep problem. You can use parentheses to group different operations. Recall that according to the **order of operations**, you perform operations in parentheses first.

 Math On the Spot
my.hrw.com

EXAMPLE 1 Problem Solving

COMMON CORE 6.NS.1

Jon is cooking enough lentils for lentil barley soup and lentil salad. The lentil barley soup recipe calls for $\frac{3}{4}$ cup of dried lentils. The lentil salad recipe calls for $1\frac{1}{2}$ cups of dried lentils. Jon has a $\frac{1}{8}$-cup scoop. How many scoops of dried lentils will Jon need to have enough for the soup and the salad?

 Analyze Information

Identify the important information.

- Jon needs $\frac{3}{4}$ cup of dried lentils for soup and $1\frac{1}{2}$ cups for salad.
- Jon has a $\frac{1}{8}$-cup scoop.
- You need to find the total number of many scoops of lentils he needs.

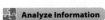 **Formulate a Plan**

You can use the expression $\left(\frac{3}{4} + 1\frac{1}{2}\right) \div \frac{1}{8}$ to find the number of scoops of dried lentils Jon will need for the soup and the salad.

 Solve

Follow the order of operations. Perform the operations in parentheses first.

First add to find the total amount of dried lentils Jon will need.

$$\frac{3}{4} + 1\frac{1}{2} = \frac{3}{4} + \frac{3}{2}$$
$$= \frac{3}{4} + \frac{6}{4}$$
$$= \frac{9}{4}$$
$$= 2\frac{1}{4}$$

John needs $2\frac{1}{4}$ cups of lentils.

Jon needs $2\frac{1}{4}$ cups of dried lentils for both the soup and the salad.

To find how many $\frac{1}{8}$-cup scoops he needs, divide the total amount of dried lentils into groups of $\frac{1}{8}$.

$$2\frac{1}{4} \div \frac{1}{8} = \frac{9}{4} \div \frac{1}{8}$$
$$= \frac{9}{4} \times \frac{8}{1}$$
$$= \frac{9 \times \cancel{8}^{2}}{\cancel{4} \times 1}$$
$$= \frac{18}{1} = 18$$

Simplify before multiplying using the GCF.

Jon will need 18 scoops of dried lentils to have enough for both the lentil barley soup and the lentil salad.

 Justify and Evaluate

You added $\frac{3}{4}$ and $1\frac{1}{2}$ first to find the total number of cups of lentils. Then you divided the sum by $\frac{1}{8}$ to find the number of $\frac{1}{8}$-cup scoops.

 Personal Math Trainer
Online Assessment and Intervention
my.hrw.com

YOUR TURN

1. Before conducting some experiments, a scientist mixes $\frac{1}{2}$ gram of Substance A with $\frac{3}{4}$ gram of Substance B. If the scientist uses $\frac{1}{8}$ gram of the mixture for each experiment, how many experiments can be conducted? _____ 10

Guided Practice

1. An art student uses a roll of wallpaper to decorate two gift boxes. The student will use $1\frac{1}{3}$ yards of paper for one box and $\frac{5}{6}$ yard of paper for the other box. The paper must be cut into pieces that are $\frac{1}{6}$ yard long. How many pieces will the student cut to use for the gift boxes? (Example 1) _____ 13

? ESSENTIAL QUESTION CHECK-IN

2. How can you solve a multistep problem that involves fractions?

Decide which operations to use; follow the order of operations.

DIFFERENTIATE INSTRUCTION

Critical Thinking

Challenge students to find the missing numbers in the following problems. Have them check their answers.

1. $\frac{3}{4} \div \square = 3\frac{3}{4}$ $\frac{1}{8}$

2. $\square \div \frac{5}{6} = 1\frac{4}{5}$ $1\frac{1}{2}$

3. $2\frac{1}{2} \div \square = 1\frac{3}{7}$ $1\frac{3}{4}$

4. $\square \div 2\frac{1}{10} = 1\frac{2}{3}$ $3\frac{1}{2}$

Multiple Representations

Show students two ways to evaluate $\frac{1}{2}(0.7)$:

$$\frac{1}{2}(0.7) = 0.5 \cdot 0.7 = 0.35$$

$$\frac{1}{2}(0.7) = \frac{1}{2} \cdot \frac{7}{10} = \frac{7}{20}$$

Show that $\frac{7}{20} = 0.35$ by dividing: $20\overline{)7.00}$ (0.35). Have students find each of the following products both ways and show that the results are equal in each case.

1. $\frac{1}{2}(0.3) \frac{3}{20} = 0.15$ 2. $\frac{1}{5}(0.4) \frac{2}{25} = 0.08$

3. $\frac{3}{4}(0.1) \frac{3}{40} = 0.075$ 4. $1\frac{1}{2}(0.2) \frac{3}{10} = 0.3$

Additional Resources

Differentiated Instruction includes:

- Reading Strategies
- Success for English Learners **ELL**
- Reteach
- Challenge **PRE-AP**

Elaborate

Talk About It
Summarize the Lesson

 Ask: How can you solve problems that involve both fractions and mixed numbers when multiplication and/or division is required? Convert the mixed number to an improper fraction before multiplying and/or dividing.

GUIDED PRACTICE

Engage with the Whiteboard

For Exercise 2, have students identify the important information and write an expression to represent each situation on the whiteboard. Then have the students solve the problems using the order of operations.

Evaluate

GUIDED AND INDEPENDENT PRACTICE

COMMON CORE 6.NS.1

Concepts and Skills	Practice
Example 1 Solving Problems with Rational Numbers	Exercises 1, 3–10

Exercise	Depth of Knowledge (D.O.K.)	COMMON CORE Mathematical Practices	
3–10	**2** Skills/Concepts	**MP.1** Problem Solving	
11–12	**3** Strategic Thinking **H.O.T.**	**MP.2** Reasoning	
13	**3** Strategic Thinking **H.O.T.**	**MP.4** Modeling	

Additional Resources

Differentiated Instruction includes:

• Leveled Practice worksheets

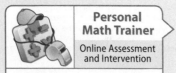

Personal Math Trainer
Online Assessment and Intervention

Online homework assignment available

 my.hrw.com

4.4 LESSON QUIZ

COMMON CORE 6.NS.1

1. Liam has $8\frac{3}{4}$ gallons of paint. He wants to use $\frac{2}{5}$ of the paint to paint his living room. How many gallons of paint will Liam use?

Lesson Quiz available online

 my.hrw.com

Answer
1. $3\frac{1}{2}$ gallons

4.4 Independent Practice

COMMON CORE 6.NS.1

3. Naomi has earned $54 mowing lawns the past two days. She worked $2\frac{1}{2}$ hours yesterday and $4\frac{1}{4}$ hours today. If Naomi is paid the same amount for every hour she works, how much does she earn per hour to mow lawns? (Example 2)

$8 per hour

4. An art teacher has $1\frac{1}{2}$ pounds of red clay and $\frac{3}{4}$ pound of yellow clay. The teacher mixes the red clay and yellow clay together. Each student in the class needs $\frac{1}{8}$ pound of the clay mixture to finish the assigned art project for the class. How many students can get enough clay to finish the project?

18 students

5. A hairstylist schedules $\frac{1}{4}$ hour to trim a customer's hair and $\frac{1}{6}$ hour to style the customer's hair. The hairstylist plans to work $3\frac{1}{3}$ hours each day for 5 days each week. How many appointments can the hairstylist schedule each week if each customer must be trimmed and styled?

40 appointments

6. A picture framer has a thin board $10\frac{1}{12}$ feet long. The framer notices that $2\frac{3}{8}$ feet of the board is scratched and cannot be used. The rest of the board will be used to make small picture frames. Each picture frame needs $1\frac{2}{3}$ feet of the board. At most, how many complete picture frames can be made?

4 picture frames

7. Jim's backyard is a rectangle that is $15\frac{5}{6}$ yards long and $10\frac{2}{5}$ yards wide. Jim buys sod in pieces that are $1\frac{1}{3}$ yards long and $1\frac{1}{3}$ yards wide. How many pieces of sod will Jim need to buy to cover his backyard with sod?

93 pieces

8. Eva wants to make two pieces of pottery. She needs $\frac{3}{5}$ pound of clay for one piece and $\frac{7}{10}$ pound of clay for the other piece. She has three bags of clay that weigh $\frac{4}{5}$ pound each. How many bags of clay will Eva need to make both pieces of pottery? How many pounds of clay will she have left over?

$1\frac{5}{8}$ bags; $1\frac{1}{10}$ pounds left over

9. Mark wants to paint a mural. He has $1\frac{1}{3}$ gallons of yellow paint, $1\frac{1}{4}$ gallons of green paint, and $\frac{7}{8}$ gallon of blue paint. Mark plans to use $\frac{3}{4}$ gallon of each paint color. How many gallons of paint will he have left after painting the mural?

$1\frac{5}{24}$ gallons

10. Trina works after school and on weekends. She always works three days each week. This week she worked $2\frac{3}{4}$ hours on Monday, $3\frac{3}{5}$ hours on Friday, and $5\frac{1}{2}$ hours on Saturday. Next week she plans to work the same number of hours as this week, but will work for the same number of hours each day. How many hours will she work on each day?

$3\frac{19}{20}$ hr

FOCUS ON HIGHER ORDER THINKING

Work Area

11. Represent Real-World Problems Describe a real-world problem that can be solved using the expression $29 \div \left(\frac{3}{8} + \frac{5}{6}\right)$. Find the answer in the context of the situation.

Sample answer: A person taking a test averages $\frac{3}{8}$ minute to read a question and $\frac{5}{6}$ minute to answer the question. It takes the person 29 minutes to answer all of the questions. How many questions are on the test? 24 questions

12. Justify Reasoning Indira and Jean begin their hike at 10 a.m. one morning. They plan to hike from the $2\frac{2}{5}$-mile marker to the $8\frac{1}{10}$-mile marker along the trail. They plan to hike at an average speed of 3 miles per hour. Will they reach the $8\frac{1}{10}$-mile marker by noon? Explain your reasoning.

Yes; they will hike a distance of $8\frac{1}{10} - 2\frac{2}{5} = 5\frac{7}{10}$ miles. At an average speed of 3 miles per hour, they will hike this distance in $5\frac{7}{10} \div 3 = 1\frac{9}{10}$ hours. Noon is 2 hours from 10 a.m., so they will reach the $8\frac{1}{10}$-mile marker before noon.

13. Multiple Representations You are measuring walnuts for banana-walnut oatmeal and a spinach and walnut salad. You need $\frac{3}{8}$ cup of walnuts for the oatmeal and $\frac{3}{4}$ cup of walnuts for the salad. You have a $\frac{1}{4}$-cup scoop. Describe two different ways to find how many scoops of walnuts you will need.

Sample answer: Add $\frac{3}{8} + \frac{3}{4} = 1\frac{1}{8}$ to find the total amount of walnuts needed. Then divide $1\frac{1}{8} \div \frac{1}{4} = 4\frac{1}{2}$ to find how many scoops. Or, divide $\frac{3}{8} \div \frac{1}{4} = 1\frac{1}{2}$ scoops for the oatmeal and divide $\frac{3}{4} \div \frac{1}{4} = 3$ scoops for the salad. Then add $1\frac{1}{2} + 3 = 4\frac{1}{2}$.

EXTEND THE MATH PRE-AP

Activity available online my.hrw.com

Activity Kyle is hanging a new painting in his house. He knows that the painting is twice as wide as it is tall. The painting is $\frac{1}{4}$ as tall as the wall he is hanging it on. If the wall is $8\frac{4}{5}$ feet high, what are the dimensions of the painting in inches?

$52\frac{4}{5}$ inches wide by $26\frac{2}{5}$ inches tall

Ready to Go On?

Assess Mastery

Use the assessment on this page to determine if students have mastered the concepts and standards covered in this module.

 **RtI** Response to Intervention

Intervention	Enrichment

Access Ready to Go On? assessment online, and receive instant scoring, feedback, and customized intervention or enrichment.

Online and Print Resources

Differentiated Instruction
- Reteach worksheets
- Reading Strategies **ELL**
- Success for English Learners **ELL**

Differentiated Instruction
- Challenge worksheets **PRE-AP**
- Extend the Math **PRE-AP** Lesson Activities in TE

Additional Resources

Assessment Resources includes:
- Leveled Module Quizzes

Ready to Go On?

4.1 Applying GCF and LCM to Fraction Operations

Solve.

1. $\frac{4}{5} \times \frac{3}{4}$ ____ $\frac{3}{5}$

2. $\frac{5}{7} \times \frac{9}{10}$ ____ $\frac{9}{14}$

3. $\frac{3}{8} + 2\frac{1}{2}$ ____ $2\frac{7}{8}$

4. $1\frac{3}{5} - \frac{5}{6}$ ____ $\frac{23}{30}$

4.2 Dividing Fractions

Divide.

5. $\frac{1}{3} \div \frac{7}{9}$ ____ $\frac{3}{7}$

6. $\frac{1}{3} \div \frac{5}{8}$ ____ $\frac{8}{15}$

7. Luci cuts a board that is $\frac{3}{4}$ yard long into pieces that are $\frac{3}{8}$ yard long. How many pieces does she cut? ____ 2

4.3 Dividing Mixed Numbers

Divide.

8. $3\frac{1}{3} \div \frac{2}{3}$ ____ 5

9. $1\frac{7}{8} \div 2\frac{2}{5}$ ____ $\frac{25}{32}$

10. $4\frac{1}{4} \div 4\frac{1}{2}$ ____ $\frac{17}{18}$

11. $8\frac{1}{3} \div 4\frac{2}{7}$ ____ $1\frac{17}{18}$

4.4 Solving Multistep Problems with Fractions and Mixed Numbers

12. Jamal hiked on two trails. The first trail was $5\frac{1}{3}$ miles long, and the second trail was $1\frac{3}{4}$ times as long as the first trail. How many miles did Jamal hike? ____ $14\frac{2}{3}$ miles

? ESSENTIAL QUESTION

13. Describe a real-world situation that is modeled by dividing two fractions or mixed numbers.

Sample answer: You want to divide $3\frac{3}{4}$ pounds of grapes into bags that hold $\frac{3}{4}$ pound each. Divide $3\frac{3}{4}$ by $\frac{3}{4}$ to find that you can fill 5 bags.

Common Core Standards

Lesson	Exercises	Common Core Standards
4.1	1–4	**6.NS.4**
4.2	5–7	**6.NS.1**
4.3	8–11	**6.NS.1**
4.4	12	**6.NS.1**

Assessment Readiness

Assessment Readiness Tip Encourage students to check their answers to multiplication problems by using division, and to division problems by using multiplication, before filling in the answer bubble.

Item 3 Students should divide their answer by $\frac{9}{7}$ to check it. If the answer is correct, they should find the quotient to be the initial value of 133 pennies.

Item 7 Students need to know that area is the product of the length and width. Since students need to divide to find the width, they should multiply their answer by $12\frac{1}{2}$ and confirm that the area is $103\frac{1}{8}$ square feet.

Avoid Common Errors

Item 4 Students may apply the Commutative Property incorrectly and find answer choice B to be another form of the expression. Remind them that the Commutative Property applies only to addition and multiplication, not subtraction or division.

Item 6 Students may take the reciprocal of just the fractional part of the mixed number and find answer C to be the reciprocal. Remind them that mixed numbers must be changed into improper fractions before their reciprocals can be found.

Additional Resources

Personal Math Trainer

Online Assessment and Intervention

my.hrw.com

Selected Response

1. Two sides of a rectangular fence are $5\frac{5}{8}$ feet long. The other two sides are $6\frac{1}{4}$ feet long. What is the perimeter?

Ⓐ $11\frac{7}{8}$ feet   Ⓑ 13 feet

Ⓒ $23\frac{3}{4}$ feet   Ⓓ $35\frac{5}{32}$ feet

2. Which shows the GCF of 18 and 24 with $\frac{18}{24}$ in simplest form?

Ⓐ GCF: 3; $\frac{3}{4}$

Ⓑ GCF: 3; $\frac{6}{8}$

Ⓒ GCF: 6; $\frac{3}{4}$

Ⓓ GCF: 6; $\frac{6}{8}$

3. A jar contains 133 pennies. A bigger jar contains $1\frac{2}{7}$ times as many pennies. What is the value of the pennies in the bigger jar?

Ⓐ $1.49   Ⓑ $1.52

Ⓒ $1.68   Ⓓ $1.71

4. Which of these is the same as $\frac{3}{5} \div \frac{4}{7}$?

Ⓐ $\frac{3}{5} \div \frac{7}{4}$

Ⓑ $\frac{4}{7} \div \frac{3}{5}$

Ⓒ $\frac{3}{5} \times \frac{4}{7}$

Ⓓ $\frac{3}{5} \times \frac{7}{4}$

5. Andy has $6\frac{2}{3}$ quarts of juice. How many $\frac{2}{3}$-cup servings can he pour?

Ⓐ $4\frac{4}{9}$ Ⓑ 6

Ⓒ 7   Ⓓ 10

6. What is the reciprocal of $3\frac{3}{7}$?

Ⓐ $\frac{7}{24}$ Ⓑ $\frac{3}{7}$

Ⓒ $\frac{7}{3}$ Ⓓ $\frac{24}{7}$

7. A rectangular patio has a length of $12\frac{1}{2}$ feet and an area of $103\frac{1}{8}$ square feet. What is the width of the patio?

Ⓐ $4\frac{1}{8}$ feet

Ⓑ $8\frac{1}{4}$ feet

Ⓒ $16\frac{1}{2}$ feet

Ⓓ 33 feet

8. Which number is greater than the absolute value of $-\frac{3}{8}$?

Ⓐ $-\frac{5}{8}$

Ⓑ $-\frac{1}{8}$

Ⓒ $\frac{1}{4}$

Ⓓ 0.5

Mini-Task

9. Jodi is cutting out pieces of paper that measure $8\frac{1}{2}$ inches by 11 inches from a larger sheet of paper that has an area of 1,000 square inches

  a. What is the area of each piece of paper that Jodi is cutting out?

    $93\frac{1}{2}$ square inches

  b. What is the greatest possible number of pieces of paper that Jodi can cut out of the larger sheet?

    10

© Houghton Mifflin Harcourt Publishing Company

Common Core Standards

Items	Grade 6 Standards	Mathematical Practices
1	6.NS.1	MP.4
2	6.NS.4	MP.7
3	6.NS.1	MP.4
4	6.NS.1	MP.2
5	6.NS.1	MP.4
6*	6.NS.1	MP.6, MP.7
7	6.NS.1	MP.4
8	6.NS.1	MP.2
9	6.NS.1	MP.4, MP.5

* Item integrates mixed review concepts from previous modules or a previous course.

Operations with Decimals

 ESSENTIAL QUESTION

How can you use operations with decimals to solve real-world problems?

You can represent real-world quantities as decimals, and then solve the problems using the appropriate operation(s).

© Houghton Mifflin Harcourt Publishing Company • Image Credits: ©PhotoDisc/ Getty Images

Real-World Video

The gravitational force on Earth's moon is less than the gravitational force on Earth. You can calculate your weight on the moon by multiplying your weight on Earth by a decimal.

my.hrw.com

GO DIGITAL

my.hrw.com

my.hrw.com	**Math On the Spot**	**Animated Math**	**Personal Math Trainer**
Go digital with your write-in student edition, accessible on any device.	Scan with your smart phone to jump directly to the online edition, video tutor, and more.	Interactively explore key concepts to see how math works.	Get immediate feedback and help as you work through practice sets.

Are You Ready?

Assess Readiness

Use the assessment on this page to determine if students need intensive or strategic intervention for the module's prerequisite skills.

RtI

Response to Intervention

Personal Math Trainer

Online Assessment and Intervention

Intervention	Enrichment

Access Are You Ready? assessment online, and receive instant scoring, feedback, and customized intervention or enrichment.

Online and Print Resources

Skills Intervention worksheets
- Skill 14 Represent Decimals
- Skill 41 Multiply Decimals by Powers of 10
- Skill 53 Words for Operations

Differentiated Instruction
- Challenge worksheets **PRE-AP**
- Extend the Math **PRE-AP** Lesson Activities in TE

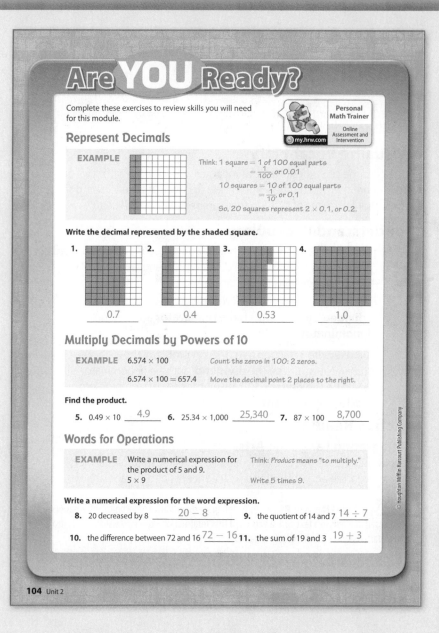

Are YOU Ready?

Complete these exercises to review skills you will need for this module.

Personal Math Trainer
Online Assessment and Intervention
my.hrw.com

Represent Decimals

EXAMPLE

Think: 1 square = 1 of 100 equal parts
$= \frac{1}{100}$, or 0.01

10 squares = 10 of 100 equal parts
$= \frac{1}{10}$, or 0.1

So, 20 squares represent 2×0.1, or 0.2.

Write the decimal represented by the shaded square.

1. 0.7   2. 0.4   3. 0.53   4. 1.0

Multiply Decimals by Powers of 10

EXAMPLE 6.574×100 Count the zeros in 100: 2 zeros.

$6.574 \times 100 = 657.4$ Move the decimal point 2 places to the right.

Find the product.

5. 0.49×10 ___4.9___   6. $25.34 \times 1,000$ ___25,340___   7. 87×100 ___8,700___

Words for Operations

EXAMPLE Write a numerical expression for the product of 5 and 9.   Think: *Product* means "to multiply."
5×9 Write 5 times 9.

Write a numerical expression for the word expression.

8. 20 decreased by 8 ___$20 - 8$___   9. the quotient of 14 and 7 ___$14 \div 7$___

10. the difference between 72 and 16 ___$72 - 16$___ 11. the sum of 19 and 3 ___$19 + 3$___

© Houghton Mifflin Harcourt Publishing Company

PROFESSIONAL DEVELOPMENT VIDEO

Author Juli Dixon models successful teaching practices as she explores multiplying and dividing decimals in an actual sixth-grade classroom.

Professional Development

my.hrw.com

GO DIGITAL
my.hrw.com

Online Teacher Edition
Access a full suite of teaching resources online—plan, present, and manage classes and assignments.

ePlanner
Easily plan your classes and access all your resources online.

Interactive Answers and Solutions
Customize answer keys to print or display in the classroom. Choose to include answers only or full solutions to all lesson exercises.

Interactive Whiteboards
Engage students with interactive whiteboard-ready lessons and activities.

Personal Math Trainer: Online Assessment and Intervention
Assign automatically graded homework, quizzes, tests, and intervention activities. Prepare your students with updated practice tests aligned with Common Core.

Reading Start-Up

Have students complete the activities on this page by working alone or with others.

Visualize Vocabulary

The chart helps students review vocabulary associated with division to prepare them to multiply and divide decimals. If time allows, discuss any other attributes of division that can be added to the chart.

Understand Vocabulary

Use the following explanation to help students learn the review words. Writing examples of fractions and division problems as you explain may help students understand the vocabulary.

> The **fraction bar** means "**divided by**." You can read $\frac{3}{4}$ as 3 **divided by** 4, where 3 is the **numerator** and 4 is the **denominator**.

> If you rewrite a fraction as a division problem, the numerator would be the **dividend**, and the denominator would be the **divisor**. The answer to the division problem is called the **quotient**.

Active Reading

Integrating Language Arts

Students can use these reading and note-taking strategies to help them organize and understand new concepts and vocabulary.

COMMON CORE **ELA-Literacy.RST.6-8.7** Integrate quantitative or technical information expressed in words in a text with a version of that information expressed visually (e.g., in a flowchart, diagram, model, graph, or table).

Additional Resources

Differentiated Instruction
- Reading Strategies **ELL**

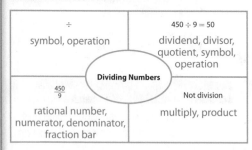

Reading Start-Up

Visualize Vocabulary

Use the ✔ words to complete the chart. You may put more than one word in each section.

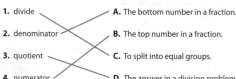

Vocabulary

Review Words
  decimal *(decimal)*
✔ denominator *(denominador)*
  divide *(dividir)*
✔ dividend *(dividendo)*
✔ divisor *(divisor)*
✔ fraction bar *(barra de fracciones)*
✔ multiply *(multiplicar)*
✔ numerator *(numerador)*
✔ operation *(operación)*
✔ product *(producto)*
✔ quotient *(cociente)*
✔ rational number *(número racional)*
✔ symbol *(símbolo)*
  whole number *(número entero)*

÷ symbol, operation	$450 \div 9 = 50$ dividend, divisor, quotient, symbol, operation
$\frac{450}{9}$ rational number, numerator, denominator, fraction bar	Not division multiply, product

Center: **Dividing Numbers**

Understand Vocabulary

Match the term on the left to the definition on the right.

1. divide
2. denominator
3. quotient
4. numerator

A. The bottom number in a fraction.
B. The top number in a fraction.
C. To split into equal groups.
D. The answer in a division problem.

Active Reading

Booklet Before beginning the module, create a booklet to help you learn the concepts in this module. Write the main idea of each lesson on its own page of the booklet. As you study each lesson, record examples that illustrate the main idea and make note of important details. Refer to your finished booklet as you work on assignments and study for tests.

Module 5 **105**

Before	In this module	After
Students understand multiplication and division: • multiply whole numbers and fractions • divide whole numbers and fractions	Students learn to multiply and divide positive rational numbers fluently: • multiply decimals • divide decimals • solve problems involving multiplication and division of fractions and decimals	Students will connect rational numbers and integers: • multiply rational numbers fluently • divide rational numbers fluently

Unpacking the Standards

Use the examples on the page to help students know exactly what they are expected to learn in this module.

Common Core Standards

Content Areas

 The Number System—6.NS

Compute fluently with multi-digit numbers and find common factors and multiples.

Go online to see a complete unpacking of the Common Core Standards.

my.hrw.com

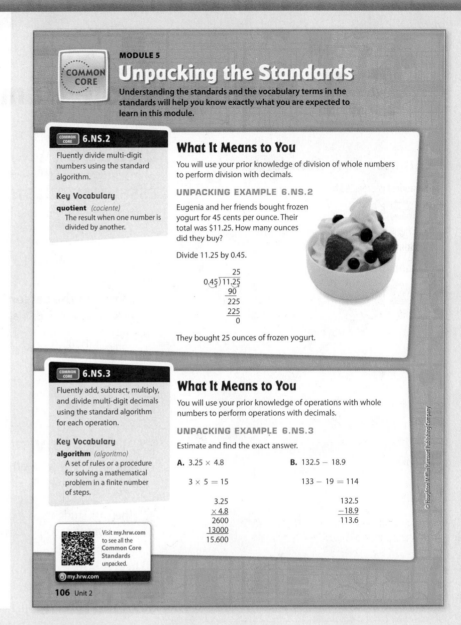

MODULE 5

COMMON CORE

Unpacking the Standards

Understanding the standards and the vocabulary terms in the standards will help you know exactly what you are expected to learn in this module.

COMMON CORE 6.NS.2

Fluently divide multi-digit numbers using the standard algorithm.

Key Vocabulary

quotient *(cociente)*
The result when one number is divided by another.

What It Means to You

You will use your prior knowledge of division of whole numbers to perform division with decimals.

UNPACKING EXAMPLE 6.NS.2

Eugenia and her friends bought frozen yogurt for 45 cents per ounce. Their total was $11.25. How many ounces did they buy?

Divide 11.25 by 0.45.

$$
\begin{array}{r}
25 \\
0.45\overline{)11.25} \\
\underline{90} \\
225 \\
\underline{225} \\
0
\end{array}
$$

They bought 25 ounces of frozen yogurt.

COMMON CORE 6.NS.3

Fluently add, subtract, multiply, and divide multi-digit decimals using the standard algorithm for each operation.

Key Vocabulary

algorithm *(algoritmo)*
A set of rules or a procedure for solving a mathematical problem in a finite number of steps.

Visit my.hrw.com to see all the Common Core Standards unpacked.

my.hrw.com

What It Means to You

You will use your prior knowledge of operations with whole numbers to perform operations with decimals.

UNPACKING EXAMPLE 6.NS.3

Estimate and find the exact answer.

A. 3.25×4.8

$3 \times 5 = 15$

$$
\begin{array}{r}
3.25 \\
\times 4.8 \\
\hline
2600 \\
13000 \\
\hline
15.600
\end{array}
$$

B. $132.5 - 18.9$

$133 - 19 = 114$

$$
\begin{array}{r}
132.5 \\
-18.9 \\
\hline
113.6
\end{array}
$$

106 Unit 2

Common Core Standards	Lesson 5.1	Lesson 5.2	Lesson 5.3	Lesson 5.4	Lesson 5.5
6.NS.2 Fluently divide mulit-digit numbers using the standard algorithm.	COMMON CORE				
6.NS.3 Fluently add, subtract, multiply, and divide multi-digit decimals using the standard algorithm for each operation.		COMMON CORE	COMMON CORE	COMMON CORE	COMMON CORE

5.1 Dividing Whole Numbers

Common Core Standards

The student is expected to:

 6.NS.2

Fluently divide multi-digit numbers using the standard algorithm.

Mathematical Practices

 MP.6 Precision

Engage

ESSENTIAL QUESTION

How do you divide multi-digit whole numbers? Starting from left to right in the dividend, divide the divisor into the dividend to get the first number in the quotient. Multiply this digit by the divisor and subtract the resulting product from the dividend. Then bring down the number in the dividend and repeat this process until all the numbers in the dividend have been divided.

Motivate the Lesson

Ask: You want to display your stamp collection using display sheets that can hold 30 stamps. If you have 1,080 stamps in your collection, how many display sheets will you need? Begin the Explore Activity to find out how to solve this type of problem.

Explore

EXPLORE ACTIVITY

Engage with the Whiteboard

 Write the following numbers on the whiteboard:

256,341   968,398   1,245,172   2,045,917

Then ask students to round each number to the tens, hundreds, thousands, ten thousands, and hundred thousands place. Compare the results and discuss the rules for rounding with the class.

Explain

EXAMPLE 1

Connect Vocabulary **ELL**

Review the terms *divisor*, *dividend*, and *quotient* as they relate to the numbers used in this problem and their placement in the problem. Explain that the dividend is the number being divided into, the divisor is the number you are using to divide, and the quotient is the answer to the division problem.

Questioning Strategies **CC** **Mathematical Practices**

• How could you check your answer? Multiply the quotient by the divisor. If your answer is correct, it should equal the dividend.

YOUR TURN

Avoid Common Errors

Some students may have difficulty keeping a long division problem organized. Encourage them to use graph paper for setting up and working their division problems. Have them write each digit in a separate square to maintain the alignment of columns and rows.

ADDITIONAL EXAMPLE 1
Approximately 14,730 people visited the mall during a 15-day period. On average, how many people visited the mall each day? 982 people

 Interactive Whiteboard
Interactive example available online

 my.hrw.com

Dividing Whole Numbers

COMMON CORE 6.NS.2
...Divide multi-digit numbers using the standard algorithm....

? **ESSENTIAL QUESTION**

How do you divide multi-digit whole numbers?

EXPLORE ACTIVITY Real World | COMMON CORE 6.NS.2

Estimating Quotients

You can use estimation to predict the quotient of multi-digit whole numbers.

A local zoo had a total of 98,464 visitors last year. The zoo was open every day except for three holidays. On average, about how many visitors did the zoo have each day?

A To estimate the average number of visitors per day, you can divide the total number of visitors by the number of days. To estimate the quotient, first estimate the dividend by rounding the number of visitors to the nearest ten thousand.

quotient
divisor)‾ dividend

98,464 rounded to the nearest ten thousand is _____100,000_____.

B There were 365 days last year. How many

days was the petting zoo open? _____362_____

C Estimate the divisor by rounding the number of days that the zoo was open to the nearest hundred.

____362____ rounded to the nearest hundred is ____400____.

D Estimate the quotient. __100,000__ ÷ __400__ = __250__

The average number of visitors per day last year was about __250__.

Reflect

1. How can you check that your quotient is correct?

Multiply the divisor and the quotient; if this product is equal to the dividend, then the quotient is correct.

2. **Critical Thinking** Do you think that your estimate is greater than or less than the actual answer? Explain.

Sample answer: Less than; the divisor was rounded up.

Math On the Spot
© my.hrw.com

Using Long Division

The exact average number of visitors per day at the zoo in the Explore Activity is the quotient of 98,464 and 362. You can use long division to find this quotient.

EXAMPLE 1 Real World | COMMON CORE 6.NS.2

A local zoo had a total of 98,464 visitors last year. The zoo was open every day except three holidays? On average, how many visitors did the zoo have each day?

STEP 1 362 is greater than 9 and 98, so divide 984 by 362. Place the first digit in the quotient in the hundreds place. Multiply 2 by 362 and place the product under 984. Subtract.

$$
\begin{array}{r}
2 \\
362\overline{)98,464} \\
-72\ 4 \\
\hline
26\ 0
\end{array}
$$

> **Math Talk**
> Mathematical Practices
>
> How does the estimate from the Explore Activity compare to the actual average number of visitors per day?

The estimate is less than the actual average.

STEP 2 Bring down the tens digit. Divide 2,606 by 362. Multiply 7 by 362 and place the product under 2,606. Subtract.

$$
\begin{array}{r}
27 \\
362\overline{)98,464} \\
-72\ 4 \\
\hline
26\ 06 \\
-25\ 34 \\
\hline
72
\end{array}
$$

STEP 3 Bring down the ones digit. Divide the ones.

$$
\begin{array}{r}
272 \\
362\overline{)98,464} \\
-72\ 4 \\
\hline
26\ 06 \\
-25\ 34 \\
\hline
724 \\
-724 \\
\hline
0
\end{array}
$$

The average number of visitors per day last year was 272.

Personal Math Trainer
Online Assessment and Intervention
© my.hrw.com

YOUR TURN

Find each quotient.

3. 34,989 ÷ 321 _____109_____   4. 73,375 ÷ 125 _____587_____

PROFESSIONAL DEVELOPMENT

CC ## Integrate Mathematical Practices MP.6

This lesson provides an opportunity to address the Mathematical Practices standard that calls for students to attend to precision. Throughout this lesson, students need to use precision whether dividing, estimating, or interpreting the remainders to solve both real-world and mathematical problems involving long division.

Math Background

The long division used by students today is related to a fifteenth century method that is sometimes referred to using an Italian phrase *a danda*, which means "by giving." In this method, a partial product is found, and then the next digit in the dividend is brought down and "given" to the remainder. One of the earliest printed books illustrating this method dates from the 1490s.

EXAMPLE 2

Connect Vocabulary ELL

The term *remainder* is used in this example. Remind students that in this context, "remainder" means the number of books left over.

Questioning Strategies CC **Mathematical Practices**

- Which value represents the dividend Which represents the divisor? The dividend is 1,850 and the divisor is 12.

- Suppose Callie packs 10 books in each box. Will she have any books left over? How do you know? No; $1,850 \div 10 = 185$, with no remainder.

YOUR TURN

Avoid Common Errors

Exercise 7 Some students interchange the divisor and dividend when translating a problem in the form $a \div b$ into the form $b \overline{)a}$. Remind students that the number after the division sign, $\div$, or the number outside the division house, $\overline{)}$, is always the divisor.

Elaborate

Talk About It
Summarize the Lesson

 Ask: What steps should be used when dividing large numbers? Start from left to right in the dividend, divide the divisor into the dividend to get the first digit in the quotient. Multiply this digit by the divisor and subtract the resulting product from the dividend. Then bring down the next number and repeat the process.

GUIDED PRACTICE

Engage with the Whiteboard

For Exercises 2–4, have students complete the division problems on the whiteboard. Ask them to explain their reasoning.

Avoid Common Errors

Exercises 1, 5–10 Some students interchange the divisor and dividend when translating a problem in the form $a \div b$ into the form $b \overline{)a}$. Remind students that the number after the division sign, $\div$, or the number outside the division house, $\overline{)}$, is always the divisor.

Exercise 11 Point out to students that this problem is asking for an estimate, not an exact answer. Remind them to round each number appropriately.

Dividing with a Remainder

Suppose you and your friend want to divide 9 polished rocks between you so that you each get the same number of polished rocks. You will each get 4 rocks with 1 rock left over. You can say that the quotient 9 ÷ 2 has a remainder of 1.

EXAMPLE 2 Real World

COMMON CORE 6.NS.2

Callie has 1,850 books. She must pack them into boxes to ship to a bookstore. Each box holds 12 books. How many boxes will she need to pack all of the books?

Divide 1,850 by 12.

```
      154 R2
12)1,850
   −12
     65
    −60
     50
    −48
      2
```

The quotient is 154, remainder 2. You can write 154 R2.

Reflect

5. **Interpret the Answer** What does the remainder mean in this situation?

After packing 154 boxes, there will be 2 books left over.

6. **Interpret the Answer** How many boxes does Callie need to pack the books? Explain.

155; an extra box is needed for the 2 books left over.

YOUR TURN

Divide.

7. 5,796 ÷ 25 _231 R21_

8. 67)3,098 _46 R16_

9. A museum gift shop manager wants to put 1,578 polished rocks into small bags to sell as souvenirs. If the shop manager wants to put 15 rocks in each bag, how many complete bags can be filled? How many rocks will be left over? _105 bags; 3 rocks left over_

Math On the Spot
my.hrw.com

My Notes

Personal Math Trainer
Online Assessment and Intervention
my.hrw.com

---

1. Estimate: 31,969 ÷ 488 (Explore Activity)

Round the numbers and then divide.

31,969 ÷ 488 = _30,000_ ÷ _500_ = _60_

Divide. (Example 1, Example 2)

2. 3,072 ÷ 32 = _96_

```
      96
32)3,072
  −288
    192
   −192
      0
```

3. 4,539 ÷ 51 = _89_

```
      89
51)4,539
  −408
    459
   −459
      0
```

4. 9,317 ÷ 95 = _98 R7_

```
      98
95)9,317
  −855
    767
   −760
      7
```

5. 2,226 ÷ 53 = _42_

6. Divide 4,514 by 74. _61_

7. 3,493 ÷ 37 = _94 R15_

8. 2,001 ÷ 83 = _24 R9_

9. 39,751 ÷ 313 = _127_

10. 35,506 ÷ 438 = _81 R28_

11. During a food drive, a local middle school collected 8,982 canned food items. Each of the 28 classrooms that participated in the drive donated about the same number of items. Estimate the number of items each classroom donated. (Explore Activity)

300 items

12. A theater has 1,120 seats in 35 equal rows. How many seats are in each row? (Example 1)

32 seats

13. There are 1,012 souvenir paperweights that need to be packed in boxes. Each box will hold 12 paperweights. How many boxes will be needed? (Example 2)

85 boxes

? ESSENTIAL QUESTION CHECK-IN

14. What steps do you take to divide multi-digit whole numbers?

Start from left to right in the dividend, and divide the divisor into the dividend to get the first digit in the quotient. Multiply this digit by the divisor and subtract the resulting product from the dividend. Then bring down the next number and repeat the process.

DIFFERENTIATE INSTRUCTION

Kinesthetic Experience

Have students work in groups of three or four. Give each group a set of index cards labeled 0–9. Have the groups mix and place the cards face down in a pile. Students should then draw four cards to make a dividend and two cards to make a divisor. Have students do the division individually. Group members should compare answers and work a problem together if they do not all get the same quotient.

Cognitive Strategies

Some students may have difficulty remembering the steps of the division algorithm—divide, multiply, subtract, bring down, then repeat. Have students make a study sheet with the steps for the division algorithm.

Additional Resources

Differentiated Instruction includes:

• Reading Strategies
• Success for English Learners **ELL**
• Reteach
• Challenge **PRE-AP**

5.1 LESSON QUIZ

 6.NS.2

Divide.

1. 4,183 ÷ 47

2. 52,114 ÷ 71

3. 62,152 ÷ 342

4. Lisa has 2,134 buttons that need to be sorted equally into 12 jars. How many buttons will be in each jar?

5. There are 3,863 shirts to pack into boxes that hold 120 shirts. How many boxes will be needed if all the shirts have to be packed in a box?

Lesson Quiz example available online

⏻ my.hrw.com

Answers

1. 89

2. 734

3. 181 R250

4. 177 buttons

5. 33 boxes

Evaluate

GUIDED AND INDEPENDENT PRACTICE

 6.NS.2

Concepts and Skills	Practice
Explore Activity Estimating Quotients	Exercises 1, 11
Example 1 Using Long Division	Exercises 2–3, 5–6, 9, 12, 15, 17, 20, 21, 24
Example 2 Dividing with a Remainder	Exercises 4, 7, 8, 10, 13, 16, 18, 19, 22, 23

Exercise	Depth of Knowledge (D.O.K.)		COMMON CORE Mathematical Practices
15–22	**2** Skills/Concepts		**MP.6** Precision
23–24	**2** Skills/Concepts		**MP.4** Modeling
25	**3** Strategic Thinking	H.O.T.	**MP.4** Modeling
26–27	**3** Strategic Thinking	H.O.T.	**MP.2** Reasoning
28	**2** Skills/Concepts		**MP.4** Modeling
29	**2** Skills/Concepts		**MP.3** Logic
30	**3** Strategic Thinking	H.O.T.	**MP.4** Modeling
31–32	**3** Strategic Thinking	H.O.T.	**MP.3** Logic
33	**3** Strategic Thinking	H.O.T.	**MP.2** Reasoning

Additional Resources

Differentiated Instruction includes:

• Leveled Practice worksheets

5.1 Independent Practice

COMMON CORE 6.NS.2

Personal Math Trainer
Online Assessment and Intervention
my.hrw.com

Divide.

15. $44{,}756 \div 167 = $ _____ 268

16. $87{,}628 \div 931 = $ _____ 94 R114

17. $66{,}253 \div 317 = $ _____ 209

18. $76{,}255 \div 309 = $ _____ 246 R241

19. $50{,}779 \div 590 = $ _____ 86 R39

20. $97{,}156 \div 107 = $ _____ 908

21. $216{,}016 \div 368 = $ _____ 587

22. $107{,}609 \div 72 = $ _____ 1,494 R41

23. Emilio has 8,450 trees to plant in rows on his tree farm. He will plant 125 trees per row. How many full rows of trees will he have? Explain.

67 rows; $8{,}450 \div 125 = 67$ R75 so he will have 67 full rows and one partial row of 75 trees.

24. Camilla makes and sells jewelry. She has 8,160 silver beads and 2,880 black beads to make necklaces. Each necklace will contain 85 silver beads and 30 black beads. How many necklaces can she make? 96 necklaces

25. During a promotional weekend, a state fair gives a free admission to every 175th person who enters the fair. On Saturday, there were 6,742 people attending the fair. On Sunday, there were 5,487 people attending the fair. How many people received a free admission over the two days?

69 people

26. How is the quotient $80{,}000 \div 2{,}000$ different from the quotient $80{,}000 \div 200$ or $80{,}000 \div 20$?

$80{,}000 \div 2{,}000 = 40$ is one tenth of $80{,}000 \div 200 = 400$, which is one tenth of $80{,}000 \div 20 = 4{,}000$.

27. Given that $9{,}554 \div 562 = 17$, how can you find the quotient $95{,}540 \div 562$?

The quotient is 10 times greater because the dividend is 10 times greater; $95{,}540 \div 562 = 170$.

28. **Earth Science** The diameter of the Moon is about 3,476 kilometers. The distance from Earth to the Moon is about 384,400 kilometers. About how many moons could be lined up in a row between Earth and the Moon? Round to the nearest whole number.

111 moons

Diameter 3,476 km

© Houghton Mifflin Harcourt Publishing Company

---

29. **Vocabulary** Explain how you could check the answer to a division question in which there is a remainder.

Multiply the quotient and the divisor, then add the remainder to the product. If the division was done correctly, the result will equal the dividend.

30. Yolanda is buying a car with a base price of $16,750. She must also pay the options, fees, and taxes shown. The car dealership will give her 48 months to pay off the entire amount. Yolanda can only afford to pay $395 each month. Will she be able to buy the car? Explain.

No; the total cost of the car is $16{,}750 + $2{,}295 = $19,045. If she pays $395 per month it will take $19{,}045 \div 395 = 48$ R85 or 49 months to pay off the car, more than the car dealership will allow.

Jackson Auto Dealer	
4-door sedan	
base price	$16,750
options	$ 500
fees	$ 370
taxes	$ 1,425

H.O.T. FOCUS ON HIGHER ORDER THINKING

31. **Check for Reasonableness** Is 40 a reasonable estimate of a quotient for $78{,}114 \div 192$? Explain your reasoning.

No; 78,114 is about 80,000 and 192 is about 200; $80{,}000 \div 200 = 400$, and 40 isn't close to 400.

32. **Critique Reasoning** Harrison predicted that the actual quotient for $57{,}872 \div 305$ will be less than the estimate $60{,}000 \div 300 = 200$. Is Harrison correct? Explain how Harrison arrived at his prediction (without dividing the actual numbers).

Yes; in the estimated quotient, the dividend increased and the divisor decreased, which will result in a quotient greater than the actual quotient.

33. **Make a Prediction** In preparation for a storm, the town council buys 13,750 pounds of sand to fill sandbags. Volunteers are trying to decide whether to fill bags that can hold 25 pounds of sand or bags that can hold 50 pounds of sand. Will they have more or fewer sandbags if they fill the 25-pound bags? How many more or fewer? Explain your reasoning.

More; the whole amount is divided into smaller portions, so there will be more bags; since 25 is half of 50, they will have twice as many bags.

Work Area

© Houghton Mifflin Harcourt Publishing Company

EXTEND THE MATH PRE-AP

Activity available online my.hrw.com

Activity Make a separate index card for each item in the table. Stack the index cards in four groups: context, dividend, divisor, and containers. Have students work in groups of four. Have one student from each group pick a card from a different group. Then have the students write a real-world problem using the information on the index cards they selected. When they are ready, have the groups exchange the problems and solve them. Ask students to critique each other's work offering suggestions.

Eggs	16,234	22	Boxes
Pieces of Candy	7,654	25	Bags
Pennies	19,213	42	Jars
Stickers	321,114	111	Baskets

5.2 Adding and Subtracting Decimals

Common Core Standards

The student is expected to:

 6.NS.3

Fluently add, subtract, multiply, and divide multi-digit decimals using the standard algorithm for each operation.

Mathematical Practices

 MP.2 Reasoning

ADDITIONAL EXAMPLE 1
Kelly ran 6.2 miles last week and 10.95 miles this week. How many miles did she run in all? 17.15 miles

 Interactive Whiteboard
Interactive example available online

 my.hrw.com

Engage

ESSENTIAL QUESTION

How do you add and subtract decimals? Align decimal numbers on the decimal points so the place-value positions line up, then add or subtract as you would whole numbers.

Motivate the Lesson

Ask: Suppose you have $50, how much change would you receive if you bought a DVD that cost $27.99? Begin Explore Activity 1 to see how to solve this type of problem.

Explore

EXPLORE ACTIVITY

Engage with the Whiteboard

Show a decimal grid on the whiteboard. Have a volunteer shade the grid to represent the sum 0.32 + 0.45. Have students use different colored pencils for each decimal. Point out to students that 100 − (the sum) is the same as the number of blocks left unshaded on the grid. Repeat with the sum 0.53 + 0.30.

Explain

EXAMPLE 1

Connect Vocabulary ELL

Remind students that decimal numbers represent combinations of whole numbers and numbers between whole numbers. The place-value chart can help them to understand, write, and compare decimal numbers. The values to the left of the decimal point are the whole numbers (thousands, hundreds, tens, and ones). The values to the right of the decimal point are the parts (tenths, hundredths, thousandths, ten-thousandths, etc.).

Questioning Strategies CC Mathematical Practices

• In Step 2, why was a zero added to 4.7? You use a zero as a placeholder so that both numbers have the same number of digits after their decimal points.

YOUR TURN

Avoid Common Errors

Students may try to align decimal numbers to the right instead of on the decimal point when adding in a vertical format. Remind them that the place-value positions in each number must line up.

LESSON
5.2

Adding and
Subtracting Decimals

COMMON CORE 6.NS.3
Fluently add [and] subtract...
decimals using the standard
algorithm....

? **ESSENTIAL QUESTION**

How do you add and subtract decimals?

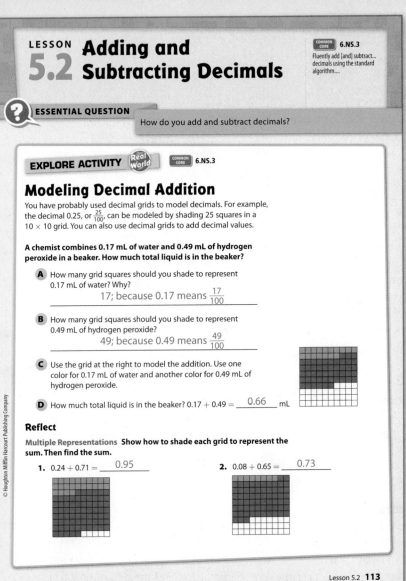

EXPLORE ACTIVITY Real World   COMMON CORE 6.NS.3

Modeling Decimal Addition

You have probably used decimal grids to model decimals. For example, the decimal 0.25, or $\frac{25}{100}$, can be modeled by shading 25 squares in a 10×10 grid. You can also use decimal grids to add decimal values.

A chemist combines 0.17 mL of water and 0.49 mL of hydrogen peroxide in a beaker. How much total liquid is in the beaker?

A How many grid squares should you shade to represent 0.17 mL of water? Why?

17; because 0.17 means $\frac{17}{100}$

B How many grid squares should you shade to represent 0.49 mL of hydrogen peroxide?

49; because 0.49 means $\frac{49}{100}$

C Use the grid at the right to model the addition. Use one color for 0.17 mL of water and another color for 0.49 mL of hydrogen peroxide.

D How much total liquid is in the beaker? 0.17 + 0.49 = _____0.66_____ mL

Reflect

Multiple Representations Show how to shade each grid to represent the sum. Then find the sum.

1. 0.24 + 0.71 = _____0.95_____

2. 0.08 + 0.65 = _____0.73_____

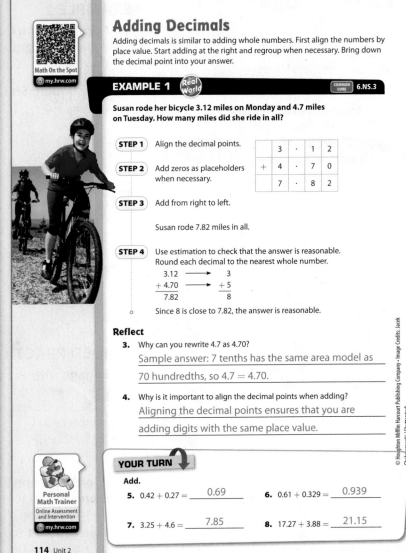

Math On the Spot
my.hrw.com

Adding Decimals

Adding decimals is similar to adding whole numbers. First align the numbers by place value. Start adding at the right and regroup when necessary. Bring down the decimal point into your answer.

EXAMPLE 1 Real World   COMMON CORE 6.NS.3

Susan rode her bicycle 3.12 miles on Monday and 4.7 miles on Tuesday. How many miles did she ride in all?

STEP 1 Align the decimal points.

STEP 2 Add zeros as placeholders when necessary.

	3	.	1	2
+	4	.	7	0
	7	.	8	2

STEP 3 Add from right to left.

Susan rode 7.82 miles in all.

STEP 4 Use estimation to check that the answer is reasonable. Round each decimal to the nearest whole number.

$$\begin{array}{r} 3.12 \\ + 4.70 \\ \hline 7.82 \end{array} \longrightarrow \begin{array}{r} 3 \\ + 5 \\ \hline 8 \end{array}$$

Since 8 is close to 7.82, the answer is reasonable.

Reflect

3. Why can you rewrite 4.7 as 4.70?

Sample answer: 7 tenths has the same area model as 70 hundredths, so 4.7 = 4.70.

4. Why is it important to align the decimal points when adding?

Aligning the decimal points ensures that you are adding digits with the same place value.

Personal
Math Trainer
Online Assessment
and Intervention
my.hrw.com

YOUR TURN

Add.

5. 0.42 + 0.27 = _____0.69_____

6. 0.61 + 0.329 = _____0.939_____

7. 3.25 + 4.6 = _____7.85_____

8. 17.27 + 3.88 = _____21.15_____

PROFESSIONAL DEVELOPMENT

CC Integrate Mathematical Practices MP.2

This lesson provides an opportunity to address the Mathematical Practices standard that calls for students to reason abstractly and quantitatively. Students will be adding and subtracting decimals using estimation to check the reasonableness of their solutions. Reasoning is applied throughout this lesson as students make decisions about the accuracy of their work as they compare their estimations to their actual solutions.

Math Background

Consider the fractional form of a problem such as 4.8 + 3.76 to help students understand why it is possible to align decimal points and add zeros to the right of decimals without changing their values.

$$4.8 + 3.76 = 4\frac{8}{10} + 3\frac{76}{100} = 4\frac{80}{100} + 3\frac{76}{100}$$

Showing the sum in this format relates directly to the addition of the decimals 4.80 and 3.76 and shows why the zero can be written to the right of the 8 without changing the value of the decimal.

EXAMPLE 2

Focus on Math Connections

Remind students that when you are finding the difference between two numbers always place the larger number on top.

Questioning Strategies CC Mathematical Practices

• In Step 3, why is regrouping necessary? You need to regroup because 2 > 1. So, it is necessary to regroup a one as 10 tenths. After you regroup, you can subtract 2 from 11 to get 9.

Elaborate

Talk About It

Summarize the Lesson

Ask: What are the most important things to remember when adding or subtracting decimals? Sample answers: Align the decimal points, use zeros as placeholders so the decimals have the same number of place values, add or subtract from right to left, and regroup when necessary.

GUIDED PRACTICE

Engage with the Whiteboard

For Exercises 1–2, have students shade the grids to represent each sum on the whiteboard. Have them use two different colored markers to show each number clearly.

For Exercises 3–8, have students show how to estimate each sum on the whiteboard. Have them explain their choice of values when rounding.

Avoid Common Errors

Exercises 10–11 Remind students to use zeros as placeholders so that the numbers have the same number of place values.

Exercises 9–14 Students may try to align decimal numbers to the right instead of on the decimal point when adding or subtracting in a vertical format. Remind them that the place-value positions in each number must line up.

Subtracting Decimals

The procedure for subtracting decimals is similar to the procedure for adding decimals.

EXAMPLE 2   6.NS.3

A Mia is 160.2 centimeters tall. Rosa is 165.1 centimeters tall. How much taller is Rosa than Mia?

STEP 1 Align the decimal points.

STEP 2 Add zeros as placeholders when necessary.

STEP 3 Subtract from right to left, regrouping when necessary.

	1	6	5	.	1
−	1	6	0	.	2
			4	.	9

Rosa is 4.9 centimeters taller than Mia.

To check that your answer is reasonable, you can estimate. Round each decimal to the nearest whole number.

$$165.1 \longrightarrow 165$$
$$-160.2 \longrightarrow -160$$
$$4.9 5$$

Since 5 is close to 4.9, the answer is reasonable.

B Matthew throws a discus 58.7 meters. Zachary throws the discus 56.12 meters. How much farther did Matthew throw the discus?

STEP 1 Align the decimal points.

STEP 2 Add zeros as placeholders when necessary.

STEP 3 Subtract from right to left, regrouping when necessary.

	5	8	.	7	0
−	5	6	.	1	2
		2	.	5	8

Matthew threw the discus 2.58 meters farther than Zachary.

To check that your answer is reasonable, you can estimate. Round each decimal to the nearest whole number.

$$58.7 \longrightarrow 59$$
$$-56.12 \longrightarrow -56$$
$$2.58 3$$

Since 3 is close to 2.58, the answer is reasonable.

My Notes

Add your answer to the number being subtracted; if your answer is correct, this sum will be the number that is subtracted from.

Math Talk
Mathematical Practices

How can you check a subtraction problem?

Shade the grid to find each sum. (Explore Activity)

1. 0.72 + 0.19 = __0.91__

2. 0.38 + 0.4 = __0.78__

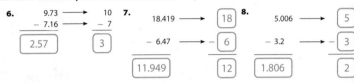

Add. Check that your answer is reasonable. (Example 1)

3.
$$54.87 \longrightarrow 55$$
$$+ 7.48 \longrightarrow + 7$$
$$62.35 62$$

4.
$$2.19 \longrightarrow \boxed{2}$$
$$+ 34.92 \longrightarrow + \boxed{35}$$
$$\boxed{37.11} \boxed{37}$$

5.
$$0.215 \longrightarrow \boxed{0}$$
$$+ 3.74 \longrightarrow + \boxed{4}$$
$$\boxed{3.955} \boxed{4}$$

Subtract. Check that your answer is reasonable. (Example 2)

6.
$$9.73 \longrightarrow 10$$
$$- 7.16 \longrightarrow - 7$$
$$\boxed{2.57} \boxed{3}$$

7.
$$18.419 \longrightarrow \boxed{18}$$
$$- 6.47 \longrightarrow - \boxed{6}$$
$$\boxed{11.949} \boxed{12}$$

8.
$$5.006 \longrightarrow \boxed{5}$$
$$- 3.2 \longrightarrow - \boxed{3}$$
$$\boxed{1.806} \boxed{2}$$

Add or subtract. (Example 1, Example 2)

9. 17.2 + 12.9 = __30.1__

10. 28.341 + 37.5 = __65.841__

11. 25.36 − 2.004 = __23.356__

12. 15.52 − 8.17 = __7.35__

13. 25.68 + 12 = __37.68__

14. 150.25 − 78 = __72.25__

15. Perry connects a blue garden hose and a green garden hose to make one long hose. The blue hose is 16.5 feet. The green hose is 14.75 feet. How long is the combined hose? (Example 1) __31.25 feet__

16. Keisha has $20.08 in her purse. She buys a book for $8.72. How much does she have left? (Example 2) __$11.36__

 ESSENTIAL QUESTION CHECK-IN

17. How is adding and subtracting decimals similar to adding and subtracting whole numbers?

You align the digits by place value when you add or subtract decimals, just as you align digits for whole numbers.

DIFFERENTIATE INSTRUCTION

Home Connection

Have students look through newspaper ads, at home or in the library, for items that, when combined, total less than $50. Have them subtract their totals from $50 to find out how much change they would receive.

Sample answer: I found shoes for $12.95, a CD for $13.98, and a skateboard for $19.49. The total cost is $46.42. The amount of change I would get from $50.00 is $3.58.

Critical Thinking

Have students solve a magic square with decimals. A magic square is a square array of numbers in which each row, column, and diagonal have the same sum. Have students find the missing numbers in the following magic square. The sum is 10.2.

0.3	7.1	0.5	2.3
5.3	1.1	3.7	0.1
1.7	1.3	4.1	3.1
2.9	0.7	1.9	4.7

Additional Resources

Differentiated Instruction includes:

- Reading Strategies
- Success for English Learners **ELL**
- Reteach
- Challenge **PRE-AP**

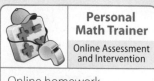

5.2 LESSON QUIZ

 6.NS.3

Add or subtract.

1. $55.867 + 25.6$

2. $8.71 - 4.306$

3. $86 - 9.71$

4. $3.22 + 45.006 + 51.9$

5. Trey has $19.76 in his wallet. He buys a pack of gum for $1.79 and a bottle of water for $2.34. How much money does Trey have left?

Lesson Quiz example available online

 my.hrw.com

Answers

1. 81.467

2. 4.404

3. 76.29

4. 100.126

5. $15.63

Evaluate

GUIDED AND INDEPENDENT PRACTICE

COMMON CORE 6.NS.3

Concepts and Skills	Practice
Explore Activity Modeling Decimal Addition	Exercises 1–2
Example 1 Adding Decimals	Exercises 3–5, 9–10, 13, 15
Example 2 Subtracting Decimals	Exercises 6–8, 11–12, 14, 16

Exercise	Depth of Knowledge (D.O.K.)	COMMON CORE Mathematical Practices
18–25	**2** Skills/Concepts	**MP.2** Reasoning
26–30	**2** Skills/Concepts	**MP.4** Modeling
31	**3** Strategic Thinking **H.O.T.**	**MP.2** Reasoning
32	**3** Strategic Thinking **H.O.T.**	**MP.7** Using Structure
33–34	**4** Extended Thinking **H.O.T.**	**MP.3** Logic

Additional Resources

Differentiated Instruction includes:

• Leveled Practice worksheets

5.2 Independent Practice

Personal
Math Trainer

Online
Assessment and
Intervention
my.hrw.com

Add or subtract.

18. $28.6 - 0.975 =$ _____ 27.625

19. $5.6 - 0.105 =$ _____ 5.495

20. $7.03 + 33.006 =$ _____ 40.036

21. $57.42 + 4 + 1.602 =$ _____ 63.022

22. $2.25 + 65.47 + 2.333 =$ _____ 70.053

23. $18.419 - 6.47 =$ _____ 11.949

24. $83 - 12.76 =$ _____ 70.24

25. $102.01 - 95.602 =$ _____ 6.408

26. Multiple Representations Ursula wrote the sum $5.815 + 6.021$ as a sum of two mixed numbers.

a. What sum did she write? _____ $5\frac{815}{1,000} + 6\frac{21}{1,000}$

b. Compare the sum of the mixed numbers to the sum of the decimals. _____ $11\frac{836}{1,000} = 11.836$

Use the café menu to answer 27–29.

27. Stephen and Jahmya are having lunch. Stephen buys a garden salad, a veggie burger, and lemonade. Jahmya buys a fruit salad, a toasted cheese sandwich, and a bottle of water. Whose lunch cost more? How much more?

_____ Jahmya; $0.54 more

28. Jahmya wants to leave $1.75 as a tip for her server. She has a $20 bill. How much change should she receive after paying for her food and leaving a tip?

_____ $9.38

29. What If? In addition to his meal, Stephen orders a fruit salad for take-out, and wants to leave $2.25 as a tip for his server. He has a $10 bill and a $5 bill. How much change should he receive after paying for his lunch, the fruit salad, and the tip?

_____ $1.53

30. A carpenter who is installing cabinets uses thin pieces of material called shims to fill gaps. The carpenter uses four shims to fill a gap that is 1.2 centimeters wide. Three of the shims are 0.75 centimeter, 0.125 centimeter, and 0.09 centimeter wide. What is the width of the fourth shim?

_____ 0.235 centimeter

Café Menu

Garden Salad **$2.29**
Fruit Salad **$2.89**

Veggie Burger **$4.75**
Toasted Cheese Sandwich
$4.59

Bottle of Water **$1.39**
Lemonade **$1.29**

---

31. A CD of classical guitar music contains 5 songs. The length of each song is shown in the table.

Track 1	Track 2	Track 3	Track 4	Track 5
6.5 minutes	8 minutes	3.93 minutes	4.1 minutes	5.05 minutes

a. Between each song is a 0.05-minute break. How long does it take to listen to the CD from the beginning of the first song to the end of the last song? _____ 27.78 minutes

b. What If? Juan wants to buy the CD from an Internet music site. He downloads the CD onto a disc that can hold up to 60 minutes of music. How many more minutes of music can he still buy after downloading the CD? _____ 32.22 minutes

H.O.T. **FOCUS ON HIGHER ORDER THINKING**

32. Analyze Relationships Use the decimals 2.47, 9.57, and 7.1 to write two different addition facts and two different subtraction facts.

$2.47 + 7.1 = 9.57; 7.1 + 2.47 = 9.57; 9.57 - 2.47 = 7.1;$

$9.57 - 7.1 = 2.47$

33. Communicate Mathematical Ideas The Commutative Property of Addition states that you can change the order of addends in a sum. The Associative Property of Addition states that you can change the grouping of addends in a sum. Use an example to show how the Commutative Property of Addition and the Associative Property of Addition apply to adding decimals.

Sample answer: The sum of $2.55 + (3.72 + 1.45) = 2.55$

$+ 5.17 = 7.72$. Using the Commutative Property, the

sum can be written as $2.55 + (1.45 + 3.72) = 7.72$, and

using the Associative Property, the sum can be written

as $(2.55 + 1.45) + 3.72 = 7.72$.

34. Critique Reasoning Indira predicts that the actual difference of $19 - 7.82$ will be greater than the estimate of $19 - 8 = 11$. Is Indira correct? Explain how Indira might have arrived at that prediction without subtracting the actual numbers.

Yes. The number being subtracted is rounded up.

Subtracting a greater number results in a smaller

difference than the actual difference.

Work Area

EXTEND THE MATH PRE-AP

Activity available online my.hrw.com

Activity Have students create a brief menu with 10 items and prices. Then have them exchange menus and select 3–4 items to purchase for a meal. Next, have students find the total cost of the meal including tax and a tip. Finally, have students determine the amount of change they would receive if they had $50 to pay for their meal.

Students can also be encouraged to bring in take-out menus from area restaurants to use for this activity.

LESSON
5.3 Multiplying Decimals

Common Core Standards

The student is expected to:

 The Number System—6.NS.3

Fluently add, subtract, multiply and divide multi-digit decimals using the standard algorithm for each operation.

Mathematical Practices

 MP.5 Using Tools

ADDITIONAL EXAMPLE 1
Wanda wants to buy 4.35 pounds of chicken salad. The grocery store sells chicken salad for $2.29 a pound. How much does the chicken salad cost?
$9.96

 Interactive Whiteboard
Interactive example available online

 my.hrw.com

Engage

ESSENTIAL QUESTION

How do you multiply decimals? Sample answer: First, multiply as you do whole numbers and then place the decimal point in the product. The number of decimal places in the product equals the sum of the number of decimal places in the factors.

Motivate the Lesson
Ask: Potato salad costs $1.29 per pound at the deli counter. About how much do you think 4.5 pounds of potato salad will cost? Begin the Explore Activity to learn how to multiply two decimals.

Explore

EXPLORE ACTIVITY 1

Focus on Modeling CC Mathematical Practices
In B, make sure students understand that the model shows the whole part as large unit squares and the decimal part as smaller rectangles and tiny squares. Each smaller rectangle represents a tenth of a unit square, and each tiny square represents a hundredth of a unit square.

Explain

EXAMPLE 1

Avoid Common Errors
When multiplying decimals, students sometimes try to place decimal points in partial products. Remind students to complete the entire multiplication before placing the decimal point in the final product.

Questioning Strategies CC Mathematical Practices
• Why does the answer have only two decimal places when there should be three decimals based on the multiplication? Money is usually written to two decimals, or to the nearest penny.

• If the third decimal place had a number other than zero, how would you round the number in the hundredths place? A number greater than or equal to 5 rounds the hundredths place up, and a number less than 5 rounds the hundredths place down.

5.3 Multiplying Decimals

COMMON CORE 6.NS.3
Fluently...multiply...
multi-digit decimals using
the standard algorithm....

? ESSENTIAL QUESTION
How do you multiply decimals?

EXPLORE ACTIVITY   COMMON CORE 6.NS.3

Modeling Decimal Multiplication

Use decimal grids or area models to find each product.

A 0.3 × 0.5

0.3 × 0.5 represents 0.3 of 0.5. Shade 5 *rows* of the decimal grid to represent 0.5.

Shade 0.3 of each 0.1 that is already shaded

to represent 0.3 of ___0.5___.

___15___ square(s) are double-shaded.

This represents ___15___ hundredth(s), or 0.15.

0.3 × 0.5 = ___0.15___

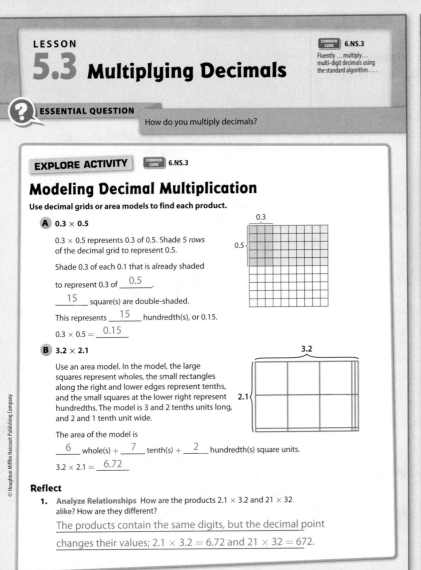

0.3

0.5

B 3.2 × 2.1

Use an area model. In the model, the large squares represent wholes, the small rectangles along the right and lower edges represent tenths, and the small squares at the lower right represent hundredths. The model is 3 and 2 tenths units long, and 2 and 1 tenth unit wide.

3.2

2.1

The area of the model is

___6___ whole(s) + ___7___ tenth(s) + ___2___ hundredth(s) square units.

3.2 × 2.1 = ___6.72___

Reflect

1. **Analyze Relationships** How are the products 2.1 × 3.2 and 21 × 32 alike? How are they different?

   The products contain the same digits, but the decimal point

   changes their values; 2.1 × 3.2 = 6.72 and 21 × 32 = 672.

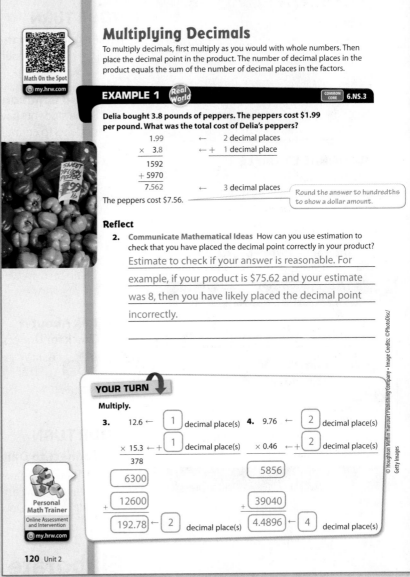

Math On the Spot
my.hrw.com

Multiplying Decimals

To multiply decimals, first multiply as you would with whole numbers. Then place the decimal point in the product. The number of decimal places in the product equals the sum of the number of decimal places in the factors.

EXAMPLE 1 Real World   COMMON CORE 6.NS.3

Delia bought 3.8 pounds of peppers. The peppers cost $1.99 per pound. What was the total cost of Delia's peppers?

```
    1.99      ←    2 decimal places
  × 3.8       ← +  1 decimal place
   1592
 + 5970
   7.562      ←    3 decimal places
```

The peppers cost $7.56.

> *Round the answer to hundredths to show a dollar amount.*

Reflect

2. **Communicate Mathematical Ideas** How can you use estimation to check that you have placed the decimal point correctly in your product?

   Estimate to check if your answer is reasonable. For

   example, if your product is $75.62 and your estimate

   was 8, then you have likely placed the decimal point

   incorrectly.

YOUR TURN

Multiply.

3.   12.6 ← ⬜1 decimal place(s)
   × 15.3 ← + ⬜1 decimal place(s)
      378
    ⬜6300
   + ⬜12600
   ⬜192.78 ← ⬜2 decimal place(s)

4.   9.76 ← ⬜2 decimal place(s)
   × 0.46 ← + ⬜2 decimal place(s)
     ⬜5856
   + ⬜39040
   ⬜4.4896 ← ⬜4 decimal place(s)

Personal Math Trainer
Online Assessment and Intervention
my.hrw.com

PROFESSIONAL DEVELOPMENT

CC Integrate Mathematical Practices MP.5

This lesson provides an opportunity to address this Mathematical Practice standard. It calls for students to select tools, including real objects, manipulatives, paper and pencil, and technology as appropriate, to solve problems. In the Explore Activity, students use decimal grids to represent decimals and identify the product of two decimals. Students use pencil and paper to multiply decimals in Example 1. And in Example 2 students focus on estimating to check the reasonableness of their answers.

Math Background

Multiplying decimals is similar to multiplying whole numbers, except for the extra step of correctly placing the decimal point. Simply count the number of *decimal places* in the factors being multiplied. Then place the decimal point so that the number of *decimal places* in the product is same as the total number in the factors.

Note that the term *decimal places* refers to the places to the *right* of the decimal point: tenths, hundredths, thousandths, and so on.

YOUR TURN

Engage with the Whiteboard

 Have students make a decimal grid to model the problems and check their work.

Avoid Common Errors

Some students have trouble placing the decimal point in the final product. Remind students to count from right to left when placing the decimal point in the final product.

EXAMPLE 2

Questioning Strategies CC Mathematical Practices

- Since grass can grow at different rates at different times of the year or in different locations, what does the rate of 3.75 inches per month mean? The rate of 3.75 inches per month represents an average rate of growth.

- When estimating, if you round both of the factors up, what can you say about your estimated answer? Your estimate will be greater than the actual product, because you multiplied two greater numbers.

Talk About it
Check for Understanding

Ask: When do you think estimation can be helpful? When an approximate answer is all that is needed, or when it is a good idea to check for a mistake, such as incorrect decimal placement in a product

YOUR TURN

Connect to Daily Life CC Mathematical Practices

For Exercise 7, have students estimate the answer before finding the product. Consider discussing how estimation can be a useful tool for planning everyday activities, such as budgeting an allowance or scheduling work/study time.

Elaborate

Talk About It
Summarize the Lesson

Ask: How do you multiply decimals? Multiply decimals as you do whole numbers and then place the decimal point by counting the total number of decimal places in the factors.

GUIDED PRACTICE

Engage with the Whiteboard

 For Exercises 3–10, have students underline and count each decimal place to find the number of decimal places in the answer. This activity can be performed before starting any multiplication.

Avoid Common Errors

Exercises 3–8 If students have difficulty placing the decimal point in the final product, remind them to count from right to left when placing the decimal point in the final product.

Exercises 9–10 Remind students that answers involving money should be rounded to the nearest hundredth.

Estimating to Check Reasonableness

In Example 1, you used estimation to check whether the decimal point was placed correctly in the product. You can also use estimation to check that your answer is reasonable.

EXAMPLE 2 COMMON CORE 6.NS.3

Blades of grass grow 3.75 inches per month. If the grass continues to grow at this rate, how much will the grass grow in 6.25 months?

$$\begin{array}{r} 3.75 \leftarrow \text{2 decimal places} \\ \times\ 6.25 \leftarrow +\ \text{2 decimal places} \\ \hline 1875 \\ 7500 \\ +\ 225000 \\ \hline 23.4375 \leftarrow \text{4 decimal places} \end{array}$$

The grass will grow 23.4375 inches in 6.25 months.

Estimate to check whether your answer is reasonable.

Round 3.75 to the nearest whole number. __4__

Round 6.25 to the nearest whole number. __6__

Multiply the whole numbers. __4__ × __6__ = 24

The answer is reasonable because 24 is close to 23.4375.

YOUR TURN

Multiply.

5.
$$\begin{array}{r} 7.14 \\ \times\ 6.78 \\ \hline 5712 \\ \boxed{49980} \\ \boxed{428400} \\ +\ \\ \hline \boxed{48.4092} \end{array}$$

6.
$$\begin{array}{r} 11.49 \\ \times\ 8.27 \\ \hline \boxed{8043} \\ \boxed{22980} \\ \boxed{919200} \\ +\ \\ \hline \boxed{95.0223} \end{array}$$

7. Rico bicycles at an average speed of 15.5 miles per hour. What distance will Rico bicycle in 2.5 hours? __38.75__ miles

8. Use estimation to show that your answer to **7** is reasonable. Sample answer: Round 15.5 to 15 and 2.5 to 3; 15 × 3 = 45; 45 is close to 38.75.

Math On the Spot
my.hrw.com

Animated Math
my.hrw.com

My Notes

Personal Math Trainer
Online Assessment and Intervention
my.hrw.com

---

1. Use the grid to multiply 0.4 × 0.7. (Explore Activity)

0.4 × 0.7 = __0.28__

2. Draw an area model to multiply 1.1 × 2.4. (Explore Activity)

1.1 × 2.4 = __2.64__

Multiply. (Example 1 and Example 2)

3. 0.18 × 0.06 = __0.0108__

4. 35.15 × 3.7 = __130.055__

5. 0.96 × 0.12 = __0.1152__

6. 62.19 × 32.5 = __2,021.175__

7. 3.4 × 4.37 = __14.858__

8. 3.762 × 0.66 = __2.48292__

9. Chan Hee bought 3.4 pounds of coffee that cost $6.95 per pound. How much did he spend on coffee? $ __23.63__

10. Adita earns $9.40 per hour working at an animal shelter. How much money will she earn for 18.5 hours of work? $ __173.90__

Catherine tracked her gas purchases for one month.

11. How much did Catherine spend on gas in week 2? $ __29.21__

12. How much more did she spend in week 4 than in week 1? $ __1.06__

Week	Gallons	Cost per gallon ($)
1	10.4	2.65
2	11.5	2.54
3	9.72	2.75
4	10.6	2.70

 ESSENTIAL QUESTION CHECK-IN

13. How can you check the answer to a decimal multiplication problem?
Divide the product by one of the decimals. The quotient should be the other decimal value.

DIFFERENTIATE INSTRUCTION

Visual Cues

Have students use a colored pencil to write the number of decimal places next to each factor. Have them write the sum of these numbers next to the space in which they would write the answer. This helps students who forget to place the decimal or forget to add the decimal places for each factor.

Critical Thinking

Review how a decimal changes when it is multiplied by 10, 100, and 1,000. Then have students find rules for multiplying by 0.1, 0.01, and 0.001. They should see that the decimal point moves but the digits stay the same.

When multiplying by
0.1, the decimal point moves left one place;
0.01, the decimal point moves left two places;
0.001, the decimal point moves left three places.

Zeros may be needed after the decimal point, as they are needed before the decimal point of numbers multiplied by 10, 100, and 1,000. For example, 12.3 × 0.001 = 0.0123.

Additional Resources

Differentiated Instruction includes:
- Reading Strategies
- Success for English Learners **ELL**
- Reteach
- Challenge **PRE-AP**

5.3 LESSON QUIZ

6.NS.3

Multiply.

1. 11.3×20.5

2. 0.12×0.04

3. 0.3×4.24

4. Anna earns $13.75 per hour and worked 20.5 hours last week. How much did she earn last week?

5. Silka swims at an average speed of 0.35 miles per hour. About what distance will Silka swim in 2.8 hours?

6. Luis uses 1.6 liters of gasoline each hour he spends mowing lawns. How much gas does he use in 5.8 hours?

Lesson Quiz example available online

 my.hrw.com

Answers

1. 231.65

2. 0.0048

3. 1.272

4. $281.88

5. 1 mile

6. 9.28 liters

Evaluate

GUIDED AND INDEPENDENT PRACTICE

6.NS.3

Concepts & Skills	Practice
Explore Activity Modeling Decimal Multiplication	Exercises 1–2
Example 1 Multiplying Decimals	Exercises 3–12, 20–23
Example 2 Estimating to Check Reasonableness	Exercises 14–18, 26

Exercise	Depth of Knowledge (D.O.K.)	Mathematical Practices
14–16	**2** Skills/Concepts	**MP.4** Modeling
17–19	**2** Skills/Concepts	**MP.5** Using Tools
20–21	**2** Skills/Concepts	**MP.4** Modeling
22	**3** Strategic Thinking **H.O.T.**	**MP.3** Logic
23–25	**2** Skills/Concepts	**MP.5** Using Tools
26	**3** Strategic Thinking **H.O.T.**	**MP.6** Precision
27	**3** Strategic Thinking **H.O.T.**	**MP.7** Using Structure
28	**3** Strategic Thinking **H.O.T.**	**MP.4** Modeling
29	**3** Strategic Thinking **H.O.T.**	**MP.8** Patterns

Additional Resources

Differentiated Instruction includes:

• Leveled Practice Worksheets

5.3 Independent Practice

COMMON CORE 6.NS.3

Personal Math Trainer

Online Assessment and Intervention

my.hrw.com

Make a reasonable estimate for each situation.

14. A gallon of water weighs 8.354 pounds. Simon uses 11.81 gallons of water while taking a shower. About how many pounds of water did Simon use?

96 pounds

15. A snail moves at a speed of 2.394 inches per minute. If the snail keeps moving at this rate, about how many inches will it travel in 7.489 minutes?

14 inches

16. Tricia's garden is 9.87 meters long and 1.09 meters wide. What is the area of her garden?

10 m²

Kaylynn and Amanda both work at the same store. The table shows how much each person earns, and the number of hours each person works in a week.

	Wage	Hours worked per week
Kaylynn	$8.75 per hour	37.5
Amanda	$10.25 per hour	30.5

17. Estimate how much Kaylynn earns in a week.

$342

18. Estimate how much Amanda earns in a week.

$310

19. Calculate the exact difference between Kaylynn and Amanda's weekly salaries.

$15.50

20. Victoria's printer can print 8.804 pages in one minute. If Victoria prints pages for 0.903 minutes, about how many pages will she have?

9 pages

A taxi charges a flat fee of $4.00 plus $2.25 per mile.

21. How much will it cost to travel 8.7 miles? _____ $23.58 _____

22. Multistep How much will the taxi driver earn if he takes one passenger 4.8 miles and another passenger 7.3 miles? Explain your process.

$35.23; Sample answer: Multiply each distance driven by 2.25, add 4 to each product, and then add the two sums.

Lesson 5.3 **123**

Kay goes for several bike rides one week. The table shows her speed and the number of hours spent per ride.

	Speed (in miles per hour)	Hours Spent on Bike
Monday	8.2	4.25
Tuesday	9.6	3.1
Wednesday	11.1	2.8
Thursday	10.75	1.9
Friday	8.8	3.75

23. How many miles did Kay bike on Thursday?

20.425 miles

24. On which day did Kay bike a whole number of miles?

Friday

25. What is the difference in miles between Kay's longest bike ride and her shortest bike ride?

14.425 miles

26. Check for Reasonableness Kay estimates that Wednesday's ride was about 3 miles longer than Tuesday's ride. Is her estimate reasonable? Explain.

Yes; on Wednesday she rode about 11 miles per hour for about 3 hours, and 11 × 3 = 33. On Tuesday she rode about 10 miles per hour for about 3 hours, and 10 × 3 = 30.

H.O.T. FOCUS ON HIGHER ORDER THINKING

Work Area

27. Explain the Error To estimate the product 3.48 × 7.33, Marisa multiplied 4 × 8 to get 32. Explain how she can make a closer estimate.

3.48 is closer to 3 and 7.33 is closer to 7; 3 × 7 = 21

28. Represent Real-World Problems A jeweler buys gold jewelry and resells the gold to a refinery. The jeweler buys gold for $1,235.55 per ounce, and then resells it for $1,376.44 per ounce. How much profit does the jeweler make from buying and reselling 73.5 ounces of gold?

$10,355.42

29. Problem Solving To find the weight of the gold in a 22 karat gold object, multiply the object's weight by 0.917. To find the weight of the gold in an 18 karat gold object, multiply the object's weight by 0.583. A 22 karat gold statue and a 14 karat gold statue both weigh 73.5 ounces. Which one contains more gold? How much more gold does it contain?

The 22 karat gold statue; 24.549 ounces

18 kt
(typo)

124 Unit 2

EXTEND THE MATH PRE-AP

Activity available online my.hrw.com

Activity Another method for multiplying decimals is called lattice multiplication. This method uses a grid system to enable users to simplify the multiplication and add the products diagonally. Demonstrate this method and then have students find the answer to the following multiplication: 3.2 × 2.8. 8.96

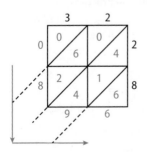

LESSON
5.4 Dividing Decimals

Common Core Standards

The student is expected to:

 The Number System—6.NS.3

Fluently add, subtract, multiply, and divide multi-digit decimals using the standard algorithm for each operation.

Mathematical Practices

 MP.2 Reasoning

ADDITIONAL EXAMPLE 1
Dana, Elaine, and Eli eat lunch in a restaurant. The bill is $27.75. If they share the bill equally, how much will each person pay?

$9.25

 Interactive Whiteboard
Interactive example available online

 my.hrw.com

Engage

....

ESSENTIAL QUESTION

How do you divide decimals? Sample answer: If necessary, first multiply the dividend and the divisor by the same power of 10 so that the divisor is a whole number. Then divide as you would normally do when dividing a number by a whole number, placing the decimal point in the quotient directly above the decimal point in the dividend.

Motivate the Lesson

Ask: You are saving $3.75 each week to buy a DVD that costs $26.79, including tax. For how many weeks will you need to save? Begin the Explore Activity to find out how to divide decimals.

Explore

....

EXPLORE ACTIVITY

Engage with the Whiteboard

 For A, have a student show how 3 equal groups can be formed using the given shaded model by circling each group with a different color.

Focus on Modeling **CC** Mathematical Practices

Make sure students understand the partially shaded grid in A shows 39 hundredths, and 39 hundredths divided by 3 is 13 hundredths. So the quotient is 2 complete grids plus 13 hundredths of a grid, or 2.13.

Explain

....

EXAMPLE 1

Connect Vocabulary **ELL**

Remind students that in a division problem the **dividend** is the number to be divided, the **divisor** is the number you are dividing by, and the **quotient** is the result. Divisors, dividends, and quotients in this lesson may be whole numbers or decimal numbers.

Questioning Strategies **CC** Mathematical Practices

• What rule can you write to explain the correct placement of a decimal in a quotient when a decimal is divided by a whole number, as in A? Place the decimal point in the quotient directly above the decimal point in the dividend.

• Explain why multiplication is a logical way to check the answer in B. Multiplication is the inverse operation for division. So, $14 \times 10.99 = 153.86$.

YOUR TURN

Avoid Common Errors

When dividing decimals, students sometimes align digits incorrectly and produce an answer that has the decimal point in the wrong place. Have students use grid paper (or lined paper turned sideways) to help align the digits correctly.

5.4 Dividing Decimals

COMMON CORE 6.NS.3
Fluently...divide multi-digit decimals using the standard algorithm....

? ESSENTIAL QUESTION

How do you divide decimals?

EXPLORE ACTIVITY COMMON CORE 6.NS.3

Modeling Decimal Division

Use decimal grids to find each quotient.

A 6.39 ÷ 3

Shade grids to model 6.39. Separate the model into 3 equal groups.

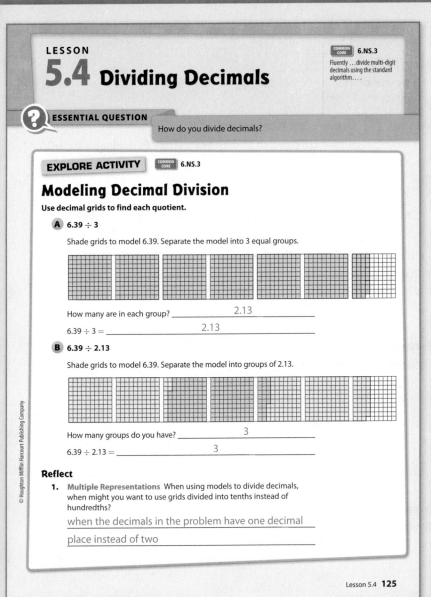

How many are in each group? _____ 2.13

6.39 ÷ 3 = _____ 2.13

B 6.39 ÷ 2.13

Shade grids to model 6.39. Separate the model into groups of 2.13.

How many groups do you have? _____ 3

6.39 ÷ 2.13 = _____ 3

Reflect

1. **Multiple Representations** When using models to divide decimals, when might you want to use grids divided into tenths instead of hundredths?

when the decimals in the problem have one decimal

place instead of two

Math On the Spot
© my.hrw.com

My Notes

Dividing Decimals by Whole Numbers

Dividing decimals is similar to dividing whole numbers. When you divide a decimal by a whole number, the placement of the decimal point in the quotient is determined by the placement of the decimal in the dividend.

EXAMPLE 1 Real World

COMMON CORE 6.NS.3

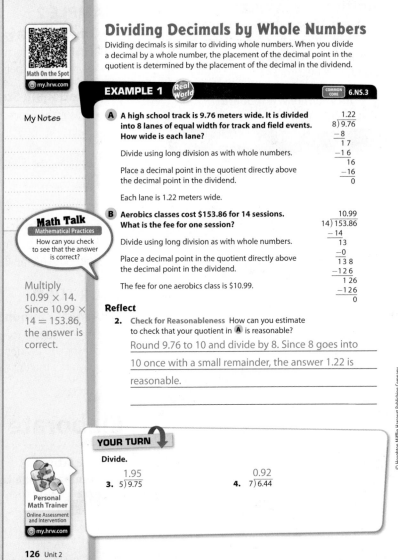

A A high school track is 9.76 meters wide. It is divided into 8 lanes of equal width for track and field events. How wide is each lane?

$$\begin{array}{r} 1.22 \\ 8\overline{)9.76} \\ -8 \\ \hline 1\,7 \\ -1\,6 \\ \hline 16 \\ -16 \\ \hline 0 \end{array}$$

Divide using long division as with whole numbers.

Place a decimal point in the quotient directly above the decimal point in the dividend.

Each lane is 1.22 meters wide.

Math Talk
Mathematical Practices

How can you check to see that the answer is correct?

Multiply 10.99 × 14. Since 10.99 × 14 = 153.86, the answer is correct.

B Aerobics classes cost $153.86 for 14 sessions. What is the fee for one session?

$$\begin{array}{r} 10.99 \\ 14\overline{)153.86} \\ -14 \\ \hline 13 \\ -0 \\ \hline 13\,8 \\ -126 \\ \hline 1\,26 \\ -1\,26 \\ \hline 0 \end{array}$$

Divide using long division as with whole numbers.

Place a decimal point in the quotient directly above the decimal point in the dividend.

The fee for one aerobics class is $10.99.

Reflect

2. **Check for Reasonableness** How can you estimate to check that your quotient in **A** is reasonable?

Round 9.76 to 10 and divide by 8. Since 8 goes into

10 once with a small remainder, the answer 1.22 is

reasonable.

Personal Math Trainer
Online Assessment and Intervention
© my.hrw.com

YOUR TURN

Divide.

3. $5\overline{)9.75}$ → 1.95

4. $7\overline{)6.44}$ → 0.92

PROFESSIONAL DEVELOPMENT

CC Integrate Mathematical Practices MP.2

This lesson provides an opportunity to address this Mathematical Practice standard. It calls for students to create and use multiple representations to organize, record, and communicate mathematical ideas. In the Explore Activity, students use decimal grids to model and solve decimal division. In Examples 1 and 2, students use math symbols to represent decimal division. Thus, students are learning and using multiple representations to represent decimal division.

Math Background

The Hindu-Arabic numerals 1 through 9 that we use today are based on older symbols known to have been used as early as 250 B.C.E. By 595 C.E., all numbers were written using the symbols for 1 through 9. The place in which each symbol was written gave the number its value. The symbol that was written in an empty place, zero, was believed to have been first used in 876 C.E.

EXAMPLE 2

Connect Vocabulary ELL

Remind students that a **power of 10** is a number such as 10, 100, 1,000, or 10,000 that results from 10 being multiplied by itself.

Questioning Strategies CC Mathematical Practices

• How is the procedure for finding $3.25 \div 0.5$ different from the procedure for finding $3.25 \div 5$? For $3.25 \div 5$, you can divide as with whole numbers and place the decimal point in the quotient. For $3.25 \div 0.5$, it is necessary to multiply the divisor and dividend by the same power of 10 before doing the division.

• How do you know what power of ten to multiply the divisor and dividend by? Multiply both numbers by the least power of ten that will make the divisor a whole number.

Focus on Critical Thinking CC Mathematical Practices

Point out to students that multiplying the divisor and the dividend by the same number does not change the quotient. For example, $42 \div 6 = 7$; $420 \div 60 = 7$; $4,200 \div 600 = 7$.

YOUR TURN

Avoid Common Errors

Some students may position the decimal point in the quotient before multiplying the divisor and dividend by a power of ten. Remind them that the decimal point is positioned only after multiplication by a power of ten has occurred.

Elaborate

Talk About It
Summarize the Lesson

Ask: How do you divide decimals? To divide a decimal by a whole number, divide as with two whole numbers and place the decimal point in the quotient. To divide a decimal by a decimal, multiply the divisor and the dividend by the same power of 10 to make the divisor an a whole number, divide as with whole numbers, and then place the decimal point in the quotient.

GUIDED PRACTICE

Engage with the Whiteboard

For Exercises 2–3, have a student move the decimal point the same number of places in the divisor and the dividend. Then have another student place the decimal point in its correct position above the long division bar before any division steps are performed.

Avoid Common Errors

Exercises 2–4 Some students may position the decimal point in the quotient before multiplying the divisor and the dividend by a power of ten. Remind them that the decimal point is positioned only after multiplication by a power of ten has occurred.

Exercises 7–14 Some students interchange the divisor and the dividend when translating a problem of the form $a \div b$ into the form $b\overline{)a}$. Remind them that the number after the division sign, $\div$, or the number outside the division house, $\overline{)}$, is always the divisor.

Dividing a Decimal by a Decimal

When dividing a decimal by a decimal, first change the divisor to a whole number by multiplying by a power of 10. Then multiply the dividend by the same power of 10.

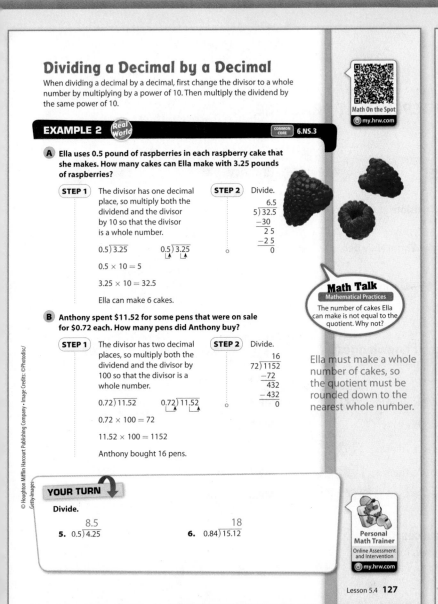

EXAMPLE 2 *Real World*

COMMON CORE 6.NS.3

A Ella uses 0.5 pound of raspberries in each raspberry cake that she makes. How many cakes can Ella make with 3.25 pounds of raspberries?

STEP 1 The divisor has one decimal place, so multiply both the dividend and the divisor by 10 so that the divisor is a whole number.

$$0.5\overline{)3.25}$$

$$0.5 \times 10 = 5$$

$$3.25 \times 10 = 32.5$$

Ella can make 6 cakes.

STEP 2 Divide.

```
      6.5
  5)32.5
    -30
      2 5
     -2 5
        0
```

B Anthony spent $11.52 for some pens that were on sale for $0.72 each. How many pens did Anthony buy?

STEP 1 The divisor has two decimal places, so multiply both the dividend and the divisor by 100 so that the divisor is a whole number.

$$0.72\overline{)11.52}$$

$$0.72 \times 100 = 72$$

$$11.52 \times 100 = 1152$$

Anthony bought 16 pens.

STEP 2 Divide.

```
      16
 72)1152
    -72
    432
   -432
      0
```

Math Talk
Mathematical Practices

The number of cakes Ella can make is not equal to the quotient. Why not?

Ella must make a whole number of cakes, so the quotient must be rounded down to the nearest whole number.

YOUR TURN

Divide.

5. $0.5\overline{)4.25}$ → 8.5

6. $0.84\overline{)15.12}$ → 18

Math On the Spot
my.hrw.com

Personal Math Trainer
Online Assessment and Intervention
my.hrw.com

Guided Practice

Divide. (Explore Activity, Examples 1 and 2)

1. $4\overline{)29.5}$ __7.375__

2. $3.1\overline{)10.261}$ __3.31__

3. $2.4\overline{)16.8}$ __7__

4. $0.96\overline{)0.144}$ __0.15__

5. $38.5 \div 0.5 =$ __77__

6. $23.85 \div 9 =$ __2.65__

7. $5.6372 \div 0.17 =$ __33.16__

8. $8.19 \div 4.2 =$ __1.95__

9. $66.5 \div 3.5 =$ __19__

10. $0.234 \div 0.78 =$ __0.3__

11. $78.74 \div 12.7 =$ __6.2__

12. $36.45 \div 0.09 =$ __405__

13. $90 \div 0.36 =$ __250__

14. $18.88 \div 1.6 =$ __11.8__

15. Corrine has 9.6 pounds of trail mix to divide into 12 bags. How many pounds of trail mix will go in each bag? __0.8 pound__

16. Michael paid $11.48 for sliced cheese at the deli counter. The cheese cost $3.28 per pound. How much cheese did Michael buy? __3.5 pounds__

17. A four-person relay team completed a race in 72.4 seconds. On average, what was each runner's time? __18.1 seconds__

18. Elizabeth has a piece of ribbon that is 4.5 meters long. She wants to cut it into pieces that are 0.25 meter long. How many pieces of ribbon will she have? __18__

19. Lisa paid $43.95 for 16.1 gallons of gasoline. What was the cost per gallon, rounded to the nearest hundredth? __$2.73 per gallon__

20. One inch is equivalent to 2.54 centimeters. How many inches are there in 50.8 centimeters? __20 inches__

? ESSENTIAL QUESTION CHECK-IN

21. When you are dividing two decimals, how can you check whether you have divided the decimals correctly?

Multiply the divisor by the quotient. The product should match the dividend.

DIFFERENTIATE INSTRUCTION

Visual Cues

If students are having difficulty keeping division problems organized, encourage them to use graph paper for setting up and working on the problems. Have them write each digit in a separate square to maintain the alignment of columns and rows.

Students also can use lined paper turned sideways to help align the digits correctly if they don't have graph paper.

Kinesthetic Experience

Have students work in groups of three or four. Give each group a set of index cards labeled 0–9. Have the groups mix and place the cards face down in a pile. Students should then draw three cards to make a dividend and two cards to make a divisor. Have students take turns determining where to place decimal points in each number and then do the division individually. Group members should compare answers and work a problem together if they do not get the same quotient.

Additional Resources

Differentiated Instruction includes:
- Reading Strategies
- Success for English Learners **ELL**
- Reteach
- Challenge **PRE-AP**

Divide.

1. $7\overline{)0.91}$

2. $0.6\overline{)1.38}$

3. $0.08\overline{)9.6}$

4. $33.475 \div 0.65$

5. $2.46 \div 12.3$

6. Corrine bought 8.4 pounds of almonds. She divided them into 30 snack-size bags. How many pounds are in each bag?

Lesson Quiz example available online

⊙ my.hrw.com

Answers

1. 0.13
2. 2.3
3. 120
4. 51.5
5. 0.2
6. 0.28 pound

Evaluate

GUIDED AND INDEPENDENT PRACTICE

COMMON CORE **6.NS.3**

Concepts & Skills	Practice
Explore Activity Modeling Decimal Division	Exercises 1, 6
Example 1 Dividing Decimals by Whole Numbers	Exercises 1, 6, 15, 22–23
Example 2 Dividing a Decimal by a Decimal	Exercises 2–5, 7–14, 16–20, 24–26, 28–31

Exercise	Depth of Knowledge (D.O.K.)	COMMON CORE Mathematical Practices
22–24	**2** Skills/Concepts	**MP.4** Modeling
25	**3** Strategic Thinking H.O.T.	**MP.3** Logic
26–31	**2** Skills/Concepts	**MP.5** Using Tools
32	**3** Strategic Thinking H.O.T.	**MP.4** Modeling
33	**3** Strategic Thinking H.O.T.	**MP.7** Using Structure
34	**3** Strategic Thinking H.O.T.	**MP.8** Patterns

Additional Resources

Differentiated Instruction includes:

• Leveled Practice Worksheets

5.4 Independent Practice

 COMMON CORE 6.NS.3

Personal Math Trainer
Online Assessment and Intervention
my.hrw.com

Use the table for 22 and 23.

Custom Printing Costs				
Quantity	25	50	75	100
Mugs	$107.25	$195.51	$261.75	$329.00
T-shirts	$237.50	$441.00	$637.50	$829.00

22. What is the price per mug for 25 coffee mugs? _____ $4.29

23. Find the price per T-shirt for 75 T-shirts. _____ $8.50

A movie rental website charges $5.00 per month for membership and $1.25 per movie.

24. How many movies did Andrew rent this month if this month's bill was $16.25? _____ 9 movies

25. Marissa has $18.50 this month to spend on movie rentals.

   a. How many movies can she view this month? _____ 10 movies

   b. **Critique Reasoning** Marisa thinks she can afford 11 movies in one month. What mistake could she be making?

   She could be rounding 10.8 up to 11, but she doesn't have enough money for 11 movies.

Victoria went shopping for ingredients to make a stew. The table shows the weight and the cost of each of the ingredients that she bought.

Ingredient	Weight (in pounds)	Cost
Potatoes	6.3	$7.56
Carrots	8.5	$15.30
Beef	4	$9.56
Bell peppers	2.50	$1.25

26. What is the price for one pound of bell peppers? _____ $0.50

27. Which ingredient costs the most per pound? _____ beef

28. **What If?** If carrots were $0.50 less per pound, how much would Victoria have paid for 8.5 pounds of carrots? _____ $11.05

29. Brenda is planning her birthday party. She wants to have 10.92 liters of punch, 6.5 gallons of ice cream, 3.9 pounds of fudge, and 25 guests at the birthday party.

   a. Brenda and each guest drink the same amount of punch. How many liters of punch will each person drink? _____ 0.42

   b. Brenda and each guest eat the same amount of ice cream. How many gallons of ice cream will each person eat? _____ 0.25

   c. Brenda and each guest eat the same amount of fudge. How many pounds of fudge will each person eat? _____ 0.15

To make costumes for a play, Cassidy needs yellow and white fabric that she will cut into strips. The table shows how many yards of each fabric she needs, and how much she will pay for those yards.

Fabric	Yards	Cost
Yellow	12.8	$86.40
White	9.5	$45.60

30. Which costs more per yard, the yellow fabric or the white fabric? _____ yellow

31. Cassidy wants to cut the yellow fabric into strips that are 0.3 yards wide. How many strips of yellow fabric can Cassidy make? _____ 42

H.O.T. FOCUS ON HIGHER ORDER THINKING

32. **Problem Solving** Eight friends purchase various supplies for a camping trip and agree to share the total cost equally. They spend $85.43 on food, $32.75 on water, and $239.66 on other items. How much does each person owe? _____ $44.73

33. **Analyze Relationships** Constance is saving money to buy a new bicycle that costs $195.75. She already has $40 saved and plans to save $8 each week. How many weeks will it take her to save enough money to purchase the bicycle? _____ 20 weeks

34. **Represent Real-World Problems** A grocery store sells twelve bottles of water for $13.80. A convenience store sells ten bottles of water for $11.80. Which store has the better buy? Explain.

The grocery store; each bottle costs $1.15, while each bottle at the convenience store costs $1.18.

EXTEND THE MATH **PRE-AP**
Activity available online my.hrw.com

Activity Write a decimal division word problem with no hundredths.

Sample answer: Lana uses 0.2 pounds of peaches in each mini-pie she makes. How many mini-pies can she make with 2.5 pounds of peaches? 2.5 ÷ 0.2 = 12.5, so she can make 12 mini-pies.

Decide whether or not grids divided into tenths would be useful to help solve it. Explain your reasoning.

Grids divided into tenths would be useful to represent this kind of problem, since there are no hundredths in the dividend or the divisor.

Common Core Standards

The student is expected to:

 The Number System—6.NS.3

Fluently add, subtract, multiply, and divide multi-digit decimals using the standard algorithm for each operation.

Mathematical Practices

 MP.1 Problem Solving

ADDITIONAL EXAMPLE 1
Leila earned $40.50 raking leaves in two days? She worked 2.75 hours yesterday and 1.75 hours today. If Leila was paid the same amount for every hour she works, how much did she earn per hour? $9 per hour

 Interactive Whiteboard
Interactive example available online

 my.hrw.com

ADDITIONAL EXAMPLE 2
William wants to buy a new skateboard that costs $48.80. He has saved $\frac{1}{4}$ of the amount necessary. How much money has he saved? $12.20

 Interactive Whiteboard
Interactive example available online

 my.hrw.com

Engage

ESSENTIAL QUESTION

How can you solve problems involving multiplication and division of fractions and decimals? Sample answer: First, write both numbers in the same form, either fractions or decimals. Then multiply or divide the numbers.

Motivate the Lesson
Ask: Suppose you are buying party favors for a birthday party and you have $25.50 to spend. If each favor cost $1.50 how many favors can you buy? Begin Example 1 to see how to divide decimals to find out.

Explore

Engage with the Whiteboard
Using a visual model may help students remember how to find fraction and decimal equivalents. Draw a number line from −5 to 5 on the whiteboard. Plot some common fractions and decimals, such as −0.20, 0.25, $-\frac{1}{3}$, $\frac{1}{2}$, −0.5, $\frac{3}{4}$, $1\frac{1}{2}$, and $-2\frac{1}{4}$. Then ask students to write the decimal or fraction equivalent for each rational number.

Explain

EXAMPLE 1

Focus on Math Connections
Remind students that when the divisor is a decimal, they should multiply both the divisor and the dividend by the same power of ten to make the divisor a whole number.

Questioning Strategies CC Mathematical Practices
• In Formulate a Plan, why is it necessary to add 2.5 and 4.25 before dividing? To find Naomi's hour rate, you need to divide by the total number of hours she worked.

YOUR TURN

Avoid Common Errors
Some students interchange the divisor and dividend when translating a problem in the form $a \div b$ into the form $b\overline{)a}$. Remind students that the number after the division sign, ÷, or the number outside the division house, $\overline{)}$, is always the divisor.

EXAMPLE 2

Connect Vocabulary ELL
Discuss how a **multipart question** is a question with related parts, such as an exercise with parts labeled A and B. Point out that since Roz got $\frac{1}{2}$ of the parts correct, the question must have had an even number of parts, such as 2 or 4.

Questioning Strategies CC Mathematical Practices
• How could you check to if your answer is reasonable? Round 37.5 to 38. Half of 38 is 19, so 18.75 is a reasonable answer.

YOUR TURN

Questioning Strategies CC Mathematical Practices
• Why might it be practical to use decimals? Money is usually expressed as decimals.

LESSON 5.5 Applying Operations with Rational Numbers

COMMON CORE 6.NS.3
Fluently add, subtract, multiply, and divide multi-digit decimals....

? ESSENTIAL QUESTION How can you solve problems involving multiplication and division of fractions and decimals?

Interpreting a Word Problem

When you solve a word problem involving rational numbers, you often need to think about the problem to decide which operations to use.

EXAMPLE 1 Problem Solving
COMMON CORE 6.NS.3

Naomi earned $54 mowing lawns in two days. She worked 2.5 hours yesterday and 4.25 hours today. If Naomi was paid the same amount for every hour she works, how much did she earn per hour?

Analyze Information

Identify the important information.
• Naomi made $54 mowing lawns.
• Naomi worked 2.5 hours yesterday and 4.25 hours today.
• You are asked to find how much she earned per hour.

Formulate a Plan

• The total amount she earned divided by the total hours she worked gives the amount she earns per hour.
• Use the expression $54 \div (2.5 + 4.25)$ to find the amount she earned per hour.

Solve

Follow the order of operations.

$(2.5 + 4.25) = 6.75$ Add inside parentheses.

$54 \div 6.75 = 8$ Divide.

Naomi earned $8 per hour mowing lawns.

Justify and Evaluate

You added 2.5 and 4.25 first to find the total number of hours worked. Then you divided 54 by the sum to find the amount earned per hour.

Lesson 5.5 **131**

Personal Math Trainer Online Assessment and Intervention · my.hrw.com

Math On the Spot · my.hrw.com

YOUR TURN

1. Casey buys 6.2 yards of blue fabric and 5.4 yards of red fabric. If the blue and red fabric cost the same amount per yard, and Casey pays $58 for all of the fabric, what is the cost per yard?

$5 per yard

Converting Fractions and Decimals to Solve Problems

Recall that you can use a number line to find equivalent fractions and decimals. If a fraction and a decimal are equivalent, they are represented by the same point on a number line.

EXAMPLE 2 Real World
COMMON CORE 6.NS.3

Each part of a multipart question on a test is worth the same number of points. The whole question is worth 37.5 points. Roz got $\frac{1}{2}$ of the parts of a question correct. How many points did Roz receive?

Solution 1

STEP 1 Convert the decimal to a fraction greater than 1.

$\frac{1}{2} \times 37.5 = \frac{1}{2} \times \frac{75}{2}$ Write 37.5 as $37\frac{1}{2}$, or $\frac{75}{2}$.

STEP 2 Multiply. Write the product in simplest form.

$\frac{1}{2} \times \frac{75}{2} = \frac{75}{4} = 18\frac{3}{4}$ Roz received $18\frac{3}{4}$ points.

Solution 2

STEP 1 Convert the fraction to a decimal.

$\frac{1}{2} \times 37.5 = 0.5 \times 37.5$

STEP 2 Multiply.

$0.5 \times 37.5 = 18.75$ Roz received 18.75 points.

Yes; $18\frac{3}{4}$ and 18.75 are equivalent.

Math Talk Mathematical Practices
Do the solutions give the same result? Explain.

YOUR TURN

2. The bill for a pizza was $14.50. Charles paid for $\frac{3}{5}$ of the bill. Show two ways to find how much he paid.

He paid $\frac{29}{2} \times \frac{3}{5} = 8\frac{7}{10}$ dollars or $14.5 \times 0.6 = $8.70.

132 Unit 2

DIFFERENTIATE INSTRUCTION

Number Sense

Students often know common decimal and fractional equivalents. However, decimals greater than one can be confusing. Point out that the digits to the *left* of the decimal are the whole-number part of the mixed-number equivalent, while the digits to the *right* are the fractional part of the mixed-number equivalent.

$$12.75 = 12\frac{3}{4}$$
$$-53.60 = -53\frac{3}{5}$$

Kinesthetic Experience

Have students work in groups of three or four. Give each group a set of index cards labeled 0–9. Have the groups mix and place the cards face down in a pile. Students should then draw three cards to make a dividend and two cards to make a divisor. Have students take turns determining where to place the decimal points in each number and then do the division individually. Group members should compare answers and work a problem together if they do not all get the same quotient.

Additional Resources

Differentiated Instruction includes:
• Reading Strategies
• Success for English Learners **ELL**
• Reteach
• Challenge **PRE-AP**

Applying Operations with Rational Numbers **132**

Elaborate

Talk About It
Summarize the Lesson

 Ask: How can you solve problems that include both fractions and decimals? Convert either the fractions or the decimals so that all the numbers are expressed in the same form. Then perform the necessary computations according to the order of operations.

GUIDED PRACTICE

Engage with the Whiteboard

 For Exercises 1–2, have students identify the important information and write an expression to represent each situation on the whiteboard. Then have the students solve the problems using the order of operations.

5.5 LESSON QUIZ

6.NS.3

Elaine bought $3\frac{4}{5}$ pounds of apples for $1.99 per pound, $\frac{3}{4}$ pound of pears for $2.25 per pound, and $3\frac{2}{3}$ pounds of bananas for $1.75 per pound.

1. What did Elaine spend on apples?

2. What did Elaine spend on pears?

3. What did Elaine spend on bananas?

4. If Elaine brought a $20 bill to the store, how much change did she get?

5. Orlando earned $92.25 washing windows on the weekend. He worked 3.5 hours on Saturday and 6.75 hours on Sunday. If Orlando charges the same amount for every hour he works, how much does he earn per hour?

Lesson Quiz example available online

Answers
1. $7.56   **4.** $4.33

2. $1.69   **5.** $9 per hour

3. $6.42

Evaluate

GUIDED AND INDEPENDENT PRACTICE

6.NS.3

Concepts & Skills	Practice
Example 1 Interpreting a Word Problem	Exercise 1
Example 2 Converting Fractions and Decimals to Solve Problems	Exercise 2

Exercise	Depth of Knowledge (D.O.K.)	COMMON CORE Mathematical Practices
3–7	**2** Skills/Concepts	**MP.4** Modeling
8	**3** Strategic Thinking **H.O.T.**	**MP.2** Reasoning
9–10	**2** Skills/Concepts	**MP.1** Problem Solving
11	**3** Strategic Thinking **H.O.T.**	**MP.4** Modeling
12	**3** Strategic Thinking **H.O.T.**	**MP.3** Logic
13	**3** Strategic Thinking **H.O.T.**	**MP.2** Reasoning

Additional Resources
Differentiated Instruction includes:
• Leveled Practice worksheets

CC CLUSTER CONNECTION **Exercises 12–13** combine concepts from the Common Core cluster "Compute fluently with multi-digit numbers and find common factors and multiples."

5.5 Guided Practice

1. Bob and Cheryl are taking a road trip that is 188.3 miles. Bob drove $\frac{5}{7}$ of the total distance. How many miles did Bob drive? (Example 1)

$134\frac{1}{2}$ miles

2. The winner of a raffle will receive $\frac{3}{4}$ of the $530.40 raised from raffle ticket sales. How much money will the winner get? (Example 2)

$397.80

5.5 Independent Practice

COMMON CORE 6.NS.3

Personal Math Trainer
Online Assessment and Intervention
my.hrw.com

3. Chanasia has 8.75 gallons of paint. She wants to use $\frac{2}{5}$ of the paint to paint her living room. How many gallons of paint will Chanasia use?

$3\frac{1}{2}$ gallons

4. Harold bought 3 pounds of red apples and 4.2 pounds of green apples from a grocery store, where both kinds of apples are $1.75 a pound. How much did Harold spend on apples?

$12.60

Samuel and Jason sell cans to a recycling center that pays $0.40 per pound of cans. The table shows the number of pounds of cans that they sold for several days.

Day	Samuel's cans (pounds)	Jason's cans (pounds)
Monday	16.2	11.5
Tuesday	11.8	10.7
Wednesday	12.5	7.1

5. Samuel wants to use his earnings from Monday and Tuesday to buy some batteries that cost $5.60 each. How many batteries can Samuel buy? Show your work.

$(16.2 + 11.8) \times 0.40 = 11.2; 11.2 \div 5.60 = 2$ batteries

6. Jason wants to use his earnings from Monday and Tuesday for online movie rentals. The movies cost $2.96 each to rent. How many movies can Jason rent? Show your work.

$(11.5 + 10.7) \times 0.40 = 8.88; 8.88 \div 2.96 = 3$ movies

7. **Multistep** Samuel and Jason spend $\frac{3}{4}$ of their combined earnings from Wednesday to buy a gift. How much do they spend? Is there enough left over from Wednesday's earnings to buy a card that costs $3.25? Explain.

$5.88; No. They earned $7.84 on Wednesday.

$7.84 - 5.88 = 1.96$, so they don't have enough money.

8. **Multiple Representations** Give an example of a problem that could be solved using the expression $9.5 \times (8 + 12.5)$. Solve your problem.

Sample problem: Nestor charged $9.50 an hour to rake leaves. He worked 8 hours one week and 12.5 hours the next. How much did Nestor earn raking leaves?

Answer: He earned $194.75.

Tony and Alice are trying to reduce the amount of television they watch. For every hour they watch television, they have to put $2.50 into savings. The table shows how many hours of television Tony and Alice have watched in the past two months.

	Hours watched in February	Hours watched in March
Tony	35.4	18.2
Alice	21.8	26.6

9. Tony wants to use his savings at the end of March to buy video games. The games cost $35.75 each. How many games can Tony buy?

3 games

10. Alice wants to use her savings at the end of the two months to buy concert tickets. If the tickets cost $17.50 each, how many can she buy?

6 tickets

H.O.T. FOCUS ON HIGHER ORDER THINKING

Work Area

11. **Represent Real-World Problems** A caterer prepares three times as many pizzas as she usually prepares for a large party. The caterer usually prepares 5 pizzas. The caterer also estimates that each party guest will eat $\frac{1}{3}$ of a pizza. Write an expression that represents this situation. How many party guests will the pizzas serve?

$(5 \times 3) \div \frac{1}{3}; 45$

Nadia charges $7.50 an hour for babysitting. She babysits 18.5 hours the first week of the month and 20 hours the second week of the month.

12. **Explain the Error** To find her total earnings for those two weeks, Nadia writes $7.5 \times 18.5 + 20 = 158.75. Explain her error. Show the correct solution.

She should have used parentheses to group the addition to find the total number of hours first.

$7.5 \times (18.5 + 20) = 7.5 \times 38.5 = 288.75

13. **What If?** Suppose Nadia raises her rate by $0.75 an hour. How many hours would she need to work to earn the same amount of money she made in the first two weeks of the month? Explain.

$35; $7.50 + $0.75 = $8.25; $288.75 \div $8.25 = 35$

EXTEND THE MATH PRE-AP
Activity available online my.hrw.com

Activity Gina ate $\frac{2}{3}$ cup of lowfat yogurt. The serving size listed on the container is 6 ounces, or $\frac{3}{4}$ cup. How many servings did Gina eat? There are 100 calories in one serving. How many calories did Gina eat?

Gina ate $\frac{8}{9}$ of a serving, which is about 88.9 calories.

Ready to Go On?

Assess Mastery

Use the assessment on this page to determine if students have mastered the concepts and standards covered in this module.

 **Response to Intervention**

Personal Math Trainer
Online Assessment and Intervention
⏻ my.hrw.com

Intervention	Enrichment

Access Ready to Go On? assessment online, and receive instant scoring, feedback, and customized intervention or enrichment.

Online and Print Resources

Differentiated Instruction
• Reteach worksheets
• Reading Strategies **ELL**
• Success for English Learners **ELL**

Differentiated Instruction
• Challenge worksheets **PRE-AP**
• Extend the Math **PRE-AP** Lesson Activities in TE

Additional Resources

Assessment Resources includes:
• Leveled Module Quizzes

MODULE QUIZ

Ready to Go On?

Personal Math Trainer
Online Assessment and Intervention
my.hrw.com

5.1 Dividing Whole Numbers

1. Landon is building new bookshelves for his bookstore's new mystery section. Each shelf can hold 34 books. There are 1,265 mystery books. How many shelves will he need to build? _____ 38 _____

5.2 Adding and Subtracting Decimals

2. On Saturday Keisha ran 3.218 kilometers. On Sunday she ran 2.41 kilometers. How much farther did she run on Saturday than on Sunday? _____ 0.808 kilometers

5.3 Multiplying Decimals

3. Marta walked at 3.9 miles per hour for 0.72 hours. How far did she walk? _____ 2.808 miles

Multiply.

4. 0.07×1.22 _____ 0.0854 _____ **5.** 4.7×2.65 _____ 12.455

5.4 Dividing Decimals

Divide.

6. $64 \div 0.4$ _____ 160 _____ **7.** $4.7398 \div 0.26$ _____ 18.23

8. $26.73 \div 9$ _____ 2.97 _____ **9.** $4 \div 3.2$ _____ 1.25

5.5 Applying Multiplication and Division of Rational Numbers

10. Doors for the small cabinets are 11.5 inches long. Doors for the large cabinets are 2.3 times as long as the doors for the small cabinets. How many large doors can be cut from a board that is $10\frac{1}{2}$ feet long? _____ 4 doors

❓ ESSENTIAL QUESTION

11. Describe a real-world situation that could be modeled by dividing two rational numbers.
Sample answer: Finding how many $\frac{1}{4}$ cup servings of rice are in a 4.75 cup container.

Module 5 **135**

© Houghton Mifflin Harcourt Publishing Company

Common Core Standards

Lesson	Exercises	Common Core Standards
5.1	1	**6.NS.2**
5.2	2	**6.NS.3**
5.3	3–5	**6.NS.3**
5.4	6–9	**6.NS.3**
5.5	10	**6.NS.3**

Assessment Readiness

Assessment Readiness Tip Students can use estimation to eliminate some or all of the answer choices.

Item 2 0.4 is close to 0.5, and 4.2 is close to 4. The answer should be approximately 0.5 × 4 = 2. Students can eliminate choices B, C, and D.

Item 7 0.55 is close to 0.5, and 1.4 is close is 1.5. Keri walks approximately 0.5 × .5 + 0.75 × 2 = 2.5 + 1.5 = 4 km per week. Students can eliminate choices A and D.

Avoid Common Errors

Item 3 Students may make the mistake of multiplying the two quantities instead of dividing them. Remind them that although they must multiply the number of pounds by the price per pound to find the total cost, they must do the opposite to find the number of pounds purchased.

Item 8 Students may read the last question quickly and may think the question refers to the unit price and who paid more per candle rather than realize the difference asked for is the difference between two amounts. Remind them to read each part of the question carefully to be sure what each step requires them to do.

Additional Resources

Personal Math Trainer

Online Assessment and Intervention

my.hrw.com

MODULE 5 MIXED REVIEW
COMMON CORE
Assessment Readiness

Personal Math Trainer
Online Assessment and Intervention
my.hrw.com

Selected Response

1. Delia has 493 stamps in her stamp collection. She can put 16 stamps on each page of an album. How many pages can she fill completely?

   (A) 30 pages   (C) 31 pages
   (B) 32 pages   (D) 33 pages

2. Sumeet uses 0.4 gallon of gasoline each hour mowing lawns. How much gas does he use in 4.2 hours?

   (A) 1.68 gallons
   (B) 3.8 gallons
   (C) 13 gallons
   (D) 16 gallons

3. Sharon spent $3.45 on sunflower seeds. The price of sunflower seeds is $0.89 per pound. How many pounds of sunflower seeds did Sharon buy?

   (A) 3.07 pounds
   (B) 3.88 pounds
   (C) 4.15 pounds
   (D) 4.34 pounds

4. How many 0.4-liter glasses of water does it take to fill up a 3.4-liter pitcher?

   (A) 1.36 glasses   (C) 8.2 glasses
   (B) 3.8 glasses   (D) 8.5 glasses

5. Each paper clip is $\frac{3}{4}$ of an inch long and costs $0.02. Exactly enough paper clips are laid end to end to have a total length of 36 inches. What is the total cost of these paper clips?

   (A) $0.36   (C) $0.96
   (B) $0.54   (D) $1.20

6. Nelson Middle School raised $19,950 on ticket sales for its carnival fundraiser last year at $15 per ticket. If the school sells the same number of tickets this year but charges $20 per ticket, how much money will the school make?

   (A) $20,600   (C) $26,600
   (B) $21,600   (D) $30,600

7. Keri walks her dog every morning. The length of the walk is 0.55 kilometer on each weekday. On each weekend day, the walk is 1.4 times as long as a walk on a weekday. How many kilometers does Keri walk in one week?

   (A) 2.75 kilometers
   (B) 3.85 kilometers
   (C) 4.29 kilometers
   (D) 5.39 kilometers

Mini-Task

8. To prepare for a wedding, Aiden bought 60 candles. He paid $0.37 for each candle. His sister bought 170 candles at a sale where she paid $0.05 less for each candle than Aiden did.

   a. How much did Aiden spend on candles?
      $22.20

   b. How much did Aiden's sister spend on candles?
      $54.40

   c. Who spent more on candles? How much more?
      Aiden's sister; $32.20 more

Common Core Standards

Items	Grade 6 Standards	Mathematical Practices
1*	6.NS.2	MP.4
2	6.NS.3	MP.4
3	6.NS.3	MP.4
4	6.NS.3	MP.4
5	6.NS.3	MP.4
6	6.NS.2	MP.4
7	6.NS.3	MP.4
8	6.NS.3	MP.4

* Item integrates mixed review concepts from previous modules.

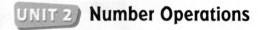

Study Guide Review

Vocabulary Development

Integrating Language Arts

Encourage students to practice using the unit vocabulary as they talk and write about mathematics. Understanding vocabulary will aid their understanding of the concepts.

 ELA-Literacy.RST.6-8.4 Determine the meaning of symbols, key terms, and other domain-specific words and phrases as they are used in a specific scientific or technical context relevant to grades 6–8 texts and topics.

MODULE 4 Operations with Fractions

 6.NS.1, 6.NS.4

Key Concepts

• The product of two proper fractions is less than each of the fractions. *(Lesson 4.1)*
• When multiplying mixed numbers, rewrite mixed numbers as fractions greater than 1 before multiplying numerators and denominators. *(Lessons 4.1, 4.2)*
• To find the reciprocal of a fraction, switch the numerator and the denominator. *(Lesson 4.3)*
• To divide fractions and mixed numbers, write any mixed numbers as fractions greater than 1, find the reciprocal of the second fraction, and multiply the numerators and denominators. *(Lessons 4.3, 4.4)*

MODULE 5 Operations with Decimals

6.NS.2, 6.NS.3

Key Concepts

• When a quotient is not a whole number, the question you are answering or the problem you are solving will give you a clue about what the remainder means. *(Lesson 5.1)*
• If you can add and subtract whole numbers, you can add and subtract decimals. Remember to pay attention to place value and line up the decimals. *(Lesson 5.2)*
• The number of decimal places in the product of decimals is the sum of the decimal places in the factors. *(Lesson 5.3)*
• To divide a decimal by a decimal, multiply both the divisor and the dividend by a power of 10 to make the divisor a whole number. *(Lesson 5.4)*
• To multiply or divide a fraction by a decimal, write both as fractions or as decimals. *(Lesson 5.5)*

Study Guide Review

MODULE 4 Operations with Fractions

Key Vocabulary
reciprocals (recíprocos)

? ESSENTIAL QUESTION

How can you use operations with fractions to solve real-world problems?

EXAMPLE 1

Add.

$\frac{7}{9} + \frac{5}{12}$ — The LCM of 9 and 12 is 36.

$\frac{7 \times 4}{9 \times 4} + \frac{5 \times 3}{12 \times 3}$ — Use the LCM to make fractions with common denominators.

$\frac{28}{36} + \frac{15}{36} = \frac{43}{36}$ — Simplify.

$\frac{43}{36} = 1\frac{7}{36}$

Subtract.

$\frac{9}{10} - \frac{5}{6}$ — The LCM of 10 and 6 is 30.

$\frac{9 \times 3}{10 \times 3} - \frac{5 \times 5}{6 \times 5}$ — Use the LCM to make fractions with common denominators.

$\frac{27}{30} - \frac{25}{30} = \frac{2}{30}$ — Simplify.

$\frac{2}{30} = \frac{1}{15}$

EXAMPLE 2

Multiply.

A. $\frac{4}{5} \times \frac{1}{8}$

$\frac{4 \times 1}{5 \times 8} = \frac{4}{40}$ — Multiply numerators. Multiply denominators.

$\frac{4 \div 4}{40 \div 4} = \frac{1}{10}$ — Simplify by dividing by the GCF.

B. $2\frac{1}{4} \times \frac{1}{5}$

$\frac{9}{4} \times \frac{1}{5}$ — Rewrite the mixed number as a fraction greater than 1.

$\frac{9 \times 1}{4 \times 5} = \frac{9}{20}$ — Multiply numerators. Multiply denominators.

EXAMPLE 3

Divide.

A. $\frac{2}{7} \div \frac{1}{2}$

$\frac{2}{7} \times \frac{2}{1}$ — Rewrite the problem as multiplication using the reciprocal of the second fraction.

$\frac{2 \times 2}{7 \times 1} = \frac{4}{7}$ — Multiply numerators. Multiply denominators.

B. $2\frac{1}{3} \div 1\frac{3}{4}$

$\frac{7}{3} \div \frac{7}{4}$ — Write both mixed numbers as improper fractions.

$\frac{\overset{1}{\cancel{7}} \times 4}{3 \times \cancel{7}_{1}} = \frac{4}{3}$ — Multiply by the reciprocal of the second fraction.

$1\frac{1}{3}$ — Simplify: $\frac{4}{3} = 1\frac{1}{3}$

EXERCISES

Add. Write the answer in simplest form. (Lesson 4.1)

1. $\frac{3}{8} + \frac{4}{5}$ ___ $1\frac{7}{40}$

2. $1\frac{9}{10} + \frac{3}{4}$ ___ $2\frac{13}{20}$

3. $\frac{2}{8} + \frac{6}{12}$ ___ $\frac{3}{4}$

Subtract. Write the answer in simplest form. (Lesson 4.1)

4. $1\frac{3}{7} - \frac{4}{5}$ ___ $\frac{22}{35}$

5. $\frac{7}{8} - \frac{5}{12}$ ___ $\frac{11}{24}$

6. $3\frac{5}{10} - \frac{4}{8}$ ___ 3

Multiply. Write the answer in simplest form. (Lesson 4.1)

7. $\frac{1}{7} \times \frac{4}{5}$ ___ $\frac{4}{35}$

8. $\frac{5}{6} \times \frac{2}{3}$ ___ $\frac{5}{9}$

9. $\frac{3}{7} \times \frac{14}{15}$ ___ $\frac{2}{5}$

10. $1\frac{1}{3} \times \frac{5}{8}$ ___ $\frac{5}{6}$

11. $1\frac{2}{9} \times 1\frac{1}{2}$ ___ $1\frac{5}{6}$

12. $2\frac{1}{7} \times 3\frac{2}{3}$ ___ $7\frac{6}{7}$

Divide. Write the answer in simplest form. (Lessons 4.2, 4.3)

13. $\frac{3}{7} \div \frac{2}{3}$ ___ $\frac{9}{14}$

14. $\frac{1}{8} \div \frac{3}{4}$ ___ $\frac{1}{6}$

15. $1\frac{1}{5} \div \frac{1}{4}$ ___ $4\frac{4}{5}$

16. On his twelfth birthday, Ben was $4\frac{3}{4}$ feet tall. On his thirteenth birthday, Ben was $5\frac{3}{8}$ feet tall. How much did Ben grow between his twelfth and thirteenth birthdays? (Lesson 4.1)

___ $\frac{5}{8}$ of a foot

17. Ron had 20 apples. He used $\frac{2}{5}$ of the apples to make pies. How many apples did Ron use for pies? (Lesson 4.4)

8 apples

18. The area of a rectangular garden is $38\frac{1}{4}$ square meters. The width of the garden is $4\frac{1}{2}$ meters. Find the length of the garden. (Lesson 4.4)

$8\frac{1}{2}$ meters

MODULE 5 Operations with Decimals

Key Vocabulary
order of operations (orden de las operaciones)

? ESSENTIAL QUESTION

How can you use operations with decimals to solve real-world problems?

EXAMPLE 1

To prepare for a race, Lloyd ran every day for two weeks. He ran a total of 67,592 meters. Lloyd ran the same distance every day. He took a two-day rest and then started running again. The first day after his rest, he ran the same distance plus 1,607.87 meters more. How far did Lloyd run that day?

Step 1 Divide to see how far Lloyd ran every day during the two weeks.

$14\overline{)67,592}$ $4,828$

Lloyd ran 4,828 meters a day.

Step 2 Add 1,607.87 to 4,828 to find out how far Lloyd ran the first day after his rest.

$\begin{array}{r} 1,607.87 \\ + 4,828.00 \\ \hline 6,435.87 \end{array}$

Lloyd ran 6,435.87 meters that day.

Unit 2 Performance Tasks

The Performance Tasks provide students with the opportunity to apply concepts from this unit in real-world problem situations.

CAREERS IN MATH

Chef In Performance Task Item 1, students can see how a chef uses mathematics on the job.

SCORING GUIDES FOR PERFORMANCE TASKS

1. MATHEMATICAL PRACTICES   **MP.4, MP.5**

Task	Possible Points (Total: 6)
a	**1 point** for correct answer: $1\frac{1}{2}$ servings
b	**1 point** for correct answer: $\frac{4}{3}$
c	**2 points** for correct answers: 1 pound chicken, $3\frac{1}{3}$ cups tomato sauce, $1\frac{1}{3}$ teaspoons oregano, $\frac{2}{3}$ teaspoon hot sauce
d	**2 points** for correct answer and explanation: No, he cannot measure these ingredients exactly, because neither $\frac{1}{2}$ nor $\frac{1}{4}$ will divide evenly into $1\frac{1}{3}$ or $\frac{2}{3}$.

2. MATHEMATICAL PRACTICES   **MP.2, MP.4**

Task	Possible Points (Total: 6)
a	**1 point** for the correct answer, and **1 point** for showing work: Height $= 1\frac{1}{2} \div 2\frac{1}{4} = \frac{3}{2} \cdot \frac{4}{9} = \frac{2}{3}$ yard
b	**1 point** for explanation: The area of one yellow rectangle is the width $\times$ height, and the height is $\frac{2}{3}$ yard, found in part **a**. **1 point** for finding the total area of the two yellow bars: Area $= 2 \cdot \frac{2}{3} \cdot \frac{3}{4} = 1$ square yard
c	**1 point** for finding the dimensions of the banner plus yellow bars: Width $= 2 \cdot \frac{3}{4} + 2\frac{1}{4} = \frac{6}{4} + \frac{9}{4} = \frac{15}{4} = 3\frac{3}{4}$ yards; Height $= \frac{2}{3}$ yard **1 point** for finding the area: Area $= 3\frac{3}{4} \times \frac{2}{3} = \frac{15}{4} \times \frac{2}{3} = \frac{5}{2} = 2\frac{1}{2}$ square yards

EXAMPLE 2

Rebecca bought 2.5 pounds of red apples. The apples cost $0.98 per pound. What was the total cost of Rebecca's apples?

$$
\begin{array}{r}
2.5 \quad \leftarrow \quad \text{1 decimal place} \\
\times\ .98 \quad \leftarrow\ +\text{2 decimal places} \\
\hline
200 \\
+\ 2250 \\
\hline
2.450 \quad \leftarrow \quad \text{3 decimal places}
\end{array}
$$

The apples cost $2.45.

EXAMPLE 3

Rashid spent $37.29 on gas for his car. Gas was $3.39 per gallon. How many gallons did Rashid purchase?

Step 1 The divisor has two decimal places, so multiply both the dividend and the divisor by 100 so that the divisor is a whole number:

$3.39\overline{)37.29}$ $339\overline{)3729}$

Step 2 Divide:

$$
\begin{array}{r}
11 \\
339\overline{)3729} \\
-339 \\
\hline
339 \\
-339 \\
\hline
0
\end{array}
$$

Rashid purchased 11 gallons of gas.

EXERCISES

Add. (Lesson 5.2)

1. $12.24 + 3.9$ __16.14__ **2.** $0.986 + 0.342$ __1.328__ **3.** $2.479 + 0.31$ __2.789__

Subtract. (Lesson 5.2)

4. $6.19 - 3.05$ __3.14__ **5.** $7.285 - 0.975$ __6.31__ **6.** $14.31 - 13.41$ __0.9__

Multiply. (Lesson 5.3)

7. $\begin{array}{r}12\\ \times 0.4\end{array}$ __4.8__ **8.** $\begin{array}{r}0.15\\ \times\ 9.1\end{array}$ __1.365__ **9.** $\begin{array}{r}3.12\\ \times 0.25\end{array}$ __0.78__

Divide. (Lessons 5.1, 5.4)

10. $78,974 \div 21$ __3,760 R14__ **11.** $19,975 \div 25$ __799__ **12.** $67,396 \div 123$ __547 R115__

13. $5\overline{)64.5}$ __12.9__ **14.** $0.6\overline{)25.2}$ __42__ **15.** $2.1\overline{)36.75}$ __17.5__

16. A pound of rice crackers costs $2.88. Matthew purchased $\frac{1}{4}$ pound of crackers. How much did he pay for the crackers? (Lesson 5.5) __$0.72__

---

1. **CAREERS IN MATH** | Chef | Chef Alonso is creating a recipe called Spicy Italian Chicken with the following ingredients: $\frac{3}{4}$ pound chicken, $2\frac{1}{2}$ cups tomato sauce, 1 teaspoon oregano, and $\frac{1}{2}$ teaspoon of his special hot sauce.

a. Chef Alonso wants each serving of the dish to include $\frac{1}{2}$ pound of chicken. How many $\frac{1}{2}$ pound servings does this recipe make?

$1\frac{1}{2}$ servings

b. What is the number Chef Alonso should multiply the amount of chicken by so that the recipe will make 2 full servings, each with $\frac{1}{2}$ pound of chicken?

$\frac{4}{3}$

c. Use the multiplier you found in part **b** to find the amount of all the ingredients in the new recipe.

1 pound chicken, $3\frac{1}{3}$ cups tomato sauce, $1\frac{1}{3}$ tsp oregano, $\frac{2}{3}$ tsp hot sauce

d. Chef Alonso only has three measuring spoons: 1 teaspoon, $\frac{1}{2}$ teaspoon, and $\frac{1}{4}$ teaspoon. Can he measure the new amounts of oregano and hot sauce exactly? Explain why or why not.

No; none of these teaspoon amounts divide evenly into $1\frac{1}{3}$ or $\frac{2}{3}$.

2. Amira is painting a rectangular banner $2\frac{1}{4}$ yards wide on a wall in the cafeteria. The banner will have a blue background. Amira has enough blue paint to cover $1\frac{1}{2}$ square yards of wall.

a. Find the height of the banner if Amira uses all of the blue paint. Show your work.

$\frac{2}{3}$ yd; $1\frac{1}{2} \div 2\frac{1}{4} = \frac{2}{3}$

b. The school colors are blue and yellow, so Amira wants to add yellow rectangles on the left and right sides of the blue rectangle. The yellow rectangles will each be $\frac{3}{4}$ yard wide and the same height as the blue rectangle. What will be the total area of the two yellow rectangles? Explain how you found your answer.

1 square yard; multiply the height of one rectangle by its width, then multiply the answer by 2.

c. What are the dimensions of the banner plus yellow rectangles? What is the total area? Show your work.

Width: $\frac{3}{4} + 2\frac{1}{4} + \frac{3}{4} = 3\frac{3}{4}$; Height: $\frac{2}{3}$ from part a; Area $= \frac{15}{4} \times \frac{2}{3} = \frac{5}{2} = 2\frac{1}{2}$ square yards

MIXED REVIEW

Assessment Readiness

Assessment Readiness Tip Students can highlight the last sentence to find the question being asked, then look back at the rest of the item to find the information needed to answer the question.

Item 1 Students may incorrectly stop solving this problem after dividing the total length by the length of each paper clip, which would lead them to choose answer choice B. Highlighting the last sentence helps them remember that they are looking for the cost, so they need to multiply 64 by $0.03 before answering.

Avoid Common Errors

Item 10 Some students may make mistakes when converting fractions in the mixed numbers to fractions with a common denominator. Remind students to multiply both the denominator and numerator.

Item 12 Because all three numbers are not carried out to the hundredths place, some students may make mistakes in addition. They may line up the numbers to the right. Remind them to line up the decimal points when adding.

Common Core Standards

Items	Grade 6 Standards	Mathematical Practices
1	6.NS.1	**MP.4** Modeling
2	6.NS.1	**MP.6** Precision
3	6.NS.1	**MP.4** Modeling
4	6.NS.3	**MP.4** Modeling
5*	6.NS.5	**MP.2** Reasoning
6*	6.NS.6a	**MP.2** Reasoning
7	6.NS.3	**MP.4** Modeling
8	6.NS.3	**MP.4** Modeling
9	6.NS.3	**MP.4** Modeling
10	6.NS.3	**MP.4** Modeling
11	6.NS.1	**MP.4** Modeling
12	6.NS.2	**MP.4** Modeling
13	6.NS.3	**MP.4** Modeling
14	6.NS.1, 6.NS.3	**MP.4** Modeling
15	6.NS.1, 6.NS.2, 6.NS.3	**MP.4** Modeling

* Item integrates mixed review concepts from previous modules or a previous course.

Assessment Readiness

Personal Math Trainer

Online Assessment and Intervention

my.hrw.com

Selected Response

1. Each paper clip is $\frac{7}{8}$ of an inch long and costs $0.03. Exactly enough paper clips are laid end to end to have a total length of 56 inches. What is the total cost of these paper clips?

Ⓐ $0.49   Ⓒ $1.47

Ⓑ $0.64   Ⓓ $1.92

2. Which of these is the same as $\frac{8}{9} \div \frac{2}{3}$?

Ⓐ $\frac{8}{9} \div \frac{3}{2}$ Ⓒ $\frac{8}{9} \times \frac{2}{3}$

Ⓑ $\frac{2}{3} \div \frac{8}{9}$ Ⓓ $\frac{8}{9} \times \frac{3}{2}$

3. A rectangular tabletop has a length of $4\frac{3}{4}$ feet and an area of $11\frac{7}{8}$ square feet. What is the width of the tabletop?

Ⓐ $1\frac{1}{16}$ feet

Ⓑ $2\frac{1}{2}$ feet

Ⓒ $4\frac{1}{4}$ feet

Ⓓ $8\frac{1}{2}$ feet

4. Dorothy types 120 words per minute. How many words does Dorothy type in 1.75 minutes?

Ⓐ 150 words

Ⓑ 180 words

Ⓒ 200 words

Ⓓ 210 words

5. What is the opposite of 17?

Ⓐ −17

Ⓑ $-\frac{1}{17}$

Ⓒ $\frac{1}{17}$

Ⓓ 17

6. What is the absolute value of −36?

Ⓐ −36

Ⓑ 0

Ⓒ 6

Ⓓ 36

7. Noelle has $\frac{5}{6}$ of a yard of purple ribbon and $\frac{9}{10}$ of a yard of pink ribbon. How much ribbon does she have altogether?

Ⓐ $1\frac{11}{15}$ yards   Ⓒ $2\frac{1}{5}$ yards

Ⓑ $1\frac{4}{5}$ yards   Ⓓ $1\frac{14}{16}$ yards

8. Apples are on sale for $1.20 a pound. Logan bought $\frac{3}{4}$ of a pound. How much money did he spend on apples?

Ⓐ $0.75   Ⓒ $0.90

Ⓑ $0.80   Ⓓ $1.00

9. Samantha bought 4.5 pounds of pears. Each pound cost $1.68. How much did Samantha spend in all?

Ⓐ $7.52   Ⓒ $8.40

Ⓑ $7.56   Ⓓ $75.60

10. Gillian earns $7.50 an hour babysitting on the weekends. Last week she babysat for 2.2 hours on Saturday and 3.5 hours on Sunday. How much did Gillian earn?

Ⓐ $4.25   Ⓒ $42.75

Ⓑ $40.25   Ⓓ $427.50

11. Luis made some trail mix. He mixed $4\frac{2}{3}$ cups of popcorn, $1\frac{1}{4}$ cups of peanuts, $1\frac{1}{3}$ cups of raisins, and $\frac{3}{4}$ cup of sunflower seeds. He gave 5 of his friends an equal amount of trail mix each. How much did each friend get?

Ⓐ $1\frac{2}{3}$ cups   Ⓒ $1\frac{3}{4}$ cups

Ⓑ $1\frac{2}{3}$ cups   Ⓓ 2 cups

12. Emily cycled 20.25 miles over 4 days last week. She cycled the same amount each day. How many miles did Emily cycle each day to the nearest hundredth?

Ⓐ 5.01 miles   Ⓒ 5.60 miles

Ⓑ 5.06 miles   Ⓓ 5.65 miles

13. Landon drove 103.5 miles on Tuesday, 320.75 miles on Wednesday, and 186.30 miles on Thursday. How far did Landon drive all three days combined?

Ⓐ 61.55 miles   Ⓒ 610.55 miles

Ⓑ 610.055 miles   Ⓓ 6,105.5 miles

Mini Task

14. Carl earns $3.25 per hour walking his neighbor's dogs. He walks them $\frac{1}{3}$ of an hour in the morning and $\frac{1}{2}$ of an hour in the afternoon.

a. How much time does Carl spend dog walking every day?

$\frac{5}{6}$ hour

b. How much time does Carl spend dog walking in a week?

$5\frac{5}{6}$ hours

c. Ten minutes is equal to $\frac{1}{6}$ of an hour. How many minutes does Carl work dog walking each week?

350 minutes

d. How much money does Carl earn each week?

$18.96

15. The city zoo had an equal number of visitors on Saturday and Sunday. In all, 32,096 people visited the zoo that weekend. How many visited each day?

16,048

a. On Saturday, $\frac{1}{8}$ of the people who visited were senior citizens, $\frac{1}{8}$ were infants, $\frac{1}{4}$ were children, and $\frac{1}{2}$ were adults. How many of each group visited the zoo on Saturday?

Senior Citizens: ___2,006___

Infants: ___2,006___

Children: ___4,012___

Adults: ___8,024___

b. On Sunday, $\frac{1}{16}$ of the people who visited were senior citizens, $\frac{3}{16}$ were infants, $\frac{3}{8}$ were children, and $\frac{3}{8}$ were adults. How many of each group visited the zoo on Sunday?

Senior Citizens: ___1,003___

Infants: ___3,009___

Children: ___6,018___

Adults: ___6,018___

c. The chart shows how much each type of ticket costs.

Type of Ticket	Cost
Infants	Free
Children Over 2	$4.50
Adults	$7.25
Senior Citizens	$5.75

d. How much money did the zoo make on Saturday? Show your work.

$($0 \times 2{,}006) + ($4.50 \times 4{,}012) +$

$($5.75 \times 2{,}006) + ($7.25 \times 8{,}024)$

$= $0 + $18{,}054 + $11{,}534.50$

$+ $58{,}174 = $87{,}762.50$

e. How much did the zoo make on Sunday?

$($0 \times 3{,}009) + ($4.50 \times 6{,}018) +$

$($5.75 \times 1{,}003) + ($7.25 \times 6{,}018)$

$= $0 + $27{,}081 + $5{,}767.25$

$+ $43{,}630.50 = $76{,}478.75$

Proportionality: Ratios and Rates

Contents

Unit Pacing Guide

45-Minute Classes

Module 6

DAY 1	DAY 2	DAY 3	DAY 4	DAY 5
Lesson 6.1	Lesson 6.1	Lesson 6.2	Lesson 6.2	Lesson 6.3

DAY 6	DAY 7	DAY 8		
Lesson 6.3	Lesson 6.3	Ready to Go On? Assessment Readiness		

Module 7

DAY 1	DAY 2	DAY 3	DAY 4	DAY 5
Lesson 7.1	Lesson 7.1	Lesson 7.1	Lesson 7.2	Lesson 7.2

DAY 6	DAY 7	DAY 8	DAY 9	DAY 10
Lesson 7.3	Lesson 7.3	Lesson 7.4	Lesson 7.4	Ready to Go On? Assessment Readiness

Module 8

DAY 1	DAY 2	DAY 3	DAY 4	DAY 5
Lesson 8.1	Lesson 8.1	Lesson 8.2	Lesson 8.2	Lesson 8.3

DAY 6	DAY 7	DAY 8	DAY 9	
Lesson 8.3	Lesson 8.3	Ready to Go On? Assessment Readiness	Study Guide Assessment Readiness	

90-Minute Classes

Module 6

DAY 1	DAY 2	DAY 3	DAY 4	
Lesson 6.1	Lesson 6.2	Lesson 6.3	Ready to Go On? Assessment Readiness	

Module 7

DAY 1	DAY 2	DAY 3	DAY 4	DAY 4
Lesson 7.1	Lesson 7.2	Lesson 7.3	Lesson 7.4	Ready to Go On? Assessment Readiness

Module 8

DAY 1	DAY 2	DAY 3	DAY 4	DAY 5
Lesson 8.1	Lesson 8.2	Lesson 8.3	Ready to Go On? Assessment Readiness	Study Guide Assessment Readiness

Program Resources

⏻ Plan

Online Teacher Edition

Access a full suite of teaching resources online—plan, present, and manage classes, assignments, and activities.

ePlanner Easily plan your classes, create and view assignments, and access all program resources with your online, customizable planning tool.

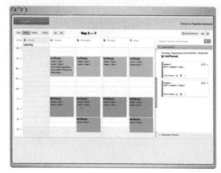

Professional Development Videos

Author Juli Dixon models successful teaching practices and strategies in actual classroom settings.

 QR Codes Scan with your smart phone to jump directly from your print book to online videos and other resources.

Teacher's Edition

Support students with point-of-use Questioning Strategies, teaching tips, resources for differentiated instruction, additional activities, and more.

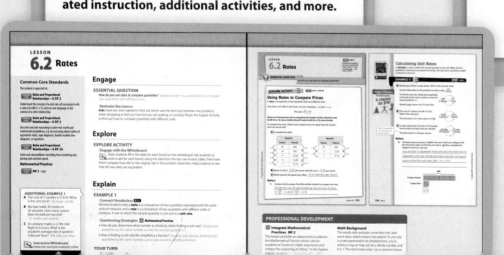

⏻ Engage and Explore

Real-World Videos Engage students with interesting and relevant applications of the mathematical content of each module.

 Animated Math Online interactive simulations, tools, and games help students actively learn and practice key concepts.

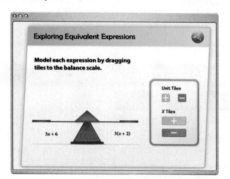

Explore Activities

Students interactively explore new concepts using a variety of tools and approaches.

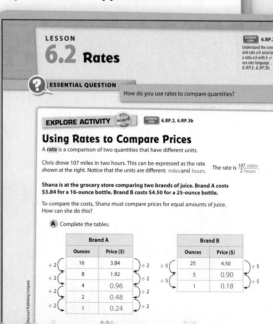

LESSON
6.2 Rates

COMMON CORE **6.RP.2**
Understand the concept of a unit rate a/b associated with a ratio a:b with b ≠ 0, and use rate language.... Also 6.RP.3, 6.RP.3b

? ESSENTIAL QUESTION

How do you use rates to compare quantities?

EXPLORE ACTIVITY Real World · COMMON CORE 6.RP.2, 6.RP.3b

Using Rates to Compare Prices

A **rate** is a comparison of two quantities that have different units.

Chris drove 107 miles in two hours. This can be expressed as the rate shown at the right. Notice that the units are different: miles and hours. The rate is $\frac{107 \text{ miles}}{2 \text{ hours}}$.

Shana is at the grocery store comparing two brands of juice. Brand A costs $3.84 for a 16-ounce bottle. Brand B costs $4.50 for a 25-ounce bottle.

To compare the costs, Shana must compare prices for equal amounts of juice. How can she do this?

A Complete the tables.

Brand A	
Ounces	Price ($)
16	3.84
8	1.92
4	0.96
2	0.48
1	0.24

(÷2, ÷2, ÷2, ÷2)

Brand B	
Ounces	Price ($)
25	4.50
5	0.90
1	0.18

(÷5, ÷5)

⏻ Teach

Math On the Spot video tutorials, featuring program authors Dr. Edward Burger and Martha Sandoval-Martinez, accompany every example in the textbook and give students step-by-step instructions and explanations of key math concepts.

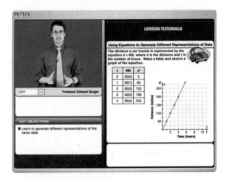

Present engaging content on a multitude of devices, including tablets and interactive whiteboards.

Continually monitor and assess student progress with integrated formative assessment.

Look for exercises indicated with this icon to build connections among standards within Common Core clusters.

Differentiated Instruction Print Resources

Support all learners with Differentiated Instruction Resources, including

- **Leveled Practice and Problem Solving**
- **Reteach**
- **Reading Strategies**
- **Success for English Learners**
- **Challenge**

⏻ Assessment and Intervention

The **Personal Math Trainer** provides online practice, homework, assessments, and intervention. Monitor student progress through reports and alerts. Create and customize assignments aligned to specific lessons or standards.

- **Practice** – With dynamic items and assignments, students get unlimited practice on key concepts supported by guided examples, step-by-step solutions, and video tutorials.

- **Assessments** – Choose from course assignments or customize your own based on course content, standards, difficulty levels, and more.

- **Homework** – Students can complete online homework with a wide variety of problem types, including the ability to enter expressions, equations, and graphs. Let the system automatically grade homework, so you can focus where your students need help the most!

- **Intervention** – Let the Personal Math Trainer automatically prescribe a targeted, personalized intervention path for your students.

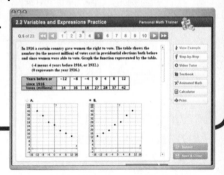

Raise the bar with homework and practice that incorporates higher-order thinking and mathematical processes in every lesson.

Assessment Readiness

Prepare students for success on tests of the Common Core Standards with practice at every module and unit.

Assessment Resources

Tailor assessments to meet the needs of all your classes and students, including

- **Leveled Module Quizzes**
- **Leveled Unit Tests**
- **Unit Performance Tasks**
- **Placement, Diagnostic, and Quarterly Benchmark Tests**

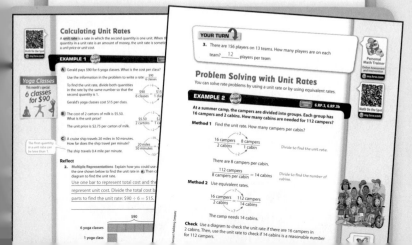

Math Background

Ratios 6.RP.1, 6.RP.3
LESSON 6.1

A *ratio* is a comparison of two quantities using division. In a classroom with 12 girls and 16 boys, the ratio of girls to boys is 12 to 16. The ratio may also be written as 12:16 or $\frac{12}{16}$. As with fractions, equivalent ratios name the same comparison, and you can find equivalent ratios by multiplying or dividing both terms of a ratio by the same nonzero number. Thus, 12:16 is equivalent to 3:4.

It is helpful for students to have different ways of describing and picturing ratios. For example, the above ratio can be interpreted as follows: "For every 3 girls in the class, there are 4 boys." This can also be represented visually as in the figure.

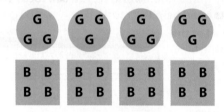

Solving Problems with Proportions 6.RP.3
LESSON 7.2

A *proportion* is a statement that two ratios are equal. Compare the two ratios in the proportion $\frac{2}{5} = \frac{x}{15}$. The denominator of $\frac{2}{5}$ must be multiplied by 3 to get the denominator of $\frac{x}{15}$. In order for the ratio to be equivalent, the numerators must be related in the same way as the denominators. So, multiply 2 by 3 to find the numerator x. This yields $x = 2 \cdot 3 = 6$.

The proportion $\frac{2}{5} = \frac{x}{15}$ can also be solved visually using a figure like the one below. Start by representing the known ratio $\frac{2}{5}$. Make copies of this representation to create a new ratio whose second term is 15. The resulting figure shows that the first term of the new ratio must be 6.

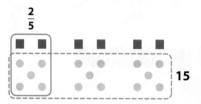

Conversion Factors 6.RP.3d
LESSON 7.3

Conversion factors are an efficient tool for converting units. They are used to perform conversions within the customary system (for example, inches to feet or pounds to ounces). They may also be used for conversions within the metric system or for conversions between systems.

A *conversion factor* is a fraction that is equal to one, such that the numerator and denominator of the fraction consist of equivalent measures. For example, a conversion factor that relates feet and yards is $\frac{3\,\text{ft}}{1\,\text{yd}}$. Since 3 ft = 1 yd, the fraction is equal to 1. The fraction may also be written as $\frac{1\,\text{yd}}{3\,\text{ft}}$. To convert units, multiply by the conversion factor that causes units to cancel. For example, to convert 36 ft to yards, use $\frac{1\,\text{yd}}{3\,\text{ft}}$ as shown: $36\,\text{ft} = 36\,\cancel{\text{ft}} \cdot \frac{1\,\text{yd}}{3\,\cancel{\text{ft}}} = \frac{36}{3}\,\text{yd} = 12\,\text{yd}$.

Understanding Percent 6.RP.3c
LESSON 8.1

Early in the first century C.E., the Roman emperor Augustus placed a tax of $\frac{1}{100}$ on all goods sold at auction. Other tax rates were based on fractions that were easily compared to hundredths. By the fifteenth century, it was common to use 100 as a base for business computations, and an early form of the familiar percent symbol (%) came into use.

It's easy to see why percents were so useful in these early business applications. Imagine comparing two tax rates: $\frac{21}{300}$ and $\frac{3}{50}$. It's not immediately obvious which rate is greater. Expressed as percents, however, the rates are 7% and 6%, respectively.

Students should understand that *percent* means "per hundred." That is, percents compare numbers to 100, so that 12% means "12 out of 100" or $\frac{12}{100}$. This can be represented by shading 12 of the 100 squares on a 10-by-10 grid. Students can use this representation to help them develop a mental image of 12%. For example, suppose 12% of a state park is a redwood forest. This means that if the area of the entire park were represented by 100 squares, 12 of the squares would be covered with redwood trees.

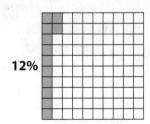

12%

Using Percents 6.RP.3, 6.RP.3c
LESSON 8.3

Tips are commonly calculated as a percentage of a bill. Tips are a useful real-world application of percents. There are several methods of estimating a standard 15% tip. One way is to find 10% + 5%. Move the decimal point of the amount of the bill one place left to find 10%. Then divide that amount by 2 to find 5%. A second method makes use of the fact that 15% $\approx \frac{1}{7}$.

As a result, a 15% tip can be estimated by tipping $1 for every $7 spent. For a bill of $27, for example, the tip should be approximately $4 because $27 $\approx$ $28, and $28 ÷ 7 = $4.

Common benchmarks can also be used to estimate tips.

Bill	$10	$20	$30
Tip	$1.50	$3.00	$4.50

For example, you can see from the table that a 15% tip for a bill of $18 should be a bit less than $3.00.

Percent Problems 6.RP.3, 6.RP.3c
LESSON 8.3

The above discussion suggests a way to use proportions to understand percents. For example, suppose the area of the state park is 50,000 acres. As shown at left, if the area of the entire park were represented by 100 squares, 12 of the squares would be covered with redwood trees. This leads to the relationship $\frac{12}{100} = \frac{x}{50,000}$, where x is the number of acres of redwoods. Solving the proportion shows that 6,000 acres of the park are covered in redwoods.

Generalizing these ideas yields the proportion $\frac{n}{100} = \frac{part}{whole}$, where $\frac{n}{100} = n\%$. Students can use this proportion to solve problems in which they are given two of the three pieces of information (the percent, the part, and the whole). However, for students to be successful with percent problems, they must become adept at identifying the percent, the part, and the whole in a variety of situations.

The percent is generally the easiest to identify because it is accompanied by the word *percent* or the symbol %. Another key element in percent problems is the word *of*. Both parts and percents are often given in terms *of the whole*.

Once students can identify the percent, the part, and the whole in a problem, they can substitute the known values into the proportion and solve for the unknown.

Proportionality: Ratios and Rates

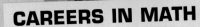

CAREERS IN MATH

Residential Builder A residential builder, also called a homebuilder, specializes in the construction of residences that range from single-family custom homes to buildings that contain multiple housing units, such as apartments and condominiums. Residential builders use math in numerous ways, such as blueprint reading, measuring and scaling, using ratios and rates to calculate the amounts of different building materials needed, and estimating costs for jobs.

If you are interested in a career as a residential builder, you should study these mathematical subjects:

- Algebra
- Geometry
- Business Math
- Technical Math

Research other careers that require using ratios and rates, and measuring and scaling.

Unit 3 Performance Task

At the end of the unit, check out how **residential builders** use math.

© Houghton Mifflin Harcourt Publishing Company • Image Credits: Alexander Hafemann/Photographer's Choice/Getty Images

Careers in Math

Residential Builder

A residential builder should be able to calculate dimensions and create estimates of necessary materials and labor costs. You will learn more about this in the Performance Tasks at the end of the unit.

For more information about careers in mathematics as well as various mathematics appreciation topics, visit the American Mathematical Society at www.ams.org

Vocabulary Preview

Use the puzzle to give students a preview of important concepts in this unit. Students may work individually, in pairs, or in groups.

Unit Resources

Go online to access all your unit resources.

my.hrw.com

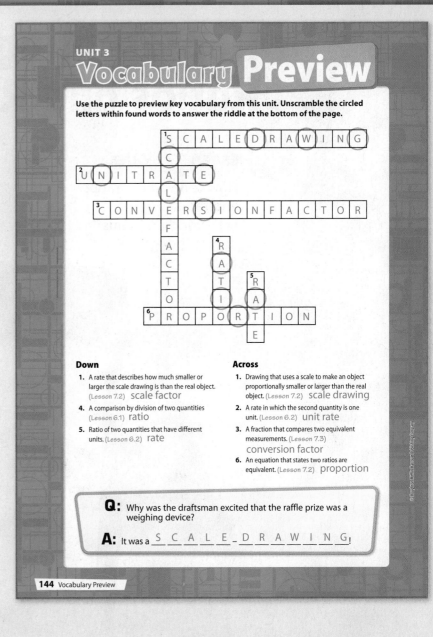

UNIT 3
Vocabulary Preview

Use the puzzle to preview key vocabulary from this unit. Unscramble the circled letters within found words to answer the riddle at the bottom of the page.

Down

1. A rate that describes how much smaller or larger the scale drawing is than the real object. (Lesson 7.2) scale factor
4. A comparison by division of two quantities (Lesson 6.1) ratio
5. Ratio of two quantities that have different units. (Lesson 6.2) rate

Across

1. Drawing that uses a scale to make an object proportionally smaller or larger than the real object. (Lesson 7.2) scale drawing
2. A rate in which the second quantity is one unit. (Lesson 6.2) unit rate
3. A fraction that compares two equivalent measurements. (Lesson 7.3) conversion factor
6. An equation that states two ratios are equivalent. (Lesson 7.2) proportion

Q: Why was the draftsman excited that the raffle prize was a weighing device?

A: It was a S C A L E _ D R A W I N G !

144 Vocabulary Preview

Before	In this Unit	After
Students understand ratio and percent: • write a ratio as a fraction • represent a percent as part of a hundred • relate fractions, decimals, and percents	Students will learn about: • ratios and proportions • rates and unit rates • converting units within a measurement system • fractions, decimals, and percents	Students will connect: • rates and proportionality • relationships between proportions and percent • proportionality in geometry

Representing Ratios and Rates

COMMON CORE

ESSENTIAL QUESTION

How can you use ratios and rates to solve real-world problems?

You can use given information about real-world situations to write ratios and rates, and then use them to find additional information about the situations.

© Houghton Mifflin Harcourt Publishing Company • Image Credits: Anne-Marie Palmer / Alamy

ⓘ my.hrw.com

Real-World Video

Scientists studying sand structures determined that the perfect sand and water mixture is equal to 1 bucket of water for every 100 buckets of sand. This recipe can be written as the ratio $\frac{1}{100}$.

GO DIGITAL

my.hrw.com

my.hrw.com

Go digital with your write-in student edition, accessible on any device.

Math On the Spot

Scan with your smart phone to jump directly to the online edition, video tutor, and more.

Animated Math

Interactively explore key concepts to see how math works.

Personal Math Trainer

Get immediate feedback and help as you work through practice sets.

Are You Ready?

Assess Readiness

Use the assessment on this page to determine if students need intensive or strategic intervention for the module's prerequisite skills.

RtI
Response to Intervention

Personal Math Trainer
Online Assessment and Intervention
 my.hrw.com

Intervention	Enrichment
Access Are You Ready? assessment online, and receive instant scoring, feedback, and customized intervention or enrichment.	

Online and Print Resources

Skills Intervention worksheets
- Skill 19 Simplify Fractions
- Skill 24 Write Equivalent Fractions

Differentiated Instruction
- Challenge worksheets **PRE-AP**
- Extend the Math **PRE-AP** Lesson Activities in TE

Are YOU Ready?

Complete these exercises to review skills you will need for this module.

Personal Math Trainer
Online Assessment and Intervention
my.hrw.com

Simplify Fractions

EXAMPLE Simplify $\frac{15}{24}$.

15: 1, ③, 5, 15   List all the factors of the numerator and denominator.
24: 1, 2, ③, 4, 6, 8, 12, 24   Circle the greatest common factor (GCF).

$\frac{15 \div 3}{24 \div 3} = \frac{5}{8}$ Divide the numerator and denominator by the GCF.

Write each fraction in simplest form.

1. $\frac{6}{9}$ $\frac{2}{3}$
2. $\frac{4}{10}$ $\frac{2}{5}$
3. $\frac{15}{20}$ $\frac{3}{4}$
4. $\frac{20}{24}$ $\frac{5}{6}$
5. $\frac{16}{56}$ $\frac{2}{7}$
6. $\frac{45}{72}$ $\frac{5}{8}$
7. $\frac{18}{60}$ $\frac{3}{10}$
8. $\frac{32}{72}$ $\frac{4}{9}$

Write Equivalent Fractions

EXAMPLE $\frac{6}{8} = \frac{6 \times 2}{8 \times 2}$ Multiply the numerator and denominator by the same number to find an equivalent fraction.
$= \frac{12}{16}$

$\frac{6}{8} = \frac{6 \div 2}{8 \div 2}$ Divide the numerator and denominator by the same number to find an equivalent fraction.
$= \frac{3}{4}$

Write the equivalent fraction.

9. $\frac{12}{15} = \frac{\boxed{4}}{5}$
10. $\frac{5}{6} = \frac{\boxed{25}}{30}$
11. $\frac{16}{24} = \frac{4}{\boxed{6}}$
12. $\frac{3}{9} = \frac{\boxed{21}}{63}$

13. $\frac{15}{40} = \frac{\boxed{3}}{8}$
14. $\frac{18}{30} = \frac{\boxed{6}}{10}$
15. $\frac{48}{64} = \frac{12}{\boxed{16}}$
16. $\frac{2}{7} = \frac{18}{\boxed{63}}$

PROFESSIONAL DEVELOPMENT VIDEO

Author Juli Dixon models successful teaching practices as she explores ratio and rate concepts in an actual sixth-grade classroom.

Professional Development
my.hrw.com

GO DIGITAL
my.hrw.com

 Online Teacher Edition
Access a full suite of teaching resources online—plan, present, and manage classes and assignments.

 ePlanner
Easily plan your classes and access all your resources online.

 Interactive Answers and Solutions
Customize answer keys to print or display in the classroom. Choose to include answers only or full solutions to all lesson exercises.

 Interactive Whiteboards
Engage students with interactive whiteboard-ready lessons and activities.

 Personal Math Trainer: Online Assessment and Intervention
Assign automatically graded homework, quizzes, tests, and intervention activities. Prepare your students with updated practice tests aligned with Common Core.

Reading Start-Up

Have students complete the activities on this page by working alone or with others.

Visualize Vocabulary

The chart helps students review vocabulary associated with multiplication and division, and prepares them to use rates and ratios. If time allows, discuss any other attributes of multiplication and division that can be added to the chart.

Understand Vocabulary

Use the following explanation to help students learn the preview words.

> A unit is a single item or a measure, such as inches, ounces, or liters. When shopping, it helps to find **unit rates**, or how much one unit costs. For example, if you know that 2 movie tickets cost $14, then you can figure out the unit rate, which is $7 for one ticket.

Active Reading

Integrating Language Arts

Students can use these reading and note-taking strategies to help them organize and understand new concepts and vocabulary.

COMMON CORE **ELA-Literacy.RST.6-8.7** Integrate quantitative or technical information expressed in words in a text with a version of that information expressed visually (e.g., in a flowchart, diagram, model, graph, or table).

Additional Resources

Differentiated Instruction

• Reading Strategies **ELL**

Reading Start-Up

Visualize Vocabulary

Use the ✔ words to complete the chart. Choose the review words that describe multiplication and division.

Understanding Multiplication and Division		
Symbol	**Operation**	**Term for the answer**
×	multiply	product
÷	divide	quotient

Understand Vocabulary

Match the term on the left to the definition on the right.

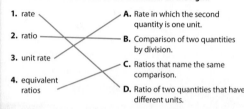

1. rate
2. ratio
3. unit rate
4. equivalent ratios

A. Rate in which the second quantity is one unit.
B. Comparison of two quantities by division.
C. Ratios that name the same comparison.
D. Ratio of two quantities that have different units.

Vocabulary

Review Words
colon *(dos puntos)*
denominator *(denominador)*
✔ divide *(dividir)*
fraction bar *(barra de fracciones)*
✔ multiply *(multiplicar)*
numerator *(numerador)*
✔ product *(producto)*
quantity *(cantidad)*
✔ quotient *(cociente)*
term *(término)*

Preview Words
equivalent ratios *(razones equivalentes)*
rate *(tasa)*
ratio *(razón)*
unit rate *(tasa unitaria)*

Active Reading

Two-Panel Flip Chart Create a two-panel flip chart, to help you understand the concepts in this module. Label one flap "Ratios" and the other flap "Rates." As you study each lesson, write important ideas under the appropriate flap. Include information about unit rates and any sample equations that will help you remember the concepts when you look back at your notes.

© Houghton Mifflin Harcourt Publishing Company

Before	**In this module**	**After**
Students understand ratios:	Students understand proportional relationships:	Students will connect:
• write a ratio as a fraction	• represent ratios with concrete models	• rates and unit rates
• write equivalent ratios	• write ratios and find equivalent ratios	• constant rates of change given a table, verbal description, equation, or graph
	• use rates and unit rates to compare quantities	
	• apply qualitative and quantitative reasoning to solve prediction and comparison of real-world problems involving ratios and rates	

Unpacking the Standards

Use the examples on this page to help students know exactly what they are expected to learn in this module.

Common Core Standards

Content Areas

COMMON CORE Ratios and Proportional Reasoning—6.RP

Understand ratio concepts and use ratio reasoning to solve problems.

Go online to see a complete unpacking of the Common Core Standards.

my.hrw.com

MODULE 6

Unpacking the Standards

Understanding the standards and the vocabulary terms in the standards will help you know exactly what you are expected to learn in this module.

COMMON CORE 6.RP.3

Use ratio and rate reasoning to solve real-world and mathematical problems, e.g., by reasoning about tables of equivalent ratios, tape diagrams, double number line diagrams, or equations.

Key Vocabulary

ratio *(razón)*
A comparison of two quantities by division.

rate *(tasa)*
A ratio that compares two quantities measured in different units.

equivalent ratios *(razones equivalentes)*
Ratios that name the same comparison.

What It Means to You

You will use equivalent ratios to solve real-world problems involving ratios and rates.

UNPACKING EXAMPLE 6.RP.3

A group of 10 friends is in line to see a movie. The table shows how much different groups will pay in all. Predict how much the group of 10 will pay.

Number in group	3	5	6	12
Amount paid ($)	15	25	30	60

The ratios are all the same.

$$\frac{3}{15} = \frac{1}{5} \qquad \frac{6}{30} = \frac{1}{5} \qquad \frac{5}{25} = \frac{1}{5} \qquad \frac{12}{60} = \frac{1}{5}$$

Find the denominator that gives a ratio equivalent to $\frac{1}{5}$ for a group of 10.

$$\frac{10}{?} = \frac{1}{5} \quad \rightarrow \quad \frac{10 \div 10}{50 \div 10} = \frac{1}{5} \quad \rightarrow \quad \frac{10}{50} = \frac{1}{5}$$

A group of 10 will pay $50.

COMMON CORE 6.RP.3b

Solve unit rate problems including those involving unit pricing and constant speed.

Key Vocabulary

unit rate *(tasa unitaria)*
A rate in which the second quantity in the comparison is one unit.

Visit my.hrw.com to see all the Common Core Standards unpacked.

my.hrw.com

What It Means to You

You will solve problems involving unit rates by division.

UNPACKING EXAMPLE 6.RP.3b

A 2-liter bottle of spring water costs $2.02. A 3-liter bottle of the same water costs $2.79. Which is the better deal?

2-liter bottle

$\dfrac{\$2.02}{2 \text{ liters}}$

$\dfrac{\$2.02 \div 2}{2 \text{ liters} \div 2}$

$\dfrac{\$1.01}{1 \text{ liter}}$

3-liter bottle

$\dfrac{\$2.79}{3 \text{ liters}}$

$\dfrac{\$2.79 \div 3}{3 \text{ liters} \div 3}$

$\dfrac{\$0.93}{1 \text{ liter}}$

The 3-liter bottle is the better deal.

Common Core Standards	Lesson 6.1	Lesson 6.2	Lesson 6.3
6.RP.1 Understand the concept of a ratio and use ratio language to describe a ratio relationship between two quantities.	COMMON CORE		
6.RP.2 Understand the concept of a unit rate a/b associated with a ratio a:b with $b \neq 0$, and use rate language in the context of a ratio relationship.		COMMON CORE	
6.RP.3 Use ratio and rate reasoning to solve real-world and mathematical problems, e.g., by reasoning about tables of equivalent ratios, tape diagrams, double number line diagrams, or equations.	COMMON CORE	COMMON CORE	COMMON CORE
6.RP.3a Make tables of equivalent ratios relating quantities with whole-number measurements, find missing values in the tables, and plot the pairs of values on the coordinate plane. Use tables to compare ratios.	COMMON CORE		COMMON CORE
6.RP.3b Solve unit rate problems including those involving unit pricing and constant speed.		COMMON CORE	

© Houghton Mifflin Harcourt Publishing Company

LESSON
6.1 Ratios

ADDITIONAL EXAMPLE 1

Dean's Pencil Box

5 pencils

2 erasers

3 pens

12 markers

24 crayons

The contents of Dean's pencil box are shown. Write each ratio below in three different ways.

pencils to erasers 5:2, 5 to 2, $\frac{5}{2}$

total items to markers 46:12, 46 to 12, $\frac{46}{12}$

 Interactive Whiteboard
Interactive example available online

 my.hrw.com

Engage

ESSENTIAL QUESTION

How do you use ratios to compare two quantities? Sample answer: You can use multiplication to compare two quantities. The terms of a ratio have a multiplicative relationship.

Motivate the Lesson

Ask: Have you ever heard the term *ratio*? If so, in what context? Begin the Explore Activity to find out.

Explore

EXPLORE ACTIVITY

Engage with the Whiteboard

Have students make a model for C on the whiteboard. Then have students make predictions for how many star-shaped beads would be needed for 5 moon beads and 8 moon beads. Ask students to write a rule that they can use to find the number of star beads for any number of moon beads.

Explain

EXAMPLE 1

Focus on Communication

Point out to students that the three different ways of writing ratios all represent the same comparison. Also point out that a ratio can compare a part to a part, a part to a whole, or a whole to a part. Give examples of each.

Questioning Strategies [CC] Mathematical Practices

• In A, if you write the ratio for 8 comedies to 3 dramas, is it the same ratio as 3 dramas to 8 comedies? No. The order of the terms is important. Compare $\frac{8}{2} > \frac{2}{8}$ and you can see that $\frac{8}{2} > \frac{2}{8}$, which is $4 > \frac{1}{4}$.

• How can you compare two ratios? Write them as fractions with common denominators.

• How can you simplify a ratio? Write the ratio as a fraction and simplify.

YOUR TURN

Avoid Common Errors

Some students may not understand that the order of the terms in a ratio is important. Remind students that they must use the order provided in the exercise to write the ratio correctly.

Integrating Language Arts [ELL]

Encourage a broad class discussion on Reflect Exercise 4. English learners will benefit from hearing and participating in classroom discussions.

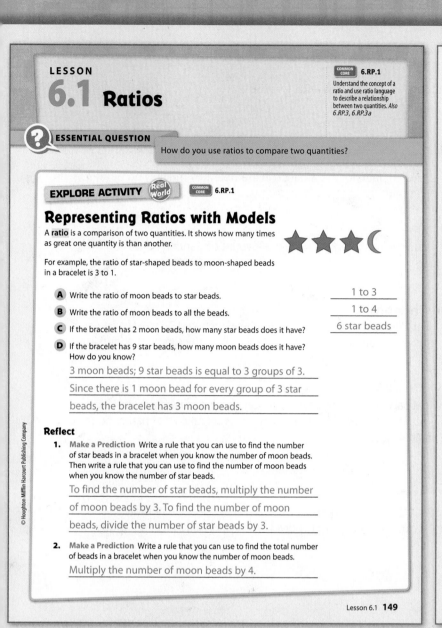

LESSON
6.1 Ratios

COMMON CORE 6.RP.1
Understand the concept of a ratio and use ratio language to describe a relationship between two quantities. *Also* 6.RP.3, 6.RP.3a

? ESSENTIAL QUESTION

How do you use ratios to compare two quantities?

EXPLORE ACTIVITY (Real World) | **COMMON CORE** 6.RP.1

Representing Ratios with Models

A **ratio** is a comparison of two quantities. It shows how many times as great one quantity is than another.

For example, the ratio of star-shaped beads to moon-shaped beads in a bracelet is 3 to 1.

A Write the ratio of moon beads to star beads. — 1 to 3

B Write the ratio of moon beads to all the beads. — 1 to 4

C If the bracelet has 2 moon beads, how many star beads does it have? — 6 star beads

D If the bracelet has 9 star beads, how many moon beads does it have? How do you know?

3 moon beads; 9 star beads is equal to 3 groups of 3.

Since there is 1 moon bead for every group of 3 star

beads, the bracelet has 3 moon beads.

Reflect

1. **Make a Prediction** Write a rule that you can use to find the number of star beads in a bracelet when you know the number of moon beads. Then write a rule that you can use to find the number of moon beads when you know the number of star beads.

To find the number of star beads, multiply the number

of moon beads by 3. To find the number of moon

beads, divide the number of star beads by 3.

2. **Make a Prediction** Write a rule that you can use to find the total number of beads in a bracelet when you know the number of moon beads.

Multiply the number of moon beads by 4.

Lesson 6.1 **149**

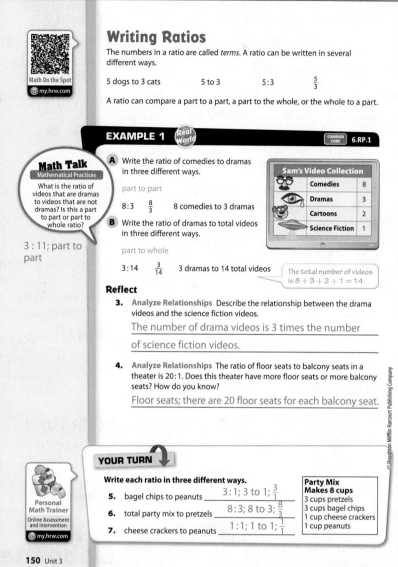

Writing Ratios

The numbers in a ratio are called *terms*. A ratio can be written in several different ways.

5 dogs to 3 cats   5 to 3   5:3 $\frac{5}{3}$

A ratio can compare a part to a part, a part to the whole, or the whole to a part.

EXAMPLE 1 (Real World) | **COMMON CORE** 6.RP.1

A Write the ratio of comedies to dramas in three different ways.

part to part

8:3 $\frac{8}{3}$ 8 comedies to 3 dramas

B Write the ratio of dramas to total videos in three different ways.

part to whole

3:14 $\frac{3}{14}$ 3 dramas to 14 total videos

The total number of videos is $8 + 3 + 2 + 1 = 14.$

Sam's Video Collection	
Comedies	8
Dramas	3
Cartoons	2
Science Fiction	1

Math Talk
Mathematical Practices
What is the ratio of videos that are dramas to videos that are not dramas? Is this a part to part or part to whole ratio?

3 : 11; part to part

Reflect

3. **Analyze Relationships** Describe the relationship between the drama videos and the science fiction videos.

The number of drama videos is 3 times the number

of science fiction videos.

4. **Analyze Relationships** The ratio of floor seats to balcony seats in a theater is 20:1. Does this theater have more floor seats or more balcony seats? How do you know?

Floor seats; there are 20 floor seats for each balcony seat.

YOUR TURN

Write each ratio in three different ways.

5. bagel chips to peanuts ___ 3:1; 3 to 1; $\frac{3}{1}$

6. total party mix to pretzels ___ 8:3; 8 to 3; $\frac{8}{3}$

7. cheese crackers to peanuts ___ 1:1; 1 to 1; $\frac{1}{1}$

Party Mix
Makes 8 cups
3 cups pretzels
3 cups bagel chips
1 cup cheese crackers
1 cup peanuts

150 Unit 3

PROFESSIONAL DEVELOPMENT

CC Integrate Mathematical Practices MP.4

This lesson provides an opportunity to address the Mathematical Practice standard that calls for students to "model with mathematics." In the Explore Activity and Example 2, students write and simplify ratios to solve real-world mathematical problems, such as determining the number of items needed to make jewelry or the amounts of ingredients needed to extend a recipe. This helps students to understand that ratios are used in everyday life.

Math Background

Ancient mathematicians used ratios primarily in geometry—for the comparison of lengths of segments and of areas.

The Golden Ratio, equal to $\frac{1 + \sqrt{5}}{2} \approx 1.618$, was considered by the ancient Greeks to be an ideal, pleasing ratio for the length and width of a rectangle. Rectangles with dimensions in this ratio appear throughout Greek art and architecture. The overall dimensions of the Parthenon are in the Golden Ratio, and the same ratio is repeated many times throughout the structure.

EXAMPLE 2

Questioning Strategies Mathematical Practices

- Can you find equivalent ratios by adding or subtracting the same number from both terms of a ratio? No; adding or subtracting the same number from both terms of a ratio, unlike multiplying or dividing by the same number, makes changes in the numbers or quantities being compared and therefore also in the relationship between the terms.

- Can you write an equivalent ratio for the situation in Example 1 by multiplying by −2? No. Since ratios are comparisons of real-world quantities, negative quantities make no sense. (e.g., It doesn't make any sense to compare −6 cups of cranberry juice to −4 cups of apple juice.)

- What is the multiplicative relationship between the amount of cranberry juice and the amount of apple juice? The amount of cranberry juice is 1.5 times the amount of apple juice.

Engage with the Whiteboard

Have students make a model for Example 2 on the whiteboard. Then have students model each equivalent ratio in the table and explain how the model changed from the previous model.

Connect Vocabulary ELL

Stress proper mathematical language to avoid confusion. Remind students that the two numbers in a ratio are called *terms* and that equivalent ratios are ratios that name the same comparison as the original ratio.

YOUR TURN

Avoid Common Errors

Remind students to multiply or divide *both* terms of a ratio by the same number to find equivalent ratios. Point out that multiplying or dividing only one term does not produce an equivalent ratio.

Elaborate
....

Talk About It
Summarize the Lesson

Ask: Why are ratios good tools to use for comparing quantities with the same units, such as ingredients in a recipe? A ratio shows the relationship between two quantities. Equivalent ratios can keep this relationship unchanged while the amounts of each quantity are increased or decreased as needed for recipes.

GUIDED PRACTICE

Engage with the Whiteboard

For Exercises 5–6, have students draw a model for each exercise on the whiteboard and explain how to write the ratio in three different ways.

Avoid Common Errors

Exercises 1–6 Some students may not understand that the order of the terms in a ratio is important. Remind students that they must use the order provided in the exercise to write the ratio correctly.

Exercises 7–9 Remind students to multiply or divide *both* terms of a ratio by the same number to find equivalent ratios. Point out that multiplying or dividing only one term does not produce an equivalent ratio.

Equivalent Ratios

Equivalent ratios are ratios that name the same comparison. You can find equivalent ratios by using a table or by multiplying or dividing both terms of a ratio by the same number. So, equivalent ratios have a multiplicative relationship.

$$\frac{2}{7} \xrightarrow{\times 2} \frac{4}{14} \qquad \frac{8}{24} \xrightarrow{\div 4} \frac{2}{6}$$

A ratio with terms that have no common factors is said to be in simplest form.

EXAMPLE 2   Real World

6.RP.3, 6.RP.3a

You make 5 cups of punch by mixing 3 cups of cranberry juice with 2 cups of apple juice. How much cranberry juice and how much apple juice do you need to make four times the original recipe?

Method 1 Use a table.

STEP 1 Make a table comparing the number of cups of cranberry juice and apple juice needed to make two times, three times, and four times the original recipe.

> Multiply both terms of the original ratio by the same number to find an equivalent ratio.

$$3 \times 2 \qquad 3 \times 3 \qquad 3 \times 4$$

Cranberry Juice	3	6	9	12
Apple Juice	2	4	6	8

$$2 \times 2 \qquad 2 \times 3 \qquad 2 \times 4$$

STEP 2 Write the original ratio and the ratio that shows the amount of cranberry juice and apple juice needed to make four times the original recipe.

$$\frac{3}{2} = \frac{12}{8}$$

You will need 12 cups of cranberry juice and 8 cups of apple juice.

Method 2 Multiply both terms of the ratio by the same number.

STEP 1 Write the original ratio in fraction form.

$$\frac{3}{2}$$

STEP 2 Multiply the numerator and denominator by the same number.

To make four times the original recipe, multiply by 4.

$$\frac{3}{2} \xrightarrow{\times 4} \frac{12}{8}$$

To make four times the original recipe, you will need 12 cups of cranberry juice and 8 cups of apple juice.

My Notes

Math Talk
Mathematical Practices

The ratio of apple juice to grape juice in a recipe is 8 cups to 10 cups. What is this ratio in simplest form? Explain.

4 to 5; divide 8 and 10 by their GCF, 2.

YOUR TURN

Personal Math Trainer
Online Assessment and Intervention
my.hrw.com

Write three ratios equivalent to the given ratio. Sample answers are given.

8. $\frac{8}{10}$ $\frac{4}{5}, \frac{16}{20}, \frac{12}{15}$

9. $\frac{5}{2}$ $\frac{10}{4}, \frac{15}{6}, \frac{20}{8}$

Guided Practice

The number of dogs compared to the number of cats in an apartment complex is represented by the model shown. (Explore Activity)

1. Write a ratio that compares the number of dogs to the number of cats. **1 to 5**

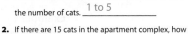 

2. If there are 15 cats in the apartment complex, how many dogs are there?

   $15 \div$ **5** $=$ **3** **dogs**

3. How many cats are there if there are 5 dogs in the apartment complex?

   $5 \times$ **5** $=$ **25** **cats**

4. The only pets in the apartment complex are cats and dogs. If there are 10 dogs, how many *pets* are there? **60 pets**

The contents of Dana's box of muffins are shown. Write each ratio in three different ways. (Example 1)

Dana's Dozen Muffins
5 corn
4 bran
2 banana nut
1 blueberry

5. banana nut muffins to corn muffins 2 to 5; 2 : 5; $\frac{2}{5}$

6. corn muffins to total muffins 5 to 12; 5 : 12; $\frac{5}{12}$

Vocabulary Write three equivalent ratios for the given ratio. Sample answers are given. Circle the simplest form of the ratio. (Example 2)

7. $\frac{10}{12}$ $\left(\frac{5}{6}\right)\frac{20}{24}, \frac{25}{30}$

8. $\frac{14}{2}$ $\left(\frac{7}{1}\right)\frac{21}{3}, \frac{28}{4}$

9. $\frac{8}{14}$ $\left(\frac{4}{7}\right)\frac{8}{14}, \frac{12}{21}, \frac{16}{28}$

? ESSENTIAL QUESTION CHECK-IN

10. Use an example to describe the multiplicative relationship between two equivalent ratios.

    The ratios $\frac{2}{5}$ and $\frac{4}{10}$ are equivalent. Each term in $\frac{4}{10}$ is two times the corresponding term in $\frac{2}{5}$.

DIFFERENTIATE INSTRUCTION

Cooperative Learning

Have students work in groups to find equivalent ratios. Groups toss two number cubes. The lesser number becomes the numerator of a ratio, and the greater number becomes the denominator. If the numbers are the same, the number is both the numerator and the denominator. Each group member names one equivalent ratio. Then have each group write the ratios in order from least denominator to greatest denominator.

Critical Thinking

Have pairs of students find the missing terms to make each group of ratios form equivalent ratios.

1. $\frac{5}{8}, \frac{?}{64}, \frac{60}{?}$ $\frac{5}{8}, \frac{40}{64}, \frac{60}{96}$

2. $\frac{?}{21}, \frac{5}{?}, \frac{75}{105}$ $\frac{15}{21}, \frac{5}{7}, \frac{75}{105}$

3. $\frac{4}{?}, \frac{32}{72}, \frac{52}{?}$ $\frac{4}{9}, \frac{32}{72}, \frac{52}{117}$

Have students explain the strategies they used to find their answers.

Additional Resources

Differentiated Instruction includes:

• Reading Strategies
• Success for English Learners **ELL**
• Reteach
• Challenge **PRE-AP**

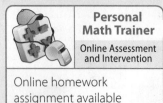

6.1 LESSON QUIZ

 6.RP.1

Ann's trail mix recipe is shown below.

Ann's Trail Mix Recipe
5 cups oats
3 cups seeds
1 cup nuts
2 cups raisins

1. Write the ratio of oats to seeds in three different ways.

2. Write the ratio of nuts to raisins in three different ways.

3. Write the ratio of oats to total cups of ingredients in three different ways.

4. Make a table to find three equivalent ratios for the ratio of oats to raisins.

5. Find three equivalent ratios for the ratio of nuts to oats.

Lesson Quiz available online

 my.hrw.com

Answers

1. 5 to 3, 5:3, $\frac{5}{3}$

2. 1 to 2, 1:2, $\frac{1}{2}$

3. 5 to 11, 5:11, $\frac{5}{11}$

4. The ratio is 5:2; Sample table:

Oats	5	10	15	20
Raisins	2	4	6	8

5. Sample answer: $\frac{2}{10}, \frac{3}{15}, \frac{5}{25}$

Evaluate

GUIDED AND INDEPENDENT PRACTICE

COMMON CORE 6.RP.1, 6.RP.3, 6.RP.3a

Concepts & Skills	Practice
Explore Activity Representing Ratios with Models	Exercises 1–4
Example 1 Writing Ratios	Exercises 5–6, 15
Example 2 Equivalent Ratios	Exercises 7–9, 11–14, 16–17

Exercise	Depth of Knowledge (D.O.K.)	**COMMON CORE** Mathematical Practices
11–12	**2** Skills/Concepts	**MP.4** Modeling
13–14	**2** Skills/Concepts	**MP.5** Using Tools
15	**3** Strategic Thinking H.O.T.	**MP.3** Logic
16	**2** Skills/Concepts	**MP.4** Modeling
17–18	**3** Strategic Thinking H.O.T.	**MP.7** Using Structure
19	**3** Strategic Thinking H.O.T.	**MP.3** Logic
20	**3** Strategic Thinking H.O.T.	**MP.7** Using Structure
21	**3** Strategic Thinking H.O.T.	**MP.3** Logic

Additional Resources

Differentiated Instruction includes:

• Leveled Practice Worksheets

6.1 Independent Practice

COMMON CORE 6.RP.1, 6.RP.3, 6.RP.3a

Personal Math Trainer
Online Assessment and Intervention
my.hrw.com

Write three ratios equivalent to the ratio described in each situation.

11. The ratio of cups of water to cups of milk in a recipe is 1 to 3.

2 to 6, 3 to 9, 4 to 12

12. The ratio of boys to girls on the bus is $\frac{20}{15}$.

$\frac{4}{3}, \frac{40}{30}, \frac{100}{75}$

13. In each bouquet of flowers, there are 4 roses and 6 white carnations. Complete the table to find how many roses and carnations there are in 4 bouquets of flowers.

Roses	4	8	12	16	20
Carnations	6	12	18	24	30

16 roses and 24 carnations

14. Ed is using the recipe shown to make fruit salad. He wants to use 30 diced strawberries in his fruit salad. How many bananas, apples, and pears should Ed use in his fruit salad?

12 bananas, 9 apples, and 18 pears

Fruit Salad Recipe
4 bananas, diced
3 apples, diced
6 pears, diced
10 strawberries, diced

15. A collector has 120 movie posters and 100 band posters. She wants to sell 24 movie posters but still have her poster collection maintain the same ratio of 120:100. If she sells 24 movie posters, how many band posters should she sell? Explain.

20; her current ratio of movie posters to band posters

is 120:100. If she sells 24 movie posters, she will have 96 left.

120:100 = 96:80, so she should sell 20 movie posters.

16. Bob needs to mix 2 cups of orange juice concentrate with 3.5 cups of water to make orange juice. Bob has 6 cups of concentrate. How much orange juice can he make?

16.5 cups

17. Multistep The ratio of North American butterflies to South American butterflies at a butterfly park is 5:3. The ratio of South American butterflies to European butterflies is 3:2. There are 30 North American butterflies at the butterfly park.

a. How many South American butterflies are there? 18

b. How many European butterflies are there? 12

18. Sinea and Ren are going to the carnival next week. The table shows the amount that each person spent on snacks, games, and souvenirs the last time they went to the carnival.

	Snacks	Games	Souvenirs
Sinea	$5	$8	$12
Ren	$10	$8	$20

a. Sinea wants to spend money using the same ratios as on her last trip to the carnival. If she spends $26 on games, how much will she spend on souvenirs? $39

b. Ren wants to spend money using the same ratios as on his last trip to the carnival. If he spends $5 on souvenirs, how much will he spend on snacks? $2.50

c. What If? Suppose Sinea and Ren each spend $40 on snacks, and each person spends money using the same ratios as on their last trip. Who spends more on souvenirs? Explain.

Sinea; Sinea's ratio of snack money to souvenir

money is 5:12, which is equivalent to 40:96. Ren's

ratio is 10:20, which is equivalent to 40:80.

H.O.T. FOCUS ON HIGHER ORDER THINKING

Work Area

19. Multiple Representations The diagram compares the ratio of girls in the chorus to boys in the chorus. What is the ratio of girls to boys? If there are 50 students in the chorus, how many are girls and how many are boys?

3:2; 30 girls and 20 boys

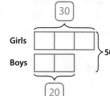

20. Analyze Relationships How is the process of finding equivalent ratios like the process of finding equivalent fractions?

In both processes you multiply or divide the terms, or

numerator and denominator, by the same number.

21. Explain the Error Tina says that 6:8 is equivalent to 36:64. What did Tina do wrong?

Tina multiplied 6 by 6 to get 36 and 8 by 8 to get 64. She

should have multiplied both terms by the same number.

EXTEND THE MATH PRE-AP

Activity available online my.hrw.com

Activity The Richmond Bakery is celebrating its 10th anniversary by offering 2 cupcakes for $3. Andy constructs this table for quick reference at the front counter. He's in a hurry and makes mistakes. Find his errors and correct them with equivalent ratios to complete the table. Write the corrected ratios. 6:9, 10:15, 12:18, and 14:21

Number of Cupcakes	2	4	6	8	10	12	14
Total Cost ($)	3	6	7	12	14	16	20

6.2 Rates

Common Core Standards

The student is expected to:

 Ratio and Proportional Relationships—6.RP.2

Understand the concept of a unit rate *a/b* associated with a ratio *a:b* with *b ≠ 0*, and use rate language in the context of a ratio relationship.

 Ratio and Proportional Relationships—6.RP.3

Use ratio and rate reasoning to solve real-world and mathematical problems, e.g. by reasoning about tables of equivalent ratios, tape diagrams, double number line diagrams, or equations.

 Ratio and Proportional Relationships—6.RP.3b

Solve unit rate problems including those involving unit pricing and constant speed.

Mathematical Practices

 MP.3 Logic

ADDITIONAL EXAMPLE 1

A The cost of 3 candles is $19.50. What is the unit price? $6.50 per candle

B Michael walks 30 meters in 20 seconds. How many meters does he walk per second? 1.5 meters per second

C An airplane makes a 2,748-mile flight in 6 hours. What is the airplane's average rate of speed in miles per hour? 458 miles per hour

 Interactive Whiteboard
Interactive example available online

 my.hrw.com

Engage

ESSENTIAL QUESTION

How do you use rates to compare quantities? Sample answer: You use multiplication or division to compare two quantities with different units.

Motivate the Lesson

Ask: Have you ever wanted to find out which of two products was the better buy, or how fast you are walking or running? Begin the Explore Activity to find out how to compare quantities with different units.

Explore

EXPLORE ACTIVITY

Engage with the Whiteboard

Have students fill in the table for each brand on the whiteboard. Ask students to write a rate for each brand, using the data from the last row of each table. Then have them compare that rate to the original rate in the problem statement. Help students to see that the two rates are equivalent.

Explain

EXAMPLE 1

Connect Vocabulary ELL

Remind students that a **ratio** is a comparison of two quantities expressed with the *same* units of measure, and a **rate** is a comparison of two quantities with *different* units of measure. A rate in which the second quantity is one unit is a **unit rate**.

Questioning Strategies CC Mathematical Practices

• How do you determine what number to divide by when finding a unit rate? Divide both quantities by the same number so that the second quantity is 1.

• How is finding a unit rate like simplifying a fraction? You find unit rates by dividing both quantities by the same number, just as you would to simplify a fraction.

Avoid Common Errors

When writing unit rates as fractions, some students might have difficulty determining which quantities should be the numerator and the denominator. Point out that *per* means "for each" or "apiece." The quantity after *per* is the denominator. For example, "cost per photograph" means $\frac{\text{cost}}{\text{number of photographs}}$.

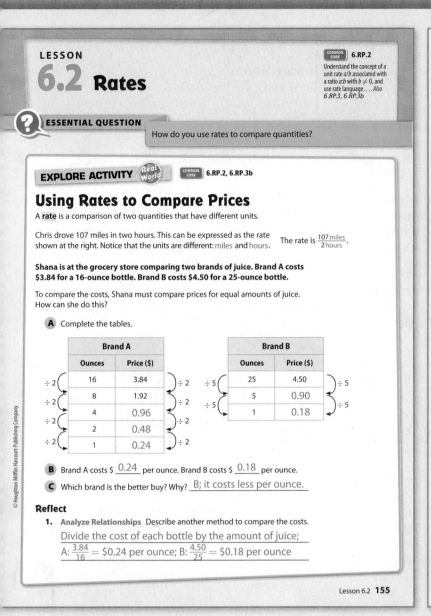

LESSON 6.2 Rates

COMMON CORE 6.RP.2
Understand the concept of a unit rate a/b associated with a ratio $a:b$ with $b \neq 0$, and use rate language.... Also 6.RP.3, 6.RP.3b

? ESSENTIAL QUESTION

How do you use rates to compare quantities?

EXPLORE ACTIVITY Real World   COMMON CORE 6.RP.2, 6.RP.3b

Using Rates to Compare Prices

A **rate** is a comparison of two quantities that have different units.

Chris drove 107 miles in two hours. This can be expressed as the rate shown at the right. Notice that the units are different: miles and hours.   The rate is $\frac{107 \text{ miles}}{2 \text{ hours}}$.

Shana is at the grocery store comparing two brands of juice. Brand A costs $3.84 for a 16-ounce bottle. Brand B costs $4.50 for a 25-ounce bottle.

To compare the costs, Shana must compare prices for equal amounts of juice. How can she do this?

A Complete the tables.

Brand A	
Ounces	Price ($)
16	3.84
8	1.92
4	0.96
2	0.48
1	0.24

÷ 2 (between each row on both sides)

Brand B	
Ounces	Price ($)
25	4.50
5	0.90
1	0.18

÷ 5 (between each row on both sides)

B Brand A costs $ __0.24__ per ounce. Brand B costs $ __0.18__ per ounce.

C Which brand is the better buy? Why? __B; it costs less per ounce.__

Reflect

1. **Analyze Relationships** Describe another method to compare the costs.
   Divide the cost of each bottle by the amount of juice;
   A: $\frac{3.84}{16} = \$0.24$ per ounce; B: $\frac{4.50}{25} = \$0.18$ per ounce

---

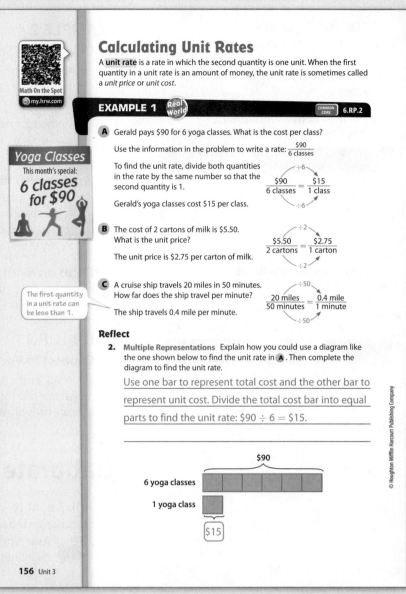

Math On the Spot
my.hrw.com

Calculating Unit Rates

A **unit rate** is a rate in which the second quantity is one unit. When the first quantity in a unit rate is an amount of money, the unit rate is sometimes called a *unit price* or *unit cost*.

EXAMPLE 1 Real World   COMMON CORE 6.RP.2

A Gerald pays $90 for 6 yoga classes. What is the cost per class?

Use the information in the problem to write a rate: $\frac{\$90}{6 \text{ classes}}$

To find the unit rate, divide both quantities in the rate by the same number so that the second quantity is 1.

$\frac{\$90}{6 \text{ classes}} = \frac{\$15}{1 \text{ class}}$ ÷6

Gerald's yoga classes cost $15 per class.

B The cost of 2 cartons of milk is $5.50. What is the unit price?

$\frac{\$5.50}{2 \text{ cartons}} = \frac{\$2.75}{1 \text{ carton}}$ ÷2

The unit price is $2.75 per carton of milk.

C A cruise ship travels 20 miles in 50 minutes. How far does the ship travel per minute?

$\frac{20 \text{ miles}}{50 \text{ minutes}} = \frac{0.4 \text{ mile}}{1 \text{ minute}}$ ÷50

The ship travels 0.4 mile per minute.

The first quantity in a unit rate can be less than 1.

Yoga Classes
This month's special:
6 classes for $90

Reflect

2. **Multiple Representations** Explain how you could use a diagram like the one shown below to find the unit rate in **A**. Then complete the diagram to find the unit rate.

   Use one bar to represent total cost and the other bar to represent unit cost. Divide the total cost bar into equal parts to find the unit rate: $90 ÷ 6 = $15.

   $90
   6 yoga classes
   1 yoga class
   $15

PROFESSIONAL DEVELOPMENT

CC Integrate Mathematical Practices MP.3

This lesson provides an opportunity to address the Mathematical Practice standard that calls for students to "construct viable arguments and critique the reasoning of others." In the Explore Activity, students compare prices by writing values in tables and analyzing the results of calculations expressed in symbols and units of measure. Then, in the Examples, students use unit rates to compare quantities that have different units. In this way, students start to learn how to construct arguments and critique the reasoning of others.

Math Background

The words *ratio* and *rate* come from the Latin word *ratus*, which means "calculation." A unit rate is a rate expressed in its simplest form, *a* to *b*, where *a* may or may not be a whole number and *b* is 1. The terms have only 1 as a common factor.

Many real-world situations involve the use of rate tables. By ordering the data, rate tables make it easy to find unit rates. A table provides a clear picture of the comparisons between quantities and their different units. For instance, the Explore Activity shows tables for comparing quantities in ounces and prices in dollars.

EXAMPLE 2

Questioning Strategies [CC] **Mathematical Practices**

- In Method 1, why do you need to find the unit rate first? Because you need to know how many campers can be housed in one cabin before you can determine how many cabins you will need for 112 campers (e.g., 112 campers ÷ 8 campers per cabin = 14 cabins).

- In Method 2, how do you determine what number to multiply by? You need to multiply the numerator and denominator of the given rate by a number that will make the numerator of the equivalent rate 112 campers (e.g., 16 campers × 7 = 112 campers).

Engage with the Whiteboard

Have students make another model of this situation on the whiteboard. Encourage students to make groups based on the unit rate until they have the correct number of campers per cabin. Discuss with students why modeling this situation depended on their knowing the unit rate.

Focus on Math Concepts [CC] **Mathematical Practices**

Remind students that just as you can write equivalent ratios, you can write equivalent rates by multiplying or dividing *both* terms of a rate *by the same number.*

YOUR TURN

Connect to Vocabulary [ELL]

Some students might have difficulty determining which quantities should be the numerator and the denominator when writing rates. Point out common phrases that indicate division, such as *"miles per gallon," "miles per hour,"* and *"cost per dollar."*

Elaborate

Talk About It
Summarize the Lesson

Ask: Why are unit rates helpful for showing the relationship between two quantities with different units of measure? Give an example. Unit rates make it easier to compare rates. Look at the Explore Activity. Brand A appeared to be the better buy because $3.84 < $4.50. However, when you compare the unit costs, you find that Brand A actually costs more per ounce, $0.24 > $0.18.

GUIDED PRACTICE

Engage with the Whiteboard

For Exercises 1–2, have students extend the table by inserting and completing a Unit Price column to the right of the Price column. Then discuss how unit rates are used not only to evaluate buying situations but also to sell products such as cars.

Avoid Common Errors

Exercise 1 Remind students that they want to find the unit rate of price to size, *not* size to price. Emphasize that the order of terms in a rate does make a difference.

Exercise 2 Point out to students that in this problem *better buy* means the *lowest* unit price. This information is not shown on the table and must be calculated.

3. There are 156 players on 13 teams. How many players are on each team? ___12___ players per team

Problem Solving with Unit Rates

You can solve rate problems by using a unit rate or by using equivalent rates.

EXAMPLE 2

COMMON CORE 6.RP.3, 6.RP.3b

At a summer camp, the campers are divided into groups. Each group has 16 campers and 2 cabins. How many cabins are needed for 112 campers?

Method 1 Find the unit rate. How many campers per cabin?

$$\frac{16\ campers}{2\ cabins} = \frac{8\ campers}{1\ cabin}$$
Divide to find the unit rate.

There are 8 campers per cabin.

$$\frac{112\ campers}{8\ campers\ per\ cabin} = 14\ cabins$$
Divide to find the number of cabins.

Method 2 Use equivalent rates.

$$\frac{16\ campers}{2\ cabins} = \frac{112\ campers}{14\ cabins}$$

The camp needs 14 cabins.

Check Use a diagram to check the unit rate if there are 16 campers in 2 cabins. Then, use the unit rate to check if 14 cabins is a reasonable number for 112 campers.

16 campers

2 cabins

8 campers   8 campers

The unit rate of 8 campers per cabin is reasonable. You can multiply 14 cabins by 8 campers per cabin to find that there would be enough room for 112 campers.

Personal Math Trainer
Online Assessment and Intervention
my.hrw.com

Math On the Spot
my.hrw.com

Animated Math
my.hrw.com

Personal Math Trainer
Online Assessment and Intervention
my.hrw.com

YOUR TURN

4. Petra jogs 3 miles in 27 minutes. At this rate, how long would it take her to jog 5 miles? Show your work.

45 minutes, $\frac{27\ minutes \div 3}{3\ miles \div 3} = \frac{9\ minutes}{1\ mile}$. The unit rate is

9 minutes per mile. $\frac{9\ minutes \times 5}{1\ mile \times 5} = \frac{45\ minutes}{5\ miles}$

Guided Practice

Mason's favorite brand of peanut butter is available in two sizes. Each size and its price are shown in the table. Use the table for 1 and 2. (Explore Activity)

1. What is the unit rate for each size of peanut butter?

Regular: $ ___0.21___ per ounce

Family size: $ ___0.19___ per ounce

	Size (oz)	Price ($)
Regular	16	3.36
Family Size	40	7.60

2. Which size is the better buy? ___family size___

3. Martin charges $10 for every 5 bags of leaves he rakes. Last weekend, he raked 24 bags of leaves. How much money did he earn? (Example 1)

___$48___ for 24 bags of leaves

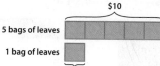
$10
5 bags of leaves
1 bag of leaves
$2

Find the unit rate. (Example 1)

4. Lisa walked 48 blocks in 3 hours.

___16___ blocks per hour

5. Gordon types 1,800 words in 25 minutes.

___72___ words per minute

6. A particular frozen yogurt has 75 calories in 2 ounces. How many calories are in 8 ounces of the yogurt? (Example 2)

___300 calories___

7. The cost of 10 oranges is $1. What is the cost of 5 dozen oranges? (Example 2)

___$6___

 ESSENTIAL QUESTION CHECK-IN

8. How can you use a rate to compare the costs of two boxes of cereal that are different sizes?

Divide the cost of each box by the size of the box in ounces to find the unit cost per ounce. Compare unit costs.

DIFFERENTIATE INSTRUCTION

Cooperative Learning

Provide prices for different packages of competitive products from several stores, for example, 24 oz for $4.80 or 36 oz for $5.40. Have students work in pairs to find the unit rate for each item and to determine which items are the best buys. Then have pairs compare their work and explain their steps.

Kinesthetic Experience

Have students choose to do something that they can count in one minute, such as hopping on one foot or tapping a pencil eraser on the desk. Have students keep track of the number of times they perform the action in one minute, and write the number they counted as a ratio with 1 minute in the denominator. Help them to see that for the first activity (hopping on one foot), one unit is hops and the other unit is minutes, and for the second activity (tapping a pencil eraser on the desk), one unit is taps and the other unit is minutes.

Other per-minute activities you could choose: number of words read, number of jumping jacks, number of books you can stack.

Additional Resources

Differentiated Instruction includes:

- Reading Strategies
- Success for English Learners **ELL**
- Reteach
- Challenge **PRE-AP**

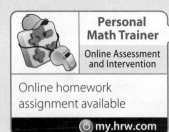
6.2 LESSON QUIZ

 6.RP.2

The table shows the available sizes and prices of Henry's favorite movie popcorn. Use the table to answer questions 1 and 2.

	Size (cups)	Price ($)
Regular	8	4
Large	15	6

1. What is the unit rate for each size?

2. Which size is the better buy?

3. Rita charges $60 for 5 tutoring sessions. What is the cost per session?

4. A package of 12 pens costs $3.60. What is the cost per pen?

5. A train travels 40 miles in 65 minutes. To the nearest tenth of a mile, how far does the train travel per minute?

Lesson Quiz available online

⏻ my.hrw.com

Answers

1. regular: 0.50; large: 0.40

2. large

3. $12

4. $0.30

5. 0.62 mile

Evaluate

GUIDED AND INDEPENDENT PRACTICE

 6.RP.2, 6.RP.3, 6.RP.3b

Concepts & Skills	Practice
Explore Activity Using Rates to Compare Prices	Exercises 1–2
Example 1 Calculating Unit Rates	Exercises 3–6, 9–10, 13, 16–18
Example 2 Problem Solving with Unit Rates	Exercises 7, 14–15, 16–17

Exercise	Depth of Knowledge (D.O.K.)		COMMON CORE Mathematical Practices
9–11	**2** Skills/Concepts		**MP.4** Modeling
12	**3** Strategic Thinking	H.O.T.	**MP.3** Logic
13–15	**2** Skills/Concepts		**MP.5** Using Tools
16	**3** Strategic Thinking	H.O.T.	**MP.7** Using Structure
17	**3** Strategic Thinking	H.O.T.	**MP.7** Using Structure
18	**3** Strategic Thinking	H.O.T.	**MP.3** Logic
19	**3** Strategic Thinking	H.O.T.	**MP.7** Using Structure

Additional Resources

Differentiated Instruction includes:

• Leveled Practice Worksheets

CC CLUSTER CONNECTION **Exercise 13** combines concepts from the Common Core cluster "Understand ratio concepts and use ratio reasoning to solve problems."

6.2 Independent Practice

COMMON CORE 6.RP.2, 6.RP.3, 6.RP.3b

Personal Math Trainer

Online Assessment and Intervention

my.hrw.com

Taryn and Alastair both mow lawns. Each charges a flat fee to mow a lawn. The table shows the number of lawns mowed in the past week, the time spent mowing lawns, and the money earned.

	Number of Lawns Mowed	Time Spent Mowing Lawns (in hours)	Money Earned
Taryn	9	7.5	$112.50
Alastair	7	5	$122.50

9. How much does Taryn charge to mow a lawn? ___$12.50 per lawn___

10. How much does Alastair charge to mow a lawn? ___$17.50 per lawn___

11. Who earns more per hour, Taryn or Alastair? ___Alastair___

12. **What If?** If Taryn and Alastair want to earn an additional $735 each, how many additional hours will each spend mowing lawns? Explain.

Taryn will spend 49 hours, Alastair will spend 30 hours;

Taryn earns $112.50 ÷ 7.5 hours = $15 per hour, and

735 ÷ 15 = 49. Alastair earns $122.50 ÷ 5 hours =

$24.50 per hour, and 735 ÷ 24.50 = 30.

13. **Multistep** Tomas makes balloon sculptures at a circus. In 180 minutes, he uses 252 balloons to make 36 identical balloon sculptures.

a. How many minutes does it take to make one balloon sculpture? How many balloons are used in one sculpture?

5 minutes; 7 balloons

b. What is Tomas's unit rate for balloons used per minute?

$1\frac{2}{5}$ balloons per minute

c. Complete the diagram to find out how many balloons he will use in 10 minutes.

14 balloons

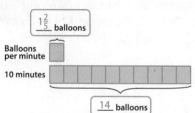

$1\frac{2}{5}$ balloons

Balloons per minute

10 minutes

14 balloons

---

14. Abby can buy an 8-pound bag of dog food for $7.40 or a 4-pound bag of the same dog food for $5.38. Which is the better buy?

8-pound bag

15. A bakery offers a sale price of $3.50 for 4 muffins. What is the price per dozen?

$10.50

16. Mrs. Jacobsen wants to order toy instruments to give as prizes to her music students. The table shows the prices for various order sizes.

	25 items	50 items	80 items
Whistles	$21.25	$36.00	$60.00
Kazoos	$10.00	$18.50	$27.20

a. What is the difference between the highest unit price for whistles and the lowest unit price for whistles?

$0.13 per whistle

b. What is the highest unit price per kazoo?

$0.40 per kazoo

c. **Persevere in Problem Solving** If Mrs. Jacobsen wants to buy the item with the lowest unit price, what item should she order and how many of that item should she order?

80 kazoos

H.O.T. FOCUS ON HIGHER ORDER THINKING

Work Area

17. **Draw Conclusions** There are 2.54 centimeters in 1 inch. How many centimeters are there in 1 foot? in 1 yard? Explain your reasoning.

There are 12 inches in 1 foot, and 2.54 × 12 =

30.48 centimeters per foot; there are 3 feet per yard, so

30.48 cm × 3 = 91.44 centimeters per yard.

18. **Critique Reasoning** A 2-pound box of spaghetti costs $2.50. Philip says that the unit cost is $\frac{2}{2.50}$ = $0.80 per pound. Explain his error.

Philip compared pounds to dollars and found the

weight per dollar. The correct unit cost is $\frac{$2.50}{2\ pounds}$ =

$1.25 per pound.

19. **Look for a Pattern** A grocery store sells three different quantities of sugar. A 1-pound bag costs $1.10, a 2-pound bag costs $1.98, and a 3-pound bag costs $2.85. Describe how the unit cost changes as the quantity of sugar increases.

The unit costs are $1.10 per pound for a 1-pound bag,

$0.99 per pound for a 2-pound bag, and $0.95 per

pound for a 3-pound bag. The unit cost decreases as the

quantity of sugar increases.

EXTEND THE MATH PRE-AP

Activity available online my.hrw.com

Activity A carpenter installed 10 windows in 4 hours. A second carpenter installed 15 windows in 5 hours. A third carpenter installed 50 windows in 20 hours.

- Draw a 4-column rate table to display this information. Include a column for Unit Rate on the table.

- Which carpenter is working at the fastest rate? second carpenter; 3 windows per hour

- Who has the next fastest rate? Explain. The first and the third carpenters are tied for the next fastest rate—2.5 windows per hour.

Carpenter	Windows	Time (hours)	Unit Rate (windows per hour)
1	10	4	2.5
2	15	5	3
3	50	20	2.5

LESSON
6.3 Using Ratios and Rates to Solve Problems

Common Core Standards

The student is expected to:

 Ratio and Proportional Relationships—6.RP.3

Use ratio and rate reasoning to solve real-world and mathematical problems, e.g. by reasoning about tables of equivalent ratios, tape diagrams, double number line diagrams, or equations.

 Ratio and Proportional Relationships—6.RP.3a

Make tables of equivalent ratios relating quantities with whole-number measurements, find missing values in the table, and plot the pairs of values on the coordinate plane. Use tables to compare ratios.

Mathematical Practices

 MP.6 Precision

ADDITIONAL EXAMPLE 1
A cookie recipe calls for 1 cup of raisins and 2 cups of flour. When Alex made a batch of cookies, he used 2 cups of raisins and 3 cups of flour. Did Alex use the correct ratio of raisins to flour? Support your opinion. No, the ratios are not the same; $\frac{1}{2} = \frac{3}{6}$ and $\frac{2}{3} = \frac{4}{6}$.

 Interactive Whiteboard
Interactive example available online

 my.hrw.com

Engage

ESSENTIAL QUESTION

How can you use ratios and rates to make comparisons and predictions? Sample answer: You can find equivalent ratios or rates with the same first or second terms to compare or make predictions.

Motivate the Lesson
Ask: Have you ever wanted a way to compare the amount of ingredients in different recipes, or predict how long it will take to get to a destination? Begin the Explore Activity to find out how to use ratios to compare quantities.

Explore

EXPLORE ACTIVITY 1

Focus on Reasoning CC Mathematical Practices

Point out to students that there is another way to determine which recipe makes stronger lemonade—they could extend the tables until they find a column in each table where the two recipes have the same amount of lemonade concentrate. The recipe with less water in that column has the stronger flavor. Ask students to find the ratios and check that this method results in the same answer as in D.

Explain

EXAMPLE 1

Connect Vocabulary ELL

Remind students that **equivalent** means "equal." Emphasize that in an **equivalent ratio** the *relationship* between the terms in each of the ratios is the same.

Questioning Strategies CC Mathematical Practices
• How is finding equivalent ratios like finding equivalent fractions? To find equivalent ratios or equivalent fractions, you multiply or divide by a form of 1.

YOUR TURN

Avoid Common Errors
Remind students to multiply or divide *both* terms of a ratio by the same number to find equivalent ratios. Point out that multiplying or dividing only one term does not produce an equivalent ratio.

Talk About It
Check for Understanding
Ask: How can you compare ratios to solve Exercise 2? Write a ratio with denominator 12 that is equivalent to $\frac{2}{3}$. If the numerator is 7, the ratios are equivalent. Otherwise, they are not.

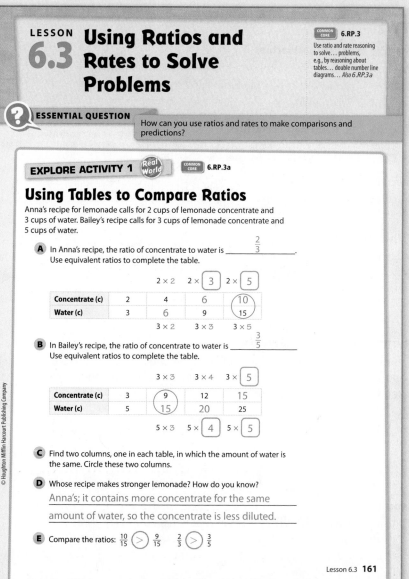

LESSON 6.3 Using Ratios and Rates to Solve Problems

COMMON CORE 6.RP.3
Use ratio and rate reasoning to solve… problems, e.g., by reasoning about tables… double number line diagrams… *Also 6.RP.3a*

? ESSENTIAL QUESTION
How can you use ratios and rates to make comparisons and predictions?

EXPLORE ACTIVITY 1 *Real World* **COMMON CORE 6.RP.3a**

Using Tables to Compare Ratios

Anna's recipe for lemonade calls for 2 cups of lemonade concentrate and 3 cups of water. Bailey's recipe calls for 3 cups of lemonade concentrate and 5 cups of water.

A In Anna's recipe, the ratio of concentrate to water is $\dfrac{2}{3}$. Use equivalent ratios to complete the table.

	2×2	$2 \times \boxed{3}$	$2 \times \boxed{5}$
Concentrate (c)	2	4	6	⑩
Water (c)	3	6	9	⑮
	3×2	3×3	3×5

B In Bailey's recipe, the ratio of concentrate to water is $\dfrac{3}{5}$. Use equivalent ratios to complete the table.

	3×3	3×4	$3 \times \boxed{5}$
Concentrate (c)	3	⑨	12	15
Water (c)	5	⑮	20	25
	5×3	$5 \times \boxed{4}$	$5 \times \boxed{5}$

C Find two columns, one in each table, in which the amount of water is the same. Circle these two columns.

D Whose recipe makes stronger lemonade? How do you know?

Anna's; it contains more concentrate for the same

amount of water, so the concentrate is less diluted.

E Compare the ratios: $\dfrac{10}{15} \bigcirc> \dfrac{9}{15}$ $\dfrac{2}{3} \bigcirc> \dfrac{3}{5}$

Lesson 6.3 **161**

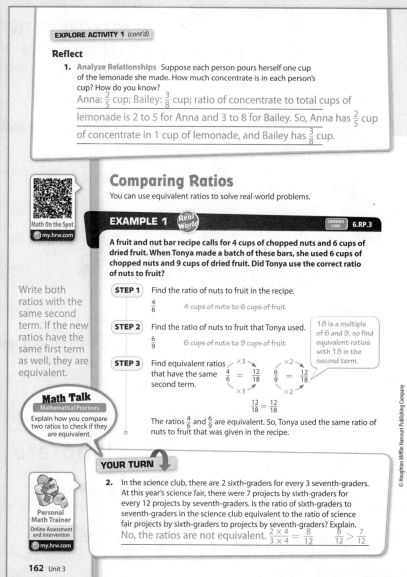

EXPLORE ACTIVITY 1 *(cont'd)*

Reflect

1. **Analyze Relationships** Suppose each person pours herself one cup of the lemonade she made. How much concentrate is in each person's cup? How do you know?

Anna: $\dfrac{2}{5}$ cup; Bailey: $\dfrac{3}{8}$ cup; ratio of concentrate to total cups of

lemonade is 2 to 5 for Anna and 3 to 8 for Bailey. So, Anna has $\dfrac{2}{5}$ cup

of concentrate in 1 cup of lemonade, and Bailey has $\dfrac{3}{8}$ cup.

Math On the Spot
my.hrw.com

Comparing Ratios

You can use equivalent ratios to solve real-world problems.

EXAMPLE 1 *Real World* **COMMON CORE 6.RP.3**

A fruit and nut bar recipe calls for 4 cups of chopped nuts and 6 cups of dried fruit. When Tonya made a batch of these bars, she used 6 cups of chopped nuts and 9 cups of dried fruit. Did Tonya use the correct ratio of nuts to fruit?

Write both ratios with the same second term. If the new ratios have the same first term as well, they are equivalent.

STEP 1 Find the ratio of nuts to fruit in the recipe.
$\dfrac{4}{6}$ *4 cups of nuts to 6 cups of fruit*

STEP 2 Find the ratio of nuts to fruit that Tonya used.
$\dfrac{6}{9}$ *6 cups of nuts to 9 cups of fruit*

> 18 is a multiple of 6 and 9, so find equivalent ratios with 18 in the second term.

STEP 3 Find equivalent ratios that have the same second term.
$\dfrac{4}{6} \overset{\times 3}{\underset{\times 3}{=}} \dfrac{12}{18}$ $\dfrac{6}{9} \overset{\times 2}{\underset{\times 2}{=}} \dfrac{12}{18}$

$\dfrac{12}{18} = \dfrac{12}{18}$

The ratios $\dfrac{4}{6}$ and $\dfrac{6}{9}$ are equivalent. So, Tonya used the same ratio of nuts to fruit that was given in the recipe.

Math Talk
Mathematical Practices
Explain how you compare two ratios to check if they are equivalent.

YOUR TURN

Personal Math Trainer
Online Assessment and Intervention
my.hrw.com

2. In the science club, there are 2 sixth-graders for every 3 seventh-graders. At this year's science fair, there were 7 projects by sixth-graders for every 12 projects by seventh-graders. Is the ratio of sixth-graders to seventh-graders in the science club equivalent to the ratio of science fair projects by sixth-graders to projects by seventh-graders? Explain.

No, the ratios are not equivalent. $\dfrac{2 \times 4}{3 \times 4} = \dfrac{8}{12}$ $\dfrac{8}{12} > \dfrac{7}{12}$

162 Unit 3

PROFESSIONAL DEVELOPMENT

CC Integrate Mathematical Practices MP.4

This lesson provides an opportunity to address the Mathematical Practice standard that calls for students to "communicate precisely." In this lesson students use symbols, tables, and double number lines to model relationships between quantities in ratios and to find equivalent rates. They employ these multiple representations to compare numbers, solve problems, and make predictions in real-world situations.

Math Background

In many ways, ratios look and behave like fractions. But it is important to note the ways in which ratios are *not* the same as fractions. Ratios can represent part-to-whole or part-to-part relationships. Fractions represent part-to-whole relationships. For example, if there are 2 lemons and 3 oranges in a bowl, the ratio of lemons to oranges is $\dfrac{2}{3}$ (part-to-part). This relationship cannot be represented with a fraction because a lemon is not part of an orange. However, the ratio of lemons to all of the fruit in the bowl is $\dfrac{2}{5}$ (part-to-whole). This relationship can be represented by a fraction because $\dfrac{2}{5}$ of the fruit in the bowl is lemons.

EXPLORE ACTIVITY 2

Focus on Modeling CC Mathematical Practices

Some students may not have seen a double number line before. Explain to students that a double number line represents rates, such as miles per hour, and that each pair of points on a double number line is an equivalent ratio.

Questioning Strategies CC Mathematical Practices

• How can you use a double number line to make predictions? Plot a series of equivalent ratios on the number lines to find equivalent ratios and make predictions.

• How would you extend the double number line? Multiplying each term in the first ratio by the same number produces the next ratio on the number lines. Multiply by 2, 3, 4, 5, and so on.

Engage with the Whiteboard

Have students extend the double number lines to 14 hours. Discuss how to find the miles driven in 12 hours and 14 hours. Have students show their calculations.
$112 \cdot 6 = 672, 2 \cdot 6 = 12; 112 \cdot 7 = 784, 2 \cdot 7 = 14$

REFLECT

Focus on Connections CC Mathematical Practices

Make sure that students understand the connections between the original rate, 15 minutes for 2 math problems, and the points 15 and 2 on the double number line so that they understand how to extend the double number line to include points such as 30 and 4.

Elaborate
....

Talk About It
Summarize the Lesson

Ask: How can using ratios and rates help to solve problems? Equivalent ratios and rates keep the relationship between their terms the same. This property is useful for solving problems with changing quantities and for predicting outcomes.

GUIDED PRACTICE

Engage with the Whiteboard

For Exercise 3, have a student complete the given double number line on the whiteboard. Have another student extend the number lines beyond 5 minutes, and write additional number pairs such as 196 words for 7 minutes. Then have students explain how they found each new number pair.

Avoid Common Errors

Exercises 1–2 Remind students to multiply or divide *both* terms of a ratio by the same number to find equivalent ratios. Point out that multiplying or dividing only one term does not produce an equivalent ratio.

EXPLORE ACTIVITY 2 COMMON CORE 6.RP.3

Using Rates to Make Predictions

You can represent rates on a double number line to make predictions.

Janet drives from Clarkson to Humbolt in 2 hours. Suppose Janet drives for 10 hours. If she maintains the same driving rate, can she drive more than 600 miles? Justify your answer.

The double number line shows the number of miles Janet drives in various amounts of time.

Miles	0	112	224	336	448	560
Hours	0	2	4	6	8	10

A Explain how Janet's rate for two hours is represented on the double number line.

The ratio of the distance to the time at each interval along the double number line is equivalent to Janet's rate of $\frac{112 \text{ miles}}{2 \text{ hours}}$.

B Describe the relationship between Janet's rate for two hours and the other rates shown on the double number line.

Both terms in the original rate are multiplied by the same number to find the equivalent rates.

C Complete the number line.

D At this rate, can Janet drive more than 600 miles in 10 hours? Explain.

No; at this rate, she will drive 560 miles in 10 hours.

Reflect

3. In fifteen minutes, Lena can finish 2 math homework problems. How many math problems can she finish in 75 minutes? Use a double number line to find the answer.

Minutes	0	15	30	45	60	75
Problems	0	2	4	6	8	10

Lena can finish 10 problems in 75 minutes.

4. How is using a double number line similar to finding equivalent ratios?

You multiply or divide both terms by the same number.

© Houghton Mifflin Harcourt Publishing Company

Guided Practice

1. Celeste is making fruit baskets for her service club to take to a local hospital. The directions say to fill the boxes using 5 apples for every 6 oranges. Celeste is filling her baskets with 2 apples for every 3 oranges. (Explore Activity 1)

a. Complete the tables to find equivalent ratios.

Apples	5	10	15	20
Oranges	6	12	18	24

Apples	2	4	6	8
Oranges	3	6	9	12

b. Compare the ratios. Is Celeste using the correct ratio of apples to oranges?

$\frac{5}{6} > \frac{4}{6}$; No, Celeste is not using the correct ratio of apples to oranges.

2. Neha used 4 bananas and 5 oranges in her fruit salad. Daniel used 7 bananas and 9 oranges. Did Neha and Daniel use the same ratio of bananas to oranges? If not, who used the greater ratio of bananas to oranges? (Example 1)

No; Neha used the greater ratio of bananas to oranges.

3. Tim is a first grader and reads 28 words per minute. Assuming he maintains the same rate, use the double number line to find how many words he can read in 5 minutes. (Explore Activity 2)

Words	0	28	56	84	112	140
Minutes	0	1	2	3	4	5

Tim can read 140 words in 5 minutes.

4. A cafeteria sells 30 drinks every 15 minutes. Predict how many drinks the cafeteria sells every hour. (Explore Activity 2)

On average, the cafeteria sells 120 drinks per hour.

? ESSENTIAL QUESTION CHECK-IN

5. Explain how to compare two ratios.

Find equivalent ratios that have the same second term. Then compare the first terms.

© Houghton Mifflin Harcourt Publishing Company

DIFFERENTIATE INSTRUCTION

Multiple Representations

Have students describe their use of tables and double number lines to make predictions. Discuss similarities and differences.

Method 1: I wrote the terms of equivalent ratios in table columns to compare the ratios of ingredients in two recipes.

Method 2: I labeled the terms of equivalent ratios on double number lines that started from 0 to predict how long it would take to drive a distance at a given rate.

In both methods, you write equivalent ratios or rates by multiplying the terms of a ratio or rate by the same number.

Communicating Math

Write the following terms on the board. Then have students match each term with its corresponding example. Ask them to be as specific as possible and to use each term only once. Ask them to explain their choices.

Ratio	d	a. 120 miles per 3 hours
Rate	a	b. 15 feet per second
Unit rate	b	c. $1.15 per pound
Unit price	c	d. 4:2

A ratio is a comparison of two quantities with the same units. A rate is a comparison of two quantities with different units. A unit rate is a rate in which the second quantity is 1. A unit price is a unit rate involving the cost of an item.

Additional Resources

Differentiated Instruction includes:

• Reading Strategies
• Success for English Learners **ELL**
• Reteach
• Challenge **PRE-AP**

6.3 LESSON QUIZ

 6.RP.3, 6.RP.3a

1. Philip's granola directions call for 3 oz of nuts to every 4 oz of raisins. He uses 2 oz of nuts to every 3 oz of raisins. Is Philip using the correct ratio of nuts to raisins? Complete the tables to help you find the answer.

Nuts	3	6	**9**	12
Raisins	4	8	**12**	16

Nuts	2	4	6	**8**
Raisins	3	6	9	**12**

2. A recipe calls for 2 cups of oats and 4 cups of flour. Alicia makes a larger batch, mixing 4 cups of oats and 6 cups of flour. Did she use the same ratio of oats to flour shown in the original recipe? Justify your answer.

3. Write an inequality to compare the ratios $\frac{2}{4}$ and $\frac{5}{6}$.

4. Ellen can read 3 pages in 7 minutes. Rob can read 8 pages in 14 minutes. Who is the faster reader? Justify your answer.

5. Mark runs 5 miles in 40 minutes. If he continues at the same rate, can he run 14 miles in 120 minutes?

Lesson Quiz available online

Answers

1. No. Philip is not using the correct ratio of nuts to raisins; $\frac{3}{4} > \frac{2}{3}$.

2. No; 2 to 4 is equivalent to 6 to 12, and 4 to 6 is equivalent to 8 to 12.

3. $\frac{2}{4} < \frac{5}{6}$

4. Rob; $\frac{8}{14} = \frac{4}{7}$ and $\frac{4}{7} > \frac{3}{7}$.

5. Yes. If Mark runs at the same rate, he will run 15 mi in 120 min; $\frac{15}{120} > \frac{14}{120}$.

Evaluate

GUIDED AND INDEPENDENT PRACTICE

 6.RP.3, 6.RP.3a

Concepts & Skills	Practice
Explore Activity 1 Using Tables to Compare Ratios	Exercise 1
Example 1 Comparing Ratios	Exercises 2, 6, 10
Explore Activity 2 Using Rates to Make Predictions	Exercises 3–4, 7–9, 11–14

Exercise	Depth of Knowledge (D.O.K.)	COMMON CORE Mathematical Practices
6	**3** Strategic Thinking H.O.T.	**MP.4** Modeling
7–9	**2** Skills/Concepts	**MP.4** Modeling
10	**3** Strategic Thinking H.O.T.	**MP.7** Using Structure
11–14	**2** Skills/Concepts	**MP.4** Modeling
15	**3** Strategic Thinking H.O.T.	**MP.5** Using Tools
16	**3** Strategic Thinking H.O.T.	**MP.3** Logic
17	**3** Strategic Thinking H.O.T.	**MP.7** Using Structure
18	**3** Strategic Thinking H.O.T.	**MP.3** Logic

Additional Resources

Differentiated Instruction includes:

• Leveled Practice Worksheets

6.3 Independent Practice

COMMON CORE 6.RP.3, 6.RP.3a

Personal Math Trainer

Online Assessment and Intervention

my.hrw.com

6. Gina's art teacher mixes 9 pints of yellow paint with 6 pints of blue paint to create green paint. Gina mixes 4 pints of yellow paint with 3 pints of blue paint. Did Gina use the same ratio of yellow paint to blue paint instructed by her teacher? Explain.

No, Gina did not use the same ratio as her teacher. 9 to 6

is not equivalent to 4 to 3.

7. The Suarez family paid $15.75 for 3 movie tickets. How much would they have paid for 12 tickets?

$63

8. A grocery store sells snacks by weight. A six-ounce bag of mixed nuts costs $3.60. Predict the cost of a two-ounce bag.

$1.20

9. The Martin family's truck gets an average of 25 miles per gallon. Predict how many miles they can drive using 7 gallons of gas.

175 miles

10. Multistep The table shows two cell phone plans that offer free minutes for each given number of paid minutes used. Pablo has Plan A and Sam has Plan B.

a. What is Pablo's ratio of free to paid minutes?

$\frac{2}{10} = \frac{1}{5}$

b. What is Sam's ratio of free to paid minutes?

$\frac{8}{25}$

	Cell Phone Plans	
	Plan A	**Plan B**
Free minutes	2	8
Paid minutes	10	25

c. Does Pablo's cell phone plan offer the same ratio of free to paid minutes as Sam's? Explain.

No. $\frac{1}{5} = \frac{5}{25}$. Since $\frac{8}{25} > \frac{5}{25}$, Sam's ratio is greater than

Pablo's.

11. Consumer Math A store has apples on sale for $3.00 for 2 pounds. How many pounds of apples can you buy for $9? If an apple is approximately 5 ounces, how many apples can you buy for $9? Explain your reasoning.

6 pounds; 19 apples; $\frac{\$3.00}{2 \text{ pounds}} = \frac{\$1.50}{1 \text{ pound}}$, $\frac{\$1.50 \times 6}{1 \text{ pound} \times 6} = \frac{\$9.00}{6 \text{ pounds}}$,

1 pound = 16 ounces, so 6 pounds $\times \frac{16 \text{ ounces}}{1 \text{ pound}} = 96$ ounces;

96 ounces $\div \frac{5 \text{ ounces}}{1 \text{ apple}} = 19.2$ apples.

12. Science Grass can grow up to six inches in a week depending on temperature, humidity, and time of year. At this rate, how tall will grass grow in 24 days?

approximately 20.6 inches

13. A town in east Texas received 10 inches of rain in two weeks. If it kept raining at this rate for a 31-day month, how much rain did the town receive?

approximately 22 inches

14. One patterned blue fabric sells for $15.00 every two yards, and another sells for $37.50 every 5 yards. Do these fabrics have the same unit cost? Explain.

Yes, they both cost $7.50 a yard.

H.O.T. FOCUS ON HIGHER ORDER THINKING

15. Problem Solving Complete each ratio table.

6	12	18	24
4.5	9	13.5	18

80.8	40.4	20.2	10.1
1,024	512	256	128

16. Represent Real-World Problems Write a real-world problem that compares the ratios 5 to 9 and 12 to 15.

Sample problem: In Tim's snack mix, the ratio of bagel chips to pretzels is 5 to 9. Sharon's snack mix has a ratio of 12 bagel chips to 15 pretzels. Which mix has the greater ratio of bagel chips to pretzels?

17. Analyze Relationships Explain how you can be sure that all the rates you have written on a double number line are correct.

All of the rates should be equivalent to each other. One way to check that they are equivalent is to divide the top term by the bottom term. All of the quotients will be equal if the rates are all correct.

18. Paul can choose to be paid $50 for a job, or he can be paid $12.50 per hour. Under what circumstances should he choose the hourly wage? Explain.

He should choose the hourly wage if the job lasts more than 4 hours. If he works less than 4 hours, he will make more than $12.50 per hour; if he works more than 4 hours, he will make less than $12.50 per hour.

Work Area

EXTEND THE MATH PRE-AP

Activity available online my.hrw.com

Activity Each time Leslie puts gas in her car, she records the mileage and the amount of gas needed to fill the gas tank to check her miles per gallon rate.

	1	2	3	4	5	6
Distance (mi)	341	285	326	210	244	223
Gas (gal)	13.3	11.5	12.8	9	9.9	10.2

What was her best miles per gallon rate and when did it occur? What was her worst miles per gallon rate and when did it occur?

best: about 25.6 miles per gallon at 1; worst: about 21.9 miles per gallon at 6

Ready to Go On?

Assess Mastery

Use the assessment on this page to determine if students have mastered the concepts and standards covered in this module.

Response to Intervention

Intervention	Enrichment

Access Ready to Go On? assessment online, and receive instant scoring, feedback, and customized intervention or enrichment.

Personal Math Trainer
Online Assessment and Intervention
my.hrw.com

Online and Print Resources

Differentiated Instruction
- Reteach worksheets
- Reading Strategies **ELL**
- Success for English Learners **ELL**

Differentiated Instruction
- Challenge worksheets
  PRE-AP
- Extend the Math **PRE-AP**
  Lesson Activities in TE

Additional Resources

Assessment Resources includes:
- Leveled Module Quizzes

Ready to Go On?

Personal Math Trainer
Online Assessment and Intervention
my.hrw.com

6.1 Ratios

Use the table to find each ratio.

1. white socks to brown socks $\frac{8}{5}$

2. blue socks to nonblue socks $\frac{4}{19}$

3. black socks to all of the socks $\frac{6}{23}$

Color of socks	white	black	blue	brown
Number of socks	8	6	4	5

4. Find two ratios equivalent to the ratio in Exercise 1.
   Sample answer: $\frac{16}{10}, \frac{24}{15}$

6.2 Rates

Find each rate.

5. Earl runs 75 meters in 30 seconds. How many meters does Earl run per second? **2.5 meters**

6. The cost of 3 scarves is $26.25. What is the unit price? **$8.75 per scarf**

6.3 Using Ratios and Rates to Solve Problems

7. Danny charges $35 for 3 hours of swimming lessons. Martin charges $24 for 2 hours of swimming lessons. Who offers a better deal? **Danny**

8. There are 32 female performers in a dance recital. The ratio of men to women is 3:8. How many men are in the dance recital? **12 men**

 ESSENTIAL QUESTION

9. How can you use ratios and rates to solve problems?
   Sample answer: Compare ratios and rates by finding equivalent ratios and rates with a common second term; make predictions by finding a unit rate and multiplying by the unit rate.

© Houghton Mifflin Harcourt Publishing Company

Common Core Standards

Lesson	Exercises	Common Core Standards
6.1	1–4	**6.RP.1, 6.RP.3, 6.RP.3a**
6.2	5–6	**6.RP.2, 6.RP.3, 6.RP.3b**
6.3	7–8	**6.RP.3, 6.RP.3a**

Assessment Readiness

Item 1 Students are given four ratios and asked to find the three that are equivalent. If they simplify the ratios, they will find that all but C have $\frac{2}{3}$ as their simplest form.

Item 7 Students are asked to find an equivalent ratio to 5 cups of beans and 2 cups of carrots. This ratio is already in simplest form, so if they simplify each of the answer choices they will find which one is equivalent. Choices A and D can be eliminated easily, as both are already in simplest form and neither is equivalent to the given ratio. If students simplify choices B and C, they will find that choice B is equivalent to 5 cups of beans and 2 cups of carrots.

Avoid Common Errors

Item 5 Some students may find the unit rate and think it is the answer, when they really need the distance for 2 minutes. Remind students to check their response to make sure they have answered the right question.

Item 9 Some students may find the ratio of the distance run to the distance biked, rather than realizing that they need to find the sum to get the total distance. Remind students to read the question carefully to make sure they are comparing the correct quantities.

Additional Resources

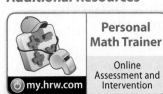

Personal Math Trainer
Online Assessment and Intervention
my.hrw.com

MODULE 6 MIXED REVIEW
COMMON CORE
Assessment Readiness

Personal Math Trainer
Online Assessment and Intervention
my.hrw.com

Selected Response

1. Which ratio is **not** equivalent to the other three?

Ⓐ $\frac{2}{3}$ Ⓒ $\frac{12}{15}$

Ⓑ $\frac{6}{9}$ Ⓓ $\frac{18}{27}$

2. A lifeguard received 15 hours of first aid training and 10 hours of cardiopulmonary resuscitation (CPR) training. What is the ratio of hours of CPR training to hours of first aid training?

Ⓐ 15:10   Ⓒ 10:15

Ⓑ 15:25   Ⓓ 25:15

3. Jerry bought 4 DVDs for $25.20. What was the unit rate?

Ⓐ $3.15   Ⓒ $6.30

Ⓑ $4.20   Ⓓ $8.40

4. There are 1,920 fence posts used in a 12-kilometer stretch of fence. How many fence posts are used in 1 kilometer of fence?

Ⓐ 150   Ⓒ 155

Ⓑ 160   Ⓓ 180

5. Sheila can ride her bicycle 6,000 meters in 15 minutes. How far can she ride her bicycle in 2 minutes?

Ⓐ 400 meters   Ⓒ 800 meters

Ⓑ 600 meters   Ⓓ 1,000 meters

6. Lennon has a checking account. He withdrew $130 from an ATM Tuesday. Wednesday he deposited $240. Friday he wrote a check for $56. What was the total change in Lennon's account?

Ⓐ −$74   Ⓒ $184

Ⓑ $54   Ⓓ $226

7. Cheyenne is making a recipe that uses 5 cups of beans and 2 cups of carrots. Which combination below uses the same ratio of beans to carrots?

Ⓐ 10 cups of beans and 3 cups of carrots

Ⓑ 10 cups of beans and 4 cups of carrots

Ⓒ 12 cups of beans and 4 cups of carrots

Ⓓ 12 cups of beans and 5 cups of carrots

8. $\frac{5}{8}$ of the 64 musicians in a music contest are guitarists. Some of the guitarists play jazz solos, and the rest play classical solos. The ratio of the number of guitarists playing jazz solos to the total number of guitarists in the contest is 1:4. How many guitarists play classical solos in the contest?

Ⓐ 10   Ⓒ 16

Ⓑ 30   Ⓓ 48

Mini-Task

9. Mikaela is competing in a race in which she both runs and rides a bicycle. She runs 5 kilometers in 0.5 hour and rides her bicycle 20 kilometers in 0.8 hour.

a. At the rate given, how many kilometers can Mikaela run in 1 hour?

10 kilometers

b. At the rate given, how many kilometers can Mikaela bike in 1 hour?

25 kilometers

c. If Mikaela runs for 1 hour and bikes for 1 hour at the rates given, how far will she travel?

35 kilometers

Common Core Standards

Items	Grade 6 Standards	Mathematical Practices
1	6.RP.1	MP.7, MP.8
2	6.RP.1	MP.4
3	6.RP.2	MP.4
4*	6.NS.2, 6.RP.3	MP.4, MP.7, MP.8
5	6.RP.2, 6.RP.3	MP.4, MP.7, MP.8
6*	6.NS.3, 6.RP.3	MP.4
7	6.RP.3	MP.4, MP.7, MP.8
8	6.RP.2, 6.RP.3	MP.4
9	6.RP.2, 6.RP.3	MP.4, MP.7, MP.8

* Item integrates mixed review concepts from previous modules or a previous course.

Applying Ratios and Rates

 MODULE 7

COMMON CORE

 ESSENTIAL QUESTION

How can you use ratios and rates to solve real-world problems?

You can use ratios and rates to make tables and graphs that represent real-world situations, and then use them to solve problems.

  my.hrw.com

Real-World Video

Chefs use lots of measurements when preparing meals. If a chef needs more or less of a dish, he can use ratios to scale the recipe up or down. Using proportional reasoning, the chef keeps the ratios of all ingredients constant.

© Houghton Mifflin Harcourt Publishing Company • Image Credits: ©Bravo/ Contributor/Getty Images

 GO DIGITAL

my.hrw.com

 my.hrw.com

Go digital with your write-in student edition, accessible on any device.

 Math On the Spot

Scan with your smart phone to jump directly to the online edition, video tutor, and more.

 Animated Math

Interactively explore key concepts to see how math works.

 Personal Math Trainer

Get immediate feedback and help as you work through practice sets.

Are You Ready?

Assess Readiness

Use the assessment on this page to determine if students need intensive or strategic intervention for the module's prerequisite skills.

  **Response to Intervention**

Intervention	Enrichment
Access Are You Ready? assessment online, and receive instant scoring, feedback, and customized intervention or enrichment.	

Personal Math Trainer
Online Assessment and Intervention
⏻ my.hrw.com

Online and Print Resources

Skills Intervention worksheets
- Skill 69 Graph Ordered Pairs (First Quadrant)
- Skill 24 Write Equivalent Fractions
- Skill 7 Multiples

Differentiated Instruction
- Challenge worksheets **PRE-AP**
- Extend the Math **PRE-AP** Lesson Activities in TE

 Are YOU Ready?

Complete these exercises to review skills you will need for this module.

 Personal Math Trainer
Online Assessment and Intervention

Graph Ordered Pairs (First Quadrant)

EXAMPLE

To graph A(2, 7), start at the origin.
Move 2 units right.
Then move 7 units up.
Graph point A(2, 7).

Graph each ordered pair on the coordinate plane above.

1. $B(9, 6)$ **2.** $C(0, 2)$ **3.** $D(6, 10)$ **4.** $E(3, 4)$

Write Equivalent Fractions

EXAMPLE $\frac{14}{21} = \frac{14 \times 2}{21 \times 2} = \frac{28}{42}$ Multiply the numerator and denominator by the same number to find an equivalent fraction.
$\frac{14}{21} = \frac{14 \div 7}{21 \div 7} = \frac{2}{3}$ **Divide** the numerator and denominator by the same number to find an equivalent fraction.

Write the equivalent fraction.

5. $\frac{6}{8} = \frac{24}{32}$ **6.** $\frac{4}{6} = \frac{8}{12}$ **7.** $\frac{1}{8} = \frac{7}{56}$ **8.** $\frac{9}{12} = \frac{3}{4}$

9. $\frac{5}{9} = \frac{25}{45}$ **10.** $\frac{5}{6} = \frac{20}{24}$ **11.** $\frac{36}{45} = \frac{12}{15}$ **12.** $\frac{20}{36} = \frac{10}{18}$

Multiples

EXAMPLE List the first five multiples of 4.
$4 \times 1 = 4$
$4 \times 2 = 8$ Multiply 4 by the numbers 1, 2,
$4 \times 3 = 12$ 3, 4, and 5.
$4 \times 4 = 16$
$4 \times 5 = 20$

List the first five multiples of each number.

13. 3 _6, 9, 12, 15_   **14.** 7 _14, 21, 28, 35_   **15.** 8 _16, 24, 32, 40_

PROFESSIONAL DEVELOPMENT VIDEO

 Author Juli Dixon models successful teaching practices as she applies ratios and rates to solve problems in an actual sixth-grade classroom.

 Professional Development
⏻ my.hrw.com

GO DIGITAL
my.hrw.com

 Online Teacher Edition
Access a full suite of teaching resources online—plan, present, and manage classes and assignments.

 ePlanner
Easily plan your classes and access all your resources online.

 Interactive Answers and Solutions
Customize answer keys to print or display in the classroom. Choose to include answers only or full solutions to all lesson exercises.

 Interactive Whiteboards
Engage students with interactive whiteboard-ready lessons and activities.

 Personal Math Trainer: Online Assessment and Intervention
Assign automatically graded homework, quizzes, tests, and intervention activities. Prepare your students with updated practice tests aligned with Common Core.

Applying Ratios and Rates   **170**

Reading Start-Up

Have students complete the activities on this page by working alone or with others.

Visualize Vocabulary

The decision tree helps students review the concepts and steps necessary to compare unit rates.

Understand Vocabulary

Use the following explanation to help students learn the preview words.

People are able to draw large objects like houses and roller coasters in correct **proportion** by creating a **scale drawing**.

One important part of a scale drawing is the scale used. The **scale** represents the degree to which the object in the drawing has been reduced in size compared to the original.

Active Reading

Integrating Language Arts

Students can use these reading and note-taking strategies to help them organize and understand new concepts and vocabulary.

COMMON CORE **ELA-Literacy.RST.6-8.7** Integrate quantitative or technical information expressed in words in a text with a version of that information expressed visually (e.g., in a flowchart, diagram, model, graph, or table).

Additional Resources

Differentiated Instruction

• Reading Strategies **ELL**

Reading Start-Up

Visualize Vocabulary

Use the ✔ words to complete the graphic.

Comparing Unit Rates

Single item
unit

↓

Ratio of two quantities that have different units
rate

→ Rate in which the second quantity is one unit
unit rate

↓

Numbers that follow a rule
pattern

Vocabulary

Review Words
equivalent ratios *(razones equivalentes)*
factor *(factor)*
graph *(gráfica)*
✔ pattern *(patrón)*
point *(punto)*
✔ rate *(tasa)*
ratio *(razón)*
✔ unit *(unidad)*
✔ unit rate *(tasa unitaria)*

Preview Words
conversion factor *(factor de conversión)*
proportion *(proporción)*
scale *(escala)*
scale drawing *(dibujo a escala)*

Understand Vocabulary

Complete the sentences using the preview words.

1. A _____conversion factor_____ is a rate that compares two equivalent measurements.

2. In a scale drawing, the _____scale_____ describes how the dimensions in the actual object compare to the dimensions in the drawing.

Active Reading

Tri-Fold Before beginning the module, create a tri-fold to help you learn the concepts and vocabulary in this module. Fold the paper into three sections. Label one column "Rates and Ratios," the second column "Proportions," and the third column "Converting Measurements." Complete the tri-fold with important vocabulary, examples, and notes as you read the module.

Before	In this module	After
Students understand proportional relationships: • identify and write equivalent ratios • determine whether two ratios form a proportion	Students understand proportional relationships: • compare additive and multiplicative relationships • represent mathematical and real-world problems involving ratios and rates using tables and graphs • solve problems with proportions • convert units within a measurement system	Students will connect: • constant rates of change given a table, verbal description, equation, or graph • the use of ratios and proportions to convert measurements • the constant of proportionality to real-world situations

Unpacking the Standards

Use the examples on the page to help students know exactly what they are expected to learn in this module.

Common Core Standards

Content Areas

 Ratios and Proportional Reasoning—6.RP

Understand ratio concepts and use ratio reasoning to solve problems.

> **Go online to see a complete unpacking of the Common Core Standards.**
>
> ⏻ my.hrw.com

 MODULE 7

Unpacking the Standards

Understanding the standards and the vocabulary terms in the standards will help you know exactly what you are expected to learn in this module.

COMMON CORE 6.RP.3

Use ratio and rate reasoning to solve real-world and mathematical problems, e.g., by reasoning about tables of equivalent ratios, tape diagrams, double number line diagrams, or equations.

Key Vocabulary

ratio *(razón)*
A comparison of two quantities by division.

rate *(tasa)*
A ratio that compares two quantities measured in different units.

What It Means to You

You will use ratios and rates to solve real-world problems such as those involving proportions.

UNPACKING EXAMPLE 6.RP.3

The distance from Austin to Dallas is about 200 miles. How far apart will these cities appear on a map with the scale of $\frac{1 \text{ in.}}{50 \text{ mi}}$?

$$\frac{1 \text{ inch}}{50 \text{ miles}} = \frac{\blacksquare \text{ inches}}{200 \text{ miles}} \qquad \text{Write the scale as a unit rate.}$$

$$\frac{1 \text{ inch} \times 4}{50 \text{ miles} \times 4} = \frac{\blacksquare \text{ inches}}{200 \text{ miles}} \qquad 200 \text{ is a common denominator.}$$

$$\blacksquare = 4$$

Austin and Dallas are 4 inches apart on the map.

COMMON CORE 6.RP.3d

Use ratio reasoning to convert measurement units; manipulate and transform units appropriately when multiplying or dividing quantities.

Key Vocabulary

unit rate *(tasa unitaria)*
A rate in which the second quantity in the comparison is one unit.

What It Means to You

You will use unit rates to convert measurement units.

UNPACKING EXAMPLE 6.RP.3d

The Washington Monument is about 185 yards tall. This height is almost equal to the length of two football fields. About how many feet is this?

$$185 \text{ yd} \cdot \frac{3 \text{ ft}}{1 \text{ yd}}$$
$$= \frac{185 \text{ yd}}{1} \cdot \frac{3 \text{ ft}}{1 \text{ yd}}$$
$$= 555 \text{ ft}$$

The Washington Monument is about 555 feet tall.

> Visit my.hrw.com to see all the **Common Core Standards** unpacked.
>
> ⏻ my.hrw.com

172 Unit 3

Common Core Standards	Lesson 7.1	Lesson 7.2	Lesson 7.3	Lesson 7.4
6.RP.3 Use ratio and rate reasoning to solve real-world and mathematical problems, e.g., by reasoning about tables of equivalent ratios, tape diagrams, double number line diagrams, or equations.	COMMON CORE	COMMON CORE		COMMON CORE
6.RP.3a Make tables of equivalent ratios relating quantities with whole-number measurements, find missing values in the tables, and plot the pairs of values on the coordinate plane. Use tables to compare ratios.	COMMON CORE			
6.RP.3b Solve unit rate problems including those involving unit pricing and constant speed.	COMMON CORE	COMMON CORE		
6.RP.3d Use ratio reasoning to convert measurement units; manipulate and transform units appropriately when multiplying or dividing quantities.			COMMON CORE	COMMON CORE

Common Core Standards

The student is expected to:

 Ratio and Proportional Relationships—6.RP.3a

Make tables of equivalent ratios relating quantities with whole-number measurements, find missing values in the tables, and plot the pairs of values on the coordinate plane. Use tables to compare ratios. *Also 6.RP.3, 6.RP.3b*

Mathematical Practices

 MP.4 Modeling

Engage

ESSENTIAL QUESTION

How can you represent real-world problems involving ratios and rates with tables and graphs? Sample answer: Find equivalent ratios and rates to make a table. Then use the table columns to make ordered pairs. Finally, graph the ordered pairs and connect the points with a line.

Motivate the Lesson

Ask: A faucet leaks 668 milliliters of water in 8 minutes. How many milliliters of water does the faucet leak per minute? Begin the Explore Activity to find out how to use a table to solve problems involving ratios and rates.

Explore

EXPLORE ACTIVITY 1

Focus on Communication

Ask students to read the problem statement and circle the key pieces of information. Have them consider the phrase *for every* and describe what this means and how the ratios relate to this phrase. Students should notice that this indicates a ratio of distilled water to ammonia.

Explain

EXPLORE ACTIVITY 2

Engage with the Whiteboard

Have students plot each point on the coordinate plane and then draw the line on the whiteboard. Discuss whether the origin should be included on the graph by having students consider how much distilled water should be added when there is no ammonia.

Focus on Reasoning

Have students consider what would happen to a point if its ratio were calculated incorrectly. Lead them to understand that the point would not fall on the line as the other points do.

Questioning Strategies [CC] Mathematical Practices

• Does the graphed line go through the origin (0, 0)? Yes How do you know? When we draw a line through the graphed points, it appears to go through (0, 0). And it is reasonable that both values are 0. The pattern in the table (1 mL of ammonia has 50 mL of distilled water) also can be used to show that (0, 0) satisfies the pattern.

• How could you use the table to predict how much ammonia would be used with 225 mL of distilled water? Think: $200 < 225 < 250$, so between 4 and 5 mL of ammonia would be used. Then notice that the difference between 200 and 225 is 25 and the distance between 225 and 250 is 25. Since the differences are the same, 225 is halfway between 200 and 250. So, 4.5 mL of ammonia would be used with 225 mL of distilled water.

• If the graph were continued, would the point (9, 450) be on the graph? How do you know? Yes; $\frac{450}{9}$ is equivalent to $\frac{50}{1}$.

LESSON 7.1 Ratios, Rates, Tables, and Graphs

 COMMON CORE **6.RP.3a**

Make tables of equivalent ratios ..., find missing values in the tables, and plot the pairs of values on the coordinate plane. ... *Also 6.RP.3, 6.RP.3b*

? ESSENTIAL QUESTION

How can you represent real-world problems involving ratios and rates with tables and graphs?

EXPLORE ACTIVITY 1   COMMON CORE **6.RP.3, 6.RP.3a**

Finding Ratios from Tables

Students in Mr. Webster's science classes are doing an experiment that requires 250 milliliters of distilled water for every 5 milliliters of ammonia. The table shows the amount of distilled water needed for various amounts of ammonia.

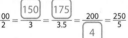

Ammonia (mL)	2	3	3.5	4	5
Distilled water (mL)	100	150	175	200	250

A Use the numbers in the first column of the table to write a ratio of distilled water to ammonia. $\frac{100}{2}$

B How much distilled water is used for 1 milliliter of ammonia? 50 mL

Use your answer to write another ratio of distilled water to ammonia. $\frac{50}{1}$

C The ratios in **A** and **B** are (equivalent/not equivalent.)

D How can you use your answer to **B** to find the amount of distilled water to add to a given amount of ammonia?

Sample answer: Multiply the amount of ammonia by $\frac{50}{1}$, or 50.

E Complete the table. What are the equivalent ratios shown in the table?

$$\frac{100}{2} = \frac{150}{3} = \frac{175}{3.5} = \frac{200}{4} = \frac{250}{5}$$

Reflect

1. **Look for a Pattern** When the amount of ammonia increases by 1 milliliter, the amount of distilled water increases by 50 milliliters. So 6 milliliters of ammonia requires 300 milliliters of distilled water.

Math Talk
Mathematical Practices

Is the relationship between the amount of ammonia and the amount of distilled water additive or multiplicative? Explain.

Multiplicative; the amount of distilled water is 50 times the amount of ammonia.

Lesson 7.1 **173**

EXPLORE ACTIVITY 2   COMMON CORE **6.RP.3a**

Graphing with Ratios

A Copy the table from Explore Activity 1 that shows the amounts of ammonia and distilled water.

Ammonia (mL)	2	3	3.5	4	5
Distilled water (mL)	100	150	175	200	250

B Write the information in the table as ordered pairs, Use the amount of ammonia as the *x*-coordinates and the amount of distilled water as the *y*-coordinates.

(2, 100) (3, 150), (3.5, 175), (4, 200), (5, 250)

Graph the ordered pairs. Because fractions and decimals can represent amounts of chemicals, connect the points.

Describe your graph. a line

C For each ordered pair that you graphed, write the ratio of the *y*-coordinate to the *x*-coordinate. $\frac{100}{2}$, $\frac{150}{3}$, $\frac{175}{3.5}$, $\frac{200}{4}$, $\frac{250}{5}$

D The ratio of distilled water to ammonia is $\frac{50}{1}$. How are the ratios in **C** related to this ratio? They are equivalent.

E The point (2.5, 125) is on the graph but not in the table. The ratio of the *y*-coordinate to the *x*-coordinate is $\frac{125}{2.5}$. How is this ratio related to the ratios in **C** and **D**? They are equivalent.

2.5 milliliters of ammonia requires 125 milliliters of distilled water.

F **Conjecture** What do you think is true for every point on the graph?

Sample answer: The *y*-coordinate is the correct amount of water for the amount of ammonia given by the *x*-coordinate.

Reflect

2. **Communicate Mathematical Ideas** How can you use the graph to find the amount of distilled water to use for 4.5 milliliters of ammonia?

Find the point on the graph whose *x*-coordinate is 4.5. The *y*-coordinate of that point is the milliliters of distilled water.

174 Unit 3

PROFESSIONAL DEVELOPMENT

CC Integrate Mathematical Processes MP.4

This lesson provides an opportunity to address this Mathematical Practice standard. It calls for students to communicate mathematical ideas using multiple representations as appropriate. In Explore Activity 1, students use tables to model a relationship between the amount of ammonia and the amount of distilled water used in an experiment. In Explore Activity 2, students then use graphs to model the same relationship shown in Explore Activity 1. Finally, in Example 1, students use a table and a graph to model the relationship between the speed and time it takes an express train to travel to Washington, D.C.

Math Background

Time is *continuous*, so distance and speed are based upon a continuous quantity that can be any nonnegative amount. Other situations involve *discrete* quantities. In Example 1, if the quantities were total cost and number of shirts, the number of shirts would be a discrete quantity. Only whole numbers make sense for the situation.

Although a line on a graph could be used to show the trend, the actual graph is restricted to a set of discrete points.

ADDITIONAL EXAMPLE 1
The number of carats of a gemstone and the mass of the gemstone in grams are related quantities. Complete the table to show the mass of a ruby in grams for various measures in carats. Then graph the information from the table.

Carats	2.5	5	7.5	10
Mass in grams	0.5	1	1.5	2

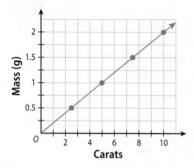

 Interactive Whiteboard
Interactive example available online

 my.hrw.com

 Animated Math
Representing
Unit Rates

Students connect unit rates to equivalent rates using this interactive graph.

 my.hrw.com

EXAMPLE 1

Focus on Math Connections CC Mathematical Practices
Remind students that the formula $d = rt$ can be used to find the distance, rate, or time of an object moving at a constant speed. You can solve for any part as long as you know the other two.

Questioning Strategies CC Mathematical Practices
• Why do you think we find the rate of distance to time, not time to distance? because distance depends upon the amount of travel time

Focus on Modeling CC Mathematical Practices
Discuss the situation and the train's journey. Have students consider whether all of the points on the line make sense in the problem situation and how long the train can realistically keep a constant speed. Note that when the Webster family exits the train, the speed is 0 miles per hour.

YOUR TURN

Avoid Common Errors
Students may try to multiply the given number in each cell by 4 to complete the table. This works only when time is given. When the amount of water is given, as in column 4, students need to *divide* by 4 to find the time.

Talk About It
Check for Understanding
 Ask: How do you complete a table that has a proportional relationship between quantities? Use two quantities that are given in the same column of the table, find their ratio or rate, and then multiply or divide both terms by the same number to find equivalent ratios or rates.

Elaborate
....

Talk About It
Summarize the Lesson
Ask: How can you use ratios and rates to represent the relationship between two quantities using tables and graphs? Sample answer: Find equivalent ratios and rates to make a table. Then use the table columns to make ordered pairs. Finally, graph the ordered pairs and connect the points with a line.

GUIDED PRACTICE

Engage with the Whiteboard
For Exercises 1, 3, and 5, have students fill in the tables on the whiteboard.
For Exercises 2, 4, and 5, have students plot the ordered pairs on the provided graph.

Avoid Common Errors
Exercise 5 Students may connect the points on the graph with a line. Have students consider whether there can be a fraction of a box of candles before graphing.

Representing Rates with Tables and Graphs

You can use tables and graphs to represent real-world problems involving equivalent rates.

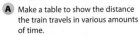

EXAMPLE 1

COMMON CORE 6.RP.3a, 6.RP.3b

The Webster family is taking an express train to Washington, D.C. The train travels at a constant speed and makes the trip in 2 hours.

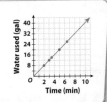

A Make a table to show the distance the train travels in various amounts of time.

STEP 1 Write a ratio of distance to time to find the rate.

$$\frac{distance}{time} = \frac{120 \text{ miles}}{2 \text{ hours}} = \frac{60 \text{ miles}}{1 \text{ hour}} = 60 \text{ miles per hour}$$

STEP 2 Use the unit rate to make a table.

Time (h)	2	3	3.5	4	5
Distance (mi)	120	180	210	240	300

B Graph the information from the table.

STEP 1 Write ordered pairs. Use Time as the x-coordinates and Distance as the y-coordinates.

(2, 120), (3, 180), (3.5, 210), (4, 240), (5, 300)

STEP 2 Graph the ordered pairs and connect the points.

YOUR TURN

3. A shower uses 12 gallons of water in 3 minutes. Complete the table and graph.

Time (min)	2	3	3.5	5	6.5
Water used (gal)	8	12	14	20	26

Math On the Spot
my.hrw.com

Animated Math
my.hrw.com

Personal Math Trainer
Online Assessment and Intervention
my.hrw.com

Lesson 7.1 **175**

---

1. The ratio of oxygen atoms to sulfur atoms in sulfur dioxide is always the same. The table shows the numbers of atoms in different quantities of sulfur dioxide. Complete the table. (Explore Activity 1)

Sulfur atoms	6	9	21	27
Oxygen atoms	12	18	42	54

What are the equivalent ratios shown in the table?

$$\frac{12}{6} = \frac{18}{9} = \frac{42}{21} = \frac{54}{27}$$

2. Use the table in Exercise 1 to graph the relationship between sulfur atoms and oxygen atoms. (Explore Activity 2)

3. Stickers are made with the same ratio of width to length. A sticker 2 inches wide has a length of 4 inches. Complete the table. (Explore Activity 1)

Width (in.)	2	4	7	8
Length (in.)	4	8	14	16

What are the equivalent ratios shown in the table?

$$\frac{2}{4} = \frac{4}{8} = \frac{7}{14} = \frac{8}{16}$$

4. Graph the relationship between the width and the length of the stickers from Exercise 3. (Explore Activity 2)

5. Five boxes of candles contain a total of 60 candles. Each box holds the same number of candles. Complete the table and graph the relationship. (Example 1)

Boxes	5	8	10
Candles	60	96	120

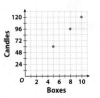

? ESSENTIAL QUESTION CHECK-IN

6. How do you represent real-world problems involving ratios and rates with tables and graphs?

Sample answer: Find equivalent ratios and rates to make a table with different amounts of each quantity. Then use the table columns to make ordered pairs, graph the ordered pairs, and if it makes sense, connect the points with a line.

DIFFERENTIATE INSTRUCTION

Curriculum Integration: Physical Education

Sports statistics provide many examples of ratios and rates.

Several commonly used sports ratios or rates:
- RBI (baseball)
- free-throws to attempted free-throws (basketball)
- pass/run (football)

Have students find sports data online or in newspapers, and then ask them to make tables and graphs to display a player's progress.

Visual Cues

If students have difficulty in making a graph from a table, have them write the ratios using a colon. Then they can plot the ratios as points on the graph by using the first number of each ratio for the distance along one axis and the second number of each ratio for the distance on the second axis.

1	2	3	4
2	4	6	8

For example, the ratios from the table above can be written as 1:2, 2:4, 3:6, and 4:8, which then become (1, 2), (2, 4), (3, 6), and (4, 8).

Additional Resources

Differentiated Instruction includes:
- Reading Strategies
- Success for English Learners **ELL**
- Reteach
- Challenge **PRE-AP**

7.1 LESSON QUIZ

 6.RP.3a

1. Are the ratios equivalent? Explain.

Protein (g)	24	28
Calories	96	112

2. Four gallons of gasoline cost $14. Complete the table.

Gallons				6
Cost ($)	3.5	7	14	

3. How much does each gallon of gasoline cost?

4. Make a graph of the relationship.

5. How much does the cost increase if the number of gallons is increased from 6 to 8?

Lesson Quiz available online

 my.hrw.com

Answers

1. Yes; $\frac{96}{24} = 4$ and $\frac{112}{28} = 4$

2.

Gallons	1	2	4	6
Cost ($)	3.5	7	14	21

3. $3.50

4.

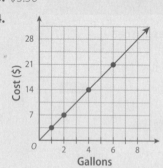

5. The cost increases by $7.

Evaluate

GUIDED AND INDEPENDENT PRACTICE

 6.RP.3, 6.RP.3a, 6.RP.3b

Concepts & Skills	Practice
Explore Activity 1 Finding Ratios from Tables	Exercises 1, 3
Explore Activity 2 Graphing with Ratios	Exercises 2, 4
Example 1 Representing Rates with Tables and Graphs	Exercises 5, 7–15

Exercise	Depth of Knowledge (D.O.K.)		**Mathematical Practices**
7–8	2 Skills/Concepts		**MP.4** Modeling
9	3 Strategic Thinking	H.O.T.	**MP.3** Logic
10	2 Skills/Concepts		**MP.5** Using Tools
11	2 Skills/Concepts		**MP.4** Modeling
12	3 Strategic Thinking	H.O.T.	**MP.7** Using Structure
13	3 Strategic Thinking	H.O.T.	**MP.3** Logic
14	3 Strategic Thinking	H.O.T.	**MP.7** Using Structure
15	3 Strategic Thinking	H.O.T.	**MP.3** Logic
16	3 Strategic Thinking	H.O.T.	**MP.2** Reasoning
17	3 Strategic Thinking	H.O.T.	**MP.3** Logic

Additional Resources

Differentiated Instruction includes:

• Leveled Practice worksheets

 CLUSTER CONNECTION **Exercises 7–12** combine concepts from the Common Core cluster "Understand ratio concepts and use ratio reasoning to solve problems."

7.1 Independent Practice

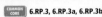 COMMON CORE 6.RP.3, 6.RP.3a, 6.RP.3b

 Personal Math Trainer
Online Assessment and Intervention
my.hrw.com

The table shows information about the number of sweatshirts sold and the money collected at a fundraiser for school athletic programs. For Exercises 7–12, use the table.

Sweatshirts sold	3	5	8	9	12
Money collected ($)	60	100	160	180	240

7. Find the rate of money collected per sweatshirt sold. Show your work.

$$\frac{\text{money collected}}{\text{sweatshirts sold}} = \frac{\$60}{3 \text{ sweatshirts}} = \frac{\$20}{1 \text{ sweatshirt}} = \$20 \text{ per sweatshirt sold}$$

8. Use the unit rate to complete the table.

9. Explain how to graph information from the table.

Write the information in the table as ordered pairs, with Sweatshirts sold being the *x*-coordinate and Money collected the *y*-coordinate. Then, graph the ordered pairs.

10. Write the information in the table as ordered pairs. Graph the relationship from the table.
(3, 60), (5, 100), (8, 160), (9, 180), (12, 240)

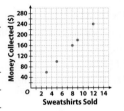

11. **What If?** How much money would be collected if 24 sweatshirts were sold? Show your work.

$480; the rate is $20 per sweatshirt sold, so multiply the number of sweatshirts by $\frac{20}{1}$, or 20, 24 × $20 = $480.

12. **Analyze Relationships** Does the point (5.5, 110) make sense in this context? Explain.

The point does not make sense. The *x*-coordinate of 5.5 means that 5.5 sweatshirts were sold, but it does not make sense to sell half of a sweatshirt.

13. **Communicate Mathematical Ideas** The table shows the distance Randy drove on one day of her vacation. Find the distance Randy would have gone if she had driven for one more hour at the same rate. Explain how you solved the problem.

Time (h)	1	2	3	4	5
Distance (mi)	55	110	165	220	275

330 mi; Find the unit rate, 55 miles per hour. Multiply 6 × 55 = 330.

Use the graph for Exercises 14–15.

14. **Analyze Relationships** How many weeks correspond to 56 days? Explain.

8 weeks; the *x*-value paired with 56 days is 8 weeks.

15. **Represent Real-World Problems** What is a real-life relationship that might be described by the graph?

Sample answer: the number of days that are in any number of weeks

H.O.T. FOCUS ON HIGHER ORDER THINKING

Work Area

16. **Make a Conjecture** Complete the table. Then find the rates $\frac{\text{distance}}{\text{time}}$ and $\frac{\text{time}}{\text{distance}}$.

Time (min)	1	2	5	20
Distance (m)	5	10	25	100

$$\frac{\text{distance}}{\text{time}} = \frac{5}{1}, \frac{10}{2}, \frac{25}{5}, \frac{100}{20}$$

$$\frac{\text{time}}{\text{distance}} = \frac{1}{5}, \frac{2}{10}, \frac{5}{25}, \frac{20}{100}$$

a. Are the $\frac{\text{time}}{\text{distance}}$ rates equivalent? Explain.

Yes; each is equal to $\frac{1}{5}$ min/m.

b. Suppose you graph the points (time, distance) and your friend graphs (distance, time). How will your graphs be different?

Sample answer: My graph will have time on the horizontal axis and distance on the vertical axis. My friend's will have the axes reversed.

17. **Communicate Mathematical Ideas** To graph a rate or ratio from a table, how do you determine the scales to use on each axis?

Sample answer: Find the maximum value for each quantity in the table. Then, choose a scale for each axis that will display that maximum value but not much more.

EXTEND THE MATH PRE-AP

Activity available online my.hrw.com

Activity Examine the graph. Decide whether it is the graph of a proportional relationship, and justify your answer.

No; the ratio of the *y*-coordinate to the *x*-coordinate is not constant.

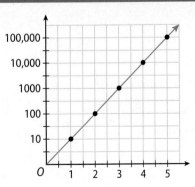

Name another point that would use the same relationship as that shown on the graph. How did you find it?

(6, 1,000,000); As each *x*-coordinate increases by 1, each *y*-coordinate is multiplied by 10.

What would this graph look like if the numbers on the vertical axis were evenly spaced multiples of 20,000?

The graph would show a curve that begins close to the horizontal axis and then rises very quickly.

Common Core Standards

The student is expected to:

 Ratio and Proportional Relationships—6.RP.3

Use ratio and rate reasoning to solve real-world and mathematical problems, e.g. by reasoning about tables of equivalent ratios, tape diagrams, double number line diagrams, or equations.

 Ratio and Proportional Relationships—6.RP.3b

Solve unit rate problems including those involving unit pricing and constant speed.

Mathematical Practices

 MP.7 Using Structure

ADDITIONAL EXAMPLE 1

For every 2 text messages that Anna sends, Kim sends 5. How many text messages would Anna send if Kim sends 40 messages? 16 text messages

 Interactive Whiteboard
Interactive example available online

 my.hrw.com

ADDITIONAL EXAMPLE 2

Ben can do 50 sit-ups in 3 minutes. At that rate, how many sit-ups can he do in 12 minutes? 200 sit-ups

 Interactive Whiteboard
Interactive example available online

 my.hrw.com

Engage

ESSENTIAL QUESTION

How can you solve problems with proportions? Sample answer: Write a proportion that includes one unknown quantity. Find equivalent ratios or rates to find the unknown quantity.

Motivate the Lesson

Ask: A carpenter can build 1 doghouse in 1 day. How many doghouses can 12 carpenters build in 20 days? Begin Example 1 to find out how to solve problems using proportions.

Explore

Engage with the Whiteboard

Ask students to write examples of equal ratios (e.g., $\frac{1}{4}$ and $\frac{4}{16}$) on the whiteboard to review equivalent ratios. Then write pairs of ratios with an unknown quantity in place of one number (e.g., $\frac{3}{8}$ and $\frac{\blacksquare}{16}$) on the whiteboard. Tell students that the ratios are equal, and then ask them to think of numbers that would make each pair of ratios equivalent.

Explain

EXAMPLE 1

Focus on Critical Thinking CC **Mathematical Practices**

Point out to students that the box in Steps 1 and 2 represents an unknown quantity.

Questioning Strategies CC **Mathematical Practices**

• In Step 2, how do you know which number to multiply the numerator and denominator by? The common denominator is 20, and $5 \cdot 4 = 20$. So, you need to multiply by 4.

• In Step 2, how do you know the answer is $8? Since the denominators are the same, the numerators must be equal.

YOUR TURN

Avoid Common Errors

Remind students that in a proportion the units must be in the same order in both ratios.

EXAMPLE 2

Questioning Strategies CC **Mathematical Practices**

• What makes 36 minutes divided by 3 miles a rate, but not a unit rate? 36 divided by 3 compares two different measurements (minutes per mile). Because the second term is 3, not 1, the rate is not a unit rate.

Avoid Common Errors

Remind students that a rate is a comparison of two quantities that have different units of measure and that the answer is not complete unless it has a unit.

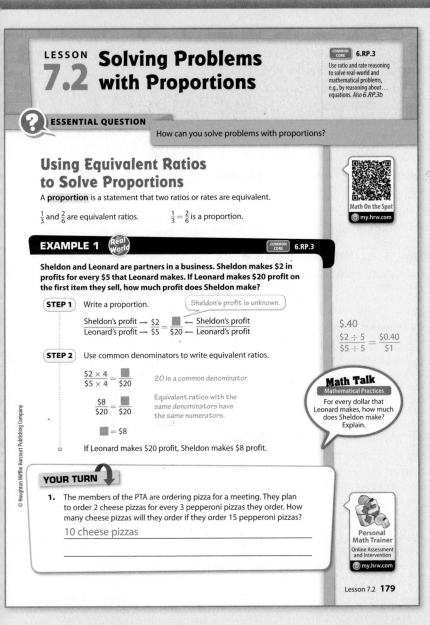

LESSON 7.2 Solving Problems with Proportions

COMMON CORE 6.RP.3

Use ratio and rate reasoning to solve real-world and mathematical problems, e.g., by reasoning about... equations. *Also 6.RP.3b*

? ESSENTIAL QUESTION

How can you solve problems with proportions?

Using Equivalent Ratios to Solve Proportions

A **proportion** is a statement that two ratios or rates are equivalent.

$\frac{1}{3}$ and $\frac{2}{6}$ are equivalent ratios. $\frac{1}{3} = \frac{2}{6}$ is a proportion.

Math On the Spot
my.hrw.com

EXAMPLE 1 Real World

COMMON CORE 6.RP.3

Sheldon and Leonard are partners in a business. Sheldon makes $2 in profits for every $5 that Leonard makes. If Leonard makes $20 profit on the first item they sell, how much profit does Sheldon make?

STEP 1 Write a proportion.   [Sheldon's profit is unknown.]

Sheldon's profit → $\frac{\$2}{\$5} = \frac{\blacksquare}{\$20}$ ← Sheldon's profit
Leonard's profit →   ← Leonard's profit

STEP 2 Use common denominators to write equivalent ratios.

$\frac{\$2 \times 4}{\$5 \times 4} = \frac{\blacksquare}{\$20}$ *20 is a common denominator.*

$\frac{\$8}{\$20} = \frac{\blacksquare}{\$20}$ *Equivalent ratios with the same denominators have the same numerators.*

$\blacksquare = \$8$

If Leonard makes $20 profit, Sheldon makes $8 profit.

$.40
$\frac{\$2 \div 5}{\$5 \div 5} = \frac{\$0.40}{\$1}$

Math Talk
Mathematical Practices

For every dollar that Leonard makes, how much does Sheldon make? Explain.

YOUR TURN

1. The members of the PTA are ordering pizza for a meeting. They plan to order 2 cheese pizzas for every 3 pepperoni pizzas they order. How many cheese pizzas will they order if they order 15 pepperoni pizzas?

   10 cheese pizzas

Personal Math Trainer
Online Assessment and Intervention
my.hrw.com

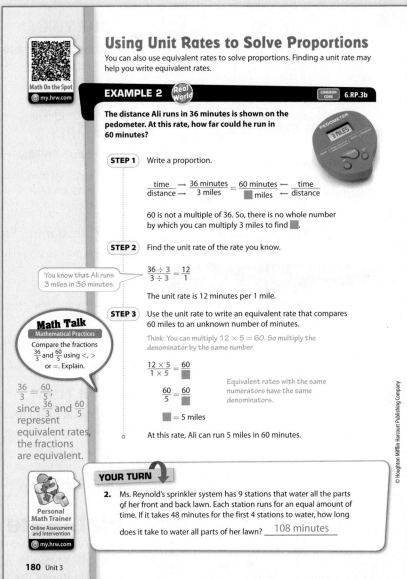

Using Unit Rates to Solve Proportions

You can also use equivalent rates to solve proportions. Finding a unit rate may help you write equivalent rates.

Math On the Spot
my.hrw.com

EXAMPLE 2 Real World

COMMON CORE 6.RP.3b

The distance Ali runs in 36 minutes is shown on the pedometer. At this rate, how far could he run in 60 minutes?

STEP 1 Write a proportion.

$\frac{time}{distance} \rightarrow \frac{36\ minutes}{3\ miles} = \frac{60\ minutes}{\blacksquare\ miles} \leftarrow \frac{time}{distance}$

60 is not a multiple of 36. So, there is no whole number by which you can multiply 3 miles to find $\blacksquare$.

STEP 2 Find the unit rate of the rate you know.

[You know that Ali runs 3 miles in 36 minutes.]

$\frac{36 \div 3}{3 \div 3} = \frac{12}{1}$

The unit rate is 12 minutes per 1 mile.

STEP 3 Use the unit rate to write an equivalent rate that compares 60 miles to an unknown number of minutes.

Think: You can multiply 12 × 5 = 60. So multiply the denominator by the same number.

$\frac{12 \times 5}{1 \times 5} = \frac{60}{\blacksquare}$

$\frac{60}{5} = \frac{60}{\blacksquare}$ *Equivalent rates with the same numerators have the same denominators.*

$\blacksquare = 5$ miles

At this rate, Ali can run 5 miles in 60 minutes.

Math Talk
Mathematical Practices

Compare the fractions $\frac{36}{3}$ and $\frac{60}{5}$ using <, > or =. Explain.

$\frac{36}{3} = \frac{60}{5}$, since $\frac{36}{3}$ and $\frac{60}{5}$ represent equivalent rates, the fractions are equivalent.

YOUR TURN

2. Ms. Reynold's sprinkler system has 9 stations that water all the parts of her front and back lawn. Each station runs for an equal amount of time. If it takes 48 minutes for the first 4 stations to water, how long does it take to water all parts of her lawn? ___108 minutes___

Personal Math Trainer
Online Assessment and Intervention
my.hrw.com

PROFESSIONAL DEVELOPMENT

CC Integrate Mathematical Practices MP.7

This lesson provides an opportunity to address the Mathematical Practice which calls for students to "look for and make use of structure." Students use the concepts of equivalent ratios and common denominators to write and solve proportions. They then use proportional reasoning to compute unit rates and find equivalent ratios. Finally, they apply their understanding of rates and proportions to use scale drawings and scale factors to find actual distances from maps.

Math Background

A proportion is an equation that states that two ratios are equivalent. The method for solving a proportion, such as $\frac{x}{3} = \frac{5}{8}$, is the same method used for solving any equation. For example, multiply both sides of the proportion by 3 · 8, or 24. This step is justified by the Multiplication Property of Equality. The resulting equation, $8x = 15$, can be solved by dividing both sides by 8 (Division Property of Equality). Thus, $x = 1.875$.

YOUR TURN

Focus on Reasoning [CC] Mathematical Practices

Explain how you might solve this problem with mental math. Sample answer: Use your knowledge of basic multiplication facts to form the equivalent ratios. Since you know that 48 is 12 times 4, you need to find the number that is 12 times 9, which is 108.

EXAMPLE 3

Focus on Math Connections [CC] Mathematical Practices

Have you ever been to a museum? If you have, you've probably seen a replica of an airplane or a train or an insect. All of these were created using scale factors. Scale factors allow you to proportionally shrink or enlarge an object.

Questioning Strategies [CC] Mathematical Practices

• How can you tell if a scale factor will enlarge or shrink an object?
A scale factor greater than 1 will make the model bigger than the original object, while a scale factor less than 1 will make the model smaller than the original object.

• What is the difference between a scale factor and a scale drawing? A scale drawing is a drawing of an object that is not the same size as the object but is proportional to the actual object. A scale factor is a rate that describes how much smaller or larger the scale drawing is than the real object.

YOUR TURN

Focus on Critical Thinking [CC] Mathematical Practices

Point out that map scales vary depending on the size of the area being mapped and the size of a map. An inch on an 11 × 17 inch map of a small town would represent a smaller distance than an inch on an 11 × 17 inch map of a state or country.

Elaborate

Talk About It
Summarize the Lesson

💬 **Ask:** How can you use proportions to solve a problem? Write a proportion that includes one unknown quantity. Find equivalent ratios or rates to find the unknown quantity.

GUIDED PRACTICE

Engage with the Whiteboard
For Exercises 3–8, have students write the proportions associated with each exercise on the whiteboard. Then discuss whether the proportions are correct before having students solve for the unknown quantity.

Avoid Common Errors
Exercises 3–8 Some students may write incorrect proportions. Remind students that in a proportion the units must be in the same order in both ratios.

Using Proportional Relationships to Find Distance on a Map

A **scale drawing** is a drawing of a real object that is proportionally smaller or larger than the real object. A **scale** describes how the dimensions in the objects compare.

A map is a scale drawing. The measurements on a map are in proportion to the actual distances. If 1 inch on a map equals an actual distance of 2 miles, the scale is 1 inch = 2 miles. You can write a scale as a rate to solve problems.

Math On the Spot
my.hrw.com

EXAMPLE 3 Real World   COMMON CORE 6.RP.3b

The distance between two schools on Lehigh Avenue is shown on the map. What is the actual distance between the schools?

STEP 1 Write a proportion.

$$\frac{2 \text{ miles}}{1 \text{ inch}} = \frac{\blacksquare \text{ miles}}{3 \text{ inches}}$$ Write the scale as a unit rate.

STEP 2 Write an equivalent rate to find the missing number.

$$\frac{2 \text{ miles} \times 3}{1 \text{ inch} \times 3} = \frac{6 \text{ miles}}{3 \text{ inches}}$$

So, in Step 1, the missing number is 6.

The actual distance between the two schools is 6 miles.

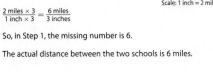

Scale: 1 inch = 2 miles

YOUR TURN

3. The distance between Sandville and Lewiston is shown on the map. What is the actual distance between the towns?

50 miles

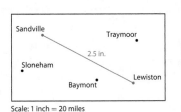

Scale: 1 inch = 20 miles

Personal Math Trainer
Online Assessment and Intervention
my.hrw.com

Lesson 7.2 **181**

Find the unknown value in each proportion. (Example 1)

1. $\frac{3}{5} = \frac{\blacksquare}{30}$

$$\frac{3 \times \boxed{6}}{5 \times \boxed{6}} = \frac{\boxed{18}}{30}$$

2. $\frac{4}{10} = \frac{\blacksquare}{5}$

$$\frac{4 \div \boxed{2}}{10 \div \boxed{2}} = \frac{\boxed{2}}{5}$$

Solve using equivalent ratios. (Example 1)

3. Leila and Jo are two of the partners in a business. Leila makes $3 in profits for every $4 that Jo makes. If Jo makes $60 profit on the first item they sell, how much profit does Leila make? ___$45___

4. Hendrick wants to enlarge a photo that is 4 inches wide and 6 inches tall. The enlarged photo keeps the same ratio. How tall is the enlarged photo if it is 12 inches wide? ___18 inches tall___

Solve using unit rates. (Example 2)

5. A person on a moving sidewalk travels 21 feet in 7 seconds. The moving sidewalk has a length of 180 feet. How long will it take to move from one end of the sidewalk to the other?

___60 seconds___

6. In a repeating musical pattern, there are 56 beats in 7 measures. How many measures are there in 104 beats?

___13 measures___

7. Contestants in a dance-a-thon rest for the same amount of time every hour. A couple rests for 25 minutes in 5 hours. How long did they rest in 8 hours?

___40 minutes___

8. Frances gets 6 paychecks in 12 weeks. How many paychecks does she get in 52 weeks?

___26 paychecks___

9. What is the actual distance between Gendet and Montrose? (Example 3)

___24 kilometers___

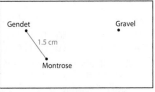

Scale: 1 centimeter = 16 kilometers

? ESSENTIAL QUESTION CHECK-IN

10. How do you solve problems with proportions?

Sample answer: Write a proportion that includes one unknown quantity. Find equivalent ratios or rates to find the unknown quantity.

182 Unit 3

DIFFERENTIATE INSTRUCTION

Manipulatives

Provide centimeter cubes (or something similar) and four cups to pairs of students. Instruct them to place 3 cubes in a cup and write the corresponding rate: $\frac{3 \text{ cubes}}{1 \text{ cup}}$. Ask students to find how many cubes they would need to make 4 cups, based on the same rate. Next, have them write the two ratios as a proportion. After solving the proportion, students can model the solution by placing 3 cubes in 3 additional cups for a total of 12 cubes. Repeat with other ratios and/or different numbers of cups.

Curriculum Integration: Social Studies

Give each student a map or an atlas. Have them use the map's scale to calculate actual distances between cities or other landmarks. Have students show how they wrote and solved each proportion to find each distance.

Additional Resources

Differentiated Instruction includes:

• Reading Strategies
• Success for English Learners **ELL**
• Reteach
• Challenge **PRE-AP**

7.2 LESSON QUIZ

 6.RP.3

1. Li can walk 2 miles in 45 minutes. At that rate, how far can she walk in 135 minutes?

2. The cooking club makes 3 chicken burritos for every 4 beef burritos they prepare. How many chicken burritos do they make if they prepare 24 beef burritos?

3. Luisa earns $20 for walking 4 dogs. How much would she earn for each dog?

4. On a map, Highmount is 5 inches from Pine Hill. If the map scale is 1 inch = 3 miles, what is the actual distance between the towns?

Lesson Quiz available online

 my.hrw.com

Answers

1. 6 miles
2. 18 chicken burritos
3. $5 per dog
4. 15 miles

Evaluate

GUIDED AND INDEPENDENT PRACTICE

 6.RP.3, 6.RP.3b

Concepts & Skills	Practice
Example 1 Using Equivalent Ratios to Solve Proportions	Exercises 1–4, 12, 13, 15, 18
Example 2 Using Unit Rates to Solve Proportions	Exercises 5–8, 15–16
Example 3 Using Proportional Relationships to Find Distance on a Map	Exercises 9, 11, 14

Exercise	Depth of Knowledge (D.O.K.)	Mathematical Practices
11	**3** Strategic Thinking **H.O.T.**	**MP.2** Reasoning
12–14	**2** Skills/Concepts	**MP.5** Using Tools
15	**3** Strategic Thinking **H.O.T.**	**MP.3** Logic
16–17	**2** Skills/Concepts	**MP.4** Modeling
18–20	**3** Strategic Thinking **H.O.T.**	**MP.7** Using Structure
21	**3** Strategic Thinking **H.O.T.**	**MP.2** Reasoning

Additional Resources

Differentiated Instruction includes:

• Leveled Practice Worksheets

7.2 Independent Practice

COMMON CORE 6.RP.3, 6.RP.3b

Personal Math Trainer

my.hrw.com

Online Assessment and Intervention

11. The scale of the map is missing. The actual distance from Liberty to West Quall is 72 miles, and it is 6 inches on the map.

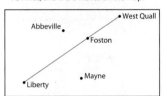

- West Quall
- Abbeville
- Foston
- Mayne
- Liberty

a. What is the scale of the map?

1 inch = 12 miles

b. Foston is between Liberty and West Quall and is 4 inches from Liberty on the map. How far is Foston from West Quall?

24 miles

12. A punch recipe says to mix 4 cups pineapple juice, 8 cups orange juice, and 12 cups seltzer in order to make 18 servings of punch.

a. How many cups of each ingredient do you need to make 108 cups of punch?

18 cups pineapple juice

36 cups orange juice

54 cups seltzer

b. How many servings can be made from 108 cups of punch? 81 servings

c. For every cup of seltzer you use, how much orange juice do you use?

$\frac{2}{3}$ cup

13. On an airplane, there are two seats on the left side in each row and three seats on the right side. There are 90 seats on the right side of the plane.

a. How many seats are on the left side of the plane? 60 seats

b. How many seats are there altogether? 150 seats

14. Carrie and Krystal are taking a road trip from Greenville to North Valley. Each person has her own map, and the scales on the maps are different.

a. On Carrie's map, Greenville and North Valley are 4.5 inches apart. The scale on her map is 1 inch = 20 miles. How far is Greenville from North Valley?

90 miles

b. The scale on Krystal's map is 1 inch = 18 miles. How far apart are Greenville and North Valley on Krystal's map?

5 inches

15. **Multistep** A machine can produce 27 inches of ribbon every 3 minutes. How many feet of ribbon can the machine make in one hour? Explain.

45 ft; there are 60 minutes in an hour, so $\frac{27 \text{ in.} \times 20}{3 \text{ min} \times 20} = \frac{540 \text{ in.}}{60 \text{ min}}$. To find the number of feet in 540 inches, divide by 12; 540 ÷ 12 = 45.

Marta, Loribeth, and Ira all have bicycles. The table shows the number of miles of each rider's last bike ride, as well as the time it took each rider to complete the ride.

	Distance of Last Ride (in miles)	Time Spent on Last Bike Ride (in minutes)
Marta	8	80
Loribeth	6	42
Ira	15	75

16. What is Marta's unit rate, in minutes per mile? $\frac{10 \text{ min.}}{1 \text{ mile}}$

17. Whose speed was the fastest on their last bike ride? Ira

18. If all three riders travel for 3.5 hours at the same speed as their last ride, how many total miles will the 3 riders travel altogether? Explain.

93 miles; 3.5 h = 210 min; Marta travels at a rate of 10 min/mi, so she travels 21 miles. Loribeth travels at a rate of 7 min/mi, so she travels 30 miles. Ira travels at a rate of 5 min/mi, so he travels 42 miles. 21 + 30 + 42 = 93 miles

19. **Critique Reasoning** Jason watched a caterpillar move 10 feet in 2 minutes. Jason says that the caterpillar's unit rate is 0.2 feet per minute. Is Jason correct? Explain.

No, the caterpillar's unit rate should be 5 feet per minute.

H.O.T. FOCUS ON HIGHER ORDER THINKING

20. **Analyze Relationships** If the number in the numerator of a unit rate is 1, what does this indicate about the equivalent unit rates? Give an example.

Sample answer: The numerator and denominator will have the same numbers. Example: $\frac{1 \text{ mi}}{1 \text{ s}} = \frac{17 \text{ mi}}{17 \text{ s}}$

21. **Multiple Representations** A boat travels at a constant speed. After 20 minutes, the boat has traveled 2.5 miles. The boat travels a total of 10 miles to a bridge.

a. Graph the relationship between the distance the boat travels and the time it takes.

b. How long does it take the boat to reach the bridge? Explain how you found it.

80 minutes; draw a line through the points (0, 0) and (20, 2.5). 80 is the x-coordinate of the point on the line where the y-coordinate is 10.

Work Area

EXTEND THE MATH PRE-AP

Activity available online my.hrw.com

Activity Work in a small group to make a scale drawing of your classroom. Follow these steps:

1. Measure the length and width of your classroom and record the measurements.

2. Choose a sensible scale so that your drawing will fit on a sheet of paper. (You may need to use trial and error.)

3. Measure the lengths and widths of a few classroom objects, such as desks, tables, and shelves. Write down these measurements.

4. Stand in a corner of the room and measure the distance to each of the objects you chose in Step 3. Record these distances.

5. Make your drawing, using your scale. Draw the objects where they belong. Then share your drawing with classmates.

Check that students' drawings are reasonably accurate. Have a group member explain how the group determined the map scale it used.

ADDITIONAL EXAMPLE 1

A Emma bought a 5-pound bag of apples. Use a proportion to convert 5 pounds to ounces. *80 ounces*

B The mass of a hummingbird is 4,000 milligrams. Use a proportion to convert 4,000 milligrams to grams. *4 grams*

 Interactive Whiteboard
Interactive example available online

 my.hrw.com

Engage

ESSENTIAL QUESTION

How do you convert units within a measurement system? Sample answer: Use a model, a proportion, or a conversion factor to convert units.

Motivate the Lesson

Ask: How much will it cost to build a fence that is 24 feet long if it costs $20 to build a fence that is 3 yards long? Begin the Explore Activity to find out how to convert units within a measurement system.

Explore

EXPLORE ACTIVITY

Focus on Patterns CC Mathematical Practices

Another way to explain measurement conversion is to use patterns. Guide students to see the pattern in Step 1, which is that for every increase of 1 yard, the number of feet increases by 3. Have students make a table to show the pattern in a different format.

Explain

EXAMPLE 1

Connect to Daily Life

Discuss with students that units of measure are used often in everyday life. In the United States, customary units are used at the grocery store and the gas pump, while metric units are used in science and medicine. Point out that most other countries use metric units exclusively.

Questioning Strategies CC Mathematical Practices

• In A, how do you write the proportion? Think of what you are changing: pounds to ounces. There are 16 ounces per pound, so use $\frac{16\ oz}{1\ lb}$.

• In A, Step 2, why do you multiply the numerator by 3? You need to write $\frac{16}{1}$ as an equivalent ratio with a denominator of 3, so you need to multiply both the numerator and the denominator by 3.

Engage with the Whiteboard

Have students go to the whiteboard to make a model, as in the Explore Activity, to show 3 pounds subdivided into ounces. Use this activity for a check of arithmetic work.

Integrating Language Arts ELL

Encourage English learners to take notes on new terms or concepts and to write them in familiar language.

Converting Within Measurement Systems

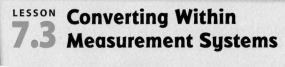

COMMON CORE 6.RP.3d

Use ratio reasoning to convert measurement units; manipulate and transform units appropriately when multiplying or dividing quantities. *Also 6.RP.3*

? ESSENTIAL QUESTION

How do you convert units within a measurement system?

EXPLORE ACTIVITY Real World
COMMON CORE 6.RP.3d

Using a Model to Convert Units

The two most common systems of measurement are the customary system and the metric system. You can use a model to convert from one unit to another within the same measurement system.

STEP 1 Use the model to complete each statement below.

1 yard = 3 feet

2 yards = __6__ feet

3 yards = __9__ feet

4 yards = __12__ feet

STEP 2 Rewrite your answers as ratios.

$\dfrac{6 \text{ feet}}{2 \text{ yards}} = \dfrac{3 \text{ feet}}{1 \text{ yard}}$ $\dfrac{9 \text{ feet}}{3 \text{ yards}} = \dfrac{3 \text{ feet}}{1 \text{ yard}}$ $\dfrac{12 \text{ feet}}{4 \text{ yards}} = \dfrac{3 \text{ feet}}{1 \text{ yard}}$

Since 1 yard = 3 feet, the ratio of feet to yards in any measurement is always $\frac{3}{1}$. This means any ratio forming a proportion with $\frac{3}{1}$ can represent a ratio of feet to yards.

$\frac{3}{1} = \frac{12}{4}$, so 12 feet = __4__ yards. $\frac{3}{1} = \frac{54}{18}$, so __54__ feet = 18 yards.

Reflect

1. **Communicate Mathematical Ideas** How could you draw a model to show the relationship between feet and inches?

   Sample answer: Draw a bar representing 1, 2, 3, and

   4 feet. Above it, draw bars with each foot divided into

   12 equal pieces, and label the pieces 12, 24, 36, and 48.

Math On the Spot
my.hrw.com

Converting Units Using Proportions and Unit Rates

You can use ratios and proportions to convert both customary and metric units. Use the table below to convert from one unit to another within the same measurement system.

Customary Measurements		
Length	**Weight**	**Capacity**
1 ft = 12 in. 1 yd = 36 in. 1 yd = 3 ft 1 mi = 5,280 ft 1 mi = 1,760 yd	1 lb = 16 oz 1 T = 2,000 lb	1 c = 8 fl oz 1 pt = 2 c 1 qt = 2 pt 1 qt = 4 c 1 gal = 4 qt

Metric Measurements		
Length	**Mass**	**Capacity**
1 km = 1,000 m 1 m = 100 cm 1 cm = 10 mm	1 kg = 1,000 g 1 g = 1,000 mg	1 L = 1,000 mL

EXAMPLE 1 Real World
COMMON CORE 6.RP.3d

A What is the weight of a 3-pound human brain in ounces?

Use a proportion to convert 3 pounds to ounces.

Use $\frac{16 \text{ ounces}}{1 \text{ pound}}$ to convert pounds to ounces.

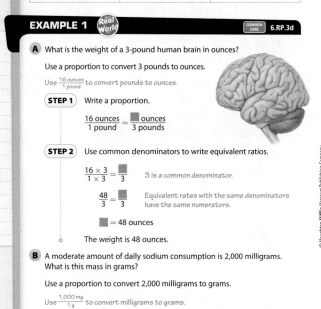

STEP 1 Write a proportion.

$\dfrac{16 \text{ ounces}}{1 \text{ pound}} = \dfrac{\blacksquare \text{ ounces}}{3 \text{ pounds}}$

STEP 2 Use common denominators to write equivalent ratios.

$\dfrac{16 \times 3}{1 \times 3} = \dfrac{\blacksquare}{3}$ 3 is a common denominator.

$\dfrac{48}{3} = \dfrac{\blacksquare}{3}$ Equivalent rates with the same denominators have the same numerators.

$\blacksquare$ = 48 ounces

The weight is 48 ounces.

B A moderate amount of daily sodium consumption is 2,000 milligrams. What is this mass in grams?

Use a proportion to convert 2,000 milligrams to grams.

Use $\frac{1,000 \text{ mg}}{1 \text{ g}}$ to convert milligrams to grams.

My Notes

PROFESSIONAL DEVELOPMENT

CC Integrate Mathematical Processes MP.4

This lesson provides an opportunity to address this Mathematical Practice standard. It calls for students to apply mathematics to problems arising in everyday life, society, and the workplace. In Examples 1 and 2, students convert both customary and metric measures in real-world problems, such as converting the weight of the average human brain from pounds to ounces and the average daily sodium consumption from milligrams to grams. They also convert units of capacity to solve everyday issues, such as how many quarts of milk to buy.

Math Background

Dimensional analysis is a useful technique for solving problems, especially in science classes. Converting factors and canceling units are at the heart of dimensional analysis. The technique focuses on using unit factors multiplied together. Many unit factors can be multiplied together without changing the value. For example, to find the number of seconds (*s*) in June, a month with 30 days, multiply:

$$s = \frac{30 \text{ days}}{1 \text{ month}} \times \frac{24 \text{ hours}}{1 \text{ day}} \times \frac{60 \text{ minutes}}{1 \text{ hour}} \times \frac{60 \text{ seconds}}{1 \text{ minute}}$$

$$= 2,592,000$$

YOUR TURN

Focus on Reasoning [CC] Mathematical Practices

Point out to students that when going from the larger unit *yards* to the smaller unit *inches*, the number of inches will be greater than the number of yards because there are 36 inches in 1 yard.

Engage with the Whiteboard

Have a student draw a door and then draw a horizontal dotted line to divide it in half. Have another student label the top half 1 yd = 36 in. Have another student label the bottom half in the same way. This will help students see why there must be more inches than yards in the conversion.

EXAMPLE 2

Questioning Strategies [CC] Mathematical Practices

• In Step 1, when writing the conversion factor, how do you decide which unit goes on the top? Write the unit you are converting *to* on the top.

• In Step 2, why do we cross out the gallons? 2 gallons is the same as $\frac{2 \text{ gallons}}{1}$. When a unit is in the numerator of one term and the denominator of the other, you can simplify the units by crossing them out because $\frac{\text{gallon}}{\text{gallon}} = 1$.

Multiple Representations [CC] Mathematical Practices

Use the conversion rate 4 quarts to 1 gallon to make a table showing the pattern of increasing by 4 quarts for each increase of 1 gallon. Draw a sketch to model the pattern.

YOUR TURN

Focus on Critical Thinking [CC] Mathematical Practices

Remind students that in the metric system, the value of each place is 10 times greater than the value to its right. When you convert one unit of measure to another, you can multiply or divide by a power of 10.

Elaborate

....

Talk About It
Summarize the Lesson

 Ask: What do using a conversion rate and forming a proportion have in common for converting units? When you convert a measure by using a unit rate, you are forming a proportion.

GUIDED PRACTICE

Engage with the Whiteboard

For Exercise 2, have a student extend the given model to 12 quarts.

Avoid Common Errors

Exercises 5–8 Remind students that metric conversions involve a power of 10 and that the decimal point moves one place (to the right or left, depending on whether you are multiplying or dividing) for each 0 in the power of 10.

STEP 1 Write a proportion.

$$\frac{1{,}000 \text{ mg}}{1 \text{ g}} = \frac{2{,}000 \text{ mg}}{\blacksquare \text{ g}}$$

STEP 2 Write equivalent ratios.

Think: You can multiply $1{,}000 \times 2 = 2{,}000$. So multiply the denominator by the same number.

$$\frac{1{,}000 \times 2}{1 \times 2} = \frac{2{,}000}{\blacksquare}$$

$$\frac{2{,}000}{2} = \frac{2{,}000}{\blacksquare}$$

Equivalent ratios with the same numerators have the same denominators.

$\blacksquare = 2$ grams

The mass is 2 grams.

YOUR TURN

2. The height of a doorway is 2 yards. What is the height of the doorway in inches? ___72 inches___

Math Talk
Mathematical Practices

How would you convert 3 liters to milliliters?

Solve the proportion
$$\frac{1 \text{ L}}{1{,}000 \text{ mL}} = \frac{3 \text{ L}}{? \text{ mL}}.$$

Personal Math Trainer
Online Assessment and Intervention
my.hrw.com

Converting Units by Using Conversion Factors

Another way to convert measurements is by using a conversion factor. A **conversion factor** is a ratio comparing two equivalent measurements.

EXAMPLE 2 Real World   COMMON CORE 6.RP.3d

Elena wants to buy 2 gallons of milk but can only find quart containers for sale. How many quarts does she need?

You are converting to quarts from gallons.

STEP 1 Find the conversion factor.

Write 4 quarts = 1 gallon as a ratio: $\frac{4 \text{ quarts}}{1 \text{ gallon}}$

STEP 2 Multiply the given measurement by the conversion factor.

$2 \text{ gallons} \cdot \frac{4 \text{ quarts}}{1 \text{ gallon}} = \blacksquare \text{ quarts}$

$2 \text{ gallons} \cdot \frac{4 \text{ quarts}}{1 \text{ gallon}} = 8 \text{ quarts}$ Cancel the common unit.

Elena needs 8 quarts of milk.

Math On the Spot
my.hrw.com

YOUR TURN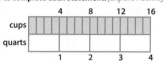

Personal Math Trainer
Online Assessment and Intervention
my.hrw.com

3. An oak tree is planted when it is 250 centimeters tall. What is this height in meters? ___2.5 meters___

Guided Practice

Use the model below to complete each statement. (Explore Activity 1)

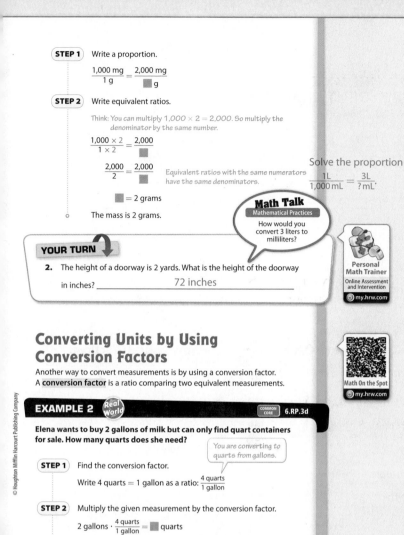

1. $\frac{4}{1} = \frac{12}{3}$, so 12 cups = ___3___ quarts

2. $\frac{4}{1} = \frac{48}{12}$, so ___48___ cups = 12 quarts

Use ratios and proportions to solve. (Example 1)

3. Mary Catherine makes 2 gallons of punch for her party. How many cups of punch did she make?
___32 cups___

4. An African elephant weighs 6 tons. What is the weight of the elephant in pounds?
___12,000 pounds___

5. The distance from Jason's house to school is 0.5 kilometer. What is this distance in meters?
___500 meters___

6. The mass of a moon rock is 3.5 kilograms. What is the mass of the moon rock in grams?
___3,500 grams___

Use a conversion factor to solve. (Example 2)

7. $1.75 \text{ grams} \cdot \frac{1{,}000 \text{ mg}}{1 \text{ g}} = $ ___1,750 mg___

8. $27 \text{ millimeters} \cdot \frac{1 \text{ cm}}{10 \text{ mm}} = $ ___2.7 cm___

9. A package weighs 96 ounces. What is the weight of the package in pounds?
___6 pounds___

10. A jet flies at an altitude of 52,800 feet. What is the height of the jet in miles?
___10 miles___

? ESSENTIAL QUESTION CHECK-IN

11. How do you convert units within a measurement system?
___Sample answer: Use a model, proportion, or a___
___conversion factor.___

DIFFERENTIATE INSTRUCTION

Home Connection

Have students create a table like the one below. Ask them to find 4 items at home that have a given measure. Have them record this information in the table and then calculate and record an equivalent measure in a different unit.

Item	Given Measure	Equivalent Measure
Box of cereal	12 ounces	$\frac{3}{4}$ pound
Milk	1 gallon	4 quarts
Tomato paste	6 ounces	$\frac{3}{4}$ cup
Noodles	8 ounces	$\frac{1}{2}$ pound

Graphic Organizer

Have students copy the following diagram into their notebooks to help them remember how to convert between metric units.

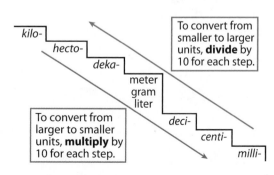

Additional Resources

Differentiated Instruction includes:

- Reading Strategies
- Success for English Learners **ELL**
- Reteach
- Challenge **PRE-AP**

7.3 LESSON QUIZ

COMMON CORE 6.RP.3d

Use unit rates to solve.

1. Hailey has 48 inches of ribbon. How many feet of ribbon does she have?

2. Noah bought 2.5 kilograms of colored tile chips for a mosaic art project. What is the mass of the tile chips in grams?

Use a conversion factor to solve.

3. A package of books weighs 72 ounces. What is the weight of the package in pounds?

4. The length of a park is 250 meters. What is the length of the park in kilometers?

Lesson Quiz available online

 my.hrw.com

Answers

1. 4 feet

2. 2,500 grams

3. 4.5 pounds; conversion factor: $\frac{1 \text{ lb}}{16 \text{ oz}}$

4. 0.25 kilometers; conversion factor: $\frac{0.001 \text{ km}}{1 \text{ m}}$

Evaluate

GUIDED AND INDEPENDENT PRACTICE

COMMON CORE 6.RP.3, 6.RP.3d

Concepts & Skills	Practice
Explore Activity Using a Model to Convert Units	Exercises 1–2
Example 1 Converting Units by Using Proportions and Unit Rates	Exercises 3–6, 13–15, 17
Example 2 Converting Units by Using Conversion Factors	Exercises 7–10, 12

Exercise	Depth of Knowledge (D.O.K.)		**COMMON CORE** Mathematical Practices
12–13	**2** Skills/Concepts		**MP.4** Modeling
14	**3** Strategic Thinking	H.O.T.	**MP.3** Logic
15	**3** Strategic Thinking	H.O.T.	**MP.3** Logic
16	**2** Skills/Concepts		**MP.7** Using Structure
17	**2** Skills/Concepts		**MP.4** Modeling
18	**3** Strategic Thinking	H.O.T.	**MP.3** Logic
19	**3** Strategic Thinking	H.O.T.	**MP.7** Using Structure
20–21	**3** Strategic Thinking	H.O.T.	**MP.3** Logic
22	**3** Strategic Thinking	H.O.T.	**MP.7** Using Structure

Additional Resources

Differentiated Instruction includes:

• Leveled Practice worksheets

7.3 Independent Practice

 6.RP.3d

12. What is a conversion factor that you can use to convert gallons to pints? How did you find it?

$\frac{8 \text{ pints}}{1 \text{ gallon}}$; Sample answer: 1 gallon = 4 quarts and 1 quart = 2 pints

13. Three friends each have some ribbon. Carol has 42 inches of ribbon, Tino has 2.5 feet of ribbon, and Baxter has 1.5 yards of ribbon. Express the total length of ribbon the three friends have in inches, feet and yards.

___126___ inches = ___10.5___ feet = ___3.5___ yards

14. Suzanna wants to measure a board, but she doesn't have a ruler to measure with. However, she does have several copies of a book that she knows is 17 centimeters tall.

a. Suzanna lays the books end to end and finds that the board is the same length as 21 books. How many centimeters long is the board?

357 centimeters

b. Suzanna needs a board that is at least 3.5 meters long. Is the board long enough? Explain.

Yes; the board is 357 centimeters, which can be converted to 3.57 meters. 3.57 > 3.5, so Suzanna's board is long enough.

Sheldon needs to buy 8 gallons of ice cream for a family reunion. The table shows the prices for different sizes of two brands of ice cream.

	Price of small size	Price of large size
Cold Farms	$2.50 for 1 pint	$4.50 for 1 quart
Cone Dreams	$4.25 for 1 quart	$9.50 for 1 gallon

15. Which size container of Cold Farm ice cream is the better deal for Sheldon? Explain.

The large size; 64 pints of Cold Farm ice cream cost $2.50 × 64 = $160, and 32 quarts of Cold Farm ice cream cost $4.50 × 32 = $144.

16. Multistep Which size and brand of ice cream is the best deal?

gallon size of Cone Dreams

---

17. In Beijing in 2008, the Women's 3,000 meter Steeplechase became an Olympic event. What is this distance in kilometers? ___3 kilometers___

18. How would you convert 5 feet 6 inches to inches? Sample answer: Convert 5 feet to 60 inches. Then add 6 inches.

H.O.T. FOCUS ON HIGHER ORDER THINKING

19. Analyze Relationships A Class 4 truck weighs between 14,000 and 16,000 pounds.

a. What is the weight range in tons? between 7 tons and 8 tons

b. If the weight of a Class 4 truck is increased by 2 tons, will it still be classified as a Class 4 truck? Explain.

No; the lightest Class 4 truck weighs 7 tons. 7 tons + 2 tons = 9 tons, which is outside the range for a Class 4 truck.

20. Persevere in Problem Solving A football field is shown at right.

Work Area

a. What are the dimensions of a football field in feet?

360 feet by 160 feet

$53\frac{1}{3}$ yd

120 yd

b. A chalk line is placed around the perimeter of the football field. What is the length of this line in feet?

1,040 feet

c. About how many laps around the perimeter of the field would equal 1 mile? Explain.

5 laps; 1 mile is 5,280 feet, and 5,280 divided by 1,040 is about 5.08.

21. Look for a Pattern What is the result if you multiply a number of cups by $\frac{8 \text{ fl oz}}{1 \text{ cup}}$ and then multiply the result by $\frac{1 \text{ cup}}{8 \text{ fl oz}}$? Give an example.

You get the original number. Example: 2 cups · $\frac{8 \text{ fl oz}}{1 \text{ cup}}$ = 16 fl oz, 16 fl oz · $\frac{1 \text{ cup}}{8 \text{ fl oz}}$ = 2 cups

22. Make a Conjecture 1 hour = 3,600 seconds and 1 mile = 5,280 feet. Make a conjecture about how you could convert a speed of 15 miles per hour to feet per second. Then convert.

Sample answer: Convert 15 miles to 79,200 feet, then use $\frac{1 \text{ hour}}{3,600 \text{ seconds}}$ to convert 1 hour to 3,600 seconds. Finally, simplify $\frac{79,200 \text{ ft}}{3,600 \text{ sec}}$ to 22 feet per second.

EXTEND THE MATH   PRE-AP

Activity available online ⏻ my.hrw.com

Activity Present the example at right. Explain that an adult tiger weighs between 350 and 600 pounds, so the choice of 400 pounds is somewhat arbitrary.

Challenge students to work in pairs to create their own unique unit of measure. Have them write three problems involving their unit of measure. Post the problems on a bulletin board and challenge other students to solve the problems.

Tiger as a unit of weight

1 tiger = 400 pounds

1. What is the weight in tigers of a car that weighs 2,800 pounds? 7 tigers

2. A box of apples weighs $\frac{1}{10}$ tiger. What is its weight in pounds? 40 pounds

3. An elephant seal weighs 16 tigers. What is its weight in tons? 3.2 tons

Common Core Standards

The student is expected to:

 Ratio and Proportional Relationships—6.RP.3b

Use ratio reasoning to convert measurement units; manipulate and transform units appropriately when multiplying or dividing quantities. *Also 6.RP.3, 6.RP.3b*

Mathematical Practices

 MP.4 Modeling

ADDITIONAL EXAMPLE 1
While making soup, Jenna added 148 milliliters of broth. About how many fluid ounces does she add to her soup? Jenna adds about 5 fluid ounces to her soup.

 Interactive Whiteboard
Interactive example available online

⏻ my.hrw.com

Engage

ESSENTIAL QUESTION

How can you use ratios and proportions to convert measurements? Sample answer: Use a table of equivalent measures to set up a conversion factor, and multiply by it to convert one unit to another.

Motivate the Lesson

Ask: About how many centimeters long is an 11-inch sheet of paper? Take a guess. Begin the Explore Activity to find out.

Explore

EXPLORE ACTIVITY

Connect Multiple Representations CC **Mathematical Practices**

Point out to students that because the table shows how many metric units are equivalent to one of each customary unit, using the values shown, a table can be created to show how many customary units are equivalent to one of each metric unit.

Explain

EXAMPLE 1

Avoid Common Errors

Students sometimes use the wrong conversion factor, using the inverse of the correct ratio. Encourage students to make sure the units that they are converting from are in the denominator of the conversion factor.

Questioning Strategies CC **Mathematical Practices**

• Which unit is larger, inches or centimeters? Justify your answer. One inch is greater than 1 centimeter because it takes about 2.54 centimeters to make 1 inch.

• What do you look at in the conversion table to know which unit is larger? Compare the number of metric units to 1. If the number is greater than 1, then the customary unit is larger. If the number is less than 1, then the metric unit is larger.

YOUR TURN

Talk About It
Check for Understanding

 Ask: Why multiply 6 quarts by $\frac{0.946\ \text{liter}}{1\ \text{quart}}$ to convert to liters? When the equivalency, 1 quart ≈ 0.946 liter, is written as the ratio, $\frac{0.946\ \text{liter}}{1\ \text{quart}}$, and multiplied by $\frac{6\ \text{quarts}}{1}$, the "quarts" units cancel, resulting in 5.676 liters.

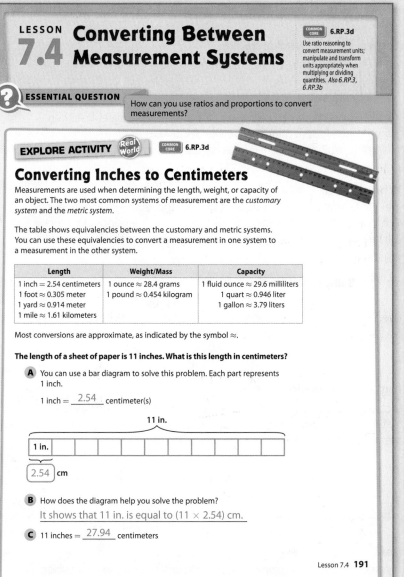

Converting Between Measurement Systems

COMMON CORE 6.RP.3d

Use ratio reasoning to convert measurement units; manipulate and transform units appropriately when multiplying or dividing quantities. Also 6.RP.3, 6.RP.3b

ESSENTIAL QUESTION How can you use ratios and proportions to convert measurements?

EXPLORE ACTIVITY (Real World) COMMON CORE 6.RP.3d

Converting Inches to Centimeters

Measurements are used when determining the length, weight, or capacity of an object. The two most common systems of measurement are the *customary system* and the *metric system*.

The table shows equivalencies between the customary and metric systems. You can use these equivalencies to convert a measurement in one system to a measurement in the other system.

Length	Weight/Mass	Capacity
1 inch = 2.54 centimeters	1 ounce ≈ 28.4 grams	1 fluid ounce ≈ 29.6 milliliters
1 foot ≈ 0.305 meter	1 pound ≈ 0.454 kilogram	1 quart ≈ 0.946 liter
1 yard ≈ 0.914 meter		1 gallon ≈ 3.79 liters
1 mile ≈ 1.61 kilometers		

Most conversions are approximate, as indicated by the symbol ≈.

The length of a sheet of paper is 11 inches. What is this length in centimeters?

A You can use a bar diagram to solve this problem. Each part represents 1 inch.

1 inch = __2.54__ centimeter(s)

11 in.

1 in.										

2.54 cm

B How does the diagram help you solve the problem?

It shows that 11 in. is equal to (11 × 2.54) cm.

C 11 inches = __27.94__ centimeters

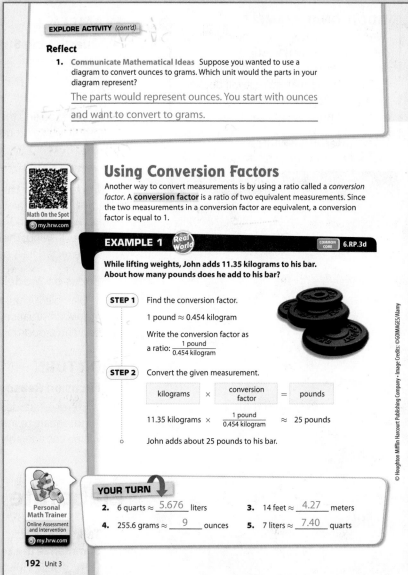

EXPLORE ACTIVITY (cont'd)

Reflect

1. **Communicate Mathematical Ideas** Suppose you wanted to use a diagram to convert ounces to grams. Which unit would the parts in your diagram represent?

   The parts would represent ounces. You start with ounces and want to convert to grams.

Using Conversion Factors

Another way to convert measurements is by using a ratio called a *conversion factor*. A **conversion factor** is a ratio of two equivalent measurements. Since the two measurements in a conversion factor are equivalent, a conversion factor is equal to 1.

Math On the Spot my.hrw.com

EXAMPLE 1 (Real World) COMMON CORE 6.RP.3d

While lifting weights, John adds 11.35 kilograms to his bar. About how many pounds does he add to his bar?

STEP 1 Find the conversion factor.

1 pound ≈ 0.454 kilogram

Write the conversion factor as a ratio: $\frac{1 \text{ pound}}{0.454 \text{ kilogram}}$

STEP 2 Convert the given measurement.

kilograms	×	conversion factor	=	pounds

$11.35 \text{ kilograms} \times \frac{1 \text{ pound}}{0.454 \text{ kilogram}} \approx 25 \text{ pounds}$

John adds about 25 pounds to his bar.

YOUR TURN

Personal Math Trainer
Online Assessment and Intervention
my.hrw.com

2. 6 quarts ≈ __5.676__ liters
3. 14 feet ≈ __4.27__ meters
4. 255.6 grams ≈ __9__ ounces
5. 7 liters ≈ __7.40__ quarts

© Houghton Mifflin Harcourt Publishing Company • Image Credits: ©GOIMAGES/Alamy

---

PROFESSIONAL DEVELOPMENT

CC Integrate Mathematical Practices MP.4

This lesson provides an opportunity to address this Mathematical Practice standard. It calls for students to apply mathematics to problems arising in everyday life, society, and the workplace. Students use a variety of mathematical methods to convert between systems to find the length of a piece of paper, to find the mass of weights used in weight lifting, to determine the cost of paving a driveway, and to find the area of a flower bed in square meters when given its dimensions in feet. Students apply mathematics to convert units from one system to another in these and other real-world situations.

Math Background

The metric system is based upon powers of 10. Metric measures generally use decimals instead of fractions, which are common in customary measures. The basic metric units of length, mass, and capacity are the meter, gram, and liter. Mass is not the same as weight. Weight depends on Earth's gravitational field, while mass does not. So the mass of an object would not change when taken to the Moon but its weight would change because the force of gravity on the Moon is less than on Earth. In the customary system, students need to identify the difference between ounces, in weight, and *fluid* ounces, in volume.

EXAMPLE 2

Questioning Strategies [CC] **Mathematical Practices**

- How is the conversion method used in Example 2 different from the one used in Example 1? A proportion is used in Example 2, while a direct multiplication by a conversion factor is used in Example 1.

- Could you find the area in square meters by calculating the area in square feet first, then setting up a proportion with the foot to meter conversion factor? No. Square feet and square meters are different units than feet and meters, so they would need a different conversion factor.

Engage with the Whiteboard

In the margin next to Example 2, invite a student to draw the rectangle and label its length and width in feet. Then have another student add the dimensions in meters to the drawing. This will help students visualize the situation and reinforce the fact that the same rectangle is being measured by two different units.

Focus on Modeling [CC] **Mathematical Practices**

In Example 2, students use information from the table to create a proportion that models a real-world situation. Use a meterstick to help students visualize that about 0.3 m is 1 ft and how the proportion contains two equivalent ratios that each represent 1.

YOUR TURN

Focus on Reasoning [CC] **Mathematical Practices**

In Exercise 7, students convert the dimensions to feet and then find the area. Compare a 1-foot square to a 1-meter square to help students reason that the number of square feet will be considerably greater than the number of square meters in the flower bed.

Elaborate

Talk About It
Summarize the Lesson

 Ask: How do you know that the conversion ratios you write using the information in the table in the Explore Activity will be unit rates? Each conversion rate shows what 1 customary unit is equivalent to in the metric system. For example, the number of gallons equivalent to 3.79 liters is 1. So, 3.79 liters per gallon is a unit rate.

GUIDED PRACTICE

Engage with the Whiteboard

 Have students complete the bar diagrams by adding the corresponding measures. Point out that each measure includes a number and a unit.

Avoid Common Errors
Exercise 4 Remind students that the conversion factor is 1 pound per 0.454 kilogram. Since 0.454 is less than 1, the answer will be less than 4 kilograms.

Exercises 5–12 After working several conversion problems, students may attempt to remember the conversion factors instead of finding them in the table. Tell them that it's a good idea to check conversion factors in the table until they are fully memorized.

Using Proportions to Convert Measurements

You can also convert a measurement from one unit to another by using a proportion. First write the conversion factor as a ratio, then multiply by a form of 1 to generate an equivalent ratio. Recall that two equal ratios form a proportion.

Proportions: $\frac{3 \text{ inches}}{2 \text{ feet}} = \frac{6 \text{ inches}}{4 \text{ feet}}$ $\frac{5}{10} = \frac{1}{2}$

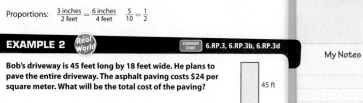

EXAMPLE 2   Real World   COMMON CORE   6.RP.3, 6.RP.3b, 6.RP.3d

Bob's driveway is 45 feet long by 18 feet wide. He plans to pave the entire driveway. The asphalt paving costs $24 per square meter. What will be the total cost of the paving?

STEP 1   First find the dimensions of the driveway in meters.

Convert each measurement to meters.
Use 1 foot ≈ 0.305 meter.

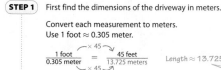

$\frac{1 \text{ foot}}{0.305 \text{ meter}} = \frac{45 \text{ feet}}{13.725 \text{ meters}}$ Length ≈ 13.725 meters

$\frac{1 \text{ foot}}{0.305 \text{ meter}} = \frac{18 \text{ feet}}{5.49 \text{ meters}}$ Width ≈ 5.49 meters

The length and width are approximate because the conversion between feet and meters is approximate.

STEP 2   Find the area in square meters.

Area = length × width
= 13.725 × 5.49
= 75.35 square meters

STEP 3   Now find the total cost of the paving.

square meters × cost per square meter = total cost
75.35   × $24   = $1,808.40

Reflect

6.   Error Analysis Yolanda found the area of Bob's driveway in square meters as shown. Explain why Yolanda's answer is incorrect.

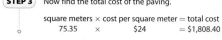

Area = 45 × 18 = 810 square feet

810 square feet × $\frac{0.305 \text{ meter}}{1 \text{ foot}}$ ≈ 247.1 square meters

Yolanda's conversion factor is used to convert feet to meters, not square feet to square meters.

45 ft

18 ft

My Notes

Math Talk
Mathematical Practices

How much does the paving cost per square foot? Explain.

About $2.23 per square foot. The cost per square foot is the quotient of the total cost ($1,808.40) and the area in square feet (45 × 18 = 810 square feet.)

Math On the Spot
my.hrw.com

Personal Math Trainer
Online Assessment and Intervention
my.hrw.com

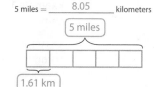

YOUR TURN

7. A flower bed is 2 meters wide and 3 meters long. What is the area of the flower bed in square feet? Round your converted dimensions and your final answer to the nearest hundredth.

__64.55__ square feet

Guided Practice

Complete each diagram to solve the problem. (Explore Activity)

1. Kate ran 5 miles. How far did she run in kilometers?

5 miles = ___8.05___ kilometers

5 miles

1.61 km

2. Alex filled a 5-gallon jug with water. How many liters of water are in the container?

5 gallons ≈ ___18.95___ liters

5 gallons

3.79 L

Use a conversion factor to convert each measurement. (Example 1 and 2)

3. A ruler is 12 inches long. What is the length of this ruler in centimeters?

___30.48___ centimeters

4. A kitten weighs 4 pounds. What is the approximate mass of the kitten in kilograms?

___1.816___ kilograms

Use a proportion to convert each measurement. (Example 2)

5. 20 yards ≈ ___18.28___ meters

6. 12 ounces ≈ ___339.6___ grams

7. 5 quarts ≈ ___4.73___ liters

8. 400 meters ≈ ___437.64___ yards

9. 10 liters ≈ ___2.64___ gallons

10. 137.25 meters ≈ ___450___ feet

11. 165 centimeters ≈ ___64.96___ inches

12. 10,000 kilometers ≈ ___6,211___ miles

?   ESSENTIAL QUESTION CHECK-IN

13. Write a proportion that you can use to convert 60 inches to centimeters.

$\frac{1 \text{ inch}}{2.54 \text{ centimeters}} = \frac{60 \text{ inches}}{x \text{ centimeters}}$; x = 152.4 cm

---

DIFFERENTIATE INSTRUCTION

Cooperative Learning

Have students get more comfortable with comparing the two systems of measurement by quizzing each other on which unit is greater, the customary or the metric.

Student 1: Which is greater, 1 gallon or 1 liter?

Student 2: 1 gallon

Student 2: Which is smaller, 1 gram or 1 ounce?

Student 1: 1 gram

Critical Thinking

Point out to students that in Example 2, the ratios $\frac{45 \text{ feet}}{13.725 \text{ meters}}$ and $\frac{18 \text{ feet}}{5.49 \text{ meters}}$ are equal to each other. Ask students to examine this claim, discuss why it is true, and justify it with a logical argument. Sample answer: Both are equal to the ratio $\frac{1 \text{ foot}}{0.305 \text{ meter}}$, so by the transitive property they are equal to each other. Or, assume they are equal, then use cross multiplication to show that they are equal.

Additional Resources

Differentiated Instruction includes:

• Reading Strategies

• Success for English Learners **ELL**

• Reteach

• Challenge **PRE-AP**

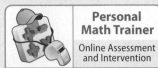
7.4 LESSON QUIZ

COMMON CORE **6.RP.3d**

1. Mindy's paper cup holds 6 fluid ounces. How many milliliters is this? Complete the diagram to solve the problem.

6 fluid ounces

29.6 mL

Tell which measure is greater.

2. 20 ounces or 20 grams

3. 60 gallons or 60 liters

4. A bag of potatoes weighs 15 pounds. How many kilograms is this?

5. You want to measure the length of a ribbon in inches. You only have a centimeter ruler. The length of the ribbon is 16 cm. Is the ribbon longer or shorter than 16 inches? How many inches long is it?

Lesson Quiz available online

🕐 my.hrw.com

Answers

1. 177.6 milliliters

2. 20 ounces

3. 60 gallons

4. 6.81 kg

5. shorter than 16 inches; about 6.3 inches

Evaluate

GUIDED AND INDEPENDENT PRACTICE

COMMON CORE **6.RP.3, 6.RP.3b, 6.RP.3d**

Concepts & Skills	Practice
Explore Activity Converting Inches to Centimeters	Exercises 1, 2, 15
Example 1 Using Conversion Factors	Exercises 3–4, 25–27
Example 2 Using Proportions to Convert Measurements	Exercises 3–13, 23, 24

Exercise	Depth of Knowledge (D.O.K.)		COMMON CORE Mathematical Practices
15–25	**2** Skills/Concepts		**MP.4** Modeling
26	**2** Skills/Concepts		**MP.5** Using Tools
27	**2** Skills/Concepts		**MP.4** Modeling
28	**3** Strategic Thinking	H.O.T.	**MP.3** Logic
29	**3** Strategic Thinking	H.O.T.	**MP.4** Modeling
30	**2** Skills/Concepts		**MP.4** Modeling
31	**3** Strategic Thinking	H.O.T.	**MP.4** Modeling
32	**3** Strategic Thinking	H.O.T.	**MP.4** Modeling
33	**3** Strategic Thinking	H.O.T.	**MP.4** Modeling
34	**3** Strategic Thinking	H.O.T.	**MP.7** Using Structure
35	**3** Strategic Thinking	H.O.T.	**MP.8** Patterns

Additional Resources

Differentiated Instruction includes:

• Leveled Practice worksheets

7.4 Independent Practice

COMMON CORE 6.RP.3, 6.RP.3b, 6.RP.3d

Personal Math Trainer

Online Assessment and Intervention

my.hrw.com

Tell which measure is greater.

14. Six feet or two meters two meters

15. One inch or one centimeter one inch

16. One yard or one meter one meter

17. One mile or one kilometer one mile

18. One ounce or one gram one ounce

19. One quart or one liter one liter

20. 10 pounds or 10 kilograms 10 kilograms

21. Four liters or one gallon four liters

22. Two miles or three kilometers two miles

23. What is the limit in kilograms?

weight limit for checked baggage: 50 pounds

22.7 kg

24. What is the speed limit in miles per hour?

55 km/h

about 34 mi/h

25. Which container holds more, a half-gallon milk jug or a 2-liter juice bottle?

2-liter juice bottle

26. The label on a can of lemonade gives the volume as 12 fl oz, or 355 mL. Verify that these two measurements are nearly equivalent.

$12 \text{ fl oz} \times \frac{29.6 \text{ mL}}{1 \text{ fl oz}} = 355.2 \approx 355$

27. The mass of a textbook is about 1.25 kilograms. About how many pounds is this?

2.75 pounds

28. Critique Reasoning Michael estimated his mass as 8 kilograms. Is his estimate reasonable? Justify your answer.

No; 8 kilograms ≈ 17.6 pounds

29. Your mother bought a three-liter bottle of water. When she got home, she discovered a small leak in the bottom and asked you to find a container to transfer the water into. All you could find were two half-gallon jugs.

a. Will your containers hold all of the water?

Yes; Two half-gallon containers will hold one gallon, which is about 3.79 liters.

b. What If? Suppose an entire liter of water leaked out in the car. In that case, would you be able to fit all of the remaining water into one of the half-gallon jugs?

No; A gallon jug can hold 3.79 liters, so a half-gallon jug would hold half of that, which is only 1.895 liters.

30. The track team ran a mile and a quarter during their practice. How many kilometers did the team run? 2.0125 km

31. A countertop is 16 feet long and 3 feet wide.

a. What is the area of the countertop in square meters? 4.47

b. Tile costs $28 per square meter. How much will it cost to cover the countertop with new tile? $ 125.16

32. At a school picnic, your teacher asks you to mark a field every ten yards so students can play football. The teacher accidentally gave you a meter stick instead of a yard stick. How far apart in meters should you mark the lines if you still want them to be in the right places?

Mark a line every 9.14 meters, or every 9 m and 14 cm.

33. You weigh a gallon of 2% milk in science class and learn that it is approximately 8.4 pounds. You pass the milk to the next group, and then realize that your teacher wanted an answer in kilograms, not pounds. Explain how you can adjust your answer without weighing the milk again. Then give the weight in kilograms.

Multiply the number of pounds by 0.454; 3.8 kg

H.O.T. FOCUS ON HIGHER ORDER THINKING

34. Analyze Relationships Annalisa, Keiko, and Stefan want to compare their heights. Annalisa is 64 inches tall. Stefan tells her, "I'm about 7.5 centimeters taller than you." Keiko knows she is 1.5 inches shorter than Stefan. Give the heights of all three people in both inches and centimeters to the nearest half unit.

Estimates may vary due to rounding. Sample answers:

Annalisa: 64 inches, about 162.5 centimeters; Stefan: about 67 inches, about 170 centimeters; Keiko: about 65.5 inches, about 166.5 centimeters

35. Communicate Mathematical Ideas Mikhael wanted to rewrite the conversion factor "1 yard ≈ 0.914 meter" to create a conversion factor to convert meters to yards. He wrote "1 meter ≈ _____." Tell how Mikhael should finish his conversion, and explain how you know.

1 meter ≈ 1.094 yards; Dividing 1 yard by 0.914 m gives the rate of yards per meter: $\frac{1 \text{ yard}}{0.914 \text{ meter}} \approx \frac{1}{0.914}$ or 1.094 yards per meter.

Work Area

EXTEND THE MATH PRE-AP

Activity available online my.hrw.com

Activity Find five or more package labels for which the dimensions, weight/mass, or capacity are given in both customary and metric units. Use what you know about conversion factors to see how much the values have been rounded. Can you find any mistakes?

Sample answers:

Bottle of water: 16.9 fl oz (500 mL); 500 mL has been rounded down. It would be more accurate to say 500.29 mL.

Can of tomatoes: 14.9 oz (411 g); 411 g is a mistake. 14.9 oz converts to 423.16 g.

Jar of hazelnut spread: 2 lb 2 oz (1 kg); 1 kg is rounded down. It would be more accurate to say 1.0084 kg.

Envelopes: $4\frac{1}{8} \times 9\frac{1}{2}$ inches (10.4 × 24.1 cm); The dimensions 10.4 × 24.1 cm have been rounded down. It would be more accurate to say 10.4775 × 24.13 cm.

Ready to Go On?

Assess Mastery

Use the assessment on this page to determine if students have mastered the concepts and standards covered in this module.

Response to Intervention

Intervention	Enrichment

Personal Math Trainer
Online Assessment and Intervention
my.hrw.com

Access Ready to Go On? assessment online, and receive instant scoring, feedback, and customized intervention or enrichment.

Online and Print Resources

Differentiated Instruction
• Reteach worksheets
• Reading Strategies **ELL**
• Success for English Learners **ELL**

Differentiated Instruction
• Challenge worksheets **PRE-AP**
• Extend the Math **PRE-AP** Lesson Activities in TE

Additional Resources

Assessment Resources includes:
• Leveled Module Quizzes

Ready to Go On?

Personal Math Trainer
Online Assessment and Intervention
my.hrw.com

7.1 Ratios, Rates, Tables, and Graphs

1. Charlie runs laps around a track. The table shows how long it takes him to run different numbers of laps. How long would it take Charlie to run 5 laps?

Number of Laps	2	4	6	8	10
Time (min)	10	20	30	40	50

__25 minutes__

7.2 Solving Proportionality Problems

2. Emily is entering a bicycle race for charity. Her mother pledges $0.40 for every 0.25 mile she bikes. If Emily bikes 15 miles, how much will her mother donate? __$24__

3. Rob is saving to buy a new MP3 player. For every $15 he earns babysitting, he saves $6. On Saturday, Rob earned $75 babysitting. How much money did he save? __$30__

7.3 Within Measurement Systems
Convert each measurement.

4. 18 meters = __1,800__ centimeters
5. 5 pounds = __80__ ounces
6. 6 quarts = __192__ fluid ounces
7. 9 liters = __9,000__ milliliters

7.4 Converting Between Measurement Systems
Convert each measurement.

8. 5 inches = __12.7__ centimeters
9. 198.9 grams ≈ __7__ ounces
10. 8 gallons ≈ __30.32__ liters
11. 12 feet ≈ __3.66__ meters

? ESSENTIAL QUESTION

12. Write a real-world problem that could be solved using a proportion.
__Sample answer: Sheila travels 110 miles in 2 hours.__
__At this rate, how far will she travel in 6 hours?__

Common Core Standards

Lesson	Exercises	Common Core Standards
7.1	1	**6.RP.3, 6.RP.3a, 6.RP.3b**
7.2	2–3	**6.RP.3, 6.RP.3b**
7.3	4–7	**6.RP.3d**
7.4	8–11	**6.RP.3, 6.RP.3b, 6.RP.3d**

Assessment Readiness

Assessment Readiness Tip Students can use the given answer choices and work backwards to eliminate incorrect answer choices.

Item 4 Students can evaluate each choice to see if it answers the question. Choice A can be eliminated because 2 miles is half of 4 miles which would be 28 minutes. Choice B is halfway between 2 miles and 4 miles, or halfway between 28 minutes and 56 minutes which is 42 minutes. Choice B is the correct answer. Since B is the correct answer, the student can stop evaluating the choices.

Item 5 Students can look at the pattern in the table. The top number increases by 5 while the bottom number increases by 2. Choice A can be eliminated because while 25 will be the next number in the top row, the next number in the bottom row will be 10. Choice B is the correct answer.

Avoid Common Errors

Item 1 Some students plot coordinate points backward. They move upward from the origin before moving to the right. Remind students to run before they jump; i.e., the coordinate plane's *x*-value represents movement to the right, and the *y*-value represents movement upward.

Item 6 Since all of the measurements are in the same units, some students may pair the wrong quantities together. Remind students to read the problem carefully and circle or underline the quantities to help ensure correct matches.

Additional Resources

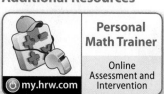

Personal Math Trainer

Online Assessment and Intervention

my.hrw.com

COMMON CORE

MODULE 7 MIXED REVIEW

Assessment Readiness

Personal Math Trainer

Online Assessment and Intervention

my.hrw.com

Selected Response

1. The graph below represents the distance Manuel walks over several hours.

Which is an ordered pair on the line?

Ⓐ (2.5, 14) Ⓒ (2.25, 12)
Ⓑ (1.25, 5) Ⓓ (1.5, 9)

2. Jonah's house and his grandparents' house are 8,046.72 meters apart. What is this distance in miles?

Ⓐ 4 miles Ⓒ 7 miles
Ⓑ 5 miles Ⓓ 8 miles

3. Megan is making bracelets to sell to earn money for the local animal shelter. It takes her $\frac{1}{4}$ hour to pick out all the beads and $\frac{1}{10}$ hour to string them. This week, she only has $5\frac{1}{4}$ hours to make bracelets. How many bracelets will Megan be able to make?

Ⓐ 10 bracelets Ⓒ 15 bracelets
Ⓑ 12 bracelets Ⓓ 21 bracelets

4. Rosa can run 4 miles in 56 minutes. How many miles does Rosa run if she runs for 42 minutes?

Ⓐ 2 miles Ⓒ 3.5 miles
Ⓑ 3 miles Ⓓ 5 miles

5. The table below shows the number of petals and leaves for different numbers of flowers.

Petals	5	10	15	20
Leaves	2	4	6	8

How many petals are present when there are 12 leaves?

Ⓐ 25 petals Ⓒ 35 petals
Ⓑ 30 petals Ⓓ 36 petals

6. A recipe calls for 3 cups of sugar and 9 cups of water. How many cups of water should be used with 2 cups of sugar?

Ⓐ 3 cups Ⓒ 6 cups
Ⓑ 4 cups Ⓓ 8 cups

Mini-Task

7. The unlabeled graph shows the relationship between two customary units of measure. Only two pairs of units can be represented by the graph.

a. Determine the possible pairs of units.
cups and quarts; quarts and
gallons

b. Describe the relationship for each pair.
There are 4 cups in 1 quart
and 4 quarts in 1 gallon.

Common Core Standards

Items	Grade 6 Standards	Mathematical Practices
1	6.RP.3a	MP.4
2	6.RP.3d	MP.2
3*	6.RP.3b	MP.4
4	6.RP.3b	MP.4
5	6.RP.3b	MP.4
6	6.RP.3d	MP.4
7	6.RP.3d	MP.2

* Item integrates mixed review concepts from previous modules or a previous course.

Percents

ESSENTIAL QUESTION

How can you use percents to solve real-world problems?

You can use percents to find a part of a real-world quantity when you know the whole and a percent, and find the whole of a quantity when you know a part and a percent.

Real-World Video

When you eat at a restaurant, your bill will include sales tax for most items. It is customary to add a tip for your server in many restaurants. Both taxes and tips are calculated as a percent of the bill.

my.hrw.com

© Houghton Mifflin Harcourt Publishing Company

GO DIGITAL
my.hrw.com

my.hrw.com

Go digital with your write-in student edition, accessible on any device.

Math On the Spot

Scan with your smart phone to jump directly to the online edition, video tutor, and more.

Animated Math

Interactively explore key concepts to see how math works.

Personal Math Trainer

Get immediate feedback and help as you work through practice sets.

Are You Ready?

Assess Readiness

Use the assessment on this page to determine if students need intensive or strategic intervention for the module's prerequisite skills.

Response to Intervention

Intervention	Enrichment

Access Are You Ready? assessment online, and receive instant scoring, feedback, and customized intervention or enrichment.

Personal Math Trainer

Online Assessment and Intervention

my.hrw.com

Online and Print Resources

Skills Intervention worksheets
- Skill 24 Write Equivalent Fractions
- Skill 40 Decimal Operations (Multiplication)
- Skill 44 Multiply Fractions

Differentiated Instruction
- Challenge worksheets **PRE-AP**
- Extend the Math **PRE-AP** Lesson Activities in TE

Are YOU Ready?

Complete these exercises to review skills you will need for this module.

Personal Math Trainer
Online Assessment and Intervention
my.hrw.com

Write Equivalent Fractions

EXAMPLE
$\frac{9}{12} = \frac{9 \times 4}{12 \times 4} = \frac{36}{48}$ Multiply the numerator and denominator by the same number to find an equivalent fraction.
$\frac{9}{12} = \frac{9 \div 3}{12 \div 3} = \frac{3}{4}$ Divide the numerator and denominator by the same number to find an equivalent fraction.

Write the equivalent fraction.

1. $\frac{9}{18} = \frac{3}{6}$
2. $\frac{4}{6} = \frac{12}{18}$
3. $\frac{25}{30} = \frac{5}{6}$
4. $\frac{12}{15} = \frac{36}{45}$

5. $\frac{15}{24} = \frac{5}{8}$
6. $\frac{24}{32} = \frac{6}{8}$
7. $\frac{50}{60} = \frac{10}{12}$
8. $\frac{5}{9} = \frac{20}{36}$

Multiply Fractions

EXAMPLE
$\frac{5}{12} \times \frac{3}{10} = \frac{1}{12_4} \times \frac{1}{10_2}$ Divide by the common factors.
$= \frac{1}{8}$ Simplify.

Multiply. Write each product in simplest form.

9. $\frac{3}{8} \times \frac{4}{11} = \frac{3}{22}$
10. $\frac{8}{15} \times \frac{5}{6} = \frac{4}{9}$
11. $\frac{7}{12} \times \frac{3}{14} = \frac{1}{8}$

12. $\frac{9}{20} \times \frac{4}{5} = \frac{9}{25}$
13. $\frac{7}{10} \times \frac{20}{21} = \frac{2}{3}$
14. $\frac{8}{18} \times \frac{9}{20} = \frac{1}{5}$

Decimal Operations (Multiplication)

EXAMPLE
$\begin{array}{r} 1.6 \\ \times 0.3 \\ \hline 0.48 \end{array}$ Multiply as you would with whole numbers.
Count the total number of decimal places in the factors.
Place the decimal point that number of places in the product.

Multiply.

15. 20×0.25 5
16. 0.3×16.99 5.097
17. 0.2×75 15

18. 5.5×1.1 6.05
19. 11.99×0.8 9.592
20. 7.25×0.5 3.625

21. 4×0.75 3
22. 0.15×12.50 1.875
23. 6.5×0.7 4.55

PROFESSIONAL DEVELOPMENT VIDEO

Author Juli Dixon models successful teaching practices as she explores percents in an actual sixth-grade classroom.

Professional Development

my.hrw.com

GO DIGITAL
my.hrw.com

 Online Teacher Edition
Access a full suite of teaching resources online—plan, present, and manage classes and assignments.

 ePlanner
Easily plan your classes and access all your resources online.

Interactive Answers and Solutions
Customize answer keys to print or display in the classroom. Choose to include answers only or full solutions to all lesson exercises.

 Interactive Whiteboards
Engage students with interactive whiteboard-ready lessons and activities.

 Personal Math Trainer: Online Assessment and Intervention
Assign automatically graded homework, quizzes, tests, and intervention activities. Prepare your students with updated practice tests aligned with Common Core.

Reading Start-Up

Have students complete the activities on this page by working alone or with others.

Visualize Vocabulary

The main idea web helps students review vocabulary associated with fractions and decimals, and prepare for finding percents. After students complete the web, discuss the vocabulary as a class.

Understand Vocabulary

Use the following explanations to help students learn the preview words.

>**Percents** are used often in everyday life. In school, grades are usually calculated as a percent of 100. For example, 90% means 90 out of 100. Other examples of percents include discounts in stores. For example, a store may have a 50% discount on clothes.

Active Reading

Integrating Language Arts

Students can use these reading and note-taking strategies to help them organize and understand new concepts and vocabulary.

COMMON CORE **ELA-Literacy.RST.6-8.7** Integrate quantitative or technical information expressed in words in a text with a version of that information expressed visually (e.g., in a flowchart, diagram, model, graph, or table).

Additional Resources

Differentiated Instruction

• Reading Strategies **ELL**

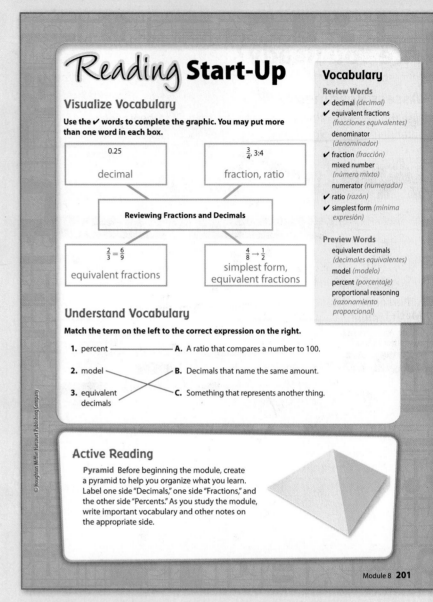

Reading Start-Up

Visualize Vocabulary

Use the ✔ words to complete the graphic. You may put more than one word in each box.

0.25		$\frac{3}{4}$, 3:4
decimal		fraction, ratio

Reviewing Fractions and Decimals

$\frac{2}{3} = \frac{6}{9}$		$\frac{4}{8} \rightarrow \frac{1}{2}$
equivalent fractions		simplest form, equivalent fractions

Understand Vocabulary

Match the term on the left to the correct expression on the right.

1. percent ——————— **A.** A ratio that compares a number to 100.

2. model **B.** Decimals that name the same amount.

3. equivalent decimals **C.** Something that represents another thing.

Vocabulary

Review Words
✔ decimal *(decimal)*
✔ equivalent fractions *(fracciones equivalentes)*
  denominator *(denominador)*
✔ fraction *(fracción)*
  mixed number *(número mixto)*
  numerator *(numerador)*
✔ ratio *(razón)*
✔ simplest form *(mínima expresión)*

Preview Words
  equivalent decimals *(decimales equivalentes)*
  model *(modelo)*
  percent *(porcentaje)*
  proportional reasoning *(razonamiento proporcional)*

Active Reading

Pyramid Before beginning the module, create a pyramid to help you organize what you learn. Label one side "Decimals," one side "Fractions," and the other side "Percents." As you study the module, write important vocabulary and other notes on the appropriate side.

Module 8 **201**

© Houghton Mifflin Harcourt Publishing Company

Before	**In this module**	**After**
Students understand fractions, decimals, and percents: • relate fractions to percents and percents to decimals • find the percent of a number	Students relate fractions, decimals, and percents: • represent percents with concrete models and fractions • generate equivalent forms of fractions, decimals, and percents using real-world problems • solve real-world problems involving percent	Students will connect solving real-world problems involving percent: • solve problems involving percent increase, percent decrease, and percent of change • solve markup and markdown problems • find sales tax, total cost, simple interest

Unpacking the Standards

Use the examples on the page to help students know exactly what they are expected to learn in this module.

Common Core Standards

Content Areas

 Ratios and Proportional Reasoning—6.RP

Understand ratio concepts and use ratio reasoning to solve problems.

Go online to see a complete unpacking of the Common Core Standards.

🔵 my.hrw.com

 MODULE 8

Unpacking the Standards

Understanding the standards and the vocabulary terms in the standards will help you know exactly what you are expected to learn in this module.

COMMON CORE 6.RP.3c

Find a percent of a quantity as a rate per 100 (e.g., 30% of a quantity means $\frac{30}{100}$ times the quantity); solve problems involving finding the whole, given a part and the percent.

Key Vocabulary

Percent *(porcentaje)*
A ratio comparing a number to 100.

What It Means to You

You will learn to write numbers in various forms, including fractions, decimals, and percents.

UNPACKING EXAMPLE 6.RP.3c

Little brown bats flap their wings about $\frac{3}{4}$ as fast as pipistrelle bats do. How fast does the little brown bat flap its wings as a percent of the pipistrelle bat's wing flap rate?

$\frac{3}{4} = 3 = 3 \div 4 = 0.75$ Divide the numerator by the denominator.

$0.75 = 75\%$ Move the decimal point 2 places to the right.

COMMON CORE 6.RP.3c

Find a percent of a quantity as a rate per 100 (e.g., 30% of a quantity means $\frac{30}{100}$ times the quantity); solve problems involving finding the whole, given a part and the percent.

What It Means to You

You will solve problems involving percent.

UNPACKING EXAMPLE 6.RP.3c

About 67% of a person's total (100%) body weight is water. If Cameron weights 90 pounds, about how much of his weight is water?

67% of 90

$\frac{67}{100} \cdot 90$

$= \frac{67}{100} \cdot \frac{90}{1}$

$= 60.3$

About 60.3 pounds of Cameron's weight is water.

Visit **my.hrw.com** to see all the Common Core Standards unpacked.

🔵 my.hrw.com

202 Unit 3

© Houghton Mifflin Harcourt Publishing Company • Image Credits: ©Ted Kinsman/ScienceSource

---

Common Core Standards	Lesson 8.1	Lesson 8.2	Lesson 8.3
6.RP.3 Use ratio and rate reasoning to solve real-world and mathematical problems, e.g., by reasoning about tables of equivalent ratios, tape diagrams, double number line diagrams, or equations.		COMMON CORE	COMMON CORE
6.RP.3c Find a percent of a quantity as a rate per 100 (e.g., 30% of a quantity means 30/100 times the quantity); solve problems involving finding the whole, given a part and the percent.	COMMON CORE		COMMON CORE

LESSON
8.1 Understanding Percent

Common Core Standards

The student is expected to:

 Ratios and Proportional Relationships—6.RP.3c

Find a percent of a quantity as a rate per 100 (e.g., 30% of a quantity means 30/100 times the quantity); solve problems involving finding the whole, given a part and the percent.

Mathematical Practices

 MP.2 Reasoning

Engage

ESSENTIAL QUESTION

How can you write a ratio as a percent? Sample answer: Write the ratio as an equivalent fraction with a denominator of 100. Then write the percent.

Motivate the Lesson

Ask: A goalie stopped 9 out of 10 shots on goal during a soccer game. What percent of the shots did the goalie stop? Begin the Explore Activity to find out how to write a ratio as a percent.

Explore

EXPLORE ACTIVITY 1

Connect Vocabulary ELL

Point out to students that because **percent** means "per hundred," 100% means "100 out of 100." This is why 100% is often used to mean "all" or "the whole thing." Also, explain that any percent less than 100% represents a part of a whole (e.g., 25% means "25 out of 100").

Integrating the ELPS ELL

You may want to pair up English learners with a partner for Explore Activity 1 to help them develop their language skills.

Explain

EXPLORE ACTIVITY 2

Engage with the Whiteboard

Have students make a 10 × 10 grid representing $\frac{1}{4}$ next to the bar model of $\frac{1}{4}$ on the whiteboard. Ask students to compare and contrast the models. Have them discuss which model they would prefer to use and why.

Questioning Strategies CC Mathematical Practices

• When making bar models using ratios, how do you know how many pieces to use in your model and how many pieces to shade? The denominator of the ratio tells you how many pieces you need in the model. The numerator tells you how many pieces to shade.

• How can you write a percent as a ratio? Write the percent as a fraction with a denominator of 100. Then write the fraction in simplest terms.

• How can you represent 100% with a bar model? Since 100% is $\frac{100}{100} = 1$, you would shade the entire bar.

8.1 Understanding Percent

COMMON CORE **6.RP.3c**

Find a percent of a quantity as a rate per 100 (e.g., 30% of a quantity means 30/100 times the quantity); ...

? ESSENTIAL QUESTION

How can you write a ratio as a percent?

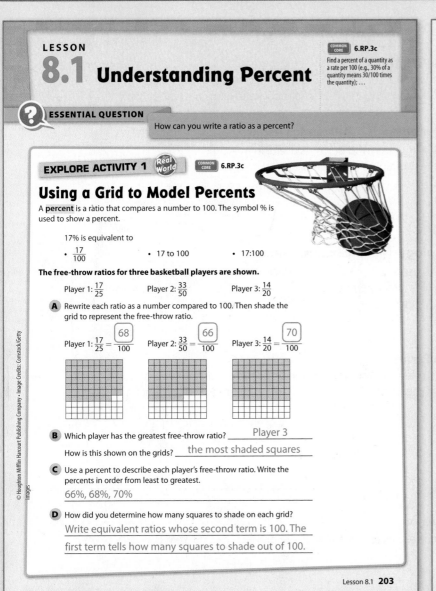

EXPLORE ACTIVITY 1 Real World | COMMON CORE **6.RP.3c**

Using a Grid to Model Percents

A **percent** is a ratio that compares a number to 100. The symbol % is used to show a percent.

17% is equivalent to

- $\frac{17}{100}$
- 17 to 100
- 17:100

The free-throw ratios for three basketball players are shown.

Player 1: $\frac{17}{25}$ Player 2: $\frac{33}{50}$ Player 3: $\frac{14}{20}$

A Rewrite each ratio as a number compared to 100. Then shade the grid to represent the free-throw ratio.

Player 1: $\frac{17}{25} = \frac{68}{100}$ Player 2: $\frac{33}{50} = \frac{66}{100}$ Player 3: $\frac{14}{20} = \frac{70}{100}$

B Which player has the greatest free-throw ratio? _____Player 3_____

How is this shown on the grids? ___the most shaded squares___

C Use a percent to describe each player's free-throw ratio. Write the percents in order from least to greatest.

66%, 68%, 70%

D How did you determine how many squares to shade on each grid?

Write equivalent ratios whose second term is 100. The first term tells how many squares to shade out of 100.

Lesson 8.1   **203**

EXPLORE ACTIVITY 2 | COMMON CORE **6.RP.3c**

Connecting Fractions and Percents

You can use a percent bar model to model a ratio expressed as a fraction and to find an equivalent percent.

A Use a percent bar model to find an equivalent percent for $\frac{1}{4}$.

Draw a model to represent 100 and divide it into fourths. Shade $\frac{1}{4}$.

0   $\frac{1}{4}$ 1
0%   25 %   100%

$\frac{1}{4}$ of 100 = 25, so $\frac{1}{4}$ of 100% = _____25%_____

Tell which operation you can use to find $\frac{1}{4}$ of 100.

Then find $\frac{1}{4}$ of 100%. ___multiplication; $\frac{1}{4} \cdot 100\% = 25\%$___

B Use a percent bar model to find an equivalent percent for $\frac{1}{3}$.

Draw a model and divide it into thirds. Shade $\frac{1}{3}$.

0   $\frac{1}{3}$ 1
0% $33\frac{1}{3}$%   100%

$\frac{1}{3}$ of 100 = $33\frac{1}{3}$, so $\frac{1}{3}$ of 100% = _____$33\frac{1}{3}$_____ %

Tell which operation you can use to find $\frac{1}{3}$ of 100.

Then find $\frac{1}{3}$ of 100%. ___multiplication; $\frac{1}{3} \cdot 100\% = 33\frac{1}{3}\%$___

Reflect

1. **Critique Reasoning** Jo says she can find the percent equivalent of $\frac{3}{4}$ by multiplying the percent equivalent of $\frac{1}{4}$ by 3. How can you use a percent bar model to support this claim?

Shade three $\frac{1}{4}$ sections to show $\frac{3}{4}$. Since $\frac{1}{4} = 25\%$,

$\frac{3}{4} = 3 \cdot 25\% = 75\%$.

PROFESSIONAL DEVELOPMENT

CC Integrate Mathematical Practices MP.2

This lesson provides an opportunity to address this Mathematical Practice standard. It calls for students to create and use representations to organize and communicate mathematical ideas. In the Explore Activities, students represent percents as fractions with a denominator of 100 and model them with both a 10 × 10 grid and a bar model. In Example 1, students use number lines to relate a fraction to its equivalent percent. Thus, students create and use multiple representations of ratios and percents.

Math Background

The percent symbol, %, has evolved over time. Manuscripts from the fifteenth century show percent symbolized as "per $\frac{o}{c}$," which is an abbreviation of the Latin phrase *per cento*. By the middle of the seventeenth century, percent had begun to be symbolized by "per $\frac{o}{o}$." Later, the word *per* was dropped, leaving only the symbol $\frac{o}{o}$. The percent symbol we use today is a direct descendant of $\frac{o}{o}$.

EXAMPLE 1

Engage with the Whiteboard

 Have students add $\frac{1}{5}$ and its equivalent percent to the model on the whiteboard. Then ask students to show 80% on the model and explain its relationship to $\frac{1}{5}$.

Questioning Strategies 🆒 Mathematical Practices

• Why are benchmark fractions and percents useful in math? Benchmark fractions and percents can be used as a point of reference in determining an estimate.

• Give an example to show when you might estimate to find a percent. When a percent is close to a benchmark percent and you don't need an exact answer, you can estimate. For example, 52% is close to 50%, so you can say, "about 50%."

Focus on Technology 🆒 Mathematical Practices

Demonstrate how to use a calculator to find a decimal equivalent of a fraction and then express it a percent. For example, enter 3, press ÷, enter 10, press =. The screen will display 0.3, which is equivalent to $\frac{3}{10} = \frac{30}{100} = 30\%$.

YOUR TURN

Avoid Common Errors

Exercise 4 Some students may not understand that the required answer should be an estimate. Stress to students that "about" refers to an estimate based on benchmark fractions and percents.

Elaborate

Talk About It
Summarize the Lesson

 Ask: What does *percent* mean? Percent compares a part to a whole. The whole equals 100, so 40% means 40 out of 100.

GUIDED PRACTICE

Engage with the Whiteboard

 In Exercise 1, have students fill in the boxes to write the ratio as a percent. Then have a student shade the 10 × 10 grid to represent the percent. In Exercise 2, have a student fill in the equivalent percent for $\frac{1}{5}$ and then shade the appropriate section(s) of the bar model.

Avoid Common Errors

Exercises 3–5 Some students may use the percent that is equivalent to the unit fraction benchmark as their answer. Direct them to look at the numerator of the given fraction and use it as a multiplier.

Exercise 6 Some students may not recognize 40% as a benchmark percent equivalent to $\frac{2}{5}$. Direct them to the double number line with Example 1 and point out that 10% is equivalent to $\frac{1}{10}$. 10% × 4 = 40% and $\frac{1}{10} \times 4 = \frac{4}{10}$ which simplifies to $\frac{2}{5}$.

Using Benchmarks and Proportional Reasoning

You can use certain *benchmark* percents to write other percents and to estimate fractions.

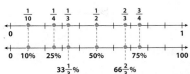

EXAMPLE 1

COMMON CORE 6.RP.3c

A Find an equivalent percent for $\frac{3}{10}$.

STEP 1 Write $\frac{3}{10}$ as a multiple of a benchmark fraction.

$$\frac{3}{10} = 3 \cdot \frac{1}{10} \qquad \text{Think: } \frac{3}{10} = \frac{1}{10} + \frac{1}{10} + \frac{1}{10}$$

STEP 2 Find an equivalent percent for $\frac{1}{10}$.

$$\frac{1}{10} = 10\% \qquad \text{Use the number lines to find the equivalent percent for } \frac{1}{10}.$$

STEP 3 Multiply.

$$\frac{3}{10} = 3 \cdot \frac{1}{10} = 3 \cdot 10\% = 30\%$$

B 76% of the students at a middle school bring their own lunch. About what fraction of the students bring their own lunch?

STEP 1 Note that 76% is close to the benchmark 75%.

STEP 2 Find a fraction equivalent for 75%:

$$75\% = \frac{3}{4}$$

About $\frac{3}{4}$ of the students bring their own lunch.

Math Talk
Mathematical Practices

Explain how you could use equivalent ratios to write $\frac{3}{10}$ as a percent.

Multiply $\frac{3}{10}$ by $\frac{10}{10}$ to get $\frac{30}{100}$, or 30%.

YOUR TURN

Use a benchmark to find an equivalent percent for each fraction.

2. $\frac{9}{10}$ _____ 90% **3.** $\frac{2}{5}$ _____ 40%

4. 64% of the animals at an animal shelter are dogs. About what fraction of the animals at the shelter are dogs?

about $\frac{2}{3}$

Guided Practice

1. Shade the grid to represent the ratio $\frac{9}{25}$. Then find a percent equivalent to the given ratio. (Explore Activity 1)

$$\frac{9 \times \boxed{4}}{25 \times \boxed{4}} = \frac{\boxed{36}}{100} = \underline{\quad 36\% \quad}$$

2. Use the percent bar model to find the missing percent. (Explore Activity 2)

0%   100%

$\boxed{20}$ %

Identify a benchmark you can use to find an equivalent percent for each ratio. Then find the equivalent percent. (Example 1)

3. $\frac{6}{10}$ Benchmark: $\dfrac{1}{\boxed{10}}$

60%

4. $\frac{2}{4}$ Benchmark: $\dfrac{\boxed{1}}{4}$

50%

5. $\frac{4}{5}$ Benchmark: $\dfrac{\boxed{1}}{5}$

80%

6. 41% of the students at an art college want to be graphic designers. About what fraction of the students want to be graphic designers? (Example 1)

about $\frac{2}{5}$

? ESSENTIAL QUESTION CHECK-IN

7. How do you write a ratio as a percent?

Write the ratio as a fraction. Then write an equivalent fraction with a denominator of 100 and change the fraction to a percent.

DIFFERENTIATE INSTRUCTION

Kinesthetic Experience

Have students work in pairs to model percents and write them as fractions. Give each pair a set of 10 × 10 grids and two number cubes. One student rolls both number cubes and writes the numbers rolled as a percent. For example, a student who rolls a 5 and a 6 would write 56%. The other student shades a grid to model the percent and writes the percent as a fraction. The first student checks the other's work. Students continue, taking turns.

Curriculum Integration

Ask students to think of as many examples as they can of words that contain the base word *cent*, which is another word for penny and a Latin root meaning *hundred*. Some examples are *century*, *centipede*, *centimeter*, and *centennial*. Have volunteers look up the words in the dictionary and share the definitions with the class. Discuss each word's connection with the number 100.

Additional Resources

Differentiated Instruction includes:
- Reading Strategies
- Success for English Learners **ELL**
- Reteach
- Challenge **PRE-AP**

8.1 LESSON QUIZ

COMMON CORE **6.RP.3c**

1. Shade the grid to represent $\frac{20}{25}$. Then find a percent equivalent to the given ratio.

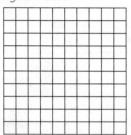

2. Use the percent bar model to find the missing percent.

0    $\frac{7}{10}$ 1

0%   ?   100%

3. Identify a benchmark you can use to find an equivalent percent for $\frac{4}{10}$.

4. Of all students who tried out for volleyball, 83% made the team. About what fraction of the students who tried out did *not* make the team? Explain your answer.

Lesson Quiz available online

Answers

1.

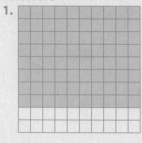

80%

2.

0    $\frac{7}{10}$ 1

0%   70%   100%

70%

Evaluate

GUIDED AND INDEPENDENT PRACTICE

COMMON CORE **6.RP.3c**

Concepts & Skills	Practice
Explore Activity 1 Using a Grid to Model Percents	Exercises 1, 8–9
Explore Activity 2 Connecting Fractions and Percents	Exercises 2, 10–11, 15–16
Example 1 Using Benchmarks and Proportional Reasoning	Exercises 3–6, 14–15

Exercise	Depth of Knowledge (D.O.K.)	COMMON CORE Mathematical Practices	
8–9	**2** Skills/Concepts	**MP.2** Reasoning	
10–11	**2** Skills/Concepts	**MP.4** Modeling	
12–13	**2** Skills/Concepts	**MP.7** Using Structure	
14	**3** Strategic Thinking H.O.T.	**MP.3** Logic	
15	**2** Skills/Concepts	**MP.5** Using Tools	
16	**3** Strategic Thinking H.O.T.	**MP.4** Modeling	
17–18	**3** Strategic Thinking H.O.T.	**MP.8** Patterns	

Additional Resources

Differentiated Instruction includes:

• Leveled Practice Worksheets

3. $\frac{1}{10}; \frac{1}{10} \cdot 4 = 10\% \cdot 4 = 40\%$

4. about $\frac{1}{5}$; Sample answer: 83% is close to 80%; if about 80% made the team, then about 100% − 80% = 20% did not make the team. 20% = $\frac{20}{100}$, which simplifies to $\frac{1}{5}$.

8.1 Independent Practice

 6.RP.3c

Personal Math Trainer
Online Assessment and Intervention
my.hrw.com

Shade the grid to represent the ratio. Then find the missing number.

8. $\frac{23}{50} = \frac{46}{100}$

9. $\frac{11}{20} = \frac{55}{100}$

10. Mark wants to use a grid like the ones in Exercises 1 and 2 to model the percent equivalent of the fraction $\frac{2}{3}$. How many grid squares should he shade? What percent would his model show?
$66\frac{2}{3}$ squares; $66\frac{2}{3}$%

11. The ratios of saves for a baseball pitcher to the number of save opportunities are given for three relief pitchers: $\frac{9}{10}, \frac{4}{5}, \frac{17}{20}$. Write each ratio as a percent. Order the percents from least to greatest.
$\frac{9}{10} = 90\%, \frac{4}{5} = 80\%, \frac{17}{20} = 85\%$; 80%, 85%, 90%

Circle the greater quantity.

12. $\frac{1}{3}$ of a box of Corn Krinkles

(50% of a box of Corn Krinkles)

13. (30% of your minutes are used up)

$\frac{1}{4}$ of your minutes are used up

14. **Multiple Representations** Explain how you could write 35% as the sum of two benchmark percents or as a multiple of a percent.
$35\% = 25\% + 10\%$ or $35\% = 7 \cdot 5\%$

15. Use the percent bar model to find the missing percent.

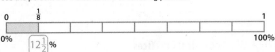

0    $\frac{1}{8}$ 1

0% $12\frac{1}{2}$%   100%

© Houghton Mifflin Harcourt Publishing Company

---

16. **Multistep** Carl buys songs and downloads them to his computer. The bar graph shows the numbers of each type of song he downloaded last year.

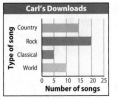

Carl's Downloads

a. What is the total number of songs Carl downloaded last year?
50

b. What fraction of the songs were country? Find the fraction for each type of song. Write each fraction in simplest form and give its percent equivalent.
Country: $\frac{3}{10} = 30\%$; Rock: $\frac{2}{5} = 40\%$; Classical: $\frac{1}{10} = 10\%$;
World: $\frac{1}{5} = 20\%$

H.O.T. FOCUS ON HIGHER ORDER THINKING

Work Area

17. **Critique Reasoning** Marcus bought a booklet of tickets to use at the amusement park. He used 50% of the tickets on rides, $\frac{1}{3}$ of the tickets on video games, and the rest of the tickets in the batting cage. Marcus says he used 10% of the tickets in the batting cage. Do you agree? Explain.
No; the percent benchmark for $\frac{1}{3}$ is $33\frac{1}{3}$%, so he used
$50\% + 33\frac{1}{3} = 83\frac{1}{3}\%$ on rides and games. $100\% - 83\frac{1}{3}\%$
$= 16\frac{2}{3}\%$ for the batting cage.

18. **Look for a Pattern** Complete the table.

Fraction	$\frac{1}{5}$	$\frac{2}{5}$	$\frac{3}{5}$	$\frac{4}{5}$	$\frac{5}{5}$	$\frac{6}{5}$
Percent	20%	40%	60%	80%	100%	120%

a. **Analyze Relationships** What is true when the numerator and denominator of the fraction are equal? What is true when the numerator is greater than the denominator?
The percent is equal to 100; the percent is greater than 100.

b. **Justify Reasoning** What is the percent equivalent of $\frac{3}{2}$? Use a pattern like the one in the table to support your answer.
150%; the pattern is $\frac{1}{2} = 50\%$, $\frac{2}{2} = 100\%$, $\frac{3}{2} = 150\%$.

© Houghton Mifflin Harcourt Publishing Company

EXTEND THE MATH PRE-AP

Activity available online my.hrw.com

Activity Have students work in pairs to model percents and write equivalent fractions.

Student 1: Write 3 percents less than 100% on separate index cards.

Student 2: Write 3 percents greater than 100% on separate index cards.

- Place the cards face down in two piles: one for each student's cards.
- Students flip over one percent card from each pile. Each student then models the difference between the larger percent and the smaller percent on 10 × 10 grids.
- Students compare their shaded grids and calculate equivalent fractions.

Challenge students to explain when they will need two 10 × 10 grids to model a difference.

LESSON
8.2 Percents, Fractions, and Decimals

Common Core Standards

The student is expected to:

 Ratios and Proportional Relationships—6.RP.3

Use ratio and rate reasoning to solve real-world and mathematical problems, e.g., by reasoning about tables of equivalent ratios, tape diagrams, double number line diagrams, or equations.

Mathematical Practices

 MP.4 Modeling

Engage

ESSENTIAL QUESTION

How can you write equivalent percents, fractions, and decimals? Sample answer: Any decimal or percent can be written as a fraction with a denominator of 100. Any fraction can be written as a decimal by dividing the numerator by the denominator. Any decimal can be written as a percent by multiplying by 100 and inserting a percent symbol.

Explore

Motivate the Lesson

Ask: Have you ever seen a sign that said "50% off" or one that said "$\frac{1}{2}$ off"? Which is a better sale? Remind students that to compare two numbers, both need to be in the same form. Have students rewrite 50% and $\frac{1}{2}$ as fractions with the same denominator and compare the numbers. Students should conclude that the two numbers are equivalent. Repeat the activity with another pair of numbers, such as 20% and $\frac{1}{4}$.

Explain

EXAMPLE 1

Focus on Math Communication **Mathematical Practices**

Point out to students that they could write the percent as a decimal first and then write the decimal as a fraction in simplest form. Either method would provide the same results.

Questioning Strategy

• In Step 2, you wrote 35% as a fraction in simplest form. How can you check your answer? You can divide 7 by 20. The result will be the same as the answer in Step 3, 0.35.

EXPLORE ACTIVITY

Engage with the Whiteboard

 Have students fill in the boxes and shade the model for each part on the whiteboard.

Questioning Strategies **Mathematical Practices**

• Why do we need two grids for B and C? Because the decimal/percent in both parts is larger than 100%, the model will need one grid to represent the whole number part and a second grid to represent the "parts out of a hundred."

Focus on Math Connections **Mathematical Practices**

Point out to students that percents less than 100% can be represented by fractions and that percents greater than 100% can be represented by mixed numbers.

Percents, Fractions, and Decimals

COMMON CORE 6.RP.3
Use ratio and rate reasoning to solve real-world and mathematical problems,...

? ESSENTIAL QUESTION

How can you write equivalent percents, fractions, and decimals?

Writing Percents as Decimals and Fractions

You can write a percent as an equivalent fraction or as an equivalent decimal. Equivalent percents, decimals, and fractions all represent equal parts of the same whole.

Math On the Spot
my.hrw.com

EXAMPLE 1 Real World

COMMON CORE 6.RP.3

Lorenzo spends 35% of his budget on rent for his apartment. Write this percent as a fraction and as a decimal.

STEP 1 Write the percent as a fraction.

$35\% = \frac{35}{100}$ *Percent means per 100.*

STEP 2 Write the fraction in simplest form.

$$\frac{35}{100} = \frac{35}{100} \begin{matrix} \div 5 \\ \\ \div 5 \end{matrix} = \frac{7}{20}$$

STEP 3 Write the percent as a decimal.

$35\% = \frac{35}{100}$ *Write the fraction equivalent of 35%.*

$= 0.35$ *Write the decimal equivalent of $\frac{35}{100}$.*

So, 35% written as a fraction is $\frac{7}{20}$ and written as a decimal is 0.35.

Math Talk
Mathematical Practices

Explain why both the numerator and denominator in Step 2 are divided by 5.

5 is the GCF of 35 and 100, so dividing both numerator and denominator by 5 gives an equivalent fraction in simplest form.

YOUR TURN

Write each percent as a fraction and as a decimal.

1. 15% $\frac{3}{20}$, 0.15   2. 48% $\frac{12}{25}$, 0.48

3. 80% $\frac{4}{5}$, 0.8   4. 75% $\frac{3}{4}$, 0.75

5. 36% $\frac{9}{25}$, 0.36   6. 40% $\frac{2}{5}$, 0.4

Personal Math Trainer
Online Assessment and Intervention
my.hrw.com

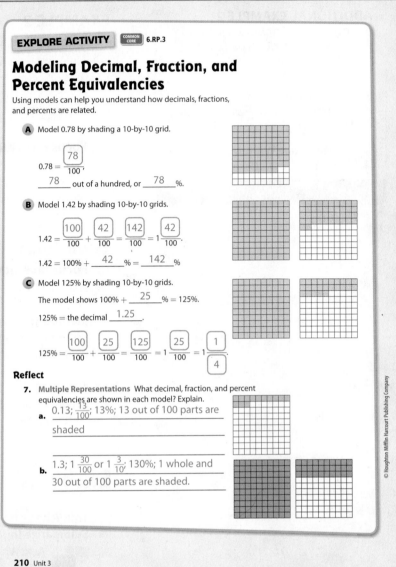

EXPLORE ACTIVITY   **COMMON CORE 6.RP.3**

Modeling Decimal, Fraction, and Percent Equivalencies

Using models can help you understand how decimals, fractions, and percents are related.

A Model 0.78 by shading a 10-by-10 grid.

$0.78 = \frac{\boxed{78}}{100}$,

$\underline{78}$ out of a hundred, or $\underline{78}$ %.

B Model 1.42 by shading 10-by-10 grids.

$1.42 = \frac{\boxed{100}}{100} + \frac{\boxed{42}}{100} = \frac{\boxed{142}}{100} = 1\frac{\boxed{42}}{100}$.

$1.42 = 100\% + \underline{42}\% = \underline{142}\%$

C Model 125% by shading 10-by-10 grids.

The model shows $100\% + \underline{25}\% = 125\%$.

$125\% =$ the decimal $\underline{1.25}$.

$125\% = \frac{\boxed{100}}{100} + \frac{\boxed{25}}{100} = \frac{\boxed{125}}{100} = 1\frac{\boxed{25}}{100} = 1\frac{\boxed{1}}{\boxed{4}}$.

Reflect

7. **Multiple Representations** What decimal, fraction, and percent equivalencies are shown in each model? Explain.

   a. 0.13; $\frac{13}{100}$; 13%; 13 out of 100 parts are shaded

   b. 1.3; $1\frac{30}{100}$ or $1\frac{3}{10}$; 130%; 1 whole and 30 out of 100 parts are shaded.

PROFESSIONAL DEVELOPMENT

CC Integrate Mathematical Practices MP.4

This lesson provides an opportunity to address this Mathematical Practice standard. It calls for students to communicate mathematical ideas using multiple representations as appropriate. In this lesson, students use multiple representations of numbers as they convert between three equivalent forms (i.e., fractions, decimals, and percents) as well as model decimals and percents on 10 × 10 grids.

Math Background

Some other symbols that are related to the percent sign are the *permille* "per thousand" sign, ‰ and the *permyriad* "per ten thousand" sign, ‱.

Permille is used to express small percentages, such as salinity. For example, the average salinity of seawater is 35‰.

The more commonly used permyriad is called a *basis point* and is used mostly to report differences in interest rates of less than 1% a year. For example, a change in an interest rate from 3.25% to 3.23% could be described as decreasing by 2 basis points.

EXAMPLE 2

Questioning Strategies Mathematical Practices

• In A, is there a different method you could use to convert the decimal equivalent to the percent equivalent? Yes, you could use mental math to divide 96 and 200 by 2 to get $\frac{48}{100}$ or 0.48 and just move the decimal point two places to the right and add a percent sign.

• In B, are 12.5% and $12\frac{1}{2}$% the same? Justify your answer. Yes, because 0.5 is equal to $\frac{1}{2}$.

Focus on Critical Thinking Mathematical Practices

For B, Step 2, discuss why a decimal number, such as 0.125, can be expressed as an equivalent percent just by moving the decimal point 2 places to the right. If necessary, explain that percent relates to hundreds and that "moving the decimal 2 places to the right" is the same as dividing by 100 to get two decimal places.

YOUR TURN

Focus on Math Connections Mathematical Practices

Point out to students that there are two methods for converting fractions to decimals and percents.

Method 1: If the denominator is a factor or multiple of 100, it is easy to rewrite the fraction with a denominator of 100. If the denominator is 100, just write the numerator with a percent sign to get the percent. To get the decimal equivalent, remove the percent sign, divide by 100, and move the decimal point two places to the left.

Method 2: If the denominator is not a factor of 100, divide the numerator by the denominator to get the decimal equivalent. Then multiply by 100, moving the decimal point two places to the right, and add a percent sign to get the percent equivalent.

Elaborate

Talk About It
Summarize the Lesson

Ask: Why can you write a percent as a fraction and as a decimal? because *percent* means "per 100" and each form indicates a way to represent "parts out of 100"

GUIDED PRACTICE

Engage with the Whiteboard

For Exercises 2–3, have students shade the grids and then write the percent and fraction equivalents on the whiteboard.

Avoid Common Errors

Exercise 1 Remind students that if they write a percent as a fraction with a denominator of 100, they need to write the fraction in simplest form, if possible.

Exercises 4–5 Some students may not realize which operation would be easier to use when converting between the three forms. Encourage students to look at the denominator of each fraction to check if it is a factor or multiple of 100. If so, they should use multiplication. If not, they should use division.

Writing Fractions as Decimals and Percents

You can write some fractions as percents by writing an equivalent fraction with a denominator of 100. This method is useful when the fraction has a denominator that is a factor or a multiple of 100. If a fraction does not have a denominator that is a factor or multiple of 100, you can use long division.

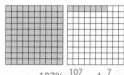

EXAMPLE 2 Real World   COMMON CORE 6.RP.3

A 96 out of 200 animals treated by a veterinarian are horses. Write $\frac{96}{200}$ as a decimal and as a percent.

> Notice that the denominator is a multiple of 100.

STEP 1 Write an equivalent fraction with a denominator of 100.

$\frac{96}{200} = \frac{48}{100}$ Divide both the numerator and denominator by 2.

STEP 2 Write the decimal equivalent.

$\frac{48}{100} = 0.48$

STEP 3 Write the percent equivalent.

$\frac{48}{100} = 48\%$ Percent means per 100.

> Notice that the denominator is not a factor or multiple of 100.

B $\frac{1}{8}$ of the animals treated by the veterinarian are dogs. Write $\frac{1}{8}$ as a decimal and as a percent.

STEP 1 Use long division to divide the numerator by the denominator.

$\frac{1}{8} = 8\overline{)1.000}$
```
    0.125
8 )1.000
   − 8
     20
   − 16
      40
    − 40
       0
```
Add a decimal point and zeros to the right of the numerator as needed.

The decimal equivalent of $\frac{1}{8}$ is 0.125.

STEP 2 Write the decimal as a percent.

$0.125 = \frac{125}{1,000}$ Write the fraction equivalent of the decimal.

$\frac{125}{1,000} = \frac{12.5}{100}$ (÷ 10)   Write an equivalent fraction with a denominator of 100.

$\frac{12.5}{100} = 12.5\%$ Write as a percent.

The percent equivalent of $\frac{1}{8}$ is 12.5%.

YOUR TURN

Write each fraction as a decimal and as a percent.

8. $\frac{9}{25}$ _____0.36, 36%_____   9. $\frac{7}{8}$ _____0.875, 87.5%_____

Guided Practice

1. Helene spends 12% of her budget on transportation expenses. Write this percent as a fraction and as a decimal. (Example 1)
   $\frac{3}{25}$; 0.12

Model the decimal. Then write percent and fraction equivalents.
(Explore Activity)

2. 0.53

53%; $\frac{53}{100}$

3. 1.07

107%; $\frac{107}{100} = 1\frac{7}{100}$

Write each fraction as a decimal and as a percent. (Example 2)

4. $\frac{7}{20}$ of the packages _____0.35; 35%_____   5. $\frac{3}{8}$ of a pie _____0.375; 37.5%_____

? ESSENTIAL QUESTION CHECK-IN

6. How does the definition of *percent* help you write fraction and decimal equivalents?

   Percent means "per 100," so any percent can be written as a fraction with a denominator of 100, and then be written in simplest form. Any fraction can be written as a decimal by dividing the numerator by the denominator.

DIFFERENTIATE INSTRUCTION

Critical Thinking

Have students divide the following list into sets of three equivalent numbers:

$\frac{1}{4}$, 75%, 0.40, $\frac{1}{8}$, 40%, 0.50, $\frac{2}{5}$, 25%, 0.75, $\frac{1}{2}$, 12.5%, 0.25, $\frac{3}{4}$, 50%, and 0.125

Have each student trade with another student to check results.

$\frac{1}{4}$, 25%, 0.25; 75%, 0.75, $\frac{3}{4}$; 0.40, 40%, $\frac{2}{5}$; $\frac{1}{8}$, 12.5%, 0.125; 0.50, $\frac{1}{2}$, 50%

Cooperative Learning

Prepare sets of number cards that contain three equivalent numbers, for example:

| 30% | $\frac{3}{10}$ | 0.30 |

Distribute the numbers randomly so that each student gets a card. Have each student find the two students who have equivalent numbers. Then have the students stand in groups of three, forming a human number line (three deep) to show the numbers in increasing order from left to right.

Additional Resources

Differentiated Instruction includes:

- Reading Strategies
- Success for English Learners **ELL**
- Reteach
- Challenge **PRE-AP**

8.2 LESSON QUIZ

 6.RP.3

Write each percent as a fraction and as a decimal.

1. 20% of the books

2. 65% of the students

3. 350% increase in sales

Write each fraction as a decimal and as a percent.

4. $\frac{144}{200}$ of the tickets

5. $\frac{225}{100}$ of last year's cost

6. Chloe answered 42 of the 50 questions correctly. Express this amount as a percent and a decimal.

Lesson Quiz available online

 my.hrw.com

Answers

1. $\frac{1}{5}$, 0.2

2. $\frac{13}{20}$, 0.65

3. $3\frac{1}{2}$, 3.5

4. 0.72, 72%

5. 2.25, 225%

6. 84%, 0.84

Evaluate

GUIDED AND INDEPENDENT PRACTICE

 6.RP.3

Concepts & Skills	Practice
Example 1 Writing Percents as Decimals and Fractions	Exercises 1, 7–12
Explore Activity Modeling Decimal, Fraction, and Percent Equivalencies	Exercises 2–3, 15–16
Example 2 Writing Fractions as Decimals and Percents	Exercises 4–5, 13–17

Exercise	Depth of Knowledge (D.O.K.)	Mathematical Practices
7–15	**2** Skills/Concepts	**MP.5** Using Tools
16–17	**2** Skills/Concepts	**MP.4** Modeling
18–19	**2** Skills/Concepts	**MP.2** Reasoning
20–21	**3** Strategic Thinking H.O.T.	**MP.3** Logic
22	**3** Strategic Thinking H.O.T.	**MP.4** Modeling
23	**3** Strategic Thinking H.O.T.	**MP.6** Precision
24	**3** Strategic Thinking H.O.T.	**MP.7** Using Structure

Additional Resources

Differentiated Instruction includes:

• Leveled Practice Worksheets

8.2 Independent Practice

COMMON CORE 6.RP.3

Personal Math Trainer

Online Assessment and Intervention

my.hrw.com

Write each percent as a fraction and as a decimal.

7. 72% full

$\frac{18}{25}$; 0.72

8. 25% successes

$\frac{1}{4}$; 0.25

9. 500% increase

$\frac{500}{100} = \frac{5}{1}$; 5

10. 5% tax

$\frac{1}{20}$; 0.05

11. 37% profit

$\frac{37}{100}$; 0.37

12. 165% improvement

$\frac{165}{100} = 1\frac{65}{100} = 1\frac{13}{20}$; 1.65

Write each fraction as a decimal and as a percent.

13. $\frac{5}{8}$ of an inch

0.625, 62.5%

14. $\frac{258}{300}$ of the contestants

0.86, 86%

15. $\frac{350}{100}$ of the revenue

3.5, 350%

16. The poster shows how many of its games the football team has won so far. Express this information as a fraction, a percent, and as a decimal.

GO TEAM!

12 out of 15 wins!

$\frac{12}{15} = \frac{4}{5}$; 80%, 0.8

17. Justine answered 68 questions correctly on an 80-question test. Express this amount as a fraction, percent, and decimal.

$\frac{68}{80} = \frac{17}{20}$; 85%, 0.85

Each diagram is made of smaller, identical pieces. Tell how many pieces you would shade to model the given percent.

18. 75% ____12____

19. 25% ____6____

20. **Multiple Representations** At Brian's Bookstore, 0.3 of the shelves hold mysteries, 25% of the shelves hold travel books, and $\frac{7}{20}$ of the shelves hold children's books. Which type of book covers the most shelf space in the store? Explain how you arrived at your answer.

children's books; $0.3 = \frac{3}{10} = \frac{6}{20}$; $25\% = \frac{25}{100} = \frac{5}{20}$; $\frac{5}{20} < \frac{6}{20} < \frac{7}{20}$

Work Area

H.O.T. FOCUS ON HIGHER ORDER THINKING

21. **Critical Thinking** A newspaper article reports the results of an election between two candidates. The article says that Smith received 60% of the votes and that Murphy received $\frac{1}{3}$ of the votes. A reader writes in to complain that the article cannot be accurate. What reason might the reader have to say this?

If all the votes were for Smith or Murphy, then 60% plus $33\frac{1}{3}\%$ (the percent equivalent of $\frac{1}{3}$) should equal 100%. But $60\% + 33\frac{1}{3}\% = 93\frac{1}{3}\%$.

22. **Represent Real-World Problems** Evan budgets $2,000 a month to spend on living expenses for his family. Complete the table to express the portion spent on each cost as a percent, fraction, and decimal.

	Food: $500	Rent: $1,200	Transportation: $300
Fraction	$\frac{1}{4}$	$\frac{3}{5}$	$\frac{3}{20}$
Percent	25%	60%	15%
Decimal	0.25	0.6	0.15

23. **Communicate Mathematical Ideas** Find the sum of each row in the table. Explain why these sums make sense.

1, 100%, 1; the fractions and decimals should add up to 1. The percents should add up to 100%. In each case, the three addends represent parts of Evan's $2,000.

24. **Explain the Error** Your friend says that 14.5% is equivalent to the decimal 14.5. Explain why your friend is incorrect by comparing the fractional equivalents of 14.5% and 14.5.

$14.5\% = \frac{14.5}{100} = \frac{145}{1000} = \frac{29}{200}$; $14.5 = 14\frac{29}{200} = 14\frac{1}{2}$; $\frac{29}{200} < 14\frac{1}{2}$

© Houghton Mifflin Harcourt Publishing Company

EXTEND THE MATH PRE-AP

Activity available online my.hrw.com

Activity Have students research local data that are presented as percents. Also have them find data that is presented as decimals and/or fractions. Students should discuss the merits of using each number format.

A common use of percents is in residential home sales, to show price changes.

Have students complete the table by working *backward* to find the original price.

HINT: They can use what they know about writing percents as fractions.

	Purchase price	Percent	Original price
Mr. Garcia	$120,000	125%	$150,000
Ms. Johnson	$70,000	150%	$105,000
Mrs. Wilson	$125,000	110%	$137,500
Mr. Miller	$95,000	80%	$76,000

LESSON
8.3 Solving Percent Problems

ADDITIONAL EXAMPLE 1

A Use proportional reasoning to find 46% of 50. Show how you set up the proportion.

$23; 46\% = \frac{46}{100}, \frac{46}{100} = \frac{?}{50}$

 Interactive Whiteboard
Interactive example available online

 my.hrw.com

Engage

ESSENTIAL QUESTION

How do you use percents to solve problems? Sample answer: You can solve percent problems by writing a proportion and solving for the unknown quantity.

Motivate the Lesson

Ask: Have you ever seen an advertisement for an item you wanted to buy but didn't know if you had enough money to pay for the item including the sales tax? Begin the Explore Activity to find out how to use a proportion to find what the total price would be.

Explore

EXPLORE ACTIVITY

Focus on Patterns **CC** Mathematical Practices

Point out to students that for every 100 gloves in the shipment, the number of left-handed gloves increases by 30. Help students to see the pattern. Show how this pattern relates to the bar model.

Total gloves	100	200	300	400
Left-handed gloves	30	60	90	120

Explain

EXAMPLE 1

Focus on Multiple Representations **CC** Mathematical Practices

Students now have two ways to find a percent of a number. They can use a model or proportional reasoning (multiplication).

Questioning Strategies **CC** Mathematical Practices

- In A, Step 1, why do you put the 25 in the denominator instead of in the numerator? The problem says 28% of 25. So, 25 is the whole, not the part.

- In A, Step 2, how do you know which factor to multiply by? Explain. Think: What number do I need to multiply the denominator, 25, by to get 100? The answer is 4. So, I multiply both the numerator and denominator of the fraction on the left side of the equal sign by 4.

Focus on Technology

Discuss with students how they might use a calculator to find a percent of a number. Guide students to see that they can write the percent as a decimal and then multiply the given whole number by the decimal. For example, 20% of 360 = 360 × 0.2 = 72. Most calculators also have a % key. You can enter 360, press ×, enter 20, and press %.

Solving Percent Problems

COMMON CORE 6.RP.3c

Find a percent of a quantity ...; solve problems involving finding the whole, given a part and the percent. Also 6.RP.3

ESSENTIAL QUESTION

How do you use percents to solve problems?

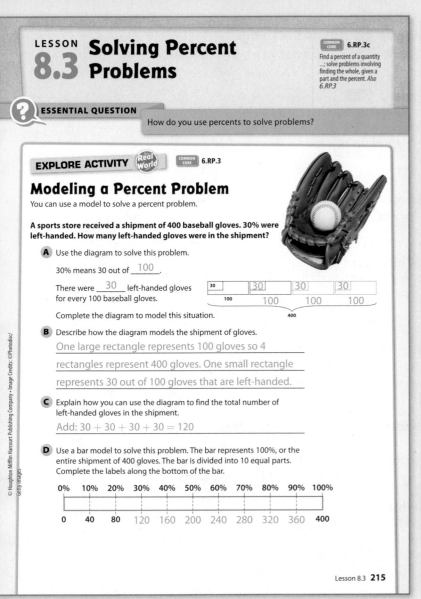

EXPLORE ACTIVITY Real World

COMMON CORE 6.RP.3

Modeling a Percent Problem

You can use a model to solve a percent problem.

A sports store received a shipment of 400 baseball gloves. 30% were left-handed. How many left-handed gloves were in the shipment?

A Use the diagram to solve this problem.

30% means 30 out of ___100___.

There were ___30___ left-handed gloves for every 100 baseball gloves.

| 30 | | 30 | 30 | 30 |

100   100   100   100

400

Complete the diagram to model this situation.

B Describe how the diagram models the shipment of gloves.

One large rectangle represents 100 gloves so 4 rectangles represent 400 gloves. One small rectangle represents 30 out of 100 gloves that are left-handed.

C Explain how you can use the diagram to find the total number of left-handed gloves in the shipment.

Add: 30 + 30 + 30 + 30 = 120

D Use a bar model to solve this problem. The bar represents 100%, or the entire shipment of 400 gloves. The bar is divided into 10 equal parts. Complete the labels along the bottom of the bar.

| 0% | 10% | 20% | 30% | 40% | 50% | 60% | 70% | 80% | 90% | 100% |

0   40   80   120   160   200   240   280   320   360   400

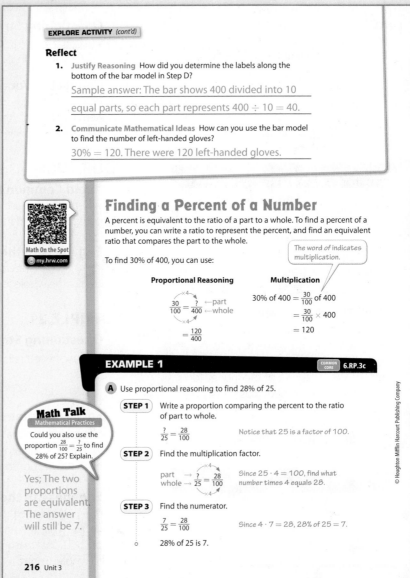

EXPLORE ACTIVITY (cont'd)

Reflect

1. **Justify Reasoning** How did you determine the labels along the bottom of the bar model in Step D?

   Sample answer: The bar shows 400 divided into 10 equal parts, so each part represents 400 ÷ 10 = 40.

2. **Communicate Mathematical Ideas** How can you use the bar model to find the number of left-handed gloves?

   30% = 120. There were 120 left-handed gloves.

Finding a Percent of a Number

A percent is equivalent to the ratio of a part to a whole. To find a percent of a number, you can write a ratio to represent the percent, and find an equivalent ratio that compares the part to the whole.

To find 30% of 400, you can use:

The word *of* indicates multiplication.

Proportional Reasoning

$\frac{30}{100} = \frac{?}{400}$ ←part ←whole

$= \frac{120}{400}$

Multiplication

30% of 400 = $\frac{30}{100}$ of 400

$= \frac{30}{100} \times 400$

$= 120$

EXAMPLE 1 COMMON CORE 6.RP.3c

A Use proportional reasoning to find 28% of 25.

STEP 1 Write a proportion comparing the percent to the ratio of part to whole.

$\frac{?}{25} = \frac{28}{100}$ Notice that 25 is a factor of 100.

STEP 2 Find the multiplication factor.

part → whole → $\frac{?}{25} = \frac{28}{100}$ Since 25 · 4 = 100, find what number times 4 equals 28.

STEP 3 Find the numerator.

$\frac{7}{25} = \frac{28}{100}$ Since 4 · 7 = 28, 28% of 25 = 7.

28% of 25 is 7.

Math Talk
Mathematical Practices

Could you also use the proportion $\frac{28}{100} = \frac{?}{25}$ to find 28% of 25? Explain.

Yes; The two proportions are equivalent. The answer will still be 7.

Math On the Spot
my.hrw.com

PROFESSIONAL DEVELOPMENT

CC Integrate Mathematical Practices MP.4

This lesson provides an opportunity to address this Mathematical Practice standard. It calls for students to apply mathematics to problems arising in everyday life, society, and the workplace. The Explore Activity and the three Examples use percents to solve real-world problems involving the number of left-handed baseball gloves in a shipment of baseball gloves, the amount of money spent on new computer equipment, the percent of students who own a pet, the percent of students who like to sing solos, and the number of high-definition TVs ordered.

Math Background

Proportional reasoning is the ability to compare two things using multiplicative comparisons. In this lesson, that means using ratios and proportions to find an unknown quantity. There are three types of problems. In each, you write a proportion and solve it for the unknown quantity.

Finding a percent of a number $\frac{30}{100} = \frac{n}{80}$

Finding a percent given a part and a whole $\frac{p}{100} = \frac{24}{80}$

Finding a whole given a part and a percent $\frac{30}{100} = \frac{24}{n}$

Questioning Strategies Mathematical Practices

• In C, the percent is 5%. What is the part and what is the whole? The part is 9, and the whole is 180.

Connect to Vocabulary ELL

Point out to students that the direction line in B asks for the fraction form of the percent. Remind students that a percent can be written as a fraction or as a decimal. Notice that C asks for the decimal form of the percent.

YOUR TURN

Avoid Common Errors

When students use a proportion to solve a problem, remind them to be sure they are comparing the part to the whole in both ratios.

Engage with the Whiteboard

Have students write a proportion comparing the percent to the ratio of the part to the whole for each exercise. Ask them to explain their reasoning.

EXAMPLE 2

Questioning Strategies CC Mathematical Practices

• How can you tell which number is the whole and which is the part? The problem says "spent $2,000," so $2,000 is the whole, and "Of this money, $120 was used" shows that $120 is part of the $2,000.

Focus on Communication CC Mathematical Practices

Show students that in Step 3 they also can find the percent by writing the fraction $\frac{120}{2,000}$ with a denominator of 100. Show students that $\frac{120 \div 20}{2,000 \div 20} = \frac{6}{100}$ and that once they have the proportion $\frac{?}{100} = \frac{6}{100}$ it's easy to see that the percent is 6%.

Engage with the Whiteboard

Write the proportions $\frac{30}{100} = \frac{\blacksquare}{80}$ and $\frac{\blacksquare}{100} = \frac{24}{80}$ on the whiteboard. Then ask students what the unknown quantity is in each proportion. Help students to see that with proportional reasoning the proportion is always going to compare part to whole with part to whole. Contrast the part that changed in Examples 1 and 2.

YOUR TURN

Avoid Common Errors

If students have difficulty recognizing the part and the whole, remind them to look for key terms, such as *out of* or *of* which indicate the whole.

B Multiply by a fraction to find 35% of 60.

STEP 1 Write the percent as a fraction.

35% of $60 = \frac{35}{100}$ of 60

STEP 2 Multiply.

$\frac{35}{100}$ of $60 = \frac{35}{100} \times 60$

$= \frac{2,100}{100}$

$= 21$ Simplify.

35% of 60 is 21.

C Multiply by a decimal to find 5% of 180.

STEP 1 Write the percent as a decimal.

$5\% = \frac{5}{100} = 0.05$

STEP 2 Multiply.

$180 \times 0.05 = 9$

5% of 180 is 9.

Reflect

3. **Analyze Relationships** In **B**, the percent is 35%. What is the part and what is the whole?

   21 is the part and 60 is the whole.

   _____

4. **Communicate Mathematical Ideas** Explain how to use proportional reasoning to find 35% of 600.

   Write the percent as a ratio and write an equivalent ratio

   comparing the unknown part to 600: $\frac{35}{100} = \frac{?}{600}$.

   $100 \times 6 = 650$ so multiply $35 \times 6 = 210$.

   35% of 600 is 210.

Animated Math
© my.hrw.com

YOUR TURN

Find the percent of each number.

5. 38% of 50 ____19____   6. 27% of 300 ____81____   7. 60% of 75 ____45____

Personal Math Trainer
Online Assessment and Intervention
© my.hrw.com

Math On the Spot
© my.hrw.com

Find a Percent Given a Part and a Whole

You can use proportional reasoning to solve problems in which you need to find a percent.

EXAMPLE 2   COMMON CORE 6.RP.3

The school principal spent $2,000 to buy some new computer equipment. Of this money, $120 was used to buy some new keyboards. What percent of the money was spent on keyboards?

STEP 1 Since you want to know the part of the money spent on keyboards, compare the part to the whole.

part → $120
whole → $2,000

STEP 2 Write a proportion comparing the percent to the ratio of part to whole.

part → $\frac{?}{100} = \frac{120}{2,000}$ ← part
whole →   ← whole

STEP 3 Find the multiplication factor.

$\frac{?}{100} = \frac{120}{2,000}$ (×20)   Since $100 \times 20 = 2,000$, find what number times 20 equals 120.

STEP 4 Find the numerator.

$\frac{6}{100} = \frac{120}{2,000}$ Since $20 \times 6 = 120$, the percent is 6%.

The principal spent 6% of the money on keyboards.

Reflect

8. **Communicate Mathematical Ideas** Write 57% as a ratio. Which part of the ratio represents the part and which part represents the whole? Explain.

   $\frac{57}{100}$; 100% of a value is the whole amount so 100%

   represents the whole; 57% is the part, which is equal to

   57 out of 100 or 0.57.

Personal Math Trainer
Online Assessment and Intervention
© my.hrw.com

YOUR TURN

9. Out of the 25 students in Mrs. Green's class, 19 have a pet. What percent of the students in Mrs. Green's class have a pet? ____76%____

DIFFERENTIATE INSTRUCTION

Home Connection

Have students look for advertisements or newspaper articles that show or mention a percent. Ask them to write a problem to go with the percent they find and to solve the problem with their parents. Post the problems and their solutions on a bulletin board.

Sample:

News item: 57% percent of college freshmen are women.
Problem: If there are 200 college students and 57% of them are women, how many of the students are women? 114 women

Critical Thinking

Present the following question to the class:

In Mrs. Landau's math class, 18 students prefer to do their homework before dinner. In Mr. Velaz's class, 20 students prefer to do their homework before dinner. Does this mean that a higher percent of the students in Mr. Velaz's class prefer to do homework before dinner? Explain your reasoning.

Not necessarily; percent is a ratio comparing two numbers, the part and the whole. The total number of students in each class must be known in order to compare the percentages.

Additional Resources

Differentiated Instruction includes:

- Reading Strategies
- Success for English Learners **ELL**
- Reteach
- Challenge **PRE-AP**

Solving Percent Problems   **218**

EXAMPLE 3

Questioning Strategies [CC] **Mathematical Practices**

• How can you tell what the part is and what the whole is in this problem? The problem includes the phrases "of the students" and "of the choir," both of which refer to a part, so the whole is unknown.

• How is the proportion in Example 1 different from this proportion? In Example 1, the unknown quantity is the part, which is in the numerator. In this problem, the unknown quantity is the whole, which is in the denominator.

Focus on Math Connections [CC] **Mathematical Practices**

Ask students for another way they could estimate to check for reasonableness. For example, 24% is about 25% and 25% × 4 = 100%. This means that the whole is about 4 times the part, or 12 × 4 = 48, which is reasonably close to 50.

YOUR TURN

Avoid Common Errors

Exercise 11 Some students may simply multiply 6 × 30%. Remind students to look for key terms that will help them to identify the parts. "Of" is before the blank, so the whole is unknown. This means that 6 is the part and the percent is 30%.

Elaborate

. . . .

Talk About It
Summarize the Lesson

 Ask: What ratios do you use to solve percent problems using a proportion? You use two part-to-whole ratios to make the proportion.

GUIDED PRACTICE

Engage with the Whiteboard

 For Exercise 1, have students complete the labeling on the bar model on the whiteboard. Have them explain their reasoning.

Avoid Common Errors

Exercise 2 Some students may put the 65% in the wrong box. Remind them that the denominator for percent is always 100.

Exercise 3 Some students may try to multiply both the numerator and the denominator by 180. Remind them that you can write any integer as a ratio with a denominator of 1.

Exercise 4 When solving a problem by using proportional reasoning, students may reverse the proportion. Remind them that the whole is always the denominator.

Finding a Whole Given a Part and a Percent

You can use proportional reasoning to solve problems in which you know a part and a percent and need to find the whole.

 Math On the Spot
my.hrw.com

EXAMPLE 3

COMMON CORE 6.RP.3c

Twelve of the students in the school choir like to sing solos. These 12 students make up 24% of the choir. How many students are in the choir?

STEP 1 Since you want to know the total number of students in the choir, compare the part to the whole.

part → 12
whole → ?

STEP 2 Write a proportion comparing the percent to the ratio of part to whole.

part → $\frac{12}{?} = \frac{24}{100}$ ← part
whole →   ← whole

You know that 12 students represent 24%.

STEP 3 Find the multiplication factor.

$\frac{12}{?} = \frac{24}{100}$ (×2)

Since 12 × 2 = 24, find what number times 2 equals 100.

STEP 4 Find the denominator.

$\frac{12}{50} = \frac{24}{100}$ Since 50 × 2 = 100, the denominator is 50.

There are 50 students in the choir.

Math Talk
Mathematical Practices

Suppose 10 more students join the choir. None of them are soloists. What percent are soloists now?

20%

Reflect

10. **Check for Reasonableness** In Example 3, 24% is close to 25%. How could you use this fact to check that 50 is a reasonable number for the total number of students in the choir?

To check that 12 is 24% of the answer 50, you could

find 25% of 50, which is 12.5. Since 12.5 is close to 12,

the answer is reasonable.

 YOUR TURN

11. 6 is 30% of ___20___.

12. 15% of ___500___ is 75.

Personal Math Trainer
Online Assessment and Intervention
my.hrw.com

---

1. A store has 300 televisions on order, and 80% are high definition. How many televisions on order are high definition? Use the bar model and complete the bottom of the bar. (Explore Activity)

0%	10%	20%	30%	40%	50%	60%	70%	80%	90%	100%
0	30	60	90	120	150	180	210	240	270	300

___240___ televisions are high definition.

2. Use proportional reasoning to find 65% of 200. (Example 1)

part → $\boxed{65}$
whole → $\frac{}{100} = \frac{?}{\boxed{200}}$ ← part
                          ← whole

65% of 200 is ___130___.

3. Use multiplication to find 5% of 180. (Example 1)

$\frac{5}{100}$ of 180 = $\frac{5}{100}$ $\boxed{\times}$ 180

= $\frac{\boxed{900}}{100}$ = $\boxed{9}$

5% of 180 is ___9___.

4. Alana spent $21 of her $300 paycheck on a gift. What percent of her paycheck was spent on the gift? (Example 2)

part → $\frac{?}{\boxed{100}} = \frac{\$\boxed{21}}{\$\boxed{300}}$ ← part
whole →   ← whole

Alana spent ___7%___ of her paycheck on the gift.

5. At Pizza Pi, 9% of the pizzas made last week had extra cheese. If 27 pizzas had extra cheese, how many pizzas in all were made last week? (Example 3)

part → $\boxed{9}$
whole → $\frac{}{100} = \frac{27}{?}$ ← part
                        ← whole

There were ___300___ pizzas made last week.

 ESSENTIAL QUESTION CHECK-IN

6. How can you use proportional reasoning to solve problems involving percent?

Read the problem to see whether you need to find a

part of a whole, a whole, or a percent. Then use the

proportion, $\frac{\text{part}}{\text{whole}} = \frac{\text{percent part}}{\text{percent whole}}$ to find the unknown

quantity.

8.3 LESSON QUIZ

 6.RP.3c

Find the percent of each number.

1. 17% of 200 books

2. 35% of 80 letters

3. 85% of 540 sales

Use proportional reasoning to complete each sentence. Show how you set up the proportion.

4. 12% of ___ shirts is 36 shirts.

5. 104 tests is ___% of 160 tests.

6. 16% of ___ cookies is 44 cookies.

Use any method to solve.

7. Nicholas has a collection of books. He has 115 fantasy and science-fiction books. These books are 46% of his collection. How many books does he have in his collection?

Lesson Quiz available online

 my.hrw.com

Answers

1. 34 books

2. 28 letters

3. 459 sales

4. 300; $\frac{12}{100} = \frac{36}{?}$

5. 65%; $\frac{104}{160} = \frac{?}{100}$

6. 275; $\frac{16}{100} = \frac{44}{?}$

7. 250 books

Evaluate

GUIDED AND INDEPENDENT PRACTICE

COMMON CORE 6.RP.3, 6.RP.3c

Concepts & Skills	Practice
Explore Activity Modeling a Percent Problem	Exercise 1
Example 1 Finding a Percent of a Number	Exercises 2–3, 7–12, 23, 26, 28
Example 2 Finding a Percent Given a Part and a Whole	Exercises 4, 13–16, 24
Example 3 Finding a Whole Given a Part and a Percent	Exercises 5, 17–22, 25, 27

Exercise	Depth of Knowledge (D.O.K.)	**COMMON CORE** Mathematical Practices
7–22	**2** Skills/Concepts	**MP.5** Using Tools
23–28	**2** Skills/Concepts	**MP.4** Modeling
29	**3** Strategic Thinking **H.O.T.**	**MP.3** Logic
30	**3** Strategic Thinking **H.O.T.**	**MP.4** Modeling
31	**3** Strategic Thinking **H.O.T.**	**MP.7** Using Structure

Additional Resources

Differentiated Instruction includes:

• Leveled Practice Worksheets

CC CLUSTER CONNECTION   **Exercise 30** combines concepts from the Common Core cluster "Understand ratio concepts and use ratio reasoning to solve problems."

8.3 Independent Practice

COMMON CORE 6.RP.3, 6.RP.3c

Personal Math Trainer
Online Assessment and Intervention
my.hrw.com

Find the percent of each number.

7. 64% of 75 tiles
48 tiles

8. 20% of 70 plants
14 plants

9. 32% of 25 pages
8 pages

10. 85% of 40 e-mails
34 e-mails

11. 72% of 350 friends
252 friends

12. 5% of 220 files
11 files

Complete each sentence.

13. 4 students is __20__ % of 20 students.

14. 2 doctors is __8__ % of 25 doctors.

15. __70__ % of 50 shirts is 35 shirts.

16. __75__ % of 200 miles is 150 miles.

17. 4% of __1,400__ days is 56 days.

18. 60 minutes is 20% of __300__ minutes.

19. 80% of __40__ games is 32 games.

20. 360 kilometers is 24% of __1,500__ kilometers.

21. 75% of __20__ peaches is 15 peaches.

22. 9 stores is 3% of __300__ stores.

23. At a shelter, 15% of the dogs are puppies. There are 60 dogs at the shelter.
How many are puppies? __9__ puppies

24. Carl has 200 songs on his MP3 player. Of these songs, 24 are country songs. What percent of Carl's songs are country songs? __12%__

25. **Consumer Math** The sales tax in the town where Amanda lives is 7%. Amanda paid $35 in sales tax on a new stereo. What was the price of the stereo? __$500__

26. **Financial Literacy** Ashton is saving money to buy a new bike. He needs $120 but has only saved 60% so far. How much more money does Ashton need to buy the scooter? __$48__

27. **Consumer Math** Monica paid sales tax of $1.50 when she bought a new bike helmet. If the sales tax rate was 5%, how much did the store charge for the helmet before tax? __$30__

28. Use the circle graph to determine how many hours per day Becky spends on each activity.

School: __6__ hours

Eating: __2.4__ hours

Sleep: __9.6__ hours

Homework: __2.4__ hours

Free time: __3.6__ hours

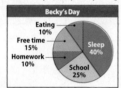

Becky's Day
Eating 10%
Free time 15%
Homework 10%
Sleep 40%
School 25%

© Houghton Mifflin Harcourt Publishing Company

H.O.T. FOCUS ON HIGHER ORDER THINKING

Work Area

29. **Multistep** Marc ordered a rug. He gave a deposit of 30% of the cost and will pay the rest when the rug is delivered. If the deposit was $75, how much more does Marc owe? Explain how you found your answer.
$175; sample answer: I used the equation $\frac{30}{100} = \frac{75}{?}$ to find the cost of the rug, $250. Since Marc made a $75 deposit, I subtracted $250 − $75 to find out what he owes, $175.

30. **Earth Science** Your weight on different planets is affected by gravity. An object that weighs 150 pounds on Earth weighs only 56.55 pounds on Mars. The same object weighs only 24.9 pounds on the Moon.

a. What percent of an object's Earth weight is its weight on Mars and on the Moon?
Mars: 37.7%; Moon: 16.6%

b. Suppose x represents an object's weight on Earth. Write two expressions: one that you can use to find the object's weight on Mars and another that you can use to write the object's weight on the Moon.
Mars: 0.377x; Moon: 0.166x

c. The space suit Neil Armstrong wore when he stepped on the Moon for the first time weighed about 180 pounds on Earth. How much did it weigh on the Moon?
about 29.88 pounds

d. **What If?** If you could travel to Jupiter, your weight would be 236.4% of your Earth weight. How much would Neil Armstrong's space suit weigh on Jupiter?
about 425.52 pounds

31. **Explain the Error** Your friend used the proportion $\frac{25}{100} = \frac{50}{?}$ to find 25% of 50 and says that the answer is 200. Explain why your friend is incorrect and find the correct answer.
To find 25% of 50, 50 represents the whole and you want to find the part, so the correct proportion is $\frac{25}{100} = \frac{?}{50}$. Then 25% of 50 is 12.5.

© Houghton Mifflin Harcourt Publishing Company

EXTEND THE MATH PRE-AP

Activity available online my.hrw.com

Activity The sales tax rate in Texas has increased over time. Have students choose two items, one costing less than $10 and one costing more than $1,000, and have them use a calculator to find the amount of sales tax for the item during each time period.

Note: Local areas impose *additional* local sales tax, so sales tax rates vary by locale.

Sample answers are shown in the table.

Texas Sales Tax Rate History

Year Rate Began	Rate	Calculator $8.00	Computer $1,200
1961	2%	$0.16	$24
1968	3%	$0.24	$36
1969	3.25%	$0.26	$39
1971	4%	$0.32	$48
1984	4.125%	$0.33	$49.50
Jan 1987	5.25%	$0.42	$63
Oct 1987	6%	$0.48	$72
1990	6.25%	$0.50	$75

Ready to Go On?

Assess Mastery

Use the assessment on this page to determine if students have mastered the concepts and standards covered in this module.

  Response to Intervention

Intervention	Enrichment

Access Ready to Go On? assessment online, and receive instant scoring, feedback, and customized intervention or enrichment.

Personal Math Trainer
Online Assessment and Intervention
my.hrw.com

Online and Print Resources

Differentiated Instruction
- Reteach worksheets
- Reading Strategies **ELL**
- Success for English Learners **ELL**

Differentiated Instruction
- Challenge worksheets
  PRE-AP
- Extend the Math **PRE-AP**
  Lesson Activities in TE

Additional Resources

Assessment Resources includes:
- Leveled Module Quizzes

Ready to Go On?

Personal Math Trainer
Online Assessment and Intervention
my.hrw.com

8.1 Understanding Percent

Shade the grid and write the equivalent percent for each fraction.

1. $\frac{19}{50}$ ___38%___

2. $\frac{13}{20}$ ___65%___

8.2 Percents, Fractions, and Decimals

Write each number in two equivalent forms.

3. $\frac{3}{5}$ ___60%, 0.6___

4. 62.5% ___0.625, $\frac{5}{8}$___

5. 0.24 ___24%, $\frac{6}{25}$___

6. $\frac{31}{50}$ ___62%, 0.62___

7. Selma spent $\frac{7}{10}$ of her allowance on a new backpack. What percent of her allowance did she spend? ___70%___

8.3 Solving Percent Problems

Complete each sentence.

8. 12 is 30% of ___40___.

9. 45% of 20 is ___9___.

10. 18 is ___60___ % of 30.

11. 56 is 80% of ___70___.

12. A pack of cinnamon-scented pencils sells for $4.00. What is the sales tax rate if the total cost of the pencils is $4.32? ___8%___

? ESSENTIAL QUESTION

13. How can you solve problems involving percents?
To find a percent of a number, multiply the number by the fraction or decimal equivalent of the percent. To find an unknown percent or part, solve a proportion comparing the percent to the ratio of part to whole.

© Houghton Mifflin Harcourt Publishing Company

Module 8 **223**

Common Core Standards

Lesson	Exercises	Common Core Standards
8.1	1–2	**6.RP.3c**
8.2	3–7	**6.RP.3**
8.3	8–12	**6.RP.3, 6.RP.3c**

Assessment Readiness

Assessment Readiness Tip Students should always read each question carefully to identify key words or phrases, such as *not* or *incorrectly*, to help identify what the question is really asking.

Item 2 Students who do not read the problem carefully may choose A, C, or D, all of which are equal to one-fourth of 52. If students first write one-fourth as a decimal or fraction, they will quickly see that choice B is the correct answer.

Item 7 Students should highlight the word *incorrectly* to remind themselves that the answer is the decimal equivalent of 7 out of 50, not 43 out of 50, so they can eliminate choices C and D quickly.

Avoid Common Errors

Item 5 Students may get this problem backwards, thinking that 40 is the whole, rather than the part and choosing A. Remind students that *of* translates to multiplication, so they are looking for the product of 40% and $270.

Item 8 Some students may not understand that the ratio 1:3 means that 3 out of 4 bagels are plain bagels. For part A, they may write the fraction $\frac{1}{3}$ and for part B, just divide 1 by 3 and write 33% as their answer instead of 75%.

Additional Resources

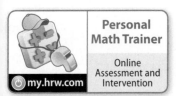

Personal Math Trainer

Online Assessment and Intervention

my.hrw.com

 COMMON CORE

MODULE 8 MIXED REVIEW

Assessment Readiness

 Personal Math Trainer

Online Assessment and Intervention

my.hrw.com

Selected Response

1. What percent does this shaded grid represent?

- (A) 42%
- (B) 48%
- (C) 52%
- (D) 58%

2. Which expression is **not** equal to one fourth of 52?

- (A) $0.25 \cdot 52$
- (B) 4% of 52
- (C) $52 \div 4$
- (D) $\frac{52}{4}$

3. Approximately $\frac{4}{5}$ of U.S. homeowners have a cell phone. What percent of homeowners do **not** have a cell phone?

- (A) 20%
- (B) 45%
- (C) 55%
- (D) 80%

4. The ratio of rock music to total CDs that Ella owns is $\frac{25}{40}$. Paolo has 50 rock music CDs. The ratio of rock music to total CDs in his collection is equivalent to the ratio of rock music to total CDs in Ella's collection. How many CDs do they own?

- (A) 65
- (B) 80
- (C) 120
- (D) 130

5. Gabriel saves 40% of his monthly paycheck for college. He earned $270 last month. How much money did Gabriel save for college?

- (A) $96
- (B) $108
- (C) $162
- (D) $180

6. Forty children from an after-school club went to the matinee. This is 25% of the children in the club. How many children are in the club?

- (A) 10
- (B) 160
- (C) 200
- (D) 900

7. Dominic answered 43 of the 50 questions on his spelling test correctly. Which decimal represents the fraction of problems he answered incorrectly?

- (A) 0.07
- (B) 0.14
- (C) 0.86
- (D) 0.93

Mini-Task

8. Jen bought some sesame bagels and some plain bagels. The ratio of the number of sesame bagels to the number of plain bagels is 1:3.

a. What fraction of the bagels are plain?

$\frac{3}{4}$

b. What percent of the bagels are plain?

75%

c. If Jill bought 2 dozen bagels, how many of each type of bagel did she buy?

18 plain and 6 sesame

© Houghton Mifflin Harcourt Publishing Company

Common Core Standards

Items	Grade 6 Standards	Mathematical Practices
1	6.RP.3	MP.4, MP.2
2	6.RP.3	MP.2, MP.7
3*	6.RP.3, 6.NS.3	MP.4
4	6.RP.3	MP.4
5	6.RP.3c	MP.4
6	6.RP.3c	MP.4, MP.5
7	6.RP.3c	MP.4
8	6.RP.3	MP.4, MP.5, MP.7

* Item integrates mixed review concepts from previous modules.

Study Guide Review

Vocabulary Development

Integrating Language Arts

Encourage students to practice using the unit vocabulary as they talk and write about mathematics. Understanding vocabulary will aid their understanding of the concepts.

 ELA-Literacy.RST.6-8.4 Determine the meaning of symbols, key terms, and other domain-specific words and phrases as they are used in a specific scientific or technical context relevant to grades 6–8 texts and topics.

MODULE 6 Representing Ratios and Rates

 6.RP.1, 6.RP.2, 6.RP.3, 6.RP.3a, 6.RP.3b

Key Concepts

• A ratio is the comparison of two quantities expressed with the same units. *(Lesson 6.1)*
• A rate is a comparison of two quantities that have different units, and a unit rate has a denominator of 1. *(Lesson 6.2)*
• You can use equivalent ratios to solve real-world problems. *(Lesson 6.3)*

MODULE 7 Applying Ratios and Rates

6.RP.3, 6.RP.3a, 6.RP.3b, 6.RP.3d

Key Concepts

• You can represent real-world problems involving ratios and rates using tables and graphs. *(Lesson 7.1)*
• A proportion is a statement that two ratios or rates are equivalent. *(Lesson 7.2)*
• You can use rates and proportions to convert one unit of measurement to another within the same measurement system. *(Lesson 7.3)*
• You can use tables and conversion factors to convert between measurement systems. *(Lesson 7.4)*

Study Guide Review

Representing Ratios and Rates

Key Vocabulary

equivalent ratios (*razones equivalentes*)

rate (*tasa*)

ratio (*razón*)

unit rate (*tasa unitaria*)

? ESSENTIAL QUESTION

How can you use ratios and rates to solve real-world problems?

EXAMPLE 1

Tina pays $45.50 for 13 boxes of wheat crackers. What is the unit price?

$$\frac{\$45.50}{13 \text{ boxes}} = \frac{\$3.50}{1 \text{ box}}$$

The unit price is $3.50 per box of crackers.

EXAMPLE 2

A trail mix recipe calls for 3 cups of raisins and 4 cups of peanuts. Mitt made trail mix for a party and used 5 cups of raisins and 6 cups of peanuts. Did Mitt use the correct ratio of raisins to peanuts?

$$\frac{3 \text{ cups of raisins}}{4 \text{ cups of peanuts}}$$

The ratio of raisins to peanuts in the recipe is $\frac{3}{4}$.

$$\frac{5 \text{ cups of raisins}}{6 \text{ cups of peanuts}}$$

Mitt used a ratio of $\frac{5}{6}$.

$$\frac{3}{4} \times \frac{3}{3} = \frac{9}{12} \qquad \frac{5}{6} \times \frac{2}{2} = \frac{10}{12} \qquad \frac{9}{12} < \frac{10}{12}$$

Mitt used a higher ratio of raisins to peanuts in his trail mix.

EXERCISES

Write three equivalent ratios for each ratio. (Lesson 7.1) Sample answers given.

1. $\frac{18}{6}$ 36:12, 9:3, 3:1

2. $\frac{5}{45}$ $\frac{1}{9}, \frac{10}{90}, \frac{2}{18}$

3. $\frac{3}{5}$ $\frac{6}{10}, \frac{9}{15}, \frac{12}{20}$

4. To make a dark orange color, Ron mixes 3 ounces of red paint with 2 ounces of yellow paint. Write the ratio of red paint to yellow paint three ways. (Lesson 7.1) 3:2, 3 to 2, $\frac{3}{2}$

5. A box of a dozen fruit tarts costs $15.00. What is the cost of one fruit tart?

(Lesson 7.2) $1.25

Compare the ratios. (Lesson 7.3)

6. $\frac{2}{5}$ $<$ $\frac{3}{4}$

7. $\frac{9}{2}$ $>$ $\frac{10}{7}$

8. $\frac{2}{11}$ $<$ $\frac{3}{12}$

9. $\frac{6}{7}$ $<$ $\frac{8}{9}$

Applying Ratios and Rates

Key Vocabulary

conversion factor (*factor de conversión*)

proportion (*proporción*)

scale (*escala*)

scale drawing (*dibujo a escala*)

? ESSENTIAL QUESTION

How can you use ratios and rates to solve real-world problems?

EXAMPLE 1

A. Jessica earns $5 for each dog she walks. Complete the table, describe the rule, and tell whether the relationship is additive or multiplicative. Then graph the ordered pairs on a coordinate plane.

Number of dogs	1	2	3	4	5
Profit ($)	5	10	15	20	25

Jessica's profit is the number of dogs walked multiplied by $5. The relationship is multiplicative.

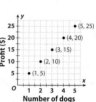

B. A veterinarian tells Lee that his dog should have a 35 centimeter collar. What is this measurement in inches?

Use the conversion factor 1 inch = 2.54 centimeters, written as the rate $\frac{1 \text{ in.}}{2.54 \text{ cm}}$.

$$35 \text{ cm} \cdot \frac{1 \text{ in.}}{2.54 \text{ cm}} \approx 13.78$$

The collar should be about 14 inches.

EXERCISES

1. Thaddeus already has $5 saved. He wants to save more to buy a book. Complete the table, and graph the ordered pairs on the coordinate graph. (Lessons 8.1, 8.2)

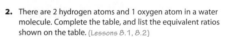

New savings	4	6	8	10
Total savings	9	11	13	15

2. There are 2 hydrogen atoms and 1 oxygen atom in a water molecule. Complete the table, and list the equivalent ratios shown on the table. (Lessons 8.1, 8.2)

Hydrogen atoms	8	12	16	20
Oxygen atoms	4	6	8	10

$$\frac{8}{4} = \frac{12}{6} = \frac{16}{8} = \frac{20}{10}$$

3. Sam can solve 30 multiplication problems in 2 minutes. How many can he solve in 20 minutes? (Lesson 8.3)

300 multiplication problems

MODULE 8 Percents

 6.RP.3, 6.RP.3c

Key Concepts
- A percent is a ratio that compares a number to 100. *(Lesson 8.1)*
- Any percent can be written as an equivalent fraction and an equivalent decimal. *(Lesson 8.2)*
- You can use proportional reasoning to solve problems that involve percents. *(Lesson 8.3)*

Unit 3 Performance Tasks

The Performance Tasks provide students with the opportunity to apply concepts from this unit in real-world problem situations.

CAREERS IN MATH

Residential Builder In Performance Task Item 1, students can see how a residential builder uses mathematics on the job.

SCORING GUIDES FOR PERFORMANCE TASKS

1. MATHEMATICAL PRACTICES MP.2, MP.4

Task	Possible Points (Total: 6)
a	**1 point** for explanation: The cost per square foot is the unit cost, so I need to divide the price by the number of square feet. **1 point** for correct answer: $\frac{\$38.50}{350\,\text{ft}^2} = \$0.11/\text{ft}^2$
b	**1 point** for correct number of gallons and **1 point** for explanation: $\frac{1\,\text{gallon}}{350\,\text{ft}^2} \cdot \frac{825\,\text{ft}}{1} \approx 2.36$ gallons; since she cannot buy part of a gallon, she should buy 3 gallons.

2. MATHEMATICAL PRACTICES MP.2, MP.4, MP.8

Task	Possible Points (Total: 6)
a	**1 point** for correct answer: No, the sheet does not satisfy the requirements. **1 point** for correct justification, for example: $920 \div 5 = 184$, which is less than $190\,\text{g/m}^2$. **1 point** for finding the correct measure: $190 \times 5 = 950\,\text{g}$
b	**2 points** for correctly finding **option 2** to be the best choice, and **1 point** for correct justification: **Option 1** has only about $183\,\text{g/m}^2$ of flannel, and **option 2** costs about $\$6.36/\text{yd}^2$, while option 3 costs $\$8/\text{yd}^2$.

4. A male Chihuahua weighs 5 pounds. How many ounces does he weigh? (Lesson 8.4)

80 ounces

 **Percents**

 ESSENTIAL QUESTION

How can you use percents to solve real-world problems?

EXAMPLE 1

Find an equivalent percent for $\frac{7}{10}$.

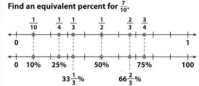

$\frac{7}{10} = 7 \cdot \frac{1}{10}$ $\frac{7}{10} = 7 \cdot 10\%$ $\frac{7}{10} = 70\%$

Find an equivalent percent for $\frac{1}{5}$.

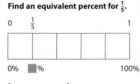

$\frac{1}{5}$ of 100 = 20, so $\frac{1}{5}$ of 100% = 20%

$\frac{1}{5} = 20\%$

EXAMPLE 2

Thirteen of the 50 states in the United States do not touch the ocean. Write $\frac{13}{50}$ as a decimal and a percent.

$\frac{13}{50} = \frac{26}{100}$ $\frac{26}{100} = 0.26$ $0.26 = 26\%$ $\frac{13}{50} = 0.26 = 26\%$

EXAMPLE 3

Buckner put $60 of his $400 paycheck into his savings account. Find the percent of his paycheck that Buckner saved.

$\frac{60}{400} = \frac{?}{100}$ $\frac{60 \div 4}{400 \div 4} = \frac{15}{100}$ Buckner saved 15% of his paycheck.

EXERCISES

Write each fraction as a decimal and a percent. (Lessons 9.1, 9.2)

1. $\frac{3}{4}$ — 0.75, 75%   **2.** $\frac{7}{20}$ — 0.35, 35%   **3.** $\frac{8}{5}$ — 1.6, 160%

Complete each statement. (Lessons 9.1, 9.2)

4. 25% of 200 is 50.   **5.** 16 is 80% of 20.   **6.** 21 is 70% of 30.

---

7. 42 of the 150 employees at Carlo's Car Repair wear contact lenses. What percent of the employees wear contact lenses? (Lesson 9.3) 28%

8. Last week at Best Bargain, 75% of the computers sold were laptops. If 340 computers were sold last week, how many were laptops? (Lesson 9.3) 255 laptops

Unit 3 Performance Tasks

1. **CAREERS IN MATH** | Residential Builder Kaylee, a residential builder, is working on a paint budget for a custom-designed home she is building. A gallon of paint costs $38.50, and its label says it covers about 350 square feet.

a. Explain how to calculate the cost of paint per square foot. Find this value. Show your work.

Divide the cost by the number of square feet: $38.50 ÷ 350 square feet = $0.11/square foot.

b. Kaylee measured the room she wants to paint and calculated a total area of 825 square feet. If the paint is only available in one-gallon cans, how many cans of paint should she buy? Justify your answer.

825 ÷ 350 ≈ 2.36; since she cannot buy part of a gallon, she should buy 3 gallons.

2. Davette wants to buy flannel sheets. She reads that a weight of at least 190 grams per square meter is considered high quality.

a. Davette finds a sheet that has a weight of 920 grams for 5 square meters. Does this sheet satisfy the requirement for high-quality sheets? If not, what should the weight be for 5 square meters? Explain.

No; 920 ÷ 5 = 184; it should be at least 190 × 5 = 950 grams.

b. Davette finds 3 more options for flannel sheets:

Option 1: 1,100 g of flannel in 6 square meters, $45

Option 2: 1,260 g of flannel in 6.6 square meters, $42

Option 3: 1,300 g of flannel in 6.5 square meters, $52

She would like to buy the sheet that meets her requirements for high quality and has the lowest price per square meter. Which option should she buy? Justify your answer.

Option 2; option 1 is not high quality flannel (~183g/m²), and option 2 costs less per square meter (~$6.36) than option 3 ($8).

Additional Resources

Personal Math Trainer

Online Assessment and Intervention

my.hrw.com

Assessment Resources

- Leveled Unit Tests: A, B, C, D
- Performance Assessment

MIXED REVIEW

Assessment Readiness

Assessment Readiness Tip Students can work backwards, checking answer choices individually instead of solving the problem directly.

Item 6 Students can write each answer choice as a fraction with a denominator of 100 and then compare it to the diagram.

Item 8 Students can multiply each answer choice by the size of the glasses (0.6 liter) and see which gives the answer of 4.5 liters. Students may find this easier than dividing decimals to find the answer directly.

Avoid Common Errors

Item 2 Some students perform the reverse operation for problems of this type. Instead of multiplying by 100, they will divide by 100 and get answer choice A. Remind students to check that their answers make sense. Does it make sense that 0.15 centimeter is equivalent to 15 meters?

Item 9 Some students will order the numbers from least to greatest out of habit. Remind students to always read the questions carefully to be sure they are answering the right question.

Common Core Standards

Items	Grade 6 Standards	Mathematical Practices
1	6.RP.1	MP.4
2	6.RP.3d	MP.8
3	6.RP.1	MP.4
4	6.RP.3a	MP.4, MP.6
5	6.RP.3a	MP.2, MP.4
6	6.RP.3c	MP.2
7	6.RP.3c	MP.4
8*	6.NS.3	MP.4
9*	6.NS.7	MP.5
10	6.RP.3d	MP.8
11	6.RP.3b, 6.RP.3d	MP.4, MP.8
12	6.RP.2, 6.RP.3b, 6.RP.3d	MP.4
13	6.RP.2	MP.4

* Item integrates mixed review concepts from previous modules or a previous course.

Assessment Readiness

Personal
Math Trainer

Online
Assessment and
Intervention

my.hrw.com

Selected Response

1. The deepest part of a swimming pool is 12 feet deep. The shallowest part of the pool is 3 feet deep. What is the ratio of the depth of the deepest part of the pool to the depth of the shallowest part of the pool?

Ⓐ 4:1

Ⓑ 12:15

Ⓒ 1:4

Ⓓ 15:12

2. How many centimeters are in 15 meters?

Ⓐ 0.15 centimeters

Ⓑ 1.5 centimeters

Ⓒ 150 centimeters

Ⓓ 1,500 centimeters

3. Barbara can walk 3,200 meters in 24 minutes. How far can she walk in 3 minutes?

Ⓐ 320 meters

Ⓑ 400 meters

Ⓒ 640 meters

Ⓓ 720 meters

4. The table below shows the number of windows and panes of glass in the windows.

Windows	2	3	4	5
Panes	12	18	24	30

Which represents the number of panes?

Ⓐ windows × 5

Ⓑ windows × 6

Ⓒ windows + 10

Ⓓ windows + 15

5. The graph below represents Donovan's speed while riding his bike.

Which would be an ordered pair on the line?

Ⓐ (1, 3)

Ⓑ (2, 2)

Ⓒ (6, 4)

Ⓓ (9, 3)

 Hot Tip! Read the graph or diagram as closely as you read the actual test question. These visual aids contain important information.

6. Which percent does this shaded grid represent?

Ⓐ 42%

Ⓑ 48%

Ⓒ 52%

Ⓓ 58%

7. Ivan saves 20% of his monthly paycheck for music equipment. He earned $335 last month. How much money did Ivan save for music equipment?

Ⓐ $65

Ⓑ $67

Ⓒ $70

Ⓓ $75

8. How many 0.6-liter glasses can you fill up with a 4.5-liter pitcher?

Ⓐ 1.33 glasses

Ⓑ 3.9 glasses

Ⓒ 7.3 glasses

Ⓓ 7.5 glasses

9. Which shows the integers in order from greatest to least?

Ⓐ 22, 8, 7, 2, −11

Ⓑ 2, 7, 8, −11, 22

Ⓒ −11, 2, 7, 8, 22

Ⓓ 22, −11, 8, 7, 2

10. How do you convert 15 feet to centimeters?

Ⓐ Multiply 15 ft by $\frac{1 \text{ ft}}{12 \text{ in.}}$ and $\frac{2.54 \text{ cm}}{1 \text{ in.}}$.

Ⓑ Multiply 15 ft by $\frac{1 \text{ ft}}{12 \text{ in.}}$ and $\frac{1 \text{ in.}}{2.54 \text{ cm}}$.

Ⓒ Multiply 15 ft by $\frac{12 \text{ in.}}{1 \text{ ft}}$ and $\frac{2.54 \text{ cm}}{1 \text{ in.}}$.

Ⓓ Multiply 15 ft by $\frac{12 \text{ in.}}{1 \text{ ft}}$ and $\frac{1 \text{ cm}}{2.54 \text{ in.}}$.

Mini Task

11. Claire and Malia are training for a race.

a. Claire runs 10 km in 1 hour. How many kilometers does she run in half an hour? in $2\frac{1}{2}$ hours?

5 km; 25 km

b. Malia runs 5 miles in 1 hour. How many miles does she run in half an hour? in $2\frac{1}{2}$ hours?

$2\frac{1}{2}$ mi; $12\frac{1}{2}$ mi

c. On Tuesday, Claire and Malia both ran for $2\frac{1}{2}$ hours. Who ran the farther distance?

Claire

12. A department store is having a sale.

a. Malcolm bought 6 bowls for $13.20. What is the unit rate?

$2.20 per bowl

b. The store is having a promotion. For every 8 glasses you buy, you get 3 free plates. Malcolm got 9 free plates. How many glasses did he buy?

24 glasses

c. The unit rate of the glasses was $1.80 per glass. How much did Malcolm spend on glasses?

$43.20

13. A recipe calls for 6 cups of water and 4 cups of flour.

a. What is the ratio of water to flour?

6 to 4

b. If the recipe is increased to use 6 cups of flour, how much water should be used?

9 cups

c. If the recipe is decreased to use 2 cups of water, how much flour should be used?

$1\frac{1}{3}$ cups of flour

Contents

Unit Pacing Guide

45-Minute Classes

Module 9

DAY 1	DAY 2	DAY 3	DAY 4	DAY 5
Lesson 9.1	Lesson 9.1	Lesson 9.2	Lesson 9.2	Lesson 9.2

DAY 6	DAY 7	DAY 8		
Lesson 9.3	Lesson 9.3	Ready to Go On? Assessment Readiness		

Module 10

DAY 1	DAY 2	DAY 3	DAY 4	DAY 5
Lesson 10.1	Lesson 10.1	Lesson 10.2	Lesson 10.2	Lesson 10.3

DAY 6	DAY 7	DAY 8	DAY 9	
Lesson 10.3	Lesson 10.3	Ready to Go On? Assessment Readiness	Study Guide Assessment Readiness	

90-Minute Classes

Module 9

DAY 1	DAY 2	DAY 3	DAY 4	
Lesson 9.1	Lesson 9.2	Lesson 9.3	Ready to Go On? Assessment Readiness	

Module 10

DAY 1	DAY 2	DAY 3	DAY 4	DAY 5
Lesson 10.1	Lesson 10.2	Lesson 10.3	Ready to Go On? Assessment Readiness	Study Guide Assessment Readiness

Program Resources

⏻ Plan

Online Teacher Edition

Access a full suite of teaching resources online—plan, present, and manage classes, assignments, and activities.

ePlanner Easily plan your classes, create and view assignments, and access all program resources with your online, customizable planning tool.

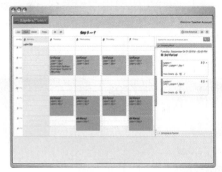

Professional Development Videos

Author Juli Dixon models successful teaching practices and strategies in actual classroom settings.

QR Codes Scan with your smart phone to jump directly from your print book to online videos and other resources.

Teacher's Edition

Support students with point-of-use Questioning Strategies, teaching tips, resources for differentiated instruction, additional activities, and more.

⏻ Engage and Explore

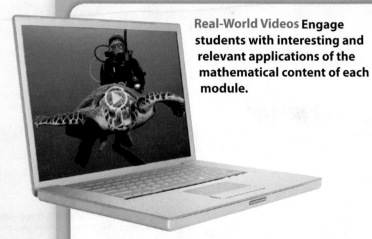

Real-World Videos Engage students with interesting and relevant applications of the mathematical content of each module.

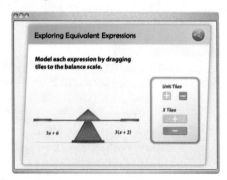

Animated Math Online interactive simulations, tools, and games help students actively learn and practice key concepts.

Explore Activities

Students interactively explore new concepts using a variety of tools and approaches.

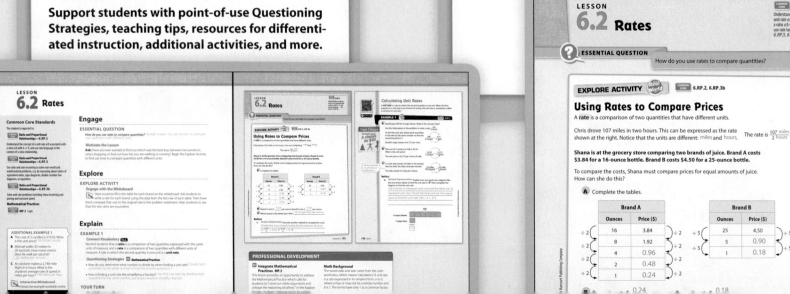

Image Credits: ©Rich Carey/Shutterstock.com; (c) ©Juli Dixon

⏻ Teach

 Math On the Spot video tutorials, featuring program authors Dr. Edward Burger and Martha Sandoval-Martinez, accompany every example in the textbook and give students step-by-step instructions and explanations of key math concepts.

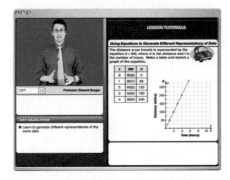

Present engaging content on a multitude of devices, including tablets and interactive whiteboards.

 Continually monitor and assess student progress with integrated formative assessment.

CC CLUSTER CONNECTION Look for exercises indicated with this icon to build connections among standards within Common Core clusters.

Differentiated Instruction Print Resources

Support all learners with Differentiated Instruction Resources, including

- **Leveled Practice and Problem Solving**
- **Reteach**
- **Reading Strategies**
- **Success for English Learners**
- **Challenge**

⏻ Assessment and Intervention

The **Personal Math Trainer** provides online practice, homework, assessments, and intervention. Monitor student progress through reports and alerts. Create and customize assignments aligned to specific lessons or standards.

- **Practice** – With dynamic items and assignments, students get unlimited practice on key concepts supported by guided examples, step-by-step solutions, and video tutorials.
- **Assessments** – Choose from course assignments or customize your own based on course content, standards, difficulty levels, and more.
- **Homework** – Students can complete online homework with a wide variety of problem types, including the ability to enter expressions, equations, and graphs. Let the system automatically grade homework, so you can focus where your students need help the most!
- **Intervention** – Let the Personal Math Trainer automatically prescribe a targeted, personalized intervention path for your students.

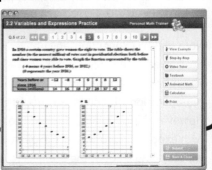

H.O.T. Raise the bar with homework and practice that incorporates higher-order thinking and mathematical processes in every lesson.

COMMON CORE
Assessment Readiness
Prepare students for success on tests of the Common Core Standards with practice at every module and unit.

Assessment Resources

Tailor assessments to meet the needs of all your classes and students, including

- **Leveled Module Quizzes**
- **Leveled Unit Tests**
- **Unit Performance Tasks**
- **Placement, Diagnostic, and Quarterly Benchmark Tests**

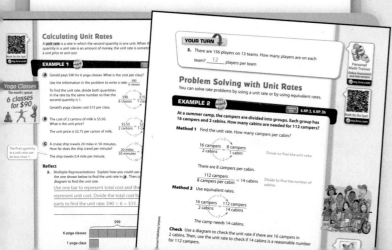

Math Background

Exponents 6.EE.1
LESSON 9.1

The term *exponent* dates to 1544, when it was introduced by the German mathematician Michael Stifel in his work *Arithmetica Integra*. The book includes the following table.

0	1	2	3	4	5	6	7	8
1	2	4	8	16	32	64	128	256

Although Stifel did not use the term *power*, today we recognize the table as a list of the powers of 2. That is, $2^0 = 1$, $2^1 = 2$, $2^2 = 4$, and so on.

A number written as a power, such as 2^3, consists of two parts, the *base* (in this case, 2) and the *exponent* (in this case, 3). A power indicates repeated multiplication, and the exponent tells how many times the base is to be used as a factor. Thus, $2^3 = 2 \times 2 \times 2 = 8$.

Note that by convention, any nonzero number raised to the power 0 is defined to be 1. That is, $a^0 = 1$ for any $a \neq 0$. This may seem counterintuitive to students, since repeated multiplication with no factors might suggest a value of 0. However, this definition is needed so that operations with exponents produce the expected results. Students will learn more about the use of zero as an exponent and negative numbers as exponents in future math courses.

Order of Operations 6.EE.1
LESSON 9.3

Students may wonder why an order of operations is needed or who decided what the order should be. However, they should come to understand that just as the order of the words in a sentence is important to the sentence's meaning, the order of operations is essential to the meaning or value of a mathematical expression. Mathematicians decided on an order of operations so that they could communicate more easily.

One common misconception about the order of operations results from the mnemonic PEMDAS (Parentheses, Exponents, Multiply, Divide, Add, Subtract). If students use this mnemonic, they may perform all multiplication before division instead of performing the operations of multiplication and division from left to right as they occur in the expression.

For example, students may simplify the expression $5 \cdot 6 \div 3 \cdot 10$ by performing all multiplication first, which gives an incorrect answer of 1. If the expression is simplified by multiplying and dividing from left to right, the correct answer of 100 is obtained.

A similar misconception may occur with addition and subtraction.

An alternative mnemonic is one that separates the operations into a clearer four-step hierarchy, as shown.

$$\boxed{\begin{array}{l} P \\ E \\ MD \\ AS \end{array}}$$

This mnemonic also emphasizes that exponents come before the other operations. For example, students may simplify the expression $3 - 2^3$ by adding first then raising the sum to the power, which gives an incorrect answer of 125. If the expression is simplified correctly, the answer is 11.

Writing Expressions 6.EE.2, 6.EE.2a
LESSON 10.1

One of the overarching themes of middle school mathematics is that there are multiple ways to represent mathematical ideas. As students make the transition to algebra, they should become more and more fluent in working among multiple representations such as graphs, equations, and tables. Lesson 10.1 introduces students to two of the most important representations they will use: words and expressions.

Translating English phrases into algebraic symbols can be challenging for many students. Some students may attempt a translation that preserves the order of the words, and this does not always work, particularly when subtraction is involved. For example, a student might translate the phrase "3 less than x" as $3 - x$. This student correctly connected the words "less than" with the operation of subtraction, but placed the 3 and the variable x in the wrong order.

Students who have difficulty translating words to expressions sometimes benefit from considering how they would write a purely numerical expression. For example, a student is likely to recognize the error in translating "3 less than 7" as $3 - 7$. Since the variable x stands for a number, the same logic applies in recognizing that $3 - x$ is an incorrect translation of "3 less than x."

Generating Equivalent Expressions 6.EE.3
LESSON 10.3

A *binary operation* is an arithmetic operation on two numbers. For example, addition, subtraction, multiplication, and division are all binary operations because they give rules for operating on a pair of numbers.

A binary operation is *commutative* if the order of the two numbers does not affect the result. Addition and multiplication are commutative, whereas subtraction and division are not.

Binary operations only tell us how to put two numbers together, so additional information is needed when an operation is used to combine three or more numbers, such as $8 + 4 + 7$. An operation is *associative* if you can group the numbers in any order without affecting the answer. Addition and multiplication are associative. For example, the Associative Property of Addition says that to simplify $8 + 4 + 7$, the 8 and 4 may be added first, or the 4 and 7 may be added first. In other words, $(8 + 4) + 7 = 8 + (4 + 7)$.

It is instructive to consider an operation that is not associative, such as subtraction. In this case, the grouping of the numbers affects the result: $(11 - 7) - 3 \neq 11 - (7 - 3)$. Therefore, to simplify an expression without parentheses, such as $11 - 7 - 3$, additional rules are needed, and this is where the order of operations comes into play.

A third property, the Distributive Property, explains how addition and multiplication work together. The property can be illustrated through an area model, as shown in the figure.

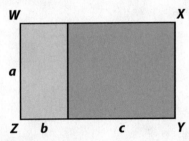

The area of rectangle *WXYZ* is equal to the product of its length and its width, or $a(b + c)$.

The area of rectangle *WXYZ* is also equal to the area of the lighter rectangle plus the area of the darker rectangle, or $ab + ac$. Setting the two area expressions equal gives $a(b + c) = ab + ac$.

Students sometimes wonder why complex names like Commutative Property of Addition are needed for "obvious" statements like $2 + 3 = 3 + 2$. As they begin to develop more sophisticated algebraic thinking, students should understand that these properties provide the logical foundations of algebra and justify the steps that are used in simplifying algebraic expressions.

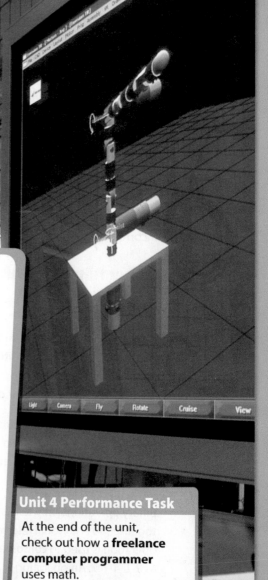

Equivalent Expressions

MODULE 9

Generating Equivalent Numerical Expressions

COMMON CORE 6.EE.1

MODULE 10

Generating Equivalent Algebraic Expressions

COMMON CORE 6.EE.2a, 6.EE.2b, 6.EE.2c, 6.EE.3, 6.EE.4, 6.EE.6

CAREERS IN MATH

Freelance Computer Programmer
A computer programmer translates commands into code, a language that a computer understands. Programmers work on a variety of tasks, from creating computer games to testing software. A freelance programmer doesn't work for a specific company; this gives the freelancer more flexibility with his or her work schedule. Computer programmers use mathematical logic when writing or altering code.

If you are interested in a career as a computer programmer, you should study these mathematical subjects:

- Algebra
- Geometry
- Trigonometry
- Calculus
- Discrete Math

Research other careers that require the understanding of mathematical logic.

Unit 4 Performance Task

At the end of the unit, check out how a **freelance computer programmer** uses math.

Careers in Math

Freelance Computer Programmer

Freelance computer programmers are people who can work for themselves, determining their own schedule, in a variety of tasks that incorporate writing or altering code. Programmers work on a variety of tasks, from creating computer games to testing software. You will learn more about this in the Performance Tasks at the end of this unit.

For more information about careers in mathematics as well as various mathematics appreciation topics, visit the American Mathematical Society at www.ams.org

Vocabulary Preview Puzzle

Use the puzzle to give students a preview of important concepts in this unit. Students may work individually, in pairs, or in groups.

Unit Resources

Go online to access all your unit resources.

my.hrw.com

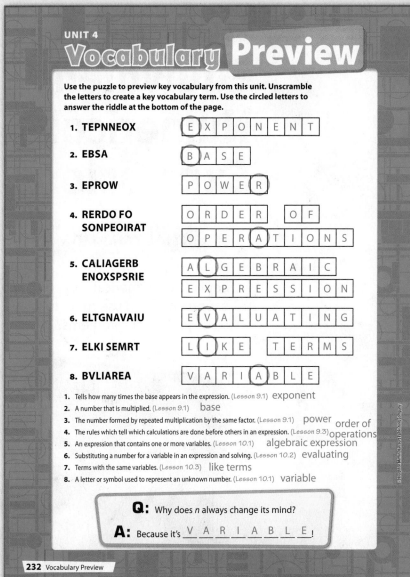

UNIT 4
Vocabulary Preview

Use the puzzle to preview key vocabulary from this unit. Unscramble the letters to create a key vocabulary term. Use the circled letters to answer the riddle at the bottom of the page.

1. TEPNNEOX (E) X P O N E N T
2. EBSA (B) A S E
3. EPROW P O W E (R)
4. RERDO FO SONPEOIRAT O R D E R O F O P E R (A) T I O N S
5. CALIAGERB ENOXSPSRIE A L (G) E B R A I C E X P R E S S I O N
6. ELTGNAVAIU E (V) A L U A T I N G
7. ELKI SEMRT L (I) K E T E R M S
8. BVLIAREA V A R I (A) B L E

1. Tells how many times the base appears in the expression. (Lesson 9.1) exponent
2. A number that is multiplied. (Lesson 9.1) base
3. The number formed by repeated multiplication by the same factor. (Lesson 9.1) power
4. The rules which tell which calculations are done before others in an expression. (Lesson 9.3) order of operations
5. An expression that contains one or more variables. (Lesson 10.1) algebraic expression
6. Substituting a number for a variable in an expression and solving. (Lesson 10.2) evaluating
7. Terms with the same variables. (Lesson 10.3) like terms
8. A letter or symbol used to represent an unknown number. (Lesson 10.1) variable

Q: Why does *n* always change its mind?

A: Because it's V A R I A B L E !

Before	In this Unit	After
Students understand how to:	Students will learn about:	Students will:
• write mathematical expressions	• generating equivalent numerical expressions	• use variables to represent quantities in a real-world or mathematical problem
• evaluate mathematical expressions	• generating equivalent algebraic expressions	• construct simple equations and inequalities to solve problems by reasoning about the quantities

Generating Equivalent Numerical Expressions

 ESSENTIAL QUESTION

How can you generate equivalent numerical expressions and use them to solve real-world problems?

You can represent real-world problems with numerical expressions and simplify the expressions by applying rules relating to exponents, prime factorization, and order of operations.

Real-World Video

Assume that you post a video on the internet. Two of your friends view it, then two friends of each of those view it, and so on. The number of views is growing exponentially. Sometimes we say the video went viral.

my.hrw.com

GO DIGITAL
my.hrw.com

my.hrw.com
Go digital with your write-in student edition, accessible on any device.

Math On the Spot
Scan with your smart phone to jump directly to the online edition, video tutor, and more.

Animated Math
Interactively explore key concepts to see how math works.

Personal Math Trainer
Get immediate feedback and help as you work through practice sets.

Are You Ready?

Assess Readiness

Use the assessment on this page to determine if students need intensive or strategic intervention for the module's prerequisite skills.

 **RtI** **Response to Intervention**

Personal Math Trainer

Online Assessment and Intervention

 my.hrw.com

Intervention	Enrichment

Access Are You Ready? assessment online, and receive instant scoring, feedback, and customized intervention or enrichment.

Online and Print Resources

Skills Intervention worksheets
- Skill 34 Whole Number Operations
- Skill 35 Use Repeated Multiplication
- Skill 38 Division Facts

Differentiated Instruction
- Challenge worksheets **PRE-AP**
- Extend the Math **PRE-AP** Lesson Activities in TE

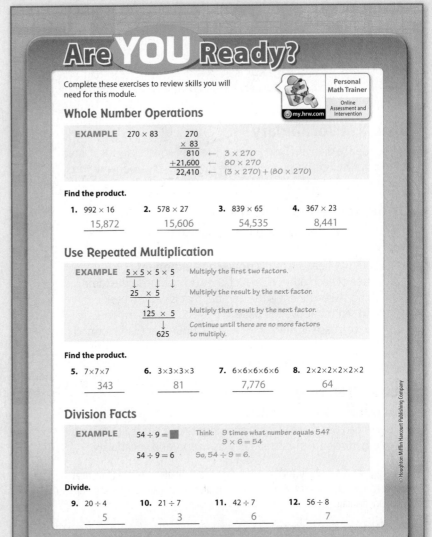

Are YOU Ready?

Complete these exercises to review skills you will need for this module.

Personal Math Trainer
Online Assessment and Intervention
my.hrw.com

Whole Number Operations

EXAMPLE 270×83

$$\begin{array}{r} 270 \\ \times\ 83 \\ \hline 810 \\ +21,600 \\ \hline 22,410 \end{array}$$
← 3×270
← 80×270
← $(3 \times 270) + (80 \times 270)$

Find the product.

1. 992×16
   15,872

2. 578×27
   15,606

3. 839×65
   54,535

4. 367×23
   8,441

Use Repeated Multiplication

EXAMPLE $5 \times 5 \times 5 \times 5$

Multiply the first two factors.

25×5

Multiply the result by the next factor.

125×5

Multiply that result by the next factor.

625

Continue until there are no more factors to multiply.

Find the product.

5. $7 \times 7 \times 7$
   343

6. $3 \times 3 \times 3 \times 3$
   81

7. $6 \times 6 \times 6 \times 6 \times 6$
   7,776

8. $2 \times 2 \times 2 \times 2 \times 2 \times 2$
   64

Division Facts

EXAMPLE $54 \div 9 = \blacksquare$ Think: 9 times what number equals 54?
$9 \times 6 = 54$

$54 \div 9 = 6$ So, $54 \div 9 = 6$.

Divide.

9. $20 \div 4$
   5

10. $21 \div 7$
    3

11. $42 \div 7$
    6

12. $56 \div 8$
    7

© Houghton Mifflin Harcourt Publishing Company

234 Unit 4

PROFESSIONAL DEVELOPMENT VIDEO

Author Juli Dixon models successful teaching practices as she explores equivalent numerical expressions in an actual sixth-grade classroom.

Professional Development

my.hrw.com

GO DIGITAL my.hrw.com

 Online Teacher Edition
Access a full suite of teaching resources online—plan, present, and manage classes and assignments.

 ePlanner
Easily plan your classes and access all your resources online.

 Interactive Answers and Solutions
Customize answer keys to print or display in the classroom. Choose to include answers only or full solutions to all lesson exercises.

 Interactive Whiteboards
Engage students with interactive whiteboard-ready lessons and activities.

 Personal Math Trainer: Online Assessment and Intervention
Assign automatically graded homework, quizzes, tests, and intervention activities. Prepare your students with updated practice tests aligned with Common Core.

Generating Equivalent Numerical Expressions   **234**

Reading Start-Up

Have students complete the activities on this page by working alone or with others.

Visualize Vocabulary

The sequence diagram helps students review vocabulary associated with factorization and prepares them to work with exponents. After students complete the diagram, discuss the vocabulary as a class.

Understand Vocabulary

Use the following explanation to help students learn the preview words.

> You may hear the terms **power** and **exponent** used in place of each other. However, they do not mean the same thing. An exponent is the number that is written beside and slightly above the **base**. It tells you how many times to use the base as a factor. A power is a number that is formed by repeated multiplication by the same factor (the base) and can be represented as the base with an exponent.

Active Reading

Integrating Language Arts

Students can use these reading and note-taking strategies to help them organize and understand new concepts and vocabulary.

COMMON CORE **ELA-Literacy.RST.6-8.7** Integrate quantitative or technical information expressed in words in a text with a version of that information expressed visually (e.g., in a flowchart, diagram, model, graph, or table).

Additional Resources

Differentiated Instruction

• Reading Strategies **ELL**

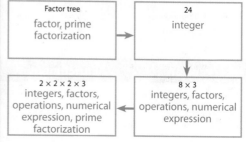

Reading Start-Up

Vocabulary

Review Words
✔ factor *(factor)*
  factor tree *(árbol de factores)*
✔ integers *(entero)*
✔ numerical expression *(expresión numérica)*
✔ operations *(operaciones)*
✔ prime factorization *(factorización prima)*
  repeated multiplication *(multiplicación repetida)*
  simplified expression *(expresión simplificada)*

Preview Words
  base *(base)*
  exponent *(exponente)*
  order of operations *(orden de las operaciones)*
  power *(potencia)*

Visualize Vocabulary

Use the ✔ words to complete the graphic. You may put more than one word in each box.

Reviewing Factorization

Factor tree	→	24
factor, prime factorization		integer

2 × 2 × 2 × 3	←	8 × 3
integers, factors, operations, numerical expression, prime factorization		integers, factors, operations, numerical expression

Understand Vocabulary

Complete the sentences using the preview words.

1. A number that is formed by repeated multiplication by the same factor is a _____power_____ .

2. A rule for simplifying expressions is _____order of operations_____ .

3. The _____base_____ is a number that is multiplied. The number that indicates how many times this number is used as a factor is the _____exponent_____ .

Active Reading

Three-Panel Flip Chart Before beginning the module, create a three-panel flip chart to help you organize what you learn. Label each flap with one of the lesson titles from this module. As you study each lesson, write important ideas like vocabulary, properties, and formulas under the appropriate flap.

© Houghton Mifflin Harcourt Publishing Company

Before	**In this module**	**After**
Students understand:	Students will learn to:	Students will connect:
• operations with whole numbers, decimals, and fractions	• generate equivalent numerical expressions using exponents	• order of operations and numerical expressions
• prime numbers	• generate equivalent numerical expressions using prime factorization	• numerical and algebraic expressions
• order of operations	• simplify numerical expressions using the order of operations	

Unpacking the Standards

Use the examples on this page to help students know exactly what they are expected to learn in this module.

Common Core Standards

Content Areas

 **Expressions and Equations—6.EE**

Apply and extend previous understandings of arithmetic to algebraic expressions.

Go online to see a complete unpacking of the Common Core Standards.

my.hrw.com

 MODULE 9

Unpacking the Standards

Understanding the standards and the vocabulary terms in the standards will help you know exactly what you are expected to learn in this module.

COMMON CORE 6.EE.1

Write and evaluate numerical expressions involving whole-number exponents.

Key Vocabulary

exponent *(exponente)*
The number that indicates how many times the base is used as a factor.

order of operations *(orden de las operaciones)* A rule for evaluating expressions: first perform the operations in parentheses, then compute powers and roots, then perform all multiplication and division from left to right, and then perform all addition and subtraction from left to right.

What It Means to You

You will simplify numerical expressions using the order of operations.

UNPACKING EXAMPLE 6.EE.1

Ellen is playing a video game in which she captures frogs. There were 3 frogs onscreen, but the number of frogs doubled every minute when she went to get a snack. She returned after 4 minutes and captured 7 frogs. Write an expression for the number of frogs remaining. Simplify the expression.

3×2	number of frogs after 1 minute
$3 \times 2 \times 2$	number of frogs after 2 minutes
$3 \times 2 \times 2 \times 2$	number of frogs after 3 minutes
$3 \times 2 \times 2 \times 2 \times 2$	number of frogs after 4 minutes

Since 3 and 2 are prime numbers, $3 \times 2 \times 2 \times 2 \times 2$ is the prime factorization of the number of frogs remaining.

$3 \times 2 \times 2 \times 2 \times 2$ can be written with exponents as 3×2^4.

The expression $3 \times 2^4 - 7$ is the number of frogs remaining after Ellen captured the 7 frogs.

Use the order of operations to simplify $3 \times 2^4 - 7$.

$$3 \times 2^4 - 7 = 3 \times 16 - 7$$
$$= 48 - 7$$
$$= 41$$

41 frogs remain.

Visit my.hrw.com to see all the Common Core Standards unpacked.

my.hrw.com

236 Unit 4

Common Core Standards	Lesson 9.1	Lesson 9.2	Lesson 9.3
6.EE.1 Write and evaluate numerical expressions involving whole-number exponents.	COMMON CORE	COMMON CORE	COMMON CORE

LESSON
9.1 Exponents

ADDITIONAL EXAMPLE 1
Use an exponent to write each expression.

A $7 \times 7 \times 7 \times 7 \times 7 \times 7$ 7^6

B $\frac{2}{3} \times \frac{2}{3} \times \frac{2}{3} \times \frac{2}{3} \times \frac{2}{3}$ $\left(\frac{2}{3}\right)^5$

 Interactive Whiteboard
Interactive example available online

Engage

ESSENTIAL QUESTION

How do you use exponents to represent numbers? Sample answer: You can use exponents to represent repeated multiplication. For example, in $5 \times 5 \times 5 \times 5$, the number 5 is multiplied 4 times, so you can represent it as 5^4.

Motivate the Lesson

Ask: Have you ever heard the terms *squared* or *cubed*? Both of those expressions are used to describe exponents. Do you know what 3 squared means? Take a guess. Begin the Explore Activity to find out.

Explore

EXPLORE ACTIVITY

Engage with the Whiteboard

Have students fill in the table on the whiteboard. Extend the table to include 8 hours, and have students fill in the table for 5, 6, 7, and 8 hours. Ask students if they could predict the total number of bacteria for hour 12 and hour 20. Discuss a rule that students could use to make those kinds of predictions.

Explain

EXAMPLE 1

Connect Vocabulary ELL

Students may know other definitions of the words *raised* and *base*. Point out that in math, **raised** means "to multiply by itself," and **base** can mean "the foundation," or that on which something is built. In 2^4, you build on the base 2 by multiplying it by itself 4 times.

Questioning Strategies CC Mathematical Practices

• In B, why is the base $\frac{4}{5}$ in parentheses in the power $\left(\frac{4}{5}\right)^4$? The base is in parentheses to show that the entire fraction is used for repeated multiplication, not just the numerator.

• Can a power have a base and an exponent that are the same number? Justify your answer. Yes; for example, $6 \times 6 \times 6 \times 6 \times 6 \times 6 = 6^6$.

YOUR TURN

Avoid Common Errors

Students may want to find the product for each expression. Review the direction line. They are not asked to simplify the expression, but to write it in exponential form.

Talk About It
Check for Understanding

 Ask: What is the difference between the two numbers in a power? The first number is the base, which is the number that is multiplied. The second number is the exponent, which tells how many times the base is multiplied by itself.

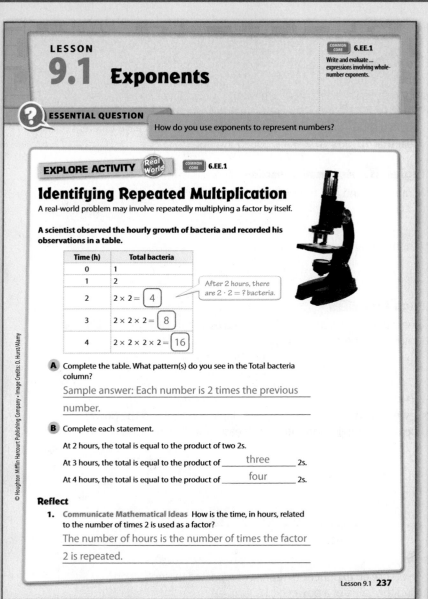

9.1 Exponents

COMMON CORE 6.EE.1
Write and evaluate ... expressions involving whole-number exponents.

? ESSENTIAL QUESTION

How do you use exponents to represent numbers?

EXPLORE ACTIVITY Real World | COMMON CORE 6.EE.1

Identifying Repeated Multiplication

A real-world problem may involve repeatedly multiplying a factor by itself.

A scientist observed the hourly growth of bacteria and recorded his observations in a table.

Time (h)	Total bacteria
0	1
1	2
2	$2 \times 2 =$ ☐ 4
3	$2 \times 2 \times 2 =$ ☐ 8
4	$2 \times 2 \times 2 \times 2 =$ ☐ 16

After 2 hours, there are 2 · 2 = ? bacteria.

A Complete the table. What pattern(s) do you see in the Total bacteria column?

Sample answer: Each number is 2 times the previous number.

B Complete each statement.

At 2 hours, the total is equal to the product of two 2s.

At 3 hours, the total is equal to the product of ___three___ 2s.

At 4 hours, the total is equal to the product of ___four___ 2s.

Reflect

1. **Communicate Mathematical Ideas** How is the time, in hours, related to the number of times 2 is used as a factor?

   The number of hours is the number of times the factor 2 is repeated.

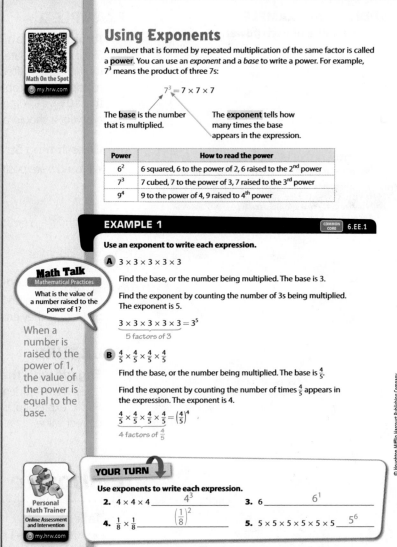

Math On the Spot
my.hrw.com

Using Exponents

A number that is formed by repeated multiplication of the same factor is called a **power**. You can use an *exponent* and a *base* to write a power. For example, 7^3 means the product of three 7s:

$$7^3 = 7 \times 7 \times 7$$

The **base** is the number that is multiplied.

The **exponent** tells how many times the base appears in the expression.

Power	How to read the power
6^2	6 squared, 6 to the power of 2, 6 raised to the 2nd power
7^3	7 cubed, 7 to the power of 3, 7 raised to the 3rd power
9^4	9 to the power of 4, 9 raised to 4th power

EXAMPLE 1

COMMON CORE 6.EE.1

Use an exponent to write each expression.

A $3 \times 3 \times 3 \times 3 \times 3$

Find the base, or the number being multiplied. The base is 3.

Find the exponent by counting the number of 3s being multiplied. The exponent is 5.

$$\underbrace{3 \times 3 \times 3 \times 3 \times 3}_{\text{5 factors of 3}} = 3^5$$

B $\frac{4}{5} \times \frac{4}{5} \times \frac{4}{5} \times \frac{4}{5}$

Find the base, or the number being multiplied. The base is $\frac{4}{5}$.

Find the exponent by counting the number of times $\frac{4}{5}$ appears in the expression. The exponent is 4.

$$\underbrace{\frac{4}{5} \times \frac{4}{5} \times \frac{4}{5} \times \frac{4}{5}}_{\text{4 factors of } \frac{4}{5}} = \left(\frac{4}{5}\right)^4$$

Math Talk
Mathematical Practices

What is the value of a number raised to the power of 1?

When a number is raised to the power of 1, the value of the power is equal to the base.

Personal Math Trainer
Online Assessment and Intervention
my.hrw.com

YOUR TURN

Use exponents to write each expression.

2. $4 \times 4 \times 4$ ___4^3___   3. 6 ___6^1___

4. $\frac{1}{8} \times \frac{1}{8}$ ___$\left(\frac{1}{8}\right)^2$___   5. $5 \times 5 \times 5 \times 5 \times 5 \times 5$ ___5^6___

PROFESSIONAL DEVELOPMENT

CC Integrate Mathematical Practices MP.2

This lesson provides an opportunity to address the Mathematical Practices standard that calls for students to reason abstractly and quantitatively. Students first use tables to identify patterns involving repeated multiplication. They then use exponents to rewrite expressions that involve repeated multiplication. Finally, students find the value of expressions that are written with exponents. This process helps students understand multiple ways to represent and use exponents.

Math Background

The use of the terms *squared* and *cubed* is directly related to the measurements of area and volume. The area of a square with sides 5 units long is found by multiplying, 5×5, or 5^2, or 5 squared. The volume of a cube with sides 5 units long is found by multiplying, $5 \times 5 \times 5$, or 5^3, or 5 cubed.

EXAMPLE 2

Avoid Common Errors
Since powers relate to multiplication, students may confuse powers with simple multiplication. After students evaluate each power, have them compare it to a simple multiplication problem to show that the two are not equal. For example, when they find that $10^4 = 10,000$, ask them to find $10 \times 4 = 40$. Since the two expressions have different answers, it should be clear that 10^4 and 10×4 are not equivalent.

Questioning Strategies Mathematical Practices
- If a and b are positive numbers and $a > b$, which is greater: 2^a or 2^b? Explain. 2^a; If the exponent a is greater than the exponent b, students find that the base 2 is used as a factor more times.

- If c and d are positive numbers and $c > d$, which is greater: c^3 or d^3? Explain. c^3; The exponent with the greater base has to be greater if the exponent is the same. For example: $5^3 = 5 \times 5 \times 5 = 125$, while $4^3 = 4 \times 4 \times 4 = 64$.

Integrating Language Arts ELL
Encourage English learners to use the active reading strategies and the illustrated, bilingual glossary as they encounter new terms and concepts.

YOUR TURN

Engage with the Whiteboard
Have students rewrite each power as repeated multiplication. Seeing the power expressed as repeated multiplication can make it easier for students to find the correct value.

Elaborate

Talk About It
Summarize the Lesson

Ask: How can you use an exponent to represent repeated multiplication? How can you find the value of a power? You can write a repeated multiplication, such as $2^3 = 2 \times 2 \times 2$. To find the value of a power, rewrite the expression without using exponents by multiplying the base the number of times shown in the exponent—for example, $5^4 = 5 \times 5 \times 5 \times 5 = 625$.

GUIDED PRACTICE

Engage with the Whiteboard
For Exercise 1, have students complete the table on the whiteboard. Discuss different methods students may have for finding the value of each power, such as using parentheses to group the repeated multiplication or multiplying the value of the previous power by 5.

Avoid Common Errors
Exercises 2–5 Remind students that their answers should be expressed as a power, not as the product of a repeated multiplication.

Exercises 6–20 Some students may multiply a base by its exponent instead of using the base as a factor the number of times indicated by the exponent. Remind them that 4^3 means that 4 is used as a factor 3 times ($4 \times 4 \times 4$).

Exercise 15 If students get the answer 8, remind them that the Property of Zero as an Exponent states that the value of *any* nonzero number raised to the power of 0 is 1.

Finding the Value of a Power

To find the value of a power, remember that the exponent indicates how many times to use the base as a factor.

Math On the Spot
my.hrw.com

Property of Zero as an Exponent

The value of any nonzero number raised to the power of 0 is 1.

Example: $5^0 = 1$

EXAMPLE 2 — COMMON CORE 6.EE.1

Find the value of each power.

A 10^4

Identify the base and the exponent.
The base is 10, and the exponent is 4.

Evaluate: $10^4 = 10 \times 10 \times 10 \times 10 = 10,000$

B 0.4^3

Identify the base and the exponent.
The base is 0.4, and the exponent is 3.

Evaluate: $0.4^3 = 0.4 \times 0.4 \times 0.4 = 0.064$

C $\left(\frac{3}{5}\right)^0$

Identify the base and the exponent.
The base is $\frac{3}{5}$, and the exponent is 0.

Evaluate.

$\left(\frac{3}{5}\right)^0 = 1$ Any number raised to the power of 0 is 1.

D $\left(\frac{2}{3}\right)^2$

Identify the base and the exponent.
The base is $\frac{2}{3}$, and the exponent is 2.

Evaluate.

$\left(\frac{2}{3}\right)^2 = \left(\frac{2}{3}\right) \times \left(\frac{2}{3}\right) = \frac{4}{9}$

Math Talk
Mathematical Practices

Is the value of 2^3 the same as the value of 3^2? Explain.

$2^3 = 2 \cdot 2 \cdot 2 = 8$ and $3^2 = 3 \cdot 3 = 9$, so the values are not the same.

YOUR TURN

Find the value of each power.

6. 3^4 ___81___   **7.** $(1)^9$ ___1___   **8.** $\left(\frac{2}{5}\right)^3$ ___$\frac{8}{125}$___   **9.** 12^2 ___144___

Personal Math Trainer
Online Assessment and Intervention
my.hrw.com

Lesson 9.1 **239**

Guided Practice

1. Complete the table. (Explore Activity 1)

Exponential form	Product	Simplified product
5^1	5	5
5^2	5×5	25
5^3	$5 \times 5 \times 5$	125
5^4	$5 \times 5 \times 5 \times 5$	625
5^5	$5 \times 5 \times 5 \times 5 \times 5$	3,125

Use an exponent to write each expression. (Example 1)

2. $6 \times 6 \times 6$ ___6^3___

    3 factors of 6

3. $10 \times 10 \times 10 \times 10 \times 10 \times 10 \times 10$ ___10^7___

4. $\frac{3}{4} \times \frac{3}{4} \times \frac{3}{4} \times \frac{3}{4} \times \frac{3}{4}$ ___$\left(\frac{3}{4}\right)^5$___

5. $\frac{7}{9} \times \frac{7}{9} \times \frac{7}{9} \times \frac{7}{9} \times \frac{7}{9} \times \frac{7}{9} \times \frac{7}{9} \times \frac{7}{9}$ ___$\left(\frac{7}{9}\right)^8$___

Find the value of each power. (Example 2)

6. 8^3 ___512___   **7.** 7^4 ___2,401___   **8.** 10^3 ___1,000___

9. $\left(\frac{1}{4}\right)^2$ ___$\frac{1}{16}$___   **10.** $\left(\frac{1}{3}\right)^3$ ___$\frac{1}{27}$___   **11.** $\left(\frac{6}{7}\right)^2$ ___$\frac{36}{49}$___

12. 0.8^2 ___0.64___   **13.** 0.5^3 ___0.125___   **14.** 1.1^2 ___1.21___

15. 8^0 ___1___   **16.** 12^1 ___12___   **17.** $\left(\frac{1}{2}\right)^0$ ___1___

18. $(13)^2$ ___169___   **19.** $\left(\frac{2}{5}\right)^2$ ___$\frac{4}{25}$___   **20.** 0.9^2 ___0.81___

? ESSENTIAL QUESTION CHECK-IN

21. How do you use an exponent to represent a number such as 16?

You use an exponent to write a number that can be written as a product of equal factors.

$16 = 4 \times 4$ (or $2 \times 2 \times 2 \times 2$), so it can be written as 4^2 (or 2^4).

240 Unit 4

DIFFERENTIATE INSTRUCTION

Kinesthetic Experience

To help students remember the meaning of the base and the exponent in a power, have them use graph paper or square tiles to construct models of the squares of whole numbers 1–10. Label the models as shown below. A visual representation of a square number can help students remember that exponents represent repeated multiplication of the same factor.

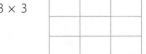

$3^2 = 3 \times 3$

Critical Thinking

Have students explore multiplication of numbers written as powers. Partners can work together to find the values of pairs of expressions such as these:

$3^2 \cdot 3^3$ and $3^1 \cdot 3^4$

$2^2 \cdot 2^4$ and $2^3 \cdot 2^3$

$4^3 \cdot 4^3$ and $4^1 \cdot 4^5$

243 and 243; 64 and 64; 4,096 and 4,096; The values of both expressions in each pair are the same. The base is used the same number of times in each pair. The exponents in each pair have equal sums. You can add the exponents to multiply powers with the same base, for example, $2^2 \cdot 2^4 = 2^6$.

Additional Resources

Differentiated Instruction includes:

- Reading Strategies
- Success for English Learners **ELL**
- Reteach
- Challenge **PRE-AP**

Exponents **240**

9.1 LESSON QUIZ

6.EE.1

Use exponents to write each expression.

1. $\frac{3}{7} \times \frac{3}{7} \times \frac{3}{7}$

2. $0.9 \times 0.9 \times 0.9 \times 0.9$

Find the value of each power.

3. 7^4

4. $\left(\frac{3}{4}\right)^3$

Lesson Quiz available online

 my.hrw.com

Answers

1. $\left(\frac{3}{7}\right)^3$

2. 0.9^4

3. $2,401$

4. $\frac{27}{64}$

Evaluate

GUIDED AND INDEPENDENT PRACTICE

6.EE.1

Concepts & Skills	Practice
Explore Activity Identifying Repeated Multiplication	Exercises 1, 38–44
Example 1 Using Exponents	Exercises 2–5, 22–37
Example 2 Finding the Value of a Power	Exercises 6–20, 38–44

Exercise	Depth of Knowledge (D.O.K.)	Mathematical Practices
22–37	**2** Skills/Concepts	**MP.5** Using Tools
38–39	**2** Skills/Concepts	**MP.4** Modeling
40	**2** Skills/Concepts	**MP.2** Reasoning
41–42	**2** Skills/Concepts	**MP.4** Modeling
43	**2** Skills/Concepts	**MP.2** Reasoning
44	**3** Strategic Thinking **H.O.T.**	**MP.7** Using Structure
45	**3** Strategic Thinking **H.O.T.**	**MP.3** Logic
46–47	**3** Strategic Thinking **H.O.T.**	**MP.7** Using Structure
48	**3** Strategic Thinking **H.O.T.**	**MP.3** Logic

Additional Resources

Differentiated Instruction includes:

• Leveled Practice worksheets

9.1 Independent Practice

COMMON CORE 6.EE.1

Personal Math Trainer

Online Assessment and Intervention

my.hrw.com

Write the missing exponent.

22. $100 = 10^{\boxed{2}}$

23. $8 = 2^{\boxed{3}}$

24. $25 = 5^{\boxed{2}}$

25. $27 = 3^{\boxed{3}}$

26. $\frac{1}{169} = \left(\frac{1}{13}\right)^{\boxed{2}}$

27. $14 = 14^{\boxed{1}}$

28. $32 = 2^{\boxed{5}}$

29. $\frac{64}{81} = \left(\frac{8}{9}\right)^{\boxed{2}}$

Write the missing base.

30. $1,000 = \boxed{10}^{3}$

31. $256 = \boxed{4}^{4}$

32. $16 = \boxed{2}^{4}$

33. $9 = \boxed{3}^{2}$

34. $\frac{1}{9} = \left(\boxed{\frac{1}{3}}\right)^{2}$

35. $64 = \boxed{8}^{2}$

36. $\frac{9}{16} = \left(\boxed{\frac{3}{4}}\right)^{2}$

37. $729 = \boxed{9}^{3}$

For Exercises 38–42, write the answer with and without using an exponent.

38. Hadley's softball team has a phone tree in case a game is canceled. The coach calls 3 players. Then each of those players calls 3 players, and so on. How many players will be notified during the third round of calls?

3^3 players, or 27 players

39. Tim is reading a book. On Monday he reads 3 pages. On each day after that, he reads 3 times the number of pages that he read on the previous day. How many pages does he read on Thursday?

3^4 pages, or 81 pages

40. The square tile shown has a side length of 10.5 inches. What power can you write to represent the area of the tile? Write the power as an expression with a base and an exponent, and then find the area of the square.

$10.5^2 = 10.5 \times 10.5 = 110.25$ in^2

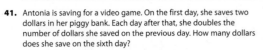

41. Antonia is saving for a video game. On the first day, she saves two dollars in her piggy bank. Each day after that, she doubles the number of dollars she saved on the previous day. How many dollars does she save on the sixth day?

2^6 dollars, or $64

42. A certain colony of bacteria triples in length every 10 minutes. Its length is now 1 millimeter. How long will it be in 40 minutes?

3^4 mm, or 81 mm

43. Which power can you write to represent the volume of the cube shown? Write the power as an expression with a base and an exponent, and then find the volume of the cube.

$\left(\frac{1}{3}\right)^3 = \frac{1}{3} \times \frac{1}{3} \times \frac{1}{3} = \frac{1}{27}$ in.^{3}

44. Write a power represented with a positive base and a positive exponent whose value is less than the base.

Sample answer: $0.3^2 = 0.09; 0.3 > 0.09$

$\frac{1}{3}$ in.

Work Area

H.O.T. FOCUS ON HIGHER ORDER THINKING

45. Communicate Mathematical Ideas What is the value of 1 raised to the power of any exponent? What is the value of 0 raised to the power of any nonnegative nonzero exponent? Explain.

The value of 1 raised to any power is 1. 1 multiplied by itself any number of times is 1. The value of 0 raised to any power is 0. 0 multiplied by itself any number of times is still 0.

46. Look for a Pattern Find the values of the powers in the following pattern: $10^1, 10^2, 10^3, 10^4$.... Describe the pattern, and use it to evaluate 10^6 without using multiplication.

Sample answer: 10; 100; 1,000; 10,000.... Each term in the pattern is a 1 followed by the same number of zeros as the exponent. $10^6 = 1,000,000$

47. Critical Thinking Some numbers can be written as powers of different bases. For example, $81 = 9^2$ and $81 = 3^4$. Write the number 64 using three different bases.

$2^6, 4^3$, and 8^2

48. Justify Reasoning Oman said that it is impossible to raise a number to the power of 2 and get a value less than the original number. Do you agree with Oman? Justify your reasoning.

Sample answer: Disagree; the product of a number between 0 and 1 and itself is less than the original number. For example, $\frac{1}{2} \times \frac{1}{2} = \frac{1}{4}$, and $\frac{1}{4} < \frac{1}{2}$.

EXTEND THE MATH PRE-AP

Activity available online my.hrw.com

Activity Every integer can be written as the sum of square numbers. For example:

Sum of 2 squares: $20 = 4^2 + 2^2$
Sum of 3 squares: $24 = 4^2 + 2^2 + 2^2$

Some integers, such as 22, can be written as the sum of square numbers more than one way.

Sum of 3 squares: $22 = 3^2 + 3^2 + 2^2$
Sum of 4 squares: $22 = 4^2 + 2^2 + 1^2 + 1^2$

- Write the integers 8, 13, and 18 as the sum of 2 squares. $8 = 2^2 + 2^2$; $13 = 3^2 + 2^2$; $18 = 3^2 + 3^2$

- Can you write the number 36 as the sum of squares in more than one way?
  Yes; $36 = 3^2 + 3^2 + 3^2 + 3^2 = 9 + 9 + 9 + 9$; $36 = 4^2 + 4^2 + 2^2 = 16 + 16 + 4$

- Write a number on one side of an index card and on the reverse write the number as a sum of squares. Challenge a classmate to write the number. For example:

Write 62 as the sum of 3 squares.	$1^2 + 5^2 + 6^2$

9.2 Prime Factorization

Common Core Standards

The student is expected to:

 Expressions and Equations—6.EE.1

Write and evaluate numerical expressions involving whole-number exponents.

Mathematical Practices

 MP.2 Reasoning

> **ADDITIONAL EXAMPLE 1**
> Rayshawn is designing a mural. The mural must have an area of 42 square yards. What are the possible whole number lengths and widths for the mural? The possible lengths and widths are listed:
>
> | Length (yd) | 42 | 21 | 14 | 7 |
> |---|---|---|---|---|
> | Width (yd) | 1 | 2 | 3 | 6 |
>
> **Interactive Whiteboard**
> *Interactive example available online*
>
> ⏻ my.hrw.com

> **Animated Math**
> **Prime Factorization**
>
> Students use an interactive factor tree to find prime factors of composite numbers.
>
> ⏻ my.hrw.com

Engage

ESSENTIAL QUESTION

How do you write the prime factorization of a number? Sample answer: Use a factor tree or a ladder diagram to find the prime factorization of the number, then write the prime factorization using exponents.

Explore

Motivate the Lesson

Ask students to name two numbers that can be multiplied to get a specific product. For example, you might ask them to name two numbers that can be multiplied to get 28 (1 and 28; 2 and 14; 4 and 7). Repeat the process using 36.

Explain

EXAMPLE 1

Focus on Reasoning **Mathematical Practices**

Point out to students that you can tell when you have found all the factors of a number when the factor pairs start to repeat.

Questioning Strategies **Mathematical Practices**

• For any number, which numbers are always factors? 1 and the number itself.

• Is it possible for a number to have all even factors? No; 1 is a factor for all numbers.

YOUR TURN

Avoid Common Errors

Remind students that when they list the factors of a number they should always begin with 1 and end with the number itself.

EXPLORE ACTIVITY 1

Connect Vocabulary **ELL**

Remind students that a **prime number** is a number with exactly 2 factors, 1 and itself, and a **composite number** is a number that has more than 2 factors.

Engage with the Whiteboard

Have students make alternate factor trees for 240 on the whiteboard, next to the given factor tree. Have students start with the following pairs: 8 and 30; 24 and 10; and 12 and 20. Point out to students that while the order of the factors in a factor tree may differ, the prime factors of a number are always the same.

Questioning Strategies **CC** Mathematical Practices

• When choosing the first factor pair for the branches of the factor tree for 240, does one of the factors have to be a prime number? Explain. No. A factor tree can start with any factor pair.

LESSON 9.2 Prime Factorization

COMMON CORE 6.EE.1
Write and evaluate numerical expressions involving whole-number exponents

? ESSENTIAL QUESTION

How do you write the prime factorization of a number?

Finding Factors of a Number

Whole numbers that are multiplied to find a product are called factors of that product. A number is divisible by its factors. For example, 4 and 2 are factors of 8 because $4 \cdot 2 = 8$, and 8 is divisible by 4 and by 2.

Math On the Spot
my.hrw.com

EXAMPLE 1 Real World

COMMON CORE Prep for 6.EE.1

Ana wants to build a rectangular garden with an area of 24 square feet. What are the possible whole number lengths and widths of the garden?

STEP 1 Recall that area = length · width. For Ana's garden, 24 ft² = length · width.

STEP 2 List the factors of 24 in pairs. List each pair only once.

$24 = 1 \cdot 24$
$24 = 2 \cdot 12$
$24 = 3 \cdot 8$
$24 = 4 \cdot 6$

$4 \cdot 6 = 6 \cdot 4$, so you only list $4 \cdot 6$.

You can also use a diagram to show the factor pairs.

1 2 3 4 6 8 12 24

The factors of 24 are 1, 2, 3, 4, 6, 8, 12, 24.

STEP 3 The possible lengths and widths are:

Length (ft)	24	12	8	6
Width (ft)	1	2	3	4

Math Talk
Mathematical Practices

Give an example of a whole number that has exactly two factors. What type of number has exactly two factors?

Sample answer: 13; its factors are 1 and 13; prime number

YOUR TURN

List all the factors of each number.

1. 21   1, 3, 7, 21
2. 37   1, 37
3. 42   1, 2, 3, 6, 7, 14, 21, 42
4. 30   1, 2, 3, 5, 6, 10, 15, 30

Personal Math Trainer
Online Assessment and Intervention
my.hrw.com

Lesson 9.2 **243**

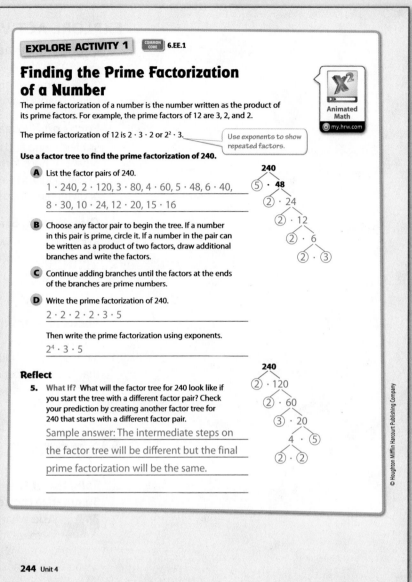

EXPLORE ACTIVITY 1

COMMON CORE 6.EE.1

Animated Math
my.hrw.com

Finding the Prime Factorization of a Number

The prime factorization of a number is the number written as the product of its prime factors. For example, the prime factors of 12 are 3, 2, and 2.

The prime factorization of 12 is $2 \cdot 3 \cdot 2$ or $2^2 \cdot 3$.

Use exponents to show repeated factors.

Use a factor tree to find the prime factorization of 240.

A List the factor pairs of 240.

$1 \cdot 240, 2 \cdot 120, 3 \cdot 80, 4 \cdot 60, 5 \cdot 48, 6 \cdot 40,$
$8 \cdot 30, 10 \cdot 24, 12 \cdot 20, 15 \cdot 16$

B Choose any factor pair to begin the tree. If a number in this pair is prime, circle it. If a number in the pair can be written as a product of two factors, draw additional branches and write the factors.

C Continue adding branches until the factors at the ends of the branches are prime numbers.

D Write the prime factorization of 240.

$2 \cdot 2 \cdot 2 \cdot 2 \cdot 3 \cdot 5$

Then write the prime factorization using exponents.

$2^4 \cdot 3 \cdot 5$

Reflect

5. **What If?** What will the factor tree for 240 look like if you start the tree with a different factor pair? Check your prediction by creating another factor tree for 240 that starts with a different factor pair.

Sample answer: The intermediate steps on the factor tree will be different but the final prime factorization will be the same.

244 Unit 4

PROFESSIONAL DEVELOPMENT

CC Integrate Mathematical Practices MP.2

This lesson provides an opportunity to address this Mathematical Practice standard. It calls for students to create and use representations to organize, record, and communicate mathematical ideas. Students use diagrams and factor trees to organize factor pairs of a number to find prime factorizations. They also use ladder diagrams to find prime factorizations, with the "ladder" as the means of recording and communicating the prime factorization.

Math Background

Ancient Greeks started to study prime numbers circa 300 B.C.E. They observed that there were an infinite number of prime numbers and that there were irregular gaps between successive prime numbers.

In 1984, Samuel Yates coined the term *titanic prime*. He used this term to refer to any prime number with 1,000 digits or more. When he first defined a titanic prime, only 110 of them were known. Today more than 110,000 titanic primes have been identified.

EXPLORE ACTIVITY 2

Engage with the Whiteboard

Have students complete the ladder diagram starting with different combinations of prime factors. Point out to students that while the order in which they used the prime factors may differ, the prime factors of a number are always the same.

Focus on Modeling [CC] Mathematical Practices

Students who find mental math difficult may find ladder diagrams to be challenging. Model other methods for dividing by 2, such as using long division or a calculator, to show that the ladder diagram is a useful organizational tool. Emphasize that they can use a combination of division methods when using ladder diagrams.

Questioning Strategies [CC] Mathematical Practices

• How do you know when 2 is a factor of a number? How do you know when 2 is *not* a factor of a number? Even numbers have 2 as a factor. Odd numbers do not.

• Why do you have to divide by prime numbers when using the ladder diagram? The divisors on the left show the prime factorization, so all of them must be prime numbers.

Focus on Communication [CC] Mathematical Practices

Discuss with students ways to check that $2 \cdot 3 \cdot 3 \cdot 3$ is the prime factorization of 54. Students should understand that they can check their work two ways: by making sure that every number in the prime factorization is prime and by multiplying the expression $2 \cdot 3 \cdot 3 \cdot 3$ to verify that the product is 54.

Elaborate

Talk About It
Summarize the Lesson

Ask: What is the prime factorization of a number, and how can you find the prime factorization of a number? The prime factorization of a number is an expression that shows the number as the product of its prime factors. You can use a factor tree or a ladder diagram to find the prime factorization of a number.

GUIDED PRACTICE

Engage with the Whiteboard

For Exercises 1–2, have students draw a diagram to list the factors of each number on the whiteboard.

For Exercise 5, have students make several different factor trees on the whiteboard.

Avoid Common Errors

Exercise 3 Remind students that you can tell when you have found all the factors of a number when the factor pairs start to repeat and that writing factor pairs in order makes it easier to check that all the factor pairs are listed.

Exercises 4–7 Remind students that they can check their work by multiplying their answer for the prime factorization to make sure the product is the original number.

EXPLORE ACTIVITY 2 — COMMON CORE 6.EE.1

Using a Ladder Diagram

A ladder diagram is another way to find the prime factorization of a number.

Use a ladder diagram to find the prime factorization of 132.

A Write 132 in the top "step" of the ladder. Choose a prime factor of 132 to write next to the step with 132. Choose 2. Divide 132 by 2 and write the quotient 66 in the next step of the ladder.

B Now choose a prime factor of 66. Write the prime factor next to the step with 66. Divide 66 by that prime factor and write the quotient in the next step of the ladder.

C Keep choosing prime factors, dividing, and adding to the ladder until you get a quotient of 1.

D What are the prime factors of 132? How can you tell from the ladder diagram?

The prime factors are 2, 2, 3, and 11. They are written to the left of the steps of the ladder.

E Write the prime factorization of 132 using exponents.

$2^2 \cdot 3 \cdot 11$

Reflect

6. Complete a factor tree and a ladder diagram to find the prime factorization of 54.

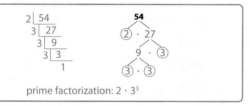

prime factorization: $2 \cdot 3^3$

7. **Communicate Mathematical Ideas** If one person uses a ladder diagram and another uses a factor tree to write a prime factorization, will they get the same result? Explain.

Yes; there is only one unique prime factorization for every integer greater than 1.

Guided Practice

Use a diagram to list the factor pairs of each number. (Example 1)

1. 18   1   2   3   6   9   18

1, 2, 3, 6, 9, 18

2. 52   1   2   4   13   26   52

1, 2, 4, 13, 26, 52

3. Karl needs to build a stage that has an area of 72 square feet. The length of the stage should be longer than the width. What are the possible whole number measurements for the length and width of the stage? (Example 1)

Complete the table with possible measurements of the stage.

Length	72	36	24	18	12	9
Width	1	2	3	4	6	8

Use a factor tree to find the prime factorization of each number. (Explore Activity 1)

4. 402

$2 \cdot 3 \cdot 67$

5. 36

$2^2 \cdot 3^2$

Use a ladder diagram to find the prime factorization of each number. (Explore Activity 2)

6. 64   2 | 64
　　　　　2 | 32
　　　　　2 | 16
　　　　　2 | 8
　　　　　2 | 4
　　　　　2 | 2
　　　　　　 1

2^6

7. 27   3 | 27
　　　　　3 | 9
　　　　　3 | 3
　　　　　　 1

$3 \cdot 3 \cdot 3$ or 3^3

? ESSENTIAL QUESTION CHECK-IN

8. Tell how you know when you have found the prime factorization of a number.

Sample answer: when all the factors are prime and their product is the original number

---

DIFFERENTIATE INSTRUCTION

Kinesthetic Experience

Students can use a method called the sieve of Eratosthenes to help identify prime numbers. Start with a 10 × 10 grid showing the numbers 1 to 100. Cross out 1, because 1 is not a prime number. Circle 2 because it is prime. Then cross out all multiples of 2, because multiples of 2 are not prime. Circle the next prime number, 3, and cross out all multiples of 3. Repeat the process until all numbers are circled or crossed out. Students can refer to this chart when deciding whether a number is prime or composite.

Critical Thinking

Discuss with students how the prime factorization of a number can be used to find all the factors of a number, by using the Associative and Commutative properties. For example, the prime factorization of 30 is $2 \cdot 3 \cdot 5$, which can be expressed as $2 \cdot (3 \cdot 5)$, $(2 \cdot 3) \cdot 5$, or $(2 \cdot 5) \cdot 3$.

When you multiply the numbers inside the parentheses, the expressions simplify to $2 \cdot (15)$, $(6) \cdot 5$, and $(10) \cdot 3$.

These numbers along with the factor pair $1 \cdot 30$, give all the factors for 30: 1, 2, 3, 5, 6, 10, 15, 30.

Additional Resources

Differentiated Instruction includes:

• Reading Strategies

• Success for English Learners **ELL**

• Reteach

• Challenge **PRE-AP**

9.2 LESSON QUIZ

COMMON CORE **6.EE.1**

1. Find all the factors of 54.

2. Find the prime factorization of 54, and then write it using exponents.

3. Find all the factors of 60.

4. Find the prime factorization of 60, and then write it using exponents.

5. Chanasia has 30 beads. She wants to put them in boxes, so that each box will contain the same whole number of beads. Use factors to list all the different ways she can put the beads into boxes.

Lesson Quiz available online

 my.hrw.com

Answers

1. 1, 2, 3, 6, 9, 18, 27, 54

2. $2 \times 3 \times 3 \times 3 = 2 \cdot 3^3$

3. 1, 2, 3, 4, 5, 6, 10, 12, 15, 20, 30, 60

4. $2 \times 2 \times 3 \times 5 = 2^2 \cdot 3 \cdot 5$

5. 1 box with 30 beads
2 boxes with 15 beads each
3 boxes with 10 beads each
5 boxes with 6 beads each
6 boxes with 5 beads each
10 boxes with 3 beads each
15 boxes with 2 beads each
30 boxes with 1 bead each

Evaluate

GUIDED AND INDEPENDENT PRACTICE

 6.EE.1

Concepts & Skills	Practice
Example 1 Finding Factors of a Number	Exercises 1–3, 9–10
Explore Activity 1 Finding the Prime Factorization of a Number	Exercises 4–5, 12–15, 17–19
Explore Activity 2 Using a Ladder Diagram	Exercises 6–7, 16

Exercise	Depth of Knowledge (D.O.K.)	COMMON CORE Mathematical Practices
9	**2** Skills/Concepts	**MP.4** Modeling
10	**2** Skills/Concepts	**MP.4** Modeling
11	**3** Strategic Thinking H.O.T.	**MP.3** Logic
12–15	**2** Skills/Concepts	**MP.5** Using Tools
16	**3** Strategic Thinking H.O.T.	**MP.6** Precision
17	**3** Strategic Thinking H.O.T.	**MP.5** Using Tools
18	**3** Strategic Thinking H.O.T.	**MP.6** Precision
19	**3** Strategic Thinking H.O.T.	**MP.7** Using Structure
20	**3** Strategic Thinking H.O.T.	**MP.3** Logic
21–22	**3** Strategic Thinking H.O.T.	**MP.7** Using Structure

Additional Resources

Differentiated Instruction includes:

• Leveled Practice Worksheets

9.2 Independent Practice

COMMON CORE 6.EE.1

Personal Math Trainer

Online Assessment and Intervention

my.hrw.com

9. **Multiple Representations** Use the grid to draw three different rectangles so that each has an area of 12 square units and they all have different widths. What are the dimensions of the rectangles?

$1 \times 12; 2 \times 6; 3 \times 4$

10. Brandon has 32 stamps. He wants to display the stamps in rows, with the same number of stamps in each row. How many different ways can he display the stamps? Explain.

6 different ways; 1 row of 32 stamps; 2 rows of 16; 4 rows of 8; 32 rows of 1; 16 rows of 2; 8 rows of 4

11. **Communicate Mathematical Ideas** How is finding the factors of a number different from finding the prime factorization of a number?

When you find the factors of a number, you find all factors, some of which are prime; when you find the prime factorization, you find only the prime factors.

Find the prime factorization of each number.

12. 891 ___$3^4 \cdot 11$___   **13.** 504 ___$2^3 \cdot 3^2 \cdot 7$___

14. 23 ___23___   **15.** 230 ___$2 \cdot 5 \cdot 23$___

16. The number 2 is chosen to begin a ladder diagram to find the prime factorization of 66. What other numbers could have been used to start the ladder diagram for 66? How does starting with a different number change the diagram?

3 and 11 can be chosen because they are prime factors. The intermediate steps would be different, but the prime factorization is the same.

17. **Critical Thinking** List five numbers that have 3, 5, and 7 as prime factors.

Sample answer: 105, 315, 525, 735, 945

18. In a game, you draw a card with three consecutive numbers on it. You can choose one of the numbers and find the sum of its prime factors. Then you can move that many spaces. You draw a card with the numbers 25, 26, 27. Which number should you choose if you want to move as many spaces as possible? Explain.

26; the prime factors of 25 are 5 and 5, the prime factors of 26 are 2 and 13, and the prime factors of 27 are 3, 3, and 3. The sums are 10, 15, and 9. The greatest sum is 15, so choose 26 to move 15 spaces.

19. **Explain the Error** When asked to write the prime factorization of the number 27, a student wrote $9 \cdot 3$. Explain the error and write the correct answer.

9 is not a prime number; prime factorization of $27 = 3^3$.

H.O.T. FOCUS ON HIGHER ORDER THINKING

20. **Communicate Mathematical Ideas** Explain why it is possible to draw more than two different rectangles with an area of 36 square units, but it is not possible to draw more than two different rectangles with an area of 15 square units. The sides of the rectangles are whole numbers.

36 has five factor pairs, so five different rectangles can be drawn. 15 has only two factor pairs, so only two different rectangles can be drawn.

21. **Critique Reasoning** Alice wants to find all the prime factors of the number you get when you multiply $17 \cdot 11 \cdot 13 \cdot 7$. She thinks she has to use a calculator to perform all the multiplications and then find the prime factorization of the resulting number. Do you agree? Why or why not?

Disagree; the factors that are being multiplied are all prime numbers, so the prime factorization of the number is $17 \cdot 13 \cdot 11 \cdot 7$.

22. **Look for a Pattern** Ryan wrote the prime factorizations shown below. If he continues this pattern, what prime factorization will he show for the number one million? What prime factorization will he show for one billion?

$10 = 5 \cdot 2$

$100 = 5^2 \cdot 2^2$

$1,000 = 5^3 \cdot 2^3 = 1,000$

one million: $5^6 \cdot 2^6$; one billion: $5^9 \cdot 2^9$

Work Area

EXTEND THE MATH (PRE-AP)

Activity available online my.hrw.com

Activity In mathematics, a **perfect number** is a number that is equal to the sum of all its factors (excluding the number itself).

The number 6 is an example of a perfect number. The factors of 6 are 1, 2, 3, and 6. The sum of the factors excluding 6 is $1 + 2 + 3 = 6$.

- Find the next largest perfect number, and show why it is perfect.
  28; the factors of 28 are 1, 2, 4, 7, 14, and 28, and $1 + 2 + 4 + 7 + 14 = 28$.

- A student claims that 128 is a perfect number. Prove or disprove the student's claim.
  False; The factors of 128 are 1, 2, 4, 8, 16, 32, 64, and 128. Their sum, excluding the number itself, is 127.

- Another student says that 496 is a perfect number. Prove or disprove the student's claim. True; The factors of 496 are 1, 2, 4, 8, 16, 31, 62, 124, 248, and 496. Their sum, excluding the number itself, is 496.

Common Core Standards

The student is expected to:

 Expressions and Equations—6.EE.1

Write and evaluate numerical expressions involving whole-number exponents.

Mathematical Practices

 MP.5 Using Tools

Engage

ESSENTIAL QUESTION

How do you use the order of operations to simplify expressions with exponents? Sample answer: Find the value of any expressions within parentheses first. Then evaluate all powers. Then multiply or divide in order from left to right, and finally, add or subtract in order from left to right.

Motivate the Lesson

Ask: Have you ever tried to simplify an expression such as $35 + 20(12^2 \div 9)$? Try it. Need help? Begin the Explore Activity to find out how to use the order of operations.

Explore

EXPLORE ACTIVITY

Engage with the Whiteboard

 Write the expression $2 + 3 \times 4$ on the whiteboard. Point out to students that this expression could have two different results (14 or 20) without guidelines to show which operation should be performed first. Show students that the correct solution is 14 based on the fact that $3 \times 4 = 4 + 4 + 4$. Thus the expression $2 + 3 \times 4$ can be written as $2 + 4 + 4 + 4$, which equals 14. Now write the expressions $36 - 18 \div 6$ and $7 + 24 \div 6 \times 2$ on the whiteboard and ask the students to solve them. After a few minutes, have students come up to the whiteboard and solve the equations, showing all the steps. Discuss the solutions with the class. Answers: 33 and 15

Explain

EXAMPLE 1

Avoid Common Errors

Students may find it easier to perform operations from left to right as they appear in an expression, rather than use the order of operations. Remind students that using the order of operations correctly ensures that everyone who simplifies the same expression will get the same answer.

Questioning Strategies CC Mathematical Practices

• Can you use the order of operations with expressions that have no parentheses? Explain. Yes. The order of operations tells the order in which operations should be performed but does not require that an expression include parentheses, exponents, or all the operations.

• Are the expressions $3 + 5 \cdot 2$ and $3 + (5 \cdot 2)$ equivalent? Explain. Yes. In both expressions $5 \cdot 2$ should be evaluated first, and then 3 should be added to the product.

YOUR TURN

Talk About It
Check for Understanding

 Ask: In the expression $220 - 450 \div 3^2$, which operation should you perform first? Explain. Evaluate the power. This expression has no parentheses so the first operation to perform is to evaluate the powers.

ADDITIONAL EXAMPLE 1
Simplify each expression.

A $30 - 3 \times 2^3$ 6

B $128 \div (4 \times 2)^2$ 2

C $40 - \dfrac{32}{(7 - 5)^3}$ 36

Interactive Whiteboard
Interactive example available online

⏻ my.hrw.com

9.3 Order of Operations

COMMON CORE 6.EE.1
Write and evaluate … expressions involving whole-number exponents.

❓ ESSENTIAL QUESTION
How do you use the order of operations to simplify expressions with exponents?

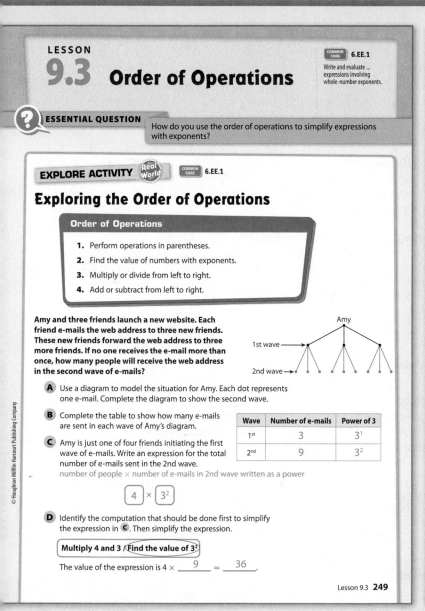

EXPLORE ACTIVITY *Real World*   **COMMON CORE** 6.EE.1

Exploring the Order of Operations

Order of Operations

1. Perform operations in parentheses.
2. Find the value of numbers with exponents.
3. Multiply or divide from left to right.
4. Add or subtract from left to right.

Amy and three friends launch a new website. Each friend e-mails the web address to three new friends. These new friends forward the web address to three more friends. If no one receives the e-mail more than once, how many people will receive the web address in the second wave of e-mails?

A Use a diagram to model the situation for Amy. Each dot represents one e-mail. Complete the diagram to show the second wave.

B Complete the table to show how many e-mails are sent in each wave of Amy's diagram.

Wave	Number of e-mails	Power of 3
1st	3	3^1
2nd	9	3^2

C Amy is just one of four friends initiating the first wave of e-mails. Write an expression for the total number of e-mails sent in the 2nd wave.

number of people × number of e-mails in 2nd wave written as a power

$$\boxed{4} \times \boxed{3^2}$$

D Identify the computation that should be done first to simplify the expression in **C**. Then simplify the expression.

$\boxed{\text{Multiply 4 and 3} / \text{Find the value of } 3^2}$

The value of the expression is $4 \times \underline{\quad 9 \quad} = \underline{\quad 36 \quad}$.

Lesson 9.3 **249**

Reflect

1. In **B**, why does it makes sense to write the numbers of e-mails as powers? What is the pattern for the number of e-mails in each wave for Amy?

   Sample answer: By writing the values as powers, you can see the exponent is equal to the wave number. The pattern would be 3^1, 3^2, 3^3, 3^4, and so on.

Math On the Spot my.hrw.com

Simplifying Numerical Expressions

A numerical expression is an expression involving numbers and operations. You can use the order of operations to simplify numerical expressions.

EXAMPLE 1   **COMMON CORE** 6.EE.1

Simplify each expression.

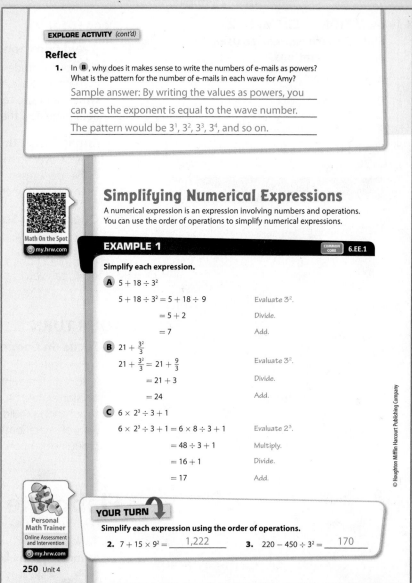

A $5 + 18 \div 3^2$

$5 + 18 \div 3^2 = 5 + 18 \div 9$	Evaluate 3^2.
$= 5 + 2$	Divide.
$= 7$	Add.

B $21 + \dfrac{3^2}{3}$

$21 + \dfrac{3^2}{3} = 21 + \dfrac{9}{3}$	Evaluate 3^2.
$= 21 + 3$	Divide.
$= 24$	Add.

C $6 \times 2^3 \div 3 + 1$

$6 \times 2^3 \div 3 + 1 = 6 \times 8 \div 3 + 1$	Evaluate 2^3.
$= 48 \div 3 + 1$	Multiply.
$= 16 + 1$	Divide.
$= 17$	Add.

Personal Math Trainer
Online Assessment and Intervention
my.hrw.com

YOUR TURN

Simplify each expression using the order of operations.

2. $7 + 15 \times 9^2 = \underline{\quad 1{,}222 \quad}$

3. $220 - 450 \div 3^2 = \underline{\quad 170 \quad}$

250 Unit 4

PROFESSIONAL DEVELOPMENT

CC Integrate Mathematical Practices MP.5

This lesson provides an opportunity to address the Mathematical Practices standard that calls for students to use appropriate tools strategically. Students work with pencil and paper using the order of operations to simplify expressions. Since use of the order of operations can involve many steps, students use mental math and number sense in situations such as finding the sum of two numbers with unlike signs and raising a negative number to a positive power.

Math Background

A History of Mathematical Notations by Florian Cajori describes the history of various mathematical symbols. According to Cajori, parentheses and brackets have been used as grouping symbols since the sixteenth century. A work published in 1556, *General trattato di numeri e misure* by Niccolò Tartaglia, is one of the first works in which parentheses are used. Brackets have been found in a manuscript edition of *Algebra,* by Rafael Bombelli which dates back to 1550.

EXAMPLE 2

Avoid Common Errors

Point out to students that some symbols have more than one purpose. Parentheses can indicate multiplication and/or act as grouping symbols. The fraction bar is a grouping symbol and also can indicate division. Remind students to read expressions carefully to determine how the symbols are being used.

Engage with the Whiteboard

 Cover up the blue text in each part and have students circle the operation to be performed for each step on the whiteboard. Ask students to explain their choices. Then discuss the choices with the class.

Questioning Strategies   CC   Mathematical Practices

- In A, what operation would you perform first if there were no parenthetical groupings? You would evaluate the power first.

- In C, can you evaluate the expression $\frac{4^2}{2}$ the same as 2^2? No. You cannot simplify the fraction before you have evaluated 4^2.

YOUR TURN

Focus on Communication

Some students may think that all multiplication is done before division and all addition is done before subtraction. Remind them that this is not the case. Multiplication and division should be done from left to right as ordered in the problem. Similarly, addition and subtraction should be done from left to right as ordered in the problem. Stress that these pairs of operations should be performed in the order they occur unless they are within grouping symbols.

Elaborate

· ·

Talk About It
Summarize the Lesson

💬 **Ask:** Why is it important to use the order of operations? The order of operations is important because correctly using the order or operations ensures that everyone who simplifies the same expression will get the same answer.

GUIDED PRACTICE

Engage with the Whiteboard

 For Exercise 1, have students complete the diagram on the whiteboard. Then have them number the branches at each level to show the numbers of each type of fish that can be formed.

Avoid Common Errors

Exercises 2–3 Remind students that when they work with an expression that has both multiplication and division, they should perform the operation that occurs first in the equation from left to right.

Exercises 4–5 Remind students that when an expression inside parentheses has more than one operation, they need to perform those operations according to the order of operations.

Using Exponents with Grouping Symbols

Remember to perform operations inside parentheses first when you simplify expressions.

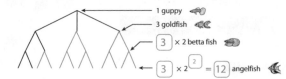

Math On the Spot
my.hrw.com

EXAMPLE 2 COMMON CORE 6.EE.1

Simplify each expression using the order of operations.

A $4 \times (9 \div 3)^2$

$4 \times (9 \div 3)^2 = 4 \times 3^2$	Perform operations inside parentheses.
$= 4 \times 9$	Evaluate 3^2.
$= 36$	Multiply.

B $5^3 + (12 - 2)^2$

$5^3 + (12 - 2)^2 = 5^3 + 10^2$	Perform operations inside parentheses.
$= 125 + 100$	Evaluate powers.
$= 325$	Add.

C $8 + \frac{(12 - 8)^2}{2}$

$8 + \frac{(12 - 8)^2}{2} = 8 + \frac{4^2}{2}$	Perform operations inside parentheses.
$= 8 + \frac{16}{2}$	Evaluate 4^2.
$= 8 + 8$	Divide.
$= 16$	Add.

Reflect

4. **Critique Reasoning** John wants to simplify the expression $(5 + 3)^2$. As a first step, he writes $5^2 + 3^2$. Will he get the correct value for the expression? If not, what should he do to simplify the expression?

No; $5^2 + 3^2 = 25 + 9 = 36$, which is incorrect. John

needs to follow the order of operations and first add

inside the parentheses: $(5 + 3)^2 = 8^2 = 64$.

YOUR TURN

Simplify each expression using the order of operations.

5. $5 \times (20 \div 4)^2 = $ _____ 125

6. $8^2 - (5 + 2)^2 = $ _____ 15

7. $7 - \frac{(63 \div 9)^2}{7} = $ _____ 0

Personal Math Trainer
Online Assessment and Intervention
my.hrw.com

---

1. In a video game, a guppy that escapes a net turns into three goldfish. Each goldfish can turn into two betta fish. Each betta fish can turn into two angelfish. Complete the diagram and write the number of fish at each stage. Write and evaluate an expression for the number of angelfish that can be formed from one guppy. (Explore Activity)

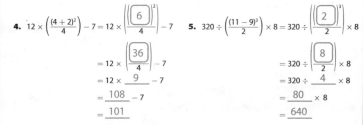

1 guppy
3 goldfish
3 × 2 betta fish
3 × 2² = 12 angelfish

$3 \times 2^2 = 12$ angelfish

Complete to simplify each expression. (Examples 1 and 2)

2. $89 - 4^2 \times 4 + 12 = 89 - \underline{16} \times 4 + 12$

$= 89 - \underline{64} + 12$

$= \underline{25} + 12$

$= \underline{37}$

3. $6 \times (36 \div 12)^2 + 8 = 6 \times (\underline{3})^2 + 8$

$= 6 \times \underline{9} + 8$

$= \underline{54} + 8$

$= \underline{62}$

4. $12 \times \left(\frac{(4 + 2)^2}{4}\right) - 7 = 12 \times \left(\frac{\boxed{6}^2}{4}\right) - 7$

$= 12 \times \left(\frac{\boxed{36}}{4}\right) - 7$

$= 12 \times \underline{9} - 7$

$= \underline{108} - 7$

$= \underline{101}$

5. $320 \div \left(\frac{(11 - 9)^3}{2}\right) \times 8 = 320 \div \left(\frac{\boxed{2}^3}{2}\right) \times 8$

$= 320 \div \left(\frac{\boxed{8}}{2}\right) \times 8$

$= 320 \div \underline{4} \times 8$

$= \underline{80} \times 8$

$= \underline{640}$

? ESSENTIAL QUESTION CHECK-IN

6. How do you use the order of operations to simplify expressions with exponents?

Find the value of any expressions within parentheses first.

Then evaluate all powers. Then multiply or divide from

left to right, and finally add or subtract from left to right.

DIFFERENTIATE INSTRUCTION

Cooperative Learning

Have students work in groups to decide which operation signs to use to make the number sentences true. They may need to use operations more than once in each number sentence.

1. Operation signs: $+, -, \cdot$

$12 \square 4 \square 6 \square 3 \square 7 = 37$

$12 \cdot 4 - 6 \cdot 3 + 7 = 37$

2. Operation signs: $+, -, \div$

$18 \square 2 \square 24 \square 12 \square 4 = 22$

$18 + 2 - 24 \div 12 + 4 = 22$

Cognitive Strategies

Students may be familiar with the abbreviation PEMDAS (or **P**lease **E**xcuse **M**y **D**ear **A**unt **S**ally) even before being introduced to the order of operations. But its abbreviation may give the impression that multiplication is always done before division and that addition is always done before subtraction. You may wish to present the mnemonic as P E M/D A/S

The slashes between the M and the D, and the A and the S, can help students remember that from left to right either operation can be performed first.

Additional Resources

Differentiated Instruction includes:

- Reading Strategies
- Success for English Learners **ELL**
- Reteach
- Challenge **PRE-AP**

Order of Operations **252**

Personal Math Trainer

Online Assessment and Intervention

Online homework assignment available

 my.hrw.com

9.3 LESSON QUIZ

COMMON CORE 6.EE.1

Simplify each expression using the order of operations.

1. $3 + (7 - 5)^2 \times 6$

2. $\frac{2^5}{(4 + 4)} \times 2$

3. $8 - 6 \div 2 + 3 \times 5$

4. $7 \times 3 - 15 \div 5$

5. $8 + 2(1 + 12 \div 2)^2$

Lesson Quiz available online

 my.hrw.com

Answers

1. 27

2. 8

3. 20

4. 18

5. 57

Evaluate

GUIDED AND INDEPENDENT PRACTICE

 6.EE.1

Concepts & Skills	Practice
Explore Activity Using the Order of Operations	Exercise 1
Example 1 Simplifying Numerical Expressions	Exercises 2–3, 7–12, 13–16
Example 2 Using Exponents with Grouping Symbols	Exercises 2, 4–6, 9

Exercise	Depth of Knowledge (D.O.K.)	COMMON CORE Mathematical Practices
7–12	**2** Skills/Concepts	**MP.5** Using Tools
13	**3** Strategic Thinking **H.O.T.**	**MP.7** Using Structure
14	**3** Strategic Thinking **H.O.T.**	**MP.3** Logic
15–16	**2** Skills/Concepts	**MP.4** Modeling
17–19	**3** Strategic Thinking **H.O.T.**	**MP.7** Using Structure

Additional Resources

Differentiated Instruction includes:

• Leveled Practice worksheets

 Exercise 17 combines concepts from the Common Core cluster "Apply and extend previous understandings of arithmetic to algebraic expressions."

9.3 Independent Practice

COMMON CORE 6.EE.1

Personal Math Trainer
Online Assessment and Intervention
my.hrw.com

Simplify each expression using the order of operations.

7. $5 \times 2 + 3^2$ _____19_____

8. $15 - 7 \times 2 + 2^3$ _____9_____

9. $(11 - 8)^3 - 2 \times 6$ _____15_____

10. $6 + 3(13 - 2) - 5^2$ _____14_____

11. $12 + \frac{9^2}{3}$ _____39_____

12. $\frac{8 + 6^2}{11} + 7 \times 2$ _____18_____

13. **Explain the Error** Jay simplified the expression $3 \times (3 + 12 \div 3) - 4$. For his first step, he added $3 + 12$ to get 15. What was Jay's error? Find the correct answer.

Jay worked inside the parentheses first, but he should have performed the division $12 \div 3 = 4$ first; 17.

14. **Multistep** A clothing store has the sign shown in the shop window. Pani sees the sign and wants to buy 3 shirts and 2 pairs of jeans. The cost of each shirt before the discount is $12, and the cost of each pair of jeans is $19 before the discount.

SALE Today ONLY
$3 off every purchase!

a. Write and simplify an expression to find the amount Pani pays if a $3 discount is applied to her total.

$3 \times 12 + 2 \times 19 - 3$; $71

b. Pani says she should get a $3 discount on the price of each shirt and a $3 discount on the price of each pair of jeans. Write and simplify an expression to find the amount she would pay if this is true.

$3 \times (12 - 3) + 2 \times (19 - 3)$; $59

c. **Analyze Relationships** Why are the amounts Pani pays in **a** and **b** different?

In **a**, the $3 discount is applied 1 time; in **b** it is applied 5 times.

d. If you were the shop owner, how would you change the sign? Explain.

Sample answer: If the shop owner wants to make more money, the sign should say "$3 off your entire purchase." If customers can take the discount off every item, a lot more money is discounted from each purchase.

---

15. Ellen is playing a video game in which she captures butterflies. There are 3 butterflies onscreen, but the number of butterflies doubles every minute. After 4 minutes, she was able to capture 7 of the butterflies.

a. **Look for a Pattern** Write an expression for the number of butterflies after 4 minutes. Use a power of 2 in your answer.

$3 \times 2 \times 2 \times 2 \times 2 = 3 \times 2^4$

b. Write an expression for the number of butterflies remaining after Ellen captured the 7 butterflies. Simplify the expression.

$3 \times 2^4 - 7 = 3 \times 16 - 7 = 48 - 7 = 41$; 41 butterflies remain.

16. Show how to write, evaluate and simplify an expression to represent and solve this problem: Jeff and his friend each text four classmates about a concert. Each classmate then texts four students from another school about the concert. If no one receives the message more than once, how many students from the other school receive a text about the concert?

$2 \times 4^2 = 32$; 32 students receive a text.

H.O.T. FOCUS ON HIGHER ORDER THINKING

Work Area

17. **Geometry** The figure shown is a rectangle. The green shape in the figure is a square. The blue and white shapes are rectangles, and the area of the blue rectangle is 24 square inches.

2 in.
6 in.

a. Write an expression for the area of the entire figure that includes an exponent. Then find the area.

$6^2 + 2 \times 6 + 24 = 72$ square inches

b. Find the dimensions of the entire figure.

8 in. by 9 in.

18. **Explain the Error** Rob and Lila try to simplify $18 \times 4^2 + (9 - 3)^2$. Rob simplifies the expression and gets 360. Lila simplifies it and gets 324. Which student is correct? What error did the other student make?

Lila is correct. Rob squared each of the numbers in the parentheses and then subtracted, instead of subtracting first and then squaring the difference.

19. **Persevere in Problem Solving** Use parentheses to make this statement true: $8 \times 4 - 2 \times 3 + 8 \div 2 = 25$

$8 \times 4 - (2 \times 3 + 8) \div 2$

EXTEND THE MATH PRE-AP

Activity available online my.hrw.com

Activity The expression $(4 \times 4 - 4) \times 4$ uses exactly 4 fours. When simplified, its value is 48.

- Write 10 expressions that use exactly 4 fours and that equal one of the numbers 0 to 9. Use what you know about the order of operations to write the expressions. You can use addition, subtraction, multiplication, division, parentheses, and exponents in the expressions.

- Justify the expressions you have written by showing how to simplify them.

Possible answers:

$4 + 4 - 4 - 4 = 0$ $\qquad$ $(4 + 4) \div (4 + 4) = 1$

$4 \div 4 + 4 \div 4 = 2$ $\qquad$ $(4 + 4 + 4) \div 4 = 3$

$4 - (4 - 4) \times 4 = 4$ $\qquad$ $\left(\frac{4}{4}\right)^4 + 4 = 5$

$4 + \frac{(4 + 4)}{4} = 6$ $\qquad$ $4 + 4 - \left(\frac{4}{4}\right) = 7$

$\frac{(4 \times 4)}{4} + 4 = 8$ $\qquad$ $4 + 4 + \left(\frac{4}{4}\right) = 9$

Ready to Go On?

Assess Mastery

Use the assessment on this page to determine if students have mastered the concepts and standards covered in this module.

RtI — **Response to Intervention**

Intervention	Enrichment

Access Ready to Go On? assessment online, and receive instant scoring, feedback, and customized intervention or enrichment.

Personal Math Trainer
Online Assessment and Intervention
my.hrw.com

Online and Print Resources

Differentiated Instruction
- Reteach worksheets
- Reading Strategies **ELL**
- Success for English Learners **ELL**

Differentiated Instruction
- Challenge worksheets **PRE-AP**
- Extend the Math **PRE-AP** Lesson Activities in TE

Additional Resources

Assessment Resources includes:
- Leveled Module Quizzes

Ready to Go On?

Personal Math Trainer
Online Assessment and Intervention
my.hrw.com

9.1 Exponents

Find the value of each power.

1. 7^3 ___343___   2. 9^2 ___81___   3. $\left(\frac{7}{9}\right)^2$ ___$\frac{49}{81}$___   4. $\left(\frac{1}{2}\right)^6$ ___$\frac{1}{64}$___

5. $\left(\frac{2}{3}\right)^3$ ___$\frac{8}{27}$___   6. $\left(\frac{1}{3}\right)^4$ ___$\frac{1}{81}$___   7. 12^0 ___1___   8. 1.4^2 ___1.96___

9.2 Prime Factorization

Find the factors of each number.

9. 96 ___1, 2, 3, 4, 6, 8, 12, 16, 24, 32, 48, 96___

10. 120 ___1, 2, 3, 4, 5, 6, 8, 10, 12, 15, 20, 24, 30, 40, 60, 120___

Find the prime factorization of each number.

11. 58 ___2×29___   12. 212 ___$2^2 \times 53$___

13. 2,800 ___$2^4 \times 5^2 \times 7$___   14. 900 ___$2^2 \times 3^2 \times 5^2$___

9.3 Order of Operations

Simplify each expression using the order of operations.

15. $(21 - 3) \div 3^2$ ___2___   16. $7^2 \times (6 \div 3)$ ___98___

17. $17 + 15 \div 3 - 2^4$ ___6___   18. $(8 + 56) \div 4 - 3^2$ ___7___

19. The nature park has a pride of 7 adult lions and 4 cubs. The adults eat 6 pounds of meat each day and the cubs eat 3 pounds. Simplify $7 \times 6 + 4 \times 3$ to find the amount of meat consumed each day by the lions. ___54 pounds___

 **ESSENTIAL QUESTION**

20. How do you use numerical expressions to solve real-world problems?
Write an expression to model the situation. Simplify the expression using the order of operations. First perform operations in parentheses, then find the value of each power, multiply or divide from left to right, and finally add or subtract from left to right.

Common Core Standards

Lesson	Exercises	Common Core Standards
9.1	1–8	**6.EE.1**
9.2	9–14	**6.EE.1**
9.3	15–19	**6.EE.1**

Assessment Readiness

Assessment Readiness Tip Students can use logic to eliminate some or all of the answer choices.

Item 5 Students can eliminate choices B, C, and D because they all have numbers that are not prime in the product expression. This leaves choice A as the correct answer.

Item 8 Students can eliminate choices A and B because they have numbers that are not prime in the product expression.

Avoid Common Errors

Item 3 Students sometimes will answer an order of operations question simply by completing the operations from left to right. Remind students to perform operations in parentheses first.

Item 7 Some students may see that 3.6 appears four times and then choose choice A. Remind them that multiplication is repeated addition and that exponents are needed to represent repeated multiplication.

Additional Resources

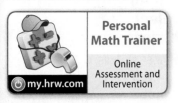

Personal Math Trainer
Online Assessment and Intervention
my.hrw.com

MODULE 9 MIXED REVIEW
Assessment Readiness
COMMON CORE

Personal Math Trainer
Online Assessment and Intervention
my.hrw.com

Selected Response

1. Which expression has a value that is less than the base of that expression?

(A) 2^3

(B) $\left(\frac{5}{6}\right)^2$

(C) 3^2

(D) 4^4

2. After the game the coach bought 9 chicken meals for $5 each and 15 burger meals for $6 each. What percent of the total amount the coach spent was used for the chicken meals?

(A) $33\frac{1}{3}\%$

(B) 45%

(C) $66\frac{2}{3}\%$

(D) 90%

3. Which operation should you perform first when you simplify $175 - (8 + 45 \div 3) \times 7$?

(A) addition

(B) division

(C) multiplication

(D) subtraction

4. For a game, three people are chosen in the first round. Each of those people chooses 3 people in the second round, and so on. How many people are chosen in the sixth round?

(A) 18

(B) 216

(C) 243

(D) 729

5. Which expression shows the prime factorization of 100?

(A) $2^2 \times 5^2$ (C) 10^{10}

(B) 10×10 (D) $2 \times 5 \times 10$

6. Which number has only two factors?

(A) 21   (C) 25

(B) 23   (D) 27

7. Which expression is equivalent to $3.6 \times 3.6 \times 3.6 \times 3.6$?

(A) 3.6×4 (C) $3^4 \times 6^4$

(B) 36^3 (D) 3.6^4

8. Which expression gives the prime factorization of 80?

(A) $2^4 \times 10$

(B) $2 \times 5 \times 8$

(C) $2^3 \times 5$

(D) $2^4 \times 5$

Mini-Task

9. George wants to put carpeting in a rectangular living room and a square bedroom. The length and width of the living room is 12 feet by 18 feet. One side of the square bedroom is 13 feet. It will cost $3.50 per square foot to carpet the rooms.

a. Write an expression that can be used to find the total amount George will pay for carpeting.

$(12 \times 18 + 13^2) \times 3.50$

b. Evaluate the expression. How much will George pay for the carpeting?

$1,347.50

© Houghton Mifflin Harcourt Publishing Company

Common Core Standards

Items	Grade 6 Standards	Mathematical Practices
1	6.EE.1	MP.7
2*	6.EE.1, 6.RP.3c	MP.4
3	6.EE.1	MP.5
4	6.EE.1	MP.4, MP.7
5	6.EE.1	MP.2
6	6.EE.1	MP.7
7	6.EE.1	MP.2
8	6.EE.1	MP.2
9	6.EE.1	MP.5

* Item integrates mixed review concepts from previous modules or a previous course.

Generating Equivalent Algebraic Expressions

You can model real-world problems with variable expressions, then use algebraic rules to solve the problems.

 ESSENTIAL QUESTION

How can you generate equivalent algebraic expressions and use them to solve real-world problems?

Real-World Video

Carpenters use formulas to calculate a project's materials supply. Sometimes formulas can be written in different forms. The perimeter of a rectangle can be written as $P = 2(l + w)$ or $P = 2l + 2w$.

my.hrw.com

GO DIGITAL

my.hrw.com

my.hrw.com

Go digital with your write-in student edition, accessible on any device.

Math On the Spot

Scan with your smart phone to jump directly to the online edition, video tutor, and more.

Animated Math

Interactively explore key concepts to see how math works.

Personal Math Trainer

Get immediate feedback and help as you work through practice sets.

© Houghton Mifflin Harcourt Publishing Company • Image Credits: ©Lloyd Sutton/ Alamy

Are You Ready?

Assess Readiness

Use the assessment on this page to determine if students need intensive or strategic intervention for the module's prerequisite skills.

 **RtI** **Response to Intervention**

Personal Math Trainer
Online Assessment and Intervention
⏻ my.hrw.com

Intervention	Enrichment

Access Are You Ready? assessment online, and receive instant scoring, feedback, and customized intervention or enrichment.

Online and Print Resources

Skills Intervention worksheets
- Skill 50 Use of Parentheses
- Skill 53 Words for Operations
- Skill 54 Evaluate Expressions

Differentiated Instruction
- Challenge worksheets **PRE-AP**
- Extend the Math **PRE-AP** Lesson Activities in TE

Are YOU Ready?

Complete these exercises to review skills you will need for this module.

Personal Math Trainer
Online Assessment and Intervention
⏻ my.hrw.com

Use of Parentheses

EXAMPLE $(6 + 4) \times (3 + 8 + 1) = 10 \times 12$ *Do the operations inside parentheses first.*

$= 120$ *Multiply.*

Evaluate.

1. $11 + (20 - 13)$ $\underline{18}$

2. $(10 - 7) - (14 - 12)$ $\underline{1}$

3. $(4 + 17) - (16 - 9)$ $\underline{14}$

4. $(23 - 15) - (18 - 13)$ $\underline{3}$

5. $8 \times (4 + 5 + 7)$ $\underline{128}$

6. $(2 + 3) \times (11 - 5)$ $\underline{30}$

Words for Operations

EXAMPLE Write a numerical expression for the quotient of 20 and 5.   *Think: Quotient means to divide.*

$20 \div 5$ *Write 20 divided by 5.*

Write a numerical expression for the word expression.

7. the difference between 42 and 19 $\underline{42 - 19}$

8. the product of 7 and 12 $\underline{7 \times 12}$

9. 30 more than 20 $\underline{20 + 30}$

10. 100 decreased by 77 $\underline{100 - 77}$

Evaluate Expressions

EXAMPLE Evaluate $2(5) - 3^2$.

$2(5) - 3^2 = 2(5) - 9$ *Evaluate exponents.*
$= 10 - 9$ *Multiply.*
$= 1$ *Subtract.*

Evaluate the expression.

11. $3(8) - 15$ $\underline{9}$

12. $4(12) + 11$ $\underline{59}$

13. $3(7) - 4(2)$ $\underline{13}$

14. $4(2 + 3) - 12$ $\underline{8}$

15. $9(14 - 5) - 42$ $\underline{39}$

16. $7(8) - 5(8)$ $\underline{16}$

PROFESSIONAL DEVELOPMENT VIDEO

Author Juli Dixon models successful teaching practices as she explores equivalent algebraic expressions in an actual sixth-grade classroom.

Professional Development
⏻ my.hrw.com

GO DIGITAL my.hrw.com

 Online Teacher Edition
Access a full suite of teaching resources online—plan, present, and manage classes and assignments.

 ePlanner
Easily plan your classes and access all your resources online.

Interactive Answers and Solutions
Customize answer keys to print or display in the classroom. Choose to include answers only or full solutions to all lesson exercises.

 Interactive Whiteboards
Engage students with interactive whiteboard-ready lessons and activities.

 Personal Math Trainer: Online Assessment and Intervention
Assign automatically graded homework, quizzes, tests, and intervention activities. Prepare your students with updated practice tests aligned with Common Core.

Reading Start-Up

Have students complete the activities on this page by working alone or with others.

Visualize Vocabulary

The graphic organizer will help students to review concepts related to simplifying expressions. If time allows, discuss as a class the mnemonic **P**lease **E**xcuse **M**y **D**ear **A**unt **S**ally for order of operations (**P**arentheses, **E**xponent, **M**ultiplication, **D**ivision, **A**ddition, **S**ubtraction).

Understand Vocabulary

Use the following explanation to help students learn the preview words.

> **Variable** is an antonym of **constant**. *Variable* means "changeable"; something that is constant does not change. In math, a variable is a letter or symbol that represents a number. A letter is used because the number is unknown, and it may vary. A constant is a numeral, not a letter. For an expression to be an **algebraic expression**, it must contain at least one variable.

Active Reading

Integrating Language Arts

Students can use these reading and note-taking strategies to help them organize and understand new concepts and vocabulary.

COMMON CORE **ELA-Literacy.RST.6-8.7** Integrate quantitative or technical information expressed in words in a text with a version of that information expressed visually (e.g., in a flowchart, diagram, model, graph, or table).

Additional Resources

Differentiated Instruction

• Reading Strategies **ELL**

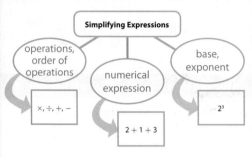

Reading Start-Up

Visualize Vocabulary

Use the review words to complete the graphic. You may put more than one word in each oval.

Simplifying Expressions

- operations, order of operations
- numerical expression
- base, exponent

$\times, \div, +, -$

$2 + 1 + 3$

2^3

Understand Vocabulary

Complete the sentences using the preview words.

1. An expression that contains at least one variable is an _____ algebraic expression _____.

2. A part of an expression that is added or subtracted is a ___ term ___.

3. A ___ constant ___ is a specific number whose value does not change.

Vocabulary

Review Words
- base *(base)*
- exponent *(exponente)*
- numerical expression *(expresión numérica)*
- operations *(operaciones)*
- order of operations *(orden de las operaciones)*

Preview Words
- algebraic expression *(expresión algebraica)*
- coefficient *(coeficiente)*
- constant *(constante)*
- equivalent expression *(expresión equivalente)*
- evaluating *(evaluar)*
- like terms *(términos semejantes)*
- term *(término, en una expresión)*
- variable *(variable)*

Active Reading

Key-Term Fold Before beginning the module, create a key-term fold to help you learn the vocabulary in this module. Write the highlighted vocabulary words on one side of the flap. Write the definition for each word on the other side of the flap. Use the key-term fold to quiz yourself on the definitions used in this module.

Module 10 **259**

Before	In this module	After
Students understand: • operations with whole numbers, decimals, and fractions • order of operations • properties of operations: inverse, identity, commutative, associative, and distributive properties	Students will learn to: • determine if two expressions are equivalent using concrete models, pictorial models, and algebraic representations • evaluate algebraic expressions for the given value of a variable • generate equivalent expressions using the properties of operations: inverse, identity, commutative, associative, and distributive properties	Students will connect: • numerical and algebraic expressions • variables and symbols to translate words into math

Unpacking the Standards

Use the examples on this page to help students know exactly what they are expected to learn in this module.

Common Core Standards

Content Areas

 Expressions and Equations—6.EE.1

Apply and extend previous understandings of arithmetic to algebraic expressions.

Go online to see a complete unpacking of the Common Core Standards.

⏱ my.hrw.com

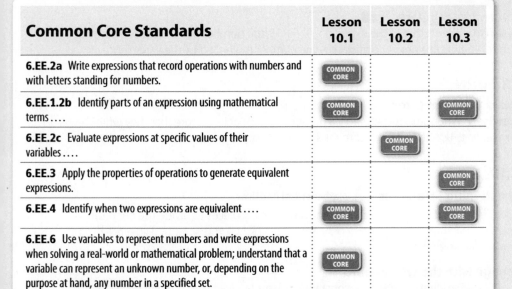

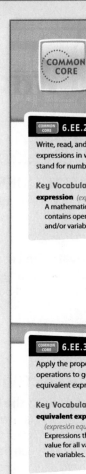

COMMON CORE

MODULE 10

Unpacking the Standards

Understanding the standards and the vocabulary terms in the standards will help you know exactly what you are expected to learn in this module.

COMMON CORE 6.EE.2

Write, read, and evaluate expressions in which letters stand for numbers.

Key Vocabulary

expression (*expresión*)
A mathematical phrase that contains operations, numbers, and/or variables.

What It Means to You

You will use models to compare expressions.

UNPACKING EXAMPLE 6.EE.2

On a math quiz, Tina scored 3 points more than Yolanda. Juan scored 2 points more than Yolanda and earned 2 points as extra credit.

Write expressions for the numbers of points that Juan and Tina scored. Use y to represent the number of points that Yolanda scored.

Tina's points: $y + 3$
Juan's points: $y + 2 + 2$

Suppose Yolanda scored 82 points. Use the expressions to find the number of points Tina and Juan scored.

Tina's points: $y + 3 = 82 + 3 = 85$ points
Juan's points: $y + 2 + 2 = 82 + 2 + 2 = 86$ points

COMMON CORE 6.EE.3

Apply the properties of operations to generate equivalent expressions.

Key Vocabulary

equivalent expressions
(*expresión equivalente*)
Expressions that have the same value for all values of the variables.

What It Means to You

You will use the properties of operations to find an equivalent expression.

UNPACKING EXAMPLE 6.EE.3

William earns $13 an hour working at a movie theater. He worked h hours in concessions and three times as many hours at the ticket counter. Write and simplify an expression for the amount of money William earned.

$13 \cdot$ hours at concessions $+ \$13 \cdot$ hours at ticket counter

$13h + 13(3h)$

$13h + 39h$ — Multiply $13 \cdot 3h$.

$h(13 + 39)$ — Distributive Property

$52h$ — Simplify.

Visit my.hrw.com to see all the Common Core Standards unpacked.

⏱ my.hrw.com

260 Unit 4

© Houghton Mifflin Harcourt Publishing Company • Image Credits: Erik Dreyer/Getty Images

---

Common Core Standards	Lesson 10.1	Lesson 10.2	Lesson 10.3
6.EE.2a Write expressions that record operations with numbers and with letters standing for numbers.	COMMON CORE		
6.EE.1.2b Identify parts of an expression using mathematical terms	COMMON CORE		COMMON CORE
6.EE.2c Evaluate expressions at specific values of their variables		COMMON CORE	
6.EE.3 Apply the properties of operations to generate equivalent expressions.			COMMON CORE
6.EE.4 Identify when two expressions are equivalent	COMMON CORE		COMMON CORE
6.EE.6 Use variables to represent numbers and write expressions when solving a real-world or mathematical problem; understand that a variable can represent an unknown number, or, depending on the purpose at hand, any number in a specified set.	COMMON CORE		

LESSON
10.1 Modeling and Writing Expressions

Common Core Standards

The student is expected to:

 Expressions and Equations—6.EE.2a

Write expressions that record operations with numbers and with letters standing for numbers.

 Expressions and Equations—6.EE.6

Use variables to represent numbers and write expressions when solving a real-world or mathematical problem; understand that a variable can represent an unknown number, or, depending on the purpose at hand, any number in a specified set.

Also 6.EE.2b, 6.EE.4

Mathematical Practices

 MP.2 Reasoning

ADDITIONAL EXAMPLE 1
Write a phrase for each algebraic expression.

$\frac{z}{5}$ the quotient of z and 5

$9 + y$ 9 more than y

 Interactive Whiteboard
Interactive example available online

⏻ my.hrw.com

ADDITIONAL EXAMPLE 2
Use a bar model to represent each expression.

$5 + y$

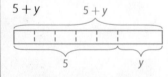

Interactive Whiteboard
Interactive example available online

⏻ my.hrw.com

Engage

ESSENTIAL QUESTION

How can you write algebraic expressions and use models to decide if expressions are equivalent? Sample answer: Write or model the variables, constants, and operations to represent each expression. Then compare the expressions or models.

Motivate the Lesson
Ask: Is a quarter the same as 5 nickels? as 25 pennies? How can you describe something in different ways but not change its value? Begin the Explore Activity to find out.

Explore

EXPLORE ACTIVITY

Engage with the Whiteboard
Write the expressions $w + 25$, $d - 12$, $3x + 5y + 12$, and $2d^2 - 1$ on the whiteboard. Then have students identify the variables and the constants. Point out to students that any letter can be used to represent an unknown quantity but using the first letter of the word being represented can help them remember what the variable stands for.

Explain

EXAMPLE 1

Questioning Strategies CC Mathematical Practices
• Does it matter which letter you choose when writing an algebraic expression? No. You can choose any letter, but mathematicians often choose the last letters of the alphabet (e.g., x, y, and z) to represent variables.

Connect Vocabulary ELL
Explain to students that in the expression $8x + 15$, the number 8 is a coefficient and the number 15 is a constant. A coefficient is the number multiplied by the variable, x.

YOUR TURN

Avoid Common Errors
Exercise 1 When students multiply a number by a variable, be sure that they write the number first: $4x$, not $x4$. It's easier to read and understand.

EXAMPLE 2

Questioning Strategies CC Mathematical Practices
• On the bar model for B, how do you know how many pieces to divide the bar into? The expression $\frac{z}{3}$ means "z divided into 3 parts," so you know you need to divide the bar into 3 equal parts.

Engage with the Whiteboard
Have students change the constant in Example 2A and/or 2B. Then have students draw a model to represent the new expression. Ask volunteers to explain their models to the class, and then ask the class if the students are correct.

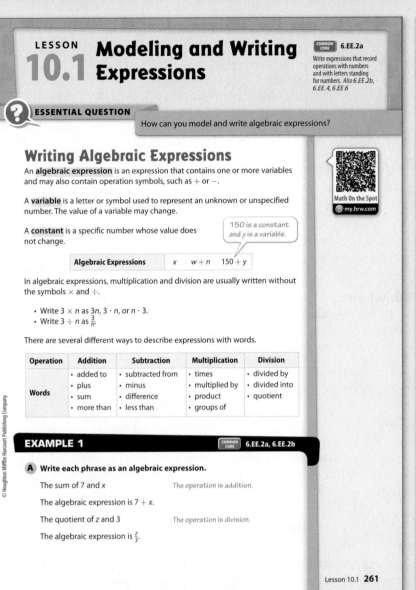

LESSON 10.1 Modeling and Writing Expressions

COMMON CORE 6.EE.2a
Write expressions that record operations with numbers and with letters standing for numbers. *Also 6.EE.2b, 6.EE.4, 6.EE.6*

ESSENTIAL QUESTION
How can you model and write algebraic expressions?

Writing Algebraic Expressions

An **algebraic expression** is an expression that contains one or more variables and may also contain operation symbols, such as $+$ or $-$.

A **variable** is a letter or symbol used to represent an unknown or unspecified number. The value of a variable may change.

A **constant** is a specific number whose value does not change.

> 150 is a constant and *y* is a variable.

| Algebraic Expressions | x | $w + n$ | $150 + y$ |

In algebraic expressions, multiplication and division are usually written without the symbols $\times$ and $\div$.

- Write $3 \times n$ as $3n$, $3 \cdot n$, or $n \cdot 3$.
- Write $3 \div n$ as $\frac{3}{n}$.

There are several different ways to describe expressions with words.

Operation	Addition	Subtraction	Multiplication	Division
Words	• added to • plus • sum • more than	• subtracted from • minus • difference • less than	• times • multiplied by • product • groups of	• divided by • divided into • quotient

EXAMPLE 1
COMMON CORE 6.EE.2a, 6.EE.2b

A Write each phrase as an algebraic expression.

The sum of 7 and *x*   *The operation is addition.*

The algebraic expression is $7 + x$.

The quotient of *z* and 3   *The operation is division.*

The algebraic expression is $\frac{z}{3}$.

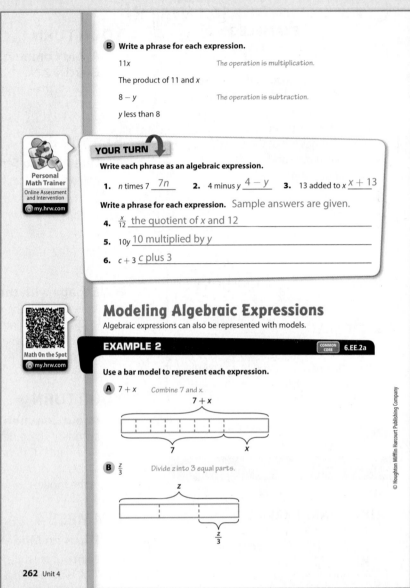

B Write a phrase for each expression.

$11x$ *The operation is multiplication.*

The product of 11 and *x*

$8 - y$ *The operation is subtraction.*

y less than 8

YOUR TURN

Write each phrase as an algebraic expression.

1. *n* times 7 ___$7n$___   2. 4 minus *y* ___$4 - y$___   3. 13 added to *x* ___$x + 13$___

Write a phrase for each expression. **Sample answers are given.**

4. $\frac{x}{12}$ ___the quotient of *x* and 12___

5. $10y$ ___10 multiplied by *y*___

6. $c + 3$ ___*c* plus 3___

Modeling Algebraic Expressions

Algebraic expressions can also be represented with models.

EXAMPLE 2
COMMON CORE 6.EE.2a

Use a bar model to represent each expression.

A $7 + x$ *Combine 7 and x.*

$$7 + x$$

$$7 \qquad x$$

B $\frac{z}{3}$ *Divide z into 3 equal parts.*

$$z$$

$$\frac{z}{3}$$

PROFESSIONAL DEVELOPMENT

Integrate Mathematical Practices MP.2

This lesson provides an opportunity to address the Mathematical Practices standard that calls for students to reason abstractly and quantitatively. In this lesson, students use symbols and bar models to represent expressions. They employ these multiple representations to compare algebraic expressions and solve problems in real-world situations.

Math Background

François Viète (1540–1603) was a lawyer in France who devoted his spare time to mathematics. In his book *In artem analyticam isagoge*, he introduced the idea of using vowels for variables and using consonants for constants. This was an important step toward modern algebra. Although Viète also used $+$ and $-$, he had no symbol for equality. To write "equals," he would use the Latin word *aequatur*. Viète is sometimes called the Father of Algebra.

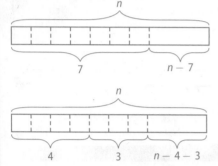

YOUR TURN

Avoid Common Errors

Exercise 7 Some students may try to model $t - 2$ as an addition equation. Remind students that for subtraction expressions, they must "take away" the 2 from the whole, *not* add to it.

EXAMPLE 3

Questioning Strategies CC Mathematical Practices

- How can you know which operation to use to solve the problem? Read the problem carefully. Katriana and Andrew "spent" or "took away" money from the money they started the day with. These words describe subtraction.

- In Step 1, what do the labels on the model represent? The variable x represents the amount of money Katriana started with, the 5 represents the money she spent, and $x - 5$ represents the money she has left.

Engage with the Whiteboard

Have students compare the models from Step 1 and Step 2 on the whiteboard by substituting values (e.g. $10, $14, $17, etc.) for x. Then stress that two expressions are equivalent when they name the same number, regardless of which value is substituted into them.

YOUR TURN

Avoid Common Errors

If students have difficulty with drawing the models, encourage them to circle the information for Tina in one color and for Juan in a different color. Then remind them to look at the list of ways to describe math operations to determine the operation they should use in the models.

EXAMPLE 4

Focus on Modeling

Point out to students that to model real-world situations with expressions, they need to look for words that indicate the action that is taking place. For example, *putting parts together* indicates addition while *separating into equal groups* indicates division. Encourage students to become familiar with the expressions provide before Example 1 when modeling real-world situations.

Questioning Strategies CC Mathematical Practices

- In A, how does the word *group* indicate multiplication? Group means a number of persons gathered together. Since we don't know how many, it is an unknown quantity which can be represented by a variable.

YOUR TURN

Avoid Common Errors

Remind students that the order of variable and the constant is important in division expressions. For example, $\frac{d}{4}$ is not the same as $\frac{4}{d}$.

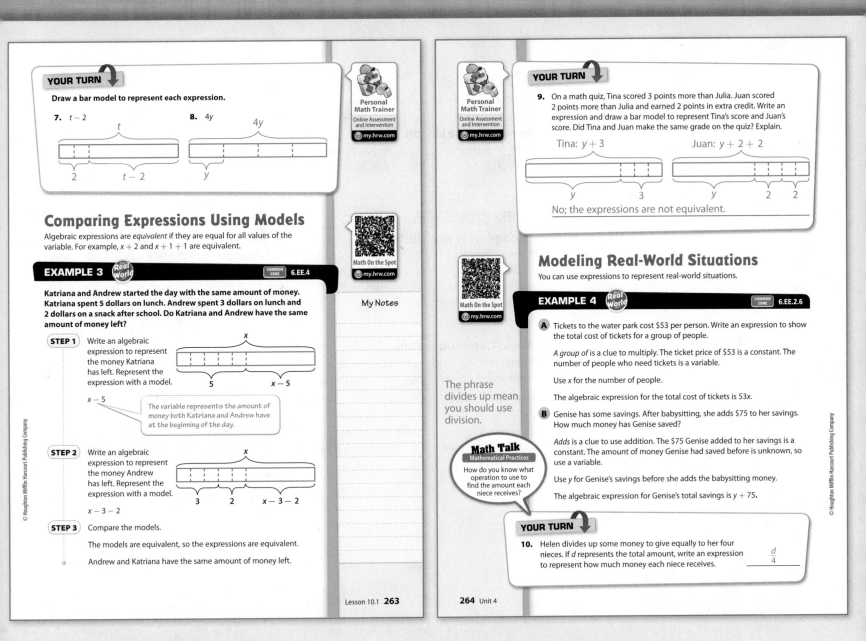

Draw a bar model to represent each expression.

7. $t - 2$

8. $4y$

Personal Math Trainer
Online Assessment and Intervention
my.hrw.com

Comparing Expressions Using Models

Algebraic expressions are *equivalent* if they are equal for all values of the variable. For example, $x + 2$ and $x + 1 + 1$ are equivalent.

EXAMPLE 3   Real World   COMMON CORE 6.EE.4

Math On the Spot
my.hrw.com

Katriana and Andrew started the day with the same amount of money. Katriana spent 5 dollars on lunch. Andrew spent 3 dollars on lunch and 2 dollars on a snack after school. Do Katriana and Andrew have the same amount of money left?

STEP 1 Write an algebraic expression to represent the money Katriana has left. Represent the expression with a model.

$x - 5$

> The variable represents the amount of money both Katriana and Andrew have at the beginning of the day.

STEP 2 Write an algebraic expression to represent the money Andrew has left. Represent the expression with a model.

$x - 3 - 2$

STEP 3 Compare the models.

The models are equivalent, so the expressions are equivalent.

Andrew and Katriana have the same amount of money left.

My Notes

Personal Math Trainer
Online Assessment and Intervention
my.hrw.com

9. On a math quiz, Tina scored 3 points more than Julia. Juan scored 2 points more than Julia and earned 2 points in extra credit. Write an expression and draw a bar model to represent Tina's score and Juan's score. Did Tina and Juan make the same grade on the quiz? Explain.

Tina: $y + 3$ Juan: $y + 2 + 2$

No; the expressions are not equivalent.

Modeling Real-World Situations

You can use expressions to represent real-world situations.

Math On the Spot
my.hrw.com

EXAMPLE 4   Real World   COMMON CORE 6.EE.2.6

A Tickets to the water park cost $53 per person. Write an expression to show the total cost of tickets for a group of people.

A group of is a clue to multiply. The ticket price of $53 is a constant. The number of people who need tickets is a variable.

Use x for the number of people.

The algebraic expression for the total cost of tickets is $53x$.

B Genise has some savings. After babysitting, she adds $75 to her savings. How much money has Genise saved?

Adds is a clue to use addition. The $75 Genise added to her savings is a constant. The amount of money Genise had saved before is unknown, so use a variable.

Use y for Genise's savings before she adds the babysitting money.

The algebraic expression for Genise's total savings is $y + 75$.

The phrase divides up mean you should use division.

Math Talk
Mathematical Practices

How do you know what operation to use to find the amount each niece receives?

10. Helen divides up some money to give equally to her four nieces. If d represents the total amount, write an expression to represent how much money each niece receives.

$\dfrac{d}{4}$

© Houghton Mifflin Harcourt Publishing Company

Elaborate

Talk About It
Summarize the Lesson

Ask: How can you find out whether algebraic expressions are equivalent? Draw models of each expression and then compare them. If the models are equivalent, the expressions are equivalent.

GUIDED PRACTICE

Engage with the Whiteboard

For Exercise 3, have students circle the variable and the constant in $y + 12$. Then have them write three different algebraic expressions that are equivalent to $y + 12$ on the whiteboard. Sample answer: $y + 3 + 9$; $y + 4 + 8$; $y + 5 + 7$

For Exercise 6, have students complete the bar models for each city on the whiteboard and then explain their reasoning.

Avoid Common Errors

Exercise 1 Remind students that the order of the variable and the constant is important in subtraction expressions, $y - 3$ is not the same as $3 - y$.

Exercise 2 When students multiply a number by a variable, be sure that they write the number first: $2p$, not $p2$. It's easier to read and understand.

Exercise 5 Some students may try to model $m \div 4$ as an addition equation. Remind students that for division expressions, they must "divide" the whole into parts, not add to it.

Write each phrase as an algebraic expression. (Example 1)

1. 3 less than y _____ $y - 3$

2. The product of 2 and p _____ $2p$

Write a phrase for each algebraic expression. (Example 1) Sample answers are given.

3. $y + 12$ _____ 12 added to y

4. $\frac{p}{10}$ _____ 10 divided into p

5. Draw a bar model to represent the expression $m \div 4$. (Example 2)

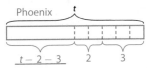

$$\frac{m}{4}$$

At 6 p.m., the temperature in Phoenix, AZ, t, is the same as the temperature in Tucson, AZ. By 9 p.m., the temperature in Phoenix has dropped 2 degrees and in Tucson it has dropped 4 degrees. By 11 p.m., the temperature in Phoenix has dropped another 3 degrees. (Example 3)

6. Represent each city's temperature at 11 p.m. with an algebraic expression and a bar model.

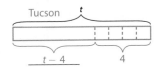

Phoenix t Tucson t

$t - 2 - 3$ 2   3 $t - 4$ 4

7. Are the expressions that represent the temperatures in the two cities equivalent? Justify your answer.

No; the models show that the temperature in Phoenix is 1 degree less than the temperature in Tucson.

8. Noelle bought some boxes of water bottles for a picnic. Each box contained 24 bottles of water. If c is the number of boxes, write an expression to show how many bottles of water Noelle bought. (Example 4)

$24c$

? ESSENTIAL QUESTION CHECK-IN

9. Give an example of a real-world situation that could be represented by an algebraic expression.

Sample answer: You earned $15 on Monday and will earn more money tomorrow. $15 + d$, where d is the money you earn tomorrow, represents your total earnings for the two days.

10.1 Independent Practice

COMMON CORE 6.EE.2a, 6.EE.2b, 6.EE.4, 6.EE.2.6

Personal Math Trainer
Online Assessment and Intervention
my.hrw.com

10. Write an algebraic expression with the constant 7 and the variable y.

Sample answer: $7 + y$

Write each phrase as an algebraic expression.

11. n divided by 8 _____ $\frac{n}{8}$

12. p multiplied by 4 _____ $4p$

13. b plus 14 _____ $b + 14$

14. 90 times x _____ $90x$

15. a take away 16 _____ $a - 16$

16. k less than 24 _____ $24 - k$

17. 3 groups of w _____ $3w$

18. the sum of 1 and q _____ $1 + q$

19. the quotient of 13 and z _____ $\frac{13}{z}$

20. c added to 45 _____ $45 + c$

21. 8 less than w _____ $w - 8$

Write a phrase in words for each algebraic expression. Sample answers given.

22. $m + 83$ _____ 83 added to m

23. $42s$ _____ 42 times s

24. $\frac{9}{d}$ _____ 9 divided by d

25. $t - 29$ _____ t minus 29

26. $2 + g$ _____ g more than 2

27. $11x$ _____ the product of 11 and x

28. $\frac{h}{12}$ _____ the quotient of h and 12

29. $5 - k$ _____ k less than 5

Sarah and Noah work at Read On Bookstore and get paid the same hourly wage. The table shows their work schedule for last week.

Read On Bookstore Work Schedule (hours)			
	Monday	Tuesday	Wednesday
Sarah	5	3	
Noah			8

30. Write an expression that represents Sarah's total pay last week. Represent her hourly wage with w. _____ $5w + 3w$

31. Write an expression that represents Noah's total pay last week. Represent his hourly wage with w. _____ $8w$

32. Are the expressions equivalent? Did Sarah and Noah earn the same amount last week? Use models to justify your answer.

Yes; Check students' models.

33. Mia buys 3 gallons of gas that costs d dollars per gallon. Bob buys g gallons of gas that costs $3 per gallon.

   a. Write an expression for the amount Mia pays for gas. _____ $3d$

   b. Write an expression for the amount Bob pays for gas. _____ $3g$

   c. What do the numeral and the variable represent in each expression?

In Mia's expression, the numeral is the number of gallons and variable is the cost per gallon; in Bob's, the numeral is the cost per gallon and the variable is the number of gallons he buys.

DIFFERENTIATE INSTRUCTION

Cognitive Strategies

Ask students for the meanings of the words *variable* and *constant* in a context such as the following:

> The air temperature in the desert was quite *variable* yesterday; it was cold overnight and warm during the day.

> The temperature at the equator was *constant* for 24 hours.

Explain that the words have the same meaning in mathematics. A *constant* is a value that does not change, such as the number 5, and a *variable* is a symbol for a quantity that is not fixed, such as x.

Cooperative Learning

Have students work in pairs to draw models of balance scales. Instruct pairs to take turns writing simple expressions and drawing circles to represent them on the balance pans on each side of the scale. Then ask each student to write and illustrate two sets of equivalent expressions that balance when arranged on the scales. Invite pairs to explain how they chose their arrangements of circles.

Additional Resources

Differentiated Instruction includes:

- Reading Strategies
- Success for English Learners **ELL**
- Reteach
- Challenge **PRE-AP**

10.1 LESSON QUIZ

COMMON CORE 6.EE.2a, 6.EE.4

1. Write each phrase as an algebraic expression:

z times 5   6 plus n

2. Write a phrase for each algebraic expression:

8y $\frac{6}{m}$

3. Use a bar model to represent $4 + m$.

4. Jan and Jackie check out the same number of library books. Jan turns in 4 books after 3 weeks. Jackie returns 2 books that week and 4 books later. Write algebraic expressions and draw bar models to represent the books Jan and Jackie have left. Do they have the same number of books left? Justify your answer.

Lesson Quiz available online

 my.hrw.com

Answers

1. $5z, 6 + n$

2. 8 multiplied by y, 6 divided by m

3.

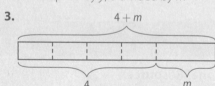

4. No. Sample answer: The expressions are not equivalent. If $b =$ the number of books each checked out, Jan's books $= b - 4$ and Jackie's books $= b - 2 - 4$.

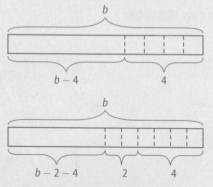

Evaluate

GUIDED AND INDEPENDENT PRACTICE

COMMON CORE 6.EE.2a, 6.EE.2b, 6.EE.4, 6.EE.6

Concepts & Skills	Practice
Example 1 Writing Algebraic Expressions	Exercises 1–4, 8, 11–20, 32–37a and b
Example 2 Modeling Algebraic Expressions	Exercises 5–6
Example 3 Comparing Expressions Using Models	Exercises 7, 31, 37c, 46
Example 4 Modeling Real-World Situations	Exercises 8–9, 29–30, 32–42, 45

Exercise	Depth of Knowledge (D.O.K.)	**COMMON CORE** Mathematical Practices
10	**2** Skills/Concepts	**MP.7** Using Structure
11–33	**2** Skills/Concepts	**MP.5** Using Tools
34–41	**2** Skills/Concepts	**MP.4** Modeling
42	**3** Strategic Thinking **H.O.T.**	**MP.4** Modeling
43	**3** Strategic Thinking **H.O.T.**	**MP.3** Logic
44	**3** Strategic Thinking **H.O.T.**	**MP.2** Reasoning
45	**3** Strategic Thinking **H.O.T.**	**MP.4** Modeling
46	**3** Strategic Thinking **H.O.T.**	**MP.7** Using Structure

Additional Resources

Differentiated Instruction includes:

• Leveled Practice worksheets

34. The student council is asking people to donate money for the new park outside the school. Everyone who makes the suggested donation amount will be given a bracelet. If everyone donates the suggested amount, and b bracelets are given away, what algebraic expression represents the total amount collected in donations?

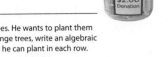

_____ $2b$ _____

35. Mr. Delgado has some young orange trees. He wants to plant them in 46 rows. If t is the total number of orange trees, write an algebraic expression to represent how many trees he can plant in each row.

_____ $\dfrac{t}{46}$ _____

36. There are 15 violinists in the orchestra this year. Next year, two violinists will leave and some new violinists will join the orchestra. If v is the number of violinists who will join the orchestra, write an expression to represent the number of violinists in the orchestra next year.

_____ $15 - 2 + v$ or $13 + v$ _____

37. Jill, Meg, and Beth are sisters. Jill is 2 years younger than Meg. Beth is half as old as Meg. Let m represent Meg's age. Write two other algebraic expressions based on this situation. Tell what each expression represents, and what the variable stands for in each expression.

$m - 2$ represents Jill's age where m is Meg's age; $\dfrac{m}{2}$

represents Beth's age where m is Meg's age.

38. **Multistep** Will, Hector, and Lydia volunteered at the animal shelter in March and April. The table shows the number of hours Will and Hector volunteered in March. Let x represent the number of hours Lydia volunteered in March.

March Volunteering	
Will	3 hours
Hector	5 hours

a. Will's volunteer hours in April were equal to his March volunteer hours plus Lydia's March volunteer hours. Write an expression to represent Will's volunteer hours in April.

_____ $3 + x$ _____

b. Hector's volunteer hours in April were equal to 2 hours less than his March volunteer hours plus Lydia's March volunteer hours. Write an expression to represent Hector's volunteer hours in April.

_____ $5 - 2 + x$ _____

c. Did Will and Hector volunteer the same number of hours in April?

Explain. Yes; the expressions are equivalent.

39. The town of Rayburn received 6 more inches of snow than the town of Greenville. Let g represent the amount of snow in Greenville. Write an algebraic expression to represent the amount of snow in Rayburn.

_____ $g + 6$ _____

40. Abby baked 48 dinner rolls and divided them evenly into bags. Let b represent the number of bags. Write an algebraic expression to represent the number of dinner rolls in each bag.

$\dfrac{48}{b}$

41. Eli is driving at a speed of 55 miles per hour. Let h represent the number of hours that Eli drives at this speed. Write an algebraic expression to represent the number of miles that Eli travels during this time.

$55h$

H.O.T. **FOCUS ON HIGHER ORDER THINKING**

42. **Multistep** Bob's Bagels offers two breakfast options, as shown.

a. Let x represent the number of customers who order coffee and a bagel. How much money will Bob's Bagels make from these orders?

_____ $3x$ _____

b. Let y represent the number of customers who order tea and a breakfast sandwich. How much money will Bob's Bagels make from

these orders? _____ $5y$ _____

c. Write an algebraic expression for the total amount Bob's Bagels will make from all the coffee and bagel orders and from all the tea and

breakfast sandwich orders. _____ $3x + 5y$ _____

43. **Represent Real-World Problems** The number of shoes in a closet is s.

a. How many pairs of shoes are in the closet? Explain.

$\dfrac{s}{2}$; There are half as many pairs of shoes as there are total shoes.

b. **What If?** Suppose one of the pairs is missing a shoe. How many

shoes are in the closet? _____ $s - 1$ shoes _____

44. **Problem Solving** Write an expression that has three terms, two different

variables, and one constant. Sample answer: $2x - 8y + 7$

45. **Represent Real-World Problems** Describe a situation that can be modeled by the expression $x - 8$.

Sample answer: Sam started the day with a box of

pencils. During the day he gave out 8 pencils.

46. **Critique Reasoning** Ricardo says that the expression $y + 4$ is equivalent to the expression $1y + 4$. Is he correct? Explain.

Sample answer: Yes; $1y$ is the product of 1 and y. Since 1

times any number is equal to the number, $1 \cdot y = y$. The

expression $y + 4$ is equivalent to $1y + 4$.

Work Area

EXTEND THE MATH **PRE-AP**

Activity available online 🔘 my.hrw.com

Activity Each season the Ravens and the Hawks baseball teams play the same number of games. So far this year, the Ravens have played 3 games at home and 4 games on the road. The Hawks have played 5 games at home and 3 games on the road. Roberto drew these bar models and says that the Hawks have more games left to play in the season than the Ravens do. Is he correct? If not, what did he do incorrectly when he represented the given information?

Ravens: $g - 5 - 3$

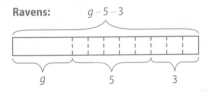

g 5   3

Hawks: $g - 3 - 4$

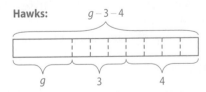

g 3   4

No, Roberto is not correct. He mixed up the data and mislabeled both models. 1) The tops of both bars should be labeled as g, the variable that stands for games left to play. 2) The Ravens model should have the labels $g - 3 - 4$, 3, and 4. 3) The Hawks model should have the labels $g - 5 - 3$, 5, and 3. Comparing the corrected models shows that the expressions are not equivalent: $7 < 8$. So, the Ravens have one more game to play than the Hawks do.

Common Core Standards

The student is expected to:

 Expressions and Equations—6.EE.2c

Evaluate expressions at specific values of their variables. Include expressions that arise from formulas used in real-world problems. Perform arithmetic operations, including those involving whole-number exponents, in the conventional order when there are no parentheses to specify a particular order (Order of Operations).

Mathematical Practices

 MP.6 Precision

ADDITIONAL EXAMPLE 1
Evaluate each expression for the given value of the variable.

A $b - 7; b = 16$ 9

B $\frac{28}{m}; m = 4$ 7

C $0.2t; t = 1.6$ 0.32

D $8s; s = \frac{1}{2}$ 4

 Interactive Whiteboard
Interactive example available online

⏻ my.hrw.com

ADDITIONAL EXAMPLE 2
Evaluate each expression for the given value of the variable.

A $6(y - 6); y = 9$ 18

B $6y - 6; y = 9$ 48

C $n - y + x; n = 5; y = 3; x = 4$ 6

D $y^2 - 2y; y = 7$ 35

E $4y - 3; y = 7$ 25

 Interactive Whiteboard
Interactive example available online

⏻ my.hrw.com

Engage

ESSENTIAL QUESTION

How can you use the order of operations to evaluate algebraic expressions? Sample answer: Substitute the given value for the variable in the expression and then use the order of operations to find the value of the resulting numerical expression.

Motivate the Lesson
Ask: How can you evaluate an expression that includes an unknown value? Begin Example 1 to find out.

Explore

Engage with the Whiteboard

 Write the expression $2(4 + x) - 5$ on the whiteboard. Ask a student to evaluate the expression for $x = 2$. Then ask the student to explain his/her reasoning. Ask the class if the student's work and reasoning are correct. If students have difficulty understanding which operation to perform first, review the order of operations.

Explain

EXAMPLE 1

Focus on Math Connections ㏄ Mathematical Practices
C and D involve an expression with a *coefficient*, a number that is multiplied by the variable. In the expression $0.5y$, the coefficient is 0.5.

Questioning Strategies ㏄ Mathematical Practices
• How might including or changing a coefficient in one of the expressions affect its value? Including or changing a coefficient could increase or decrease the value depending on the expression. In A, for example, if the coefficient 2 were inserted then the solution would increase to 21. In B, inserting the coefficient 2 would decrease the solution to 1.

YOUR TURN

Talk About It
Check for Understanding

 Ask: How do you evaluate an expression for a given variable? Substitute the given value for the variable in the expression. Then perform the operations, using the order of operations to find the value of the expression.

EXAMPLE 2

Focus on Math Connections ㏄ Mathematical Practices
Remind students of the correct order of operations (parentheses, exponents, multiplication/division, addition/subtraction) and the mnemonic device *PEMDAS*.

Questioning Strategies ㏄ Mathematical Practices
• The answers to A and B are not the same, even though the expressions are very similar. Why? The parentheses in $4(x - 4)$ mean that you subtract first. There are no parentheses in $4x - 4$, so you multiply first.

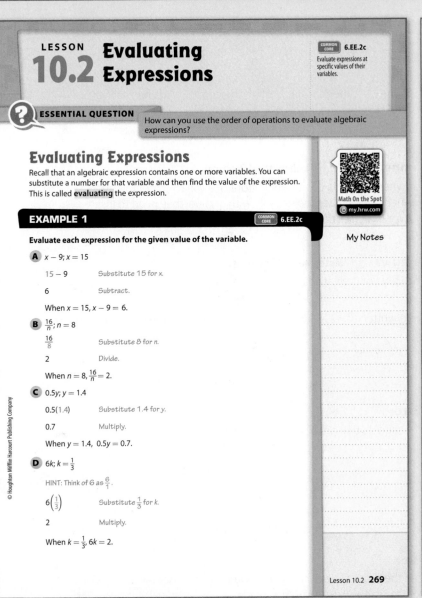

LESSON 10.2 Evaluating Expressions

COMMON CORE 6.EE.2c
Evaluate expressions at specific values of their variables.

? ESSENTIAL QUESTION
How can you use the order of operations to evaluate algebraic expressions?

Evaluating Expressions

Recall that an algebraic expression contains one or more variables. You can substitute a number for that variable and then find the value of the expression. This is called **evaluating** the expression.

EXAMPLE 1
COMMON CORE 6.EE.2c

Evaluate each expression for the given value of the variable.

A $x - 9; x = 15$

$15 - 9$ Substitute 15 for x.

6 Subtract.

When $x = 15$, $x - 9 = 6$.

B $\frac{16}{n}; n = 8$

$\frac{16}{8}$ Substitute 8 for n.

2 Divide.

When $n = 8$, $\frac{16}{n} = 2$.

C $0.5y; y = 1.4$

$0.5(1.4)$ Substitute 1.4 for y.

0.7 Multiply.

When $y = 1.4$, $0.5y = 0.7$.

D $6k; k = \frac{1}{3}$

HINT: Think of 6 as $\frac{6}{1}$.

$6\left(\frac{1}{3}\right)$ Substitute $\frac{1}{3}$ for k.

2 Multiply.

When $k = \frac{1}{3}$, $6k = 2$.

My Notes

© Houghton Mifflin Harcourt Publishing Company

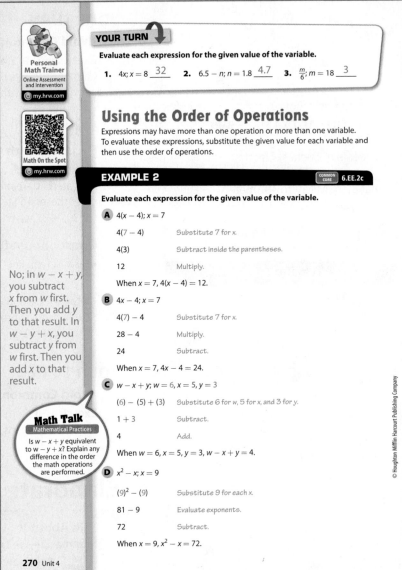

Personal Math Trainer
Online Assessment and Intervention
my.hrw.com

Math On the Spot
my.hrw.com

YOUR TURN

Evaluate each expression for the given value of the variable.

1. $4x; x = 8$ 32   **2.** $6.5 - n; n = 1.8$ 4.7   **3.** $\frac{m}{6}; m = 18$ 3

Using the Order of Operations

Expressions may have more than one operation or more than one variable. To evaluate these expressions, substitute the given value for each variable and then use the order of operations.

EXAMPLE 2
COMMON CORE 6.EE.2c

Evaluate each expression for the given value of the variable.

A $4(x - 4); x = 7$

$4(7 - 4)$ Substitute 7 for x.

$4(3)$ Subtract inside the parentheses.

12 Multiply.

When $x = 7$, $4(x - 4) = 12$.

B $4x - 4; x = 7$

$4(7) - 4$ Substitute 7 for x.

$28 - 4$ Multiply.

24 Subtract.

When $x = 7$, $4x - 4 = 24$.

C $w - x + y; w = 6, x = 5, y = 3$

$(6) - (5) + (3)$ Substitute 6 for w, 5 for x, and 3 for y.

$1 + 3$ Subtract.

4 Add.

When $w = 6, x = 5, y = 3$, $w - x + y = 4$.

D $x^2 - x; x = 9$

$(9)^2 - (9)$ Substitute 9 for each x.

$81 - 9$ Evaluate exponents.

72 Subtract.

When $x = 9$, $x^2 - x = 72$.

No; in $w - x + y$, you subtract x from w first. Then you add y to that result. In $w - y + x$, you subtract y from w first. Then you add x to that result.

Math Talk
Mathematical Practices

Is $w - x + y$ equivalent to $w - y + x$? Explain any difference in the order the math operations are performed.

© Houghton Mifflin Harcourt Publishing Company

PROFESSIONAL DEVELOPMENT

CC Integrate Mathematical Practices MP.6

This lesson provides an opportunity to address the Mathematical Practices standard that calls for students to attend to precision. In each Example and Exercise, students use mathematical ideas and language, including the order of operations, to evaluate algebraic expressions by substituting given values for variables. Students then evaluate real-world expressions such as formulas for finding surface area and volume and converting Celsius temperatures to Fahrenheit.

Math Background

We translate (or write) words into algebraic expressions by using a consistent, universally understood system. This system has evolved over thousands of years. Archaeological records indicate that Babylonian mathematicians had developed prose-based algebra by 2000 B.C.E.

The adoption of symbols to represent operations was also part of this evolution. The symbols $+$ and $-$ can be traced to Johann Widman (1498); the symbol $\cdot$ can be traced to Gottfried Leibniz (1698); and the symbol $\div$ can be traced to Johann Heinrich Rahn (1659).

YOUR TURN

Avoid Common Errors

Exercises 7–9 Watch for students who substitute the wrong value for the variable. Caution students to be sure that they are substituting the correct value for each variable in expressions with more than one variable.

EXAMPLE 3

Focus on Math Connections   **Mathematical Practices**

Remind students that when there is a coefficient in front of a variable, multiplication is indicated. Therefore, when they replace the variable with a value, they need to insert parentheses. In Step 2, for example, the expression 1.8c + 32 should be written as 1.8(30) + 32 when substituting 30 for c.

Questioning Strategies **Mathematical Practices**

- How do you find the value of the variable c? Read the text of the problem carefully. The value of the variable is given in the last sentence.

- If the expression were written as 32 + 1.8c, would you still perform the multiplication first? Explain. Addition is associative, so changing the order of the terms does not change the expression in any way. You still need to do the multiplication before the addition.

YOUR TURN

Avoid Common Errors

Exercise 10 Remind students that an exponent tells how many times to use the base as a factor, so x^3 means $x \cdot x \cdot x$, not 3x.

Elaborate

Talk About It
Summarize the Lesson

Ask: How can the order of operations help you evaluate algebraic expressions? When an expression contains more than one operation, the order of operations tells which operation to perform first.

GUIDED PRACTICE

Engage with the Whiteboard

For Exercises 7–8, have students circle all the important information provided, including key words that indicate operations, on the whiteboard. Then have them write an expression to represent each problem. Finally, have them complete the steps to evaluate each problem.

Avoid Common Errors

Exercise 2 Remind students that when there is a coefficient in front of a variable, multiplication is indicated. Therefore, when they replace the variable with a value, they need to insert parentheses.

Exercises 3, 5 Remind students that the fraction bar is another way to represent division.

YOUR TURN

Evaluate each expression for $n = 5$.

4. $3(n + 1)$ ___18___ **5.** $4(n - 4) + 14$ ___18___ **6.** $6n + n^2$ ___55___

Evaluate each expression for $a = 3$, $b = 4$, and $c = 6$.

7. $ab - c$ ___6___ **8.** $bc + 5a$ ___39___ **9.** $a^3 - (b + c)$ ___17___

Evaluating Real-World Expressions

You can evaluate expressions to solve real-world problems.

EXAMPLE 3 (Real World)   COMMON CORE 6.EE.2c

The expression $1.8c + 32$ gives the temperature in degrees Fahrenheit for a given temperature in degrees Celsius c. Find the temperature in degrees Fahrenheit that is equivalent to $30\,°C$.

STEP 1 Find the value of c.

$c = 30\,°C$

STEP 2 Substitute the value into the expression.

$1.8c + 32$

$1.8(30) + 32$ Substitute 30 for c.

$54 + 32$ Multiply.

86 Add.

$86\,°F$ is equivalent to $30\,°C$.

YOUR TURN

10. The expression $6x^2$ gives the surface area of a cube, and the expression x^3 gives the volume of a cube, where x is the length of one side of the cube. Find the surface area and the volume of a cube with a side length of 2 m.

$S =$ ___24___ m^2; $V =$ ___8___ m^3

11. The expression $60m$ gives the number of seconds in m minutes. How many seconds are there in 7 minutes?

___420___ seconds

Personal Math Trainer
Online Assessment and Intervention
my.hrw.com

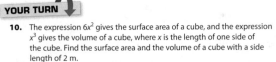
Math On the Spot
my.hrw.com

Guided Practice

Evaluate each expression for the given value(s) of the variable(s).
(Examples 1 and 2)

1. $x - 7$; $x = 23$ ___16___ **2.** $3a - b$; $a = 4$, $b = 6$ ___6___

3. $\frac{8}{t}$; $t = 4$ ___2___ **4.** $9 + m$; $m = 1.5$ ___10.5___

5. $\frac{1}{2}w + 2$; $w = \frac{1}{9}$ ___$2\frac{1}{18}$___ **6.** $5(6.2 + z)$; $z = 3.8$ ___50___

7. The table shows the prices for games in Bella's soccer league. Her parents and grandmother attended a soccer game. How much did they spend if they all went together in one car? (Example 3)

Women's Soccer Game Prices	
Student tickets	$6
Nonstudent tickets	$12
Parking	$5

a. Write an expression that represents the cost of one carful of nonstudent soccer fans. Use x as the number of people who rode in the car and attended the game.

___$12x + 5$___ is an expression that represents the cost of one carful of nonstudent soccer fans.

b. Since there are three attendees, evaluate the expression $12x + 5$ for $x = 3$.

$12(\underline{3}) + 5 = \underline{36} + 5 = \underline{41}$

The family spent ___$41___ to attend the game.

8. Stan wants to add trim all around the edge of a rectangular tablecloth that measures 5 feet long by 7 feet wide. The perimeter of the rectangular tablecloth is twice the length added to twice the width. How much trim does Stan need to buy? (Example 3)

a. Write an expression that represents the perimeter of the rectangular tablecloth. Let l represent the length of the tablecloth and w represent its width. The expression would be ___$2w + 2l$___.

b. Evaluate the expression $P = 2w + 2l$ for $l = 5$ and $w = 7$.

$2(\underline{7}) + 2(\underline{5}) = 14 + \underline{10} = \underline{24}$

Stan bought ___24 feet___ of trim to sew onto the tablecloth.

? ESSENTIAL QUESTION CHECK-IN

9. How do you know the correct order in which to evaluate algebraic expressions?

Substitute for the variables and follow the order of
operations that you would use for a numerical expression.

DIFFERENTIATE INSTRUCTION

Home Connection

Have students record real-world math situations they experience at home, using both words and mathematical symbols.

Sample answer: Mom works out for the same length of time each day. How long does she work out in a week? $7t$, where t represents the length of time she works out each day.

Cooperative Learning

Have students work in groups to solve a magic square. A magic square is an array of numbers in which each row, column, and diagonal has the same sum. Ask students if the array below is a magic square if $x = 4$; if $x = 6$; or if $x = 0$.

$x + 7$	x	$2x + 1$
$x + 2$	$0.5x + 6$	$x + 6$
$3x - 5$	$3x$	$x + 1$

The array is a magic square if $x = 4$, but not if $x = 6$ or if $x = 0$.

Additional Resources

Differentiated Instruction includes:

- Reading Strategies
- Success for English Learners **ELL**
- Reteach
- Challenge **PRE-AP**

10.2 LESSON QUIZ

 6.EE.2c

Evaluate each expression for the given value(s) of the variable(s).

1. $a + 6$; $a = 2$

2. $\frac{16}{g}$; $g = 4$

3. $7(m - 6)$; $m = 8$

4. $7m - 6$; $m = 8$

5. $s - k + x$; $s = 7, k = 4, x = 6$

6. The expression $4g$ gives the number of quarts in g gallons. How many quarts are there in 4 gallons?

Lesson Quiz available online

 my.hrw.com

Answers

1. 8

2. 4

3. 14

4. 50

5. 9

6. 16 quarts

Evaluate

GUIDED AND INDEPENDENT PRACTICE

 6.EE.2c

Concepts & Skills	Practice
Example 1 Evaluating Expressions	Exercises 1–6
Example 2 Using the Order of Operations	Exercises 1–6, 13
Example 3 Evaluating Real-World Expressions	Exercises 7–8, 10–12, 14, 16

Exercise	Depth of Knowledge (D.O.K.)		COMMON CORE Mathematical Practices
10–12	**2** Skills/Concepts		**MP.4** Modeling
13	**3** Strategic Thinking	H.O.T.	**MP.3** Logic
14–16	**3** Strategic Thinking	H.O.T.	**MP.4** Modeling
17	**3** Strategic Thinking	H.O.T.	**MP.3** Logic
18	**3** Strategic Thinking	H.O.T.	**MP.7** Using Structure

Additional Resources

Differentiated Instruction includes:

• Leveled Practice worksheets

10.2 Independent Practice

COMMON CORE 6.EE.2c

Personal Math Trainer

Online Assessment and Intervention

my.hrw.com

10. The table shows ticket prices at the Movie 16 theater. Let a represent the number of adult tickets, c the number of children's tickets, and s the number of senior citizen tickets.

Movie 16 Ticket Prices	
Adults	$8.75
Children	$6.50
Seniors	$6.50

a. Write an expression for the total cost of the three types of tickets.

$8.75a + 6.5c + 6.5s$ or $8.75a + 6.5(c + s)$

b. The Andrews family bought 2 adult tickets, 3 children's tickets, and 1 senior ticket. Evaluate your expression in part a to find the total cost of the tickets.

$8.75(2) + 6.5(3) + 6.5(1) =$

$8.75(2) + 6.5(3 + 1) = \$43.50$

c. The Spencer family bought 4 adult tickets and 2 children's tickets. Did they spend the same as the Andrews family? Explain.

No; $8.75(4) + 6.5(2) = \$48.00$

11. The area of a triangular sail is given by the expression $\frac{1}{2}bh$, where b is the length of the base and h is the height. What is the area of a triangular sail in a model sailboat when $b = 12$ inches and $h = 7$ inches?

$A = \underline{42}$ in.^{2}

12. Ramon wants to balance his checking account. He has $2,340 in the account. He writes a check for $140. He deposits a check for $268. How much does Ramon have left in his checking account? $\underline{\$2,468}$

13. Look for a Pattern Evaluate the expression $6x - x^2$ for $x = 0, 1, 2, 3, 4, 5,$ and 6. Use your results to fill in the table and describe any pattern that you see.

x	0	1	2	3	4	5	6
$6x - x^2$	0	5	8	9	8	5	0

The value of $6x - x^2$ increases from 0 at $x = 0$ to 9 at $x = 3$, then decreases back to 0 at $x = 6$. Also, the values are the same for $x = 0$ and 6, for $x = 1$ and 5, and for $x = 2$ and 4.

14. The kinetic energy (in joules) of a moving object can be calculated from the expression $\frac{1}{2}mv^2$, where m is the mass of the object in kilograms and v is its speed in meters per second. Find the kinetic energy of a 0.145-kg baseball that is thrown at a speed of 40 meters per second.

$E = \underline{116}$ joules

15. The area of a square is given by x^2, where x is the length of one side. Mary's original garden was in the shape of a square. She has decided to double the area of her garden. Write an expression that represents the area of Mary's new garden. Evaluate the expression if the side length of Mary's original garden was 8 feet.

$2(x^2)$; $2(64) = 128$ square feet

16. The volume of a pyramid with a square base is given by the expression $\frac{1}{3}s^2h$, where s is the length of a side of the base and h is the height. Find the volume of a pyramid with a square base of side length 24 feet and a height of 30 feet.

$V = \underline{5,760 \text{ ft}^3}$

H.O.T. FOCUS ON HIGHER ORDER THINKING

Work Area

17. Draw Conclusions Consider the expressions $3x(x - 2) + 2$ and $2x^2 + 3x - 12$.

a. Evaluate each expression for $x = 2$ and for $x = 7$. Based on your results, do you know whether the two expressions are equivalent? Explain.

For $x = 2$, each expression has a value of 2. For $x = 7$, each expression has a value of 107. These results suggest that the expressions may be equivalent but do not prove that the expressions are equivalent.

b. Evaluate each expression for $x = 5$. Based on your results, do you know whether the two expressions are equivalent? Explain.

For $x = 5$, the 1st expression has a value of 47 and the 2nd expression has a value of 53. Because the values are different, the expressions are not equivalent.

18. Critique Reasoning Marjorie evaluated the expression $3x + 2$ for $x = 5$ as shown:

$$3x + 2 = 35 + 2 = 37$$

What was Marjorie's mistake? What is the correct value of $3x + 2$ for $x = 5$?

$3x$ means that 3 should be multiplied by the value of x; 17

EXTEND THE MATH PRE-AP

Activity available online my.hrw.com

Activity Harold has a globe that has a diameter of 10 inches. He builds a globe with a radius twice as long as his original globe. Use the formulas below to find the surface area and the volume of the new globe. Use $\pi = 3.14$. Explain your process and show your work.

Surface Area (SA) of a sphere $= 4\pi r^2$, where r is the radius of the sphere. Volume (V) of a sphere $= \frac{4}{3}\pi r^3$, where r is the radius of the sphere.

Sample answer: First, find the radius of the new globe. The diameter of the original globe is 10 inches, so its radius is $10 \div 2 = 5$ inches. The radius of the new globe is twice as long: 5 inches $\times 2 = 10$ inches. Then use $r = 10$ inches as the value to substitute for r in each formula.

SA of new globe is $4\pi r^2 \approx 4(3.14)(10)^2 \approx 4(3.14)(100) \approx 4(314) \approx 1,256$ in^2;

V of new globe is $\frac{4}{3}\pi r^3 \approx \frac{4}{3}(3.14)(10)^3 \approx \frac{4}{3}(3.14)(1,000) \approx \frac{4}{3}(3,140) \approx 4,186\frac{2}{3}$ in^3

Common Core Standards

The student is expected to:

 Expressions and Equations—6.EE.3

Apply the properties of operations to generate equivalent expressions.

 Expressions and Equations—6.EE.2b

Identify parts of an expression using mathematical terms (sum, term, product, factor, quotient, coefficient); view one or more parts of an expression as a single entity.

 Expressions and Equations—6.EE.4

Identify when two expressions are equivalent (i.e. when the two expressions name the same number regardless of which value is substituted into them).

Mathematical Practices

 MP.2 Reasoning

Engage

ESSENTIAL QUESTION

How can you identify and write equivalent expressions? Sample answer: Substitute the same value into each expression and compare the results, or simplify each expression to see if they are equivalent.

Motivate the Lesson

Ask: Are the expressions $3x + 8$ and $2x + 14$ equivalent expressions for $x = 6$? Begin the Explore Activity to find out.

Explore

EXPLORE ACTIVITY 1

Focus on Critical Thinking **CC** Mathematical Practices

Point out to students that even though expressions share an element, such as $5x$, and include the same operation, they are not necessarily equivalent expressions. For example, x^2 and x^3 have the same base and look similar but they are not equivalent; $x^2 = x \cdot x$ and $x^3 = x \cdot x \cdot x$.

Explain

EXPLORE ACTIVITY 2

Focus on Modeling **CC** Mathematical Practices

Point out that the number and arrangement of the algebra tiles models each expression. The first model shows three groups of 1 variable plus 2 ones, and the second model shows 3 variables plus 6 ones. Discuss with students why the two algebraic expressions are equivalent.

Questioning Strategies **CC** Mathematical Practices

• Earlier, you used counters to make models. How are algebra tiles similar to counters? How are they different? Both counters and algebra tiles are used the same way, one tile or counter for each number being added. The difference is that algebra tiles have an x (variable) tile used to represent an unknown quantity, while counters represent +1.

• Which two characteristics do you look for in the models to decide whether the two expressions are equivalent? The models of both expressions should have 1) an equal number of x tiles and 2) an equal number of +1-tiles.

ESSENTIAL QUESTION

How can you identify and write equivalent expressions?

EXPLORE ACTIVITY 1 | COMMON CORE **6.EE.4**

Identifying Equivalent Expressions

One way to test whether two expressions might be equivalent is to evaluate them for the same value of the variable.

Match the expressions in List A with their equivalent expressions in List B.

List A	List B
$5x + 65$	$5x + 1$
$5(x + 1)$	$5x + 5$
$1 + 5x$	$5(13 + x)$

A Evaluate each of the expressions in the lists for $x = 3$.

List A	List B
$5(3) + 65 = \boxed{80}$	$5(3) + 1 = \boxed{16}$
$5(3 + 1) = \boxed{20}$	$5(3) + 5 = \boxed{20}$
$1 + 5(3) = \boxed{16}$	$5(13 + 3) = \boxed{80}$

B Which pair(s) of expressions have the same value for $x = 3$?
$5(x + 1)$ and $5x + 5$; $1 + 5x$ and $5x + 1$; $5x + 65$ and $5(13 + x)$

C How could you further test whether the expressions in each pair are equivalent?
Sample answer: Evaluate for several other values of x.

D Do you think the expressions in each pair are equivalent? Why or why not?
Sample answer: Yes; it appears that they will always have the same value.

EXPLORE ACTIVITY 1 *(cont'd)*

Reflect

1. **Error Analysis** Lisa evaluated the expressions $2x$ and x^2 for $x = 2$ and found that both expressions were equal to 4. Lisa concluded that $2x$ and x^2 are equivalent expressions. How could you show Lisa that she is incorrect?
Evaluate the expressions for a different value of x; for example, when $x = 1$, $2x = 2$ and $x^2 = 1$.

EXPLORE ACTIVITY 2 | COMMON CORE **6.EE.3**

Modeling Equivalent Expressions

You can also use models to determine if two expressions are equivalent. *Algebra tiles* are one way to model expressions.

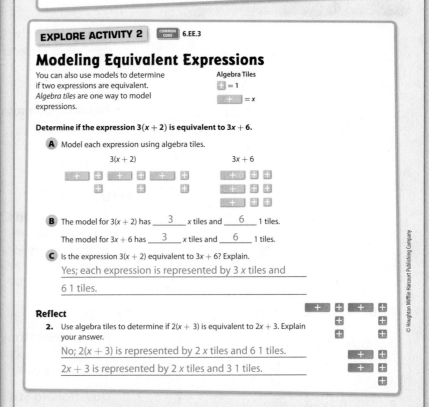

Algebra Tiles
$\boxed{+} = 1$
$\boxed{\ +\ } = x$

Determine if the expression $3(x + 2)$ is equivalent to $3x + 6$.

A Model each expression using algebra tiles.

$3(x + 2)$ $3x + 6$

B The model for $3(x + 2)$ has ___3___ x tiles and ___6___ 1 tiles.
The model for $3x + 6$ has ___3___ x tiles and ___6___ 1 tiles.

C Is the expression $3(x + 2)$ equivalent to $3x + 6$? Explain.
Yes; each expression is represented by 3 x tiles and 6 1 tiles.

Reflect

2. Use algebra tiles to determine if $2(x + 3)$ is equivalent to $2x + 3$. Explain your answer.
No; $2(x + 3)$ is represented by 2 x tiles and 6 1 tiles.
$2x + 3$ is represented by 2 x tiles and 3 1 tiles.

PROFESSIONAL DEVELOPMENT

CC Integrate Mathematical Practices MP.2

This lesson provides an opportunity to address the Mathematical Practices standard that calls for students to reason abstractly and quatitatively. In this lesson's Explore Activities and Examples, students use words and operational symbols as well as algebra tiles to identify, represent, and compare algebraic expressions and to generate equivalent expressions.

Math Background

Algebraic expressions are equivalent if they simplify to the same value. The Commutative, Associative, Distributive, and Identity properties give rules about how to rewrite an expression without changing its value.

$x + (3x + 2) + (2x + 3)$	
$x + 3x + (2 + 2x) + 3$	Associative
$x + 3x + (2x + 2) + 3$	Commutative
$(x + 3x + 2x) + (2 + 3)$	Associative
$x(1 + 3 + 2) + (2 + 3)$	Distributive
$x(6) + (5)$	Addition
$6x + 5$	Commutative

EXAMPLE 1

Questioning Strategies Mathematical Practices

• How does the Commutative Property of Addition allow you to rewrite an expression without changing its value? You can change the order of the terms in an addition expression.

• How do you know which properties of operations may help you identify equivalent expressions? Look at the operational symbols that appear in the given expressions. Apply properties of operations that relate to those symbols.

Engage with the Whiteboard

Have students circle the operational symbol in Example 1 and write an equivalent expression on the whiteboard. Then have students draw a model of each expression, using algebra tiles to show that the expressions are equivalent.

Focus on Communication Mathematical Practices

Make sure students understand that the properties of operations are rules about how to rewrite expressions by rearranging and combining terms without changing the value of the expression.

YOUR TURN

Avoid Common Errors

If students have difficulty determining which property to use, remind them to begin by identifying the operation used in the given expression. Then they should look at the list of properties to see which properties apply to that operation. Point out that a given expression may have more than one equivalent expression, as more than one property can be applied.

EXAMPLE 2

Focus on Reasoning Mathematical Practices

Invite students to examine the pairs of expressions in A and B. Discuss why the order of elements in expressions is important when comparing for equivalence.

Questioning Strategies Mathematical Practices

• In A, how does the Distributive Property enable you to determine that the expressions are equivalent without evaluating them? The Distributive Property states that multiplying a number by a difference, as in $3(x - 2)$, is the same as multiplying each number in the difference and subtracting the products: $(3)(x) - (3)(2) = 3x - 6$.

YOUR TURN

Engage with the Whiteboard

For Exercises 6–7, have students use algebra tiles to draw a model of each expression on the whiteboard. Then have students explain whether the expressions are equivalent or not.

Writing Equivalent Expressions Using Properties

Properties of operations can be used to identify equivalent expressions.

Properties of Operations	Examples
Commutative Property of Addition: When adding, changing the order of the numbers does not change the sum.	$3 + 4 = 4 + 3$
Commutative Property of Multiplication: When multiplying, changing the order of the numbers does not change the product.	$2 \times 4 = 4 \times 2$
Associative Property of Addition: When adding more than two numbers, the grouping of the numbers does not change the sum.	$(3 + 4) + 5 = 3 + (4 + 5)$
Associative Property of Multiplication: When multiplying more than two numbers, the grouping of the numbers does not change the product.	$(2 \times 4) \times 3 = 2 \times (4 \times 3)$
Distributive Property: Multiplying a number by a sum or difference is the same as multiplying by each number in the sum or difference and then adding or subtracting.	$6(2 + 4) = 6(2) + 6(4)$ $8(5 - 3) = 8(5) - 8(3)$
Identity Property of Addition: Adding zero to a number does not change its value.	$9 + 0 = 9$
Identity Property of Multiplication: Multiplying a number by one does not change its value.	$1 \times 7 = 7$

EXAMPLE 1 — COMMON CORE 6.EE.3

Use a property to write an expression that is equivalent to $x + 3$.

The operation in the expression is addition.

You can use the Commutative Property of Addition to write an equivalent expression: $x + 3 = 3 + x$.

YOUR TURN

For each expression, use a property to write an equivalent expression. Tell which property you used. Sample answers given.

3. $(ab)c = $ _$a(bc)$; Associative Property of Multiplication_

4. $3y + 4y = $ _$(3 + 4)y$; Distributive Property_

5. 6×7 _7×6; Commutative Property of Multiplication_

Math On the Spot
my.hrw.com

Animated Math
my.hrw.com

Personal Math Trainer
Online Assessment and Intervention
my.hrw.com

Lesson 10.3 **277**

Identifying Equivalent Expressions Using Properties

EXAMPLE 2 — COMMON CORE 6.EE.3

Use the properties of operations to determine if the expressions are equivalent.

A $3(x - 2)$; $3x - 6$

$3(x - 2) = 3x - 6$ — Distributive Property

$3(x - 2)$ and $3x - 6$ are equivalent expressions.

B $2 + x$; $\frac{1}{2}(4 + x)$

$\frac{1}{2}(x + 4) = \frac{1}{2}x + 2$ — Distributive Property

$= 2 + \frac{1}{2}x$ — Commutative Property

$2 + x$ does not equal $2 + \frac{1}{2}x$.

They are not equivalent expressions.

YOUR TURN

Use the properties of operations to determine if the expressions are equivalent.

6. $6x - 8$; $2(3x - 5)$
   $2(3x - 5) = 6x - 10$;
   not equivalent

7. $2 - 2 + 5x$; $5x$
   $2 - 2 + 5x = 5x$;
   equivalent

8. Jamal bought 2 packs of stickers and 8 individual stickers. Use x to represent the number of stickers in a pack of stickers and write an expression to represent the number of stickers Jamal bought. Is the expression equivalent to $2(4 + x)$? Check your answer with algebra tile models.

   Jamal bought $2x + 8$ stickers. $2(4 + x) = 8 + 2x = 2x + 8$; yes

Personal Math Trainer
Online Assessment and Intervention
my.hrw.com

278 Unit 4

DIFFERENTIATE INSTRUCTION

Visual Cues

Point out to students that it is often helpful to use colored pencils to identify like terms before combining them.

Have students identify the like terms in the following expressions.

1. $a + 2b + 2a + b + 2c$ — Like terms: a and $2a$, $2b$ and b

2. $18 + 2d^3 + 5d + 3d^3 - 2d^2$ — Like terms: $2d^3$ and $3d^3$

3. $5x^3 + 3y + 7x^3 - 2y - 4x^2$ — Like terms: $5x^3$ and $7x^3$, $3y$ and $2y$

Cognitive Strategies

A fun way for students to remember how to combine like terms is to name the variable part of like terms. For example, for the expression $2a + 5b + 4a$, students can name variable a apples and variable b bananas. Thus, 2 apples + 5 bananas + 4 apples = 6 apples + 5 bananas = $6a + 5b$.

Additional Resources

Differentiated Instruction includes:

- Reading Strategies
- Success for English Learners **ELL**
- Reteach
- Challenge **PRE-AP**

EXAMPLE 3

Connect Vocabulary ELL

Stress the use of correct mathematical terminology. The parts of an expression that are separated by + or − signs, such as $3x$ and $5x$ in the expression $3x + 5x$, are called *terms*. Terms that have identical variable parts are *like terms*. In the expression $3x + 5x$, $3x$ and $5x$ are like terms. The properties of operations allow you to rearrange and combine like terms.

Questioning Strategies CC Mathematical Practices

• In B, why do you have to apply the Distributive Property before adding like terms? Because of the order of operations, you need to multiply before you can add.

• In C, why does $y + 7y$ equal $8y$? Because y is $1y$, so $1y + 7y = (1 + 7)y = 8y$.

YOUR TURN

Avoid Common Errors

Exercise 11 Students may neglect to add single variables. Remind them that b is $1b$, so adding b to another b-term increases the coefficient by 1.

Elaborate

Talk About It
Summarize the Lesson

 Ask: How do properties of operations help you to write equivalent expressions? Properties of operations allow me to write an expression in different ways without changing its value. I can use the properties to form equivalent expressions by regrouping, reordering, and combining terms.

GUIDED PRACTICE

Engage with the Whiteboard

For Exercise 1, have students rewrite each expression on the whiteboard by substituting 5 for y and then simplifying the expressions.
For Exercise 2, ask a student to circle the part of the model that shows that the two expressions are not equivalent on the whiteboard.

Avoid Common Errors

Exercises 3–4 If students have difficulty determining which property to use, remind them to begin by identifying the operation used in the given expression. Then they should look at the list of properties to see which properties apply to that operation.

Exercises 5–6 Remind students that when they apply the Distributive Property they must distribute the constant or variable that is *outside* the parentheses to each term that is *inside* the parentheses.

Exercise 8 Students may neglect to add single variables. Remind them that $-x$ is $-1x$, so adding $-x$ to another x-term decreases the coefficient by 1.

Generating Equivalent Expressions

Parts of an algebraic expression		
terms	The parts of the expression that are separated by + or − signs	$12 + 3y^2 + 4x + 2y^2 + 4$
coefficients	Numbers that are multiplied by at least one variable	$12 + 3y^2 + 4x + 2y^2 + 4$
like terms	Terms with the same variable(s) raised to the same power(s)	$12 + 3y^2 + 4x + 2y^2 + 4$

When an expression contains like terms, you can use properties to combine the like terms and write an equivalent expression.

Math On the Spot
my.hrw.com

EXAMPLE 3   COMMON CORE 6.EE.3, 6.EE.2b

Combine like terms.

A $6x^2 - 4x^2$ ⎯⎯⎯⎯⎯ ($6x^2$ and $4x^2$ are like terms.)

$6x^2 - 4x^2 = x^2(6 - 4)$	Distributive Property
$= x^2(2)$	Subtract inside the parentheses.
$= 2x^2$	Commutative Property of Multiplication

$6x^2 - 4x^2 = 2x^2$

B $3a + 2(b + 5a)$

$3a + 2(b + 5a) = 3a + 2b + 2(5a)$	Distributive Property
$= 3a + 2b + (2 \cdot 5)a$	Associative Property of Multiplication
$= 3a + 2b + 10a$	Multiply 2 and 5.
$= 3a + 10a + 2b$	Commutative Property of Addition
$= (3 + 10)a + 2b$	Distributive Property
$= 13a + 2b$	Add inside the parentheses.

$3a + 2(b + 5a) = 13a + 2b$

Math Talk
Mathematical Practices

Write 2 terms that can be combined with $7y^4$.

Sample answers: y^4 and $6y^4$

C $y + 11x + 7y - 7x$ ⎯⎯⎯⎯⎯ (y and 7y are like terms; 11x and 7x are like terms.)

$y + 11x + 7y - 7x = y + 7y + 11x - 7x$	Commutative Property
$= (1 + 7)y + (11 - 7)x$	Distributive Property
$= 8y + 4x$	Simplify inside parentheses.

$y + 11x + 7y - 7x = 8y + 4x$

Lesson 10.3 **279**

YOUR TURN

Personal Math Trainer
Online Assessment and Intervention
my.hrw.com

Combine like terms.

9. $8y - 3y = $ ___5y___   **10.** $6x^2 + 4(x^2 - 1) = $ $10x^2 - 4$

11. $4a^5 - 2a^5 + 4b + b = $ **12.** $8m + 14 - 12 + 4n = $
___$2a^5 + 5b$___   ___$8m + 2 + 4n$___

Guided Practice

1. Evaluate each of the expressions in the list for $y = 5$. Then, draw lines to match the expressions in List A with their equivalent expressions in List B.
(Explore Activity 1)

List A	List B
$4 + 4y = $ ___24___	$4y - 4 = $ ___16___
$4(y - 1) = $ ___16___	$4(y + 1) = $ ___24___
$4y + 1 = $ ___21___	$1 + 4y = $ ___21___

2. Determine if the expressions are equivalent by comparing the models. (Explore Activity 2) ___not equivalent___

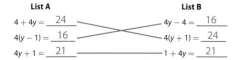

$x + 4$ $2(x + 2)$

For each expression, use a property to write an equivalent expression. Tell which property you used. (Example 1) Sample answers are given.

3. $ab = $ ___ba___
___Commutative Prop. of Mult.___

4. $5(3x - 2) = $ ___$5(3x) - 5(2)$___
___Distributive Prop.___

Use the properties of operations to determine if each pair of expressions is equivalent. (Example 2)

5. $\frac{1}{2}(4 - 2x)$; $2 - 2x$ ___not equivalent___

6. $\frac{1}{2}(6x - 2)$; $3 - x$ ___not equivalent___

Combine like terms. (Example 3)

7. $32y + 12y = $ ___$44y$___

8. $12 + 3x - x - 12 = $ ___$2x$___

? ESSENTIAL QUESTION CHECK-IN

9. Describe two ways to write equivalent algebraic expressions.

___Use properties of operations or combine like terms___

_____

280 Unit 4

10.3 LESSON QUIZ

 6.EE.2b, 6.EE.3, 6.EE.4

1. Use one of the properties of operations to write an expression that is equivalent to $4 + m$. Tell which property you used.

Use the properties of operations to determine if the expressions are equivalent.

2. $3 + y; \frac{1}{3}(6 + y)$

3. $4(y - 3); 4y - 12$

Combine like terms.

4. $9y^2 - 6y^2$

5. $5c + 4(d + 6c)$

6. $x + 10y - 4y + 4x$

Lesson Quiz available online

 my.hrw.com

Answers

1. $m + 4$; Commutative Property of Addition

2. not equivalent

3. equivalent

4. $3y^2$

5. $29c + 4d$

6. $5x + 6y$

Evaluate

GUIDED AND INDEPENDENT PRACTICE

 6.EE.2b, 6.EE.3, 6.EE.4

Concepts & Skills	Practice
Explore Activity 1 Identifying Equivalent Expressions	Exercise 1
Explore Activity 2 Modeling Equivalent Expressions	Exercises 2, 14
Example 1 Writing Equivalent Expressions Using Properties	Exercises 3–4, 10–13, 27–29
Example 2 Identifying Equivalent Expressions Using Properties	Exercises 5–6, 25
Example 3 Generating Equivalent Expressions	Exercises 7–8, 15–24, 26

Exercise	Depth of Knowledge (D.O.K.)	Mathematical Practices
10–24	**2** Skills/Concepts	**MP.5** Using Tools
25	**3** Strategic Thinking **H.O.T.**	**MP.3** Logic
26–27	**2** Skills/Concepts	**MP.4** Modeling
28–29	**2** Skills/Concepts	**MP.2** Reasoning
30	**3** Strategic Thinking **H.O.T.**	**MP.7** Using Structure
31	**3** Strategic Thinking **H.O.T.**	**MP.3** Logic
32	**3** Strategic Thinking **H.O.T.**	**MP.7** Using Structure

Additional Resources

Differentiated Instruction includes:

• Leveled Practice worksheets

CC CLUSTER CONNECTION **Exercise 25** combines concepts from the Common Core cluster "Apply and extend previous understandings of arithmetic to algebraic expressions."

10.3 Independent Practice

COMMON CORE 6.EE.2b, 6.EE.3, 6.EE.4

Personal Math Trainer

my.hrw.com

Online Assessment and Intervention

For each expression, use a property to write an equivalent expression. Tell which property you used. Sample answers given.

10. $cd =$ _____ dc _____
Commutative Prop. of Mult.

11. $x + 13 =$ _____ $13 + x$ _____
Commutative Prop. of Addition

12. $4(2x - 3) =$ _____ $4(2x) - 4(3)$ _____
Distributive Prop.

13. $2 + (a + b) =$ _____ $(2 + a) + b$ _____
Associative Prop. of Addition

14. Draw algebra tile models to prove that $4 + 8x$ and $4(2x + 1)$ are equivalent.

$4 + 8x$ $4(2x + 1)$

Combine like terms.

15. $7x^4 - 5x^4 =$ _____ $2x^4$

16. $32y + 5y =$ _____ $37y$

17. $6b + 7b - 10 =$ _____ $13b - 10$

18. $2x + 3x + 4 =$ _____ $5x + 4$

19. $y + 4 + 3(y + 2) =$ _____ $4y + 10$

20. $7a^2 - a^2 + 16 =$ _____ $6a^2 + 16$

21. $3y^2 + 3(4y^2 - 2) =$ _____ $15y^2 - 6$

22. $z^2 + z + 4z^3 + 4z^2 =$ _____ $4z^3 + 5z^2 + z$

23. $0.5(x^4 - 3) + 12 =$ _____ $0.5x^4 + 10.5$

24. $\frac{1}{4}(16 + 4p) =$ _____ $4 + p$

25. **Justify Reasoning** Determine whether $3x + 12 + x$ is equivalent to $4(3 + x)$. Use properties of operations to justify your answer.

Yes. Apply the Distributive Property: $4(3 + x) = 12 + 4x = 12 + 3x + x$.

Apply the Commutative Property: $12 + 3x + x = 3x + 12 + x$.

26. William earns $13 an hour working at a movie theater. Last week he worked h hours at the concession stand and three times as many hours at the ticket counter. Write and simplify an expression for the amount of money William earned last week.

$13h + 13(3h) = 13h + 39h = 52h$

27. **Multiple Representations** Use the information in the table to write and simplify an expression to find the total weight of the medals won by the top medal-winning nations in the 2012 London Olympic Games. The three types of medals have different weights.

2012 Summer Olympics			
	Gold	Silver	Bronze
United States	46	29	29
China	38	27	23
Great Britain	29	17	19

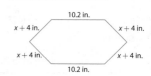

$(46 + 38 + 29)g + (29 + 27 + 17)s + (29 + 23 + 19)b;$
$113g + 73s + 71b$

Write an expression for the perimeters of each given figure. Simplify the expression.

28. _____ $6x + 10$ mm _____

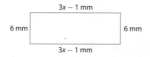

$3x - 1$ mm

6 mm   6 mm

$3x - 1$ mm

29. _____ $36.4 + 4x$ in. _____

10.2 in.

$x + 4$ in. $x + 4$ in.

$x + 4$ in. $x + 4$ in.

10.2 in.

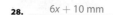

H.O.T. **FOCUS ON HIGHER ORDER THINKING**

Work Area

30. **Problem Solving** Examine the algebra tile model.

a. Write two equivalent expressions for the model. $4 + 6x;\ 2(2 + 3x)$

b. **What If?** Suppose a third row of tiles identical to the ones above is added to the model. How does that change the two expressions?

The expressions become $6 + 9x$ and $3(2 + 3x)$.

31. **Communicate Mathematical Ideas** Write an example of an expression that cannot be simplified, and explain how you know that it cannot be simplified.

$3x^2 - 4x + 7$; It does not have any like terms.

32. **Problem Solving** Write an expression that is equivalent to $8(2y + 4)$ that can be simplified.

Sample answer: $2(8y + 16)$

EXTEND THE MATH PRE-AP

Activity available online my.hrw.com

Activity During a basketball game, Joelle scored 8 points on free throws. She also scored 2 points for each inside shot and 3 points for each outside shot she made. Joelle made n inside shots and s outside shots during the game. Write six equivalent expressions for the total number of points Joelle scored. Which properties of operations did you use to identify equivalent expressions?

Sample answer:
Commutative Property of Addition: $8 + 2n + 3s$, $8 + 3s + 2n$, $2n + 3s + 8$, $2n + 8 + 3s$;
Distributive Property and Commutative Property of Addition: $2(4 + n) + 3s$,
$3s + 2(4 + n)$

Ready to Go On?

Assess Mastery

Use the assessment on this page to determine if students have mastered the concepts and standards covered in this module.

Response to Intervention

Intervention	Enrichment

Access Ready to Go On? assessment online, and receive instant scoring, feedback, and customized intervention or enrichment.

Online and Print Resources

Personal Math Trainer

Online Assessment and Intervention

my.hrw.com

Differentiated Instruction
- Reteach worksheets
- Reading Strategies **ELL**
- Success for English Learners **ELL**

Differentiated Instruction
- Challenge worksheets **PRE-AP**
- Extend the Math **PRE-AP** Lesson Activities in TE

Additional Resources

Assessment Resources includes:
- Leveled Module Quizzes

Ready to Go On?

10.1 Modeling and Writing Expressions

Write each phrase as an algebraic expression.

1. p divided by 6 $\quad \dfrac{p}{6}$

2. 65 less than j $\quad j - 65$

3. the sum of 185 and h $\quad 185 + h$

4. the product of 16 and g $\quad 16g$

5. Let x represent the number of television show episodes that are taped in a season. Write an expression for the number of episodes taped in 4 seasons. $\quad 4x$

10.2 Evaluating Expressions

Evaluate each expression for the given value of the variable.

6. $8p; p = 9 \quad 72$

7. $11 + r; r = 7 \quad 18$

8. $4(d + 7); d = 2 \quad 36$

9. $\dfrac{60}{m}; m = 5 \quad 12$

10. To find the area of a triangle, you can use the expression $b \times h \div 2$, where b is the base of the triangle and h is its height. What is the area of a triangle with a base of 6 and a height of 8? $\quad 24$

10.3 Generating Equivalent Expressions

11. Draw lines to match the expressions in List A with their equivalent expressions in List B.

List A	List B
$7x + 14$	$7(1 + x)$
$7 + 7x$	$7x - 7$
$7(x - 1)$	$7(x + 2)$

? ESSENTIAL QUESTION

12. How can you solve problems involving equivalent expressions?

Sample answer: Model the expressions with bar models or algebra tiles to determine if the expressions are equivalent; Write equivalent expressions using properties of operations and order of operations.

Module 10 **283**

Common Core Standards

Lesson	Exercises	Common Core Standards
10.1	1–5	6.EE.2a, 6.EE.2b, 6.EE.4, 6.EE.6
10.2	6–10	6.EE.2c
10.3	11	6.EE.2b, 6.EE.3, 6.EE.4

Assessment Readiness

Assessment Readiness Tip Students can circle or underline key words and phrases to identify important information.

Item 1 Students should underline the word *product*. Product means the operation used is multiplication. Thus, students can quickly see that choice C is the correct answer.

Item 3 Students should underline the phrase *divided them evenly among p pages*. Since the operation used is division, students can eliminate choices A and B, and then check the order of division in the two remaining answer choices to reveal that choice D is the correct answer.

Avoid Common Errors

Item 5 Some students may forget that $7w$ means the product of 7 and the variable and mistakenly substitute 9 for w to make the number 79. Remind students that the variable in a term is multiplied by the coefficient.

Item 6 Caution students to read the question carefully. Some students may not realize that this question is asking for how many pages Katie has left to read and may indicate that choice D is correct.

Additional Resources

Personal Math Trainer
Online Assessment and Intervention
my.hrw.com

MODULE 10 MIXED REVIEW
Assessment Readiness
COMMON CORE

Personal Math Trainer
Online Assessment and Intervention
my.hrw.com

Selected Response

1. Which expression represents the product of 83 and x?

   Ⓐ $83 + x$

   Ⓑ $83 \div x$

   Ⓒ $83x$

   Ⓓ $83 - x$

2. Which phrase describes the algebraic expression $\frac{r}{9}$?

   Ⓐ the product of r and 9

   Ⓑ the quotient of r and 9

   Ⓒ 9 less than r

   Ⓓ r more than 9

3. Rhonda was organizing photos in a photo album. She took 60 photos and divided them evenly among p pages. Which algebraic expression represents the number of photos on each page?

   Ⓐ $p - 60$ Ⓒ $\frac{p}{60}$

   Ⓑ $60 - p$ Ⓓ $\frac{60}{p}$

4. Using the algebraic expression $4n + 6$, what is the greatest whole-number value of n that will give you a result less than 100?

   Ⓐ 22   Ⓒ 24

   Ⓑ 23   Ⓓ 25

5. Evaluate $7w - 14$ for $w = 9$.

   Ⓐ 2

   Ⓑ 18

   Ⓒ 49

   Ⓓ 77

6. Katie has read 32% of a book. If she has read 80 pages, how many more pages does Katie have left to read?

   Ⓐ 40

   Ⓑ 170

   Ⓒ 200

   Ⓓ 250

7. The expression $12(x + 4)$ represents the total number of CDs Mei bought in April and May at $12 each. Which property is applied to write the equivalent expression $12x + 48$?

   Ⓐ Associative Property of Addition

   Ⓑ Associative Property of Multiplication

   Ⓒ Commutative Property of Multiplication

   Ⓓ Distributive Property

Mini-Task

8. You can convert a temperature given in degrees Celsius to a Fahrenheit temperature by using the expression $9x \div 5 + 32$, where x is the Celsius temperature.

   a. Water freezes when the temperature is 0 °C. At what Fahrenheit temperature does water freeze? _____ 32 °F

   b. Water boils at 100 °C. At what temperature does water boil in degrees Fahrenheit? _____ 212 °F

   c. The temperature of some water is 15 °C. What is the Fahrenheit temperature? _____ 59 °F

Common Core Standards

Items	Grade 6 Standards	Mathematical Practices
1	6.EE.2a	MP.2
2	6.EE.2a	MP.2
3	6.EE.2a	MP.4, MP.2
4	6.EE.2c	MP.7
5	6.EE.2c	MP.2
6*	6.EE.6, 6.NS.3	MP.4
7	6.EE.2c	MP.4
8	6.EE.6	MP.4, MP.2

* Item integrates mixed review concepts from previous modules or a previous course.

Study Guide Review

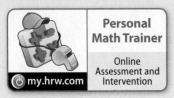
Vocabulary Development

Integrating Language Arts

Encourage students to practice using the unit vocabulary as they talk and write about mathematics. Understanding vocabulary will aid their understanding of the concepts.

 ELA-Literacy.RST.6-8.4 Determine the meaning of symbols, key terms, and other domain-specific words and phrases as they are used in a specific scientific or technical context relevant to grades 6–8 texts and topics.

MODULE 9 Generating Equivalent Numerical Expressions

COMMON CORE 6.EE.1

Key Concepts

- Use exponents to show repeated addition and find the value of exponential expressions. *(Lesson 9.1)*
- Find the prime factorization of a number. *(Lessons 9.2)*
- Simplify expressions using the order of operations. *(Lesson 9.3)*

MODULE 10 Generating Equivalent Algebraic Expressions

COMMON CORE 6.EE.2a, 6.EE.2b, 6.EE.2c, 6.EE.3, 6.EE.4, 6.EE.6

Key Concepts

- Write algebraic expressions for verbal phrases and verbal phrases for algebraic expressions. *(Lesson 10.1)*
- Evaluate algebraic expressions. *(Lesson 10.2)*
- Determine if two algebraic expressions are equivalent and combine like terms to simplify an algebraic expression. *(Lesson 10.3)*

Study Guide Review

MODULE 9 ## Generating Equivalent Numerical Expressions

Key Vocabulary
base *(base (en numeración))*
exponent *(exponente)*
order of operations *(orden de las operaciones)*
power *(potencia)*

? ESSENTIAL QUESTION

How can you generate equivalent numerical expressions and use them to solve real-world problems?

EXAMPLE 1

Find the value of each power.

A. 0.9^2

$0.9^2 = 0.9 \times 0.9 = 0.81$

B. 18^0

Any number raised to the power of 0 is 1.

$18^0 = 1$

C. $\left(\frac{1}{4}\right)^4$

$\left(\frac{1}{4}\right)^4 = \left(\frac{1}{4}\right)\left(\frac{1}{4}\right)\left(\frac{1}{4}\right)\left(\frac{1}{4}\right) = \frac{1}{256}$

EXAMPLE 2

Find the prime factorization of 60.

$$
\begin{array}{r|l}
2 & 60 \\
2 & 30 \\
3 & 15 \\
5 & 5 \\
& 1
\end{array}
$$

$60 = 2 \times 2 \times 3 \times 5$

$60 = 2^2 \times 3 \times 5$

The prime factorization of 60 is $2^2 \times 3 \times 5$.

EXAMPLE 3

Simplify each expression.

A. $4 \times (2^3 + 5)$

$= 4 \times (8 + 5)$ $2^3 = 8$

$= 4 \times 13$ Add.

$= 52$ Multiply.

B. $27 \div 3^2 \times 6$

$= 27 \div 9 \times 6$ $3^2 = 9$

$= 3 \times 6$ Divide.

$= 18$ Multiply.

EXERCISES

Use an exponent to write each expression. (Lesson 9.1)

1. 3.6×3.6 ___3.6^2___

2. $9 \times 9 \times 9 \times 9$ ___9^4___

3. $\frac{4}{5} \times \frac{4}{5} \times \frac{4}{5}$ ___$\left(\frac{4}{5}\right)^3$___

Find the value of each power. (Lesson 9.1)

4. 12^0 ___1___

5. 13^2 ___169___

6. $\left(\frac{2}{7}\right)^3$ ___$\frac{8}{343}$___

7. 0.4^2 ___0.16___

8. $\left(\frac{4}{9}\right)^1$ ___$\frac{4}{9}$___

9. 0.7^3 ___0.343___

Find the prime factorization of each number. (Lesson 9.2)

10. 75 ___$5^2 \times 3$___

11. 29 ___1×29___

12. 168 ___$2^3 \times 3 \times 7$___

13. Eduardo is building a sandbox that has an area of 84 square feet. What are the possible whole number measurements for the length and width of the sandbox? (Lesson 9.2)

___1, 84; 2, 42; 3, 28; 4, 21; 6, 14; 7, 12___

Simplify each expression. (Lesson 9.3)

14. $2 \times 5^2 - (4 + 1)$ ___45___

15. $\frac{22 - (3^2 + 4)}{12 \div 4}$ ___3___

MODULE 10 ## Generating Equivalent Algebraic Expressions

Key Vocabulary
algebraic expression *(expresión algebraica)*
coefficients *(coeficiente)*
constant *(contante)*
equivalent expressions *(expresión equivalente)*
evaluating *(evaluar)*
term *(término (en una expresión))*

? ESSENTIAL QUESTION

How can you generate equivalent algebraic expressions and use them to solve real-world problems?

EXAMPLE 1

Evaluate each expression for the given values of the variables.

A. $2(x^2 - 9); x = 5$

$2(5^2 - 9)$ $5^2 = 25$

$= 2(16)$ Subtract.

$= 32$ Multiply.

When $x = 5$, $2(x^2 - 9) = 32$.

B. $w + y^2 + 3w; w = 2, y = 6$

$2 + 6^2 + 3(2)$ $6^2 = 36$

$= 2 + 36 + 6$ Multiply.

$= 44$ Add.

When $w = 2$ and $y = 6$, $w + y^2 + 3w = 44$.

EXAMPLE 2

Determine whether the algebraic expressions are equivalent:
$5(x + 2)$ **and** $10 + 5x$.

$5(x + 2) = 5x + 10$ Distributive Property

$= 10 + 5x$ Commutative Property

$5(x + 2)$ is equal to $10 + 5x$. They are equivalent expressions.

Unit 4 Performance Tasks

The Performance Tasks provide students with the opportunity to apply concepts from this unit in real-world problem situations.

CAREERS IN MATH

Freelance Computer Programmer In Performance Task Item 1, students can see how a freelance computer programmer uses mathematics on the job.

SCORING GUIDES FOR PERFORMANCE TASKS

1. MATHEMATICAL PRACTICES **MP.1, MP.4**

Task	Possible Points (Total: 6)
a	**1 point** for correctly writing an expression for the formula: $2^n - 1$
b	**2 points** for correct answer: 65,535 golden keys
c	**1 point** for correctly writing an expression for number of bits: 14×2^8 **2 points** for correct answer: 3,584 bits

2. MATHEMATICAL PRACTICES **MP.1, MP.4, MP.7**

Task	Possible Points (Total: 6)
a	**1 point** for correctly writing an expression for the number of pictures: $p = 14^3$ **2 points** for correct answer: 2,744 pictures
b	**1 point** for correctly writing an expression for the number of pictures: $p = \dfrac{14^3}{2}$ **2 points** for correct answer: 1,372 pictures

Write each phrase as an algebraic expression. (Lesson 10.1)

1. x subtracted from 15 _____ $15 - x$

2. 12 divided by t _____ $\dfrac{12}{t}$

3. 4 groups of y _____ $4y$

4. the sum of z and 7 _____ $z + 7$

Write a phrase for each algebraic expression. (Lesson 10.1) Sample answers are given.

5. $8p$ _____ the product of 8 and p

6. $s + 7$ _____ the sum of s and 7

Evaluate each expression for the given values of the variables.
(Lesson 10.2)

7. $8z + 3$; $z = 8$ _____ 67

8. $3(7 + x^2)$; $x = 2$ _____ 33

9. $s - 5t + s^2$; $s = 4$, $t = -1$ _____ 25

10. $x - y^3$; $x = -7$, $y = 3$ _____ -34

11. The expression $\frac{1}{2}(h)(b_1 + b_2)$ gives the area of a trapezoid, with b_1 and b_2 representing the two base lengths of a trapezoid and h representing the height. Find the area of a trapezoid with base lengths 4 in. and 6 in. and a height of 8 in. (Lesson 10.2) _____ 40 in^2

Determine if the expressions are equivalent. (Lesson 10.3)

12. $7 + 7x$; $7\left(x + \frac{1}{7}\right)$ _____ not equivalent

13. $2.5(3 + x)$; $2.5x + 7.5$ _____ equivalent

Combine like terms. (Lesson 10.3)

14. $3m - 6 + m^2 - 5m + 1$ _____ $m^2 - 2m - 5$

15. $7x + 4(2x - 6)$ _____ $15x - 24$

16. $b^2 + 3 + 2b^2 + 4 - 7$ _____ $3b^2$

17. $3(p + 5) - 8 + 11p$ _____ $14p + 7$

Unit 4 Performance Tasks

1. **CAREERS IN MATH** Freelance Computer Programmer

Antonio is a freelance computer programmer. In his work, he often uses the power of 2^n to find the number of ways bits (or units of information) can be arranged. The n often stands for the number of bits.

a. Antonio is working on programming a new video game called *Millie's Quest*. In the game, the main character, Millie, collects golden keys to help her in her quest. Antonio wants to write a formula to show that Millie can collect one less key than the highest number of bits that can be arranged in the system. What formula can he use?

_____ $2^n - 1$

b. If Antonio is working with a 16-bit system, how many golden keys can Millie collect?

_____ 65,535 golden keys

c. Antonio is also working on a new spreadsheet program. The program takes up 14 bytes of memory. If each byte is equal to 8 bits, how many bits is Antonio's program? Show your work.

_____ $14 \times 2^8 = 14 \times 256 = 3{,}584$ bits

2. Hannah just bought a new camera. In January she took 14 pictures. The number of pictures she took doubled each month for three months.

a. How many pictures did Hannah take in March? Write and solve an expression with an exponent to show how many pictures she took.

_____ $p = 14^3$; 2,744 pictures

b. In April, Hanna took half the number of pictures she took in March. Her brother Jack thinks she took the same number of pictures in April that she did in February. Hanna knew he was incorrect. Write and solve an expression to show why Hannah is right.

In February, Hannah took 14^2, or 196 pictures. In April, Hannah took 1,372 pictures: $p = \dfrac{14^3}{2} = 1{,}372$ pictures

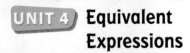

MIXED REVIEW

MIXED REVIEW

Assessment Readiness

Additional Resources

Personal Math Trainer

Online Assessment and Intervention

my.hrw.com

Assessment Resources
- Leveled Unit Tests: A, B, C, D
- Performance Assessment

Assessment Readiness Tip Remind students that they may need to complete more than one step when solving real-world problems.

Item 6 Students will need to determine how many 15 second increments are in 2 minutes and to use their knowledge of exponents to solve.

Avoid Common Errors

Item 8 Remind students to multiply before adding or subtracting when evaluating expressions.

Common Core Standards

Items	Grade 6 Standards	Mathematical Practices
1	**6.EE.1**	**MP.2** Reasoning
2	**6.EE.2c**	**MP.2** Reasoning
3	**6.EE.2a**	**MP.2** Reasoning
4	**6.EE.1**	**MP.2** Reasoning
5	**6.EE.2a**	**MP.2** Reasoning
6	**6.EE.2c**	**MP.1** Problem Solving
7	**6.EE.1**	**MP.2** Reasoning
8	**6.EE.2a**	**MP.2** Reasoning
9	**6.EE.2c**	**MP.2** Reasoning
10	**6.RP.3a**	**MP.2** Reasoning
11	**6.RP.3c**	**MP.1** Problem Solving
12*	**6.NS.7**	**MP.2** Reasoning
13	**6.EE.2**	**MP.1** Problem Solving
14	**6.EE.1, 6.EE.2**	**MP.1** Problem Solving
15	**6.EE.1, 6.EE.2**	**MP.1** Problem Solving

* Item integrates mixed review concepts from previous modules or a previous course.

COMMON CORE

Assessment Readiness

Personal Math Trainer

my.hrw.com
Online Assessment and Intervention

Selected Response

1. Which expression is equivalent to $2.3 \times 2.3 \times 2.3 \times 2.3 \times 2.3$?

Ⓐ 2.3×5

Ⓑ 23^5

Ⓒ $2^5 \times 3^5$

Ⓓ 2.3^5

2. Which operation should you perform first when you simplify $63 - (2 + 54 \times 6) \div 5$?

Ⓐ addition

Ⓑ division

Ⓒ multiplication

Ⓓ subtraction

3. Sheena was organizing items in a scrapbook. She took 25 photos and divided them evenly between p pages. Which algebraic expression represents the number of photos on each page?

Ⓐ $p - 25$

Ⓑ $25 - p$

Ⓒ $\frac{p}{25}$

Ⓓ $\frac{25}{p}$

4. Which is another way to write $7 \times 7 \times 7 \times 7$?

Ⓐ 7^4

Ⓑ $7(4)$

Ⓒ 28

Ⓓ 4^7

5. Angela earns x dollars an hour. On Friday, she worked 6 hours. On Saturday, she worked 8 hours. Which expression shows how much she earned both days?

Ⓐ $6x + 8$

Ⓑ $8x \times 6x$

Ⓒ $(6 + 8)x$

Ⓓ $\frac{6 + 8}{x}$

6. Marcus is doing a science experiment in which he measures the rate at which bacteria multiply. Every 15 seconds, the bacteria double in number. If there are 10 bacteria now, how many will there be in 2 minutes?

Ⓐ 160 bacteria

Ⓑ 256 bacteria

Ⓒ 1,280 bacteria

Ⓓ 2,560 bacteria

7. The prime factorization of which number is $2^5 \times 5$?

Ⓐ 50

Ⓑ 125

Ⓒ 160

Ⓓ 500

8. Which expression has a value of 36 when $x = 4$ and $y = 7$?

Ⓐ $2xy$

Ⓑ $2x + 4y$

Ⓒ $6y - x$

Ⓓ $12x - 2y$

Hot Tip!

When possible, use logic to eliminate at least two answer choices.

9. What should you do first to simplify the expression $(4^3 + 9) \div 76 + 5$?

Ⓐ Add 4 and 9.

Ⓑ Add 76 and 5.

Ⓒ Multiply $4 \times 4 \times 4$.

Ⓓ Divide $(4^3 + 9)$ by 76.

10. Which ratio is equivalent to 4:10?

Ⓐ $\frac{2}{5}$

Ⓑ $\frac{8}{10}$

Ⓒ $\frac{12}{16}$

Ⓓ $\frac{16}{10}$

11. Travis and Paula went to lunch. Travis ordered a sandwich for $7.50, and Paula ordered a burger for $5.25. After lunch, they left a 15% tip for their waiter. How much money did they spend altogether?

Ⓐ $12.75

Ⓑ $14.66

Ⓒ $15.95

Ⓓ $16.00

12. Which shows the following numbers in order from greatest to least?

$$1.5, \frac{2}{4}, \frac{4}{2}, 1.05$$

Ⓐ $\frac{4}{2}, 1.5, 1.05, \frac{2}{4}$

Ⓑ $1.05, 1.5, \frac{2}{4}, \frac{4}{2}$

Ⓒ $\frac{4}{2}, \frac{2}{4}, 1.5, 1.05$

Ⓓ $1.05, \frac{4}{2}, \frac{2}{4}, 1.5$

Mini-Tasks

13. For every bag of trail mix the local Scout Guide troop sells, they earn $0.45.

a. Write an expression to represent this situation.

$$\$0.45 \times t$$

b. Sarah sold 52 bags of trail mix. How much did she earn for her troop?

$$\$0.45 \times 52 = \$23.40$$

c. Let x represent the total number of bags of trail mix sold by Sarah's troop. Write an expression to show what percentage of bags Sarah sold.

$$\frac{52}{x} \times 100$$

14. Robert is replacing sod in two square-shaped areas of his backyard. One side of the first area is 7.5 feet. One side of the other area is 5.7 feet. The sod costs y dollars per square foot.

a. Write an expression to show how much Robert will spend on sod.

$$(7.5^2 + 5.7^2)y$$

b. If the sod costs $3.25 per square foot, about how much will Robert spend to put sod down in both areas of his backyard? Round to the nearest dollar.

$$(7.5^2 + 5.7^2)\$3.25 = 288.405; \$288$$

15. Jose wants to find how many gallons of water he needs to fill his cube-shaped aquarium. One side of his aquarium is 4 feet long.

a. Write and solve an expression to find the volume of Jose's aquarium.

$$V = 4^3, V = 64 \text{ cubic feet}$$

b. One cubic foot is equal to 7.48 gallons of water. How many gallons of water does Jose need to fill his aquarium? Round to the nearest gallon.

$$64 \times 7.48 = 478.72, 479 \text{ gallons}$$

UNIT 5

Equations and Inequalities

Contents

Unit Pacing Guide

45-Minute Classes

Module 11

DAY 1	DAY 2	DAY 3	DAY 4	DAY 5
Lesson 11.1	Lesson 11.1	Lesson 11.2	Lesson 11.2	Lesson 11.2

DAY 6	DAY 7	DAY 8	DAY 9	DAY 10
Lesson 11.3	Lesson 11.3	Lesson 11.3	Lesson 11.4	Lesson 11.4

DAY 11				
Ready to Go On? Assessment Readiness				

Module 12

DAY 1	DAY 2	DAY 3	DAY 4	DAY 5
Lesson 12.1	Lesson 12.1	Lesson 12.2	Lesson 12.2	Lesson 12.2

DAY 6	DAY 7	DAY 8	DAY 9	DAY 10
Lesson 12.3	Lesson 12.3	Lesson 12.4	Lesson 12.4	Lesson 12.4

DAY 11	DAY 12			
Ready to Go On? Assessment Readiness	Study Guide Assessment Readiness			

90-Minute Classes

Module 11

DAY 1	DAY 2	DAY 3	DAY 4	DAY 5
Lesson 11.1	Lesson 11.2	Lesson 11.3	Lesson 11.4	Ready to Go On? Assessment Readiness

Module 12

DAY 1	DAY 2	DAY 3	DAY 4	DAY 5
Lesson 12.1	Lesson 12.2	Lesson 12.3	Lesson 12.4	Ready to Go On? Assessment Readiness

DAY 6				
Study Guide Assessment Readiness				

Program Resources

⏻ Plan

Online Teacher Edition

Access a full suite of teaching resources online—plan, present, and manage classes, assignments, and activities.

ePlanner Easily plan your classes, create and view assignments, and access all program resources with your online, customizable planning tool.

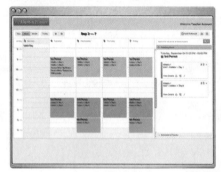

Professional Development Videos

Author Juli Dixon models successful teaching practices and strategies in actual classroom settings.

QR Codes Scan with your smart phone to jump directly from your print book to online videos and other resources.

Teacher's Edition

Support students with point-of-use Questioning Strategies, teaching tips, resources for differentiated instruction, additional activities, and more.

⏻ Engage and Explore

Real-World Videos Engage students with interesting and relevant applications of the mathematical content of each module.

Animated Math Online interactive simulations, tools, and games help students actively learn and practice key concepts.

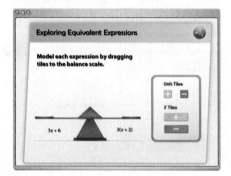

Explore Activities

Students interactively explore new concepts using a variety of tools and approaches.

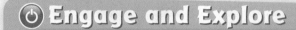

Image Credits: ©Rich Carey/Shutterstock.com; (c) ©Juli Dixon

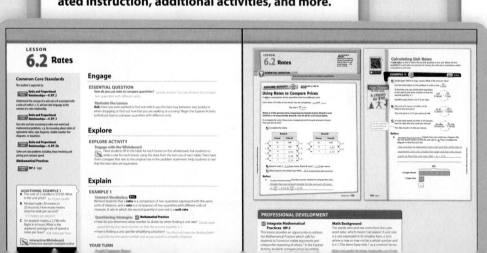

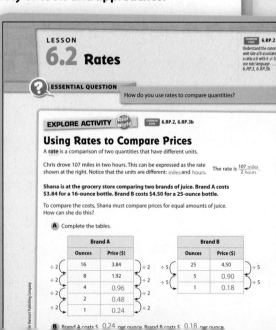

LESSON

6.2 Rates

6.RP.2
Understand the concept of a unit rate a/b associated with a ratio a:b with $b \neq 0$, and use rate language . . . . Also 6.RP.3, 6.RP.3b

ESSENTIAL QUESTION

How do you use rates to compare quantities?

EXPLORE ACTIVITY 6.RP.2, 6.RP.3b

Using Rates to Compare Prices

A **rate** is a comparison of two quantities that have different units.

Chris drove 107 miles in two hours. This can be expressed as the rate shown at the right. Notice that the units are different: miles and hours. The rate is $\frac{107 \text{ miles}}{2 \text{ hours}}$

Shana is at the grocery store comparing two brands of juice. Brand A costs \$3.84 for a 16-ounce bottle. Brand B costs \$4.50 for a 25-ounce bottle.

To compare the costs, Shana must compare prices for equal amounts of juice. How can she do this?

A Complete the tables.

Brand A	
Ounces	Price (\$)
16	3.84
8	1.92
4	0.96
2	0.48
1	0.24

÷ 2 (applied between each row on both columns)

Brand B	
Ounces	Price (\$)
25	4.50
5	0.90
1	0.18

÷ 5 (applied between each row on both columns)

B Brand A costs \$ 0.24 per ounce. Brand B costs \$ 0.18 per ounce.

Teach

 Math On the Spot video tutorials, featuring program authors Dr. Edward Burger and Martha Sandoval-Martinez, accompany every example in the textbook and give students step-by-step instructions and explanations of key math concepts.

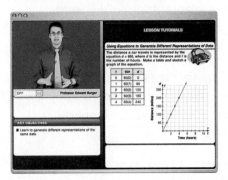

Present engaging content on a multitude of devices, including tablets and interactive whiteboards.

 Continually monitor and assess student progress with integrated formative assessment.

 Look for exercises indicated with this icon to build connections among standards within Common Core clusters.

Differentiated Instruction Print Resources

Support all learners with Differentiated Instruction Resources, including

- **Leveled Practice and Problem Solving**
- **Reteach**
- **Reading Strategies**
- **Success for English Learners**
- **Challenge**

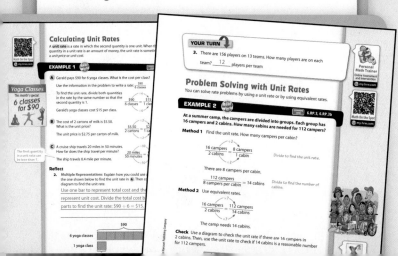

Assessment and Intervention

 The **Personal Math Trainer** provides online practice, homework, assessments, and intervention. Monitor student progress through reports and alerts. Create and customize assignments aligned to specific lessons or standards.

- **Practice** – With dynamic items and assignments, students get unlimited practice on key concepts supported by guided examples, step-by-step solutions, and video tutorials.

- **Assessments** – Choose from course assignments or customize your own based on course content, standards, difficulty levels, and more.

- **Homework** – Students can complete online homework with a wide variety of problem types, including the ability to enter expressions, equations, and graphs. Let the system automatically grade homework, so you can focus where your students need help the most!

- **Intervention** – Let the Personal Math Trainer automatically prescribe a targeted, personalized intervention path for your students.

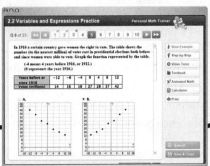

 Raise the bar with homework and practice that incorporates higher-order thinking and mathematical processes in every lesson.

 Assessment Readiness
Prepare students for success on tests of the Common Core Standards with practice at every module and unit.

Assessment Resources

Tailor assessments to meet the needs of all your classes and students, including

- **Leveled Module Quizzes**
- **Leveled Unit Tests**
- **Unit Performance Tasks**
- **Placement, Diagnostic, and Quarterly Benchmark Tests**

Equations and Inequalities **291D**

Math Background

Writing Equations 6.EE.7
LESSON 11.1

Students must be able to translate English phrases and sentences into algebraic symbols. To avoid misunderstandings, there are conventions we all use when translating from words to math. The phrase "*the difference of* 3 *and* 7" translates to $3 - 7$.

An *equation* is a mathematical statement that two quantities are equal. An equation may involve only numbers, as in $6 + 5 = 11$, or may have algebraic expressions, as in $2x = 6$. When an equation contains one variable, the *solution* of the equation is a value of the variable that makes the equation true.

For instance, $x = 3$ is the solution of $2x = 6$ since $2(3) = 6$ is a true statement.

An equation such as $2x = 6$ is sometimes called an *open sentence*. That is, it is neither true nor false until additional information (i.e., a value of x) is given. When x is replaced by a value that is a solution, the open sentence becomes a true statement. If the given value of x is not a solution, the open sentence becomes a false statement.

Students should know that an equation may have no solutions, one solution, more than one solution, or infinitely many solutions. For example, the equation $x + 5 = 2 + x + 3$ has infinitely many solutions. Every real number is a solution of this equation. Such an equation is called an *identity*.

Solving Equations 6.EE.5, 6.EE.7
LESSONS 11.2 to 11.3

An equation is like a scale that is perfectly balanced. The quantities on both sides have exactly the same weight. When two quantities a and b cause a scale to balance, the same quantity c can be added to both sides of the scale while preserving the balance. Applying this idea to equations yields the **Addition Property of Equality**: If $a = b$, then $a + c = b + c$.

Similarly, it is possible to subtract the same quantity c from both sides of the scale and preserve the balance. Applying this idea to equations gives the **Subtraction Property of Equality**: If $a = b$, then $a - c = b - c$.

The **Multiplication Property of Equality** states that multiplying each side of an equation by the same nonzero number produces a new equation that has the same solutions as the original. In other words, if $a = b$ and $c \neq 0$, then $ac = bc$. (Strictly speaking, multiplying both sides by a constant $c = 0$ results in a true equation, $0 = 0$, but this is not useful because we lose whatever information the original equation contained.)

The **Division Property of Equality** states that dividing each side of an equation by the same nonzero number produces a new equation that has the same solutions as the original. That is, if $a = b$ and $c \neq 0$, then $\frac{a}{c} = \frac{b}{c}$.

Relationships Between Two Variables 6.EE.9
LESSONS 12.2 to 12.3

The relationship between two quantities or variables is one of the fundamental ideas of algebra and a concept that students will investigate again and again in future mathematics courses. In many such relationships, one variable depends on the other and it is considered the *dependent variable*. The other is the *independent variable*. For example, the cost of buying apples for $.75 per apple depends on the number of apples bought. Cost is the dependent variable and number of apples is the independent variable. The table illustrates this relationship.

Number of apples	1	2	3	4
Cost	0.75	1.50	2.25	3.00

Independent variables are often represented by the letter x, and dependent variables are represented by the letter y. The relationship above may be written in the form of an equation $y = 0.75x$.

As students make the transition from arithmetic to algebra, it is especially important for them to become comfortable switching among multiple representations of algebraic relationships. The above example shows how a relationship may be represented by words, by a table, or by an equation.

You can also represent relationships with a graph.

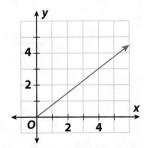

One of the key ideas of algebra is that the graph of an equation is exactly the set of ordered pairs that are solutions of the equation. In other words, once students have made a table of values, plotted points, and graphed a line, they should recognize that they can find additional solutions of the equation by finding ordered pairs that lie on the line. Likewise, a point that does not lie on the line, such as (6, 3), cannot be a solution of the equation. This is easily verified by substituting the values $x = 6$ and $y = 3$ in the equation: $3 \stackrel{?}{=} (0.75)(6)$. The resulting equation, $3 = 4.5$, is not true, so (6, 3) is not a solution.

Equations and Inequalities

MODULE 11

Equations and Relationships

COMMON CORE 6.EE.5, 6.EE.6, 6.EE.7

MODULE 12

Relationships in Two Variables

COMMON CORE 6.NS.6, 6.NS.6b, 6.EE.9

CAREERS IN MATH

Botanist A botanist is a biologist who studies plants. Botanists use math to analyze data and create models of biological organisms and systems. They use these models to make predictions. They also use statistics to determine correlations. If you are interested in a career in botany, you should study these mathematical subjects:

- Algebra
- Trigonometry
- Probability and Statistics
- Calculus

Research other careers that require the analysis of data and use of mathematical models.

Unit 5 Performance Task

At the end of the unit, check out how **botanists** use math.

Careers in Math

Botanist

A botanist is a biologist who specializes in plant studies. Botanists use math in many ways, including the application of statistics to analyze data, determine correlations, and utilize mathematical models to explain results.

For more information about careers in mathematics as well as various mathematics appreciation topics, visit the American Mathematical Society at www.ams.org

Vocabulary Preview Puzzle

Use the puzzle to give students a preview of important concepts in this unit. Students may work individually, in pairs, or in groups.

Unit Resources

Go online to access all your unit resources.

my.hrw.com

UNIT 5
Vocabulary Preview

Use the puzzle to preview key vocabulary from this unit. Unscramble the circled letters within found words to answer the riddle at the bottom of the page.

```
T O Y H S D F P P O T H T J J
N E S S V L E B C N R V N N F
E K O P X U C D A A N I U P N
D O F J S F P R Y O Q H G C I
N F P Z O E D U I N V Z W I N
E B N U A A T T Z O Q C C J N
P S O X U F U A D C P Z H L P
E D X Q X L D L N V J S A V K
D E P Z O M E A Q I O Q X W B
N O W S S H Z W T Y D Q E B T
I R U T L O O P R S S R S J A
Z H X R H O P L Y C U X O Q C
U B X F U B Y H J F K P U O E
S B F Q O E K Y K P H C S N C
L F W W Z T V F O P U H U U B
```

- A word that describes a variable that depends on another variable. (Lesson 12.2) independent
- A value of the variable that makes the equation true. (Lesson 11.1) solution
- The numbers in an ordered pair. (Lesson 12.1) coordinates
- The point where the axes intersect to form the coordinate plane. (Lesson 12.1) origin
- One of the four regions into which the x- and y-axes divide the coordinate plane. (Lesson 12.1) quadrant
- The two number lines that intersect at right angles to form a coordinate plane. (Lesson 12.1) axes

Q: Why did the paper rip when the student tried to stretch out the horizontal axis of his graph?

A: Too much X _ T E N S I O N !

Before	In this Unit	After
Students understand how to: • represent real-world and mathematical problems by graphing points in the first quadrant of the coordinate plane, and interpret coordinate values of points in the context of the situation	Students will learn about: • writing and solving one-step equations and inequalities • rational numbers as locations on number lines • signs of numbers in ordered pairs as indicating locations in quadrants of the coordinate plane	Students will: • use variables to represent quantities in a real-world or mathematical problem • solve multistep real-life and mathematical problems posed with positive and negative rational numbers in any form

Equations and Relationships

COMMON CORE

 ESSENTIAL QUESTION

How can you use equations and relationships to solve real-world problems?

You can model real-world problems with equations, then use algebraic rules to solve the equations.

Real-World Video

Suppose a world weightlifting record is w pounds. To find how many more pounds m must be lifted to set a new record of n pounds, you can use the equation $n = w + m$.

my.hrw.com

GO DIGITAL

my.hrw.com

my.hrw.com

Go digital with your write-in student edition, accessible on any device.

Math On the Spot

Scan with your smart phone to jump directly to the online edition, video tutor, and more.

Animated Math

Interactively explore key concepts to see how math works.

Personal Math Trainer

Get immediate feedback and help as you work through practice sets.

Are You Ready?

Assess Readiness

Use the assessment on this page to determine if students need intensive or strategic intervention for the module's prerequisite skills.

 **Response to Intervention**

Personal Math Trainer
Online Assessment and Intervention
⏻ my.hrw.com

Intervention	Enrichment
Access Are You Ready? assessment online, and receive instant scoring, feedback, and customized intervention or enrichment.	

Online and Print Resources

Skills Intervention worksheets
- Skill 54 Evaluate Expressions
- Skill 56 Connect Words and Equations

Differentiated Instruction
- Challenge worksheets **PRE-AP**
- Extend the Math **PRE-AP** Lesson Activities in TE

Personal Math Trainer
Online Assessment and Intervention

Are YOU Ready?

Complete these exercises to review skills you will need for this module.

Evaluate Expressions

EXAMPLE   Evaluate $8(3+2) - 5^2$

$8(3+2) - 5^2 = 8(5) - 5^2$ Perform operations inside parentheses first.
$= 8(5) - 25$ Evaluate exponents.
$= 40 - 25$ Multiply.
$= 15$ Subtract.

Evaluate the expression.

1. $4(5 + 6) - 15$ ___29___
2. $8(2 + 4) + 16$ ___64___
3. $3(14 - 7) - 16$ ___5___
4. $6(8 - 3) + 3(7 - 4)$ ___39___
5. $10(6 - 5) - 3(9 - 6)$ ___1___
6. $7(4 + 5 + 2) - 6(3 + 5)$ ___29___
7. $2(8 + 3) + 4^2$ ___38___
8. $7(14 - 8) - 6^2$ ___6___
9. $8(2 + 1)^2 - 4^2$ ___56___

Connect Words and Equations

EXAMPLE   The product of a number and 4 is 32.
The product of x and 4 is 32.   Represent the unknown with a variable.
$4 \times x$ is 32.   Determine the operation.
$4 \times x = 32$.   Determine the placement of the equal sign.

Write an algebraic equation for the word sentence.

10. A number increased by 7.9 is 8.3. $x + 7.9 = 8.3$
11. 17 is the sum of a number and 6. $17 = x + 6$
12. The quotient of a number and 8 is 4. $x \div 8 = 4$
13. 81 is three times a number. $81 = 3x$
14. The difference between 31 and a number is 7. $31 - x = 7$
15. Eight less than a number is 19. $x - 8 = 19$

294 Unit 5

PROFESSIONAL DEVELOPMENT VIDEO

Author Juli Dixon models successful teaching practices as she explores equation concepts in an actual sixth-grade classroom.

Professional Development
⏻ my.hrw.com

DIGITAL
my.hrw.com

 Online Teacher Edition
Access a full suite of teaching resources online—plan, present, and manage classes and assignments.

 ePlanner
Easily plan your classes and access all your resources online.

 Interactive Answers and Solutions
Customize answer keys to print or display in the classroom. Choose to include answers only or full solutions to all lesson exercises.

 Interactive Whiteboards
Engage students with interactive whiteboard-ready lessons and activities.

 Personal Math Trainer: Online Assessment and Intervention
Assign automatically graded homework, quizzes, tests, and intervention activities. Prepare your students with updated practice tests aligned with Common Core.

Reading Start-Up

Have students complete the activities on this page by working alone or with others.

Visualize Vocabulary

The main idea web will help students review vocabulary and concepts related to algebraic expressions. Ask students to think of other algebraic expressions and their components and share them with the class, making sure to identify the variable, coefficient, terms, and constant in each expression.

Understand Vocabulary

Use the following explanations to help students learn the preview words.

The words *expression* and *equation* are not synonyms. An **algebraic expression** is a mathematical statement that contains one or more variables. An **equation** is a mathematical statement stating that two expressions are equal. You **evaluate** an expression and **solve** an equation.

Active Reading

Integrating Language Arts

Students can use these reading and note-taking strategies to help them organize and understand new concepts and vocabulary.

COMMON CORE **ELA-Literacy.RST.6-8.7** Integrate quantitative or technical information expressed in words in a text with a version of that information expressed visually (e.g., in a flowchart, diagram, model, graph, or table).

Additional Resources

Differentiated Instruction

• Reading Strategies **ELL**

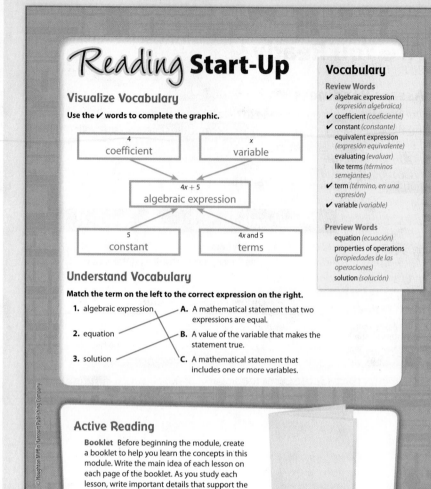

Reading Start-Up

Visualize Vocabulary

Use the ✔ words to complete the graphic.

4 — coefficient
x — variable
4x + 5 — algebraic expression
5 — constant
4x and 5 — terms

Understand Vocabulary

Match the term on the left to the correct expression on the right.

1. algebraic expression
2. equation
3. solution

A. A mathematical statement that two expressions are equal.
B. A value of the variable that makes the statement true.
C. A mathematical statement that includes one or more variables.

Vocabulary

Review Words
✔ algebraic expression (*expresión algebraica*)
✔ coefficient (*coeficiente*)
✔ constant (*constante*)
equivalent expression (*expresión equivalente*)
evaluating (*evaluar*)
like terms (*términos semejantes*)
✔ term (*término, en una expresión*)
✔ variable (*variable*)

Preview Words
equation (*ecuación*)
properties of operations (*propiedades de las operaciones*)
solution (*solución*)

Active Reading

Booklet Before beginning the module, create a booklet to help you learn the concepts in this module. Write the main idea of each lesson on each page of the booklet. As you study each lesson, write important details that support the main idea, such as vocabulary and formulas. Refer to your finished booklet as you work on assignments and study for tests.

Module 11 **295**

Before	In this module	After
Students understand: • operations with rational numbers • properties of operations: inverse, identity, commutative, associative, and distributive properties	Students will learn to: • write one-variable, one-step equations to represent constraints or conditions within problems • model and solve one-variable, one-step equations that represent problems • write corresponding real-world problems given one-variable, one-step equations • write inequalitites	Students will learn how to: • write one-variable, two-step equations to represent real-world problems • write a real-world problem to represent a one-variable, two-step equation • solve one-variable, two-step equations

Unpacking the Standards

Use the examples on this page to help students know exactly what they are expected to learn in this module.

Common Core Standards

Content Areas

COMMON CORE **Expressions and Equations—6.EE**

Reason about and solve one-variable equations and inequalities

Go online to see a complete unpacking of the Common Core Standards.

⏻ my.hrw.com

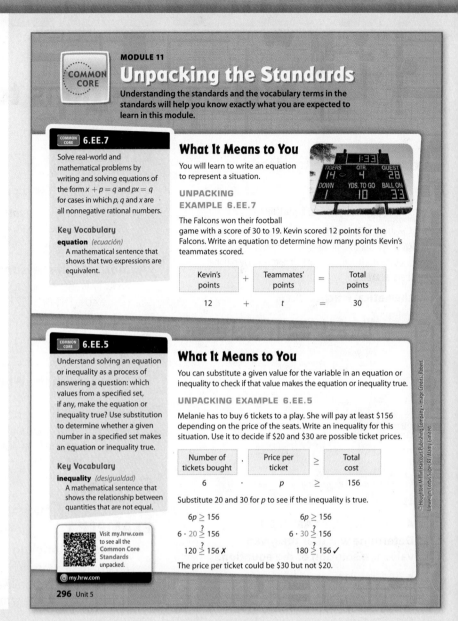

MODULE 11
Unpacking the Standards

Understanding the standards and the vocabulary terms in the standards will help you know exactly what you are expected to learn in this module.

COMMON CORE 6.EE.7

Solve real-world and mathematical problems by writing and solving equations of the form $x + p = q$ and $px = q$ for cases in which p, q and x are all nonnegative rational numbers.

Key Vocabulary

equation *(ecuación)*
A mathematical sentence that shows that two expressions are equivalent.

What It Means to You

You will learn to write an equation to represent a situation.

UNPACKING EXAMPLE 6.EE.7

The Falcons won their football game with a score of 30 to 19. Kevin scored 12 points for the Falcons. Write an equation to determine how many points Kevin's teammates scored.

Kevin's points		Teammates' points		Total points
12	+	t	=	30

COMMON CORE 6.EE.5

Understand solving an equation or inequality as a process of answering a question: which values from a specified set, if any, make the equation or inequality true? Use substitution to determine whether a given number in a specified set makes an equation or inequality true.

Key Vocabulary

inequality *(desigualdad)*
A mathematical sentence that shows the relationship between quantities that are not equal.

Visit my.hrw.com to see all the Common Core Standards unpacked.

⏻ my.hrw.com

What It Means to You

You can substitute a given value for the variable in an equation or inequality to check if that value makes the equation or inequality true.

UNPACKING EXAMPLE 6.EE.5

Melanie has to buy 6 tickets to a play. She will pay at least $156 depending on the price of the seats. Write an inequality for this situation. Use it to decide if $20 and $30 are possible ticket prices.

Number of tickets bought		Price per ticket		Total cost
6	·	p	≥	156

Substitute 20 and 30 for p to see if the inequality is true.

$6p \geq 156$ $\qquad$ $6p \geq 156$

$6 \cdot 20 \overset{?}{\geq} 156$ $\qquad$ $6 \cdot 30 \overset{?}{\geq} 156$

$120 \overset{?}{\geq} 156$ ✗ $\qquad$ $180 \overset{?}{\geq} 156$ ✓

The price per ticket could be $30 but not $20.

Common Core Standards	Lesson 11.1	Lesson 11.2	Lesson 11.2	Lesson 11.4
6.EE.5 Understand solving an equation or inequality as a process of answering a question: which values from a specified set, if any, make the equation or inequality true? Use substitution to determine whether a given number in a specified set makes an equation or inequality true.	COMMON CORE	COMMON CORE	COMMON CORE	COMMON CORE
6.EE.6 Use variables to represent numbers and write expressions when solving a real-world or mathematical problem; understand that a variable can represent an unknown number, or, depending on the purpose at hand, any number in a specified set.	COMMON CORE	COMMON CORE	COMMON CORE	COMMON CORE
6.EE.7 Solve real-world and mathematical problems by writing and solving equations of the form $x + p = q$ and $px = q$, for cases in which p, q, and x are all non-negative rational numbers.	COMMON CORE	COMMON CORE	COMMON CORE	
6.EE.8 Write an inequality of the form $x > c$ or $x < c$ to represent a constraint or condition in a real-world or mathematical problem. Recognize that inequalities of the form $x > c$ or $x < c$ have infinitely many solutions; represent solutions of such inequalities on number line diagrams.				COMMON CORE

LESSON
11.1 Writing Equations to Represent Situations

Common Core Standards

The student is expected to:

 Expressions and Equations—6.EE.7

Solve real-world and mathematical problems by writing and solving equations of the form $x + p = q$ and $px = q$ for cases in which p, q, and x are all nonnegative rational numbers. *Also 6.EE.5, 6.EE.6*

Mathematical Practices

 MP.4 Modeling

ADDITIONAL EXAMPLE 1
Determine whether the given value is a solution of the equation.

A $x + 15 = 10; x = 5$ no

B $\frac{m}{3} = 11; m = 33$ yes

C $5n = 42; x = 7$ no

 Interactive Whiteboard
Interactive example available online

⏻ my.hrw.com

ADDITIONAL EXAMPLE 2
Eli is y years old. His 9-year-old cousin Jen is 4 years younger than he is. Write an equation to represent this situation.

Sample answer: $y - 4 = 9$

 Interactive Whiteboard
Interactive example available online

⏻ my.hrw.com

Engage

ESSENTIAL QUESTION

How do you write equations and determine whether a number is a solution of an equation? Write a statement that links two expressions with an equals sign. Substitute a number for the variable and simplify. If the final statement is true, the number is a solution.

Motivate the Lesson

Ask: Ty wants to buy a video game. He has $57, which is $38 less than he needs. Does the game cost $90 or $95? Begin Example 1 to find out how to solve this problem.

Explore

Engage with the Whiteboard

Write $x + 4$ and $x + 4 = 9$ on the whiteboard. Ask students how they differ. Explain the difference between an *expression* and an *equation*. Then have students model both sides of the equation, using algebra tiles on the whiteboard. Ask them what x must represent for the two sides to be equal. Tell them that $x = 5$ is the *solution* of the equation.

Explain

EXAMPLE 1

Focus on Modeling [CC] **Mathematical Practices**

Explain to students that an equation is like a balanced scale. Just as the weights on both sides of a balanced scale are exactly the same, the expressions on both sides of an equation represent exactly the same value. Show examples of equations on a balance scale.

Questioning Strategies [CC] **Mathematical Practices**

• In A, why is $x = 6$ a solution of the equation? because the resulting statement, $15 = 15$, is a true statement In B, why is $y = 8$ not a solution of the equation? because the resulting statement, $2 = 32$, is a false statement

YOUR TURN

Avoid Common Errors

Watch for students who substitute the given value incorrectly. Caution students to double-check their work for accuracy.

EXAMPLE 2

Questioning Strategies [CC] **Mathematical Practices**

• Could you write another equation to represent the situation? Yes. I can write the equation $p = $ Total points $-$ Mark's points or $p = 46 - 17$ because subtraction is the opposite of addition.

YOUR TURN

Focus on Critical [CC] **Thinking Mathematical Practices**

Point out that any letter can be used as a variable. In Ex. 7, c is convenient because it represents Craig's age, but x or n or any other letter could be used, as well.

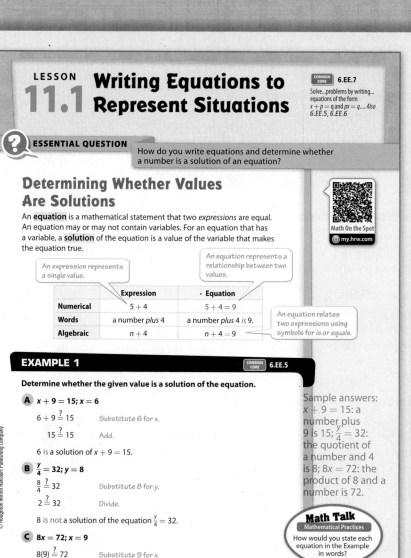

11.1 Writing Equations to Represent Situations

COMMON CORE 6.EE.7

Solve...problems by writing... equations of the form $x + p = q$ and $px = q$.... *Also 6.EE.5, 6.EE.6*

? ESSENTIAL QUESTION

How do you write equations and determine whether a number is a solution of an equation?

Determining Whether Values Are Solutions

An **equation** is a mathematical statement that two *expressions* are equal. An equation may or may not contain variables. For an equation that has a variable, a **solution** of the equation is a value of the variable that makes the equation true.

An expression represents a single value.

An equation represents a relationship between two values.

	Expression	Equation
Numerical	$5 + 4$	$5 + 4 = 9$
Words	a number *plus* 4	a number *plus* 4 *is* 9.
Algebraic	$n + 4$	$n + 4 = 9$

An equation relates two expressions using symbols for *is* or *equals*.

EXAMPLE 1

COMMON CORE 6.EE.5

Determine whether the given value is a solution of the equation.

A $x + 9 = 15; x = 6$

$6 + 9 \overset{?}{=} 15$ Substitute 6 for x.

$15 \overset{?}{=} 15$ Add.

6 is a solution of $x + 9 = 15$.

B $\frac{y}{4} = 32; y = 8$

$\frac{8}{4} \overset{?}{=} 32$ Substitute 8 for y.

$2 \overset{?}{=} 32$ Divide.

8 is not a solution of the equation $\frac{y}{4} = 32$.

C $8x = 72; x = 9$

$8(9) \overset{?}{=} 72$ Substitute 9 for x.

$72 \overset{?}{=} 72$ Multiply.

9 is a solution of $8x = 72$.

Sample answers:
$x + 9 = 15$: a number plus 9 is 15; $\frac{y}{4} = 32$: the quotient of a number and 4 is 8; $8x = 72$: the product of 8 and a number is 72.

Math Talk

Mathematical Practices

How would you state each equation in the Example in words?

Lesson 11.1 **297**

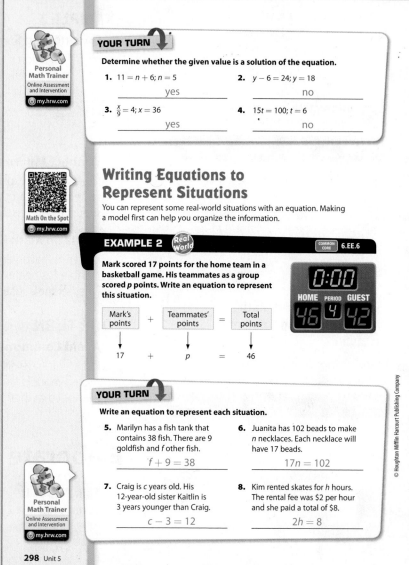

YOUR TURN

Determine whether the given value is a solution of the equation.

1. $11 = n + 6; n = 5$ yes

2. $y - 6 = 24; y = 18$ no

3. $\frac{x}{9} = 4; x = 36$ yes

4. $15t = 100; t = 6$ no

Writing Equations to Represent Situations

You can represent some real-world situations with an equation. Making a model first can help you organize the information.

EXAMPLE 2 Real World

COMMON CORE 6.EE.6

Mark scored 17 points for the home team in a basketball game. His teammates as a group scored p points. Write an equation to represent this situation.

Mark's points	+	Teammates' points	=	Total points
17	+	p	=	46

YOUR TURN

Write an equation to represent each situation.

5. Marilyn has a fish tank that contains 38 fish. There are 9 goldfish and f other fish.

$f + 9 = 38$

6. Juanita has 102 beads to make n necklaces. Each necklace will have 17 beads.

$17n = 102$

7. Craig is c years old. His 12-year-old sister Kaitlin is 3 years younger than Craig.

$c - 3 = 12$

8. Kim rented skates for h hours. The rental fee was $2 per hour and she paid a total of $8.

$2h = 8$

298 Unit 5

PROFESSIONAL DEVELOPMENT

CC Integrate Mathematical Practices MP.4

This lesson provides an opportunity to address the Mathematical Practice which calls for students to apply the mathematics they know to solve problems arising in everyday life. Students begin by distinguishing equations from expressions. Then they determine whether a given number is a solution of the equation. Next, students write equations that represent real-world situations expressed in words. Finally, students use substitution to check whether a value for a variable makes an equation true.

Math Background

The equals sign, which first appeared about 450 years ago, is a relatively new math concept. The term *equation* comes from a Latin word meaning "to set equal."

There are, essentially, four types of equations:

- True equation: $2 + 3 = 5$
- False equation: $3 + 4 = 8$
- Conditional equation: $y - 6 = 7$ (not true for all values)
- Identity: $3n + 5n = 8n$ (true for all values)

Animated Math
Modeling Equations

Students model equations using interactive algebra tiles.

⏻ my.hrw.com

EXAMPLE 3

Questioning Strategies [CC] Mathematical Practices

- Is the equation $x - 47 = 18$ true? Explain. The equation is true only when $x = 65$. An equation is a balanced mathematical statement, and only the correct solution will maintain the balance.

- How can you check your answer by using a different mathematical operation? Add $18 and $47 to find the original amount on the card. You should get $65.

Connect Multiple Representations [CC] Mathematical Practices

Have students explain why adding $18 to $47 to check that $65 is the answer will yield the same result as subtracting $47 from $65 to see that $18 is the money left over. Students should recognize that addition and subtraction are inverse operations.

Focus on Math Connections

Point out that an equals sign with a question mark above ($\overset{?}{=}$) is used immediately after a variable has been substituted by a number. This symbol indicates that it is not yet known whether the equation is true or false.

YOUR TURN

Avoid Common Errors

If students have difficulty writing equations to represent the situation, encourage them to make a model, like the one in Example 3, to organize the information. Then remind students to check that their solution makes the original equation true.

Elaborate

Talk About It
Summarize the Lesson

 Ask: How do you know when a number is a solution to an equation? When the number is substituted for the variable, it makes the equation true. An equation is true when the values of the expressions on opposite sides of the equals sign are the same.

GUIDED PRACTICE

Engage with the Whiteboard

For Exercises 1–2, have students fill in the boxes and determine whether the given values are solutions to the equations.

For Exercise 13, have a student circle the important information in the problem statement on the whiteboard. Then have another student complete the model for the word equation and write the equation next to the model.

Avoid Common Errors

Exercises 3–12 Watch for students who substitute the given value incorrectly. Caution students to double-check their work for accuracy.

Exercises 14–16 If students have difficulty writing equations to represent the word problems, encourage them to make a model, like the one in Example 3, to organize the information. Then remind students to check that their solution makes the original equation true.

Writing an Equation and Checking Solutions

You can substitute a given value for the variable in a real-world equation to check if that value makes sense for the situation.

Math On the Spot
my.hrw.com

EXAMPLE 3 Real World

COMMON CORE 6.EE.7

Sarah used a gift card to buy $47 worth of groceries. Now she has $18 left on her gift card. Write an equation to represent this situation. Use your equation to determine whether Sarah had $65 or $59 on the gift card before buying groceries.

STEP 1 Write a word equation based on the situation.

| Amount on card | − | Amount spent | = | Amount left on card |

STEP 2 Rewrite the equation using a variable for the unknown quantity and the given values for the known quantities.

Let x be the amount on the card.

| Amount on card | − | Amount spent | = | Amount left on card |
| x | − | 47 | = | 18 |

> The amount spent and the amount left on the card are the known quantities. Substitute those values in the equation.

STEP 3 Substitute 65 and 59 for x to see which equation is true.

$$x - 47 = 18 \qquad x - 47 = 18$$
$$65 - 47 \overset{?}{=} 18 \qquad 59 - 47 \overset{?}{=} 18$$
$$18 \overset{?}{=} 18 \qquad 12 \overset{?}{=} 18$$

The amount on Sarah's gift card before she bought groceries was $65.

Reflect

9. **What If?** Suppose Sarah has $12 left on her gift card. How would this change the equation and the final answer?

The equation would be $x - 47 = 12$; the original

amount would be $59.

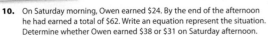
YOUR TURN

10. On Saturday morning, Owen earned $24. By the end of the afternoon he had earned a total of $62. Write an equation represent the situation. Determine whether Owen earned $38 or $31 on Saturday afternoon.

Sample equation: $x + 24 = 62$; $38

Animated Math
my.hrw.com

Personal Math Trainer
Online Assessment and Intervention
my.hrw.com

Determine whether the given value is a solution of the equation. (Example 1)

1. $23 = x - 9$; $x = 14$ ___no___

$$23 \overset{?}{=} \boxed{14} - 9$$
$$23 \overset{?}{=} \boxed{5}$$

2. $\frac{n}{13} = 4$; $n = 52$ ___yes___

$$\frac{\boxed{52}}{13} \overset{?}{=} 4$$
$$\boxed{4} \overset{?}{=} 4$$

3. $14 + x = 46$; $x = 32$ ___yes___

4. $17y = 85$; $y = 5$ ___yes___

5. $25 = \frac{k}{5}$; $k = 5$ ___no___

6. $2.5n = 45$; $n = 18$ ___yes___

7. $21 = m + 9$; $m = 11$ ___no___

8. $21 - h = 15$; $h = 6$ ___yes___

9. $d - 4 = 19$; $d = 15$ ___no___

10. $5 + x = 47$; $x = 52$ ___no___

11. $w - 9 = 0$; $w = 9$ ___yes___

12. $5q = 31$; $q = 13$ ___no___

13. Each floor of a hotel has r rooms. On 8 floors, there are a total of 256 rooms. Write an equation to represent this situation. (Example 2)

| Number of floors | × | Number of rooms on each floor | = | Total number of rooms |

$8r = 256$

14. In the school band, there are 5 trumpet players and f flute players. There are twice as many flute players as there are trumpet players. (Example 2)

Sample answer: $\frac{f}{2} = 5$

15. Pedro bought 8 tickets to a basketball game. He paid a total of $208. Write an equation to determine whether each ticket cost $26 or $28. (Example 3)

Sample equation: $8x = 208$; $26

16. The high temperature was 92 °F. This was 24 °F higher than the overnight low temperature. Write an equation to determine whether the low temperature was 62 °F or 68 °F. (Example 3)

Sample equation: $x + 24 = 92$; 68 °F

? ESSENTIAL QUESTION CHECK-IN

17. Tell how you can determine whether a number is a solution of an equation.

Substitute the number for the variable and simplify. If the

final statement is true, the number is a solution.

DIFFERENTIATE INSTRUCTION

Visual Cues

Display a set of pan balance scales. For each of the following equations, write the left side over the left scale and the right side over the right scale. Ask what the value of the variable must be for the scales to remain balanced.

1. $x + 3 = 7$ $x = 4$
2. $t - 5 = 3$ $t = 8$
3. $4y = 28$ $y = 7$
4. $\frac{w}{2} = 6$ $w = 12$

Critical Thinking

Give students the following problem to solve.

> Rebecca has 17 one-dollar bills. Courtney has 350 nickels. Do the two girls have the same amount of money?

Remind students that to compare quantities, they need to use the same units.

$17 \neq 350 \div 20$; No, they do not have the same amount of money.

Additional Resources

Differentiated Instruction includes:

- Reading Strategies
- Success for English Learners **ELL**
- Reteach
- Challenge **PRE-AP**

Personal Math Trainer

Online Assessment and Intervention

Online homework assignment available

 my.hrw.com

11.1 LESSON QUIZ

COMMON CORE 6.EE.5, 6.EE.6, 6.EE.7

Determine whether the given value is a solution of the equation. Write yes or no.

1. $w - 7 = 20$; $w = 13$

2. $15t = 120$; $t = 8$

3. $\frac{y}{12} = 2$; $y = 24$

4. $5 = x + 5$; $x = 10$

5. In a choir there are 16 altos and s sopranos. There are twice as many sopranos as altos. Write an equation to represent this situation.

6. Jerome is one-third the age of his aunt, who is 51 years old. Write an equation to determine whether Jerome is 14 or 17.

Lesson Quiz available online

 my.hrw.com

Answers

1. no

2. yes

3. yes

4. no

5. $\frac{s}{2} = 16$

6. $3x = 51$; Jerome is 17 years old.

Evaluate

GUIDED AND INDEPENDENT PRACTICE

COMMON CORE 6.EE.5, 6.EE.6, 6.EE.7

Concepts & Skills	Practice
Example 1 Determining Whether Values Are Solutions	Exercises 1–12
Example 2 Writing Equations to Represent Situations	Exercises 13–14, 18–21, 24–25
Example 3 Writing an Equation and Checking Solutions	Exercises 15–16, 26

Exercise	Depth of Knowledge (D.O.K.)	**COMMON CORE** Mathematical Practices
18–20	**2** Skills/Concepts	**MP.4** Modeling
21	**3** Strategic Thinking **H.O.T.**	**MP.3** Logic
22	**2** Skills/Concepts	**MP.7** Using Structure
23	**3** Strategic Thinking **H.O.T.**	**MP.4** Modeling
24	**3** Strategic Thinking **H.O.T.**	**MP.3** Logic
25–26	**3** Strategic Thinking **H.O.T.**	**MP.2** Reasoning
27–29	**3** Strategic Thinking **H.O.T.**	**MP.3** Logic

Additional Resources

Differentiated Instruction includes:

• Leveled Practice Worksheets

11.1 Independent Practice

COMMON CORE 6.EE.5, 6.EE.6, 6.EE.7

Personal Math Trainer
Online Assessment and Intervention
my.hrw.com

18. Andy is one-fourth as old as his grandfather, who is 76 years old. Write an equation to determine whether Andy is 19 or 22 years old.

$4n = 76$; 19 years old

19. A sleeping bag weighs 8 pounds. Your backpack and sleeping bag together weigh 31 pounds. Write an equation to determine whether the backpack without the sleeping bag weighs 25 or 23 pounds.

$x + 8 = 31$; 23 pounds

20. Halfway through a bus route, 23 students have been dropped off and 48 students remain on the bus. Write an equation to determine whether there are 61 or 71 students on the bus at the beginning of the route.

$x - 23 = 48$; 71 students

21. Write an equation that involves multiplication, contains a variable, and has a solution of 5. Then write another equation that has the same solution and the same variable and numbers but uses division.

Sample answer: $4x = 20$;

$20 \div x = 4$ or $x = 20 \div 4$

22. **Vocabulary** How are expressions and equations different?

Sample answer: An expression represents one value and an equation is a statement that two expressions are equivalent.

23. **Multistep** Alan has partially completed a table showing the distances between his town, Greenville, and two other towns.

Distance between Greenville and Nearby Towns (miles)	
Parker	29
Hadley	?

a. The distance between Hadley and Greenville is 13 miles less than the distance between Parker and Greenville. Write two equations that compare the distance between Hadley and Greenville and the distance between Parker and Greenville. Tell what your variable represents.

$29 - 13 = x$; $13 + x = 29$; the distance between Hadley and Greenville.

b. Alan says the distance from Hadley to Greenville is 16 miles. Is he correct? Explain.

Yes; 16 is a solution of the equations in **a**.

24. **Explain the Error** A problem states that Ursula earns $9 per hour. To write an expression that tells how much money Ursula earns for h hours, Joshua wrote $\frac{9}{h}$. Sarah wrote $9h$. Whose expression is correct and why?

Sarah is correct because the earnings are the number of hours times the amount per hour, or $9h$.

25. **Communicate Mathematical Ideas** A dog weighs 44 pounds and the veterinarian thinks it needs to lose 7 pounds. Mikala wrote the equation $x + 7 = 44$ to represent the situation. Kirk wrote the equation $44 - x = 7$. Which equation is correct? Can you write another equation that represents the situation?

Both equations are correct. Another correct equation is $44 - 7 = x$.

26. **Multiple Representations** The table shows the ages of Cindy and her dad.

Dad's Age	Cindy's Age
28 years old	2 years old
36 years old	10 years old
?	18 years old

a. Write an equation that relates Cindy's age to her dad's age when Cindy is 18. Tell what the variable represents.

$x - 26 = 18$; the age of Cindy's dad

b. Determine if 42 is a solution to the equation. Show your work.

No; $42 - 26 = 16$; 16 is not equal to 18.

c. Explain the meaning of your answer in part **b**.

Cindy's father will not be 42 when she is 18.

 FOCUS ON HIGHER ORDER THINKING

Work Area

27. **Critical Thinking** In the school band, there are 4 trumpet players and f flute players. The total number of trumpet and flute players is 12. Are there twice as many flute players as trumpet players? Explain.

Yes, because $4 + f = 12$ means there are 8 flute players, and 8 is twice 4.

28. **Problem Solving** Ronald paid $162 for 6 tickets to a basketball game. During the game he noticed that his friend paid $130 for 5 tickets. The price of each ticket was $26. Was Ronald overcharged? Explain.

Yes, Ronald was overcharged because $6(26) = 156$ and $156 < 162$.

29. **Communicate Mathematical Ideas** Tariq said you can write an equation by setting an expression equal to itself. Would an equation like this be true? Explain.

Yes, setting an expression equal to itself forms an equation that will always be true regardless of the value of the variable(s) or numbers in the expression.

EXTEND THE MATH PRE-AP

Activity available online ⊙ my.hrw.com

Activity Following the release of the hit movie *Attack of the Giant Muffins*, muffin fever spread across the country. This resulted in a contest to choose the plot of the sequel *Attack of the Giant Muffins, Part 2*.

The table shows the number of contest entries from some towns in one state.

Town	Entries
Hillville	40
Dos Rios	30
High Corn	105
Moose	n
Ho-Hum	25

Write an equation for each statement.

1. The sum of the number of entries from Hillville and Moose was 90. $n + 40 = 90$

2. The difference between the number of Moose entries and Ho-Hum entries was 25.
$n - 25 = 25$

3. The total number of entries is 5 times the number of Moose entries. $5n = 250$

11.2 Addition and Subtraction Equations

Common Core Standards

The student is expected to:

 Expressions and Equations—6.EE.7

Solve real-world and mathematical problems by writing and solving equations of the form $x + p = q$ and $px = q$ for cases in which p, q and x are all nonnegative rational numbers. *Also 6.EE.5, 6.EE.6*

Mathematical Practices

 MP.2 Reasoning

ADDITIONAL EXAMPLE 1

Solve the equation $y + 8 = 22$. Graph the solution on a number line. $y = 14$

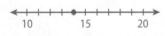

Interactive Whiteboard
Interactive example available online

 my.hrw.com

Engage

ESSENTIAL QUESTION

How do you solve equations that contain addition and subtraction? Sample answer: Apply the inverse operation—subtraction for addition equations and addition for subtraction equations—to both sides of the equation.

Motivate the Lesson

Ask: Does anyone have a puppy? Have you noticed how fast they grow? Begin the Explore Activity to find out how to model one puppy's weight gain, using an equation and algebra tiles.

Explore

EXPLORE ACTIVITY

Focus on Modeling CC Mathematical Practices

Remind students that an equation is like a balanced scale. If you increase or decrease the weights by the same amount on both sides, the scale will remain in balance. Emphasize that students must remove the same number of tiles from *both* sides of the mat.

Explain

EXAMPLE 1

Focus on Math Connections CC Mathematical Practices

Remind students that subtraction is the inverse, or opposite, of addition. If an equation contains addition, solve it by subtracting from both sides to "undo" the addition.

Questioning Strategies CC Mathematical Practices

• Would you solve $15 + a = 26$ differently from $a + 15 = 26$? No, because addition is commutative, and the order of the variable and the added number does not change the process of subtracting 15 from both sides.

• How can you use substitution to check an answer to an addition equation? Substitute the value for the variable into the original equation and simplify. If the result is a true statement, the value is the solution.

• Why is the graph only a single point? because there is only one solution to the equation

YOUR TURN

Avoid Common Errors

Watch for students who perform the inverse operation of subtraction only on the side with the variable. Stress that to keep the equation "balanced" the same amount must be taken away from each side.

Addition and Subtraction Equations

COMMON CORE 6.EE.7
Solve real-world and mathematical problems by writing and solving equations of the form $x + p = q$.... Also 6.EE.5, 6.EE.6

? ESSENTIAL QUESTION
How do you solve equations that contain addition or subtraction?

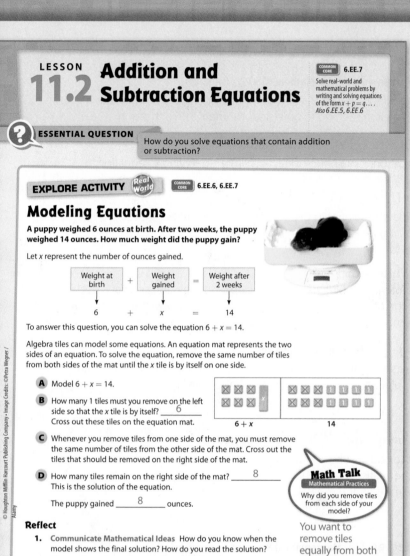

EXPLORE ACTIVITY Real World
COMMON CORE 6.EE.6, 6.EE.7

Modeling Equations

A puppy weighed 6 ounces at birth. After two weeks, the puppy weighed 14 ounces. How much weight did the puppy gain?

Let x represent the number of ounces gained.

Weight at birth	+	Weight gained	=	Weight after 2 weeks
6	+	x	=	14

To answer this question, you can solve the equation $6 + x = 14$.

Algebra tiles can model some equations. An equation mat represents the two sides of an equation. To solve the equation, remove the same number of tiles from both sides of the mat until the x tile is by itself on one side.

A Model $6 + x = 14$.

B How many 1 tiles must you remove on the left side so that the x tile is by itself? ___6___
Cross out these tiles on the equation mat.

$6 + x$ 14

C Whenever you remove tiles from one side of the mat, you must remove the same number of tiles from the other side of the mat. Cross out the tiles that should be removed on the right side of the mat.

D How many tiles remain on the right side of the mat? ___8___
This is the solution of the equation.

The puppy gained ___8___ ounces.

Math Talk
Mathematical Practices

Why did you remove tiles from each side of your model?

You want to remove tiles equally from both sides to keep the equation balanced.

Reflect

1. **Communicate Mathematical Ideas** How do you know when the model shows the final solution? How do you read the solution?

The x tile is alone on one side of the mat. The solution is the number of small tiles on the other side.

Using Subtraction to Solve Equations

Removing the same number of tiles from each side of an equation mat models subtracting the same number from both sides of an equation.

Subtraction Property of Equality

You can subtract the same number from both sides of an equation, and the two sides will remain equal.

When an equation contains addition, solve by subtracting the same number from both sides.

EXAMPLE 1
COMMON CORE 6.EE.5

Solve the equation $a + 15 = 26$. Graph the solution on a number line.

$a + 15 = 26$ Notice that the number 15 is added to a.

$$\begin{array}{r} a + 15 = 26 \\ -15 \quad -15 \\ \hline a \quad = 11 \end{array}$$ Subtract 15 from both sides of the equation.

Check: $a + 15 = 26$

$11 + 15 \overset{?}{=} 26$ Substitute 11 for a.

$26 \overset{?}{=} 26$ Add on the left side.

Graph the solution on a number line.

5 6 7 8 9 10 11 12 13 14 15

Reflect

2. **Communicate Mathematical Ideas** How do you decide which number to subtract from both sides?

Subtract the number added to the variable so that the variable is isolated, or alone, on one side of the equation.

YOUR TURN

3. Solve the equation $5 = w + 1.5$.
Graph the solution on a number line.

−5 −4 −3 −2 −1 0 1 2 3 4 5

$w = $ ___3.5___

Personal Math Trainer
Online Assessment and Intervention
my.hrw.com

PROFESSIONAL DEVELOPMENT

CC Integrate Mathematical Practices MP.2

This lesson provides an opportunity to address this Mathematical Practice standard. It calls for students to create and use representations to organize, record, and communicate mathematical ideas. Students use algebra tiles and number lines to model the solutions to one-step equations. They proceed to solve algebraic equations symbolically by using inverse operations to isolate the variable. They then apply the algebraic method to solve equations representing real-world situations.

Math Background

In *Elements, Book I*, Euclid listed five axioms that he called "common notions."

1. Things which are equal to the same thing are also equal to one another.

2. If equals be added to equals, the wholes are equal.

3. If equals be subtracted from equals, the remainders are equal.

4. Things which coincide with one another are equal to one another.

5. The whole is greater than the part.

305 Lesson 11.2

EXAMPLE 2

Focus on Math Connections CC Mathematical Practices

Remind students that addition and subtraction are inverse operations. If an equation contains subtraction, solve it by adding to both sides to "undo" the subtraction.

Questioning Strategies CC Mathematical Practices

- How is solving an equation containing subtraction similar to solving an equation containing addition? Solve both types of equations by using the inverse operation to get the variable by itself on one side of the equation.

- Does it make sense that the solution is greater than 18? Explain. Yes. The equation indicates that subtracting 21 from some numbers gives an answer of 18, so the solution must be greater than 18.

Engage with the Whiteboard

 Cover up the sentences in blue next to each step of the solution and have students write a description of what is happening in each step. Then have the students graph the solution on the number line.

Focus on Modeling CC Mathematical Practices

Guide students to see that it makes sense to draw only the needed portion of the number line when graphing a solution, especially when the numbers are large.

YOUR TURN

Focus on Math Connections CC Mathematical Practices

Remind students that to add or subtract fractions with different denominators, it is necessary to rewrite the fractions with a common denominator. A fraction greater than 1 should be written as a mixed number for ease of graphing.

EXAMPLE 3

Questioning Strategies CC Mathematical Practices

- How do you know that $x + 60 = 180$ is the correct equation to use to find the value of x? The two angles shown in the drawing are supplementary.

- Does the sketch of the unknown angle x appear to be twice 60°? Explain. Yes. If I divide x into two halves, the two angles appear to have measures that are similar to the 60° angle.

Focus on Math Connections CC Mathematical Practices

Have students explain what will be true about an unknown angle whose supplement has measure less than 90°. Elicit that it will be an obtuse angle. Then ask the same question about angles whose supplements have measures greater than 90°.

YOUR TURN

Focus on Math Connections CC Mathematical Practices

Point out to students that the angle represented here is a right angle and that a right angle measures exactly 90°. Remind them that if the sum of the measures of two angles is 90°, the two angles are complementary angles. This information should help students to write and solve an equation to find the measure of the unknown angle.

EXAMPLE 4

Connect to Daily Life CC Mathematical Practices

Point out to students that the equation has decimals containing hundredths and that money is commonly represented as decimals containing hundredths. Thus, a good real-world application for this equation would be a situation involving money. Encourage students to brainstorm situations from everyday life that could make sense.

Using Addition to Solve Equations

When an equation contains subtraction, solve by adding the same number to both sides.

> ### Addition Property of Equality
> You can add the same number to both sides of an equation, and the two sides will remain equal.

Math On the Spot
my.hrw.com

EXAMPLE 2 COMMON CORE 6.EE.5

Solve the equation $y - 21 = 18$. **Graph the solution on a number line.**

$y - 21 = 18$ Notice that the number 21 is subtracted from y.

$$\begin{array}{r} y - 21 = 18 \\ +21 \quad +21 \\ \hline y \quad = 39 \end{array}$$

Add 21 to both sides of the equation.

Check: $y - 21 = 18$

$39 - 21 \overset{?}{=} 18$ Substitute 39 for y.

$18 \overset{?}{=} 18$ Subtract.

Graph the solution on a number line.

35 36 37 38 39 40 41 42 43 44 45

Reflect

4. **Communicate Mathematical Ideas** How do you know whether to add on both sides or subtract on both sides when solving an equation?

   If the equation contains addition, subtract. If the equation contains subtraction, add.

> ### YOUR TURN
> 5. Solve the equation $h - \frac{1}{2} = \frac{3}{4}$.
>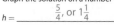
>   -2   -1   0   1   2
>   Graph the solution on a number line.
> $h = \frac{5}{4}$, or $1\frac{1}{4}$

Personal Math Trainer
Online Assessment and Intervention
my.hrw.com

Solving Equations that Represent Geometric Concepts

You can write equations to represent geometric relationships.

Recall that a straight line has an angle measure of 180°. Two angles whose measures have a sum of 180° are called supplementary angles. Two angles whose measures have a sum of 90° are called complementary angles.

EXAMPLE 3 COMMON CORE 6.EE.7, 6.EE.6

Find the measure of the unknown angle.

STEP 1 Write the information in the boxes.

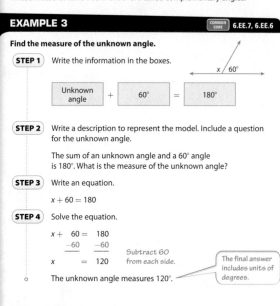

| Unknown angle | + | 60° | = | 180° |

STEP 2 Write a description to represent the model. Include a question for the unknown angle.

The sum of an unknown angle and a 60° angle is 180°. What is the measure of the unknown angle?

STEP 3 Write an equation.

$x + 60 = 180$

STEP 4 Solve the equation.

$$\begin{array}{r} x + 60 = 180 \\ -60 \quad -60 \\ \hline x \quad = 120 \end{array}$$

Subtract 60 from each side.

> The final answer includes units of degrees.

The unknown angle measures 120°.

> ### YOUR TURN
> 6. Write and solve an equation to find the measure of the unknown angle.
> $x + 65 = 90; x = 25°$
>
>   65°
>
> 7. Write and solve an equation to find the complement of an angle that measures 42°.
> $x + 42 = 90; x = 48°$

Math On the Spot
my.hrw.com

Personal Math Trainer
Online Assessment and Intervention
my.hrw.com

DIFFERENTIATE INSTRUCTION

Critical Thinking

Present the magic square shown below. Explain that the sum of any three numbers added across, down, or diagonally should have the same sum.

Have students write and solve equations to fill in the table. The magic sum for this square is 465.

248	31	186
93	155	217
124	279	62

Cognitive Strategies

Have students work with a partner to create "mind-reading" puzzles that depend upon inverse operations to return to the original number. The following puzzle is an example. Pick a number.

1. Add 4.   5. Subtract 4.
2. Subtract 1.   6. Add 5.
3. Add 7.   7. Subtract 7.
4. Subtract 5.   8. Add 1.

Your answer is the number you started with.

Additional Resources

Differentiated Instruction includes:

- Reading Strategies
- Success for English Learners **ELL**
- Reteach
- Challenge **PRE-AP**

- Using number sense, what can you determine about the value of x, given that the sum of two numbers is 25? The value of x will be less than 25.

- How else could you write the equation to solve for x? Explain. Sample answer: You could write $x + 21.79 = 25$; addition is commutative, so $x + 21.79 = 21.79 + x$.

- How is the question in a real-world problem related to its equation? The question asks about the value of the variable.

YOUR TURN

Focus on Communication **CC** Mathematical Practices

Guide students to write problems that use sensible data, and have them explain, step by step, how to solve their equations. Challenge each student to create original word problems based on unique situations.

Elaborate

Talk About It
Summarize the Lesson

Ask: How do you solve and check an equation containing only addition or only subtraction? You apply the inverse operation—subtraction for addition equations and addition for subtraction equations—to both sides of the equation.

GUIDED PRACTICE

Engage with the Whiteboard

For Exercise 1, have a student complete the verbal model on the whiteboard and then draw a model with algebra tiles below the verbal model. Ask students to provide an explanation of the solution.

Avoid Common Errors

Exercises 2–6 Remind students to use the inverse operation of subtraction to undo addition or addition to undo subtraction.

Exercise 7 Remind students to begin by identifying the angle they are using, as right, straight, or obtuse so that they will know what angle measure to use in their equation.

Writing Real-World Problems for a Given Equation

You can write a real-world problem for a given equation. Examine each number and mathematical operation in the equation.

Math On the Spot
my.hrw.com

EXAMPLE 4 | Real World | COMMON CORE 6.EE.7

Write a real-world problem for the equation $21.79 + x = 25$. Then solve the equation.

$21.79 + x = 25$

STEP 1 Examine each part of the equation.

x is the unknown or quantity we are looking for.

21.79 is added to x.

$= 25$ means that after adding 21.79 and x, the result is 25.

STEP 2 Write a real-world situation that involves *adding* two quantities.

Joshua wants to buy his mother flowers and a card for Mother's Day. Joshua has $25 to spend and selects roses for $21.79. How much can he spend on a card?

STEP 3 Solve the equation.

$$\begin{array}{r} 21.79 + x = 25 \\ -21.79 \qquad -21.79 \\ \hline x = 3.21 \end{array}$$

Joshua can spend $3.21 on a Mother's Day card.

> **Math Talk**
> Mathematical Practices
> How is the question in a real-world problem related to its equation?

The question asks about the value of the variable.

> The final answer includes units of money in dollars.

Reflect

8. What If? How might the real-world problem change if the equation was $x - 21.79 = 25$ and you still used roses for 21.79?

21.79 is subtracted from the unknown value, and the result would remain 25. The variable would be the total amount of money and 25 would the amount of money available after buying roses.

YOUR TURN

9. Write a real-world problem for the equation $x - 100 = 40$. Then solve the equation.

Check students' problems. $x = 140$

Personal Math Trainer
Online Assessment and Intervention
my.hrw.com

Guided Practice

1. A total of 14 guests attended a birthday party. Three friends stayed after the party to help clean up. How many left when the party ended? (Explore Activity)

a. Let x represent the number of guests who left when the party ended.

b.

Number that left at end of party		Number that stayed to clean		Total at party
x	$+$	3	$=$	14

c. Draw algebra tiles to model the equation.

11 friends left when the party ended.

Solve each equation. Graph the solution on a number line. (Examples 1 and 2)

2. $2 = x - 3$ $x = \underline{5}$

$$-5\ -4\ -3\ -2\ -1\ \ 0\ \ 1\ \ 2\ \ 3\ \ 4\ \ 5$$

3. $s + 12.5 = 14$ $s = \underline{1.5}$

$$-5\ -4\ -3\ -2\ -1\ \ 0\ \ 1\ \ 2\ \ 3\ \ 4\ \ 5$$

Solve each equation. (Examples 1 and 2)

4. $h + 6.9 = 11.4$

$h = \underline{4.5}$

5. $82 + p = 122$

$p = \underline{40}$

6. $n + \frac{1}{2} = \frac{7}{4}$

$n = \underline{\frac{5}{4}}$

7. Write and solve an equation to find the measure of the unknown angle. (Example 3)

$x + 45 = 180;\ x = 135°$

8. Write a real-world problem for the equation $x - 75 = 200$. Then solve the equation. (Example 4)

Check students' answers; $x = 275$

? ESSENTIAL QUESTION CHECK-IN

9. How do you solve equations that contain addition or subtraction?

You apply the inverse operation—subtraction for addition equations and addition for subtraction equations—to both sides of the equation.

11.2 LESSON QUIZ

COMMON CORE **6.EE.7**

Solve each equation.

1. $y + 8.3 = 12.7$

2. $w - 14 = 23$

3. $6 + x = 18$

4. $t - 1.9 = 15.7$

5. $\frac{1}{2} = a - \frac{5}{4}$

6. Ellie spent $88.79 at the computer store. She then had $44.50 left to buy a cool hat. How much money did she originally have? Write and solve an equation to answer the question.

7. Write a real-world problem for the equation $x + 12 = 35$. Then solve the equation.

Lesson Quiz available online

 my.hrw.com

Answers

1. $y = 4.4$

2. $w = 37$

3. $x = 12$

4. $t = 17.6$

5. $a = \frac{7}{4}$

6. $x - \$88.79 = \$44.50$; $x = \$133.29$

7. Check students' answers; $x = 23$

Evaluate

GUIDED AND INDEPENDENT PRACTICE

COMMON CORE **6.EE.5, 6.EE.6, 6.EE.7**

Concepts & Skills	Practice
Explore Activity Modeling Equations	Exercise 1
Example 1 Using Subtraction to Solve Equations	Exercises 2–6, 10, 12–14
Example 2 Using Addition to Solve Equations	Exercises 2–6, 11, 15–16
Example 3 Solving Equations that Represent Geometric Concepts	Exercise 7
Example 4 Writing Real-World Problems for a Given Equation	Exercises 8, 17

Exercise	Depth of Knowledge (D.O.K.)	COMMON CORE Mathematical Practices
10–16	**2** Skills/Concepts	**MP.4** Modeling
17–18	**3** Strategic Thinking H.O.T.	**MP.7** Using Structure
19	**3** Strategic Thinking H.O.T.	**MP.4** Modeling
20	**3** Strategic Thinking H.O.T.	**MP.3** Logic
21	**3** Strategic Thinking H.O.T.	**MP.8** Patterns

Additional Resources

Differentiated Instruction includes:

• Leveled Practice Worksheets

11.2 Independent Practice

Personal Math Trainer
Online Assessment and Intervention
my.hrw.com

COMMON CORE 6.EE.5, 6.EE.6, 6.EE.7

Write and solve an equation to answer each question.

10. A wildlife reserve had 8 elephant calves born during the summer and now has 31 total elephants. How many elephants were in the reserve before summer began?

Sample answer: $e + 8 = 31$; 23 elephants

11. My sister is 14 years old. My brother says that his age minus twelve is equal to my sister's age. How old is my brother?

Sample answer: $14 = b - 12$; $b = 26$

12. Kim bought a poster that cost $8.95 and some colored pencils. The total cost was $21.35. How much did the colored pencils cost?

Sample answer: $x + 8.95 = 21.35$; $12.40

13. The Acme Car Company sold 37 vehicles in June. How many compact cars were sold in June?

Acme Car Company – June Sales	
Type of car	**Number sold**
SUV	8
Compact	?

Sample answer: $x + 8 = 37$; 29 compact cars

14. Sandra wants to buy a new MP3 player that is on sale for $95. She has saved $73. How much more money does she need?

Sample answer: $73 + b = 95$ or $95 - b = 73$; $22

15. Ronald spent $123.45 on school clothes. He counted his money and discovered that he had $36.55 left. How much money did he originally have?

Sample answer: $m - 123.45 = 36.55$; $160

16. Brita withdrew $225 from her bank account. After her withdrawal, there was $548 left in Brita's account. How much money did Brita have in her account before the withdrawal?

Sample answer: $548 = t - 225$; $t = 773

17. **Represent Real-World Problems** Write a real-world situation that can be represented by $15 + c = 17.50$. Then solve the equation and describe what your answer represents for the problem situation.

Check students' answers. $c = 2.50$

18. **Critique Reasoning** Paula solved the equation $7 + x = 10$ and got 17, but she is not certain if she got the correct answer. How could you explain Paula's mistake to her?

Paula added the 7 to 10 instead of subtracting. She should have subtracted 7 from both sides of the equation and found that $x = 3$.

H.O.T. FOCUS ON HIGHER ORDER THINKING

Work Area

19. **Multistep** A grocery store is having a sale this week. If you buy a 5-pound bag of apples for the regular price, you can get another bag for $1.49. If you buy a 5-pound bag of oranges at the regular price, you can get another bag for $2.49.

Grocery Prices	
	Regular price
5-pound bag of apples	$2.99
5-pound bag of oranges	$3.99

a. Write an equation to find the discount for each situation using a for the amount of the discount for apples and r for the amount of the discount for oranges.

$1.49 + a = 2.99$; $2.49 + r = 3.99$

b. Which fruit has a greater discount? Explain.

Both a and r are equal to $1.50, so the discount is the same.

20. **Critical Thinking** An orchestra has twice as many woodwind instruments as brass instruments. There are a total of 150 brass and woodwind instruments.

a. Write two different addition equations that describe this situation. Use w for woodwinds and b for brass.

$w + b = 150$; $w = b + b = 2b$

b. How many woodwinds and how many brass instruments satisfy the given information?

$w = 100$; $b = 50$

21. **Look for a Pattern** Assume the following: $a + 1 = 2$, $b + 10 = 20$, $c + 100 = 200$, $d + 1,000 = 2,000$, ...

a. Solve each equation for each variable.

$a = 1$; $b = 10$, $c = 100$, $d = 1,000$, ...

b. What pattern do you notice between the variables?

Every variable is ten times the one before it.

c. What would be the value of g if the pattern continues?

$g = 1,000,000$

EXTEND THE MATH PRE-AP

Activity available online ⏻ my.hrw.com

Activity Use the code shown in the table below to send messages.

A	B	C	D	E	F	G	H	I	J	K	L	M
1	2	3	4	5	6	7	8	9	10	11	12	13

N	O	P	Q	R	S	T	U	V	W	X	Y	Z
14	15	16	17	18	19	20	21	22	23	24	25	26

- Write a short secret message on a piece of paper.
- Use the chart to find the number that matches each letter of your message. Write the number above each letter in your message.
- To send your message in code, write a series of equations on a separate piece of paper. Use n as your variable and write the equations in the same order as the letters appear in your message. For example, for the letter G, $n = 7$. You might write $n + 5 = 12$.
- Trade equations and decode classmates' messages.

LESSON
11.3 Multiplication and Division Equations

Common Core Standards

The student is expected to:

 Expressions and Equations—6.EE.5

Understand solving an equation or inequality as a process of answering a question: which values from a specified set, if any, make the equation or inequality true? Use substitution to determine whether a given number in a specified set makes an equation or inequality true.

 Expressions and Equations—6.EE.6

Use variables to represent numbers and write expressions when solving a real-world or mathematical problem; understand that a variable can represent an unknown number, or, depending on the purpose at hand, any number in a specified set.

 Expressions and Equations—6.EE.7

Solve real-world and mathematical problems by writing and solving equations of the form $x + p = q$ and $px = q$ for cases in which p, q, and x are all non-negative rational numbers.

Mathematical Practices

 MP.5 Using Tools

ADDITIONAL EXAMPLE 1
Solve each equation. Graph the solution on a number line.

A $6y = 24$ $y = 4$

$-5 \qquad 0 \qquad 5$

B $27 = 9z$ $z = 3$

$-5 \qquad 0 \qquad 5$

 Interactive Whiteboard
Interactive example available online

 my.hrw.com

Engage

ESSENTIAL QUESTION

How do you solve equations that contain multiplication or division? Sample answer: You apply the inverse operation—division for multiplication equations and multiplication for division equations—to both sides of the equation.

Motivate the Lesson

Ask: How many of you like to bake? Can you imagine writing an equation to calculate the ingredients you need? Begin the Explore Activity to see an example for a cookie recipe.

Explore

EXPLORE ACTIVITY

Engage with the Whiteboard

For B, have a student circle the remaining two groups of the model on the whiteboard. Then have students fill in the answer for C and the final answer. Ask how the model helped them understand the problem.

Explain

EXAMPLE 1

Focus on Math Connections CC Mathematical Practices
Remind students that division is the inverse, or opposite, of multiplication. To solve an equation that contains multiplication, use division to "undo" the multiplication.

Questioning Strategies CC Mathematical Practices

• How will you know what number to divide both sides of an equation by in order to solve it? Divide both sides by the number that the variable is multiplied by.

• Why must you divide *both* sides of the equation by the same number? You do so to maintain the equality, or the balance, of the equation.

Focus on Critical Thinking CC Mathematical Practices

Challenge students to describe how solving a multiplication equation is similar to solving an addition or subtraction equation. Students should indicate that the same inverse operation must be applied to both sides of the equation, leaving the variable isolated on one side of the equation.

YOUR TURN

Avoid Common Errors
Watch for students who multiply both sides of the equation when they should divide. Remind students to be certain they are using the inverse operation and to check their answers.

Multiplication and Division Equations

COMMON CORE 6.EE.5
Understand solving an equation...as a process of answering a question: which values...make the equation... true? *Also 6.EE.6, 6.EE.7*

ESSENTIAL QUESTION

How do you solve equations that contain multiplication or division?

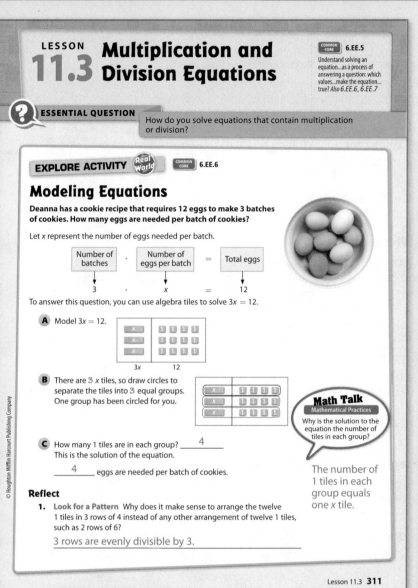

EXPLORE ACTIVITY Real World   **COMMON CORE 6.EE.6**

Modeling Equations

Deanna has a cookie recipe that requires 12 eggs to make 3 batches of cookies. How many eggs are needed per batch of cookies?

Let x represent the number of eggs needed per batch.

Number of batches	·	Number of eggs per batch	=	Total eggs
3	·	x	=	12

To answer this question, you can use algebra tiles to solve $3x = 12$.

A Model $3x = 12$.

B There are 3 x tiles, so draw circles to separate the tiles into 3 equal groups. One group has been circled for you.

C How many 1 tiles are in each group? ____4____
This is the solution of the equation.

____4____ eggs are needed per batch of cookies.

Math Talk
Mathematical Practices

Why is the solution to the equation the number of tiles in each group?

The number of 1 tiles in each group equals one x tile.

Reflect

1. **Look for a Pattern** Why does it make sense to arrange the twelve 1 tiles in 3 rows of 4 instead of any other arrangement of twelve 1 tiles, such as 2 rows of 6?

3 rows are evenly divisible by 3.

Math On the Spot
my.hrw.com

Using Division to Solve Equations

Separating the tiles on both sides of an equation mat into an equal number of groups models dividing both sides of an equation by the same number.

Division Property of Equality

You can divide both sides of an equation by the same nonzero number, and the two sides will remain equal.

When an equation contains multiplication, solve by dividing both sides of the equation by the same nonzero number.

EXAMPLE 1   **COMMON CORE 6.EE.5**

Solve each equation. Graph the solution on a number line.

A $9a = 54$

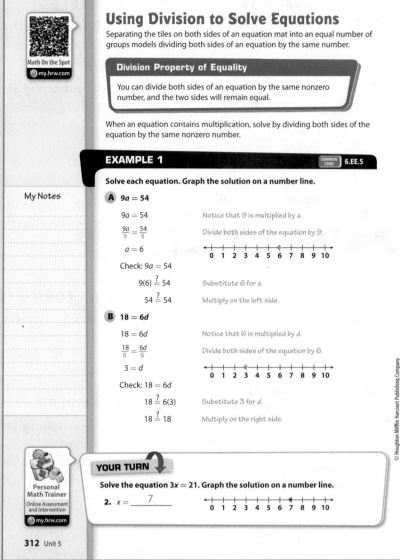

$9a = 54$ — Notice that 9 is multiplied by a.

$\dfrac{9a}{9} = \dfrac{54}{9}$ — Divide both sides of the equation by 9.

$a = 6$

Check: $9a = 54$

$9(6) \stackrel{?}{=} 54$ — Substitute 6 for a.

$54 \stackrel{?}{=} 54$ — Multiply on the left side.

B $18 = 6d$

$18 = 6d$ — Notice that 6 is multiplied by d.

$\dfrac{18}{6} = \dfrac{6d}{6}$ — Divide both sides of the equation by 6.

$3 = d$

Check: $18 = 6d$

$18 \stackrel{?}{=} 6(3)$ — Substitute 3 for d.

$18 \stackrel{?}{=} 18$ — Multiply on the right side.

My Notes

Personal Math Trainer
Online Assessment and Intervention
my.hrw.com

YOUR TURN

Solve the equation $3x = 21$. Graph the solution on a number line.

2. $x =$ ____7____

PROFESSIONAL DEVELOPMENT

CC Integrate Mathematical Practices MP.5

This lesson provides an opportunity to address the Mathematical Practice that calls for students to use appropriate tools strategically. Students first use number sense to identify which inverse operation they should use to isolate the variable on one side of an equation. They then use pencil and paper to solve equations, to check their solutions by using substitution, and to graph the solutions on a number line. In Example 3, students use number sense to translate words to algebraic equations. Students should be encouraged to use mental math to check their answers.

Math Background

Division is defined as multiplication by the reciprocal. To solve $3x = 15$, for example, we could multiply both sides by $\frac{1}{3}$, which would be equivalent to dividing both sides by 3. While most students would rather divide by 3 than multiply by $\frac{1}{3}$, this alternate interpretation is useful when trying to solve equations such as $\frac{2}{3}x = 4$. Dividing by $\frac{2}{3}$ is equivalent to multiplying by $\frac{3}{2}$.

EXAMPLE 2

Focus on Math Connections CC Mathematical Practices
Remind students that multiplication and division are inverse operations. To solve an equation that contains division, use multiplication to "undo" the division.

Questioning Strategies CC Mathematical Practices
• How is solving an equation containing division similar to solving an equation containing multiplication? You solve both by using the inverse operation on both sides to get the variable by itself.

• Does it make sense that the solution is greater than 15? Yes. Since some number divided by 2 is 15, the unknown number will be greater than (double) the unknown number.

Engage with the Whiteboard
Cover up the sentences in blue next to each step of the solution in B and have students write a description of what is happening in each step on the whiteboard. Then have the students graph the solution on the number line.

YOUR TURN

Avoid Common Errors
Watch for students who divide both sides of the equation when they should multiply. Remind students to be certain that they are using the inverse operation and to check their answers.

EXAMPLE 3

Questioning Strategies CC Mathematical Practices
• Why does it make sense to express Juanita's total scrapbooking time as the decimal 2.5? How else might you express the time? You can compute easily with the number 2.5. Another way is to express the time as the mixed number $2\frac{1}{2}$ or as the fraction $\frac{5}{2}$.

• Is Julia's scrapbooking speed best described as a ratio, a rate, or a unit rate? Explain. It is a unit rate because it not only compares quantities in different units, but it also has a denominator of 1 unit.

• Suppose Juanita works at her usual rate for 6 hours one weekend. How many pages can she expect to complete? about 54 pages

Focus on Math Connections CC Mathematical Practices
In solving the problem about Juanita's scrapbooking, students need to subtract after they solve the division equation, to compare her rate last week to her usual rate. This Example not only reinforces the usefulness of the four-step problem-solving process but also prepares students for solving two-step equations—those containing more than one operation.

Integrating Language Arts ELL
Encourage English learners to take notes on new terms or concepts and to write them in familiar language.

Using Multiplication to Solve Equations

When an equation contains division, solve by multiplying both sides of the equation by the same number.

Multiplication Property of Equality

You can multiply both sides of an equation by the same number, and the two sides will remain equal.

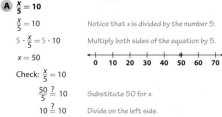

EXAMPLE 2   COMMON CORE 6.EE.5

Solve each equation. Graph the solution on a number line.

A $\frac{x}{5} = 10$

$\frac{x}{5} = 10$ Notice that x is divided by the number 5.

$5 \cdot \frac{x}{5} = 5 \cdot 10$ Multiply both sides of the equation by 5.

$x = 50$

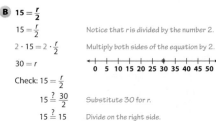

(number line: 0 10 20 30 40 50 60 70)

Check: $\frac{x}{5} = 10$

$\frac{50}{5} \overset{?}{=} 10$ Substitute 50 for x.

$10 \overset{?}{=} 10$ Divide on the left side.

B $15 = \frac{r}{2}$

$15 = \frac{r}{2}$ Notice that r is divided by the number 2.

$2 \cdot 15 = 2 \cdot \frac{r}{2}$ Multiply both sides of the equation by 2.

$30 = r$

(number line: 0 5 10 15 20 25 30 35 40 45 50)

Check: $15 = \frac{r}{2}$

$15 \overset{?}{=} \frac{30}{2}$ Substitute 30 for r.

$15 \overset{?}{=} 15$ Divide on the right side.

YOUR TURN

Solve the equation $\frac{y}{9} = 1$. Graph the solution on a number line.

3. $\frac{y}{9} = 1$

$y = \underline{\quad 9 \quad}$

(number line: 0 1 2 3 4 5 6 7 8 9 10)

Personal Math Trainer
Online Assessment and Intervention
my.hrw.com

Math Talk
Mathematical Practices

How is solving a multiplication equation similar to solving a division equation? How is it different?

Both equations are solved by applying an inverse operation to both sides of the equation. The inverse operations applied are different.

Math On the Spot
my.hrw.com

My Notes

Lesson 11.3 **313**

Math On the Spot
my.hrw.com

Using Equations to Solve Problems

You can use equations to solve real-world problems.

EXAMPLE 3   Problem Solving   COMMON CORE 6.EE.7

Juanita is scrapbooking. She usually completes about 9 pages per hour. One night last week she completed pages 23 through 47 in 2.5 hours. Did she work at her average rate?

Analyze Information

Identify the important information.
- Worked for 2.5 hours
- Starting page: 23   Ending page: 47
- Scrapbooking rate: 9 pages per hour

Formulate a Plan

- Solve an equation to find the number of pages Juanita can expect to complete.
- Compare the number of pages Juanita can expect to complete with the number of pages she actually completed.

Solve

Let n represent the number of pages Juanita can expect to complete in 2.5 hours if she works at her average rate of 9 pages per hour.

Write an equation.

$\frac{n}{2.5} = 9$ Write the equation.

$2.5 \cdot \frac{n}{2.5} = 2.5 \cdot 9$ Multiply both sides by 2.5.

$n = 22.5$

Juanita can expect to complete 22.5 pages in 2.5 hours.

Juanita completed pages 23 through 47, a total of 25 pages. Because $25 > 22.5$, she worked faster than her expected rate.

Justify and Evaluate

You used an equation to find the number of pages Juanita could expect to complete in 2.5 hours if she worked at her average rate. You found that she could complete 22.5 pages.

Since 22.5 pages is less than the 25 pages Juanita completed, she worked faster than her average rate.

The answer makes sense, because Juanita completed 25 pages in 2.5 hours, which is equivalent to a rate of 10 pages in 1 hour. Since $10 > 9$, you know that she worked faster than her average rate.

314 Unit 5

DIFFERENTIATE INSTRUCTION

Number Sense

Have students use a fraction bar to indicate division of both sides of the equation. This provides an easy visual check to compare the coefficient of the variable and the number chosen for dividing both sides of the equation.

Kinesthetic Experience

Give each group of students a set of nine cards numbered 1–9. On signal, each group picks a card at random and passes it to a different group. The number on this card becomes the divisor in a division equation. On a second signal, each group passes a different card to the same group, and this card becomes the quotient. Each group solves their equation, using the following form: $(x \div \text{first card}) = (\text{second card})$. The first group to solve their equation wins.

Additional Resources

Differentiated Instruction includes:
- Reading Strategies
- Success for English Learners **ELL**
- Reteach
- Challenge **PRE-AP**

YOUR TURN

Focus on Reasoning CC Mathematical Practices

In this multistep problem, students first need to find the total number of cards Roberto started with. Have students describe why $\frac{x}{5} = 9$ is the correct equation for finding that number.

EXAMPLE 4

Focus on Reasoning CC Mathematical Practices

Encourage students to begin by analyzing the equation and using number sense to find situations from everyday life that could make sense. For example, if an equation contained decimals, a situation involving money would most likely be a good real-world situation.

Questioning Strategies CC Mathematical Practices

• Using number sense, what can you determine about the value of x given that the product of two numbers is 72? That the value of x will be less than 72.

• How is the question in a real-world problem related to its equation? The question asks about the value of the variable.

YOUR TURN

Focus on Communication CC Mathematical Practices

Guide students to write problems that use sensible data, and have them explain step by step how to solve their equations. Challenge each student to create original word problems based on unique situations.

Elaborate

Talk About It
Summarize the Lesson

 Ask: How do you solve equations that contain multiplication or division? You apply the inverse operation—division for multiplication equations and multiplication for division equations—to both sides of the equation.

GUIDED PRACTICE

Engage with the Whiteboard

For Exercise 1, have students complete the verbal model on the whiteboard and then draw a model with algebra tiles below the verbal model. Ask students to explain their reasoning.

Avoid Common Errors

Exercises 2–3 Remind students to use the inverse operation of division to undo multiplication or multiplication to undo division.

Exercise 4 Remind students that the formula for area of a rectangle is $A = l \cdot w$.

YOUR TURN

4. Roberto is dividing his baseball cards equally among himself, his brother, and his 3 friends. Roberto was left with 9 cards. How many cards did Roberto give away? Write and solve an equation to solve the problem.

Sample answer: $\frac{x}{5} = 9$; $x = 45$; Roberto gave away

$45 - 9 = 36$ cards.

Personal
Math Trainer
Online Assessment
and Intervention
my.hrw.com

Writing Real-World Problems

You can write a real-world problem for a given equation.

EXAMPLE 4 COMMON CORE 6.EE.7

Math On the Spot
my.hrw.com

Write a real-world problem for the equation $8x = 72$. Then solve the problem.

STEP 1 Examine each part of the equation.

x is the unknown value you want to find.

8 is multiplied by x.

$= 72$ means that after multiplying 8 and x, the result is 72.

STEP 2 Write a real-world situation that involves multiplying two quantities.

A hot air balloon flew at 8 miles per hour. Write and solve a multiplication equation to find out how many hours the balloon traveled if it covered a distance of 72 miles.

STEP 3 Use the equation to solve the problem.

$8x = 72$

$\frac{8x}{8} = \frac{72}{8}$ *Divide both sides by 8.*

$x = 9$

The balloon traveled for 9 hours.

YOUR TURN

5. Write a real-world problem for the equation $11x = 385$. Then solve the problem.

Check students' problems; $x = 35$

Personal
Math Trainer
Online Assessment
and Intervention
my.hrw.com

---

1. Caroline ran 15 miles in 5 days. She ran the same distance each day. Write and solve an equation to determine the number of miles she ran each day. (Explore Activity)

a. Let x represent the ___number of miles run each day___.

b.

Number of days	·	Number of miles run each day	=	Total number of miles
5	·	x	=	15

c. Draw algebra tiles to model the equation.
Caroline ran ___3___ miles each day.

Solve each equation. Graph the solution on a number line.
(Examples 1 and 2)

2. $x \div 3 = 3$; $x =$ ___9___

0 1 2 3 4 5 6 7 8 9 10

3. $4x = 32$; $x =$ ___8___

0 1 2 3 4 5 6 7 8 9 10

4. The area of the rectangle shown is 24 square inches. How much longer is its length than its width? (Example 3)

6 in.

w

$24 = 6w$; $w = 4$ inches; length is 2 inches longer than the width

5. Write a real-world problem for the equation $15w = 45$. Then solve the problem. (Example 4)

Check students' problems; $w = 3$.

? ESSENTIAL QUESTION CHECK-IN

6. How do you solve equations that contain multiplication or division?

You apply the inverse operation—division for multiplication equations and multiplication for division equations—to both sides of the equation.

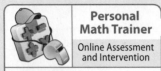

Personal Math Trainer

Online Assessment and Intervention

Online homework assignment available

 my.hrw.com

11.3 LESSON QUIZ

 6.EE.5, 6.EE.7

Solve each equation.

1. $\frac{x}{4} = 12.5$

2. $8w = 120$

3. $6 = \frac{z}{4.5}$

4. $20 = 2.5m$

5. The area of a rectangle is 48 square inches. The length is 8 inches. What is the measure of its width? Write and solve an equation.

Lesson Quiz available online

 my.hrw.com

Answers

1. $x = 50$

2. $w = 15$

3. $z = 27$

4. $m = 8$

5. Sample answer: $8x = 48$; $x = 6$ in.

Evaluate

GUIDED AND INDEPENDENT PRACTICE

COMMON CORE 6.EE.5, 6.EE.6, 6.EE.7

Concepts & Skills	Practice
Explore Activity Modeling Equations	Exercise 1
Example 1 Using Division to Solve Equations	Exercise 3
Example 2 Using Multiplication to Solve Equations	Exercise 2
Example 3 Using Equations to Solve Problems	Exercises 4, 6–12
Example 4 Writing Real-Word Problems	Exercises 5, 13–14

Exercise	Depth of Knowledge (D.O.K.)		**COMMON CORE** Mathematical Practices
7–13	**2** Skills/Concepts		**MP.4** Modeling
14	**3** Strategic Thinking	**H.O.T.**	**MP.5** Using Tools
15	**3** Strategic Thinking	**H.O.T.**	**MP.7** Using Structure
16	**3** Strategic Thinking	**H.O.T.**	**MP.3** Logic
17–19	**3** Strategic Thinking	**H.O.T.**	**MP.7** Using Structure

Additional Resources

Differentiated Instruction includes:

• Leveled Practice worksheets

 Exercise 18 combines concepts from the Common Core cluster "Reason about and solve one-variable equations and inequalities."

Name _____ Class _____ Date _____

Personal Math Trainer
Online Assessment and Intervention
my.hrw.com

In 7–13, write and solve an equation to answer each question. Sample answers are given.

7. Jorge baked cookies for his math class's end-of-year party. There are 28 people in Jorge's math class including Jorge and his teacher. Jorge baked enough cookies for everyone to get 3 cookies each. How many cookies did Jorge bake?

$\frac{c}{28} = 3$; 84 cookies

8. Sam divided a rectangle into 8 congruent rectangles that each have the area shown. What is the area of the rectangle before Sam divided it?

Area = 5 cm²		

$\frac{a}{8} = 5$; 40 square centimeters

9. Carmen participated in a read-a-thon. Mr. Cole pledged $4.00 per book and gave Carmen $44. How many books did Carmen read?

$4k = 44$; 11 books

10. Lee drove 420 miles and used 15 gallons of gasoline. How many miles did Lee's car travel per gallon of gasoline?

$15m = 420$; 28 mi/gal

11. On some days, Melvin commutes 3.5 hours per day to the city for business meetings. Last week he commuted for a total of 14 hours. How many days did he commute to the city?

$3.5d = 14$; 4 days

12. Dharmesh has a square garden with a perimeter of 132 feet. Is the area of the garden greater than 1,000 square feet?

s
□ s

$4s = 132$; $s = 33$ ft;

$33 \times 33 = 1,089$ square feet

Yes, the area of the garden is greater than 1,000 square feet.

13. Ingrid walked her dog and washed her car. The time she spent walking her dog was one-fourth the time it took her to wash her car. It took Ingrid 14 minutes to walk the dog. How long did it take Ingrid to wash her car?

$\frac{w}{4} = 14$; 56 minutes

14. **Representing Real-World Problems** Write and solve a problem involving money that can be solved with a multiplication equation.

Sample answer: Jayne earned $168 for babysitting over 6 weeks. If she earned the same amount each week, how much did she earn for one week?

$6x = 168$; $x = \$28$

15. **Representing Real-World Problems** Write and solve a problem involving money that can be solved with a division equation and has a solution of 1,350.

Sample answer: Marcy split her income from last week equally between paying her student loans, rent, and savings. She put $450 in savings. How much did Marcy earn last week? $\frac{x}{3} = 450$, $x = 1,350$; Marcy earned $1,350 last week.

H.O.T. FOCUS ON HIGHER ORDER THINKING

16. **Communicating Mathematical Ideas** Explain why $7 \cdot \frac{x}{7} = x$. How does your answer help you solve a division equation such as $\frac{x}{7} = 2$?

$\frac{x}{7}$ is equivalent to $\frac{1}{7} \cdot x$. So, multiplying $7 \cdot \frac{x}{7}$ is the same as multiplying $7 \cdot \frac{1}{7} \cdot x$, which equals $1x$, or x. When you solve $\frac{x}{7} = 2$, you multiply both sides by 7 to get $x = 14$.

17. **Critical Thinking** A number tripled and tripled again is 729. What is the number? Show your work.

$3(3x) = 729$; $9x = 729$; $x = 81$; the number is 81.

18. **Multistep** Andre has 4 times as many model cars as Peter, and Peter has one-third as many model cars as Jade. Andre has 36 model cars.

a. Write and solve an equation to find how many model cars Peter has.

$4p = 36$; $p = 9$; Peter has 9 model cars.

b. Using your answer from part **a**, write and solve an equation to find how many model cars Jade has.

$\frac{1}{3}j = 9$; $j = 27$; Jade has 27 model cars.

19. **Persevere in Problem Solving** The area of a rectangle is 42 square inches and one side is 12 inches long. Find the perimeter of the rectangle. Show your work.

31 inches; $42 = 12 \cdot x$, where x is the length of the other side of the rectangle; $x = 3.5$. So, perimeter $= 2(12) + 2(3.5) = 31$ inches.

Work Area

© Houghton Mifflin Harcourt Publishing Company

EXTEND THE MATH PRE-AP
Activity available online my.hrw.com

Activity Here is one way you can name 14, using four 7s and common arithmetic operations:

$$\frac{7 \times 7}{7} + 7$$

Use four 7s and the signs for common operations to name each given number.

1. $2 = $ _____

2. $3 = $ _____

3. $4 = $ _____

4. $5 = $ _____

Sample solutions: 1. $\frac{7}{7} + \frac{7}{7}$ 2. $\frac{7+7+7}{7}$ 3. $\frac{77}{7} - 7$ 4. $7 - \frac{7+7}{7}$

11.4 Writing Inequalities

Common Core Standards

The student is expected to:

 Expressions and Equations—6.EE.5

Understand solving an equation or inequality as a process of answering a question: which values from a specified set, if any, make the equation or inequality true? Use substitution to determine whether a given number in a specified set makes an equation or inequality true.

 Expressions and Equations—6.EE.6

Use variables to represent numbers and write expressions when solving a real-world or mathematical problem; understand that a variable can represent an unknown number, or, depending on the purpose at hand, any number in a specified set.

 Expressions and Equations—6.EE.8

Write an inequality of the form $x > c$ or $x < c$ to represent a constraint or condition in a real-world or mathematical problem. Recognize that inequalities of the form $x > c$ or $x < c$ have infinitely many solutions; represent solutions of such inequalities on number line diagrams.

Mathematical Practices

 MP.2 Reasoning

ADDITIONAL EXAMPLE 1
Graph the solutions of each inequality. Check the solutions.

A $b \geq -4$

Sample check: $-1 \geq -4$

B $-3 > s$

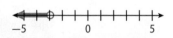

Sample check: $-3 > -5$

 Interactive Whiteboard
Interactive example available online

 my.hrw.com

Engage

ESSENTIAL QUESTION

How can you use inequalities to represent real-world constraints or conditions? Sample answer: You can choose a letter to represent the variable value in the situation and then use one of the inequality symbols to describe its range of values.

Motivate the Lesson

Ask: If you know the lowest and highest temperatures recorded for yesterday, how could you describe yesterday's temperature at any given time of day? For example, what could you say about the temperature at noon? Begin the Explore Activity to find out.

Explore

EXPLORE ACTIVITY

Engage with the Whiteboard

Have students graph $-2\ °F$ on the number line on the whiteboard and then graph $-1\ °F$, $0\ °F$, $3\ °F$, $5\ °F$, and $6\ °F$ in a different color on the same number line. Then have them write inequalities comparing each of the temperatures from B to $-2\ °F$ on the whiteboard. Students will see that all five temperatures are *greater than* $-2\ °F$. Ask students to compare some of the numbers to the left of -2 as well, so that they use both the $>$ and $<$ symbols.

Explain

EXAMPLE 1

Focus on Communication CC Mathematical Practices

Remind students that when a variable is less than a given number, all the values to the left of the given number on the number line make that inequality true. They are all solutions of the inequality. For example, if $x < 4$, then every number less than 4 is a solution.

Questioning Strategies CC Mathematical Practices

- What is the difference between the graph of $y \leq 4$ and the graph of $y < 4$? In the first graph, 4 is included in the solution set. In the second graph, 4 is not included in the solution set.

- What is the difference between using a solid circle and an open circle? A solid circle includes the number at that point; an open circle does not.

- How do you know when to use a solid circle or an open circle? A solid circle is used to represent $\leq$ or $\geq$ on a graph; an open circle is used to represent $<$ or $>$ on a graph.

- How can you check that the graph of an inequality is correct? Pick a point on the shaded portion of the graph. Any point selected should make the inequality a true inequality.

11.4 Writing Inequalities

COMMON CORE 6.EE.8

Write an inequality...to represent a constraint or condition in a real-world or mathematical problem.... Also 6.EE.5, 6.EE.6

? ESSENTIAL QUESTION How can you use inequalities to represent real-world constraints or conditions?

EXPLORE ACTIVITY
Real World   **COMMON CORE** 6.EE.8, 6.EE.5

Using Inequalities to Describe Quantities

You can use inequality symbols with variables to describe quantities that can have many values.

Symbol	Meaning	Word Phrases
$<$	Is less than	Fewer than, below
$>$	Is greater than	More than, above
$\leq$	Is less than or equal to	At most, no more than
$\geq$	Is greater than or equal to	At least, no less than

A The lowest temperature ever recorded in Florida was $-2\,°F$. Graph this temperature on the number line.

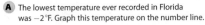

B The temperatures $0\,°F$, $3\,°F$, $6\,°F$, $5\,°F$, and $-1\,°F$ have also been recorded in Florida. Graph these temperatures on the number line.

C How do the temperatures in **B** compare to -2? How can you see this relationship on the number line?

They are all greater than -2. All of the temperatures are located to the right of -2.

D How many other numbers have the same relationship to -2 as the temperatures in **B** ? Give some examples.

infinitely many; any number greater than -2; sample answer: 1, 2, 8.5, 10

E Suppose you could graph all of the possible answers to **D** on a number line. What would the graph look like?

a ray extending to the right of -2, but not including -2

F Let x represent all the possible answers to **D**.

Complete this inequality: $x \boxed{>} -2$

Math On the Spot
my.hrw.com

Yes; yes; both numbers make the inequality true.

Math Talk
Mathematical Practices
Is $-4\frac{1}{4}$ a solution of $y \leq -3$? Is -5.6?

Graphing the Solutions of an Inequality

A **solution of an inequality** that contains a variable is any value of the variable that makes the inequality true. For example, 7 is a solution of $x > -2$, since $7 > -2$ is a true statement.

EXAMPLE 1
COMMON CORE 6.EE.5

Graph the solutions of each inequality. Check the solutions.

A $y \leq -3$

STEP 1 Draw a solid circle at -3 to show that -3 is a solution.

STEP 2 Shade the number line to the left of -3 to show that numbers less than -3 are solutions.

Use a solid circle for an inequality that uses $\geq$ or $\leq$.

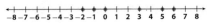

STEP 3 Check your solution.

Choose a number that is on the shaded section of the number line, such as -4. Substitute -4 for y.

$-4 \leq -3$ -4 is less than -3, so -4 is a solution.

B $1 < m$

STEP 1 Draw an empty circle at 1 to show that 1 is not a solution.

STEP 2 Shade the number line to the right of 1 to show that numbers greater than 1 are solutions.

Use an open circle for an inequality that uses $>$ or $<$.

STEP 3 Check your answer.
Substitute 2 for m.

$1 < 2$ 1 is less than 2, so 2 is a solution.

Reflect

1. **Critique Reasoning** Inez says you can rewrite $1 < m$ as $m > 1$. Do you agree?

Yes; The two inequalities have the same solutions.

2. **Analyze Relationships** How is $x < 5$ different from $x \leq 5$?

For $x < 5$, 5 is not a solution and is not included in the graph. For $x \leq 5$, 5 is a solution and is included.

PROFESSIONAL DEVELOPMENT

CC Integrate Mathematical Practices MP.2

This lesson provides an opportunity to address the Mathematical Practice standard which calls for students to reason abstractly and quantitatively. In the Explore Activity and the Examples, students use number lines, word expressions, and mathematical symbols to express inequalities. They use graphs to represent inequalities and to determine if a given number is a solution.

Math Background

Inequalities have a number of properties, including the Transitive Property of Inequality. This property states that for any real numbers $a, b, c,$

if $a > b$ and $b > c$, then $a > c$.
if $a < b$ and $b < c$, then $a < c$.
if $a > b$ and $b = c$, then $a > c$.
if $a < b$ and $b = c$, then $a < c$.

This may seem like common sense, but the Transitive Property is not necessarily true in daily life. If Team A defeats Team B, and Team B defeats Team C, you can't assume that Team A will defeat Team C.

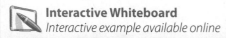
YOUR TURN

Avoid Common Errors

If students have trouble determining which side of the number line to shade, remind them that the inequality sign always points to the lesser of two numbers. Since $t \leq -4$, they should shade the number line to the left of −4, because the numbers decrease to the left on a number line.

EXAMPLE 2

Focus on Reasoning CC Mathematical Practices

Point out to students that sometimes a problem may provide clues and facts that you must use to find a solution. Encourage them to use logical reasoning to solve this kind of problem. For example, in A, tell students that the first step is to identify key words or phrases that indicate operations or relationships. Then they can proceed to write an inequality.

Questioning Strategies CC Mathematical Practices

• In A, how do you know which operation to use to write the inequality? The word *sum* indicates addition.

• In A, how do you know which inequality symbol to use? The phrase *greater than* indicates the symbol >.

• In B, how do you know which inequality symbol to use? The phrase *keeps the temperature below 5 °C* tells me that the temperature is less than 5, which indicates that the symbol < should be used.

YOUR TURN

Avoid Common Errors

Exercise 3 Some students may read the problem quickly and use > instead of $\geq$. Encourage them to begin by underlining the key words or phrases before trying to graph the inequality.

Elaborate

Talk About It
Summarize the Lesson

Ask: How can you make sure you have graphed an inequality correctly? Test one of the values on the shaded part of the number line. If it makes the inequality true, the number line is correct. Check the inequality symbol and be sure that you have used an open or closed circle as called for by the symbol.

GUIDED PRACTICE

Engage with Whiteboard

For Exercise 3, have students begin by underlining the key words or phrases on the whiteboard and then write an inequality, using the same method shown in Example 2. Finally, ask students to graph the inequality on the number line.

Avoid Common Errors

Exercises 1 and 2 Some students may shade in the wrong direction when they attempt to graph the solution set of an inequality, such as $1 \leq x$. Reading $1 \leq x$ as "x is greater than or equal to 1" serves as a reminder to shade to the right.

Exercise 4 Some students may have difficulty determining which inequality symbol to use. Encourage them to begin by underlining key words or phrases before graphing the inequality.

3. Graph the solution of the inequality $t \leq -4$.

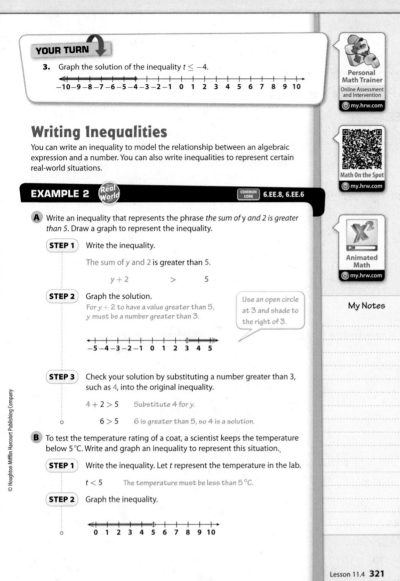

Writing Inequalities

You can write an inequality to model the relationship between an algebraic expression and a number. You can also write inequalities to represent certain real-world situations.

EXAMPLE 2

COMMON CORE 6.EE.8, 6.EE.6

A Write an inequality that represents the phrase *the sum of y and 2 is greater than 5*. Draw a graph to represent the inequality.

STEP 1 Write the inequality.

The sum of y and 2 is greater than 5.

$$y + 2 \qquad > \qquad 5$$

STEP 2 Graph the solution.

For $y + 2$ to have a value greater than 5, y must be a number greater than 3.

Use an open circle at 3 and shade to the right of 3.

STEP 3 Check your solution by substituting a number greater than 3, such as 4, into the original inequality.

$4 + 2 > 5$ Substitute 4 for y.

$6 > 5$ 6 is greater than 5, so 4 is a solution.

B To test the temperature rating of a coat, a scientist keeps the temperature below 5 °C. Write and graph an inequality to represent this situation.

STEP 1 Write the inequality. Let t represent the temperature in the lab.

$t < 5$ The temperature must be less than 5 °C.

STEP 2 Graph the inequality.

Personal Math Trainer
Online Assessment and Intervention
my.hrw.com

Math On the Spot
my.hrw.com

Animated Math
my.hrw.com

My Notes

Personal Math Trainer
Online Assessment and Intervention
my.hrw.com

4. Write an inequality that represents the phrase *the sum of 1 and y is greater than or equal to 3* . Check to see if $y = 1$ is a solution.

$1 + y \geq 3$; $y = 1$ is not a solution because $1 + 1$ is not greater than or equal to 3.

Write and graph an inequality to represent each situation.

5. The temperature in February was at most 6 °F. _____ $t \leq 6$

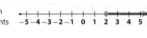

6. Each package must weigh more than 2 ounces. _____ $w > 2$

Guided Practice

1. Graph $1 \leq x$. Use the graph to determine which of these numbers are solutions of the inequality: $-1, 3, 0, 1$ (Explore Activity and Example 1)

_____ 3, 1

2. Graph $-3 > z$. Check the graph using substitution. (Example 1)

3. Write an inequality that represents the phrase "the sum of 4 and x is greater than 6." Draw a graph that represents the inequality, and check your solution. (Example 2)

$4 + x > 6$

4. During hibernation, a garter snake's body temperature never goes below 3 °C. Write and graph an inequality that represents this situation. (Example 2)

Let t be temperature in °C; $t \geq 3$

ESSENTIAL QUESTION CHECK-IN

5. Write an inequality to represent this situation: Nina wants to take at least $15 to the movies. How did you decide which inequality symbol to use?

$d \geq 15$, where d represents the dollar amount Nina wants to take. "At least" means she wants to take $15 or more than $15.

DIFFERENTIATE INSTRUCTION

Critical Thinking

Have students work together to consider absolute-value inequalities, such as $|x| < 2$.

First have students find numbers that make the inequality true. Then have them use the numbers to sketch a graph of what they think the solution should be.

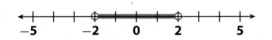

Cooperative Learning

Have students work in groups of 4. Have each group make a set of inequality symbol cards, a variable card, and 6 number cards (3 negative numbers and 3 positive numbers). Have the students take turns using the cards to create an inequality, such as this one:

Then have the groups record the inequalities and graph them on a number line.

Additional Resources

Differentiated Instruction includes:

• Reading Strategies

• Success for English Learners **ELL**

• Reteach

• Challenge **PRE-AP**

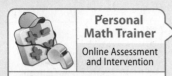

11.4 LESSON QUIZ

 COMMON CORE 6.EE.5, 6.EE.8

Graph each inequality.

1. $a \leq -2$

2. $n < 4$

3. $h > -1.5$

4. $t \leq 3$

Write an inequality that matches the number line model. Use x for the variable.

5.

6.

7.

8.

9. The weight of a package is at least 2.5 pounds. Write an inequality to represent this situation.

Lesson Quiz available online

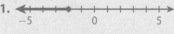
Answers

1.

2.

3.

4.

5. $x \leq -5$

6. $x > -1$

7. $x \geq -0.5$

8. $x < 2$

9. $x \geq 2.5$

Evaluate

GUIDED AND INDEPENDENT PRACTICE

COMMON CORE 6.EE.5, 6.EE.6, 6.EE.8

Concepts & Skills	Practice
Explore Activity Using Inequalities to Describe Quantities	Exercise 1
Example 1 Graphing the Solutions of an Inequality	Exercises 1–2, 6–11, 16–19
Example 2 Writing Inequalities	Exercises 3–4, 12–15, 16–19

Exercise	Depth of Knowledge (D.O.K.)	COMMON CORE Mathematical Practices
6	**2** Skills/Concepts	**MP.7** Using Structure
7–15	**2** Skills/Concepts	**MP.2** Reasoning
16	**2** Skills/Concepts	**MP.7** Using Structure
17–19	**2** Skills/Concepts	**MP.4** Modeling
20	**3** Strategic Thinking **H.O.T.**	**MP.3** Logic
21–22	**3** Strategic Thinking **H.O.T.**	**MP.7** Using Structure

Additional Resources

Differentiated Instruction includes:

• Leveled Practice worksheets

11.4 Independent Practice

COMMON CORE 6.EE.5, 6.EE.6, 6.EE.8

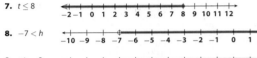

Personal Math Trainer

Online Assessment and Intervention

my.hrw.com

6. Which of the following numbers are solutions to $x \geq 0$?

$-5, 0.03, -1, 0, 1.5, -6, \frac{1}{2}$ _____ $0.03, 0, 1.5, \frac{1}{2}$

Graph each inequality.

7. $t \leq 8$

8. $-7 < h$

9. $x \geq -9$

10. $n > 2.5$

11. $-4\frac{1}{2} > x$

Write an inequality that matches the number line model.

12. $x > 6$

13. $x \leq -3$

14. $x < 1.5$

15. $x \geq -3.5$

16. A child must be at least 48 inches tall to ride a roller coaster.

  a. Write and graph an inequality to represent this situation.

  $c \geq 48$

  b. Can a child who is 46 inches tall ride the roller coaster? Explain.

  No; 46 is not greater than or equal to 48.

Write and graph an inequality to represent each situation.

17. The stock is worth at least $14.50. _____ $s \geq 14.5$

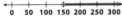

18. The temperature is less than 3.5 °F. _____ $t < 3.5$

19. The goal of the fundraiser is to make more than $150. _____ $g > 150$

H.O.T. FOCUS ON HIGHER ORDER THINKING

Work Area

20. **Communicate Mathematical Ideas** Explain how to graph the inequality $8 \geq y$.

Sample answer: Make a solid circle at 8 because of the inequality symbol, greater than or equal to. Then shade in the numbers to the left of 8, which are the numbers that make y less than 8.

21. **Represent Real-World Problems** The number line shows an inequality. Describe a real-world situation that the inequality could represent.

Sample answer: Steve has more than $2.75 in his wallet.

22. **Critique Reasoning** Natasha is trying to represent the following situation with a number line model: There are fewer than 5 students in the cafeteria. She has come up with two possible representations, shown below. Which is the better representation, and why?

Sample answer: The number line that shows only 1, 2, 3, and 4 as solutions is correct. In this example, it does not make sense to have negative numbers of students or fractional parts of students.

EXTEND THE MATH PRE-AP

Activity available online my.hrw.com

Activity The four graphs at right show constraints on both ends of the graph. Challenge students to describe each graph in words and with an inequality statement. Tell them that graphs C and D describe the solutions for a single variable and that they should use the word "or" to describe these situations.

A x is greater than -2 and less than 3: $-2 < x < 3$

B x is greater than -2 and is less than or equal to 3; $-2 < x \leq 3$

C x is less than -2 or x is greater than 3; $-2 > x$ or $x > 3$

D x is less than or equal to -2 or x is greater than or equal to 3; $-2 \geq x$ or $x \geq 3$

A

B

C

D

Ready to Go On?

Assess Mastery

Use the assessment on this page to determine if students have mastered the concepts and standards covered in this module.

 **Response to Intervention**

Intervention	Enrichment

Access Ready to Go On? assessment online, and receive instant scoring, feedback, and customized intervention or enrichment.

Online and Print Resources

Personal Math Trainer
Online Assessment and Intervention
⏻ my.hrw.com

Differentiated Instruction
• Reteach worksheets
• Reading Strategies **ELL**
• Success for English Learners **ELL**

Differentiated Instruction
• Challenge worksheets **PRE-AP**
• Extend the Math **PRE-AP** Lesson Activities in TE

Additional Resources

Assessment Resources includes:
• Leveled Module Quizzes

Ready to Go On?

Personal Math Trainer
Online Assessment and Intervention
ⓒ my.hrw.com

11.1 Writing Equations to Represent Situations

Determine whether the given value is a solution of the equation.

1. $\frac{b}{12} = 5$; $b = 60$ _____ yes   **2.** $7w = 87$; $w = 12$ _____ no

Write an equation to represent the situation.

3. The number of eggs in the refrigerator e decreased by 5 equals 18.
$e - 5 = 18$

11.2 Addition and Subtraction Equations

Solve each equation.

4. $r - 38 = 9$ _____ $r = 47$ **5.** $h + 17 = 40$ _____ $h = 23$

6. $n + 75 = 155$ _____ $n = 80$ **7.** $q - 17 = 18$ _____ $q = 35$

11.3 Multiplication and Division Equations

Solve each equation.

8. $8z = 112$ _____ $z = 14$ **9.** $\frac{d}{14} = 7$ _____ $d = 98$

10. $\frac{f}{28} = 24$ _____ $f = 672$ **11.** $3a = 57$ _____ $a = 19$

11.4 Writing Inequalities

Write an inequality to represent each situation, then graph the solutions.

12. There are fewer than 8 gallons of gas in the tank. _____ $f < 8$

0 1 2 3 4 5 6 7 8 9 10

13. There are at least 3 slices of bread left in the bag. _____ $p \geq 3$

0 1 2 3 4 5 6 7 8 9 10

? ESSENTIAL QUESTION

14. How can you solve problems involving equations that contain addition, subtraction, multiplication, or division?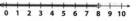
Write an equation for the situation. Then apply the inverse operation to get the variable alone on one side of the equation.

© Houghton Mifflin Harcourt Publishing Company

Common Core Standards

Lesson	Exercises	Common Core Standards
11.1	1–3	**6.EE.5, 6.EE.6, 6.EE.7**
11.2	4–7	**6.EE.5, 6.EE.6, 6.EE.7**
11.3	8–11	**6.EE.5, 6.EE.6, 6.EE.7**
11.4	12–13	**6.EE.5, 6.EE.6, 6.EE.8**

Assessment Readiness

Assessment Readiness Tip Instead of solving equations directly, students can work backward by substituting answers into given equations to see if they are correct.

Item 7 Students can try substituting the answers in the equation in order. When they try choice A, they should find that the result is a true equation, indicating that this is the correct solution.

Item 8 Students can write the equation $17x = 680$ to represent the situation and then start substituting answers in the equation to find which answer makes the sentence true. Choices A and B result in false equations, but choice C results in $680 = 680$. Thus, choice C is the correct answer.

Avoid Common Errors

Item 1 Some students will see the word *times*, automatically think of multiplication, and quickly pick choice B. Encourage them to read carefully to identify all key words or phrases such as *more times*, which indicates addition, not multiplication.

Item 4 Some students may select choice A because they looked only at the endpoint of the circle and the direction the arrow was pointing and didn't pay attention to whether or not the circle was solid or open. Remind them that they need to analyze art or diagrams carefully to fully understand them.

Additional Resources

Personal Math Trainer
Online Assessment and Intervention
my.hrw.com

COMMON CORE

MODULE 11 MIXED REVIEW
Assessment Readiness

Personal Math Trainer
Online Assessment and Intervention
my.hrw.com

Selected Response

1. Kate has gone up to the chalkboard to do math problems 5 more times than Andre. Kate has gone up 11 times. Which equation represents this situation?

Ⓐ $a - 11 = 5$
Ⓑ $5a = 11$
Ⓒ $a - 5 = 11$
Ⓓ $a + 5 = 11$

2. For which equation is $y = 7$ a solution?

Ⓐ $7y = 1$
Ⓑ $18 = 11 + y$
Ⓒ $y + 7 = 0$
Ⓓ $\frac{y}{2} = 14$

3. Which is an equation?

Ⓐ $17 + x$ Ⓒ $20x = 200$
Ⓑ $45 \div x$ Ⓓ $90 - x$

4. The temperature never rose above 6 °F on Friday. Which number line could represent this situation?

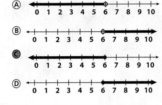

5. Becca hit 7 more home runs than Beverly. Becca hit 21 home runs. How many home runs did Beverly hit?

Ⓐ 3   Ⓒ 21
Ⓑ 14   Ⓓ 28

6. Jeordie spreads out a rectangular picnic blanket with an area of 42 square feet. Its width is 6 feet. Which equation could you use to find its length?

Ⓐ $6x = 42$ Ⓒ $\frac{6}{x} = 42$
Ⓑ $42 - x = 6$ Ⓓ $6 + x = 42$

7. What is a solution to the equation $6t = 114$?

Ⓐ $t = 19$ Ⓒ $t = 120$
Ⓑ $t = 108$ Ⓓ $t = 684$

8. The area of a rectangular deck is 680 square feet. The deck's width is 17 feet. What is its perimeter?

Ⓐ 40 feet   Ⓒ 114 feet
Ⓑ 57 feet   Ⓓ 228 feet

Mini-Task

9. Sylvia earns $7 per hour at her afterschool job. After working one week, she received a paycheck for $91.

a. Write and solve an equation to find the number of hours Sylvia worked to earn $91.

<u>   13   </u>

b. The greatest number of hours Sylvia can work in any week is 15. Write an inequality to represent this statement.

<u> $h \leq 15$ </u>

c. What is the greatest amount of money Sylvia can earn in one week?

<u> $105   </u>

Common Core Standards

Items	Grade 6 Standards	Mathematical Practices
1	6.EE.6	MP.4
2	6.EE.5	MP.5
3	6.EE.5	MP.7
4*	6.EE.5, 6.EE.8, 6.NS.6	MP.6
5	6.EE.5, 6.EE.7	MP.4, MP.7
6	6.EE.6	MP.4, MP.7
7	6.EE.7	MP.5
8	6.EE.5, 6.EE.7	MP.4, MP.7
9	6.EE.7, 6.EE.8	MP.4, MP.7

* Item integrates mixed review concepts from previous modules or a previous course.

Relationships in Two Variables

 ESSENTIAL QUESTION

How can you use relationships in two variables to solve real-world problems?

You can use tables, graphs, and equations in two variables to model real-world problems, then use these representations to solve the problems.

Real-World Video

A two-variable equation can represent an animal's distance over time. A graph can display the relationship between the variables. You can graph two or more animals' data to visually compare them.

 my.hrw.com

GO DIGITAL

my.hrw.com

 my.hrw.com

Go digital with your write-in student edition, accessible on any device.

 Math On the Spot

Scan with your smart phone to jump directly to the online edition, video tutor, and more.

 Animated Math

Interactively explore key concepts to see how math works.

 Personal Math Trainer

Get immediate feedback and help as you work through practice sets.

© Houghton Mifflin Harcourt Publishing Company • Image Credits: Blickwinkel/Alamy

Are You Ready?

Assess Readiness

Use the assessment on this page to determine if students need intensive or strategic intervention for the module's prerequisite skills.

 **RtI** **Response to Intervention**

 Personal Math Trainer

Online Assessment and Intervention

⏻ my.hrw.com

Intervention	Enrichment

Access Are You Ready? assessment online, and receive instant scoring, feedback, and customized intervention or enrichment.

Online and Print Resources

Skills Intervention worksheets
- Skill 36 Multiplication Facts
- Skill 69 Graph Ordered Pairs (First Quadrant)

Differentiated Instruction
- Challenge worksheets **PRE-AP**
- Extend the Math **PRE-AP** Lesson Activities in TE

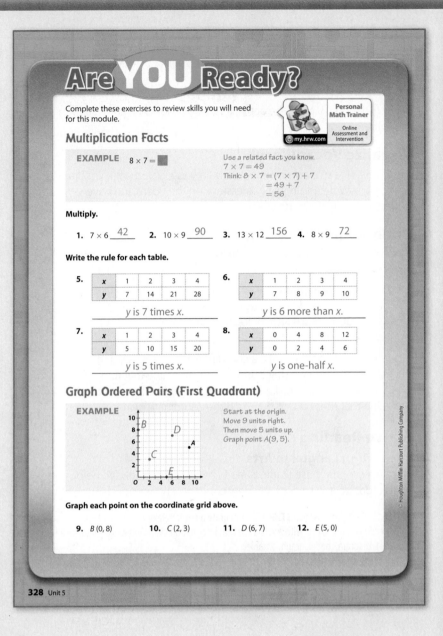

Are YOU Ready?

Complete these exercises to review skills you will need for this module.

 Personal Math Trainer

Online Assessment and Intervention

⏻ my.hrw.com

Multiplication Facts

EXAMPLE $8 \times 7 = \blacksquare$

Use a related fact you know.
$7 \times 7 = 49$
Think: $8 \times 7 = (7 \times 7) + 7$
$= 49 + 7$
$= 56$

Multiply.

1. 7×6 __42__ **2.** 10×9 __90__ **3.** 13×12 __156__ **4.** 8×9 __72__

Write the rule for each table.

5.

x	1	2	3	4
y	7	14	21	28

y is 7 times x.

6.

x	1	2	3	4
y	7	8	9	10

y is 6 more than x.

7.

x	1	2	3	4
y	5	10	15	20

y is 5 times x.

8.

x	0	4	8	12
y	0	2	4	6

y is one-half x.

Graph Ordered Pairs (First Quadrant)

EXAMPLE

Start at the origin.
Move 9 units right.
Then move 5 units up.
Graph point A(9, 5).

Graph each point on the coordinate grid above.

9. B (0, 8) **10.** C (2, 3) **11.** D (6, 7) **12.** E (5, 0)

© Houghton Mifflin Harcourt Publishing Company

PROFESSIONAL DEVELOPMENT VIDEO

Author Juli Dixon models successful teaching practices as she explores graphing in the coordinate plane in an actual sixth-grade classroom.

 Professional Development ⏻ my.hrw.com

GO DIGITAL my.hrw.com

 Online Teacher Edition
Access a full suite of teaching resources online—plan, present, and manage classes and assignments.

ePlanner
Easily plan your classes and access all your resources online.

Interactive Answers and Solutions
Customize answer keys to print or display in the classroom. Choose to include answers only or full solutions to all lesson exercises.

 Interactive Whiteboards
Engage students with interactive whiteboard-ready lessons and activities.

Personal Math Trainer: Online Assessment and Intervention
Assign automatically graded homework, quizzes, tests, and intervention activities. Prepare your students with updated practice tests aligned with Common Core.

Reading Start-Up

Have students complete the activities on this page by working alone or with others.

Visualize Vocabulary

The chart helps students review vocabulary associated with algebraic expressions. Write additional expressions on the board and have students identify the parts of each expression.

Understand Vocabulary

Use the following explanations to help students learn the preview words.

A **coordinate plane** is formed by two number lines that intersect at right angles. Coordinate planes are used in geographic maps and for locating images on computer screens.

The two lines that make a coordinate plane are called the **axes**. The **x-axis** is the horizontal number line that runs left to right on the coordinate plane. The **y-axis** is the vertical line that runs up and down on the coordinate plane.

Active Reading

Integrating Language Arts

Students can use these reading and note-taking strategies to help them organize and understand new concepts and vocabulary.

COMMON CORE **ELA-Literacy.RST.6-8.7** Integrate quantitative or technical information expressed in words in a text with a version of that information expressed visually (e.g., in a flowchart, diagram, model, graph, or table).

Additional Resources

Differentiated Instruction

• Reading Strategies **ELL**

Reading Start-Up

Visualize Vocabulary

Use the ✔ words to complete the chart.

Parts of the Algebraic Expression 14 + 3x		
Definition	**Mathematical Representation**	**Review Word**
A specific number whose value does not change	14	constant
A number that is multiplied by a variable in an algebraic expression	3	coefficient
A letter or symbol used to represent an unknown	x	variable

Understand Vocabulary

Complete the sentences using the preview words.

1. The numbers in an ordered pair are _____coordinates_____.

2. A _____coordinate plane_____ is formed by two number lines that intersect at right angles.

Vocabulary

Review Words
✔ coefficient (*coeficiente*)
✔ constant (*constante*)
   equation (*ecuación*)
   negative number (*número negativo*)
   positive number (*número positivo*)
   scale (*escala*)
✔ variable (*variable*)

Preview Words
   axes (*ejes*)
   coordinate plane (*plano cartesiano*)
   coordinates (*coordenadas*)
   dependent variable (*variable dependiente*)
   independent variable (*variable independiente*)
   ordered pair (*par ordenado*)
   origin (*origen*)
   quadrants (*cuadrante*)
   x-axis (*eje x*)
   x-coordinate (*coordenada x*)
   y-axis (*eje y*)
   y-coordinate (*coordenada y*)

Active Reading

Layered Book Before beginning the module, create a layered book to help you learn the concepts in this module. Label each flap with lesson titles from this module. As you study each lesson, write important ideas such as vocabulary and formulas under the appropriate flap. Refer to your finished layered book as you work on exercises from this module.

Before	**In this module**	**After**
Students understand:	Students will learn to:	Students will connect:
• how to recognize the difference between additive and multiplicative numerical patterns given in a table or graph	• identify independent and dependent quantities from tables and graphs	• tables and verbal descriptions with a linear relationship
• how to graph a relationship on a number line	• write an equation that represents the relationship between independent and dependent quantities from a table	• graphs and equations with a linear relationship
• how to identify and locate ordered pairs of whole numbers in the first quadrant	• represent a given situation using verbal descriptions, tables, graphs, and equations in the form $y = kx$ or $y = x + b$	• ordered pairs with an equation
	• graph points in all four quadrants using ordered pairs of rational numbers	

Unpacking the Standards

Use the examples on this page to help students know exactly what they are expected to learn in this module.

Common Core Standards

Content Areas

 Expressions and Equations—6.EE

Represent and analyze quantitative relationships between dependent and independent variables.

> **Go online to see a complete unpacking of the Common Core Standards.**
>
> ⏻ my.hrw.com

MODULE 12

Unpacking the Standards

Understanding the standards and the vocabulary terms in the standards will help you know exactly what you are expected to learn in this module.

COMMON CORE 6.EE.9

Use variables to represent two quantities in a real-world problem that change in relationship to one another; write an equation to express one quantity, thought of as the dependent variable, in terms of the other quantity, thought of as the independent variable. ...

Key Vocabulary

equation *(ecuación)*
A mathematical sentence that shows that two expressions are equivalent.

What It Means to You

You will learn to write an equation that represents the relationship in a table.

UNPACKING EXAMPLE 6.EE.9

Emily has a dog-walking service. She charges a daily fee of $7 to walk a dog twice a day. Create a table that shows how much Emily earns for walking 1, 6, 10, and 15 dogs. Write an equation that represents the situation.

Dogs walked	1	6	10	15
Earnings ($)	7	42	70	105

Earnings is 7 times the number of dogs walked. Let the variable e represent earnings and the variable d represent the number of dogs walked.

$$e = 7 \times d$$

COMMON CORE 6.EE.9

...Analyze the relationship between the dependent and independent variables using graphs and tables, and relate these to the equation.

Key Vocabulary

coordinate plane
(plano cartesiano)
A plane formed by the intersection of a horizontal number line called the *x*-axis and a vertical number line called the *y*-axis.

 Visit my.hrw.com to see all the Common Core Standards unpacked.

⏻ my.hrw.com

330 Unit 5

What It Means to You

You can use words, a table, a graph, or an equation to model the same mathematical relationship.

UNPACKING EXAMPLE 6.EE.9

The equation $y = 4x$ represents the total cost y for x games of miniature golf. Make a table of values and a graph for this situation.

Number of games, x	1	2	3	4
Total cost ($), y	4	8	12	16

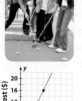

Common Core Standards	Lesson 12.1	Lesson 12.2	Lesson 12.3	Lesson 12.4
6.NS.6b Understand signs of numbers in ordered pairs as indicating locations in quadrants of the coordinate plane....	COMMON CORE			
6.NS.6c Find and position integers and other rational numbers on ... number line diagram; find and position pairs of integers and other rational numbers on a coordinate plane.	COMMON CORE			
6.NS.8 Solve real-world and mathematical problems by graphing points in all four quadrants of the coordinate plane. Include use of coordinates and absolute value to find distances between points with the same first coordinate or the same second coordinate.	COMMON CORE			
6.EE.9 Use variables to represent two quantities in a real-world problem that change in relationship to one another; write an equation to express one quantity, thought of as the dependent variable, in terms of the other quantity, thought of as the independent variable. Analyze the relationship between the dependent and the independent variables using graphs and tables....		COMMON CORE	COMMON CORE	COMMON CORE

LESSON
12.1 Graphing on the Coordinate Plane

Common Core Standards

The student is expected to:

 **The Number System—
6.NS.6c**

Find and position integers and other rational numbers on a horizontal or vertical number line diagram; find and position pairs of integers and other rational numbers on a coordinate plane. *Also 6.NS.6, 6.NS.6b, 6.NS.8*

Mathematical Practices

 MP.2 Reasoning

ADDITIONAL EXAMPLE 1
Identify the coordinates of each point. Name the quadrant where each point is located.

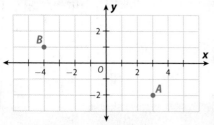

A: (3, −2), IV; *B*: (−4, 1), II

 Interactive Whiteboard
Interactive example available online

 my.hrw.com

ADDITIONAL EXAMPLE 2
Graph and label *P*(0, −2), *Q*(−4, 1.5), and *R*(3.5, 0) on the coordinate plane.

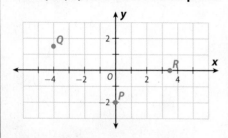

 Interactive Whiteboard
Interactive example available online

 my.hrw.com

Engage

ESSENTIAL QUESTION

How do you locate and name points in the coordinate plane? Sample answer: Points in the coordinate plane are located and named by positions to the left or right of the origin first, then above or below the origin. The order of the coordinates is important.

Motivate the Lesson
Ask: Have you ever tried to find a city or town by its location on a map grid? Maps are like a coordinate plane. Begin Example 1 to find out how to locate a point on a coordinate plane.

Explore

Engage with the Whiteboard

To introduce students to the four-quadrant coordinate plane, sketch a simple "treasure map" with a coordinate plane on the whiteboard. Mark a point for "Start" at the origin and a point for "Treasure" in Quadrant I. Ask students to draw a path to the treasure using the grid lines and then to describe the path in words, such as, "Walk east 3 steps. Then walk north 5 steps." Repeat several times with new coordinates for the "Treasure."

Explain

EXAMPLE 1

Focus on Communication [CC] **Mathematical Practices**
Point out to students that coordinates describe a location in relation to the origin, so it is important to always start at the origin when identifying the coordinates of a point.

Questioning Strategies [CC] **Mathematical Practices**
• Is point (2, 3) the same as point (3, 2)? Explain. No, they are not the same point. Point (2, 3) lies 2 units to the right of the origin and 3 units up, while point (3, 2) lies 3 units to the right and 2 units up.

YOUR TURN

Avoid Common Errors
Students may give incorrect coordinates for a point because they transposed the *x*- and *y*-coordinates. Remind students that the *x*-coordinate is the first number in an ordered pair.

EXAMPLE 2

Connect Vocabulary [ELL]
Some students may have difficulty remembering what the *x*- and *y*-coordinates mean in an ordered pair. Encourage students to think of plotting points as physical movements, run and jump. The *x*-coordinate tells how far to run to the right or left, and the *y*-coordinate tells how far to jump up or down. So, when plotting points, students should always "run before they jump."

Questioning Strategies [CC] **Mathematical Practices**
• Describe how graphing the point (0, −3) is similar to graphing the point (−3, 0). How is it different? Sample answer: They are similar because you start at the origin and move three units to graph each point. They are different because in (0, −3), you move down from the origin. In (−3, 0), you move left from the origin.

LESSON 12.1 Graphing on the Coordinate Plane

6.NS.6c

...find and position pairs of integers and other rational numbers on a coordinate plane. *Also 6.NS.6, 6.NS.6b, 6.NS.8*

? ESSENTIAL QUESTION

How do you locate and name points in the coordinate plane?

Naming Points in the Coordinate Plane

A **coordinate plane** is formed by two number lines that intersect at right angles. The point of intersection is 0 on each number line.

- The two number lines are called the **axes**.
- The horizontal axis is called the **x-axis**.
- The vertical axis is called the **y-axis**.
- The point where the axes intersect is called the **origin**.
- The two axes divide the coordinate plane into four **quadrants**.

An **ordered pair** is a pair of numbers that gives the location of a point on a coordinate plane. The first number tells how far to the right (positive) or left (negative) the point is located from the origin. The second number tells how far up (positive) or down (negative) the point is located from the origin.

The numbers in an ordered pair are called **coordinates**. The first number is the **x-coordinate** and the second number is the **y-coordinate**.

EXAMPLE 1

6.NS.6c, 6.NS.6b

Identify the coordinates of each point. Name the quadrant where each point is located.

Point *A* is 1 unit *left* of the origin, and 5 units *down*. It has *x*-coordinate −1 and *y*-coordinate −5, written (−1, −5). It is located in Quadrant III.

Point *B* is 2 units *right* of the origin, and 3 units *up*. It has *x*-coordinate 2 and *y*-coordinate 3, written (2, 3). It is located in Quadrant I.

Lesson 12.1 **331**

Math On the Spot
my.hrw.com

Reflect

1. If both coordinates of a point are negative, in which quadrant is the point located? _____III_____

2. Describe the coordinates of all points in Quadrant I.
   Both coordinates are positive.

3. **Communicate Mathematical Ideas** Explain why (−3, 5) represents a different location than (3, 5).
   The *x*-coordinate in (−3, 5) is −3 which will be to the left of the origin. The *x*-coordinate in (3, 5) is 3 which will be to the right of the origin.

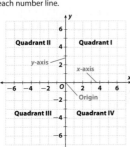

Personal Math Trainer
Online Assessment and Intervention
my.hrw.com

YOUR TURN

Identify the coordinates of each point. Name the quadrant where each point is located.

4. *G* (4, −4); IV
   E (−2, 4); II

5. *F* (3, 2); I
   H (−1, −3); III

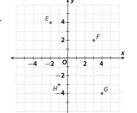

Graphing Points in the Coordinate Plane

Points that are located on the axes are not located in any quadrant. Points on the *x*-axis have a *y*-coordinate of 0, and points on the *y*-axis have an *x*-coordinate of 0.

Math On the Spot
my.hrw.com

EXAMPLE 2

6.NS.6c, 6.NS.6

Graph and label each point on the coordinate plane.
   A(−5, 2), *B*(3, 1.5), *C*(0, −3)

Point *A* is 5 units *left* and 2 units *up* from the origin.

Point *B* is 3 units *right* and 1.5 units *up* from the origin. Graph the point halfway between (3, 1) and (3, 2).

Point *C* is 3 units *down* from the origin. Graph the point on the *y*-axis.

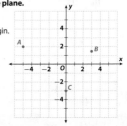

332 Unit 5

PROFESSIONAL DEVELOPMENT

CC Integrate Mathematical Practices MP.3

This lesson provides an opportunity to address this Mathematical Practice standard. It calls for students to create and use representations to organize, record, and communicate mathematical ideas. Students use coordinate planes to locate points. Then students solve a real-world problem on a coordinate plane in which the scale on each axis represents a real-world situation. In this way, students are able to connect a coordinate plane to the real world.

Math Background

The concept of the rectangular coordinate system is generally credited to French mathematician and philosopher René Descartes and, therefore, is sometimes referred to as the Cartesian plane. Every point on the plane can be located because all real numbers, not just integers, are used. The points represented by integer coordinates are sometimes called lattice points.

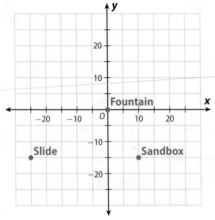

YOUR TURN

Avoid Common Errors

Students may graph the points incorrectly by using the *x*- and *y*-coordinates in the wrong order. Remind students to run before they jump.

EXAMPLE 3

Focus on Math Connections [CC] Mathematical Practices

Point out to students that the coordinate plane also indicates directions. The *x*-axis points east (to the right) and west (to the left) and the *y*-axis points north (up) and south (down). For Example 3, have students add the correct north, south, east, and west labels to the axes of the coordinate plane.

Questioning Strategies [CC] Mathematical Practices

• Describe the direction you would go from Gary's house to Jen's house. I would travel east to go from Gary's house to Jen's house.

• What would the coordinates of Gary's house be if he lived 30 miles directly east of Jen? Explain. (35, 15); Jen lives at (5, 15), so 30 miles directly east would be (35, 15).

YOUR TURN

Focus on Math Connections [CC] Mathematical Practices

Show students how to translate directions to movements by using the axes. Remind students that "20 miles south" is on the *y*-axis *below* the origin and that "20 miles west" is on the *x*-axis to the *left* of the origin. Both movements are in a negative direction, so the coordinates of Ted's home are (−20, −20). Since Ned lives "50 miles directly north of Ted's house," only the *y*-coordinate changes. Because north is a positive direction, −20 + 50 = 30. So, Ned's home is located at (−20, 30).

Elaborate

· ·

Talk About It
Summarize the Lesson

 Have students complete a graphic organizer that shows the number of each quadrant and the signs of the coordinates in each quadrant.

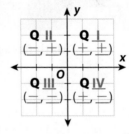

GUIDED PRACTICE

Engage with the Whiteboard

 For Exercises 1–2, have students fill in the blanks by identifying the coordinates of each point on the whiteboard. Then have them name the quadrant where each point is located. Also ask students to describe how they would graph each point.

Avoid Common Errors

Exercises 3–4, 6–7 Students may graph the points incorrectly by using the *x*- and *y*-coordinates in the wrong order. Remind students to run before they jump.

YOUR TURN

Graph and label each point on the coordinate plane.

6. $P(-4, 2)$

7. $Q(3, 2.5)$

8. $R(-4.5, -5)$

9. $S(4, -5)$

10. $T(-2.5, 0)$

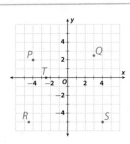

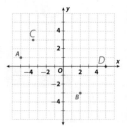

Personal Math Trainer
Online Assessment and Intervention
my.hrw.com

Reading Scales on Axes

The *scale* of an axis is the number of units that each grid line represents. So far, the graphs in this lesson have a scale of 1 unit, but graphs frequently use other units.

Math On the Spot
my.hrw.com

EXAMPLE 3 Real World

COMMON CORE 6.NS.8

The graph shows the location of a city. It also shows the location of Gary's and Jen's houses. The scale on each axis represents miles.

A Use the scale to describe Gary's location relative to the city.

Each grid square is 5 miles on a side.

Gary's house is at $(-25, 15)$, which is 25 miles west and 15 miles north of the city.

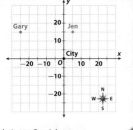

North and south are the positive and negative directions along the *y*-axis; east and west are the positive and negative directions on the *x*-axis.

B Describe the location of Jen's house relative to Gary's house.

Jen's house is located 6 grid squares to the right of Gary's house. Since each grid square is 5 miles on a side, her house is $6 \cdot 5 = 30$ miles from Gary's.

Math Talk
Mathematical Practices

How are north, south, east, and west represented on the graph in Example 3?

YOUR TURN

Use the graph in the Example.

11. Ted lives 20 miles south and 20 miles west of the city represented on the graph in Example 3. His brother Ned lives 50 miles north of Ted's house. Give the coordinates of each brother's house.

Ted $(-20, -20)$, Ned $(-20, 30)$

Personal Math Trainer
Online Assessment and Intervention
my.hrw.com

© Houghton Mifflin Harcourt Publishing Company

Identify the coordinates of each point in the coordinate plane. Name the quadrant where each point is located. (Example 1)

1. Point *A* is 5 units ___left___ of the origin and

   1 unit ___up___ from the origin.

   Its coordinates are ___$(-5, 1)$___. It is in quadrant ___II___.

2. Point *B* is ___2___ units right of the origin

   and ___3___ units down from the origin.

   Its coordinates are ___$(2, -3)$___. It is in quadrant ___IV___.

Graph and label each point on the coordinate plane above. (Example 2)

3. Point *C* at $(-3.5, 3)$

4. Point *D* at $(5, 0)$

For 5–7, use the coordinate plane shown. (Example 3)

5. Describe the scale of the graph.

   Each grid square is $\frac{1}{2}$ unit on a side.

6. Plot point *A* at $\left(-\frac{1}{2}, 2\right)$.

7. Plot point *B* at $\left(2\frac{1}{2}, -2\right)$.

8. **Vocabulary** Describe how an ordered pair represents a point on a coordinate plane. Include the terms *x*-coordinate, *y*-coordinate, and origin in your answer.

   The first number, the *x*-coordinate, tells how many units to the right or left the point is located from the origin. The second number, the *y*-coordinate, tells how many units up or down the point is located from the origin.

ESSENTIAL QUESTION CHECK-IN

9. Give the coordinates of one point in each of the four quadrants, one point on the *x*-axis, and one point on the *y*-axis.

   Sample answers: Quadrant I: (2, 5); Quadrant II (−3, 5); Quadrant III (−3, −3); Quadrant IV (5, −2). *x*-axis: (−3, 0); *y*-axis: (0, 5).

© Houghton Mifflin Harcourt Publishing Company

DIFFERENTIATE INSTRUCTION

Curriculum Integration

Have students draw coordinate grid lines on maps of Texas. Instruct students to draw the *x*- and *y*-axes through the state capital and the other lines at $\frac{1}{2}$-inch increments above, below, to the left, and to the right of the axes. Have the students label the grid lines, beginning with the axes, with the appropriate numbers and give coordinates for various cities and towns on the map.

Cooperative Learning

Have students work in three teams to play coordinate tic-tac-toe. Use a coordinate plane that is 5 units from the origin in all directions. One player on each team alternates calling out the coordinates of a point. Another player on each team locates the point and marks it on the coordinate plane. The first team to place three marks in an uninterrupted row horizontally, vertically, or diagonally wins the round.

Additional Resources

Differentiated Instruction includes:

• Reading Strategies

• Success for English Learners **ELL**

• Reteach

• Challenge **PRE-AP**

12.1 LESSON QUIZ

COMMON CORE 6.NS.6c

Use the coordinate plane shown. Each unit represents 1 city block.

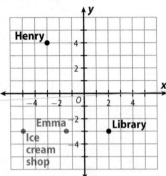

1. Write the ordered pairs that represent Henry and the library.

2. Describe Henry's location relative to the library.

3. Henry wants to meet his friend Emma at an ice cream shop before they go to the library. The ice cream shop is 7 blocks west of the library. Plot and label a point representing the ice cream shop. What are the coordinates of the point?

4. Emma describes her current location: "I'm directly west of the library, halfway to the ice cream shop." Plot and label a point representing Emma's location. What are the coordinates of the point?

Lesson Quiz available online

 my.hrw.com

Answers

1. Henry (−3, 4), Library (2, −3)

2. Henry is 5 blocks west and 7 blocks north of the library.

3. (−5, −3)

4. (−1.5, −3)

Evaluate

GUIDED AND INDEPENDENT PRACTICE

COMMON CORE 6.NS.6b, 6.NS.6c, 6.NS.8

Concepts & Skills	Practice
Example 1 Naming Points in the Coordinate Plane	Exercises 1–2, 10–13
Example 2 Graphing Points in the Coordinate Plane	Exercises 3–4, 10–13
Example 3 Reading Scales on Axes	Exercises 5–7, 14–15

Exercise	Depth of Knowledge (D.O.K.)	**COMMON CORE** Mathematical Practices
10	**2** Skills/Concepts	**MP.4** Modeling
11	**3** Strategic Thinking **H.O.T.**	**MP.7** Using Structure
12–13	**2** Skills/Concepts	**MP.4** Modeling
14–15	**2** Skills/Concepts	**MP.2** Reasoning
16	**3** Strategic Thinking **H.O.T.**	**MP.8** Patterns
17	**3** Strategic Thinking **H.O.T.**	**MP.3** Logic
18–19	**3** Strategic Thinking **H.O.T.**	**MP.7** Using Structure

Additional Resources

Differentiated Instruction includes:

• Leveled Practice Worksheets

12.1 Independent Practice

COMMON CORE 6.NS.6, 6.NS.6b, 6.NS.6c, 6.NS.8

Personal Math Trainer

Online Assessment and Intervention

my.hrw.com

For 10–13, use the coordinate plane shown. Each unit represents 1 kilometer.

10. Write the ordered pairs that represent the location of Sam and the theater.

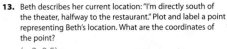
Sam: (4, 2); Theater: (−3, 5)

11. Describe Sam's location relative to the theater.

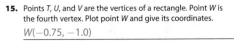
Sam is 3 km south and 7 km east of the theater.

12. Sam wants to meet his friend Beth at a restaurant before they go to the theater. The restaurant is 9 km south of the theater. Plot and label a point representing the restaurant. What are the coordinates of the point?

(−3, −4)

13. Beth describes her current location: "I'm directly south of the theater, halfway to the restaurant." Plot and label a point representing Beth's location. What are the coordinates of the point?

(−3, 0.5)

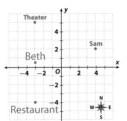

For 14–15, use the coordinate plane shown.

14. Find the coordinates of points T, U, and V.

T (0.75, −1.0); U (0.75, 1.25); V (−0.75, 1.25)

15. Points T, U, and V are the vertices of a rectangle. Point W is the fourth vertex. Plot point W and give its coordinates.

W(−0.75, −1.0)

16. **Explain the Error** Janine tells her friend that ordered pairs that have an x-coordinate of 0 lie on the x-axis. She uses the origin as an example. Describe Janine's error. Use a counterexample to explain why Janine's statement is false.

Janine is describing points that lie on the y-axis. Ordered pairs that lie on the x-axis have a y-coordinate of 0. The origin lies on the x- and y-axis. Any other point with an x-coordinate of 0, such as (0, 3), lies on the y-axis.

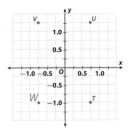

H.O.T. FOCUS ON HIGHER ORDER THINKING

Work Area

17. **Critical Thinking** Choose scales for the coordinate plane shown so that you can graph the points J(2, 40), K(3, 10), L(3, −40), M(−4, 50), and N(−5, −50). Explain why you chose the scale for each axis.

Sample answer: On the x-axis I used a scale of 1 unit for each grid square. On the y-axis I used a scale of 10 units for each grid square. ·

The x-coordinates ranged from −5 to 3, and the y-coordinates ranged from −50 to 50.

18. **Communicate Mathematical Ideas** Edgar wants to plot the ordered pair (1.8, −1.2) on a coordinate plane. On each axis, one grid square equals 0.1. Starting at the origin, how can Edgar find (1.8, −1.2)?

Count 18 grid squares to the right (in a positive direction) along the x-axis. Then count 12 grid squares down (in a negative direction).

19. **Represent Real-World Problems** Zach graphs some ordered pairs in the coordinate plane. The x-values of the ordered pairs represent the number of hours since noon, and the y-values represent the temperature at that time.

a. In which quadrants could Zach graph points? Explain your thinking.

Quadrants I and IV; time is always positive, but temperatures can be positive or negative. In quadrants I and IV, the x-coordinate is always positive, but the y-coordinate can be positive or negative.

b. In what part of the world and at what time of year might Zach collect data so that the points he plots are in Quadrant IV?

Sample answer: in a region with a cold climate during the winter

---

EXTEND THE MATH PRE-AP *Activity available online* my.hrw.com

Activity Plot the points for each set of ordered pairs below. Then connect the points in the order shown to reveal a figure. Name the figure and find its area.

Set 1: (2, 5), (2, −1), (−3, −1), (−3, 5)
Set 2: (−4, −3), (6, −3), (6, 4)
Set 3: (1, 3), (−4, 3), (−4, −2), (1, −2)

Write the coordinates for another set of points that form a figure. Find its area. Then challenge a classmate to draw the figure and find its area.

Set 1: rectangle, A = 30 square units
Set 2: triangle, A = 35 square units
Set 3: square, A = 25 square units

Independent and Dependent Variables in Tables and Graphs

Common Core Standards

The student is expected to:

 Expressions and Equations— 6.EE.9

Use variables to represent two quantities in a real-world problem that change in relationship to one another; write an equation to express one quantity, thought of as the dependent variable, in terms of the other quantity, thought of as the independent variable. Analyze the relationship between the dependent and independent variables using graphs and tables, and relate these to the equation.

Mathematical Practices

 MP.4 Modeling

Engage

ESSENTIAL QUESTION

How can you identify independent and dependent quantities from tables and graphs?
Sample answer: The dependent variable is the quantity that depends on the other variable. On a graph, the independent variable is shown on the horizontal axis and the dependent variable is shown on the vertical axis.

Motivate the Lesson

Ask: Suppose a person gets paid by the hour. What is the relationship between the amount of time the person works and the amount of money that person earns? Begin the Explore Activity to find out what independent and dependent quantities are and how to recognize them.

Explore

EXPLORE ACTIVITY 1

Connect to Vocabulary ELL

Have students describe the meaning of the following phrases: Sample answers are given.

- independently wealthy doesn't need to work for money
- Independence Day day of freedom
- working independently doesn't need help to do a job
- dependent child needs a parent
- insulin-dependent needs insulin daily
- dependent clause cannot stand alone in a sentence

Then ask students to define independent and dependent variables. An independent variable stands alone and isn't changed by the other variables. A dependent variable depends on or is changed by another variable.

Explain

EXPLORE ACTIVITY 2

Connect Multiple Representations CC Mathematical Practices
Have students complete this table, which represents the situation about the art teacher and clay, to reinforce that both a table and a graph can represent this relationship.

Clay bought by teacher (lb)	0	10	20	30
Clay available for classes (lb)	20	30	40	50

Engage with the Whiteboard

Ask a student volunteer to locate the point on the graph that shows the 50 pounds of clay that is available for the art class. Have the volunteer draw a line from the *y*-axis to the point and a line from the point to the *x*-axis. Have students repeat this process for several more values.

Independent and Dependent Variables in Tables and Graphs

 COMMON CORE **6.EE.9**
Use variables to represent two quantities in a real-world problem that change in relationship to one another; ... Analyze the relationship between the dependent and independent variables.…

? ESSENTIAL QUESTION

How can you identify independent and dependent quantities from tables and graphs?

EXPLORE ACTIVITY 1 **COMMON CORE** 6.EE.9

Identifying Independent and Dependent Quantities from a Table

Many real-world situations involve two variable quantities in which one quantity depends on the other. The quantity that depends on the other quantity is called the **dependent variable**, and the quantity it depends on is called the **independent variable**.

A freight train moves at a constant speed. The distance y in miles that the train has traveled after x hours is shown in the table.

Time x (h)	0	1	2	3
Distance y (mi)	0	50	100	150

A What are the two quantities in this situation?

time and distance

Which of these quantities depends on the other?

Distance depends on time.

What is the independent variable? _____ time, x

What is the dependent variable? _____ distance, y

B How far does the train travel each hour? _____ 50 miles

The relationship between the distance traveled by the train and the time in hours can be represented by an equation in two variables.

Distance traveled (miles)	=	Distance traveled per hour	·	Time (hours)
↓		↓		↓
y	=	50	·	x

© Houghton Mifflin Harcourt Publishing Company

EXPLORE ACTIVITY *(cont'd)*

Reflect

1. **Analyze Relationships** Describe how the value of the independent variable is related to the value of the dependent variable. Is the relationship additive or multiplicative?

The value of y is always 50 times the value of x; multiplicative.

2. What are the units of the independent variable and of the dependent variable?

independent variable: hours; dependent variable: miles.

3. A rate is used in the equation. What is the rate?

50 miles per hour

EXPLORE ACTIVITY 2 **COMMON CORE** 6.EE.9

Identifying Independent and Dependent Variables from a Graph

In Explore Activity 1, you used a table to represent a relationship between an independent variable (time) and a dependent variable (distance). You can also use a graph to show this relationship.

An art teacher has 20 pounds of clay but wants to buy more clay for her class. The amount of clay x purchased by the teacher and the amount of clay y available for the class are shown on the graph.

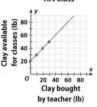

A If the teacher buys 10 more pounds of clay, how many pounds will be available for the art class? _____ 30 lb

If the art class has a total of 50 pounds of clay available, how many pounds of clay did the teacher buy?

How can you use the graph to find this information?

30 lb; find the point on the graph with a y-coordinate of 50. Then find the x-coordinate of this point, which is 30.

Clay Used in Art Class

© Houghton Mifflin Harcourt Publishing Company • Image Credits: © Hill Street Studios/Corbis

---

PROFESSIONAL DEVELOPMENT

CC Integrate Mathematical Practices MP.4

This lesson provides an opportunity to address this Mathematical Practice standard. It calls for students to communicate mathematical ideas using multiple representations as appropriate. Students use tables, graphs, equations, and language to describe and model relationships between independent and dependent variables. In this way, students use multiple representations to model real-world situations involving independent and dependent variables.

Math Background

Although the term *function* is not mentioned in this lesson, the tables in the lesson represent functions. A function is a rule that relates two quantities so that each input value corresponds to exactly one output value. When y is a function of x, x is called the independent variable and y is called the dependent variable. Whenever a value is assigned to x, a value is automatically assigned to y by an applicable rule or correspondence.

Questioning Strategies Mathematical Practices

• Why does the graph show only Quadrant I? Negative amounts do not make sense in this situation, so the values and the graph are limited to positive *x*- and *y*-values.

• Why does the graph start at (0, 20)? The art teacher had 20 pounds of clay to start with.

• As the *x*-value is increasing, what is happening to the *y*-value? The *y*-value is also increasing.

EXAMPLE 1

Engage with the Whiteboard

Have a volunteer sketch a graph of the relationship shown in the table in A. Have a second volunteer make a table of the relationship shown in the graph in B. This will help students to see that both a table and a graph can represent the same relationship.

Connect Multiple Representations Mathematical Practices

Point out to students that each of these situations can be represented by a verbal description, a table, a graph, or an equation.

Questioning Strategies

• How can the relationship in A be represented by an equation? The table begins with a *y*-value of 10, so the *y*-value always will be 10 units greater than the *x*-value. Then, as *x* increases by 1, *y* also increases by 1, resulting in the equation $y = x + 10$.

• How would you describe the relationship in A? Explain. The relationship is an additive relationship because the value of *y* is always 10 units greater than the value of *x*.

• How can the relationship in B be represented by an equation? The graph begins at the origin, so both variables begin at 0. Then, as *x* increases by 1, *y* increases by 12, resulting in the equation $y = 12x$.

• How could you check that the equation is correct for either A or B? Pick a point from either the table or the graph and substitute it into the equation. The result should be a true equation.

Focus on Reasoning Mathematical Practices

Ask students to identify the independent and dependent quantities in the following situations.

• A veterinarian must weigh an animal before determining the amount of medication it needs. independent quantity, weight of animal, dependent quantity: amount of medication

• A company charges $10 per hour to rent a jackhammer. independent quantity: time, dependent quantity: cost

Integrating the ELPS

Encourage English learners to use the active reading strategies presented at the beginning of the module.

ADDITIONAL EXAMPLE 1

A The table below shows a relationship between two variables, *x* and *y*. Describe a possible situation the table could represent. Describe the independent and dependent variables in this situation.

Independent variable, *x*	1	2	3	4
Dependent variable, *y*	8	16	24	32

Sample answer: The table could represent the amount a person earns at a rate of $8 per hour. The independent variable, *x*, is the number of hours the person works. The dependent variable, *y*, is the total earnings.

B The graph below shows a relationship between two variables, *x* and *y*. Describe a possible situation the graph could represent. Describe the independent and dependent variables.

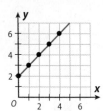

Sample answer: The graph could represent the progress of a rock climber, starting at a 2-foot height and continuing at a pace of 1 foot every second. The independent variable is the number of seconds, and the dependent variable is the total number of feet climbed after *x* seconds.

Interactive Whiteboard
Interactive example available online

B What are the two quantities in this situation?

the clay bought by the teacher and the amount of clay
available to the class

Which of these quantities depends on the other?

The amount of clay available to the class depends on
the amount of clay bought by the teacher.

What is the independent variable? ___clay bought by teacher___
What is the dependent variable? ___clay available for the class___

C The relationship between the amount of clay purchased by the teacher
and the amount of clay available to the class can be represented by an
equation in two variables.

Amount of clay available (pounds)	=	Current amount of clay (pounds)	+	Amount of clay purchased (pounds)
↓		↓		↓
y	=	20	+	x

D Describe in words how the value of the independent variable is related
to the value of the dependent variable.

The value of y is always 20 units greater than the
value of x.

Reflect

4. In this situation, the same units are used for the independent and
dependent variables. How is this different
from the situation involving the train in the first Explore?

The other situation involves two different units

(miles and hours).

5. **Analyze Relationships** Tell whether the relationship between the
independent variable and the dependent variable is a multiplicative or
an additive relationship.

additive

6. What are the units of the independent variable, and what are the units
of the dependent variable?

independent variable: ___pounds___ ; dependent variable: ___pounds___

Math On the Spot
my.hrw.com

Describing Relationships Between Independent and Dependent Variables

Thinking about how one quantity depends on another helps you identify which
quantity is the independent variable and which quantity is the dependent
variable. In a graph, the independent variable is usually shown on the
horizontal axis and the dependent variable on the vertical axis.

EXAMPLE 1   COMMON CORE **6.EE.9**

A The table shows a relationship between two variables, x and y. Describe
a possible situation the table could represent. Describe the independent
and dependent variables in the situation.

Independent variable, x	0	1	2	3
Dependent variable, y	10	11	12	13

As x increases by 1, y increases by 1. The relationship is additive.
The value of y is always 10 units greater than the value of x.

The table could represent Jina's savings if she starts with $10 and adds $1
to her savings every day.

The independent variable, x, is the number of days she has
been adding money to her savings.
The dependent variable, y, is her savings after x days.

B The graph shows a relationship between two variables.
Describe a possible situation that the graph could
represent. Describe the independent and dependent
variables.

As x increases by 1, y increases by 12. The relationship
is multiplicative. The value of y is always 12 times the value of x.

The graph could represent the number of eggs in cartons
that each hold 12 eggs.

The independent variable, x, is the number of cartons.
The dependent variable, y, is the total number of eggs.

Reflect

7. What are other possible situations that the table and graph in the
Examples could represent?

Sample answer table: Paul has 10 DVDs and buys more.

Independent: number of DVDs he buys; dependent:

number he has after he buys x DVDs. Graph: 12 photos

fit on each page of a yearbook. Independent: number of

pages; dependent: total number of photos on x pages.

![hands icon]

DIFFERENTIATE INSTRUCTION

Curriculum Integration

Music: The notes you hear played by a musical
instrument are an example of a dependent
relationship. For example, a clarinet's pitch at a
particular moment depends on the number of
holes covered by the musician. A harp's pitch
depends on the length of the string being
plucked.

Cooperative Learning

One way to remember which is the independent variable and which is the dependent
variable is to use the names of the two variables
in a sentence that makes sense. For example:

Dollars Earned depends on *Hours Worked*,
but *Hours Worked* does not depend on
Dollars Earned. So, *Dollars Earned* must be
the dependent variable and *Hours Worked*
must be the independent variable.

Additional Resources

Differentiated Instruction includes:

- Reading Strategies
- Success for English Learners **ELL**
- Reteach
- Challenge **PRE-AP**

YOUR TURN

Avoid Common Errors

If students have difficulty distinguishing between independent and dependent variables, remind them that the independent variable causes a change in the dependent variable, while the dependent variable could not cause a change in the independent variable.

Elaborate

Talk About It
Summarize the Lesson

Ask: How do you know which is the dependent variable and which is the independent variable in a table or graph? In a table, the independent variable usually is represented by the variable x. The dependent variable usually is represented by the variable y. On a graph, the independent variable usually is shown on the horizontal axis and the dependent variable on the vertical axis.

GUIDED PRACTICE

Engage with the Whiteboard

For Exercises 1–2, have a student sketch the graph to represent the table on the whiteboard. Have the student explain how to know which quantity should be represented by the x-axis and which by the y-axis.

For Exercise 3, have a student volunteer label the axes on the graph to represent the real-world situation suggested by the student.

Avoid Common Errors

Exercise 3 If students have difficulty determining whether a relationship is additive or multiplicative, remind them that in a multiplicative relationship the graph will pass through the origin, but in an additive relationship the graph will not pass through the origin.

Exercise 4 Remind students that if the independent variable is on the horizontal axis of a graph, the dependent variable is on the vertical axis of the graph.

YOUR TURN

Describe real-world values that the variables could represent. Describe the relationship between the independent and dependent variables.

8.

x	0	1	2	3
y	15	16	17	18

Sample answer: Bridget's grandmother gave her a collection of 15 perfume bottles. Bridget adds one bottle per week to the collection. The independent variable is the number of weeks. The dependent variable is the number of perfume bottles in her collection. The value of y is always 15 units greater than the value of x.

9.

x	0	1	2	3	4
y	0	16	32	48	64

Sample answer: Colin created a website to sell T-shirts that are printed with funny slogans. He makes $16 per T-shirt. The independent variable is the number of T-shirts he sells, and the dependent variable is his profit in dollars. As the independent variable increases by 1, the dependent variable increases by 16.

10.

Sample answer: Tickets to the school musical cost $3 each. The independent variable is the number of tickets purchased, and the dependent variable is the total cost. The value of y is always 3 times the value of x.

Guided Practice

1. A boat rental shop rents paddleboats for a fee plus an additional cost per hour. The cost of renting for different numbers of hours is shown in the table.

Time (hours)	0	1	2	3
Cost ($)	10	11	12	13

What is the independent variable, and what is the dependent variable? How do you know? (Explore Activity 1)

Time is the independent variable and cost is the dependent variable, because cost depends on the number of hours rented.

2. A car travels at a constant rate of 60 miles per hour. (Explore Activity 1)

Time x (h)	0	1	2	3
Distance y (mi)	0	60	120	180

a. Complete the table.

b. What is the independent variable, and what is the dependent?

Time is the independent variable and distance is the dependent variable.

c. Describe how the value of the independent variable is related to the value of the dependent variable.

The value of y is always 60 times the value of x.

Use the graph to answer the questions.

3. Describe in words how the value of the independent variable is related to the value of the dependent variable. (Explore Activity 2)

The value of the dependent variable is 5 times the value of the independent variable.

4. Describe a real-world situation that the graph could represent. (Example 1)

Sample answer: The graph could represent the total cost y of buying x carnival tickets for $5 each.

? ESSENTIAL QUESTION CHECK-IN

5. How can you identify the dependent and independent variables in a real-world situation modeled by a graph?

Sample answer: The dependent variable is the quantity that depends on the other variable. On a graph, the independent variable is usually shown on the horizontal axis and the dependent variable on the vertical axis.

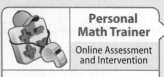

12.2 LESSON QUIZ

 6.EE.9

The graph below shows the relationship between the number of tickets Lisa is ordering for a raffle and the cost. Use the graph to answer questions 1–3.

Lisa's Ticket Order

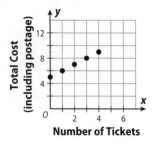

1. What are the dependent and independent variables?

2. Is the relationship between the two variables additive or multiplicative?

3. Describe the relationship between the two quantities in words.

Use the table for question 4.

x	0	1	2	3	4
y	0	7	14	21	28

4. Describe a possible situation that can be represented by the table. Identify the dependent and independent variables in this situation.

Lesson Quiz available online

 my.hrw.com

Answers

1. Independent variable, *x*, is the number of tickets bought; dependent variable, *y*, is the total cost.

2. It is an additive relationship.

3. The total cost is the number of tickets bought plus $5 for postage for the tickets.

Evaluate

GUIDED AND INDEPENDENT PRACTICE

 6.EE.9

Concepts & Skills	Practice
Explore Activity 1 Identifying Independent and Dependent Quantities from a Table	Exercises 1–2, 7
Explore Activity 2 Identifying Independent and Dependent Variables from a Graph	Exercises 3, 6, 8
Example 1 Describing Relationships Between Independent and Dependent Variables	Exercises 4, 6

Exercise	Depth of Knowledge (D.O.K.)	COMMON CORE Mathematical Practices
6	**2** Skills/Concepts	**MP.4** Modeling
7	**3** Strategic Thinking **H.O.T.**	**MP.7** Using Structure
8–9	**3** Strategic Thinking **H.O.T.**	**MP.3** Logic
10	**3** Strategic Thinking **H.O.T.**	**MP.8** Patterns

Additional Resources

Differentiated Instruction includes:

• Leveled Practice Worksheets

4. Sample answer: Parking at the airport costs $7 per day. Independent variable, *x*, is the number of days a vehicle is parked; dependent variable, *y*, is the total cost for parking.

12.2 Independent Practice

COMMON CORE 6.EE.9

6. The graph shows the relationship between the hours a soccer team practiced after the season started and their total practice time for the year.

a. How many hours did the soccer team practice before the season began?

  6 hours

b. What are the two quantities in this situation?

  hours practiced during the season and total practice time for year

c. What are the dependent and independent variables?

  independent: hours practiced during season;
  dependent: total practice time for year

d. Is the relationship between the variables additive or multiplicative? Explain.

  Additive; the total practice increases by 1 hour as the practice time during the season increases by 1 hour.

e. **Analyze Relationships** Describe the relationship between the quantities in words.

  Total practice time for the year is 6 hours more than practice time during the season.

7. **Multistep** Teresa is buying glitter markers to put in gift bags. The table shows the relationship between the number of gift bags and the number of glitter markers she needs to buy.

Number of gift bags, x	0	1	2	3
Number of markers, y	0	5	10	15

a. What is the dependent variable? ___number of markers___

b. What is the independent variable? ___number of gift bags___

c. Is the relationship additive or multiplicative? Explain.

  The relationship is multiplicative because y increases by a factor of 5 as x increases by 1.

d. Describe the relationship between the quantities in words.

  The number of glitter markers is 5 times the number of gift bags.

8. Ty borrowed $500 from his parents. The graph shows how much he owes them each month if he pays back a certain amount each month.

Ty's Loan Payments

a. Describe the relationship between the number of months and the amount Ty owes. Identify an independent and dependent variable and explain your thinking.

  Ty starts out owing $500 and every month the amount he owes decreases by $50; independent variable: number months; dependent variable: amount he owes; the amount he owes depends on the number of months he has been paying.

b. How long will it take Ty to pay back his parents?

  10 months

H.O.T. FOCUS ON HIGHER ORDER THINKING

Work Area

9. **Error Analysis** A discount store has a special: 8 cans of juice for a dollar. A shopper decides that since the number of cans purchased is 8 times the number of dollars spent, the cost is the independent variable and the number of cans is the dependent variable. Do you agree? Explain.

  Sample answer: I disagree because the amount a shopper pays depends on the number of cans purchased. So, the number of cans is the independent variable, and cost is the dependent variable.

10. **Analyze Relationships** Provide an example of a real-world relationship where there is no clear independent or dependent variable. Explain.

  Sample answer: Andrea is 4 years older than Lisa. You could say that Andrea's age depends on Lisa's because you can add 4 to Lisa's age. You can also say that Lisa's age depends on Andrea's age because you can subtract 4 from Lisa's age.

EXTEND THE MATH PRE-AP

Activity available online my.hrw.com

Introduce students to independent and dependent variables in situations that involve decimals or fractions. For example:

Gina is charged $0.15 for each text message that she sends.

1. What is the independent variable?   a

  a. number of texts sent

  b. charge per text

  c. total amount charged for texting

2. What is the dependent variable?   c

  a. number of texts sent

  b. charge per text

  c. total amount charged for texting

3. Write an equation that expresses the situation.

  Let b be the amount of Gina's bill.

  Let s be the number of texts sent.

  $b = 0.15s$

12.3 Writing Equations from Tables

Common Core Standards

The student is expected to:

 Expressions and Equations—6.EE.9

Use variables to represent two quantities in a real-world problem that change in relationship to one another; write an equation to express one quantity, thought of as the dependent variable, in terms of the other quantity, thought of as the independent variable. Analyze the relationship between the dependent and independent variables using graphs and tables, and relate these to the equation.

Mathematical Practices

 MP.1 Problem Solving

ADDITIONAL EXAMPLE 1
Write an equation that expresses y in terms of x.

A

x	1	2	3	4	5
y	3	6	9	12	15

$y = 3x$

B

x	2	4	6	8	10
y	7	9	11	13	15

$y = x + 5$

 Interactive Whiteboard
Interactive example available online

⏻ my.hrw.com

 Animated Math
Writing Equations from Tables

Students generate patterns with an interactive model, record the data in a table, and write equations to represent the pattern.

⏻ my.hrw.com

Engage

ESSENTIAL QUESTION

How can you use an equation to show a relationship between two variables? Use a table to find the relationship between the two variables. Use that relationship to write an equation.

Motivate the Lesson

Ask students to imagine a hot dog stand that charges $3 per hot dog. How much would 4 hot dogs cost? 30 hot dogs? Begin the Explore Activity to find out how to write an equation that will help you predict the total cost for any number of hot dogs.

Explore

EXPLORE ACTIVITY

Focus on Patterns **Mathematical Practices**

Point out to students that to write an equation from the data in the table, they need to look for a pattern in the data. First, they should look for changes in both the input values and the output values. Then they need to see how the changes are related. For example:

$$8 = 8 \cdot 1$$
$$16 = 8 \cdot 2$$
$$24 = 8 \cdot 3$$

So, the pattern is $y = 8 \cdot x$, where x is the number of dogs walked and y is the amount of money earned.

Explain

EXAMPLE 1

Focus on Reasoning **CC** Mathematical Practices

In A, point out to students that the y-value is always less than the x-value. Therefore, the operation in the equation must be subtraction, division, or multiplication by a factor that is less than 1. In B, point out to students that the y-value is always more than the x-value. Therefore, the operation in the equation must be addition or multiplication by a factor that is greater than 1.

Questioning Strategies **CC** Mathematical Practices

• For A, how can you write an equation that expresses x in terms of y? I can compare the x- and y-values and find that each x-value is twice the corresponding y-value, which gives me the equation $x = 2y$.

YOUR TURN

Engage with the Whiteboard

For Exercises 2–5, have students write a pattern on the whiteboard for each table. Then have them use the pattern to write an equation to represent each table. Ask students to explain their reasoning.

12.3 Writing Equations from Tables

COMMON CORE 6.EE.9

...write an equation to express one quantity, thought of as the dependent variable, in terms of the other quantity, thought of as the independent variable. ...

 ESSENTIAL QUESTION How can you use an equation to show a relationship between two variables?

 EXPLORE ACTIVITY Real World COMMON CORE 6.EE.9

Writing an Equation to Represent a Real-World Relationship

Many real-world situations involve two variable quantities in which one quantity depends on the other. This type of relationship can be represented by a table. You can also use an equation to model the relationship.

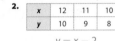

The table shows how much Amanda earns for walking 1, 2, or 3 dogs. Use the table to determine how much Amanda earns per dog. Then write an equation that models the relationship between number of dogs walked and earnings. Use your equation to complete the table.

Dogs walked	1	2	3	5	10	20
Earnings	$8	$16	$24	$40	$80	$160

For 1 dog, Amanda earns 1 · 8 = $8. For 2 dogs, she earns 2 · 8 = $16.

A For each column, compare the number of dogs walked and earnings. What is the pattern?

Each earnings amount is 8 times the corresponding number of dogs walked.

B Based on the pattern, Amanda earns $ __8__ for each dog she walks.

C Write an equation that relates the number of dogs Amanda walks to the amount she earns. Let e represent earnings and d represent dogs.

$$e = 8 \cdot d$$

D Use your equation to complete the table for 5, 10, and 20 walked dogs.

E Amanda's earnings depend on the number of dogs walked .

Reflect

1. **What If?** If Amanda changed the amount earned per dog to $11, what equation could you write to model the relationship between number of dogs walked and earnings? $e = 11 \cdot d$

Math On the Spot
my.hrw.com

Writing an Equation Based on a Table

The relationship between two variables where one variable depends on the other can be represented in a table or by an equation. An equation expresses the dependent variable in terms of the independent variable.

When there is no real-world situation to consider, we usually say x is the independent variable and y is the dependent variable. The value of y depends on the value of x.

Animated Math
my.hrw.com

EXAMPLE 1

COMMON CORE 6.EE.9

Write an equation that expresses y in terms of x.

A

x	1	2	3	4	5
y	0.5	1	1.5	2	2.5

STEP 1 Compare the x- and y-values to find a pattern.

Each y-value is $\frac{1}{2}$, or 0.5 times, the corresponding x-value.

STEP 2 Use the pattern to write an equation expressing y in terms of x.

$$y = 0.5x$$

B

x	2	4	6	8	10
y	5	7	9	11	13

STEP 1 Compare the x- and y-values to find a pattern.

Each y-value is 3 more than the corresponding x-value.

STEP 2 Use the pattern to write an equation expressing y in terms of x.

$$y = x + 3$$

Substitute each value of x in the equation. If the equation is correct, the result is the corresponding y-value.

Math Talk
Mathematical Practices

How can you check that your equations are correct?

YOUR TURN

For each table, write an equation that expresses y in terms of x.

2.

x	12	11	10
y	10	9	8

$$y = x - 2$$

3.

x	10	12	14
y	25	30	35

$$y = 2.5x$$

4.

x	5	4	3
y	10	9	8

$$y = x + 5$$

5.

x	0	1	2
y	0	2	4

$$y = 2x$$

Personal Math Trainer
Online Assessment and Intervention
my.hrw.com

PROFESSIONAL DEVELOPMENT

CC Integrate Mathematical Practices

This lesson provides an opportunity to address Mathematical Practices **MP.4,** which calls for students to "model with mathematics." Students use verbal descriptions to make tables and draw graphs that represent real-life situations. They also represent information from graphs by using tables and equations; and represent equations by using tables and graphs.

Math Background

A rule that relates the x- and y-values in a table also can be called a relation. A relation describes a function if, for each x-value (input), there is only one y-value (output).

There are several different ways to describe the variables of a function:

Independent Variable	Dependent Variable
x-value	y-value
Domain	Range
Input	Output
x	$f(x)$

EXAMPLE 2

Focus on Reasoning CC Mathematical Practices

Point out to students that sometimes a problem may provide clues and facts that you must use to find a solution. Encourage students to begin by identifying the important information. They can underline or circle the information in the problem statement.

Engage with the Whiteboard

 Have students extend the table on the whiteboard, continuing with sale prices of $400 through $1,200 in increments of $100. Then have students find the donation amount for these sale prices. After they have completed the table, ask students to identify any patterns in the table.

Questioning Strategies

- What is the independent variable in this situation? the dependent variable? The independent variable is the sale price of a painting. The dependent variable is the amount donated to charity.

- How else could you solve this problem? Use proportional reasoning. For instance, consider $\frac{50}{200} = \frac{d}{1,200}$. Because $1,200 \div 200 = 6$, multiply 50 by 6: $d = 300$.

YOUR TURN

Avoid Common Errors

If students have difficulty identifying the independent and dependent variables, remind them to begin by using the given information to make a table and then look for a pattern.

Elaborate

....

Talk About It
Summarize the Lesson

Ask: How can you use a table to write an equation that represents the relationship in the table? In the table, find the relationship between the independent and dependent variables. Then write the equation that represents the relationship.

GUIDED PRACTICE

Engage with the Whiteboard

For Exercises 1–2, have students write a pattern on the whiteboard for each table. Then have students use the pattern to write an equation to represent each table. Ask students to explain their reasoning.

For Exercise 5, have students fill in the missing information in the table on the whiteboard. Then have them identify the pattern and write an equation.

Avoid Common Errors

Exercises 1–4 Some students may write an equation that expresses x in terms of y instead of y in terms of x. Remind them that the form of the equation should be $y = kx$ or $y = x + b$.

Exercise 5 If students have difficulty identifying the independent and dependent variables, remind them to begin by using the given information to make a table and then look for a pattern.

Using Tables and Equations to Solve Problems

You can use tables and equations to solve real-world problems.

Math On the Spot
my.hrw.com

EXAMPLE 2 Problem Solving

COMMON CORE 6.EE.9

A certain percent of the sale price of paintings at a gallery will be donated to charity. The donation will be $50 if a painting sells for $200. The donation will be $75 if a painting sells for $300. Find the amount of the donation if a painting sells for $1,200.

Analyze Information

You know the donation amount when the sale price of a painting is $200 and $300. You need to find the donation amount if a painting sells for $1,200.

Formulate a Plan

You can make a table to help you determine the relationship between sale price and donation amount. Then you can write an equation that models the relationship. Use the equation to find the unknown donation amount.

Solve

Make a table.

Sale price ($)	200	300
Donation amount ($)	50	75

> One way to determine the relationship between sale price and donation amount is to find the percent.

$$\frac{50}{200} = \frac{50 \div 2}{200 \div 2} = \frac{25}{100} = 25\% \qquad \frac{75}{300} = \frac{75 \div 3}{300 \div 3} = \frac{25}{100} = 25\%$$

Write an equation. Let p represent the sale price of the painting. Let d represent the donation amount to charity.

The donation amount is equal to 25% of the sale price.

> p is the independent variable; its value does not depend on any other value. d is the dependent variable; its value depends on the price of the painting.

$d = 0.25 \cdot p$

Find the donation amount when the sale price is $1,200.

$d = 0.25 \cdot p$

$d = 0.25 \cdot 1,200$ Substitute $1,200 for the sale price of the painting.

$d = 300$ Simplify to find the donation amount.

When the sale price is $1,200, the donation to charity is $300.

Justify and Evaluate

Substitute values from the table for p and d to check that they are solutions of the equation $d = 0.25 \cdot p$. Then check your answer of $300 by substituting for d and solving for p.

$d = 0.25 \cdot p$	$d = 0.25 \cdot p$	$d = 0.25 \cdot p$
$d = 0.25 \cdot 200$	$d = 0.25 \cdot 300$	$300 = 0.25 \cdot p$
$d = 50$ ✓	$d = 75$ ✓	$p = 1,200$ ✓

Personal Math Trainer
Online Assessment and Intervention
my.hrw.com

YOUR TURN

6. When Ryan is 10, his brother Kyle is 15. When Ryan is 16, Kyle will be 21. When Ryan is 21, Kyle will be 26. Write and solve an equation to find Kyle's age when Ryan is 52.

Ryan	10	16	21
Kyle	15	21	26

$k = r + 5$; 57 years old

Guided Practice

Write an equation to express y in terms of x. (Explore Activity, Example 1)

1.

x	10	20	30	40
y	6	16	26	36

$y = x - 4$

2.

x	0	1	2	3
y	0	4	8	12

$y = 4x$

3.

x	4	6	8	10
y	7	9	11	13

$y = x + 3$

4.

x	12	24	36	48
y	2	4	6	8

$y = \frac{x}{6}$

5. Jameson downloaded one digital song for $1.35, two digital songs for $2.70, and 5 digital songs for $6.75. Write and solve an equation to find the cost to download 25 digital songs. (Example 2)

Songs downloaded	1	2	5	10
Total cost ($)	1.35	2.70	6.75	13.50

Number of songs = n; Cost = _____ $c = 1.35n$

The total cost of 25 songs is _____ $33.75

? ESSENTIAL QUESTION CHECK-IN

6. Explain how to use a table to write an equation that represents the relationship in the table.

Compare the x- and y-values to find a pattern. Use the pattern to write an equation expressing y in terms of x.

DIFFERENTIATE INSTRUCTION

Curriculum Integration

Discuss the relationship between Celsius temperature and Kelvin temperature. Show students the following table and ask them to write an equation to convert from degrees Celsius to degrees Kelvin.

Celsius (°C)	Kelvin (°K)
−100	173
−50	223
0	273
50	323
100	373

$K = C + 273$

Cognitive Strategies

Some students may find it helpful to include a "Process" column in a table to help them identify patterns. Have students complete the table below.

x	Process	y
−3	$-2 = -3 + 1$	−2
−2	$-1 = -2 + 1$	−1
−1	$0 = -1 + 1$	0
0	$1 = 0 + 1$	1
1	$2 = 1 + 1$	2
2	$3 = 2 + 1$	3

Each value of y is one more than the value of x.

Additional Resources

Differentiated Instruction includes:

- Reading Strategies
- Success for English Learners **ELL**
- Reteach
- Challenge **PRE-AP**

12.3 LESSON QUIZ

 6.EE.9

Write an equation that expresses y in terms of x.

1.

x	1	2	3	4	5
y	5	10	15	20	25

2.

x	10	20	30	40	50
y	7	17	27	37	47

3. Jaime bought 2 puzzles for $5.00 and 3 puzzles for $7.50. Write and solve an equation to find the cost of 15 puzzles.

4. A balloon rises to 100 feet in 4 minutes and 125 feet in 5 minutes. Write and solve an equation to find the distance the balloon rises in 8 minutes.

Lesson Quiz available online

 my.hrw.com

Answers

1. $y = 5x$

2. $y = x - 3$

3. $c = 2.50 \cdot p$; $37.50

4. $d = 25m$; 200 feet

Evaluate

GUIDED AND INDEPENDENT PRACTICE

 6.EE.9

Concepts & Skills	Practice
Explore Activity Writing an Equation to Represent a Real-World Relationship	Exercises 1–4, 8, 11
Example 1 Writing an Equation Based on a Table	Exercises 1–4, 9–10
Example 2 Using Tables and Equations to Solve Problems	Exercises 5, 11

Exercise	Depth of Knowledge (D.O.K.)	COMMON CORE Mathematical Practices
7	**3** Strategic Thinking **H.O.T.**	**MP.7** Using Structure
8	**2** Skills/Concepts	**MP.4** Modeling
9–10	**3** Strategic Thinking **H.O.T.**	**MP.8** Patterns
11	**3** Strategic Thinking **H.O.T.**	**MP.4** Modeling
12	**3** Strategic Thinking **H.O.T.**	**MP.3** Logic
13–14	**3** Strategic Thinking **H.O.T.**	**MP.7** Using Structure
15	**3** Strategic Thinking **H.O.T.**	**MP.6** Precision

Additional Resources

Differentiated Instruction includes:

• Leveled Practice worksheets

12.3 Independent Practice

COMMON CORE 6.EE.9

Personal Math Trainer

my.hrw.com
Online Assessment and Intervention

7. Vocabulary What does it mean for an equation to express *y* in terms of *x*?

The variable *y* is on one side of the equation. The expression
on the other side of the equation shows the relationship
between *x* and *y*.

8. The length of a rectangle is 2 inches more than twice its width.

Write an equation relating the length *l* of the rectangle to its width *w*.

$$l = 2w + 2$$

9. Look for a Pattern Compare the *y*-values in the table to the corresponding *x*-values. What pattern do you see? How is this pattern used to write an equation that represents the relationship between the *x*- and *y*-values?

x	20	24	28	32
y	5	6	7	8

The *y*-value is $\frac{1}{4}$ of the *x*-value. Write an equation that
relates *y* to $\frac{1}{4}$ of *x*.

10. Explain the Error A student modeled the relationship in the table with the equation *x* = 4*y*. Explain the student's error. Write an equation that correctly models the relationship.

x	2	4	6	8
y	8	16	24	32

The student switched the variables; *y* = 4*x*

11. Multistep Marvin earns $8.25 per hour at his summer job. He wants to buy a video game system that costs $206.25.

a. Write an equation to model the relationship between number of hours worked *h* and amount earned *e*.

$$e = 8.25h$$

b. Solve your equation to find the number of hours Marvin needs to work in order to afford the video game system.

206.25 = 8.25*h*; 25 = *h*; 25 hours

12. Communicate Mathematical Ideas For every hour that Noah studies, his test score goes up 3 points. Explain which is the independent variable and which is the dependent variable. Write an equation modeling the relationship between hours studied *h* and the increase in Noah's test score *s*.

Independent: hours studied; its value does not depend on
another variable; dependent: test score; its value depends
on the number of hours that Noah studies; *s* = 3*h*

H.O.T. FOCUS ON HIGHER ORDER THINKING

Work Area

13. Make a Conjecture Compare the *y*-values in the table to the corresponding *x*-values. Determine whether there is an additive relationship or a multiplicative relationship between *x* and *y*. If possible, write an equation modeling the relationship. If, not explain why.

x	1	3	5	7
y	3	6	8	21

Not possible; there is no consistent pattern between the
y-values and corresponding *x*-values.

14. Represent Real-World Problems Describe a real-world situation in which there is an additive or multiplicative relationship between two quantities. Make a table that includes at least three pairs of values. Then write an equation that models the relationship between the quantities.

Sample answer: The distance Yasmine traveled in miles
is equal to 50 times the number of hours she drove;
d = 50 × *t* (multiplicative relationship).

Time (h)	2	3	4	5
Distance (mi)	100	150	200	250

15. Critical Thinking Georgia knows that there is either an additive or multiplicative relationship between *x* and *y*. She only knows a single pair of data values. Explain whether Georgia has enough information to write an equation that models the relationship between *x* and *y*.

No; with only one pair of values, Georgia cannot tell
whether the relationship is additive or multiplicative, so
she cannot write an equation for the relationship.

EXTEND THE MATH PRE-AP

Activity available online my.hrw.com

Activity To introduce the idea of relationships that are not purely additive or multiplicative, have students find the *y*-values in the following tables. Remind them to use the order of operations. Have them compare and contrast these relationships with additive and multiplicative relationships.

1. $y = 2x + 1$

x	0	1	2	3
y	1	3	5	7

2. $y = 3x - 2$

x	1	2	3	4
y	1	4	7	10

3. $y = \frac{1}{2}x + 3$

x	0	2	4	6
y	3	4	5	6

4. $y = \frac{1}{3}x - 1$

x	3	6	9	12
y	0	1	2	3

LESSON 12.4 Representing Algebraic Relationships in Tables and Graphs

Common Core Standards

The student is expected to:

 Expressions and Equations—6.EE.9

Use variables to represent two quantities in a real-world problem that change in relationship to one another; write an equation to express one quantity, thought of as the dependent variable, in terms of the other quantity, thought of as the independent variable. Analyze the relationship between the dependent and independent variables using graphs and tables, and relate these to the equation.

Mathematical Practices

 MP.4 Modeling

Engage

ESSENTIAL QUESTION

How can you use verbal descriptions, tables, and graphs to represent algebraic relationships? Sample answer: You can make a table from the verbal description and then make a graph from the ordered pairs in the table. From a graph, you can make a table and write an equation.

Motivate the Lesson
Ask: Have you ever thought about running in a marathon? Do you know how many kilometers you could run in an hour? in two hours? Begin Explore Activity 1 to find out how to make a table and a graph to estimate how far you could run in a given period of time.

Explore

EXPLORE ACTIVITY 1
Connect Multiple Representations CC Mathematical Practices
Point out to students that the ordered pairs from each table are used to make the graphs. However, after the lines are drawn on the graphs, they represent a more complete picture of the relationship than the tables do because all nonnegative real numbers, not just whole numbers, are included in the graph.

Explain

EXPLORE ACTIVITY 2
Focus on Math Connections CC Mathematical Practices
Point out to students that when finding an equation from a graph, it is easier to first make a table of values from the graph. Then they can look for a pattern for the equation.

Questioning Strategies CC Mathematical Practices
• Is the relationship additive or multiplicative? Explain how you know. The relationship is additive, because the line drawn through the points does not go through the origin.

• Explain how you can find the entrance fee for the museum from the graph. The starting point of the graph is (0, 5). This ordered pair represents the cost of Cherise's expenses at the museum without any purchases at the gift shop, so it represents the entrance fee, $5.

Engage with the Whiteboard
Ask a student volunteer to complete the table and identify the pattern. Then have the student write the equation to represent the total amount spent at the museum gift shop. Finally, discuss with the class what the independent and dependent variables are.

Representing Algebraic Relationships in Tables and Graphs

COMMON CORE 6.EE.9
...Analyze the relationship between the dependent and independent variables using graphs and tables, and relate these to the equation.

How can you use verbal descriptions, tables, and graphs to represent algebraic relationships?

EXPLORE ACTIVITY 1 Real World | COMMON CORE 6.EE.9

Representing Algebraic Relationships

Angie's walking speed is 5 kilometers per hour, and May's is 4 kilometers per hour. Show how the distance each girl walks is related to time.

A For each girl, make a table comparing time and distance.

Time (h)	0	1	2	3	4
Angie's distance (km)	0	5	10	15	20

> For every hour Angie walks, she travels 5 km.

Time (h)	0	1	2	3	4
May's distance (km)	0	4	8	12	16

> For every hour May walks, she travels 4 km.

B For each girl, make a graph showing her distance y as it depends on time x. Plot points from the table and connect them with a line. Write an equation for each girl that relates distance y to time x.

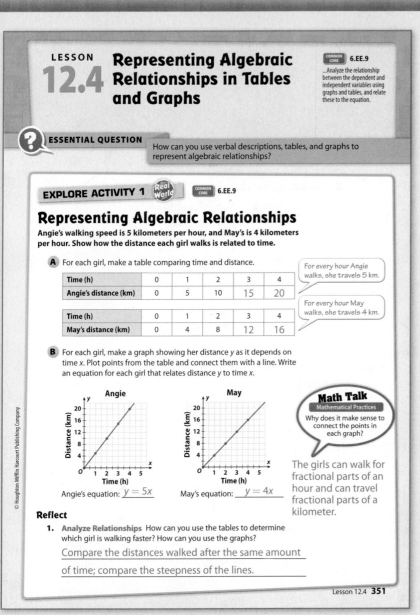

Angie's equation: $y = 5x$

May's equation: $y = 4x$

Math Talk
Mathematical Practices

Why does it make sense to connect the points in each graph?

The girls can walk for fractional parts of an hour and can travel fractional parts of a kilometer.

Reflect

1. **Analyze Relationships** How can you use the tables to determine which girl is walking faster? How can you use the graphs?

Compare the distances walked after the same amount of time; compare the steepness of the lines.

EXPLORE ACTIVITY 2 Real World | COMMON CORE 6.EE.9

Writing an Equation from a Graph

Cherise pays the entrance fee to visit a museum, then buys souvenirs at the gift shop. The graph shows the relationship between the total amount she spends at the museum and the amount she spends at the gift shop. Write an equation to represent the relationship.

A Read the ordered pairs from the graph. Use them to complete a table comparing total spent y to amount spent at the gift shop x.

Gift shop amount ($)	0	5	10	15	20
Total amount ($)	5	10	15	20	25

B What is the pattern in the table?

The total amount is $5 more than the gift shop amount.

C Write an equation that expresses the total amount spent, y, in terms of the amount spent at the gift shop, x.

$y = x + 5$

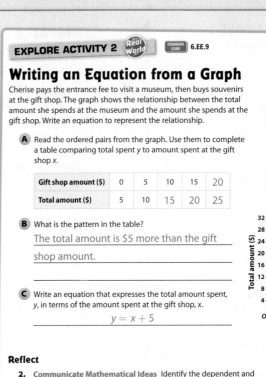

Reflect

2. **Communicate Mathematical Ideas** Identify the dependent and independent quantities in this situation.

Dependent: total amount spent; independent: amount spent at the gift shop

3. **Multiple Representations** Draw a line through the points on the graph. Find the point that represents Cherise spending $18 at the gift shop. Use this point to find the total she would spend if she spent $18 at the gift shop. Then use your equation from **C** to verify your answer.

Check students' graphs; (18, 23); $23; 23 = 18 + 5; 23 = 23

PROFESSIONAL DEVELOPMENT

CC Integrate Mathematical Practices MP.4

This lesson provides an opportunity to address this Mathematical Practices standard. It calls for students to model with mathematics. Students use verbal descriptions to make tables and draw graphs that represent real-life situations. They also represent information from graphs by using tables and equations; and represent equations by using tables and graphs.

Math Background

The equations in this lesson are linear equations. A *linear equation* is an equation whose solutions fall on a line on a coordinate plane. All solutions of a particular linear equation fall on the line, and all the points on the line are solutions of the equation. Linear equations have constant slope. In the slope-intercept form, $y = mx + b$, m is the slope and b is the y-intercept.

Linear equations fit into the general category of polynomial equations. Linear equations are called first-degree equations, because the greatest power of x is 1.

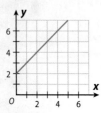
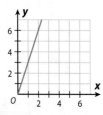

EXAMPLE 1

Talk About It
Check for Understanding

Ask: Can the points on the graphs only have whole number coordinates? Explain your answer. No, the coordinates can be any pair of rational numbers that satisfies the equation. For example, (0.5, 1.5) is on the graph of $y = x + 1$. Limits on the values of the variables in equations are usually the result of real-world situations.

Questioning Strategies **CC** **Mathematical Practices**

- How can you plot points on the graph in A other than the ones in the table? Choose numbers on the x-axis other than the ones in the table. Add 1 to each value of x, and plot the points (x, y) that you produce.

- How can you plot points on the graph in B other than the ones in the table? Choose numbers on the x-axis other than the ones in the table. Multiply each value of x by 2, and plot the points (x, y) that you produce.

YOUR TURN

Avoid Common Errors
Students may plot the points in the table but forget to draw a line connecting the points. Remind them that they must connect the points with a line for the graph to be correctly drawn.

Elaborate

Talk About It
Summarize the Lesson

Ask: How can you use tables and graphs to represent algebraic relationships? You can make a table from the verbal description and then make a graph from the ordered pairs in the table. From a graph, you can make a table and write an equation.

GUIDED PRACTICE

Engage with the Whiteboard
For Exercises 1–2, have students complete the table and graph the points on the coordinate grid on the whiteboard. Then have another student identify the pattern and write the equation.

Avoid Common Errors
Exercises 1–2 Students may plot the points in the table but forget to draw a line connecting the points. Remind them that they must connect the points with a line for the graph to be drawn correctly.

Graphing an Equation

An ordered pair (x, y) that makes an equation like $y = x + 1$ true is called a **solution** of the equation. The graph of an equation represents all the ordered pairs that are solutions.

EXAMPLE 1

COMMON CORE **6.EE.9**

Graph each equation.

A $y = x + 1$

STEP 1 Make a table of values. Choose some values for x and use the equation to find the corresponding values for y.

STEP 2 Plot the ordered pairs from the table.

STEP 3 Draw a line through the plotted points to represent all of the ordered pair solutions of the equation.

x	x + 1 = y	(x, y)
1	1 + 1 = 2	(1, 2)
2	2 + 1 = 3	(2, 3)
3	3 + 1 = 4	(3, 4)
4	4 + 1 = 5	(4, 5)
5	5 + 1 = 6	(5, 6)

Math Talk
Mathematical Practices

Is the ordered pair (3.5, 4.5) a solution of the equation $y = x + 1$? Explain.

Yes; (3.5, 4.5) is on the graph. You can substitute for the variables in the equation to check.

B $y = 2x$

STEP 1 Make a table of values. Choose some values for x and use the equation to find the corresponding values for y.

STEP 2 Plot the ordered pairs from the table.

STEP 3 Draw a line through the plotted points to represent all of the ordered pair solutions of the equation.

x	2x = y	(x, y)
1	2 × 1 = 2	(1, 2)
2	2 × 2 = 4	(2, 4)
3	2 × 3 = 6	(3, 6)
4	2 × 4 = 8	(4, 8)
5	2 × 5 = 10	(5, 10)

YOUR TURN

4. Graph $y = x + 2.5$.

x	x + 2.5 = y	(x, y)
0	0 + 2.5 = 2.5	(0, 2.5)
1	1 + 2.5 = 3.5	(1, 3.5)
2	2 + 2.5 = 4.5	(2, 4.5)
3	3 + 2.5 = 5.5	(3, 5.5)

Guided Practice

Frank mows lawns in the summer to earn extra money. He can mow 3 lawns every hour he works. (Explore Activity 1 and Explore Activity 2)

1. Make a table to show the relationship between the number of hours Frank works, x, and the number of lawns he mows, y. Graph the relationship and write an equation. Label the axes of your graph.

Hours worked	Lawns mowed
0	0
1	3
2	6
3	9

$y = 3x$

Graph $y = 1.5x$. (Example 1)

2. Make a table to show the relationship.

x	0	1	2	3
y	0	1.5	3	4.5

3. Plot the points and draw a line through them.

? ESSENTIAL QUESTION CHECK-IN

4. How can a table represent an algebraic relationship between two variables?

It shows pairs of values that satisfy the relationship.

DIFFERENTIATE INSTRUCTION

Cooperative Learning

Have students work in pairs to write an equation with two variables. Each equation should involve addition. Collect students' equations and randomly redistribute them. Have the students make tables for the equations and write solutions of the equations as ordered pairs. Then have the students graph the equations.

Modeling

Draw an equilateral triangle and a square, each with a side length of 6 inches, on the chalkboard. Have students find the perimeter of each. Ask students to come up with a formula for the perimeter of an equilateral triangle and a square. Then have students make a table and a graph for each formula.

Additional Resources

Differentiated Instruction includes:

- Reading Strategies
- Success for English Learners **ELL**
- Reteach
- Challenge **PRE-AP**

Personal
Math Trainer
Online Assessment
and Intervention

Online homework
assignment available

 my.hrw.com

12.4 LESSON QUIZ

 6.EE.9

The graph shows the number of bracelets Olivia can make in an hour.

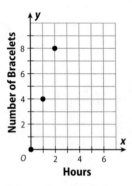

1. Read the ordered pairs from the graph to make a table.

2. Write an equation to model the relationship.

The equation $y = x + 2$ represents the total cost of doing x loads of laundry at a laundromat in dollars, including buying a box of detergent.

3. Make a table that represents the relationship between number of loads and total cost.

4. Make a graph showing the relationship.

Lesson Quiz available online

 my.hrw.com

Answers

1.

Number of hours	0	1	2
Number of bracelets	0	4	8

2. $y = 4x$

3.

Number of loads	0	1	2	3
Total cost ($)	2	3	4	5

Evaluate

GUIDED AND INDEPENDENT PRACTICE

 6.EE.9

Concepts & Skills	Practice
Explore Activity 1 Representing Algebraic Relationships	Exercise 1
Explore Activity 2 Writing an Equation from a Graph	Exercises 1, 5–7
Example 1 Graphing an Equation	Exercises 2–3, 8–9, 11

Exercise	Depth of Knowledge (D.O.K.)	Mathematical Practices
5–6	**2** Skills/Concepts	**MP.4** Modeling
7	**3** Strategic Thinking H.O.T.	**MP.7** Using Structure
8–9	**2** Skills/Concepts	**MP.2** Reasoning
10	**3** Strategic Thinking H.O.T.	**MP.3** Logic
11	**3** Strategic Thinking H.O.T.	**MP.7** Using Structure
12	**3** Strategic Thinking H.O.T.	**MP.3** Logic
13–14	**3** Strategic Thinking H.O.T.	**MP.7** Using Structure

Additional Resources

Differentiated Instruction includes:

• Leveled Practice worksheets

CC CLUSTER CONNECTION **Exercise 11** combines concepts from the Common Core cluster "Represent and analyze quantitative relationships between dependent and independent variables."

4.

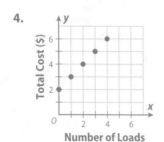

12.4 Independent Practice

 6.EE.9

Personal
Math Trainer
Online
Assessment and
Intervention
my.hrw.com

Students at Mills Middle School are required to work a certain number of community service hours. The table shows the numbers of additional hours several students worked beyond their required hours, as well as the total numbers of hours worked.

5. Read the ordered pairs from the graph to make a table.

Additional hours	0	5	10	15	20
Total hours	20	25	30	35	40

6. Write an equation that expresses the total hours in terms of the additional hours.

$y = x + 20$

7. **Analyze Relationships** How many community service hours are students required to work? Explain.

20 hours; when 0 additional hours are worked, the total is 20 hours.

Beth is using a map. Let x represent a distance in centimeters on the map. To find an actual distance y in kilometers, Beth uses the equation $y = 8x$.

8. Make a table comparing a distance on the map to the actual distance.

Map distance (cm)	1	2	3	4	5
Actual distance (km)	8	16	24	32	40

9. Make a graph that compares the map distance to the actual distance. Label the axes of the graph.

10. **Critical Thinking** The actual distance between Town A and Town B is 64 kilometers. What is the distance on Beth's map? Did you use the graph or the equation to find the answer? Why?

8 cm; sample answer: I used the equation because the scales on the graph don't extend far enough.

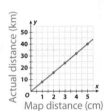

11. **Multistep** The equation $y = 9x$ represents the total cost y for x movie tickets. Label the axes of the graph.

a. Make a table and a graph to represent the relationship between x and y.

Number of tickets, x	1	2	3	4	5
Total cost ($), y	9	18	27	36	45

b. **Critical Thinking** In this situation, which quantity is dependent and which is independent? Justify your answer.

Dependent: total cost; independent: number of tickets; the total cost depends on how many tickets were purchased.

c. **Multiple Representations** Eight friends want to go see a movie. Would you prefer to use an equation, a table, or a graph to find the cost of 8 movie tickets? Explain how you would use your chosen method to find the cost.

Sample answer: an equation; substitute 8 for x in $y = 9x$ to get $y = 9(8) = \$72$.

H.O.T. FOCUS ON HIGHER ORDER THINKING

12. **Critical Thinking** Suppose you graph $y = 5x$ and $y = x + 500$ on the same coordinate plane. Which line will be steeper? Why?

The graph of $y = 5x$ will be steeper because y increases more rapidly for each value of x.

13. **Persevere in Problem Solving** Marcus plotted the points (0, 0), (6, 2), (18, 6), and (21, 7) on a graph. He wrote an equation for the relationship. Find another ordered pair that could be a solution of Marcus's equation. Justify your answer.

Sample answer: (30, 10); every y value is $\frac{1}{3}$ of the x value. So, $10 = \frac{1}{3}(30)$.

14. **Error Analysis** The cost of a personal pizza is $4. A drink costs $1. Anna wrote the equation $y = 4x + 1$ to represent the relationship between total cost y of buying x meals that include one personal pizza and one drink. Describe Anna's error and write the correct equation.

Anna's equation does not show that every meal includes both a pizza and a drink; the correct equation is $y = 5x$.

Work Area

EXTEND THE MATH PRE-AP

Activity available online my.hrw.com

Activity Ask students if they know that you can find the approximate temperature by listening to snowy tree crickets chirp. The chirp rate of the cricket varies by temperature. The hotter it is, the more chirps per minute. The temperature in °F can be approximated by multiplying the number of chirps in one minute by $\frac{1}{4}$ and adding 40. Write the equation that represents this situation. Then, make a table of values to approximate the temperature for 20, 40, 60, 80, and 100 chirps per minute.

$t = \frac{1}{4}c + 40$, where t is the Fahrenheit temperature and c is the number of chirps in a minute

c	20	40	60	80	100
t	45	50	55	60	65

Ready to Go On?

Assess Mastery

Use the assessment on this page to determine if students have mastered the concepts and standards covered in this module.

Response to Intervention

Personal Math Trainer
Online Assessment and Intervention

⏻ my.hrw.com

Intervention	Enrichment

Access Ready to Go On? assessment online, and receive instant scoring, feedback, and customized intervention or enrichment.

Online and Print Resources

Differentiated Instruction
- Reteach worksheets
- Reading Strategies **ELL**
- Success for English Learners **ELL**

Differentiated Instruction
- Challenge worksheets **PRE-AP**
- Extend the Math **PRE-AP** Lesson Activities in TE

Additional Resources

Assessment Resources includes:
- Leveled Module Quizzes

Ready to Go On?

Personal Math Trainer
Online Assessment and Intervention
⏻ my.hrw.com

12.1 Graphing on the Coordinate Plane

Graph each point on the coordinate plane.

1. $A(-2, 4)$
2. $B(3, 5)$
3. $C(6, -4)$
4. $D(-3, -5)$
5. $E(7, 2)$
6. $F(-4, 6)$

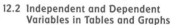

12.2 Independent and Dependent Variables in Tables and Graphs

7. Jon buys packages of pens for $5 each. Identify the independent and dependent variables in the situation.

independent: number of packages; dependent: total cost

12.3 Writing Equations from Tables

Write an equation that represents the data in the table.

8.

x	3	5	8	10
y	21	35	56	70

$y = 7x$

9.

x	5	10	15	20
y	17	22	27	32

$y = x + 12$

12.4 Representing Algebraic Relationships in Tables and Graphs

Graph each equation.

10. $y = x + 3$

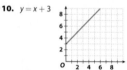

11. $y = 5x$

? ESSENTIAL QUESTION

12. How can you write an equation in two variables to solve a problem?
Decide which variable depends on the other. Use a table to find the relationship between the variables and write an equation.

Common Core Standards

Lesson	Exercises	Common Core Standards
12.1	1–6	**6.NS.6, 6.NS.6b, 6.NS.6c, 6.NS.8**
12.2	7	**6.EE.9**
12.3	8–9	**6.EE.9**
12.4	10–11	**6.EE.9**

Assessment Readiness

Assessment Readiness Tip Some items are called context-based items, which means the student has to examine each answer choice in order to determine the correct answer.

Item 2 If students don't remember that for every point in quadrant II the *x*-coordinate is a negative number and the *y*-coordinate is a positive number, they may need to plot each point to see that choice C is the correct answer.

Item 5 To find the point that the graph of $y = 10 + x$ does not pass through, students may need to graph each point on a coordinate grid to see that choice C is the correct answer.

Avoid Common Errors

Item 1 Students may forget what the first and second numbers in an ordered pair mean. Remind students that the first number is the *x*-coordinate, and the second is the *y*-coordinate.

Item 4 Students often will get the independent and dependent quantities backward in problems, thereby choosing A for the answer. Remind students that the dependent quantity *depends* on the independent quantity. Therefore, the number of points earned *depends* on the number of prizes captured.

Additional Resources

Personal Math Trainer

Online Assessment and Intervention

my.hrw.com

MODULE 12 MIXED REVIEW

Assessment Readiness

COMMON CORE

Personal Math Trainer

Online Assessment and Intervention

my.hrw.com

Selected Response

1. What are the coordinates of point *G* on the coordinate grid below?

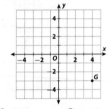

Ⓐ (4, 3)　　Ⓒ (−4, 3)
Ⓑ (4, −3)　　Ⓓ (−4, −3)

2. A point is located in quadrant II of a coordinate plane. Which of the following could be the coordinates of that point?

Ⓐ (−5, −7)　　Ⓒ (−5, 7)
Ⓑ (5, 7)　　Ⓓ (5, −7)

3. Matt had 5 library books. He checked 1 additional book out every week without returning any books. Which equation describes the number of books he has, *y*, after *x* weeks?

Ⓐ $y = 5x$　　Ⓒ $y = 1 + 5x$
Ⓑ $y = 5 − x$　　Ⓓ $y = 5 + x$

4. Stewart is playing a video game. He earns the same number of points for each prize he captures. He earned 1,200 points for 6 prizes, 2,000 points for 10 prizes, and 2,600 points for 13 prizes. Which is the dependent variable in the situation?

Ⓐ the number of prizes captured
Ⓑ the number of points earned
Ⓒ the number of hours
Ⓓ the number of prizes available

5. Which point is *not* on the graph of the equation $y = 10 + x$?

Ⓐ (0, 10)　　Ⓒ (8, 2)
Ⓑ (3, 13)　　Ⓓ (5, 15)

6. Amy gets paid by the hour. Her sister helps. As shown, Amy gives her sister part of her earnings. Which equation represents Amy's pay when her sister's pay is $13?

Amy's pay in dollars	10	20	30	40
Sister's pay in dollars	2	4	6	8

Ⓐ $y = \frac{13}{5}$　　Ⓒ $5 = 13y$
Ⓑ $13 = \frac{x}{5}$　　Ⓓ $13 = 5x$

Mini-Task

7. The table compares the ages, in years, of two cousins.

Ann's age, *x*	4	8	12
Tom's age, *y*	8	12	16

a. Write an equation that compares Tom's and Ann's ages.

$y = x + 4$

b. Draw a graph to represent the equation.

Common Core Standards

Items	Grade 6 Standards	Mathematical Practices
1	6.NS.6c	MP.2
2	6.NS.6b	MP.7
3*	6.EE.2a, 6.EE.9	MP.4
4	6.EE.9	MP.4
5*	6.EE.2c, 6.NS.8	MP.7
6	6.EE.9	MP.2, MP.4
7	6.NS.8, 6.NS.6c	MP.4, MP.7

* Item integrates mixed review concepts from previous modules or a previous course.

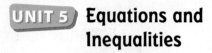
Study Guide Review

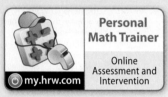
Vocabulary Development

Integrating Language Arts

Encourage students to practice using the unit vocabulary as they talk and write about mathematics. Understanding vocabulary will aid their understanding of the concepts.

 ELA-Literacy.RST.6-8.4 Determine the meaning of symbols, key terms, and other domain-specific words and phrases as they are used in a specific scientific or technical context relevant to grades 6–8 texts and topics.

MODULE 11 Equations and Relationships

 6.EE.5, 6.EE.6, 6.EE.7, 6.EE.8

Key Concepts
• An equation is a mathematical statement that two expressions are equal, which, if it includes a variable, has a solution. *(Lesson 11.1)*
• Both sides of an equation remain equal after adding, or subtracting, the same number from both sides. *(Lesson 11.2)*
• Both sides of an equation remain equal after multiplying, or dividing, both sides by the same number. *(Lesson 11.3)*

MODULE 12 Relationships in Two Variables

6.EE.6, 6.EE.6b, 6.EE.6c, 6.EE.8, 6.EE.9

Key Concepts
• An ordered pair is a pair of numbers in the form (x, y) that gives the location of a point on a coordinate plane. *(Lesson 12.1)*
• The quantity that depends on the other quantity is called the dependent variable, and the quantity it depends on is called the independent variable. *(Lesson 12.2)*
• Tables and graphs can be used to represent the relationship between an independent and dependent variable. *(Lesson 12.4)*

Study Guide Review

MODULE 11 Equations and Relationships

> **Key Vocabulary**
> equation (*ecuación*)
> solution (*solución*)
> solution of an inequality (*solución de una desigualdad*)

? ESSENTIAL QUESTION

How can you use equations and relationships to solve real-world problems?

EXAMPLE 1

Determine if the given value is a solution of the equation.

A. $r - 5 = 17; r = 12$

$12 - 5 \stackrel{?}{=} 17$ Substitute.

$7 \neq 17$

12 is not a solution of $r - 5 = 17$.

B. $\frac{x}{6} = 7; x = 42$

$\frac{42}{6} \stackrel{?}{=} 7$ Substitute.

$7 = 7$

42 is a solution of $\frac{x}{6} = 7$.

EXAMPLE 2

Solve each equation. Check your answer.

A. $y - 12 = 10$

$\underline{+12}\quad \underline{+12}$ Add 12 to both sides.

$y = 22$

Check: $22 - 12 \stackrel{?}{=} 10$ Substitute.

$10 = 10$

B. $5p = 30$

$\frac{5p}{5} = \frac{30}{5}$ Divide both sides by 5.

$p = 6$

Check: $5(6) \stackrel{?}{=} 30$ Substitute.

$30 = 30$

EXAMPLE 3

Write and graph an inequality to represent each situation.

A. There are at least 5 gallons of water in an aquarium.

$g \geq 5$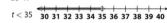

B. The temperature today will be less than 35 °F.

$t < 35$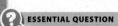

EXERCISES

Determine whether the given value is a solution of the equation. (Lesson 11.1)

1. $7x = 14; x = 3$ _____no_____   **2.** $y + 13 = 17; y = 4$ _____yes_____

Write an equation to represent the situation. (Lesson 11.1)

3. Don has three times as much money as his brother, who has $25. _____$\frac{d}{3} = 25$_____

4. There are *s* students enrolled in Mr. Rodriguez's class. There are 6 students absent and 18 students present today. _____$s - 6 = 18$_____

Solve each equation. Check your answer. (Lessons 11.2, 11.3)

5. $p - 5 = 18$ _____$p = 23$_____   **6.** $9q = 18.9$ _____$q = 2.1$_____

7. $3.5 + x = 7$ _____$x = 3.5$_____   **8.** $\frac{2}{7} = 2x$ _____$x = \frac{1}{7}$_____

9. Sonia used $12.50 to buy a new journal. She has $34.25 left in her savings account. How much money did Sonia have before she bought the journal? Write and solve an equation to solve the problem. (Lesson 11.2) _____$x - 12.50 = 34.25;\ \$46.75$_____

Write and graph an inequality to represent each situation. (Lesson 11.4)

10. The company's stock is worth less than $2.50 per share. _____$s < 2.5$_____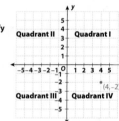

11. Tina got a haircut, and her hair is still at least 15 inches long. _____$h \geq 15$_____

MODULE 12 Relationships in Two Variables

> **Key Vocabulary**
> axes (*ejes*)
> coordinate plane (*plano cartesiano*)
> coordinates (*coordenadas*)
> ordered pair (*par ordenado*)
> origin (*origen*)
> quadrants (*cuadrantes*)
> x-axis (*eje x*)

? ESSENTIAL QUESTION

How can you use relationships in two variables to solve real-world problems?

EXAMPLE 1

Graph the point (4, −2) and identify the quadrant where it is located.

$(4, -2)$ is located 4 units to the right of the origin and 2 units down from the origin.

$(4, -2)$ is in quadrant IV.

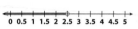

Unit 5 Performance Tasks

The Performance Tasks provide students with the opportunity to apply concepts from this unit in real-world problem situations.

CAREERS IN MATH

Botanist In Performance Task Item 1, students can see how a botanist uses mathematics on the job.

SCORING GUIDES FOR PERFORMANCE TASKS

1. MATHEMATICAL PRACTICES **MP.4, MP.7**

Task	Possible Points (Total: 6)
a	**1 point** for correctly writing the expression: $205 + 2d$
b	**1 point** for correctly setting the expression: $205 + 2d = 235$ **1 point** for correct answer: 15 days
c	**1 point** for the correct expression for Suntracker: $195 + 2.5d$ **1 point** for determining the heights of each sunflower variety after 22 days: Suntracker: $h = 195 + 2.5(22) = 250$ Sunny Yellow: $h = 205 + 2(22) = 249$ **1 point** for stating that Suntracker is taller.

2. MATHEMATICAL PRACTICES **MP.4**

Task	Possible Points (Total: 6)
a	**1 point** for correctly defining a variable: Let w = the number of hours Vernon practiced soccer over the weekend. **1 point** for the correct equation: $4\frac{1}{3} + w = 5\frac{3}{4}$
b	**1 point** for correctly finding the LCM, 12, and showing how to find it. Students can use a number line, a list of multiples, or prime factorization to find the LCM. $4 = 2 \times 2; 3 = 3;$ LCM $= 2 \times 2 \times 3 = 12$
c	**1 point** for correctly solving the equation: $w = 1\frac{5}{12}$ **1 point** for showing the stepped-out solution to the equation. **1 point** for correctly interpreting the equation in terms of the problem: Vernon practiced $1\frac{5}{12}$ hours over the weekend.

EXAMPLE 2

Tim is paid $8 more than the number of bags of peanuts he sells at the baseball stadium. The table shows the relationship between the money Tim earns and the number of bags of peanuts Tim sells. Identify the independent and dependent variables, and write an equation that represents the relationship.

Bags of peanuts, x	0	1	2	3
Money earned, y	8	9	10	11

The number of bags is the independent variable, and the money Tim earns is the dependent variable.

The equation $y = x + 8$ expresses the relationship between the number of bags Tim sells and the amount he earns.

EXERCISES

Graph and label each point on the coordinate plane. (Lesson 12.1)

1. (4, 4)

2. (−3, −1)

3. (−1, 4)

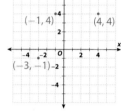

Use the graph to answer the questions. (Lesson 12.2)

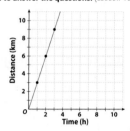

4. What is the independent variable? _____ time _____

5. What is the dependent variable? _____ distance _____

6. Describe the relationship between the independent variable and the dependent variable.

   The dependent variable is 3 times the independent variable.

---

7. Use the data in the table to write an equation to express y in terms of x. Then graph the equation. (Lessons 12.3, 12.4)

x	0	1	2	3
y	4	5	6	7

$y = x + 4$

Unit 5 Performance Tasks

1. **CAREERS IN MATH** | Botanist Dr. Adama is a botanist. She measures the daily height of a particular variety of sunflower, Sunny Yellow, beginning when the sunflower is 60 days old. At 60 days, the height of the sunflower is 205 centimeters. Dr. Adama finds that the growth rate of this sunflower is 2 centimeters per day after the first 60 days.

   a. Write an expression to represent the sunflower's height after d days. _____ $205 + 2d$ _____

   b. How many days does it take for the sunflower to reach 235 centimeters? Show your work.

      15 days; $235 = 205 + 2d$; $30 = 2d$; $15 = d$

   c. The Suntracker grows at a rate of 2.5 centimeters per day after the first 60 days. If this sunflower is 195 centimeters tall when it is 60 days old, write an expression to represent Suntracker's height after d days. Which sunflower will be taller after 22 days, or when it is 82 days old? Explain how you found your answer.

      Suntracker: $195 + 2.5d$; after 22 days: Suntracker: $h = 195 + 2.5(22)$
      $= 250$; Sunny Yellow: $h = 205 + 2(22) = 249$. Suntracker is taller.

2. Vernon practiced soccer $5\frac{3}{4}$ hours this week. He practiced $4\frac{1}{3}$ hours on weekdays and the rest over the weekend.

   a. Write an equation that represents the situation. Define your variable.

      Let $w =$ the number of hours Vernon practiced soccer over the
      weekend; $4\frac{1}{3} + w = 5\frac{3}{4}$

   b. What is the least common multiple of the denominators of $5\frac{3}{4}$ and $4\frac{1}{3}$? Show your work.

      Using prime factorization: $4 = 2 \times 2$; $3 = 3$; LCM $= (2)(2)(3) = 12$

   c. Solve the equation and interpret the solution. Show your work.

      $4\frac{1}{3} + w = 5\frac{3}{4}$; $4\frac{4}{12} + w = 5\frac{9}{12}$; $w = 5\frac{9}{12} - 4\frac{4}{12} = 1\frac{5}{12}$

      Vernon practiced $1\frac{5}{12}$ hours over the weekend.

Assessment Readiness

Additional Resources

Personal Math Trainer

Online Assessment and Intervention

my.hrw.com

Assessment Resources
- Leveled Unit Tests: A, B, C, D
- Performance Assessment

Assessment Readiness Tip Students should always read each question carefully to identify key words or phrases, such as *no more than,* to help identify what the question is really asking.

Item 5 Students should underline the phrase *no more than*; it will help them to realize that *n* cannot be larger than 7, but it can be equal to 7. This will help them choose the correct inequality.

Item 7 Students who do not read the problem carefully may choose B because they see the word *times.* But reading carefully they will see the phrase "3 more *times* than," which will reveal choice D as the correct answer.

Avoid Common Errors

Item 8 Some students may fail to pay attention to the direction in which the graph is pointing. As a result, they may choose answer choice A because it includes the number 4.4 in the solution. Remind students that the direction of the inequality is as important as its endpoint.

Item 11 Some students may choose D as the correct answer because they have made a mistake when placing the decimals. Remind students to pay close attention to place value when they are working with decimals.

Common Core Standards

Items	Grade 6 Standards	Mathematical Practices
1	**6.EE.5**	**MP.2** Reasoning
2	**6.EE.7**	**MP.2** Reasoning
3	**6.EE.8**	**MP.4** Modeling
4	**6.EE.5**	**MP.2** Reasoning
5	**6.EE.8**	**MP.4** Modeling
6	**6.EE.8**	**MP.4** Modeling
7	**6.EE.5**	**MP.4** Modeling
8	**6.EE.8**	**MP.2** Reasoning
9	**6.EE.9**	**MP.4** Modeling
10*	**6.RP.3, 6.NS.1**	**MP.7** Using Structure
11*	**6.NS.3**	**MP.7** Using Structure
12	**6.EE.6**	**MP.4** Modeling
13	**6.EE.9**	**MP.4** Modeling

* Item integrates mixed review concepts from previous modules or a previous course.

Assessment Readiness

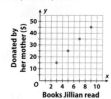

Personal Math Trainer

my.hrw.com

Online Assessment and Intervention

1. Using the expression $7x = 3y$, if y is 35, what is x?

- Ⓐ 15
- Ⓑ 21
- Ⓒ 35
- Ⓓ 105

2. Bruce has 97 sports cards. 34 of them are football cards. Which equation can be used to find the number of sports cards y that are not football cards?

- Ⓐ $97 + 34 = y$
- Ⓑ $y + 97 = 34$
- Ⓒ $34 + y = 97$
- Ⓓ $y - 97 = 34$

3. The overnight temperature in Tampa never reached below 40 °F during November. Which inequality shows that?

- Ⓐ $x < 40$
- Ⓑ $x > 40$
- Ⓒ $x = 40$
- Ⓓ $x \geq 40$

4. Truman puts money into his savings account every time he gets paid. The table below shows how much he saves.

Amount Truman is paid	$15	$30	$45
Amount Truman saves	$1.50	$3	$4.50

Which of the following equations can be used to find the amount m Truman saves when he is paid $20?

- Ⓐ $m = 20(0.10)$
- Ⓒ $0.10m = 20$
- Ⓑ $20m = 0.10$
- Ⓓ $m = \frac{10}{20}$

5. No more than 7 copies of a newspaper are left in the newspaper rack. Which inequality represents this situation?

- Ⓐ $n < 7$
- Ⓑ $n \leq 7$
- Ⓒ $n > 7$
- Ⓓ $n \geq 7$

6. For which of the inequalities below is $v = 4$ a solution?

- Ⓐ $v + 5 \geq 9$
- Ⓑ $v + 5 > 9$
- Ⓒ $v + 5 \leq 8$
- Ⓓ $v + 5 < 8$

7. Sarah has read aloud in class 3 more times than Joel. Sarah has read 9 times. Which equation represents this situation?

- Ⓐ $j - 9 = 3$
- Ⓑ $3j = 9$
- Ⓒ $j - 3 = 9$
- Ⓓ $j + 3 = 9$

8. The number line below represents the solution to which inequality?

- Ⓐ $m > 4.4$
- Ⓑ $m > 5$
- Ⓒ $m < 4.4$
- Ⓓ $m < 4$

When possible, use logic to eliminate at least two answer choices.

9. Brian is playing a video game. He earns the same number of points for each star he picks up. He earned 2,400 points for 6 stars, 4,000 points for 10 stars, and 5,200 points for 13 stars. Which is the independent variable in the situation?

- Ⓐ the number of stars picked up
- Ⓑ the number of points earned
- Ⓒ the number of hours played
- Ⓓ the number of stars available

10. Which ratio is **not** equivalent to the other three?

- Ⓐ $\frac{2}{5}$
- Ⓒ $\frac{6}{15}$
- Ⓑ $\frac{12}{25}$
- Ⓓ $\frac{18}{45}$

11. One inch is about 2.54 centimeters. About how many centimeters is 4.5 inches?

- Ⓐ 1.8 centimeters
- Ⓑ 11.4 centimeters
- Ⓒ 13.7 centimeters
- Ⓓ 114 centimeters

Mini-Tasks

12. Dana, Neil, and Frank are siblings. Dana is the oldest.

a. Frank's age is one-fourth of Dana's age. Write an equation to represent Frank's age f if Dana's age is d years.
$$f = \frac{d}{4}$$

b. Neil's age is one-half of the difference between Dana's and Frank's ages. Write an equation to represent Neil's age n in terms of Dana's age d.
$$n = \frac{1}{2}\left(d - \frac{d}{4}\right)$$

c. Use the equations to find Neil's and Frank's ages if Dana is 16 years old.

Frank: 4 years old

Neil: 6 years old

13. Jillian is participating in a book reading contest to raise funds for her local library. For every book Jillian reads, her mother pledged to make a donation.

a. The table shows how much Jillian's mother will donate. Find the pattern, and finish the table.

Books Jillian reads	3	5	7	9
Money Jillian's mother donates	$15	$25	$35	$45

b. Write an equation showing the pattern from the table. Identify the variables.

$y = 5x$, $x =$ books read,

$y =$ money donated by Jillian's

mother

c. Graph the equation.

© Houghton Mifflin Harcourt Publishing Company

UNIT 6

Relationships in Geometry

Contents

Unit Pacing Guide

45-Minute Classes

Module 13

DAY 1	DAY 2	DAY 3	DAY 4	DAY 5
Lesson 13.1	Lesson 13.1	Lesson 13.2	Lesson 13.2	Lesson 13.2

DAY 6	DAY 7	DAY 8	DAY 9	DAY 10
Lesson 13.3	Lesson 13.3	Lesson13.4	Lesson13.4	Ready to Go On? Assessment Readiness

Module 14

DAY 1	DAY 2	DAY 3	DAY 4	DAY 5
Lesson 14.1	Lesson 14.1	Lesson 14.2	Lesson 14.2	Ready to Go On? Assessment Readiness

Module 15

DAY 1	DAY 2	DAY 3	DAY 4	DAY 5
Lesson 15.1	Lesson 15.1	Lesson 15.2	Lesson 15.2	Lesson 15.3

DAY 6	DAY 7	DAY 8		
Lesson 15.3	Ready to Go On? Assessment Readiness	Study Guide Assessment Readiness		

90-Minute Classes

Module 13

DAY 1	DAY 2	DAY 3	DAY 4	DAY 5
Lesson 13.1	Lesson 13.2	Lesson 13.3	Lesson 13.4	Ready to Go On? Assessment Readiness

Module 14

DAY 1	DAY 2	DAY 3		
Lesson 14.1	Lesson 14.2	Ready to Go On? Assessment Readiness		

Module 15

DAY 1	DAY 2	DAY 3	DAY 4	DAY 5
Lesson 15.1	Lesson 15.2	Lesson 15.3	Ready to Go On? Assessment Readiness	Study Guide Assessment Readiness

Program Resources

Plan

Online Teacher Edition

Access a full suite of teaching resources online—plan, present, and manage classes, assignments, and activities.

ePlanner Easily plan your classes, create and view assignments, and access all program resources with your online, customizable planning tool.

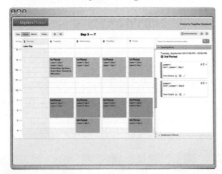

Professional Development Videos

Author Juli Dixon models successful teaching practices and strategies in actual classroom settings.

QR Codes Scan with your smart phone to jump directly from your print book to online videos and other resources.

Teacher's Edition

Support students with point-of-use Questioning Strategies, teaching tips, resources for differentiated instruction, additional activities, and more.

Engage and Explore

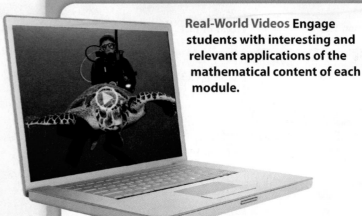

Real-World Videos Engage students with interesting and relevant applications of the mathematical content of each module.

Animated Math Online interactive simulations, tools, and games help students actively learn and practice key concepts.

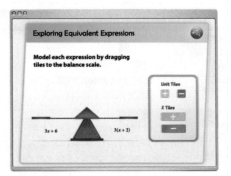

Explore Activities

Students interactively explore new concepts using a variety of tools and approaches.

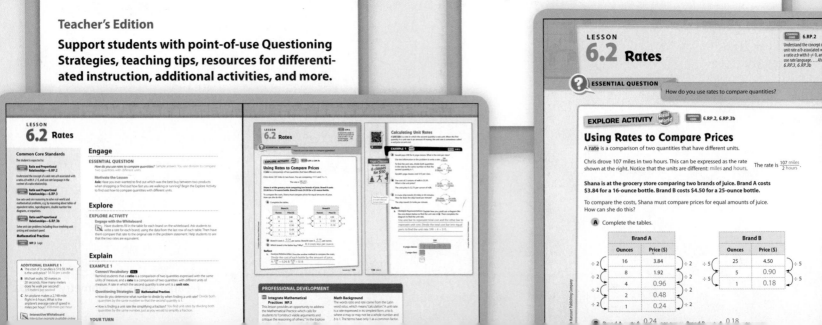

⏻ Teach

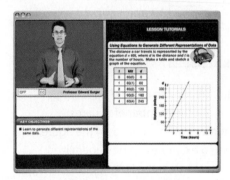 **Math On the Spot** video tutorials, featuring program authors Dr. Edward Burger and Martha Sandoval-Martinez, accompany every example in the textbook and give students step-by-step instructions and explanations of key math concepts.

 Present engaging content on a multitude of devices, including tablets and interactive whiteboards.

 Continually monitor and assess student progress with integrated formative assessment.

 Look for exercises indicated with this icon to build connections among standards within Common Core clusters.

Differentiated Instruction Print Resources

Support all learners with Differentiated Instruction Resources, including

- **Leveled Practice and Problem Solving**
- **Reteach**
- **Reading Strategies**
- **Success for English Learners**
- **Challenge**

⏻ Assessment and Intervention

The Personal Math Trainer provides online practice, homework, assessments, and intervention.
   Monitor student progress through reports and alerts. Create and customize assignments aligned to specific lessons or standards.

- **Practice** – With dynamic items and assignments, students get unlimited practice on key concepts supported by guided examples, step-by-step solutions, and video tutorials.
- **Assessments** – Choose from course assignments or customize your own based on course content, standards, difficulty levels, and more.
- **Homework** – Students can complete online homework with a wide variety of problem types, including the ability to enter expressions, equations, and graphs. Let the system automatically grade homework, so you can focus where your students need help the most!
- **Intervention** – Let the Personal Math Trainer automatically prescribe a targeted, personalized intervention path for your students.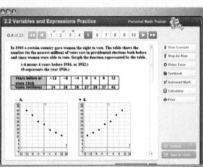

 Raise the bar with homework and practice that incorporates higher-order thinking and mathematical processes in every lesson.

 Assessment Readiness
Prepare students for success on tests of the Common Core Standards with practice at every module and unit.

Assessment Resources

Tailor assessments to meet the needs of all your classes and students, including

- **Leveled Module Quizzes**
- **Leveled Unit Tests**
- **Unit Performance Tasks**
- **Placement, Diagnostic, and Quarterly Benchmark Tests**

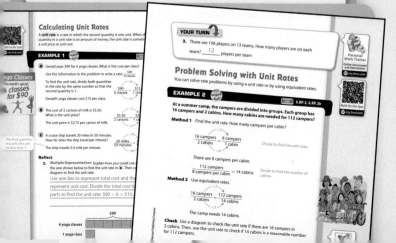

Math Background

Area 6.G.1
LESSON 13.1

When you measure the length of a line segment, you begin with a unit length and determine how many of the unit lengths are needed to cover the segment without gaps or overlaps. A unit length is simply a length that measures 1 unit, such as 1 inch, 1 centimeter, or 1 mile. To find the length of line segment $\overline{AB}$ shown below, you can use 1 cm as the unit length and see by comparison against this benchmark that the length of the line segment is 4 cm.

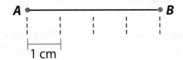

Area is defined and measured in much the same way. The definition of area begins with a definition of a unit square. A *unit square* is a square whose sides have length 1 unit. The area of a unit square is defined to be one square unit.

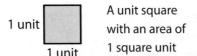

Just as a one-unit segment may be used as a standard for measuring length, a unit square may be used as a standard for measuring area. In particular, the *area* of a plane figure is defined to be the number of nonoverlapping unit squares needed to cover the figure.

Consider a rectangle with sides of length 3 cm and 4 cm. Clearly, this rectangle may be covered by exactly 12 unit squares, each of which has side lengths of 1 cm. In other words, the area of the rectangle is 12 cm².

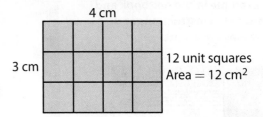

The number of unit squares needed to cover the rectangle can be counted by multiplying the number of squares across the figure by the number of squares down the figure. In other words, the preceding example can be generalized to show that the area of a rectangle is the length of its base time its height, or $A = bh$. Students should understand that this familiar formula for the area of a rectangle is the starting point for developing all other area formulas.

Geometry on the Coordinate Plane 6.NS.8, 6.G.3
LESSON 14.1 to LESSON 14.2

Representing geometric figures on a coordinate plane is a skill students will need in later courses. To find the length of a segment, students must understand that distance is always a positive number. Students first learn how to find lengths of horizontal and vertical segments, applying what they know about absolute value and distance on a number line. For example, the length of the vertical segment that connects the points (0, 0) and (0, −5) is |−5|, or 5 units. The length of the vertical segment connecting (0, 2) and (0, −5) is |2| + |−5| = 7 units. Once students know how to find lengths of horizontal and vertical segments, they can use such lengths to solve problems involving perimeter and area of figures plotted on a coordinate plane.

Nets and Surface Area 6.G.4
LESSON 15.1

The surface area of a three-dimensional figure is the sum of the areas of all the surfaces of the figure. Note that surface area is measured in square units, like any other area. Students are sometimes confused about this because they associate cubic units with three-dimensional figures. However, they should understand that a surface is actually two-dimensional. Nets can help students appreciate this fact.

A *net* is a diagram of the surfaces of a three-dimensional figure that can be cut out and folded to form the three-dimensional figure. Nets are a natural link between two-dimensional figures and three-dimensional figures, so it is often beneficial for students to draw and cut out nets as part of a hands-on approach to surface area.

Nets also offer excellent opportunities for visualization. For example, as students work with nets, they may need to decide whether two nets are identical. To make this decision, students will need to flip, turn, and slide the nets in their "mind's eye." The two nets for a cube shown below are identical since the net on the left can be turned clockwise to form the net on the right.

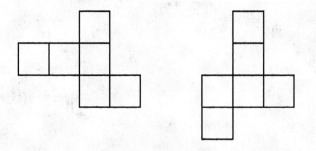

Students should be aware that nets for three-dimensional figures are generally not unique. For example, there are 11 distinct nets that can be folded to form a cube.

Volume 6.G.2
LESSON 15.2

In the same way that the area of a plane figure is the number of nonoverlapping unit squares needed to cover the figure, the volume of a three-dimensional figure is the number of nonoverlapping unit cubes needed to fill the figure. As shown below, a unit cube is a cube whose length, width, and height are all one unit.

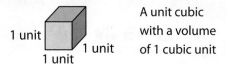

1 unit
1 unit
1 unit

A unit cubic with a volume of 1 cubic unit

The volume of a unit cube is 1 cubic unit. Thus, a three-dimensional figure that can be filled by exactly 12 unit cubes has a volume of 12 cubic units. In the case of a rectangular prism, the number of unit cubes contained in the figure may be counted by multiplying the length times the width times the height, or, more generally, by multiplying the area of the base times the height.

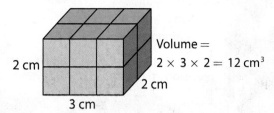

2 cm
3 cm
2 cm

Volume = $2 \times 3 \times 2 = 12$ cm^3

The general formula for volume of a prism is $V = Bh$, where B is the area of the base and h is the height. The formula for B depends on the shape of the base. The concept of volume when represented as $V = Bh$ can be demonstrated by stacking thin congruent objects such as playing cards to form a prism.

Relationships in Geometry

MODULE 13

Area and Polygons

COMMON CORE 6.G.1, 6.EE.7

MODULE 14

Distance and Area in the Coordinate Plane

COMMON CORE 6.NS.6b, 6.NS.8, 6.G.3

MODULE 15

Surface Area and Volume of Solids

COMMON CORE 6.G.2, 6.G.4, 6.EE.7

CAREERS IN MATH

Theater Set Construction A person who works in theater set construction works with the set designer to create scenery and needs technical precision when scaling and building sets based on the dimensions of the models.

If you are interested in a career in theater set construction, you should study these mathematical subjects:
- Geometry
- Algebra
- Trigonometry

Research other careers that require technical precision in scaling and building models.

Unit 6 Performance Task

At the end of the unit, check out how **theater set construction** workers use math.

Careers in Math

Theater Set Construction

Theater set construction workers often use 3-D drafting and modeling software, for which solid foundation in mathematics is essential. You will learn more about the geometry of set building in the Performance Tasks at the end of the unit.

For more information about careers in mathematics as well as various mathematics appreciation topics, visit the American Mathematical Society at www.ams.org

Vocabulary Preview

Use the puzzle to give students a preview of important concepts in this unit. Students may work individually, in pairs, or in groups.

Unit Resources

Go online to access all your unit resources.

my.hrw.com

Before	In this Unit	After
Students understand: • properties of triangles and quadrilaterals • how to solve problems involving area and volume using concrete or pictorial models	Students will learn about: • triangles and their properties • area of geometric figures • surface area and volume of right rectangular prisms	Students will learn about: • polygons and their properties • angle pair relationships • circumference and area of a circle • area of composite figures • volume and surface area of prisms and pyramids

Area and Polygons

COMMON CORE

ESSENTIAL QUESTION

How can you find the area of an irregular polygon using area formulas?

Sample answer: First, break the irregular polygon into shapes whose areas you can find using familiar formulas. The sum of these areas is the area of the polygon.

LESSON 13.1
Area of Quadrilaterals
 COMMON CORE 6.G.1

LESSON 13.2
Area of Triangles
 COMMON CORE 6.G.1

LESSON 13.3
Solving Area Equations
COMMON CORE 6.G.1, 6.EE.7

LESSON 13.4
Area of Polygons
COMMON CORE 6.G.1

Real-World Video

Quilting, painting, and other art forms use familiar geometric shapes, such as triangles and rectangles. To buy enough supplies for a project, you need to find or estimate the areas of each shape in the project.

my.hrw.com

GO DIGITAL

my.hrw.com

my.hrw.com

Go digital with your write-in student edition, accessible on any device.

Math On the Spot

Scan with your smart phone to jump directly to the online edition, video tutor, and more.

Animated Math

Interactively explore key concepts to see how math works.

Personal Math Trainer

Get immediate feedback and help as you work through practice sets.

Are You Ready?

Assess Readiness

Use the assessment on this page to determine if students need intensive or strategic intervention for the module's prerequisite skills.

 RtI **Response to Intervention**

Intervention	Enrichment

Access Are You Ready? assessment online, and receive instant scoring, feedback, and customized intervention or enrichment.

 **Personal Math Trainer**
Online Assessment and Intervention
⏻ my.hrw.com

Online and Print Resources

Skills Intervention worksheets
- Skill 57 Inverse Operations
- Skill 72 Metric Units
- Skill 85 Area of Squares and Rectangles

Differentiated Instruction
- Challenge worksheets **PRE-AP**
- Extend the Math **PRE-AP** Lesson Activities in TE

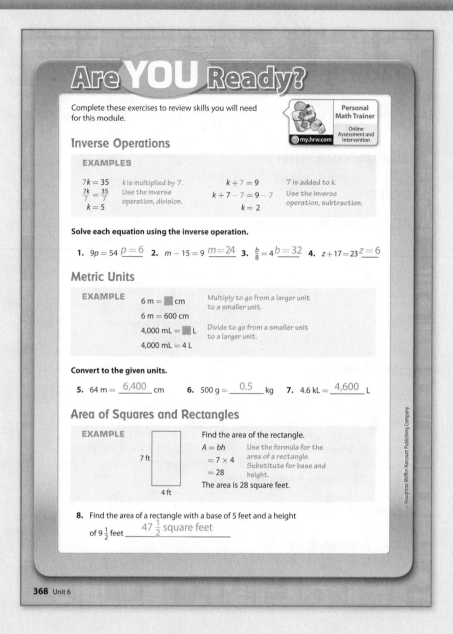

Are YOU Ready?

Complete these exercises to review skills you will need for this module.

 Personal Math Trainer
Online Assessment and Intervention
⏻ my.hrw.com

Inverse Operations

EXAMPLES

$7k = 35$	k is multiplied by 7.	$k + 7 = 9$	7 is added to k.
$\frac{7k}{7} = \frac{35}{7}$	Use the inverse operation, division.	$k + 7 - 7 = 9 - 7$	Use the inverse operation, subtraction.
$k = 5$		$k = 2$	

Solve each equation using the inverse operation.

1. $9p = 54$ $\underline{p = 6}$ 2. $m - 15 = 9$ $\underline{m = 24}$ 3. $\frac{b}{8} = 4$ $\underline{b = 32}$ 4. $z + 17 = 23$ $\underline{z = 6}$

Metric Units

EXAMPLE

6 m = ▪ cm — Multiply to go from a larger unit to a smaller unit.
6 m = 600 cm

4,000 mL = ▪ L — Divide to go from a smaller unit to a larger unit.
4,000 mL = 4 L

Convert to the given units.

5. 64 m = $\underline{6,400}$ cm   6. 500 g = $\underline{0.5}$ kg   7. 4.6 kL = $\underline{4,600}$ L

Area of Squares and Rectangles

EXAMPLE

7 ft, 4 ft (rectangle)

Find the area of the rectangle.
$A = bh$ — Use the formula for the area of a rectangle.
$= 7 \times 4$ — Substitute for base and height.
$= 28$
The area is 28 square feet.

8. Find the area of a rectangle with a base of 5 feet and a height of $9\frac{1}{2}$ feet $\underline{47\frac{1}{2} \text{ square feet}}$

PROFESSIONAL DEVELOPMENT VIDEO

 Author Juli Dixon models successful teaching practices as she explores solving area and volume equations in an actual sixth-grade classroom.

 Professional Development
⏻ my.hrw.com

G⏻ DIGITAL
my.hrw.com

 Online Teacher Edition
Access a full suite of teaching resources online—plan, present, and manage classes and assignments.

 ePlanner
Easily plan your classes and access all your resources online.

 Interactive Answers and Solutions
Customize answer keys to print or display in the classroom. Choose to include answers only or full solutions to all lesson exercises.

 Interactive Whiteboards
Engage students with interactive whiteboard-ready lessons and activities.

 Personal Math Trainer: Online Assessment and Intervention
Assign automatically graded homework, quizzes, tests, and intervention activities. Prepare your students with updated practice tests aligned with Common Core.

Reading Start-Up

Have students complete the activities on this page by working alone or with others.

Visualize Vocabulary

The graphic organizer helps students review the different types of polygons.

Understand Vocabulary

Use the following explanation to help students learn the preview words.

A quadrilateral is any shape with four sides. Several shapes can be quadrilaterals. A **parallelogram** is a four-sided shape with two pairs of parallel sides. A **rhombus** is a parallelogram with four equal side lengths. A **trapezoid** has only one pair of parallel sides.

Active Reading

Integrating Language Arts

Students can use these reading and note-taking strategies to help them organize and understand new concepts and vocabulary.

COMMON CORE **ELA-Literacy.RST.6-8.7** Integrate quantitative or technical information expressed in words in a text with a version of that information expressed visually (e.g., in a flowchart, diagram, model, graph, or table).

Additional Resources

Differentiated Instruction

• Reading Strategies **ELL**

Reading Start-Up

Visualize Vocabulary

Use the ✔ words to complete the graphic. You will put one word in each oval.

Types of Polygons

triangle — hexagon — quadrilateral

has 3 sides and 3 angles

has 6 sides and 6 angles

has 4 sides

Vocabulary

Review Words
✔ hexagon (hexágono)
✔ polygon (polígono regular)
  quadrilateral (cuadrilátero)
  rectangular prism (prisma rectangular)
  regular polygon (polígono)
  right triangle (triángulo rectángulo)
✔ triangle (triángulo)

Preview Words
  parallelogram (paralelogramo)
  rhombus (rombo)
  trapezoid (trapecio)

Understand Vocabulary

Match the term on the left to the correct expression on the right.

1. parallelogram

2. trapezoid

3. rhombus

A. A quadrilateral in which all sides are congruent and opposite sides are parallel.

B. A quadrilateral in which opposite sides are parallel and congruent.

C. A quadrilateral in which two sides are parallel.

Active Reading

Pyramid Before beginning the module, create a pyramid to help you organize what you learn. Label each side with one of the lesson titles from this module. As you study each lesson, write important ideas like vocabulary, properties, and formulas on the appropriate side.

Module 13 **369**

Before	In this module	After
Students understand:	Students will learn how to:	Students will connect:
• properties of triangles and quadrilaterals	• model area formulas for parallelograms, trapezoids, and rhombuses by decomposing and rearranging parts of these shapes	• circumference and area of a circle
• how to solve problems involving area and volume using concrete or pictorial models	• model area formulas for triangles by decomposing and rearranging parts of shapes	• area of triangles and quadrilaterals and area of composite figures
	• write equations that represent problems related to the area of rectangles, parallelograms, trapezoids, and triangles where dimensions are positive rational numbers	• volume of prisms and pyramids
	• write equations that represent problems related to the volume of right rectangular prisms where dimensions are positive rational numbers	

Unpacking the Standards

Use the examples on this page to help students know exactly what they are expected to learn in this module.

Common Core Standards

Content Areas

 Geometry—6.G

Solve real-world and mathematical problems involving area, surface area, and volume.

Go online to see a complete unpacking of the Common Core Standards.

my.hrw.com

MODULE 13

Unpacking the Standards

Understanding the standards and the vocabulary terms in the standards will help you know exactly what you are expected to learn in this module.

COMMON CORE 6.G.1

Find the area of right triangles, other triangles, special quadrilaterals, and polygons by composing into rectangles or decomposing into triangles and other shapes; apply these techniques in the context of solving real-world and mathematical problems.

What It Means to You

You will use the formula for the area of a figure to write an equation that can be used to solve a problem.

UNPACKING EXAMPLE 6.G.1

The Hudson Middle School wrestling team won the state tournament and was awarded a triangular pennant to display in the school gymnasium. The pennant has an area of 2.25 square meters. The base of the pennant is 1.5 meters long. Write an equation to find the height of the pennant.

$A = \frac{1}{2}bh$
$2.25 = \frac{1}{2}(1.5)h$
$2.25 = 0.75h$

An equation to find the height of the pennant is $2.25 = 0.75h$.

COMMON CORE 6.G.1

Find the area of right triangles, other triangles, special quadrilaterals, and polygons by composing into rectangles or decomposing into triangles and other shapes; apply these techniques in the context of solving real-world and mathematical problems.

What It Means to You

You will use formulas to find the area of irregular polygons.

UNPACKING EXAMPLE 6.G.1

John is measuring his room for new carpet. Find the area of the room.

Find the area of the rectangle.

$A = bh = 15 \times 6 = 90 \ ft^2$

Find the area of the square.

$A = s^2 = 6^2 = 36 \ ft^2$

The total area is $90 \ ft^2 + 36 \ ft^2 = 126 \ ft^2$.

Visit my.hrw.com to see all the Common Core Standards unpacked.

my.hrw.com

370 Unit 6

© Houghton Mifflin Harcourt Publishing Company

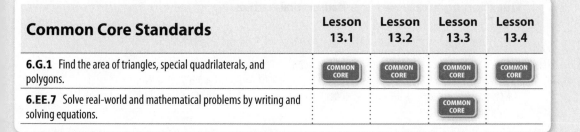

Common Core Standards	Lesson 13.1	Lesson 13.2	Lesson 13.3	Lesson 13.4
6.G.1 Find the area of triangles, special quadrilaterals, and polygons.	COMMON CORE	COMMON CORE	COMMON CORE	COMMON CORE
6.EE.7 Solve real-world and mathematical problems by writing and solving equations.			COMMON CORE	

Common Core Standards

The student is expected to:

 Geometry—6.G.1

Find the area of right triangles, other triangles, special quadrilaterals, and polygons by composing into rectangles or decomposing into triangles and other shapes; apply these techniques in the context of solving real-world and mathematical problems.

Mathematical Practices

 MP.3 Logic

ADDITIONAL EXAMPLE 1

A section of a patio is in the shape of a trapezoid. What is the area of this section of the patio?

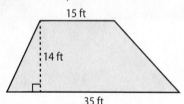

350 square feet

 Interactive Whiteboard
Interactive example available online

 my.hrw.com

 Animated Math
Finding Area Formulas

Students explore area formulas for parallelograms and trapezoids by manipulating interactive figures.

 my.hrw.com

Engage

ESSENTIAL QUESTION

How can you find the areas of parallelograms, rhombuses, and trapezoids? Use the area formulas for each figure. For a parallelogram, use $A = bh$. For a rhombus, use $A = \frac{1}{2}d_1d_2$. For a trapezoid, use $A = \frac{1}{2}h(b_1 + b_2)$. Substitute the known dimensions and solve the equation.

Motivate the Lesson

Ask: Have you ever seen a kite sailing high in the sky and wondered how much material you would need to make a kite that shape? Begin the Explore Activity to find out.

Explore

EXPLORE ACTIVITY

Focus on Math Connections [CC] **Mathematical Practices**

Remind students that a rectangle is a special type of parallelogram that has four 90° angles. Make sure they understand that the area formula for a parallelogram, $A = bh$, also applies to a rectangle. The length and width of a rectangle are its base length and height.

Explain

EXAMPLE 1

Connect Vocabulary [ELL]

Point out to students that in the term b_1, the number 1 is called a subscript. It is read as "b sub-one" or "b-one."

Questioning Strategies [CC] **Mathematical Practices**

• How do you find the height of a trapezoid? The height of a trapezoid is measured along a segment perpendicular to both bases. It is usually shown as a dashed segment with a right angle symbol one end.

• How can you tell that a quadrilateral is a trapezoid rather than a parallelogram? A trapezoid is a quadrilateral with only one pair of parallel sides. A parallelogram has two pairs.

YOUR TURN

Engage with the Whiteboard

Have students sketch and label a trapezoid next to the problem statement on the whiteboard. Then have them write the formula for the area of a trapezoid and substitute the given values for the bases and the height. Have students write out all the steps of their calculation on the whiteboard as a visual check that their answer is correct.

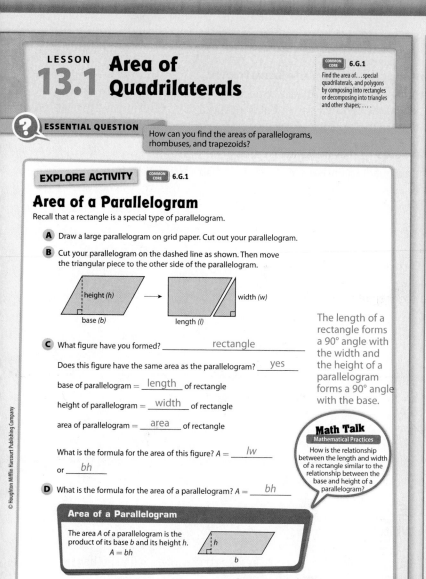

Area of Quadrilaterals

COMMON CORE 6.G.1
Find the area of...special quadrilaterals, and polygons by composing into rectangles or decomposing into triangles and other shapes; ....

ESSENTIAL QUESTION

How can you find the areas of parallelograms, rhombuses, and trapezoids?

EXPLORE ACTIVITY   COMMON CORE 6.G.1

Area of a Parallelogram

Recall that a rectangle is a special type of parallelogram.

A Draw a large parallelogram on grid paper. Cut out your parallelogram.

B Cut your parallelogram on the dashed line as shown. Then move the triangular piece to the other side of the parallelogram.

C What figure have you formed? _____rectangle_____

Does this figure have the same area as the parallelogram? _____yes_____

base of parallelogram = _____length_____ of rectangle

height of parallelogram = _____width_____ of rectangle

area of parallelogram = _____area_____ of rectangle

What is the formula for the area of this figure? $A = $ _____lw_____

or _____bh_____

D What is the formula for the area of a parallelogram? $A = $ _____bh_____

The length of a rectangle forms a 90° angle with the width and the height of a parallelogram forms a 90° angle with the base.

Math Talk
Mathematical Practices

How is the relationship between the length and width of a rectangle similar to the relationship between the base and height of a parallelogram?

Area of a Parallelogram

The area A of a parallelogram is the product of its base b and its height h.

$$A = bh$$

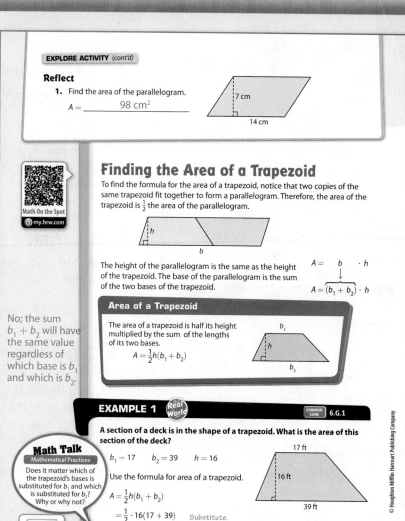

Reflect

1. Find the area of the parallelogram.

$A = $ _____98 cm²_____

7 cm
14 cm

Math On the Spot
my.hrw.com

Finding the Area of a Trapezoid

To find the formula for the area of a trapezoid, notice that two copies of the same trapezoid fit together to form a parallelogram. Therefore, the area of the trapezoid is $\frac{1}{2}$ the area of the parallelogram.

The height of the parallelogram is the same as the height of the trapezoid. The base of the parallelogram is the sum of the two bases of the trapezoid.

$$A = b \cdot h$$
$$\downarrow$$
$$A = (b_1 + b_2) \cdot h$$

No; the sum $b_1 + b_2$ will have the same value regardless of which base is b_1 and which is b_2.

Area of a Trapezoid

The area of a trapezoid is half its height multiplied by the sum of the lengths of its two bases.

$$A = \frac{1}{2}h(b_1 + b_2)$$

EXAMPLE 1 Real World   COMMON CORE 6.G.1

A section of a deck is in the shape of a trapezoid. What is the area of this section of the deck?

$b_1 = 17$ $b_2 = 39$ $h = 16$

Use the formula for area of a trapezoid.

$A = \frac{1}{2}h(b_1 + b_2)$

$= \frac{1}{2} \cdot 16(17 + 39)$ Substitute.

$= \frac{1}{2} \cdot 16(56)$ Add inside the parentheses.

$= 8 \cdot 56$ Multiply $\frac{1}{2}$ and 16.

$= 448$ square feet   Multiply.

17 ft
16 ft
39 ft

Math Talk
Mathematical Practices

Does it matter which of the trapezoid's bases is substituted for b_1 and which is substituted for b_2? Why or why not?

Animated Math
my.hrw.com

PROFESSIONAL DEVELOPMENT

CC Integrate Mathematical Practices MP.3

This lesson provides an opportunity to address this Mathematical Practice standard. It calls for students to display, explain, and justify mathematical ideas and arguments using precise mathematical language in written or oral communication. In this lesson's Explore Activity and Examples, students use symbols, geometric labels, definitions, and consistent and precise language to determine and describe the areas of parallelograms, trapezoids, and rhombuses.

Math Background

The formula for the area of a trapezoid is explained in the lesson by forming a parallelogram with two congruent trapezoids. An alternate method is to use a diagonal of a trapezoid to form two triangles.

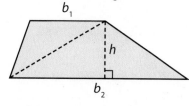

b_1

h

b_2

The area of the trapezoid is the sum of the areas of two triangles that share the same height:

$$A = \frac{1}{2}b_1h + \frac{1}{2}b_2h = \frac{1}{2}h(b_1 + b_2)$$

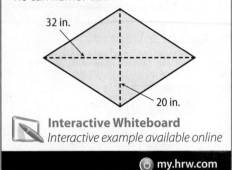
EXAMPLE 2

Focus on Math Connections [CC] Mathematical Practices

Point out to students that a rhombus is actually a special type of parallelogram. Recall that in a parallelogram each pair of opposite sides is equal in length. With a rhombus, all four sides are the same length. It therefore has all the properties of a parallelogram.

Questioning Strategies [CC] Mathematical Practices

• How can you tell that a quadrilateral is a rhombus rather than a trapezoid? In a rhombus, all sides have equal length and opposite sides are parallel. In a trapezoid, the sides do not all have equal length and exactly one pair of sides is parallel.

YOUR TURN

Avoid Common Errors

Remind students that the area of a rhombus is *half* the product of the lengths of its *diagonals*, not its base or height.

Elaborate

Talk About It
Summarize the Lesson

Ask: How are the area of a trapezoid and the area of a parallelogram related? Two copies of the same trapezoid can be fitted together to form a parallelogram that has the same height and whose base length is the sum of the lengths of the bases of the parallelogram. Therefore, the area of a trapezoid is $\frac{1}{2}$ the area of this parallelogram.

GUIDED PRACTICE

Engage with the Whiteboard

For Exercises 1–3, have students identify the parts of each figure by labeling them as height, base₁, base₂, diagonal₁, or diagonal₂, as appropriate for each figure. Then have them fill in the blanks and find the area for each figure.

Avoid Common Errors

Exercise 2 Remind students that the area of a trapezoid is *half* the product of its height and the *sum* of its two bases.

Exercise 3 Remind students that the area of a rhombus is *half* the product of the lengths of its *diagonals*.

2. Another section of the deck is also shaped like a trapezoid. For this section, the length of one base is 27 feet, and the length of the other base is 34 feet. The height is 12 feet. What is the area of this section of the deck? $A = $ _____ 366 _____ ft²

Personal Math Trainer
Online Assessment and Intervention
my.hrw.com

Finding the Area of a Rhombus

A **rhombus** is a quadrilateral in which all sides are congruent and opposite sides are parallel. A rhombus can be divided into four triangles that can then be rearranged into a rectangle.

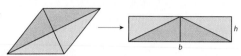

Math On the Spot
my.hrw.com

The base of the rectangle is the same length as one of the diagonals of the rhombus. The height of the rectangle is $\frac{1}{2}$ the length of the other diagonal.

$A = b \cdot h$
$\downarrow \quad \downarrow$
$A = d_1 \cdot \frac{1}{2}d_2$

Area of a Rhombus

The area of a rhombus is half of the product of its two diagonals.

$A = \frac{1}{2}d_1d_2$

EXAMPLE 2 Real World

COMMON CORE 6.G.1

Cedric is constructing a kite in the shape of a rhombus. The spars of the kite measure 15 inches and 24 inches. How much fabric will Cedric need for the kite?

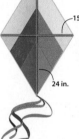
15 in.
24 in.

To determine the amount of fabric needed, find the area of the kite.

$d_1 = 15 \qquad d_2 = 24$

Use the formula for area of a rhombus.

$A = \frac{1}{2}d_1d_2$

$= \frac{1}{2}(15)(24)$ Substitute.

$= 180$ square inches   Multiply.

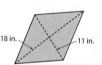
Personal Math Trainer
Online Assessment and Intervention
my.hrw.com

Find the area of each rhombus.

3. $d_1 = 35$ m; $d_2 = 12$ m
$A = $ _____ 210 _____ m²

4. $d_1 = 9.5$ in.; $d_2 = 14$ in.
$A = $ _____ 66.5 _____ in²

5. $d_1 = 10$ m; $d_2 = 18$ m
$A = $ _____ 90 _____ m²

6. $d_1 = 8\frac{1}{4}$ ft; $d_2 = 40$ ft
$A = $ _____ 165 _____ ft²

Guided Practice

1. Find the area of the parallelogram. (Explore Activity)

$A = bh$

$= (\underline{13})(\underline{9})$

$= \underline{117}$ in²

9 in.
13 in.

2. Find the area of the trapezoid. (Example 1)

$A = \frac{1}{2}h(b_1 + b_2)$

$= \frac{1}{2}\left(\boxed{14}\right)\left(\boxed{9} + \boxed{15}\right)$

$= \underline{168}$ cm²

9 cm
14 cm
15 cm

3. Find the area of the rhombus. (Example 2)

$A = \frac{1}{2}d_1d_2$

$= \frac{1}{2}\left(\boxed{18}\right)\left(\boxed{11}\right)$

$= \underline{99}$ in²

18 in.
11 in.

? ESSENTIAL QUESTION CHECK-IN

4. How can you find the areas of parallelograms, rhombuses, and trapezoids?

Sample answer: For a parallelogram, use the formula $A = bh$. For a rhombus, use the formula $A = \frac{1}{2}d_1d_2$. For a trapezoid, use the formula $A = \frac{1}{2}h(b_1 + b_2)$. Substitute the known dimensions and solve the equation.

DIFFERENTIATE INSTRUCTION

Graphic Organizers

Have students construct a three-column table of information about the areas of quadrilaterals. The first column lists names of the figures: parallelogram, trapezoid, and rhombus. The second column has formulas for the areas. The third column shows drawings of the figures with labels for their bases, heights, and diagonals. Students can refer to the lesson to check their work.

World History

The English word *rhombus*, first used in the 1560s, comes from the Latin *rhombus*, derived from *rhombos*, the ancient Greek word meaning "something that spins, a top."

Additional Resources

Differentiated Instruction includes:

- Reading Strategies
- Success for English Learners **ELL**
- Reteach
- Challenge **PRE-AP**

13.1 LESSON QUIZ

COMMON CORE **6.G.1**

1. Find the area of the parallelogram.

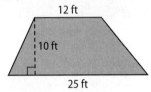

5 cm

10 cm

2. What is the area of a parallelogram that has a base of $4\frac{1}{2}$ in. and a height of $2\frac{1}{4}$ in.?

3. An attic wall is in the shape of a trapezoid. What is the area of the wall?

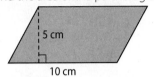

12 ft

10 ft

25 ft

4. The bases of a trapezoid are 24 cm and 32 cm. Its height is 16 cm. What is the area of the trapezoid?

5. Renaldo designs a tabletop in the shape of a rhombus. The tabletop diagonals measure 5 feet and 8 feet. How much wood will Renaldo need for the tabletop?

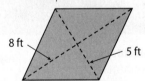

8 ft

5 ft

Lesson Quiz available online

🔵 my.hrw.com

Answers

1. 50 cm²

2. $10\frac{1}{8}$ in²

3. 185 ft²

4. 448 cm²

5. 20 square feet of wood

Evaluate

GUIDED AND INDEPENDENT PRACTICE

COMMON CORE **6.G.1**

Concepts and Skills	Practice
Explore Activity Area of a Parallelogram	Exercises 1, 5–6, 13, 15
Example 1 Finding the Area of a Trapezoid	Exercises 2, 7–8, 11, 14
Example 2 Finding the Area of a Rhombus	Exercises 3, 9–10, 12

Exercise	Depth of Knowledge (D.O.K.)	COMMON CORE Mathematical Practices
5–10	**2** Skills/Concepts	**MP.5** Using Tools
11–13	**2** Skills/Concepts	**MP.4** Modeling
14	**3** Strategic Thinking H.O.T.	**MP.3** Logic
15	**3** Strategic Thinking H.O.T.	**MP.1** Problem Solving
16	**3** Strategic Thinking H.O.T.	**MP.7** Using Structure
17	**3** Strategic Thinking H.O.T.	**MP.3** Logic
18	**3** Strategic Thinking H.O.T.	**MP.4** Modeling

Additional Resources

Differentiated Instruction includes:

• Leveled Practice Worksheets

13.1 Independent Practice

COMMON CORE 6.G.1

5. Find the area of the parallelogram.

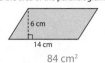

6 cm
14 cm

84 cm²

6. What is the area of a parallelogram that has a base of $12\frac{3}{4}$ in. and a height of $2\frac{1}{2}$ in.?

$31\frac{7}{8}$ in²

7. Find the area of the trapezoid.

42 in.
24 in.
36 in.

936 in²

8. The bases of a trapezoid are 11 meters and 14 meters. Its height is 10 meters. What is the area of the trapezoid?

125 m²

9. Find the area of the rhombus.

16 m
9 m

72 m²

10. The diagonals of a rhombus are 21 m and 32 m. What is the area of the rhombus?

336 m²

11. The seat of a bench is in the shape of a trapezoid with bases of 6 feet and 5 feet and a height of 1.5 feet. What is the area of the seat?

8.25 ft²

12. A kite in the shape of a rhombus has diagonals that are 25 inches long and 15 inches long. What is the area of the kite?

187.5 in²

13. A window in the shape of a parallelogram has a base of 36 inches and a height of 45 inches. What is the area of the window?

1,620 in²

14. Communicate Mathematical Ideas Find the area of the figure. Explain how you found your answer.

10 ft
6 ft
12 ft
18 ft

Area of rectangle = 12 · 18 =
216 ft² Area of trapezoid =
$\frac{1}{2}$ · 6(10 + 18) = 84 ft²
Total area = 216 + 84 = 300 ft²

15. Multistep A parking space shaped like a parallelogram has a base of 17 feet and a height is 9 feet. A car parked in the space is 16 feet long and 6 feet wide. How much of the parking space is not covered by the car?

57 ft²

H.O.T. FOCUS ON HIGHER ORDER THINKING

16. Critique Reasoning Simon says that to find the area of a trapezoid, you can multiply the height by the top base and the height by the bottom base. Then add the two products together and divide the sum by 2. Is Simon correct? Explain your answer.

Yes; Simon uses the Distributive Property to multiply each base by the height. Then he finds the sum. Multiplying by $\frac{1}{2}$ is the same as dividing by 2.

17. Multistep The height of a trapezoid is 8 in. and its area is 96 in.² One base of the trapezoid is 6 inches longer than the other base. What are the lengths of the bases? Explain how you found your answer.

9 in. and 15 in.; use the formula for the area of a trapezoid. Substitute 96 for A and 8 for h and simplify the equation to find $24 = (b_1 + b_2)$. Use guess and check to find two numbers that add to 24 with one number 6 more than the other and get 9 and 15.

18. Multiple Representations The diagonals of a rhombus are 12 in. and 16 in. long. The length of a side of the rhombus is 10 in. What is the height of the rhombus? Explain how you found your answer.

9.6 in.; use the formula $A = \frac{1}{2}d_1d_2$ to find the area of the rhombus, which is 96 in². Since a rhombus is a parallelogram, use the formula for the area of a parallelogram to find the height of the rhombus: $96 = 10(h)$, so $h = 9.6$.

Work Area

EXTEND THE MATH PRE-AP

Activity available online 🕐 my.hrw.com

Activity The area of a trapezoid is 160 square inches. One base of the trapezoid is 8 inches longer than the other base. The sum of the bases is 32 inches. What is the height? What are the lengths of the bases? Explain how you found your answers.

10 in.; 12 in. and 20 in.; Use the formula for the area of a trapezoid. Substitute 160 for A and 32 for $b_1 + b_2$ and simplify the equation to find $h = 10$. Use guess and check to find two numbers ($b_1 + b_2$) that add to 32 with one number 8 more than the other and get 12 and 20.

13.2 Area of Triangles

Common Core Standards

The student is expected to:

 Geometry—6.G.1

Find the area of right triangles, other triangles, special quadrilaterals, and polygons by composing into rectangles or decomposing into triangles and other shapes; apply these techniques in the context of solving real-world and mathematical problems.

Mathematical Practices

 MP.2 Reasoning

ADDITIONAL EXAMPLE 1
Find the area of each triangle.

A

12 m

30 m

180 m²

B

6 in.

14 in.

42 in²

Interactive Whiteboard
Interactive example available online

🔴 my.hrw.com

Engage

ESSENTIAL QUESTION

How do you find the area of a triangle? Use the formula $A = \frac{1}{2}bh$. Substitute the known dimensions into the formula and solve the equation.

Motivate the Lesson
Ask: How can you use what you know about the area of a rectangle to find the area of a right triangle? Begin the Explore Activity to find out.

Explore

EXPLORE ACTIVITY 1

Focus on Modeling [CC] Mathematical Practices

On a piece of graph paper, have students draw a rectangle. Then have them cut along the diagonal to form 2 congruent right triangles. Have them match up the two equal parts. This shows that the diagonal cuts any rectangle into equal right triangles.

Explain

EXPLORE ACTIVITY 2

Focus on Reasoning [CC] Mathematical Practices

Ask students if the formula is true for any triangle. Have them try the activity using use acute triangles and obtuse triangles to see if they get the same results. Show students that the formula works for all triangles regardless of size or shape.

EXAMPLE 1

Connect Vocabulary [ELL]

Stress the use of proper terminology when talking about triangles. A triangle has three angles called vertices. The base can be any one of the three sides. The height of the triangle is the perpendicular distance from a vertex to the opposite side of the triangle.

Questioning Strategies [CC] Mathematical Practices

• How can you tell which dimension is the height? The height is the perpendicular distance from a vertex to the opposite side, called the base of the triangle. On diagrams, a dashed line is often used to represent this segment.

• Why is area expressed in square units? Area is a measure of the space inside a two-dimensional figure. For this reason, area is always measured in square units.

13.2 Area of Triangles

COMMON CORE 6.G.1

Find the area of right triangles, other triangles, ... by composing into rectangles ...

? ESSENTIAL QUESTION

How do you find the area of a triangle?

EXPLORE ACTIVITY 1 **COMMON CORE** 6.G.1

Area of a Right Triangle

A Draw a large rectangle on grid paper.

What is the formula for the area of a rectangle? $A = $ _____ bh _____

B Draw one diagonal of your rectangle.

The diagonal divides the rectangle into _____ two right triangles _____.

Each one represents _____ half _____ of the rectangle.

Use this information and the formula for area of a rectangle to write a formula for the area of a right triangle. $A = $ _____ $\frac{1}{2} bh$ _____

Reflect

1. **Communicate Mathematical Ideas** In the formula for the area of a right triangle, what do b and h represent?

_____ the lengths of the sides that form the right angle _____

EXPLORE ACTIVITY 2 **COMMON CORE** 6.G.1

Area of a Triangle

A Draw a large triangle on grid paper. Do not draw a right triangle.

B Cut out your triangle. Then trace around it to make a copy of your triangle. Cut out the copy.

C Cut one of your triangles into two pieces by cutting through one angle directly across to the opposite side. Now you have three triangles — one large triangle and two smaller right triangles.

Lesson 13.2 **377**

EXPLORE ACTIVITY 2 *(cont'd)*

When added together, the areas of the two smaller triangles equal the _____ area _____ of the large triangle.

D Arrange the three triangles into a rectangle.

What fraction of the rectangle does the large triangle represent? _____ $\frac{1}{2}$ _____

The area of the rectangle is $A = bh$. What is the area of the large triangle? $A = $ _____ $\frac{1}{2} bh$ _____

How does this formula compare to the formula for the area of a right triangle that you found in Explore Activity 1?

_____ They are the same. _____

Reflect

2. **Communicate Mathematical Ideas** What type of angle is formed by the base and height of a triangle?

_____ right angle _____

Finding the Area of a Triangle

Area of a Triangle

The area A of a triangle is half the product of its base b and its height h.

$$A = \frac{1}{2} bh$$

EXAMPLE 1 **COMMON CORE** 6.G.1

Find the area of each triangle.

A

$b = 20$ meters $h = 8$ meters

$A = \frac{1}{2} bh$

$= \frac{1}{2} (20 \text{ meters}) (8 \text{ meters})$ Substitute.

$= 80$ square meters   Multiply.

378 Unit 6

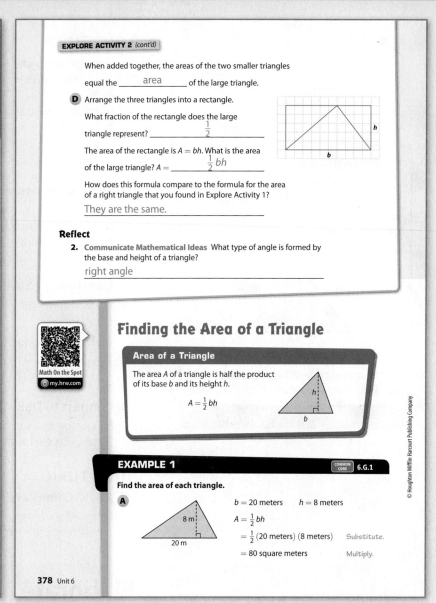

PROFESSIONAL DEVELOPMENT

CC Integrate Mathematical Practices MP.2

This lesson provides an opportunity to address this Mathematical Practice standard. It calls for students to create and use representations to organize, record, and communicate mathematical ideas. In the Explore Activities, students draw and cut out triangles on grid paper to derive area formulas for triangles. In Examples 1 and 2, students use words, symbols, diagrams, and the area formula to represent and calculate the areas of triangles. They then apply the area formula to solve real-world problems.

Math Background

Heron, a mathematician in ancient Alexandria, developed a formula for finding the area of a triangle from the length of its sides. Heron's Formula is

$$A = \sqrt{s(s - a)(s - b)(s - c)}, \text{ where } s = \frac{a + b + c}{2}$$

In the formula, s stands for the semi-perimeter, or one-half the perimeter, of the triangle, and a, b, and c are the lengths of the sides.

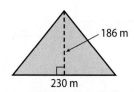

EXAMPLE 2

Focus on Reasoning CC Mathematical Practices

Point out to students that when working with word problems, they need to read the problems carefully to identify all the important information. Encourage students to circle or highlight the important information before trying to substitute the numbers into the formula.

Questioning Strategies CC Mathematical Practices

• How can you tell which dimension is the base? The base is always a side of the triangle. The height must be perpendicular to the base.

• What happens to the area of a triangle when the base is doubled and the height remains the same? Explain. The area doubles. Since $A = \frac{1}{2}bh$, doubling the base would result in the equation $A = \frac{1}{2}(2b)h = bh$, which is twice the original area.

Connect to Daily Life CC Mathematical Practices

Encourage students to share and draw examples of different types of triangles they have come in contact with at home, at school, or elsewhere in the community.

YOUR TURN

Avoid Common Errors

Some students may forget to write the units in their answer. Remind them that their answer is not complete without the units.

Elaborate

Talk About It
Summarize the Lesson

 Ask: How do you find the area of a triangle? Use the formula $A = \frac{1}{2}bh$. Substitute the known dimensions into the formula and solve the equation.

GUIDED PRACTICE

Engage with the Whiteboard

For Exercises 1 or 2, have students double the length of a base or height and then calculate the new areas. Compare and contrast the resulting areas.

Avoid Common Errors

Exercises 1–2 Some students are often tempted to find the area of a triangle by mentally multiplying the base by the height, forgetting to multiply by $\frac{1}{2}$. Encourage them to write the equation before they do any calculations.

Find the area of each triangle.

B

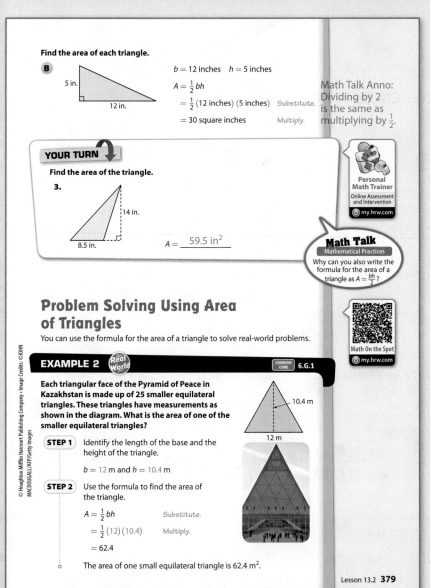

5 in.
12 in.

$b = 12$ inches $\quad h = 5$ inches

$A = \frac{1}{2} bh$

$\quad = \frac{1}{2}(12 \text{ inches})(5 \text{ inches})$ Substitute.

$\quad = 30$ square inches   Multiply.

Math Talk Anno: Dividing by 2 is the same as multiplying by $\frac{1}{2}$.

YOUR TURN

Find the area of the triangle.

3.

14 in.

8.5 in.

$A = \underline{\quad 59.5 \quad} \text{ in}^2$

Personal Math Trainer
Online Assessment and Intervention
my.hrw.com

Math Talk
Mathematical Practices

Why can you also write the formula for the area of a triangle as $A = \frac{bh}{2}$?

Math On the Spot
my.hrw.com

Problem Solving Using Area of Triangles

You can use the formula for the area of a triangle to solve real-world problems.

EXAMPLE 2   Real World

COMMON CORE   6.G.1

Each triangular face of the Pyramid of Peace in Kazakhstan is made up of 25 smaller equilateral triangles. These triangles have measurements as shown in the diagram. What is the area of one of the smaller equilateral triangles?

10.4 m

12 m

STEP 1   Identify the length of the base and the height of the triangle.

$b = 12$ m and $h = 10.4$ m

STEP 2   Use the formula to find the area of the triangle.

$A = \frac{1}{2} bh$ Substitute.

$\quad = \frac{1}{2}(12)(10.4)$ Multiply.

$\quad = 62.4$

The area of one small equilateral triangle is 62.4 m².

Reflect

4. **Persevere in Problem Solving** What is the total area of one face of the pyramid? What is the total surface area of the faces of the pyramid, not counting the bottom? (Hint: the bottom of the pyramid is a square.)

One face of the pyramid has an area of $62.4 \times 25 =$ 1,560 m². All four faces of the pyramid have a total area of $1,560 \times 4 = 6,240$ m².

Personal Math Trainer
Online Assessment and Intervention
my.hrw.com

YOUR TURN

5. Amy needs to order a shade for a triangular-shaped window that has a base of 6 feet and a height of 4 feet. What is the area of the shade?

12 ft²

Guided Practice

Find the area of each triangle. (Explore Activities 1 and 2, Example 1)

1.

8 in.
14 in.

$A = \frac{1}{2} bh$

$\quad = \frac{1}{2}(\underline{\;14\;})(\underline{\;8\;})$

$\quad = \underline{\;56\;} \text{ in}^2$

2. A pennant in the shape of a triangle has a base of 12 inches and a height of 30 inches. What is the area of the pennant? (Example 2)

$A = \frac{1}{2} bh$

$\quad = \frac{1}{2}(\underline{\;12\;})(\underline{\;30\;})$

$\quad = \underline{\;180\;} \text{ in}^2$

GO COYOTES!

? ESSENTIAL QUESTION CHECK-IN

3. How do you find the area of a triangle?

Use the formula $A = \frac{1}{2} bh$. Substitute the known dimensions into the formula and solve the equation.

DIFFERENTIATE INSTRUCTION

Cooperative Learning

Have students work in small groups to draw a triangle whose lengths have whole number measures that fit onto a standard sheet of graph paper. Have students cut out the triangle and use the formula to show that any of the sides can serve as the base. Groups can draw a rectangle around the triangle on another sheet of graph paper to find the height of the triangle for each base.

Critical Thinking

Have students plot the geometric figure with vertices (3, 5), (2, 5), (4, 4), (5, 2), and (−1, 2) on a coordinate plane. Then have them find the area of the figure. They can divide the shape into any combination of rectangles, trapezoids, and triangles to find the area. 9 square units

Additional Resources

Differentiated Instruction includes:

- Reading Strategies
- Success for English Learners **ELL**
- Reteach
- Challenge **PRE-AP**

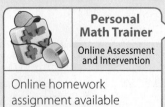

13.2 LESSON QUIZ

 6.G.1

Find the area of each triangle.

1.

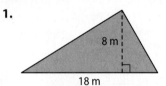

8 m

18 m

2.

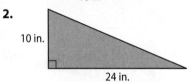

10 in.

24 in.

3.

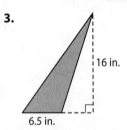

16 in.

6.5 in.

4. The Philadelphia Museum of Art's triangular pediment has the measurements shown in the diagram. What is its area?

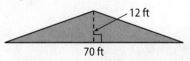

12 ft

70 ft

5. Julia wants to paint a triangular wall in her attic. The wall has a height of 2 m and a base of 4 m. What is the area of the wall?

Lesson Quiz available online

 my.hrw.com

Answers

1. 72 m²

2. 120 in²

3. 52 in²

4. 420 ft²

5. 4 m²

Evaluate

GUIDED AND INDEPENDENT PRACTICE

 COMMON CORE 6.G.1

Concepts and Skills	Practice
Explore Activity 1 Area of a Right Triangle	Exercises 1, 5, 9, 12
Explore Activity 2 Area of a Triangle	Exercise 1
Example 1 Finding the Area of a Triangle	Exercises 1, 4, 6–8
Example 2 Problem Solving Using Area of Triangles	Exercises 2, 10–14

Exercise	Depth of Knowledge (D.O.K.)		**COMMON CORE** Mathematical Practices
4–9	**2** Skills/Concepts		**MP.5** Using Tools
10–12	**2** Skills/Concepts		**MP.4** Modeling
13–15	**3** Strategic Thinking	H.O.T.	**MP.3** Logic
16–17	**3** Strategic Thinking	H.O.T.	**MP.7** Using Structure

Additional Resources

Differentiated Instruction includes:

• Leveled Practice Worksheets

Name _____ Class _____ Date _____

13.2 Independent Practice

COMMON CORE 6.G.1

Personal Math Trainer
Online Assessment and Intervention
my.hrw.com

Find the area of each triangle.

4.

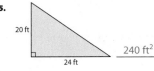
10 cm
15 cm

75 cm²

5.

20 ft
24 ft

240 ft²

6.

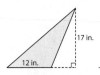
17 in.
12 in.

102 in²

7.

18 ft
32 ft

288 ft²

8. What is the area of a triangle that has a base of $15\frac{1}{4}$ in. and a height of 18 in.?

$137\frac{1}{4}$ in²

9. A right triangle has legs that are 11 in. and 13 in. long. What is the area of the triangle?

71.5 in²

10. A triangular plot of land has the dimensions shown in the diagram. What is the area of the land?

300 km²

20 km
30 km

11. The front part of a tent has the dimensions shown in the diagram. What is the area of this part of the tent?

20 ft²

5 ft
8 ft

12. **Multistep** The sixth-grade art students are making a mosaic using tiles in the shape of right triangles. Each tile has leg measures of 3 centimeters and 5 centimeters. If there are 200 tiles in the mosaic, what is the area of the mosaic?

1,500 cm²

13. **Critique Reasoning** Monica has a triangular piece of fabric. The height of the triangle is 15 inches and the triangle's base is 6 inches. Monica says that the area of the fabric is 90 in². What error did Monica make? Explain your answer.

Monica forgot to multiply by $\frac{1}{2}$.

The area of the fabric is 45 in².

14. **Multistep** Wayne is going to paint the side of the house shown in the diagram. What is the area that will be painted? Explain how you found your answer.

Area of rectangle = 25 · 12 = 300 ft²

Area of triangle = $\frac{1}{2}$(25)(8) = 100 ft²

Total area = 300 + 100 = 400 ft²

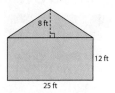
8 ft
12 ft
25 ft

H.O.T. FOCUS ON HIGHER ORDER THINKING

15. **Communicate Mathematical Ideas** Explain how the areas of a triangle and a parallelogram with the same base and height are related.

You can draw a diagonal in the parallelogram, forming two congruent triangles with the same base and height as the parallelogram. So, the area of the triangle is half the area of a parallelogram.

16. **Analyze Relationships** A rectangle and a triangle have the same area. If their bases are the same lengths, how do their heights compare? Justify your answer.

The height of the triangle is twice the height of the rectangle. If both the rectangle and triangle have an area of 20 in² and both have a base of 10 in., the rectangle would have a height of 2 in. since 10 · 2 = 20. The triangle would have a height of 4 in. since $\frac{1}{2}$(10)(4) = 20.

17. **What If?** A right triangle has an area of 18 square inches.

a. If the triangle is an isosceles triangle, what are the lengths of the legs of the triangle?

6 in.

b. If the triangle is not an isosceles triangle, what are all the possible lengths of the legs, if the lengths are whole numbers?

1 in. and 36 in., 2 in. and 18 in., 3 in. and 12 in., 4 in. and 9 in.

Work Area

© Houghton Mifflin Harcourt Publishing Company

EXTEND THE MATH PRE-AP

Activity available online my.hrw.com

Activity Terry calculates how much wood he needs to build the deck shown in the diagram. He says the area is 600 ft². What error did Terry make? Find the correct area and explain your answer.

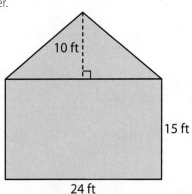
10 ft
15 ft
24 ft

Terry forgot to multiply by $\frac{1}{2}$ to find the area of the triangle.

Area of rectangle = 24 · 15 = 360 ft². Area of triangle = $\frac{1}{2}$ · 24 · 10 = 120 ft². So the total area = 360 + 120 = 480 ft².

13.3 Solving Area Equations

Common Core Standards

The student is expected to:

 Geometry—6.G.1

Find the area of right triangles, other triangles, special quadrilaterals, and polygons by composing into rectangles or decomposing into triangles and other shapes; apply these techniques in the context of solving real-world and mathematical problems. *Also 6.EE.7*

Mathematical Practices

 MP.1 Problem Solving

ADDITIONAL EXAMPLE 1

The Weston highway department built a triangular traffic island on the expressway. The base of the island is 3.5 feet long. It has an area of 17.5 square feet. What is the height of the traffic island? 10 ft

 Interactive Whiteboard
Interactive example available online

 my.hrw.com

ADDITIONAL EXAMPLE 2

A cross section of an attic is shaped like a trapezoid. It has an area of 37.4 square meters. One base is 6.4 meters and the other base is 12.3 meters long. What is the height of the cross section? 4 meters

 Interactive Whiteboard
Interactive example available online

 my.hrw.com

Engage

ESSENTIAL QUESTION

How do you use equations to solve problems about area of rectangles, parallelograms, trapezoids, and triangles? Use the area formula for the figure to write an equation. Solve the equation to find the missing dimension or area of the figure.

Motivate the Lesson

Ask: Have you ever wondered how to figure out how much paint you need to cover a surface? Begin Example 1 to find out.

Explore

Engage with the Whiteboard

Have students sketch and label a rectangle, parallelogram, trapezoid, and triangle on the whiteboard. Then have them write the area formula for each figure. Finally, have them compare and contrast the formulas.

Explain

EXAMPLE 1

Focus on Reasoning CC Mathematical Practices

Encourage students to circle or highlight the important information before trying to substitute the numbers into the formula.

Questioning Strategies CC Mathematical Practices

• Why does the answer have feet when area is measured in square feet? The answer is the height. It is one dimension of the figure so its measure is one-dimensional.

EXAMPLE 2

Focus on Communication

Draw trapezoids on the board. Ask students to point out the bases and heights. Remind students that trapezoids have two parallel and unequal bases.

Questioning Strategies

• Could you have solved this equation differently? Yes, after substituting, I could have multiplied each side by 2 to eliminate the fraction. Then added and divided both sides by 14.8.

YOUR TURN

Avoid Common Errors

If students have difficulty identifying the important information, encourage them to make a sketch to help them identify the dimensions given in the problem.

LESSON
13.3
Solving Area Equations

COMMON CORE 6.G.1
Find the area of right triangles, other triangles, special quadrilaterals, and polygons...; apply these techniques in the context of solving...problems. Also 6.EE.7

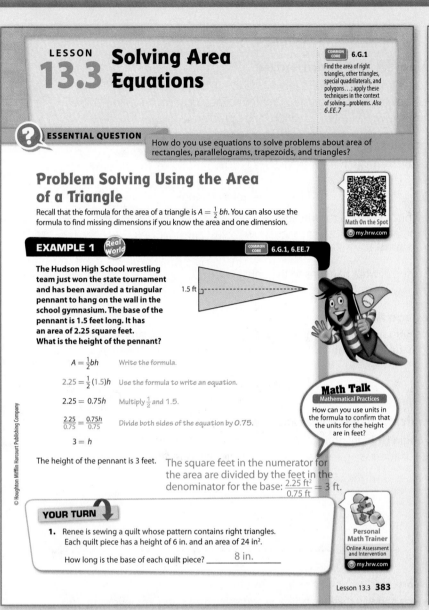

? **ESSENTIAL QUESTION**

How do you use equations to solve problems about area of rectangles, parallelograms, trapezoids, and triangles?

Problem Solving Using the Area of a Triangle

Recall that the formula for the area of a triangle is $A = \frac{1}{2}bh$. You can also use the formula to find missing dimensions if you know the area and one dimension.

EXAMPLE 1 (Real World)

COMMON CORE 6.G.1, 6.EE.7

The Hudson High School wrestling team just won the state tournament and has been awarded a triangular pennant to hang on the wall in the school gymnasium. The base of the pennant is 1.5 feet long. It has an area of 2.25 square feet. What is the height of the pennant?

1.5 ft

$A = \frac{1}{2}bh$ Write the formula.

$2.25 = \frac{1}{2}(1.5)h$ Use the formula to write an equation.

$2.25 = 0.75h$ Multiply $\frac{1}{2}$ and 1.5.

$\frac{2.25}{0.75} = \frac{0.75h}{0.75}$ Divide both sides of the equation by 0.75.

$3 = h$

The height of the pennant is 3 feet.

Math Talk
Mathematical Practices

How can you use units in the formula to confirm that the units for the height are in feet?

The square feet in the numerator for the area are divided by the feet in the denominator for the base: $\frac{2.25 \text{ ft}^2}{0.75 \text{ ft}} = 3 \text{ ft}$.

YOUR TURN

1. Renee is sewing a quilt whose pattern contains right triangles. Each quilt piece has a height of 6 in. and an area of 24 in².

   How long is the base of each quilt piece? _____8 in._____

Personal Math Trainer
Online Assessment and Intervention
my.hrw.com

Math On the Spot
my.hrw.com

Writing Equations Using the Area of a Trapezoid

You can use the formula for area of a trapezoid to write an equation to solve a problem.

EXAMPLE 2 (Real World)

COMMON CORE 6.G.1, 6.EE.7

A garden in the shape of a trapezoid has an area of 44.4 square meters. One base is 4.3 meters long and the other base is 10.5 meters long. The height of the trapezoid is the width of the garden. How wide is the garden?

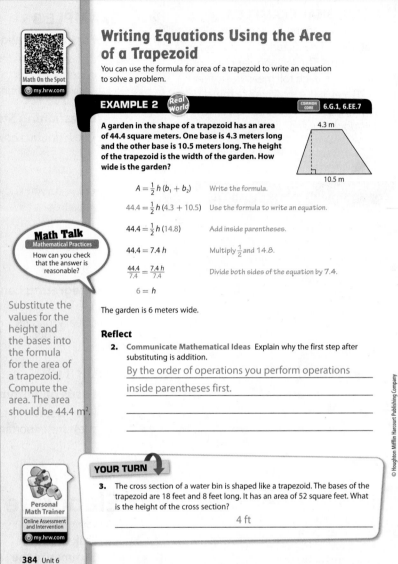

4.3 m

10.5 m

$A = \frac{1}{2}h(b_1 + b_2)$ Write the formula.

$44.4 = \frac{1}{2}h(4.3 + 10.5)$ Use the formula to write an equation.

$44.4 = \frac{1}{2}h(14.8)$ Add inside parentheses.

$44.4 = 7.4h$ Multiply $\frac{1}{2}$ and 14.8.

$\frac{44.4}{7.4} = \frac{7.4h}{7.4}$ Divide both sides of the equation by 7.4.

$6 = h$

The garden is 6 meters wide.

Math Talk
Mathematical Practices

How can you check that the answer is reasonable?

Substitute the values for the height and the bases into the formula for the area of a trapezoid. Compute the area. The area should be 44.4 m².

Reflect

2. **Communicate Mathematical Ideas** Explain why the first step after substituting is addition.

   By the order of operations you perform operations

   inside parentheses first.

   _____

   _____

YOUR TURN

3. The cross section of a water bin is shaped like a trapezoid. The bases of the trapezoid are 18 feet and 8 feet long. It has an area of 52 square feet. What is the height of the cross section?

   4 ft

Personal Math Trainer
Online Assessment and Intervention
my.hrw.com

PROFESSIONAL DEVELOPMENT

CC Integrate Mathematical Practices MP.1

This lesson provides an opportunity to address this Mathematical Practice standard. It calls for students to use a problem-solving model that incorporates analyzing given information, formulating a plan, determining a solution, and evaluating the reasonableness of the solution. Students use a four-step problem-solving model in solving Example 3. Then, in Guided Practice, students apply that model to multistep problems in real-world situations involving the areas of a triangle, a trapezoid, and a rectangle.

Math Background

The four-step problem-solving model derives from the principles presented in *How to Solve It* (1945) by Hungarian mathematician George Pólya. He noticed that students often struggled with math problems because they didn't understand the problem. Thus, he encouraged teachers to ask students questions such as: Do you understand all of the words used in the problem? What are you asked to find or show? Can you make a diagram that might help you understand the problem? Is there enough information to enable you to find a solution?

EXAMPLE 3

Focus on Reasoning CC Mathematical Practices

Discuss with students why analyzing information and formulating a plan are especially important steps to do before solving multistep problems. Encourage students to begin by circling or highlighting the important information in the problem.

Questioning Strategies CC Mathematical Practices

• How do you know which equation to write for Step 1? When the fabric is unrolled, it will be a rectangle measuring 2.5 feet by 15 feet. I need to find how many feet of fabric each roll contains, so I need to use the formula for the area of a rectangle, $A = lw$.

• How do you know which equation to write for Step 2? From Step 1, I know that each roll of fabric has 37.5 ft^2 of fabric. What I need to find now is how many rolls of fabric I need. Since I need 200 ft^2 of fabric for the curtain, I need to divide 200 ft^2 by 37.5 ft^2.

• When you divide in Step 2, what happens to the units? The units cancel out, so all I'm left with is $5\frac{1}{3}$.

Integrating Language Arts ELL

Be sure English learners understand that the rolls of fabric mentioned in Example 3 are actually long rectangular pieces of fabric. You may want to demonstrate by unrolling a roll of paper towels.

YOUR TURN

Focus on Communication CC Mathematical Practices

Remind students to begin by highlighting the important information in the problem. Then stress the importance of addressing each step of the 4-step plan one at a time when solving multistep problems.

Elaborate

Talk About It
Summarize the Lesson

Ask: What steps can you take to approach and solve area problems involving rectangles, trapezoids, parallelograms, and triangles? Analyze the given information and make a plan that includes writing equations for the figure's area. Solve the equation(s) for the area or for the unknown dimension. Check that your results match the question and are reasonable.

GUIDED PRACTICE

Engage with the Whiteboard

For Exercises 1–2, have students circle or highlight the important information in the problem on the whiteboard. Ask them to draw diagrams to model the bandana and desktop, labeling heights and bases. Then have them find the unknown dimension of each figure.

Avoid Common Errors

Exercises 1–3 Encourage students to follow a step-by-step approach—without skipping steps—to avoid confusion and errors when they solve area problems.

Exercise 2 Make sure students remember that the area of a trapezoid is *half* the sum of its bases times the height.

Solving Multistep Problems

You can write and solve equations that represent real-world problems related to relationships in geometry.

Math On the Spot
my.hrw.com

EXAMPLE 3 Problem Solving

COMMON CORE 6.G.1

John and Mary are using rolls of fabric to make a rectangular stage curtain for their class play. The rectangular piece of fabric on each roll measures 2.5 feet by 15 feet. If the area of the curtain is 200 square feet, what is the least number of rolls they need?

Analyze Information

Rewrite the question as a statement.
- Find the least number of rolls of fabric needed to cover an area of 200 ft².

List the important information.
- Each roll of fabric is a 2.5 foot by 15 foot rectangle.
- The area of the curtain is 200 square feet.

Formulate a Plan

Write an equation to find the area of each roll of fabric.

Use the area of the curtain and the area of each roll to write an equation to find the least number of rolls.

Solve

STEP 1 Write an equation to find the area of each roll of fabric.

$A = lw$

$A = 15 \cdot 2.5$

$A = 37.5 \text{ ft}^2$

STEP 2 Write an equation to find the least number of rolls.

$n = 200 \div 37.5$

$n = 5\frac{1}{3}$

STEP 3 The problem asks for the least number of rolls needed. Since 5 rolls will not be enough, they will need 6 rolls to make the curtain.

John and Mary will need 6 rolls of fabric to make the curtain.

Justify and Evaluate

The area of each roll is about 38 ft². Since 38 ft² · 6 = 228 ft², the answer is reasonable.

Personal Math Trainer
Online Assessment and Intervention
my.hrw.com

YOUR TURN

4. A parallelogram-shaped field in a park needs sod. The parallelogram has a base of 21.5 meters and a height of 18 meters. The sod is sold in pallets of 50 square meters. How many pallets of sod are needed to fill the field?

8 pallets

Guided Practice

1. A triangular bandana has an area of 70 square inches. The height of the triangle is $8\frac{3}{4}$ inches. Write and solve an equation to find the length of the base of the triangle. (Example 1)

   $70 = \frac{1}{2}\left(8\frac{3}{4}\right)b$; 16 inches

2. The top of a desk is shaped like a trapezoid. The bases of the trapezoid are 26.5 and 30 centimeters long. The area of the desk is 791 square centimeters. The height of the trapezoid is the width of the desk. Write and solve an equation to find the width of the desk. (Example 2)

   $791 = \frac{1}{2}h(26.5 + 30)$; 28 centimeters

3. Taylor wants to paint his rectangular deck that is 42 feet long and 28 feet wide. A gallon of paint covers about 350 square feet. How many gallons of paint will Taylor need to cover the entire deck? (Example 3)

   Write an equation to find the ___area___ of the deck.

   Write and solve the equation.

   $A = 42(28) = 1,176 \text{ ft}^2$

   Write an equation to find the ___number of gallons of paint___.

   Write and solve the equation.

   $n = 1,176 \div 350 = 3.36$

   Taylor will need ___4___ gallons of paint.

? ESSENTIAL QUESTION CHECK-IN

4. How do you use equations to solve problems about area of rectangles, parallelograms, trapezoids, and triangles?

   Use the formula for the area of the figure to write an equation. Then solve the equation to find the missing dimension or the area of the figure.

DIFFERENTIATE INSTRUCTION

Critical Thinking

Remind students that not all quadrilaterals are parallelograms. For example, a rectangle, a square, and a rhombus are parallelograms, but a trapezoid is not.

The formula for finding the area of a parallelogram will work for any of the special parallelograms: square, rectangle, and rhombus. However, the formula does not work for the trapezoid.

Auditory Cues

Students who have difficulty visualizing how the area formulas work may benefit from discussing them. Ask leading questions such as "How can you find the height?" and "Which segment is the base?" when you are presenting the area formulas so that students can express their reasoning aloud to one another.

Additional Resources

Differentiated Instruction includes:
- Reading Strategies
- Success for English Learners **ELL**
- Reteach
- Challenge **PRE-AP**

13.3 LESSON QUIZ

6.G.1

1. A ship's triangular signal flag has a base of 8 inches and an area of 64 square inches. What is the height of the signal flag?

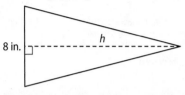

2. A section in a stained glass window is shaped like a right triangle. The section has a height of 7.5 cm. If the area of the section of glass is 17.25 cm², how long is the base of the section?

3. A park is shaped like a trapezoid. It has an area of 7.2 square miles. One base is 1.2 miles, and the other base is 2.4 miles long. What is the height of the trapezoid?

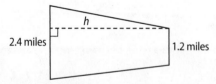

4. Mel and Kenneth want to refinish the community center gym floor. The rectangular floor is 15.2 m wide and 25.6 m long. If each gallon of polyurethane covers about 180 square meters, how many gallons should Mel and Kenneth buy?

Lesson Quiz available online

 my.hrw.com

Answers

1. 16 in.

2. 4.6 cm

3. 4 mi

4. 3 gal

387 Lesson 13.3

Evaluate

GUIDED AND INDEPENDENT PRACTICE

6.G.1, 6.EE.7

Concepts and Skills	Practice
Example 1 Problem Solving Using the Area of a Triangle	Exercises 1, 6, 9, 11–12
Example 2 Writing Equations Using the Area of a Trapezoid	Exercises 2, 7, 12, 14
Example 3 Solving Multistep Problems	Exercises 3, 5, 8, 10–12

Exercise	Depth of Knowledge (D.O.K.)	COMMON CORE Mathematical Practices
5–8	**2** Skills/Concepts	**MP.4** Modeling
9–13	**2** Skills/Concepts	**MP.7** Using Structure
14	**3** Strategic Thinking H.O.T.	**MP.3** Logic
15	**3** Strategic Thinking H.O.T.	**MP.7** Using Structure
16	**3** Strategic Thinking H.O.T.	**MP.1** Problem Solving

Additional Resources

Differentiate Instruction includes:

• Leveled Practice Worksheets

YOUR TURN

Find the area of each polygon.

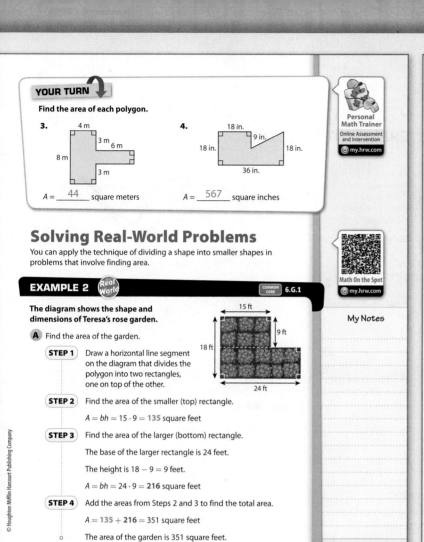

3.

4 m
3 m
6 m
8 m
3 m

$A =$ ___44___ square meters

4.

18 in.
9 in.
18 in.
18 in.
36 in.

$A =$ ___567___ square inches

Solving Real-World Problems

You can apply the technique of dividing a shape into smaller shapes in problems that involve finding area.

EXAMPLE 2 *Real World*   COMMON CORE **6.G.1**

The diagram shows the shape and dimensions of Teresa's rose garden.

15 ft
9 ft
18 ft
24 ft

A Find the area of the garden.

STEP 1 Draw a horizontal line segment on the diagram that divides the polygon into two rectangles, one on top of the other.

STEP 2 Find the area of the smaller (top) rectangle.

$A = bh = 15 \cdot 9 = 135$ square feet

STEP 3 Find the area of the larger (bottom) rectangle.

The base of the larger rectangle is 24 feet.

The height is $18 - 9 = 9$ feet.

$A = bh = 24 \cdot 9 = 216$ square feet

STEP 4 Add the areas from Steps 2 and 3 to find the total area.

$A = 135 + 216 = 351$ square feet

The area of the garden is 351 square feet.

B Teresa wants to buy mulch for her garden. One bag of mulch covers 12 square feet. How many bags will she need?

$\frac{351 \text{ square feet}}{12 \text{ square feet}} = 29.25$ *Divide to find the number of bags needed.*

Teresa will need to buy 30 bags of mulch.

Personal Math Trainer — Online Assessment and Intervention — my.hrw.com

Math On the Spot — my.hrw.com

My Notes

Lesson 13.4 **391**

Personal Math Trainer — Online Assessment and Intervention — my.hrw.com

YOUR TURN

5. The diagram shows the floor plan of a hotel lobby. Carpet costs $3 per square foot. How much will it cost to carpet the lobby?

$3,348

30 ft
15.5 ft
42 ft
15.5 ft
30 ft

Guided Practice

1. In the diagram, the area of the large square is 1 square unit. Two diagonal segments divide the square into four equal-sized triangles. Two of these triangles are divided into smaller red and blue triangles that all have the same height and base length. Find the area of a red triangle. (Explore Activity)

_____ $\frac{1}{8}$ square unit _____

Find the area of each polygon. (Example 1)

2.

4 ft
10 ft
14 ft
18 ft

$A =$ ___112___ square feet

3.

16 m
10 m
8 m
20 m

$A =$ ___196___ square meters

4. Jess is painting a giant arrow on a playground. Find the area of the giant arrow. If one can of paint covers 100 square feet, how many cans should Jess buy? (Example 2)

___240 square feet; 3 cans of paint___

5 ft
18 ft
24 ft
10 ft
5 ft

? ESSENTIAL QUESTION CHECK-IN

5. How can you find the area of a polygon that is not one for which you know an area formula?

Sample answer: You can break the large polygon into shapes such as rectangles and triangles, and then find the area of each of the smaller shapes using an area formula. Add the areas to find the area of the polygon.

392 Unit 6

DIFFERENTIATE INSTRUCTION

Cooperative Learning

Have students work in pairs to find areas of composite figures. Each student draws a figure on a sheet of graph paper. Students trade figures with their partners; divide the figures into squares, rectangles, triangles, parallelograms, and trapezoids; find the areas of the individual figures; and find the total area of each composite figure.

Critical Thinking

Divide students into groups, and ask them to draw a composite figure that could be solved using subtraction rather than addition. When complete, have the groups present their figures and a solution to the class.

For example, in the figure below, you would subtract the area of the triangle from the area of the rectangle.

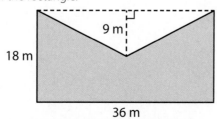

9 m
18 m
36 m

Additional Resources

Differentiated Instruction includes:

- Reading Strategies
- Success for English Learners **ELL**
- Reteach
- Challenge **PRE-AP**

Area of Polygons **392**

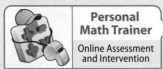
13.4 LESSON QUIZ

 6.G.1

1. What is the area of the polygon?

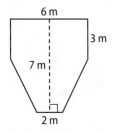

6 m
3 m
7 m
2 m

2. The diagram shows the shape of Jane's backyard. Find the area of Jane's backyard.

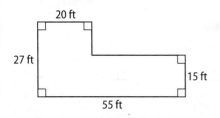

20 ft
27 ft
15 ft
55 ft

3. Jane wants to plant grass seed in her yard. If it costs $0.75 per square foot for grass seed, how much will Jane spend?

Lesson Quiz example available online

⏱ my.hrw.com

Answers

1. 34 m²

2. 1,065 ft²

3. $798.75

Evaluate

GUIDED AND INDEPENDENT PRACTICE

 6.G.1

Concepts & Skills	Practice
Explore Activity Finding Areas Using Tangrams	Exercise 1
Example 1 Finding Areas of Polygons	Exercises 2–3
Example 2 Solving Real-World Problems	Exercises 4, 6–9

Exercise	Depth of Knowledge (D.O.K.)	Mathematical Practices
6–8	**2** Skills/Concepts	**MP.4** Modeling
9–10	**3** Strategic Thinking **H.O.T.**	**MP.2** Reasoning
11	**4** Extended Thinking **H.O.T.**	**MP.2** Reasoning

Additional Resources

Differentiated Instruction includes:

• Leveled Practice worksheets

CC **CLUSTER CONNECTION**

Exercise 10 combines concepts from the Common Core cluster "Solve real-world and mathematical problems involving area, surface area, and volume."

13.4 Independent Practice

COMMON CORE 6.G.1

Personal Math Trainer

Online Assessment and Intervention

my.hrw.com

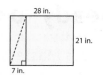

6. Alice wants to put wall-to-wall carpeting in a small room with the floor plan shown.

a. Alice says she can find the area of the room by dividing the floor plan into two trapezoids. Show how she can divide the floor plan into two trapezoids. Then find the area using her method.

$\frac{1}{2} \times (7.5 + 15)(5) + \frac{1}{2} \times (10 + 5)(7.5) = 112.5$ square feet

b. Describe another way to find the area.

Sample answer: Divide the floor plan into two rectangles: $5 \times 15 + 7.5 \times 5 = 112.5$ square feet

c. How much will Alice pay for carpet that costs $4.50 per square foot?

$506.25

7. Hal's backyard has a patio, a walkway, and a garden.

a. About what percent of the total area of Hal's backyard is the area taken up by the patio, walkway, and garden? Round to the nearest whole percent.

about 60%

b. One longer side of Hal's backyard lies next to the back of his house. Hal wants to build a fence that costs $9.75 per foot around the other three sides. How much will Hal spend on his new fence?

$321.75

8. The students in a furniture-making class make a tabletop shaped like the figure shown.

a. What is the area of the tabletop?

26 square feet

b. One of the students wants to make a tabletop shaped like a right triangle. This tabletop will have the same area as the tabletop shown. What are a set of possible lengths for the sides of the tabletop that meet in a right angle? Explain.

Sample answer: 13 feet and 4 feet; the sides that meet at a right angle are the height and base of the triangle; $A = \frac{1}{2} \times 13 \times 4 = 26$ square feet.

9. **Multistep** Cho is making banners shaped like triangles out of a rectangular piece of fabric. She cuts out two triangular banners as shown.

a. What is the area of a triangular banner?

73.5 square inches

b. What are the dimensions of the fabric left over after Cho cuts out the two banners?

21 inches by 21 inches

c. What is the maximum number of banners that Cho can cut out from the fabric? Will she use all the fabric?

8 banners; yes

H.O.T. FOCUS ON HIGHER ORDER THINKING

Work Area

10. **Persevere in Problem Solving** The base of a parallelogram is 8 units, and the height is 5 units. A segment divides the parallelogram into two identical trapezoids. The height of each trapezoid is 5 units. Draw the parallelogram and the two trapezoids on the grid shown. Then find the area of one of the trapezoids.

Sample answer shown.

20 square units

11. **Persevere in Problem Solving** The figure shown is a square with a triangular hole cut into one side. The ratio of the height h of the triangle to a side length of the square is 7 to 8. The ratio of the base b of the triangle to the side length of the square is 1 to 2. If the area of the square is 64 square inches, what is the area of the shaded part of the square? Show your work.

50 square inches; since the square's area is 64 square inches, its side length must be 8 inches: $8 \cdot 8 = 64$. So, the height of the triangle is 7 inches because the ratio h to the side length of the square is 7 : 8. The base of the triangle is 4 inches because 4 to 8 is equivalent to 1 to 2. The area of the shaded part $= 64 - \left(\frac{1}{2} \cdot 4 \cdot 7\right) = 50$ in².

EXTEND THE MATH PRE-AP

Activity available online my.hrw.com

Activity Have students solve this problem.

Brian cut a rectangle out of cardboard. The ratio of the length to the width was 4 : 3. Then Brian cut a square with side lengths of 3 centimeters from the corner of the rectangle. He removed the cardboard square and found that the area of the remaining figure was 99 square centimeters. What were the dimensions of the original rectangle?

12 cm by 9 cm

Ready to Go On?

Assess Mastery

Use the assessment on this page to determine if students have mastered the concepts and standards covered in this module.

  **Response to Intervention**

Intervention	Enrichment
Access Ready to Go On? assessment online, and receive instant scoring, feedback, and customized intervention or enrichment.	

Personal Math Trainer
Online Assessment and Intervention
my.hrw.com

Online and Print Resources

Differentiated Instruction
- Reteach worksheets
- Reading Strategies **ELL**
- Success for English Learners **ELL**

Differentiated Instruction
- Challenge worksheets **PRE-AP**
- Extend the Math **PRE-AP** Lesson Activities in TE

Additional Resources

Assessment Resources includes:
- Leveled Module Quizzes

Ready to Go On?

Personal Math Trainer
Online Assessment and Intervention
my.hrw.com

13.1 Area of Quadrilaterals

1. Find the area of the figure.

$\underline{\hspace{2cm} 215 \text{ yd}^2 \hspace{2cm}}$

$12\frac{1}{2}$ yd
$17\frac{1}{5}$ yd

13.2 Area of Triangles

2. Find the area of the triangle.

$\underline{\hspace{2cm} 119 \text{ ft}^2 \hspace{2cm}}$

14 ft
17 ft

13.3 Solving Area Equations

3. A triangular pane of glass has a height of 30 inches and an area of 270 square inches. What is the length of the base of the pane?

$\underline{\hspace{2cm} 18 \text{ inches} \hspace{2cm}}$

4. A tabletop in the shape of a trapezoid has an area of 6,550 square centimeters. Its longer base measures 115 centimeters, and the shorter base is 85 centimeters. What is the height?

$\underline{\hspace{2cm} 65.5 \text{ centimeters} \hspace{2cm}}$

13.4 Area of Polygons

5. Find the area of the polygon.

$\underline{\hspace{1cm} 45 \hspace{1cm}}$ square centimeters

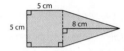
5 cm
5 cm
8 cm

? **ESSENTIAL QUESTION**

6. How can you find the area of an irregular polygon using area formulas?

Sample answer: First, break the irregular polygon into shapes whose areas you can find using familiar formulas. The sum of these areas is the area of the polygon.

© Houghton Mifflin Harcourt Publishing Company

Common Core Standards

Lesson	Exercises	Common Core Standards
13.1	1	**6.G.1**
13.2	2	**6.G.1**
13.3	3–4	**6.G.1, 6.EE.7**
13.4	5	**6.G.1**

Assessment Readiness

Assessment Readiness Tip Some items are called context-based items, which means the student has to examine each answer choice in order to determine the correct answer.

Item 4 Students need to look at each choice to find the equation that has the given information used correctly. Area of a trapezoid = $\frac{1}{2}h(b_1 + b_2)$, so given $b_1 = 63$, $b_2 = 27$, and $A = 1{,}575$, students should recognize that choice A, $45h = 1{,}575$, is the correct answer.

Avoid Common Errors

Item 1 Some students are often tempted to find the area of a rhombus by simply multiplying the lengths of the diagonals. Remind them that the equation for the area of a rhombus is $A = \frac{1}{2}d_1 d_2$, so they need to multiply the product of the diagonals by one-half.

Item 2 Some students will see the phrase "the value of h is $\frac{3}{4}$" and automatically substitute $\frac{3}{4}$ for h in the equation $A = \frac{1}{2}bh$. Remind them that they need to read the problem carefully to see that "the value of h is $\frac{3}{4}$ times the side length that is labeled on the figure" (4.8 mm) or 3.6 mm.

Additional Resources

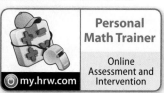

Personal Math Trainer

Online Assessment and Intervention

my.hrw.com

Selected Response

1. The lengths of the diagonals of the rhombus are given. What is the area of the rhombus?

23 in.

28 in.

- Ⓐ $161\ \text{in}^2$
- Ⓑ $322\ \text{in}^2$
- Ⓒ $644\ \text{in}^2$
- Ⓓ $966\ \text{in}^2$

2. In the triangle below, the value of h is $\frac{3}{4}$ the side length that is labeled on the figure. What is the area of the triangle?

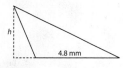

h

4.8 mm

- Ⓐ $3.6\ \text{mm}^2$
- Ⓑ $6.4\ \text{mm}^2$
- Ⓒ $8.64\ \text{mm}^2$
- Ⓓ $17.28\ \text{mm}^2$

3. Tim is designing a logo. The logo is a polygon whose shape is a square attached to an equilateral triangle. The square and the equilateral triangle have side lengths of 2 centimeters, and the equilateral triangle has a height of about 1.7 cm. Find the area of the logo.

- Ⓐ $1.7\ \text{cm}^2$
- Ⓑ $4\ \text{cm}^2$
- Ⓒ $5.7\ \text{cm}^2$
- Ⓓ $7.4\ \text{cm}^2$

4. The trapezoid below has an area of $1{,}575\ \text{cm}^2$.

63 cm

27 cm

Which equation could you solve to find the height of the trapezoid?

- Ⓐ $45h = 1{,}575$
- Ⓑ $90h = 1{,}575$
- Ⓒ $850.5h = 1{,}575$
- Ⓓ $1{,}701h = 1{,}575$

Mini-Task

5. Cindy is designing a rectangular fountain in the middle of a courtyard. The rest of the courtyard will be covered in stone.

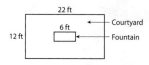

22 ft

6 ft ← Courtyard

12 ft ← Fountain

The part of the courtyard that will be covered in stone has an area of 246 square feet.

a. What is the width of the fountain?

3 feet

b. What fraction of the area of the courtyard will be occupied by the fountain?

$\frac{3}{44}$

Common Core Standards

Items	Grade 6 Standards	Mathematical Practices
1	6.G.1	MP.2
2*	6.G.1, 6.EE.7, 6.NS.3	MP.2
3*	6.G.1, 6.EE.7, 6.NS.3	MP.4
4	6.G.1	MP.7
5	6.G.1, 6.EE.7	MP.4

* Item integrates mixed review concepts from previous modules or a previous course.

Distance and Area in the Coordinate Plane

 ESSENTIAL QUESTION

What steps might you take to solve a polygon problem given the coordinates of its vertices?

Plot the polygon on a grid using its vertices, and use absolute value to find the lengths of the sides; these lengths can be substituted into area formulas.

LESSON 14.1
Distance in the Coordinate Plane
COMMON CORE 6.NS.6b, 6.NS.8

LESSON 14.2
Polygons in the Coordinate Plane
COMMON CORE 6.G.3

Real-World Video

Many cities are designed on a grid. You can use the lengths of blocks to calculate perimeters and areas just like on a coordinate plane.

 my.hrw.com

© Houghton Mifflin Harcourt Publishing Company • Image Credits: © Balefire/Shutterstock.com

GO DIGITAL
my.hrw.com

my.hrw.com	**Math On the Spot**	**Animated Math**	**Personal Math Trainer**
Go digital with your write-in student edition, accessible on any device.	Scan with your smart phone to jump directly to the online edition, video tutor, and more.	Interactively explore key concepts to see how math works.	Get immediate feedback and help as you work through practice sets.

Are You Ready?

Assess Readiness

Use the assessment on this page to determine if students need intensive or strategic intervention for the module's prerequisite skills.

Response to Intervention

Intervention	Enrichment

Access Are You Ready? assessment online, and receive instant scoring, feedback, and customized intervention or enrichment.

Personal Math Trainer

Online Assessment and Intervention

my.hrw.com

Online and Print Resources

Skills Intervention worksheets
- Skill 69 Graph Ordered Pairs
- Skill 76 Identify Polygons

Differentiated Instruction
- Challenge worksheets **PRE-AP**
- Extend the Math **PRE-AP** Lesson Activities in TE

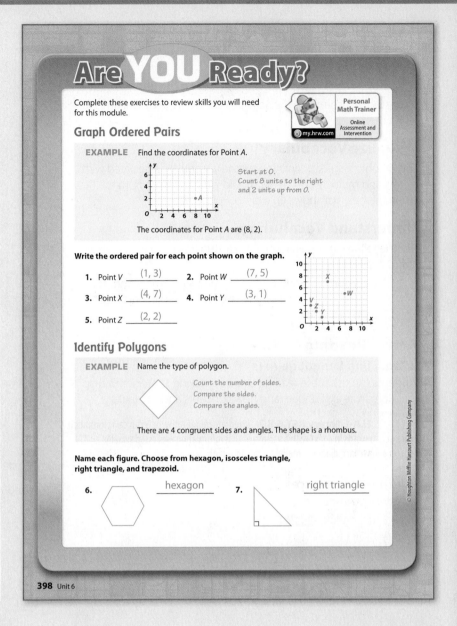

Are YOU Ready?

Complete these exercises to review skills you will need for this module.

Personal Math Trainer
Online Assessment and Intervention
my.hrw.com

Graph Ordered Pairs

EXAMPLE Find the coordinates for Point A.

Start at O.
Count 8 units to the right and 2 units up from O.

The coordinates for Point A are (8, 2).

Write the ordered pair for each point shown on the graph.

1. Point V __(1, 3)__
2. Point W __(7, 5)__
3. Point X __(4, 7)__
4. Point Y __(3, 1)__
5. Point Z __(2, 2)__

Identify Polygons

EXAMPLE Name the type of polygon.

Count the number of sides.
Compare the sides.
Compare the angles.

There are 4 congruent sides and angles. The shape is a rhombus.

Name each figure. Choose from hexagon, isosceles triangle, right triangle, and trapezoid.

6. __hexagon__
7. __right triangle__

PROFESSIONAL DEVELOPMENT VIDEO

Author Juli Dixon models successful teaching practices as she explores finding distance in the coordinate plane in an actual sixth-grade classroom.

Professional Development

my.hrw.com

GO DIGITAL
my.hrw.com

Online Teacher Edition
Access a full suite of teaching resources online—plan, present, and manage classes and assignments.

ePlanner
Easily plan your classes and access all your resources online.

Interactive Answers and Solutions
Customize answer keys to print or display in the classroom. Choose to include answers only or full solutions to all lesson exercises.

Interactive Whiteboards
Engage students with interactive whiteboard-ready lessons and activities.

Personal Math Trainer: Online Assessment and Intervention
Assign automatically graded homework, quizzes, tests, and intervention activities. Prepare your students with updated practice tests aligned with Common Core.

Reading Start-Up

Have students complete the activities on this page by working alone or with others.

Visualize Vocabulary

This graphic helps students review the vocabulary associated with factors and multiples. Students should write the word from the Review List in the box that shows an example of the word.

Understand Vocabulary

Use the following explanation to help students learn the preview words.

> A **polygon** is formed by line segments that meet only at their endpoints. The point where two line segments meet is called a **vertex.**

Active Reading

Integrating Language Arts

Students can use these reading and note-taking strategies to help them organize and understand new concepts and vocabulary.

COMMON CORE **ELA-Literacy.RST.6-8.7** Integrate quantitative or technical information expressed in words in a text with a version of that information expressed visually (e.g., in a flowchart, diagram, model, graph, or table).

Additional Resources

Differentiated Instruction

- Reading Strategies **ELL**

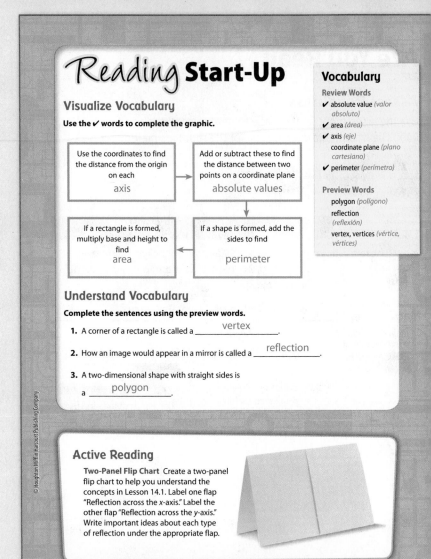

Before	In this module	After
Students understand that distance between two points can be measured on a coordinate plane: • find and position ordered pairs of integers and other rational numbers on a coordinate plane • classify polygons	Students will learn how to: • use absolute value to find distances between points in the coordinate plane • solve problems that involve drawing polygons in the coordinate plane and finding the length of a side	Students will connect distance on the coordinate plane to scale drawings: • solve problems involving scale drawings of geometric figures including computing actual lengths

Unpacking the Standards

Use the examples on the page to help students know exactly what they are expected to learn in this module.

Common Core Standards

Content Areas

 6.NS

Apply and extend previous understandings of numbers to the system of rational numbers.

 6.G

Solve real-world and mathematical problems involving area, surface area, and volume.

Go online to see a complete unpacking of the Common Core Standards.

⏻ my.hrw.com

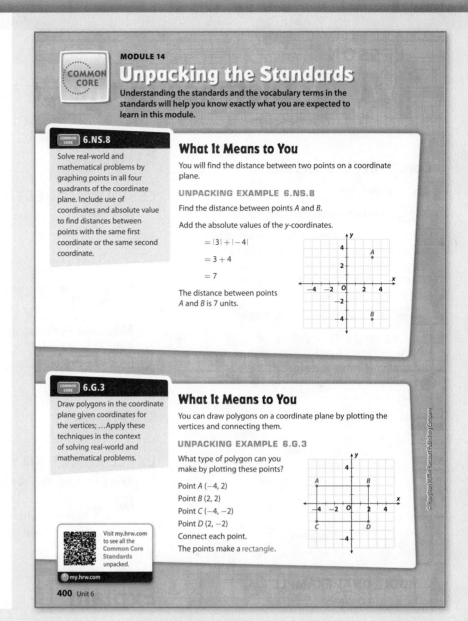

MODULE 14

Unpacking the Standards

Understanding the standards and the vocabulary terms in the standards will help you know exactly what you are expected to learn in this module.

COMMON CORE 6.NS.8

Solve real-world and mathematical problems by graphing points in all four quadrants of the coordinate plane. Include use of coordinates and absolute value to find distances between points with the same first coordinate or the same second coordinate.

What It Means to You

You will find the distance between two points on a coordinate plane.

UNPACKING EXAMPLE 6.NS.8

Find the distance between points A and B.

Add the absolute values of the y-coordinates.

$$= |3| + |-4|$$
$$= 3 + 4$$
$$= 7$$

The distance between points A and B is 7 units.

COMMON CORE 6.G.3

Draw polygons in the coordinate plane given coordinates for the vertices; …Apply these techniques in the context of solving real-world and mathematical problems.

Visit my.hrw.com to see all the Common Core Standards unpacked.

⏻ my.hrw.com

What It Means to You

You can draw polygons on a coordinate plane by plotting the vertices and connecting them.

UNPACKING EXAMPLE 6.G.3

What type of polygon can you make by plotting these points?

Point A (−4, 2)
Point B (2, 2)
Point C (−4, −2)
Point D (2, −2)
Connect each point.
The points make a rectangle.

Common Core Standards	Lesson 14.1	Lesson 14.2
6.NS.6b Understand signs of numbers in ordered pairs as indicating locations in quadrants of the coordinate plane; recognize that when two ordered pairs differ only by signs, the locations of the points are related by reflections across one or both axes.	COMMON CORE	
6.NS.8 Solve real-world and mathematical problems by graphing points in all four quadrants of the coordinate plane. Include use of coordinates and absolute value to find distances between points with the same first coordinate or the same second coordinate.	COMMON CORE	
6.G.3 Draw polygons in the coordinate plane given coordinates for the vertices; use coordinates to find the length of a side joining points with the same first coordinate or same second coordinate. Apply these techniques in the context of solving real-world and mathematical problems.		COMMON CORE

Common Core Standards

The student is expected to:

 The Number System—6.NS.8

Solve real-world and mathematical problems by graphing points in all four quadrants of the coordinate plane. Include use of coordinates and absolute value to find distances between points with the same first coordinate or the same second coordinate.

 The Number System—6.NS.6b

Understand signs of numbers in ordered pairs as indicating locations in quadrants of the coordinate plane; recognize that when two ordered pairs differ only by signs, the locations of the points are related by reflections across one or both axes.

Mathematical Practices

 MP.3 Logic

ADDITIONAL EXAMPLE 1
Find each distance.

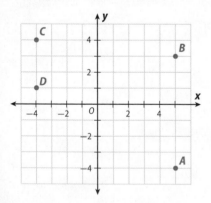

A What is the distance between point A and point B? 7 units

B What is the distance between point C and point D? 3 units

 Interactive Whiteboard
Interactive example available online

 my.hrw.com

Engage

ESSENTIAL QUESTION

How can you use absolute value to find the distance between two points with the same x- or y-coordinates? To find the distance between two points that have the same x-coordinates, find the distance between the y-coordinates. If the y-coordinates have the same sign, find the difference of their absolute values. If the y-coordinates have different signs, find the sum of their absolute values. Use the same process to find the distance between two points that have the same y-coordinates by finding the distance between the x-coordinates.

Motivate the Lesson

Ask: What is a reflection? How can you reflect a point across an axis on a coordinate plane? Begin the Explore Activity to find out.

Explore

EXPLORE ACTIVITY

Engage with the Whiteboard

Review how to locate and graph ordered pairs on a coordinate plane. Then have students locate and graph points on a coordinate plane. Then have students find the distance between pairs of points by counting the grid spaces between them.

Explain

EXAMPLE 1

Connect Vocabulary ELL

Remind students that the absolute value of a number is its distance from 0 on the number line. Relate the x- and y-axes to number lines, and show students how to find the distance from a point to the x-axis. Finally, remind students that the absolute value of a number can never be negative as it is a measure of distance.

Questioning Strategies CC Mathematical Practices

• If the x-coordinates of two points are the same, how do you know whether to add or subtract the absolute values of the y-coordinates to find the distance between the two points? Sample answer: If the y-coordinates have the same sign, you find the difference between the absolute values. If the y-coordinates have different signs, you find the sum of the absolute values.

YOUR TURN

Avoid Common Errors

If students have difficulty getting started, encourage them to graph each pair of points on a coordinate plane before trying to find the distance.

Distance in the Coordinate Plane

COMMON CORE 6.NS.8

Solve...problems by graphing points....Include use of coordinates and absolute value to find distances between points... Also 6.NS.6b

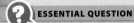

? **ESSENTIAL QUESTION** How can you use absolute value to find the distance between two points with the same *x*- or *y*-coordinates?

EXPLORE ACTIVITY 1 COMMON CORE 6.NS.6b

Reflecting in the Coordinate Plane

A point on a coordinate plane can be *reflected* across an axis. The **reflection** is located on the opposite side of the axis, at the same distance from the axis.

> Hold your paper up to the light if necessary to see the reflection.

Draw a coordinate plane on graph paper. Label both axes from −10 to 10.

A Graph (3, −2). Then fold your coordinate plane along the *y*-axis and find the reflection of (3, −2). Record the coordinates of the new point in the table.

B Unfold your coordinate plane. Then fold it along the *x*-axis and find the reflection of (3, −2). Record the coordinates of the new point in the table.

C Choose three additional points and repeat **A** and **B**.
Sample answers given.

Point	Reflected across *y*-axis	Reflected across *x*-axis
(3, −2)	(−3, −2)	(3, 2)
(3, 5)	(−3, 5)	(3, −5)
(−2, 6)	(2, 6)	(−2, −6)
(−3, 8)	(3, 8)	(−3, −8)

Reflect

1. What is the relationship between the coordinates of a point and the coordinates of its reflection across each axis?

    across *y*-axis: opposite *x*-coordinate and same *y*-coordinate as the original point; across *x*-axis: same *x*-coordinate and opposite *y*-coordinate as the original point

2. **Conjecture** A point is reflected across the *y*-axis. Then the reflected point is reflected across the *x*-axis. How will the coordinates of the final point be related to the coordinates of the original point?

    Both coordinates will be the opposites of the coordinates of the original point.

Math On the Spot
my.hrw.com

Finding Distances in the Coordinate Plane

You can also use absolute values to find distances between two points that have the same *x*-coordinates or the same *y*-coordinates on a coordinate plane.

EXAMPLE 1 COMMON CORE 6.NS.6b

Find each distance.

A What is the distance between point *A* and point *B*?

STEP 1 Find the distance between point *A* and the *x*-axis.

The *y*-coordinate is 3, so point *A* is |3| units from the *x*-axis.

STEP 2 Find the distance between point *B* and the *x*-axis.

The *y*-coordinate of *B* is −2, so point *B* is |−2| = 2 units from the *x*-axis.

STEP 3 Find the sum of the distances.

Distance from *A* to *B* = |3| + |−2| = 3 + 2 = 5 units.

B What is the distance between point *D* and point *C*?

STEP 1 Find the distance between point *D* and the *y*-axis.

Point *D* is |−5| = 5 units from the *y*-axis.

STEP 2 Find the distance between point *C* and the *y*-axis.

Point *C* is |−1| = 1 unit from the *y*-axis.

STEP 3 Find the distance between *C* and *D* by finding this difference:

Distance of *D* from the *y*-axis − distance of *C* from the *y*-axis

|−5| − |−1| = 4 units

Math Talk
Mathematical Practices

How is the distance between a point and its reflection across an axis related to the distance between the point and the axis? Explain.

The distance between a point and its reflection across an axis is twice the distance between the original point and the axis, because a point and its reflection across an axis are the same distance from the axis.

Personal Math Trainer
Online Assessment and Intervention
my.hrw.com

YOUR TURN

Find the distance between each pair of points.

3. *E*(−4, 7) and *F*(5, 7) ___9 units___

4. *G*(0, −5) and *H*(0, −10) ___5 units___

PROFESSIONAL DEVELOPMENT

CC Integrate Mathematical Practices MP.3

This lesson provides an opportunity to address the Mathematical Practices standard that calls for students to construct viable arguments and critique the reasoning of others. Throughout this lesson, students are asked to explain and justify questions dealing with finding the distance between two points and reflecting a point across an axis using precise mathematical language in written form. They also make conjectures about the coordinates of points that are reflected more than once.

Math Background

In this lesson, students use absolute value to find distances between points that can be connected by horizontal or vertical line segments in a coordinate plane. In a later course, using students will use the Distance Formula to find the distance between any two points in a coordinate plane.

In a coordinate plane, the distance from (x_1, y_1) to (x_2, y_2) is $d = \sqrt{(x_2 - x_1)^2 + (y_2 - y_1)^2}$.

EXAMPLE 2

Focus on Reasoning CC **Mathematical Practices**

Point out to students that sometimes a problem may provide clues and facts that you must use to find a solution. Encourage students to begin by identifying the important information. They can underline or circle the information in the problem statement.

Questioning Strategies CC **Mathematical Practices**

• Why is it important to calculate the distance first when determining how long it takes for the truck to travel from one location to another? If you do not calculate the distance, you will have two variables in the formula and it would not be possible to solve. To find any value in the distance formula, you must know the other two.

Engage with the Whiteboard

Have a student volunteer place a different location vertically from M on the coordinate grid. Then ask the students to calculate the time to get to this new location given a speed of 60 miles per hour.

YOUR TURN

Remind students that they have to find the distance traveled before they can use the distance formula to find how much time the trip took.

Elaborate

Talk About It
Summarize the Lesson

Ask: How do you use absolute value to find the distance between two points that have the same y-coordinates but different x-coordinates? If both x-coordinates have the same sign, find the difference of their absolute values to find the distance between the points. If the x-coordinates have different signs, find the sum of their absolute values.

GUIDED PRACTICE

Engage with the Whiteboard

For Exercises 3–4, have students fill in the coordinates on the whiteboard and then calculate the distance. For Exercises 5–6, have students plot the reflection of points C and D on the coordinate grid on the whiteboard.

Avoid Common Errors

Exercises 1–2 Watch out for students who reflect across the incorrect axis. Remind them to read the question carefully to make sure they are answering the correct question.

Exercise 8 Point out to students that this relationship is proportional. Instead of using a distance formula, have them use a proportion: $\frac{1 \text{ block}}{3 \text{ minutes}} = \frac{7 \text{ blocks}}{x \text{ minutes}}$.

Solving Distance Problems

You can solve problems using the distance between points on a grid.

Math On the Spot
my.hrw.com

EXAMPLE 2 *Problem Solving*

COMMON CORE 6.NS.8

The coordinate plane represents a map. Each grid unit represents 20 miles. A retail company has warehouses at M(−70, 10) and N(50, 10). How long does it take a truck that drives 40 miles per hour to travel from warehouse M to warehouse N?

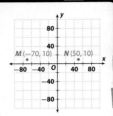

Analyze Information

Identify the important information.

- One warehouse is located at M(−70, 10). The other is at N(50, 10).
- A truck drives from M to N at a speed of 40 miles per hour.

Formulate a Plan

- Find the distance between M and N by adding the absolute values of the x-coordinates of the points.
- Find the time it takes the truck to drive this distance by using the relationship, distance = rate · time.

Solve

Add the absolute values of the x-coordinates to find the distance between point M and point N on the grid.

$$|-70| + |50| = 70 + 50 = 120$$

The warehouses are 120 miles apart.

The truck drives 120 miles at 40 mi/h. Because 120 = 40(3), it takes the truck 3 hours to travel from M to N.

Justify and Evaluate

You found the sum of the absolute values of the x-coordinates to find the horizontal distance on the grid. Then you used distance = rate · time to find the time it takes to drive that distance.

YOUR TURN

5. A store is located at P(50, −30). How long will it take a truck driving at 50 miles per hour to drive from warehouse N to this store?

  0.8 hrs, or 48 minutes

Personal Math Trainer
Online Assessment and Intervention
my.hrw.com

---

1. The point (5, −2) is reflected across the x-axis. What are the coordinates of the reflection? (Explore Activity)

  (5, 2)

2. The point (−6, 8) is reflected across the y-axis. What are the coordinates of the reflection? (Explore Activity)

  (6, 8)

Use the coordinate plane. (Example 1)

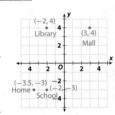

3. The distance between point A and point B is

  $$\boxed{5} + \boxed{-2} = \boxed{5} + \boxed{2} = \boxed{7}$$ units.

4. The distance between point A and point C is

  $$\boxed{5} - \boxed{1} = \boxed{5} - \boxed{1} = \boxed{4}$$ units.

5. Plot the reflection of point C across the y-axis. What is the distance between point C and its reflection? ____ 2 units

6. Plot the reflection of point A across the x-axis. What is the distance of the reflection from the x-axis? ____ 3 units

Use the map shown. Each grid on the map represents 1 city block. (Example 2)

7. Yoko walks from the library to the mall. How many city blocks does she walk? ____ 5 blocks

8. If Yoko walks 1 block in 3 minutes, how long does it take her to walk from the school to the library? How long does it take her to walk from home to school?

  21 minutes; 4.5 minutes

ESSENTIAL QUESTION CHECK-IN

9. How do you use absolute value to find the distance between two points that have the same x-coordinates but different y-coordinates?

  If both y-coordinates have the same sign, find the difference of their absolute values to find the distance between the points. If the y-coordinates have different signs, find the sum of their absolute values.

DIFFERENTIATE INSTRUCTION

Connect to Daily Life

Reflections occur often in real-world situations. Ask students to describe real-world examples of reflections such as looking in a mirror.

Sample answers: the image of trees on a lake represents a reflection, or the image of a building or monument in a reflecting pool.

Visual Cues

Give students enlarged coordinate grids, and have them graph points and reflect the points across the x- and y-axis.

Tell students to use a ruler to help align the points across the axes. Have them use colored pencils or markers to show each reflection.

If this is used as a class project, have students share their work with the class.

Additional Resources

Differentiated Instruction includes:

- Reading Strategies
- Success for English Learners **ELL**
- Reteach
- Challenge **PRE-AP**

14.1 LESSON QUIZ

 6.NS.6b, 6.NS.8

1. The point $(-9, 2)$ is reflected across the x-axis. What are the coordinates of the reflection?

2. What is the distance between the points $(8, -4)$ and $(-5, -4)$?

3. What is the distance between the points $(-7, -5)$ and $(-7, -8)$?

4. A truck travels from warehouse A at $(-4, 8)$ to warehouse B at $(-4, -1)$. If each unit represents 20 miles and the truck is traveling 60 miles per hour, how long will it take the truck to travel this distance?

Lesson Quiz available online

 my.hrw.com

Answers

1. $(-9, -2)$

2. 13 units

3. 3 units

4. 3 hours

Evaluate

GUIDED AND INDEPENDENT PRACTICE

 6.NS.6b, 6.NS.8

Concepts and Skills	Practice
Explore Activity Reflecting Points in the Coordinate Plane	Exercises 1–2, 10–15
Example 1 Finding Distances in the Coordinate Plane	Exercises 3–6, 12–15
Example 2 Solving Distance Problems	Exercises 7–8, 16–18

Exercise	Depth of Knowledge (D.O.K.)	**COMMON CORE** Mathematical Practices
10–15	**2** Skills/Concepts	**MP.5** Using Tools
16	**2** Skills/Concepts	**MP.4** Modeling
17	**2** Skills/Concepts	**MP.1** Problem Solving
18	**2** Skills/Concepts	**MP.4** Modeling
19	**3** Strategic Thinking H.O.T.	**MP.2** Reasoning
20	**3** Strategic Thinking H.O.T.	**MP.3** Logic
21	**3** Strategic Thinking H.O.T.	**MP.7** Use Structure
22	**3** Strategic Thinking H.O.T.	**MP.3** Logic

Additional Resources

Differentiated Instruction includes:

• Leveled Practice Worksheets

14.1 Independent Practice

COMMON CORE 6.NS.6b, 6.NS.8

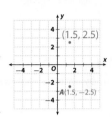

Personal Math Trainer

Online Assessment and Intervention

my.hrw.com

Use the coordinate plane.

10. Plot the reflection of point *A* across the *x*-axis. What are the coordinates of the reflection of point *A* across the *x*-axis? What is the distance between point *A* and its reflection?

(1.5, 2.5); 5 units

11. How can you plot the reflection of point *A* across the *y*-axis? Give the coordinates of the reflection across the *y*-axis, and tell how many units the reflection is from point *A*.

Place another point on the other side of the

y-axis the same distance from the *y*-axis as

point *A*; (−1.5, −2.5); 3 units

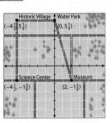

(1.5, 2.5)

A(1.5, −2.5)

Find the coordinates of each point after the described reflection. Give the distance between each point and its reflection.

12. *R*(−5, 8) is reflected across the *x*-axis. ____(−5, −8); 16 units

13. *S*(−7, −3) is reflected across the *y*-axis. ____(7, −3); 14 units

14. *T*(8, 2) is reflected across the *x*-axis. ____(8, −2); 4 units

15. *U*(2.4, −1) is reflected across the *y*-axis ____(−2.4, −1); 4.8 units

Pedro uses a coordinate system to map the locations of some tourist locations in a large city. Each grid unit represents one mile.

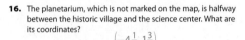

Historic Village (−4½, 5½)   Water Park (0, 5½)

Science Center (−4½, −1¾)   Museum (2, −1¾)

16. The planetarium, which is not marked on the map, is halfway between the historic village and the science center. What are its coordinates?

$\left(-4\frac{1}{2}, 1\frac{3}{4}\right)$

17. Pedro wants to walk from the historic village to the science center. Then he will walk from the science center to the museum. If he walks at a speed of $4\frac{1}{2}$ miles per hour, how long will it take him?

3 hours

18. Pedro is staying at a hotel whose location is a reflection across the *x*-axis of the museum's location. What are the coordinates of the location of Pedro's hotel?

$\left(2, 1\frac{3}{4}\right)$

H.O.T. **FOCUS ON HIGHER ORDER THINKING**

Work Area

19. Communicate Mathematical Ideas Deirdre plotted a point *D* in Quadrant IV. After she reflected the point across an axis, the reflection was in Quadrant III. Give possible coordinates for point *D* and its reflection, and tell why you chose these coordinates.

Sample answer: (4, −2) reflected across the *y*-axis to

(−4, −2). I chose this point because it has to have a

positive *x*-coordinate and a negative *y*-coordinate to be

in Quadrant IV. To reflect a point from Quadrant IV to

Quadrant III, you have to reflect across the *y*-axis.

20. Explain the Error Jason plotted the points (4, 4) and (−4, −4) on a coordinate plane. He says that the distance between the two points is 8 units because |4| + |−4| = 8. What mistake is Jason making?

The method Jason is using only works if the two points have

the same *x*-coordinate or the same *y*-coordinate. In this case,

the two points have different *x*- and different *y*-coordinates.

21. Look for a Pattern A point is reflected over the *x*-axis and then reflected again over the *y*-axis. Will the coordinates after these two reflections be the same or different if the point is first reflected over the *y*-axis and then over the *x*-axis? Use an example to support your answer.

The same; if you first reflect (2, 3) over the *x*-axis, you get

(2, −3) for the new coordinates. Then, when you reflect

(2, −3) over the *y*-axis, you get (−2, −3) for the new

coordinates. If you first reflect (2, 3) over the *y*-axis, you

get (−2, 3). When you reflect (−2, 3) over the *x*-axis, you

get (−2, −3) for the new coordinates.

22. Explain the Error Bentley states that the distance between *R*(−8, −3.5) and *S*(−8, −12) is |−12| + |−3.5| = 15.5 units. Is Bentley correct? Explain your answer. If Bentley is not correct, explain how to find the correct distance between the points.

Bentley is not correct; the two points are on the same

side of the axis, one above the other. So Bentley should

not have added the absolute values, he should have

subtracted them. |−12| − |−3.5| = 8.5 units

EXTEND THE MATH PRE-AP

Activity available online my.hrw.com

Activity Graph the reflection of quadrilateral *ABCD* across the *x*-axis. Then graph the reflected quadrilateral across the *y*-axis, and list the final coordinates.

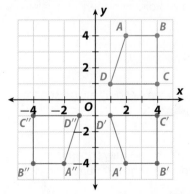

A″(−2, −4)
B″(−4, −4)
C″(−4, −1)
D″(−1, −1)

LESSON
14.2 Polygons in the Coordinate Plane

Common Core Standards

The student is expected to:

 Geometry—6.G.3

Draw polygons in the coordinate plane given coordinates for the vertices: use coordinates to find the length of a side joining points with the same first coordinate or the same second coordinate. Apply these techniques in the context of solving real-world and mathematical problems.

Mathematical Practices

 MP.2 Reasoning

ADDITIONAL EXAMPLE 1
The grid shows the path Lisa followed when she walked from her home (0, 1) to various locations and back home again. If each grid square represents one block, how many blocks did Lisa walk? 22 blocks

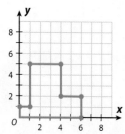

 Interactive Whiteboard
Interactive example available online

 Animated Math
Perimeter and Area of Polygons

Students explore perimeter and area of various polygons on the coordinate plane.

Engage

ESSENTIAL QUESTION

How can you solve problems by drawing polygons in the coordinate plane? Plot the polygons on the coordinate plane, find the length of the sides of the polygon, use known formulas to find area and perimeter, and convert from grid units to other units if given.

Motivate the Lesson
Ask: How can you plot polygons in a coordinate plane? Begin the Explore Activity to find out.

Explore

EXPLORE ACTIVITY

Engage with the Whiteboard
 Have students plot the points $E(-4, 5)$, $F(-2, 6)$, $G(2, 5)$, $H(2, -1)$, and $J(-3, -1)$ in a coordinate plane. Have them connect the points in order to form a polygon. Ask them to identify the shape and relate the shape to the number of vertices and the number of sides. (The shape is a pentagon with 5 vertices and 5 sides.)

Explain

EXAMPLE 1

Connect Vocabulary ELL
Remind students that the perimeter of a polygon is the distance around the figure. The space inside the figure is the area.

Questioning Strategies CC Mathematical Practices

• How could you find the total amount Tommy walked if each block length is equal to 0.25 mile? Multiply the total perimeter of 22 blocks by 0.25 mile.

• Explain how to find the perimeter of any polygon in a coordinate plane. Find the length of each side of the polygon, then add all the sides together. The sum is the perimeter.

YOUR TURN

Engage with the Whiteboard
 Have students plot the points given in the problem on a coordinate grid on the whiteboard. Then have them find the distances.

Avoid Common Errors
Watch out for students who may plot a point incorrectly because they transposed the *x*- and *y*-coordinates. Remind students that the *x*-coordinate is the first number in an ordered pair.

Polygons in the Coordinate Plane

COMMON CORE 6.G.3
Draw polygons in the coordinate plane;... find the length of a side... in the context of solving... problems.

? ESSENTIAL QUESTION

How can you solve problems by drawing polygons in the coordinate plane?

EXPLORE ACTIVITY Real World | COMMON CORE 6.G.3

Polygons in the Coordinate Plane

A **polygon** is a closed plane figure formed by three or more line segments that meet only at their endpoints. A **vertex** is the point where two sides of a polygon meet. The *vertices* of a polygon can be represented as ordered pairs, and the polygon can then be drawn in the coordinate plane.

Sheila wants to make a pattern of two different tile shapes on a floor. She first graphs the shapes on a coordinate plane.

A Plot these points to form one of the tile shapes:

$A(3, 5)$, $B(4, 6)$, $C(5, 5)$, $D(4, 4)$

Connect the points in order.

The polygon formed is a(n) ___square___.

B Plot these points to form the other tile shape:

$P(-5, 2)$, $Q(-4, 3)$, $R(0, 3)$, $S(1, 2)$,

$T(1, -2)$, $U(0, -3)$, $V(-4, -3)$, $W(-5, -2)$

Connect the points in order.

The polygon formed is a(n) ___octagon___.

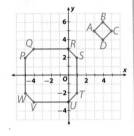

Reflect

1. How is the number of vertices related to the number of sides of the polygon and to the type of polygon? Give two examples.

They are the same; the number of vertices can be used to classify the polygon; examples: a polygon with 3 vertices is a triangle and a polygon with 6 vertices is a hexagon.

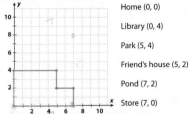

Math On the Spot
my.hrw.com

Finding Perimeter in the Coordinate Plane

You can use what you know about finding lengths in the coordinate plane to find the perimeter of a polygon.

EXAMPLE 1 Real World | COMMON CORE 6.G.3

The grid shows the path Tommy followed when he walked from his home at (0, 0) to various locations and back home again. If each grid square represents one block, how many blocks did he walk?

Home (0, 0)
Library (0, 4)
Park (5, 4)
Friend's house (5, 2)
Pond (7, 2)
Store (7, 0)

Math Talk
Mathematical Practices

How do you find the distance between two points in the same quadrant that have the same *x*-coordinate?

Subtract the absolute values of the *y*-coordinates.

STEP 1 Find each distance. Each grid unit represents one block.

Tommy's home (0, 0) to the library (0, 4) is $|4| - 0 = 4 - 0 = 4$ blocks.

The library (0, 4) to the park (5, 4) is $|5| - 0 = 5 - 0 = 5$ blocks.

The park (5, 4) to Tommy's friend's house (5, 2) is $|4| - |2| = 4 - 2 = 2$ blocks.

Tommy's friend's house (5, 2) to the pond (7, 2) is $|7| - |5| = 7 - 5 = 2$ blocks.

The pond (7, 2) to the store (7, 0) is $|2| - 0 = 2 - 0 = 2$ blocks.

The store (7, 0) to Tommy's home (0, 0) is $|7| - 0 = 7 - 0 = 7$ blocks.

STEP 2 Find the sum of the distances.

Tommy walked $4 + 5 + 2 + 2 + 2 + 7 = 22$ blocks.

Personal Math Trainer
Online Assessment and Intervention
my.hrw.com

YOUR TURN

2. Suppose the next day Tommy walks from his home to the mall at (0, 8), and then walks to a movie theater at (7, 8). After leaving the theater Tommy walks to the store at (7, 0) before returning home.

How far does he walk? ___30___ blocks

PROFESSIONAL DEVELOPMENT

CC Integrate Mathematical Practices MP.2

This lesson provides an opportunity to address the Mathematical Practices standard that calls for students to reason abstractly and quantitatively. Throughout this lesson, students are using their reasoning skills as they find distances on a coordinate plane or subdivide polygons that do not have known area formulas into smaller polygons that have known area formulas.

Math Background

In this lesson, students are applying many of the concepts they have explored previously, such as perimeter and area, to the coordinate plane. In order to find the side lengths or the dimensions needed to calculate area or perimeter, they will need to use the methods taught in the previous lesson on calculating distance in the coordinate plane.

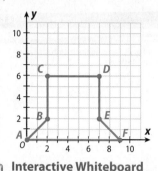
EXAMPLE 2

Connect Vocabulary ELL
Remind students that the area of a figure is the number of unit squares in a figure. The formula for the area of a rectangle or a parallelogram is $A = bh$, where b is the length of the base and h is the height.

Questioning Strategies CC Mathematical Practices
- Why can't you use the length of the segment connecting points A and B for the height of the parallelogram? The segment used to measure the height needs to be perpendicular to the base, and segment AB is not perpendicular to segment AF.

- How is finding the area of the rectangle different from finding the area of the parallelogram? All the sides in a rectangle are perpendicular whereas, in a parallelogram the sides are not necessarily perpendicular. You need to draw a perpendicular segment from the base of the parallelogram to the opposite side to find the height.

YOUR TURN

Engage with the Whiteboard
Have a student plot, label, and connect the points on a coordinate grid on the whiteboard. Then have another student subdivide the polygon into two quadrilaterals with known area formulas. Then have the students use the area formulas to find the area of the given polygon.

Elaborate

Talk About It
Summarize the Lesson
Ask: How is finding the area of a figure plotted in a coordinate plane similar to finding the perimeter of the figure? How is it different? For both, you need to find dimensions of the figure. To find the area or the perimeter of a rectangle, for example, you need to find the length and width. To find the perimeter of the rectangle, you find the sum of all the side lengths. To find the area, you find the product of the length and the width.

GUIDED PRACTICE

Engage with the Whiteboard
For Exercises 1–3, have a student plot, label, and connect the given points on the coordinate plane on the whiteboard. Then have other students fill in the blanks for Exercises 1–3 on the whiteboard.

Avoid Common Errors
Exercises 1, 4 Watch out for students who may plot a point incorrectly because they transposed the x- and y-coordinates. Remind students that the x-coordinate is the first number in an ordered pair.

Finding Area in the Coordinate Plane

You can use familiar area formulas to find areas of polygons in the coordinate plane.

Math On the Spot
my.hrw.com

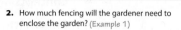

EXAMPLE 2 Real World

COMMON CORE 6.G.3

Caleb is planning a new deck for his house. He graphs the deck as polygon *ABCDEF* on a coordinate plane in which each grid unit represents one foot. The vertices of the polygon are *A*(1, 0), *B*(3, 2), *C*(3, 5), *D*(8, 5), *E*(8, 2), and *F*(6, 0). What is the area of Caleb's deck?

STEP 1 Graph the vertices, and connect them in order.

Draw a horizontal dashed line segment to divide the polygon into two quadrilaterals—a rectangle and a parallelogram.

STEP 2 Find the area of the rectangle using the length of segment *BE* as the base *b* and the length of segment *BC* as the height *h*.

$b = |8| - |3| = 5$ feet $\qquad h = |5| - |2| = 3$ feet

$A = bh = 5 \cdot 3 = 15$ square feet

STEP 3 Find the area of the parallelogram using the length of segment *AF* as the base. Use the length of a segment from *F*(6, 0) to the point (6, 2) as the height *h*.

$b = |6| - |1| = 5$ feet $\qquad h = |2| - 0 = 2$ feet

$A = bh = 5 \cdot 2 = 10$ square feet

STEP 4 Add the areas to find the total area of the deck.

$A = 15 + 10 = 25$ square feet

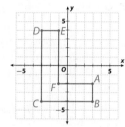

YOUR TURN

3. The vertices of a polygon are *L*(1, 2), *M*(1, 6), *N*(7, 6), *O*(7, 2), *P*(5, 0), and *Q*(3, 0). Graph the polygon. Then find its area.

$A = \underline{\quad 32 \quad}$ square units

Personal Math Trainer
Online Assessment and Intervention
my.hrw.com

Guided Practice

A gardener uses a coordinate grid to design a new garden. The gardener uses polygon *WXYZ* on the grid to represent the garden. The vertices of this polygon are *W*(3, 3), *X*(−3, 3), *Y*(−3, −3), and *Z*(3, −3). Each grid unit represents one yard.

1. Graph the points, and connect them in order. What is the shape of the garden? (Explore Activity)

   square

2. How much fencing will the gardener need to enclose the garden? (Example 1)

   Each side of the garden is $\underline{\quad 6 \quad}$ yards in length.

   The gardener will need $\underline{\quad 24 \quad}$ yards of fencing to enclose the garden.

3. What is the area of the garden? (Example 2)

   36 square yards

4. A clothing designer makes letters for varsity jackets by graphing the letters as polygons on a coordinate plane. One of the letters is polygon *ABCDEF*. The vertices of this polygon are *A*(3, −2), *B*(3, −4), *C*(−3, −4), *D*(−3, 4), *E*(−1, 4), and *F*(−1, −2). Each grid unit represents one inch. Graph the points on the coordinate plane, and connect them in order. Identify the letter formed. Then find its area. (Example 2)

   L; 24 square inches

? ESSENTIAL QUESTION CHECK-IN

5. How can you use a coordinate plane to solve perimeter and area problems?

   Plot the polygon on the coordinate plane, find the length of the sides of the polygon, use known formulas to find area and perimeter, and convert from grid units to other units if necessary.

DIFFERENTIATE INSTRUCTION

Multiple Representations

Have students use graph paper to find as many different rectangles as possible that have a perimeter of 16 units and then calculate the area of each. Then have them find as many different rectangles as possible that have an area of 24 square units and calculate the perimeter of each. Finally, have them describe any patterns they notice in the tables.

Kinesthetic Experience

Have students find the perimeters and areas of figures in and around their classroom. Then have them figure out what the perimeters and areas of those items would be if the dimensions were halved and tripled. Students can record their findings and share them with the class.

Additional Resources

Differentiated Instruction includes:
- Reading Strategies
- Success for English Learners **ELL**
- Reteach
- Challenge **PRE-AP**

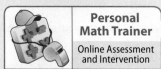

14.2 LESSON QUIZ

 6.G.3

1. The vertices of a polygon are $A(0, 4)$, $B(5, 4)$, $C(5, -3)$, and $D(0, -3)$. Graph the vertices and connect them in order. What is the perimeter of the polygon?

2. The vertices of a polygon are $A(4, -3)$, $B(1, 2)$, $C(1, 6)$, $D(7, 6)$, and $E(7, 2)$. Graph the polygon. What is the area of this polygon?

3. The vertices of a quadrilateral are $M(-4, 2)$, $N(6, 2)$, $P(6, -4)$, and $Q(-4, -4)$. Graph the quadrilateral. Then find the perimeter and area.

Lesson Quiz available online

 my.hrw.com

Answers

1.

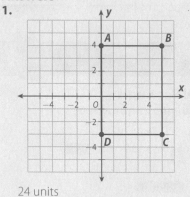

24 units

Evaluate

GUIDED AND INDEPENDENT PRACTICE

 6.G.3

Concepts and Skills	Practice
Explore Activity Polygons in the Coordinate Plane	Exercise 1
Example 1 Finding Perimeter in the Coordinate Plane	Exercise 2
Example 2 Finding Area in the Coordinate Plane	Exercises 3–4

Exercise	Depth of Knowledge (D.O.K.)	Mathematical Practices
6–7	**2** Skills/Concepts	**MP.2** Reasoning
8	**2** Skills/Concepts	**MP.4** Modeling
9	**3** Strategic Thinking **H.O.T.**	**MP.2** Reasoning
10	**3** Strategic Thinking **H.O.T.**	**MP.6** Precision
11–12	**3** Strategic Thinking **H.O.T.**	**MP.2** Reasoning

Additional Resources

Differentiated Instruction includes:

• Leveled Practice Worksheets

CC CLUSTER CONNECTION **Exercise 9** combines concepts from the Common Core cluster "Solve real-world and mathematical problems involving area, surface area, and volume."

2.

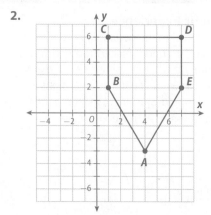

39 square units

3.

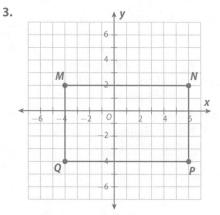

$P = 32$ units; $A = 60$ square units

14.2 Independent Practice

COMMON CORE 6.G.3

Personal
Math Trainer

Online
Assessment and
Intervention

my.hrw.com

6. A graphic designer creates letters for wall art by first graphing the letters as polygons on a coordinate plane. One of the letters is polygon *MNOPQRSTUV* with vertices *M*(2, 1), *N*(2, 9), *O*(7, 9), *P*(7, 7), *Q*(4, 7), *R*(4, 6), *S*(6, 6), *T*(6, 4), *U*(4, 4), and *V*(4, 1). Each grid unit represents one inch.

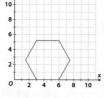

a. Graph the points on the coordinate plane, and connect them in order. What letter is formed? _____F_____

b. The designer will use decorative tape to paint the outline of the letter on a wall. How many inches of tape are needed? __30 inches__

c. How much space does the letter cover on the wall? __26 square inches__

d. How did you find your answer to c? Use the name(s) of shapes in your answer.

Sample answer: I divided the letter into four rectangles and added their areas.

7. **Vocabulary** The polygon shown is a regular polygon since all sides have equal length and all angles have equal measure.

a. The polygon is a regular ____hexagon____.

b. What is the perimeter of the polygon? ____18 units____

c. A line can divide the figure into two identical four-sided polygons. Each polygon has two bases, and one base is twice the length of the other base. Identify the polygon, and give its perimeter.

____trapezoid; 15 units____

8. Jean wants to put furniture in her clubhouse. She drew a floor plan of the clubhouse, as shown. Each grid unit represents one foot.

a. Which polygon names the shape of the floor?

____hexagon____

b. How many feet of baseboard are needed to go around the entire clubhouse?

____24 feet____

c. How much carpet is needed for the clubhouse floor?

____25 square feet____

---

9. **Persevere in Problem Solving** To find the area of triangle *ABC*, Jen first drew a square around the figure. Two sides of the square passed through the points *B* and *C*. The other two sides met at point *A*. Draw Jen's square, and explain how you can use it to find the area of triangle *ABC*.

The sides of the square are also the

sides of three right triangles. Find the area of the square,

and find the area of each triangle. Area of triangle *ABC* =

Area of square − area of the other triangles = 25 −

[(0.5)(2)(5) + (0.5)(2)(3) + (0.5)(3)(5)] = 9.5 square units

10. **Communicate Mathematical Ideas** The coordinates *A*(5, −2), *B*(3, −1), *C*(−4, −4), *D*(−3, 8), and *E*(−1, 4) form the vertices of a polygon when they are connected in order from *A* through *E*. Classify the polygon without plotting the points. Explain your answer.

Pentagon; five points are used to plot the polygon on a

grid, so there will be five line segments connecting the

points, and there will be five vertices. A figure with five

sides and five vertices is a pentagon.

11. **Explain the Error** Josh's teacher draws a regular octagon on a coordinate plane. One side has endpoints at (1, 5) and (4, 5). Josh says he can't find the perimeter of the octagon because he can only find lengths of horizontal and vertical segments. He says he can't find the lengths of the slanted sides of the octagon. What mistake is Josh making? What is the perimeter of the octagon?

The octagon is a regular octagon, so all the sides will

have the same length as the side whose endpoints are

given. Since that side length = |4| − |1| = 3 units, the

perimeter of the octagon is 8(3) = 24 units.

12. **Critical Thinking** Give coordinates for the vertices of a triangle that could have an area of 35 square units. Prove that your triangle fits the description by finding its area.

Sample answer: Vertices at (0, 0), (0, 7), and (0, 10);

Area = (0.5)(7)(10) = 35 square units

EXTEND THE MATH PRE-AP

Activity available online ⊙ my.hrw.com

Activity Have students draw their initials on grid paper using polygons. See Exercise 6 in the Independent Practice for an example of how to draw a letter on a coordinate grid. Make sure students draw block letters that use no diagonal segments or curved parts. Then have them find the total perimeter and area of their initials. They can decorate their letters and post them in the classroom.

Ready to Go On?

Assess Mastery

Use the assessment on this page to determine if students have mastered the concepts and standards covered in this module.

Personal Math Trainer

Online Assessment and Intervention

⏻ my.hrw.com

Intervention	Enrichment

Access Are You Ready? assessment online, and receive instant scoring, feedback, and customized intervention or enrichment.

Online and Print Resources

Differentiated Instruction
- Reteach worksheets
- Reading Strategies **ELL**
- Success for English Learners **ELL**

Differentiated Instruction
- Challenge worksheets **PRE-AP**
- Extend the Math **PRE-AP** Lesson Activities in TE

Additional Resources

Assessment Resources includes:
- Leveled Module Quizzes

Ready to Go On?

14.1 Distance in the Coordinate Plane

1. Reflect *A* across the *x*-axis. Label the reflection as *N*, and give its coordinates on the graph.

2. Reflect *B* across the *x*-axis. Label the reflection as *M*, and give its coordinates on the graph.

3. The distance between *A* and *N* is **2 units**.

4. Suppose the graph represents a map in which each grid unit equals 1 mile. If a school is located at *B* and a library is located at *N*, what is the distance between the school and the library? **5 miles**

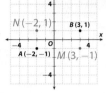

Find the coordinates of the point for each reflection.

5. $(-5, 7)$ across the *x*-axis **$(-5, -7)$**   6. $(2, 5.5)$ across the *y*-axis **$(-2, 5.5)$**

Find the distance between each pair of points.

7. $(1, 1)$ and $(1, -2)$ **3** units   8. $(-2, 3)$ and $(-4, 3)$ **2** units

14.2 Polygons in the Coordinate Plane

9. On the coordinate plane shown, each grid unit represents 10 feet. Polygon *QRST* has vertices $Q(10, 20)$, $R(-10, 20)$, $S(-10, -10)$, and $T(10, -10)$, and represents the floor plan of a room. Find the perimeter and area of the room.

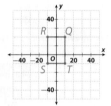

perimeter = 100 feet; area = 600 square feet

? ESSENTIAL QUESTION

10. Suppose you are given the coordinates of the vertices of a polygon. What steps could you take to solve a problem involving the polygon's area?
Plot the polygon on a grid using its vertices, and use absolute value to find the lengths of the sides; these lengths can be used to find the area.

Common Core Standards

Lesson	Exercises	Common Core Standards
14.1	1–8	6.NS.6b, 6.NS.8
14.2	9	6.G.3

Assessment Readiness

MODULE 14 MIXED REVIEW

Assessment Readiness

COMMON CORE

Personal Math Trainer

Online Assessment and Intervention

my.hrw.com

Selected Response

1. Which point is a reflection of point R across the x-axis?

Ⓐ Point A   Ⓒ Point C
Ⓑ Point B   Ⓓ Point D

2. Which point is a reflection of (12, −8) across the y-axis on a coordinate plane?

Ⓐ (−12, −8)   Ⓒ (8, 12)
Ⓑ (−8, 12)   Ⓓ (12, 8)

3. What is the distance between points J and L on the grid?

Ⓐ 1.5 units   Ⓒ 3 units
Ⓑ 2 units   Ⓓ 3.5 units

4. What is the greatest common factor of 12 and 30?

Ⓐ 2   Ⓒ 6
Ⓑ 3   Ⓓ 12

5. What is the distance between two points located at (−6, 2) and (−6, 8) on a coordinate plane?

Ⓐ 4 units   Ⓒ 10 units
Ⓑ 6 units   Ⓓ 12 units

6. Which is the sum of $\frac{1}{12} + \frac{3}{8}$?

Ⓐ $\frac{1}{6}$ Ⓒ $\frac{11}{48}$
Ⓑ $\frac{1}{5}$ Ⓓ $\frac{11}{24}$

Mini-Task

7. An artist is laying out the design for a wall hanging on a coordinate plane. She uses polygon EFGH with vertices E(4, 4), F(−4, 4), G(−4, −4), and H(4, −4) to represent the finished piece. Each unit on the grid represents two feet.

a. Plot the polygon on the grid, and classify its shape.

Name of Polygon: _____square_____

b. How much area will the art cover on a wall? _____64 square feet_____

Common Core Standards

Items	Grade 6 Standards	Mathematical Practices
1	6.NS.6b	MP.2
2	6.NS.6b	MP.2
3	6.G.3, 6.NS.6b	MP.2
4*	6.NS.4	MP.5
5	6.G.3, 6.NS.6b	MP.2
6*	6.NS.1	MP.5
7	6.G.3, 6.NS.8	MP.4

* Item integrates mixed review concepts from previous modules or a previous course.

Surface Area and Volume of Solids

ESSENTIAL QUESTION

How can a model help you to solve surface area and volume problems?

A net of the figure makes it easier to see the faces and find their areas when finding surface area; a drawing of the figure makes it easier to choose a base and see the height when finding the volume.

LESSON 15.1

Nets and Surface Area

COMMON CORE 6.G.4

LESSON 15.2

Volume of Rectangular Prisms

COMMON CORE 6.G.2

LESSON 15.3

Solving Volume Equations

COMMON CORE 6.EE.7, 6.G.2

Real-World Video

Surface area and volume can be important considerations when constructing or repairing buildings or other structures.

⏻ my.hrw.com

GO DIGITAL

my.hrw.com

my.hrw.com

Go digital with your write-in student edition, accessible on any device.

Math On the Spot

Scan with your smart phone to jump directly to the online edition, video tutor, and more.

Animated Math

Interactively explore key concepts to see how math works.

Personal Math Trainer

Get immediate feedback and help as you work through practice sets.

Are You Ready?

Assess Readiness

Use the assessment on this page to determine if students need intensive or strategic intervention for the module's prerequisite skills.

 **RtI** Response to Intervention

Personal Math Trainer
Online Assessment and Intervention
⏻ my.hrw.com

Intervention	Enrichment
Access Are You Ready? assessment online, and receive instant scoring, feedback, and customized intervention or enrichment.	

Online and Print Resources

Skills Intervention worksheets
- Skill 50 Use of Parentheses
- Skill 85 Area of Squares, Rectangles, Triangles

Differentiated Instruction
- Challenge worksheets **PRE-AP**
- Extend the Math **PRE-AP** Lesson Activities in TE

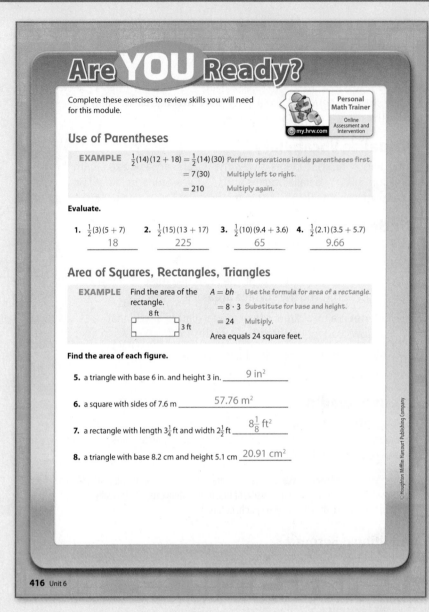

Are YOU Ready?

Complete these exercises to review skills you will need for this module.

Personal Math Trainer
⏻ my.hrw.com
Online Assessment and Intervention

Use of Parentheses

EXAMPLE $\frac{1}{2}(14)(12 + 18) = \frac{1}{2}(14)(30)$ Perform operations inside parentheses first.

$= 7(30)$ Multiply left to right.

$= 210$ Multiply again.

Evaluate.

1. $\frac{1}{2}(3)(5 + 7)$ 18

2. $\frac{1}{2}(15)(13 + 17)$ 225

3. $\frac{1}{2}(10)(9.4 + 3.6)$ 65

4. $\frac{1}{2}(2.1)(3.5 + 5.7)$ 9.66

Area of Squares, Rectangles, Triangles

EXAMPLE   Find the area of the rectangle.

8 ft

3 ft

$A = bh$ Use the formula for area of a rectangle.

$= 8 \cdot 3$ Substitute for base and height.

$= 24$ Multiply.

Area equals 24 square feet.

Find the area of each figure.

5. a triangle with base 6 in. and height 3 in. 9 in^2

6. a square with sides of 7.6 m 57.76 m^2

7. a rectangle with length $3\frac{1}{4}$ ft and width $2\frac{1}{2}$ ft $8\frac{1}{8} \text{ ft}^2$

8. a triangle with base 8.2 cm and height 5.1 cm 20.91 cm^2

PROFESSIONAL DEVELOPMENT VIDEO

Author Juli Dixon models successful teaching practices as she explores the concepts of finding surface area and volume of solids in an actual sixth-grade classroom.

 Professional Development
⏻ my.hrw.com

GO DIGITAL
my.hrw.com

 Online Teacher Edition
Access a full suite of teaching resources online—plan, present, and manage classes and assignments.

 ePlanner
Easily plan your classes and access all your resources online.

 Interactive Answers and Solutions
Customize answer keys to print or display in the classroom. Choose to include answers only or full solutions to all lesson exercises.

 Interactive Whiteboards
Engage students with interactive whiteboard-ready lessons and activities.

 Personal Math Trainer: Online Assessment and Intervention
Assign automatically graded homework, quizzes, tests, and intervention activities. Prepare your students with updated practice tests aligned with Common Core.

Reading Start-Up

Have students complete the activities on this page by working alone or with others.

Visualize Vocabulary

This graphic helps students review the vocabulary associated with the area formulas for parallelograms and triangles. Students should write the word from the Review List in the box that belongs in the blank.

Understand Vocabulary

Use the following explanations to help students learn the preview words.

> Finding the total area of all the faces of a three-dimensional figure is finding the **surface area** of that solid.
>
> A **net** is a two-dimensional model [flat] of a solid that allows you to see all the faces of the solid.
>
> A **pyramid** is a solid that has faces that are triangle-shaped.

Active Reading

Integrating Language Arts

Students can use these reading and note-taking strategies to help them organize and understand new concepts and vocabulary.

COMMON CORE **ELA-Literacy.RST.6-8.7** Integrate quantitative or technical information expressed in words in a text with a version of that information expressed visually (e.g., in a flowchart, diagram, model, graph, or table).

Additional Resources

Differentiated Instruction
- Reading Strategies **ELL**

Reading Start-Up

Visualize Vocabulary

Use review words to complete the graphic.

Shape	Area Formula
parallelogram	$A = b \times$ __height__
triangle	$A = \frac{1}{2} \times$ __base__ $\times h$

Vocabulary

Review Words
- area *(área)*
- base *(base)*
- height *(altura)*
- rectangular prism *(prisma rectangular)*
- volume *(volumen)*

Preview Words
- net *(plantilla)*
- pyramid *(pirámide)*
- surface area *(área total)*

Understand Vocabulary

Complete the sentences using the preview words.

1. The total area of all the faces of a three-dimensional figure is called the __surface area__.

2. A model that looks like an unfolded three-dimensional figure is a __net__.

3. A three-dimensional shape with a polygon for a base and triangles for sides is a __pyramid__.

Active Reading

Booklet Before beginning the module, create a booklet to help you learn the concepts in this module. Write the main idea of each lesson on each page of the booklet. As you study each lesson, write important details that support the main idea, such as vocabulary and important steps in solving problems. Refer to your finished booklet as you work on assignments and study for tests.

© Houghton Mifflin Harcourt Publishing Company

Before	In this module	After
Students will have explored volume to: • recognize volume as an attribute of solid figures and understand concepts of volume measurement • measure volumes by counting unit cubes, using cubic cm, cubic in., cubic ft, and improvised units • relate volume to the operations of multiplication and addition and solve real-world and mathematical problems involving prisms and composite solids made of prisms	In this module, students will: • identify nets and use nets to find the surface area of a solid • calculate the volume of rectangular solids and use volume equations to solve problems	Students will solve real-world and mathematical problems involving: • area, volume, and surface area of two- and three-dimensional objects composed of triangles, quadrilaterals, polygons, cubes, and right prisms

Unpacking the Standards

Use the examples on the page to help students know exactly what they are expected to learn in this module.

Common Core Standards

Content Areas

Solve real-world and mathematical problems involving area, surface area, and volume.

Go online to see a complete unpacking of the Common Core Standards.

ⓟ my.hrw.com

 MODULE 15

Unpacking the Standards

Understanding the standards and the vocabulary terms in the standards will help you know exactly what you are expected to learn in this module.

COMMON CORE 6.G.2

Find the volume of a right rectangular prism with fractional edge lengths by packing it with unit cubes of the appropriate unit fraction edge lengths, and show that the volume is the same as would be found by multiplying the edge lengths of the prism. Apply the formulas $V = lwh$ and $V = bh$ to find volumes of right rectangular prisms with fractional edge lengths in the context of solving real-world and mathematical problems.

What It Means to You

You will use the formula for the volume of a rectangular prism.

UNPACKING EXAMPLE 6.G.2

Jala has an aquarium in the shape of a rectangular prism. The dimensions of the base of the aquarium are $1\frac{1}{4}$ feet by $\frac{1}{2}$ foot, and the height is $\frac{3}{4}$ foot. Find the volume of the aquarium.

$$V = l \cdot w \cdot h$$
$$= 1\frac{1}{4} \cdot \frac{1}{2} \cdot \frac{3}{4}$$
$$= \frac{5}{4} \cdot \frac{1}{2} \cdot \frac{3}{4}$$
$$= \frac{15}{32}$$

The volume of the aquarium is $\frac{15}{32}$ cubic foot.

COMMON CORE 6.G.4

Represent three-dimensional figures using nets made up of rectangles and triangles, and use the nets to find the surface area of these figures. ...

What It Means to You

You will use a net to find the surface area of a square pyramid.

UNPACKING EXAMPLE 6.G.4

Meg drew a net to find the surface area of a square pyramid.

Square face: $A = b \times h = 16$ square inches

Triangular face: $A = \frac{1}{2} b \times h = 6$ square inches

Total of the areas:
$16 + (4 \times 6) = 40$ square inches

The surface area is 40 square inches.

4 in. 3 in.

Visit my.hrw.com to see all the Common Core Standards unpacked.

ⓟ my.hrw.com

418 Unit 6

Common Core Standards	Lesson 15.1	Lesson 15.2	Lesson 15.2
6.EE.7 Solve real-world and mathematical problems by writing and solving equations of the form $x + p = q$ and $px = q$ for cases in which p, q and x are all nonnegative rational numbers.			COMMON CORE
6.G.2 Find the volume of a right rectangular prism with fractional edge lengths by packing it with unit cubes of the appropriate unit fraction edge lengths, and show that the volume is the same as would be found by multiplying the edge lengths of the prism. Apply the formulas $V = lwh$ and $V = bh$ to find volumes of right rectangular prisms with fractional edge lengths in the context of solving real-world and mathematical problems.		COMMON CORE	COMMON CORE
6.G.4 Represent three-dimensional figures using nets made up of rectangles and triangles, and use the nets to find the surface area of these figures.	COMMON CORE		

LESSON
15.1 Nets and Surface Area

ADDITIONAL EXAMPLE 1
Use a net to find the surface area of the square pyramid. 132 cm²

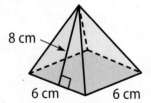

8 cm

6 cm   6 cm

 Interactive Whiteboard
Interactive example available online

 my.hrw.com

Engage

ESSENTIAL QUESTION

How can you use nets to find surface areas? A net shows a three-dimensional shape as two-dimensional shapes, which makes it easier to find the area of each face.

Motivate the Lesson
Ask: How many of you have every wrapped a present? Have you ever wondered how to figure out how much wrapping paper you need? Begin the Explore Activity to find out.

Explore

EXPLORE ACTIVITY

Focus on Modeling CC Mathematical Practices
Show students an empty cereal box. Rip the seams so the box will lie flat. Tell the students that the box was a rectangular prism with six faces. Also, tell them that the flattened box can be considered a net and represents the surface area of the box. The surface area determines how much cardboard is needed to make the box.

Explain

EXAMPLE 1

Focus on Modeling CC Mathematical Practices
Point out to students that if they draw the net for any figure on graph paper, they can count the squares to estimate the surface area of the figure before they actually do the calculations.

Questioning Strategies CC Mathematical Practices
• How do the triangular faces of a square pyramid compare? All four triangular faces are congruent, so they have the same area.

• How are the triangular faces of a rectangular pyramid different from the triangular faces of a square pyramid? Not all four faces are congruent. Two faces will have a different slant height from the other two faces.

YOUR TURN

Engage with a Whiteboard
Have a student volunteer draw and label the net on the whiteboard. Then have another student write expressions for the areas of the four triangles and the area of the base before performing the calculations. Then have another student write the answer on the whiteboard.

Questioning Strategies CC Mathematical Practices
• What type of pyramid is this? a square pyramid How many faces does this pyramid have? There are 5 faces.

• What shapes are used in the net? There are 4 congruent triangles and 1 square.

LESSON 15.1 Nets and Surface Area

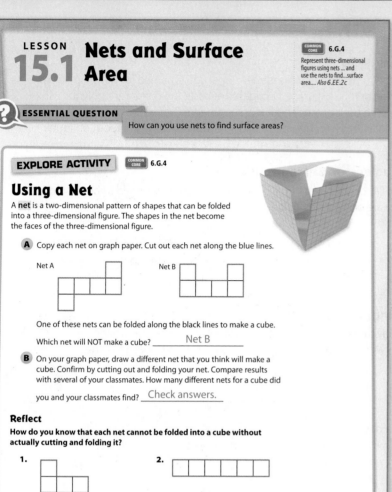

COMMON CORE 6.G.4

Represent three-dimensional figures using nets ... and use the nets to find...surface area.... Also 6.EE.2c

? ESSENTIAL QUESTION

How can you use nets to find surface areas?

EXPLORE ACTIVITY COMMON CORE 6.G.4

Using a Net

A **net** is a two-dimensional pattern of shapes that can be folded into a three-dimensional figure. The shapes in the net become the faces of the three-dimensional figure.

A Copy each net on graph paper. Cut out each net along the blue lines.

Net A   Net B

One of these nets can be folded along the black lines to make a cube.

Which net will NOT make a cube? __Net B__

B On your graph paper, draw a different net that you think will make a cube. Confirm by cutting out and folding your net. Compare results with several of your classmates. How many different nets for a cube did you and your classmates find? __Check answers.__

Reflect

How do you know that each net cannot be folded into a cube without actually cutting and folding it?

1.

The net has only 5 faces, but a cube has 6.

2.

The net folds into a "loop" of squares with no top or bottom.

Lesson 15.1 **419**

EXPLORE ACTIVITY (cont'd)

3. What shapes will appear in a net for a rectangular prism that is not a cube? How many of these shapes will there be?

rectangles; 6

Surface Area of a Pyramid

The **surface area** of a three-dimensional figure is the sum of the areas of its faces. A net can be helpful when finding surface area.

A **pyramid** is a three-dimensional figure whose base is a polygon and whose other faces are triangles that meet at a point. A pyramid is identified by the shape of its base.

EXAMPLE 1 COMMON CORE 6.G.4

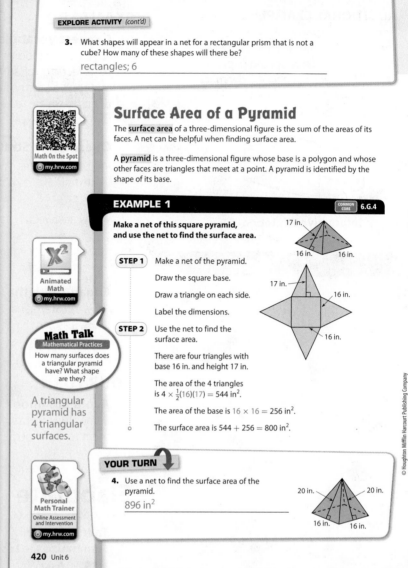

Make a net of this square pyramid, and use the net to find the surface area.

STEP 1 Make a net of the pyramid.

Draw the square base.

Draw a triangle on each side.

Label the dimensions.

STEP 2 Use the net to find the surface area.

There are four triangles with base 16 in. and height 17 in.

The area of the 4 triangles is $4 \times \frac{1}{2}(16)(17) = 544$ in^2.

The area of the base is $16 \times 16 = 256$ in^2.

The surface area is $544 + 256 = 800$ in^2.

Math Talk
Mathematical Practices

How many surfaces does a triangular pyramid have? What shape are they?

A triangular pyramid has 4 triangular surfaces.

YOUR TURN

4. Use a net to find the surface area of the pyramid.

896 in^2

420 Unit 6

PROFESSIONAL DEVELOPMENT

CC Integrate Mathematical Practices MP.6

This lesson provides an opportunity to address the Mathematical Practices standard that calls for students to attend to precision. Throughout this lesson, students are drawing nets and calculating surface area. They need to be careful when labeling the dimensions of the nets. They also need to calculate accurately and efficiently when finding the surface area of a given figure.

Math Background

A **net** is a two-dimensional pattern of shapes that can be folded into a three-dimensional figure. The shapes in the net become the faces of the three-dimensional figure. You can use the net to find the surface area of the three-dimensional figure by adding up the areas of the faces.

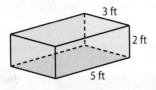

EXAMPLE 2

Connect Vocabulary ELL

Point out to students that a **prism** is a three-dimensional figure named for the shape of its base; rectangular, square, or triangular. The two identical bases are congruent polygons. In this book, all the prisms are right prisms and it is assumed that the faces of a prism that are not its bases are rectangles. In a later geometry course, students will learn about oblique prisms.

Questioning Strategies CC Mathematical Practices

• How many faces does a square prism have? 6 faces How many faces need to be covered with foil? 5 faces Why are only 5 faces being covered? The bottom face will be touching the floor and will not need to be covered with foil.

• How are a rectangular prism and a rectangular pyramid similar? How are they different? Both are three-dimensional shapes, and both have faces that are polygons. Prisms have two bases; pyramids only have one base. Rectangular prisms have 6 faces while rectangular pyramids have 5 faces.

Engage with the Whiteboard

 In Step 1, have a student volunteer draw and label the net on the whiteboard. Discuss the net with the class, confirming its shape and the labeling of the measurements.

YOUR TURN

Avoid Common Errors

Some students may omit faces when finding the surface area of solid figures. Encourage them to either begin by drawing a net or by listing the faces.

Elaborate

....

Talk About It
Summarize the Lesson

Ask: What is a net, and how does it help us find surface area? A net is a two-dimensional representation of a three-dimensional figure. We can use it to find the area of each face and then use the sum of all the areas to find the surface area of the figure.

GUIDED PRACTICE

Engage with the Whiteboard

For Exercise 3, have students draw and label a net on the whiteboard. Then have them write expressions for bases and sides before calculating the areas.

Avoid Common Errors

Exercises 1, 3 Some students may omit faces when finding the surface area of solid figures. Encourage them to either begin by drawing a net or by listing the faces.

Exercises 1–3 Remind students to look at the shape of each face and then choose the most appropriate formula to calculate its area.

Surface Area of a Prism

A **prism** is a three-dimensional figure with two identical and parallel bases that are polygons. The other faces are rectangles. A prism is identified by the shape of its base.

EXAMPLE 2

COMMON CORE 6.G.4

A sculpture sits on pedestal in the shape of a square prism. The side lengths of a base of the prism are 3 feet. The height of the prism is 4 feet. The museum director wants to cover all but the underside of the pedestal with foil that costs $0.22 per square foot. How much will the foil cost?

STEP 1 Use a net to show the faces that will be covered with foil.

Draw the top.

Draw the faces of the prism that are connected to the top.

You don't need to include the bottom of the pedestal.

	Back		Right
4 ft	4 ft	4 ft	side
4 ft	3 ft	4 ft	
3 ft	Top	3 ft	
Left	3 ft	4 ft	
side	Front	4 ft	

STEP 2 Use the net to find the area that will be covered with foil.

Area of top = $3 \cdot 3 = 9$ ft^2

The other four faces are identical.

Area of four faces = $4 \cdot 3 \cdot 4 = 48$ ft^2

Area to be covered = $9 + 48 = 57$ ft^2

STEP 3 Find the cost of the foil.

$57 \cdot \$0.22 = \$12.54$

The foil will cost $12.54.

Reflect

5. Critical Thinking What shapes would you see in the net of a triangular prism?

two identical triangles and three rectangles

My Notes

Personal Math Trainer
Online Assessment and Intervention
my.hrw.com

YOUR TURN

6. The figure shown is a triangular prism. How much would it cost to cover the bases and the other three faces with foil that costs $0.22 per square foot?

_$7.92_

Guided Practice

A square pyramid is shown.

1. The figure has ____1____ square base and ____4____ triangular faces. (Explore Activity)

2. Find the surface area. (Example 1)

The area of the base is ___36___ square inches.

The area of the four faces is ___48___ square inches.

The surface area is ___84___ square inches.

3. Yolanda makes wooden boxes for a crafts fair. She makes 100 boxes like the one shown, and she wants to paint all the outside faces. (Example 2)

a. Find the surface area of one box.

248 square inches

b. Find the total surface area of 100 boxes.

24,800 square inches

c. One can of paint will cover 14,000 square inches. How many cans of paint will Yolanda need to buy?

2 cans

? ESSENTIAL QUESTION CHECK-IN

4. How is a net useful when finding the surface area of prisms and pyramids?

A net shows the three-dimensional figure as flat and
two-dimensional, which makes it easier to visualize the
shapes of the surfaces and add up their areas.

DIFFERENTIATE INSTRUCTION

Manipulatives

Some students may have difficulty interpreting a drawing of a prism. Give these students three-dimensional models to help them identify the bases and sides. You may also wish to have them use the models to trace the faces when drawing their nets.

Modeling

Give students the nets for several three-dimensional figures on graph paper. Have them cut out the nets and assemble them to make models of the figures. Students can then use the graph paper squares to estimate the surface area before computing the actual surface area. Comparing their actual answers with the estimates will help them determine whether their answers are reasonable.

Additional Resources

Differentiated Instruction includes:

• Reading Strategies
• Success for English Learners **ELL**
• Reteach
• Challenge **PRE-AP**

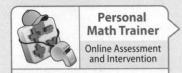

15.1 LESSON QUIZ

COMMON CORE **6.G.4**

1. What shape does this net represent? What is its surface area?

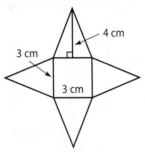

3 cm

4 cm

3 cm

3 cm

2. Find the surface area.

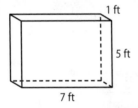

1 ft

5 ft

7 ft

3. Lauren bought a rectangular box that is 6 inches long, 10 inches wide, and 4 inches high. She wants to cover it in fabric. The fabric costs $0.25 per square inch. How much will the fabric cost?

Lesson Quiz available online

Answers

1. square pyramid; 33 square centimeters

2. 94 square feet

3. $62

Evaluate

GUIDED AND INDEPENDENT PRACTICE

COMMON CORE 6.G.4

Concepts & Skills	Practice
Explore Activity Using a Net	Exercise 1
Example 1 Surface Area of a Pyramid	Exercise 2
Example 2 Surface Area of a Prism	Exercises 3, 5–9

Exercise	Depth of Knowledge (D.O.K.)	**COMMON CORE** Mathematical Practices
5–8	**2** Skills/Concepts	**MP.4** Modeling
9	**2** Skills/Concepts	**MP.2** Reasoning
10	**2** Skills/Concepts	**MP.4** Modeling
11	**2** Skills/Concepts	**MP.6** Precision
12–13	**3** Strategic Thinking	**MP.3** Logic

Additional Resources

Differentiated Instruction includes:

• Leveled Practice Worksheets

CC CLUSTER CONNECTION **Exercise 12** combines concepts from the Common Core cluster "Solve real-world and mathematical problems involving area, surface area, and volume."

15.1 Independent Practice

COMMON CORE 6.G.4

Personal Math Trainer

Online Assessment and Intervention

my.hrw.com

5. Use a net to find the surface area of the cereal box.

Total surface area: _____272 in²_____

6. Inez bought a shipping container at a packaging store. She measured the dimensions shown.

a. Sketch a net of the shipping container, and label the dimensions.

b. Find the surface area of the shipping container.

180 square inches

7. Raj builds a side table in the shape of a cube. Each edge of the cube measures 20 inches. Raj wants to cover the top and four sides of the table with ceramic tiles. Each tile has an edge length of 5 inches. How many tiles will he need?

80 tiles

8. Santana wants to cover a gift box shaped like a rectangular prism with foil. The foil costs $0.03 per square inch. Santana has a choice between Box A which is 8 inches long, 3 inches wide, and 6 inches high, and Box B which is 10 inches long, 3 inches wide, and 4 inches high. Which box will be less expensive to cover with foil, and by how much?

Box B will cost $0.48 less than Box A.

9. **Vocabulary** Name a three-dimensional shape that has four triangular faces and one rectangular face. Name a three-dimensional shape that has three rectangular faces and two triangular faces.

rectangular pyramid; triangular prism

10. Victor wrapped the gift box shown with adhesive paper (with no overlaps). How much paper did he use?

236 in²

Lesson 15.1 **423**

11. **Communicate Mathematical Ideas** Describe how you approach a problem involving surface area. What do you do first? What are some strategies you can use?

Sample answer: Decide whether the figure is a prism or a pyramid, and what the shapes of the bases and faces are. Make a net of the figure, and label the dimensions. Use appropriate area formulas to find the areas of the faces, and then find the sum of the areas.

H.O.T. FOCUS ON HIGHER ORDER THINKING

Work Area

12. **Persevere in Problem Solving** A pedestal in a craft store is in the shape of a triangular prism. The bases are right triangles with side lengths of 12 centimeters, 16 centimeters, and 20 centimeters. The store owner wraps a piece of rectangular cloth around the pedestal, but does not cover the identical bases of the pedestal with cloth. The area of the cloth is 192 square centimeters.

a. What is the distance around the base of the pedestal? How do you know?

48 centimeters; the base is a triangle with perimeter 12 + 16 + 20 cm.

b. What is the height of the pedestal? How did you find your answer?

4 centimeters; Sample answer: The cloth is a rectangle whose longer side is 48 centimeters long; the width is the height of the pedestal; 192 ÷ 48 = 4 cm.

13. **Critique Reasoning** Robert sketches two rectangular prisms, A and B. Prism A's side lengths are 5 centimeters, 6 centimeters, and 7 centimeters. Prism B's side lengths were twice those of prism A's: 10 centimeters, 12 centimeters, and 14 centimeters. Robert says the surface area of prism B is twice the surface area of prism A. Is he correct? If he is not, how many times as great as prism A's surface area is prism B's surface area? Show your work.

Robert is incorrect; Surface area of A is 30 + 30 + 42 + 42 + 35 + 35 = 214 square centimeters. Surface area of B is 120 + 120 + 168 + 168 + 140 + 140 = 856 square centimeters. B's surface area is 4 times as great as A's.

424 Unit 6

EXTEND THE MATH PRE-AP

Activity available online my.hrw.com

Activity Find the surface area of the rectangular prism shown with a rectangular-prism-shaped hole all the way through it.

2,592 cm²

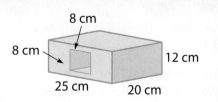

15.2 Volume of Rectangular Prisms

Common Core Standards

The student is expected to:

 Geometry—6.G.2

Find the volume of a right rectangular prism with fractional edge lengths by packing it with unit cubes of the appropriate unit fraction edge lengths, and show that the volume is the same as would be found by multiplying the edge lengths of the prism. Apply the formulas $V = lwh$ and $V = bh$ to find volumes of right rectangular prisms with fractional edge lengths in the context of solving real-world and mathematical problems.

Mathematical Practices

 MP.4 Modeling

ADDITIONAL EXAMPLE 1
Find the volume of the rectangular prism. 77 cubic centimeters

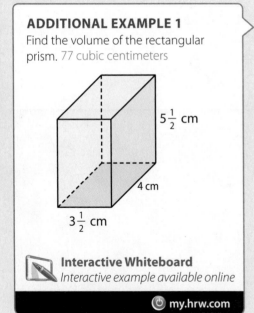

$5\frac{1}{2}$ cm

4 cm

$3\frac{1}{2}$ cm

Interactive Whiteboard
Interactive example available online

⏻ my.hrw.com

Engage

ESSENTIAL QUESTION

How do you find the volume of a rectangular prism? Use the formula $V = lwh$, where l is the length, w is the width, and h is the height.

Motivate the Lesson
Ask: Have you ever wondered how to find the volume of a rectangular aquarium or terrarium? Begin the Explore Activity to find out how to find the volume of a rectangular prism.

Explore

EXPLORE ACTIVITY

Focus on Modeling [CC] Mathematical Practices

Use centimeter cubes to build a rectangular prism that is 4 centimeters long, 2 centimeters wide, and 2 centimeters high. Explain to students that the volume of a three-dimensional figure is the number of cubes it can hold. Show them that you can find the volume of the rectangular prism by counting the cubes or by multiplying the lengths of the edges.

EXAMPLE 1

Focus on Math Connections [CC] Mathematical Practices

Point out to students that the process of finding the volume of a three-dimensional figure is similar to the process of finding the area of a two-dimensional figure, except that now you are multiplying three dimensions. Also, point out that volume is measured in cubic units and area is measured in square units.

Questioning Strategies [CC] Mathematical Practices

• Does the order in which you multiply the dimensions of the prism matter? No. Multiplication is commutative which means that you can multiply numbers in any order and get the same result.

• Describe another way to find the volume of the prism. You can first find the area of the base and then multiply by the height, $V = Bh$.

Connect Vocabulary [ELL]

Make sure that students understand the distinction between the **base** of a prism and the base of a rectangle or parallelogram. In the formula $V = Bh$, B represents the area of a base. In the formula $A = bh$, b represents the length of the base of a rectangle or parallelogram.

YOUR TURN

Avoid Common Errors
Some students may multiply the fraction parts and whole number parts separately when multiplying. Remind them that this method results in an incorrect product, and emphasize that mixed numbers must first be written as improper fractions before multiplying.

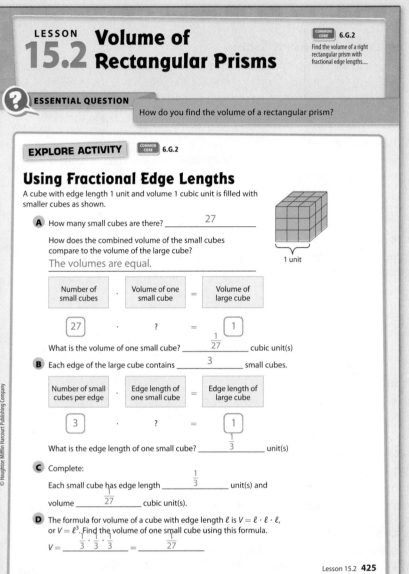

LESSON 15.2 Volume of Rectangular Prisms

COMMON CORE 6.G.2
Find the volume of a right rectangular prism with fractional edge lengths....

? ESSENTIAL QUESTION

How do you find the volume of a rectangular prism?

EXPLORE ACTIVITY   COMMON CORE 6.G.2

Using Fractional Edge Lengths

A cube with edge length 1 unit and volume 1 cubic unit is filled with smaller cubes as shown.

A How many small cubes are there? _____27_____

How does the combined volume of the small cubes compare to the volume of the large cube?
The volumes are equal.

1 unit

Number of small cubes	·	Volume of one small cube	=	Volume of large cube
27	·	?	=	1

What is the volume of one small cube? _____$\frac{1}{27}$_____ cubic unit(s).

B Each edge of the large cube contains _____3_____ small cubes.

Number of small cubes per edge	·	Edge length of one small cube	=	Edge length of large cube
3	·	?	=	1

What is the edge length of one small cube? _____$\frac{1}{3}$_____ unit(s).

C Complete:

Each small cube has edge length _____$\frac{1}{3}$_____ unit(s) and

volume _____$\frac{1}{27}$_____ cubic unit(s).

D The formula for volume of a cube with edge length ℓ is $V = \ell \cdot \ell \cdot \ell$, or $V = \ell^3$. Find the volume of one small cube using this formula.

$V = \underline{\frac{1}{3} \cdot \frac{1}{3} \cdot \frac{1}{3}} = \underline{\frac{1}{27}}$

Lesson 15.2 **425**

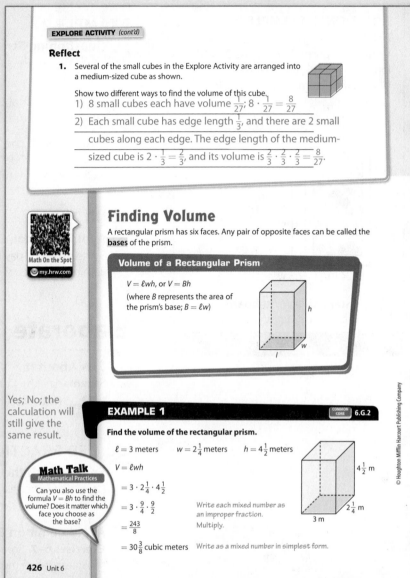

EXPLORE ACTIVITY (cont'd)

Reflect

1. Several of the small cubes in the Explore Activity are arranged into a medium-sized cube as shown.

Show two different ways to find the volume of this cube.
1) 8 small cubes each have volume $\frac{1}{27}$; $8 \cdot \frac{1}{27} = \frac{8}{27}$

2) Each small cube has edge length $\frac{1}{3}$, and there are 2 small cubes along each edge. The edge length of the medium-sized cube is $2 \cdot \frac{1}{3} = \frac{2}{3}$, and its volume is $\frac{2}{3} \cdot \frac{2}{3} \cdot \frac{2}{3} = \frac{8}{27}$.

Finding Volume

A rectangular prism has six faces. Any pair of opposite faces can be called the **bases** of the prism.

Math On the Spot
my.hrw.com

Volume of a Rectangular Prism

$V = \ell w h$, or $V = Bh$
(where B represents the area of the prism's base; $B = \ell w$)

Yes; No; the calculation will still give the same result.

EXAMPLE 1   COMMON CORE 6.G.2

Find the volume of the rectangular prism.

Math Talk
Mathematical Practices
Can you also use the formula $V = Bh$ to find the volume? Does it matter which face you choose as the base?

$\ell = 3$ meters $w = 2\frac{1}{4}$ meters $h = 4\frac{1}{2}$ meters

$V = \ell w h$

$= 3 \cdot 2\frac{1}{4} \cdot 4\frac{1}{2}$

$= 3 \cdot \frac{9}{4} \cdot \frac{9}{2}$ Write each mixed number as an improper fraction.

$= \frac{243}{8}$ Multiply.

$= 30\frac{3}{8}$ cubic meters   Write as a mixed number in simplest form.

$4\frac{1}{2}$ m
$2\frac{1}{4}$ m
3 m

426 Unit 6

PROFESSIONAL DEVELOPMENT

CC Integrate Mathematical Practices MP.4

This lesson provides an opportunity to address the Mathematical Practices standard that calls for students to model with mathematics. Throughout this lesson, students use tools such as diagrams and formulas to solve problems arising in everyday life and society.

Math Background

When students first learned about the exponent 2, they were told that an expression like 5^2 is read "five squared." That is related to the fact that a square with sides of length 5 units has an area of 5^2, or 25 square units.

Similarly, an expression like 6^3 can be related to a cube whose sides have a length of 6 units. By the formula for the volume of a rectangular prism, this cube has a volume of $6 \times 6 \times 6$, or 6^3 cubic units. Just as the model of a square illustrates why we refer to 5^2 as "five squared," the model of a cube illustrates why we refer to 6^3 as "six cubed."

© Houghton Mifflin Harcourt Publishing Company

Volume of Rectangular Prisms **426**

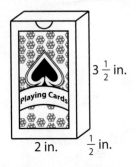

EXAMPLE 2

Questioning Strategies   **CC** Mathematical Practices

- Could another face be used as the base of the prism? Give an example. Yes; for example, if the base is the $13\frac{1}{2} \times 16$ inch face, then $B = 216$ and h would be $25\frac{1}{2}$; $216 \times 25\frac{1}{2} = 5{,}508$.

- If you were to double the length, width, or height of the terrarium, how would the volume be affected? If you double one dimension of the terrarium, the volume doubles as well.

Engage with the Whiteboard

 Have a student find the volume using the formula $V = lwh$ on the whiteboard. Then explain to students that the two formulas are equivalent by showing that $B = lw$.

YOUR TURN

Avoid Common Errors

Some students may forget to write the units or may write square units to represent volume. Remind students that cubic units, not square units, are used to measure volume.

Elaborate

Talk About It
Summarize the Lesson

 Ask: Describe two ways you can find the volume of a rectangular prism. Find the area of one base and multiply by the height, or use the formula $V = lwh$.

GUIDED PRACTICE

Engage with the Whiteboard

For Exercises 3-4, have students fill in the blanks and calculate the volumes of each prism. Ask students to find the volume using both formulas as a check.

Avoid Common Errors

Exercises 6–7 Some students may multiply the fraction parts and whole number parts separately when multiplying. Remind them that this method results in an incorrect product, and emphasize that mixed numbers must first be written as improper fractions before multiplying.

YOUR TURN

Find the volume of each rectangular prism.

2.

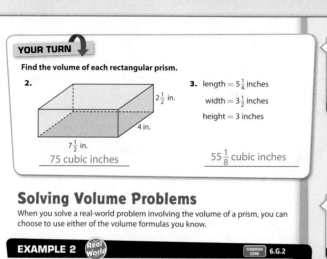

$2\frac{1}{2}$ in.

$7\frac{1}{2}$ in.

4 in.

75 cubic inches

3. length = $5\frac{1}{4}$ inches

width = $3\frac{1}{2}$ inches

height = 3 inches

$55\frac{1}{8}$ cubic inches

Personal
Math Trainer
Online Assessment
and Intervention
my.hrw.com

Solving Volume Problems

When you solve a real-world problem involving the volume of a prism, you can choose to use either of the volume formulas you know.

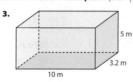
Math On the Spot
my.hrw.com

EXAMPLE 2   Real World

COMMON CORE **6.G.2**

A terrarium is shaped like a rectangular prism. The prism is $25\frac{1}{2}$ inches long, $13\frac{1}{2}$ inches wide, and 16 inches deep. What is the volume of the terrarium?

STEP 1 Choose one side to be the base, and find its area.

$B = 25\frac{1}{2} \times 13\frac{1}{2}$ Use the $25\frac{1}{2}$-inch by $13\frac{1}{2}$-inch face as the base.

$= \frac{51}{2} \times \frac{27}{2}$

$= \frac{1,377}{4}$

> The area of the base is $\frac{1,377}{4}$ square inches. You need to perform another operation, so you don't need to write this value as a mixed number.

STEP 2 Find the volume.

$V = Bh$

$= \frac{1,377}{4} \times 16$ Substitute $\frac{1,377}{4}$ for B and 16 for h.

$= \frac{1,377}{1\cancel{4}} \times \frac{\cancel{16}^{4}}{1}$ Simplify before multiplying.

$= 5,508$

The volume of the terrarium is 5,508 cubic inches.

YOUR TURN

4. A rectangular swimming pool is 15 meters long, $10\frac{1}{2}$ meters wide, and $2\frac{1}{2}$ meters deep. What is its volume?

$393\frac{3}{4}$ cubic meters

Personal
Math Trainer
Online Assessment
and Intervention
my.hrw.com

Lesson 15.2 **427**

Guided Practice

A large cube is made up of smaller unit cubes as shown on the right. Each small cube has an edge length of $\frac{1}{2}$ unit. (Explore Activity)

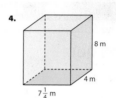

1. Each edge of the large cube is ___2___ units.

2. The volume of the large cube is ___8___ cubic units.

Find the volume of each prism. (Example 1)

3.

5 m

3.2 m

10 m

$V = \underline{\ 10\ } \times \underline{\ 3.2\ } \times \underline{\ 5\ }$

$= \underline{\ 160\ }$ cubic meters

4.

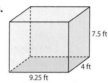

8 m

4 m

$7\frac{1}{4}$ m

$B = \underline{\ 7\frac{1}{4}\ } \times \underline{\ 4\ } = \underline{\ 29\ }$ m^2

$V = \underline{\ 232\ }$ cubic meters

5.

7.5 ft

9.25 ft

4 ft

$V = \underline{\ 277.5\ }$ cubic feet

6.

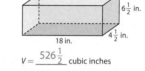

$6\frac{1}{2}$ in.

$4\frac{1}{2}$ in.

18 in.

$V = \underline{\ 526\frac{1}{2}\ }$ cubic inches

7. A cereal box is $8\frac{1}{2}$ inches long, $3\frac{1}{2}$ inches wide, and 12 inches high. What is the volume of the box? (Example 2) ___357 cubic inches___

? ESSENTIAL QUESTION CHECK-IN

8. Which two formulas can you use to find the volume of a rectangular prism? Why are these two formulas equivalent?

$V = lwh$ and $V = Bh$; The area of the base, B, is really lw (length times width), and since both B and lw are multiplied by h, the two are equivalent.

428 Unit 6

DIFFERENTIATE INSTRUCTION

Manipulatives

Have students bring a box, such as a cereal box or cracker box, from home. Have them find the volume of the box. Make a table of the dimensions and volumes on the board. Then ask students if two rectangular prisms can have different heights but the same volume. Ask them to explain their reasoning. Sample answer: Yes, it is possible for two rectangular prisms to have different heights but the same volume. For example, a prism with a 2 × 3 unit base and a height of 2 units has the same volume (12 units^3) as a prism with a 6 × 2 unit base and a height of 1 unit.

Critical Thinking

Have students build a variety of prisms using centimeter cubes. Ask students to count the cubes to find the height, area of the base, and volume of each prism and to record the data in a table as shown.

Area of base	Height	Volume

Ask students to find a relationship between the area of the base, the height, and the volume. Sample answer: The volume is the product of the area of the base and the height, or $V = Bh$.

Additional Resources

Differentiated Instruction includes:

• Reading Strategies

• Success for English Learners **ELL**

• Reteach

• Challenge **PRE-AP**

15.2 LESSON QUIZ

 6.G.2

1. A rectangular prism is 20 inches long, 10 inches wide, and 15 inches high. What is the volume of the prism?

2. What is the volume of a rectangular prism with a length of $2\frac{1}{2}$ inches, a width of $4\frac{1}{4}$ inches, and a height of 3 inches?

3. Find the volume of a rectangular prism with a base that has an area of 22 cm² and a height of 8 cm.

4. A classroom is $32\frac{1}{2}$ feet long, 30 feet wide, and $7\frac{1}{2}$ feet high. What is the volume of the classroom?

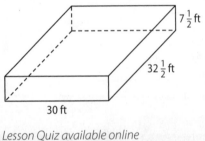

Lesson Quiz available online

 my.hrw.com

Answers

1. 3,000 cubic inches

2. $31\frac{7}{8}$ cubic inches

3. 176 cm³

4. 6.72 ft³, 1.6 ft

Evaluate

GUIDED AND INDEPENDENT PRACTICE

COMMON CORE 6.G.2

Concepts and Skills	Practice
Explore Activity Using Fractional Edge Lengths	Exercises 1–2
Example 1 Finding Volume	Exercises 3–6
Example 2 Solving Volume Problems	Exercises 7, 9–10, 12–15

Exercise	Depth of Knowledge (D.O.K.)	COMMON CORE Mathematical Practices
9–10	**2** Skills/Concepts	**MP.4** Modeling
11	**3** Strategic Thinking **H.O.T.**	**MP.2** Reasoning
12–13	**2** Skills/Concepts	**MP.4** Modeling
14	**3** Strategic Thinking **H.O.T.**	**MP.2** Reasoning
15	**2** Skills/Concepts	**MP.4** Modeling
16–17	**3** Strategic Thinking **H.O.T.**	**MP.2** Reasoning
18	**3** Strategic Thinking **H.O.T.**	**MP.6** Precision
19	**3** Strategic Thinking **H.O.T.**	**MP.2** Reasoning

Additional Resources

Differentiated Instruction includes:

• Leveled Practice Worksheets

15.2 Independent Practice

COMMON CORE 6.G.2

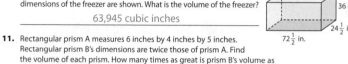

Personal Math Trainer
Online Assessment and Intervention
my.hrw.com

9. A block of wood measures 4.5 inches by 3.5 inches by 7 inches. What is the volume of the block of wood?

110.25 cubic inches

10. A restaurant buys a freezer in the shape of a rectangular prism. The dimensions of the freezer are shown. What is the volume of the freezer?

63,945 cubic inches

36 in.
$24\frac{1}{2}$ in.
$72\frac{1}{2}$ in.

11. Rectangular prism A measures 6 inches by 4 inches by 5 inches. Rectangular prism B's dimensions are twice those of prism A. Find the volume of each prism. How many times as great is prism B's volume as prism A's volume?

A: 120 in³; B: 960 in³; 8 times as great

12. Leticia has a small paper weight in the shape of a rectangular prism. The dimensions of the paper weight are shown. What is the volume of the paper weight?

$58\frac{7}{16}$ cubic centimeters

5 cm
$2\frac{3}{4}$ cm
$4\frac{1}{4}$ cm

13. A company is designing a juice box. The box is in the shape of a rectangular prism. The base of the box is $6\frac{1}{2}$ inches by $2\frac{1}{2}$ inches, and the box is 4 inches high. If juice fills 90% of the box's volume, find the volume of juice in the box.

58.5 cubic inches

14. **Science** Density is the amount of mass in a certain volume of an object. To find the density in grams per cubic centimeter of a substance you can use this relationship:

$$\text{Density} = \frac{\text{mass in grams}}{\text{volume in cubic centimeters}}$$

A gold bar that is 16 centimeters by 2.5 centimeters by 5 centimeters has a density of 19.3 grams per cubic centimeter. What is the mass of the gold bar?

3,860 grams

15. A suitcase is a rectangular prism whose dimensions are $1\frac{1}{4}$ feet by $1\frac{3}{4}$ feet by $1\frac{1}{4}$ feet. Find the volume of the suitcase.

$2\frac{47}{64}$ cubic feet

© Houghton Mifflin Harcourt Publishing Company • Image Credits:

16. The Smith family is moving and needs to decide on the size of the moving truck they should rent.

a. A moving van rents for $94.50 per day, and a small truck rents for $162 per day. Based on the amount of space inside the van or truck, which is the better deal? Explain your answer.

They cost the same per unit volume; the van's volume is 378 ft³, so the cost is $0.25 per ft³ and the small truck volume is 648 ft³, so the cost is $0.25 per ft³.

Inside Dimensions of Trucks			
Type	Length (ft)	Width (ft)	Height (ft)
Van	$10\frac{1}{2}$	6	6
Small Truck	12	8	$6\frac{3}{4}$
Large Truck	20	$8\frac{3}{4}$	$8\frac{1}{2}$

b. How much greater is the volume of the large truck than the volume of the small truck?

839.5 cubic feet

c. The family estimates that they need about 1,100 cubic feet to move their belongings. What should they rent?

the large truck

H.O.T. FOCUS ON HIGHER ORDER THINKING

Work Area

17. **Persevere in Problem Solving** A cube has a volume of $\frac{1}{512}$ cubic meter. What is the length of each side of the cube? Explain your thinking.

$\frac{1}{8}$ m; find a fraction that, when multiplied by itself 3 times, equals $\frac{1}{512}$.

18. **Communicate Mathematical Ideas** Think about two rectangular prisms, one labeled prism P and one labeled prism Q.

a. Suppose the bases of the prisms have the same area, but the height of prism Q is twice the height of prism P. How do the volumes compare?

The volume of Q is twice the volume of P.

b. Suppose the area of the base of prism Q is twice the area of the base of prism P. How do the volumes compare?

The volume of Q is twice the volume of P.

19. **Critical Thinking** The dimensions of a rectangular prism are $3\frac{1}{4}$ feet by $2\frac{1}{2}$ feet by 5 feet. Lee found the volume by multiplying $12\frac{1}{2}$ by $3\frac{1}{4}$. Lola found the volume by multiplying $16\frac{1}{4}$ by $2\frac{1}{2}$. Who is correct? Explain.

Both are correct. Lee used the $2\frac{1}{2}$ by 5-foot face as the base and $3\frac{1}{4}$ as the height, then multiplied the base area, $12\frac{1}{2}$, by the height. Lola used the $3\frac{1}{4}$ by 5-foot face as the base and $2\frac{1}{2}$ as the height, then multiplied the base area, $16\frac{1}{4}$, by the height.

© Houghton Mifflin Harcourt Publishing Company

EXTEND THE MATH PRE-AP

Activity available online ⊙ my.hrw.com

Activity A 5-inch section of a hollow brick measures 12 inches tall and 8 inches wide on the outside. The brick is 1 inch thick. Find the volume of the brick, not the hollow interior.

180 in³

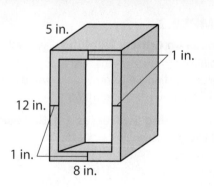

5 in.
1 in.
12 in.
1 in.
8 in.

LESSON
15.3 Solving Volume Equations

Common Core Standards

The student is expected to:

 Expressions and Equations—6.EE.7

Solve real-world and mathematical problems by writing and solving equations of the form $x + p = q$ and $px = q$ for cases in which p, q, and x are all nonnegative rational numbers.

 Geometry—6.G.2

Find the volume of a right rectangular prism with fractional edge lengths by packing it with unit cubes of the appropriate unit fraction edge lengths, and show that the volume is the same as would be found by multiplying the edge lengths of the prism. Apply the formulas $V = lwh$ and $V = bh$ to find volumes of right rectangular prisms with fractional edge lengths in the context of solving real-world and mathematical problems.

Mathematical Practices

 MP.6 Precision

ADDITIONAL EXAMPLE 1
Abby has a shoebox with a volume of 609 cubic inches. The length of the shoebox is 14.5 inches, and the width is 7 inches. What is the height of the shoebox? 6 in.

 Interactive Whiteboard
Interactive example available online

⏻ my.hrw.com

ADDITIONAL EXAMPLE 2
One cubic foot of oil equals approximately 0.2 barrel and weighs approximately 55 pounds.

A rectangular oil storage tank holds 210 barrels of oil. It is 7 feet wide and has a height of 10 feet. What is the length of the tank? 15 ft

 Interactive Whiteboard
Interactive example available online

 ⏻ my.hrw.com

Engage

ESSENTIAL QUESTION
How do you write equations to solve problems involving volume of rectangular prisms?
Sample answer: Use $V = lwh$ to write an equation. Substitute known values and solve.

Motivate the Lesson
Ask: Have you ever wondered about the volume of a swimming pool, or how much water it takes to fill an aquarium? Begin Example 1 to find out.

Explore

Engage with the Whiteboard
 Make a model of a rectangular prism using cubes ($4 \times 2 \times 3$) on the whiteboard. Ask students how many cubes make up this prism. Tell them they have just found the volume of the prism. Then tell them that they can also use $V = lwh$ to find the volume.

Explain

EXAMPLE 1

Focus on Math Connections CC **Mathematical Practices**
Point out to students that finding a missing dimension in a problem involving volume is similar to finding an unknown value using an area formula.

Questioning Strategies
• How do you know what operation to use? The formula for volume is a multiplication equation, so you will need to use division to find any one of the missing dimensions.

YOUR TURN

Avoid Common Errors
Remind students that dividing by a number is the same as multiplying by its reciprocal.

EXAMPLE 2

Focus on Critical Thinking CC **Mathematical Practices**
Point out to students that just as with problems involving area, you can use the formula for volume to find a missing or unknown dimension. The process is the same; you just have an additional variable to work with.

Questioning Strategies CC **Mathematical Practices**
• In Step 1, why is 30 gallons divided by 7.5 gallons per cubic foot? To find the length of the aquarium in cubic feet, you need to express 30 gallons as a measure in cubic feet. To do so, you need to divide 30 gallons by the conversion factor, 7.5 gallons per cubic foot.

YOUR TURN

Avoid Common Errors
Remind students that they must first convert the amount of water the aquarium holds to cubic feet before they can find the width of the aquarium.

LESSON 15.3 Solving Volume Equations

COMMON CORE 6.G.2

... Apply the formulas $V = \ell wh$ and $V = bh$ ... in the context of solving real-world and mathematical problems. Also 6.EE.7

 ESSENTIAL QUESTION How do you write equations to solve problems involving volume of rectangular prisms?

Writing Equations Using the Volume of a Rectangular Prism

You can use the formula for the volume of a rectangular prism to write an equation. Then solve the equation to find missing measurements for a prism.

EXAMPLE 1

COMMON CORE 6.G.2, 6.EE.7

Samuel has an ant farm with a volume of 375 cubic inches. The width of the ant farm is 2.5 inches and the length is 15 inches. What is the height of Samuel's ant farm?

$V = \ell wh$ Write the formula.

$375 = 15 \cdot 2.5 \cdot h$ Use the formula to write an equation.

$375 = 37.5h$ Multiply.

$\dfrac{375}{37.5} = \dfrac{37.5h}{37.5}$ Divide both sides of the equation by 37.5.

$10 = h$

The height of the ant farm is 10 inches.

Reflect

1. **Communicate Mathematical Ideas** Explain how you would find the solution to Example 1 using the formula $V = Bh$.

Multiply 15×2.5 to find B, 37.5. Then divide the volume, 375, by 37.5.

YOUR TURN

2. Find the height of this rectangular prism, which has a volume of $\frac{15}{16}$ cubic feet.

The height is $\frac{5}{2}$ ft or $2\frac{1}{2}$ ft.

  $\frac{3}{4}$ ft $\frac{1}{2}$ ft

Solving Multistep Problems

One cubic foot of water equals approximately 7.5 gallons and weighs approximately 62.43 pounds.

EXAMPLE 2

COMMON CORE 6.G.2, 6.EE.7

The classroom aquarium holds 30 gallons of water. It is 0.8 feet wide and has a height of 2 feet. Find the length of the aquarium.

STEP 1 Find the volume of the classroom aquarium in cubic feet.

$\dfrac{30 \text{ gallons}}{7.5 \text{ gallons per cubic foot}} = 4$ cubic feet

> Divide the total number of gallons by the unit rate to find the number of cubic feet.

STEP 2 Find the length of the aquarium.

$4 = \ell \cdot 0.8 \cdot 2$ Use the formula $V = \ell wh$ to write an equation.

$4 = \ell(1.6)$ Multiply.

$\dfrac{4}{1.6} = \dfrac{\ell(1.6)}{1.6}$ Divide both sides of the equation by 1.6.

$2.5 = \ell$

The length of the aquarium is 2.5 feet.

Math Talk
Mathematical Practices

How much does the water in the classroom aquarium weigh? Explain.

249.72 pounds; one cubic foot weighs 62.43 pounds.
$62.43 \times 4 = 249.72$

YOUR TURN

3. An aquarium holds 33.75 gallons of water. It has a length of 2 feet and a height of 1.5 feet. What is the width of the aquarium? ___1.5 feet___

Guided Practice

1. Use an equation to find the width of the rectangular prism. (Example 1)

$6,336 = 16(18)w$; $w = 22$ centimeters

$V = 6,336 \text{ cm}^3$
18 cm
16 cm
? cm

2. One clay brick weighs 5.76 pounds. The brick is 8 inches long and $2\frac{1}{4}$ inches wide. If the clay weighs 0.08 pounds per cubic inch, what is the volume of the brick? Find the height of the brick. (Example 2)

$V = 72 \text{ in}^3$; 4 inches

DIFFERENTIATE INSTRUCTION

Home Connection

Students may be unfamiliar with the volumes of rectangular prisms commonly found in their homes. Point out, for example, that they can calculate the volumes of items such as a juice box, a cereal box, a container of milk, a jewelry box, or even a rectangular cake. Ask students to select an item they can find at home, and have them estimate the volume of that item. Then have them share their work with the class. Make a list of all the items students choose.

Critical Thinking

Ask: How does increasing the area of a base of a rectangular prism affect its volume if the prism's height remains the same? Explain and give an example. Sample answer: If the area of the base increases, the volume also increases because $V = Bh = lwh$. For example, doubling the area doubles the volume. Increasing the length of a side of the base also increases the area, so the volume becomes greater as well (e.g., If a prism is 5 in. × 4 in. × 3 in., $V = 60$ in³, but If the width (4 in.) becomes 5 in., then $V = 75$ in³.).

Additional Resources

Differentiated Instruction includes:

- Reading Strategies
- Success for English Learners **ELL**
- Reteach
- Challenge **PRE-AP**

15.3 LESSON QUIZ

 6.EE.7, 6.G.2

1. The volume of a prism is 48 cubic centimeters. If the length is 2 centimeters and the width is 4 centimeters, what is the height?

2. Jeremy has a wooden box that has a volume of 160,000 cubic centimeters. The length of the box is 80 cm, and the height is 40 cm. What is the width of the box?

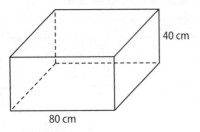

40 cm

80 cm

3. One cubic foot of water equals approximately 7.5 gallons. A rectangular restaurant sink holds 50.4 gallons of water. It has a length of 3 ft and a height of 1.4 ft. What is the volume of the sink? What is the width of the sink?

Lesson Quiz available online

ⓜ **my.hrw.com**

Answers

1. 6 cm

2. 50 cm

3. 6.72 ft³, 1.6 ft

Elaborate

Talk About It
Summarize the Lesson

Ask: How can you use equations to solve problems involving the volume of right rectangular prisms? Use $A = lwh$, the formula for the volume of a rectangular prism, to write an equation. Then substitute known values for variables into the equation and solve for the unknown dimension.

GUIDED PRACTICE

Engage with the Whiteboard

For Exercise 2, have students circle or highlight the important information in the problem on the whiteboard. Ask them to sketch the figure, labeling known dimensions. Then have them find the height of the brick and explain their reasoning.

Avoid Common Errors

Exercise 2 Remind students that they must first convert the volume of the brick from pounds to cubic inches before they can find the height of the brick.

Evaluate

GUIDED AND INDEPENDENT PRACTICE

 6.EE.7, 6.G.2

Concepts & Skills	Practice
Example 1 Writing Equations Using the Volume of a Rectangular Prism	Exercises 1, 3–5
Example 2 Solving Multistep Problems	Exercises 2, 6–10

Exercise	Depth of Knowledge (D.O.K.)	**Mathematical Practices**
3–6	**2** Skills/Concepts	**MP.4** Modeling
7	**2** Skills/Concepts	**MP.3** Logic
8–9	**2** Skills/Concepts	**MP.4** Modeling
10	**2** Skills/Concepts	**MP.3** Logic
11	**3** Strategic Thinking H.O.T.	**MP.4** Modeling
12	**3** Strategic Thinking H.O.T.	**MP.7** Using Structure
13	**3** Strategic Thinking H.O.T.	**MP.2** Reasoning
14	**3** Strategic Thinking H.O.T.	**MP.3** Logic

Additional Resources

Differentiated Instruction includes:

• Leveled Practice Worksheets

15.3 Independent Practice

COMMON CORE 6.EE.7, 6.G.2

Personal
Math Trainer
Online
Assessment and
Intervention
my.hrw.com

3. Jala has an aquarium in the shape of a rectangular prism with the dimensions shown. What is the height of the aquarium?

Height = ___12.4 inches___

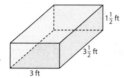
V = 3,758.75 cubic inches
12.5 in.
24.25 in.
?

4. The area of the base of a rectangular juice box is $4\frac{1}{2}$ square inches. If the volume of the box is 18 cubic inches, how tall is the box?

Height = ___4 inches___

5. A box of cereal is shaped like a rectangular prism. The box is 20 centimeters long and 30 centimeters high. Its volume is 3,600 cubic centimeters. Find the width of the box.

Width = ___6 centimeters___

6. About 7.5 gallons of water fill up 1 cubic foot of space. How many gallons of water will fill a goldfish pool shaped like the prism shown?

$118\frac{1}{8}$ gallons

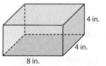
$1\frac{1}{2}$ ft
$3\frac{1}{2}$ ft
3 ft

7. **Physical Science** A small bar of gold measures 40 mm by 25 mm by 2 mm. One cubic millimeter of gold weighs about 0.0005 ounce. Find the volume in cubic millimeters and the weight in ounces of this small bar of gold.

The volume of the bar is 2,000 cubic millimeters, and the weight of the bar is 1 ounce.

8. **History** A typical stone on the lowest level of the Great Pyramid in Egypt was a rectangular prism 5 feet long by 5 feet high by 6 feet deep and weighed 15 tons. What was the volume of the average stone? How much did one cubic foot of this stone weigh?

150 cubic feet; 0.1 ton

9. Hank has cards that are 8 inches by 4 inches. A stack of these cards fits inside the box shown and uses up 32 cubic inches of volume. How tall is the stack of cards? What percent of the box's volume is taken up by the cards?

1 inch; 25%

4 in.
4 in.
8 in.

10. A freshwater fish is healthiest when there is at least 1 gallon of water for every inch of its body length. Roshel wants to put a goldfish that is about $2\frac{1}{2}$ inches long in her tank. Roshel's tank is 7 inches long, 5 inches wide, and 7 inches high. The volume of 1 gallon of water is about 231 cubic inches.

a. How many gallons of water would Roshel need for the fish? 2.5 gallons

b. What is the volume of Roshel's tank? 245 cubic inches

c. Is her fish tank large enough for the fish? Explain. No, the fish would need 577.5 cubic inches of water.

H.O.T. FOCUS ON HIGHER ORDER THINKING

Work Area

11. **Multistep** Larry has a clay brick that is 7 inches long, 3.5 inches wide, and 1.75 inches thick, the same size as the gold stored in Fort Knox in the form of gold bars. Find the volume of this brick. If the weight of the clay in the brick is 0.1 pound per cubic inch and the weight of the gold is 0.7 pound per cubic inch, find the weight of the brick and the gold bar. Round all answers the nearest tenth.

Volume of the brick or bar = ___42.9___ cubic inches

Weight of the brick = ___4.3___ pounds

Weight of the gold bar = ___30.0___ pounds

12. **Represent Real-World Problems** Luisa's toaster oven, which is in the shape of a rectangular prism, has a base that is 55 cm long by 40 cm wide. It is 30 cm high. Luisa wants to buy a different oven with the same volume but a smaller length, so it will fit better on her kitchen counter. What is a possible set of dimensions for this different oven?

Sample answer: If the base area B and the height h are the same, the volume will also be the same. The length could be 50 cm, the width 44 cm, and the height 30 cm.

13. **Multiple Representations** Use the formula $V = Bh$ to write a different version of this formula that you could use to find the area of the base B of a rectangular prism if you know the height h and the volume V. Explain what you did to find this equation.

Begin with $V = Bh$ and divide both sides of the equation by h to get $B = \frac{V}{h}$.

14. **Communicate Mathematical Ideas** The volume of a cube is 27 cubic inches. What is the length of an edge? Explain.

3 inches; $3 \cdot 3 \cdot 3 = 27$

EXTEND THE MATH PRE-AP

Activity available online my.hrw.com

Activity Jeff's new tent is shaped like a triangular prism. Each triangular face of the prism has a base length of 4.5 feet and a height of 4 feet. The height of the prism is 6.5 feet. What is the volume of the tent? Explain.

58.5 ft³; use the formula, $V = Bh$. For a triangular prism, B = area of the triangular base $= \frac{1}{2}bh = \frac{1}{2}(4.5 \cdot 4$ ft$) = 9$ ft². The height of the prism is 6.5 ft. So, $V = 9 \cdot 6.5 = 58.5$ ft³.

The volume of Jeff's old tent was 46.8 cubic feet. How many times as great as the volume of the old tent is the volume of the new one?

1.25 times as great

Ready to Go On?

Assess Mastery

Use the assessment on this page to determine if students have mastered the concepts and standards covered in this module.

RtI Response to Intervention

Intervention	Enrichment

Access Are You Ready? assessment online, and receive instant scoring, feedback, and customized intervention or enrichment.

Online and Print Resources

Differentiated Instruction
- Reteach worksheets
- Reading Strategies **ELL**
- Success for English Learners **ELL**

Differentiated Instruction
- Challenge worksheets **PRE-AP**
- Extend the Math **PRE-AP** Lesson Activities in TE

Additional Resources

Assessment Resources includes:
- Leveled Module Quizzes

Ready to Go On?

15.1 Nets and Surface Area

A square pyramid is shown sitting on its base.

1. Draw the net of the pyramid.

2. The surface area of the pyramid is ___336___ square centimeters.

15.2 Volume of Rectangular Prisms

Find the volume of each rectangular prism.

3.

$V = $ ___$414\frac{9}{16}$___ cubic meters

4.

$V = $ ___$73\frac{1}{8}$___ cubic feet

15.3 Solving Volume Equations

Find the volume of each rectangular prism.

5. The volume inside a rectangular storage room is 2,025 cubic feet. The room is 9 feet high. Find the area of the floor. ___$225\ ft^2$___

6. An aquarium holds 11.25 cubic feet of water, and is 2.5 feet long and 1.5 feet wide. What is its depth? ___3 ft___

❓ ESSENTIAL QUESTION

7. How can a model help you to solve surface area and volume problems?
A net shows faces and helps you find surface area; a drawing helps you choose a base and height when finding volume.

Common Core Standards

Lesson	Exercises	Common Core Standards
15.1	1–2	6.G.4
15.2	3–4	6.G.2
15.3	5–6	6.EE.7, 6.G.2

Assessment Readiness

Item 1 If students have difficulty getting started, encourage them to draw a net of the figure to help them see the faces of the prism. If they do they will see that there are six faces for this figure.

Item 3 If students have difficulty getting started, encourage them to draw a net of the figure to help them see the faces of the prism. If they do they will see that there are five faces for this figure.

Avoid Common Errors

Item 2 Some students may solve for the volume of one compartment and quickly select choice A. Remind students to read the problem carefully to be sure they are answering the correct question. Point out that there are 12 compartments in the tray, and they need to find the volume of all 12 compartments.

Item 5 If students have difficulty getting started, encourage them to draw a diagram first. Then they should be able to choose the correct formula to find the surface area of the rectangular prism.

Additional Resources

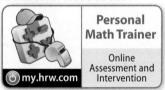

Personal Math Trainer
Online Assessment and Intervention
my.hrw.com

MODULE 15 **MIXED REVIEW**

COMMON CORE

Assessment Readiness

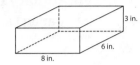

Personal Math Trainer
Online Assessment and Intervention
my.hrw.com

Selected Response

1. Indira is wrapping the box below. How much wrapping paper does she need?

3 in.
6 in.
8 in.

- (A) 34 in.^{2}
- (C) 144 in.^{2}
- (B) 90 in.^{2}
- (D) 180 in.^{2}

2. Colin has an ice cube tray with 12 identical compartments. Each compartment is a prism that is 4 centimeters long, 3 centimeters wide, and 3 centimeters high. Given that 1 cubic centimeter holds 1 milliliter of water, how many milliliters of water can the tray hold?

- (A) 36 mL
- (C) 432 mL
- (B) 66 mL
- (D) 792 mL

3. A store manager set up a cardboard display to advertise a new brand of perfume. The display is a square pyramid whose base is 18 inches on each side. The height of each triangular face of the pyramid is 12 inches. How much cardboard was used to make the display?

- (A) 516 in^2
- (C) 756 in^2
- (B) 612 in^2
- (D) 1,080 in^2

4. Which expression is equivalent to $24 + 32$?

- (A) $8 \times (3 + 4)$
- (B) $8 \times (3 + 32)$
- (C) $6 \times (4 + 32)$
- (D) $6 \times (4 + 6)$

5. A bathtub in the shape of a rectangular prism is 5 feet long, $3\frac{1}{2}$ feet wide, and $4\frac{1}{4}$ feet high. How much water could the tub hold?

- (A) $14\frac{7}{8}$ ft^3
- (C) $74\frac{3}{8}$ ft^3
- (B) $25\frac{1}{2}$ ft^3
- (D) $87\frac{1}{2}$ ft^3

6. The point $(-1.5, 2)$ is reflected across the y-axis, What are the coordinates of the point after the reflection?

- (A) $(-1.5, -2)$
- (C) $(2, -1.5)$
- (B) $(1.5, 2)$
- (D) $(2, 1.5)$

Mini-Task

7. An cardboard box is open at one end and is shaped like a square prism missing one of its square bases. The volume of the prism is 810 cubic inches, and its height is 10 inches.

a. What is the length of each side of the base? _____ 9 inches _____

b. Draw a net of the box.

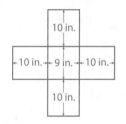

10 in.
←10 in.→←9 in.→←10 in.→
10 in.

c. How much cardboard is used for the box?

_____ 441 square feet _____

© Houghton Mifflin Harcourt Publishing Company

Common Core Standards

Items	Grade 6 Standards	Mathematical Practices
1	6.G.4, 6.EE.7	MP.4
2	6.G.2, 6.EE.7	MP.4
3	6.G.4, 6.EE.7	MP.4
4*	6.EE.3	MP.7
5	6.G.2, 6.EE.7	MP.4
6*	6.NS.8	MP.2
7	6.G.2, 6.G.4	MP.4

* Item integrates mixed review concepts from previous modules or a previous course.

Study Guide Review

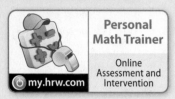
Vocabulary Development

Integrating Language Arts

Encourage students to practice using the unit vocabulary as they talk and write about mathematics. Understanding vocabulary will aid their understanding of the concepts.

COMMON CORE **ELA-Literacy.RST.6-8.4** Determine the meaning of symbols, key terms, and other domain-specific words and phrases as they are used in a specific scientific or technical context relevant to grades 6–8 texts and topics.

MODULE 13 Area and Polygons

COMMON CORE **6.G.1, 6.EE.7**

Key Concepts
- The area A of a parallelogram is the product of its base b and its height h, $A = bh$. *(Lesson 13.1)*
- The area of a rhombus is half of the product of its two diagonals, $A = \frac{1}{2}d_1d_2$. *(Lesson 13.1)*
- The area A of a triangle is half the product of its base b and its height h, $A = \frac{1}{2}bh$. *(Lesson 13.2)*
- The area of a trapezoid is half its height multiplied by the sum of the lengths of its two bases, $A = \frac{1}{2}h(b_1 + b_2)$. *(Lesson 13.4)*
- You can find the area of a polygon by breaking the polygon into smaller shapes. *(Lesson 13.4)*

MODULE 14 Distance and Area in the Coordinate Plane

COMMON CORE **6.G.3, 6.NS.6b, 6.NS.8**

Key Concepts
- A point on a coordinate plane can be reflected across an axis. *(Lesson 14.1)*
- The vertices of a polygon can be represented as ordered pairs. The polygon can then be drawn in the coordinate plane. *(Lesson 14.2)*

Study Guide Review

Key Vocabulary
parallelogram *(paralelogramo)*
rhombus *(rombo)*
trapezoid *(trapecio)*

? ESSENTIAL QUESTION

How can you use area and volume equations to solve real-world problems?

EXAMPLE 1

Find the area of the trapezoid.

4 in.

10 in.

7 in.

$A = \frac{1}{2}(h)(b_1 + b_2)$

$A = \frac{1}{2}(10)(7 + 4)$

$A = 55$ in²

EXAMPLE 2

Find the area of Jorge's backyard.

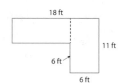

18 ft

11 ft

6 ft

6 ft

Find the area of the first rectangle.	Find the area of the second rectangle.
$A = bh$	$A = bh$
$A = 12(5)$	$A = 6(11)$
$A = 60$ square feet	$A = 66$ square feet

Total area of yard = 60 + 66 = 126 square feet

EXERCISES

Find the area of each figure. *(Lessons 13.1, 13.2)*

1.

24 in.

12 in.

___288 in²___

2.

5 cm

10 cm

10 cm

___75 cm²___

Find the missing measurement. *(Lesson 13.3)*

3.

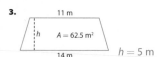

11 m

h

$A = 62.5$ m²

14 m

___$h = 5$ m___

4.

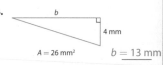

b

4 mm

$A = 26$ mm²

___$b = 13$ mm___

Key Vocabulary
polygon *(polígono)*
reflection *(reflexión)*
vertex, vertices *(vértice, vértices)*

? ESSENTIAL QUESTION

What steps might you take to solve a polygon problem given the coordinates of its vertices?

EXAMPLE 1

Find the distance between points A and B on the coordinate plane.

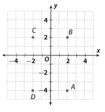

Find the distance between point A and the x-axis.

The y-coordinate is -4. The absolute value represents the distance.

$|-4| = 4$ The distance is 4 units.

Find the distance between point B and the x-axis.

The y-coordinate is 2. The distance is 2 units.

Add the two distances to find the distance between the two points.

$4 + 2 = 6$ The distance between points A and B is 6 units.

EXAMPLE 2

Find the area of the rectangle whose vertices are the points on the coordinate plane in Example 1.

Use the distance between points A and B in Example 1 as the height.

height = 6 units

Find the distance between points A and D and use it as the base.

Distance from A to $D = |-2| + 2 = 2 + 2 = 4$

base = 4 units

Find the area.

$A = bh = 4 \cdot 6 = 24$ square units

EXERCISES

Find the distance between the two points.

1. Z and Y ___8 units___

2. X and Y ___14 units___

3. W and X ___14 units___

4. Find the area of rectangle $XYZV$. ___112 units²___

MODULE 15 Surface Area and Volume of Solids

 6.G.2, 6.G.4, 6.EE.7

Key Concepts
- The surface area of a three-dimensional figure is the sum of the areas of its faces. A net can be helpful when finding surface area. *(Lesson 15.1)*
- A rectangular prism has six faces. Any pair of opposite faces can be called the bases of the prism. *(Lesson 15.2)*
- The volume V of a rectangular prism is the product of its length l, its width w, and its height h, $V = lwh$. *(Lesson 15.3)*

Unit 6 Performance Tasks

The Performance Tasks provide students with the opportunity to apply concepts from this unit in real-world problem situations.

CAREERS IN MATH

Theater Set Construction In Performance Task Item 1, students can see how a person working in theater set construction uses mathematics on the job.

SCORING GUIDES FOR PERFORMANCE TASKS

1. MATHEMATICAL PRACTICES **MP.4, MP.3**

Task	Possible Points (Total: 5)
a	**2 points** for answer and work: $\frac{1}{2}(1.5 \text{ ft})(1 \text{ ft}) + \frac{1}{2}(2 \text{ ft})(1.5 \text{ ft}) + \frac{1}{2}(1 \text{ ft})(0.75 \text{ ft}) + (0.75 \text{ ft})(5 \text{ ft}) =$ $0.75 \text{ ft}^2 + 1.5 \text{ ft}^2 + 0.375 \text{ ft}^2 + 3.75 \text{ ft}^2 = 6.375 \text{ ft}^2$
b	**1 point** for each correct answer and work: pyramid area: $0.75 \text{ ft}^2 + 1.5 \text{ ft}^2 + 0.375 \text{ ft}^2 = 2.625 \text{ ft}^2$ pyramid paint: $2(2.625 \text{ ft}^2)\left(\frac{1 \text{ quart}}{45 \text{ ft}^2}\right) = 0.12$ quart base area: 3.75 ft^2; base paint: $2(3.75 \text{ ft}^2)\left(\frac{1 \text{ quart}}{45 \text{ ft}^2}\right) = 0.17$ quart

Surface Area and Volume of Solids

? ESSENTIAL QUESTION

How can a model help you solve surface area and volume problems?

EXAMPLE 1

Draw a net and find the surface area of the pyramid.

8 cm
4 cm

8 cm
4 cm

Find the area of the square base.

$A = bh$

$A = 4 \cdot 4$

$A = 16 \text{ cm}^2$

Find the area of one triangle and multiply by four.

$A = \frac{1}{2}bh$

$A = \frac{1}{2}(4 \cdot 8)$

$A = 16 \text{ cm}^2$

The area of the 4 triangles is $4 \cdot 16 = 64 \text{ cm}^2$.

The total surface area of the pyramid is $16 \text{ cm}^2 + 64 \text{ cm}^2 = 80 \text{ cm}^2$.

EXAMPLE 2

A cubic centimeter of gold weighs approximately 19.32 grams. Find the weight of a brick of gold that has a height of 6 centimeters, width of 3 centimeters, and length of 8 centimeters.

8 cm
6 cm
3 cm

$V = lwh$

$V = 8(3)(6)$

$V = 144 \text{ cm}^3$

The weight of the gold is 144×19.32 grams, which is 2,782.08 grams.

EXERCISES

Draw a net to find the surface area of each solid shape. (Lesson 15.1)

1.

7 in.
5 in.
3 in.

_____142 in²_____

2.

14 cm

8 cm

_____288 in²_____

Find the volume of each rectangular prism. (Lesson 15.2)

3.

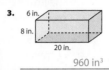

6 in.
8 in.
20 in.

_____960 in³_____

4. A rectangular prism with a width of 7 units, a length of 8 units, and a height of 2 units _____112 cubic units_____

Unit 6 Performance Tasks

1. CAREERS IN MATH | **Theater Set Construction** Ahmed and Karina are building scenery of the Egyptian pyramids out of plywood for a community play. The pyramids are represented by triangles on a rectangular base. The diagram shows the measurements of the piece of scenery.

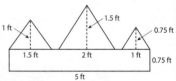

1 ft
1.5 ft
0.75 ft
1.5 ft
2 ft
1 ft
0.75 ft
5 ft

a. How many square feet of plywood is in the scenery? Show your work.

$\frac{1}{2}(1.5 \text{ ft})(1 \text{ ft}) + \frac{1}{2}(2 \text{ ft})(1.5 \text{ ft}) + \frac{1}{2}(1 \text{ ft})(0.75 \text{ ft}) + (0.75 \text{ ft})(5 \text{ ft}) =$

$0.75 \text{ ft}^2 + 1.5 \text{ ft}^2 + 0.375 \text{ ft}^2 + 3.75 \text{ ft}^2 = 6.375 \text{ ft}^2$

b. The pyramids (the triangles) will be painted gray, and the base (the rectangle) will be painted black. How much of each paint color will they use, if one quart covers 45 square feet? Only one side of the model needs to be painted, but two coats of paint will be needed. Show your work. Round to the nearest hundredth of a square foot.

pyramid area: $0.75 \text{ ft}^2 + 1.5 \text{ ft}^2 + 0.375 \text{ ft}^2 = 2.625 \text{ ft}^2$;

pyramid paint: $2(2.625 \text{ ft}^2)\left(\frac{1 \text{ quart}}{45 \text{ ft}^2}\right) = 0.12$ quart;

base area: 3.75 ft^2; base paint: $2(3.75 \text{ ft}^2)\left(\frac{1 \text{ quart}}{45 \text{ ft}^2}\right) = 0.17$ quart

MIXED REVIEW

Assessment Readiness

Assessment Readiness Tip Students can use the provided chart to find formulas they may have forgotten.

Item 4 A glance at the formula chart will remind the students that the area of a triangle is half the base times the height. Encourage students to look at the chart for even basic problems to help avoid careless errors.

Item 5 Students can substitute the lengths of the two bases in the formula for the area of a trapezoid from the formula chart, simplify, and then compare their equation to the given equations to reveal that choice A is the correct answer.

Avoid Common Errors

Item 8 Students may forget that every whole number except 0 and 1 has at least two factors. Remind them that even a prime number has two factors, itself and 1.

Item 11 Some students may transpose the *x*- and *y*-coordinates. Remind students that the *y*-coordinate is the second number in an ordered pair.

Common Core Standards

Items	Grade 6 Standards	Mathematical Practices
1	6.G.1	**MP.2** Reasoning
2	6.G.1, 6.EE.7	**MP.2** Reasoning
3	6.G.1	**MP.5** Using Tools
4	6.G.1	**MP.5** Using Tools
5	6.G.1, 6.EE.7	**MP.2** Reasoning
6	6.G.1, 6.EE.7	**MP.2** Reasoning
7*	6.EE.2a	**MP.2** Reasoning
8*	6.NS.3	**MP.7** Using Structure
9*	6.NS.6a	**MP.7** Using Structure
10	6.G.4	**MP.1** Problem Solving
11	6.G.1	**MP.4** Modeling

* Item integrates mixed review concepts from previous modules or a previous course.

Assessment Readiness

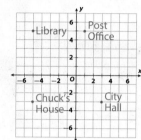
Personal Math Trainer
Online Assessment and Intervention
my.hrw.com

Selected Response

1. Jessie has a piece of cardboard that is 8.5 inches by 11 inches. She makes a picture frame with the cardboard by cutting out a 4 inch by 4 inch square from the center of the cardboard. What is the area of the frame?

- Ⓐ 16 in²
- Ⓒ 93.5 in²
- Ⓑ 77.5 in²
- Ⓓ 118.5 in²

2. Jermaine is ordering a piece of glass in the shape of a trapezoid to create a patio table top. Each square foot of glass costs $25. The trapezoid has base lengths of 5 feet and 3 feet and a height of 4 feet. What is the cost of the glass?

- Ⓐ $400
- Ⓒ $800
- Ⓑ $437.50
- Ⓓ $1,500

3. What is the area of a trapezoid that has bases measuring 19 centimeters and 23 centimeters, and a height of 14 centimeters?

- Ⓐ 105 square centimeters
- Ⓑ 266 square centimeters
- Ⓒ 294 square centimeters
- Ⓓ 322 square centimeters

4. What is the area of the triangle shown below?

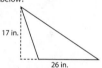

17 in.

26 in.

- Ⓐ 110.5 square inches
- Ⓑ 221 square inches
- Ⓒ 442 square inches
- Ⓓ 884 square inches

5. The trapezoid below has an area of 475 square meters.

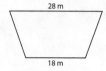

28 m

18 m

Which equation could you solve to find the height of the trapezoid?

- Ⓐ $23h = 475$
- Ⓑ $252h = 475$
- Ⓒ $46h = 475$
- Ⓓ $504h = 475$

6. A rectangular prism has a volume of 1,500 cubic centimeters. It has a length of 34 centimeters and a width of 22 centimeters. Which equation could be solved to find the height of the rectangular prism?

- Ⓐ $374h = 1,500$
- Ⓑ $28h = 1,500$
- Ⓒ $748h = 1,500$
- Ⓓ $56h = 1,500$

7. Which expression represents the sum of 59 and x?

- Ⓐ $59 + x$
- Ⓑ $59 \div x$
- Ⓒ $59x$
- Ⓓ $59 - x$

8. Which number has more than two factors?

- Ⓐ 19
- Ⓑ 23
- Ⓒ 25
- Ⓓ 29

9. Which of the following statements about rational numbers is **not** correct?

- Ⓐ All whole numbers are also rational numbers.
- Ⓑ All integers are also rational numbers.
- Ⓒ All rational numbers can be written in the form $\frac{a}{b}$.
- Ⓓ Rational numbers cannot be negative.

Mini-Tasks

10. Lisa bought a tank for her hermit crab. The tank can hold 1,331 cubic inches of water and includes a top. The base of the aquarium is a square. The height of the aquarium is 11 inches.

a. What is the length of each side of the base of the tank?

11 inches

b. What shape is Lisa's tank?

cube

c. Draw a net of the tank.

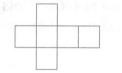

d. What is the surface area of the tank?

726 in²

11. Chuck is making a map of his neighborhood. Each grid unit represents one city block. He uses the following coordinates, with north being the direction of the positive y-axis.

Library: $(-5, 5)$
Chuck's house: $(-5, -3)$
City Hall: $(3, -3)$

a. Plot each point on the coordinate grid below.

b. How far does Chuck live from the library and from City Hall?

8 blocks; 8 blocks

c. Chuck decided to add the post office to his map. The post office is 6 blocks east of the library. What are the coordinates of the post office? Plot the post office on the coordinate grid.

(1, 5)

d. If you connect the points on the map, what shape do you make?

trapezoid

e. What is the area of the shape in **d**? Use square blocks as the unit.

56 square blocks

UNIT 7

Measurement and Data

Contents

Unit Pacing Guide

45-Minute Classes

Module 16

DAY 1	DAY 2	DAY 3	DAY 4	DAY 5
Lesson 16.1	Lesson 16.1	Lesson 16.1	Lesson 16.2	Lesson 16.2

DAY 6	DAY 7	DAY 8	DAY 9	DAY 10
Lesson 16.2	Lesson 16.3	Lesson 16.3	Lesson 16.4	Lesson 16.4

DAY 11	DAY 12	DAY 13	DAY 14	DAY 15
Lesson 16.4	Lesson 16.5	Lesson 16.5	Ready to Go On? Assessment Readiness	Study Guide Assessment Readiness

90-Minute Classes

Module 16

DAY 1	DAY 2	DAY 3	DAY 4	DAY 5
Lesson 16.1	Lesson 16.2	Lesson 16.3	Lesson 16.4	Lesson 16.5

DAY 6	DAY 7
Ready to Go On? Assessment Readiness	Study Guide Assessment Readiness

Program Resources

Plan

Online Teacher Edition

Access a full suite of teaching resources online—plan, present, and manage classes, assignments, and activities.

ePlanner Easily plan your classes, create and view assignments, and access all program resources with your online, customizable planning tool.

Professional Development Videos

Author Juli Dixon models successful teaching practices and strategies in actual classroom settings.

QR Codes Scan with your smart phone to jump directly from your print book to online videos and other resources.

Teacher's Edition

Support students with point-of-use Questioning Strategies, teaching tips, resources for differentiated instruction, additional activities, and more.

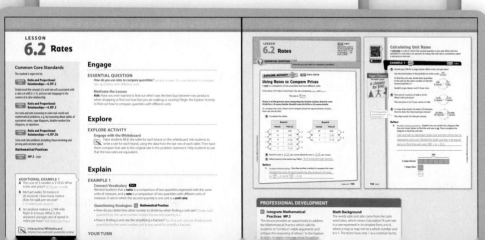

Engage and Explore

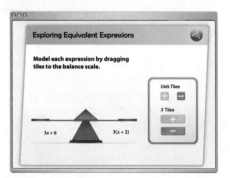

Real-World Videos Engage students with interesting and relevant applications of the mathematical content of each module.

Animated Math Online interactive simulations, tools, and games help students actively learn and practice key concepts.

Exploring Equivalent Expressions

Model each expression by dragging tiles to the balance scale.

$3x + 6$ $3(x + 2)$

Explore Activities

Students interactively explore new concepts using a variety of tools and approaches.

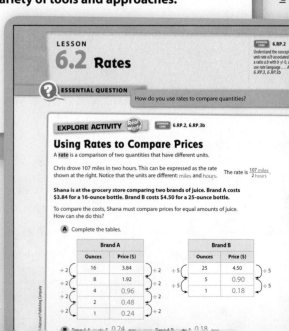

LESSON
6.2 Rates

COMMON CORE 6.RP.2
Understand the concept of a unit rate a/b associated with a ratio $a:b$ with $b \neq 0$, and use rate language.... Also 6.RP.3, 6.RP.3b

? ESSENTIAL QUESTION

How do you use rates to compare quantities?

EXPLORE ACTIVITY (Real World)   COMMON CORE 6.RP.2, 6.RP.3b

Using Rates to Compare Prices

A **rate** is a comparison of two quantities that have different units.

Chris drove 107 miles in two hours. This can be expressed as the rate shown at the right. Notice that the units are different: miles and hours.   The rate is $\frac{107 \text{ miles}}{2 \text{ hours}}$

Shana is at the grocery store comparing two brands of juice. Brand A costs $3.84 for a 16-ounce bottle. Brand B costs $4.50 for a 25-ounce bottle.

To compare the costs, Shana must compare prices for equal amounts of juice. How can she do this?

A Complete the tables.

Brand A	
Ounces	Price ($)
16	3.84
8	1.92
4	0.96
2	0.48
1	0.24

Brand B	
Ounces	Price ($)
25	4.50
5	0.90
1	0.18

Teach

Math On the Spot video tutorials, featuring program authors Dr. Edward Burger and Martha Sandoval-Martinez, accompany every example in the textbook and give students step-by-step instructions and explanations of key math concepts.

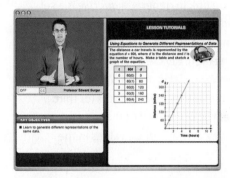

Present engaging content on a multitude of devices, including tablets and interactive whiteboards.

Math Talk

Continually monitor and assess student progress with integrated formative assessment.

CC CLUSTER CONNECTION

Look for exercises indicated with this icon to build connections among standards within Common Core clusters.

Differentiated Instruction Print Resources

Support all learners with Differentiated Instruction Resources, including

- Leveled Practice and Problem Solving
- Reteach
- Reading Strategies
- Success for English Learners
- Challenge

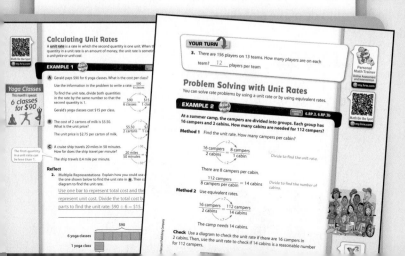

Assessment and Intervention

The **Personal Math Trainer** provides online practice, homework, assessments, and intervention. Monitor student progress through reports and alerts. Create and customize assignments aligned to specific lessons or standards.

- **Practice** – With dynamic items and assignments, students get unlimited practice on key concepts supported by guided examples, step-by-step solutions, and video tutorials.
- **Assessments** – Choose from course assignments or customize your own based on course content, standards, difficulty levels, and more.
- **Homework** – Students can complete online homework with a wide variety of problem types, including the ability to enter expressions, equations, and graphs. Let the system automatically grade homework, so you can focus where your students need help the most!
- **Intervention** – Let the Personal Math Trainer automatically prescribe a targeted, personalized intervention path for your students.

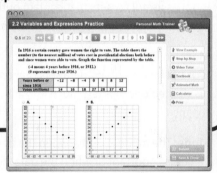

H.O.T.

Raise the bar with homework and practice that incorporates higher-order thinking and mathematical processes in every lesson.

COMMON CORE

Assessment Readiness

Prepare students for success on tests of the Common Core Standards with practice at every module and unit.

Assessment Resources

Tailor assessments to meet the needs of all your classes and students, including

- Leveled Module Quizzes
- Leveled Unit Tests
- Unit Performance Tasks
- Placement, Diagnostic, and Quarterly Benchmark Tests

Math Background

Measures of Center 6.SP.5c
LESSON 16.1

The mean, median, and mode are three ways of summarizing a data set by using a single value. With this goal in mind, students may wonder which measure best represents a particular set of data. Although there is no definitive answer to this question, there are cases in which one measure is clearly more effective at describing a data set than the others. Some general guidelines for choosing a measure to describe a data set can be established.

Mean: The mean (or average) takes every data value into account, is easy to calculate, and works well for describing data sets that are normally distributed. (In a data set that is normally distributed, the graph of the distribution is a bell-shaped curve with the mean at the center.) The mean is not as useful for sets that contain outliers because the outliers can have a large effect on the mean.

Median: The median is also easy to calculate. The median is useful for describing data sets that are not normally distributed because it is much less affected by outliers than the mean.

Mode: The mode is useful when the frequency of data values is important or when the data cluster around multiple values. Among the mean, median, and mode, only the mode can be used to summarize a set of nonnumerical data, such as favorite colors.

Each measure provides a slightly different perspective on a data set. The clearest understanding of a data set is generally obtained when all three measures are considered as a group.

Students should recognize that the mean of a data set need not be one of the data values. The same is true of the median. For example, the data set {10, 20} has a mean and median of 15. On the other hand, the mode, if it exists, must be one of the values in the data set.

Box Plots 6.SP.4
LESSON 16.3

The American statistician John Tukey introduced the box-and-whisker plot (also called a box plot) in his 1977 book *Exploratory Data Analysis*. A box-and-whisker plot is based on the idea of a quartile (from the Latin word *quartilis*, meaning one-fourth). In general, a *quartile* is a set of three values that divide a data set into four equal parts, with each part containing one-fourth of the data set. The second quartile, or *median*, divides the data set in half. The *lower quartile* (or first quartile) is the median of the lower half of the data set, and the *upper quartile* (or third quartile) is the median of the upper half of the data set. Note that the quartiles may or may not be values in the data set.

A box-and-whisker plot shows how data are distributed by depicting the quartiles on a number line. Vertical segments show the three quartiles, and a rectangle groups the data between the lower and upper quartiles. The "whiskers" extend from the minimum data value to the lower quartile and from the upper quartile to the maximum value.

As an example, consider this set of test scores: {71, 74, 83, 80, 70, 80, 100, 82, 76, 72}. Listing the scores in ascending order makes it easy to identify the quartiles.

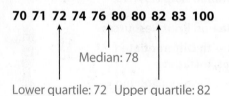

Turning this into a box-and-whisker plot offers a valuable perspective on the data. The box shows that much of the data are clustered between 72 and 82, while the long whisker on the right side of the plot shows that 100 is an outlier.

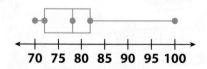

Outliers and Interquartile Range 6.SP.2
LESSON 16.4

At this level, students are introduced to outliers in general terms as values that are very different from the other values in a data set. A common and more specific definition of outliers involves the *interquartile range* (IQR) of a data set.

The IQR is the difference between the first and third quartiles of the data. The *first quartile* is the median of the lower half of the data set, and the *third quartile* is the median of the upper half of the data set.

An outlier is often defined as a value that is less than the lower quartile or greater than the upper quartile by an amount that is 1.5 times as great as the IQR. An example is given below.

Data: 5 6 7 8 9 10 20

First quartile: 6

Third quartile: 10

IQR: $10 - 6 = 4$

Any value less than $6 - 1.5(4) = 0$ or greater than $10 + 1.5(4) = 16$ is an outlier. Therefore, by the definition given above, 20 is an outlier for this data set.

An outlier can have a great effect on the mean of a data set. A visual presentation can help students understand this idea. In particular, when data values are plotted on a number line, the mean is the point at which the data set balances. The figure shows how changing one value in a data set to become an outlier affects the mean.

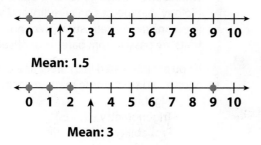

Histograms 6.SP.4, 6.SP.5
LESSON 16.5

A histogram can be considered a special type of bar graph. A histogram displays data that have a quantitative (that is, numerical) independent variable. The values that may be taken by the independent variable are organized into equal intervals, or bins. The height of each bar shows the frequency of data values that fall into each interval.

The choice of the interval size can greatly affect the appearance of a histogram. For example, consider the following data set that shows the ages of the members of a museum tour group: {15, 17, 20, 35, 36, 37, 38, 48, 50, 62, 62, 69, 71, 72}. The two histograms display the data using two different interval sizes for the independent variable.

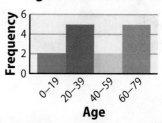

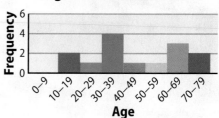

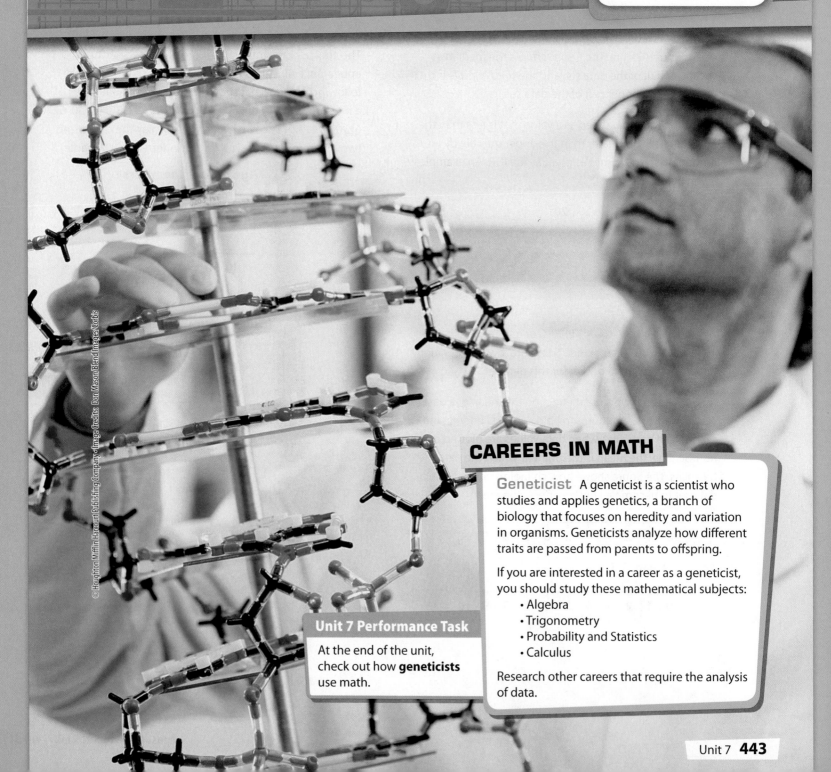

CAREERS IN MATH

Geneticist A geneticist is a scientist who studies and applies genetics, a branch of biology that focuses on heredity and variation in organisms. Geneticists analyze how different traits are passed from parents to offspring.

If you are interested in a career as a geneticist, you should study these mathematical subjects:
- Algebra
- Trigonometry
- Probability and Statistics
- Calculus

Research other careers that require the analysis of data.

Unit 7 Performance Task

At the end of the unit, check out how **geneticists** use math.

Careers in Math

Geneticist

A geneticist uses probability and statistics to analyze and predict genetically inherited traits in a population. You will learn more about genetic variation and the mathematics used in the Performance Tasks at the end of the unit.

For more information about careers in mathematics as well as various mathematics appreciation topics, visit the American Mathematical Society at www.ams.org

Vocabulary Preview

Use the puzzle to give students a preview of important concepts in this unit. Students may work individually, in pairs, or in groups.

Unit Resources

Go online to access all your unit resources.

my.hrw.com

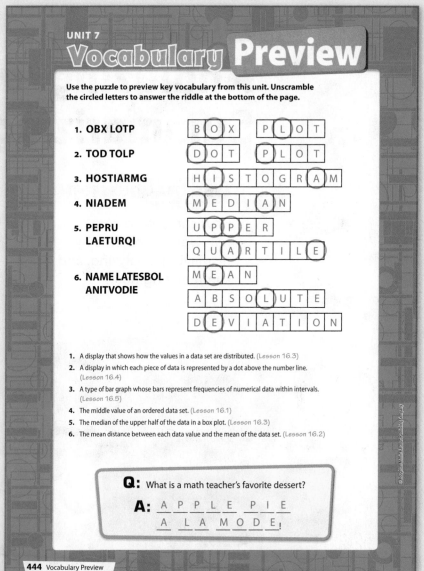

UNIT 7
Vocabulary Preview

Use the puzzle to preview key vocabulary from this unit. Unscramble the circled letters to answer the riddle at the bottom of the page.

1. **OBX LOTP** — B O X   P L O T
2. **TOD TOLP** — D O T   P L O T
3. **HOSTIARMG** — H I S T O G R A M
4. **NIADEM** — M E D I A N
5. **PEPRU LAETURQI** — U P P E R   Q U A R T I L E
6. **NAME LATESBOL ANITVODIE** — M E A N   A B S O L U T E   D E V I A T I O N

1. A display that shows how the values in a data set are distributed. (Lesson 16.3)
2. A display in which each piece of data is represented by a dot above the number line. (Lesson 16.4)
3. A type of bar graph whose bars represent frequencies of numerical data within intervals. (Lesson 16.5)
4. The middle value of an ordered data set. (Lesson 16.1)
5. The median of the upper half of the data in a box plot. (Lesson 16.3)
6. The mean distance between each data value and the mean of the data set. (Lesson 16.2)

Q: What is a math teacher's favorite dessert?

A: A P P L E   P I E   A L A M O D E !

Before	In this Unit	After
Students understand: • how to collect and organize data • how to find measures of center • how to use and analyze graphs	Students will learn about: • numeric data • representing numeric data graphically • interpreting numeric data from a dot plot, box plot, or histogram • categorical data	Students will learn about: • ways to compare two sets of data • ways to analyze data about a population • choosing an appropriate display for a set of data

Displaying, Analyzing, and Summarizing Data

ESSENTIAL QUESTION

How can you solve real-world problems by displaying, analyzing, and summarizing data?

You can calculate measures of center, measures of spread, and other measures of the data, and use them to better understand the problems.

Real-World Video

Biologists collect data on different animals. They can describe the data using measures of center or spread, and by displaying the data in plots or graphs, they may see trends related to the animal population.

⏻ my.hrw.com

© Houghton Mifflin Harcourt Publishing Company • Image Credits: ©Rich Carey/Shutterstock.com

GO DIGITAL

my.hrw.com

my.hrw.com

Go digital with your write-in student edition, accessible on any device.

Math On the Spot

Scan with your smart phone to jump directly to the online edition, video tutor, and more.

Animated Math

Interactively explore key concepts to see how math works.

Personal Math Trainer

Get immediate feedback and help as you work through practice sets.

Are You Ready?

Assess Readiness

Use the assessment on this page to determine if students need intensive or strategic intervention for the module's prerequisite skills.

 **RtI** **Response to Intervention**

Intervention	Enrichment

Access Are You Ready? assessment online, and receive instant scoring, feedback, and customized intervention or enrichment.

Personal Math Trainer
Online Assessment and Intervention
my.hrw.com

Online and Print Resources

Skills Intervention worksheets
- Skill 39 Remainders
- Skill 94 Read Bar Graphs

Differentiated Instruction
- Challenge worksheets **PRE-AP**
- Extend the Math **PRE-AP** Lesson Activities in TE

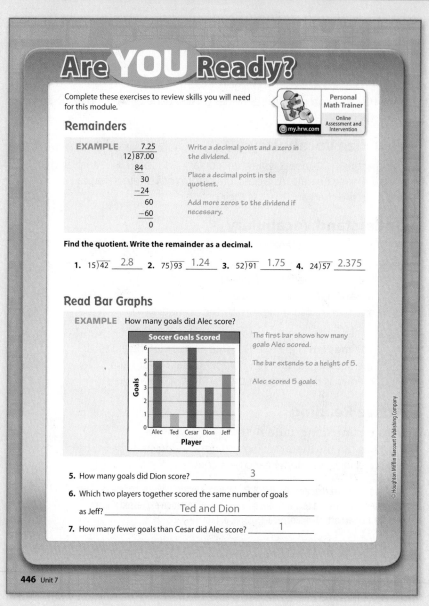

Are YOU Ready?

Complete these exercises to review skills you will need for this module.

 Personal Math Trainer Online Assessment and Intervention

my.hrw.com

Remainders

EXAMPLE

$$12\overline{)87.00}$$ quotient 7.25

84

30

−24

60

−60

0

Write a decimal point and a zero in the dividend.

Place a decimal point in the quotient.

Add more zeros to the dividend if necessary.

Find the quotient. Write the remainder as a decimal.

1. $15\overline{)42}$ __2.8__
2. $75\overline{)93}$ __1.24__
3. $52\overline{)91}$ __1.75__
4. $24\overline{)57}$ __2.375__

Read Bar Graphs

EXAMPLE How many goals did Alec score?

Soccer Goals Scored

The first bar shows how many goals Alec scored.

The bar extends to a height of 5.

Alec scored 5 goals.

5. How many goals did Dion score? __3__

6. Which two players together scored the same number of goals as Jeff? __Ted and Dion__

7. How many fewer goals than Cesar did Alec score? __1__

© Houghton Mifflin Harcourt Publishing Company

PROFESSIONAL DEVELOPMENT VIDEO

Author Juli Dixon models successful teaching practices as she explores how to summarize data in an actual sixth-grade classroom.

 Professional Development

my.hrw.com

G⊙ DIGITAL my.hrw.com

Online Teacher Edition
Access a full suite of teaching resources online—plan, present, and manage classes and assignments.

ePlanner
Easily plan your classes and access all your resources online.

Interactive Answers and Solutions
Customize answer keys to print or display in the classroom. Choose to include answers only or full solutions to all lesson exercises.

Interactive Whiteboards
Engage students with interactive whiteboard-ready lessons and activities.

Personal Math Trainer: Online Assessment and Intervention
Assign automatically graded homework, quizzes, tests, and intervention activities. Prepare your students with updated practice tests aligned with Common Core.

Reading Start-Up

Have students complete the activities on this page by working alone or with others.

Visualize Vocabulary

The chart helps students review vocabulary associated with analyzing and summarizing data. As a class, brainstorm other terms that can be added to the chart and discuss their definitions.

Understand Vocabulary

Use the following explanations to help students learn the preview words.

Students sometimes confuse mean and median. The **mean**, or average, is calculated by adding all of the values and then dividing the sum by the number of values in the data set.

The **median** is the middle value of an ordered data set. If the data set has an even number of data values, the median is the average of the middle two data values.

Active Reading

Integrating Language Arts

Students can use these reading and note-taking strategies to help them organize and understand new concepts and vocabulary.

COMMON CORE **ELA-Literacy.RST.6-8.7** Integrate quantitative or technical information expressed in words in a text with a version of that information expressed visually (e.g., in a flowchart, diagram, model, graph, or table).

Additional Resources

Differentiated Instruction
• Reading Strategies **ELL**

Reading Start-Up

Visualize Vocabulary

Use the review words to complete the chart.

Introduction to Statistics		
Definition	**Example**	**Review word**
A group of facts	The grades of all of the students in a school	data
A tool used to gather information from individuals	A questionnaire given to all students to find the number of hours each student spends studying in 1 week	survey
A value that summarizes a set of unequal values, found by addition and division	Results of the survey show that students typically spend 5 hours a week studying	average

Understand Vocabulary

Complete the sentences using the preview words.

1. The average of a data set is the _____mean_____.
2. The _____median_____ is the middle value of a data set.
3. The number or category that occurs most frequently in a data set is the _____mode_____.

© Houghton Mifflin Harcourt Publishing Company

Vocabulary

Review Words
average (*promedio*)
data (*datos*)
survey (*encuesta*)

Preview Words
box plot (*diagrama de caja*)
categorical data (*datos categóricos*)
dot plot (*diagrama de puntos*)
histogram (*histograma*)
interquartile range (*rango entre cuartiles*)
lower quartile (*cuartil inferior*)
✔ mean (*media*)
mean absolute deviation (MAD) (*desviación absoluta media, (DAM)*)
✔ median (*mediana*)
measure of center (*medida central*)
measure of spread (*medida de dispersión*)
✔ mode (*moda*)
range (*rango*)
statistical question (*pregunta estadística*)
upper quartile (*cuartil superior*)

Active Reading

Layered Book Before beginning the module, create a layered book to help you learn the concepts in this module. Label each flap with lesson titles from this module. As you study each lesson, write important ideas, such as vocabulary and formulas under the appropriate flap. Refer to your finished layered book as you work on exercises from this module.

Before	**In this module**	**After**
Students understand:	Students will learn how to:	Students will learn about:
• how to find the mean, median, and mode of a set of data • how to represent data in frequency tables, bar graphs, dot plots	• represent numeric data graphically, including dot plots, histograms, and box plots • use graphical representations of numeric data to describe the center, spread, and shape of a data distribution • summarize numeric data with numerical summaries, including the mean and median and the range and interquartile range (IQR) • interpret numeric data summarized in dot plots, histograms, and box plots • summarize categorical data with numerical and graphical summaries, including mode and relative frequency tables	• information presented in the form of a graph or plot • ways to compare two sets of data • ways to analyze data about a population

Unpacking the Standards

Use the examples on this page to help students know exactly what they are expected to learn in this module.

Common Core Standards

Content Areas

 Statistics and Probability—6.SP.2

Summarize and describe distributions.

Go online to see a complete unpacking of the Common Core Standards.

my.hrw.com

 MODULE 16

Unpacking the Standards

Understanding the standards and the vocabulary terms in the standards will help you know exactly what you are expected to learn in this module.

COMMON CORE 6.SP.5C

Summarize numerical data sets in relation to their context, such as by giving quantitative measures of center (median and/or mean) and variability (interquartile range and/or mean absolute deviation), as well as describing any overall pattern and any striking deviations from the overall pattern with reference to the context in which the data were gathered.

What It Means to You

You will use measures of center to describe a data set.

UNPACKING EXAMPLE 6.SP.5C

Several students' scores on a history test are shown. Find the mean score and the median score. Which measure better describes the typical score for these students? Explain.

History Test Scores

| 73 | 48 | 88 | 90 | 90 | 81 | 83 |

Mean: $\frac{73 + 48 + 88 + 90 + 90 + 81 + 83}{7} = \frac{553}{7} = 79$

To find the median, write the data values in order from least to greatest and find the middle value.
Median: 48 73 81 (83) 88 90 90

The median better describes the typical score. The mean is affected by the low score of 48.

COMMON CORE 6.SP.4

Display numerical data in plots on a number line, including dot plots, histograms, and box plots.

What It Means to You

You will interpret the data from a dot plot, histogram, or box plot.

UNPACKING EXAMPLE 6.SP.4

Kim has started rating each movie she sees using a scale of 1 to 10 on an online site. She made a histogram that shows how she rated the movies. What does the shape of the distribution tell you about the movies Kim has rated?

Of the 15 movies that Kim rated, she rated almost half a 7 or an 8 and did not generally give extreme ratings.

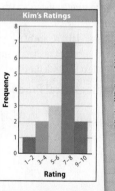

Visit my.hrw.com to see all the Common Core Standards unpacked.

my.hrw.com

Common Core Standards	Lesson 16.1	Lesson 16.2	Lesson 16.3	Lesson 16.4	Lesson 16.5
6.SP.1 Recognize a statistical question as one that anticipates variability in the data related to the question....				COMMON CORE	
6.SP.3 Recognize that a measure of center for a numerical data set summarizes all of its values with a single number, while a measure of variation describes how its values vary....	COMMON CORE				
6.SP.4 Display numerical data in plots on a number line, including dot plots, histograms, and box plots.			COMMON CORE	COMMON CORE	COMMON CORE
6.SP.5 Summarize numerical data sets in relation to their context...	COMMON CORE				COMMON CORE
6.SP.5c Summarize numerical data sets ... by giving quantitative measures of center (median and/or mean) and variability... as well as describing any overall pattern and any striking deviations....	COMMON CORE	COMMON CORE	COMMON CORE	COMMON CORE	
6.SP.5d Summarize numerical data sets ... by relating the choice of measures of center and variability to the shape of the data distribution and the context....	COMMON CORE				COMMON CORE

© Houghton Mifflin Harcourt Publishing Company

LESSON 16.1 Measures of Center

Common Core Standards

The student is expected to:

 Statistics and Probability—6.SP.5

Summarize numerical data sets in relation to their context, such as by:

a. Reporting the number of observations.

b. Describing the nature of the attribute under investigation, including how it was measured and its units of measurement.

c. Giving quantitative measures of center (median and/or mean) and variability (interquartile range and/or mean absolute deviation), as well as describing any overall pattern and any striking deviations from the overall pattern with reference to the context in which the data were gathered.

d. Relating the choice of measures of center and variability to the shape of the data distribution and the context in which the data were gathered. *Also 6.SP.3*

Mathematical Practices

 MP.4 Modeling

ADDITIONAL EXAMPLE 1

A A nurse records the heights, in inches, of several students. Find the median of the heights.

62, 55, 64, 58, 60, 55, 59, 57, 61, 57, 64

59 inches

B A teacher records the test scores of several students. Find the median score.

74, 82, 70, 80, 72, 76, 71, 75, 78, 72

74.5

 Interactive Whiteboard
Interactive example available online

 my.hrw.com

Engage

ESSENTIAL QUESTION

How can you use measures of center to describe a data set? Sample answer: Since a measure of center describes a typical value from the data set, you can use either the mean or median to represent or describe the data.

Motivate the Lesson

Ask: Have you ever wondered how a baseball player's batting average was calculated? Or how a miles-per-gallon average for a car is calculated? Begin Explore Activity 1 to find out how to calculate and use measures of center.

Explore

EXPLORE ACTIVITY 1

Connect Multiple Representations **CC** Mathematical Practices

Be certain that students are able to connect the models and the equations that give the mean. Point out to students that the counters in A are used in both B and C. In B, the counters are rearranged so each group has the same number. In C, the addends are the number of counters as shown in A.

Explain

EXAMPLE 1

Connect Vocabulary **ELL**

To help students distinguish the terms *median* and *mean*, give them another definition of median: a strip of land in the center of a road that separates the lanes of traffic going in opposite directions. Point out that just as a median divides a road down its center, the median of a data set divides the data values in two at the center.

Questioning Strategies **CC** Mathematical Practices

- When ordering a set of data, must you list numbers that repeat? Yes. The median is the middle value of a given set of data, so every value must be listed, even if it is repeated, to get an accurate center value.

- Would the median be the same if you ordered the data from greatest to least? Yes, the middle of the data is still in the same place.

- A data set is composed of all whole numbers. Will the median of the data set always be a whole number? No. When a data set has two middle values, the median is an average of those values and may or may not be a whole number.

- In B, how would replacing the data value 77 with 65 affect the median? Explain. It would have no effect on the median, as the median describes the central position in a set of data. Extreme values, either very small or very large, would not influence the central data.

16.1 Measures of Center

COMMON CORE **6.SP.5**
Summarize numerical data sets in relation to their context, ... Also 6.SP.3, 6.SP.5a, 6.SP.5b, 6.SP.5c, 6.SP.5d

? ESSENTIAL QUESTION

How can you use measures of center to describe a data set?

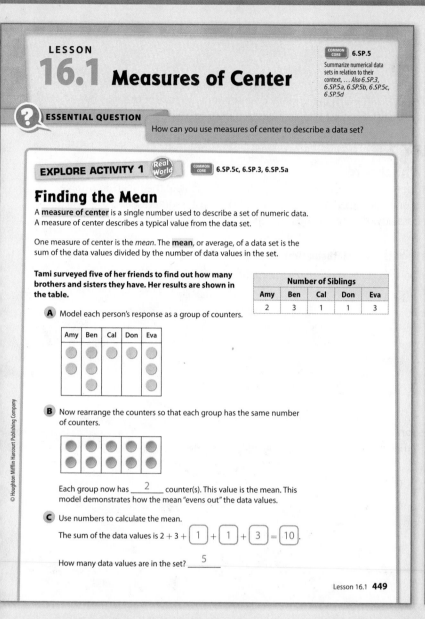

EXPLORE ACTIVITY 1 Real World   COMMON CORE **6.SP.5c, 6.SP.3, 6.SP.5a**

Finding the Mean

A **measure of center** is a single number used to describe a set of numeric data. A measure of center describes a typical value from the data set.

One measure of center is the *mean*. The **mean**, or average, of a data set is the sum of the data values divided by the number of data values in the set.

Tami surveyed five of her friends to find out how many brothers and sisters they have. Her results are shown in the table.

Number of Siblings				
Amy	Ben	Cal	Don	Eva
2	3	1	1	3

A Model each person's response as a group of counters.

B Now rearrange the counters so that each group has the same number of counters.

Each group now has ___2___ counter(s). This value is the mean. This model demonstrates how the mean "evens out" the data values.

C Use numbers to calculate the mean.

The sum of the data values is $2 + 3 + \boxed{1} + \boxed{1} + \boxed{3} = \boxed{10}$.

How many data values are in the set? ___5___

EXPLORE ACTIVITY 1 (cont'd)

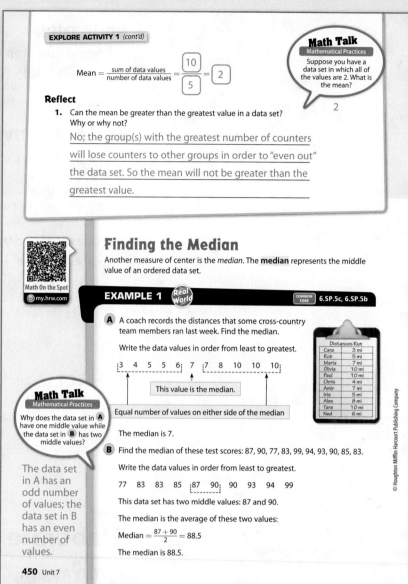

$$\text{Mean} = \frac{\text{sum of data values}}{\text{number of data values}} = \frac{\boxed{10}}{\boxed{5}} = \boxed{2}$$

Math Talk
Mathematical Practices

Suppose you have a data set in which all of the values are 2. What is the mean?

2

Reflect

1. Can the mean be greater than the greatest value in a data set? Why or why not?

No; the group(s) with the greatest number of counters will lose counters to other groups in order to "even out" the data set. So the mean will not be greater than the greatest value.

Finding the Median

Another measure of center is the *median*. The **median** represents the middle value of an ordered data set.

Math On the Spot
my.hrw.com

EXAMPLE 1 Real World   COMMON CORE **6.SP.5c, 6.SP.5b**

A A coach records the distances that some cross-country team members ran last week. Find the median.

Write the data values in order from least to greatest.

3 4 5 5 6 │ 7 │ 7 8 10 10 10

This value is the median.

Equal number of values on either side of the median

The median is 7.

Distances Run	
Cara	3 mi
Rob	5 mi
Maria	7 mi
Olivia	10 mi
Paul	10 mi
Chris	4 mi
Amir	7 mi
Iris	5 mi
Alex	8 mi
Tara	10 mi
Ned	6 mi

Math Talk
Mathematical Practices

Why does the data set in **A** have one middle value while the data set in **B** has two middle values?

The data set in A has an odd number of values; the data set in B has an even number of values.

B Find the median of these test scores: 87, 90, 77, 83, 99, 94, 93, 90, 85, 83.

Write the data values in order from least to greatest.

77 83 83 85 │87 90│ 90 93 94 99

This data set has two middle values: 87 and 90.

The median is the average of these two values:

$\text{Median} = \frac{87 + 90}{2} = 88.5$

The median is 88.5.

PROFESSIONAL DEVELOPMENT

CC Integrate Mathematical Practices MP.4

This lesson provides an opportunity to address this Mathematical Practice standard. It calls for students to apply mathematics to problems arising in everyday life, society, and the workplace. In the Explore Activities and in Example 1, students apply mean and median to situations involving distances traveled by a cross-country team, teenager salaries, number of minutes exercised, and final exam scores. Thus, students apply mean and median to real-world situations found in everyday life or society using models and using pencil and paper.

Math Background

The mean and median are the two most commonly used measures of center, or central tendency. The mean, often called the *average*, is found by dividing the sum of values by the number of values. The median is the value that is physically in the middle of an ordered data set.

The mean of a data set may be affected by the presence of outliers. An outlier is a data value that is significantly higher or lower than the other values. For data that include outliers, the median may better represent the "typical" value.

YOUR TURN

Avoid Common Errors

Students may forget to list 8 two times when ordering the data values. Suggest that they count the total number of numbers in the original data set and then count the number of numbers in their reordered list. Each list should include the same number of data points.

EXPLORE ACTIVITY 2

Engage with the Whiteboard

In A, have a student fill in the boxes, find the sum, and calculate the mean. In B, have another volunteer write the data values in order from least to greatest and then circle the median. Then discuss how the mean and median differ.

Questioning Strategies CC Mathematical Practices

- In A, why is the symbol ≈ used when finding the mean? Sample answer: 2,455 is not divisible by 7. Since the data represents money, the answer is rounded to hundredths.

- How will data values that are unusually large or small compared to the rest of the data affect the mean? If the value(s) are much larger than the other values, the mean will be larger than the center values. If the value(s) are much smaller than the other values, the mean will be smaller than the center values.

REFLECT

Talk About It
Summarize the Lesson

Ask: Which data value in Exercise 4 greatly affects the mean? Explain why.
99; Sample answer: The score of 99 is more than 20 points higher than any of the other exam scores, so it raises the mean to 76.4, which is greater than the four other scores.

Elaborate

Talk About It
Summarize the Lesson

Ask: Which measure of center best describes the following data? Explain why.
Jared's points scored in basketball games: 12, 20, 32, 8, 14, 11, 15. The median best describes the data. The mean is 16 and the median is 14. The mean is affected by the value 32 and is larger than the central numbers in the data.

GUIDED PRACTICE

Engage with the Whiteboard

For Exercise 1, have students make a model using counters to represent this situation and show how finding the average evens out the data set on the whiteboard. Then have students find the mean using arithmetic. Compare and contrast the two methods.

Avoid Common Errors

Exercise 2 Students might choose one of the two center numbers in an even number of values as the median. Remind students that in this case, the median is the average of the two middle values.

Reflect

2. What If? Which units are used for the data in **A**? If the coach had recorded some distances in kilometers and some in miles, can you still find the median of the data? Explain.

Miles; no, not unless the coach converts all the data to the same units.

YOUR TURN

3. Charlotte recorded the number of minutes she spent exercising in the past ten days: 12, 4, 5, 6, 8, 7, 9, 8, 2, 1. Find the median of the data.

median = 6.5 minutes

Personal Math Trainer
Online Assessment and Intervention
my.hrw.com

EXPLORE ACTIVITY 2   COMMON CORE 6.SP.5d, 6.SP.5c

Comparing the Mean and the Median

The mean and median of a data set may be equal, very close to each other, or very different from each other. For data sets where the mean and median differ greatly, one likely describes the data set better than the other.

The monthly earnings of several teenagers are $200, $320, $275, $250, $750, $350, and $310.

A Find the mean.

$$\frac{200 + 320 + 275 + 250 + 750 + 350 + 310}{7} = \frac{2,455}{7} \approx 350.71$$

B Write the data values in order from least to greatest and find the median.

200 250 275 ⟨310⟩ 320 350 750

C The mean and the median differ by about $ __40__ . Why?

The mean is affected by the data value 750, which is much greater than the other data values. The median is not affected by this value.

D Which measure of center better describes the typical monthly earnings for this group of teenagers—the mean or the median? Explain.

Median; The mean is greater than all but one of the data values. The median is a more central value.

Lesson 16.1 **451**

EXPLORE ACTIVITY 2 (cont'd)

Reflect

4. Communicate Mathematical Ideas Luka's final exam scores for this semester are 70, 72, 99, 72, and 69. Find the mean and median. Which is a better description of Luka's typical exam score? Explain your thinking.

Mean = 76.4; median = 72; median; the median is closer in value to most of the data values than the mean.

Guided Practice

1. Spencer surveyed five of his friends to find out how many pets they have. His results are shown in the table. What is the mean number of pets? (Explore Activity 1)

Number of Pets				
Lara	**Cody**	**Sam**	**Ella**	**Maria**
3	5	2	4	1

$$\text{Mean} = \frac{\text{sum of data values}}{\text{number of data values}} = \frac{15}{5} = 3$$

The mean number of pets is __3__

2. The following are the weights, in pounds, of some dogs at a kennel: 36, 45, 29, 39, 51, 49. (Example 1)

a. Find the median. __42__

b. Suppose one of the weights were given in kilograms. Can you still find the median? Explain.

No; only if you convert all the weights to the same units.

3. a. Find the mean and the median of this data set: 9, 6, 5, 3, 28, 6, 4, 7. (Explore Activity 2)

mean: 8.5; median: 6

b. Which better describes the data set, the mean or the median? Explain.

The median; sample answer: the median is closer to most of the data values than the mean is.

? ESSENTIAL QUESTION CHECK-IN

4. How can you use measures of center to describe a data set?

Sample answer: The mean and median can be used to represent or summarize the data.

452 Unit 7

DIFFERENTIATE INSTRUCTION

Home Connection

Have students search through a newspaper or magazine at home with a family member to find a set of data, such as prices of houses, high temperatures, or points scored by the players on a sports team. Students can then find the mean and median for the data set.

Communicating Math

Have students develop a presentation that compares and contrasts the mean and median of a data set. Students can work alone or in groups. The presentation should include a written description of how to calculate the value of each measure as well as graphics that the students think would be helpful.

Additional Resources

Differentiated Instruction includes:

- Reading Strategies
- Success for English Learners **ELL**
- Reteach
- Challenge **PRE-AP**

16.1 LESSON QUIZ

COMMON CORE **6.SP.5c**

The ages of the student volunteers at an event are 13, 11, 12, 15, 16, 11, 12, 14, 15, and 11.

1. Find the mean age of the students.

2. Find the median age of the students.

The lengths of the pieces of lumber that a carpenter has are shown in the table.

2 ft	3 ft	6 ft
1.5 ft	4.5 ft	1 ft

3. Find the mean length.

4. Find the median length.

5. Suppose the data value 3 yards is added to the table above. What should you do before finding the mean and median lengths for the new data set?

6. If the data value 9 feet is added to the data set, which would better describe the data set, the mean or the median? Explain.

Lesson Quiz available online

 my.hrw.com

Answers

1. 13

2. 12.5

3. 3 ft

4. 2.5 ft

5. Convert 3 yards to 9 feet.

6. Median. Sample answer: Since 9 feet is 3 feet greater than any of the other values, it will raise the mean. So, the median will be closer to most of the data values.

Evaluate

GUIDED AND INDEPENDENT PRACTICE

 COMMON CORE **6.SP.3, 6.SP.5, 6.SP.5a, 6.SP.5b, 6.SP.5c, 6.SP.5d**

Concepts & Skills	Practice
Explore Activity 1 Finding the Mean	Exercises 1, 6–7, 10
Example 1 Finding the Median	Exercises 2, 6–7, 10
Explore Activity 2 Comparing the Mean and the Median	Exercises 3, 8, 11

Exercise	Depth of Knowledge (D.O.K.)	COMMON CORE Mathematical Practices
5–7	**2** Skills/Concepts	**MP.4** Modeling
8	**3** Strategic Thinking **H.O.T.**	**MP.7** Using Structure
9	**3** Strategic Thinking **H.O.T.**	**MP.7** Using Structure
10	**2** Skills/Concepts	**MP.4** Modeling
11	**3** Strategic Thinking **H.O.T.**	**MP.7** Using Structure
12	**3** Strategic Thinking **H.O.T.**	**MP.7** Using Structure
13	**3** Strategic Thinking **H.O.T.**	**MP.3** Logic
14	**3** Strategic Thinking **H.O.T.**	**MP.7** Using Structure

Additional Resources

Differentiated Instruction includes:

• Leveled Practice Worksheets

16.1 Independent Practice

COMMON CORE 6.SP.3, 6.SP.5, 6.SP.5a, 6.SP.5b, 6.SP.5c, 6.SP.5d

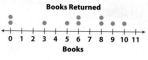

Personal Math Trainer

my.hrw.com Online Assessment and Intervention

Several students in Ashton's class were randomly selected and asked how many text messages they sent yesterday. Their answers were 1, 0, 10, 7, 13, 2, 9, 15, 0, 3.

5. How many students were asked? How do you know?

Ten students were asked, because there are 10 data values in the list.

6. Find the mean and the median for these data.

Mean = ___6___   Median = ___5___

The points scored by a basketball team in its last 6 games are shown. Use these data for 7 and 8.

Points Scored					
73	77	85	84	37	115

7. Find the mean score and the median score.

Mean = ___78.5___   Median = ___80.5___

8. Which measure better describes the typical number of points scored? Explain.

Sample answer: Both describe the number of points equally well.

Some people were asked how long it takes them to commute to work. Use the data for 9–11.

9. What units are used for the data? What should you do before finding the mean and median number of minutes?

Minutes and hours; convert all times to minutes.

16 min	5 min
7 min	8 min
14 min	12 min
0.5 hr	1 hr

10. Find the mean and median number of minutes.

Mean = ___19___   Median = ___13___

11. Which measure do you think is more typical of the data?

Median; it is closer to most of the data values; the data value for 1 hr (60 min) raises the mean.

H.O.T. FOCUS ON HIGHER ORDER THINKING

Work Area

12. Critique Reasoning For two weeks, the school librarian recorded the number of library books returned each morning. The data are shown in the dot plot. The librarian found the mean number of books returned each morning.

Books Returned

0 1 2 3 4 5 6 7 8 9 10 11
Books

$$\frac{8+6+10+5+9+8+3+6}{8} = \frac{55}{8} \approx 6.9$$

Is this the correct mean of this data set? If not, explain and correct the answer.

No; the sum is correct, but the sum should be divided by 10, not by 8. The mean is 5.5.

13. Critical Thinking Lauren's scores on her math tests are 93, 91, 98, 100, 95, 92, and 96. What score could Lauren get on her next math test so that the mean and median remain the same? Explain your answer.

95; sample answer: the mean and the median of Lauren's scores are both 95. If she gets 95 on the next math test, the mean and median will remain at 95.

14. Persevere in Problem Solving Yuko wants to take a job selling cars. Since she will get a commission for every car she sells, she finds out the sale price of the last four cars sold at each company.

Company A: $16,000; $20,000; $25,000; $35,000;

Company B: $21,000, $23,000, $36,000, $48,000

a. Find the mean selling price at each company.

mean: Company A, $24,000; Company B, $32,000

b. Find the median selling price at each company.

median: Company A, $22,500; B, $29,500

c. Communicate Mathematical Ideas At either company, Yuko will get paid a commission of 20% of the sale price of each car she sells. Based on the data, where do you recommend she take a job? Why?

Answers may vary. Sample answer: Company B: both the mean and the median are greater at Company B, so Yuko will make a greater commission.

EXTEND THE MATH PRE-AP

Activity available online my.hrw.com

Activity Challenge students to use the given clues to identify the data values for the following sets of data.

1. There are 4 whole numbers in a data set. The mean of the data set is 67. Three of the data values are 56, 63, and 70. What is the fourth data value?

2. There are 7 whole numbers in a data set. The least number is 9, and the greatest number is 20. The mean and median are both 14. What numbers could be the values in the data set?

3. Develop a Challenge question similar to one of the questions above, and challenge a classmate to find the answer.

Answers

1. 79

2. Sample answer: 9, 12, 13, 14, 15, 15, 20

3. Questions will vary.

LESSON
16.2 Mean Absolute Deviation

ADDITIONAL EXAMPLE 1

A carpenter wants to hire an assistant. He is interviewing Robert and Tanya to see who is more precise at cutting lumber. Each person was told to cut 10 pieces of wood, and the lengths of their cuts in feet are given below. Whose cuts had less variability in length?

Robert: 2.3, 2.4, 2.3, 2.5, 2.5, 2.8, 2.4, 2.5, 2.3, 2.5

Tanya: 2.0, 2.2, 2.1, 2.4, 2.3, 2.4, 2.6, 2.5, 2.4, 2.3

The MAD for Robert is 0.11 ft, and the MAD for Tanya is 0.14 ft, so Robert's cuts had less variability in length.

 Interactive Whiteboard
Interactive example available online

 my.hrw.com

 Animated Math
Mean Absolute Deviation

Students use a graphical representation of data to visualize distance from the mean and explore mean absolute deviation.

 my.hrw.com

Engage

ESSENTIAL QUESTION

How can you determine and use the mean absolute deviation of a set of data points?
Sample answer: The mean absolute deviation is the mean of the distances between the data values and the mean of the data set. The MAD can be used to quantify the spread in the data set.

Motivate the Lesson

Ask: How many statistical measures do you know that can describe a data set? List the different statistical measures you know before you start the Explore Activity.

Explore

EXPLORE ACTIVITY

Focus on Modeling **CC** **Mathematical Practices**

When finding the distance from the mean, students may want to assign the distance either a negative or positive value, depending on whether the mean was greater than or less than the value from the data set. Remind students that distance is always positive, so all values in the table will be positive.

Explain

EXAMPLE 1

Connect Vocabulary **ELL**

Relate the math term *mean absolute deviation* to the math term *absolute value*. Students should remember that the absolute value is the distance between a number and 0, and the MAD is the mean distance between each data value and the mean of the data set.

Questioning Strategies

• In Example 1, why is the mean not sufficient to answer the chicken farmer's question about which set had less variability? The mean does not tell you how close values in a set are to each other.

• To find the MAD, you must find the mean of the data and then the mean of the absolute deviations. Will the number you divide by to find the mean and the MAD be the same number in both cases? Explain. Yes; each data value and absolute deviation are associated with the same data set, so the divisor used to find the means will be the same in both cases.

Engage with the Whiteboard

In Step 2, cover up the distances from the mean and have students complete each table. Discuss different ways to find each distance, such as mental math or by using pencil and paper.

LESSON 16.2 Mean Absolute Deviation

COMMON CORE 6.SP.5c

Summarize numerical data sets in relation to their context, such as by giving quantitative measures of ...variability (...mean absolute deviation)....

? ESSENTIAL QUESTION

How can you determine and use the mean absolute deviation of a set of data points?

EXPLORE ACTIVITY **COMMON CORE 6.SP.5c**

Understanding Mean Absolute Deviation

A **measure of variability** is a single number used to describe the spread of a data set. It can also be called a measure of spread. One measure of variability is the **mean absolute deviation (MAD)**, which is the mean of the distances between the data values and the mean of the data set.

The data represent the height, in feet, of various buildings. Find the mean absolute deviation for each data set.

A 60, 58, 54, 56, 63, 65, 62, 59, 56, 58

Calculate the mean. Round to the nearest whole number.

$$\frac{60 + 58 + 54 + 56 + 63 + 65 + 62 + 59 + 56 + 58}{10} \approx 59$$

Complete the table.

Height (ft)	60	58	54	56	63	65	62	59	56	58
Distance from mean	1	1	5	3	4	6	3	0	3	1

Calculate the MAD by finding the mean of the values in the second row of the table. Round to the nearest whole number.

$$\frac{1 + 1 + 5 + 3 + 4 + 6 + 3 + 0 + 3 + 1}{10} \approx 3$$

B 46, 47, 56, 48, 46, 52, 57, 52, 45

Find the mean. Round to the nearest whole number.

$$\frac{46 + 47 + 56 + 48 + 46 + 52 + 57 + 52 + 45}{9} \approx 50$$

EXPLORE ACTIVITY (cont'd)

Complete the table.

Height (ft)	46	47	56	48	46	52	57	52	45
Distance from mean	4	3	6	2	4	2	7	2	5

Calculate the MAD. Round to the nearest whole number.

$$\frac{4 + 3 + 6 + 2 + 4 + 2 + 7 + 2 + 5}{9} \approx 4$$

Reflect

1. **Analyze Relationships** Compare the MADs. How do the MADs describe the distribution of the heights in each group?

The MAD in part B is greater; the heights in part B are

spread out more from the mean than the heights in part A.

Math Talk
Mathematical Practices

What is the difference between a measure of center and a measure of variability?

A measure of center is a number that indicates where the "middle" or center of a data set is, while a measure of variability is a number that indicates how much the data are spread out from the center of the data.

Math On the Spot
my.hrw.com

Using Mean Absolute Deviation

The mean absolute deviation can be used to answer statistical questions in the real world. Many of these questions may have implications for the operation of various businesses.

EXAMPLE 1 **COMMON CORE 6.SP.5c**

A chicken farmer wants her chickens to all have about the same weight. She is trying two types of feed to see which type produces the best results. All the chickens in Pen A are fed Premium Growth feed, and all the chickens in Pen B are fed Maximum Growth feed. The farmer records the weights of the chickens in each pen in the tables below. Which chicken feed produces less variability in weight?

Pen A: Premium Growth Weights (lb)									
5.8	6.1	5.5	6.6	7.3	5.9	6.3	5.7	6.8	7.1

Pen B: Maximum Growth Weights (lb)									
7.7	7.4	5.4	7.8	6.1	5.2	7.5	7.9	6.3	5.6

STEP 1 Find the mean weight of the chickens in each pen. Round your answers to the nearest tenth.

Pen A: $\frac{5.8 + 6.1 + 5.5 + 6.6 + 7.3 + 5.9 + 6.3 + 5.7 + 6.8 + 7.1}{10} \approx 6.3$

Pen B: $\frac{7.7 + 7.4 + 5.4 + 7.8 + 6.1 + 5.2 + 7.5 + 7.9 + 6.3 + 5.6}{10} \approx 6.7$

PROFESSIONAL DEVELOPMENT

CC Integrate Mathematical Practices MP.5

This lesson provides an opportunity to address the Mathematical Practices standard that calls for students to use appropriate tools strategically. Students use paper and pencil to find the mean absolute deviation for two sets of data. Then students use the AVERAGE and AVEDEV functions on a spreadsheet program to find the mean and the MAD of a data set.

Math Background

The mean absolute deviation is just one example of an absolute deviation. Another example is the similarly named median absolute deviation, which is the median of the distances between the data values and the median of the data set.

YOUR TURN

Avoid Common Errors

Using two sets of data makes it easy for students to mix up the data sets part way through a problem. To focus on one set of data at a time, have students calculate the MAD for waiter A, then have them calculate the MAD for waiter B.

EXAMPLE 2

Questioning Strategies

- Can the mean paper width of each machine be used to see which machine did a better job? Explain. The mean paper width cannot be used; the mean of Machine A is 8.4998 inches and the mean of Machine B is 8.5002 inches, which makes both the same amount away from the intended paper size of 8.5 inches.

- What would be the MAD of a paper-cutting machine that always cuts paper with a width of exactly 8.500 inches? Explain. 0; every piece of cut paper measures 8.500 inches, so the mean value is 8.500 inches. The difference between 8.500 and 8.500 is 0, and the mean of a set of 0s is 0.

Focus on Technology CC Mathematical Practices

In Example 2, students need to make sure they are entering the formulas correctly to ensure that the question can be solved by the spreadsheet. Explain that using two cells separated by a colon instructs the spreadsheet to use those cells and all cells in between them as the input of the function.

STEP 2 Find the distance from the mean for each of the weights.

The distances from the mean for Pen A are the distance of each weight from 6.3 lb.

Pen A: Premium Growth									
Weight (lb)	5.8	6.1	5.5	6.6	7.3	5.9	6.3	5.7	6.8	7.1
Distance from mean	0.5	0.2	0.8	0.3	1.0	0.4	0	0.6	0.5	0.8

The distances from the mean for Pen B are the distance of each weight from 6.7 lb.

Pen B: Maximum Growth									
Weight (lb)	7.7	7.4	5.4	7.8	6.1	5.2	7.5	7.9	6.3	5.6
Distance from mean	1.0	0.7	1.3	1.1	0.6	1.5	0.8	1.2	0.4	1.1

STEP 3 Calculate the MAD for the chickens in each pen. Round your answers to the nearest tenth.

Pen A: $\dfrac{0.5 + 0.2 + 0.8 + 0.3 + 1.0 + 0.4 + 0 + 0.6 + 0.5 + 0.8}{10} \approx 0.5$ lb

Pen B: $\dfrac{1.0 + 0.7 + 1.3 + 1.1 + 0.6 + 1.5 + 0.8 + 1.2 + 0.4 + 1.1}{10} \approx 1.0$ lb

Since Pen A's MAD is less, Premium Growth feed produces less variability in weight.

YOUR TURN

2. Two waiters at a cafe each served 10 large fruit smoothies. The amount in each large smoothie is shown below. Which waiter's smoothies showed less variability?

Amounts in Waiter A's Large Smoothies (oz)									
19.1	20.1	20.9	19.6	20.9	19.5	19.2	19.4	20.3	20.9

Amounts in Waiter B's Large Smoothies (oz)									
20.1	19.6	20.0	20.5	19.8	20.0	20.1	19.7	19.9	20.4

The MAD for Waiter A is 0.6 oz, and the MAD for Waiter B is 0.2 oz, so Waiter B's smoothies showed less variability.

Animated Math
© my.hrw.com

No; For example, in the Explore Activity, the data set with the smaller mean had more variability.

Math Talk
Mathematical Practices
Will a smaller mean always signal less variability?

Math On the Spot
© my.hrw.com

My Notes

Personal Math Trainer
Online Assessment and Intervention
© my.hrw.com

Using a Spreadsheet to Find MAD

Spreadsheets can be used to find the mean absolute deviation of a data set.

EXAMPLE 2 Real World   COMMON CORE 6.SP.5c

A paper mill is testing two paper-cutting machines. Both are set to produce pieces of paper with a width of 8.5 inches. The actual widths of 8 pieces of paper cut by each machine are shown. Use a spreadsheet to determine which machine has less variability and, thus, does a better job.

Widths of Pieces of Paper Cut by Machine A (in.)							
8.502	8.508	8.499	8.501	8.492	8.511	8.505	8.491

Widths of Pieces of Paper Cut by Machine B (in.)							
8.503	8.501	8.498	8.499	8.498	8.504	8.496	8.502

STEP 1 Enter the data values for Machine A into row 1 of a spreadsheet, using cells A to H.

	A	B	C	D	E	F	G	H
1	8.502	8.508	8.499	8.501	8.492	8.511	8.505	8.491
2								
3								

STEP 2 Enter "mean = " into cell A2 and the formula =AVERAGE(A1:H1) into cell B2.

	A	B	C	D	E	F	G	H
1	8.502	8.508	8.499	8.501	8.492	8.511	8.505	8.491
2	mean =	8.501125						
3								

STEP 3 Enter "MAD = " into cell A3 and the formula =AVEDEV(A1:H1) into cell B3.

	A	B	C	D	E	F	G	H
1	8.502	8.508	8.499	8.501	8.492	8.511	8.505	8.491
2	mean =	8.501125						
3	MAD =	0.005375						

The MAD for Machine A is about 0.0054 in.

STEP 4 Repeat Steps 1–3 with the data values for Machine B.

	A	B	C	D	E	F	G	H
1	8.503	8.501	8.498	8.499	8.498	8.504	8.496	8.502
2	mean =	8.500125						
3	MAD =	0.002375						

The MAD for Machine B is about 0.0024 in.

Machine B has less variability, so it does a better job.

DIFFERENTIATE INSTRUCTION

Technology

Discuss with students what formulas can be typed into a spreadsheet that would produce the same results as the AVERAGE and AVEDEV functions. Have students write formulas that refer to specific cells and use the basic operators. Remind students that the order of operations is to be used in any formulas they enter into a spreadheet.

Critical Thinking

Have students predict which set of songs will have less variability in length: songs from their own personal collection, or songs played on the radio. Students can research the length of a sample of songs that are played on the radio and calculate the mean absolute deviation. Then have students calculate the MAD for a sample of songs from their personal collection.

Additional Resources

Differentiated Instruction includes:

- Reading Strategies
- Success for English Learners **ELL**
- Reteach
- Challenge **PRE-AP**

YOUR TURN

Talk About It
Check for Understanding

Ask: How can you use a spreadsheet to find the MAD of a set of data? Input the data, one cell at a time, starting in cell A1 and moving to the right. Use the AVERAGE function to have the spreadsheet calculate the mean, and use the AVEDEV function to have the spreadsheet calculate the mean absolute deviation.

Elaborate

Talk About It
Summarize the Lesson

Ask: What steps do you take to find the mean absolute deviation of a data set? First, find the mean of the data set by adding all the values and dividing by the number of values. Then, subtract to find the distance each value is from the mean. Finally, find the mean of the distances by dividing the sum of the distances by the number of values.

GUIDED PRACTICE

Engage with the Whiteboard

 Have a student volunteer add a second row to the table in Exercise 1. Have another student fill in the distance from the mean for each value in the new row.

Avoid Common Errors

Exercise 1 Remind students that distance is always positive, so all distances from the mean will be positive numbers.

Exercise 2 Remind students that AVERAGE and AVEDEV are different spreadsheet functions and that each needs to be entered into the correct cell.

YOUR TURN

3. Two aspirin-making devices are set to make tablets containing 0.35 gram of aspirin. The actual amounts in 8 tablets from each device are shown. Use a spreadsheet to determine which device has less variability.

Personal
Math Trainer
Online Assessment
and Intervention
@ my.hrw.com

Amounts of Aspirin in Tablets Made by Device A (g)							
0.353	0.351	0.350	0.352	0.349	0.348	0.350	0.346

Amounts of Aspirin in Tablets Made by Device B (g)							
0.349	0.341	0.347	0.358	0.359	0.354	0.339	0.343

A: MAD ≈ 0.0017; B: MAD ≈ 0.0063; A has less variability.

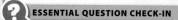

Guided Practice

1. A bus route takes about 45 minutes. The company's goal is a MAD of less than 0.5 minute. One driver's times for 9 runs of the route are shown. Did the bus driver meet the goal? (Explore Activity and Example 1)

Times to Complete Bus Route (min)								
44.2	44.9	46.1	45.8	44.7	45.2	45.1	45.3	44.6

a. Calculate the mean of the bus times. ___45.1 min___

b. Calculate the MAD to the nearest tenth. ___0.4 min___

The bus driver (**did**/ did not) meet the company's goal.

2. Below are a different driver's times on the same route. Find the mean and the MAD using a spreadsheet. Enter the data values into row 1 using cells A to I. Enter "mean =" into cell A2 and "MAD =" into cell A3. (Example 2)

Times to Complete Bus Route (min)								
44.4	43.8	45.6	45.9	44.1	45.6	44.0	44.9	45.8

The mean is ___44.9___ minutes, and the MAD is ___0.733333___ minutes.

This time, the bus driver (did /**did not**) meet the company's goal.

? **ESSENTIAL QUESTION CHECK-IN**

3. What is the mean absolute deviation and what does it tell you about data sets?

It is the mean of the distances between the data values and the mean of the data set. It can tell you how spread out from the mean the data values are.

16.2 Independent Practice

COMMON CORE 6.SP.5c

Personal
Math Trainer
Online
Assessment and
Intervention
@ my.hrw.com

Frank wants to know how many people live in each household in his town. He conducts a random survey of 10 people and asks how many people live in their household. His results are shown in the table.

Number of People per Household									
1	6	2	4	4	3	5	5	2	8

4. Calculate the mean number of people per household. ___4 people___

5. Calculate the MAD of the number of people per household. ___1.6 people___

6. What conclusions can you draw about the "typical" number of people in each household? Explain.

Sample answer: The average is 4, but the number of people varies greatly because the MAD is almost half the mean. For the sample, there is not really a typical household size.

Teachers are being trained to standardize the scores they give to students' essays. The same essay was scored by 10 different teachers at the beginning and at the end of their training. The results are shown in the tables.

Scores for Essay at Beginning of Teachers' Training									
76	81	85	79	89	86	84	80	88	79

Scores for Essay at End of Teachers' Training									
79	82	84	81	77	85	82	80	78	83

7. Calculate the MADs for the teachers' scores. Did the teachers make progress in standardizing their scores?

The MAD at the beginning of the training was about 3.7, and at the end, it was about 2.1, so they made progress in standardizing their scores.

8. **What If?** What would it mean if the teachers had a MAD of 0?

If the teachers had a MAD of 0, it would mean all their scores were the same.

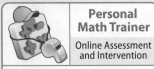

16.2 LESSON QUIZ

 6.SP.5c

An engineer is testing two designs for a catapult. She wants the catapult to launch objects 150 feet. The engineer records the distances in feet for 10 trials for the two designs, shown below.

Catapult A: 144, 154, 148, 147, 150, 150, 156, 151, 153, 151

Catapult B: 150, 148, 149, 151, 153, 152, 150, 144, 152, 153

1. Calculate the mean absolute deviation for Catapult A.

2. Calculate the mean absolute deviation for Catapult B.

3. Which catapult has less variability? Explain.

A restaurant owner orders tomatoes from 2 different farms. The weights of a random sample of 10 tomatoes from each farm are shown below in ounces.

Culver Farm: 3.1, 4.3, 5.2, 4.9, 3.8, 4.1, 4.3, 3.9, 4.3, 3.2

Jonesville Farm: 4.1, 5.5, 4.9, 5.4, 4.9, 5.1, 5.9, 5.2, 4.8, 5.1

4. Calculate the mean absolute deviation for tomatoes from Culver Farm.

5. Calculate the mean absolute deviation for tomatoes from Jonesville Farm.

6. Which tomatoes have less variability? Explain.

Lesson Quiz available online

my.hrw.com

Evaluate

GUIDED AND INDEPENDENT PRACTICE

 6.SP.5c

Concepts & Skills	Practice
Explore Activity Understanding Mean Absolute Deviation	Exercises 1, 4–5, 7–8
Example 1 Using Mean Absolute Deviation	Exercises 1, 4–5, 7–8
Example 2 Using a Spreadsheet to Find MAD	Exercises 2, 9–10

Exercise	Depth of Knowledge (D.O.K.)		Mathematical Practices
4–10	**2** Skills/Concepts		**MP.4** Modeling
11–12	**3** Strategic Thinking H.O.T.		**MP.7** Using Structure
13	**3** Strategic Thinking H.O.T.		**MP.3** Logic
14	**3** Strategic Thinking H.O.T.		**MP.7** Using Structure
15	**3** Strategic Thinking H.O.T.		**MP.3** Logic

Additional Resources

Differentiated Instruction includes:

• Leveled Practice Worksheets

 Exercises 9–11 combine concepts from the Common Core cluster "Develop understanding of statistical variability."

Answers

1. 2.6 feet

2. 2.0 feet

3. Catapult B has the smaller MAD, so Catapult B has less variability.

4. 0.49 ounce

5. 0.332 ounce

6. The tomatoes from Jonesville Farm have a lower MAD, so they have less variability.

The annual rainfall for Austin, Texas, and San Antonio, Texas, in each of the years from 2002 to 2011 are shown in the tables. Use the data for 9–11.

Annual Rainfall for Austin, Texas (in.)									
36.00	21.41	52.27	22.33	34.70	46.95	16.07	31.38	37.76	19.68

Annual Rainfall for San Antonio, Texas (in.)									
46.27	28.45	45.32	16.54	21.34	47.25	13.76	30.69	37.39	17.58

9. Use a spreadsheet to find the mean for the two cities' annual rainfalls. In which city does it rain more in a year, on average?

The mean for Austin is 31.855 in., while the mean for San Antonio is 30.459 in. Therefore, on average, it rains more in Austin in a year.

10. Use your spreadsheet to find the MADs. Use the MADs to compare the distribution of annual rainfall for the two cities.

The MAD for Austin is 9.681 in., while the MAD for San Antonio is 10.925 in. The annual rainfall for San Antonio varies more from the mean than the rainfall for Austin.

11. Make a Conjecture Does the information allow you to predict how the future amounts of rainfall for the two cities will compare? Explain.

Sample answer: Over many years, you should get more rainfall in Austin, but in any particular year, you can't predict which city will get more rainfall due to the variability.

12. Critical Thinking The life spans of 10 adult mayflies have a mean of 4 hours and a MAD of 2 hours. Fill in the table with possible values for the life spans. You can use the same value more than once. Sample answer:

Life Spans of Ten Mayflies (h)									
1	1	2	2	4	4	4	6	6	10

Can any one of the 10 mayflies in the group live for 1 full day? Justify your answer.

No; 24 hours deviates 20 from the mean. Because the MAD is 2 and there are 10 mayflies, this means no other mayfly could deviate from 4. But that would increase the mean to 6.

Work Area

13. Multistep In a spreadsheet, before entering any data values, first enter "mean =" into cell A2 and the formula =AVERAGE(A1:J1) into cell B2. Next, enter "MAD =" into cell A3 and the formula =AVEDEV(A1:J1) into cell B3. You should see #DIV/0! in cell B2 and #NUM! in cell B3 as shown. Now do the following:

a. Enter "1" into cell A1. What do you get for the mean and the MAD of the data set? Explain why this makes sense.

The mean is 1, and the MAD is 0. Because 1 is the only data value, it is the mean of the data set and does not deviate from the mean.

b. Enter "2" into cell B1. What do you get for the mean and the MAD of the data set this time? Explain why this makes sense.

The mean is 1.5, and the MAD is 0.5. $1 + 2 = 3$, and $3 \div 2 = 1.5$. Also, both 1 and 2 are 0.5 away from 1.5.

c. Enter the numbers 3 through 10 into cells C1 to J1 and watch the mean and the MAD change. Do they increase, decrease, or stay the same? Explain why this makes sense.

They increase. The values are getting larger, so the mean should increase, and they are getting more spread out, so the MAD should increase.

14. Make a Conjecture Each of the values in a data set is increased by 10. Does this affect the MAD of the data set? Why or why not?

No, it does not affect the MAD of the data set because the mean also increases by 10, so the distance of each data value from the mean remains the same.

15. What If? Suppose a data set contains all whole numbers. Would the MAD for the data set also be a whole number? Explain.

No; the MAD is a mean of the distances of the various data values from the mean. When you find the MAD, you may not get a whole number value.

EXTEND THE MATH PRE-AP

Activity available online ⏻ my.hrw.com

There are five numbers in a set: 10, 14, 15, 18, and 21. There are ten subsets that can be made using exactly three of the numbers in the set. For example (10, 14, 21) is a three-number subset. Find all three-number subsets that have a mean absolute deviation that is a whole number. (10, 14, 15), (10, 14, 21), and (15, 18, 21); the MAD for every three-number subset is shown below. The MADs that are not whole numbers are rounded to the nearest tenth.

Subset	Mean Absolute Deviation	Subset	Mean Absolute Deviation
(10, 14, 15)	2	(10, 18, 21)	4.2
(10, 14, 18)	2.7	(14, 15, 18)	1.6
(10, 14, 21)	4	(14, 15, 21)	2.9
(10, 15, 18)	2.9	(14, 18, 21)	2.4
(10, 15, 21)	3.8	(15, 18, 21)	2

LESSON
16.3 Box Plots

Engage

ESSENTIAL QUESTION

How can you use a box plot and measures of spread to describe a data set? Sample answer: You can draw a box plot to display the spread of the data set, find the range of the data, or find the interquartile range to describe the spread of the middle half of the data.

Motivate the Lesson

Ask: How could you describe how the heights of a group of students compare using a diagram? Begin Example 1 to find out how to make a box plot to organize data.

Explore

Connect to Daily Life CC Mathematical Practices

Have students stand in line in order of their heights from shortest to tallest. If there are an even number of students, have one student step out of line to be a helper. Ask the student who represents the median to step forward. Then ask the students on each end to step forward. Tell students that they will learn how to use these data points to build a box plot.

Explain

EXAMPLE 1

Connect Vocabulary ELL

A *box plot* is sometimes called a *box-and-whisker plot*. The box shows the lower quartile, the median, and the upper quartile, and the whiskers are drawn from the box to the least and greatest data values. The ends, the least and greatest values, are often called the *extremes*.

Questioning Strategies CC Mathematical Practices

• If the data set had an odd number of values, where do you place the median? In the middle of the two halves. It is not included in either half of the data.

YOUR TURN

Avoid Common Errors

Students may draw the plot incorrectly because they do not understand the scale on the number line. They may find it helpful to label each tick mark (i.e., using 72, 76, and so on).

EXAMPLE 2

Engage with the Whiteboard

Have a student draw lines from the Group A box plot to the number line to show how to read the upper and lower quartiles from the number line. Then have the student find the difference between the values. Have another student do the same for Group B. Tell students that those are the IQRs of each group and explain how to use the IQRs to compare the ages in each group.

Questioning Strategies CC Mathematical Practices

• If the IQR for a data set were very small, what would this tell you about the data set? The middle half of the data values are clustered close together.

16.3 Box Plots

COMMON CORE 6.SP.4

Display numerical data in plots on a number line, including ... box plots. *Also* 6.SP.5c

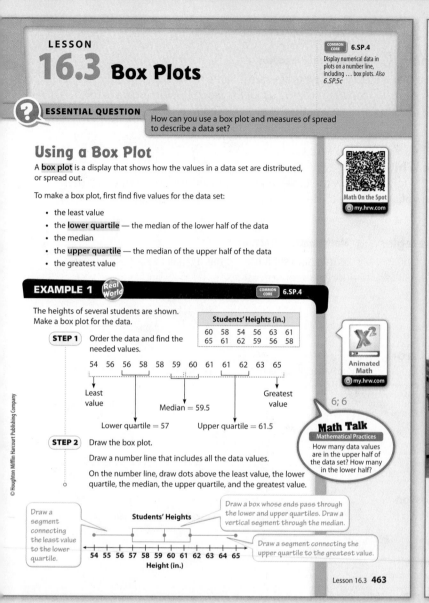

? ESSENTIAL QUESTION

How can you use a box plot and measures of spread to describe a data set?

Using a Box Plot

A **box plot** is a display that shows how the values in a data set are distributed, or spread out.

To make a box plot, first find five values for the data set:

- the least value
- the **lower quartile** — the median of the lower half of the data
- the median
- the **upper quartile** — the median of the upper half of the data
- the greatest value

EXAMPLE 1 Real World

COMMON CORE 6.SP.4

The heights of several students are shown. Make a box plot for the data.

Students' Heights (in.)

60	58	54	56	63	61
65	61	62	59	56	58

STEP 1 Order the data and find the needed values.

54 56 56 58 58 59 60 61 61 62 63 65

Least value

Median = 59.5

Greatest value

Lower quartile = 57   Upper quartile = 61.5

STEP 2 Draw the box plot.

Draw a number line that includes all the data values.

On the number line, draw dots above the least value, the lower quartile, the median, the upper quartile, and the greatest value.

Draw a segment connecting the least value to the lower quartile.

Draw a box whose ends pass through the lower and upper quartiles. Draw a vertical segment through the median.

Draw a segment connecting the upper quartile to the greatest value.

Students' Heights

54 55 56 57 58 59 60 61 62 63 64 65
Height (in.)

Math Talk
Mathematical Practices

How many data values are in the upper half of the data set? How many in the lower half?

6; 6

Lesson 16.3 **463**

Reflect

1. In the example, what percent of the data values are included in the box portion? What percent are included in each of the "whiskers" on the ends of the box? 50%; 25%; 25%

YOUR TURN

2. The daily high temperatures for some days last month are shown. Make a box plot of the data.

Daily High Temperatures (°F)

85	78	92	88	78	84
80	94	89	75	79	83

70 74 78 82 86 90 94 98
Daily High Temperatures, °F

Finding the Interquartile Range

A **measure of spread** is a single number that describes the spread of a data set. One measure of spread is the *interquartile range*. The **interquartile range (IQR)** is the difference of the upper quartile and the lower quartile.

EXAMPLE 2 Real World

COMMON CORE 6.SP.5c

The box plots compare the ages of dancers in two different dance troupes.

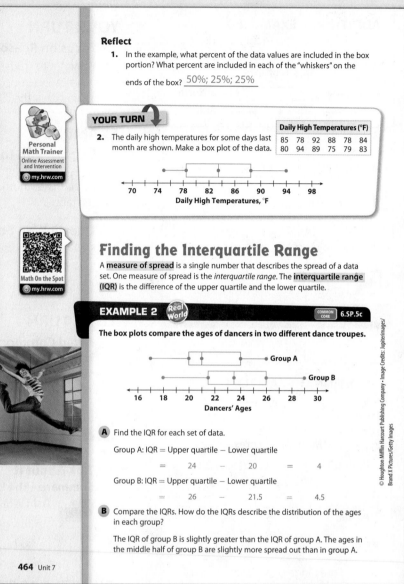

16 18 20 22 24 26 28 30
Dancers' Ages

Group A
Group B

A Find the IQR for each set of data.

Group A: IQR = Upper quartile − Lower quartile

= 24 − 20 = 4

Group B: IQR = Upper quartile − Lower quartile

= 26 − 21.5 = 4.5

B Compare the IQRs. How do the IQRs describe the distribution of the ages in each group?

The IQR of group B is slightly greater than the IQR of group A. The ages in the middle half of group B are slightly more spread out than in group A.

464 Unit 7

PROFESSIONAL DEVELOPMENT

CC Integrate Mathematical Practices MP.2

This lesson provides an opportunity to address this Mathematical Practice standard. It calls for students to create and use representations to organize, record, and communicate mathematical ideas. Students create box plots to organize and record numeric data in a way that makes it easy to see how values in the data set are distributed.

Math Background

The American mathematician John W. Tukey introduced the box plot in 1977. A box plot shows the median, the quartiles, and the extremes of a set of data: 50% of the data are in the box, and each of the "whiskers" on the ends of the box represents 25% of the data. Because not all of the data values are shown in a box plot, only the median, quartile values, and extremes can be read from the plot.

YOUR TURN

Focus on Reasoning CC Mathematical Practices

Point out to students that since the box plots are on the same number line, and the box on the plot for Group A is longer than the box on the plot for Group B, it is reasonable to assume that the IQR for Group A is greater than the IQR for Group B.

EXAMPLE 3

Engage with the Whiteboard

Ask a volunteer to write below the table: range = greatest value − least value. Then have another volunteer circle the least and greatest value in each data set and find the range.

Questioning Strategies CC Mathematical Practices

• What you can say about the values in a data set if the set has a small range? If the range is small, then there is little difference between the values of the individual items in the data set.

YOUR TURN

Avoid Common Errors

Watch for students who have difficulty organizing the data. Encourage students to use a number line to help them order the numbers.

Elaborate

Talk About It
Summarize the Lesson

Ask: What two measures describe the spread of a data set? How do you find each measure? The range describes the spread of a data set, and the IQR describes the spread of data around the median. The range is the difference between the greatest and least values. The IQR is the difference between the upper and lower quartiles.

GUIDED PRACTICE

Engage with the Whiteboard

For Exercise 1, have a student order the data from least to greatest on the whiteboard. Then have another student identify the median, upper quartile, and lower quartile. Finally, have a third student draw the box plot. Then ask the class to find the IQR and the range.

Avoid Common Errors

Exercise 2 If a student's answer is not a whole number, the student probably calculated the mean, not the median. Remind them that the median is the middle value in a data set.

Exercises 3–4 If students try to include the median in either the lower or upper quartiles, remind them that when there is an odd number of values, the median is the middle value and does not belong in either quartile.

YOUR TURN

3. The box plots compare the weekly earnings of two groups of salespeople from different clothing stores. Find and compare the IQRs of the box plots.

Weekly Earnings ($)

Group A IQR = $700. Group B IQR = $450. Group A's IQR is greater, so the salaries in the middle 50% for group A are more spread out than those for group B.

Personal Math Trainer
Online Assessment and Intervention
my.hrw.com

Math Talk Anno: Find the difference of the greatest and least values.

Math On the Spot
my.hrw.com

Finding the Range

Another measure that describes the spread of a set of data is the *range*. The **range** is the difference of the greatest value and the least value in a set of data.

EXAMPLE 3   Real World   COMMON CORE   6.SP.5c

The data sets show the ages of the players on two professional baseball teams. Find the range of each set of data.

Team A	36, 27, 28, 31, 39, 39, 28, 29, 24, 29, 30, 31, 29, 29, 28, 29, 31, 29, 32, 25, 37, 21, 26, 33, 29
Team B	25, 25, 26, 30, 27, 24, 29, 21, 27, 28, 26, 27, 25, 31, 22, 23, 29, 28, 25, 26, 28, 30, 23, 28, 29

STEP 1 Arrange the data sets in order from least to greatest.

Team A: 21, 24, 25, 26, 27, 28, 28, 28, 29, 29, 29, 29, 29, 29, 30, 31, 31, 31, 32, 33, 36, 37, 39, 39

Team B: 21, 22, 23, 23, 24, 25, 25, 25, 26, 26, 26, 27, 27, 27, 28, 28, 28, 28, 29, 29, 29, 30, 30, 31

STEP 2 Find the range of the data. Subtract the least value from the greatest value in each data set.

Team A: 39 − 21 = 18

Team B: 31 − 21 = 10

The range of ages for team A is 18 years, while the range of ages for team B is 10 years.

Math Talk
Mathematical Practices
How can you find the range of a set of data represented by a box plot?

YOUR TURN

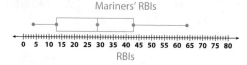

Personal Math Trainer
Online Assessment and Intervention
my.hrw.com

4. Find the range of each set of data. Which city's data has a greater range?

Average Monthly High Temperature (°F)	
Miami, FL	76, 78, 80, 83, 87, 90, 91, 91, 89, 86, 82, 78, 84
Chicago, IL	31, 35, 47, 59, 70, 80, 84, 82, 75, 62, 48, 35, 59

Miami = 15, Chicago = 53; Chicago

Guided Practice

The RBIs (runs batted in) for 15 players from the 2010 Seattle Mariners are shown. Use this data set for 1–7.

Mariners' RBIs
15 51 35 25 58 33 64
43 33 29 14 13 11 4 10

1. Order the data from least to greatest. (Example 1)
   4 10 11 13 14 15 25 29 33 33 35 43 51 58 64

2. Find the median. (Example 1) __29__

3. Find the lower quartile. (Example 1) __13__

4. Find the upper quartile. (Example 1) __43__

5. Make a box plot for the data. (Example 1)

Mariners' RBIs

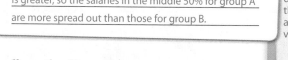

RBIs

6. Find the IQR. (Example 2) __30__

7. Find the range. (Example 3) __60__

? ESSENTIAL QUESTION CHECK-IN

8. How is the range of a set of data different from the IQR?

   The range of a set of data is the difference of the greatest and least values in the data set. The IQR is the difference of the upper and lower quartiles.

DIFFERENTIATE INSTRUCTION

Cognitive Strategies

Explain the concept of median to students in a different context. Tell them to visualize an interstate highway and its median splitting the highway lanes into halves. Then point out that the median of a set of data has the same function. It splits a set of data into two equal parts. Then the upper and lower quartiles further divide the data on each side.

Manipulatives

Write the data values from a data set on index cards. Have students place the cards in numerical order on a flat surface. Arrange the cards to determine the least value, lower quartile, median, upper quartile, and greatest value. Then use the cards to illustrate that although each quartile contains 25% of the data values, the range of data values in each quartile almost always varies.

Additional Resources

Differentiated Instruction includes:

• Reading Strategies

• Success for English Learners **ELL**

• Reteach

• Challenge **PRE-AP**

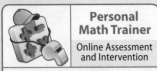

16.3 LESSON QUIZ

COMMON CORE 6.SP.5c

Use the data for the books each class donated for a book drive.

Books Donated					
28	15	39	43	27	22
50	36	41	37	21	25

1. Find the median.

2. Find the lower quartile.

3. Find the upper quartile.

4. Make a box plot of the data.

5. Find the IQR.

6. Find the range.

Lesson Quiz available online

 my.hrw.com

Answers

1. 32

2. 23

3. 41

4.

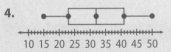

5. 18

6. 35

Evaluate

GUIDED AND INDEPENDENT PRACTICE

COMMON CORE 6.SP.4, 6.SP.5c

Concepts & Skills	Practice
Example 1 Using a Box Plot	Exercises 1–5, 9–12
Example 2 Finding the Interquartile Range	Exercises 6, 13, 15
Example 3 Finding the Range	Exercises 7, 14, 16

Exercise	Depth of Knowledge (D.O.K.)	**COMMON CORE** Mathematical Practices
9	**2** Skills/Concepts	**MP.2** Reasoning
10	**2** Skills/Concepts	**MP.4** Modeling
11–12	**3** Strategic Thinking **H.O.T.**	**MP.7** Using Structure
13–14	**2** Skills/Concepts	**MP.4** Modeling
15–17	**3** Strategic Thinking **H.O.T.**	**MP.7** Using Structure
18	**3** Strategic Thinking **H.O.T.**	**MP.6** Precision

Additional Resources

Differentiated Instruction includes:

• Leveled Practice Worksheets

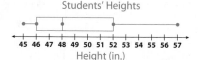

COMMON CORE 6.SP.4, 6.SP.5c

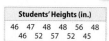

Personal Math Trainer
Online Assessment and Intervention
my.hrw.com

For 9–12, use the data set of the heights of several different students.

Students' Heights (in.)
46 47 48 48 56 48
46 52 57 52 45

9. Draw a box plot of the data.

Students' Heights

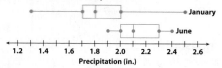

45 46 47 48 49 50 51 52 53 54 55 56 57
Height (in.)

10. How many students are included in the data set? _____11_____

11. What method could have been used to collect the data?

Sample answer: Students could have measured each others' heights.

12. **Represent Real-World Problems** What other data could you collect from the students to create a box plot? Provide several examples with units of measurement, if applicable.

Sample answers: test scores, shoe sizes, ages (years)

For 13–15, use the box plots of the total precipitation for the same group of cities for the months of January and June.

January

June

1.2   1.4   1.6   1.8   2.0   2.2   2.4   2.6
Precipitation (in.)

13. Calculate the IQR for each month.

January = __0.3__ inches   June = __0.3__ inches

14. Calculate the range for each month.

January = __1.2__ inches   June = __0.5__ inches

15. Compare the IQRs. What can you conclude about the two data sets?

The IQRs are the same. The spreads of the middle 50% of the data values are the same for the two data sets.

16. Compare the ranges. What can you conclude about the two data sets?

The range for January is more than twice as great as the range for June.

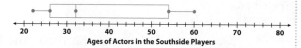

FOCUS ON HIGHER ORDER THINKING

Work Area

17. **Analyze Relationships** Can two box plots have the same range and IQR and yet represent completely different data? Explain.

Yes; sample explanation: One data set could range from 100 to 150, and another data set could range from 10 to 60. Both have a range of 50. The first data set could have quartiles at 120 and 130 and the second data set at 20 and 30, with both IQRs equal to 10.

18. **Multiple Representations** Matthew collected data about the ages of the actors in two different community theater groups. He drew a box plot for one of the sets of data.

20   30   40   50   60   70   80
Ages of Actors in the Southside Players

Ages of Actors in the Northside Players	71, 62, 63, 21, 63, 39, 25, 26, 30

a. Find the median, range, and IQR for each set of data.

Theater Group	Median	Range	IQR
Northside Players	39	50	37.5
Southside Players	32	38	28

b. Suppose you were to draw a second box plot for the Northside Players using the same number line as for the Southside Players. Which box plot would be longer overall? Which would have the longest box portion?

The box plot for the Northside Players will be longer overall because the data have a greater range. It will also have a longer box portion because the IQR is greater.

c. **Critique Reasoning** Mandy assumes that because nine data values are shown for the Northside Players, nine data values were used to make the box plot for the Southside Players. Explain why this is not necessarily true.

All box plots show only five values: the greatest and least values, the median, and the quartiles. You can't tell from looking at a box plot how many values were in the original data set.

EXTEND THE MATH PRE-AP

Activity available online my.hrw.com

Activity Challenge students to find data values that could be in a data set by using clues found in the following information.

- There are 12 data values in a data set.
- The median of the data set is 12.
- The mean of the data set is 11.
- The range of the data set is 12.
- The least data value is 5.

1. Find the possible values that could be in this set.

2. Draw a box plot that represents the data set.

3. **Extend** Find another set of values that could be in this data set. Explain what method you used.

1. Sample answer: 5, 8, 8, 9, 9, 12, 12, 12, 12, 13, 15, 17

2. Box plots should match data.

3. Students may see that they can easily find a different set by changing a pair of numbers on opposite sides of the median using opposite operations. For example, they could change one 8 to 9, and change the 15 to 14.

LESSON
16.4 Dot Plots and Data Distribution

ADDITIONAL EXAMPLE 1

The coach of the soccer team records the number of goals scored by the team during the season. Use the data to make a dot plot.

3, 4, 4, 10, 6, 5, 2, 5, 4, 2, 3, 4, 5, 0, 6

 Interactive Whiteboard
Interactive example available online

 my.hrw.com

Engage

ESSENTIAL QUESTION

How can you summarize and display numeric data? Sample answer: You can summarize numeric data using measures of center such as mean and median or measures of spread such as range. You can display numeric data on box plots or dot plots.

Motivate the Lesson

Ask: How tall is an average maple tree? Does this question have more than one answer? Is this a statistical question? Begin the Explore Activity to find out.

Explore

Focus on Communication

Help students distinguish between **statistical** and **nonstatistical** questions. Statistical questions are questions that have more than one answer, such as "What is the average weight of a dog?" Nonstatistical questions are questions that can have only one answer, such as "How far is it from Austin to Dallas?"

Explain

EXAMPLE 1

Connect Vocabulary [ELL]

Point out to students that the *frequency* of a data value is the number of times it occurs in the data set, and the distribution of a data set shows the spread of the values.

Questioning Strategies [CC] Mathematical Practices

• How do you know which numbers to use on a number line for a dot plot? Find the range of the data. Then make a number line that includes the range.

• How are a dot plot and a box plot similar? How are they different? Similar: Both displays use a number line to represent numerical data, and both show the distribution of the data. Different: In a dot plot, you see every data value. In a box plot, you see the how the data are distributed around the median.

YOUR TURN

Engage with the Whiteboard

For Exercise 4, have a student label the number line on the whiteboard. Then have another student complete the the dot plot. Ask the class to confirm that the plot is correct or challenge the placement of a dot. Then discuss frequency.

Avoid Common Errors

Remind students that the number of data values shown on a dot plot should be the same as the number of data values in the given data set.

COMMON CORE 6.SP.4

Display numerical data in plots on a number line, including dot plots.... Also 6.SP.1, 6.SP.2, 6.SP.5c, 6.SP.5d

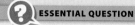 **ESSENTIAL QUESTION**

How can you summarize and display numeric data?

 **EXPLORE ACTIVITY** COMMON CORE 6.SP.1

Variable Data and Statistical Questions

The question "How much does a typical cat weigh?" is an example of a statistical question. A **statistical question** is a question that has many different, or variable, answers.

A Decide whether each of the situations below could yield variable data.

1. Your sister wants to know the typical weight for an adult cat.

___variable___

2. You want to know how tall your friend is. ___not variable___

3. You want to know how far your house is from school. ___not variable___

4. A car owner wants to know how much money people usually pay

for a new tire. ___variable___

5. How many students were in line for lunch at the cafeteria today

at 12:30? ___not variable___

B For which of the situations in part **A** can you write a statistical question? Write questions for these situations.

1 and 4; 1. How much does a typical adult cat weigh?

4. How much does a tire usually cost?

Reflect

1. Choose one of the questions you wrote in part **B**. How might you find answers to this question? What units would you use for the answers?

Sample answers: 1. Weigh a sample of adult cats and find the mean

or median weight in pounds. 4. Ask people who recently bought a

tire how much they paid in dollars, and find the mean or median.

 Math On the Spot

my.hrw.com

Making a Dot Plot

Statistical questions are answered by collecting and analyzing data. One way to understand a set of data is to make a visual display. A **dot plot** is a visual display in which each piece of data is represented by a dot above a number line. A dot plot shows the frequency of each data value.

EXAMPLE 1 Real World COMMON CORE 6.SP.4

A baseball team manager records the number of runs scored by the team in each game for several weeks. Use the data to make a dot plot.

1, 3, 1, 7, 2, 0, 11, 2, 2, 3, 1, 3, 4, 2, 2, 4, 5, 2, 6

The team usually scores between 0 and 7 runs in a game, but in one game they scored 11 runs.

STEP 1 Make a number line.
Data values range from 0 to 11, so use a scale from 0 to 11.

STEP 2 Draw a dot above the number line for each data value.

Runs Scored

Reflect

2. How many games did the team play during the season? How can you tell from looking at the dot plot?

19; there are 19 dots, each of which represents a game.

3. At how many games did the team score 2 runs or fewer? How do you know?

10 games; I counted the number of dots for the values

less than or equal to 2.

YOUR TURN

4. A different baseball team scores the following numbers of runs in its games for several weeks:
4, 4, 6, 1, 2, 4, 1, 2, 5, 3, 3, 5, 4, 2

Runs Scored

Use the data to make a dot plot. Tell how many games the team played, and identify the data value with the greatest frequency.

14 games; the value with the greatest frequency is 4;

there were 4 games in which the team scored 4 runs.

 Personal Math Trainer

Online Assessment and Intervention

my.hrw.com

PROFESSIONAL DEVELOPMENT

CC Integrate Mathematical Practices MP.3

This lesson provides an opportunity to address this Mathematical Practice standard. It calls for students to display, explain, and justify mathematical ideas and arguments using precise mathematical language in written or oral communication. Students interpret dot plots by identifying the value with the greatest frequency, outliers and any clustering of values. Students read dot plots; find mean, median and range; and describe what these measures of center and spread mean for each given situation.

Math Background

The dots in a dot plot represent individual data values, and the total number of dots in the plot is the total number of values in the data set. Displaying data in a dot plot can make it easy to interpret the characteristics of a data set, such as the *center* (the median), the *spread* (range of the data), the *shape* (Is it symmetrical or asymmetrical? Are there peaks or clusters?), and *unusual features* (gaps in the data, outliers).

EXAMPLE 2

Connect Vocabulary ELL

Point out to students that a figure is symmetric if a line can be drawn through the center to divide the figure into two parts that are mirror images of each other. Also, peaks are values with the highest frequency, and clusters are groups of values occurring closely together.

YOUR TURN

Focus on Communication CC Mathematical Practices

Ask students to describe the spread, center, and shape of the data distribution from Your Turn question 4. The data values are spread out from 1 to 6, with peaks at 2 and 4. The distribution is not symmetric because the data is not clustered around the center of the distribution. The distribution does not have an outlier.

EXAMPLE 3

Connect Vocabulary ELL

Review the meaning of *mean, median,* and *range* with the class, pointing out which measures of center are affected by outliers.

Questioning Strategies CC Mathematical Practices

• When finding the mean in A, Step 1, why do you need to include 0? In one game the team scored 0 runs, so 0 is a data value and must be included.

• Why doesn't the outlier affect the median? The median is the middle number of a data distribution and isn't affected by the numbers on either side of it.

YOUR TURN

Avoid Common Errors

Be certain students understand that that since there are 14 data values, the median is the mean of two middle values.

Interpreting a Dot Plot

A dot plot can give you a visual picture of the spread, center, and shape of a data distribution.

You can describe the spread of a data set by identifying the least and greatest values. You can also look for **outliers** which are data values that are either much greater or much less than the other data values.

You can describe the center and shape of a data set in terms of *peaks, clusters,* or *symmetry.* A symmetric distribution has approximately the same number of data values on either side of the center.

Math On the Spot
ⓜ my.hrw.com

EXAMPLE 2   COMMON CORE 6.SP.2

Describe the spread, center, and shape of each data distribution.

A The data values are spread out from 3 to 7 with no outliers.

The data has a cluster from 3 to 7 with one peak at 5, which is the center of the distribution.

The distribution is symmetric. The data values are clustered around the center of the distribution.

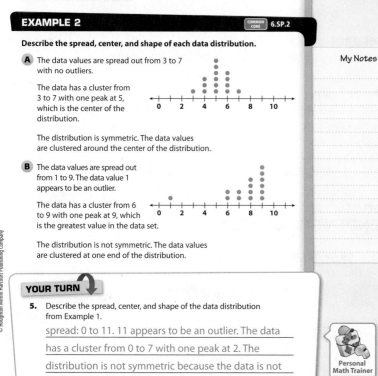

B The data values are spread out from 1 to 9. The data value 1 appears to be an outlier.

The data has a cluster from 6 to 9 with one peak at 9, which is the greatest value in the data set.

The distribution is not symmetric. The data values are clustered at one end of the distribution.

YOUR TURN

5. Describe the spread, center, and shape of the data distribution from Example 1.

spread: 0 to 11. 11 appears to be an outlier. The data

has a cluster from 0 to 7 with one peak at 2. The

distribution is not symmetric because the data is not

clustered around the center of the distribution.

Personal Math Trainer
Online Assessment and Intervention
ⓜ my.hrw.com

My Notes

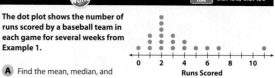
Math On the Spot
ⓜ my.hrw.com

Finding Measures from a Dot Plot

You can also find and calculate measures of center and spread from a dot plot.

EXAMPLE 3    COMMON CORE 6.SP.5d, 6.SP.5c

The dot plot shows the number of runs scored by a baseball team in each game for several weeks from Example 1.

Runs Scored

A Find the mean, median, and range of the data.

STEP 1 To find the mean, find the sum of the data values and divide by the number of data values.

$$\frac{1(0) + 3(1) + 6(2) + 3(3) + 2(4) + 1(5) + 1(6) + 1(7) + 1(11)}{19} = \frac{61}{19} \approx 3.2$$

The mean is about 3.2.

STEP 2 To find the median, count the dots from left to right until you find the middle value. You may need to find the mean of two middle values.

The median is 2.

STEP 3 To find the range, read the least and greatest values from the dot plot. Subtract the least value from the greatest.

$11 - 0 = 11$

The range is 11.

B How many runs does the team typically score in a game? Explain.

The mean number of runs is 3.2. The median number of runs is 2.

The shape of the dot plot suggests that the outlier 11 may be affecting these measures of center. To see if that is the case, find the mean and median without including the outlier. Compare these values with the original values.

STEP 1 Find the mean without including the outlier.

$$\frac{1(0) + 3(1) + 6(2) + 3(3) + 2(4) + 1(5) + 1(6) + 1(7)}{18} = \frac{50}{18} \approx 2.8$$

Without the outlier, the mean is 2.8, which is less than the original mean of 3.2.

STEP 2 Find the median without including the outlier.

Counting from left to right, the median is still 2.

Given that it is not affected by the outlier, the median may be more typical of the data. The team typically scores two runs per game.

Math Talk
Mathematical Practices

Why is the question in **B** a statistical question?

The number of runs varies from game to game.

DIFFERENTIATE INSTRUCTION

Curriculum Integration

Have students use a map of Florida and pick a city. Then have them research the local daily high and low temperatures for the last 15 days for that city. Have students write a paragraph that summarizes the temperature data they collected by incorporating measures of center and discussing symmetry, peaks, clusters, and outliers.

Cooperative Learning

Have students work in small groups. Each group is responsible for making a list of at least 5 questions that include both statistical and nonstatistical questions. Have a student from each group read their questions aloud. Students from other groups must decide if the question is statistical or nonstatistical.

Additional Resources

Differentiated Instruction includes:

- Reading Strategies
- Success for English Learners **ELL**
- Reteach
- Challenge **PRE-AP**

Elaborate

Talk About It
Summarize the Lesson

 Ask: What measures of center and spread can you find from a dot plot? You can find the mean, median, and range from a dot plot.

GUIDED PRACTICE

Engage with the Whiteboard

 For Exercise 2, have students complete the dot plot on the whiteboard.

Avoid Common Errors
Exercise 3 Remind students to include the data values of 0 when finding the mean, median, and range.

Evaluate

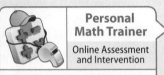

GUIDED AND INDEPENDENT PRACTICE

 COMMON CORE 6.SP.1, 6.SP.2, 6.SP.4, 6.SP.5c, 6.SP.5d

Concepts & Skills	Practice
Explore Activity Variable Data and Statistical Questions	Exercises 1, 7–10, 26
Example 1 Making a Dot Plot	Exercises 2, 11, 22
Example 2 Interpreting a Dot Plot	Exercises 4, 12–13, 19–20, 21–24
Example 3 Finding Measures from a Dot Plot	Exercises 3, 14–15, 16–18, 25

6. Find the mean, median, and range of the data from Your Turn question 4. What is the typical number of runs the team scores in a game? Justify your answer.

Mean: about 3.3, median: 3.5, range: 5; sample answer:

between 3 and 4 runs. The mean and median are close

in value, and there are no outliers.

Personal Math Trainer

Online Assessment and Intervention

my.hrw.com

Guided Practice

Tell whether the situation could yield variable data. If possible, write a statistical question. (Explore Activity)

1. The town council members want to know how much recyclable trash a typical household in town generates each week.

Variable data; sample answer: How many pounds of

recyclable trash does each household generate?

Kate asked some friends how many movies they saw last winter. Use her data for 2 and 3.

2. Make a dot plot of the data. (Example 1)

Movies Seen Last Winter
0, 1, 1, 2, 2, 3, 3, 3, 4, 4, 4, 5, 5, 5, 5, 6, 6, 7, 7, 7, 8, 8, 9, 9, 17

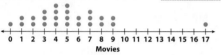

Movies

3. Find the mean, median, and range of the data. (Example 3)

Mean: about 5.2; median = 5; range = 17.

4. Describe the spread, center, and shape of the data. (Example 2)

spread: 0 to 17. 17 appears to be an outlier. The data has a cluster from 0

to 9 with peaks at 4 and 5. The distribution is not symmetric.

? ESSENTIAL QUESTION CHECK-IN

5. What are some measures of center and spread that you can find from a dot plot? How can making a dot plot help you visualize a data distribution?

Mean, median, and range; you can see whether the data are symmetric

about a central value or clustered around a different value.

16.4 Independent Practice

COMMON CORE **6.SP.1, 6.SP.2, 6.SP.4, 6.SP.5c, 6.SP.5d**

Personal Math Trainer

my.hrw.com

Online Assessment and Intervention

6. **Vocabulary** Describe how a statistical question yields an answer with variability. Give an example.

A statistical question has many

different, or variable answers.

Sample example: How old are

my friends' pets?

For 7–10, determine whether the question is a statistical question. If it is a statistical question, identify the units for the answer.

7. An antique collector wants to know the age of a particular chair in a shop.

not statistical

8. How tall do the people in your immediate and extended family tend to be?

statistical; feet and inches or

centimeters

9. How tall is Sam?

not statistical

10. How much did your classmates typically spend on music downloads last year?

statistical; dollars

For 11–14, use the following data. The data give the number of days of precipitation per month during one year in a city.

12 10 11 9 9 10 12 9 8 7 9 10

11. Make a dot plot of the data.

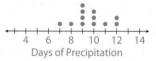

Days of Precipitation

12. What does each dot represent? How many months are represented?

the number of days of rain in

one month; 12 months

13. Describe the shape, center, and spread of the data distribution. Are there any outliers?

All the data values are between

7 and 12 days, with a peak around

9 days. There are no outliers.

14. Find the mean, median, and range of the data.

Mean: about 9.7 days; median:

9.5 days; range: 5 days

15. **What If?** During one month there were 7 days of precipitation. What if there had only been 3 days of precipitation that month? How would that change the measures of center?

The mean would change from

about 9.7 to about 9.3; the median

would stay at 9.5; the range would

change from 5 days to 9 days.

Answers

1.

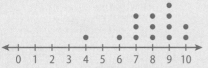

2. The data values are spread out from 4 to 10 with one peak at 9. Data value 4 appears to be an outlier. The data values are clustered around 8. The distribution is not symmetric.

3. Mean: 8; median: 8; range: 6

4. Sample answer: For this group of students, what is the typical score on the spelling quiz? The typical score is 8, since both the mean and the median are 8.

Exercise	Depth of Knowledge (D.O.K.)	COMMON CORE Mathematical Practices
6	2 Skills/Concepts	**MP.7** Using Structure
7–10	2 Skills/Concepts	**MP.7** Using Structure
11	2 Skills/Concepts	**MP.4** Modeling
12–14	2 Skills/Concepts	**MP.7** Using Structure
15	3 Strategic Thinking **H.O.T.**	**MP.7** Using Structure
16	2 Skills/Concepts	**MP.5** Using Tools
17–19	2 Skills/Concepts	**MP.7** Using Structure
20	2 Skills/Concepts	**MP.3** Logic
21	2 Skills/Concepts	**MP.7** Using Structure
22	2 Skills/Concepts	**MP.2** Reasoning
23–25	2 Skills/Concepts	**MP.7** Using Structure
26–27	3 Strategic Thinking **H.O.T.**	**MP.3** Logic
28	3 Strategic Thinking **H.O.T.**	**MP.7** Using Structure

Additional Resources
Differentiated Instruction includes:
• Leveled Practice Worksheets

CC CLUSTER CONNECTION **Exercises 28** combines concepts from the Common Core cluster "Summarize and describe distributions."

For 16–20, use the dot plot of the number of cars sold at a car dealership per week during the first half of the year.

Cars Sold

16. Find the mean, median, and range.

Mean = __10.25__   Median = __10__

Range = __17__

17. The owner of the car dealership decides to treat the value 22 as an outlier. Which measure of center or spread is affected the most if the owner removes this outlier? Explain.

The range; it changes from 17 to 10.

The mean changes from 10.25 to 9.7,

and the median does not change.

18. How many cars are sold in a typical week at the dealership? Explain.

10 cars; The mean and median

are both about 10.

19. Write an expression that represents the total number of cars sold during the first half of the year.

$5(2) + 6(2) + 7 + 8(3) + 9(2) + 10(5)$

$+ 11 + 12(3) + 13(2) + 15(2) + 22$

20. Describe the spread, center, and shape of the data distribution.

Sample answer: The data values

spread out from 5 to 22. The data

value 22 appears to be an outlier.

The data has a cluster from 5 to

15 with one peak at 10.

21. **Vocabulary** Explain how you can tell the frequency of a data value by looking at a dot plot.

Count the number of dots above

a data value.

For 22–26 use the following data. The data give the number of runs scored by opponents of the Boston Red Sox in June 2010.

4, 4, 9, 0, 2, 4, 1, 2, 11, 8, 2, 2, 5, 3, 2, 5, 6, 4, 0

22. Make a dot plot for the data.

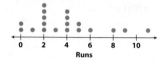

Runs

23. How many games did the Boston Red Sox play in June 2010? Explain.

19; Each dot represents one game.

24. Which data value in your dot plot has the greatest frequency? Explain what that frequency means for this data.

2 runs; 2 runs were scored against

the Red Sox in 5 games in June 2010.

25. Find the mean, median, and range of the data.

Mean: about 3.9 runs; median: 4

runs; range: 11 runs

26. What is a statistical question that you could answer using the dot plot? Answer your question and justify your response.

Sample answer: What was the typical

number of runs scored by opponents

of the Boston Red Sox in June 2010?

The mean is 3.9 and the median is 4,

so the typical number of runs is 4.

Work Area

27. A pediatrician records the ages of the patients seen in one day: 1, 2, 5, 7, 9, 17, 13, 16, 18, 12, 3, 5, 1.

a. **Explain the Error** Assuming that some of the patients are infants who are less than 1 year old, what information did the pediatrician forget to write down?

the units for the ages (years, months, weeks)

b. **Critical Thinking** Can you make a dot plot of the pediatrician's data? Can you find the mean, median, and range? Why or why not?

No; to make a dot plot or to find measures of center

and spread, the doctor needs to use the same units

for all the data.

28. **Multistep** A nurse measured a patient's heart rate at different times over several days.

Heart Rate (beats per minute)
86, 87, 89, 87, 86, 88, 90, 85, 82, 86, 83, 85, 84, 86

Heartbeats per Minute

a. Make a dot plot.

b. Describe the shape, center, and spread of the data. Then find the mean, median, range, and IQR for the data.

The data distribution is symmetric and the data values

are clustered around the median. There are no obvious

outliers. Mean = 86, median = 86, range = 8, IQR = 2

c. **What If?** The nurse collected the data when the patient was resting. How might the dot plot and the measures change if the nurse collects the data when the patient is exercising?

Sample answer: The heart rate might go up; the

mean, the range and the IQR could increase.

EXTEND THE MATH PRE-AP

Activity available online my.hrw.com

Activity The *relative frequency* of a data value is the ratio of the number of times the data item occurs in a data set to the total number of data items. Find the relative frequency of each color preference in the table. Then make a circle graph.

Color	Red	Yellow	Blue	Green	Other
Frequency	12	9	18	4	7
Relative Frequency	$\frac{12}{50} = 24\%$	$\frac{9}{50} = 18\%$	$\frac{18}{50} = 36\%$	$\frac{4}{50} = 8\%$	$\frac{7}{50} = 14\%$

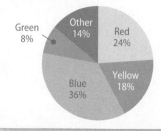

LESSON
16.5 Histograms

Common Core Standards

The student is expected to:

 Statistics and Probability—6.SP.4

Display numerical data in plots on a number line, including dot plots, histograms, and box plots.

 Statistics and Probability—6.SP.5

Summarize numerical data sets in relation to their context.

Mathematical Practices

 MP.2 Reasoning

ADDITIONAL EXAMPLE 1

A A dog walker counts and records the number of dogs at a dog park every morning at 8:00 for several days. Make a histogram of the data.

8, 2, 5, 6, 3, 4, 7, 4, 5, 3, 4, 7, 3, 1, 6, 4, 3, 2, 5, 8

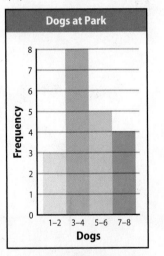

Interactive Whiteboard
Interactive example available online

⏻ my.hrw.com

Engage

ESSENTIAL QUESTION

How can you display data in a histogram? Sample answer: Order the data from least to greatest. Then organize the data in equal non-overlapping intervals. Make a bar graph where the bars touch one another and each bar has the height of a frequency of an interval.

Motivate the Lesson

Ask: How could you organize and display the temperatures of a particular city for a month to find which temperatures occur most often? Begin the Explore Activity to find out how to make a histogram to organize such data.

Explore

Focus on Modeling 🆁🅲 Mathematical Practices

Explain the similarities and differences between a bar graph and a histogram. For example, in a histogram the bars are connected, but they are separate in a bar graph; the width of each bar of a histogram shows a range. This is not true for a bar graph. The height or length of each bar in a histogram shows the frequency of the data in that interval, whereas each bar of a bar graph shows a number.

Explain

EXAMPLE 1

Connect Vocabulary 🅴🅻🅻

Point out to students that a frequency table lists items together according to the number of times, or frequency, that the items occur. Also, point out that a histogram is a bar graph that shows the frequency of data within equal intervals.

Questioning Strategies 🆁🅲 Mathematical Practices

• In Step 1, why is it important to use a frequency table to organize the data? Frequency tables show the data in intervals, so making a frequency table first makes it easier to make a histogram.

• How do you choose the intervals for a histogram? Choose intervals of equal size that cover all the data values. You can make the intervals whatever size best fits the data set.

LESSON
16.5 Histograms

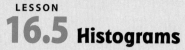

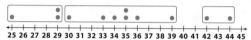

COMMON CORE 6.SP.4
Display numerical data in plots on a number line, including ... histograms.... *Also 6.SP.5*

? ESSENTIAL QUESTION
How can you display data in a histogram?

EXPLORE ACTIVITY (Real World) | COMMON CORE 6.SP.5, 6.SP.4

Grouping Data in Intervals

The members of the high-school basketball team practice free throws. Each player attempts 50 free throws. The number of free throws made by each player is listed below.

25, 29, 29, 30, 33, 34, 35, 35, 36, 39, 42, 44

A Use a dot plot to represent the data.

25 26 27 28 29 30 31 32 33 34 35 36 37 38 39 40 41 42 43 44 45

B On your dot plot, circle the dots that are in each interval of the frequency table below. Then complete the frequency table.

Interval	Frequency
20–29	3
30–39	7
40–49	2

> Enter the number of data values for the interval 30–39.

C Analyze the data. How were the data collected? How many data values are there? What are the mean, median, range, and IQR of the data?

12 players attempted 50 free throws each, and the number of free throws each player made was counted. There are 12 data values. Mean = 34.25; median = 34.5; range = 19; IQR = 6

EXPLORE ACTIVITY (cont'd)

Reflect

1. Can you use the dot plot to find the mean and the median of the data? Can you use the frequency table? Why or why not?
   Yes; no; the dot plot shows all the data values, so you can find the median and calculate the mean. The frequency table groups data into intervals, so you can't see the individual data values.

2. How do you find the number of data values in a data set from a dot plot? How can you find the number of data values from a frequency table?
   Count the number of dots; find the sum of the frequencies.

Using a Histogram

A **histogram** is a type of bar graph whose bars represent the frequencies of numeric data within intervals.

Math On the Spot
my.hrw.com

EXAMPLE 1 (Real World) | COMMON CORE 6.SP.4, 6.SP.5

A birdwatcher counts and records the number of birds at a birdfeeder every morning at 9:00 for several days.

12, 3, 8, 1, 1, 6, 10, 14, 3, 6, 2, 1, 3, 2, 7

Make a histogram of the data.

STEP 1 Make a frequency table.

Divide the data into equal-sized intervals of 4. Make a frequency table.

Interval	Frequency
1–4	8
5–8	4
9–12	2
13–16	1

STEP 2 Make a histogram.

The intervals are listed along the horizontal axis. The vertical axis shows the frequencies. For each interval, draw a bar to show the number of days in that interval. The bars should have equal widths. They should touch but not overlap.

Math Talk
Mathematical Practices
How does the histogram show the total number of days the birdwatcher counted birds?
The heights of the bars add up to 15.

Birds at Feeder

(Histogram with vertical axis "Frequency" from 0 to 12 and horizontal axis "Birds" with intervals 1–4, 5–8, 9–12, 13–16.)

PROFESSIONAL DEVELOPMENT

CC Integrate Mathematical Practices MP.2

This lesson provides an opportunity to address the Mathematical Practices standard that calls for students to reason abstractly and quantitatively. In the Explore Activity and Examples, students use data organized in frequency tables and histograms. They read and interpret the data displays, including how data values are distributed.

Math Background

The word *histogram* is from the Greek words *histos* (something set upright) + *gramma* (drawing or writing). A **histogram** is a special type of bar graph. It displays numerical data whose values are organized into equal intervals (or *bins*). The height of each bar shows the frequency of the values in that interval.

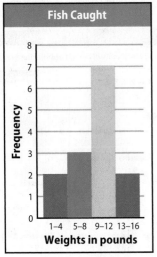

YOUR TURN

Engage with the Whiteboard

 Ask a student volunteer to make a frequency table for the data on the whiteboard. Ask the class if they could have other sized intervals for this question. Discuss pros and cons of small and large intervals with the class. Then have another student make a histogram on the whiteboard.

EXAMPLE 2

Connect Vocabulary [ELL]

Remind students to look at the least and greatest values when describing the **spread** of a data set. To describe the data distribution, they can also look at the center and shape of the data represented in a histogram.

Focus on Reasoning [CC] Mathematical Practices

- What information does the height of each bar provide? It tells the frequency for that interval.

- How can you tell that it was more likely for the birdwatcher to see a small number of birds than a large number? The bars for the intervals 1–4 and 5–8 are the highest.

YOUR TURN

Questioning Strategies [CC] Mathematical Practices

- How many movies did Kim rate? 15 movies

- How many did she give a rating of at least 7 to? 9 movies

Elaborate

....

Talk About It
Summarize the Lesson

 Ask: How is a histogram helpful in showing data? Sample answer: It displays data grouped into intervals and helps you see the overall distribution of the data.

GUIDED PRACTICE

Engage with the Whiteboard

For Exercise 2, have a student complete the frequency table on the whiteboard. Then have a second student make the histogram.

Avoid Common Errors

Exercise 3 Remind students that the height of the bar in a histogram is a frequency, not a data value. The frequency in the table gives the height of the bar for that interval.

Reflect

3. **What If?** Suppose the birdwatcher continues his observation for three more days and collects these new data values: 5, 18, and 2. How could you change the histogram to include the data?

Sample answer: Add an interval from 17–20 to show a

bar 1 unit high for the new data value of 18. Increase

the bar heights for the intervals 1–4 and 5–8 by 1.

YOUR TURN

4. Kim has started rating each movie she sees using a scale of 1 to 10 on an online site. Here are her ratings so far:

6, 9, 8, 5, 7, 4, 8, 8, 3, 7, 8, 7, 5, 1, 10

Make a histogram of the data.

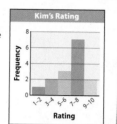

Kim's Rating

Personal Math Trainer
Online Assessment and Intervention
my.hrw.com

Analyzing a Histogram

By grouping data in intervals, a histogram gives a picture of the distribution of a data set.

EXAMPLE 2 — Real World   COMMON CORE 6.SP.5

Use the histogram from Example 1. What are some conclusions about the data that can you make from the shape of the distribution?

The highest bar is for the interval 1–4, which means that on more than half the days (8 out of 15), the birdwatcher saw only 1–4 birds. The bars decrease in height from left to right, showing that it was more likely for the birdwatcher to see a small number of birds rather than a large number on any given day.

Math On the Spot
my.hrw.com

YOUR TURN

5. Use your histogram from Your Turn 4. What are some conclusions you can make about Kim's movie ratings from the shape of the distribution?

Sample answer: Kim gave ratings of 7 or 8 to 7 of 15

movies. She gave ratings of 9 or 10 to 2 of 15 movies.

Personal Math Trainer
Online Assessment and Intervention
my.hrw.com

---

1. Wendy kept track of the number of text messages she sent each day for three weeks. Complete the frequency table. *(Explore Activity)*

0, 5, 5, 7, 11, 12, 15, 20, 22, 24, 25, 25, 27, 27, 29, 29, 32, 33, 34, 35, 35

Interval	Frequency
0–9	4
10–19	3
20–29	9
30–39	5

Ed counted the number of seats available in each cafe in his town. Use his data for 2–3.

18, 20, 22, 26, 10, 12, 16, 18, 7, 8

2. Complete the frequency table and the histogram. *(Example 1)*

Interval	Frequency
1–7	1
8–14	3
15–21	4
22–28	2

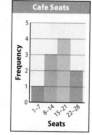

Cafe Seats

3. What are some conclusions you can make about the distribution of the data? *(Example 2)*

Sample answer: Only one cafe has less than 7 seats

available. The bars increase in height until they reach

the interval for 15–21 seats, and then they decrease in

height, showing that most cafes have 21 or fewer seats.

? ESSENTIAL QUESTION CHECK-IN

4. How can you display data in a histogram?

Order the data from least to greatest. Organize the data

in intervals of the same size, and make a bar graph of the

frequencies for each interval.

DIFFERENTIATE INSTRUCTION

Cooperative Learning

Have students work in groups to find data that they are interested in and can display using a frequency table. Ideas can include topics such as, the number of Super Bowls won by teams in the NFL or the number of Olympic medals won by different countries. Have students make a frequency table with intervals and a histogram to represent the data. Have groups present their data to the class.

Kinesthetic Experience

Have students measure and record the length in centimeters of a collection of pencils of different lengths. Then have them divide the lengths into equal-sized intervals, for example: 0–4 cm, 5–8 cm, 9–12 cm, and 13–16 cm. Then have students make a histogram of the results. Depending on the number of pencils used and the variation in their lengths, students may want to make another histogram using different intervals, and then compare the two histograms.

Additional Resources

Differentiated Instruction includes:

- Reading Strategies
- Success for English Learners **ELL**
- Reteach
- Challenge **PRE-AP**

16.5 LESSON QUIZ

6.SP.4, 6.SP.5

A running club records the ages of the club members who are running in a marathon.

32, 18, 23, 21, 40, 54, 29, 38, 25, 46, 30, 16, 36, 55, 58, 47, 16, 31, 50, 35

1. Make a frequency table and a histogram of the data.

2. Describe two things you know about the runners by looking at the distribution of the data.

Lesson Quiz available online

Answers

1. Sample answer:

Age	Frequency
10–19	3
20–29	4
30–39	6
40–49	3
50–59	4

Ages of Runners

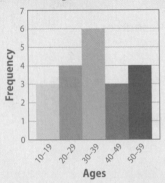

2. Sample answer: Out of 20 runners, none were younger than 10 or older than 59. The greatest number of runners were between 30 and 39 years old. There were the same number of runners between ages 10 and 29 as between 40 and 59.

Evaluate

GUIDED AND INDEPENDENT PRACTICE

6.SP.4, 6.SP.5

Concepts & Skills	Practice
Explore Activity Grouping Data in Intervals	Exercises 1–2, 5, 9
Example 1 Using a Histogram	Exercises 2, 5, 9
Example 2 Analyzing a Histogram	Exercises 3, 6–7

Exercise	Depth of Knowledge (D.O.K.)	Mathematical Practices
5	**2** Skills/Concepts	**MP.5** Using Tools
6–7	**2** Skills/Concepts	**MP.7** Using Structure
8	**3** Strategic Thinking **H.O.T.**	**MP.3** Logic
9	**3** Strategic Thinking **H.O.T.**	**MP.7** Using Structure
10	**3** Strategic Thinking **H.O.T.**	**MP.3** Logic

Additional Resources

Differentiated Instruction includes:

• Leveled Practice Worksheets

16.5 Independent Practice

COMMON CORE 6.SP.4, 6.SP.5

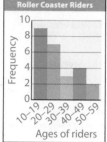

Personal Math Trainer

Online Assessment and Intervention

my.hrw.com

An amusement park employee records the ages of the people who ride the new roller coaster during a fifteen–minute period.

Ages of riders: 47, 16, 16, 35, 45, 43, 11, 29, 31, 50, 23, 18, 18, 20, 29, 17, 18, 48, 56, 24, 18, 21, 38, 12, 23.

5. Complete the frequency table. Then make a histogram of the data.

Interval	Frequency
10–19	9
20–29	7
30–39	3
40–49	4
50–59	2

Roller Coaster Riders

(histogram: Frequency vs Ages of riders)

6. Describe two things you know about the riders who are represented by the data.

Sample answer: Out of 25 riders, no riders were younger than 10 or older than 59; the greatest number of riders were between 10 and 19 years old.

7. Multiple Representations West Middle School has classes of many different sizes during first period. The number of students in each class is shown.

9, 23, 18, 14, 20, 26, 14, 18, 18, 12, 8, 13, 21, 22, 28, 10, 7, 19, 24, 20

a. Hank made a histogram using intervals of 6–10, 11–15, and so on. How many bars did his histogram have? What was the height of the highest bar? _____ 6

b. Lisa made a histogram using intervals of 0–9, 10–19, and so on. How many bars did her histogram have? What was the height of the highest bar? _____ 3 bars; 9

c. Besides a histogram, what are some other ways you could display these data?

box plot, dot plot

H.O.T. FOCUS ON HIGHER ORDER THINKING

Work Area

8. Communicate Mathematical Ideas Can you find the mean or median of a set of data from a histogram? Explain.

No; individual data values cannot be read from a histogram.

9. Multistep A theater owner keeps track of how many people come to see movies on 21 different Saturdays.

Saturday Moviegoers

Interval	Frequency
60–69	1
70–79	3
80–89	10
90–99	7

Saturday Moviegoers

(histogram: Frequency vs Number of Moviegoers)

a. Use the data to make a histogram.

b. Make a Prediction The theater owner asks, "How many moviegoers come to the theater on a typical Saturday?" What would you tell the theater owner? Use your histogram to support your answer.

Sample answer: You can expect somewhere between 80 to 99 people to come. The histogram shows that on 17 out of 21 Saturdays, the number of people who came to the theater was in that range.

c. Communicate Mathematical Ideas Is the theater owner's question a statistical question? Why or why not?

Yes; The number of people who come on Saturday varies.

10. Explain the Error Irina says she can find the range of a set of data from a histogram. Is she correct? Justify your answer.

No; Because a histogram groups data in intervals, you cannot see values in a given interval. So, you can't know the least and greatest data values.

EXTEND THE MATH PRE-AP

Activity available online my.hrw.com

Activity Explain that **cumulative frequency** is the running total of frequencies in a frequency table and can be displayed in a **cumulative frequency histogram.** The histogram looks like a bar graph that shows the data after it has been added to the previous data.

The table below shows the scores a group of students received on a math test.

Score	Frequency	Cum. frequency
61–70	3	3
71–80	5	8
81–90	12	20
91–100	9	29

1. Draw a cumulative frequency histogram using the "Score" column as the intervals.

2. Describe the shape of the cumulative frequency histogram.

1.

Score	Cumulative Frequency
61–70	3
71–80	8
81–90	20
91–100	29

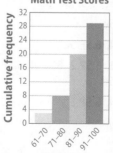

Math Test Scores

(histogram: Cumulative frequency vs Test scores)

2. Sample answer: The cumulative frequency histogram has bars that increase in height as you move to the right.

Ready to Go On?

Assess Mastery

Use the assessment on this page to determine if students have mastered the concepts and standards covered in this module.

Response to Intervention

Intervention	Enrichment

Access Ready to Go On? assessment online, and receive instant scoring, feedback, and customized intervention or enrichment.

Online and Print Resources

Differentiated Instruction
- Reteach worksheets
- Reading Strategies **ELL**
- Success for English Learners **ELL**

Differentiated Instruction
- Challenge worksheets **PRE-AP**
- Extend the Math **PRE-AP** Lesson Activities in TE

Additional Resources

Assessment Resources includes:
- Leveled Module Quizzes

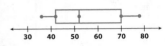 to Go On?

16.1 Measures of Center

1. Find the mean and median of these data: 2, 5, 9, 11, 17, 19.

   mean: 10.5, median: 10

16.2 Mean Absolution Deviation

2. Find the distance of each data value in Exercise 1 from the mean. Then find the mean absolute deviation of the data. 8.5, 5.5, 1.5, 0.5, 6.5, 8.5, MAD: 5.17

16.3 Box Plots

3. Make a box plot for the data set.

   | 36 | 42 | 44 | 52 | 61 | 70 | 78 |

16.4 Dot Plots and Data Distribution

A baseball team scored the following number of runs over a 10-game period: 6, 6, 8, 5, 4, 6, 4, 3, 8, 4

4. Make a dot plot for the data.

5. Find the mean, median, and range.

   mean: 5.4, median: 5.5, range: 5

16.5 Histograms

6. Make a histogram for the data set.

23	45	62	19
48	10	39	54
39	16	48	12
25	32	18	4

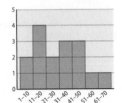

? ESSENTIAL QUESTION

7. How can you represent and summarize data in a dot plot?

   Make a number line and draw a dot above it for each data value. Summarize by describing the spread and shape of the data.

Common Core Standards

Lesson	Exercises	Common Core Standards
16.1	1	6.SP.3, 6.SP.5, 6.SP.5a, 6.SP.5b, 6.SP.5c, 6.SP.5d
16.2	2	6.SP.5c
16.3	3	6.SP.4, 6.SP.5c
16.4	4–5	6.SP.1, 6.SP.2, 6.SP.4, 6.SP.5c, 6.SP.5d
16.5	6	6.SP.4, 6.SP.5

Assessment Readiness

Assessment Readiness Tip Students should read diagrams carefully, extracting important information and writing on the diagram whenever it is helpful.

Item 1 The student can label the beginning of the box and the end of the box (20 and 35). By subtracting, students can discover the interquartile range is 15.

Item 2 To find the median, students can cross out pairs of dots, one dot at the beginning of the plot and one at the end, until they reach the middle and reveal that choice C is the correct answer.

Avoid Common Errors

Item 3 Some students may look at the diagram and quickly choose choice A, not paying attention to the inequality symbols. Remind them that ≥ and ≤ are the symbols that include the endpoints, which they need to do for this question.

Item 5 If students have difficulty getting started, remind them they must first find the mean of the values. So, they need to write the values in increasing order. Then they need to find the distance between each data value and the mean and find the average of those differences.

Additional Resources

Personal Math Trainer

Online Assessment and Intervention

⏻ my.hrw.com

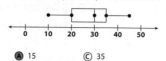

Selected Response

1. What is the interquartile range of the data represented by the box plot shown below?

Ⓐ 15   Ⓒ 35
Ⓑ 20   Ⓓ 40

The dot plot shows the ages of quiz show contestants.

20 21 22 23 24 25

2. What is the median of the data?

Ⓐ 21   Ⓒ 22
Ⓑ 21.5   Ⓓ 25

3. Which inequalities describe the possible ages of the contestants in the dot plot?

Ⓐ $a > 20$ and $a < 25$
Ⓑ $a \geq 20$ and $a \leq 25$
Ⓒ $a < 20$ and $a > 25$
Ⓓ $a \leq 20$ and $a \geq 25$

4. Suppose a new data value, 30, is included in the dot plot. Which statement describes the effect on the median?

Ⓐ The median would increase.
Ⓑ The median would decrease.
Ⓒ The median would stay the same.
Ⓓ The median would equal the mean.

5. Andrea recorded the points she scored in her last eight basketball games. What is the mean absolute deviation of the scores?

28, 32, 47, 16, 40, 35, 38, 54

Ⓐ 8.5   Ⓒ 17.75
Ⓑ 36.25   Ⓓ 38

Mini-Task

6. The frequency table shows data about how many tickets were sold by students.

Tickets Sold	Frequency
0–9	2
10–19	4
20–29	3
30–39	1

a. Use the frequency table to make a histogram.

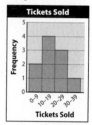

b. How many students sold tickets?

10 students

c. What percent of the students sold 20 or more tickets?

40%

Common Core Standards

Items	Grade 6 Standards	Mathematical Practices
1	6.SP.5c	MP.2
2	6.SP.5c	MP.4
3	6.SP.5d	MP.2
4	6.SP.5c	MP.2
5	6.SP.5c	MP.4
6*	6.RP.3c, 6.SP.5	MP.4

* Item integrates mixed review concepts from previous modules or a previous course.

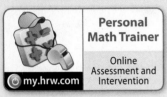

Study Guide Review

Vocabulary Development

Integrating Language Arts

Encourage students to practice using the unit vocabulary as they talk and write about mathematics. Understanding vocabulary will aid their understanding of the concepts.

 ELA-Literacy.RST.6-8.4 Determine the meaning of symbols, key terms, and other domain-specific words and phrases as they are used in a specific scientific or technical context relevant to grades 6–8 texts and topics.

MODULE 16 Displaying, Analyzing, and Summarizing Data

COMMON CORE 6.SP.1, 6.SP.2, 6.SP.3, 6.SP.4, 6.SP.5, 6.SP.5a, 6.SP.5b, 6.SP.5c, 6.SP.5d

Key Concepts

- The mean, or average, of a data set is the sum of the data values divided by the number of data values in the set. *(Lesson 16.1)*
- The median is the middle value of an ordered data set. *(Lesson 16.1)*
- The measure of spread is a single number that describes the spread of a data set. Interquartile range, or IQR, and range are two measures of spread. *(Lesson 16.4)*
- A statistical question is a question that has many different, or variable, answers. *(Lesson 16.4)*
- The frequency of a data value is the number of times it occurs in a data set. *(Lesson 16.5)*
- You can display data using box plots, dot plots, or histograms. *(Lessons 16.3, 16.4, and 16.5)*

Unit 7 Performance Tasks

The Performance Tasks provide students with the opportunity to apply concepts from this unit in real-world problem situations.

CAREERS IN MATH

Geneticist In Performance Task Item 1, students can see how a geneticist uses mathematics on the job.

SCORING GUIDES FOR PERFORMANCE TASKS

1. **MATHEMATICAL PRACTICES** **MP.3, MP.4, MP.6**

Task	Possible Points (Total: 5)
1	**1 point** for naming mean, median, range, and IQR as appropriate measures of center and variation, **1 point** for naming dot plot, box-and-whisker plot, and histogram for ways to display the data, **1 point** for stating only the dot plot and box-and-whisker plot could be used to show the measures of center and variation named earlier, and **2 points** for explaining that a histogram cannot be used because it only shows intervals from which you cannot read individual data.

Study Guide Review

Displaying, Analyzing, and Summarizing Data

Key Vocabulary

box plot (*diagrama de caja*)
categorical data (*datos categóricos*)
dot plot (*diagrama de puntos*)
histogram (*histograma*)
interquartile range (*rango entre cuartiles*)
lower quartile (*cuartil inferior*)
mean (*media*)
mean absolute deviation (MAD) (*desviación absoluta media, (DAM)*)
measure of center (*medida central*)
measure of spread (*medida de dispersión*)
median (*mediana*)
mode (*moda*)
range (*rango*)
statistical question (*pregunta estadística*)
upper quartile (*cuartil superior*)

? ESSENTIAL QUESTION

How can you solve real-world problems by displaying, analyzing, and summarizing data?

EXAMPLE 1

The ages of Thomas's neighbors are shown.

Ages of Thomas's Neighbors
30, 48, 31, 45, 42, 32, 32, 38, 34, 50, 49, 48

Make a box plot of the data.

30 31 <u>32 32</u> 34 <u>38 42</u> 45 <u>48 48</u> 49 50

Lower quartile = 32   Median = 40   Upper quartile = 48

30 32 34 36 38 40 42 44 46 48 50

EXAMPLE 2

Find the mean, median, and range of the data shown on the dot plot.

9 10 11 12 13 14 15 16 17

The mean is 13. $\frac{2(9) + 4(13) + 5(14) + 16}{12} = 13$

The median is 13.5.   9, 9, 13, 13, 13, <u>13, 14</u>, 14, 14, 14, 14, 16

The range is 7. $16 - 9 = 7$

EXAMPLE 3

Find the mean absolute deviation (MAD) of the data in Example 2. Round to the nearest tenth.

The MAD is the mean distance of each of the 12 data points from the mean, 13.

$$\frac{4+4+0+0+0+0+1+1+1+1+1+3}{12} = \frac{16}{12} \approx 1.3$$

The mean absolute deviation is approximately 1.3.

EXERCISES

1. The number of goals for the 13 players on a soccer team are 4, 9, 0, 1, 1, 2, 0, 0, 2, 8, 8, 3, 1. Find the median, lower quartile, and upper quartile. Then make a box plot for the data. (Lesson 16.3) _____ 2; 0.5; 6

0 1 2 3 4 5 6 7 8 9 10

2. The coach recorded the time it took 15 students to run a mile. The times are as follows: 9:23, 8:15, 9:23, 9:01, 6:45, 6:55, 7:20, 9:14, 6:21, 7:12, 7:34, 6:10, 9:15, 9:18. (Lesson 16.5)

Use the data to complete the frequency table. Then use the table to make a histogram.

Interval	Frequency
6–6:59	4
7–7:59	3
8–8:59	1
9–9:59	6

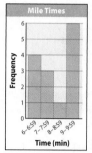

Mile Times

3. Find the mean and mean absolute deviation of the set of data. Round to the nearest hundredth. (Lesson 16.2)

Distance per day (mi) driven by Juan						
12	9	7	7	11	10	7

Mean: _____ 9 mi   Mean absolute deviation: _____ $\frac{12}{7} \approx 1.71$ mi

Unit 7 Performance Tasks

1. **CAREERS IN MATH** **Geneticist** Kinesha collects data about the heights of students in her science class. What measures of center and variation are appropriate for the data? Which of the data displays that you learned about in this unit could Keisha use to display the data? Which could be used to show the measures of center and variation you named? Explain.

Mean, median, range, IQR; dot plot, box plot, histogram; only the first two because a histogram shows intervals from which you cannot read individual values.

MIXED REVIEW

Assessment Readiness

Assessment Readiness Tip Students can use logic to eliminate some of the answer choices.

Item 1 The mean of a set of numbers is never the maximum or minimum value of the set, unless the set is made entirely of the same number. The answer choice 6.5 can be eliminated, because it is the maximum of the data set.

Item 5 A prime number has only two factors, 1 and itself. So, answer choice C can be eliminated because 10 is not prime, and answer choice D can be eliminated because 12 is not prime. The student can then evaluate the remaining expressions to find the correct answer.

Avoid Common Errors

Item 4 Some students will forget to place numbers in numerical order before looking for their median. Remind students that, to find the median, the numbers must be in order from greatest to least or least to greatest.

Item 9 Some students will forget that the ratio in the problem is set up in correlation to the wording, and so they may solve for male lions instead of female lions. Remind students that the ratio is written in the order of the wording that is used.

Common Core Standards

Items	Grade 6 Standards	Mathematical Practices
1	6.SP.3, 6.SP.5c	MP.4
2	6.SP.3, 6.SP.5c	MP.7
3	6.SP.3, 6.SP.5c	MP.7, MP.8
4	6.SP.2, 6.SP.5c	MP.4
5*	6.NS.3	MP.7
6	6.SP.4, 6.SP.5c	MP.2, MP.4, MP.7
7	6.SP.3, 6.SP.5c	MP.4
8*	6.RP.3, 6.RP.3d	MP.4, MP.7
9*	6.RP.1, 6.RP.3	MP.5
10	6.SP.3, 6.SP.4, 6.SP.5c	MP.4
11	6.SP.1, 6.SP.2, 6.SP.3	MP.4, MP.8
12	6.SP.1, 6.SP.2, 6.SP.4, 6.SP.5c	MP.4, MP.8

* Item integrates mixed review concepts from previous modules or a previous course.

Assessment Readiness

Personal Math Trainer
Online Assessment and Intervention

© my.hrw.com

Selected Response

1. Over 6 days, Jim jogged 6.5 miles, 5 miles, 3 miles, 2 miles, 3.5 miles, and 4 miles. What is the mean distance that Jim jogged?

- (A) 3.75 miles
- (C) 4.5 miles
- (B) 4 miles
- (D) 6.5 miles

Use the data set below for 2–3.

26	30	45	43	26
14	28	33	56	29

2. What is the mean of the data set?

- (A) 14
- (C) 33
- (B) 26
- (D) 46

3. What is the mean absolute deviation?

- (A) 2
- (B) 4
- (C) 6
- (D) 9

4. The ages of the volunteers at a local food bank are shown below.

34, 25, 24, 50, 18, 46, 43, 36, 32

What is the median of this set of data?

- (A) 32
- (C) 34
- (B) 33.1
- (D) 50

5. Which expression shows the prime factorization of 120?

- (A) $2^3 \times 3 \times 5$
- (B) $2 \times 3 \times 5$
- (C) 10^{12}
- (D) $2 \times 5 \times 12$

6. The dot plot shows the number of participants in each age group in a science fair.

Which of the following is **not** supported by the dot plot?

- (A) The range is 6.
- (B) The mean of the ages is about 14.4.
- (C) The mode of the ages is 13.
- (D) The median of the ages is 15.

7. Sarita recorded the distances she ran for 5 days: 5 miles, 4 miles, 5.5 miles, 4.5 miles, and 5.5 miles. What is the mean distance Sarita ran?

- (A) 4.9 miles
- (B) 5 miles
- (C) 5.1 miles
- (D) 5.5 miles

8. On a map of the city, 1 centimeter represents 2.5 miles. What distance on the map would represent 20 miles?

- (A) 6 centimeters
- (B) 8 centimeters
- (C) 12 centimeters
- (D) 18 centimeters

9. The ratio of the number of male lions to female lions in the animal reserve is 21:20. If there are 123 lions in the animal reserve, how many of the lions are female?

- (A) 40
- (C) 60
- (B) 50
- (D) 70

Mini-Tasks

10. The students in Ms. Lorenzo's class collected the following numbers of bottle caps:

10, 20, 40, 50, 30, 10, 60, 10, 20
40, 30, 30, 50, 70, 50, 70, 60, 30

a. Make a dot plot for the data.

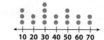

b. What is the median?

35

c. What is the mean?

37.78

11. The heights in inches of 8 students are 50, 53, 52, 68, 54, 49, 55, and 51.

a. What is the mean of the students' heights?

54 inches

b. Is there an outlier in the data set? If so, which number is the outlier?

yes, 68 inches

c. What is the mean height if the outlier is removed from the data?

52 inches

12. The data show the latest math test scores in Mr. White's class.

98	76	76	85	43
90	85	76	98	100
75	84	95	87	98
100	57	92	67	73
56	97	100	75	100

a. Draw a histogram of the data.

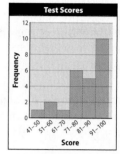

b. What is the outlier? Would removing the outlier change how the chart looks?

43; yes, if the outlier is removed, the chart would have one less column.

Glossary/Glosario

ENGLISH	SPANISH	EXAMPLES
absolute value The distance of a number from zero on a number line; shown by | |.	**valor absoluto** Distancia a la que está un número de 0 en una recta numérica. El símbolo del valor absoluto es | |.	$\|-5\| = 5$
acute angle An angle that measures greater than 0° and less than 90°.	**ángulo agudo** Ángulo que mide más do 0° y menos de 90°.	
acute triangle A triangle with all angles measuring less than 90°.	**triángulo acutángulo** Triángulo en el que todos los ángulos miden menos de 90°.	
addend A number added to one or more other numbers to form a sum.	**sumando** Número que se suma a uno o más números para formar una suma.	In the expression $4 + 6 + 7$, the numbers 4, 6, and 7 are addends.
Addition Property of Opposites The property that states that the sum of a number and its opposite equals zero.	**Propiedad de la suma de los opuestos** Propiedad que establece que la suma de un número y su opuesto es cero.	$12 + (-12) = 0$
additive inverse The opposite of a number.	**inverso aditivo** El opuesto de un número.	-4 is the additive inverse of 4.
adjacent angles Angles in the same plane that have a common vertex and a common side.	**ángulos adyacentes** Ángulos en el mismo plano que comparten un vértice y un lado.	$\angle 1$ and $\angle 2$ are adjacent angles.
algebraic expression An expression that contains at least one variable.	**expresión algebraica** Expresión que contiene al menos una variable.	$x + 8$ $4(m - b)$
algebraic inequality An inequality that contains at least one variable.	**desigualdad algebraica** Desigualdad que contiene al menos una variable.	$x + 3 > 10$ $5a > b + 3$
alternate exterior angles For two lines intersected by a transversal, a pair of angles that lie on opposite sides of the transversal and outside the other two lines.	**ángulos alternos externos** Dadas dos rectas cortadas por una transversal, par de ángulos no adyacentes ubicados en los lados opuestos de la transversal y fuera de las otras dos rectas.	$\angle 4$ and $\angle 5$ are alternate exterior angles.

alternate interior angles For two lines intersected by a transversal, a pair of nonadjacent angles that lie on opposite sides of the transversal and between the other two lines.

ángulos alternos internos Dadas dos rectas cortadas por una transversal, par de ángulos no adyacentes ubicados en los lados opuestos de la transversal y entre las otras dos rectas.

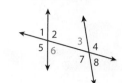

$\angle 3$ and $\angle 6$ are alternate interior angles.

---

angle A figure formed by two rays with a common endpoint called the vertex.

ángulo Figura formada por dos rayos con un extremo común llamado vértice.

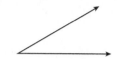

---

area The number of square units needed to cover a given surface.

área El número de unidades cuadradas que se necesitan para cubrir una superficie dada.

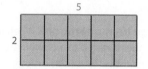

The area is 10 square units.

---

arithmetic sequence A sequence in which the terms change by the same amount each time.

sucesión aritmética Una sucesión en la que los términos cambian la misma cantidad cada vez.

The sequence 2, 5, 8, 11, 14 . . . is an arthmetic sequence.

Associative Property of Addition The property that states that for three or more numbers, their sum is always the same, regardless of their grouping.

Propiedad asociativa de la suma Propiedad que establece que agrupar tres o más números en cualquier orden siempre da como resultado la misma suma.

$2 + 3 + 8 = (2 + 3) + 8 = 2 + (3 + 8)$

Associative Property of Multiplication The property that states that for three or more numbers, their product is always the same, regardless of their grouping.

Propiedad asociativa de la multiplicación Propiedad que establece que agrupar tres o más números en cualquier orden siempre da como resultado el mismo producto.

$2 \cdot 3 \cdot 8 = (2 \cdot 3) \cdot 8 = 2 \cdot (3 \cdot 8)$

---

asymmetrical Not identical on either side of a central line; not symmetrical.

asimétrico Que no es idéntico a ambos lados de una línea central; no simétrico.

---

average The sum of the items in a set of data divided by the number of items in the set; also called *mean*.

promedio La suma de los elementos de un conjunto de datos dividida entre el número de elementos del conjunto. También se le llama *media*.

Data set: 4, 6, 7, 8, 10

Average: $\frac{4 + 6 + 7 + 8 + 10}{5} = \frac{35}{5} = 7$

---

axes The two perpendicular lines of a coordinate plane that intersect at the origin. singular: axis

ejes Las dos rectas numéricas perpendiculares del plano cartesiano que se intersecan en el origen.

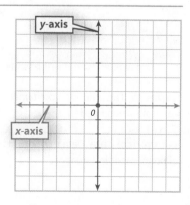

bar graph A graph that uses vertical or horizontal bars to display data.

gráfica de barras Gráfica en la que se usan barras verticales u horizontales para presentar datos.

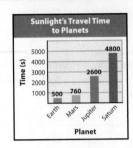

base (in numeration) When a number is raised to a power, the number that is used as a factor is the base.

base (en numeración) Cuando un número es elevado a una potencia, el número que se usa como factor es la base.

$3^5 = 3 \cdot 3 \cdot 3 \cdot 3 \cdot 3$; 3 is the base.

base (of a polygon or three-dimensional figure) A side of a polygon; a face of a three-dimensional figure by which the figure is measured or classified.

base (de un polígono o figura tridimensional) Lado de un polígono; la cara de una figura tridimensional, a partir de la cual se mide o se clasifica la figura.

bases of a cylinder   bases of a prism

base of a cone   base of a pyramid

bisect To divide into two congruent parts.

trazar una bisectriz Dividir en dos partes congruentes.

box plot A graph that shows how data are distributed by using the median, quartiles, least value, and greatest value; also called a box-and-whisker plot.

gráfica de caja Gráfica para demostrar la distribución de datos utilizando la mediana, los cuartiles y los valores menos y más grande; también llamado gráfica de mediana y rango.

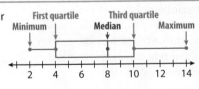

break (graph) A zigzag on a horizontal or vertical scale of a graph that indicates that some of the numbers on the scale have been omitted.

discontinuidad (gráfica) Zig-zag en la escala horizontal o vertical de una gráfica que indica la omisión de algunos de los números de la escala.

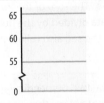

capacity The amount a container can hold when filled.

capacidad Cantidad que cabe en un recipiente cuando se llena.

categorical data Data that consists of nonnumeric information.

datos categóricos Datos que constan de información no numérica.

ENGLISH	SPANISH	EXAMPLES

Celsius A metric scale for measuring temperature in which 0°C is the freezing point of water and 100°C is the boiling point of water; also called *centigrade*.

Celsius Escala métrica para medir la temperatura, en la que 0° C es el punto de congelación del agua y 100° C es el punto de ebullición. También se llama *centígrado*.

---

center (of a circle) The point inside a circle that is the same distance from all the points on the circle.

centro (de un círculo) Punto interior de un círculo que se encuentra a la misma distancia de todos los puntos de la circunferencia.

---

center (of rotation) The point about which a figure is rotated.

centro (de una rotación) Punto alrededor del cual se hace girar una figura.

---

checking account An account at a financial institution that allows for withdrawals and deposits.

cuenta corriente Una cuenta en una institución financiera que permite para retiros y depósitos.

---

chord A line segment whose endpoints lie on a circle.

cuerda Segmento cuyos extremos se encuentran en un círculo.

---

circle The set of all points in a plane that are the same distance from a given point called the center.

círculo Conjunto de todos los puntos en un plano que se encuentran a la misma distancia de un punto dado llamado centro.

---

circle graph A graph that uses sections of a circle to compare parts to the whole and parts to other parts.

gráfica circular Gráfica que usa secciones de un círculo para comparar partes con el todo y con otras partes.

Residents of Mesa, AZ

65+ — 13% Under 18 — 27% 45–64 — 19% 18–24 — 11% 25–44 — 30%

---

circumference The distance around a circle.

circunferencia Distancia alrededor de un círculo.

Circumference

---

clockwise A circular movement in the direction shown.

en el sentido de las manecillas del reloj Movimiento circular en la dirección que se indica.

Glossary/Glosario

| --- | --- | --- |

Glossary/Glosario

ENGLISH	SPANISH	EXAMPLES
clustering A method used to estimate a sum when all addends are close to the same value.	**agrupación** Método que se usa para estimar una suma cuando todos los sumandos se aproximan al mismo valor.	27, 29, 24, and 23 all cluster around 25.
coefficient The number that is multiplied by the variable in an algebraic expression.	**coeficiente** Número que se multiplica por la variable en una expresión algebraica.	5 is the coefficient in 5*b*.
combination An arrangement of items or events in which order does not matter.	**combinación** Agrupación de objetos o sucesos en la cual el orden no es importante.	For objects *A, B, C,* and *D,* there are 6 different combinations of 2 objects: *AB, AC, AD, BC, BD, CD.*
common denominator A denominator that is the same in two or more fractions.	**denominador común** Denominador que es común a dos o más fracciones.	The common denominator of $\frac{5}{8}$ and $\frac{2}{8}$ is 8.
common factor A number that is a factor of two or more numbers.	**factor común** Número que es factor de dos o más números.	8 is a common factor of 16 and 40.
common multiple A number that is a multiple of each of two or more numbers.	**múltiplo común** Un número que es múltiplo de dos o más números.	15 is a common multiple of 3 and 5.
Commutative Property of Addition The property that states that two or more numbers can be added in any order without changing the sum.	**Propiedad conmutativa de la suma** Propiedad que establece que sumar dos o más números en cualquier orden no altera la suma.	$8 + 20 = 20 + 8$
Commutative Property of Multiplication The property that states that two or more numbers can be multiplied in any order without changing the product.	**Propiedad conmutativa de la multiplicación** Propiedad que establece que multiplicar dos o más números en cualquier orden no altera el producto.	$6 \cdot 12 = 12 \cdot 6$
compatible numbers Numbers that are close to the given numbers that make estimation or mental calculation easier.	**números compatibles** Números que están cerca de los números dados y hacen más fácil la estimación o el cálculo mental.	To estimate $7{,}957 + 5{,}009$, use the compatible numbers 8,000 and 5,000: $8{,}000 + 5{,}000 = 13{,}000$.
compensation When a number in a problem is close to another number that is easier to calculate with, the easier number is used to find the answer. Then the answer is adjusted by adding to it or subtracting from it.	**compensación** Cuando un número de un problema está cerca de otro con el que es más fácil hacer cálculos, se usa el número más fácil para hallar la respuesta. Luego, se ajusta la respuesta sumando o restando.	
complement The set of all outcomes that are not the event.	**complemento** La serie de resultados que no están en el suceso.	When rolling a number cube, the complement of rolling a 3 is rolling a 1, 2, 4, 5, or 6.

ENGLISH	SPANISH	EXAMPLES
complementary angles Two angles whose measures add to 90°.	**ángulos complementarios** Dos ángulos cuyas medidas suman 90°.	The complement of a 53° angle is a 37° angle.
composite number A number greater than 1 that has more than two whole-number factors.	**número compuesto** Número mayor que 1 que tiene más de dos factores que son números cabales.	4, 6, 8, and 9 are composite numbers.
compound inequality A combination of more than one inequality.	**desigualdad compuesta** Combinación de dos o más desigualdades.	$-2 \leq x < 10$
cone A three-dimensional figure with one vertex and one circular base.	**cono** Figura tridimensional con un vértice y una base circular.	
congruent Having the same size and shape.	**congruentes** Que tienen la misma forma y el mismo tamaño.	
congruent angles Angles that have the same measure.	**ángulos congruentes** Ángulos que tienen la misma medida.	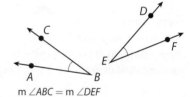 m ∠ABC = m ∠DEF
congruent figures Two figures whose corresponding sides and angles are congruent.	**figuras congruentes** Figuras que tienen el mismo tamaño y forma.	
congruent line segments Two line segments that have the same length.	**segmentos congruentes** Dos segmentos que tienen la misma longitud.	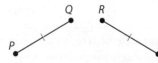
conjecture A statement that is believed to be true.	**conjetura** Enunciado que se supone verdadero.	
constant A value that does not change.	**constante** Valor que no cambia.	3, 0, π
coordinate grid A grid formed by the intersection of horizontal and vertical lines that is used to locate points.	**cuadrícula de coordenadas** Cuadrícula formada por la intersección de líneas horizontales y líneas verticales que se usan por localizar puntos.	

Glossary/Glosario

ENGLISH	SPANISH	EXAMPLES
coordinate plane A plane formed by the intersection of a horizontal number line called the *x*-axis and a vertical number line called the *y*-axis.	**plano cartesiano** Plano formado por la intersección de una recta numérica horizontal llamada eje *x* y otra vertical llamada eje *y*.	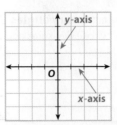
coordinates The numbers of an ordered pair that locate a point on a coordinate graph.	**coordenadas** Los números de un par ordenado que ubican un punto en una gráfica de coordenadas.	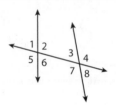 The coordinates of *B* are (−2, 3).
correspondence The relationship between two or more objects that are matched.	**correspondencia** La relación entre dos o más objetos que coinciden.	
corresponding angles (for lines) Angles in the same position formed when a third line intersects two lines.	**ángulos correspondientes (en líneas)** Ángulos en la misma posición formados cuando una tercera línea interseca dos líneas.	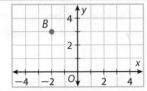 ∠1 and ∠3 are corresponding angles.
corresponding angles (in polygons) Angles in the same relative position in polygons with an equal number of sides.	**ángulos correspondientes (en polígonos)** Ángulos que se ubican en la misma posición relativa en polígonos que tienen el mismo número de lados.	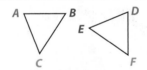 ∠A and ∠D are corresponding angles.
corresponding sides Sides in the same relative position in polygons with an equal number of sides.	**lados correspondientes** Lados que se ubican en la misma posición relativa en polígonos que tienen el mismo número de lados.	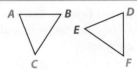 $\overline{AB}$ and $\overline{DE}$ are corresponding sides.
counterclockwise A circular movement in the direction shown.	**en sentido contrario a las manecillas del reloj** Movimiento circular en la dirección que se indica.	
credit card A plastic card issued by a financial company allowing a customer to buy goods or services on credit.	**tarjeta de crédito** Tarjeta de pago plástica que un cliente puede utilizar para comprar bienes o servicios. El cliente puede pagar por las compras a plazos, pero pagará intereses en el saldo restante.	
credit history Information about how a consumer has borrowed and repaid debt.	**historia crediticia** Información del buen manejo de dinero y pago de cuentas por parte de un cliente.	

Glossary/Glosario

ENGLISH	SPANISH	EXAMPLES
credit report A report containing detailed information on a person's credit history.	**informe crediticio** Informe que recopilan las agencias acerca de la historia crediticia de un cliente y que ayuda a los prestamistas a decidir si dan dinero a crédito a los clientes.	
credit score A number based on information in a consumer's credit report that measures an individual's creditworthiness.	**calificación crediticia** Número basado en información de un informe crediticio de un cliente. Se usa para predecir la posibilidad de que una persona se retrase en hacer pagos o que no pague una deuda.	
cross product The product of numbers on the diagonal when comparing two ratios.	**producto cruzado** El producto de los números multiplicados en diagonal cuando se comparan dos razones.	For the proportion $\frac{2}{3} = \frac{4}{6}$, the cross products are $2 \cdot 6 = 12$ and $3 \cdot 4 = 12$.
cube (geometric figure) A rectangular prism with six congruent square faces.	**cubo (figura geométrica)** Prisma rectangular con seis caras cuadradas congruentes.	
cube (in numeration) A number raised to the third power.	**cubo (en numeración)** Número elevado a la tercera potencia.	$5^3 = 5 \cdot 5 \cdot 5 = 125$
cumulative frequency The frequency of all data values that are less than or equal to a given value.	**frecuencia acumulativa** Muestra el total acumulado de las frecuencias.	
customary system The measurement system often used in the United States.	**sistema usual de medidas** El sistema de medidas que se usa comúnmente en Estados Unidos.	inches, feet, miles, ounces, pounds, tons, cups, quarts, gallons
cylinder A three-dimensional figure with two parallel, congruent circular bases connected by a curved lateral surface.	**cilindro** Figura tridimensional con dos bases circulares paralelas y congruentes, unidas por una superficie lateral curva.	

debit card An electronic card issued by a financial institution that allows a customer to access their account to withdraw cash or pay for goods and services	**tarjeta de débito** Tarjeta de pago plástica que un cliente puede usar para pagar por bienes o servicios. El dinero se retira inmediatamente de la cuenta corriente o de ahorros del cliente.	
degree The unit of measure for angles or temperature.	**grado** Unidad de medida para ángulos y temperaturas.	

© Houghton Mifflin Harcourt Publishing Company

denominator The bottom number of a fraction that tells how many equal parts are in the whole.

denominador Número de abajo en una fracción que indica en cuántas partes iguales se divide el entero.

$\frac{3}{4}$ ←—— denominator

---

dependent events Events for which the outcome of one event affects the probability of the other.

sucesos dependientes Dos sucesos son dependientes si el resultado de uno afecta la probabilidad del otro.

A bag contains 3 red marbles and 2 blue marbles. Drawing a red marble and then drawing a blue marble without replacing the first marble is an example of dependent events.

---

dependent variable The output of a function; a variable whose value depends on the value of the input, or independent variable.

variable dependiente Salida de una función; variable cuyo valor depende del valor de la entrada, o variable independiente.

For $y = 2x + 1$, y is the dependent variable: input: x output: y.

---

diagonal A line segment that connects two nonadjacent vertices of a polygon.

diagonal Segmento de recta que une dos vértices no adyacentes de un polígono.

---

diameter A line segment that passes through the center of a circle and has endpoints on the circle, or the length of that segment.

diámetro Segmento de recta que pasa por el centro de un círculo y tiene sus extremos en la circunferencia, o bien la longitud de ese segmento.

---

difference The result when one number is subtracted from another.

diferencia El resultado de restar un número de otro.

---

dimension The length, width, or height of a figure.

dimensión Longitud, ancho o altura de una figura.

---

discount The amount by which the original price is reduced.

descuento Cantidad que se resta del precio original de un artículo.

Distributive Property The property that states if you multiply a sum by a number, you will get the same result if you multiply each addend by that number and then add the products.

Propiedad distributiva Propiedad que establece que, si multiplicas una suma por un número, obtendrás el mismo resultado que si multiplicas cada sumando por ese número y luego sumas los productos.

$5(20 + 1) = 5 \cdot 20 + 5 \cdot 1$

---

dividend The number to be divided in a division problem.

dividendo Número que se divide en un problema de división.

In $8 \div 4 = 2$, 8 is the dividend.

---

divisible Can be divided by a number without leaving a remainder.

divisible Que se puede dividir entre un número sin dejar residuo.

18 is divisible by 3.

---

divisor The number you are dividing by in a division problem.

divisor El número entre el que se divide en un problema de división.

In $8 \div 4 = 2$, 4 is the divisor.

---

dot plot A visual display in which each piece of data is represented by a dot above a number line.

diagrama de puntos Despliegue visual en que cada dato se representa con un punto sobre una recta numérica.

double-bar graph A bar graph that compares two related sets of data.

gráfica de doble barra Gráfica de barras que compara dos conjuntos de datos relacionados.

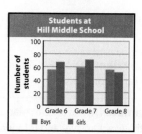

double-line graph A graph that shows how two related sets of data change over time.

gráfica de doble línea Gráfica lineal que muestra cómo cambian con el tiempo dos conjuntos de datos relacionados.

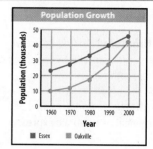

edge The line segment along which two faces of a polyhedron intersect.

arista Segmento de recta donde se intersecan dos caras de un poliedro.

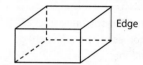

elements The words, numbers, or objects in a set.

elementos Palabras, números u objetos que forman un conjunto.

Elements of A: 1, 2, 3, 4

empty set A set that has no elements.

conjunto vacío Un conjunto que no tiene elementos.

endpoint A point at the end of a line segment or ray.

extremo Un punto ubicado al final de un segmento de recta o rayo.

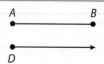

equally likely Outcomes that have the same probability.

igualmente probables Resultados que tienen la misma probabilidad de ocurrir.

When you toss a coin, the outcomes "heads" and "tails" are equally likely.

equation A mathematical sentence that shows that two expressions are equivalent.

ecuación Enunciado matemático que indica que dos expresiones son equivalentes.

$x + 4 = 7$
$6 + 1 = 10 - 3$

equilateral triangle A triangle with three congruent sides.

triángulo equilátero Triángulo con tres lados congruentes.

equivalent Having the same value.

equivalentes Que tienen el mismo valor.

equivalent expression Equivalent expressions have the same value for all values of the variables.

expresión equivalente Las expresiones equivalentes tienen el mismo valor para todos los valores de las variables.

$4x + 5x$ and $9x$ are equivalent expressions.

Glossary/Glosario

equivalent fractions Fractions that name the same amount or part.

fracciones equivalentes Fracciones que representan la misma cantidad o parte.

$\frac{1}{2}$ and $\frac{2}{4}$ are equivalent fractions.

---

equivalent ratios Ratios that name the same comparison.

razones equivalentes Razones que representan la misma comparación.

$\frac{1}{2}$ and $\frac{2}{4}$ are equivalent ratios.

---

estimate (n) An answer that is close to the exact answer and is found by rounding or other methods.

estimación (s) Una solución aproximada a la respuesta exacta que se halla mediante el redondeo u otros métodos.

---

estimate (v) To find an answer close to the exact answer by rounding or other methods.

estimar (v) Hallar una solución aproximada a la respuesta exacta mediante el redondeo u otros métodos.

---

evaluate To find the value of a numerical or algebraic expression.

evaluar Hallar el valor de una expresión numérica o algebraica.

Evaluate $2x + 7$ for $x = 3$.
$2x + 7$
$2(3) + 7$
$6 + 7$
13

---

even number A whole number that is divisible by two.

número par Un número cabal que es divisible entre dos.

---

event An outcome or set of outcomes of an experiment or situation.

suceso Un resultado o una serie de resultados de un experimento o una situación.

---

expanded form A number written as the sum of the values of its digits.

forma desarrollada Número escrito como suma de los valores de sus dígitos.

236,536 written in expanded form is $200,000 + 30,000 + 6,000 + 500 + 30 + 6$.

---

experiment In probability, any activity based on chance.

experimento En probabilidad, cualquier actividad basada en la posibilidad.

Tossing a coin 10 times and noting the number of "heads"

---

experimental probability The ratio of the number of times an event occurs to the total number of trials, or times that the activity is performed.

probabilidad experimental Razón del número de veces que ocurre un suceso al número total de pruebas o al número de veces que se realiza el experimento.

Kendra attempted 27 free throws and made 16 of them. Her experimental probability of making a free throw is $\frac{\text{number made}}{\text{number attempted}} = \frac{16}{27} \approx 0.59$.

---

exponent The number that indicates how many times the base is used as a factor.

exponente Número que indica cuántas veces se usa la base como factor.

$2^3 = 2 \cdot 2 \cdot 2 = 8$; 3 is the exponent.

---

exponential form A number is in exponential form when it is written with a base and an exponent.

forma exponencial Cuando se escribe un número con una base y un exponente, está en forma exponencial.

4^2 is the exponential form for $4 \cdot 4$.

---

expression A mathematical phrase that contains operations, numbers, and/or variables.

expresión Enunciado matemático que contiene operaciones, números y/o variables.

$6x + 1$

Glossary/Glosario

face A flat surface of a polyhedron.

cara Lado plano de un poliedro.

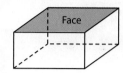

---

factor A number that is multiplied by another number to get a product.

factor Número que se multiplica por otro para hallar un producto.

7 is a factor of 21 since $7 \cdot 3 = 21$.

---

factor tree A diagram showing how a whole number breaks down into its prime factors.

árbol de factores Diagrama que muestra cómo se descompone un número cabal en sus factores primos.

$12 = 3 \cdot 2 \cdot 2$

Fahrenheit A temperature scale in which 32 °F is the freezing point of water and 212 °F is the boiling point of water.

Fahrenheit Escala de temperatura en la que 32 °F es el punto de congelación del agua y 212 °F es el punto de ebullición.

---

fair When all outcomes of an experiment are equally likely, the experiment is said to be fair.

justo Se dice de un experimento donde todos los resultados posibles son igualmente probables.

When tossing a fair coin, heads and tails are equally likely. Each has a probability of $\frac{1}{2}$.

---

formula A rule showing relationships among quantities.

fórmula Regla que muestra relaciones entre cantidades.

$A = \ell w$ is the formula for the area of a rectangle.

---

fraction A number in the form $\frac{a}{b}$, where $b \neq 0$.

fracción Número escrito en la forma $\frac{a}{b}$, donde $b \neq 0$.

---

frequency The number of times a data value occurs.

frecuencia Cantidad de veces que aparece el valor en un conjunto de datos.

In the data set 5, 6, 7, 8, 6, the data value 6 has a frequency of 2.

---

frequency table A table that lists items together according to the number of times, or frequency, that the items occur.

tabla de frecuencia Una tabla en la que se organizan los datos de acuerdo con el número de veces que aparece cada valor (o la frecuencia).

Data set: 1, 1, 2, 2, 3, 4, 5, 5, 5, 6, 6
Frequency table:

Date	Frequency
1	2
2	2
3	1
4	1
5	3
6	2

---

front-end estimation An estimating technique in which the front digits of the addends are added.

estimación por partes Técnica en la que se suman sólo los números enteros de los sumandos y luego se ajusta la suma para tener una estimación mas exacta.

Estimate $25.05 + 14.671$ with the sum $25 + 14 = 39$. The actual value is 39 or greater.

---

function An input-output relationship that has exactly one output for each input.

función Relación de entrada-salida en la que a cada valor de entrada corresponde un valor de salida.

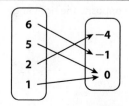

| | ENGLISH | SPANISH | EXAMPLES |

function table A table of ordered pairs that represent solutions of a function.

tabla de funciónes Tabla de pares ordenados que representan soluciones de una función.

x	3	4	5	6
y	7	9	11	13

grants Money awarded to students that does not need to be repaid.

beca Dinero que se otorga a estudiantes y el cual no se necesita devolver.

graph of an equation A graph of the set of ordered pairs that are solutions of the equation.

gráfica de una ecuación Gráfica del conjunto de pares ordenados que son soluciones de la ecuación.

greatest common factor (GCF) The largest common factor of two or more given numbers.

máximo común divisor (MCD) El mayor de los factores comunes compartidos por dos o más números dados.

The GCF of 27 and 45 is 9.

height In a triangle or quadrilateral, the perpendicular distance from the base to the opposite vertex or side. In a prism or cylinder, the perpendicular distance between the bases.

altura En un triángulo o cuadrilátero, la distancia perpendicular desde la base de la figura al vértice o lado opuesto. En un prisma o cilindro, la distancia perpendicular entre las bases.

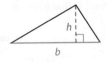

heptagon A seven-sided polygon.

heptágono Polígono de siete lados.

hexagon A six-sided polygon.

hexágono Polígono de seis lados.

histogram A bar graph that shows the frequency of data within equal intervals.

histograma Gráfica de barras que muestra la frecuencia de los datos en intervalos iguales.

hypotenuse In a right triangle, the side opposite the right angle.

hipotenusa En un triángulo rectángulo, el lado opuesto al ángulo recto.

Glossary/Glosario

Identity Property (for Addition) The property that states the sum of zero and any number is that number.

Propiedad de identidad (de la suma) Propiedad que establece que la suma de cero y cualquier número es ese número.

$7 + 0 = 7$
$-9 + 0 = -9$

Identity Property (for Multiplication) The property that states that the product of 1 and any number is that number.

Propiedad de identidad (de la multiplicación) Propiedad que establece que el producto de 1 y cualquier número es ese número.

$5 \times 1 = 5$
$-8 \times 1 = -8$

---

improper fraction A fraction in which the numerator is greater than or equal to the denominator.

fracción impropia Fracción cuyo numerador es mayor que o igual al denominador.

$\frac{5}{5}$

$\frac{7}{3}$

---

independent variable The input of a function; a variable whose value determines the value of the output, or dependent variable.

variable independiente Entrada de una función; variable cuyo valor determina el valor de la salida, o variable dependiente.

For $y = 2x + 1$, x is the dependent variable. Input: x output: y

---

indirect measurement The technique of using similar figures and proportions to find a measure.

medición indirecta La técnica de usar figuras semejantes y proporciones para hallar una medida.

---

inequality A mathematical sentence that shows the relationship between quantities that are not equal.

desigualdad Enunciado matemático que muestra una relación entre cantidades que no son iguales.

$5 < 8$
$5x + 2 \geq 12$

---

input The value substituted into an expression or function.

valor de entrada Valor que se usa para sustituir una variable en una expresión o función.

For the rule $y = 6x$, the input 4 produces an output of 24.

---

integer A member of the set of whole numbers and their opposites.

entero Un miembro del conjunto de los números cabales y sus opuestos.

$\ldots -3, -2, -1, 0, 1, 2, 3, \ldots$

---

interest The amount of money charged for borrowing or using money, or the amount of money earned by saving money.

interés Cantidad de dinero que se cobra por el préstamo o uso del dinero, o la cantidad que se gana al ahorrar dinero.

---

interquartile range (IQR) The difference of the third (upper) and first (lower) quartiles in a data set, representing the middle half of the data.

rango intercuartil (RIC) Diferencia entre el tercer cuartil (superior) y el primer cuartil (inferior) de un conjunto de datos, que representa la mitad central de los datos.

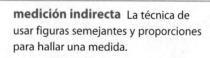

Lower half	Upper half
18, ⟨23,⟩ 28,	29, ⟨36,⟩ 42
First quartile	Third quartile

Interquartile range:
$36 - 23 = 13$

---

intersecting lines Lines that cross at exactly one point.

rectas secantes Líneas que se cruzan en un solo punto.

Glossary/Glosario

ENGLISH	SPANISH	EXAMPLES

intersection (sets) The set of elements common to two or more sets.

intersección (de conjuntos) Conjunto de elementos comunes a dos o más conjuntos.

---

interval The space between marked values on a number line or the scale of a graph.

intervalo El espacio entre los valores marcados en una recta numérica o en la escala de una gráfica.

---

inverse operations Operations that undo each other: addition and subtraction, or multiplication and division.

operaciones inversas Operaciones que se cancelan mutuamente: suma y resta, o multiplicación y división.

---

isosceles triangle A triangle with at least two congruent sides.

triángulo isósceles Triángulo que tiene al menos dos lados congruentes.

L

lateral surface In a cylinder, the curved surface connecting the circular bases; in a cone, the curved surface that is not a base.

superficie lateral En un cilindro, superficie curva que une las bases circulares; en un cono, la superficie curva que no es la base.

Lateral surface

---

least common denominator (LCD) The least common multiple of two or more denominators.

mínimo común denominador (m.c.d.) El mínimo común múltiplo de dos o más denominadores.

The LCD of $\frac{3}{4}$ and $\frac{5}{6}$ is 12.

---

least common multiple (LCM) The smallest number, other than zero, that is a multiple of two or more given numbers.

mínimo común múltiplo (m.c.m.) El menor de los múltiplos (distinto de cero) de dos o más números.

The LCM of 10 and 18 is 90.

---

like fractions Fractions that have the same denominator.

fracciones semejantes Fracciones que tienen el mismo denominador.

$\frac{5}{12}$ and $\frac{3}{12}$ are like fractions.

---

like terms Terms with the same variables raised to the same exponents.

términos semejantes Términos con las mismas variables elevadas a los mismos exponentes.

$3a^2b^2$ and $7a^2b^2$

---

line A straight path that has no thickness and extends forever.

recta Trayectoria recta que no tiene ningún grueso y que se extiende por siempre.

ℓ

---

line graph A graph that uses line segments to show how data changes.

gráfica lineal Gráfica que muestra cómo cambian los datos mediante segmentos de recta.

Marlon's Video Game Scores

Glossary/Glosario

| | ENGLISH | SPANISH | EXAMPLES |

line plot A number line with marks or dots that show frequency.

diagrama de puntos Recta numérica con marcas o puntos que indican la frecuencia.

Number of Pets

---

line of reflection A line that a figure is flipped across to create a mirror image of the original figure.

línea de reflexión Línea sobre la cual se invierte una figura para crear una imagen reflejada de la figura original.

Line of reflection

---

line of symmetry The imaginary "mirror" in line symmetry.

eje de simetría El espejo imaginario en la simetría axial.

---

line segment A part of a line between two endpoints.

segmento de recta Parte de una línea con dos extremos.

---

line symmetry A figure has line symmetry if one-half is a mirror image of the other half.

simetría axial Una figura tiene simetría axial si una de sus mitades es la imagen reflejada de la otra.

---

linear equation An equation whose solutions form a straight line on a coordinate plane.

ecuación lineal Ecuación en la que las soluciones forman una línea recta en un plano cartesiano.

$y = 2x + 1$

---

mean The sum of the items in a set of data divided by the number of items in the set; also called *average*.

media La suma de todos los elementos de un conjunto de datos dividida entre el número de elementos del conjunto.

Data set: 4, 6, 7, 8, 10

Mean: $\frac{4 + 6 + 7 + 8 + 10}{5} = \frac{35}{5} = 7$

---

mean absolute deviation (MAD) The mean distance between each data value and the mean of the data set.

desviación absoluta media (DAM) Distancia media entre cada dato y la media del conjunto de datos.

---

measure of center A measure used to describe the middle of a data set. Also called measure of central tendency.

medida central Medida que se usa para describir el centro de un conjunto de datos; la media, la mediana y la moda son medidas centrales. También se conocen como medidas de tendencia central.

---

measure of spread A measure that describes how far apart the data are distributed.

medida de dispersión Medida que describe la separación en una distribución de datos.

Glossary/Glosario

Glossary/Glosario

median The middle number or the mean (average) of the two middle numbers in an ordered set of data. | **mediana** El número intermedio o la media (el promedio) de los dos números intermedios en un conjunto ordenado de datos. | Data set: 4, 6, 7, 8, 10
Median: 7

metric system A decimal system of weights and measures that is used universally in science and commonly throughout the world. | **sistema métrico** Sistema decimal de pesos y medidas empleado universalmente en las ciencias y por lo general en todo el mundo. | centimeters, meters, kilometers, grams, kilograms, milliliters, liters

midpoint The point that divides a line segment into two congruent line segments. | **punto medio** El punto que divide un segmento de recta en dos segmentos de recta congruentes. |

B is the midpoint of $\overline{AC}$.

mixed number A number made up of a whole number that is not zero and a fraction. | **número mixto** Número compuesto por un número cabal distinto de cero y una fracción. | $5\frac{1}{8}$

mode The number or numbers that occur most frequently in a set of data; when all numbers occur with the same frequency, we say there is no mode. | **moda** Número o números más frecuentes en un conjunto de datos; si todos los números aparecen con la misma frecuencia, no hay moda. | Data set: 3, 5, 8, 8, 10
Mode: 8

multiple The product of a number and any nonzero whole number. | **múltiplo** El producto de un número y cualquier número cabal distinto de cero es un múltiplo de ese número. |

Multiplication Property of Zero The property that states that the product of any number and 0 is 0. | **Propiedad de multiplicación del cero** Propiedad que establece que el producto de cualquier número y 0 es 0. | $6 \times 0 = 0$
$-5 \times 0 = 0$

multiplicative inverse One of two numbers whose product is 1. | **inverso multiplicativo** Uno de dos números cuyo producto es igual a 1. | The multiplicative inverse of $\frac{3}{4}$ is $\frac{4}{3}$.

N

negative number A number less than zero. | **número negativo** Número menor que cero. | -2 is a negative number.

net An arrangement of two-dimensional figures that can be folded to form a polyhedron. | **plantilla** Arreglo de figuras bidimensionales que se doblan para formar un poliedro. |

10 m   10 m   6 m   6 m

numerator The top number of a fraction that tells how many parts of a whole are being considered. | **numerador** El número de arriba de una fracción; indica cuántas partes de un entero se consideran. | $\frac{3}{4} \longleftarrow$ numerator

numerical expression An expression that contains only numbers and operations. | **expresión numérica** Expresión que incluye sólo números y operaciones. | $(2 \cdot 3) + 1$

© Houghton Mifflin Harcourt Publishing Company

obtuse angle An angle whose measure is greater than 90° but less than 180°.

ángulo obtuso Ángulo que mide más de 90° y menos de 180°.

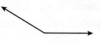

---

obtuse triangle A triangle containing one obtuse angle.

triángulo obtusángulo Triángulo que tiene un ángulo obtuso.

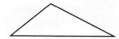

---

odd number A whole number that is not divisible by two.

número impar Un número cabal que no es divisible entre dos.

---

opposites Two numbers that are an equal distance from zero on a number line.

opuestos Dos números que están a la misma distancia de cero en una recta numérica.

5 and −5 are opposites.

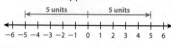

---

order of operations A rule for evaluating expressions: first perform the operations in parentheses, then compute powers and roots, then perform all multiplication and division from left to right, and then perform all addition and subtraction from left to right.

orden de las operaciones Regla para evaluar expresiones: primero se resuelven las operaciones entre paréntesis, luego se hallan las potencias y raíces, después todas las multiplicaciones y divisiones de izquierda a derecha y, por último, todas las sumas y restas de izquierda a derecha.

$3^2 − 12 ÷ 4$	Evaluate the power.
$9 − 12 ÷ 4$	Divide.
$9 − 3$	Subtract.
6	

---

ordered pair A pair of numbers that can be used to locate a point on a coordinate plane.

par ordenado Par de números que sirven para ubicar un punto en un plano cartesiano.

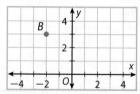

The coordinates of B are $(−2, 3)$.

---

origin The point where the *x*-axis and *y*-axis intersect on the coordinate plane; $(0, 0)$.

origen Punto de intersección entre el eje *x* y el eje *y* en un plano cartesiano: $(0, 0)$.

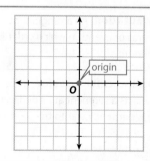

---

outcome A possible result of a probability experiment.

resultado Posible resultado de un experimento de probabilidad.

When rolling a number cube, the possible outcomes are 1, 2, 3, 4, 5, and 6.

---

outlier A value much greater or much less than the others in a data set.

valor atípico Un valor mucho mayor o menor que los demás valores de un conjunto de datos.

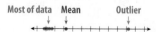

Glossary/Glosario

ENGLISH	SPANISH	EXAMPLES
output The value that results from the substitution of a given input into an expression or function.	**valor de salida** Valor que resulta después de sustituir un valor de entrada determinado en una expresión o función.	For the rule $y = 6x$, the input 4 produces an output of 24.
overestimate An estimate that is greater than the exact answer.	**estimación alta** Estimación mayor que la respuesta exacta.	100 is an overestimate for the sum $23 + 24 + 21 + 22$.

parallel lines Lines in a plane that do not intersect.	**rectas paralelas** Líneas que se encuentran en el mismo plano pero que nunca se intersecan.	
parallelogram A quadrilateral with two pairs of parallel sides.	**paralelogramo** Cuadrilátero con dos pares de lados paralelos.	
pentagon A five-sided polygon.	**pentágono** Polígono de cinco lados.	
percent A ratio comparing a number to 100.	**porcentaje** Razón que compara un número con el número 100.	$45\% = \frac{45}{100}$
perfect square A square of a whole number.	**cuadrado perfecto** El cuadrado de un número cabal.	$5^2 = 25$, so 25 is a perfect square.
perimeter The distance around a polygon.	**perímetro** Distancia alrededor de un polígono.	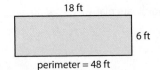 18 ft 6 ft perimeter = 48 ft
permutation An arrangement of items or events in which order is important.	**permutación** Arreglo de objetos o sucesos en el que el orden es importante.	For objects A, B, and C, there are 6 different permutations: ABC, ACB, BAC, BCA, CAB, CBA.
perpendicular bisector A line that intersects a segment at its midpoint and is perpendicular to the segment.	**mediatriz** Línea que cruza un segmento en su punto medio y es perpendicular al segmento.	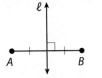 ℓ is the perpendicular bisector of $\overline{AB}$.
perpendicular lines Lines that intersect to form right angles.	**rectas perpendiculares** Líneas que al intersecarse forman ángulos rectos.	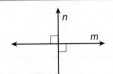

Glossary/Glosario

pi (π) The ratio of the circumference of a circle to the length of its diameter; $\pi \approx 3.14$ or $\frac{22}{7}$.

pi (π) Razón de la circunferencia de un círculo a la longitud de su diámetro; $\pi < 3.14$ ó $\frac{22}{7}$

---

plane A flat surface that has no thickness and extends forever.

plano Superficie plana que no tiene ningún grueso y que se extiende por siempre.

plane *R* or plane *ABC*

---

point An exact location that has no size.

punto Ubicación exacta que no tiene ningún tamaño.

P •

point *P*

---

polygon A closed plane figure formed by three or more line segments that intersect only at their endpoints.

polígono Figura plana cerrada, formada por tres o más segmentos de recta que se intersecan sólo en sus extremos.

---

polyhedron A three-dimensional figure in which all the surfaces or faces are polygons.

poliedro Figura tridimensional cuyas superficies o caras tienen forma de polígonos.

---

population The whole group being surveyed.

población El grupo completo que es objeto de estudio.

In a survey about eating habits of middle school students, the population is all middle school students.

---

positive number A number greater than zero.

número positivo Número mayor que cero.

2 is a positive number.

-4 -3 -2 -1 0 1 2 3 4

---

power A number produced by raising a base to an exponent.

potencia Número que resulta al elevar una base a un exponente.

$2^3 = 8$, so 2 to the 3rd power is 8.

---

prediction A guess about something that will happen in the future.

predicción Pronóstico sobre algo que puede ocurrir en el futuro.

---

prime factorization A number written as the product of its prime factors.

descomposición en factores primos Un número escrito como el producto de sus factores primos.

$10 = 2 \cdot 5$
$24 = 2^3 \cdot 3$

---

prime number A whole number greater than 1 that has exactly two factors, itself and 1.

número primo Número cabal mayor que 1 que sólo es divisible entre 1 y él mismo.

5 is prime because its only factors are 5 and 1.

---

principal The initial amount of money borrowed or saved.

capital Cantidad inicial de dinero depositada o recibida en préstamo.

---

prism A polyhedron that has two congruent, polygon-shaped bases and other faces that are all rectangles.

prisma Poliedro con dos bases congruentes con forma de polígono y caras con forma de rectángulos.

Glossary/Glosario

Glossary/Glosario

probability A number from 0 to 1 (or 0% to 100%) that describes how likely an event is to occur.

probabilidad Un número entre 0 y 1 (ó 0% y 100%) que describe qué tan probable es un suceso.

A bag contains 3 red marbles and 4 blue marbles. The probability of randomly choosing a red marble is $\frac{3}{7}$.

---

product The result when two or more numbers are multiplied.

producto Resultado de multiplicar dos o más números.

The product of 4 and 8 is 32.

---

proper fraction A fraction in which the numerator is less than the denominator.

fracción propia Fracción en la que el numerador es menor que el denominador.

$\frac{3}{4}, \frac{1}{13}, \frac{7}{8}$

---

proportion An equation that states that two ratios are equivalent.

proporción Ecuación que establece que dos razones son equivalentes.

$\frac{2}{3} = \frac{4}{6}$

---

protractor A tool for measuring angles.

transportador Instrumento para medir ángulos.

---

pyramid A polyhedron with a polygon base and triangular sides that all meet at a common vertex.

pirámide Poliedro cuya base es un polígono; tiene caras triangulares que se juntan en un vértice común.

Q

quadrant The x- and y-axes divide the coordinate plane into four regions. Each region is called a quadrant.

cuadrante El eje x y el eje y dividen el plano cartesiano en cuatro regiones. Cada región recibe el nombre de cuadrante.

Quadrant II	Quadrant I
Quadrant III	Quadrant IV

---

quartile Three values, one of which is the median, that divide a data set into fourths.

cuartil Cada uno de tres valores, uno de los cuales es la mediana, que dividen en cuartos un conjunto de datos.

First quartile   Third quartile
least value   Median   greatest value

2   4   6   8   10   12   14

---

quotient The result when one number is divided by another.

cociente Resultado de dividir un número entre otro.

In $8 \div 4 = 2$, 2 is the quotient.

R

radius A line segment with one endpoint at the center of a circle and the other endpoint on the circle, or the length of that segment.

radio Segmento de recta con un extremo en el centro de un círculo y el otro en la circunferencia, o bien la longitud de ese segmento.

range In statistics, the difference between the greatest and least values in a data set.

rango (en estadística) Diferencia entre los valores máximo y mínimo de un conjunto de datos.

rate A ratio that compares two quantities measured in different units.

tasa Una razón que compara dos cantidades medidas en diferentes unidades.

rate of change A ratio that compares the difference between two output values to the difference between the corresponding input values.

tasa de cambio Razón que compara la diferencia entre dos salidas con la diferencia entre dos entrados.

The cost of mailing a letter increased from 22 cents in 1985 to 25 cents in 1988. The rate of change was $\frac{25 - 22}{1988 - 1985} = \frac{3}{3}$

$= 1$ cent per year.

rate of interest The percent charged or earned on an amount of money; see *simple interest*.

tasa de interés Porcentaje que se cobra por una cantidad de dinero prestada o que se gana por una cantidad de dinero ahorrada; ver *interés simple*.

ratio A comparison of two quantities by division.

razón Comparación de dos cantidades mediante una división.

12 to 25, 12:25, $\frac{12}{25}$

rational number A number that can be written in the form $\frac{a}{b}$, where a and b are integers and $b \neq 0$.

número racional Número que se puede expresar como $\frac{a}{b}$, donde a y b son números enteros y $b \neq 0$.

$3, 1.75, 0.\overline{3}, -\frac{2}{3}, 0$

ray A part of a line that starts at one endpoint and extends forever in one direction.

rayo Parte de una línea que comienza en un extremo y se extiende siempre en una dirección.

D

reciprocal One of two numbers whose product is 1.

recíproco Uno de dos números cuyo producto es igual a 1.

The reciprocal of $\frac{2}{3}$ is $\frac{3}{2}$.

rectangle A parallelogram with four right angles.

rectángulo Paralelogramo con cuatro ángulos rectos.

rectangular prism A polyhedron whose bases are rectangles and whose other faces are rectangles.

prisma rectangular Poliedro cuyas bases son rectángulos y cuyas caras tienen forma de rectángulos.

reflection A transformation of a figure that flips the figure across a line.

reflexión Transformación que ocurre cuando se invierte una figura sobre una línea.

regular polygon A polygon with congruent sides and angles.

polígono regular Polígono con lados y ángulos congruentes.

|---|---|---|

relative frequency The ratio of the number of times an event or data value occurs and the total number of events or data values. | **frecuencia relativa** La razón del número de veces que ocurre un evento o dato (frecuencia) al total del número de eventos o datos. | |

repeating decimal A decimal in which one or more digits repeat infinitely. | **decimal periódico** Decimal en el que uno o más dígitos se repiten infinitamente. | $0.75757575\ldots = 0.\overline{75}$ |

rhombus A parallelogram with all sides congruent. | **rombo** Paralelogramo en el que todos los lados son congruentes. | |

right angle An angle that measures 90°. | **ángulo recto** Ángulo que mide exactamente 90°. | |

right triangle A triangle containing a right angle. | **triángulo rectángulo** Triángulo que tiene un ángulo recto. | |

rotation A transformation in which a figure is turned around a point. | **rotación** Transformación que ocurre cuando una figura gira alrededor de un punto. | |

rotational symmetry A figure that can be rotated about a point by an angle less than 360° so that the image coincides with the preimage has rotational symmetry. | **simetría de rotación** Una figura que puede rotarse alrededor de un punto en un ángulo menor de 360° de forma tal que la imagen coincide con la imagen original que tenga simetría de rotación. | |

rounding Replacing a number with an estimate of that number to a given place value. | **redondear** Sustituir un número por una estimación de ese número hasta cierto valor posicional. | 2,354 rounded to the nearest thousand is 2,000; 2,354 rounded to the nearest 100 is 2,400. |

S

sales tax A percent of the cost of an item which is charged by governments to raise money. | **impuesto sobre la venta** Porcentaje del costo de un artículo que los gobiernos cobran para recaudar fondos. | |

sample A part of a group being surveyed. | **muestra** Parte de un grupo que es objeto de estudio. | In a survey about eating habits of middle school math students, a sample is a survey of 100 randomly chosen students. |

ENGLISH	SPANISH	EXAMPLES
sample space All possible outcomes of an experiment.	**espacio muestral** Conjunto de todos los resultados posibles de un experimento.	When rolling a number cube, the sample space is 1, 2, 3, 4, 5, 6.
scale The ratio between two sets of measurements.	**escala** La razón entre dos conjuntos de medidas.	1 cm: 5 mi
scale drawing A drawing that uses a scale to make an object proportionally smaller than or larger than the real object.	**dibujo a escala** Dibujo en el que se usa una escala para que un objeto se vea proporcionalmente mayor o menor que el objeto real al que representa.	A blueprint is an example of a scale drawing.
scale model A proportional model of a three-dimensional object.	**modelo a escala** Modelo proporcional de un objeto tridimensional.	
scalene triangle A triangle with no congruent sides.	**triángulo escaleno** Triángulo que no tiene lados congruentes.	
scholarship A monetary award to a student to support their education.	**becas** Dinero que se otorga a los estudiantes en base a logros.	
scientific notation A method of writing very large or very small numbers by using powers of 10.	**notación científica** Método que se usa para escribir números muy grandes o muy pequeños mediante potencias de 10.	$12{,}560{,}000{,}000{,}000 = 1.256 \times 10^{13}$
segment A part of a line made of two endpoints and all points between them.	**segmento** Parte de una línea que consiste en dos extremos y todos los puntos entre éstos.	
sequence An ordered list of numbers.	**sucesión** Lista ordenada de números.	2, 4, 6, 8, 10, . . .
set A group of items.	**conjunto** Un grupo de elementos.	
side A line bounding a geometric figure; one of the faces forming the outside of an object.	**lado** Línea que delimita las figuras geométricas; una de las caras que forman la parte exterior de un objeto.	
significant figures The figures used to express the precision of a measurement.	**dígitos significativos** Dígitos usados para expresar la precisión de una medida.	
similar Figures with the same shape but not necessarily the same size are similar.	**semejantes** Figuras que tienen la misma forma, pero no necesariamente el mismo tamaño.	

Glossary/Glosario

ENGLISH	SPANISH	EXAMPLES
simple event An event consisting of only one outcome.	**suceso simple** Suceso que tiene sólo un resultado.	In the experiment of rolling a number cube, the event consisting of the outcome 3 is a simple event.
simple interest A fixed percent of the principal. It is found using the formula $I = Prt$, where P represents the principal, r the rate of interest, and t the time.	**interés simple** Un porcentaje fijo del capital. Se calcula con la fórmula $I = Cit$, donde C representa el capital, i, la tasa de interés y t, el tiempo.	
simplest form (of a fraction) A fraction is in simplest form when the numerator and denominator have no common factors other than 1.	**mínima expresión (de una fracción)** Una fracción está en su mínima expresión cuando el numerador y el denominador no tienen más factor común que 1.	Fraction: $\frac{8}{12}$ Simplest form: $\frac{2}{3}$
simplify To write a fraction or expression in simplest form.	**simplificar** Escribir una fracción o expresión numérica en su mínima expresión.	
simulation A model of an experiment, often one that would be too difficult or too time-consuming to actually perform.	**simulación** Representación de un experimento, por lo regular de uno cuya realización sería demasiado difícil o llevaría mucho tiempo.	
skew lines Lines that lie in different planes that are neither parallel nor intersecting.	**líneas oblicuas** Líneas que se encuentran en planos distintos, por eso no se intersecan ni son paralelas.	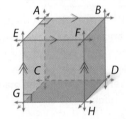
slope The constant rate of change of a line.	**pendiente** La tasa de cambio constante de una línea.	(table of x, y values with slopes shown)
solid figure A three-dimensional figure.	**cuerpo geométrico** Figura tridimensional.	
solution of an equation A value or values that make an equation true.	**solución de una ecuación** Valor o valores que hacen verdadera una ecuación.	Equation: $x + 2 = 6$ Solution: $x = 4$
solution of an inequality A value or values that make an inequality true.	**solución de una desigualdad** Valor o valores que hacen verdadera una desigualdad.	Inequality: $x + 3 \geq 10$ Solution set: $x \geq 7$

The slope example shows:

$$\begin{array}{c|ccccc} x & 0 & 1 & 4 & 6 & 7 \\ \hline y & 1 & 2 & 5 & 7 & 8 \end{array}$$

with changes $+1, +3, +2, +1$ across both rows, and $\frac{1}{1} = 1 \quad \frac{3}{3} = 1 \quad \frac{2}{2} = 1 \quad \frac{1}{1} = 1$

© Houghton Mifflin Harcourt Publishing Company

G26 Glossary/Glosario

solution set The set of values that make a statement true.

conjunto solución Conjunto de valores que hacen verdadero un enunciado.

Inequality: $x + 3 \geq 5$
Solution set: $x \geq 2$

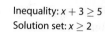

---

solve To find an answer or a solution.

resolver Hallar una respuesta o solución.

---

square (geometry) A rectangle with four congruent sides.

cuadrado (en geometría) Rectángulo con cuatro lados congruentes.

---

square (numeration) A number raised to the second power.

cuadrado (en numeración) Número elevado a la segunda potencia.

In 5^2, the number 5 is squared.

---

square number A number that is the product of a whole number and itself.

cuadrado de un número El producto de un número cabal multiplicado por sí mismo.

25 is a square number since $5^2 = 25$.

---

square root A number that is multiplied by itself to form a product is called a square root of that product.

raíz cuadrada El número que se multiplica por sí mismo para formar un producto se denomina la raíz cuadrada de ese producto.

$16 = 4 \cdot 4$ and $16 = -4 \cdot -4$, so 4 and -4 are square roots of 16.

---

standard form (in numeration) A number written using digits.

forma estándar Una forma de escribir números por medio de dígitos.

Five thousand, two hundred ten in standard form is 5,210.

---

statistical question A question that has many different, or variable, answers.

pregunta estadística Pregunta con muchas respuestas o variables diferentes.

---

straight angle An angle that measures 180°.

ángulo llano Ángulo que mide exactamente 180°.

---

subset A set contained within another set.

subconjunto Conjunto que pertenece a otro conjunto.

---

substitute To replace a variable with a number or another expression in an algebraic expression.

sustituir Reemplazar una variable por un número u otra expresión en una expresión algebraica.

---

sum The result when two or more numbers are added.

suma Resultado de sumar dos o más números.

---

supplementary angles Two angles whose measures have a sum of 180°.

ángulos suplementarios Dos ángulos cuyas medidas suman 180°.

ENGLISH

surface area The sum of the areas of the faces, or surfaces, of a three-dimensional figure.

SPANISH

área total Suma de las áreas de las caras, o superficies, de una figura tridimensional.

EXAMPLES

12 cm

6 cm

8 cm

Surface area = 2(8)(12) + 2(8)(6) + 2(12)(6) = 432cm²

term (in an expression) The parts of an expression that are added or subtracted.

término (en una expresión) Las partes de una expresión que se suman o se restan.

$3x^2 +$ $6x -$ 8

↑   ↑   ↑

Term   Term   Term

---

terminating decimal A decimal number that ends, or terminates.

decimal finito Decimal con un número determinado de posiciones decimales.

6.75

---

tessellation A repeating pattern of plane figures that completely covers a plane with no gaps or overlaps.

teselado Patrón repetido de figuras planas que cubren totalmente un plano sin superponerse ni dejar huecos.

---

theoretical probability The ratio of the number of ways an event can occur to the total number of equally likely outcomes.

probabilidad teórica Razón del numero de las maneras que puede ocurrir un suceso al número total de resultados igualmente probables.

When rolling a number cube, the theoretical probability of rolling a 4 is $\frac{1}{6}$.

---

tip The amount of money added to a bill for service; usually a percent of the bill.

propina Cantidad que se agrega al total de una factura por servicios. Por lo general, es un porcentaje del total de la factura.

---

transformation A change in the size or position of a figure.

transformación Cambio en el tamaño o la posición de una figura.

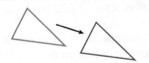

---

translation A movement (slide) of a figure along a straight line.

traslación Desplazamiento de una figura a lo largo de una línea recta.

---

trapezoid A quadrilateral with exactly one pair of parallel sides.

trapecio Cuadrilátero con un par de lados paralelos.

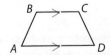

---

tree diagram A branching diagram that shows all possible combinations or outcomes of an event.

diagrama de árbol Diagrama ramificado que muestra todas las posibles combinaciones o resultados de un suceso.

trial   Each repetition or observation of an experiment.

prueba   Cada repetición u observación de un experimento.

In the experiment of rolling a number cube, each roll is one trial.

---

triangle   A three-sided polygon.

triángulo   Polígono de tres lados.

Triangle Sum Theorem   The theorem that states that the measures of the angles in a triangle add to 180°.

Teorema de la suma del triángulo   Teorema que establece que las medidas de los ángulos de un triángulo suman 180°.

---

triangular prism   A polyhedron whose bases are triangles and whose other faces are rectangles.

prisma triangular   Poliedro cuyas bases son triángulos y cuyas demás caras tienen forma de rectángulos.

U

underestimate   An estimate that is less than the exact answer.

estimación baja   Estimación menor que la respuesta exacta.

100 is an underestimate for the sum $26 + 29 + 31 + 27$.

---

union   The set of all elements that belong to two or more sets.

unión   El conjunto de todos los elementos que pertenecen a dos o más conjuntos.

---

unit conversion   The process of changing one unit of measure to another.

conversión de unidades   Proceso que consiste en cambiar una unidad de medida por otra.

---

unit rate   A rate in which the second quantity in the comparison is one unit.

tasa unitaria   Una tasa en la que la segunda cantidad de la comparación es una unidad.

10 cm per minute

---

unlike fractions   Fractions with different denominators.

fracciones distintas   Fracciones con distinto denominador.

$\frac{3}{4}$ and $\frac{1}{2}$ are unlike fractions.

V

variable   A symbol used to represent a quantity that can change.

variable   Símbolo que representa una cantidad que puede cambiar.

In the expression $2x + 3$, x is the variable.

---

variation (variability)   The spread of values in a set of data.

variación (variabilidad)   Amplitud de los valores de un conjunto de datos.

The data set {1, 5, 7, 10, 25} has greater variation than the data set {8, 8, 9, 9, 9}.

Venn diagram   A diagram that is used to show relationships between sets.

diagrama de Venn   Diagrama que muestra las relaciones entre conjuntos.

Transformations
Rotations

Glossary/Glosario

vertex (vertices) On an angle or polygon, the point where two sides intersect.

vértice (vértices) En un ángulo o polígono, el punto de intersección de dos lados.

A is the vertex of ∠*CAB*.

---

vertical angles A pair of opposite congruent angles formed by intersecting lines.

ángulos opuestos por el vértice Par de ángulos opuestos congruentes formados por líneas secantes.

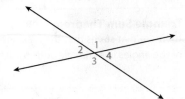

∠1 and ∠3 are vertical angles.
∠2 and ∠4 are vertical angles.

---

volume The number of cubic units needed to fill a given space.

volumen Número de unidades cúbicas que se necesitan para llenar un espacio.

4 ft
3 ft
12 ft

Volume = $3 \cdot 4 \cdot 12 = 144$ ft³

---

work-study program A program in which students are able to work at jobs on campus to make money to pay their college tuition.

programas de trabajo y estudio Programas que permiten a los estudiantes universitarios trabajar a medio tiempo y así ganar dinero para las matrículas universitarias y los gastos.

---

x-axis The horizontal axis on a coordinate plane.

eje x El eje horizontal del plano cartesiano.

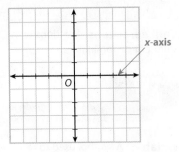

x-axis

O

---

x-coordinate The first number in an ordered pair; it tells the distance to move right or left from the origin, (0, 0).

coordenada x El primer número en un par ordenado; indica la distancia que debes avanzar hacia la izquierda o hacia la derecha desde el origen, (0, 0).

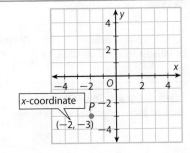

x-coordinate

P

(−2, −3)

Glossary/Glosario

y-axis The vertical axis on a coordinate plane.

eje y El eje vertical del plano cartesiano.

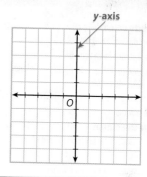

y-coordinate The second number in an ordered pair; it tells the distance to move up or down from the origin, (0, 0).

coordenada y El segundo número en un par ordenado; indica la distancia que debes avanzar hacia arriba o hacia abajo desde el origen, (0, 0).

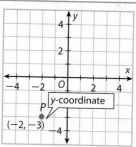

Z

zero pair A number and its opposite, which add to 0.

par nulo Un número y su opuesto, que sumados dan 0.

18 and −18

Glossary/Glosario

Index

Index

chef, 73, 140
climatologist, 1, 70
freelance computer programmer, 231, 288
geneticist, 443, 486
residential builder, 143, 228
theater set construction, 365, 440
center, measures of, 449–452, 472
centimeters, 191–192, 194, 195, 424, 429, 432, 433
Check for Reasonableness, 93, 112, 121, 124, 126, 219
chemistry, 11
clusters, 471
coefficients, 279
common factors, 31, 32, 34
on area models, 33
greatest. *See* greatest common factor (GCF)
common multiples, 38. *See also* least common multiple (LCM)
Communicate Mathematical Ideas, 12, 20, 24, 36, 40, 48, 53, 55, 59, 61, 64, 83, 90, 91, 118, 120, 177, 178, 185, 192, 196, 214, 216, 217, 218, 237, 242, 245, 247, 248, 282, 302, 303, 304, 305, 318, 324, 332, 336, 350, 375, 377, 378, 382, 384, 406, 412, 424, 430, 431, 434, 452, 454, 482
communicating math
arrange, 465
classify, 50, 52, 412
compare, 15, 16, 18, 25, 349, 350, 430, 464, 465, 467
describe, 18, 24, 40, 49, 61, 101, 135, 174, 215, 242, 280, 301, 324, 334, 335, 341, 342, 343, 350, 356, 424, 471, 473, 474, 475, 476
draw, 281, 283, 308, 322, 352, 467
estimate, 121, 123, 126
evaluate, 275, 482
explain. *Explain appears in most lessons. See, for example,* 12, 13, 19, 24, 36, 47, 52, 57, 83
give an example, 190, 319, 344
justify, 302, 355, 356, 382, 406, 473
list, 14, 16, 25, 51, 61, 243, 247
match, 275
Math Talk. *Math Talk appears in most lessons. See, for example,* 10, 14, 15, 20, 33, 48, 55, 61
order, 17, 18, 60, 61, 63, 64, 466
shade, 119, 125, 203, 206, 207, 210, 223
use an example, 118
Commutative Property, 118, 277, 278
comparisons, 15
of absolute values, 21–22
with equivalent ratios, 161–162, 164
of measures, 195
with ratios, 149, 161–162, 164
using rates, 155
complementary angles, 306
constants, 261
consumer math, 165, 221
conversion factors, 187, 192
conversions
of units using conversion factors, 187–188
of units using models, 185
of units using proportions and unit rates, 186–187

coordinate plane, 331
defined, 330
distance in, 401–406, 408
graphing on, 331–333
polygons in, 407–412
finding area, 409, 410
finding perimeter, 408
reflecting in, 401
coordinates, 292, 331
counters, 449
Critical Thinking, 52, 57, 64, 107, 214, 242, 247, 302, 310, 318, 336, 350, 355, 356, 387, 412, 430, 454, 461, 475, 476
Critique Reasoning, 18, 24, 36, 52, 64, 112, 118, 160, 184, 195, 204, 208, 248, 251, 268, 274, 309, 324, 376, 424, 454, 468
cubes
as cubic units, 425
nets for, 419
surface area of, 423
volume of, 242, 425–426, 428
cubic centimeters, 429, 432
cubic feet, 428–430, 432, 433
cubic inches, 427–429, 432, 434
cubic meters, 426–428
cubic millimeters, 433
cubic units, 425
customary system of measurement, 185, 186

D

data
displayed in histograms, 480
grouping at intervals, 477–478
mean, absolute deviation of, 455–462
decimal grids, 113–116, 119, 125
decimals
adding, 113–118
aligning decimal points, 114
converting to solve problems, 132
dividing, 125–127
equivalent, 58, 132
modeling equivalencies with fractions and percents, 210
multiplying, 119–122
ordering, 59
subtracting, 115–118
writing fractions as, 132, 211–212
writing percents as, 209
denominator, 74
dependent variables, 337–344, 346
distance
in the coordinate plane, 401–406, 408
from Earth to Moon, 111
on a map, 181
distribution, histograms and, 479, 480
Distributive Property, 33, 277, 278
dividend, 74
division
algebraic expressions for, 261
of decimals, 125–127
of equations, 312

estimating quotients, 107, 110
to find equivalent ratios, 151
of fractions, 85–89
of integers, 47–48
long, 108, 110
of mixed numbers, 91–93
of multi-digit whole numbers, 107–112
of number by factors, 243
in order of operations, 249
with remainders, 109
word problems with fractions and mixed numbers, 97–100
divisor, 74
dot plots, 470–472, 477–478
double number lines, 163, 205
Draw Conclusions, 40, 58, 96, 160, 274, 388

E

earth science, 24, 111, 222
edge length, volume and, 425–426, 428
elevation, 7
equality
addition property of, 305
division property of, 312
multiplication property of, 313
subtraction property of, 304
equations, 296, 297
adding, 305
algebraic, 261–264
checking solutions to, 299
defined, 330
dividing, 312
with greatest common factor, 32–34, 36
modeling, 303, 311
multiplying, 313
representing geometric concepts, 306
subtracting, 304
using to find area of shapes, 383–386, 390–394
using to solve real-world problems, 314–315
for volume, 431–434
writing from graphs, 352
writing from tables, 345–347
writing real-world problems for, 307
writing to represent situations, 297–299
equilateral triangles, 379
equivalent decimals, 58, 132
equivalent expressions, 260, 261, 263–264
generating, 275–279
identifying, 275–276
modeling, 261, 276
using properties to identify, 278
using properties to write, 277
equivalent fractions, 58, 132, 180
equivalent rates, 157–158
and proportions, 179
to solve proportions, 180
equivalent ratios, 148, 151–152, 193
comparisons with, 161–162, 164
multiplicative relationship between, 152
solving proportions with, 179
solving real-world problems with, 162
equivalent values, reciprocals and, 87

Index

Index

© Houghton Mifflin Harcourt Publishing Company

Index

Index